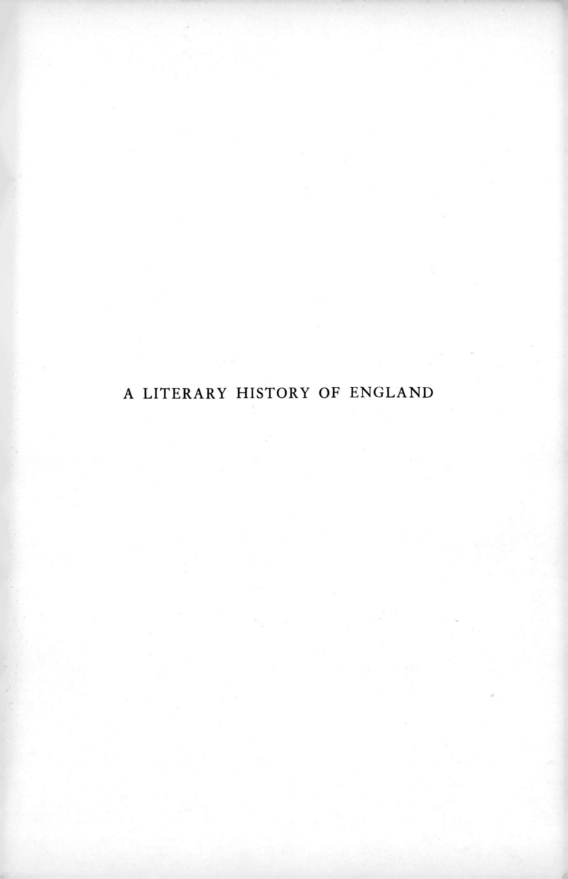

# A LITERARY HISTORY OF ENGLAND

# A LITERARY HISTORY OF ENGLAND

—VOLUME I—

## The Middle Ages (to 1500)

**KEMP MALONE**
*Johns Hopkins University*

**ALBERT C. BAUGH**
*University of Pennsylvania*

—VOLUME II—

## The Renaissance (1500–1660)

**TUCKER BROOKE**

**MATTHIAS A. SHAABER**
*University of Pennsylvania*

—VOLUME III—

## The Restoration and Eighteenth Century (1660–1789)

**GEORGE SHERBURN**

**DONALD F. BOND**
*The University of Chicago*

—VOLUME IV—

## The Nineteenth Century and After (1789–1939)

**SAMUEL C. CHEW**

**RICHARD D. ALTICK**
*The Ohio State University*

*A LITERARY HISTORY OF ENGLAND*

Second Edition

Edited by Albert C. Baugh

—————————— VOLUME IV ——————————

# THE

# NINETEENTH CENTURY
## AND AFTER
## (1789-1939)

by

SAMUEL C. CHEW

&

RICHARD D. ALTICK

LONDON

ROUTLEDGE & KEGAN PAUL LTD

*Published in Great Britain*
*by Routledge & Kegan Paul Ltd*
*Broadway House, 68–74 Carter Lane*
*London, E.C.4*

*Second Edition 1967*

*Printed in Great Britain*
*by Unwin Brothers Limited, Woking*

*SBN 7100 6131 5*

# Preface to the First Edition

The purpose of the work of which the present volume forms a part is to provide a comprehensive history of the literature of England, an account that is at once scholarly and readable, capable of meeting the needs of mature students and of appealing to cultivated readers generally. The extent of English literature is so great that no one can hope to read more than a fraction of it, and the accumulated scholarship—biographical, critical, and historical—by which writers and their works, and the forms and movements and periods of English literature have been interpreted, is so vast that no single scholar can control it. A literary history by one author, a history that is comprehensive and authoritative over the whole field, is next to impossible. Hence, the plan of the present work. A general harmony of treatment among the five contributors, rather than rigid uniformity of method, has seemed desirable, and there is quite properly some difference of emphasis in different sections. It is hoped that the approach to the different periods will seem to be that best suited to the literature concerned. The original plan brought the history to an end with the year 1939 (the outbreak of the Second World War); but delay in publication caused by the war has permitted reference to a few events of a date subsequent to 1939.

Since it is expected that those who read this history or consult it will wish for further acquaintance with the writings and authors discussed, it has been a part of the plan to draw attention, by the generous use of footnotes, to standard editions, to significant biographical and critical works, and to the most important books and articles in which the reader may pursue further the matters that interest him. A few references to very recent publications have been added in proof in an effort to record the present state of scholarly and critical opinion.

As for the present volume, all that is necessary here is to repeat the grateful acknowledgment of indebtedness for helpful suggestions made by Professor Frederick L. Jones, Professor Mary S. Gardiner, and Professor Arthur C. Sprague, and to thank readers who called attention to three or four small errors in the single-volume edition, which have here been corrected.

S. C. C.

## NOTE TO SECOND EDITION

The reception of the *Literary History of England* has been so gratifying as to call for a number of successive printings, and these have permitted minor corrections to be made. The present edition has a further aim—to bring the book in line with the most recent scholarship. Small changes have been made in the plates wherever possible, but most of the additions, factual and bibliographical, are recorded in a Supplement. The text, Supplement, and Index are correlated by means of several typographical devices. Explanations of these devices appear on each part-title page as well as at the beginning of the Supplement and the Index.

The editor regrets that the authors of Books II, III, and IV did not live to carry out the revisions of those books, but their places have been ably taken by the scholars whose names appear with theirs in the list of collaborators. It has been the desire of the editor, as well as of those who have joined him, that each of these books should remain essentially as the original author wrote it, and we believe that other scholars would concur. Any new points of view, it is hoped, are adequately represented in the Supplement.

A. C. B.

# Contents

# List of Abbreviations

| | |
|---|---|
| *AJP* | American Journal of Philology |
| *Archiv* | Archiv für das Studium der neueren Sprachen und Literaturen |
| *ARS* | Augustan Reprint Society |
| *CBEL* | Cambridge Bibliography of English Literature (4v, Cambridge, 1941) |
| *CFMA* | Les Classiques français du moyen âge |
| *CHEL* | Cambridge History of English Literature (14v, 1907–17) |
| *CL* | Comparative Literature |
| *E&S* | Essays and Studies by Members of the English Association |
| *EETS* | Early English Text Society, Original Series |
| *EETSES* | Early English Text Society, Extra Series |
| *EHR* | English Historical Review |
| *EIC* | Essays in Criticism |
| *ELH* | *ELH*, A Journal of English Literary History |
| *ELN* | English Language Notes |
| *EML Series* | English Men of Letters Series |
| *ES* | English Studies |
| *ESt* | Englische Studien |
| *GR* | Germanic Review |
| *HLQ* | Huntington Library Quarterly |
| *Hist. Litt.* | Histoire littéraire de la France (38v, 1733–1941, in progress) |
| *JAAC* | Journal of Aesthetics and Art Criticism |
| *JEGP* | Journal of English and Germanic Philology |
| *JHI* | Journal of the History of Ideas |
| *KSJ* | Keats-Shelley Journal |
| *LTLS* | (London) Times Literary Supplement |
| *MA* | Medium Ævum |
| *MLN* | Modern Language Notes |
| *MLQ* | Modern Language Quarterly |
| *MLR* | Modern Language Review |
| *MP* | Modern Philology |
| *N&Q* | Notes and Queries |
| *NCF* | Nineteenth-Century Fiction |
| *PMLA* | Publications of the Modern Language Association of America |
| *PQ* | Philological Quarterly |

| | |
|---|---|
| *REL* | Review of English Literature |
| *RES* | Review of English Studies |
| *RLC* | Revue de littérature compaŕée |
| *RR* | Romanic Review |
| *SAB* | Shakespeare Association Bulletin |
| *SATF* | Societé des anciens textes français |
| *SEL* | Studies in English Literature, 1500–1900 (Rice Univ.) |
| *SF&R* | Scholars' Facsimiles and Reprints |
| *ShS* | Shakespeare Survey |
| *SP* | Studies in Philology |
| *SQ* | Shakespeare Quarterly |
| *SRen* | Studies in the Renaissance |
| *STS* | Scottish Text Society |
| *UTQ* | University of Toronto Quarterly |
| *VP* | Victorian Poetry |
| *VS* | Victorian Studies |

# BOOK IV

## The Nineteenth Century
## and After (1789-1939)

∽ ⟋ ⟍

*Guide to reference marks*

Throughout the text of this book, a point • set beside a page number indicates that references to new critical material will be found under an identical paragraph/page number (set in **boldface**) in the BIBLIOGRAPHICAL SUPPLEMENT.

In the Index, a number preceded by an **S** indicates a paragraph/page number in the BIBLIOGRAPHICAL SUPPLEMENT.

# I

## The Background of Revolution, Repression, and Reform: 1789-1832

The forty-three years from the Fall of the Bastille (1789) to the passage of the first Reform Bill (1832) precisely cover the period in English literary history from the appearance of Blake's *Songs of Innocence* to the death of Sir Walter Scott. Commonly called the Romantic Period, it might be called the pre-Victorian, in a double sense, both chronologically as preceding the Queen's long reign and also because it saw England moving through the ordeal of the Industrial Revolution and the Napoleonic Wars to her period of dominance during the middle decades of the nineteenth century.[1]

### I

During the seventeen-eighties, under the impulsion of accelerating economic change, the champions of reform became more active. The social conscience found expression in the movement for the abolition of the slave-trade, the revision of the system of poor relief, the religious education of the poor, the mitigation of conditions in prisons and "hulks," the diminution of the national vice of intemperance, the relief of dissenters, and other good causes. But the advocates of the redress of grievances saw that their best strategy was to plead the cause of parliamentary reform—a fairer representation of the people in Parliament. The consensus, however, in the ruling classes was that particular grievances were of no consequence in comparison with the virtue of the English system as a whole. Property interests were fundamental; the people were represented in the spirit of the law even though not in the letter; and—the pragmatic argument—the old system worked.

Events in France in the summer of 1789 were watched with eager interest by Englishmen and imparted a fresh zeal to the champions of reform. "The London Revolution Society," though founded to celebrate the centenary of political liberty won in 1688, became associated in the popular mind with what was going on across the Channel; and this impression seemed to be confirmed when in November the Society sent a message of congratulation

*Agitation for Reform*

*Opponents of Burke*

---

[1] P. A. Brown, *The French Revolution in English History* (1923); A. F. Freemantle, *England in the Nineteenth Century, 1801-1805* (1929), *1806-1810* (1930); G. M. Trevelyan, *History of England* (1926), Book V, chs. IV-VII, and *English Social History* (1942), chs. XV-XVI; *Social England*, ed. H. D. Traill (1896), V chs. XIX-XX; J. M. Thompson, *English Witnesses of the French Revolution* (1938); various chapters in *The Cambridge Modern History*, VIII and IX.

to the French National Assembly on the triumph of liberty over arbitrary power. This message roused Edmund Burke to the composition of his *Reflections on the Revolution in France* (1790). The anti-revolutionary opinions so widely disseminated in this pamphlet did not go unchallenged.[2] Mary Wollstonecraft [3] (1759-1797) attacked Burke for his reliance upon the past and his contempt of the poor; but though charged with generous feeling her *Vindication of the Rights of Men* (1790) was too hastily written and too emotional to be very effective. Nor was the *Vindiciae Gallicae* (1791) of James Mackintosh [4] (1765-1832) widely influential, for it was too refined in its Whig liberalism. But the demagogic style in which Thomas Paine [5] (1737-1809) wrote *The Rights of Man* (1791) made it at once a textbook of popular radicalism. Anyone, even if unable to follow close reasoning, could comprehend his ringing assertions that "man has no property in man" and that "there is a morning of reason rising upon the world." The violence of Paine's attack upon the British monarchy was, however, prejudicial to his own cause, and he harmed it further by the crass anti-Christianity of *The Age of Reason* (1794). In contrast to this fanaticism is the cool argument in *Letters to the Right Honourable Edmund Burke* (1791) by Joseph

[2] With Burke's opponents may be associated Arthur Young (1741-1820), whose defense of the French Revolution was none the less telling for being indirect. He was already an expert observer of agricultural and social conditions and had published three *Tours* (1768-1770) through different parts of England and a *Tour in Ireland* (1780) when in 1787 he made the famous tour of which he gave an account in *Travels in France* (1792); ed. M. Bentham-Edwards (1924). By exposing the rottenness of economic conditions under the *ancien régime* this work demonstrated the inevitability of the Revolution.

[3] After early experience as a teacher (see her *Thoughts on the Education of Daughters*, 1787), Mary Wollstonecraft became literary adviser to Joseph Johnson, a publisher. Her *Original Stories* (1791) were illustrated by Blake; ed. E. V. Lucas (1906). *A Vindication of the Rights of Women* (1792) argues for equality of education for both sexes and state control of co-education. In Paris in 1792-1793 she formed an attachment with Gilbert Imlay, her principles forbidding her to marry. Their daughter, Fanny, has a part in Shelley's story. On discovering Imlay's infidelity, Mary attempted to drown herself in the Thames but was rescued. Imlay deserted her and she returned to work in Johnson's shop, where in 1796 she met William Godwin. The union between these two was regularized by marriage in 1797 in order to safeguard the legal rights of a coming child. This was a daughter, Mary, who became Shelley's second wife. At her birth Mrs. Godwin died. — *Posthumous Works*, ed. William Godwin (4v, 1798), of which the *Love Letters to Gilbert Imlay*, ed. Roger Ingpen (1908), were originally part. See William Godwin, *Memoirs of the Author of a Vindication of the Rights of Women* (1798); ed. W. C. Durant (1927) and J. M. Murry (1930); G. R. S. Taylor, *Mary Wollstonecraft* (1911); H. R. James, *Mary Wollstonecraft* (1932); G. R. Preedy, *This Shining Woman* (1937).

[4] In later years, shocked by the excesses of the revolutionists, Mackintosh came to agree entirely with Burke. But he continued to advocate parliamentary reform. His fragmentary *History of the Revolution in England* (posthumous, 1834) points forward to Macaulay. — R. J. Mackintosh, *The Life of Sir James Mackintosh* (1836).

[5] In early life Paine was an exciseman. A meeting with Benjamin Franklin in London led him to go to America in 1774. In January, 1776 he published *Common Sense*, arguing for the separation of the colonies from Britain and their union in a republic. During the American Revolution he was an energetic pamphleteer. Returning to England, he issued *Prospects on the Rubicon* (1787), pleading for friendship with France. *The Rights of Man* led to his indictment for high treason, but he escaped to France. *The Age of Reason* (1794) mingles lofty morality with rough ridicule. He returned to America in 1802 and died in New York in 1809. — *Writings*, ed. M. D. Conway (4v, 1894-1896); *Representative Selections*, ed. H. H. Clark (1944). See M. D. Conway, *The Life of Thomas Paine* (1892); M. A. Best, *Thomas Paine, Prophet and Martyr of Democracy* (1927); Hesketh Pearson, *Tom Paine, Friend of Mankind* (1937); Frank Smith, *Thomas Paine, Liberator* (1938); W. E. Woodward, *Tom Paine: America's Godfather* (1946).

Priestley [6] (1733-1804). That this first clear enunciation of the doctrine of perfectibility came from a chemist was significant, for the scientific advances of the later eighteenth century stimulated ideas of progress and social evolution. John Thelwall [7] (1764-1834) expounded his social radicalism in a miscellany of prose and verse entitled *The Peripatetic* (1793), but his direct answers to Burke were in speeches delivered in 1795 and in two pamphlets of 1796.

William Godwin [8] (1756-1836) began to write *Political Justice* in 1791, *Godwin* though it was not published till 1793. It is at once a criticism of existing *and* society, a system of social ethics, and a series of prophecies for the future. *Radicalism* Godwin shared with other radicals an optimism founded upon their confidence in the power of the human reason. Ignoring the obvious lessons which might have been drawn from the past of the very society that he criticized, he held that truth must prevail because the arguments supporting it are in the nature of the case stronger than those supporting error. Truth needs no sanction but itself. Vice is an error of judgment. Adopting the sensationalistic interpretation of Locke's theory of knowledge, Godwin believed that judgments, falsified by passion and ignorance, could be rectified by education.[9] Though, like the physical world, the mind of man is subject to necessity (the invariable sequence of cause and effect) and though the basic motive of morality is the desire for pleasure and the avoidance of pain, education can make the individual adapt his own interests to the common good. This "enlightened self-interest," which in the moral sphere cor-

---

[6] The discoverer of oxygen was a voluminous writer on natural science, metaphysics, theology, sociology, and other topics. His idea of perfectibility influenced the Marquis de Condorcet, whose *Esquisse d'un tableau historique du progrès de l'esprit humain* (1794) is one of the documents of revolutionary optimism. Priestley emigrated to America (1794) and settled in Pennsylvania, where he died.

[7] Thelwall's ideas influenced Coleridge and Wordsworth; there are definite parallels between *The Peripatetic* and *The Excursion.* — Charles Cestre, *John Thelwall* (1906).

[8] Godwin began his career as a Calvinist minister but soon adopted the principles of the "Enlightenment." He wrote much, but nothing of importance, before *Political Justice* (1793). This was followed by *Caleb Williams*, on which and on his other novels see below, ch. VIII. After the death of his first wife he married a Mrs. Clairmont, one of whose children by a former marriage was Jane ("Claire") Clairmont. In later life Godwin was in constant pecuniary difficulties, wrote many ephemeral literary and historical works, and carried on a small publishing business. — *Political Justice*, ed. and abridged by R. A. Preston (1906); C. K. Paul, *William Godwin, his Friends and Contemporaries* (2v, 1876); Raymond Gourg, *William Godwin* (Paris, 1908); H. N. Brailsford, *Shelley, Godwin and their Circle* (1913); F. K. Brown, *The Life of William Godwin* (1926); George Woodcock, *William Godwin* (1946); Sir Leslie Stephen, *English Thought in the Eighteenth Century* (ed. 1902), II. 264-281; Basil Willey, *The Eighteenth Century Background* (1940), pp. 217-239.

[9] The basic document of romantic theories of education is *De l'esprit* (1758) by Claude Adrien Helvétius. The author follows Condillac's interpretation of Locke's epistemology. The mind is at birth a *tabula rasa*; ideas come solely through sensation, the mind adding nothing but merely arranging the data of sense. Hence the supreme importance of an education which will provide the right sensations. The destructive side of Helvétius's thought is his attack upon conservatism and tradition, kings, priests, and hereditary rights. A more superficial book (which had, however, a great influence) is the Baron d'Holbach's *Système de la nature* (1770). Here the mechanistic theory of the universe coupled with the materialistic monism logically deducible from the sensationalistic interpretation of Locke results in absolute atheism. Reason is the only guide. In lieu of threats of supernatural vengeance as a sanction a right education becomes an assurance of morality. See further Daniel Mornet, *French Thought in the Eighteenth Century*, trans. L. M. Levin (1929).

responds to the "will of the majority" in the political, points forward to the Utilitarians; Jeremy Bentham had, indeed, already adumbrated it in his *Fragment on Government* (1776). Only create the right environment for a proper education, Godwin urged, and limitless development in the right direction is possible. In a well ordered society reason, not law, will maintain the social equilibrium. Men will require no political control and government will be reduced to a minimum or will altogether disappear. (It is difficult to distinguish between Godwin's theory of government and pure anarchy.) The institution of private property will not be destroyed, but men will be too reasonable to claim more than their just shares. Marriage, a form of tyranny, will disappear. The penal code and other social conventions will be reformed. This utopian vision is not a "return to nature" in accordance with the usual English interpretation of Rousseau's doctrines,[10] for Godwin advocates not innocent ignorance but virtuous wisdom. When Southey and Coleridge, influenced by *Political Justice,* devised their "pantisocratic" society, they were doubtful of the possibility of reforming their own minds, already warped by wrong education, but planned for the next generation an environment from which opportunities for evil would be shut out and only right sensations impressed upon the mind. These poets and Wordsworth moved away from Godwinian ideas; and Godwin moved away, as it were, from himself. In place of the cool, analytical theory of *Political Justice* his later books substitute a sentimental naturalism.

Though English radicalism was in close touch with Paris, English societies were not planned upon French models. "The Friends of the People" (1791) was moderate in its program of parliamentary reform, though Fox and the New Whigs, who for all their sympathy with France were not "levelers," stood aloof from it. "The London Corresponding Society" (1792), which had branches all over the country, planned to unite the common people for the purpose of making their wishes felt. But by 1792 the increasing violence of the French Revolution strengthened reaction in England. Already in 1791 a "Church and King" mob in Birmingham had burned Priestley's home and laboratory, but this riot had expressed hostility to Dissent rather than to advanced political opinion. Societies appeared dedicated to "the protection of Liberty and Property against republicans and levelers." Men who had formerly sympathized with France began to waver in their optimism. Pamphlets celebrating the blessedness of the English Constitution found ready readers. Loyal addresses flooded the government; newspapers were subsidized; informers wormed their way into radical meetings; and a heresy-hunt began.

*War with France*     When the reactionary powers of the Continent made their first attack upon France (1792), Pitt had refused to join them; but the French Convention's invitation to a general revolution of all peoples and its indiscriminate defiance of all sovereigns, coupled with the attack upon the Nether-

---

[10] The English notion of Rousseau's teaching derived primarily from the ideas in his two early *Discours* which were modified and qualified in the writings of his maturity.

lands, brought England into the war early in 1793. Pitt's object was to prevent the annexation of the Low Countries and to meet the cost of hostilities by seizing French colonies in the West Indies. After the expulsion of her army in 1794 England's military rôle on the Continent was almost negligible till the beginning of the Peninsular War in 1808. Her successes in the West Indies were purchased at a high cost in lives and money and contributed little to her ultimate victory. Her practical control of the sea after the Battle of the Nile (1798) was complete after Trafalgar (1805). But meanwhile Napoleon remained invincible on land. The Treaty of Amiens (1802) as much as recognized the oceans as England's sphere, Europe as Napoleon's. But England interpreted the treaty as setting a limit to French conquests, while Napoleon proceeded with his annexations. Consequently Amiens turned out to be but an uneasy truce. Pitt's methods of financing the war by indirect taxation (the income tax was not introduced till 1798) bore heavily upon that part of the population which could least afford to pay, and rising prices and food scarcity increased suffering and discontent. The strange remoteness from the war on the part of many members of the cultivated and wealthy classes was due in part to the fact that they were so little affected by taxation, in part to the fact that the navy was manned by means of the press-gang and there was no call for service in the army save for the short time of threatened invasion in 1805, and in part to the disaffection of the Whigs who, though alienated from France, were half-hearted in support of the war and remained aloof, enjoying a life of wealth and ease.

The outbreak of war in 1793 led to the so-called "Anti-Jacobin Terror" *Anti-* of 1794. Daniel Isaac Eaton, the publisher of the newspaper *Hog's Wash* *Jacobinism* (its name an ironical allusion to Burke's scornful phrase, "the swinish multitude"), was tried but acquitted; but in Scotland cruel sentences were imposed upon the victims of the public panic. In the autumn Horne Tooke, John Thelwall, and other radicals were brought to trial for high treason. Their advocate, Thomas Erskine, exposed the falsity of the evidence against them. Several were acquitted and the rest released without trial. Whereupon the volatile populace, which had been strongly anti-Jacobin, celebrated this triumph of freedom of speech and assembly over governmental tyranny. This outcome encouraged the societies, which had been lying low, to become active again for reform. The government countered in 1795 with acts more rigorously defining treason and prohibiting public gatherings without special authorization. To the word *Convention* events in France had attached a sinister meaning; it was feared that assemblies would attempt to overawe or even supersede Parliament. Seething unrest in Ireland, a mutiny in the fleet, and great suffering among the poor were further causes for alarm. The ministry at length suspended habeas corpus. Pitt's motives in putting into force these repressive measures have been much disputed. There seems to be little doubt that he genuinely feared sedition; but he appears to have stimulated panic as a means to rouse the country to support the war.

Freedom of the press, resting upon the Common Law, was never completely suppressed, though actions for libel and sedition were frequent. The two ablest newspapers, *The Morning Chronicle* and *The Morning Post* (for which Coleridge wrote), were bitter opponents of the ministry. Pitt, on the other hand, had the support of the two cleverest caricaturists of the day, James Gillray and Thomas Rowlandson; and in 1797-1798 George Canning, George Ellis, and J. H. Frere championed the government and defended the system of taxation in their brilliant newspaper, *The Anti-Jacobin*. The chief purpose of their satire was to contrast abstract republican philanthropy with the actual cruelties of the Jacobins. This satire was at once strengthened and lightened with parodies of those English poets who expressed sympathy with radical ideas. The contributors had also an eye for other absurdities of modern thought and fashion.[11]

With the spread of opinion hostile to France the situation eased at the turn of the century, but with the renewal of the war in 1803 fears of subversive activities were again rife. It was in this year that William Blake was brought to trial on the charge of sedition. It was difficult to advance the cause of any reform, no matter how obviously salutary it might be. The argument with which conservatives met the advocates of change was that English society, which had rejected reform, had survived, while French

[11] See *Parodies and Other Burlesque Pieces by George Canning, George Ellis and John Hookham Frere with the whole Poetry of the Anti-Jacobin*, ed. Henry Morley (1890). The most effective part of this weekly paper was the verse. In it appeared *The Needy Knife-Grinder*, by Canning and Frere, a parody on Southey; *The Loves of the Triangles*, a parody of Erasmus Darwin's *Loves of the Plants; The Progress of Man*, a parody of Richard Payne Knight's *Progress of Civil Society*; and similar pieces. Canning was the chief author of *The New Morality* which vigorously satirizes Coleridge, Southey, Paine, Priestley, and other radicals; renders Burke's ideas into verse; and closes with a lofty exhortation to Britain to be true to her noblest traditions. — George Canning (1770-1827), a young protégé of Pitt, became a great statesman. See Dorothy Marshall, *The Rise of George Canning* (1938), pp. 175-188. George Ellis (1753-1815) contributed to the *Probationary Odes for the Laureateship* (1784 and following years; collected, 1791). He is remembered also for his antiquarian studies of which the most distinguished result is his *Specimens of Early English Metrical Romances* (1805). John Hookham Frere (1769-1846) pointed the way towards Byron's *Don Juan* (see below, ch. xi) and occupied the leisure of a diplomatic career with his translation of Aristophanes (1839). See Gabrielle Festing, *J. H. Frere and his Friends* (1899); Albert Eichler, *J. H. Frere, sein Leben und seine Werke* (Vienna, 1905). — The editor of *The Anti-Jacobin* was William Gifford (1756-1826). Gifford was schooled in boyhood in hard experience but through the kindness of a philanthropist obtained an Oxford education. His stern nature found congenial stuff in the satires of Juvenal and Persius; and the latter was his model for *The Baviad* (1791) in which with a weight of learning and invective he crushed the poor butterflies who fluttered round Robert Merry, the chief "Della Cruscan" poetaster. The feeble verses of this coterie of sentimentalists had appeared in the *World* newspaper and were gathered into a volume. Gifford followed up his first attack with *The Mæviad* (1795), this time dividing his attention between his former victims and the absurdities of the contemporary stage. The harsh energy and assumption of righteous indignation in these satires are due as much to Gifford's Latin model as to any personal feeling. See J. M. Longaker, *The Della Cruscans and William Gifford* (Philadelphia, 1924). In 1809 Gifford became editor of *The Quarterly Review* where his notices of new literature were often written in the current "slashing" style. He edited Ben Jonson (1816) and John Ford (1827). See R. B. Clark, *William Gifford, Tory Satirist, Critic, and Editor* (1930). — Apart from the *Anti-Jacobin* group was Thomas James Mathias (1754-1835) whose *Pursuits of Literature* appeared in three installments, 1794-1797. In form, dialogues modeled on Pope, these satires derive in thought from Burke. Mathias denounced and ridiculed everything contaminated with revolutionary ideas. He smelt a rat in every corner and many of his corners were small and dark. Most of his victims are forgotten today. See further C. W. Previté-Orton, *Political Satire in English Poetry* (Cambridge, 1910), pp. 154-164; W. J. Courthope, *A History of English Poetry*, vi (1910), ch. vi.

society, which had welcomed it, had collapsed; and that changes were entering wedges proposed by dangerous persons who planned to "go further." The one great accomplishment of these years, the abolition of the slave trade, belongs to the interim of Tory governments when Fox headed the Ministry-of-All-the-Talents. Samuel Romilly [12] carried on his agitation for the reform of the cruel and illogical penal code under a cloud of anti-Jacobin prejudice. Sir Francis Burdett,[13] to whom Shelley dedicated *The Wandering Jew* (1810), was a leader in the attacks upon the government. Among the many victims of the policy of repression were John and Leigh Hunt, who were prosecuted in 1811 for exposing the cruelty of flogging in the army. On the same charge William Cobbett was fined and imprisoned. The trial of Daniel Isaac Eaton in 1812, on the charge of reprinting Paine's *Age of Reason,* was the occasion of Shelley's *Letter to Lord Ellenborough.* The Luddite riots of 1811 led to the Frame-Breaking Bill (1812) which made it a capital offense to destroy manufacturing machinery. Against this bill Byron delivered his maiden speech in the House of Lords. Under its terms various unfortunate victims of technological unemployment were executed in the presence of sullen crowds cowed by the military. The state of the public's nerves is shown by the fact that when in 1812 there was a strike among the Scottish weavers a panic spread over Britain. Scott wrote to Southey: "The country is mined beneath our feet." [14]

## II

The restrictions upon popular liberty were war measures, but they were *Reactions* not withdrawn after Waterloo and for years the movement for reform was *and Social* impeded because it was associated with sedition.[15] The retention of office by *Unrest* Tory governments till 1830 was at first due to the prestige of victory, but more largely to the divisions among the Whigs, who by failing to agree among themselves on a plan of parliamentary reform deprived themselves of their one chance of gaining popularity. For the misery and unrest of 1815-1817 several causes are apparent. The growth of population came partly from Irish immigration but chiefly through the decline in the infantile death-rate. Consequent upon this growth was the overcrowding in the new cities of the Midlands with all the horrors of slums and cellar-dwellings. Discharged soldiery swelled the ranks of those thrown out of work by the

[12] *Memoirs of Sir Samuel Romilly written by Himself* (3v, 1840).
[13] M. W. Patterson, *Sir Francis Burdett and His Times* (2v, 1931).
[14] Sir Walter Scott, *Letters,* ed. Sir H. J. C. Grierson, III. 125.
[15] The classical survey of English society in 1815 is Elie Halévy, *Histoire du peuple anglais au dix-neuvième siècle,* I (3 ed., 1923); Vols. II and III (1923) bring the story down to 1841. See also E. L. Woodward, *The Age of Reform, 1815-1870* (Oxford, 1938); J. H. Clapham, *Economic History of Modern Britain,* I (1930); F. O. Darvall, *Popular Disturbances and Public Order in Regency England* (1934). There is a wealth of illustrations in E. B. Chancellor, *Life in Regency and Early Victorian Times* (1927). Of Rudolph Ackermann's *The Microcosm of London* (3v, 1808-1811) with its color-plates by A. C. Pugin and Thomas Rowlandson there is a reprint (3v, 1904). This is an unrivaled evocation of the outward appearance of Regency London. See also M. J. Quinlan, *Victorian Prelude: a History of English Manners, 1700-1830* (1941).

new machinery. Hand-looms gave place to power-looms slowly—more slowly in the woolen industry than the cotton, but fast enough to cause distress. The decline in trade and fall in prices coincided with the repeal of the income tax with the consequent burden of indirect taxation upon the poor. The fall in the price of corn brought about the enactment of the Corn Laws with their "sliding scale" which afforded protection to the farmers and the landed interests at the expense of the laboring and mercantile classes. In 1816 there was destruction of machinery, agitation among the colliers, and the circulation of petitions to Parliament, and in December a great meeting at Spa Fields, organized by "Orator" Hunt,[16] was accompanied with rioting. The ministers, alarmed, suspended habeas corpus and had an act passed making seditious meetings unlawful. With a temporary revival of trade, panic subsided; but a new depression began in 1819. In August a huge crowd, estimated at 50-60,000, gathered in St. Peter's Field at Manchester to hear an address by Hunt. The crowd was orderly, but the authorities lost their heads, and when soldiers dispersed the gathering, eleven persons were killed and about four hundred wounded. This "Peterloo Massacre," which prompted Shelley to write *The Masque of Anarchy*, roused indignation even in the upper classes. The Six Acts regulating agitation, assembly, and arrest followed. Immediately afterwards came the "Cato Street Conspiracy," so called because in that street were arrested some fanatics who were plotting to blow up the cabinet. The ill repute of the Prince Regent had its share in inflaming popular feeling, as did the indifference and isolation of the Whigs with their leisured, luxurious, cultivated, and often profligate life. When divorce proceedings were brought against Queen Caroline (1820), and when at her husband's coronation (1820) she claimed the right to be crowned, popular opinion rallied round her as a symbolic victim of oppression. In the popular mind Viscount Castlereagh was associated with the policy of repression because he was the leader of the House of Commons. Actually his own interests and great achievements were in the domain of foreign affairs, in bringing back peace to Europe.[17] But his was a Tory mentality and he supported harsh measures. Hence the almost symbolic position that he occupies in the poetry of Byron and Shelley. His suicide in 1822 marked the close of the worst years of reaction.

Cobbett    The fear of the "mob," grounded upon shocked observation of the French Terror, was enhanced by the violence of radical pamphleteering. The most influential of the agitators was William Cobbett [18] (1766-1835), whose early

---

[16] Henry Hunt (1793-1835) was a disciple of Horne Tooke. In 1810 he was a fellow-prisoner with William Cobbett. In prison, to which he was sentenced after "Peterloo," he wrote his *Memoirs* (1820). He was elected to Parliament in 1830.

[17] C. K. Webster, *The Foreign Policy of Castlereagh, 1815-1822* (1934).

[18] After experience as a soldier (1784-1791) and six months in France (1792) Cobbett lived in America (1792-1800), where as "Peter Porcupine" he was a satiric pamphleteer and publisher, intensely pro-British, anti-French, and anti-Republican. He was prosecuted and fined for libel. After his return to England he veered gradually from support of the Tories towards radicalism. His imprisonment for exposing the cruelties of flogging in the army followed in 1809. On his release he became so much involved in debt that in 1817 he fled to the United States. On his return home he stood repeatedly for Parliament, was elected, 1830,

anti-Jacobinism gave way to an ardor for reform after his return from America in 1800. He began publication of *The Political Register* in 1802. In its pages and in other writings vivid observation, loud-voiced denunciation, and conviction-compelling sincerity attracted wide attention. In many journeys through the length and breadth of England, recorded in *Rural Rides* (1830), he made himself the master of the "condition of England question." Though fined and imprisoned, weighed down with debts, and compelled to exile himself for a time in the United States, he lived to become a member of the first reformed Parliament. With him in the history of the struggle for a free press may be associated two publishers. William Hone [19] (1780-1842) was tried in 1817 on the charge of sedition and blasphemy for publishing parodies on the Creed, the Litany, and the Catechism. He was acquitted. But in 1818 Richard Carlile [20] (1790-1843) was fined and imprisoned for reprinting Hone's parodies and Paine's works.

Meanwhile the tide of reform was slowly coming in. The act of 1819 limiting the hours of child labor in the cotton mills to eleven, pitiable though the concession was, was important in that it recognized the principle of parliamentary interference. Another favorable sign after 1815 was the headway made by the movement for working class education. The "Mechanics' Institutes" and similar organizations were philanthropic responses to the argument that leisure for the poor was a social evil because they had no opportunity for harmless recreation. The experiments which Robert Owen (1771-1858) had been conducting since 1800 at his mills in New Lanark near Glasgow set an example not only in the educational field but in the whole field of social amelioration. Owen's conviction that human character depended upon a right environment was the basis of the principles set forth in his *New View of Society* of which the first part appeared in 1813. His attempts to reconcile the conflict between hand labor and machinery, to organize labor, to manage a business upon a profit-sharing basis, and to establish model communities, with (at a later date) his labor exchange system and socialistic propaganda, were important influences upon the social legislation of the Victorian period and upon the social economics of John Ruskin.

*The Advance of Reform*

In the years between Waterloo and the Reform Bill the doctrines which

*Bentham*

re-elected, 1834. — Based on his *Life and Adventures of Peter Porcupine* (1798) and on autobiographical memoranda is *The Progress of a Plough-boy to a Seat in Parliament*, ed. William Reitzel (1933). See also Lewis Melville [pseudonym for L. S. Benjamin], *Life and Letters of William Cobbett* (2v, 1913); *Letters to Edward Thornton*, ed. G. D. H. Cole (1937); G. D. H. Cole, *The Life of William Cobbett* (1924); Marjorie Bowen, *Peter Porcupine, a Study of William Cobbett* (1936); M. C. Clark, *Peter Porcupine in America: the Career of William Cobbett, 1792-1800* (Philadephia, 1939); George Saintsbury, "William Cobbett," *Collected Essays and Papers* (1923), I. 268-301.

[19] F. W. Hackwood, *William Hone, His Life and Times* (1912); Augustus de Morgan, "Hone's Famous Trials," *A Budget of Paradoxes* (Chicago, 1916), I. 180-187; W. H. Wickwar, *The Struggle for the Freedom of the Press, 1819-1832* (1928).

[20] Theophila Carlile Campbell, *The Battle of the Press as told in the Story of the Life of Richard Carlile* (1899).

Jeremy Bentham [21] (1748-1832) had begun to promulgate at a much earlier date began to bear practical fruit. His theory of the pursuit of happiness is open to much question; but at a time when the social conscience was awakening, the doctrine of the "greatest happiness of the greatest number" was a criterion of practical service. It made for reforms in the direction of peace and public order. Bentham's chief concern was not with private morals but with the betterment of society. He was no revolutionary but trusted in parliamentary procedure, advocating governmental supervision but not governmental control. His was a logical rather than a historical method. For the heritage of the past he had an entire contempt unless a reason for survival could be found in a satisfactory answer to his persistent question: "What is its use?" The test of usefulness was of utmost value in the revision and codification of the law. He was especially active in the reform of criminal law; but less directly his doctrines bore upon the problem of a fairer and wider suffrage. Through his disciples, James Mill [22] (1773-1836) and John Stuart Mill [23] (1806-1873), who put much of his memoranda into final shape, he became the father of the Utilitarian school of philosophy.

*The Re-*
*form Bill*

Against this background of reform the Tories held office during the eighteen-twenties. The death of Castlereagh opened the era of George Canning's dominance (1822-1827). Canning represented a liberal Toryism which was opposed to the high Toryism of Wellington and Eldon. This division and the separation of the Whigs into three groups had the advantage that different sides of public opinion were reflected in Parliament. The prosperity of the early twenties was a support to public order and good feeling. After Canning's death, power came into the hands of the more reactionary Tories; but so great was the pressure of public opinion that they repealed the Test and Corporation Act (1828) and emancipated the Roman Catholics (1829). The pressure for parliamentary reform was led by Francis Place (1771-1854) whose tailor-shop was the rallying-ground of moderate radicalism. Place was active in gathering petitions presented to Parliament by his collaborator, Joseph Hume. The French Revolution of July, 1830 was a further incentive. There was an outbreak of strikes, violent agitation, and arrests. The Whigs' concession to the demand for a more just representation was due to their realization of the strength of popular opinion. There is no need here to repeat the familiar story of the confusion between party lines, the swift

[21] Bentham possessed private means which enabled him to pursue his interests. He studied law but was more concerned with the reform of legal abuses than with establishing a practice. His *Fragment on Government* (1776), published anonymously, was a criticism of the English Constitution and manifested both his indifference to historical considerations and his test of utility. In 1789 appeared his *Principles of Morals and Legislation*. He worked for the abolition of the system of transportation for crime, and the establishment of prisons on lines invented by himself. In 1823 he founded *The Westminster Review* as the organ of philosophic radicalism.

[22] The elder Mill collaborated with Bentham and wrote voluminously on history (*The History of India*, 1818), economics (*Elements of Political Economy*, 1821), psychology (*Analysis of the Human Mind*, 1829), and public affairs. As an economist he was a follower of David Ricardo; as a psychologist he developed associationism. In his political writings he advocated a wide extension of the franchise. He was one of the founders of the University of London (1825).

[23] On the younger Mill see below, ch. xxi.

alternations of governments, the threats uttered by the reformers, and the prophecies of disaster made by the reactionaries. In the end fifty-six boroughs were disfranchised and the membership of thirty others was reduced. Representation was given to many new centers of population. The franchise was limited to householders, copyholders, leaseholders, and freeholders. The day of manhood suffrage was still far off and the laboring classes remained in large part without direct representation. The Reform Bill of 1832 shifted the center of political power to the middle classes.

# II

## Romanticism

The French Revolution, the Napoleonic Wars, and the progress of domestic reform enlarged the boundaries and enriched the content of English romanticism,[1] but these social and political events did not initiate the movement. For its origins search must be made deep into the past, perhaps into the very nature of the human spirit. Upon that quest we cannot embark here. The word *romans* meant originally a vernacular descended from the Latin; then the literature written in the vernacular; and then the prevailing kind of that literature. The adjective *romantic* (with variants) first appeared in English in the mid-seventeenth century as a word to describe the fabulous, the extravagant, the fictitious, and the unreal. From this disrepute it was rescued during the following hundred years by being used to describe pleasing scenes and situations of the sort appearing in "romantic" fiction and poetry.[2] Gradually the term *Romanticism* came to be applied to the resurgence of instinct and emotion which the prevalent rationalism of the eighteenth century never wholly suppressed. More or less timid and tentative manifestations of this revolt against "common sense" have been recognized in the previous section of this History. The choice of the word *Romanticism* was perhaps unfortunate, because it begs the question whether there is any such single cultural phenomenon in Europe; but it is too firmly fixed to be discarded. The confusion prevalent in recent discussions of the matter may be clarified in a measure if we remember that it springs from the use of the same term for different tendencies. Romantic phenomena vary in different countries, and even within the same country no two writers are necessarily romantic in the same way or to the same degree, nor is a writer necessarily romantic in all his work or throughout his life. The term some-

---

[1] H. N. Fairchild, *The Romantic Quest* (1931), to which this chapter is especially indebted; H. N. Fairchild, Elizabeth Nitchie, and others, "Romanticism: a Symposium," *PMLA,* LV (1940). 1-60; Paul Elmer More, *The Drift of Romanticism* (1913); Irving Babbitt, *Rousseau and Romanticism* (1919); Lascelles Abercrombie, *Romanticism* (1926); F. L. Lucas, *The Decline and Fall of the Romantic Ideal* (1936); B. I. Evans, *Tradition and Romanticism* (1940); Jacques Barzun, *Romanticism and the Modern Ego* (1944); Ernest Bernbaum, *Guide through the Romantic Movement* (1930), especially pp. 438-459; Sir H. J. C. Grierson, "Classical and Romantic," in *The Background of English Literature* (1925); W. P. Ker, "Romantic Fallacies," in *The Art of Poetry* (1921); Alfred North Whitehead, "The Romantic Reaction," in *Science and the Modern World* (1925); C. H. Herford, "Romanticism in the Modern World," *E&S,* VIII (1922). 109-134; A. O. Lovejoy, "On the Discrimination of Romanticisms," *PMLA,* XXXIX (1924). 229-253. — Annual bibliographies on the Romantic Movement have been published in *ELH* (1937-49), *PQ* (1950-64), and *ELN* (1965-    )

[2] Logan P. Smith, *Four Words, S. P. E. Tract,* No. XVII (1924), pp. 3-17.

times implies a theory, a formulated code, a "school"; but in England romanticism was informal and almost wholly unattached to any doctrinaire program. Though often used of writers in rebellion against classical rules of composition, romanticism is not merely a matter of technique. It is true that many of these writers were deficient in critical control of their material, but the technical excellencies usually praised as classical may be found in association with elements of romanticism. As a recognition of the need to discriminate among many tendencies, it has been proposed that the plural *romanticisms* be employed; but other scholars, rejecting this counsel of despair, pursue the quest for some underlying principle or common denominator binding together the various phenomena of this movement of thought and emotion.

The romanticist is "amorous of the far." He seeks to escape from familiar *"Amorous* experience and from the limitations of "that shadow-show called reality" *of the Far"* which is presented to him by his intelligence. He delights in the marvelous and abnormal. To be sure, loving realistic detail and associating the remote with the familiar, he is often "true to the kindred points of heaven and home." But he is urged on by an instinct to escape from actuality, and in this escape he may range from the most trivial literary fantasy to the most exalted mysticism. His effort is to live constantly in the world of the imagination above and beyond the sensuous, phenomenal world. For him the creations of the imagination are "forms more real than living man." He practises willingly that "suspension of disbelief" which "constitutes poetic faith." In its most uncompromising form this dominance of the intuitive and the irrational over sense experience becomes mysticism—"the life which professes direct intuition of the pure truth of being, wholly independent of the faculties by which it takes hold of the illusory contaminations of this present world." [3] Wordsworth described this experience as "that serene and blessed mood" in which, "the burden of the mystery" being lightened, he "sees into the life of things." Blake, who seems to have lived almost continuously in this visionary ecstasy, affirmed that the "vegetable universe" of phenomena is but a shadow of that real world which is the Imagination. To the romanticist not the thing perceived is important but the thing imagined. But it is difficult to sustain for long this vision of the archetypal reality. The attempt to find some correspondence between actuality and desire results in joy when for fleeting moments the vision is approximated, but in despondency or despair when the realization comes that such reconciliations are impossible. Thus, Byron's Lucifer tempts Cain to revolt by forcing upon him an awareness of "the inadequacy of his state to his conceptions." [4] A sense of this contrast is expressed by Shelley in those poems in which there is a sudden fall from ecstasy into disillusionment. The same sense adds a new poignancy to the melancholy strain inherited by the romantic poets

[3] L. Abercrombie, *Romanticism*, p. 107.
[4] Byron, *Letters and Journals*, ed. Prothero, v. 470.

from their predecessors.[5] If the vision embraces the concept of perfection in this present life ("perfectibilitarianism"), the poet, becoming aware of the unattainability of this ideal here and now, tends to escape from actuality into "the innermost stronghold of his own spirit." There is a "withdrawal from outer experience in order to concentrate upon inner experience."[6] A reliance upon the life within carries with it the belief that in that life there is liberty to realize some perfection inherent in the nature of man. There is a trust in the validity of natural impulses, in "the holiness of the heart's affections."[7] At its boldest (as in Blake) the self-sufficient imagination is utterly confident. "The classical writer," it has been said,[8] "feels himself to be a member of an organized society; the romantic is in rebellion against external law. He asserts the rights of his individuality *contra mundum.*"

*Extremes of Sensibility*      With this confidence in intuition goes an expanding imaginative sensibility which in extreme instances may take exotic and disquieting forms, as in the Byronic concepts of the daemonic male and the *femme fatale.* Emphasizing the abnormal element, some scholars have singled out the morbidly erotic and deranged as distinguishing marks of romanticism, interpreting this as evidence of the part played by the less conscious impulses of the mind and noting that a larger number of English writers of the period approached the borders of insanity or went beyond, than can be accounted for on the ground of mere coincidence. That several were attracted to the theme of incest is sometimes thought to be significant.[9] Yet when all is said, there is little exploitation of perversity in English literature between 1789 and 1832 and, on the higher literary levels, little of the grotesque and bizarre. In line with this reticence is the almost unanimous refusal of the English romanticists to attract attention in vulgar fashion by outlandish pose. William Beckford, who exhibits the romantic mood in an unqualified form, says of the incestuous loves of the brother and sister in one of his tales, that there had entered into them "the ardent elixir of a too exquisite sensibility and the poison of an insatiable desire."[10] This is a memorable formula for the extremes of the romantic attitude; but to select, with Paul Elmer More,[11] as "the essential type and image of the romantic life and literature" Beckford's vision of the damned moving ever round the throne of Eblis with hands upon flaming hearts, is to generalize extravagantly, for the English genius, with its instinct to compromise, seldom pursued the primrose path the entire way to the everlasting bonfire. Is not the hunger

---

[5] See E. M. Sickels, *The Gloomy Egoist: Moods and Themes of Melancholy from Gray to Keats* (1932); Oswald Doughty, "The English Malady of the Eighteenth Century," *RES,* II (1926). 257-269.

[6] L. Abercrombie, *op. cit.,* p. 51.

[7] Keats, *Letters,* ed. M. B. Forman (1931), I. 72.

[8] J. Middleton Murry, *The Problem of Style* (1922), p. 146.

[9] On the abnormal extremes of the romantic temperament see Mario Praz, *The Romantic Agony* (1933), and for an argument based upon psychoanalytic theories of the Ego, Super-Ego, and "Reality Principle" see F. L. Lucas, *op. cit.,* chs. I and II.

[10] Beckford, "The Story of Zulkäis," *The Episodes of Vathek,* trans. by Sir F. T. Marzials (ed. 1922), p. 197.

[11] P. E. More, *op. cit.,* p. 36, referring to the final episode in *Vathek.*

for illusion balanced in the English mind by the steadying influence of common sense? Only seldom are the poet's flights of fancy taken with metaphysical seriousness; rarely is he lost in "an *O Altitudo*." The romanticist's attempts to find a rational justification for the pleasures of the imagination were misleading; but modern opponents of romanticism fall into the opposite error when they repudiate these pleasures because they belong to the realm of desire and dream.

In the romantic mood there has been detected the influence of the Oriental mind which had flowed into the West through the channels of Neo-Platonic speculation. Whereas the classical mind of Greece had sought for the Divine *Anti-intel-* in the qualities of order, restraint, and proportion, the East associated the *lectualism* Divine with the vast and vague. In Gnosticism and other ancient heresies there are elements of what many centuries later came to be called romanticism—the identification of the intellect with desire; the dominance of emotion over reason; the assertion of the Ego above the claims of society.[12] As the eighteenth century moved on, the instinctive side of personality asserted itself ever more strongly and in more individuals. The check provided by tradition, morality, and religion upon human potentialities was relaxed. Rousseau's doctrine that man, by nature good but corrupted by bad laws and customs, should be freed from these and left to the guidance of his own personality, was an impelling force.[13] The Calvinistic conviction of predestination to salvation modulated into "a sense of goodness and freedom" in the individual "which must somehow find corroboration in the nature of the universe"; and even Hume's self-destructive psychology, discrediting the very rationalism by which it worked, "gave encouragement to those who desired to believe in the truth of the unaccountable and the uncriticized." [14] This anti-intellectualism is expressed by Wordsworth when he denounces "that false secondary power by which we multiply distinctions" [15] and by Blake when he pictures Urizen at his sad and evil task of breaking up the primal unity into rational categories.[16] Again, when Keats declares that "Philosophy will clip an angel's wings," [17] we are reminded of one of Blake's emblems where purblind Reason is clipping the wings of Love.[18]

This anti-intellectualism was no sudden manifestation of a spirit of revolt; it had been swelling in volume for many years. In the thought of the predecessors of the great romantic poets there had been a tendency to view learning with suspicion as allied to vice and to commend ignorance as concomitant with virtue. The idealization of the "noble savage," the peasant, and the child had come about in greater or less degree long before Coleridge

[12] P. E. More, *op. cit.*, pp. 21-31.
[13] The influence of Rousseau upon romanticism was stressed by Irving Babbitt, *op. cit.* and by T. E. Hulme in "Romanticism and Classicism," *Speculations*, ed. Herbert Read (1924), pp. 113-140, especially p. 116.
[14] H. N. Fairchild, in his contribution to the symposium, *PMLA*, LV. 21.
[15] *The Prelude*, II. 216-217.
[16] *The First Book of Urizen*.
[17] *Lamia*, II. 234.
[18] "Aged Ignorance," *The Gates of Paradise*, Emblem XI; *Writings*, Nonesuch Edition, III.

and Southey conceived their plan to emigrate to America, and Wordsworth chose his dalesmen as fit characters for poetry, and Blake sang his *Songs of Innocence.* The confidence in the intuitive wisdom of childhood runs parallel with the exaltation of the primitive life of rustics and savages; and both are aspects of the romantic "escape" from actuality. This primitivistic tendency was one of the powerful impulses upon the revolutionary movement in France; and conversely, the same tendency received a powerful new impulse from the democratic forces let loose by the French Revolution. But obviously, sympathy with the Revolution cannot be considered an infallible "touchstone" of English romanticism since many of its elements had appeared before 1789.[19]

*The Middle Ages*

The attraction of the remote from social sophistication—the simple, the rustic, the democratic—found various forms of expression. It is a "return to nature." It is behind the cult of mountains and desert islands and the virgin lands of the New World, unstained by the slow contagion of civilization. This primitivism explains the taste for the "reliques" of ancient poetry; it is behind the romantic conception of genius and of poetry as a gift of nature, not an acquired art. With such currents of thought and feeling flowing, it was natural that the Middle Ages were regarded with a fresh sympathy, though not, be it said, with accurate understanding. It is true that there were those who, like Shelley, seeking to reshape the present in accordance with desire, did not revert to the past but pursued their ideal into a utopian future. But to others the Middle Ages offered a spiritual home, remote and vague and mysterious. The typical romanticist does not "reconstruct" the past from the substantial evidence provided by research, but fashions it anew, not as it was but as it ought to have been. The more the writer insists upon the historical accuracy of his reconstruction the less romantic is he. Under the stimulus of the Napoleonic Wars this love of the past tended to become nationalistic, with a special emphasis upon antiquarian and regionalist elements in English history. But this nationalism is an accidental characteristic of some phases of romanticism rather than a component part of the movement as a whole. The tremendous public events of the time brought out the patriotism of the older generation of romantic poets, but the younger generation remained cosmopolitan in outlook.

*The Super-natural*

The remote in place offered an appeal similar to that of the remote in time, and in innumerable cases the two attractions are combined. From castles in "the wind-grieved Apennines" the romantic imagination passed easily to those haunted castles whose magic casements opened upon the perilous seas of fairyland. The archetypal romantic poet "lures his fancy to its utmost scope." In the company of Coleridge we visit the enchanted palace of Kubla Khan, the vampire-haunted castle of Christabel, the demon-

---

[19] The direct influence of the French revolutionary philosophers upon the English romantic poets was formerly somewhat overestimated; but through Godwin and other radicals the new ideas were assimilated into English poetry. See Edward Dowden, *The French Revolution and English Literature* (1897); A. E. Hancock, *The French Revolution and the English Poets* (1899); Charles Cestre, *La révolution française et les poètes anglais* (Paris, 1906).

infested seas of the Ancient Mariner. With Keats we stand in the church-portal on Saint Mark's Eve or attend the wedding-banquet of Lycius and the lamia in the palace at Corinth. Upon the lower levels of romanticism the revolt from intellectualism and "common sense" produced mere spectre-ballads and "Gothicism," but upon the higher levels we have the true "Renaissance of Wonder" of Watts-Dunton's famous definition.[20]

The typical romanticist is a dreamer, though no single writer conforms wholly, consistently, and uninterruptedly to the type. In dreams a great significance attaches to symbolism. A wealth of symbols enriches romantic literature.[21] There is a persistent resort to suggestiveness in language, to overtones of meaning, and to the dreamy associations that attach to words.

[20] "The Renascence of Wonder in English Poetry," originally the introduction to *Chambers' Cyclopaedia of English Literature* (1903), Vol. III; reprinted with additional material in *Poetry and the Renascence of Wonder,* ed. Thomas Hake (1916).
[21] The interpretation of romantic symbolism is carried to extremes of complexity in G. Wilson Knight, *The Starlit Dome* (1941).

# III

## William Blake

### I

The first clear voice of romanticism was that of William Blake [1] (1757-1827). It was almost unheeded. There were times when the failure of his fellow-men to respond to his message moved him to indignant protest; but beneath his anger there was always an abiding happiness, for this neglect was but an incident in the warfare which his imagination waged with spiritual enemies. That the few men who recognized his genius did not comprehend his ideas and that the world passed him by was of little moment to one who knew that his works were the delight of the archangels.[2] The *Descriptive Catalogue* of his pictures closes with these noble and prophetic words:

If a man is master of his profession, he cannot be ignorant that he is so; and if he is not employed by those who pretend to encourage art, he will employ himself, and laugh in secret at the pretences of the ignorant, while he has every night ... a reward for the labours of the day such as the world cannot give, and patience and time await to give him all that the world can give.[3]

He was content with his "great task" which was "to open the immortal Eyes of Man inwards into the Worlds of Thought." [4]

---

[1] *The Writings of William Blake*, Nonesuch Edition, ed. Geoffrey Keynes (3v, 1925); *Prose and Poetry*, Nonesuch Edition (1932), complete but without textual apparatus; *Works*, ed. E. J. Ellis and W. B. Yeats (3v, 1893); *Prophetic Books*, ed. D. J. Sloss and J. P. R. Wallis (2v, 1926). — Geoffrey Keynes, *Bibliography* (1921); Mona Wilson, *Life of William Blake* (1927); Thomas Wright, *Life of William Blake* (2v, 1929); Alexander Gilchrist, *Pictor Ignotus: The Life of William Blake* (1863), ed. Ruthven Todd (Everyman's Library, 1942); Helene Richter, *William Blake* (Strassburg, 1906); Pierre Berger, *Mysticisme et Poésie: William Blake* (Paris, 1907; trans. D. H. Conner, 1914); A. C. Swinburne, *William Blake* (1868); Arthur Symons, *William Blake* (1907); E. J. Ellis, *The Real Blake* (1907); Basil de Selincourt, *William Blake* (1909); S. Foster Damon, *William Blake, his Philosophy and Symbols* (1922); H. L. Bruce, *William Blake in this World* (1926); Osbert Burdett, *William Blake* (*EML Series*, 1926); J. Middleton Murry, *William Blake* (1933); J. Bronowski, *William Blake: A Man without a Mask* (1943); M. Plowman, *Introduction to the Study of Blake* (1927); Denis Saurat, *Blake and Milton* (1920; reissued 1935); Helen C. White, *The Mysticism of William Blake* (1927); M. O. Percival, *William Blake's Circle of Destiny* (1938); Emily S. Hamblen, *On the Minor Prophecies of William Blake* (1930); Laurence Binyon, *The Engraved Designs of William Blake* (1926); Darrell Figgis, *The Paintings of William Blake* (1925); J. B. Wicksteed, *Blake's Vision of the Book of Job* (1910). Mark Schorer, *William Blake: The Politics of Vision* (1946) appeared when this chapter was in type. It presents an "anti-mystical" interpretation of Blake and relates him closely to movements of political and social thought.

[2] See the letters to Thomas Butts, January 10, 1802, and July 6, 1803; *Writings*, II. 199 and 246.

[3] *Writings*, III. 120.

[4] *Jerusalem*, 1; *Writings*, III. 169.

There are three periods in Blake's life. The first extends from his birth (November 28, 1757) to his marriage in 1782 and the publication of *Poetical Sketches* in 1783. Within the second period (1783-1803) we note especially the years 1793-1800 when he lived in Lambeth and the years 1800-1803 when he lived at Felpham on the Sussex coast. During the last period (1803-1827) he lived in London. The first is the time of his apprenticeship in poetry and the arts of design; the second, of his fully coherent powers as a poet and of his earliest mature designs; the third, of increasing extravagance in poetry followed by twenty years of almost unbroken silence, and of full power as an artist, increasing till the year of his death. Throughout it is possible to trace, sometimes clearly, sometimes obscurely, the development of his ideas. There are contradictions of detail which cannot be resolved, incoherences which no amount of exegesis has made clear; but fundamentally there are no inconsistencies; what seem to be such are alterations of emphasis.

From childhood, when he saw a tree full of angels, and his youth, when *The* in Westminster Abbey he had visions of ancient kings, to his old age, when *Visionary* he drew "spiritual portraits" of the mighty dead, he consorted with beings from the world of the imagination, rising ever higher into mystical illusion. Unlike the Christian mystics his apprehension was not of Divinity in its nameless essence but of a cloud of heavenly witnesses that compassed him about. The record of his visions is in his poems and designs. They are not drug-inspired hallucinations or literary fancies. In his youth, the stream of mystical thought in England which, flowing apart from the main current of ideas, had never wholly evaporated, was swollen by the writings of Emmanuel Swedenborg. Reading him, Blake was impelled to elaborate what he conceived to be true in the doctrines of the Church of the New Jerusalem and to refute what was false. He studied Behmenism, Rosicrucianism, and other esoteric ideas which came from Neo-Platonism, Gnosticism, and other well-springs of profound, if often confused, speculation. This reading confirmed him in his confidence in the validity of his own experiences. Into the problem of the causes of mystical phenomena we cannot enter here. Suffice it to say that they are manifested in Blake. There is that sense of the inadequacy of this world to satisfy the aspirations of the soul which in the mystic inspires, in a sort of transport, a realization here and now of the perfections of Eternity. There is the feeling of exultation and power, the sense of illumination, the confidence that the rapt soul is in the possession of absolute Truth. Mysticism not seldom challenges orthodoxy, for it claims an immediate apprehension of Truth from God unaided by any Church to which has been committed the duty of revelation. Blake belongs among those mystics who repudiate allegiance to the Church.

While Blake was an apprentice to Basire the engraver and afterwards while seeking his livelihood from the booksellers, he wrote his first poems.

Poetical
Sketches

Well-intentioned people whom he met at the home of Mrs. Henry Mathew [5] assisted him financially in the publication of *Poetical Sketches* [6] (1783). Among these some pieces of cadenced Ossianic prose are ominous of the turgid style of the "Prophetic Books." *Fair Elenor* is an exercise in the Gothic mode but of an impassioned intensity beyond the capabilities of any Gothicizer. *To the Evening Star* and the four poems on the seasons are suggestive of Collins but with exquisite faltering rhythms which sound an individual note. *King Edward the Third* is an imitation of Elizabethan tragedy crude and boyish enough but with passages of fine energy. There are echoes of Jacobean song, such as *My Silks and Fine Array,* so unexpected in the period of classical decline as to be fresh creations. In the *Mad Song* there is a boldness of metrical innovation for which nothing in contemporary poetry prepares the reader. Everywhere a freshness of utterance springs from the poet's own genius. Joy, laughter, love, and harmony are the prevailing notes. The Muses, who, forsaking poetry, had fled from England, were ready to return. A new star had risen, but there were few to watch its rising.

Innocence
and
Experience

The qualities of spontaneity and simplicity undeformed by sentimentality are more fully apparent in *Songs of Innocence* (1789). This lovely little volume enriched the resources of English prosody. [7] Blake learned from the ballads and perhaps from Chatterton the principle of "substitution" or "equivalents" and carried it beyond the limits of his models, anticipating effects of *Christabel.* There are shifting patterns, quiet modulations from one key into another, or sudden changes in metrical schemes. Accents fall upon light syllables more boldly than in Augustan poetry. Pauses in breathing take the place of missing syllables. The laughter and glee which ring and tinkle through these lyrics are indicative of Blake's personal happiness, but they also symbolize the joy in that primal unity of which the child, type of unfallen mortality, is still aware, doomed though he be to the "shades of the prison-house." As that shadow is the obverse of the light, so are the later *Songs of Experience* (1794) implicit in those of *Innocence.* For that Blake was already apprehending both sides of his thought, the negative as well as the positive, is shown by the rapidity with which *The Marriage of Heaven and Hell* [8] (1790) followed the songs of childhood.

Without qualification or reserve and with an almost terrifying downrightness this strange work denies the validity of the moral law. The god of

[5] Blake was introduced into this circle by John Flaxman, the sculptor. For his own relief and not for publication he composed *An Island in the Moon,* an amusing but incoherent and in parts very coarse satire upon the habitués of Mrs. Mathew's salon. It contains drafts of some of the *Songs of Innocence.* From one passage we learn that Blake had already devised his method of "illuminated printing."

[6] See M. R. Lowery, *Windows of the Morning* (New Haven, 1940), a critical study of *Poetical Sketches.*

[7] See George Saintsbury, *A History of English Prosody* (1910), III. 8-29.

[8] This was issued by the method of "illuminated printing" (the text as well as the illustrations engraved, and each copy colored by hand). With this method Blake had already experimented in the two tiny booklets, *There is No Natural Religion* and *All Religions are One* (both about 1789), in *Songs of Innocence,* and in *Tiriel* and *Thel,* the earliest of the "Prophetic Books."

Sinai is a jealous and evil god. Satan is the type of energy, desire, and will. Action is good; slave-morality is sin. Joy is its own justification. The antinomianism, expressed with splendor and audacity in the famous *Proverbs of Hell,* is intertwined but not completely fused with Blake's positive doctrine of the One-ness of the Human and the Divine. "Those who envy or calumniate great men hate God; for there is no other God."

In the bookshop of Joseph Johnson, Blake met Paine, Priestley, Godwin, *The Early* and Mary Wollstonecraft. He was soon alienated by their rationalism; but *Prophetic* meanwhile expositions of the new revolutionary ideas confirmed him in his *Books* own rebelliousness. In 1791 Johnson published *The French Revolution, a Prophecy.* The metrical form of this poem is the unrimed "fourteener," loosely handled but not entirely undisciplined. Blake viewed events in France as an opening episode in the cosmic warfare which would lead ultimately to the overthrow of morality and law and the triumph of instinct and freedom. From France in the throes of revolution he then turned to the triumph of revolution across the Atlantic, and in *Visions of the Daughters of Albion* and *America, a Prophecy* (both 1793) he interpreted the War of Independence symbolically. The action takes place on two planes, the natural and the supra-mundane; Washington and his colleagues consort with the strange spirits of Blake's imagination. There is some incoherence, but the general drift is clear. Orc, symbol of vital passion and desire, exults in his victory over Urizen (Reason). He tramples to dust the stony law of the commandments and scatters religion as a torn book, proclaiming that

> everything that lives is holy, life delights in life;
> Because the soul of sweet delight can never be defil'd.[9]

In *The First Book of Urizen* (1794) the metrical form is further broken down, the incoherence more pronounced, and the action more tumultuous. Violent, shapeless beings weep and shriek and roar and bellow through the abyss. Urizen finds not joy but anguish in his nefarious task of dividing and measuring time and space, breaking the primal unity into categories, setting up the reign of law, and snaring the five senses in the net of religion. *Urizen* was followed by *Europe* (1794) and *The Song and Book of Los* and its sequel *The Book of Ahania* (both 1795). In these three some of the symbolic characters and their actions have defied the ingenuity of all the commentators.

The "Lambeth Period" was at first fairly prosperous. Blake received numerous commissions to engrave the designs of other artists, and also gave drawing-lessons to a few pupils. His fecundity of invention was shown in no less than 537 designs for Young's *Night Thoughts* (1797). But in 1798 commissions fell off and he plunged into the composition of the longer "Prophetic Books." To this time belongs *The Four Zoas* (also called *Vala*) which he never engraved. This obscure chaos of dross and treasure later

[9] *America; Writings,* i. 265.

served as a reservoir of incidents and ideas drawn upon for the *Milton* and *Jerusalem.*

When penury threatened in 1799, Blake found in Thomas Butts a generous friend.[10] Through Flaxman he also met William Hayley [11] who invited him to live on his estate at Felpham. The next three years saw the tragicomedy of the relations of a great genius with a kindly but overbearing patron who had no conception of the quality of the man whom he sheltered. At first all went well; Felpham was a paradise. But as Blake found himself obliged not only to furnish designs for Hayley's books but to listen to his verses, while his own work was blandly discouraged or ignored, happiness turned to uneasiness and then into resentment. Gradually there was a spiritual restoration. He busied himself with the designs for Milton's poems and the Bible. Hayley's loyalty during the quarrel with the drunken soldier Schofield satisfied Blake that he was a friend; and when they parted in the autumn of 1803 it was upon amicable terms.

Once more in London, Blake was at first cheerfully active. He began the *Milton,* on which he worked till about 1808, and the *Jerusalem,* which occupied him intermittently till 1820. Between 1804 and 1809 there was much painting and engraving. In the ill treatment which he received from R. H. Cromek, print-seller and publisher,[12] he saw an incident in his warfare with the powers of darkness. In 1809 he issued the *Prospectus* interpreting his engraving of the Canterbury Pilgrims, and the greatest of his prose works, the *Descriptive Catalogue* for the exhibition of his paintings which he now held and which was almost completely ignored. This and other writings of the time are eloquent of his sense of neglect but also of his entire self-confidence. After the failure of the exhibition he passed into almost

complete obscurity. "I am hid," he wrote.[13] Till 1818 there are no extant letters. Hayley and even Butts disappear. Journeyman-work as an engraver supported him and his wife, and there was much painting in water-color, but save for work on *Jerusalem* there was little poetry. The view, however, that his increasing mystical tendency destroyed in him the power to write is scarcely tenable, for in 1818 he showed undiminished energy in *The Everlasting Gospel* and in the final version of *The Gates of Paradise*. New friends now appeared: John Linnel, an artist; John Varley, painter and astrologer; Henry Crabb Robinson, the diarist, who left invaluable impressions of Blake; and a group of young artists who gathered round the aging genius.[14]

---

[10] Butts was for years a steady purchaser of Blake's works. See Blake's *Letters to Thomas Butts,* facsimiles of the manuscripts, introduction by Geoffrey Keynes (1926).

[11] William Hayley (1745-1820), friend and biographer of Cowper, was a well-to-do amateur of letters, critic, poetaster (*The Triumphs of Temper* (1781) and other works), connoisseur, and something of an arbiter of taste.

[12] Cromek commissioned Blake to make the designs for Blair's *Grave* (1808) but engaged another artist to engrave the plates. He saw Blake's design for the Canterbury Pilgrims, pirated the idea, and commissioned Thomas Stothard to make a rival engraving. Blake's lampoons on Cromek were committed to a note-book and not intended for publication.

[13] An annotation to Sir Joshua Reynolds' *Discourses; Writings,* III. 5.

[14] The gentle pastoralism of Blake's designs for Thornton's edition of Virgil's *Eclogues* influenced these disciples, especially Samuel Palmer. See Laurence Binyon, *The Followers of William Blake* (1926). Palmer was a connecting link between Blake and the Pre-Raphaelites.

To the last years of intense activity in the graphic arts belong the woodcuts for Thornton's *Virgil,* the "spectral" portraits, the illustrations to the *Divine Comedy,* and the *Job.* Gradually, but in serenity and spiritual joy, Blake's health failed, and he died on August 12, 1827. The site of his grave in Bunhill Fields is unknown. Frederick Tatham, a friend of orthodox mind, destroyed the plates of his engravings and burned or dispersed his manuscripts.

## II

In the eighteenth century Gothic art was what English genius, too long *Blake's* fettered with conventions, needed and was groping after. Blake found it in *Symbolism* boyhood and it did his genius harm. His mind was undisciplined; it lacked the balance, scope, and tolerance which a classical training might have provided. Disgust with classical art (known to him only in plaster replicas of late Greco-Roman statues) closed his imagination to a whole series of traditional forms. The medieval tombs at Westminster confirmed an instinctive taste for the enormous and distorted; and from amorphous things he sought to shape his symbols. The mystic movement of his mind required metaphor; he saw not likenesses but identities. Upon an age not accustomed to think in symbols he tried to impose those of his own devising or drawn from esoteric sources. The task would have been difficult had he tried to force upon rationalists the traditional symbolism of Christianity or such august pagan symbols as Fortuna or Chronos. As it was, from the first his purpose was hopeless of success. His imagination was "in rebellion, not only against the limits of reality, but against the only means by which he could make vision visible to others." [15] He possessed his own associations but could communicate only a fraction of them, leaving scattered clues but no key to unlock all doors. He held that "that which is not too explicit is fittest for instruction, because it rouses the faculties to act." [16] But the faculties, overdriven, may lapse into lethargy. He defined "the most sublime poetry" as "Allegory addressed to the Intellectual powers while it is altogether hidden from the Corporeal Understanding." [17] But he relied too confidently upon powers not as extraordinary as his own and lacking his private key to the great secrets. "He forgets," it has been said,[18] "that he is talking to men on the earth in some language which he learnt in heavenly places." His symbolism embraces all time and space; vague, tremendous forms with uncouth and hideous names; contemporary events and people; personages of the past; continents, oceans, and points of the compass; provincial towns; districts of London; incidents in his own life. Many of the actors in his mighty drama remain mere names; from others a meaning may be wrested by care-

[15] Arthur Symons, *William Blake,* p. 217.
[16] *Writings,* II. 175.
[17] *Ibid.,* II. 246.
[18] Arthur Symons, *William Blake,* p. 84. On the distinction between single vision, twofold, three-fold, and even four-fold vision in Blake see J. W. Beach, *The Concept of Nature in Nineteenth Century Poetry* (1936), pp. 112-113.

ful collation of reference with reference. Whether the result is worth the effort is a question which the interpreters, dazzled by the light they have disclosed, are perhaps not best qualified to judge.

Upon the "wide, wallowing waves" of shifting and partially contradictory detail the main themes float apprehensibly. Blake continued to love all the forms of nature so long as they are understood to be but the phenomenal expression of the Divine Reality, and he never ceased to draw imagery from the natural world. But since "Mental Things are alone Real," there is in the later "Prophetic Books" scorn and even hatred of the symbol. Hence his disapproval of the poetry of Wordsworth who, he thought, loved the mere phenomenon and forgot the Reality of which it was but the sign. Poetry founded upon reason (Pope and Dryden); realistic art (as represented by the Venetians, Rubens, and Reynolds); rationalism (as represented by Voltaire and Rousseau); and science or "Single Vision" (of which Bacon, Newton, and Locke are the usual symbols)—all these come within the compass of Blake's indignation as agents of Urizen.

*The Cosmic Warfare*

The mythology of the "Prophetic Books" is a perversion of Milton's theodicy, reënforced from Job, the apocalyptic books of the Bible, and such texts as Eph. 6:12, from Boehme and Swedenborg, notions of the Neo-Platonic Trinity perhaps derived from the English Platonist Thomas Taylor, and from fragments of a long tradition of occultism. In this mythology Blake recounts the pre-mundane and supra-mundane origins of his beliefs. They are based upon his instinctive dualism; yet he was not a Manichee, for as boldly as the author of Isa. 45:7, he would have asserted that the Lord is responsible for both light and darkness, good and evil. "Without Contraries is no progression," he said; and "To be an Error and to be Cast out, is a part of God's design." [19] The recurrent theme is the War in Heaven, but the battlefield is on two planes: the cosmic and within the mind of man. Blake envisages the destiny of the universe but also (like Dante) the cycle through which the individual soul moves. The process is from Unity through Diversity to the restoration of Unity. Urizen (the Reason), rebelling against the Eternals, is cast out and fashions the world of Time and Space, subject to Law. He is the Creator (Blake often identifies him with Jehovah). He symbolizes discipline, rule, order, limitation, abstinence, asceticism, science, analysis, self, separation from the Unity which is God—who is the Imagination. The force and variety with which this concept is suggested account for the seeming ubiquity of evil and disharmony in Blake's visions. But against Urizen and his cohorts are arrayed the mighty opposites, symbols of Spiritual Freedom (Orc), Poetry (Los), Love (Enitharmon), Passion (Luvah), and other champions. The strategy is confused, but there is an ever-present sense of the mightiness of the issues at stake. The antinomianism is paramount, though only in *The Everlasting Gospel* (which is not a "Prophetic Book") and in short poems is it expressed with

[19] *The Marriage of Heaven and Hell; Writings,* I. 182; *A Vision of the Last Judgment; Writings,* III. 156.

no shadow of symbolism upon its clarity. But though the gratification of desire is freedom and freedom is the only good, and though the attacks upon continence, obedience, modesty, restraint, and discipline are thorough-going, yet there is a standard of conduct, a sanction: not an obligation imposed by church or state, but Love, symbolized in the Christ, the Saviour, and identified with the Imagination, Poetry, Art. (Blake seems not to have recognized that while the Kingdom of Love requires no Law, the absence of Law does not necessarily lead to the Kingdom of Love.) Every act of the sympathetic Imagination is a triumph over Urizen and a step in the conquest of Jerusalem. Thus the soul mounts the *Scala Perfectionis,* "the ever-varying spiral ascents to the heavens of heavens." [20] "Perfect Love casteth out fear." "Love is the fulfilling of the Law."

Blake is representative of the new age in the congenital enthusiasm of his *Blake's* temperament, his exquisite apprehension of beauty, his passion for freedom, *After-Fame* the largeness of his vision, the fascination which the supernatural exerted upon him, his faith in the imagination, his anti-intellectualism, his lyric thought. But, as he said, "Genius is always above the age"; and though not completely ignored he remained almost isolated in his time. Genuine interest in his poetry and (apart from a narrow circle) in his designs dates from the middle of the nineteenth century. His ideas were then found to be in harmony with new ethical and spiritual tendencies. His defiance of traditional morality was congenial to bold spirits. His view of Christ's message as one of joy was a protest against the Carlylean doctrine of renunciation and sorrow. His insistence upon what came to be called "fullness of life" was agreeable to the generation influenced by Swinburne and Pater. His non-orthodox mysticism appealed strongly to Rossetti,[21] and, later, to Yeats. His conviction that the Human and the Divine were One resembled that "Religion of Humanity" brought into England by the disciples of Auguste Comte. It is not insignificant that interest in him synchronized with the first real appreciation of Shelley and with the "discovery" of Walt Whitman by young Englishmen. In our own day Blake's realization of the force of the subconscious and his efforts to break down moral inhibitions have attracted new attention to him, with the consequence that in the spiritual chaos of the decades intervening between two wars there was a tendency to view him as a philosopher whose message the world must heed.[22] Even those who question this exalted status or deny it to him altogether acknowledge the perennial fascination which he exercises as poet and artist and man.

[20] *Europe; Writings,* I. 299.
[21] On the spiritual affinities of these two poets see Kerrison Preston, *Blake and Rossetti* (1944).
[22] Denis Saurat, *Blake and Modern Thought* (1929) and various studies of the last two decades listed in our bibliography; but not Osbert Burdett's biography, which supplies a valuable corrective.

# IV
## William Wordsworth[1]

Wordsworth's claim to preëminence among modern English poets has often been made to rest upon qualities not strictly poetical. He has been loved and revered as a far-seeing statesman, a penetrating moralist, a great critic, a philosopher, a guide and counselor to multitudes of readers. But by success in none of these rôles is a poet rightly judged. He was also a great, albeit not always dependable, artist. In recent criticism this has not always been remembered. He has been made the subject and sometimes the prey of the psychologist and the historian of ideas. The disclosure in 1916 of his French love affair provided "psychoanalytical" biographers with an explanation of his revolutionary enthusiasm, subsequent despondency, so-called "apostasy," and loss of poetic power. This explanation has not survived calm scrutiny, and today the obsession with Annette Vallon is disappearing. More important was the appearance in 1926 of the original version of *The Prelude,* a poem which had hitherto been known only as altered into conformity with the poet's later beliefs.

*The Prelude*—the autobiographical account of "the growth of a poet's mind"—is the primary subject of Wordsworthian studies. To satisfy himself of his capacity to write the philosophical poem on Man, Nature, and Society which he contemplated, Wordsworth felt the need to probe into his memories of the past, tracing the development of his powers. His record

---

[1] *Poetical Works,* ed. William Knight (11v, 1882-1886; 8v, 1896); *Poems,* ed. N. C. Smith (3v, 1908); *Poems,* ed. E. de Selincourt, I-III (1940-6), in progress, with full *apparatus criticus; Representative Poems,* ed. Arthur Beatty (1937); *The Prelude,* ed. E. de Selincourt (1926), texts of 1805-1806 and 1850; *Prose Works,* ed. W. Knight (2v, 1896); *Guide to the Lakes,* ed. E. de Selincourt (1906); *Letters of William and Dorothy Wordsworth,* ed. E. de Selincourt (6v, 1935-1939); *Literary Criticism,* ed. N. C. Smith (1905). — G. M. Harper, *William Wordsworth: His Life, Works, and Influence* (2v, 1916; revised, 1929); C. H. Herford, *Wordsworth* (1930); Herbert Read, *Wordsworth* (1930); H. I'A. Fausset, *The Lost Leader* (1933); Emile Legouis, *La Jeunesse de Wordsworth* (Paris, 1896), English trans., *The Early Life of William Wordsworth* (1897); G. W. Meyer, *Wordsworth's Formative Years* (Ann Arbor, 1943); critical studies: Walter Raleigh, *Wordsworth* (1909); Arthur Beatty, *William Wordsworth: His Doctrine and Art in their Historical Relations* (Madison, 1922); H. W. Garrod, *Wordsworth* (Oxford, 1927); Marian Mean, *Four Studies in Wordsworth* (1928); M. M. Rader, *Presiding Ideas in Wordsworth's Poetry* (1931); *Wordsworth and Coleridge: Studies,* ed. E. L. Griggs (Princeton, 1939); S. F. Gingerich, *Essays in the Romantic Poets* (1924); pp. 91-191; R. D. Havens, *The Mind of a Poet: a Study of Wordsworth's Thought with Particular Reference to "The Prelude"* (Baltimore, 1941); Basil Willey, *The Eighteenth Century Background* (1940), ch. XII; J. W. Beach, *The Concept of Nature,* chs. IV-VI; Eric Robertson, *Wordsworth and the English Lake Country* (1911); Lane Cooper, *Concordance* (1911). — *The Poetry of Dorothy Wordsworth,* ed. Hyman Eigerman (1940); *The Journals of Dorothy Wordsworth,* ed. E. de Selincourt (2v, 1941); C. M. MacLean, *Dorothy Wordsworth: the Early Years* (1932); E. de Selincourt, *Dorothy Wordsworth, a Biography* (1933). — *Letters of Dora Wordsworth,* ed. H. P. Vincent (1944).

must be used with circumspection. Though he realized the danger of con-
founding "present feelings" with those of long ago and knew that his
memory transfigured even though it did not distort actuality, yet he claimed
for the mind the position of "lord and master" over fact.[2] When "the consecration and the poet's dream" were added, incidents took on a deeper
meaning in retrospect than they had possessed when they occurred. Not
only in *The Prelude* but (with some notable exceptions in which the effect
of spontaneity strikes the reader with overwhelming force) generally
throughout his poetry he wrote from a point of view in after-time. Hence
there is much pathos in Wordsworth, but little or no command of tragedy.
He is the least dramatic of great poets. Few men and women in his pages
stand out with individualized clarity. In human portraiture as in his landscapes
he does not scrutinize minutely but selects the traits that appeal to him;
and even these he views from a distance, as it were. He has been called a
great narrative poet; but he is not, for he does not so much tell a story as
dwell upon the impression of an event or character upon himself. This self-
centeredness, to which Hazlitt and Keats called attention, might be repellent
(as, indeed, it is to some readers) were it not that he is a figure so majestical
that an understanding of his development, achievement, and decline sheds
light upon his entire epoch. To resolve the ambiguities in the record is the
task of the scholarship which traces Wordsworth's course from his neo-
classical apprenticeship to his dominant position in romanticism, from his
advocacy of revolution to his support of the established order, from his
trust in the "visionary gleam" to his meek acceptance of divine grace.

The life of William Wordsworth (1770-1850) presents no such clear-cut *The Three*
pattern as does Blake's. His own scheme of the Three Ages or stages in the *Ages*
mental history of every individual—Childhood, the age of sensation; Youth,
the age of simple ideas and emotions; Manhood, the age of complex ideas
and emotions—is too much generalized to serve as an outline. What is
discernible from a distance is the central, lofty plateau of the *decennium
mirabile* (1797-1807). The way to this height moves from his childhood in
the Lake Country, through his career as an undergraduate at Cambridge
(1787-1790) and the years of *Sturm und Drang* (1791-1795), to the years of
recovered serenity and assured purpose (1796-1797). At mid-point in the
great decade Wordsworth married and settled at Grasmere (1802) and in
the immortal *Ode* bade farewell to the visions of youth and welcomed the
consolations of the "philosophic mind." The rate and gradient of ascent are
not identical for Wordsworth as an artist and as a thinker. As a stylist he
rose slowly and awkwardly from the low level of contemporary verse till
the sudden upward movement to the heights of 1797. His progress in
thought was steadier from point to point. In the descent after 1807 the reverse of this process took place. In his thinking the decline into orthodoxy
was precipitate, while for another ten years in poetic power he remained al-

---

[2] Bennett Weaver, "Wordsworth's *Prelude*: the Poetic Function of Memory," *SP*, xxxiv
(1937). 552-563; and "Wordsworth: Forms and Images," *SP*, xxxv (1938). 433-445.

most unimpaired. Yet poems comparable to the best work of the great decade were more and more sparsely interspersed among what Wordsworth himself called (ominously) "valuable chains of thought." After 1817 the poetic decline was rapid, but till about 1835 he remained, as it were, incalculable; that is, though the reader must prepare for the worst, he can never be certain that he may not meet with poems equal almost to the best. Such, in brief, was the progress and regress which must now be traced more carefully.

*Early Poems*

In his earliest noteworthy poem, *The Vale of Esthwaite* [3] (1787), of interest only for some direct transcriptions of Westmorland scenery, Wordsworth mixed Gothicism and sentiment in the current mode. A little later he began *An Evening Walk,* which is chiefly the work of his Cambridge years. For it he borrowed material from various prose descriptions of the Lake Country [4] and also from the bucolic poets who were in fashion in France.[5] In style he adhered to the artificial idiom and vocabulary of the period and in subject conformed to the conventions of regional poetry.[6] No uninformed reader could deduce from it that already, while it was being written, Wordsworth in the summer of 1788 had become "a dedicated spirit," unconscious though he then was of the "vows" made for him; [7] and that in the summer of 1790 during a walking-tour on the Continent he had been brought into contact with revolutionary events. Of his impressions of this tour he left two major records. That written later—part of the sixth book of *The Prelude*—is more trustworthy than the earlier *Descriptive Sketches,* a conventional travel poem, composed in 1792, into which he introduced sentiments which he had not felt two years before. The conception of the Swiss as the ideal society of freemen is founded not upon his own observations but upon his reading of Ramond de Carbonnières [8] whose eloquent prose Wordsworth paraphrases closely in several places. In style *Descriptive Sketches* belongs to the school which he was afterwards to repudiate; and its mingling of history, landscape, and moral reflections is characteristic of the not very attractive genre of which it is a favorable specimen.

On leaving Cambridge early in 1791 [9] Wordsworth passed four months in London and then went for a second time to France. Here he lived till the fall of 1792, pausing but briefly in Paris and remaining for long periods

---

[3] Long thought to be lost. See Ernest de Selincourt, *The Early Wordsworth* (1936).

[4] Especially William Gilpin, *Observations on the Mountains and Lakes of Cumberland and and Westmorland* (1786).

[5] Rosset, *L'Agriculture* (1774 and 1782), Roucher, *Les Mois* (1779), Delille, *Les Jardins* (1780), and other poems.

[6] R. A. Aubin, *Topographical Poetry in the Eighteenth Century* (1936), pp. 217-219; Christopher Hussey, *The Picturesque* (1927), ch. iv: "Picturesque Travel."

[7] *The Prelude,* iv, 309-338. (All references to *The Prelude* are to the line-numbering in the text of 1850).

[8] To a lesser extent Wordsworth was also indebted to William Coxe, *Sketches of Swisserland* (1779), of which Ramond's book is a translation "augmentée des observations faites par le traducteur" (1781). See C. E. Engel, *La littérature alpestre en France et en Angleterre aux xviii^e et xix^e siècles* (Chambéry, 1930), Part ii, ch. v, and Part iii, ch. ii.

[9] On Wordsworth's environment at the University see D. A. Winstanley, *Unreformed Cambridge, a Study of Certain Aspects of the University in the Eighteenth Century* (1935).

at Orleans and Blois. The magnificent chateaux of the region stirred him *France*
to imaginative sympathy with the aristocratic life of the past, but friendship *and*
with Michel Beaupuy, an officer in the revolutionary army, brought him to *Annette*
the popular side.[10] Of the love of Wordsworth for Annette Vallon little need *Vallon*
be said.[11] To them a daughter, Caroline, was born in December, 1792. Want
of funds forced Wordsworth to return to England. His uncles, however,
refused to supply him with money or to help in any way to regularize the
liaison. War intervened and he was shut off from France,[12] though he remained in occasional communication with Annette. The view that in later
years he was plagued with remorse which he sublimated by writing poems
about forsaken women and unmarried mothers has little to commend it.[13]

But anxiety for Annette and Caroline deepened Wordsworth's despond- *Godwinism*
ency when, once more in London, he watched the Revolution degenerate
into the Reign of Terror. England's entry into the war against France
shocked him as a betrayal of the cause of liberty, and to it he ascribed the
opportunity afforded the extremists in Paris to seize the reins of power.
Under the influence of the radicals who frequented Joseph Johnson's bookshop [14] he continued work on *Guilt and Sorrow*,[15] a poem begun in 1791.
In using the Spenserian stanza instead of the couplet and in striving for
simplicity of language and syntax, Wordsworth evinced dissatisfaction with
the neo-classical tradition. The intertwined stories of a soldier's destitute
widow and of a discharged soldier who is driven by penury to crime expose
the miseries of war, the injustices of the penal code, and the wrongs inflicted
by the privileged upon the defenseless poor. This indictment of society is
Godwinian. To the same period (1793) belongs the *Letter to the Bishop of
Llandaff*,[16] which is really a reply to Burke. Bishop Richard Watson, defending the established social order, had expounded in a sermon the wisdom
and justice of God in creating rich and poor. In his noble pamphlet Wordsworth admitted that to put power into the hands of the people before they
were ready to wield it wisely might be, as the Terror showed, only a change
in the forms of tyranny. But he defended the republican principle, blaming
upon iniquitous institutions that "terrific reservoir of guilt and ignorance" [17]

[10] On the character and opinions of Michel-Armand Beaupuy see *The Prelude*, IX. 288-552.
On Wordsworth and the French Revolution see, in addition to authorities already cited, Sir
H. J. C. Grierson, *Milton and Wordsworth* (1937), ch. VII.
[11] See, in addition to all the biographies published since Professor Harper's disclosure of
the story in 1916, Émile Legouis, *William Wordsworth and Annette Vallon* (1922) and
*Wordsworth in a New Light* (1923).
[12] There is some evidence that he returned to France in the autumn of 1793. If he did so,
he ran a great risk and there is no evidence that he saw Annette. See G. M. Harper, "Did
Wordsworth Defy the Guillotine?", *The Quarterly Review*, CCXLVIII (1927). 254-264, and
letters in *LTLS*, May 1 and 29 and June 12, 1930.
[13] These poems are *The Ruined Cottage* (afterwards imbedded in *The Excursion*, I. 871-
916), *The Thorn*, and *Ruth*.
[14] Johnson published *An Evening Walk* and *Descriptive Sketches* (both 1793).
[15] This poem was repeatedly revised. The present ending with the soldier's acceptance of
his death as an expiation probably takes the place of an original condemnation of capital
punishment. See O. J. Campbell and Paul Mueschke, "Wordsworth's *Guilt and Sorrow*," *MP*,
XXIII (1926). 293-306; and R. D. Havens' comments, *RES*, III (1927). 71-73.
[16] First published in *Prose Works*, ed, Grosart, I. 3-23.
[17] *The Prelude*, X. 476-480.

which must burst and flood the land before a new order, based upon political justice, could be secured. The comments upon hereditary privileges, the laws for the protection of property, the penal code, and the miseries of war expressed the sentiments of the English radicals. It is unknown whether this letter was sent to Watson. It was not published. To have advertised an open alliance with the extremists might have cut short a career as a poet before it was well begun.

Forced by his radical convictions to suppress his patriotic instincts and to condone the Terror, Wordsworth was in an unhappy state of mind. He attempted a satire on Pitt and English society but soon abandoned it. Gradually he was tempted into the region of abstract Godwinian speculation; but reliance upon syllogistic reasoning brought him to the point where he "yielded up moral questions in despair." [18] The distrust of logic is not, however, to be understood as a repudiation of "Reason in her highest mood"; there is the same distinction which Kant had drawn and Coleridge was to draw between the "higher" reason and the understanding.[19] From the slough of despond into which he fell in 1793 Wordsworth extricated himself with painful slowness. It is impossible to trace here the course of his spiritual *"Despond-* convalescence. The transition came in the autumn of 1795 when, having *ency* settled at Racedown with his sister Dorothy,[20] he turned from France and *Corrected"* Godwin to a political philosophy more in harmony with Burke, and to the loveliness of the natural world. Dorothy's companionship and a legacy which relieved his financial anxieties played their parts in this recovery. Thwarted political enthusiasm was turned into imaginative channels; and in 1796-1797 he wrote the tragedy of *The Borderers.*[21] This laborious effort in the "German" fashion is of slight moment as drama but of much as a milestone on Wordsworth's progress. The story of the villain Oswald who, after committing a crime, banishes remorse by condemning all human feeling as weakness and thus becomes a malignant moral skeptic is intended to demonstrate that though the attempt to live by the light of reason may be a noble aspiration, yet to discard affections and "prejudices" leaves not reason but the passions supreme. The play is, moreover, not merely a negation of Godwinism but an affirmation of the reconciliation of man and nature.[22]

The poet had met Coleridge in 1795, and by the summer of 1797, when the Wordsworths moved to Alfoxden, near Nether Stowey where Coleridge lived, the friendship had ripened into intimacy. Coleridge's influence gradually "turned Wordsworth's work from fragmentary descrip-

---

[18] *The Prelude,* XI. 305.
[19] J. W. Beach, "Reason and Nature in Wordsworth," *JHI,* 1 (1940). 335-351.
[20] Bergen Evans and Hester Pinney, "Racedown and the Wordsworths," *RES,* VIII (1932). 1-18.
[21] Not published till 1842. No early draft exists to show how much it was revised. A preface, long believed to be lost, has been recovered; see E. de Selincourt, *Oxford Lectures on Poetry* (1934), pp. 157-179.
[22] O. J. Campbell and Paul Mueschke, *"The Borderers* as a Document in the History of Wordsworth's Aesthetic Development," *MP,* XXIII (1925-1926). 465-482.

tions of impressions and emotions into the expression of a comprehensive *The Influ-* philosophy."[23] Whether through this guidance or from independent *ence of* reading. Wordsworth had now absorbed the associationist philosophy of *Hartley* David Hartley's *Observations on Man*[24] (1749). This type of empiricism, which denies the existence of innate ideas, teaches that all sense impressions originate in external things. Through the power of association the simple ideas deriving from sensation combine into larger and more highly organized units. Hence the character of a man's higher ideas is determined by the character of his sensations; the "sense" is the guardian of the heart and soul of the moral being.[25] Each faculty of the mind is produced by a transformation of the faculty next below it in rank; and at the summit is the moral sense. The three-fold hierarchy of sensations, simple ideas, and complex ideas Wordsworth found to correspond to the Three Ages or stages in mental development. When he wrote of those sensations which pass from the "blood" into the "heart" (or feelings) and thence into the mind he was expounding Hartley's psychology.[26] But according to Hartley, the mind has no control over the physical or mechanical necessity by which it acts; he allows it the power of classifying ideas into categories of pleasure and pain, but nothing else. In Wordsworth's view, on the other hand, though experience may be merely passive and in that case the theory is necessitarian, this is not always the case; the influence of natural objects may depend in part upon us; we are then not merely passive recipients but "half create" that which we perceive.[27] This belief may become a claim for the superior validity of imaginative experience over the data communicated by sense. In other words, Wordsworth imposed upon associationism a Platonic principle of mystical insight—"another gift of aspect more sublime."[28]

During the year at Alfoxden Wordsworth and Coleridge, in revolt from *Lyrical* the contorted and artificial phrasing of contemporary verse, evolved the *Ballads*

[23] See the excellent review of Wordsworth's state of mind when he met Coleridge and of the immediate influence of each poet upon the other in Lawrence Hanson, *The Life of Coleridge: the Early Years* (1939), pp. 163-202. The opinion that each poet was incomplete without the other is well stated in F. W. Bateson, "Wordsworth and Coleridge," in *From Anne to Victoria*, ed. Bonamy Dobrée (1937), pp. 546-559.

[24] Wordsworth's debt to Hartley was first fully demonstrated in Arthur Beatty, *William Wordsworth: His Doctrine and Art* (1922). Beatty summarizes his argument in the introduction to his edition of *Representative Poems*. An important corrective to this view is Melvin Rader, "The Transcendentalism of William Wordsworth," MP, xxvi (1928-1929). 169-190. See also J. D. Rea, "Coleridge's Intimations of Immortality from Proclus," MP, xxvi (1928-1929). 201-213. Both articles emphasize the anti-associationist elements in Wordsworth's thought. Other influences than Hartley are brought out in N. P. Stallknecht, "Wordsworth and Philosophy," *PMLA*, xl (1925). 346-361. For the "neo-humanistic" attack upon Wordsworth's naturalism see Barry Cerf, "Wordsworth's Gospel of Nature," *PMLA* xxxvii (1922). 615-638, to which J. W. Beach offers an "Expostulation and Reply," *ibid.*, xl (1925). 346-361. See also O. J. Campbell and Paul Mueschke, "Wordsworth's Aesthetic Development, 1796-1802," *Essays and Studies in English and Comparative Literature* (Ann Arbor, 1933), pp. 1-57.

[25] *Lines Composed a Few Miles above Tintern Abbey*, lines 108-111.

[26] *Ibid.*, lines 28-29.

[27] Coleridge goes further: "We receive but what we give" (*Dejection: an Ode*, line 47).

[28] *Tintern Abbey*, lines 36-37. Compare Lascelles Abercrombie (*Romanticism*, p. 63): "The power of the unknown can only reside within. The senses can but deal with what they know."

theory (towards which Coleridge had long been moving and which had connections with associationism) that poetry should be written in "a selection from the real language of men in a state of vivid sensation"; [29] and in accordance with this theory and with Hartley's psychology they composed many of the poems on rustic and humble life collected in *Lyrical Ballads* (1798). The as yet unnamed *Prelude* was conceived to justify or, more happily, remove the misgivings which Wordsworth felt as to his strength for a yet greater task, *The Recluse, or Views on Man, Nature, and Society*. Of this the autobiographical poem was at first planned as a part; but it grew to independent proportions.[30] After a long interruption there was continuous work in 1804 and it was completed in 1805. As originally planned *The Prelude* had only five books and culminated in the "consecration" episode of 1788. But Wordsworth realized the need to carry the story through the two sojourns on the Continent, the Revolution, life in London, despondency, and release; and he added nine books more. In so doing he enriched *The Prelude* but impoverished *The Recluse* where much of this material might have been used to good advantage.

In broad outline the pattern of *The Prelude* is suggested in the *Lines Composed a Few Miles above Tintern Abbey,* the incomparably beautiful result of a walking-tour in June, 1798. This was inserted at the very end of *Lyrical Ballads with a few other Poems* [31] which Joseph Cottle of Bristol published in September. With this off their hands, the Wordsworths and Coleridge set sail for Germany. Having separated from their companion, Wordsworth and Dorothy passed a somewhat dull and lonely winter at Goslar.[32] To this period belong various narrative pieces afterwards in-

*The "Lucy"
Poems*

corporated in *The Prelude,* and the cycle of five poems commemorative of "Lucy." There has been much speculation as to her identity. Coleridge's idea that the poems reflect Wordsworth's love for Dorothy must certainly be rejected. Efforts to discover an English girl whom he had loved and lost have been fruitless. The view that "Lucy" is purely ideal and imaginary must overcome the not insuperable objection that seldom, if ever, elsewhere does Wordsworth display such objective power. It has been shown that the region of "the springs of Dove" was a commonplace in ballad topography and that the name "Lucy" was conventional in elegies. The exquisite little cycle may therefore be regarded as the poet's evocation in an uncongenial foreign city of an ideal that is simple, humble, rustic, and English.

Returning to England in the spring of 1799, the Wordsworths after some

[29] See Mrs. M. L. Greenbie, *Wordsworth's Theory of Poetic Diction* (1917).

[30] Garrod's opinion that *The Prelude* was begun at Racedown in 1797 is contested by D. H. Bishop, who holds that the beginning was at Grasmere in 1799. See D. H. Bishop, "Wordsworth's 'Hermitage,' Racedown or Grasmere?", *SP*, xxxii (1935). 483-507, and "The Origin of *The Prelude* and the Composition of Books I and II," *SP*, xxxviii (1941). 494-520.

[31] Facsimile ed. (Oxford, 1926).

[32] That the influence of German literature and culture upon Wordsworth, at this time and earlier and later, was comparatively slight is shown by M. J. Herzberg, "William Wordsworth and German Literature," *PMLA*, xl (1925). 302-345.

wandering settled at Dove Cottage on the outskirts of Grasmere.[33] In the *Grasmere* summer Wordsworth and Coleridge were engaged upon the enlarged second edition of *Lyrical Ballads* (1800) which included, besides *Michael,* the finest of the "pastorals," the preface which grew out of Wordsworth's realization that it was necessary to educate his readers by explanation as well as ex- amples of his work. Here, in a central paragraph, is a concentrated statement of his convictions and intentions: to draw material for poetry from humble and rustic life because on that social level the "essential passions" are "less under restraint"; to set forth the chosen incidents in a selection from the language really used by men; to throw over them "a certain colouring of the imagination"; and to trace in them "the primary laws of our nature."

Save for work on *The Prelude* and on the fragment of *The Recluse* which (apart from the magnificent Proem) was not published till 1888, the year 1801 was comparatively barren. The state of Coleridge's health caused in- creasing anxiety; and Wordsworth was conducting his courtship of Mary Hutchinson. But 1802 was an eventful year. *The Leech-Gatherer,* renamed *Resolution and Independence,* of which the germ is recognizable in Doro- thy's Journal in September, 1800, was composed, and the *Ode on Intimations* *1802* *of Immortality* was begun. The Peace of Amiens provided the opportunity for a final settlement with Annette Vallon; and in July Wordsworth and Dorothy met her at Calais. Association with his old love and with their child Caroline heightened by contrast the poet's devotion to his own country, and this was rendered the more ardent by his increasing distrust of Napo- leon's ambitions. The mood had found voice before his departure from England; it reached a climax at Calais; and was still strong upon him for a while after his return. Impassioned protests against Napoleon's suppres- sion of liberty in nations and individuals mingle with exhortations to Eng- land to be worthy of her past glory and of the "exultations, agonies, love, and man's unconquerable mind" which are her great allies. Yet there is a clear-sighted recognition of England's spiritual weakness. "O Grief"—not "O Joy"—he exclaims, "O Grief, that earth's best hopes rest all in thee!" These *Sonnets Dedicated to National Independence and Liberty* are a spon- taneous overflow of patriotic feeling without parallel in English literature since Milton.[34]

Wordsworth married Mary Hutchinson on October 4, 1802, and on that *Farewell to* day Coleridge published *Dejection: an Ode,* which has an obvious affinity *Childhood* to the *Ode on Intimations of Immortality.* In the latter poem the preëxistence theme, which Wordsworth probably derived from Coleridge and which is scarcely more than mythological machinery, has the unfortunate effect of falsifying the poet's characteristic view of Nature and degrading her into the rôle of a foster-mother who weans the child from recollection of the heavenly mansions whence he came. More fundamental is the theme of the

---

[33] When Dove Cottage became too small for Wordsworth's family, he moved twice and finally, in 1813, settled at Rydal Mount.

[34] Amid these patriotic utterances the only sonnet bearing directly upon Wordsworth's personal affairs is that addressed to his daughter, beginning "It is a beauteous evening."

Three Ages which relates the *Ode* to the *Tintern Abbey* lines and to *The Prelude*; and it is with certain passages in *The Prelude* in mind that it is to be interpreted. In intimacy with the natural world Wordsworth had found the corrective to despondency; the beauty of natural objects had made "sorrow and despair from ruin and from change" seem but "an idle dream." [35] These experiences of contact and response had been peculiarly vivid in childhood. His effort now was to recapture in recollection those "spots of time" [36] so that he could draw "invigorating thought from former years." [37] The consciousness that this power of immediate apprehension was passing from him he expressed with poignant foreboding:

> The soul,
> Remembering how she felt, but what she felt
> Remembering not, retains an obscure sense
> Of possible sublimity; [38]

**and** again:

> I see by glimpses now; when age comes on
> May scarcely see at all.[39]

In the light of these passages the *Ode* is seen to be a farewell to the past and an impassioned celebration of the vitality of childhood.[40] The assertion that for the lost gift of apprehension the years have brought "abundant recompense" in the consolations of the philosophic mind does not carry complete conviction.[41]

On a tour of Scotland in 1803, whence he returned with the exquisite *Highland Reaper* and other *Memorials,* Wordsworth met Sir Walter Scott, whose influence is apparent in the *Song at the Feast of Brougham Castle* (1807) and other poems. The loss at sea of his beloved brother John Wordsworth (1805) is the "deep distress" which, in the *Elegiac Stanzas on a Picture of Peele Castle,* has "humanized" the poet's soul, making him aware of the stormy reality of life which contrasts with the poetic dreams of youth. With this brother (and perhaps Beaupuy and Lord Nelson) in mind he wrote *The Character of the Happy Warrior,* and in the same mood the *Ode to Duty.* The three poems are closely related. In the *Ode to Duty* the romantic conviction of the inherent goodness of man has declined into a belief that though there are some *schöne Seelen* whom Nature "saves from wrong," most men must depend for guidance upon the sense of Duty, "stern daughter of the voice of God." The *Happy Warrior* affords a specific illustration of this doctrine.

*Duty*

These pieces, with the political sonnets, the *Memorials of a Tour in Scot-*

[35] *The Excursion,* I. 949-952.
[36] *The Prelude,* XII. 208.
[37] *Ibid.,* I. 621.
[38] *Ibid.,* II. 315-318.
[39] *Ibid.,* XII. 281-282.
[40] A. C. Babenroth, *English Childhood: Wordsworth's Treatment of Childhood in the Light of English Poetry from Prior to Crabbe* (1922).
[41] On the structure and prosody of the *Ode* see Oliver Elton, *Survey of English Literature, 1780-1830* (1920), II. 78.

*land,* and much else, were published in *Poems in Two Volumes* (1807). The collection marks the culmination of Wordsworth's work and the end of the great decade. His reading of the finished *Prelude* to Coleridge at this time thus takes on a symbolic significance: his youth is rounded out. A friendship of several years' standing with Sir George Beaumont, a wealthy patron of the arts, now furthered the drift towards conservatism, and in Coleridge's absence Wordsworth was also drawn closer to Southey, with the same consequences. The course of Napoleon's tyrannical progress through Europe had forced upon the poet a re-orientation of his political and social ideas. The change is marked in the prose tract on *The Convention of Cintra* [42] (1809) in which, while indicating with Miltonic eloquence England's place and duty in the comity of nations, Wordsworth enunciated an anti-democratic doctrine of leadership which foreshadows the "hero-worship" of Carlyle.[43] A respect for tradition which owes much to Burke, a growing affection for the past as enshrined in English institutions, awakened his sense of the political value of the ecclesiastical Establishment and a reverence for the means whereby Christianity has given formal expression to religious concepts. Trust in the inner "gleam" yielded to the acceptance of divine grace through the mediation of the Church. These changes brought to a close Wordsworth's early turbulent spiritual life. His "anticlimax" was at hand.[44] To what degree this decline—for despite special pleading [45] the fact of the decline is undeniable—was due to psychological disturbances resulting from the French love affair and its long aftermath, or to the alienation from Coleridge, or to the acceptance of conservatism, or to an awareness that the themes for poetry to which he had committed himself were exhausted, or merely to a weakening in inspiration not without parallels in the case of other poets approaching middle life, or to all these causes combined, is a debated question which does not admit of a solution acceptable to everyone. *The Decline*

The great task of the succeeding years was *The Excursion* (1814), the central portion of the never finished *Recluse*. The first two books, which were written in 1797, are fastened to what follows rather than fused with it. There is not only a shift in topography but a change in mood; the spirit of social protest and of oneness with the cause of the poor and outcast, expressed at the beginning, disappears, and in the later books Wordsworth seems to look with complacency upon their sufferings, content with the promise of a heavenly recompense for earthly trials. Such was the view of Bishop Watson whom the poet had formerly refuted so passionately. *The Excursion* exhibits a dichotomy not only in structure but in themes; there is a cleavage but awkwardly bridged between those portions which deal *The Excursion*

[42] Ed. A. V. Dicey (1915). See A. V. Dicey, *The Statesmanship of Wordsworth* (1917), a study reflecting the crisis amid which it was written but still of value.
[43] See B. H. Lehman, *Carlyle's Theory of the Hero* (Durham, N. C., 1928), pp. 138-144.
[44] See W. L. Sperry, *Wordsworth's Anti-Climax* (Cambridge, Mass., 1935).
[45] See Edith Batho, *The Later Wordsworth* (1933); Mary E. Burton, *The One Wordsworth* (Chapel Hill, 1942).

with high metaphysicalities and those which recount rather flatly the simple annals of the poor. As in the narrative, so in the style there is a jarring contrast between the homeliness of these stories and the Miltonic sublimity of the speculative passages. Wordsworth was probably insensitive to this disharmony. He heard "humanity in fields and groves pipe solitary anguish" and for this misery he offered counsel and consolation. But the transitions from the one mood to the other, from the chronicler of humble life to the rapt affirmer of immortal glory, are too abrupt. The need for modulation is not satisfied. The general pietistic tone of the poem contrasts strangely with the magnificent Proem or *Prospectus* in which the poet with mystic confidence passes Jehovah and his angels "unalarmed" and ascends to

> breathe in worlds
> To which the heaven of heavens is but a veil.

The four principal characters are but so many aspects or facets of Wordsworth himself: the Poet, who is for the most part a silent listener; the Wanderer, to whom are assigned most of the arguments supporting Christian optimism; the Pastor, who tells the stories of the departed dalesmen; and the Solitary, a disillusioned rationalist who is what Wordsworth, but for the grace of God, might have been, and whose function is to state objections to religious faith in order that they may be refuted by his companions. In the colloquies among these four Wordsworth resumes the argument advanced by Pope in the *Essay on Man*. In the vast Chain of Being man has his appointed place. The defectiveness of his faculties is appropriate to his position in the scale.[46] The principle of universal harmony, an optimistic necessitarianism, supports the argument that "what may seem ill from a restricted point of view is seen to be good by reference to the design and intention of the whole." [47] The "final causes of natural things"—that is to say, the ends which God has in mind—must be kept in view. Wordsworth widens the scope of Pope's argument, resting it not only upon experience but upon faith. He proves nothing except that he is himself convinced.[48] To apply to *The Excursion* the touchstones of great poetry recommended by Wordsworth himself is a profitable exercise of the critical intelligence. In the preface to the collected edition of his poems (1815) he listed the "powers requisite for the production of poetry." These are: Observation and Description; Sensibility; Reflection; Imagination and Fancy; Invention; and Judgment. The list is as illuminating for what is omitted as for what it contains; but if these criteria, such as they are, are applied to *The Excursion* it becomes apparent that some of these requisite powers are absent and others disproportionately relied upon.

Wordsworth followed the *Song at the Feast of Brougham Castle* (1807) with *The White Doe of Rylstone* (1815). Though these poems show some affinity to Scott's metrical romances, the resemblances to typical antiquarian

---

[46] See A. O. Lovejoy, "Optimism and Romanticism," *PMLA*, XLII (1927). 921-945.
[47] J. W. Beach, *The Concept of Nature*, p. 176.
[48] G. M. Harper, *William Wordsworth* (1916), II. 224.

poems are only superficial. Wordsworth was not interested in re-creating the past or in the action of his tales. *Brougham Castle* celebrates the advantages of a life in communion with nature; *The White Doe* exposes the futility of the life of action and recommends a wise passiveness as the cure for sorrow.[49] A new departure, foreshadowed by passages in earlier poems and supported by sympathetic allusions in *The Excursion* to the value of pagan myths as symbols of the religious imagination,[50] was made in *Laodamia* (1814) and *Dion* (1816).[51] The Virgilian tone of wistful beauty and austere melancholy in the former poem is profoundly authentic and deeply moving. In the advocacy of rational self-discipline some readers may detect a rebuke to the poet's own passionate youth. The alteration in his conception of Laodamia's fate in the other world—a "weak pity" for her in the original version giving place in the later to righteous condemnation and retribution—is indicative of the change coming over Wordsworth's temperament and outlook. In these poems Wordsworth re-created mythological poetry and established a tradition which his successors from Keats to Bridges were to follow.

The Preface of 1815 contains the memorable distinction (pointing back *Expanding* to discussions with Coleridge many years earlier and forward to the *Bio-* *Fame* *graphia Literaria*) between the Imagination, which is serious and penetrating and detects moral associations, and the Fancy, which is frivolous and arbitrary. *Peter Bell,* a poem of 1797 long withheld from publication, appeared in 1819 and provoked much ridicule. But the poet had now triumphed over earlier neglect. The expansion of his fame after 1814-1815 is shown by Leigh Hunt's estimate of him not only as the greatest of living poets but as the founder and leader of a school of naturalistic poetry which succeeded the artificial poetry of the preceding era. Among the disciples of this new school Hunt numbered not only himself but Keats; and, indeed, the influence of Wordsworth in general and of *The Excursion* in particular was strong upon Keats. It is obvious also in Shelley's poetry and for a time in Byron's. On his visits to London the reverence with which the members of Hunt's circle regarded Wordsworth as a poet was strongly tinged with dislike because of his egotism.[52] In the wider world his fame was growing as teacher and moralist; the "healing power" of his poetry was exerting a benignant influence.

The didactic and austere sonnets, *The River Duddon* (1820), derive little from regional legend, for there was little to be found, and owe to Coleridge's projected but never written poem, *The Brook,* the idea of tracing a stream from its mountain source to the sea. The metaphor of the stream

---

[49] C. B. Bradford, "Wordsworth's *White Doe of Rylstone* and Related Poems," *MP,* XXXVI (1938). 59-70.
[50] *The Excursion,* IV. 718-762; 847-887; VI. 538-547.
[51] Douglas Bush, *Mythology and the Romantic Tradition in English Poetry* (Cambridge, Mass., 1937), pp. 56-70. (Hereinafter referred to as Bush).
[52] Wordsworth saw a good deal of the painter Benjamin Robert Haydon (1786-1846) in these years and addressed three sonnets to him. The impressions of the poet in Haydon's *Autobiography and Journals* are vivid and valuable.

*The Last
Phase*

was employed to bind together the *Ecclesiastical Sonnets* [53] (1822), Wordsworth's homage to tradition and the Established Church. Gleams of the old splendor appear fitfully in both these series. Meanwhile, *Memorials of a Tour on the Continent* (1820) were laborious and solemn records and impressions of a journey through France and Italy.[54] Much time in later years was expended upon the revision of *The Prelude* and upon the preparation of successive editions of the collected works. *Yarrow Revisited* (1835) and *Poems, Chiefly of Early and Late Years* (1842) were the last new publications. During the last two decades Wordsworth's continued interest in public affairs took generally the form of a dread of change. He professed an interest in Chartism; but he opposed parliamentary reform, holding that the extension of the suffrage would put power into the hands of men who would proceed quickly to violence. He opposed the emancipation of Catholics, the secret ballot, and even the abolition of capital punishment for various minor offenses. His sister's tragic lapse into premature senility and a daughter's death were devastating blows under which his fortitude bowed. Always austere and repressed, he now drooped sadly.[55] There are many extant records of the gloom of Rydal Mount in these last years. He died on April 23, 1850, and was buried in Grasmere Churchyard.

[53] Ed. A. B. Potts (1922).
[54] A later tour (1837) which Wordsworth made in the company of Henry Crabb Robinson, the diarist, was not productive of any poetry. Robinson (1777-1867) was a friend of the entire Wordsworth-Coleridge circle and of many other celebrities of the age. In his voluminous diaries he has left invaluable records and impressions of innumerable people. See Edith J. Morley, *The Life and Times of Henry Crabb Robinson* (1935); *Correspondence with the Wordsworth Family*, ed. E. J. Morley (2v, 1927); *Henry Crabb Robinson on Books and their Writers*, ed. E. J. Morley (2v, 1938).
[55] On the death of Southey in 1843 Wordsworth accepted the post of poet laureate but on condition that he should not be expected to produce "official" poems. The only such poem published under his name was actually written by his son-in-law. — For the last phase of his life see Frederika Beatty, *William Wordsworth of Rydal Mount: an Account of the Poet and his Friends in the Last Decade* (1939).

# V

## Samuel Taylor Coleridge

The verdict passed upon Coleridge [1] that his legacy to posterity consists of "a handful of golden poems" and "a will-o'-the-wisp light to bemused thinkers" [2] is one-half disputable, but it points the contrast between the radiant months of 1797-1798 (with their afterglow in 1802) when most of the "golden poems" were written and the long years before and after when Coleridge followed the light, often flickering and uncertain, of philosophy. From his youth up he was both poet and philosopher; the "inspired Charity-boy" of Lamb's famous reminiscence [3] was "metaphysician" as well as "bard"; and though lovers of poetry may regret that the fertile gardens of Xanadu were abandoned for "the holy jungle of metaphysics," it must be remembered that Coleridge conceived as part of his life work the fructification of receptive minds. Not only through his writings but through his talk [4] he impressed his ideas upon such contemporaries as Wordsworth, Hazlitt, and De Quincey and upon younger men of promise, including even John Stuart Mill and the recalcitrant Carlyle. How fruitful was the impregnation is obvious in many fields of inquiry: in the theory and practice of literary criticism, the theory of the state, psychology, the interpretation of German

*Metaphy-sician and Bard*

[1] There is no definitive edition. *Complete Works*, ed. W. G. T. Shedd (7v, 1858); *Complete Poetical Works*, ed. E. H. Coleridge (2v, Oxford, 1912); *Biographia Literaria*, ed. John Shawcross (2v, Oxford, 1907); *Literary Remains*, ed. H. N. Coleridge (4v, 1836-1839); *Anima Poetae*, from the unpublished Note-books, ed. E. H. Coleridge (1895); *Specimens of the Table-Talk*, ed. H. N. Coleridge (2v, 1835); *Shakespearean Criticism*, ed. T. M. Raysor (2v, 1930); *Miscellaneous Criticism*, ed. T. M. Raysor (1936); *Literary Criticism*, ed. J. W. Mackail (1931), a selection; *Select Poems*, ed. A. J. George (Boston, 1905); *Select Poetry and Prose*, ed. Stephen Potter (1933); *Coleridge on Logic and Learning*, ed. A. D. Snyder (New Haven, 1929); *Treatise on Method*, ed. A. D. Snyder (1934); *Letters*, ed. E. H. Coleridge (2v, 1895); *Unpublished Letters*, ed. E. L. Griggs (2v, New Haven, 1933). — T. J. Wise, *Bibliography* (1913) and *Coleridgiana* (1919); V. W. Kennedy, *Bibliography* (Baltimore, 1935); Lawrence Hanson, *The Life of S. T. Coleridge: the Early Years* (1939); Sir Edmund Chambers, *Samuel Taylor Coleridge* (1938); J. Dykes Campbell, *Samuel Taylor Coleridge, a Narrative of the Events of his Life* (1894); H. I'A. Fausset, *Coleridge* (1926); John Charpentier, *Coleridge, the Sublime Somnambulist*, trans. by M. V. Nugent (1929); J. H. Muirhead, *Coleridge as Philosopher* (1930); A. D. Snyder, *The Critical Principle of the Reconciliation of Opposites as employed by Coleridge* (Ann Arbor, 1918); R. W. White, *The Political Thought of S. T. Coleridge* (1938); C. R. Sanders, *Coleridge and the Broad Church Movement* (Durham, N. C., 1942); *Coleridge: Studies by Several Hands*, ed. Edmund Blunden and E. L. Griggs (1934); *Wordsworth and Coleridge: Studies*, ed. E. L. Griggs (Princeton, 1939); S. F. Gingerich, *Essays in the Romantic Poets* (1924), pp. 17-87; L. W. Willoughby, "Coleridge as a Philologist," *MLR*, XXXI (1936). 176-201; Walter Graham, "Contemporary Critics of Coleridge the Poet," *PMLA*, XXXVIII (1923). 278-289.

[2] Sir Edmund Chambers, *Coleridge*, p. 331.

[3] *Essays of Elia: Christ's Hospital Five-and-Thirty Years Ago*.

[4] R. W. Armour and R. F. Howes, *Coleridge the Talker. A Series of Contemporary Descriptions and Comments* (Ithaca, N. Y., 1939). The introduction discusses Coleridge's technique as a conversationalist.

romantic philosophy, the reconciliation of Trinitarian Christianity with Neo-Platonic thought, and other speculative problems. The immense and intense, albeit undisciplined, mental activity which lay behind both the written and the spoken word has been too much obscured by the record of irresponsibility in practical affairs, of grandiose plans unrealized, of promises broken and pledges unredeemed. The friends who, yielding to the fascination of his personality, gave him financial assistance which he was all too willing to accept seem not to have considered their investment wholly unprofitable. This fact must be set against Southey's harsh strictures, Lamb's mockery of the good intentions of the "archangel somewhat damaged," the anxieties and disappointments of the Wordsworths, and Coleridge's oft-repeated self-reproaches.

Samuel Taylor Coleridge (1772-1834), the precocious and dreamy youngest son of a Devonshire clergyman, had acquired many of his lifelong traits of character by the age of ten when he entered Christ's Hospital school. Already he was willing to cadge for small sums of money; already he was planning for himself careers beyond his powers of realization. The faculty of winning friends and the need for affection and the ability to evoke it were conspicuous. At school began the friendship with Charles Lamb, life-long and but once momentarily clouded over. Already a "library cormorant" (as he later called himself), he was in the process of substantiating his later assertion that he had read almost everything and was "deep in all out of the way books." He discovered the Neo-Platonists [5] and unfolded to admiring auditors "the mysteries of Iamblicus." His earliest sonnets, feeble in sentiment, and diction, and structure, were his response to the influence of William Lisle Bowles,[6] in whose insipidities he discerned a sincere nature poetry uncontaminated by fashionable artifice. From the shackles of the contemporary mode Coleridge, however, was not himself free. His addiction to "turgid ode and tumid stanza," [7] clogged with pompous rhetoric and frigid personification, is evident in the *Destruction of the Bastille* (1789), in which he expressed radical political sentiment, and in the *Monody on the Death of Chatterton* which was later (1794) completely rewritten.

Coleridge entered Cambridge in January, 1791, with a reputation for astonishing erudition; but almost at once his career there became so erratic as to disappoint his friends. There is some evidence of fast living. There were indiscretions when he aired opinions which were republican in politics

[5] It is possible, though not proved, that Coleridge knew at this time the translations of Plotinus and Proclus by Thomas Taylor "the Platonist" (1758-1835). He read Taylor's works later, but was already able to read the Neo-Platonists in the original Greek. On Taylor, who also influenced Wordsworth, Blake, and Shelley, see F. B. Evans, "Thomas Taylor, Platonist," *PMLA*, LV (1940). 1060-1079, and authorities there cited.

[6] The Rev. W. L. Bowles (1762-1850) published in 1789 *Fourteen Sonnets* notable for simplicity of diction, purity of form, and sensitiveness of observation, though they lacked sturdiness of thought. His later, longer poems—*The Spirit of Discovery* (1804), *The Grave of the Last Saxon* (1822), and others—are forgotten. *Poetical Works*, ed. George Gilfillan (2v, 1855); Garland Greever, *A Wiltshire Parson and his Friends: the Correspondence of W. L. Bowles* (1926). For his controversy with Byron over the merits of Pope's poetry see ch. xi., note 33, below. — Coleridge was also influenced by Charlotte Smith's *Elegiac Sonnets* (1784).

[7] Byron, *English Bards and Scotch Reviewers*, line 256.

and Unitarian in theology. Debts piled up; from study he was distracted by his love for Mary Evans (whom he had met while still at school); and in December, 1793, he suddenly left the university. The serio-comic episode of his enlistment in the dragoons followed. From this predicament he was rescued by his family and reinstated in Cambridge. In the summer of 1794 came, at Oxford, the first meeting with Robert Southey. The two young *Meeting* men, both infected with radical doctrine, were soon deep in plans to emi- *with* grate to America and establish there a "pantisocratic" community free from *Southey* prejudice and tradition and based upon "the generalization of individual property." Coleridge's immoderate enthusiasm is reflected in certain sonnets on Pantisocracy and in *The Fall of Robespierre* (1794), a worthless drama composed in collaboration with Southey. The same impulsiveness took a tragic turn when, because matrimony was an essential factor in the American scheme, he affianced himself at Bristol to Sarah Fricker, the sister of the young woman to whom Southey was betrothed. When it was "too late" he learned that his love for another woman, Mary Evans, was reciprocated.[8] The reaction from high hopes which bore little relation to reality was expressed in one of the earliest and not least poignant of those many passages of self-depreciation which are not to be judged insincere merely because Coleridge evidently derived a perverse satisfaction from inditing them:

> To me hath Heaven with bounteous hand assign'd
> Energic Reason and a shaping mind,
> The daring ken of Truth, the Patriot's part,
> And Pity's sigh, that breathes the gentle heart—
> Sloth-jaundic'd all! [9]

A long though irregular connection with the newspapers began with the publication in *The Morning Chronicle* (December, 1795—January, 1796) of a dozen *Sonnets on Eminent Characters*—Pitt, Priestley, Godwin, Bowles, and others. Seeking employment, Coleridge went to London, where he lingered long, associating with Lamb and reluctant to face his responsibilities in the west of England. In July Southey practically compelled his return. The two poets lectured at Bristol—Southey on history, Coleridge on politics and religion [10]—as a means of raising money for their passage to America; but Coleridge's untrustworthiness now led to an estrangement which was not bridged over till after Southey's return from Portugal and then without a renewal of confident intimacy. Coleridge had married Miss *Marriage* Fricker in October, 1795; and shortly afterwards he toured England, lecturing and canvassing for subscriptions to a proposed journal of public affairs. Of this journal, *The Watchman,* ten issues appeared in the spring of 1796. By the impartiality of his attacks on both Godwin and Pitt Coleridge managed to alienate both radical and conservative readers. A weak will was

---

[8] *On a Discovery Made Too Late; Poetical Works,* ed. E. H. Coleridge, I. 72.
[9] *Lines on a Friend who Died of a Frenzy Fever;* lines 39-43; *Poetical Works,* I. 72.
[10] Three of Coleridge's lectures were published as tiny pamphlets: *A Moral and Political Lecture; Conciones ad populum;* and *The Plot Discovered* (all Bristol, 1795).

unequal to the drudgery involved in the undertaking; there was too much dependence for "copy" upon parliamentary reports; subscriptions fell off; and soon *The Watchman* "ceased to cry the state of the political atmosphere." At this juncture a few guineas came to hand from Joseph Cottle, who not only published but paid for Coleridge's *Poems on Various Occasions* (1796). In this volume he had intended to include *The Destiny of Nations,* which he had permitted Southey to use as part of *Joan of Arc* and which he now reclaimed and expanded; but submitting to Lamb's advice he suppressed it and it was not published till 1817 in its entirety. The most ambitious piece in the volume of 1796 is *Religious Musings* upon which Coleridge had been at work since Cambridge days. In it the French Revolution is idealized; Priestley's Unitarianism is praised; there are signs of adherence to Hartley's psychology and its implications; and a vague current of mysticism marks the drift away from Godwinian rationalism. One or two small poems, such as the *Song of the Pixies,* show a timid venturing into the realms of the glamorous where Coleridge was soon to be at home. The *Poems* were not ill received and a second edition was called for.[11]

In desultory search for congenial employment Coleridge went about the country, preaching in Unitarian chapels.[12] On one of these journeys he received word of the birth of his eldest son, Hartley, and composed a sonnet in which the Platonic idea of preëxistence points forward to Wordsworth's *Ode.* In the autumn he was in correspondence with John Thelwall, the radical; [13] and to the same period belongs his first admission that he was addicted to opium.[14] A desire to live in the country and the fantastic conviction that he could earn a livelihood by farming led him, notwithstanding the warnings of his sensible friend Thomas Poole,[15] to move into a cottage at Nether Stowey among the Quantock hills. The year 1796 closed with an *Ode to the Departing Year* in which a belief that "Divine Providence regulates into one vast harmony all the events of time, however calamitous some of them may appear to mortals," [16] struggles for expression through the conventional poetic diction.

The spring of 1797 was occupied with a tragedy undertaken on an invitation from Sheridan, the manager of Drury Lane. This was *Osorio.* The plot was adapted from part of Schiller's novel *Der Geisterseher* which was

---

[11] To the second edition (1797) were added poems by Charles Lamb and Charles Lloyd.

[12] At this time Hazlitt first met Coleridge, as he records in *My First Acquaintance with Poets.*

[13] See the famous letter to Thelwall (November, 1796) containing the self-portrait ("indolence capable of energies"); *Letters,* ed. E. H. Coleridge, 1. 178-181. Thelwall visited Coleridge at Nether Stowey.

[14] *Letters,* 1. 173 and 240. Opium had, however, been prescribed much earlier to alleviate the rheumatic pains from which Coleridge suffered from childhood.

[15] See the letter to Poole of mid-December, 1796; *Letters,* 1. 187-193. — In later years Poole was a tower of strength to Mrs. Coleridge. See *Minnow among Tritons; Mrs. S. T. Coleridge's Letters to Thomas Poole, 1799-1834,* ed. Stephen Potter (1934). See also Mrs. Henry Sandford, *Thomas Poole and his Friends* (2v, 1888). — Another loyal and generous supporter of Coleridge at a later date was Thomas Wedgwood, one of the famous family of manufacturers of pottery.

[16] Coleridge's Argument prefixed to the *Ode; Poetical Works,* ed. E. H. Coleridge, 1. 160.

soon to contribute something to *The Ancient Mariner*. The play caters to some extent to the "Gothic" taste with an incongruous but not unracteristic mingling of a politico-philosophic strain. On the ground of the obscurity of the later acts it was, after long delay, rejected. Many years later (1813) Coleridge revised it and as *Remorse* it reached the stage.

The first meeting with Wordsworth at an undetermined date late in 1795 had developed by the summer of 1797 into close friendship. Coleridge visited the Wordsworths at Racedown in June [17] and persuaded them to move to Alfoxden. The Wordsworthian influence is apparent in *This Lime-tree Bower My Prison* both in its stylistic freedom from Augustan idiom and in the heightened sensitiveness to the minutiae of the natural world. Parallels between Coleridge's poetry of the succeeding year and the contemporary entries in Dorothy's Journal show that not to her brother only (as he testified) but to Coleridge also the "exquisite sister" gave eyes and ears. During the wonderful half-year between November, 1797, and May, 1798, *The Rime of the Ancient Mariner*, the First Part of *Christabel*, and the fragment of *Kubla Khan* were composed; a projected tale, *The Wanderings of Cain*, was outlined; the theory of poetic diction was discussed; and a decision was reached as to the respective shares of the two poets in a volume to be published jointly. Wordsworth was to give "the charm of novelty to things of every day," while Coleridge's province was to be "persons and characters supernatural, or at least romantic," but with an attachment to them of "a human interest and a semblance of truth sufficient to procure for these shadows of imagination that willing suspension of disbelief for the moment, which constitutes poetic faith." [18]

For a study in "the ways of the imagination" as exemplified in the history of the composition of *The Ancient Mariner* there is abundant material in the records of Coleridge's "cormorant" reading.[19] For years a chaotic medley of ideas and images had sunk into "the deep well" of his "unconscious cerebration." An adept in recondite lore of many kinds, he had been accustomed to follow from book to book chance references to anything that attracted his all-devouring attention. In the literature of travel—from Herodotus and Strabo through Hakluyt and Purchas to Bartram and Bruce —he had found multitudes of facts and fictions about the sea in storm and calm, about tropic heat and austral cold, about phosphorescent and auroral phenomena, about strange creatures of the deep. For his never realized project of six *Hymns* to the Sun, the Moon, and the Four Elements he had been accumulating ideas of the most varied kinds, from Neo-Platonic speculations on tutelary spirits to the latest researches reported in the scientific publications of the day. At Bristol he had consorted with seafaring men. He had read of ships guided by the dead. From Schiller

*The Ancient Mariner*

[17] See the enthusiastic impressions of Wordsworth ("I feel myself a little man by his side"), *Letters*, I. 221.
[18] Coleridge, *Biographia Literaria*, beginning of ch. XIV.
[19] See J. L. Lowes, *The Road to Xanadu: A Study in the Ways of the Imagination* (1927), one of the most fascinating of all products of literary research.

and other sources his imagination had been fired by the legend of the Wandering Jew and, as we have seen, he was meditating a story upon the doom of Cain. Deep in the unconscious these and numberless other images became associated together. Wordsworth's suggestion (which he derived from an incident in George Shelvocke's *Voyage*) of the theme of retribution for the crime of slaying a bird beloved by an elemental spirit [20] acted upon all these images as a drop of chemical upon a solution held in suspense. The poem was precipitated; or rather, more accurately and changing the metaphor, the ideas, richly encrusted with associated imagery, rose to the surface of thought, there to be subjected to the conscious working of "the shaping spirit of imagination." The choice of the ballad-measure, the discussions with Wordsworth on the reform of poetic diction, and a white-hot imaginative apprehension of his subject combined to rid Coleridge of the old trammels of the Augustan style.[21] The resultant poem is the most enchanting of all evocations of the romantic spirit of wonder, winning by means of the clarity of its general design, the realism of detail, and the unanalyzable amalgam of the natural and the marvelous an unreluctant "suspension of disbelief" from every reader.

Christabel    The First Part of *Christabel* was begun after, and finished before, *The Ancient Mariner*. In the Second Part, not composed till 1800, the imaginative tension is somewhat relaxed; and despite Coleridge's assurances that he had the entire design in mind, the poem was never completed. Coleridge thought that he had invented the metre—the line consisting of four stressed and a varying number of unstressed syllables; but it is really a revival of an old form. In its tantalizing state the story has invited much speculation as to his intentions.[22] Fragments of his reading of Percy's *Reliques*, Lewis's *The Monk*, and Mrs. Radcliffe's romances went into the poem. It seems that classical ideas of the lamia and medieval ideas of the vampire, conflated in the person of Geraldine, were to be crossed with the theme of vicarious suffering as expiation for a wrong. After Coleridge settled in the Lake Country he introduced into Part II something of the traditions and landscape of Westmorland. The fire-lore which shone more luridly in the first

[20] To the summer of 1797 (and therefore several months earlier than the conception of *The Ancient Mariner* in November of that year) belongs *The Raven* (*Poetical Works*, I. 169-171), a little poem which Coleridge dismissed as "doggerel" and which is strangely unnoticed by the biographers and commentators, but which is significant because of its freedom from metrical and rhetorical conventions, its faint anticipation of the "magical" quality of Coleridge's masterpieces, and its theme—the vengeance wreaked upon a ship and its company for a wrong done to a bird.

[21] The archaisms of the version of 1798 were much reduced in number in the version of 1800 and there was less of macabre grotesquerie. The beautiful marginal glosses, though perhaps composed at an early date, did not accompany the poem till the version of 1817.

[22] Lowes did not include *Christabel* in *The Road to Xanadu* because he could not discover "the mysterious tracks from which it rose." A. H. Nethercot, *The Road to Tryermaine* (1939), has assembled much interesting erudition and comes nearest to a solution. See also B. R. McElderry, "Coleridge's Plan for Completing *Christabel*," *SP*, XXXIII (1936). 437-455; D. R. Tuttle, "*Christabel* Sources in Percy's *Reliques* and the Gothic Romance," *PMLA*, LIII (1938). 445-474.

version of *The Ancient Mariner* than in the revised form burns mysteriously in *Christabel*.[23]

In *Kubla Khan* (composed, if we accept Coleridge's statement,[24] in an opium-induced dream) the images which had been deposited in the unconscious from Coleridge's reading about subterranean rivers, pleasure-palaces, and other esoteric scenes and marvelous phenomena surged up and were expressed immediately in words without the exercise of conscious art. On waking he began to write the poem but was interrupted by an intrusive stranger, and afterwards neither the words nor the vision could be recaptured; and Coleridge, who persuaded himself that he would one day finish *Christabel*, made no effort to complete this other fragment of haunted and haunting beauty. *Kubla Khan*

Below the level of these three "golden poems" but very memorable nevertheless are other pieces of 1798: *Fire, Famine, and Slaughter*, an excoriating attack upon William Pitt; *Frost at Midnight*, close in sentiment and beauty to Wordsworth's *Tintern Abbey* lines; *The Nightingale*, with its lovely picture of the father stilling his infant's sobs by showing him the moon; *The Three Graves*, an attempt, such as Wordsworth made in *Peter Bell*, to suggest mystery and horror without recourse to the supernatural; and *France: an Ode*, a magnificent plea to Freedom for forgiveness because the poet had mistakenly identified her with revolutionary France. Over these and other things we must pass without further comment. Coleridge's greatest work as a poet was now all but done; and the long remainder of his life must here be surveyed with utmost brevity.

Before his departure for Germany (September, 1798) Coleridge had been busy with his versions of Schiller's *Piccolomini* and *The Death of Wallenstein*,[25] a task brought to completion after his return in 1799. From Germany he carried home quantities of books and the determination to devote himself to philosophy. He was now employed by *The Morning Post*, and some of his articles on public affairs attracted such wide attention that Daniel Stuart, the editor, offered him an editorial position at a handsome salary. Coleridge, however, would not commit himself to a partisan policy— or to fixed obligations. In 1800 he settled at Greta Hall on the outskirts of

[23] What sight met Christabel's gaze when Geraldine laid bare her bosom? Did she have eyes in her breasts? Compare the well-known story of Shelley's hallucination at Geneva in 1816, and the epithet "bosom-eyed" in *The Witch of Atlas*, xi. 8. Or did flames, forked-tipt like a serpent's tongue, jut from her breasts? A tradition that this was the conception may have been handed down in the Pre-Raphaelite circle and is recorded in Watts-Dunton's *Aylwin*. Or was her heart enveloped in flames, like the hearts of the damned in Beckford's *Vathek*? "Bosom-eyed" monsters occur in the travel books Coleridge had read. Whether he had read *Vathek* has never been proved but seems certain.

[24] As does Lowes, *The Road to Xanadu*, Book IV. But see Elisabeth Schneider, "The 'Dream' of *Kubla Khan*," *PMLA*, LX (1945). 784-801.

[25] P. Machule, "Coleridge's Wallensteinübersetzung," *ESt*, XXXI (1902). 182-239. Some of Coleridge's supposed mistranslations have been shown to be due to the fact that he worked from Schiller's manuscripts, which differed from the later published versions. — On the wider subject of Coleridge's relations with German thought and culture see J. L. Haney, *The German Influence on Coleridge* (Philadelphia, 1902); F. W. Stokoe, *German Influence in the English Romantic Period* (1926), pp. 89-143; A. C. Dunstan, "The German Influence on Coleridge," *MLR*, XVII (1922). 272-281, and XVIII (1923). 183-201.

*Opium*

Keswick, and prepared with Wordsworth the second edition of *Lyrical Ballads.* The opium habit had now taken firm hold upon him. Love for his wife, which had never been deep-rooted, faded and died.[26] Increasing anxiety for him found repeated expression in Dorothy Wordsworth's Journal; and at this time Wordsworth drew his portrait in the *Stanzas Written in a Copy of Thomson's "Castle of Indolence."* In October, 1802, he published his last great poem, the poignant *Dejection: an Ode* in which he lamented the loss of the faculty of response from within to the beauty of the natural world and of that "shaping spirit of Imagination" which nature had given him at his birth.[27] Desire to escape from Greta Hall and to seek health in a warmer climate led to his acceptance of a secretarial appointment at Malta, and he was absent from England for more than a year. On his return the alienation from Mrs. Coleridge drifted into a separation [28] which was none the less final because never put upon a legal basis. Henceforth he lived mostly in London. He wrote for *The Courier*; he began in 1808 the first of various courses of lectures on Shakespeare and other poets and on metaphysical topics. During nine months of 1809-1810 he issued *The Friend,* a journal of philosophical, political, and literary opinion, irregular in its dates of appearance, and often dull in its contents, though enlivened with *Satyrane's Letters,* written from Germany in 1798-1799 and afterwards included in the *Biographia Literaria.* The estrangement from Wordsworth in 1810, brought about by Basil Montague's indiscreet report of Wordsworth's confidential warning against Coleridge's habits, increased his despondency. There was, however, a constant though at first unsuccessful struggle against opium. The lectures on Shakespeare in 1812 were attended by the world of fashion and were brilliantly successful. Coleridge, who owed a good deal to Lessing

*Lectures*

and other German critics, emphasized the philosophic aspect of Shakespeare, reading more into the subject than the text always warranted and neglecting the outer form for the sake of what he held to be the inner reality. The dramas were for him a spiritual as well as an aesthetic experience.[29] In 1813-1814 he delivered four courses of lectures, mostly on literary subjects, at Bristol. Through Lord Byron's persuasion and mediation *Remorse* (the revised *Osorio*) was produced at Drury Lane (1813). A second drama, *Zapolya* (1816), was rejected. Coleridge's dark pathway was still illuminated with visionary projects. In 1814 these took the form of a great treatise on *Christianity, the One True Philosophy.* This design came to nothing—or very little; but it marks his severance from Unitarianism

[26] The tone of Coleridge's letters to his wife is generally kindly; but for cruel candor see *Unpublished Letters,* ed. E. L. Griggs, 1. 218-222.

[27] *Dejection* is closely associated with Coleridge's unhappy love for Sara Hutchinson, to which allusion is made in various poems between 1801 and 1810. See T. M. Raysor, "Coleridge and 'Asra,'" *SP,* xxvi (1929). 305-324. The original version of the ode is printed and discussed by E. de Selincourt, "Coleridge's *Dejection: an Ode,*" *E&S,* xxii (1937). 7-25.

[28] After their daughter Sara's marriage there was a partial reconciliation and from about 1822 till the end Coleridge and his wife occasionally met in London.

[29] Augustus Ralli, *History of Shakespearean Criticism* (1932), 1. 126-143. For Coleridge's relation to earlier English criticism of Shakespeare see R. W. Babcock, *The Genesis of Shakespeare Idolatry* (1931).

and acceptance of a Neo-Platonic form of Christianity. That it was intended
to be "illustrated by fragments of Autobiography" shows that he was now
contemplating another work. In 1816 he put himself under the care and
into the household of James Gillman, a physician at Highgate.[30] His determination was to submit to an anti-narcotic regimen "not only firm but
severe." In this year *Christabel* and *Kubla Khan* (both by now famous in
literary circles from recitations and manuscript copies) were published, together with *The Pains of Sleep* (written in 1803) which conveyed a picture
contrasting with the glories of Xanadu. Many more poems were assembled
in *Sibylline Leaves* (1817).

The *Biographia Literaria,* which had gone through numerous vicissitudes, Biographia
at length appeared in 1817. Despite digressions, the first volume was fairly Literaria
coherent, but in the second the plan broke down and it was expanded to
the proportions of the first only by a reprint of *Satyrane,* an acrimonious
critique of Maturin's *Bertram,* and a rambling concluding chapter. The
most important chapters are those on the Wordsworthian theory of poetic
style and those formulating a theory, based upon the Kantian distinction
between the *Vernunft* and the *Verstand* (with heavy obligations to Schelling), distinguishing between the Fancy, which is merely "a mode of Memory
emancipated from the order of time and space" and which, like Memory,
receives its material from the laws of association, and the Imagination, which
transcends sensational material and brings the mind into direct connection
with the ultimate and supersensuous reality.[31] The *Biographia* was harshly
reviewed by Hazlitt;[32] and *Blackwood's*[33] was so outrageously personal
in its attack upon Coleridge's private life that he thought of bringing suit
for libel.

In later years Coleridge renewed intercourse with Southey, was more *Last Years*
closely in touch with Wordsworth, revived for a short time the publication
of *The Friend,* delivered a last series of lectures in 1819, published a miscellany of philosophy, piety, and literary criticism entitled *Aids to Reflection*
(1825), struggled manfully and on the whole successfully with the old
enemy, opium, was almost crushed with the disgrace of his son Hartley's
expulsion from Oxford, and gathered round him disciples of the younger
generation, including Edward Irving, John Sterling, Frederick D. Maurice,
and other religious-minded liberals, who absorbed his discourses at Highgate. In 1827-1828 there was a St. Martin's-Summer revival of the poetic
instinct and he wrote *The Garden of Boccaccio* and *Love, Hope and Patience.* The moving *Epitaph* for his own grave was composed in failing
health in November, 1833. He died on July 25, 1834, and was buried in

[30] L. E. Watson, *Coleridge at Highgate* (1925); A. W. Gillman, *The Gillmans of Highgate*
(1895).
[31] I. A. Richards, *Coleridge on Imagination* (1935). For criticism of Richards' views see
F. L. Lucas, *The Decline and Fall of the Romantic Ideal* (1936), ch. IV.
[32] In the *Edinburgh Review,* August, 1817; *Collected Works,* ed. A. R. Waller and Arnold
Glover, x. 135-158.
[33] October, 1817; reprinted in *Notorious Literary Attacks,* ed. Albert Mordell (1926), pp.
20-62. The authorship has been ascribed to John Wilson, but this is doubtful.

Highgate cemetery. Southey pursued his memory, in private letters, with shocking rancor. Lamb mourned for him during the short remainder of his life. Wordsworth pronounced him "the most wonderful" man he had ever known and referred in magnificent lines to the marvelous intellectual power of

> The rapt One, of the godlike forehead,
> The heaven-eyed creature.[34]

The attempt of Coleridge's literary executors to piece together the much talked-of philosophical and religious *magnum opus* failed; but his nephew, Henry Nelson Coleridge (who married the poet's daughter, Sara [35]), gathered together the *Literary Remains* and published the fascinating record of his "Table-Talk."

[34] *Extempore Effusion on the Death of James Hogg.*
[35] See E. L. Griggs, *Coleridge Fille. A Biography of Sara Coleridge* (1940). Sara Coleridge edited many of her father's writings.

# VI

## Robert Southey, Walter Savage Landor, and Other Poets

### I

The reputation of Robert Southey [1] (1774-1843) has suffered from his *Southey* association with men of far greater genius than was his, from the mass and unevenness of his work, from his undertaking tasks in poetry beyond his powers, and from the circumstance that he is often judged simply as a poet rather than as a professional man of letters. His own self-confidence betrayed him. He was convinced that he was planting acorns which would grow into great oaks in whose shade posterity would find recreation. The trust in posterity has proved fallacious. His epics are unread and—with the doubtful exception of *Roderick*—unreadable; the historical works on Brazil and on the Peninsular War and his editions of various books [2] have been superseded; *The Doctor* may, at most, be dipped into here and there; most of the shorter poems have turned out to be ephemeral; and Southey's reputation as a poet is kept alive by a few things, such as *The Inchcape Rock, The Battle of Blenheim,* and *My Days among the Dead are Passed;* as a writer of prose by *The Life of Nelson* and perhaps *The Life of Wesley;* [3] and as a man by his connection with Wordsworth and Coleridge, his change in political opinions, and his quarrel with Lord Byron.

Yet because of his personal relationships, the early date at which he was active in revolutionary and romantic literature, the significant changes in opinion which are illustrated by his conspicuous example, and his range and choice of themes in prose and poetry he remains an important historical figure. His early life and later years are clearly divided from one another in 1803, when he settled at Keswick. Before that time he had been expelled from school; gained little from life at Oxford; been inspired by the French

---

[1] *Poetical Works* (10v, 1837-1838); *Poems,* ed. M. H. FitzGerald (Oxford, 1909), containing the longer poems except *Joan of Arc,* and a selection from the minor poems; *Select Prose,* ed. Jacob Zeitlin (1916). There is no collected edition of the prose works. *Life and Correspondence,* ed. C. C. Southey (6v, 1849-1850); *Correspondence with Caroline Bowles,* ed. Edward Dowden (Dublin, 1881); *Letters,* ed. M. H. FitzGerald (Oxford, 1912), a selection. — Edward Dowden, *Southey* (EML Series, 1874); Jack Simmons, *Southey* (1945); William Haller, *The Early Life of Robert Southey* (1917); George Saintsbury, "Southey," *Collected Essays and Papers* (1923), I. 239-268.

[2] *Amadis of Gaul,* the *Chronicle of the Cid,* Chatterton's *Poems, Specimens* of the English poets, and so forth.

[3] *The Life of Nelson,* ed. H. B. Butler (1911); *The Life of Wesley,* ed. M. H. FitzGerald (1925).

Revolution to compose an epic on *Joan of Arc* [4] (1793; published 1796) and *Wat Tyler,* a two-act drama which remained long in manuscript; met Coleridge, with whom he evolved the "pantisocratic" scheme and wrote *The Fall of Robespierre* (1794); collaborated with Robert Lovell on a volume of *Poems* (1795); traveled with an uncle in Portugal and Spain; [5] published *Minor Poems* (1797-1799); studied law half-heartedly; visited Portugal for a second time; and completed there *Thalaba the Destroyer* (1801). The radicalism of his youth had been put behind him by the time that he established himself at Keswick for the long remainder of his busy life. He accumulated a vast library and vaster stores of erudition. To the "Poet's Corner" of *The Morning Post* and to other newspapers and periodicals he contributed countless ephemeralities. *Metrical Tales* appeared in 1805. An ambitiously planned history of Portugal never materialized in entirety, but the *History of Brazil* (1810-1819) is part of it. After the initiation of *The Quarterly Review* (1809) he was for many years a regular and voluminous contributor. Meanwhile he had the epic poems long in hand. *Madoc* appeared in 1805, *The Curse of Kehama* in 1810, *Roderick the Last of the Goths* in 1814, and *A Tale of Paraguay* (of less than epic proportions) in 1825. The little masterpiece of pellucid prose, *The Life of Nelson,* belongs to 1813. In that year, on the death of Henry James Pye,[6] Southey was made poet laureate.[7] Southey's "official" poems, of which *Carmen Triumphale* for the year 1814 is the most inflated and *A Vision of Judgment* (1821) the best remembered (because of Byron's parody), are among his least happy efforts. There is space to note here only two of his miscellaneous prose works. In *Sir Thomas More, or Colloquies on the Progress and Prospects of Society* (1829), the form of which owes something to Landor's *Imaginary Conversations,* he showed his distrust in democracy and lasting desire for social betterment by urging a return from modern competition to coöperative feudalism and by stressing the helpful interdependence of medieval society. This reverence for tradition is a heritage from Burke; but William Cobbett had been writing along similar lines and Carlyle and Ruskin were soon to do so. *The Doctor* [8] (1834-1847) is an *omnium gatherum* of lore and learning, anecdote and fantasy, serious thought lightly expressed and facetiousness laboriously hammered out, all of the most various kinds. To read it entire

[4] The Christian "machinery" of the original version was discarded in the revision of 1798 and Joan became a "child of Nature," guided, like Wordsworth's Lucy, by her benign influence. Joan is of course the champion of liberty. In his preface to the final edition (1837) Southey confessed that when writing the poem he "was ignorant enough of history and of human nature to believe that a happier order of things had commenced with the independence of the United States, and would be accelerated by the French Revolution."

[5] Southey, *Letters written during a Short Residence in Spain and Portugal* (1797).

[6] H. J. Pye (1745-1813), author of *Alfred,* an epic (1801) and many other volumes of worthless verse; poet laureate, 1790-1813.

[7] The new Tory laureate was embarrassed when in 1814 Richard Carlile, the radical publisher, having obtained possession of the manuscript, piratically published *Wat Tyler,* a drama of Southey's long-since-vanished revolutionary youth. The process of Southey's change in political opinion is analogous to that of Wordsworth but less complex.

[8] Seven volumes, the last two posthumous. *Selections from The Doctor, Etc.,* ed. R. B. Johnson (n.d.).

is beyond most modern capacities; to dip into it is to discover matter both informative and entertaining. In later life Southey's career was clouded with losses and sorrows, a son dying in 1816 and a favorite daughter in 1826. His wife, who had gone insane, died in 1837. Two years later he married Caroline Bowles, whose claims to remembrance for her own literary works are of the slightest. Not long afterwards his mind began to fail, and after a period of pathetic incompetence he died in 1843.

Southey's failures or at best partial successes as a poet ought not to obscure *The Epics* the fact that he was early in many fields of romance and in some led the way followed by greater poets. In *Thalaba the Destroyer* and in *The Curse of Kehama* he penetrated into Arabia and the further East;[9] in *Madoc* into Wales and America; in *Roderick* into Spain. In the Oriental epics immense learning at second-hand, displayed in elaborate explanatory notes, is no acceptable substitute for actual experience and imaginative grasp. There are arresting episodes in both poems, such as the description of the "Hand of Glory" in *Thalaba*[10] and the pageant-like opening of *Kehama,* but they are not enough to give life to the whole. Southey's choice of metre in *Thalaba* was ill-advised.[11] The rimeless lines of varying length, contracting and expanding according to no discernible principle of either sense or form, seem but so much prose chopped up indiscriminately; the reader is constantly looking for a pattern that is not there. Southey may have been uneasy, for he introduced rimes into *Kehama*; but the objection still stands, for they are inserted so irregularly that while holding out the promise of design they fail to fulfill it. Even so, Southey was in this matter a precursor, for where he failed later poets, managing more subtly the cadences which distinguish free verse from prose, have succeeded. These undisciplined forms encouraged a volubility which was not checked when, in *Madoc,* Southey reverted to blank verse. Here, following the lead of Gray and other poets of the earliest romantic generation, Southey tells a story of barbarous Celtic violence, crossing it with traditions of the "Aztecas" of America, the land to which Madoc emigrates.[12] It is refreshing to turn from this to the clear-cut tale of Count Julian's betrayal of Spain to the Moors in revenge for the seduction of his daughter by King Roderick—an appropriate theme when Wellesley's campaigns were turning the thoughts of Englishmen to the Iberian peninsula.[13] The opening of the story with Roderick's penitence is perhaps due to Scott's treatment of the legend, and Southey owed some-

9 See A. Waechter, *Ueber Robert Southeys Orientalische Epen* (Halle, 1890).

10 Book v, stanza xxvii. Compare Scott, *The Antiquary,* ch. xvii.

11 In his preface Southey acknowledged his indebtedness to Francis Sayers of Norwich who in his *Poems* (1792) had used irregular rimeless verse. Sayers in turn derived the form from William Collins who, however, had used it in the ode *To Evening* with far more delicacy and within manageable limits.

12 This is based on the tradition (found in Hakluyt and Drayton) of Madoc's discovery of America three centuries before Columbus. — Coleridge, Pantisocracy, and Spain all have their places in *Madoc.* See H. G. Wright, "Three Aspects of Southey," *RES,* ix (1933). 37-46.

13 Compare Scott, *The Vision of Don Roderick* (1811) and Byron, *Childe Harold* (1812), I. xxxv. For the kernel of history in the legend see *The Cambridge Medieval History,* II. 48 and 265.

thing to Landor's *Count Julian*.[14] The initial situation is an arresting one
and stimulates interest in the earlier episodes to which the poem folds back.
Southey realized the tragic power of the grim tale; unfortunately his blank
verse is a slow-moving and creaking vehicle.

*The
Shorter
Poems*

From the inexhaustible resources of his learning Southey drew the materials for those of his shorter poems into which he instilled most life. He
employed the ballad-measure at a date which may have been earlier than
that at which Coleridge was writing in the same form; the question of
priority is not important because Coleridge is incomparably more skilful
than Southey. Southey's crude and jaunty anapaests owe, admittedly, something to M. G. Lewis, to whose *Tales of Wonder* he contributed. He is at
his best in ballads where the supernatural is treated lightly, with touches
of humor, or where the horrible is crossed with the grotesque. The finest
examples in these kinds are his rendering of the legend of Bishop Hatto
and the still well-known *Old Woman of Berkeley*. Something like irony is
substituted for humor in *The Well of St. Keyne* and *The Inchcape Rock*,
where the supernatural is muted though still present. In *Blenheim* the weird
and wondrous notes are not sounded. Southey's handling of even such short
pieces is seldom certain; but even the less good are of historical interest
because Southey helped to liberate romantic prosody from eighteenth-
century restrictions. In both matter and form his exploitations of the macabre
point the way towards Hood, Praed, and *The Ingoldsby Legends*. While his
acorns mouldered in the ground, these small seeds took root.

## II

*Landor*

The traditional concept of Walter Savage Landor [15] (1775-1864) as an
austere and lonely figure is founded upon the self-portraits which he liked
to draw; actually there is as little of truth in it as in the notoriously irascible
poet's proud assertion that he strove with none for none was worth his strife.
From boyhood when he won the friendship of the great scholar Samuel
Parr to old age when he was protected by Browning and received Swinburne's homage, he enjoyed the admiration of many famous men, not excluding Byron, whose satiric thrust at "that deep-mouthed Bœotian Savage
Landor" [16] is not wholly unlaudatory, and Dickens, whose caricature of
him as Boythorn in *Bleak House* is, in intention at any rate, good-natured.
Landor's wide circle of friends embraced many people who were not authors,
and in particular various gracious women to whom he offered the tribute

[14] See E. Schwichtenberg, *Southeys Roderick und Landors Count Julian* (Königsberg, 1906).
[15] *Complete Works*, ed. T. E. Welby and Stephen Wheeler (16v, 1927-1936), not absolutely
"complete"; *Poetical Works*, ed. S. Wheeler (3v, 1937). — T. J. Wise and S. Wheeler, *Bibliography* (1919); John Forster, *Walter Savage Landor* (1869); Sidney Colvin, *Landor* (*EML
Series*, 1881); Helene Richter, "Walter Savage Landor," *Anglia*, L (1926). 123-152, 317-344;
LI (1927). 1-30; H. C. Minchin, *Last Days, Letters and Conversations of Walter Savage Landor*
(1934); Malcolm Elwin, *Savage Landor* (1941); George Saintsbury, "Landor," *Essays and
Papers*, II. 110-131; Bush, pp. 229-245.
[16] *Don Juan*, XI. lix.

of his courtly verses. He was not isolated from the world (even during the years in Italy) save toward the end and then through his own fault. Nor are his writings, either poetry or prose, so much apart from the currents of the age as is sometimes said. His Jacobinism in the days when he joined the Spanish revolutionaries and hoped to live to see King George III hanged between the two archbishops was one bond of sympathy with Southey, though unlike him Landor remained loyal to his republican convictions. The Orientalism which is one strand in the fabric of his works links him to Southey, Byron, and Moore. In his evocations of the past he worked, with all the obvious dissimilarities, along lines parallel with Scott. The chastity of phrase and style in his poetry shows a connection with those minor poets in whom the tastes and traditions of the eighteenth century lived on into the nineteenth. The elaborations of his prose remind the reader, notwithstanding the differences in the harmonies, that De Quincey (one of Landor's earliest admirers) was a contemporary who likewise pulled out all the organ-stops of the language. The "marmoreal" quality of his best verse is suggestive of Keats's latest style and may have had an influence upon it. A passionate love of Italy Landor shared with Byron and Shelley, and, like them, he, an aristocratic republican, dedicated his powers to the service of the cause of Italian unity and independence. Again like these and other poets of the period, he experimented in the dramatic form. The Grecian *Idylls* point the way toward Tennyson's classical pieces; some of the dialogues approximate to forms which Browning later employed. At all these and yet other points he touches one or another of the romantics. Why, then, does he seem so solitary a figure? One reason may be found in the quarrels which marred his middle life, and the violent scandal of 1857 which forced him to leave England and left a memory of lonely exile. Another reason is that his long life embraced three literary generations, so that it is difficult to classify him with any. A third is that because he is of equal note as poet and as writer of prose it is difficult to fit him into either category.

The juvenile phase during which Landor was an imitator of older poets was quickly passed through. The tumidity of the odes in the *Poems* of 1795 is not a characteristic of his mature work. He never ceased to fancy himself as a satirist; but though almost always missing the mark, he fails in an individual way not attributable to imitation of his predecessors. Profound knowledge of Latin led him into his own path. In Clara Reeve's *Progress of Gebir Romance* [17] he discovered a story which, with free adaptations and embellishments from other sources, he fashioned into *Gebir* (1798). This he began in Latin verse, and after the publication of the English form he returned to the Latin and completed *Gebirus* (1803). The tale of ancient Egypt involves enchantments, a descent into hell, and the death of the hero in a horrifying manner. The Latinate syntax, the heavily charged style, and the

---

[17] The dialogue form of this book may have suggested to Landor the form of the *Imaginary Conversations* (see a letter by M. F. Ashley-Montague in *LTLS,* January 27, 1940). But there were older and better precedents for him to follow.

allusive indirectness of the narrative make *Gebir* a burden to read entire, consecutively. Few pieces of comparable length gain more from selection; and the selections are usually such brief passages as the famous lines on the sea-shell. The men and women of the story, for all the violence of the issues in which they are engaged, are not dynamic. They are, in Arthur Symons' apt metaphor,[18] figures in low relief—figures, one may add, upon a stele, for about them there is a death-like stillness.

*Poems by the Author of Gebir*[19] (1802) contains, along with much of interest only as anticipations of greater things to come, one short piece, *Regeneration,* in which the passion for Greek antiquity and the passion for liberty are blended as they were later to be in Byron's poetry, but with a stylistic control that is not Byronic. In succeeding years Landor, who possessed independent means, lived much in Italy, engaged in litigation and personal quarrels, and wrote a quantity of Latin verse which he later translated into English. In 1812 appeared his tragedy of *Count Julian* on the story of Don Roderick. The indirectness of Landor's approach, the intricacy of style, and the assumption that the reader can supply from his own knowledge what it is the dramatist's business to impart spoil this play beyond redemption even by the occasional passages of noble eloquence.

Imaginary Conversations

The first series of *Imaginary Conversations* (1824) was followed by others to the number of five by 1829, and more were published at later dates, the latest (save those published posthumously) in 1848. With them may be considered *The Citation and Examination of William Shakespeare* (1834) and *The Pentameron* (1837), while on the periphery of this immense mass of prose is *Pericles and Aspasia* (1836). In time the *Conversations* range from remote antiquity to Landor's own day.[20] The characters are nearly always historical. The author never intrudes himself save when he is an interlocutor; but though he is not present we have seldom any sense of impartiality, for the arguments are so managed as to reveal and support Landor's opinions. Frequently Landor draws out the thread of his verbosity finer than the staple of his argument; the style is nobler than is appropriate to the thinness of the idea; an obvious thought is swathed in metaphor; and the restrained feeling contrasts with the magniloquence with which the very restraint is expressed. Landor can be intolerably dull, as in the colloquies on statecraft and public policy; and the elephantine humor of some of his attacks upon ecclesiasticism is equally tedious. But in the best of the *Conversations* there are passion and vitality and a genuine realization of a dramatic situation, as when Achilles confronts Helen or Henry VIII Anne Boleyn. His learning and intuition harmonize when he imagines great men giving expression

---

[18] *The Romantic Movement in English Poetry* (1909), p. 179.
[19] On the poems up to 1802 see William Bradley, *The Early Poems of Landor: A Study of his Development and Debt to Milton* (1914).
[20] Their geographical distribution may be summarized by noting the arrangement adopted in Welby's edition (numerals indicate the number of conversations in each category): Greek (18), Roman (12), Italian (29), English (35), Scottish (2), Irish (5), American (3), Spanish (5), French (17), German (7), Russian (7), Oriental (8), various (4). See H. M. Flasdieck, "Landor und seine *Imaginary Conversations*," *ESt*, LVIII (1924). 390-431.

to his own serenely epicurean outlook upon life.[21] Between these philosophic dialogues and those on purely literary subjects there is no well-defined boundary. Those concerned with problems of criticism and taste are often delightful, for Landor, though whimsical and unreliable, is a stimulating guide through the world of books. Generally he introduces but two speakers, the interest being thus concentrated upon the clash of two personalities or upon their perfect accord; but in a few cases he brings on three or even four people. There are practically no "stage-directions," the *mise-en-scène* being indicated with deft touches in the dialogue or left to the reader's knowledge of the situation.

The *Pentameron* may be regarded as one of the *Conversations* extended through five days of uninterrupted leisure during which Petrarch and Boccaccio discuss life and letters with special reference to the character, thought, themes, and poetic style of Dante. But though the interlocutors are the fourteenth-century humanists, the thoughts are Landor's, for neither Petrarch nor Boccaccio can be imagined as holding such opinions of Dante as they are made to express; the disparagement is Landor's, not theirs. The homely incidents, intended to provide "relief," are not quite in keeping, though the humor is above Landor's average level. Variety of a more welcome kind is supplied in the beautiful narratives of dreams.

Landor dared even more greatly than usual when he undertook to show the youthful Shakespeare on trial before Sir Thomas Lucy for deer-stealing. The high spirits of the *Citation* make it a pleasant volume to dip into, but it is difficult to sustain attention throughout its length. Had Landor curbed his prolixity and refrained from long digressions which blur the wit and retard the action, he might have produced an almost convincing portrait of the young genius who is at once so clever, so impudent, and so eloquent. But just when we are about to believe that this is how the charming deer-stealer would have spoken, his voice falls silent and for long whiles we hear Landor speaking.

The most ambitious of all Landor's works is *Pericles and Aspasia,* not a series of conversations (though much dialogue is recorded) but of imaginary letters exchanged between Aspasia and her friend Cleone, with occasional letters from others of the Periclean circle. Into this picture of the Golden Age of Athens Landor unfortunately permitted allusions by indirection to modern England to intrude, and he committed the fundamental mistake of making Aspasia the mouthpiece for his own opinions. These concern a variety of subjects—war, politics, the drama, and (very interestingly) the Homeric question. But the disputations are so cloudy as to obscure the lovely evocations of ancient Greece. The dramatic effect of the first short, swift letters is not sustained in the sequel, save in occasional pas- *Pericles and Aspasia*

---

[21] See especially the colloquy between Scaliger and Montaigne. A comparison between this and Water Pater's portrait of Montaigne in *Gaston de Latour* brings out interesting likenesses and dissimilarities between Landor and Pater. Pater's *Imaginary Portraits* owe something to Landor; and note also the "Conversation Not Imaginary" (which is a version of one of Lucian's dialogues) in *Marius the Epicurean* (ch. xxiv).

sages such as the narrative of the plague. The book would have been better had it been one-third as long; as it is, the anthologist must do for Landor what he would not do for himself.

Turning now to Landor's poetry, we may dismiss the Neapolitan trilogy [22] with a few words. Despite warm pleadings in their behalf,[23] to peruse them is an ordeal for which the occasional passages of stately eloquence in these most shut-in of all closet dramas afford but little compensation. Landor did not know how to conduct a dramatic action. The reader is bewildered with the intricacies of the historical situation, which is rendered only the darker by the rare flashes of familiar episode, as when Boccaccio and Fiammetta cross the stage. Even the figure of the evil monk Rupert—straight out of Gothic romances but tinged with the deeper dye of Landor's anti-ecclesiastical prejudices—looms dimly through the haze of policy and words. Save momentarily and then for but a few lines, the characters all talk alike—pure Landor.

*The Shorter Poems*

Of the short poems—some of them of but relative brevity by Landorian standards, for they range in length from one line (literally) to four or five hundred—a few, such as *Rose Aylmer* and *Past Ruined Ilion Helen Lives* (that incomparable expression of the poet's pride and confidence in his art) have won universal admiration.[24] In these pieces of marmoreal loveliness Landor seems to remember that upon a monument there is room for but a short inscription. Yet there is none of the dryness of epigraphy. The heat of passion is there, though it is so firmly constricted that it cannot burst into flame. For the reader weary of the more exuberant romantics there is refreshment in this proud reticence. In elegy and courtly compliment there are never those false notes that occasionally mar Landor's prose. The *Hellenics* (1847) are more difficult to judge. The best—such as *The Death of Artemidora*—are very beautiful; but their studied quiet is suggestive of the calm of a Street of Tombs. Nowhere is the "arrestedness" of which Landor's critics have often written more apparent. These men and women, youths and maidens of ancient Hellas move slowly or not at all. The sacrificial victim approaches the altar but is not slain; the lover for all his boldness does not achieve the embrace. Though the landscape is sun-drenched, the prevailing atmosphere is of a sad serenity. Landor is master of a firmly-wrought blank verse oftener eloquent than poetic, but he is as restricted in metrical forms as in his style. In all his poetry he uses familiar traditional metres and seems never to have been tempted to experiments in prosody.

To know and love the best of Landor there is needed a sense of dedication to a heavy task. Much that is tedious and otiose must be passed through in order to discover what is perfect in its kind. He who endures—not neces-

---

[22] *Andrea of Hungary* and *Giovanna of Naples* (both together, 1839); *Fra Rupert* (1840).

[23] Notably by Oliver Elton, *Survey . . . 1780-1830*, II. 22-24.

[24] Other poems in this group are *Dirce; Mother, I Cannot Mind my Wheel; Soon, O Ianthe; From You, Ianthe, Little Troubles Pass; I Strove with None;* and *Death Stands Above Me, Whispering Low.*

sarily to the end—may find himself in the select company of those who have delighted to pay him homage.[25]

## III

Remoter than Landor from the main tendencies of the age was George *Crabbe* Crabbe [26] (1754-1832), who might have been considered in the previous section of this *History* but for the fact that the works in which his genius found full expression appeared at so late a date as to bring them into chronological relationship with the great romantic poets. Crabbe's earliest poems attracted no attention, despite his plea to the reviewers in *The Candidate* (1780); but a letter with samples of his verses won the consideration of Edmund Burke and through his influence Crabbe obtained ordination and the curacy of his native village of Aldeburgh on the Suffolk coast. Later, an accumulation of livings assured him a competency. *The Village* (1783) displayed his maturing powers. In succeeding years he wrote much and destroyed much, but with negligible exceptions published nothing till the *Poems* of 1807 in which *The Parish Register* is the principal item. Then followed *The Borough* (1810), *Tales in Verse* (1812), and *Tales of the Hall* (1819). He won a wide following and became a well-known figure in London society though his home in later life was in Wiltshire.

Admirer of Pope and arch anti-romantic though he was, Crabbe has this *Anti-ro-* in common with Wordsworth, that he brought within the horizon of poetry *manticism* the characters and social condition of poor and humble people. But while Wordsworth sought to throw "a certain colouring of imagination" over "incidents and situations" in ordinary life, Crabbe worked with absolute realism in the sphere of the lowly and the ignoble. When he portrayed loftier social circles it was generally to darken by contrast the humiliation to which privileged persons subject interlopers from the nether world. The exaggerations in his picture were due to his unflinching determination not to soften or mitigate the sordid and the squalid elements in these lowly lives. *Realism* In the poetry of his master he found justification for this realism, noting that "Pope himself had no small portion of this actuality of relation, this nudity of description, and poetry without an atmosphere." [27] In his reaction

[25] Landor's brother, Robert Eyres Landor (1781-1869), has been brought back into notice by Eric Partridge who has edited *Selections* from his poetry and prose (1927). He gains from judicious anthologizing. The beauties of his plays—*The Count Arezzi* (1824), *The Earl of Brecon, Faith's Fraud*, and *The Ferryman* (all 1841)—must otherwise be sought in a mass of gnarled, crude 'matter. Their obscurities make the effort scarcely worth while. Two pieces of elaborate prose show the attraction of ultra-romantic subjects to an austere scholar. *The Fawn of Sertorius* (1846), an attempt at historical romance based upon Plutarch, introduces a supernatural being who is the guide and companion of a Roman general. *The Fountain of Arethusa* (1848) brings together two modern explorers and the ancient ghosts whom they meet in a subterranean cavern in Derbyshire. After the opening lively narrative there is an over-plus of dialogue.

[26] *Works* (8v, 1834); *Works*, ed. A. W. Ward (3v, Cambridge, 1906). — George Crabbe (son), *The Life of the Rev. George Crabbe* (1834); René Huchon, *George Crabbe and his Times*, trans. Frederick Clarke (1907); J. H. Evans, *The Poems of George Crabbe: a Literary and Historical Study* (1933); George Saintsbury, "Crabbe," *Essays and Papers*, I. 1-25; V. H Lang, "George Crabbe and the Eighteenth Century," *ELH*, v (1938). 305-333.

[27] Preface to *Tales: Works*, ed. Ward, II. 10.

from contemporary romanticism he was hostile rather to the novel of sentiment and wild adventure than to romantic poetry, for when he became
fixed in his style and outlook the great romantic poets had not appeared. He
expressed his contempt for Gothic inventions, those "shadows of a shade"
upon which as a boy he had wasted his "sixpences and tears." [28] The particu-
larity of his realistic detail is shot through with satiric comments, though
these are not directed against recognizable individuals.

> Man's Vice and Crime I combat as I can,
> But to his God and conscience leave the Man.[29]

Nature he delineated not for her own sake but as an accessory to man, the
somber background for the tragedy of poor outcasts. Fogs and storms and,
oftener, autumnal mists and decay (as in *The Patron* [30]) are suggestive of
the hard human lot and are symbols of the death of men's hopes. A recurring note of disappointment and disillusion sounds sometimes with mere
mournful iteration but more rarely with moving power, as in the story of
the condemned felon's dream of pardon.[31] He despised the old pastoral vein
of rustic verse and the idealization of village life. There is pathos, humor,
and resignation in some of his characters; but he is pitiless to the wicked.
No sudden "conversion" ever brings one of his tales to a forced "happy
ending." There is a grim monotony in his manner, and his themes, as
Hazlitt remarked, "turn, one and all, on the same sort of teasing, helpless,
unimaginative distress." [32] Enmeshed in the particular, he rarely, if ever,
rises to a universal view of life. Stressing the consequences rather than the
causes of folly or sin, he shows himself, like Hogarth, as much a penologist
as a psychologist. Even in his more lightly ironic stories there is a sardonic
tone; and a note of morbidness was sounded when in later life he became
addicted to opium. The effect of the drug is evident in some of his poems.[33]

In structural capacity he was weak. *The Village* is but loosely held together, and the letter form adopted for various sections of *The Borough* is
inappropriate. In the preface to the *Tales* he discussed the possibility of connecting them "by some associating circumstance" in the manner of Chaucer
and Boccaccio but concluded that he could not avail himself "of the benefit
of such artificial mode of affinity." [34] For *Tales of the Hall* he did, however,
invent a simple "frame," contrived from the reunion of two long separated
brothers. Most of his poetry is written in rimed couplets; it is perhaps significant that for the two pieces in which the influence of opium is most
apparent he chose stanzaic forms. In his fidelity to harsh actuality he was

---

[28] *The Borough*, xx. 11-32; *Works*, I. 470. Compare the satiric description (*ibid.*, xx. 59-77)
of the decayed chateau through which the wind and the heroine "sweep."
[29] *The Borough*, xxiv. 450-451; *Works*, I. 524.
[30] Lines 426-433; *Works*, II. 78-79.
[31] *The Borough*, xxiii. 226-332; *Works*, I. 509-511.
[32] *The Spirit of the Age; Collected Works*, ed. Waller and Glover, IV. 352.
[33] Especially in *Sir Eustace Grey* (*Works*, I. 238-251) and *The World of Dreams* (*Works*,
III. 403-413). See Meyer Abrams, *The Milk of Paradise* (Cambridge, Mass., 1934), pp. 13-21.
[34] *Works*, II. 7.

sometimes positively unfair to life, for his eye and mind rejected those mitigating circumstances that seldom fail to soften even the unhappiest fate. Gifford was justified in protesting against Crabbe's "contempt for the *bienséances* of life, and rage for its realities." [35] This "rage" explains his most conspicuous weakness: an inability to select. Every detail must be set down, not only what adds to the effect of a scene but what the reader may claim the right to take for granted. A lack of sensitiveness to language, which is sometimes definitely vulgar, is admitted even by Crabbe's warmest admirers; and there are few passages in his verse that would lose much if recast in prose. Among his admirers have been Scott and Byron; his influence is apparent in the later realistic novel; and there are still a few to praise his "hard, human pulse, ... his plain excellence and stubborn skill." [36]

Samuel Rogers [37] (1763-1855) is of interest not for his ineffectual poems *Rogers* but because he is a typical figure in a period when taste vacillated between the old classicism and the new romanticism. His wealth enabled him to write with no thought of pleasing the public. Commencing with an *Ode to Superstition* (1786), adorned with historical allusions and formal personifications, he passed on to *The Pleasures of Memory* (1792), in which Archibald Alison's theory of the association of ideas [38] is paraphrased in polished couplets and illustrated with refined instances of the awakening of the imagination by the crowding associations of certain objects and places. In the *Epistle to a Friend* (1798) he celebrated the joys of the art-collector. For years thereafter Rogers wrote no more verses. *The Voyage of Columbus* (1812) shows an advance, or rather a change, in his poetic course; he was no longer dwelling in the sanctuary of classicism but ventured timidly forth. The abrupt and fragmentary manner of the narrative, the attempts at suggestion rather than direct representation, the adventurous theme of storms and mutiny, and the unintentionally absurd supernaturalism of the conspiracy of the gods of America to turn Columbus back, all show Rogers attempting to adapt his "Muse" to romantic tastes. In his next poem, *Jacqueline* (1813), he withdrew to the tame subject of a country maiden whose run-away match is forgiven by her father. He returned in *Human Life* (1819) to the sedately reflective manner best suited to his slender talent. *Italy* (1822), his best-known poem, is a collection of fifty-two sections of impressions and anecdotes of which five are in prose and the remainder might as well have been, though they are in blank verse. Here, with divagations, Rogers followed in the footsteps of Childe Harold from Switzerland to Venice, to Florence, and to Rome. The impressions are often sensitively set down and the tales well told, but only once, in the touching tribute to

---

[35] *The Quarterly Review,* IV (1810). 281-312 (a notice of *The Borough*).
[36] Edwin Arlington Robinson, "George Crabbe," *Collected Poems* (1922), p. 93.
[37] *Poetical Works* (1875). — *Table-Talk,* ed. Alexander Dyce (1856); G. H. Powell, *Reminiscences and Table-Talk of Samuel Rogers* (1903); P. W. Clayden, *The Early Life of Samuel Rogers* (1887) and *Rogers and his Contemporaries* (1889); R. E. Roberts, *Samuel Rogers and his Circle* (1910).
[38] Based on Hartley's psychology and set forth in *Essays on the Nature and Principles of Taste* (1790).

Byron's memory,[39] does the writing approximate to poetry. Thereafter, through the long remainder of his life, though he refurbished his verses, Rogers wrote little that was new; but he employed two artists—J. M. W. Turner and Thomas Stothard—to do what he could not do for himself: insure the survival of his poems in the memory of posterity. In their editions of *Italy* (1830) and the miscellaneous *Poems* (1834) the matchless delicacy of the vignettes reveals the technique of line-engraving at its best. Rogers was a sort of arbiter of taste in London society. He knew everybody; and to be invited to one of his famous breakfasts was an accolade. The sharpness of his wit contrasted with the gentleness of his verse. He lived long enough to be offered the laureateship on the death of Wordsworth; declining the post, he gave his voice for Tennyson.

*Campbell*     Another transitional figure was Thomas Campbell [40] (1777-1844), a Scot long resident in London. Campbell withstood the pressure of romanticism and yet was restive under classical restraint. *The Pleasures of Hope* (1799) reveals a temperament which was essentially lyrical struggling to free itself from didactic form. During travels on the Continent in 1800 he composed some of his finest martial lyrics. The outbreak of war between England and Denmark was celebrated in *The Battle of the Baltic,* a poem whose fervent splendor was not justified by an exploit of which England has long since ceased to be proud. Newspaper work, lecturing, and the editorship of *The New Monthly Magazine* supported him in London. Of several narrative poems [41] *Gertrude of Wyoming* (1809) alone retains any interest, and that not much. It stands between Beattie's *The Minstrel* and Byron's *Childe Harold* in its employment of the Spenserian stanza. The exotic American setting is a bid for popular approval; but the story of a massacre of settlers by the Indians is told with an inappropriate fastidiousness. The fire which is missing from the long poems blazes in some of the short pieces. *Ye Mariners of England* still stirs the blood; and in *Hohenlinden* Campbell expressed with memorable power the tragedy and heroism and futility of battle.[42] *The Soldier's Dream* is on a somewhat lower level, as is the once so popular ballad of *Lord Ullin's Daughter.* Two great Scottish themes, the Jacobite rising of 1745 and the gift of second-sight, are combined in *Lochiel's Warning.* These and other short things are more spontaneous (or seemingly so) than the long narratives, which Campbell polished till all the vital ruggedness appropriate to his subjects was smoothed away.

A more brilliant and popular figure in the literary circle of the Whigs was

[39] *Italy* (ed. 1830), pp. 97-99.
[40] *Complete Poetical Works,* ed. J. L. Robertson (Oxford, 1908); *Life and Letters,* ed. William Beattie (3v, 1849); J. C. Hadden, *Thomas Campbell* (Edinburgh, 1899).
[41] *Theodric: a Domestic Tale* (1824) and *The Pilgrims of Glencoe* (1842) have faded from remembrance. — Campbell wrote several biographies, of which the most ambitious, *Frederick the Great and his Times* (1842-1843), has been for long lost to sight in the shadow of Carlyle.
[42] See George Saintsbury, "English War-Songs—Campbell," *Essays and Papers,* I. 330-355. To Campbell, as to Byron, was sometimes attributed the most enduringly popular of poems inspired by Napoleonic events, *The Burial of Sir John Moore* (1816), by a young Irishman, Charles Wolfe (1791-1823), who wrote nothing else of consequence.

Thomas Moore [43] (1779-1852) in whose early work there are vestiges of *Moore* classicism while the later is entirely romantic. Moore, who was born in Dublin, came to London in 1798. A version of the *Odes of Anacreon* (1800) was followed by *The Poetical Works of the Late Thomas Little, Esq.* (1802) the insipid amatory improprieties of which gained for Moore, whose authorship was soon known, a notoriety among the prurient. In 1803-1804 he occupied an official post in Bermuda, but having left it in charge of a deputy he traveled in the United States and Canada and then returned to England. *Epistles, Odes and other Poems* (1806) contains impressions of these wanderings. He attempted formal satire in Pope's manner, but not very successfully. Installments of *Irish Melodies* began to appear in 1807 "with symphonies and accompaniments" by Sir John Stevenson and some airs composed by Moore himself. The instant success was furthered among the privileged by Moore who himself sang sweetly in fashionable drawing-rooms. The series of *Melodies* continued intermittently till 1834. Among them were sheaves of *Sacred Songs* and *National Songs*. Moore's satiric talent found an informal outlet in the political squibs and gay lampoons which, beginning in the columns of *The Morning Chronicle,* he published in seven volumes between 1812 and 1835. Of these *The Fudge Family in Paris* (1818) and *Fables for the Holy Alliance* (1823) are representative. *Lalla Rookh* was begun in 1812 and published in 1817. The deputy in Bermuda embezzled funds for which Moore was legally responsible, and between 1818 and 1822 he had to live on the Continent beyond the bailiff's reach. In Venice he associated with Byron who had been his close friend since 1812; but he was more at home in Paris. His last considerable poem was *The Loves of the Angels* (1823). Of much miscellaneous prose work his biography of Byron (1830) is the most noteworthy. In his last years senile dementia overclouded the wit and charm which for long had dazzled society.

To read Moore's poems is to feel, in his own simile, like one who treads "some banquet-hall deserted" with garlands dead and lights extinguished. His works are old-fashioned without being venerable. There are few things more pathetic than faded frivolousness and outmoded sentiment. Only a few of the "melodies"—*Believe Me, if All Those Endearing Young Charms; The Young May Moon is Beaming; Oft in the Stilly Night*—are kept in remembrance, and some of them as much for the sake of the airs as for the words. He is memorable as the first of a long line of singers of Ireland's woes; but he sang them with a sentiment too facile and superficial to be comparable to the poignant laments of the bards of Young Ireland of later date. His light-hearted nature found a proper medium for his easy Muse in the political and social lampoons which were seldom cruel (even against

[43] *Poetical Works* (9v, 1840-1842); a tenth volume, added later, contains a reprint of *The Epicurean* (1827), a philosophical romance of third-century Egypt, Moore's only attempt at prose fiction. *Memoirs, Journal and Correspondence of Thomas Moore,* ed. Lord John Russell (8v, 1853-1856); *Poetical Works,* ed. A. D. Godley (Oxford, 1910). — Stephen Gwynn, *Thomas Moore* (EML Series, 1904); W. F. Trench, *Tom Moore* (Dublin, 1934); H. M. Jones, *The Harp that Once—A Chronicle of the Life of Thomas Moore* (1937); L. A. G. Strong, *The Minstrel Boy: a Portrait of Tom Moore* (1937).

the Prince Regent) and never mean. But with the fading from memory of the occasions and persons that prompted them these things have lost their interest; scholarly commentary sits heavily upon thistledown. In *Lalla Rookh,* which was an instant success all over Europe and was translated, imitated, and turned into an opera, he rode on the crest of the wave of Orientalism which had been long gathering. The poem can still please those who enjoy large expanses of prettiness, and there is wit in it for those who have the patience to search; but there is no strength beneath the surface coloring. *The Loves of the Angels,* taken in part from the Moslem legend of Haruth and Maruth,[44] challenged comparison with Byron's *Heaven and Earth,* which appeared at exactly the same time. It tells of three "sons of God" who fell in love with "the daughters of men" with consequent punishments fitting their greater or lesser degrees of rebelliousness. As originally written, the poem derived from Gen. 6: 1-4 rather than from the *Koran,* and there was an outcry against the juxtaposition of religion and eroticism. Moore promptly "turned his angels into Turks"—that is, into Moslem angels. The episode is characteristic of a poet whose artistic conscience did not much trouble him.

# V

*Hunt*

The last poet to be considered in this chapter brings us even closer than does Moore to the younger generation of the great romantic poets. Leigh Hunt [45] (1784-1859) inherited from his father the eccentricity and improvidence which caused him endless difficulties and humiliations, and from his mother the charm and gentle courage which won him hosts of loyal friends. His first collection of poems, candidly entitled *Juvenilia* (1801), has signs of discipleship to Thomson and Collins but with a reversion in prosody from the "closed" couplet of Pope to the freer manner of Dryden. The importance of Hunt's lasting liking for run-on lines is that it influenced Keats's early poetry. While still a youth Hunt began his career as a journalist and handy-man-of-letters, contributing to periodicals conducted by his elder brother, John. In 1808 John Hunt began to issue on Sundays *The Examiner* which quickly became a formidable opponent of the Tory government.[46] For it Leigh Hunt did the literary and theatrical criticism.[47] In 1811 the

[44] Richard Laurence's translation (1823) of the Ethiopic version of *The Book of Enoch,* manuscripts of which James Bruce had discovered in Abyssinia in 1771, probably called Byron's and Moore's attention to the theme. Analogous subjects were popular among the romantic poets. James Montgomery wrote *A World before the Flood* (1813) as did Reginald Heber (*Poetical Works* (1853), pp. 93-105); George Croly wrote *The Angel of the World* (1820). Lamartine, Vigny, and Hugo wrote similar poems under Byron's influence.

[45] *Poetical Works,* ed. H. S. Milford (Oxford, 1923); *Essays and Poems,* ed. R. B. Johnson (2v, 1891); *Selections in Prose and Verse,* ed. J. H. Lobban (1909); *Prefaces,* ed. R. B. Johnson (1930); *Correspondence,* ed. Thornton Hunt (2v, 1862). — Edmund Blunden, *Leigh Hunt* (1930); Edmund Blunden, *Leigh Hunt's "Examiner" Examined* (1928); Louis Landré, *Leigh Hunt. Contribution à l'histoire du romantisme anglais* (2v, Paris, 1935-1936); Barnette Miller, *Leigh Hunt's Relations with Byron, Shelley, and Keats* (1910).

[46] Michael Roberts, "Leigh Hunt's Place in the Reform Movement, 1808-1810," *RES,* xi (1935). 58 65.

[47] He had already been theatrical critic of *The News* in 1805-1807. See the selection of his *Dramatic Essays,* ed. William Archer and R. W. Lowe (1894). Hunt, says Archer, was "the

Hunts were prosecuted for exposing the barbarities of army discipline; and in 1812 the brothers were fined and imprisoned for denouncing the Prince Regent as a rake and a liar. Meanwhile Hunt had published *The Feast of the Poets* (1811), a satire in which the chief poets of the age appear. In later editions the text and commentary were expanded and altered to suit Hunt's changing tastes.

Hunt was in prison from early in 1813 till February, 1815. He obtained permission to have his wife and children live with him, to carry on his literary work, and to receive visits from friends old and new (the latter attracted by his martyrdom). While incarcerated he published *The Descent of Liberty: a Mask* (1814) in celebration of the downfall of Napoleon, which caused Hazlitt to brand him as an apostate. After his release he lived in the "Vale of Health" in suburban Hampstead, where he was soon associating with two young admirers, Shelley and Keats. A change came over him after his emergence from prison. He held loyally to his political opinions, but he tended to withdraw into the world of books, trusting to his followers the furtherance of the cause for which he had suffered. Benevolent himself, he became increasingly dependent upon the benevolence of friends, not to the advantage of his credit in business affairs.

*The Story of Rimini* (1816) was Hunt's most ambitious bid for fame as a serious poet. The "free and idiomatic use of language" and the run-on couplets which are characteristics of this poem were of value in promoting a less austere vocabulary and metrical flexibility; but Hunt's taste was insufficiently secure to manage these liberties without adopting a jaunty and familiar style, as of a novelette, disastrously ill-suited to the tragic Dantesque matter of his narrative.[48] The effect of his slipshod vulgarity upon Keats's early style was soon realized by the younger and immeasurably greater poet, with the result that Keats gradually freed himself from Hunt's influence. The taint of low breeding gave some warrant for Lockhart's notorious attack upon the "Cockney School of Poetry" in *Blackwood's Magazine* [49] (October, 1817), though it did not excuse its brutality.

*Hunt's Prosody*

---

first writer of any note who made it his business to see and report upon all the principal theatrical events of the day." Hunt denounces the venality and incompetence of most contemporary theatrical criticism.

[48] Hunt's critical writings and conversation did much to direct the attention of Keats and other young poets to Italian literature. For interest in Italy during the preceding generation see R. Marshall, *Italy in English Literature, 1755-1815* (1934), and for Hunt's interest in Dante see Paget J. Toynbee, *Dante in English Literature from Chaucer to Cary* (2v, 1909), II. 116-164. The first published English version of the *Divine Comedy* was made by Henry Boyd: the *Inferno* (1785); the entire *Comedy* (1802), but this was not so much a translation as an expanded paraphrase. See Toynbee, I. 410-419. Boyd's version was superseded by the famous translation by the Rev. Henry Francis Cary (1772-1844). Of this the *Inferno* appeared in 1805-1806 and the entire poem in 1814 with the title: *The Vision: or Hell, Purgatory, and Paradise, of Dante Alighieri*. The work was almost unnoticed till 1818 when a recommendation of it by Coleridge in one of his lectures called attention to it. See Toynbee, I. 455-502. Cary numbered many men of letters among his friends and was on terms of intimacy with Charles Lamb. See R. W. King, *The Translator of Dante: The Life, Work, and Friendships of Henry Francis Cary* (1925).

[49] Reprinted in *Notorious Literary Attacks*, ed. Albert Mordell (1926), pp. 11-19.

*Foliage* (1818) contains, along with some admirable translations, one poem of lasting interest. This is *The Nymphs,* the foster-sister, as it were, of *Endymion.* It throws light upon the aesthetic milieu in which Keats's poem was written. The two narratives in *Hero and Leander; and Bacchus and Ariadne* (1819) show that Hunt had not learned that great subjects were beyond his capability as a poet. *The Indicator* (1819-1821), a literary weekly, contained some of Hunt's pleasantest essays, things trivial in themselves but written with the easy discursiveness of the born journalist. In 1822 Byron and Shelley invited him to join them in the project of a new quarterly to be called *The Liberal.* This ill-fated scheme brought Hunt and his family

*At Pisa* to Italy shortly before Shelley was drowned. Four issues of *The Liberal* appeared, but Byron lost heart in the undertaking and Hunt's situation in Italy became forlorn. In Florence he consorted with Landor and Hazlitt. The latter's portrait of Hunt in *The Spirit of the Age,* while candid in revealing his faults both as a writer and a man, was in the main so generous in advertising his virtues and accomplishments that it did much to cheer the now wayworn author.

*Later Years* Hunt returned to England in 1825. Obliged by necessity, he consented to publish his reminiscences of Byron at this time when there was a great demand for Byroniana. In these articles, which, with additional matter, were made into *Lord Byron and Some of his Contemporaries* (1828), Hunt, without any fundamental falsification of the truth, unwisely avenged himself for humiliations to which Byron had subjected him. The book occasioned an acrimonious quarrel with Thomas Moore.[50] Between 1830 and 1832 Hunt conducted *The Tatler,* issued in rivalry to the newly founded *Spectator.* For the loss of old friends there was partial compensation in the gain of new, among them Browning, Dickens, and Carlyle. Carlyle has left a vivid pen-sketch of Hunt and his family, concluding: "A most interesting, pitiable, lovable man, to be used kindly but with discretion."[51] Dickens' caricature of him as Harold Skimpole in *Bleak House* (1852) was not in intention unkind, but it wounded by the thoughtless implication that the dishonesty belonging to the fictitious person was a characteristic of the real prototype. In his later years a vast quantity of miscellaneous matter poured from Hunt's pen. *A Legend of Florence* (1840), a play neither better nor worse than the usual run of poetic drama, had a *succès d'estime* in his circle. In 1850 he published the most delightful of his books, the *Autobiography;*[52] and in the same year, when mentioned for the laureateship, generously supported the claims of Tennyson.

As a poet Hunt is remembered for *Abou ben Adhem,* which passes from anthology to anthology; for a few bits of graceful trivia such as *Jenny Kissed Me* (the kiss was Mrs. Carlyle's compliment to him; the verses, his to her); for the forceful indictment of militarism in *Captain Sword and Captain*

[50] Moore attacked Hunt in an unpleasant satiric fable, *The Living Dog and the Dead Lion.*
[51] J. A. Froude, *Thomas Carlyle: The First Forty Years* (ed. 1910), II. 354-355.
[52] Ed. Roger Ingpen (1903); World's Classics ed. (1928).

*Pen;* and for his serious but fortunately temporary misguidance of Keats. The issues upon which he wrote were often fine, but his spirit was seldom finely touched to them. For the sake of spontaneity he sacrificed art; for the sake of liveliness he sacrificed dignity. Grave themes generally betrayed him into falsities of taste; light themes into sentimentality and triviality. The taint of vulgarity is on most of his verse. It is less apparent in his prose because, making less effort, he stumbled less often. Most of his essays and miscellaneous prose writings have proved ephemeral; they were good journalism in their day but are of little moment in ours. He could handle acceptably, and occasionally adorn, any subject that occurred to his quick and facile fancy.

# VII

## Reviews and·Magazines: 1802-1830; The Essayists

### I

The old distinction between the "review" and the "magazine" was still in force at the beginning of the nineteenth century. The function of the former was to survey politics, literature, science, and art; the latter, as its name implied, was a storehouse of literary and antiquarian learning with an infusion of more fanciful prose and verse. *The Gentleman's Magazine,* the greatest of its kind, continued uninterruptedly till mid-Victorian times and with vicissitudes almost to our own day. It was without party affiliations and existed solely to instruct and entertain. The organs of political and religious opinions which after 1802 had to struggle against fresh, vigorous rivals had once numbered great men of letters among their occasional contributors, but in general they were written by slovenly and ill-paid hacks who as literary critics made scarcely a pretense to independence, being cowed by their editors. These in turn were dependent upon the booksellers whose wares they advertised; consequently they did not dare to criticize adversely. Criticism was not only venal but quite non-selective. Whether valuable or worthless, books that were advertised were noticed.

**The Edinburgh Review** Such, in brief, was the situation when in 1802 a new stage in the history of English periodicals began. Three young men then living in Edinburgh— Francis Jeffrey, an advocate; Henry Brougham, a barrister; and Sydney Smith, an Anglican clergyman—found themselves at one in conservative literary tastes and liberal political outlook. Alarmed by the strength of entrenched Toryism, they determined to found a review which should support the Whigs in the advocacy of reform. With Constable of Edinburgh and Longman and Rees of London as publishers and with Jeffrey as editor, they launched *The Edinburgh Review and Critical Journal* in October, 1802. In politics and literature alike the *Edinburgh* spoke as one having authority and not as the scribblers. It aimed not only to reflect but to mold political opinion in the Whig interest. But unlike the old partisan· organs, it was written by men of vigorous minds and independent judgment. Its repute was enhanced by the policy of anonymity. The voice was not that of an individual, however eminent, but of a group, a party, one-half England. The strong personality of the editor imposed a unity of tone, but the contributors wrote from conviction, not of necessity. Pay at rates hitherto unheard of commanded the services of the most distinguished talent, and though there was grumbling at editorial changes and condensations, these writers felt themselves protected by anonymity and very few severed their profitable and congenial connection. Among these few was Sir Walter Scott who, when the Whiggery of the *Edinburgh* became too disturbingly pronounced, transferred his allegiance to the *Quarterly*. But the genial independence of spirit which characterized the group is evinced by the lasting personal friendship between Scott and Jeffrey. The vigor and authoritativeness of its style, its indubitable independence, and the policy of selecting for comment only publications which possessed some value made the *Edinburgh* an instantaneous success. Its circulation rose steadily to a maximum of about 14,000 in 1818, a figure which, however, does not represent the public it reached, for copies passed from hand to hand and there was a constant demand for reprints in bound volumes.

Of the *Edinburgh* triumvirate the chief was the editor, Francis Jeffrey [1]    *Jeffrey* (1773-1850), who held his post till 1829. The tone he set was exasperating to many, yet warranted to attract attention and to impose opinion upon countless readers who desired guidance. He applied to criticism a versatile, legalistic, and dogmatic mind. He was the last considerable English critic who held to the high a priori road, bringing imaginative literature to the bar of established forms and conventions. Yet the classical tradition to which he was loyal struggled with a reluctant admiration for the new romanticism. Late in life he admitted that his early judgments of the Lake Poets were at fault, and there is wistfulness in his famous retrospective farewell to the "rich melodies" of Keats and Shelley, the "splendid strains" of Moore, and the "blazing star" of Byron.[2] The fascination which romance exercised upon this precise, sharp dogmatist is evident in his love of the lesser Elizabethan dramatists. Jeffrey was not a great critic, but he was honest, independent, and influential, and by making his *Review* a medium for critics more profound and sensitive than himself he raised the general level of the profession. His miscellaneous articles, ranging over law, politics, biography, history, travel, and other subjects, have proved ephemeral.

His colleague Henry Brougham [3] (1778-1868), afterwards Lord Chancellor, stands on the extreme periphery of literary history. Brougham's courageous    *Brougham* endeavors in the cause of political, social, and educational reform, his gifts as statesman and orator, his defects of character, and his quarrels and controversies are subjects that concern the biographer and political historian. So close was his connection with the *Edinburgh* and so large his services to it that in later years, when Macvey Napier was editor, he attempted to

[1] Afterwards (1834) Lord Jeffrey. — *Contributions to the Edinburgh Review* (4v, 1844); *Selections*, ed. L. E. Gates, (1894); *Literary Criticism*, ed. D. Nichol Smith (1910). — H. T. Cockburn, *Life of Lord Jeffrey* (1852); George Saintsbury, "Jeffrey," *Essays and Papers*, I. 79-105.
[2] *The Edinburgh Review*, L (1829). 47.
[3] *Works* (11v, Edinburgh, 1872-1873); *Life and Times of Lord Brougham Written by Himself* (3v, 1871-1872). — G. T. Garratt, *Lord Brougham* (1935); A. M. Gilbert, *The Work of Lord Brougham for Education in England* (Chambersburg, Pa., 1922); Arthur Aspinall, *Lord Brougham and the Whig Party* (Manchester, 1927).

dictate its policies and regarded it almost as his personal organ. This attitude involved him in many disputes, notoriously with his hated rival, Macaulay. Of the vast number of his contributions to the *Review* not one is read today.

*Sydney Smith*

Sydney Smith [4] (1771-1845) is one of those figures about whom it is easy to say much and difficult to say little. His famous wit is more easily discoverable in letters and anecdotes than recoverable from his formal writings, partly because it is there imbedded in the context and partly because it has faded with the issues that inspired it. This wit too frequently swelled to mere high spirits which sound coarsely rollicking to our ears; but some of his sayings and even some of his practical jokes are classics in their kind, and beneath his jesting were ardent sincerity and immense vigor dedicated to many good causes. He was the mainstay of the *Edinburgh* in its championship of a variety of reforms, from the emancipation of Catholics to changes in the game laws, from the elevation of female education to the abolition of mantraps. His powers as a satirist and advocate of reform are seen at their best in the *Letters on the Subject of the Catholics* (1808), generally known from the pseudonym on the title-page as *The Plymley Letters*.

*The Quarterly Review*

Of the contributors whom Jeffrey gathered round him by far the greatest was Sir Walter Scott. By 1806 Scott had written ten articles for the *Edinburgh,* but in that year he withdrew his support and began negotiations with John Murray for the establishment of a new review which should challenge the dominance of the Whigs and supply a counterpoise to "the disgusting and deleterious doctrines with which the most popular of these periodicals disgraces its pages." [5] Scott was offered but declined the editorship of *The Quarterly Review,* and it went to the learned but acidulous and unimaginative William Gifford [6] who impressed his own dull aridity upon the initial number (February, 1809). From this unpromising beginning there was a recovery, but though the *Quarterly* soon rivaled the *Edinburgh* in circulation and authority it was never so uniformly brilliant in style. Scott wrote frequently for it, and Southey so voluminously that Gifford regarded him as "the sheet anchor of the *Review*."

*Black-wood's*

The pontifical ponderousness of the *Quarterly* suggested the desirability of a more nimble weapon against the Whigs. This need was apparent to William Blackwood [7] of Edinburgh who desired also to promote the fortunes of his publishing house at the expense of Constable, his competitor. In 1817 *Blackwood's Edinburgh Magazine* got off to a discouraging start

[4] *Works* (4v, 1839-1840); *Selections,* ed. Ernest Rhys (1892). — Lady Holland, *Memoir of the Rev. Sydney Smith* (2v, 1855); G. W. E. Russell, *Sydney Smith,* (EML Series, 1905); André Chevrillon, *Sydney Smith et la renaissance des idées libérales en Angleterre au xix* siècle* (Paris, 1894); George Saintsbury, "Sydney Smith," *Essays and Papers,* I. 53-78.

[5] Scott to Gifford, October 25, 1808; *Letters,* ed. Grierson, II. 105.

[6] On Gifford see ch. I, n. 11, above. — A regular contributor to the *Quarterly* was Macaulay's enemy, John Wilson Croker (1780-1857), a bigoted Tory politician and atrabiliar pedant, best remembered for his edition of Boswell's *Johnson.* Croker wrote the review of Keats's *Endymion* (1818) for which the *Quarterly* has suffered merited obloquy. — The *Croker Papers,* ed. L. J. Jennings (2v, 1884); M. F. Brightfield, *John Wilson Croker* (Berkeley, 1940). See also in general Walter Graham, *Tory Criticism in the Quarterly Review, 1809-1853* (1921).

[7] M. O. Oliphant, *Annals of a Publishing House: William Blackwood* (3v, 1897).

but quickly recovered itself when the proprietor procured the services of three clever writers, John Gibson Lockhart and James Hogg (who as poets and novelists are considered later in the present work) and John Wilson [8] (1785-1854), poet, scholar, and forceful personality. A *succès de scandale* engineered by these three set the new magazine on its feet. *The Chaldee MS,* a biblical parody, subjected to ridicule the entire entourage of *The Edinburgh Review* and many other respectable personages in the northern metropolis. The point of this satire is now blunted, and it is difficult to understand why even at the time it roused much interest south of the Border; but the fact is that it took all Britain by storm. The actions for libel which resulted served merely as more advertisements for *Blackwood's.* This success fixed the tone of flippant and cruel satire which was characteristic of the magazine for many years, though after the duel which resulted in the death of John Scott, Lockhart became more seemly and the manners of the group gradually improved. In 1819 Blackwood added to his ranks the wayward Irishman, William Maginn [9] (1793-1842), scholar, wit, and improvisor of burlesques. From him may have come the suggestion for the *Noctes Ambrosianae* which began in 1822 and became a popular feature of the magazine. The chief author of these papers was, however, John Wilson. Taking its name from a public-house where the friends met together, the *Noctes* is a record of real or imaginary conversations on life and letters, enthusiastic, romantic, satirical, derisive, and rowdy by turns. In it Hogg appears *in propria persona;* Wilson in the pseudonymous guise of "Christopher North"; Maginn as "O'Doherty"; and other characters, some fictitious, others real, appear from time to time, the real people not always with their own consent. The raciness and realism of the dialogues have given them something of enduring vitality and they are still enjoyable. In this department as in all the editorial contributions a Tory flavoring was maintained; but *Blackwood's* also offered entertainment unattached to political party. It published verse and fiction.[10]

   To the success of *Blackwood's* was due a new venture, the brilliant and

---

[8] Wilson's poem *The Isle of Palms* (1812) is quietly lovely and Wordsworthian; *The City of the Plague* (1816) is a succession of dramatic episodes based upon Defoe's *Journal of the Plague Year.* His fiction is of little moment. In 1820, notwithstanding his slender qualifications and the rival candidacy of Sir William Hamilton, the Tory majority of the town council elected Wilson to the chair of moral philosophy in the University of Edinburgh. As a professor he influenced generations of students who admired the man and were indifferent to his lack of philosophic profundity. — *Works,* ed. J. F. Ferrier (12v, 1855-1858); *Essays, Critical and Imaginative* (4v, 1856); *Noctes Ambrosianae,* ed. R. S. Mackenzie (5v, 1854), containing only the *Noctes* written by Wilson, about half the total number; *Recreations of Christopher North* (2v, 1887); *Poetical Works* (Edinburgh, 1896). — Mary Gordon, *Christopher North, a Memoir of John Wilson* (2v, Edinburgh, 1862); George Saintsbury, "Wilson," *Essays and Papers,* I. 184-209.

[9] *Miscellaneous Writings* (5v, 1855-1857). — The best biography of Maginn, relieving him of the serious charges brought against him by an enemy and recently revived by Michael Sadleir, is in M. M. H. Thrall, *Rebellious Fraser's* (1934), pp. 161-244. In later life Maginn's convivial habits degenerated into confirmed drunkenness, but he deserves to be remembered for himself as well as for Lockhart's lines on "bright, broken Maginn."

[10] The popularity of this fiction is attested by three series of *Tales from Blackwood* (12v, 1858-1861; 12v, 1878-1880; 6v, 1889). Many are still readable, notably *The Iron Shroud* which may have suggested to Poe *The Pit and the Pendulum.*

**The London Magazine**

short-lived (1820-1829) *London Magazine*. Its editor, John Scott[11] (1783-1821), gathered round him a notable variety of talents, including Lamb, Hazlitt, and De Quincey. In so far as it concerned itself with politics the *London* was liberal, and its literary sympathies were with the romantic school. Its most serious rival, save *Blackwood's,* was Colburn's *New Monthly Magazine,* which was for long popular under the successive editorships of Campbell, Bulwer, Hook, and Hood. Though faintly Whig in tint, it tried to eschew politics altogether. *The Westminster Review,* a publication of graver import, was founded in 1824 as the organ of the "Philosophic Radicals" led by Bentham and the Mills.[12] It offered trenchant criticism of Whigs and Tories alike. While the great reviews pursued their equable courses the magazines which aimed to entertain came to depend more and more upon serialized fiction and thus provided one of the two media (the other being publication in the form of monthly parts) for the Victorian

**Fraser's**

novelists who were appearing upon the scene. *Fraser's Magazine,*[13] long-lived and very influential, managed to combine amusement with the serious advocacy of many reforms. Its proprietor engaged the services of William Maginn as editor. Under his pen-name of "Oliver Yorke" he is known to all readers of *Sartor Resartus;* but those who remember Carlyle's satire do not always appreciate the liberalism of the editorial mind which gave hospitality to a work of literature so new and strange as *Sartor.* With the appearance of *Fraser's* in 1830 the modern era of periodical publications may be considered to begin.[14]

## II

**Lamb**

Charles Lamb[15] (1775-1834) was born in the heart of the great city which throughout his life was his home and his delight. Though he had happy

[11] Scott had been editor of *The Champion* and had attracted attention with his brilliant impressions of Paris in 1814 and 1815 which Thackeray commended long afterwards as "famous good reading" (*The Newcomes,* ch. xxii). Among his admirers were Wordsworth and Byron. In *The London Magazine* (May, 1820) Scott attacked the Blackwood group for their satiric scurrilities. Lockhart challenged him to a duel. The quarrel was settled in so bungling a fashion that Lockhart's friend C. H. Christie imputed cowardice to Scott. Whereupon Scott challenged Christie. In the duel Scott was mortally wounded and died in a few days (February, 1821).

[12] G. L. Nesbitt, *Benthamite Reviewing: Twelve Years of the Westminster Review, 1824-1836* (1934).

[13] Among the contributors to *Fraser's* in its early days were Carlyle, Thackeray, Crofton Croker (the Irish folklorist), Hook, Galt, Lockhart, and Francis Mahony ("Father Prout"), the charming ex-Jesuit and author of *The Shandon Bells.* See M. M. H. Thrall, *Rebellious Fraser's* (1934). On its lighter side *Fraser's* was a precursor of *Punch* (founded in 1841) for which many of its staff wrote in later years.

[14] Of special studies of Victorian periodicals the most important are W. B. Thomas, *The Story of the Spectator* (1928), E. M. Everett, *The Party of Humanity: The Fortnightly Review and its Contributors, 1865-1874* (1939), L. A. Marchand, *The Athenaeum: a Mirror of Victorian Culture* (1941), and M. M. Bevington, *The Saturday Review, 1855-1868* (1941). See also E. E. Kellett, "The Press," in *Early Victorian England,* ed. G. M. Young (1934), II. 3-97, and references there given to histories of *The Times, Punch,* and so forth.

[15] *Life and Works,* ed. Alfred Ainger (12v, 1899-1900); *Works,* ed. E. V. Lucas (7v, 1903); *Works in Prose and Verse,* ed. Thomas Hutchinson (2v, Oxford, 1909); *Works,* ed. William Macdonald (12v, 1903); *Letters,* ed. E. V. Lucas (3v, 1935); *Twenty Essays of Elia,* ed. Daniel Varney (1932); *Essays and Letters,* ed. J. M. French (1937), a selection. — J. C. Thomas,

recollections of the rural holidays of his childhood, spent vacations in various parts of England, and became the friend of the great poets who made a cult of nature, he was as urban as Doctor Johnson. He told Wordsworth that he did not care if he never saw a mountain, and on a visit to Keswick he affirmed that he would not exchange Fleet Street for Skiddaw. In this indifference to nature he stands apart from all his friends.

At Christ's Hospital,[16] where he was educated, he formed a lifelong friendship with Coleridge, and through Coleridge he later met Wordsworth, whom he never ceased to regard as the greatest of living poets. On leaving school he was employed for a short time in South Sea House [17] and then, in 1792, entered upon his long career of secure routine as a clerk in East India House. Wisely he chose to depend upon this post for his livelihood and not upon his talent as a writer. Four sonnets by him appeared without his name among Coleridge's *Poems* of 1796; other pieces, this time ascribed to him, were added in the edition of 1797. He helped a friend, James White, with the ingenious skit which claimed to be *Original Letters, etc., of Sir John Falstaff* [18] (1796). There was insanity in Lamb's family, though he was himself touched with it but once, at the age of twenty. But in 1796 came the dreadful blow when his sister Mary (1764-1847) in sudden mania killed their mother. Unwilling to have Mary permanently put away, Lamb made himself for the remainder of his life responsible for her. Much of the time she was normal and shared in his literary tastes and pursuits; but at intervals, on the appearance of premonitory symptoms, she had to be consigned to an asylum. This is the melancholy background of Lamb's character and humor—and intemperance.

Through Coleridge Lamb met Charles Lloyd,[19] a Quaker with a thin poetic talent, in collaboration with whom he published a volume baldly entitled *Blank Verse* (1798). This contained his best-known poem, *Old Familiar Faces,* which in its gentle pathos and nostalgia for the past is characteristic of the author, though he was but twenty-three years old. To the same year belongs *The Tale of Rosamund Gray,* part fiction, part reminiscence, not very coherent, but delicate in its humor, descriptions, and characterizations. *John Woodvil* (1802) is a clumsily constructed and almost

*Bibliography* (1908); E. V. Lucas, *Life of Charles Lamb* (2v, 1905); F. V. Morley, *Lamb before Elia* (1932); Edmund Blunden, *Charles Lamb and his Contemporaries* (1933); A. C. Ward, *The Frolic and the Gentle: a Centenary Study of Charles Lamb* (1934); J. May Lewis, *Charles Lamb* (1934); Orlo Williams, *Charles Lamb* (1934); E. C. Johnson, *Lamb Always Elia* (1935); E. C. Ross, *The Ordeal of Bridget Elia: a Chronicle of the Lambs* (Norman, Okl., 1940); Katharine Anthony, *The Lambs* (1945); M. H. Law, *The English Familiar Essay in the Early Nineteenth Century* (Philadelphia, 1934).

[16] Edmund Blunden, "Elia and Christ's Hospital," *E&S,* xxii (1937). 37-60.

[17] To save the feelings of his elder brother John, who spent his life as a clerk there, Lamb wrote under a pseudonym when he published *Recollections of the South-Sea House,* the first of the *Essays of Elia (The London Magazine,* August, 1820). The name Elia was that of an Italian clerk who had been employed in South Sea House.

[18] Ed. C. E. Merrill (1924). — The skit was prompted by W. H. Ireland's "Shakespearean" fabrication, *Vortigern,* which had been produced in this same year, 1796.

[19] Charles Lloyd (1775-1839), author of *Edmund Oliver* (1798), a novel containing a satiric portrait of Coleridge, and of several volumes of poems for the most part feebly Wordsworthian in tone. He translated the tragedies of Vittorio Alfieri (1815).

plotless drama, but lively in movement and noble in sentiment. Its period is the Restoration and its protagonist an old parliamentarian; but in atmosphere and style it is a precursor of the "Elizabethan Revival" which Lamb, as critic and anthologist, presently did much to initiate. Between 1802 and 1804 he wrote for various newspapers and through association with ill-conditioned hacks was confirmed in his taste for alcohol. But these men were not his intimates. At his famous "Wednesday evenings," of which Hazlitt has left a vivid description, men of talent or genius forgathered and they became a notable feature of literary London.

Lamb's farce, *Mr. H———* (1806), though no worse than the general run of its kind, met with failure upon the stage. Its buffoonery—good enough for a passing jest but thin and stupid when stretched to an evening's entertainment—is a reminder of the need to distinguish between Lamb's humor, which is subtly perceptive of the incongruities of life, and his jocosity, which is a matter of puns and horseplay not always in the best of taste. His humor was known to the privileged few long before it delighted readers. His earliest public efforts to be funny were often laborious and sometimes grim, and to the end he was not always sure of himself but liable, when writing against the grain of melancholy, to strike a forced and false note. A strange streak of the sardonic, which is often overlooked in accounts of "the frolic and the gentle" Lamb, appears in some anecdotes of his behavior and in some passages in his letters.

Tales from Shake-speare

Though his name appeared alone on the title-page of *Tales from Shakespeare* (1807), actually he wrote only the six tragedies and his sister the fourteen comedies. The histories, the Roman plays, and two of the comedies were omitted. The skill with which Shakespeare's language is retained in simplified form and so carefully dovetailed into the narrative that the joints are almost invisible is matched by the exquisite tact with which the essentials of the stories are preserved yet adapted to an immature intelligence and moral sense.[20] The style, without being pastiche, is so perfectly in keeping as to suggest that these are the original tales, here recovered, whence Shakespeare derived his plots. Though addressed to children, this charming book reached an adult audience at the moment when romantic "bardolatry" was raising Shakespeare to his modern position of supreme national poet.[21] A companion book entirely by Charles, *The Adventures of Ulysses* (1808), though written with spirited directness, suffers from too close a dependence upon Chapman's *Odyssey*. In 1808 came also the *Specimens of the English Dramatic Poets who Lived about the Time of Shakespeare,* one of the finest of all anthologies. Save for an inadequate appreciation of Marlowe's genius Lamb's taste is faultless. The great scenes of Heywood, Webster, Dekker, Fletcher, Middleton, and Ford were here restored to remembrance, and

---

20 The problem which *Othello* presented Lamb solved beautifully by treating passionate love in the guise of a supreme affection which comes within the compass of a child's understanding. See Oliver Elton, *Survey . . . 1780-1830* (1920), II. 341-342.

21 On the earlier stages of this movement see R. W. Babcock, *The Genesis of Shakespeare Idolatry* (Chapel Hill, 1931).

the passages chosen were illuminated with brief comments which contain some of the best-known *obiter dicta* in English criticism.

*Mrs. Leicester's School* (1809) contains ten tales of childhood (three by Charles and seven by Mary), supposedly related by the "young ladies" of the school and set down by their teacher. In these slight, tender, delicate things memories are interwoven with fiction. Close to them is another joint work, *Poems for Children* (1809), mainly by Mary, simple little bits of moralizing but with a humor and pathos which raise them above the level of the apologues which it was then the educational mode to inflict upon the young. This was the last book the Lambs published together.

The letters of the following decade, addressed to Wordsworth, Coleridge, George Dyer, and other friends, are filled with critical comment upon contemporary poetry and older literature and are among the most precious of Lamb's writings. For the public he wrote comparatively little. In Leigh Hunt's *Reflector* were published (1811) the penetrating but somewhat labored studies of Hogarth and of Shakespeare's tragedies.[22] *Recollections of Christ's Hospital* (in *The Gentleman's Magazine,* 1813) gave promise of *Elia,* still several years off. The *Confessions of a Drunkard* (in *The Philanthropist,* 1813) was, though exaggerated, founded upon personal experience and not without serious intent. Lamb impishly reprinted it in *The London Magazine* in 1822 as a sort of pendant to De Quincey's *Confessions of an English Opium-Eater.*

To *The London Magazine* Lamb contributed between 1820 and 1825 the **"Elia"** essays signed "Elia." A first collection of these was made in 1823;[23] and *The Last Essays of Elia* (gathered from various magazines) appeared in 1833. Their descent is from the "familiar" essay of the eighteenth century, but in color and warmth they are romantic and there are closer affinities to seventeenth-century prose. Lamb had long since imitated with extraordinary fidelity the manner and mood of Robert Burton;[24] and in the essays the wide-ranging curiosity and delight in strange learning recall Burton. Some of the deliberate archaisms of style are traceable to the same source and others to Sir Thomas Browne, and in phrase and cadence and in the solemn, elaborate treatment of small things there are suggestions of Browne. The sixteen *Popular Fallacies* of the *Last Essays* were obviously imitated from the *Vulgar Errors.* Temple, Taylor, Fuller, and the "Character-Writers" were also laid under contribution. Lamb's retentive memory betrayed him at times into something like plagiarism; but what he took he made his own. He was master of a simple, direct manner when it was appropriate to his subject; but with De Quincey he was responsible for restoring to English style the elaborate harmonies of pre-Augustan prose. Like all the romantics he is self-revelatory, but there is nothing in him of the

[22] See Augustus Ralli, *A History of Shakespearean Criticism* (1932), I. 143-145.
[23] *Elia, Essays which have Appeared under that Signature in The London Magazine.*
[24] The *Fragments of Burton,* first published with *John Woodvil* (1802), were not really intended to deceive and are therefore not, properly speaking, fabrications. They include an astonishing imitation of Burtonian melancholy in the poem *Hypochondriacus.*

"egotistical-sublime." Experience had made him too clear-sighted to take any individual, least of all himself, too seriously. The admissions of his own weaknesses, follies, and prejudices are so many humorous warnings to his readers. In middle age Lamb found his most characteristic subject in the *recherche du temps perdu*. Past time is viewed through glowing mists of memory which distort the actual without entirely falsifying it. The point where fact shades into fancy is so indefinite that he is not trustworthy and does not pretend to be, for he was a pseudonymous essayist, not a sworn witness before a jury of biographers. The affection for children is rooted in memories of his own childhood, and odd characters and situations, recollected from his own youth, are the material for many of the essays. The *Humor and Pathos* prevailing mood is pathos, but Lamb is a humorist and when on the verge of sentimentality can almost always check himself with laughter, and recognizing the nearness of laughter to tears, he accomplished many of his most individual effects through this proximity. The contrast and convergence of the two moods were for him the stuff of human life.

Ill health led to his resignation from East India House in 1825. *The Superannuated Man* is a memorial of his freedom and a complaint that he now had too much time on his hands. He severed his connection with *The London Magazine,* but continued to contribute to other periodicals. *The Wife's Trial* (1827) is a comedy in blank verse founded upon Crabbe's tale, *The Confidant*. His sister's periods of insanity and his own intemperance were increasing strains upon his health. In 1830 his poems were gathered together in *Album Verses*. Some of these occasional pieces are quaint and charming; there are lovely echoes of the seventeenth-century poets; and one sonnet, *The Gypsy's Mansion,* rises far above the modest level of "album" poetry. The *Last Essays* appeared in 1833, and in the following year "the frolic and the gentle" Lamb "vanished from his humble hearth." Mary, whose remarkable personality has been too much obscured by her brother's, survived him thirteen years.

Lamb seldom permitted his profounder views of life to appear above the humorous, pathetic, and ironical surface of his writings. In religion he sympathized with the Unitarians; in politics (in so far as he had any political opinions) he was a radical with many reservations. He never pretended to frame a consistent philosophy, nor did he aim to teach or to lead; but, loving his fellow-men, he asked, if for anything, for their affection. This he won in abundance from countless friends and from generations of readers who love him not only for his writings but even more for himself.

## III

*Hazlitt*

In this matter of friendship and affection the contrast which William Hazlitt [25] presents is extraordinary. "Call me Ishmael!" he might have ex-

[25] *Complete Works,* ed. P. P. Howe (21v, 1930-1933); *Collected Works,* ed. A. R. Waller and Arnold Glover (12v, 1902-1904; Index, 1906), does not include the *Life of Napoleon* nor the pieces first assembled in *New Writings,* ed. P. P. Howe (2v, 1925 and 1927); *Essays by*

claimed. His temperament drove him into the very dissidence of dissent, sometimes into a minority of one. He was the target of scurrilous attacks and gave as good as he got. He was often contemptuous, sometimes malignant. He quarreled with all his friends save Lamb—and nearly quarreled with him. He bore misfortune not with the quiet fortitude of Lamb but morbidly, angrily, acrimoniously. His enemies gloated over his solitude and misery. Yet he was not miserable. He nursed his wrath to keep it warm and possessed a proud self-confidence in adversity. He railed against people and institutions but not against life. His story is unhappy in the telling; but on his death-bed he declared that he had had a happy life. He made his own way, was never seduced from honest conviction by considerations of worldly interest, and was no man's hireling. For all his egotism, he was passionately devoted to the rights and liberties of mankind. This devotion to freedom is the thread which binds together all his work. It explains his seemingly perverse idolatry of Napoleon, for in the downfall of this foe of the old hereditary despotisms he recognized the triumph not of liberalism but of reaction. Hazlitt's prejudices sometimes blinded him to merit. His jealousy of rank probably colored his estimate of Shelley, and instinctive hostility to a lord worked against his sympathy with Byron's liberalism. But more often his political opinions were not allowed to warp his judgment and taste as a literary critic. He detested Burke's politics but lavished praise upon him as a writer. He regarded Wordsworth as a turn-coat but also as the greatest poet of the age. He would kneel, he said, to the author of the Waverley Novels, but he would not shake hands with the Tory Sir Walter Scott.

William Hazlitt (1778-1830), the son of a nonconformist minister, passed his youth in Shropshire.[26] Characteristically, his earliest piece of writing was a letter (1791) to a Shrewsbury newspaper defending Joseph Priestley and remonstrating against the outrage done him by the Birmingham mob. With almost no regular education, he read and meditated and walked about the country. In 1798 he met Coleridge, who invited him to Nether Stowey where he met Wordsworth. These new friends shaped his course toward literature, but his ambition was to become a painter. The Peace of Amiens in 1802 afforded an opportunity to visit Paris, where he copied Titians in the Louvre and was enraptured with the works of art which

William Hazlitt, ed. P. V. D. Shelly (1924); Selected Essays, ed. Geoffrey Keynes (1930); Hazlitt on English Literature, ed. Jacob Zeitlin (1913). — Geoffrey Keynes, Bibliography (1931); P. P. Howe, The Life of William Hazlitt (1922); Augustine Birrell, William Hazlitt (EML Series, 1902); C. M. Maclean, Born under Saturn: A Biography of William Hazlitt (1944); M. H. Law, The English Familiar Essay in the Early Nineteenth Century (Philadelphia, 1934); W. P. Ker, "William Hazlitt," Collected Essays (1925), I. 242-257; George Saintsbury, "Hazlitt," Essays and Papers, I. 106-133; Virginia Woolf, "William Hazlitt," The Second Common Reader (1932), pp. 186-199; H. W. Garrod, "The Place of Hazlitt in English Criticism," The Profession of Poetry and other Lectures (Oxford, 1929), pp. 93-109; S. P. Chase, "Hazlitt as a Critic of Art," PMLA, XXXIX (1924). 179-202; P. L. Carver, "Hazlitt's Contributions to the Edinburgh Review," RES, IV (1928). 385-393.

26 He was with his family for three years in America, but was too young to absorb any memories save of the beauty of the New England country.

were the trophies of Napoleon's victories. After his return home he struggled to master his chosen profession, but though there is evidence of talent in his portrait of Lamb, in the end he abandoned the attempt. It bore fruit, however, in his writings upon art and in his friendships with Flaxman, Haydon, and Northcote.[27] Meanwhile, intercourse with Coleridge had turned his mind toward philosophy, and in 1805 he published *An Essay on the Principles of Human Action*. This has been judged amateurish, but the basic pluralism which he expounded is the key to his sporadic pronouncements upon aesthetics and prepares the reader for his catholic sympathies as a critic of art and literature.

Hazlitt's marriage (1808) to Sarah Stoddart, a friend of the Lambs, forced him to seek a livelihood as a journalist and lecturer. For years after 1813 he wrote theatrical criticisms, which were collected in *A View of the English Stage* (1818). His enthusiasm was not for the scholarship or antiquarianism of the theatre, but for the actual plays, new or revived, for the actors, for the audience, and for his own responses. To the subject of his first considerable book, the *Memoir of Thomas Holcroft* (1816), he was drawn not only by Holcroft's political radicalism but by his talent as a dramatist. Hazlitt's knowledge of the practical problems of the stage helped *Lectures* to vitalize the lectures on the *Characters of Shakespeare's Plays* (1817) in which, ignoring historical and philological research, he shared with his readers an enjoyment of Shakespeare's profound and varied panorama of human life.[28] Many short papers on miscellaneous topics, somewhat in the manner of the old "familiar" essay, were published in *The Examiner* and collected in *The Round Table* (1817). There are good things here, such as the characterization of Rousseau and the papers on Milton, but Hazlitt's expansive genius needed ampler room. This he had in the three books that followed: *Lectures on the English Poets* (1818); *Lectures on the English Comic Writers* (1819), which reached beyond the announced subject to include Montaigne, *Don Quixote,* and *Gil Blas;* and *Lectures on the Dramatic Literature of the Age of Elizabeth* (1820), which with broader sweep carried on the work begun by Lamb. *Table-Talk* (1821-1822) ranges over literature and life and contains such examples of Hazlitt's finest writing as the essays *On Going a Journey* and *On the Fear of Death*. The *Epistle to William Gifford, Esq.* (1819) is strong but distasteful. Gifford was a disagreeable person who deserved a dressing-down, but Hazlitt almost overreached himself as he poured out the vials of his spleen and hatred upon the Tory editor who had treated him so insolently.[29]

When he was at the top of his powers, Hazlitt became involved in the

---

[27] Hazlitt's *Conversations of James Northcote (The New Monthly Magazine,* 1826; ed. Edmund Gosse, 1894) made much trouble for the artist and his friends because of the record of pungent personalities.

[28] See Augustus Ralli, *A History of Shakespearean Criticism* (1932), I. 145-157; H. T. Baker, "Hazlitt as a Shakespearean Critic," *PMLA,* xlvii (1932). 191-199; G. Schnöckelborg, *A. W. Schlegels Einfluss auf William Hazlitt als Shakespeare-Kritiker* (Emsdetten, 1931).

[29] Gifford's outrageous notice of *The Round Table (The Quarterly Review,* April, 1817) is reprinted in *Notorious Literary Attacks,* ed. Albert Mordell (1926), pp. 1-10.

sordid and unhappy love affair which led him to divorce his wife and which
he recorded in *Liber Amoris* (1823). Sarah Walker, the girl with whom he    Liber
was madly enamoured, was the daughter of his landlord. A knowledge of    Amoris
her duplicity did not check the course of Hazlitt's erotomania. The frankness and power of self-analysis with which this "expense of spirit in a waste
of shame" is narrated is a reminder that Hazlitt idolized Rousseau and
that it is with the *Confessions* that this book must be compared. When he
had cleansed his bosom of this perilous stuff, he entered into a second marriage (1824) and with his new wife set out upon a Continental tour. With a
mixture of enthusiasm for art and scenery and a Smollett-like repugnance
for foreigners he contributed his impressions to *The Morning Chronicle*
and collected them in *Notes on a Journey through France and Italy* (1826).
His finest books belong to these years: *The Spirit of the Age* (1825), in
which fair-mindedness in criticism of his contemporaries is but occasionally
betrayed by his prejudices, and *The Plain Speaker; or Opinions on Books,
Men, and Things* (1826), which ranges more widely and on the whole
more serenely. In 1827 the second marriage terminated. The last years of
his life were mostly wasted upon a *Life of Napoleon* (1828-1830), intended
as a rejoinder and corrective to Scott's biography.

Hazlitt's enemies sneered at his want of education and at the narrow
limits of his reading. He admitted the truth of both charges. In youth his
reading had been random and undisciplined; in later life he came actually
to dislike reading and depended largely upon memories. Like Lamb, he
relied upon the impressions of former years. Passionate retrospection is    *Retrospec-*
a prevalent note in his essays. His early admiration for Raphael, Titian,    *tion*
Poussin, and Claude provided him with the touchstones in his criticism of
art. His emphasis upon the literary content of painting anticipated the
typical Victorian approach to art, and in his rapturous descriptions of
masterpieces as well as in his insistence upon the moral and intellectual aspects
of the arts he was a precursor of Ruskin. All this is very old-fashioned
today, but Hazlitt's enthusiasm is still infectious. The incidental utterances
on aesthetics can be reduced to coherence only with the aid of the aestheti-
cians, to whom we must leave this task.[30]

In the love of painting, literature, and natural scenery the discords of    *"Depth of*
Hazlitt's nature were resolved into harmony. His function as a critic was,    *Taste"*
he said, "to feel what is good and give reasons for the faith that is in me."
That faith was grounded upon his own convictions. He would not repeat
what other critics had written, but would "give words and intelligible symbols
to that which was never imagined or expressed before." He wished to
share his enjoyment with the many, not to keep it to himself or reserve it
for a privileged coterie. His criticism depended not upon his breadth of
knowledge but upon what Keats called his "depth of taste." How seldom
he went astray is nowhere better shown than in *The Spirit of the Age* in
which the estimates of his contemporaries more often than not indicate the

30 Elisabeth Schneider, *The Aesthetics of William Hazlitt* (Philadelphia, 1933).

direction which the judgment of posterity was to take. This holds generally for his appraisals of older literature as well.

There is a lack of serenity and composure in Hazlitt's writings, and those who seek these qualities had best turn to Lamb. There is also a want of unity. An idea starts each essay off; there is a rush of associations; and when the torrent subsides an end but not a conclusion is reached. The method of comparison is constantly employed, with one great painter or writer balanced against another or a greater enhanced by contrast with a less. In the antitheses *Style* and terse clarity of his style he is a link between the eighteenth century and Macaulay, with the lucidity and often the moderation of the one and the force and conciseness of the other. Yet as a stylist he commands a wider range. *My First Acquaintance with Poets* is as lyrically reminiscent as anything of Lamb's; *On the Feeling of Immortality in Youth* is imposingly ornate without dependence upon archaisms; *On Going to a Fight,* a theme which invited the use of slang, is loyal to pure English, yet none the less virile for its purity; the *Farewell to Essay-Writing* is charged with romantic emotionality. Whatever the style or subject, it is Hazlitt's own. Like his favorite Montaigne, he could assure the reader that his was *un livre de bonne foi.*

# IV

*De*      The vagrant and patternless life of Thomas De Quincey [31] (1785-1859)
*Quincey* is not easily summarized. When once he began to write for a living, he wrote unceasingly and on an immense variety of subjects; but almost all his works came out in periodicals where they were left till during his last decade he issued the first collected edition of his writings; and books—the to-be-expected milestones along an author's path—are in his case but three in number: *The Confessions of an English Opium-Eater* (1822); *Klosterheim* (1832), a tedious novel of the Thirty Years' War; and the negligible *Logic of Political Economy* (1844). De Quincey came of a well-to-do family and inherited a patrimony which might have launched him smoothly upon life; but being impractical in worldly affairs he soon squandered his little fortune and fell into the hands of the money-lenders. To learning he had taken with the aptitude of a genius whose native home was the intellectual sphere, and at fifteen he could converse fluently in Greek. But he ran away from school, wandered in Wales, and in 1802-1803 found himself, homeless and penniless, in London. There he was sheltered by a girl of the streets, that Ann who soon disappeared from his ken but never from his dreams.

---

[31] *Collected Writings,* ed. David Masson (14v, 1889-1890); *Uncollected Writings,* ed. James Hogg (2v, 1890); *Posthumous Works,* ed. A. H. Japp (2v, 1891); *Selected Writings,* ed. P. Van D. Stern (1939); *Confessions of an English Opium Eater* [the text of 1822] *with Notes of De Quincey's Conversations with* [Richard] *Woodhouse,* ed. Richard Garnett (1885); *Literary Criticism,* ed. H. Darbishire (1909); *A Diary of Thomas De Quincey for 1803,* ed. H. A. Eaton (1927). — J. A. Green, *Bibliography* (1908); H. A. Eaton, *Thomas De Quincey, a Biography* (1936); E. Sackville-West, *Thomas De Quincey: his Life and Work* (1936); J. C. Metcalf, *De Quincey, a Portrait* (1940); Sigmund Proctor, *Thomas De Quincey's Theory of Literature* (Ann Arbor, 1943).

In 1804 he first had recourse to opium for the relief of toothache. The habit  *Opium*
grew fast upon him and he was presently consuming enormous quantities
of the drug. For years he wrestled with the vice, sometimes victorious,
sometimes backsliding, never wholly acquiescent in its tyranny. Meanwhile
he had come to terms with his guardians and was able to pass five years
(1803-1808) at Oxford. But he left the university without a degree. Alert to
novel excellence in literature, he was one of the first men to recognize
Wordsworth's genius. He became his friend, advised him on the composition of the tract on Cintra, and saw it through the press. Notwithstanding
differences due to his tactlessness and Wordsworth's self-esteem, this friendship endured till 1834 when the publication of De Quincey's too candid
reminiscences of life at Grasmere caused a permanent separation. With
Lamb and Coleridge he was also on terms of intimacy. From 1809 till 1820
he lived at Grasmere. There, in 1816, he married Margaret Simpson, the
"dear M" of the *Confessions* and the most patient of wives. For a time he
was editor of *The Westmorland Gazette.* In 1819 he made a connection
with *Blackwood's,* and in the following year took up his abode in London
and was introduced by Lamb to the proprietors of *The London Magazine.*

At this point De Quincey's literary life really began. In the *London*
(September and October, 1821) appeared *The Confessions of an English
Opium-Eater,* which attracted wide attention and made him famous, for
though published anonymously the authorship was soon an open secret. Late
in life (1856) De Quincey enlarged it greatly. There are precious things in
the expanded version, but one needs to know also the first brief, direct narrative before it was confused with divagations. After 1825 De Quincey lived
in Edinburgh, Glasgow, and other parts of Scotland, moving from lodging-
house to lodging-house, industrious but desultory, contributing to *Blackwood's,* consorting (as the *Noctes Ambrosianae* record) with Wilson and
others of "Maga's" staff, never precisely a popular author but one for whose
writings there was a market in various periodicals. Had he possessed worldly
wisdom, the days of pecuniary stress would have been over; as it was,
though most of the time he kept himself and his large family out of misery,
he lived in an almost constant state of impecuniosity.

De Quincey's fame depends upon a small fraction of the mass of his  *Miscel-*
writings. His vast learning and all-embracing curiosity enabled him to  *laneous*
turn to his own purposes (and not always with the acknowledgements of  *Writings*
indebtedness that are customary) whatever came to hand. Like the young
Carlyle, he stimulated, while he helped to supply, the demand for translations from the German romanticists. He interpreted Kant, though he
evinced no interest in later developments of German idealism. Among
critical articles on German literature is the curiously ill-balanced estimate of
Goethe in which *Faust* is dismissed in a single sentence. To some extent
he drew from German scholarship the materials for his historical papers.
Of these *The Spanish Military Nun,* in which a groundwork of fact is richly
embroidered with fancy, is the most interesting. The chief monument of his

classical erudition is the series of biographies of *The Caesars* in which he generally restrained his tendency to discursiveness. A lifelong student of political economy, he defended the theories of Ricardo against Malthus. He wrote constantly on English literature, interweaving biography and criticism. Of the vivid and pungent impressions and reminiscences of his contemporaries [32] it must suffice to say that the candor with which they were written wounded, though to wound was far from the intention of De Quincey's childlike unworldliness. His literary criticism, with the exception of *On the Knocking on the Gate in Macbeth,* survives in fragments, often illuminating and penetrating but seldom of impressive length, sometimes incoherent, and occasionally, as in the remarks on Keats, quite perverse.

All this was far enough above the level of periodical ephemeralities to justify its being assembled into more than one collected edition, but much of it was not sufficiently far above that level to keep it in remembrance. Employing De Quincey's own familiar categories, one may dismiss most of this miscellaneous popularized and stylized erudition as belonging to that "Literature of Knowledge" which sooner or later is always superseded. In some places—in *The Revolt of the Tartars,* for example, and in passages of noble eloquence in *The Caesars*—the creative artist was at work and the erudition was so strongly impregnated with imagination as to rise into the higher category of the "Literature of Power." There the aim is not to instruct but to move. This level is attained more often in De Quincey's narratives and descriptions than in his critical and expository writings. His gift for portraiture enabled him to vitalize figures even of the far past. The nearer his own day the more vivid the portrait; and the most striking likenesses are of men who came within the compass of his own experience—Wordsworth, Coleridge, and Lamb.

*Self-revelation*   Of himself his experience was intensest, and consequently he was most able to move when he wrote about himself. He is in the company of self-revelatory romanticists. There is much to be said for the view that undue attention has been paid to De Quincey as a "damaged soul." [33] Had he not been a genius opium would not have made him one, for though the drug may destroy or perhaps stimulate talent it cannot originate. It is not always borne in mind that the *Confessions* were not a despairing farewell but a confident introduction to his literary career. Nearly forty years of industry followed the book which fastened upon him forever the soubriquet of "the Opium-Eater." Like Lamb, he shaped his recollections, unreliable in detail but true in substance, into the form of art. The splendor of his dream-narratives makes it difficult to estimate the importance of his dream-life in relation to other experiences. The later autobiographical reminiscences which developed from the *Confessions* must be known if the balance is to be redressed. Yet De Quincey will always be remembered chiefly for his ad-

[32] A convenient collection is: *Reminiscences of the English Lake Poets* (Everyman's Library, 1911).

[33] On the effects of opium upon De Quincey see Jeannette Marks. *Genius and Disaster* (1925); M. H. Abrams, *The Milk of Paradise* (Cambridge, Mass., 1934).

ventures in the world of dreams. He was not content merely to relate them, *The World* but aimed to show the stuff of actuality—the encounter with Ann; the visit *of Dreams* of the Malay at Grasmere; the first news of Waterloo; the reading of Livy; the night-journey in the stage-coach—upon which his dreams were based. Providing some of the material for modern students of abnormal psychology and anticipating some of their conclusions, he recorded the enormous distortions of time and space; the sense that stupendous issues are involved in the situations in which the dreamer finds himself; the monstrous animals; the persistent crowds and tumults; the claustrophobia. Some of these hallucinations haunted his waking intelligence; the obsession of crowds explains his furtiveness. Yet though shy and solitary and never precisely convivial, De Quincey was no misanthrope but courtly and urbane in any company.

Discursiveness, a major flaw in romantic literature, is De Quincey's besetting fault as a writer. He cannot resist the temptation to divagate. The flood-gates of erudition are always ready to burst open; and then he is swept far off his course into inlets and swamps of learning and argument. But this want of control must be distinguished from the deliberate art with which he prepares, with leisurely and, as it seems, wandering garrulity, for *Style* the great effects of his prose. The organ-stops are pulled out one by one till the music swells and rolls in amplitude, as in the great evocation of "just, subtile, and mighty Opium," or in the *Dream-Fugue* following the *Vision of Sudden Death,* or the concluding address to the Bishop of Beauvais in the *Joan of Arc,* or the three-fold description of "Our Ladies of Sorrow." In general he reserved his most elaborate style for the record of meditations and of dreams; but in somewhat less ornate form such passages occur in unexpected places, even in the biographical sketches and literary criticism. The technical means by which he accomplished his mighty effects have been often analyzed [34]—the cadenced antitheses, the balanced phrases and clauses, the cycles and epicycles of verbal elaboration. He brought his imaginings to the furthest borderland of language, where the "prose poem" impinges upon the province of music.[35] Tastes in style, which during the era of Ruskinian prose carried De Quincey to the top of his reputation, have turned against the ornate periods of which he was the greatest master since the seventeenth century; but there are signs that the winds of opinion are again shifting in his favor. It is unlikely that any fluctuation will restore nine-tenths of his writings to remembrance; but there may be a new appreciation of the remaining tenth.

[34] Excellently, though briefly, by Oliver Elton, *Survey . . . 1780-1830* (1920), II. 327-331. Comparisons with Landor are frequent in studies of De Quincey's style.

[35] De Quincey was conscious of this proximity. In the foreword to *The Vision of Sudden Death* he explains that "the ultimate object was the Dream-Fugue, as an attempt to wrestle with the utmost efforts of music in dealing with a colossal form of impassioned horror."

# VIII

## Gothic Romance and the Novel of Doctrine

### I

The antithesis suggested in the title of this chapter is, as a matter of fact, somewhat blurred, for not only was English fiction [1] during the last decade of the eighteenth century and the first decade of the nineteenth developing along other lines besides the Gothic romance and the doctrinaire novel but such categories as have been set up are ill-defined and the characteristics of one kind are often found in another. Writers whose aim is to entertain and astound often aim also to edify; and conversely, writers whose intention is starkly doctrinal often employ the technique of the romancers. Between extreme specimens of one group and another there may be nothing in common; but in general the classes tend to shade off into one another. Looked at from a distance, fiction at this time seems to be at once sentimental, doctrinal, historical, and Gothic.

Between 1790, when William Lane, the busiest caterer to the popular taste, named his publishing house "The Minerva Press," [2] and 1814, when *Waverley* appeared, so great was the flood of extravagant fiction that even today it has not all been canalized into bibliographies. The tributaries to this stream were sensational Jacobean drama, seventeenth-century romance, translations and adaptations of Prévost and the *frénétique* fiction and drama of Baculard d'Arnaud, and some native English novels. The horrors of Smollett's *Ferdinand Count Fathom* and the naïve supernaturalism of Walpole's *Castle of Otranto* had been portents; and now a current already flowing was swollen by a torrent from Germany. One result of the romantic interest in North European culture was an attention to German literature which had hitherto been practically non-existent in England. It began with translations from Klopstock and Gessner. William Taylor of Norwich [3] (1765-1836) was in Germany as early as 1781. Throughout his life he exerted

*The German Influence*

---

[1] E. A. Baker, *The History of the English Novel*, v (1934), chs. VIII and IX (hereinafter referred to as Baker); Montague Summers, *The Gothic Quest* (1939) and *A Gothic Bibliography* (1941); Edith Birkhead, *The Tale of Terror* (1921); Eino Railo, *The Haunted Castle* (1927); Mario Praz, *The Romantic Agony* (1933), ch. II, on the hero-villain; J. M. S. Tompkins, *The Popular Novel in England, 1770-1800* (1932), chs. V-VIII; A. S. Collins, *The Profession of Letters . . . 1780-1832* (1929), on the relation of authors to their publishers; R. E. Prothero (Lord Ernle), *The Light Reading of Our Ancestors* (1927); Amy Cruse, *The Englishman and his Books in the Early Nineteenth Century* (1930). The most recent general survey is Edward Wagenknecht, *Cavalcade of the English Novel* (1943), with excellent bibliographies.

[2] Dorothy Blakey, *The Minerva Press, 1790-1820* (1939), with bibliography.

[3] J. A. Robberds, *Memoir of William Taylor of Norwich* (2v, 1843).

an influence which reached from Scott to Carlyle, writing hundreds of articles on German subjects. His activities culminated in the *Historic Survey of German Poetry* (1828-1830). In 1792-1793 Matthew Gregory Lewis made a long sojourn at Weimar. Schiller's drama *Die Räuber* was translated in 1792 and attracted the enthusiastic attention of Coleridge and Scott. The following years saw many translations from the German. Typical of these is Christiane Naubert's *Herman of Unna* (1794), which contains the elements of mystery, terror, and suspense presently exploited by the English Gothicizers, and Earl Grosse's *Horrid Mysteries* (1796), which has been kept in remembrance by Jane Austen's satire.

Less extravagant, indigenous ingredients were combined with the German infusion to form Gothic romance. A distinction is to be drawn between "Terror Gothic" and "Historical Gothic." [4] The earliest English experiments in the historical novel have already received notice. Following in the steps of the pioneers came Sophia Lee (1750-1824) who did gross violence to history in *The Recess* (1785), the story of two daughters of Mary Queen of Scots by a clandestine marriage with the Duke of Norfolk. Miss Lee contributed two stories to *Canterbury Tales* (1797-1805), mainly by her sister Harriet Lee [5] (1757-1851). Jane Porter (1776-1850) adapted history to her purposes in *Thaddeus of Warsaw* (1803) and *The Scottish Chiefs* (1810), though she did not mistreat Clio so miserably as her predecessors had done. But the gain in accuracy has carried with it no gain in lasting vitality. Miss Porter's early readers found her thrilling, but her laborious adaptations of chronicle material are today as lifeless as anything in out-moded fiction.

Charlotte Smith [6] (1749-1806) is in the line of descent from Fanny Burney, but the lineage has been modified by an infiltration of romance. From her first novel, *Emmeline, the Orphan of the Castle* (1788) to *The Old Manor House* (1793), her best-known book, there is increasing attention to the scenic background. In the latter story the dilapidated mansion, deep woods, moonlight, and moaning wind are designed to harmonize with the tale. Mrs. Smith's characters are generally those of domestic fiction, but the situations in which she places them are often romantic in the extreme. She makes use of mysterious occurrences, secret passageways, and such typically Gothic themes as that of the long-lost, rightful heir. In her imagination the dissolute seducer of Richardson has taken on a Gothic gloom, and her sentimental lovers have read *The Sorrows of Werther*. Along with much senti-

[4] See Gerard Buck, *Die Vorgeschichte des historischen Romans in der modernen englischen Literatur* (1931); George Saintsbury, "The Historical Novel, 1: The Days of Ignorance," *Essays and Papers*, III. 1-20; Montague Summers, *The Gothic Quest*, ch. IV. — On a contemporary parodist of these early historical novels see J. M. S. Tompkins, "James White, Esq., a Forgotten Humourist," *RES*, III (1927). 146-156. — Ill-informed efforts to recreate the medieval scene in literature synchronized with the growing interest in Gothic architecture. See W. H. Smith, *Architecture in English Fiction* (New Haven, 1934); Kenneth Clark, *The Gothic Revival* (1928), ch. IV: "Romanticism and Archaeology."

[5] One of Harriet Lee's tales, *Kruitzner*, is of genuine power and gave Byron the plot of his tragedy, *Werner*.

[6] F. M. A. Hilbish, *Charlotte Smith, Poet and Novelist* (1941).

ment there is some satire, and occasionally she touches upon contemporary problems. *Desmond* (1792) shows her sympathy with the French Revolution, and *The Young Philosopher* (1798), the story of an idealist who is disillusioned with Europe and seeks refuge in America, reveals the influence of Rousseau. Here Mrs. Smith is close to the doctrinaire novelists; but in general she is closer to Ann Radcliffe.[7]

*Ann Radcliffe*

Mrs. Radcliffe [8] (1764-1823), a quiet lady who never had an adventure in her life, is the arch-Gothicizer of them all. After an unpromising first attempt, she produced in *A Sicilian Romance* (1790) a full-blooded horror-story of a wicked husband, imprisoned wife, and guileless daughter. Though indebted to French romancers for certain incidents,[9] she is here already mistress of her peculiar art. *The Romance of the Forest* (1791), in part derivative, relies for its effect upon the gloom of forests and Gothic ruins where villains absolute in wickedness wreak their rage upon good people who are flawlessly refined. The influence of Rousseau is apparent in Mrs. Radcliffe's descriptions of nature, and there is something of the atmosphere of the paintings of Salvator Rosa. This story was followed by Mrs. Radcliffe's masterpiece, *The Mysteries of Udolpho* (1794), in which her technique of terror by suggestion—often through strange sounds—is fully displayed. A basic rationalism forbade her to do more than touch the marvelous. The compromise adopted is never quite satisfactory, for her mysteries are often held so long in suspense that the rational explanations, when they come, fail to satisfy a curiosity which is no longer alert. It was beyond her ability, and aside from her purpose, to people her stage with convincing human beings; the dialogue put into the mouths of her characters is of a stiltedness that must be sampled to be imagined. But there is no denying the effectiveness of her tenebrous landscapes and atmosphere.

The portrait of the criminal monk, Schedoni, in her next book, *The Italian* (1797), owes something to Lewis's portrait of Ambrosio in *The Monk*; but Lewis was but repaying a debt, for Montoni in *The Mysteries of Udolpho* had given him suggestions for Ambrosio. The anti-sacerdotalism of both Mrs. Radcliffe and Lewis had deep roots in Protestant prejudice and roots of more recent growth in the attacks on the Jesuits in many Continental countries. Schedoni, with his mysterious origin, his somber mien, his pallor, his arresting eyes, the aura round him of unspeakable guilt, and the horror touched with pity which he inspires, is the type-figure of the romantic *homme fatal,* the precursor of Byron's Lara and Manfred. He dominates the story as he dominates the lovers who are caught in the toils of the Inquisition. In certain episodes a sense of spiritual wicked-

---

[7] The romances of S. E. Brydges, the antiquarian, are modeled upon Mrs. Smith's. See M. K. Woodworth, *Sir Samuel Egerton Brydges* (Oxford, 1936).

[8] See, in addition to the general authorities, A. M. Killen, *Le Roman terrifiant ou roman noir de Walpole à Ann Radcliffe* (1924); C. F. McIntyre, *Ann Radcliffe in Relation to her Time* (1920); A. A. S. Wietens, *Mrs. Radcliffe: her Relation towards Romanticism* (1926); E. Margraf, *Der Einfluss der deutschen Litteratur auf der englischen Schauerroman* (1901); Jakob Brauchli, *Die englische Schauerroman* (1928).

[9] J. R. Foster, "The Abbé Prévost and the English Novel," *PMLA,* XLII (1927). 443-464.

ness is conveyed which may still appall the sympathetic reader, keyed to the right pitch of emotion. The contrasting scenes of Neapolitan loveliness and the dark recesses of the great abbey are managed admirably. But the modern reader finds it difficult to stomach the melodrama, crudities of drawing, and incredible complexities of iniquity.

*Gaston de Blondeville,* Mrs. Radcliffe's last novel (written in 1802), is an unsuccessful compromise between Gothicism and history. Hitherto she had rejected the responsibilities assumed by the novelists who claimed to recreate an authentic past; in this story she tried to be conscientious and succeeded merely in being tedious. Moreover, she succumbed at last to the lure of the unexplained supernatural and introduced a genuine ghost. Whether because of this intrusion or because she was sensitive to Miss Austen's satire, Mrs. Radcliffe did not publish this novel and it appeared posthumously (1826).

No rationalistic scruples inhibited Matthew Gregory Lewis (1775-1818). *"Monk"* His reading of Tieck, Spiess, Musäus, and other prolific spawners of the *Lewis* macabre filled his head with fantasies of the grotesque, the horrible, and the criminal. But in his notorious romance, *The Monk* [10] (1797), a nightmare of fiendish wickedness, ghastly supernaturalism and sadistic sensuality, there is almost indubitably something else than mere literary sensationalism; it gives evidence of a psychopathic condition perhaps inherent in the extremes of the romantic temperament.[11] The crude purposes to which Lewis adapted the great themes of Faust and Ahasuerus suggest deliberate parody; but he was intensely serious, though capable only of such coarse, broad strokes in characterization and setting as make his scenes of lust and torture and rotting corpses repellent beyond description. They are even more revolting in the original version which, in fear of legal action, Lewis afterwards modified. *The Monk* still has its admirers,[12] but to most critics it is of interest only because it combines various literary traditions in a monument of romantic extravagance. Lewis won the regard of great men; Scott and Southey were contributors to his anthologies, Byron and Shelley his friends in Switzerland. On the stage his *Castle Spectre* (1798) and later pieces were successful. His death at sea on a return voyage from Jamaica, where he possessed property, is said to have been in circumstances worthy of his own spectral imagination.[13]

[10] Ed. E. A. Baker (1907); (3v, 1913).
[11] Or (to regard the matter with less gravity), *The Monk* may be considered the dream of an "oversexed" adolescent, for Lewis was only twenty when he wrote it.
[12] With Montague Summers' immoderate praise (*The Gothic Quest,* pp. 212-223) contrast the just estimate in Baker, v. 207-211. See also Eino Railo, *The Haunted Castle,* chs. II and IV.
[13] Many romances were written in imitation of *The Monk.* Edmund Montague's *The Demon of Sicily* (1807) is a specimen of extreme extravagance. Charlotte Dacre's *Zofloya, or the Moor* (1806; ed. M. Summers, 1927) is of interest for its influence on Shelley. H. J. Sarratt's *Koenigsmark the Robber, or the Terror of Bohemia* (1801) is an adaptation from the German of R. E. Raspe. Raspe put this story into the mouth of Baron Münchhausen. There is thus a connection with the famous popular saga which, beginning with Raspe's *Baron Munchausen's Narrative of his Marvellous Travels and Campaigns in Russia* (1785), received in later recensions facetious and extravagant accretions. Raspe lived in England and wrote in English. *Munchausen* is therefore entitled to be regarded as an English classic.

Mrs.
Shelley

Mary Wollstonecraft Shelley [14] (1797-1851) wrote *Frankenstein* (1817), the only novel of terror that is still famous. Gothic horrors, sentimental humanitarianism, and the current pseudo-scientific theory of vitalism or the "vital spark" are combined in the story of the man-made monster. Among Mrs. Shelley's other novels *The Last Man* (1826), on the destruction of human society by a pestilence, and *Lodore* (1835), based on the privations which the Shelleys had suffered in 1814, are of some interest for their "fictionized" portraits of Byron and Shelley.[15]

Maturin

Charles Robert Maturin [16] (1780-1824) showed himself in his first romance, *The Fatal Revenge* (1807), as a disciple of Mrs. Radcliffe; but in *The Wild Irish Boy* (1808) and *The Milesian Chief* (1812) he gave voice to Irish nationalistic feeling. His tragedy, *Bertram* (1816), won at Drury Lane a success which was deserved, for despite the accumulation of Gothic accouterments its action is swift and its emotion genuine. Then came *Melmoth the Wanderer* [17] (1820), Maturin's masterpiece and the greatest novel of the school of terror. Its structure is complicated and obscure, but there is inventive ingenuity in each of the six episodes into which it is divided. The theme of the Wandering Jew, or more broadly, of the never-ending life, which haunted the imagination of the period,[18] is impressively developed. The idea of combining the stories of Ahasuerus and Faust might have resulted in a pretentious failure, a mere variant upon *The Monk;* but *Melmoth* is not imitative, is not a failure; and it has strongly impressed various great writers.[19]

In the sub-literary depths of romanticism there were hundreds of stories in imitation of Mrs. Radcliffe, Lewis, and the horror-mongers of the Continent. Here iniquity rioted in ruined castles and dim oratories and crypts and dungeons, where monstrous villains oppressed the innocent, and ghosts walked, and demons lured their victims to destruction. But into these noisome fastnesses we need not descend.

[14] Mrs. Julian Marshall, *The Life and Letters of Mary Wollstonecraft Shelley* (2v, 1889); *Letters of Mary W. Shelley,* ed. Frederick L. Jones (2v, Norman, Okla, 1944); R. Glynn Grylls, *Mary Shelley, a Biography* (1938).

[15] W. E. Peck, "The Biographical Element in the Novels of Mary Wollstonecraft Shelley," *PMLA,* xxxvi (1923). 196-219.

[16] Nielo Idman, *Charles Robert Maturin: His Life and Works* (1923); William Scholten, *Charles Robert Maturin, the Terror Novelist* (Amsterdam, 1933).

[17] Ed. anonymously (3v, 1892), with memoir and bibliography.

[18] Lewis attached the story of the Wandering Jew loosely to the main plot of *The Monk.* The theme is used by Wordsworth, Coleridge, Godwin, and Shelley. It reappears in Thomas Medwin's poem, *Ahasuerus the Wanderer* (1823) and in George Croly's flamboyant romance, *Salathiel the Immortal* (1827). See Werner Zirus, *Der ewige Jude in der Dichtung vornehmlich in der englischen und deutschen* (Leipzig, 1928); A. M. Killen, "L'Évolution de la légende du Juif errant," *RLC,* v (1925). 5-36; Eino Railo, *op. cit.,* ch. v.

[19] Balzac's *Melmoth reconcilié* is a sort of sequel. Maturin influenced Hugo's *Han d'Islande.* Vigny, Baudelaire, and Villiers de l'Isle Adam were among the admirers of the book, as were Rossetti and Poe. Oscar Wilde after his disgrace took the pen-name of "Sebastian Melmoth" (the saint pierced with arrows associated with the doomed wanderer).

## II

Fiction in the late eighteenth century became a convenient medium for *The Novel* promulgating the new social theories which were entering England from *of Doctrine* France.[20] Rousseau's *Emile* (1762) was soon known in England, and one of its chief themes—education not by coercion but by persuasion and guidance —is found in Henry Brooke's *The Fool of Quality* (1765-1770) and is the basis of *Sandford and Merton* (1783) by Thomas Day (1748-1789). Sandford is reared close to nature with the result that he is healthy, kindly, and sensible, while Merton, having had the conventional education of a gentle-man, is a headstrong weakling. Elizabeth Inchbald [21] (1753-1821) used the *Mrs.* subject twice. *A Simple Story* (written in 1777 though not published till *Inchbald* 1791) presents the contrast between a mother who has been educated in the old fashion and a daugher who has benefited from the new ideas. What might seem unpromising material for fiction is vitalized by Mrs. Inchbald's art, which, though serene, is capable of scenes of passion and tragedy. A masculine variant of the theme is presented in her second novel, *Nature and Art* (1796). Henry, one of the protagonists, who has been brought up on "Zocotora Island," brings to English society the simplicity and candor of a child of nature, while William, the cousin who has been educated in England, is a rake and a hypocrite. Henry befriends the woman whom William has seduced and abandoned. Later, in a memorable scene, William, now a judge, sentences this unfortunate woman to death.

This novel shows the influence of Robert Bage (1728-1801), whose earlier *Bage* satiric stories must be passed over,[22] but whose last novel, *Hermsprong, or Man as He is Not* (1796), is, notwithstanding its conventionally happy end-ing, a significant indictment of society. The hero, having been reared among the Redskins, is a candid *homme sauvage* who criticizes sophisticated so-ciety in a manner which recalls the "Foreign Visitor" of Montesquieu, Lyttelton, and Goldsmith. Bage makes telling points in his exposure of the abuses perpetrated by rank and wealth. But the frankness of the hero is often both coarse and dull. Bage had little talent for characterization, and his good people and bad are scarcely more than personifications of the virtues and vices.[23]

In William Godwin's *Caleb Williams, or Things as They Are* [24] (1794) *Godwin* the antithesis is not between nature and conventionality but between the power possessed by the privileged and the helplessness of the lowly. This novel is intended to illustrate by a particular case the general indictment

20 Allene Gregory, *The French Revolution and the English Novel* (1915).
21 William McKee, *Elizabeth Inchbald* (Washington, 1935).
22 See J. M. S. Tompkins, *The Popular Novel*, pp. 194-196, for an appreciation of Bage's earlier novels as in some measure anticipating Peacock and even Thackeray.
23 With *Hermsprong* may be associated Thomas Holcroft's *Anna St. Ives* (1792) in which the revolutionary program of "perfectibility" is put into the form of fiction. The idealistic hero confounds the machinations of the aristocratic villain and in the end converts him to a better view of life.
24 Ed. E. A. Baker (1903). — On Godwin see above, ch. I.

of society which Godwin had drawn up in *Political Justice*. But far from being merely a polemic, *Caleb Williams* is an absorbingly interesting story of suspense and fear, connected with the tales of terror and even anticipating in some measure the design and technique of detective fiction. Caleb, a youthful servant, has become possessed of the secret that his master, Falkland, has committed a murder; but the social prestige of Falkland enables him to retain the mastery and pursue his victim implacably. Godwin's quite definitely Gothic *St. Leon* (1799), a pseudo-historical tale of the sixteenth century, deals clumsily with the themes of the "eternal wanderer" and the philosopher's stone. His later novels are heavy and lifeless, the narratives being burdened with philosophic disquisitions. Into *Fleetwood* (1805) he introduced his subversive opinions about marriage, but it is more important as showing that Godwin, like some of his disciples, abandoned his early opinions. He is here no longer the rationalist and necessitarian but has come under the influence of romantic anti-intellectualism and nature-worship.

*Maria Edgeworth*     The doctrinaire novel shades off into the novel of manners.[25] The novels and tales of Maria Edgeworth [26] (1767-1849) are in the line from Miss Burney but with ingredients from Day and other writers who used fiction as an instrument for reform. She points forward to both Jane Austen and Sir Walter Scott. Her social philosophy separates her from them and connects her with the reforming group; but her pictures of society have much of the shrewdness, though little of the subtlety, of Jane Austen, and her "regional" settings in Ireland suggested to Scott the possibilities of a Scottish background for fiction. From her father, Richard L. Edgeworth, she obtained not only many of her ideas on education and society but—with unfortunate consequences to her art—aid in the composition of many of her books. *The Parents' Assistant,* a series of moral tales which between 1796 and 1800 grew from one volume to six, was designed as a supplement to Mr. Edgeworth's treatise on *Practical Education* (1798). The titles of these little stories—*Forgive and Forget; Waste Not, Want Not;* and the like—indicate their quality and purpose. For a century they remained part of the nursery regimen. From these humble and utilitarian beginnings Miss Edgeworth graduated to the composition of novels of full length for readers of mature years. Yet the didacticism of her stories for children reappears in her writings for adults and would be the ruin of them were it not that, for all her faults and theories, she knew how to tell a tale, to paint scenery with minute yet interesting accuracy, and to represent the clash of characters in their social relations. Viewed as a historical novel *Castle Rackrent* (1800)

25 Amelia Opie (1769-1853), a member of Godwin's circle, wrote fiction—*Father and Daughter* (1801), *Tales of Real Life* (1813), and many other books—in which the purpose to instruct is often present but almost always subordinated to sentiment. Mrs. Opie's plots are often intricate and in some of them use is made of mystery and villainy.

26 *Novels and Tales* (18v, 1832-1833); *Novels* (12v, 1893); *Castle Rackrent* and *The Absentee,* ed. Brander Matthews, in Everyman's Library. — E. A. Edgeworth, *A Memoir of Maria Edgeworth* (3v, 1867), privately printed and very rare; A. J. C. Hare, *The Life and Letters of Maria Edgeworth* (2v, 1894); Emily Lawless, *Maria Edgeworth* (EML Series, 1904); Friedrich Michael, *Die irischen Romane von Maria Edgeworth* (Königsburg, 1918); Theodore Goodman, *Maria Edgeworth, Novelist of Reason* (1936); Baker, VI, chs. I and II.

is more accurate and vivacious than any such work of fiction before Scott. On the technical side it is a milestone in the development of the novel. The fortunes of a family through several generations are seen from the point of view of a character in the book who tells the story. This is a structural innovation of great consequence. Being almost without any tincture of her social theories, *Castle Rackrent* remains Miss Edgeworth's most attractive book. The novelettes in the first series of *Tales of Fashionable Life* (1810) require no comment, but in the second series (1812) the principal item is *The Absentee,* a long short story or short novel which many good judges reckon her masterpiece. Here London society and the life of the Irish gentry are wittily contrasted, and the scenes of low life in Ireland are contrived with much animation. There is still great vitality in the book, marred though it is by didacticism and by a conventional scale of social values. In Miss Edgeworth's later books—*Patronage* (1814), *Ormond* (1817), and others that must be passed over—the leading figures seem patterned according to a formula; only from the minor people does human nature extrude. When her sense of humor is not clogged with theory Miss Edgeworth can delineate her men and women with a minuteness of observation and a shrewdness of understanding not unworthy of Jane Austen; but she has not Miss Austen's aloofness and objectivity and finesse.

# IX

## Jane Austen

The happiest and most productive years in the life of Jane Austen [1] (1775-1817) were passed in two small towns of Hampshire. She was the seventh of the eight children of the rector of Steventon. In the Austen family there existed a sympathetic affection based upon an identity of tastes and an outlook upon life illuminated by lightly ironic detachment. Jane's juvenilia—*Love and Freindship* and the little pieces collected in *Volume the First*—are mostly burlesques and parodies written for the amusement of the family. She moved in this intimate circle throughout her uneventful life. However, her experience of provincial society gradually broadened, and she had visited Bath before, on her father's retirement, the Austens settled there in 1801. By that time she had written, besides a number of minor things, first versions of three of her novels. In the uncongenial atmosphere of Bath she accomplished little; nor were the three years (1806-1809) in Southampton, where, after her father's death, she lived with her mother, more fruitful. Not until she breathed again the congenial air of the provincial town of Chawton did the creative instinct reassert itself. There she was very active till, shortly before her death, she moved to Winchester.

*Line of Development*

Apart from *Lady Susan,* a false start from which she quickly withdrew herself, Miss Austen began as a satirist of the current sentimental mode—that romantic view of life which trusts to the dictates of the heart.[2] *Northanger Abbey* treats this theme superficially, and *Sense and Sensibility* analyzes with greater profundity the contrast between a woman who submits herself to the guidance of common sense and one who follows impulse. The theme of *Pride and Prejudice* is announced in its original title—*First*

[1] *Novels,* ed. R. W. Chapman (5v, Oxford, 1923), the definitive edition of the six novels. The juvenilia and fragments are all accessible in modern editions: *Love and Freindship* (1922; 1929); *Lady Susan* (1925); *Sanditon* (1925); *Plan of a Novel* (1926); *The Watsons* (1927); *Volume the First* (1933). *Letters,* ed. R. W. Chapman (1932).—R. W. Chapman, *Bibliography* (1929); J. E. Austen-Leigh, *A Memoir of Jane Austen* (1870), ed. R. W. Chapman (1926); Leonie Villard, *Jane Austen: sa vie et son œuvre* (Paris, 1915), trans. by Veronica Lucas as *Jane Austen: a French Appreciation* (1924); C. Linklater Thomson, *Jane Austen, a Survey* (1929); R. Brimley Johnson, *Jane Austen: Her Life, her Work, and her Critics* (1930); John Bailey, *Introductions to Jane Austen* (1931); David Rhydderch, *Jane Austen, Her Life and Art* (1932); Guy Rawlence, *Jane Austen* (1934); Lord David Cecil, *Jane Austen* (1935); Mary Lascelles, *Jane Austen and her Art* (1939); Elizabeth Jenkins, *Jane Austen, a Biography* (1939); A. C. Bradley, "Jane Austen," *E&S,* II (1911). 7-36; Baker, VI, chs. III-V. — Miss Austen was four years younger than Sir Walter Scott, but her first published novel appeared three years before, and she died three years after, the publication of *Waverley* and is therefore considered here before Scott.

[2] See J. M. S. Tompkins, "*Elinor and Marianne:* a Note on Jane Austen," *RES,* XVI (1940). 33-43.

*Impressions,* which are not to be trusted but must be corrected by experience and afterthought. In the last three novels there is no longer a preoccupation with sentimentalism. *Mansfield Park* presents the antithesis between wordliness and unworldliness. *Emma,* her most thoughtful comedy, is a study in the self-deceptions of vanity. *Persuasion,* more definitely a love story than its predecessors, develops the contrast between true love and prudential calculations. From the appended table,[3] in which the somewhat complex facts of the dates of composition, the revisions, the changes in title, and the publication of the novels are summarized, it will be seen that they fall into two groups, separated by a sterile decade. These "silent years" are accounted for by Miss Austen's discouragement; for the original version of *Northanger Abbey* a publisher had given her a pittance, but he had not issued it; and *First Impressions* had been rejected, unread. But it is a mistake to differentiate too sharply between the earlier and the later novels, for the three in the first group were subjected to revision during the years when she was engaged upon the three in the second. All that can be safely said is that the element of burlesque gradually disappeared; that in the later books there is an increasing gravity, an occasional frostiness of tone, and perhaps a suspicion of heaviness of handling; and that at the close she permitted herself a guarded display of emotion which the readers of her first books could not have expected of her.

The Austen family were, as Jane said, "great Novel-readers and not *Tastes and* ashamed of being so."[4] This reading embraced not only the classics of *Interests* eighteenth-century fiction and Fanny Burney and Maria Edgeworth; the Austens read and enjoyed, though they laughed at, Mrs. Radcliffe and other purveyors of terror and sentimentalism. From most of her predecessors Jane learned one or another of the secrets of her craft, what to do and what to avoid; but she learned more from her own practice. Her tastes, grounded upon Richardson, the essayists, Cowper, and her "dear Doctor Johnson,"[5]

---

[3] c. 1790-1793:  *Love and Freindship; Volume the First.*
Before 1796:  *Elinor and Marianne* (not extant); recast, 1797-1799, as *Sense and Sensibility;* further revision, 1809-1810; published 1811.
1792-1796(?):  *Lady Susan;* survives in a fair copy of c. 1805 or later; first published in Austen-Leigh, *Memoir,* second ed., 1871.
1796-1797:  *First Impressions* (not extant); rewritten, c. 1812, as *Pride and Prejudice;* published 1813.
1797-1798:  *Susan* (not extant); recast and much expanded as *Northanger Abbey,* 1805; posthumously published 1818.
1803:  *The Watsons* (a fragment); first published in Austen-Leigh, *Memoir,* 1871.
1811-1813:  *Mansfield Park;* published 1814.
1814-1815:  *Emma;* published towards the end of 1815 or more probably early in 1816.
1815-1816:  *Persuasion;* published posthumously 1818.
1817:  *Sanditon* (a fragment to which this title was given by the Austen family); first published from the manuscript in 1925.

[4] Jane Austen to her sister Cassandra, December 18, 1798. On Miss Austen's reading see Mona Wilson, *Jane Austen and Some of her Contemporaries* (1938), pp. 1-42.

[5] Resemblances to Johnson have been noted: her distrust in any indulgence in emotion; her penetrative honesty in observing human nature. That Johnson's influence was not uniformly fortunate is evident from those rare passages in the novels where, essaying a full and heightened style, Miss Austen gives an impression of strain.

were so much of the eighteenth century that her mind has been called "femininely Augustan." [6] She lived when the tide of romanticism was at the flood, yet was never borne upon it or even sprinkled with its foam. Not only did she not frequent literary society; she had not a single literary correspondent during her entire life. Scott's poetry entertained her—but she mocked at it. *Waverley* she admired—but reluctantly. To Wordsworth, Coleridge, and Byron she was completely indifferent. Romanticism gave her an opportunity to ridicule Mrs. Radcliffe; it affected her in no other way. There is nothing surprising in the absence of a large historical perspective and wide social view from her novels; fiction was not expected to deal with such matters. But the fact remains that even in her letters Miss Austen exhibits practically no interest in social problems and public events. The Napoleonic Wars swept past and left little trace upon her books. This lack of concern reflects the state of mind of county society. The "lower orders," portentously upsurging across the Channel, appear seldom and casually in the novels and only in their proper position as subservient to gentle folk. She never wrote the annals of the poor; she was not interested in the simple or the primitive. Collective humanity never puts in its appearance in her stories; there is no mob or any scene of public disturbance. Her people are unaffected by the drift of contemporary thought; they have no concern with abstract ideas; no anxiety about destiny disturbs them; and if death must come it will come at some indeterminate date beyond the *finis* of their story.

Weaknesses of character are the stuff from which these novels are fashioned; but there is little of positive evil. Miss Austen's sole experiment in the delineation of a thoroughly bad woman is *Lady Susan*. This story of an adventuress who schemes to sell her daughter to a rake while entrapping for herself the daughter's young lover is an advance upon Miss Austen's early burlesques of circulating-library fiction in that her intention seems to be to draw a credible bad woman in contrast to the incredible ones of popular fiction. But that it was huddled up to an abrupt conclusion [7] is a sign of her distaste for such a theme. She thought that "guilt and misery" were "odious subjects," [8] and from them she escaped quickly on the rare occasions when she had to deal with them at all. There are no adventures, properly so called, in the novels; and only in *Persuasion* is there a physical accident, external to character, which alters the course of events. In the work of few other novelists does coincidence play so small a part. She was much concerned with the effects of emotion upon human beings; but the emotion itself is almost always indicated by implication. All her plots revolve upon love; but only once (in the case of Mr. Knightley) do we hear a lover declare himself. There is no lack of knowledge of passion or of interest in it; but there is an instinctive reticence. She can be sympathetic even while seeing the ironical and satiric implications in character and situation. She

[6] F. E. Pierce, *Currents and Eddies in the English Romantic Generation* (1918), p. 310.
[7] It is not a fragment, as some writers (e.g., *CHEL*, XII. 259) call it.
[8] *Mansfield Park*, ch. XLI.

is, as one of her successors has remarked, "a mistress of much deeper emotion than appears upon the surface. She stimulates us to supply what is not there." [9] In the story of the woes of Marianne, told though it is with no blindness to absurdities, "the burning human heart" was, as George Moore maintained,[10] revealed for the first time in English fiction.

She pictured a limited part of the English scene. "Three or four Families in a Country Village is," she said, "the very thing to work upon." Her small world is that of the provincial gentry. But her oft-quoted metaphor of the "small square two inches of ivory" is too modest a self-estimate. She leaves out many aspects of experience, but what she pictures is grounded upon so comprehensive a knowledge of human nature as to universalize it; her men and women, true of their own period, are true also of all time. Wisely she stayed "within the range of her imaginative inspiration"; [11] that range was of almost the same circumference as her own personal experience. It has often been remarked that she never describes a scene in which no woman is present. She knew nothing about finance, and the prestige and power of money play little part in her stories. When her niece, writing a novel, sought counsel of her, Miss Austen wrote: "Let the Portmans [characters in the novel] go to Ireland, but as you know nothing of the Manners there, you had better not go with them." The niece should "stick to Bath" where she would be "quite at home." [12] The familiar incident of Miss Austen's correspondence with the domestic chaplain to the Prince of Wales cannot be omitted here, for it shows that even a message from royalty could not distract her from her path. The chaplain suggested that in her next novel she might delineate the character of a clergyman; and Jane, sensing that the hints which he supplied were based upon his own experience, mischievously replied that she might be equal to "the comic parts of the characters" but "not the good, the enthusiastic, the literary." Her correspondent then, with amusing insensitiveness, suggested that "any historical romance illustrative of the history of the august House of Cobourg, would just now be very interesting." But Jane was not to be enticed; she must, she felt, "go on in [her] own way." [13]

That way led her through the world of men and women in their personal relationships. She regarded them with the shrewdness and acumen of the satirist but without losing sight of moral values. There is no distortion in her perspective. She shows us the tangle resulting from conflicting personalities; we hear the jangle of incongruous temperaments. Her province is not that of somber delinquency but of venial error. The faults in her characters are mostly due to bad training or want of training in youth. In older people these are often beyond repair; but in young, especially the young lovers,

*Jane Austen's "World"*

---

[9] Virginia Woolf, *The Common Reader* (1925), p. 174.

[10] *Avowals* (1919), pp. 43-44.

[11] Lord David Cecil, *Jane Austen*, p. 8.

[12] *Letters*, p. 395.

[13] *Ibid.*, pp. 429-430, 443, 445, 451. This correspondence inspired Miss Austen to write the *Plan of a Novel* in which she burlesques those faults and falsities in fiction which she was most careful to avoid.

they are purged and done away through tribulations which are none the less poignant for being generally mere misunderstandings. Each book is thus a history of self-education and self-correction. Miss Austen proffers no counsels of perfection, for her practical idealism is content with the implied lesson that a sound education, a marriage based upon congenial dispositions as well as passion, and social decorum give the best promise of happiness in life.

*Characteri-*
*zation*
But to make "the dreary intercourse of daily life" significant a novelist must be able to create living characters. This ability Jane Austen possessed in a measure never excelled among writers of fiction. We have been made to know her people so well that when a crisis arrives they act as we expect them to act; their behavior never astonishes us.[14] Miss Austen knew them so well that she would narrate to her family incidents in their lives which do not occur in the books. *Tout comprendre c'est tout pardonner* is not a proverb to be applied unreservedly to her; she does not always forgive. But those whom she forgives she often loves. There may be truth in the tradition that it was because she "fell in love with" Catherine Morland that she expanded what was probably a mere skit upon Gothic romance into *Northanger Abbey*.[15] The element of burlesque which was probably conspicuous in the original form of *Sense and Sensibility* disappeared in the revision, and for all the sharp, satiric thrusts there is affection for the emotional Marianne. Elizabeth in *Pride and Prejudice* Miss Austen loved unreservedly, declaring her to be "as delightful a creature as ever appeared in print." [16] Emma, on the other hand, she described as "a heroine whom no one but myself will like much," [17] thus doing less than justice to her art and to her readers, for with all Emma's faults we are attracted to the self-deceived woman who is the profoundest of Miss Austen's characterizations. In *Persuasion,* where the satire is directed almost entirely against Bath society, there is nothing but sympathy for the long-parted lovers who are at length united. An unwonted self-revelatory tone, new to this most impersonal of artists, has made many readers suspect that in this book Jane Austen for once unlocked her heart.

The plots are so firmly integrated that it is impossible to isolate even the subsidiary characters (as is so easily done in Dickens). Each is part of a

---

[14] It must be admitted, however, that in some moments of strain they do not talk as we should expect. See on this point Herbert Read, *English Prose Style* (1928), pp. 119-120.

[15] Montague Summers projected an edition of the seven "horrid" novels which Miss Andrews recommended to Isabella Thorpe, but only two—*Horrid Mysteries* and *The Necromancer of the Black Forest*—appeared. See also Michael Sadleir, *The Northanger Novels: a Footnote to Jane Austen* (1927). — Before the final revision of *Northanger Abbey* in 1816 two books had appeared which may have convinced Miss Austen that the two decades intervening since she wrote her satire had not rendered it obsolete. One of these books is Sarah Green's *Romance Readers and Romance Writers* (1810), in which the heroine's head is turned by too much reading of extravagant fiction. The other is Eaton Stannard Barrett's *The Heroine* (1813; ed. Walter Raleigh, 1909), in which the satiric parody, though amusing in spots, is carried to such cruel lengths that Cherubina's plights, intended to expose her to ridicule, actually make her pitiable. On Barrett see further Edith Birkhead, *The Tale of Terror* (1921), pp. 133-137.

[16] *Letters*, p. 297.

[17] J. E. Austen-Leigh, *Memoir*, ed. R. W. Chapman, p. 157.

closely woven fabric. All are what a modern novelist has described as "three-dimensional" or "round" figures, as contrasted with "two-dimensional" or "flat" characters in which a single quality or factor is portrayed.[18] In other words, there are no throw-backs, as in Scott or Dickens, to the old-fashioned "humors." Miss Austen's men and women are seen from a thousand facets. In depicting them she very rarely introduces herself, as Fielding had done and Meredith was to do; still less does she plead with and cajole her readers as some novelists do. Direct record of dialogue and action, not interpolated comment, conveys her impressions and opinions. At times, however, the task of interpreting people and events is shared between the anonymous, impersonal, omniscient narrator and certain of her dramatis personae. Thus, we accept Elizabeth Bennett's point of view as on the whole a reflection of the author's; and in general the tangle in which the characters are enmeshed is observed from a single angle.[19]

There are qualities of Miss Austen's style—the delicate precision, the nice *Style* balance, the seeming simplicity which often masks subtlety, the lucidity and vitality and ironic wit—which remind many readers of Congreve's comedies.[20] Certainly in the neat rhythms of her dialogue the resemblance to stage-comedy is apparent; it is particularly close when she verges upon the farcical, as in the scene of Mr. Collins' proposal of marriage to Elizabeth. It has been remarked that the three-volume form in which the novels were first published brings out an analogy which is obscured in modern one-volume editions, for as in a three-act comedy there is a crescendo, a crisis, and a dénouement.[21] *Pride and Prejudice,* the most dramatic of them all, has even been analyzed into five acts.[22] Miss Austen's preference for the dramatic method involved a severe economy in the use of description; or, putting it the other way round, perhaps her slight interest in the external appearance of people or the details of places led her to adopt the dramatic method. This technique reaches perfection in *Pride and Prejudice.* In the last three books there is more description with more color and sensitiveness; but there is a corresponding loss in animation and a new sobriety of tone. *Mansfield Park* is the least dramatic of the series, and though the half dozen strands of the story are interwoven with wonderful skill, something was sacrificed along with unity of plot. In *Emma* there was a recovery of concentration, and here we have for our delight Miss Austen's greatest comic creations, Mr. Woodhouse and Miss Bates, a superbly natural pair who would be recognizably at home if we saw them on the boards. The resemblance to drama is much less marked in *Persuasion.* Here Miss Austen seems to be feeling her way towards a new technique. What seems a new

18 E. M. Forster, *Aspects of the Novel* (1927), pp. 112-113.
19 Perhaps Miss Austen abandoned the novel-in-letters because in that form the point of view necessarily shifts from writer to writer.
20 Congreve, however, she never mentions and may not have read.
21 C. L. Thomson, *Jane Austen,* p. 233.
22 Baker, vi, 84-87. Only *Pride and Prejudice* begins with a dialogue; the other openings are quietly expository.

departure in *Sanditon* may have been due to a desire to work with fresh materials, perhaps to a belief that the original vein was running thin. But this fragment had not advanced far enough at the time of her death to warrant guesses as to the direction in which it and its author's genius might have developed.[23]

Through almost all her life Jane Austen might have said, with Blake, "I am hid." Few of her books reached a second edition in her lifetime. Only towards the end were there signs of coming recognition.[24] Yet it was long retarded. The collected edition of 1833 supplied the market till 1882. From about 1890 biographies and appreciative estimates began to multiply, and the twentieth century has atoned for the neglect of most of the nineteenth. There have been many studies of her mind and art, her style and technique. There is not a fragment of her writings that has not been edited with loving care. Scholars have scrutinized and interpreted every detail of her picture of English society. Those who have made her the object of a cult have not alienated from her the wider circle of readers. The fact that she wrote comparatively little and that that little is almost always of the highest quality has resulted in the unique distinction which her reputation now enjoys, that she is the only author of her period whose works can be read, and are read, today with delight in their entirety.

[23] For some speculations on this problem see Virginia Woolf, *The Common Reader*, pp. 203-206.

[24] Especially Sir Walter Scott's article on the novels in *The Quarterly Review*, October, 1815; reprinted in *Famous Reviews*, ed. R. B. Johnson (1914).

# X

## Sir Walter Scott

### I

The genial manliness of Scott's character, his fame first as a poet and then as a novelist, the crash of his fortunes, and the heroism with which in broken health he assumed responsibility for a vast debt form a tale which has become part of the British heritage. Possessing a pattern as clear-cut as any story of his own invention, it reveals the fatal flaw in character which brings about a catastrophe, but also the strength without which there is no true tragedy.

Born into an honorable but not lofty position in a society where the *Youth* feudal tradition was still strong, Walter Scott [1] (1771-1832) cherished the ambition to become a landed aristocrat. The Scottish past, legendary and historical, whether of families or clans or regions or the entire country, fascinated him. An incurable lameness, without making him a recluse, led him to devote much time as a boy to reading. He learned Latin, French, and Italian, and later more than a smattering of German. An encyclopedic knowledge of European history was stored in his phenomenal memory. Fairy tales, Oriental fables, romances of chivalry, balladry, and folklore fed his imagination. A brief experience in the dragoons started a lifelong interest in soldiering; and the study of the law, while providing him with a profession, accounts for the legal technicalities in some of his novels and for the effectiveness of his trial scenes. His young days were not devoted wholly to libraries, for loving a life of action he rode about Scotland, drinking and gossiping with humble folk, collecting from their lips quantities

[1] *The Waverley Novels,* Abbotsford Edition (12v, 1842-1847); Border Edition, ed. Andrew Lang (48v, 1892-1894); Oxford Edition (25v, 1912); *Poetical Works* (12v, Edinburgh, 1820), with Scott's notes; Globe Edition, ed. F. T. Palgrave (1866 and reprints); Oxford Edition, ed. J. L. Robertson (1904); *Miscellaneous Prose Works* (30v, 1834-1871); *Letters,* ed. Sir H. J. C. Grierson (12v, 1932-1937); *Private Letter-Books,* ed. Wilfred Partington (1930); *Journal, 1825-1832,* ed. David Douglas (2v, 1890); *Journal, 1825-1832,* ed. J. G. Tait (3v, 1939-1947).— Greville Worthington, *Bibliography* (1930); William Ruff, *Bibliography of the Poetical Works, Transactions of the Edinburgh Bibliographical Society,* I, Part II (1937); J. C. Corson, *A Bibliography of Sir Walter Scott* (1943); J. G. Lockhart, *Memoirs of the Life of Sir Walter Scott* (7v, Edinburgh, 1837-1838); Sir H. J. C. Grierson, *Sir Walter Scott, Bart.* (1938), supplementing and correcting Lockhart. See also Sir H. J. C. Grierson, *Lang, Lockhart, and Biography* (1934); Stephen Gwynn, *Life of Sir Walter Scott* (1930); John Buchan, *Sir Walter Scott* (1932); Archibald Stalker, *The Intimate Life of Sir Walter Scott* (1921); Donald Carswell, *Scott and his Circle* (1930); Wolfgang Keller, *Walter Scott* (Münster, 1933); Lord David Cecil, *Sir Walter Scott* (1933); *Sir Walter Scott To-Day,* ed. Sir H. J. C. Grierson (1932), essays by various authors; W. H. Hudson, *Sir Walter Scott* (1901); C. A. Young, *The Waverley Novels, an Appreciation* (Glasgow, 1907); Margaret Bail, *Sir Walter Scott as a Critic of Literature* (1907); C. F. Fiske, *Epic Suggestion in the Imagery of the Waverley Novels* (New

of traditional ballads, and enlarging his knowledge of peasant types and manners, architectural antiquities, places already famous in song and story, and other places to which he would one day impart a like renown.

**Ballads**    Enthusiasm for balladry was heightened by his study of German; [2] and he "commenced poet" with a free version entitled *William and Helen* (1796), of *Lenore*, G. A. Bürger's ballad on the theme of the spectre bridegroom.[3] In 1797 he married Charlotte Carpenter.[4] He had already experienced the passion and pain of an unsuccessful love affair,[5] and he put no such ardor into his marriage, these emotions coming, as he said, but once in a lifetime. His activities as a folklorist brought Scott into touch with "Monk" Lewis, who included some of his pieces in *Tales of Wonder* (1801). Among his collaborators Scott had John Leyden, an erudite Scottish peasant, and James Hogg, the eccentric shepherd-poet. He benefited also from the counsel of Joseph Ritson.[6] The example of earlier anthologies encouraged him to prepare with Leyden the *Minstrelsy of the Scottish Border* (1802-1803) in which, along with authentic ballads, more or less retouched, were original pieces by Scott or Leyden to take the places of lost ballads. Scott admitted that he added and emended freely, and, though in this matter not perfectly lucid, he did not attempt to palm off his own compositions as genuine antiques. That the learned Ritson approved of his work should have put the question of his essential honesty beyond dispute; it has, nevertheless, been disputed.[7] An edition of the metrical romance of *Sir Tristrem*, retouched and expanded, followed in 1804.

**The Lay of the Last Minstrel**    Then came *The Lay of the Last Minstrel* (1805), which put Scott in the forefront of living poets. There was an eager public for the Gothic stuff from which its confused plot was fashioned. The "frame" in which the tale is set —an aged minstrel reciting the *Lay*—was a happy device, linking the poem to the genuine heritage of old narrative verse and helping to justify the

Haven, 1940); O. F. Emerson, "The Early Literary Life of Sir Walter Scott," *JEGP*, XXIII (1924). 28-62, 241-269, 389-417; W. P. Ker, "Scott," *Collected Essays* (1920), I. 161-179; Baker, VI, chs. VI-IX; Edwin Muir, "Sir Walter Scott," in *From Anne to Victoria*, ed. Bonamy Dobrée (1937), pp. 528-545; P. N. Landis, "The Waverley Novels, or A Hundred Years After," *PMLA*, LII (1937). 461-473.

[2] See F. W. Stokoe, *German Influence in the English Romantic Period* (Cambridge, 1926), ch. IV and appendices I-III. — In 1799 Scott published a version of Goethe's *Götz von Berlichingen*. Another drama influenced by German Gothicism is *The House of Aspen* which Scott wrote in 1799 but did not publish till 1820.

[3] A better version of *Lenore*, by William Taylor of Norwich, also appeared in 1796; and three other renderings were published in the same year.

[4] The mystery of Miss Carpenter's origin and family has been cleared up, so far as seems possible, by Grierson, *Sir Walter Scott*, ch. III.

[5] See Grierson, *op. cit.*, pp. 28-32.

[6] See B. H. Bronson, *Joseph Ritson, Scholar-at-Arms* (2v, Berkeley, 1939). On the work of Ritson and other antiquaries and anthologists see also F. E. Pierce, *Currents and Eddies in the English Romantic Generation* (1918), ch. III.

[7] See the *Minstrelsy*, ed. T. F. Henderson (1892). The case against Scott is presented in F. Elliot, *Trustworthiness of the Border Ballads* (Edinburgh, 1906) and *Further Essays on the Border Ballads* (Edinburgh, 1910). For the defense see Andrew Lang, *Sir Walter Scott and the Border Minstrelsy* (1910). See also Oliver Elton, *Survey ... 1780-1830* (1920), II. 303-304.

extravagant flights of fancy. The metre was modeled upon the ballads with some intermixture from *Christabel,* which Scott had heard recited. The carelessnesses of style, looseness of structure, and crudeness in characterization—defects easily discernible now—were not stumbling-blocks to the first readers of a poem whose vital energy carried everything before it. Scott did not at once follow up this success. While writing his next poem he was busy professionally and socially and engaged in the finest of his scholarly undertakings, the edition of Dryden (1808), and in negotiations which initiated *The Quarterly Review.* In 1808 appeared *Marmion,* a poem less varied `Marmion` in prosody than the *Lay* and more clear-cut in conception, a tale of private adventure set against the background of public events which culminated in the defeat of James IV at Flodden Field. Marmion, the lordly scoundrel, troubles our psychological scruples; but to such heroes the taste of the day was accustomed. The introductions to the several cantos, verse epistles to various friends, are not quite in keeping with the context; but their tributes to Nelson, Pitt, and Fox harmonized with the martial spirit of the narrative and roused patriotic feeling at a time when every Briton needed to have a stout heart.

In *The Lady of the Lake* (1810), which was inspired by Scott's enthusiasm `Later` for the wild country of Loch Katrine, the plot, though better managed than `Poems` the plots of the earlier poems, is subordinate to the descriptive passages, to such episodes as the stag-hunt and the gathering of the clans, and to the beautiful songs, *Rest, Warrior, Rest* and the plangent *Coronach. The Vision of Don Roderick* (1811), which preceded Southey's and Landor's versions of the legendary crime of the last of the Goths, is a *pièce d'occasion.* To its lack of interest may be in part attributed the blame for the falling off in Scott's popularity which he later ascribed wholly to the emergence of Byron. The sales of *Rokeby* (1813) were alarmingly small. Scott had no intimate knowledge of the Yorkshire setting and consequently the "thunderous, cumulative topography" [8] which is a feature of the Scottish poems is diminished. The heroine is the first of various tenderly reminiscential portraits of Scott's first love. Of more significance is the figure of Bertram, in whom we observe the characteristics of the Byronic hero-type—the somber personage compounded of crime, remorse, and magnanimity—in all its features, antedating *Lara* by a year.[9] The period is that of the Cavaliers and Roundheads; in choice and treatment of materials the poem points the way towards the historical novels. We may glance beyond Scott's shift to prose fiction to notice the remaining poems. *The Bridal of Triermain* (1813) is the first experiment by a nineteenth-century poet with the "Matter of Arthur." In it Scott virtually tells as an Arthurian story the tale of the Sleeping Beauty, thus crossing different strains of folklore with the easy

---

[8] John Buchan, *Sir Walter Scott,* p. 113.

[9] The concept, deriving in long descent from Milton's Satan and immediately from the heroes of Gothic romance, shows that "Byronism" was already prevalent when Byron availed himself of it. See Byron, *Childe Harold and other Romantic Poems,* ed. S. C. Chew (1936), pp. xxv-xxvi.

license of the medieval romancers.[10] *The Lord of the Isles* (1815), on the wanderings of Robert Bruce, adheres more closely to history than the earlier poems and is redeemed from dullness only by the fine narrative of Bannockburn. In *Harold the Dauntless* (1817) Scott made the mistake of not taking his own wild theme quite seriously and introduced an element of burlesque which consorts ill with a fierce northern saga.

*Poetic Style*    Scott's prosody, a compound of interwoven rimes in the ballad measure, of octosyllabics, and of cataracts of rime which continue sometimes for five or six lines, is at its best well adapted to the matter of the narratives, but combined with his inexhaustible memories and affluent imagination it produced stories and descriptions that are almost always too long. His finest vein is that of rapid and tumultuous action, when we hear

> sounds of insult, shame and wrong,
> And trumpets blown for wars.

In the analysis both of private motive and of those considerations of state which result in great events he is feeble, often abandoning such problems to the reader's surmise. He could manage mysteries fairly well (as that of the disguised De Wilton in *Marmion*), but he did not know the value of reticence. Overtones of meaning, the substitution of suggestion for state-ment, were beyond his powers. Only in the lyric did he curb his redundancy and often achieve a condensed poignancy. The most memorable passage in the *Lay* is the version of the *Dies Irae*. More stirringly than in any passage of narrative is the martial spirit conveyed to the reader in the *Pibroch of Donald Dhu* and in *Macgregor's Gathering;* and in *Proud Maisie* (the song in *The Heart of Midlothian*) romantic pathos is quintessentialized as it is in none of the long poems or novels.

## II

*Abbotsford*    In 1812 Scott purchased a farm on the Tweed and began not only to build Abbotsford but to acquire more and more land. Thus, through the disastrous realization of the dreams of childhood, the foundation was laid for a pyramid of debts. Involved financial obligations culminated in his ruin.[11] The first omens of the disaster which his arrangements with James Ballantyne and Archibald Constable were to bring upon him appeared as early as 1813 and emphasized the need to check the decline in popularity with efforts along new lines. Long since he had tried his hand at fiction, beginning novels on Thomas the Rhymer and on the Civil Wars.[12] In

---

[10] See Howard Maynadier, *The Arthur of the English Poets* (1907), pp. 336-340. In this same year (1813) Scott's friend Reginald Heber (1783-1826), the famous hymn-writer, was at work upon his *Morte d'Arthur*, which remained a fragment. See Maynadier, pp. 340-342.

[11] Grierson, *Sir Walter Scott,* is largely concerned with the problem of disentangling the complicated evidence and apportioning blame for the crash. Scott's folly and indiscretion, into which his social ambitions drove him, are now seen to have been more blameworthy than Lockhart admitted or Scott himself seems to have realized.

[12] In an appendix to the General Preface to the collected edition of 1829 Scott outlined the plot and printed a fragment of the romance of Thomas the Rhymer.

1805 he had begun *Waverley,* only to lay it aside, discouraged perhaps by the failure of *Queenhoo Hall* (1808), a historical romance by Joseph Strutt which, after the author's death, Scott completed and prepared for the press. The discarded manuscript was now taken up again, and in 1814 *Waverley,* *Waverley* or *'Tis Sixty Years Since* was published anonymously. Scott thought it beneath his dignity as an official of the law to attach his name to a novel; it might also cheapen his reputation as a poet and hinder him from producing tales as rapidly as, with his teeming memory and imagination, he was planning to do. Later, when *Waverley* and its successors were enormously popular, he enjoyed the mystification as to the authorship, though it cannot be denied that it involved him in falsehoods.[13]

In his youth Scott had had from elderly people first-hand reminiscences of the "Forty-five." These he used to make *Waverley* in part a "novel of manners" of the comparatively recent past. But in it history, romance, scenery, folklore, and humor are blended as they had never been before in prose fiction. The different materials are not very well fused; the plot is conventional and the hero not only feebly characterized but representative of a more refined state of society than is quite credible at the epoch and in the environment. But the success of the book was instantaneous and Scott set himself to hold the market he had won.[14] *Guy Mannering* (1815) was written in six weeks, a feat as amazing physically as intellectually. This is a picture of society rather than a historical novel. The period is recent; the setting a remote part of Scotland. The well-worn plot of the missing heir is intricate and incoherent but may be disregarded, for the story's charm lies in the vivid episodes, the brilliant drawing of the subsidiary figures, and the cheerful gusto of the telling. In *The Antiquary* (1816)[15] Scott repeated the plot of the missing heir, contriving it very clumsily and setting it in a period of which he had youthful memories. *Tales of My Landlord* (1816) contains two works, the crudely Gothic *Black Dwarf*[16] in which Scott descended to the level from which he had been rescuing romance, and the splendid *Old Mortality,* a story centering in the rising of the Covenanters in 1685. In *Rob Roy* (1818) Scott's design was, as he noted in the introduction, to contrast the "cultivated mode of life" in southern Scotland with the "wild and lawless adventures" still to be met with in the Highlands. Rob Roy is but a secondary figure in the book, overshadowed by Di Vernon;

13 From the first the authorship was apparent to good judges (Miss Austen, for example). In 1822 J. L. Adolphus, in *Letters to Richard Heber containing Critical Remarks on the Series of Novels beginning with Waverley,* arguing from the resemblances between the novels and Scott's poems, put the matter beyond all doubt—though by then few had any doubts. In the introduction to *Chronicles of the Canongate,* First Series (1825), Scott avowed himself as "the sole and unaided author of these Novels of Waverley," a fact by that time universally known.

14 The fecundity of Scott's first few years as a novelist has suggested the theory (for which there is no real evidence) that he had in hand drafts of at least six of the books which he poured out in rapid succession. See Una Pope-Hennessey's letter in *LTLS,* April 28, 1932.

15 Impressions of a visit to the Continent in 1815 were recorded in *The Field of Waterloo,* a poem, and in *Paul's Letters to his Kinsfolk,* journalistic impressions of the state of Europe. Both were published in 1816.

16 See C. O. Parsons, "The Original of the Black Dwarf," *SP,* XL (1943). 567-575.

the most winning of Scott's heroines. The second series of *Tales of My Landlord* was taken up wholly with *The Heart of Midlothian* (1818), the finest of all the Waverley Novels. In it Scott made amends to the memory of the Covenanters to whom, in *Old Mortality,* he had shown himself, if not unjust, at any rate less than sympathetic. Jeanie Deans represents the covenanting spirit among the peasantry at its noblest. Between 1817 and 1819 Scott was often ill with gall-stones. The disease was at its worst when he wrote the third series of the *Tales* (1819). *The Legend of Montrose,* on

The Bride of Lammermoor

the campaign against Argyle, is a slight thing; but *The Bride of Lammermoor* is very different not only from its companion tale but from all the other books. It was dictated during such agonies that when he read it afterwards Scott remembered not a scene or word. *The Bride* has been well described as "that masterpiece of Gothic fiction which so many had been trying to write and never succeeding." [17] It is a reversion to such stories of doom as the ballads tell, with disasters foretold by soothsayers and sped with curses dark; the violent death of bride and bridegroom; and the extinction of an ancient house.[18] Unlike Scott's other heroes, Ravenswood is the center of his story; but his tragedy is external to his character and is brought upon him by malignant fate. The comic scenes of the faithful retainer are wearisomely prolonged and so farcical as to defeat their purpose of darkening the tragedy by contrast. But the powerful portents uttered by the witch-woman have been likened, not unjustifiably, to the prophecies in *Macbeth.*

Ivanhoe

A recovery of health which, however, left Scott with but half his former physical strength, was signaled by a new departure. *Ivanhoe* (1820) [19] is his first incursion into the Middle Ages. In this romance of adventure, history is accommodated to the exigencies of the plot. In pattern *Ivanhoe* is more firmly knit than are most of the Waverley Novels; and though it was long since relegated to the category of "books for boys" (a position which it now holds very precariously), it contains episodes which, once read (and perhaps never read again), are never forgotten and characters which remain unfadingly vivid. In this year, 1820, Scott wrote far too much. The protracted and confused story of *The Monastery,* with its supernatural absurdities and lack of understanding of "monkish" ideals, gives evidence of hasty writing. Its sequel, *The Abbot,* is much better. For all the violence done to fact, this tale of Mary Queen of Scots combines history and romance in a setting of memorable charm. Scott was now advised by Constable to write a story to be called *The Armada*; but in wisely rejecting the title he relieved himself of the responsibility which would have been his had he put into the forefront of his book the quarrel with Spain. Instead, he chose as his center the apocryphal legend of the death of Amy Robsart and as his setting

---

[17] Baker, VI (1935). 168. — Consciously or unconsciously Scott took the main situation of *The Bride* from C. R. Maturin's *The Milesian Chief* (1812).

[18] See C. O. Parsons, "The Dalrymple Legend in *The Bride of Lammermoor,*" *RES,* XIX (1943). 51-58.

[19] In this year, 1820, a baronetcy was bestowed upon Scott.

a romantic spot which he had visited; and the result was *Kenilworth* (1821). *The Pirate* (1822), founded on impressions of the northern islands received in 1814 and on his interest in the Norse sagas, is second-rate work partially redeemed by fine descriptions of coast and storm. *The Fortunes of Nigel* (1822) shows us London in the reign of James I; there is very little history and consequently little violence is done to it. The evocation of the streets and crowds and iniquities of London is masterly; the opportunity to set Scottish eccentrics against a contrasting background is well exploited; and the character of the King is Scott's most careful historical portrait. Working under deplorable pressure, Scott produced a third novel in this same year: *Peveril of the Peak*. The characters and locality were unfamiliar to him; he did not grasp the complex horrors of the so-called Popish Plot; and the dull story is drawn out to intolerable length. Here we have the first evidence of Scott's decline.

Again there was recovery in *Quentin Durward* (1823), Scott's first foray into French history, based on the *Chronicles* of Philippe de Commines and dealing with the quarrel between Louis XI and Charles the Bold. It falls into the same category with *Ivanhoe,* and judgments passed upon that romance apply equally well to this. In *St. Ronan's Well* (1824) an experiment was made with a story of contemporary life, but the combination of light social satire with a tragic theme was an unhappy one and the book must be judged a failure. On a much higher plane is *Redgauntlet* (1824), the last novel of first rank. Here, reverting to a subject near to his heart, Scott showed the tragic though futile nobility of Jacobitism. The private story (such as it is) is combined with the unfounded tradition of the Young Pretender's secret visit to London. There is more of personal recollection than in any of the other books, much law which derives from the writer's experiences, and memories of his first love affair. The famous inset, *Wandering Willie's Tale,* gives to the book a peculiar prestige. This masterpiece of supernaturalism attains its effect in part by the skilful juxtaposition of the matter-of-fact and the weird and in part by the sense it conveys of mounting terror as the unhurried narrative with which it opens gives way to horror. The climax of the grisly revel is tremendous. *Tales of the Crusaders* (1825) is made up of *The Betrothed* and *The Talisman,* the former an almost negligible piece of Gothicism (though the appearance of Vanda in the haunted chamber is memorable), the latter a lively adventure-story with robust characters and brightly colored Syrian landscape.

Then, when in 1825 England plunged into an economic depression, the *Debts* crash came, and Scott found himself burdened with debt, permitted to retain some of his possessions only through the indulgence of creditors to whom he bound himself by hard conditions, and doomed to seven years of unremitting toil from which he was released only by death. In this year he began to keep the *Journal* which is one of the most moving of autobiographic documents. Turning to one of the first historical themes to attract his attention, the English Civil Wars, he had begun *Woodstock* (1826) amid anxieties but before the wrecking of his fortunes. The unusual care with which it is composed is a sign, perhaps, of his sense of responsibility to his creditors. In the first series of *Chronicles of the Canongate* (1827) he placed in an attractive frame several novelettes, of which some are inconsiderable Gothic fantasies of ghost-lore and divination while two, *The Highland Widow* and *The Two Drovers,* are little tragedies of condensed power. A second series of the *Chronicles* (1828) has as its main offering *The Fair Maid of Perth,* which interweaves a love story with a picture of the conflict between nobles and townsfolk in the Scottish Middle Ages. The psychological insight shown in the delineation of the cowardly young chief of the clan Quhele is noteworthy. Three series (1828, 1829, and 1831) of *Tales of a Grandfather* are not fiction but simplifications of Scottish and French history addressed to youthful intelligences. In *Anne of Geierstein* (1829) he returned to Franco-Burgundian history in the fifteenth century. Here the flame gives light for the last time. In *Count Robert of Paris,* a story of eleventh-century Byzantium taken largely from Gibbon, it flickers fitfully; and in *Castle Dangerous* it goes out in smoke. These last two romances appeared together as the fourth series of *Tales of My Landlord* (1832). Heart and brain had been overdriven; and with "the retinue of the world's good wishes" Scott sought health in Italy. But it was too late. He was brought back to Abbotsford to die (September 21, 1832).[20]

## III

*The Marvelous*

Scott defined romance as "a fictitious narrative in prose or verse, the interest of which turns upon marvelous and uncommon incidents," and the novel as "a fictitious narrative, differing from the romance, because the events are accommodated to the ordinary train of human events, and the modern state of society."[21] Classified accordingly, almost all his fictitious narratives are romances rather than novels. By combining direct observation and imaginative apprehension he blended elements of wonder from old romance with elements of real life into a new synthesis of historical prose romance.[22] With an inveterate taste for "bogles and brownies and

[20] From the above chronological survey the dramas and the miscellaneous prose works have been omitted. Such interest as the former still possess lies in their reflection of contemporary tastes. *The Doom of Devorgoil* (publihed 1826 but written long before) is a "melo-drama" (in the contemporary sense) with serio-comic goblins, songs, and music. *Halidon Hill* (1822) is a clearly drawn sketch from history, full of movement. *Auchindrane* is a domestic tragedy. Scott's major work as an editor, besides the Dryden (1808), is the Swift (1814), a less congenial task. He also edited several collections of letters, memoirs, and state papers. *The Border Antiquities of England and Scotland* (1817) have to do with the scenery and architecture of the region. *Letters on Demonology and Witchcraft* (1830), though a somewhat chaotic compilation, was written *con amore* and retains its interest.

[21] *Essay on Romance*, published in the Supplement to the *Encyclopædia Britannica* (1824); reprinted in *Miscellaneous Prose Works* (1827).

[22] Max Korn, "Sir Walter Scott und die Geschichte," *Anglia*, LXI (1937). 416-441. G. E. Smock, *Sir Walter Scott's Theory of the Novel*, a Cornell University dissertation, 1934, is not yet published.

lang-nebbit things frae the neist world," Scott never entirely freed himself from dependence upon the marvelous.[23] This varies in tone and atmosphere from the crudest supernaturalism [24] to such a moving evocation of awe and dread as the apparition of old Alice to Ravenswood. The many failures in this kind are partly due to Scott's failure to take the supernatural seriously. The White Lady of Avenel (a grotesque sister of Fouqué's *Undine*), which even Lockhart admitted to be a "blot" upon *The Monastery*,[25] is a shocking mixture of farce and fantasy. Elspeth the witch in *The Antiquary* and Norna of the Fitful Head in *The Pirate* are the merest pieces of theatrical clap-trap. That he had overdone this sort of thing Scott implied in the introduction to *The Fortunes of Nigel* where he promised to make no use of "dreams, or presages, or obscure allusions to future events," "not so much as the poor tick of a solitary death-watch in the wainscot."

The farther back in time the stories are placed the larger the element of *The* romance and the smaller the attention paid to "the ordinary train of human *Treatment* events." Those whose period is the eighteenth century are, for all their *of History* romantic qualities, also novels of manners, and are sometimes so advertised on title-page or in introduction. Since types and manners change slowly in Scotland, the same may be said of *Old Mortality* and *The Heart of Midlothian*. But in the fifteenth and sixteenth centuries Scott was less at home, and when we have retreated to the Middle Ages we are in a dream-world where Scott cheerfully admits that he "may have confused the manners of two or three centuries." [26] A distinction must be made between anachronisms due to insufficient knowledge or sympathy and the deliberate distortions of history designed to heighten the interest of the story. He could on occasion master a historic situation supremely well, as the Covenanters in *Old Mortality* and the Porteous Riots in *The Heart of Midlothian* bear witness. He knew as well as his critics that in *Kenilworth* events are condensed and telescoped, that Dudley's marriage to Amy Robsart was not a secret and that her death had occurred long before the period of the story; but when he made Shakespeare a figure renowned at court at a date when he was really a child he allowed himself too great a liberty. There are times when his failure to grasp a situation bewilders and exasperates his readers. The desperate confusion in *The Monastery* is a case in point; and there, too, we note his incompetence when he deals with a subject with which he has no sympathy. The monastic ideal and consequently the tragedy of its degeneracy were beyond his range. The aesthetic question is whether his offenses against Clio are of a nature to shock the sensibilities not only of a

---

[23] C. O. Colman has published many studies of Scott's use of folklore and the supernatural. See especially *N&Q*, CLXXXIV (1943). 95-97; 358-363; CLXXXV (1943). 4-9; 92-100;CLXXXVIII (1945). 2-8; 30-33; 76-77; 98-101.

[24] Such as the apparition of the Bodach Glas in *Waverley* or the wraith which appears on the battlefield in *A Legend of Montrose*.

[25] Lockhart, *Life of Scott*, ch. L. Lockhart argued that Scott erred in dwelling too long upon the phantom: "The phantom with whom we have leisure to become familiar is sure to fail." The assertion is debatable; and even a very little of the White Lady would have been too much.

[26] Introduction to *Ivanhoe*.

professional historian, like Freeman,[27] but of the usually indulgent general reader. Of profounder moment are Scott's "moral anachronisms," when he ascribes to men and women of past ages the thoughts, tastes, and emotions of his own day. In this respect he followed, probably unconsciously, the example of the rationalistic historians of the preceding age who accepted the principle of immutable natural laws which included human behavior, making the motives of men subject to the same influences in all times and places. In general he showed wisdom in relegating great historical figures to the middle distance or the background. When they are thrust forward to the footlights they are sometimes rather stagey. This is certainly true of his Mary Queen of Scots, though she is made a queenly and romantic personality. But the failure to face the problem of her guilt or innocence in the murder of Darnley makes his portrait psychologically valueless; and the inconclusive end of *The Abbot* at Langside leaves her tragedy but half told. Only once in *Kenilworth* does Queen Elizabeth rise to the height of her reputation; and Louis XI in *Quentin Durward* is a portrait verging upon caricature, unforgettable though the grotesque bigot may be. Scott's most convincing regal figure is James I in *The Fortunes of Nigel,* an eccentric pedant with a strain of vulgarity crossed with kingly dignity.

*Characteri-*
*zation*
Scott's supreme feat was to make the past alive again. His best work was done within the world he knew: the past of Scotland within about a hundred years, that, is within the memory of people he had known in his youth. It has been said that he looked on a man "as an antiquarian looks on a house." [28] He had an eye for every portion of the structure, recognizing that this characteristic was due to this inherited trait and that to that circumstance of environment. He envisaged a man as being colored by the social conditions into which he is born and of which he is heir. With the anxieties and aspirations of men and women considered as individuals he concerned himself scarcely at all; their private lives are of interest only as they are part of history. Working within these limitations he could not give a "three-dimensional" quality to his heroes and heroines; but at his best he imparted a tragic dignity to large situations: revenge, remorse, or the struggle of rival loyalties. His greatest creations usually have but a small part in the conventional plot of the story or are altogether independent of it. They belong to regions which he knew and loved. Not the ineffectual hero but Fergus MacIvor and the Baron of Bradwardine give vitality to *Waverley.* The "wax-work" protagonists of *Guy Mannering* are easily forgotten, but we remember the crowds of peasants and especially Meg Merrilies. Jonathan Oldbuck in *The Antiquary* elbows the nominal hero out of the way and shares his claim to attention only with the vagabond Edie Ochiltree. Bailie Nicol Jarvie and the lying braggart Andrew Fairservice, with their humorous vernacular,[29] are the life of *Rob Roy.* Even in *The*

[27] See the strictures on *Ivanhoe* in E. A. Freeman, *The Norman Conquest,* v, Note W.
[28] Lord David Cecil, *Sir Walter Scott,* p. 7.
[29] The dialect is generally of Scott's own district. Sometimes it is "broad"; or he may make a concession to southern readers by coloring standard English with local idioms and

*Heart of Midlothian,* where the principal characters count for more than in the general run of the novels, the most vivid figures are the criminals. Just as he made of the Scots dialect an instrument for the expression of a wide range of emotion, so Scott is always excellent when he is portraying social outcasts, treating them often humorously, but as often horrifyingly. He is, in fact, a much more convincing artist when he deals with the humorous, the eccentric, the squalid, even with the downright villainous, than when he delineates the morally irreproachable.

In a few cases Scott took pains with the structure of an entire story; but generally we remember the novels for separate episodes rather than for any total artistic effect. Innumerable scenes are greater than the stories that contain them. Sometimes these are scenes of hair-breadth escapes, as when Queen Mary escapes from Loch Leven or when Charles I appears as a fugitive. Of like kind is the scene in *Old Mortality*—one of the supreme things in the novels—when Claverhouse saves Morton from the fanatics who are attending his midnight doom. The confrontation of mighty opposites is a challenge to all Scott's powers. Scenes of action are more congenial to him than are interludes of calm. He and his public were overfond of weird and horrible episodes; but when his imagination was excited to its depths, as in the scene of the corpse-winding in *The Bride of Lammermoor,* he rose far above the level of contemporary Gothicism. The total effect was generally marred because Scott seldom conceived a unified design. He displayed a brilliant but disorderly pageant, imposing upon this vital confusion a semblance of order by means of the artificial plot. Some of the novels are too long in getting started; he seems to be letting his pen drive on while deciding what to write about. Others continue after the real story is wound up; the long anticlimax of *The Heart of Midlothian* was stitched on because the book had to be extended to the contracted length. The conventional reversal of fortune at the close of some stories is a concession to his public, Scott being one who, living to please, had to please to live.[30] An anxiety not to alienate readers resulted in the hopeless marring of *St. Ronan's Well* where last-minute changes in the plot blurred the whole point of the intrigue.[31]

*Great Scenes*

Of any profound philosophic conception of life there is no trace in Scott. He would have been bewildered had he guessed it would be sought for. There is no speculation in his eyes. His sympathies were aristocratic, almost feudal; he enjoyed the position of the bountiful laird surrounded by loyal retainers; and he delighted to pay homage to his liege lord—even though that liege was George IV. This loyalty to the House of Hanover did not

*Tastes and Sympathies*

words. Scott knew no Gaelic, and Celtic scholars have criticized his attempts to render Gaelic idiom. In the medieval romances the problem of the style of the dialogue was met by not making it so obsolete as to be incomprehensible nor so modern as to jar upon the sensibilities of the trained reader; but it was not very well solved, for the antique effects are often of the sort known as "Wardour Street English."

30 "No one shall find me rowing against the stream—I write for general amusement" (Introductory Epistle to *The Fortunes of Nigel*).

31 See Baker, VI. 194-195.

clash with the purely sentimental "Charlie-over-the-Waterism" which Borrow was later to laugh at. His sympathies were with the Cavaliers—which is why he was somewhat less than just to the Roundheads; but in dealing with history he generally avoided controversial issues, preferring to accept the current popular judgment. Love, though the major theme of his plots, is not the major theme of his books. They have to do with warfare and adventures, wild, curious and improbable, dangers by flood and field. Such subjects consorted with his taste for chivalry and "gramarye," ancient architecture, armor, heraldry, old sports and pastimes, and folk-legends. His robust interest in art and antiques was not discriminating, as the miscellaneous assortment of objects assembled at Abbotsford testified. He had little love of music save when a melody called to mind the words of songs.

*Fame*

During the last decade of his life a legion of now forgotten imitators trailed after him. His immediate contemporaries among Scottish novelists worked mostly along other lines.[32] Later came Ainsworth, Bulwer-Lytton, and G. P. R. James; then Reade and Kingsley; and much later Stevenson. The French romanticists—Vigny, Dumas, Hugo, and even (though with a difference) Merimée—were his followers in the field of the historical novel.[33] Without Scott, Manzoni's *I Promessi Sposi* is inconceivable. In Germany a school of novelists regarded him as their master, and G. M. Ebers applied his methods to stories of ancient Egypt. In England and America his reputation is probably somewhat higher today than it was a generation ago; but from the ardor of some vocal admirers one must not infer an increase in the number of his readers.[34]

[32] See ch. XVI, below.

[33] Louis Maigron, *Le roman historique à l'époque romantique: essai sur l'influence de Walter Scott* (Paris, 1898).

[34] For a survey of the fluctuations in the prestige of the novels see J. T. Hillhouse, *The Waverley Novels and their Critics* (Minneapolis, 1936).

# XI

## Lord Byron

### I

It is a commonplace of criticism to distinguish between the poetry which Byron composed before his final departure from England in 1816 and the poetry of his later years. The break in continuity was not complete. He vacillated between rationalism and romantic illusionism, between respect for convention and defiant revolt, between loyalty to the old classicism and adherence to the new fashions in poetry. There are satiric elements in his romantic poems; and, conversely, there are romantic passages in his satires.[1]

George Gordon Byron [2] (1788-1824), who at the age of ten became Lord Byron of Newstead, inherited from both sides of his ancestry an emotional

---

[1] Helene Richter, "Byron, Klassizismus und Romantik," *Anglia,* XLVIII (1924). 209-257. Miss Richter makes much of this dichotomy in her *Lord Byron: Persönlichkeit und Werk* (Halle, 1929).

[2] *Works: Poetry,* ed. E. H. Coleridge; *Letters and Journals,* ed. R. E. Prothero (13v, 1898-1904); *Poetical Works,* ed. P. E. More (1905); *Correspondence,* ed. John Murray (2v, 1922); *Don Juan and other Satirical Poems,* ed. L. I. Bredvold (1935); *Childe Harold's Pilgrimage and other Romantic Poems,* ed. S. C. Chew (1936). — T. J. Wise, *Bibliography* (2v, 1932-1933); Ethel C. Mayne, *Byron* (2v, 1912; revised, 1924); John Drinkwater, *The Pilgrim of Eternity: Byron—A Conflict* (1925); André Maurois, *Byron* (2v, Paris, 1930); Harold Nicolson, *Byron: The Last Journey, 1823-1824* (1924); Peter Quennell, *Byron: The Years of Fame* (1935) and *Byron in Italy* (1941); Ethel C. Mayne, *The Life of Lady Byron* (1929). On the Byron "Problem" see also Ralph Milbanke, Earl of Lovelace, *Astarte: A Fragment of Truth concerning . . . Lord Byron* (privately printed, 1905; ed. Mary, Countess of Lovelace, 1921); John Murray, E. H. Pember, and R. E. Prothero, *Lord Byron and his Detractors* (privately printed, 1906); Richard Edgecombe, *Byron: The Last Phase* (1909); Sir John Fox, *The Byron Mystery* (1924). Monographs on special topics: Charles du Bos, *Byron et le besoin de la fatalité* (Paris, 1929; English trans., by E. C. Mayne, 1932); W. J. Calvert, *Byron: Romantic Paradox* (Chapel Hill, 1935); S. C. Chew, *The Dramas of Lord Byron* (Göttingen, 1915); C. M. Fuess, *Lord Byron as a Satirist in Verse* (1912); C. T. Goode, *Byron as Critic* (Weimar, 1923); Dora N. Raymond, *The Political Career of Lord Byron* (1924). On Byron's reputation and influence: S. C. Chew, *Byron in England: His Fame and After-Fame* (1924); W. E. Leonard, *Byron and Byronism in America* (1905); Edmond Estève, *Byron et le romantisme français* (Paris, 1907); G. Muoni, *La Fama del Byron e il Byronismo in Italia* (Milan, 1903); Max Simhart, *Lord Byrons Einfluss auf die italienische Literatur* (Munich, 1909); Antonio Porta, *Byronismo Italiano* (Milan, 1923); W. Ochsenbein, "Die Aufnahme Lord Byrons in Deutschland," *Untersuchungen zur neueren Sprach- und Literaturgeschichte,* VI (Berne, 1905); Cedric Hentschell, *The Byronic Teuton* (1939); P. H. Churchman, "The Beginnings of Byronism in Spain," *Revue hispanique,* XXIII (1910). 333-410. Important critical estimates are: P. E. More, "The Wholesome Revival of Byron," *Atlantic Monthly,* LXXXII (1898). 801-809; W. P. Trent, "The Byron Revival," *Forum,* XXVI (1898). 242-256; George Rebec, "Byron and Morals," *International Journal of Ethics,* XIV (1903). 39-54; J. F. A. Pyre "Byron in our Day," *Atlantic Monthly,* XCIX (1907). 542-552; S. F. Gingerich, *Essays in the Romantic Poets* (1924), pp. 243-276; H. W. Garrod, *Byron: 1824-1924* (1924), a lecture; Lord Ernle (R. E. Prothero), "The Poetry of Byron," *Quarterly Rev.* CCXLI (1924). 229-263; H. M. Jones, "The Byron Centenary," *Yale Rev.* XIII (1924). 730-745; Bertrand Russell, "Byron and the Modern World," *JHI,* I (1940). 24-37. — Parts of this chapter are taken, by permission of the Odyssey Press, from the writer's introduction to the volume of selections mentioned above.

instability bordering upon madness.[3] His father, having had by a first marriage a daughter, Augusta, had married Catherine Gordon of Gight; and having depleted her small dowry, he decamped to France where he died when his only son was three years old. Congenital lameness, narrow circumstances in his childhood at Aberdeen,[4] and alternating indulgence and abuse from his mother fixed in the boy a subconscious sense of inferiority which found expression in pride, scorn, and contemptuousness. Of several precocious love affairs, one, with a cousin, Mary Chaworth, he later made famous to all the world. At Harrow he won some distinction for oratory; and at Cambridge (1805-1808), where dissipation distracted him from study, he made friends with John Cam Hobhouse[5] and with the mysterious "Thyrza" whose death in 1812 he mourned in a cycle of elegies. In 1806 his *Fugitive Pieces* appeared privately, only to be suppressed because of the impropriety of one poem. After a second false start, *Poems on Various Occasions* (1807), Byron sought a wider audience and published *Hours of Idleness* (1807). These poems, reprinted in the main from the two previous volumes, are imitative and pretentious, facile and rhetorical, commendable only for the sincere love of Highland scenery expressed in some of them. Henry Brougham's slashing criticism in *The Edinburgh Review*[6] goaded Byron to the discovery of his powers as a satirist. He kept his anger under control, proceeded slowly, and did not publish *English Bards and Scotch Reviewers* till 1809. It attracted some attention. That its author was young and injudicious was evident; but that he could polish an epigram and hit hard was undeniable.

*Youth*

*Travels in the Levant*

Shortly after this, Byron, having attained his majority and taken his seat in the House of Lords, set out with Hobhouse for the Levant. They traveled by way of Portugal and Spain, sailed to Malta and thence to Albania, and at length came to Athens.[7] There Byron celebrated the charms of Teresa Macri in *Maid of Athens,* the best known of his songs. At Smyrna he completed the first two cantos of *Childe Harold's Pilgrimage.*[8] Of a sojourn at Constantinople (May to July, 1810) we know little, for the travel poem was not carried on to this point and later gossip is mostly baseless. Hobhouse then returned home; but Byron lingered for a second stay in Athens and did not reach England till July, 1811. He brought with him the manuscripts of several poems.

[3] Of various studies of Byron's mental health-history the latest is J. H. Cassity, "Psychopathological Glimpses of Lord Byron," *Psychoanalytic Review*, XII (1925). 397-413. See also Hermann Conrad, "Byrons Vorfahren und Kindheit," *Anglia*, LI (1927). 164-173, 372-383.

[4] The early Scottish influence upon Byron is stressed in J. D. Symon, *Byron in Perspective* (1925), and in T. S. Eliot, "Byron," in *From Anne to Victoria*, ed. Bonamy Dobrée (1937), pp. 601-619.

[5] J. C. Hobhouse (1786-1869), created Lord Broughton, entered Parliament, championed reform, and was a member of Grey's, Melbourne's, and Russell's cabinets. His *Recollections of a Long Life* (2v, 1909) contains much information on Byron.

[6] January, 1808; reprinted in *Letters and Journals*, ed. Prothero, I, 344-349.

[7] Harold Spender, *Byron and Greece* (1924); Karl Brunner, "Griechenland in Byrons Dichtung," *Anglia*, LX (1936). 203-210.

[8] Hobhouse's *A Journey through Albania and other Provinces of Turkey* (1813) supplements Byron's second canto.

A friend, R. C. Dallas, was disappointed in *Hints from Horace,* a laborious sequel to *English Bards. The Curse of Minerva,* attacking Lord Elgin for the vandalism committed upon the Parthenon, was set aside because possibly actionable.[9] Dallas then read the verse narrative of Byron's travels and recognizing it to be a work of genius, persuaded the poet to consent to its publication by John Murray. Subjected to revision while passing through the press, it received the stamp of Byron's moody loneliness, intensified by the death of his mother and of two dear friends, in the months following his return to England. But he now met two influential men of letters, Rogers and Moore, and by them was introduced to the brilliant Whig society which centered in Holland House.[10] His beauty, youth, and ancient name, the romantic journey which he had accomplished, reports of his genius, and rumors of his wickedness were more than sufficient to offset his self-conscious gaucherie; and the years of his notoriety began. The morning when he "awoke and found himself famous" was March 10, 1812, when *Childe Harold's Pilgrimage* appeared. The way for it had been prepared by the people who molded literary taste; there was nothing disconcertingly novel in a narrative and reflective poem in the Spenserian stanza; the poet's rank and reputation stimulated curiosity; the Iberian setting of the first canto was of topical interest; the Levantine setting of the second appealed to the taste for Oriental travel books; [11] and the *leitmotif* of disillusioned skepticism was attractively romantic and melancholy. The crudities of these cantos are now all too obvious; but they may be still enjoyed by anyone who is stimulated by contact with a young mind of exceptional energy.

*Childe Harold*

Byron's cynicism appraised popular applause correctly, but he made the most of it while it lasted. More sought after than seeking, he passed from one love affair to another, sensual or sentimental. The most conspicuous was the liaison with Lady Caroline Lamb; the most serious was the incestuous relationship with his half-sister, Augusta Leigh. Happiness fled before him who sought to find it in pleasure. Gloom and satiety were none the less sincere for being theatrically displayed. In the midst of amatory and social triumphs he turned out the three Oriental Tales—*The Giaour, The Bride of Abydos* (both 1813), and *The Corsair* (1814), rhetorical narratives of mysterious adventure and sentimental love which are today readable only for their occasional passages of genuine poetry. In *Lara* (1814) Byron turned from the East and employed the Gothic mode for the delineation of the "Byronic" hero. The type is descended from the Miltonic Satan and the criminal heroes of Mrs. Radcliffe; but the lowering doom is

*The Oriental Tales*

[9] Privately printed (1812) and pirated in mangled form, but not included in Byron's works till after his death. The famous opening lines describing sunset on the Acropolis were transferred to *The Corsair,* Canto III.

[10] See the Countess of Airlie, *In Whig Society, 1775-1818* (1921); Lord David Cecil, *The Young Melbourne* (1939), pp. 47-80; Marjorie Villiers, *The Grand Whiggery* (1939), pp. 236-303.

[11] The best account of these is in Wallace C. Brown's as yet unpublished study, *The Gorgeous East in Fee.*

darkened by Byron's sense of predestination, and "the fire which preys on lonely bosoms" is kindled by personal guilt and remorse. The portrait of Lara has been regarded as a masterpiece of self-revelation, but the "self" revealed is to some degree a deliberate fabrication.[12]

*Marriage and Separation*

Through 1814 Byron was looking about for a wife to mend his fortunes and, perchance, his ways. His choice fell upon Anna Isabella Milbanke, who, having wisely rejected him, yielded when he addressed her a second time; and they were married on January 2, 1815. The unhappy story of the marital year does not need retelling. *Parisina* and *The Siege of Corinth* are the chief poems of this period. Byron was often drunken, saturnine, and taciturn, brutal and unfaithful to his wife. Their only child, Augusta Ada,[13] was born in December; and in January, 1816, Lady Byron left her husband.[14] Negotiations followed, but in the end Byron consented to a separation. He found revenge in two poems which piratical publishers circulated as *Poems on his Domestic Circumstances*. One was a sentimental farewell to his wife, the other a lampoon upon her female companion—both in the worst of taste. A few friends rallied round him; the romantic Jane Clairmont [15] ("Claire") offered herself as his mistress. The storm of social ostracism raged too high and in April he left England forever.

*Switzerland*

By way of Waterloo [16] and the Rhine Byron journeyed to Geneva, where he rejoined Jane Clairmont, who was living with Shelley and Mary Godwin. Association with Shelley enlarged the humanitarian sentiment to which Byron had already given expression;[17] and from Shelley came also an understanding of Wordsworth which did not last but which helped to inspire the nature feeling of the third canto of *Childe Harold* and the style of *Churchill's Grave*. Shelley and "Monk" Lewis (who joined the company at Geneva) introduced Byron to Goethe's *Faust,* with profound effect upon his imagination.[18] To the early summer belong *The Dream,* a cruel in-

[12] Compare Charles du Bos, *Byron et le besoin de la fatalité* (Paris, 1929), pp. 70-78, with T. S. Eliot's comment thereon in *From Anne to Victoria*, p. 614.

[13] Afterwards Countess of Lovelace, mother of the author of *Astarte* and mother-in-law of the poet-traveler Wilfrid Scawen Blunt.

[14] It seems clear that Lady Byron knew of the relationship which had existed between Byron and Mrs. Leigh; but having received the latter's assurances that it had been broken off before Byron's marriage, she extended her forgiveness and protection to her sister-in-law. The incest was, therefore, not the cause of the separation. So long as Lady Byron suspected (with good reason, as modern alienists hold) that her husband was insane, she was determined to remain with him; but when a physician assured her that Byron was mentally responsible for the outrages committed against her, she decided, on her father's advice, to demand a separation. Byron made a great show of "going into court" rather than submit; but when his bluff was called he capitulated.

[15] A. C. Gordon, *Allegra: the Story of Byron and Miss Clairmont* (1926).

[16] The narrative of Waterloo in *Childe Harold,* III, is followed by the most elaborate of Byron's estimates of Napoleon's character. See Gerhard Eggert, "Lord Byron und Napoleon," *Palæstra,* CLXXXVI (Leipzig, 1933).

[17] In February, 1812, Byron had spoken in the House of Lords in defense of the Nottingham frame-breakers, and in April, 1812, on behalf of the repeal of Catholic disabilities. In June, 1813, he presented a petition from an advocate of parliamentary reform who had been mishandled by the military. For a letter refusing to present a petition for the amelioration of the conditions in which debtors were detained see *The Nation* (N. Y.), CVI (1918). 473-474.

[18] See J. G. Robertson, *Goethe and Byron* (1925; *Publications of the English Goethe Society,* n.s., II); F. W. Stokoe, *German Influence in the English Romantic Period* (1926), ch. VII.

discretion against his wife and Mary Chaworth, and the *Epistle to Augusta,* in which, employing *ottava rima* for the first time, he displayed his "bleeding heart." The intense and fiery *Prometheus,* one of Byron's grandest utterances, is of a Shelleyan nobility of thought. The two poets made a voyage round Lake Leman which is recorded in *Childe Harold,* III, and in Shelley's letters and bore fruit also in *The Prisoner of Chillon.* After parting from Shelley Byron visited the Bernese Oberland. The Jungfrau and the Valley of Lauterbrunnen provided the setting for *Manfred,* a wildly Gothic drama in which Promethean and Faustian elements are combined with extravagances taken from Beckford's *Vathek,* Chateaubriand's *René,* the legend of the Wandering Jew, and remorseful memories of Augusta Leigh. In October Byron crossed the Simplon into Italy and after a stay in Milan arrived in *Italy* Venice in November.

In the licentiousness of the next few months, recorded in the most brilliant and boisterous of his letters, there was a defiance of the English "code" which betokened something like desperation. After the Carnival of 1817, when he wrote the exquisite lyric, *So we'll go no more a-roving,* Byron settled into a more regular way of life; and all the while he had not wasted himself entirely upon the society of gondoliers and their wenches but had studied Italian, read the poets, visited the galleries, and frequented the salons. Among his few English visitors was Hobhouse, with whom he went southward in April. Ferrara suggested to him *The Lament of Tasso.* By way of Florence and Umbria he came to Rome, where he completed *Manfred* and in Hobhouse's expert company surveyed the antiquities.[19] The summer was passed near Padua with Byron engaged upon the fourth canto of *Childe Harold,* that splendid panorama of human destiny inspired by Italian history. Renewed association with Shelley at this time is recorded for us in Shelley's *Julian and Maddalo.* Before the end of the year Byron had finished *Childe Harold,* and in the poetry of Luigi Pulci had found a new and very different inspiration.

## II

Byron seems never to have read William Tennant's *Anster Fair* [20] (1812), *The Mock-* the poem which introduced the Italian mock-heroic style into modern *heroic* English literature. In 1816 he had read—or looked into—Giovanni Battista Casti's *Gli Animali Parlanti* (1794-1802), a late survival of the style;[21] but he did not know *The Court and Parliament of Beasts* (1816), the version of Casti by William Stewart Rose.[22] He may have known one or two poems

[19] See Hobhouse's *Historical Illustrations of the Fourth Canto of Childe Harold* (1818).
[20] For a specimen of *Anster Fair* see Ward's *English Poets* (1892), IV, 304-308.
[21] Casti's poem is a satiric improvisation in which the conflict between the *ancien régime* and the new republicanism is transferred to the antediluvian animal world. The subject appealed to Byron's political sympathies.
[22] W. S. Rose (1775-1843) was living in Venice during Byron's sojourn there. See his letter in *ottava rima* to Byron, *Letters and Journals,* ed. Prothero, IV. 212-214. Rose translated Ariosto's *Orlando Furioso* (1823 and 1831). — Byron may have read the samples of the *Morgante Maggiore* translated by J. H. Merivale (1806-1807) and the same scholar's rendering of the

of this sort in the Venetian dialect; but the real incentive came from John Hookham Frere's mock-heroic poem entitled *Prospectus and Specimen of an intended National Work, by William and Robert Whistlecraft ... intended to comprise the most interesting particulars relating to King Arthur and his Round Table* [23] (1817). "Whistlecraft" opened Byron's eyes to the wide possibilities inherent in this kind of satire, taught him to base it upon a famous legend, and led him straight to Pulci, the "sire of the half-serious rhyme."[24] In the *Morgante Maggiore* [25] Pulci, inheriting an older Italian tradition of burlesquing the legend of Charlemagne, narrated the romantic, amorous, comic, and heroic exploits of the Paladins. Running through his vast poem is a vein of moral, political, social, and philosophical comment, generally bantering in tone but capable on occasion of profound seriousness. The connection of Pulci with Byron is direct, but a long rambling tradition must also be reckoned with which leads through Rabelais and Cervantes, Tassoni's *La Secchia Rapita,* Butler's *Hudibras,* and Boileau's *Le Lutrin,* to Pope's *Rape of the Lock* and other mock-heroic poems of the English Augustan age.

Don Juan

In the autumn of 1817 Byron first experimented in the Pulcesque vein. *Beppo,* a Venetian tale of Carnival-time, is frivolous and facetious and just sufficiently naughty to startle the prudes. By a multitude of digressions this trifle is expanded to ninety-nine stanzas. It gives a foretaste of *Don Juan.* In September, 1818, Byron wrote to Moore that he had begun a new poem "meant to be a little quietly facetious upon everything" but perhaps "too free for these very modest days." [26] This is his first allusion to his masterpiece.[27] Whence came his knowledge of the legend of Don Juan Tenorio? [28] What is the relationship between the legend and his poem? Why did he choose this subject? Almost certainly he did not know at first-hand Tirso de Molina's *El Burlador de Sevilla* (1630) or later Spanish versions of the story. Molière's tragicomedy he may have read, and he may have attended per-

---

final episode, *Orlando in Roncesvalles* (1814). For Byron's own version of the first canto of Pulci (1820) see *Poetry,* ed. Coleridge, IV. 279-309. — On the broader movement of which these translations and imitations were part see R. W. King, "Italian Influence on English, Scholarship and Literature during the Romantic Revival," *MLR,* xx (1925). 48-63, 295-304; xxi (1926). 24-33.

[23] Expanded as *The Monks and the Giants* (1818); ed. R. D. Waller (Manchester, 1926). On Frere see also above, ch. I, n. 11.

[24] *Don Juan,* IV, vi.

[25] The *Morgante* was published in 1480; the enlarged version (hence *Maggiore*) in 1482. — Byron's debt to Pulci has never been fully explored. The Satan of *The Vision of Judgment* owes something to the courtly demon Astarotte. The flight through space in *Cain* may owe a hint to Astarotte's transportation of Rinaldo from Egypt to Roncesvalles; but from Lucian to Shelley there are many magical flights in poetry and legend. Astarotte, who insists that he is a fallen angel, not a mere tricksy imp, may have given Byron a suggestion for *Heaven and Earth.* And there are other parallels.

[26] *Letters and Journals,* IV. 260.

[27] See E. F. Boyd, *Byron's Don Juan: A Critical Study* (New Brunswick, 1945); P. G. Trueblood, *The Flowering of Byron's Genius: Studies in Byron's Don Juan* (Stanford University, 1945).

[28] George Gendarme de Bévotte, *La Légende de Don Juan. Son évolution dans la littérature des origines au romantisme* (Paris, 1906); Hans Heckel, *Das Don Juan-Problem in der neueren Dichtung* (Stuttgart, 1915).

formances of Goldoni's comedy and of Mozart's opera. He had seen at
Covent Garden the pantomime in which Grimaldi, the famous clown, took
the part of Scaramouch. There is little in common between the titanic figure
of the Spanish tradition and the adventurous young rake of Byron's poem;
but the problem of how youthful innocence could develop into a personage
so formidable as the legendary Don Juan was perhaps at the back of Byron's
mind. It may be that with recollections that he had been attacked as a "Don
Juan" and a "Sardanapalus" he undertook to portray analytically these types
of licentiousness, Sardanapalus with grave sympathy, Juan with sardonic
humor. Between September, 1818, and March, 1823, Byron wrote sixteen
cantos. The first five were published anonymously by John Murray (1819
and 1821); the later cantos, declined by Murray, were published by John
Hunt (1823 and 1824). The political radicalism, blasphemy, and immorality
of the first installment occasioned a great outcry; but Byron stood his
ground.[29]

Into *Don Juan* Byron put his abundant knowledge of the world and
what wisdom he had garnered from experience. It is a brilliant picture of
life in many lands, furnished with a running commentary, satirical, sardonic,
or serious, upon men, women, and affairs. It exhibits Byron's admirable gift
of friendship; his sensual view of women; his clear-sighted superiority to
the conventions of society and the fads of the moment; his political convictions; his memories of romantic wanderings in the Levant; his titanic
questionings of the cosmos; his poetic sense of the grandeur of nature and
the contrasting pettiness of man. All life is here in its various phases of love
and joy, suffering and hate and fear. The poem is a satire on social usage,
sham and cant and humbug, pride of place, the ostentation and vanity of
glory, the wickedness and needlessness of war, the hypocrisies of conventional morality. A great variety of human beings crowd its pages, friends
and enemies [30] of Byron's, acquaintances, and strangers whom he had
passed by. It is a poem of many moods. There is more of romance and of
"the mannerly obscene" in the early cantos, of public affairs in the middle,
and of social satire in the closing episodes, where Byron's attitude towards
England is strangely tolerant, as that of a man of the world rather than of a
romantic outcast. The changes in mood are reflected in the constant surprises
in the rimes;[31] and the *ottava rima* lends itself to many tones. It is admirably
adapted to satirical purposes, for a situation can be set forth in the sestet
and the required epigrammatic verdict rendered in the couplet. But though
the serio-comic is the most characteristic mood, the evil of the world is not
sensed the less sharply because the corrective supplied is that of ridicule.
Sometimes the Comic Muse withdraws and the poem is flooded with ro-

29 S. C. Chew, *Byron in England*, ch. IV: "The Reception of Don Juan." Imitators were at
once in the field with "forged *Don Juans*," and when at Byron's death the poem was left a
fragment there were many attempts to carry it on. See *ibid.*, ch. V: "The Continuations of
*Don Juan*." A fragment of the genuine Canto XVII was first published in 1904.
30 Byron suppressed his ferocious dedication to Southey when it was decided to publish the
poem anonymously; and it first appeared after Byron's death.
31 E. Eckhardt, "Lord Byrons komische Reime," *ESt*, LXX (1935-1936). 198-208.

mantic sunshine or clouded over with philosophic speculation. *Don Juan,* a wonderful memorial to a society that has "gone glimmering through the dreams of things that were," is yet true to the enduring facts of human nature. Almost it deserves the title which some admirers have bestowed upon it—"the epic of modern life." There are signs that our own disillusioned generation has returned to it with a fresh understanding of its significance.

*Ravenna*

The five years during which Byron had *Don Juan* in hand were filled with other activities. In April, 1819, he met at Venice the Countess Teresa Guiccioli, who fell passionately in love with him. As her *cavaliere servente* he lived near her in Ravenna from December, 1819, till October, 1821. Through her brother, Count Pietro Gamba, Byron came into touch with the conspiratorial organization called the Carbonari which was working for the liberation of Italy. Political liberalism, already voiced in *Childe Harold,* found expression in *The Prophecy of Dante* (1819), in the later cantos of *Don Juan,* and in the two Venetian plays, *Marino Faliero* (1820)

*The Tragedies*

and *The Two Foscari* (1821). The story of the Doge Faliero who joined the rebels against the state of which he was titular head and whose private animus against his own social order became merged in, and subordinate to, the larger issue of freedom against tyranny, inspired Byron to some of his noblest utterances. Unfortunately, in protest against the contemporary degenerate stage (with which he later sought to come to terms in his tragedy, *Werner* [32]) and in line with his advocacy of "regularity" and classical restraint,[33] Byron took as his model the tragedies of Alfieri and composed his drama in accordance with the pseudo-classical "rules," with the consequence that the action begins at so late a point in the story that the cumulative effect of the Doge's resentment is lost.[34] The dramatization of the story of the Doge Foscari who was in duty compelled to pass sentence upon his own son is less impressive. *Sardanapalus* (1821), the most strictly regular of Byron's tragedies, is also the most poetic and personal. In the character of the last Assyrian monarch Byron discerned his own features—his sensuality and love of ease, his detestation of tyranny and wars of conquest, his skepticism and championship of free inquiry, his intellectual probity, his ability to shake off lassitude and act in a righteous cause.

*Cain*

To the Ravenna period belong the two biblical "mysteries," *Cain* and *Heaven and Earth* (both 1821). They are challenges to submissive orthodoxy and assertions of man's right to exercise the reason implanted in him. *Cain*

---

[32] Byron began *Werner* in 1815 and returned to it in 1821-1822. So lacking in the typical Byronic qualities that it has even been suspected that he did not write it, it had, nevertheless, more success upon the stage than any other of his plays. See T. H. V. Motter, "Byron's *Werner* Re-estimated," *Essays in Dramatic Literature,* ed. Hardin Craig (Princeton, 1935), pp. 243-275. See also D. V. Erdman, "Byron's Stage Fright: the History of his Ambition and Fear of Writing for the Stage," *ELH,* vi (1939). 218-243.

[33] In 1821 Byron defended Pope against the strictures in W. L. Bowles's *Invariable Principles of Poetry* (1819). See J. J. Van Rennes, *Bowles, Byron, and the Pope Controversy* (1927); *Letters and Journals,* ed. Prothero, v. 522-592.

[34] Swinburne's tragedy *Marino Faliero* (1885) was partly inspired by his sensitiveness to the defects of style and structure in Byron's. For a comparison of the two plays see S. C. Chew, *Swinburne* (1929), pp. 215-219.

owes little to the narrative in Genesis and nothing to the medieval plays on the theme. Lucifer (as Byron was careful to note) resembles the Satan of *Paradise Lost;* he stands in somewhat the same relation to Cain as does Goethe's Mephistopheles to Faust. From Pierre Bayle's *Dictionary* Byron derived various ideas, especially the Manichaean doctrine of the Two Principles, which he seems not to have fully understood. The Promethean motif, already noted in *Manfred,* reappears, for Cain is not a mere egoistic rebel but "a symbol and a sign to Mortals of their fate and force." [35] His intellect "recoils from its encumbering clay"; [36] and Lucifer brings him into the state of mind which leads to the catastrophe by showing him "infinite things and his own abasement," so that "the rage and fury against the inadequacy of his state to his conceptions" discharges itself "rather against Life, and the author of Life, than the mere living." [37] In thus interpreting his theme, the poet illuminated the very core of Byronism. Like his own Lucifer, he was one of those

> Souls who dare look the Omnipotent tyrant in
> His everlasting face, and tell him that
> His evil is not good.[38]

Reason's challenge to Omnipotence he resumed in *Heaven and Earth.*[39] This "mystery" on the subject of the loves of the sons of God for the daughters of men breaks off abruptly at the coming of the flood, probably because Byron was put to it to devise a sequel.[40]

Byron's political liberalism and his challenge to orthodoxy were behind the quarrel with Robert Southey which culminated in *The Vision of Judgment* (1821), the tremendous parody of the laureate's elegy on George III.[41] Into this little masterpiece Byron put all his "tempest-anger, tempest-mirth," his contempt for the man whom he considered a Tory renegade, his scorn of sycophancy and compromise, his hatred of reactionary despotism. With the exception of the concluding cantos of *Don Juan* this was his last great work.[42]

When the police forced the Gamba family to leave the States of the *Pisa* Church, Byron moved to Pisa. His old connection with John Murray was

---

[35] Byron, *Prometheus,* lines 45-46.
[36] Byron, *The Prophecy of Dante,* IV. 21-22.
[37] *Letters and Journals,* v. 470. Compare *Cain,* I. i. 174-178.
[38] *Cain,* I. i. 138-140. For the outcry occasioned by *Cain* and Byron's disingenuous attempt to set up an analogy with *Paradise Lost* see S. C. Chew, *Byron in England,* ch. VI: "The Reception of *Cain.*"
[39] This was rejected by Murray and published in the second number of *The Liberal* (January, 1823). On the resemblances to James Montgomery's *The World before the Flood* (1812), George Croly's *The Angel of the World* (1820), Thomas Dale's *Irad and Adah, a Tale of the Flood* (1821), and Thomas Moore's *The Loves of the Angels* (1822) see S. C. Chew, *The Dramas of Lord Byron* (Göttingen, 1915), pp. 137-140.
[40] Another fragment, written at Pisa in 1822, is *The Deformed Transformed,* a variation on the Faust theme.
[41] On the origins and development of the quarrel with Southey see *Letters and Journals,* VI. 377-399.
[42] *The Island* (1823), on the story of the mutiny of the *Bounty,* is a reversion to romantic primitivism.

severed on account of the publisher's reluctance to be associated with poems denounced for their impiety, obscenity, and seditiousness. At Shelley's invitation Leigh Hunt arrived at Pisa and the publication of a new quarterly, *The Liberal,* was initiated. Another member of the Pisan circle was Edward John Trelawny.[43] Shelley's death in July, 1822, led to the break-up of the group, and Byron rejoined the Countess Guiccioli at Genoa. He was bored, depressed, resentful of his entanglement with Hunt, aware of a falling off in his reputation in England, perhaps conscious of a decline in poetic power. In this mood he undertook the expedition to Greece. A revolt against the Ottoman overlordship had broken out in 1821 and from the Morea had spread into Attica and Albania. A wave of Philhellenism swept through Western Europe, and a group of Greek nationalists who arrived in London early in 1823 to plead for intervention succeeded in establishing a "Greek Committee" of which Trelawny was a member. Through him and other friends Byron became associated with this organization, and after months of negotiations he sailed from Genoa with Trelawny, Pietro Gamba, and other followers, in July, 1823. He went with little hope of success, believing himself to be on "a fool's errand," but liking the cause and determined to "stick to it." A long delay followed while Byron, in Cephalonia, reached a decision as to the Greek leader to whom he would throw the weight of his prestige and resources, for though there had been military victories there was political confusion among the rival native leaders. He wisely chose Prince Mavrocordatos, the ablest of them, and arrived at his headquarters at Missolonghi early in January, 1824. What followed is known to all the world: the disputes composed genially by Byron; the squalor, and unceasing rain, and hardships bravely borne; the poem written on his thirty-sixth birthday in which he looked forward to a soldier's death; the fever which struck him down; and the end, on April 19, 1824. When the news reached England a month later, animosities were almost universally forgotten and to most men it seemed as though the sun had vanished from the heaven of poetry.[44] His body was brought home and buried in the family church at Hucknall Torkard, near Newstead.

*The Last Journey*

It is difficult to pass judgment upon a poet so *divers et ondoyant* as Lord Byron. His imperfections as an artist are exaggerations of faults common to all the romanticists, and it is unnecessary to amplify his own self-condemnation: "No one has done more through negligence to corrupt the language." His impact upon the reader comes from the mass and weight of his entire work. Today his reputation as a satirist is far higher than as a writer of romantic poems; but his letters and all his poetry, save the negligible juvenilia, must be read if you would know him; and he must be known as a romanticist, representative of his own age, as well as a satirist, belated representative of the Augustans. In one mood he would have sym-

*Romance and Satire*

---

[43] On Trelawny see below, ch. xvi.

[44] See S. C. Chew, *Byron in England,* ch. xi: "The Death of Byron." For the decline in Byron's reputation, the revival of interest in the eighteen-sixties (due largely to the growth of liberal feeling), and later phases of his "after-fame" see *ibid.,* subsequent chapters.

pathized with George Meredith's ridicule of the ultra-romanticism of *Manfred*; but his readiness to turn quizzically upon his own extravagances must not be taken as a token that his tempestuous and introspective moods were insincere. He calculated the value of theatrical posturing to hold attention, but the pose was natural to him. The sense of sin in the Byronic hero comes from his own accusing conscience, and the sense of doom was part of his Calvinistic heritage. He played to perfection the rôle of *l'homme fatal* (with which some of his precursors had experimented) because it was in character. Yet to his despondency and melancholy he could apply the corrective of his cynicism and wit and reasonableness. His opinions on religion are difficult to apprehend because of his instability and two-sidedness.[45] From the Calvinism of his childhood he worked gradually through negation to a vague deism with attendant doubts about immortality illogically at variance with a strong, abiding predestinarianism. Apart from a brief period of derivative transcendentalism in 1816, he found in the natural world not God but an escape from mankind. His poetic imagery [46] is drawn *Imagery* generally from the great natural forces and phenomena, winds and sun and clouds, mountains and the sea. But though he affects to withdraw from his fellows, Byron is to a far greater degree than the other romanticists the poet of humankind. He conveys with tremendous power the majesty and desolation of history, the vanity of pomp and pride, the transitoriness of fame. And he is the poet of contemporary society, keen to discern the false and the corrupt, courageous in denunciation, yet with pity for the young and innocent and with signs of a broader tolerance towards the end.[47] Among the signs of his greatness are his refusal to placate or compromise, his honesty in facing fact, the resolution with which he kept his eyes open to evil in himself as in other men, and the steady decline in affectation and increase in sincerity of purpose as his poetry matured. As a man he will continue to present to posterity a problem which does not admit of a universally acceptable solution. As a poet he mirrored brilliantly and without distortion an absorbingly interesting world.

[45] Manfred Eimer, *Byron und der Kosmos* (Heidelberg, 1912; *Anglistische Forschungen,* xxxiv); E. M. Marjarum, *Byron as Skeptic and Believer* (Princeton, 1938).

[46] See G. Wilson Knight, *The Burning Oracle* (1939), ch. vi: "The Two Eternities: an Essay on Byron," where extravagant claims are made for the metaphysical significance of Byron's imagery.

[47] See G. R. Elliott, "Byron and the Comic Spirit," *PMLA,* xxxix (1924). 897-909.

# XII

## Percy Bysshe Shelley

### I

Consistency of purpose runs through Shelley's career.[1] In boyish letters the ideas of his maturity pulsate with embryonic life. The continuity is obscured by the contrast between the fanaticism of his undisciplined youth and the growing tolerance and moderated hopes of his last years. But the change was in strategy, not in aim. Realizing that premature direct action by reformers would defeat their ends, he came to rely upon poetry as one of the "instruments with which high spirits call the future from its cradle." [2] By gradual modulation rather than abrupt change the radical pamphleteer developed into the greatest of radical poets. The time when one phase

---

[1] *Complete Works*, Julian Edition, ed. Roger Ingpen and W. E. Peck (10v, 1926-1930); *Poems*, ed. C. D. Locock (2v, 1911); *Selected Poems, Essays, and Letters*, ed. Ellsworth Barnard (1944); *Narrative Poems*, ed. C. H. Herford (1927); *Letters*, ed. Roger Ingpen (2v, 1909); *Shelley's Lost Letters to Harriet*, ed. Leslie Hotson (1930); *Note-Books*, ed. H. B. Forman (3v, privately printed, St. Louis, 1911); *Verse and Prose from the Manuscripts*, ed. Sir J. C. E. Shelley-Rolls and Roger Ingpen (1934); *Letters of Mary W. Shelley*, ed. F. L. Jones (2v, Norman, Okla., 1944). — Bibliography in T. J. Wise, *A Shelley Library* (privately printed, 1924). Newman I. White, *Shelley* (2v, 1940), the definitive biography, and *Portrait of Shelley* (1945); Edmund Blunden, *Shelley: A Life Story* (1946); Edward Dowden, *The Life of Percy Bysshe Shelley* (2v, 1886); W. E. Peck, *Shelley: His Life and Work* (2v, 1927); Olwen W. Campbell, *Shelley and the Unromantics* (1924); Roger Ingpen, *Shelley in England* (2v, 1917); Helen Rossetti Angeli, *Shelley and His Friends in Italy* (1911); T. J. Hogg, *After Shelley: Letters to Jane Williams*, ed. Sylva Norman (1934); Thomas Medwin, *Life of Shelley*, ed. H. B. Forman (1913); *The Life of Percy Bysshe Shelley as Comprised in the Life of Shelley by T. J. Hogg, the Recollections of Shelley and Byron by E. J. Trelawny, and Memoirs of Shelley by T. L. Peacock*, introduction by Humbert Wolfe (2v, 1933); Jane, Lady Shelley, *Shelley and Mary* (4v, privately printed, 1882); R. M. Smith and others, *The Shelley Legend* (1945), on which see strictures by N. I. White, *SP*, XLIII (1946). 522-544; F. L. Jones, *PMLA*, LXI (1946). 848-890; K. N. Cameron, *JEGP*, XLV (1946). 369-379. — Critical studies: Francis Thompson, *Shelley* (1909), a famous rhapsody; Edward Dowden, Richard Garnett, and W. M. Rossetti, *Letters about Shelley* (1917), informal consultations among three Shelleyans; A. T. Strong, *Three Studies in Shelley* (1921); Floyd Stovall, *Desire and Restraint in Shelley* (Durham, N. C., 1931); Bennett Weaver, *Toward the Understanding of Shelley* (Minneapolis, 1932); B. P. Kurtz, *The Pursuit of Death* (1933); C. H. Grabo, *The Magic Plant: the Growth of Shelley's Thought* (Chapel Hill, 1936); Ellsworth Barnard, *Shelley's Religion* (Minneapolis, 1936); O. W. Firkins, *Power and Elusiveness in Shelley* (Minneapolis, 1937); A. P. Cappon, *The Scope of Shelley's Philosophic Thinking* (Chicago, 1938); Lillian Winstanley, "Platonism in Shelley," *E&S*, IV (1913). 72-100; Gingerich, *Essays in the Romantic Poets* (1924), pp. 195-239; M. A. Bald, "Shelley's Mental Progress," *E&S*, XIII (1928). 112-137; Herbert Read, *In Defence of Shelley and Other Essays* (1936), pp. 1-86; George Cowling, *Shelley and Other Essays* (Melbourne, 1936), pp. 13-108; Bush, ch. IV; Edmund Blunden, *Shelley and Keats as They Struck Their Contemporaries* (1925); N I. White, *The Unextinguished Hearth: Shelley and His Contemporary Critics* (Durham, N. C., 1938); F. C. Mason, *A Study in Shelley Criticism, 1818-1860* (Mercersburg, Pa., 1937); Henri Peyre, *Shelley et la France* (Cairo, Egypt, 1935); M. L. G. de Courten, *Shelley e l'Italia* (Milan, 1923); Solomon Liptzin, *Shelley in Germany* (1924) — F. S. Ellis, *Concordance* (1892).

[2] Shelley, *Epipsychidion*, lines 520-521.

yielded to the other cannot be determined precisely; the years 1812-1818 saw the transition.

In outline and in many romantic, distressing, or grotesque particulars the life of Percy Bysshe Shelley (1792-1822) is a familiar story. But it is hard to keep the details in mind; they involve the dreary complexities of pecuniary entanglements and the record of constant changes of abode. The fact that at times Shelley was perilously close to madness chastens amusement when we contemplate his impulsive eccentricities of conduct, his swift revulsions from affinities, his humorless resolution in translating theory into practice, the compromises into which he was forced, the contrast between his visions and reality, the contrast between his genius and the milieu whence he sprang.

His family possessed Whig convictions and recently acquired wealth. From *Boyhood* his father, Timothy Shelley, he appears to have inherited no trait of character save the stubbornness with which he held to his opinions. The life of the imagination led with the little sisters whom he charmed with weird and marvelous tales was enriched by the reading of Gothic romances, whence he derived a hatred of tyrants and a desire to emulate the rescuers of damsels in distress. His first love affair, with a cousin, Harriet Grove,[3] was conducted with an ardor as much philosophical as sentimental, for he intended that she should be the first convert to his doctrines. Her betrothal to a man whom Shelley considered "a clod of earth" was the first great disappointment in his life. At Eton this sensitive boy suffered from bullies and from the system of fagging, and his sympathy with the oppressed was deepened. He pursued his hobby of scientific experimentation, with startling immediate results and with a strong ultimate effect upon his imagination. He wrote and even had published a romance, *Zastrozzi* (1810), which was followed by another, *St. Irvyne* (1811).[4] The portrayal in them of despotic iniquity and oppressed virtue is characteristic, but they are the veriest Gothic rubbish, of no promise whatsoever. Equally worthless is *Original Poetry by Victor and Cazire*[5] (1810), written in part by Shelley's sister, Elizabeth. In *The Wandering Jew*[6] appears the figure of Ahasuerus, who was to loom large in *Queen Mab* and *Hellas*.

Shelley entered Oxford in 1810 and soon became intimate with Thomas *Oxford* Jefferson Hogg (1792-1862). The youths absorbed together the ideas of the Neo-Platonists, the French philosophers of the preceding age, the English political radicals, and contemporary writers on natural science. Shelley's childish, unthinking acceptance of orthodox religion had changed to a militant rationalism, and with rhetorical rancor he was dedicating himself to a Voltairian warfare against Christianity. In *Posthumous Fragments of*

---

[3] See *The Journal of Harriet Grove for the Years 1809-1810*, ed. Roger Ingpen (privately printed, 1932). N. I. White incorporates in his biography the portions significant for the study of Shelley.

[4] A. M. D. Hughes, "Shelley's *Zastrozzi* and *St. Irvyne*," MLR, VII (1912). 54-63.

[5] Ed. Richard Garnett (1898).

[6] Shelley's cousin, Thomas Medwin, collaborated with him on this poem. See Manfred Eimer, "Zu Shelley's Dichtung *The Wandering Jew*," *Anglia*, XXXVIII (1914). 433-476.

*Margaret Nicholson* [7] (1811) poems attacking despotism are mingled with others exploiting Gothic horrors or expressing personal melancholy. In February, 1811, appeared *The Necessity of Atheism*. This is a less blatant performance than those who know it only by its challenging title infer. It is really a brief, precise bit of dialectic culminating in the signature: "Thro' deficiency of proof, an Atheist." Shelley's expulsion from the university followed promptly, not on the ground of his authorship of the pamphlet but for contumacy in refusing to answer questions. Hogg was equally obdurate and shared his friend's fate.

Timothy Shelley mismanaged the situation in a tragicomic fashion; and his son, leading a lonely life in London, was soon in a serious plight. An interest in Elizabeth Hitchener, a Sussex schoolteacher was now developing into the attachment of two kindred souls. More ominous for the future was Shelley's concern for his sisters' beautiful young friend, Harriet West-brook, who was unhappy at school. For Shelley schools were synonymous with oppression. When Harriet threw herself upon his protection, like a knight of romance he was impelled to rescue her. An elopement followed, and their marriage in Edinburgh in August, 1811. Shelley subscribed to Godwin's anti-matrimonial theories, but (like his future father-in-law) disregarded them in practice, holding that till society was educated free love worked too great a hardship upon a woman. Leaving his wife at York under the protection of Hogg, he set out to negotiate a financial settlement with his father (which came to nothing); and in his absence Hogg treacherously attempted to seduce Harriet. When he learned of this, Shelley reasoned with Hogg and forgave him, but perfect congeniality was not for a long while, if ever, restored.

*Harriet West-brook*

The next sojourn was at Keswick. Here Shelley saw a good deal of Southey, whose poetry he admired. But repeated contacts convinced him that the elder poet was a turn-coat and time-server.[8] A letter to William Godwin established a relationship long before Shelley met him face to face.[9] Ill health at Keswick (as often afterwards) was concurrent with mental anxiety; and at this time occurred the first grave case of the hallucinations which Shelley experienced thereafter from time to time. With Harriet's elder sister, Eliza, the Shelleys set out for Ireland in February, 1812. The Irish cause was to be the starting-point of a movement to emancipate the human spirit. In Dublin Shelley issued an *Address to the Irish People* and *Proposals for an Association*. The spectacle of three young dreamers distributing tracts on street-corners has obscured the fact that the proposals were moderate in tone and scope. Shelley was aware of the perils of secret societies and mob violence, and while expressing confidence

*Ireland*

[7] The point of the hoaxing title is that twenty-five years earlier Margaret Nicholson had attempted to assassinate George III.

[8] See K. N. Cameron, "Shelley vs. Southey: New Light on an Old Quarrel," *PMLA*, LVII (1942). 489-512.

[9] See Paul Elsner, *Shelleys Abhängigkeit von William Godwins "Political Justice"* (Berlin, 1906).

that the Catholics would soon be emancipated and the Union repealed, cautioned the Irish against over-optimism; misery and crime would not disappear with the accomplishment of their immediate program. His written words were supplemented by an address to a meeting in Dublin. But the sight of the abject poverty depressed him and initial confidence gave way to discouragement. "I make myself," he wrote to Godwin, "the cause of an effect wh will take place ages after I have mouldered in the dust." [10]

They were in England again in April. Shelley occupied himself with radical propaganda in Devonshire and Wales. He read Sir James Henry Lawrence's utopian romance, *The Empire of the Nairs,* whose ideas entered into *Queen Mab* and later poems.[11] The prosecution of Daniel Eaton prompted a *Letter to Lord Ellenborough* (distributed privately) in which Shelley attacked Christianity and defended the right of free speech. In Wales he threw himself, Faust-like, into a project for the reclamation of waste land. Miss Hitchener was now a member of his household; but the belief that she was the "sister of his soul" did not long survive close association, and they parted with bitter feeling on both sides. A short stay in London, where he at last met Godwin, was followed by another sojourn in Wales, a second visit to Ireland, and a return to London.

*Queen Mab* appeared in the summer of 1813.[12] Parts of it are in the irregular rimeless verse of Southey's *Thalaba;* the rest, in blank verse, is clear and forceful radical oratory without shade or subtlety. The vision unfolded to Ianthe by the Spirit was suggested by Volney's *Les Ruines des Empires;* the harshly anti-Christian rationalism comes from Volney, Voltaire, Holbach, Paine, and Godwin. Ahasuerus, the type of sufferer from vengeful power, denounces God, the cruel tyrant who is the depraved creation of the human mind. Kings and priests are the instruments of tyranny. Other subversive doctrines are introduced. In revised form, as *The Dæmon of the World,* the least "dangerous" parts of *Queen Mab* reappeared in the *Alastor* volume (1816); but the complete poem, though subjected to repeated prosecutions, made its way in pirated editions and became a *vade mecum* among the radicals.[13] {Queen Mab}

After the birth of their daughter Ianthe, the alienation from Harriet which had begun long before kept pace with his growing attachment to Godwin's daughter Mary. Affairs moved to a crisis in June, 1814, when he eloped with Mary and in company with Jane Clairmont set off upon a fantastic {Mary Godwin}

[10] March 18, 1812; *Works,* Julian Edition, VIII. 302.
[11] Walter Graham, "Shelley and the *Empire of the Nairs,*" PMLA, XL (1925). 881-891. On the sources of certain details in *Queen Mab* see Carlos Baker, "Spenser, the Eighteenth Century, and Shelley's *Queen Mab,*" MLQ, II (1941). 81-98. See also in general D. J. MacDonald, *The Radicalism of Shelley and its Sources* (Washington, D. C., 1912).
[12] To the same period belong two pamphlets: *A Vindication of Natural Diet,* advocating vegetarianism (a subject which intrudes incongruously into *Queen Mab*), and *A Refutation of Deism,* in which Shelley employs a method of controversy vaguely anticipating the ironical attack upon revealed religion in Samuel Butler's *The Fair Haven.*
[13] N. I. White, "Shelley and the Active Radicals of the Early Nineteenth Century," So. Atl. Quar., XXIX (1930). 248-261.

journey to Switzerland. The restless trio soon returned to England. In London late in 1814 Shelley sank to the nadir of his fortunes, hounded by bailiffs, cast off by Godwin, and in constant controversy with the forsaken Harriet. All that must be said here of the tragedy of Shelley and his first wife is that though his actions were in accord with his avowed principles and were supported by an unshakable consciousness of rectitude, a "conviction of sin" such as a Christian would have confessed would not have made him a less noble man. Intercourse with Hogg and the friendship of Thomas Love Peacock were props to his mind in these dark days. Financial burdens were lightened on the death of his grandfather; but his impractical generosity in dealings with Godwin and in alleviating the poverty of others kept him till the end of his life under the shadow of debt.

*Alastor*

Shelley's depression and sense of isolation found expression in *Alastor, or the Spirit of Solitude* (1816). For the plain rhetoric of *Queen Mab* there is here substituted a delicate, elusive symbolism, employed to give to mental experiences the guise of persons, events, and the forms of nature. The Poet is the devotee of the Ideal; his journey, the quest thereof; his death, his failure to find it in the actual world.[14] That Shelley had in mind the greatness and decline of Wordsworth is likely;[15] but on its deeper levels *Alastor* is indubitably autobiographical.

*Switzerland*

The summer of 1816 was passed in Switzerland. The climate benefited Shelley's health, and association with Byron was a stimulus to both poets.[16] At this time the *Hymn to Intellectual Beauty*—to that unseen Power which consecrates all human thoughts and forms—marked a further stage in Shelley's progress from Godwinian necessitarianism towards Platonic idealism. Later in the summer Shelley visited Chamounix, where in an inn-album he subscribed himself 'ἄθεος. This audacity, reported in England with scandalous gossip about the Geneva household,[17] blackened a reputation already dark. When "Monk" Lewis joined the group, Shelley's interest was excited in Goethe and he translated some scenes from *Faust*.[18]

*The Death of Harriet*

The return to London in September was followed by a series of disasters. The suicide of Mary's half-sister, Fanny Imlay, though for it Shelley was not responsible, was none the less a shock. Harriet's suicide in November and the consequent embittering of the quarrel with the Westbrook family led to the long-drawn-out suit in Chancery which deprived the poet of the

14 B. P. Kurtz, *The Pursuit of Death*, p. 89. See also H. L. Hoffman, *An Odyssey of the Soul, Shelley's Alastor* (1933); R. D. Havens, "Shelley's *Alastor*," PMLA, XLV (1930). 1098-1115.

15 Paul Mueschke and E. L. Griggs, "Wordsworth as the Prototype of the Poet in Shelley's *Alastor*," PMLA, XLIX (1934). 229-245.

16 Manfred Eimer, *Die persönlichen Beziehungen zwischen Byron und den Shelleys* (Heidelberg, 1910); I. C. Clarke, *Shelley and Byron, a Tragic Friendship* (1934). — Byron's physician, J. W. Polidori, was a member of the group. See his *Diary, 1816*, ed. W. M. Rossetti (1911).

17 That there was a love-affair between Shelley and Jane Clairmont is argued by J. H. Smith, "Shelley and Claire Clairmont," PMLA, LIV (1939). 758-814. This theory is controverted by F. L. Jones, "Mary Shelley and Claire Clairmont," *So. Atl. Quar.*, XLII (1943). 406-412. See also R. Glynn Grylls, *Claire Clairmont* (1939).

18 On Shelley's German studies and translations from Goethe see F. W. Stokoe, *German Influence in the English Romantic Period* (1926), ch. VI and appendix IV.

custody of his two children by Harriet, Ianthe and the infant Charles. Marriage to Mary, who had borne him a son, William, and was again with child, followed quickly upon Harriet's death. Shelley's burdens increased when in February, 1817, Jane Clairmont gave birth to Byron's daughter, Allegra. Till the death of this child in 1822 he had constantly to act as mediator between the mother and Lord Byron.

Much of 1817 was spent at Marlow, near Windsor. Here the friendship and encouragement of Horace Smith [19] and Leigh Hunt [20] were of utmost value, and Shelley gradually recovered his spirits and creative energy. *Laon and Cythna,* which in slightly revised form became *The Revolt of Islam,* was now written.[21] The copious monotony and confused detail of the action of *The Revolt of Islam* repel all but the most sympathetic readers; but there are passages of lofty beauty and others of macabre horror. The story reflects the hopes and disappointments of the French Revolution; but it is intended to show—and here Shelley's optimism is in impressive contrast to Wordsworth's despondent revulsion from early confidence—that the Revolution had failed not in consequence of the ideas whence it arose but because of the violence and vengeance with which it was prosecuted. The contrast between the tolerance of this poem and the fanaticism of *Queen Mab* is a measure of the distance Shelley's thought had moved during four years. In the end the lovers die; but they are sustained by the hope that their love will endure and by a "mystical faith that annihilates the differences between fact and dream." [22]

The Revolt of Islam

Two shorter poems of the same period are *Prince Athanase,* which draws from Plato's *Convivium* the comparison between the Uranian and Pandemian Love, and *Rosalind and Helen,* which contrasts true love, unlegalized, with marriage unsanctified because without true love.[23]

In quest of a salubrious climate the Shelleys, with their son, William, an infant daughter, Clara, Jane Clairmont (who now called herself Claire), and Allegra, left England in March, 1818. Shelley was about to reach his full stature as a poet.

## II

At Pisa the Shelleys began a friendship with John and Maria Gisborne; and then, pursuing negotiations relative to Allegra, Shelley met Byron at

[19] Horace Smith (1779-1849) was co-author with his brother James Smith (1775-1839) of *Rejected Addresses* (1812), a series of clever, good-natured parodies of contemporary poets pretending to be submitted in competition for the prize offered for an address to be recited at the opening of the new Drury Lane theatre. The brothers also wrote together *Horace in London* (1813). In later life Horace Smith was the author of many historical novels. His *Gaieties and Gravities* (3v, 1826) contains the still remembered *Address to the Mummy in Belzoni's Exhibition.*

[20] R. B. Johnson, *Shelley-Leigh Hunt. How Friendship Made History* (1928).

[21] See F. L. Jones, "The Revision of *Laon and Cythna,*" *JEGP,* XXXII (1933). 366-372.

[22] B. P. Kurtz, *The Pursuit of Death,* p. 121. The close of *The Revolt of Islam* contains important evidence for the development of Shelley's ideas on immortality, on which see Kurtz, pp. 122-135. On the indebtedness to Volney's *Les Ruines* see K. N. Cameron, "A Major Source of *The Revolt of Islam,*" *PMLA,* LVI (1941). 175-206.

[23] R. D. Havens, "Rosalind and Helen," *JEGP,* XXX (1931). 218-222.

*Venice*

Venice. There Mary joined him, bringing with her the ailing baby Clara, whose death followed in a short time. Mary seems to have held Shelley responsible for this distressing loss, because he had urged her to come to Venice. A spiritual alienation and physical revulsion from her husband which she evinced may be the explanation of the long, latter portion of Shelley's *Julian and Maddalo.* The opening of this poem, a philosophical conversation-piece between Julian (Shelley) and Maddalo (Byron), is but loosely connected with what follows. It has been generally believed that the Madman's desperate story shadows forth the tragedy of Shelley and Harriet, but there are better reasons for associating it with the change in Shelley's and Mary's relations.[24] A despondency less close to insanity but scarcely less profound is expressed in the *Lines Written among the Euganean Hills,* a poem beautifully constructed around the hours of the day, evoking the loveliness of Italian landscape, and containing a magnificent tribute to Byron.

That Shelley carried his melancholy with him to the South in the winter of 1818-1819 is evident from the *Lines Written in Dejection, near Naples;* [25] but in the spring when he went to Rome there was a renewal of confidence and even a measure of happiness, as may be seen in the letters of this time to T. L. Peacock. In that "divinest climate" he resumed work upon *Pro-*

Prome-
theus
Unbound

*metheus Unbound,* which had been begun in the previous autumn, and completed the drama as originally conceived. Act IV, the cosmic choral hymn celebrating the victory of Prometheus, was written later. The prosodic triumphs of this massive yet iridescent drama range from the gentle songs of the comforting spirits, through the rhapsodic *aria,* "Life of Life," to the mighty orchestration of the fourth act. It was once the fashion to interpret Shelley's meaning in terms of formal allegory,[26] but this method is now generally discarded in favor of explications of his erudite symbolism.[27] Of this the reader must be apprised if he would wrest the meaning from *Prometheus.* Even if some of the supposed resemblances to Platonic thought and contemporary scientific theory are discounted as unconscious reminiscences, sufficient remain to indicate that Shelley aimed at a synthesis of his youthful radicalism, his mature Platonism, Christian ethics, and modern science. The fourth act, for example, certainly cannot be understood without recourse to theories of electric phenomena, vitalism, and "animal

[24] N. I. White, *Shelley,* II. 38-56. In the light of Professor White's discussion the theory of R. D. Havens, "Julian and Maddalo," *SP,* XXVII (1930). 648-653, that the Madman is drawn from Tasso must be modified though not necessarily abandoned.

[25] Light has been thrown by N. I. White, *Shelley,* II. 71-83, on the mystery of Shelley's "Neopolitan ward." According to the register of births at Naples a daughter, Elena, was born to Shelley and Mary. That this parentage was impossible at the time is certain. A review of all the possibilities supports the hypothesis that Shelley falsely affirmed the parentage of an adopted child; but Professor White's theory has not been accepted by all Shelley scholars.

[26] One form of allegorical interpretation is represented by W. M. Rossetti's lectures of 1886-1887 (*Shelley Society Papers,* I); another by V. D. Scudder in her edition of *Prometheus Unbound* (1892). For objections to these and other interpretations see N. I. White, "*Prometheus Unbound,* or Every Man His Own Allegorist," *PMLA,* XL (1925). 172-184. See also K. N. Cameron, "The Political Symbolism of *Prometheus Unbound,*" *PMLA,* LVIII (1943). 728-753.

[27] C. H. Grabo, *A Newton among Poets* (Chapel Hill, 1930) and *Prometheus Unbound: an Interpretation* (Chapel Hill, 1935).

magnetism." In *Queen Mab* the Spirit of Nature had symbolized Necessity, that is, the uninterrupted sequence of cause and effect in the intellectual and material world. But Shelley saw that by observing cause and consequence we can modify conduct and opinion through persuasion and exhortation. To do this is the poet's function, and in this sense, as he afterwards proclaimed, "poets are the unacknowledged legislators of the world." Instead of attacking institutions Shelley came to realize that evil is in man's own mind. If the will did not enchain us to evil, "we might be otherwise." [28] The titan's "unbinding" comes about through the birth of pity, the disappearance of the desire for vengeance, and repentance for evil done. The conquest of Jupiter takes place within the mind of Prometheus. Thus the overthrow of the despotic God who is the creature of man's own imagination is brought about, and the mind is united with Ideal Love. Shelley's concept of the Utopia which follows upon this union has been derided as both Godwinian and sentimental; but it needs to be observed that in the closing words of the drama there is warning as well as triumph; the Golden Age, though won, may be lost again; in the great cycle of renewal and decline the struggle may have to be resumed.

Shelley employed his symbolism to convey suggestions of ideas almost beyond the reach of language. We may pause to note a few examples.[29] By a strange distortion, images ordinarily associated with evil are often made images of good in Shelley's poetry. Thus, the serpent generally represents the good principle.[30] Meteors, which are maleficent in popular superstition, are sometimes beneficent in his imagination, though at others the word *meteor,* in the sense of marsh-light or will-o'-the-wisp, is used with an evil connotation. Metaphors of poison—the poisoned cup or chalice, or poisoned springs, or the air, or the dew—occur often; and in general an obsession with the sinister [31] is the obverse of Shelley's idealism and reflects his passionate consciousness of evil in the world. His boyish Gothic fancies and later hallucinations contributed to the charnel-house imaginings and strange associations of loveliness with terror and decay which, sometimes in swift metaphor, sometimes in elaborated symbol, darken his poems and reach a climax of horror in the ghastly garden described in *The Sensitive Plant.* A favorite symbol of evil is that of the scorpion which (as in the old emblem-books) stings itself to death; for evil is in its nature self-destroying. A symbol may have more than one meaning, even contradictory meanings. Thus, the oft-recurring image of the veil may mean hypocrisy, which hides injustice and selfishness; but "the painted veil which men call life" separates the ideal from the errors of the phenomenal world. The moon is another favorite image, sometimes employed with a Keatsian connotation, or as an

*Symbols*

28 Shelley, *Julian and Maddalo,* lines 170-172.
29 A. T. Strong, "Shelley's Symbolism," *Three Studies in Shelley,* pp. 67-106.
30 For this Shelley had the warrant of the Serpent in the Wilderness, the snake associated with Aesculapius, the serpent as the emblem of wisdom and eternity, and so forth. In *The Revolt of Islam,* I, sts. XXVI-XXXIII, the serpent struggles with the eagle. The eagle as an emblem of evil was suggested by the eagle of despotic Rome.
31 A. T. Strong, "The Sinister in Shelley," *Three Studies in Shelley,* pp. 107-147.

emblem of mutability, or with suggestions of thaumaturgic power. In *Alastor,* in Asia's song in *Prometheus,* and elsewhere we note the image of the boat, which either bears the soul or *is* the soul, and floats beyond death into the regions of the ideal. Sometimes the boat is associated with caverns, and it may be steered by a fair woman, who is Intellectual Beauty. Even in such apparently airy fantasies as *The Cloud* Shelley's poetic imagery is generally the outer covering of profound meaning.

The Cenci

*The Cenci,*[32] which was written in Leghorn in the autumn of 1819, was intended for the theatre, but though it contains a few scenes of dramatic power and of an intensity almost Websterian, it has never proved to be suited to the stage. The conflict presented between good and evil bears an obvious resemblance to *Prometheus;* Beatrice is, however, not a titanic figure but rather a representative victim of an evil society and religion. Before this tragedy was written another calamity had fallen upon Shelley and Mary—the death of their little son William. Mary was plunged into bitter despair from which she rallied slowly. In Florence Shelley received news of the "Peterloo Massacre" and was moved to compose the *Masque of Anarchy* in forceful, downright terms comprehensible to working-men.[33] An unfinished and for long unpublished prose work, the *Philosophic View of Reform* [34] (1819), confirms our impression that though extreme in the poetic statement of his ideals, Shelley was moderate in his practical program. He wrote of the widening gap between wealth and poverty created by the class of fund-holders (the "tax-eaters" of Cobbett's fulminations) who live on the interest on the public debt. He believed that this debt could be abolished by the confiscation of capital. A truly representative Parliament would provide a solution. Yet he believed that England was not yet prepared for universal suffrage, and he advocated armed insurrection only as a last resort if parliamentary action failed. Late in 1819 he wrote *Peter Bell the Third,* a satiric narrative of Wordsworth's apostasy; and he wrote also the

Ode to the West Wind

incomparable *Ode to the West Wind* in which, gathering together a wealth of symbolism already adumbrated in earlier poems, he employed not only his powers of metrical orchestration at their mightiest but also a structural art that is by no means invariably characteristic of his poetry. The adaptation of *terza rima* to a stanzaic form is no less wonderful than is the development of the symbols of wave and leaf and cloud.

Pisa

The last years of his life,[35] from the beginning of 1820, were spent in Pisa and its neighborhood. Serenity and kindliness are in the *Letter to Maria Gisborne,* in which Leigh Hunt's familiar style is used without a trace of Hunt's vulgarity; there is piercing pathos in *To a Skylark*; and there is airy loveliness in *The Witch of Atlas,* in which the theme of Intellectual

[32] See E. S. Bates, *A Study of Shelley's Drama The Cenci* (1908); *The Cenci,* ed. G. E. Woodberry (Boston, 1909); *The Stage Version of Shelley's Cenci,* ed. A. C. Hicks and R. M. Clarke (1945).
[33] This was intended for *The Examiner* but remained unpublished till 1832.
[34] Ed. T. W. Rolleston (1920).
[35] Shelley's and Mary's youngest child, Percy Florence Shelley, was born in Florence, November, 1819.

Beauty is treated with a fantastic grace hiding from all but the initiated the recondite sources of its lore.[36] How ample was Shelley's range is shown by contrasting this poem with his *Swell-Foot the Tyrant,* a satiric drama on the divorce proceedings brought against Queen Caroline. Here Shelley combined Aristophanic motifs with others suggested by contemporary caricatures and lampoons.[37] But the satire is too learned to be effective.

In the person of Emilia Viviani,[38] a lovely Italian girl "imprisoned," as   Episychi-
he fancied, in a convent-school, Shelley found for the last time in mortal   dion
form "the likeness of what is perhaps eternal," and to *la figlia della sua mente, l'amorosa idea* he addressed the impassioned rhapsody *Epipsychidion* (1821). In this poem the symbols of the sun and the moon recognizably mean Emilia and Mary respectively; other symbols are used, as Shelley hints, rather to conceal than to reveal. The invitation to Emilia to fly with him to a far-off island is not quite in keeping with the exalted Platonism of the earlier part of the poem and was perhaps an afterthought. *The Defence of Poetry* (called forth by T. L. Peacock's *Four Ages of Poetry*) is an eloquent affirmation of the supreme social and moral value of the poet.[39]
On hearing of Keats's death in February, 1821, Shelley was moved to write *Adonais,* second only to *Lycidas* among English elegies. The classical conven-   Adonais
tions of the opening stanzas are not managed quite convincingly; the self-pity in the likening of one of the mourners to a stricken deer shows that Shelley's thoughts were as much upon his own wrongs as Keats's; the curse launched against the reviewers strikes a false note; but towards its close *Adonais* rises into a sublime hymn to the eternal Principle of Beauty. Sympathy with the Greek revolutionists now bore fruit in *Hellas,* a topical drama curiously aloof from contemporary events and redeemed from mediocrity only by the splendid choruses. *The Triumph of Life,*[40] the last, unfinished poem, bears the marks of the study of Dante and especially of Petrarch's *Trionfi.* It is too fragmentary to permit speculation as to Shelley's intentions. The concept of the victims of Life is desolating in its despondency.

Byron, Trelawny, and other friends gathered round him. His last days were happy in association with Edward and Jane Williams to whom he had been introduced by Tom Medwin. To Jane he addressed a few beautiful short poems. Edward Williams shared with Shelley a love of sailing. In the summer of 1822 the Shelleys lived near Lerici on the Gulf of Spezia. Early in July he and Williams sailed to Leghorn to greet the arrival of Leigh Hunt from England. On the return voyage Shelley and Williams

[36] C. H. Grabo, *The Meaning of "The Witch of Atlas"* (Chapel Hill, 1935); E. E. Kellett, *Suggestions* (1923), pp. 109-136.
[37] N. I. White, "Shelley's *Swell-Foot the Tyrant* in Relation to Contemporary Political Satires," *PMLA,* xxxvi (1921). 332-346.
[38] E. V. Della Robbia, *Vita di una Donna* (Florence, 1936), a biography of Emilia Viviani.
[39] *Peacock's Four Ages of Poetry; Shelley's Defence of Poetry; Browning's Essay on Shelley,* ed. H. F. B. Brett-Smith (1923). The relation of Shelley's essay to Sidney's *Apologie for Poetry* is generally recognized; for the indebtedness to the discourse on poetry in Johnson's *Rasselas* see K. N. Cameron, "A New Source for Shelley's *A Defence of Poetry,*" *SP,* xxxviii (1941). 629-644.
[40] F. M. Stawell, "Shelley's Triumph of Life," *E&S,* v (1914). 104-131.

*Death*

were caught in a squall, and drowned on July 8, 1822. Some days later the bodies were washed ashore, and in the presence of Byron and Trelawny were committed to the flames. Shelley's ashes were buried in the new Protestant Cemetery in Rome. The pathetic group which had been held together by the magic of his personality dispersed.

Mary Shelley returned to England to keep alive her husband's memory in the face of the opposition of his father, who desired that he be forgotten. Under the threat of withdrawing financial support from his little grandson, Percy Florence Shelley, Timothy Shelley was able to impose the condition that there should be no biography of the poet. Mary was able to circumvent this prohibition in a measure by the publication of the *Posthumous Poems* (1824) and the *Works* (1839). Leigh Hunt and other admirers worked for the expansion of his fame. *Queen Mab* continued to make its way among the radicals, but till the publication of the Galignani edition in 1829 Shelley's other poems were difficult to procure. In that year there took place a famous debate between a group of Cambridge undergraduates (of whom Arthur Henry Hallam was one) and a group of Oxford undergraduates. Cambridge defended the merits of Shelley against the Oxford upholders of Byron. Byron's cause triumphed; but the significant fact is that the question was considered a matter for debate. The young poets had no doubts. Beddoes was Shelley's disciple; Browning hailed him as the "Sun-treader."

# XIII

## John Keats

Keats,[1] like Théophile Gautier, was "a man for whom the physical world *Thought* exists." His genius was objective and concrete, moving not so readily in the *and* world of abstract thought as in the world of imaginative realization.[2] Yet *Sensation* critics who regard him as the lover and creator of sensuous beauty are opposed by those who contend that he is a great philosophic poet.[3] The truth probably lies between these two extremes. Efforts to synthesize his ideas do not carry conviction, for later views of life would, had he lived longer, probably have been as much subject to change as had been those of earlier date. All that can be discerned clearly is the drift from romantic egocentricity towards objectivity. The problem of his development is one of the most fascinating of literary studies because of the wealth of evidence both in his poems and letters and in the records accumulated by his friends.[4]

[1] *Poetical Works and Other Writings*, Hampstead Edition, ed. M. Buxton Forman (8v, 1938), based on ed. H. Buxton Forman (5v, 1900) with additional material; *Poems*, ed. Ernest de Selincourt (1926), with admirable commentary; *Poetical Works*, ed. H. W. Garrod (1939), with full collation of texts; *Complete Poems and Selected Letters*, ed. C. DeW. Thorpe (1935); *Letters*, ed. M. B. Forman (2v, 1931). — Sir Sidney Colvin, *John Keats: His Life and Poetry, His Friends, Critics and After-Fame* (1917; revised, 1925); Amy Lowell, *John Keats* (2v, 1925); R. M. Milnes (Lord Houghton), *Life, Letters, and Literary Remains of John Keats* (2v, 1848; Everyman's Library, 1927); C. L. Finney, *The Evolution of Keats's Poetry* (2v, Cambridge, Mass., 1936), to which the present chapter is much indebted; Lucien Wolff, *John Keats, sa vie et son œuvre* (Paris, 1910); Albert Erlande, *Life of John Keats*, trans. by Marion Robinson (1929); H. I'A. Fausset, *Keats, a Study in Development* (1922); Dorothy Hewlett, *Adonais: A Life of John Keats* (Indianapolis, 1938); B. C. Williams, *Forever Young* (1943); E. V. Weller, *Autobiography of John Keats, Compiled from his Letters and Essays* (Palo Alto, Cal., 1933); Edmund Blunden, *Shelley and Keats as They Struck Their Contemporaries* (1925); Edmund Blunden, *Keats's Publisher: A Memoir of John Taylor (1781-1864)* (1936). — Among studies primarily critical, not biographical, are: C. DeW. Thorpe, *The Mind of John Keats* (1926); H. W. Garrod, *Keats* (1926); J. Middleton Murry, *Keats and Shakespeare: A Study of Keats's Poetic Life* (1925); J. M. Murry, *Studies in Keats* (1930; enlarged, 1939); W. J. Bate, *Negative Capability: the Intuitive Approach to Keats* (Cambridge, Mass., 1939) and *The Stylistic Development of Keats* (1945); A. W. Crawford, *The Genius of Keats* (1932); *John Keats Memorial Volume*, ed. G. C. Williamson (1921); Robert Bridges, "A Critical Introduction to Keats," *Collected Essays* (1929), IV, originally the introduction to Keats's *Poems* in the Muses' Library (1895); A. C. Bradley, "The Letters of Keats," *Oxford Lectures on Poetry* (1909), pp. 209-244; Bush, ch. III. — D. L. Baldwin and others, *Concordance* (Washington, D. C., 1917).

[2] This antithesis is stated in unqualified form by J. M. Murry, *Keats and Shakespeare*, p. 7.

[3] For these opposing views see Royall Snow, "Heresy concerning Keats," *PMLA*, XLIII (1928). 1142-1149, and M. E. Shipman, "Orthodoxy concerning Keats," *ibid.*, XLIV (1929). 929-934. The first effort to interpret Keats as a philosophic and not merely a sensuous poet was F. M. Owen, *John Keats* (1880). Today this view is represented in its extreme form by J. Middleton Murry. For the interpretation of Keats as a sensuous poet see H. N. Fairchild, *The Romantic Quest*, ch. XXII.

[4] Hunt, Clarke, Haydon, Dilke, Mathew, Reynolds, Severn, and other friends left their testimony. The two men to whom posterity is most indebted are Richard Woodhouse, who made manuscript collections of Keatsiana which have been used by many scholars, and Charles Armitage Brown, whose *Life of John Keats*, ed. D. H. Bodurtha and W. B. Pope, remained

The swiftness of his progress is almost without parallel in the history of the arts. There were retardations and perturbations, returning eddies which swept him upstream to points which he had left behind; but always his exalted conception of poetry made him dissatisfied with each stage as it was reached and determined to press on further. What his goal might have been we cannot say. He expressed the hope to live to write "a few great plays"; but there is little evidence to support the opinion that his true bent was towards the drama. On better grounds it may be held that with longer life he would have written more, and greater, narrative poetry, in which human characters portrayed with psychological insight would have moved before a background of romantic beauty.[5] But this is mere speculation. What we know is that in the three or four crucial years (1816-1819) there was a struggle between what Keats thought of as the Wordsworthian conception of the poet's function and what he thought of as the Shakespearean, a struggle, that is, between the opposing ideals of a reasoned humanitarianism and an objective dispassionateness of suspended judgment.

Born in London in the milieu of an humble trade but of people self-respecting and fairly well-to-do, John Keats (1795-1821) at an early age lost his father; then his mother; and then the grandmother who after his parents' death had given him a home. The terms of a trust deprived him of the share in a modest estate which would have relieved him of anxieties and perhaps prolonged his life. At school at Enfield (1803-1811) he made friends with Charles Cowden Clarke, the son of the headmaster. There are records of Keats's vivacious personality, pugnacity, sense of humor, and love of sport, but not of any special interest in literature till at the age of fifteen Clarke helped to awaken in him a love of mythology and travel-lore. In 1811 his guardian apprenticed him to an apothecary-surgeon at Edmonton.[6]

*Juvenilia*   His reading of *The Faerie Queene* resulted in 1813 in the first poem that is still extant, an *Imitation of Spenser* of little value. The influence which the poems of Mary Tighe had upon him has been exaggerated.[7] That Keats knew and admired Mrs. Tighe's *Psyche* (1805) is indubitable; but most of the parallels noted between her poetry and his are due to their common use of conventional and sentimental diction. Nothing is unimportant in tracing the development of such a genius; but the student must turn to larger treatises for the details of Keats's juvenilia. Among them is an *Ode to Apollo* in the manner of Gray, and sonnets addressed to the memory of

---

in manuscript till 1937. For the squabbles over rival claims to be Keats's first biographer see the introduction to this biography. See also *Some Letters and Miscellanies of Charles Brown,* ed. M. B. Forman (1937).

[5] This was A. C. Bradley's opinion. See *Oxford Lectures on Poetry* (1909), p. 239. For the unusual view that Keats would not have accomplished greater things had he lived see G. R. Elliott, "The Real Tragedy of Keats," PMLA, xxxvi (1921). 315-331.

[6] Sir W. Hale-White, *Keats as a Medical Student* (1925) and *Keats as Doctor and Patient* (1938).

[7] *Keats and Mary Tighe: The Poems of Mary Tighe with Parallel Passages from the Works of John Keats,* ed. E. V. Weller (1928). — A stronger and longer lasting influence was that of C. M. Wieland's romantic poem, *Oberon,* which Keats knew in William Sotheby's translation (1798). See W. W. Beyer, *Keats and the Dæmon King* (1947).

Chatterton, to Byron, and to Leigh Hunt (lately released from prison). The influence of Byron was ephemeral; that of Chatterton subtly pervasive; Hunt's for a time paramount.

In October, 1815, Keats became a medical student in the London hospitals. *Influence* A verse epistle to a friend, G. F. Mathew, is in a genre descending from *of Hunt* Drayton. For the run-on couplets with many double rimes and accented light syllables there was Elizabethan precedent as well as Hunt's example; but the displeasing colloquialisms are due to Hunt's vulgarization of the Wordsworthian principle of simplicity of diction. With the desire to emulate *The Story of Rimini* Keats began a romantic narrative, but this *Specimen of an Induction to a Poem* got no further than the title indicates, for the story refused to "come." Of *Calidore,* an offshoot from *The Faerie Queene,* only the opening episode was written. The jauntiness of the narrative shows that Hunt, not Spenser, was Keats's model. The luscious vocabulary includes some of Hunt's favorite words, notably those soft adjectives ending in *y* which for so long were blemishes on Keats's style. In the *Epistle to My Brother George,* written in August, 1816, Keats debated the choice between surgery and poetry as a profession; by September, as we learn from the *Epistle to Charles Cowden Clarke,* the die had been cast. Then suddenly, as though to put the seal upon an irrevocable decision, in October he wrote the sonnet *On First Looking into Chapman's Homer,*[8] drawing a magni- *"The* ficent simile from Robertson's narrative of Balboa's first sight of the Pacific *Realms of* Ocean and another from Bonnycastle's narrative of Herschel's discovery of *Gold"* Uranus. We feel that to the excitement of the exploration of the earth, the heavens, and the golden realms of poetry Keats was adding the ardor of the exploration of his own poetic powers. This impression connects the Chapman sonnet with *Sleep and Poetry,* upon which he was engaged in the autumn, after he and Hunt had become friends. This poem, which contains the famous description of Hunt's study at Hampstead, is the fullest expression of Keats's discipleship. Hunt's teaching is recognizable in the survey of the three schools of English poetry: the "Italian," which was dominant from Chaucer to Milton; the "French," in which a foppish and barbaric "crew" obeyed the rules dictated by Boileau; and the new, "natural" school of which Wordsworth is the master and to which Hunt and, by implication, Keats himself belong. A contrast is drawn between the poetry of natural loveliness which is presided over by "Flora and old Pan" and the poetry which reveals "the agonies, the strife of human hearts." The need to choose between the two kinds remained the burning problem in Keats's thought.[9] In a companion poem without title, beginning "I stood

---

[8] C. L. Finney, *The Evolution of Keats's Poetry,* I. 121-128; G. W. Landrum, "More concerning Chapman's Homer and Keats," *PMLA,* XLII (1927). 986-1009; B. I. Evans, "Keats's Approach to the Chapman Sonnet," *E&S,* XVI (1931). 26-52.

[9] Though Keats kept political questions almost entirely out of his poetry (unless, as some have thought, *Hyperion* reflects the French Revolution), his letters reveal liberal opinions which by no means merely echo Hunt. He sympathized with Cobbett, with the prosecuted radical publishers, and with the victims of the "Peterloo Massacre." He was opposed to the Holy Alliance and to the restored, reactionary Continental dynasties. See H. G. Wright, "Keats and Politics," *E&S,* XVIII (1933). 7-23.

tip-toe upon a little hill," Keats described the stimulus to the poetic faculty afforded by natural beauty and developed the Wordsworthian doctrine that the poets of ancient Greece were inspired by that beauty to create myths. This piece is, then, a sort of proem to *Endymion*.

Intimacy with Hunt reached a climax on the day when the two poets crowned each other with laurel. Of the effusiveness and affectation of this "intercoronation" episode Keats was soon ashamed, as he confessed in an *Ode* in which he asked forgiveness of Apollo. He had now met Benjamin Robert Haydon, the painter and art-critic, lately victorious in his battle for recognition of the Phidian workmanship and supreme aesthetic value of the Elgin marbles.[10] Haydon's efforts to emancipate the young poet from discipleship to Hunt bore first fruit in the sonnet *On Seeing the Elgin Marbles*. The first period in Keats's career was rounded out in March, 1817, when his first volume, entitled simply *Poems*,[11] was published. The few reviews, though slight, were not altogether unfavorable. Keats had progressed far enough to accept the admonition to eschew affectation and shun bad models.

Endymion

*Endymion*,[12] which marks a transitional phase in Keats's development, was written between April and October, 1817. A close study of Shakespeare's diction, style, and imagery began early in this year.[13] The study of Milton and of Dante (in Cary's translation) was encouraged by a new friend, Benjamin Bailey, a theological student, who also turned the poet's thoughts towards humanitarianism. The incubus of Hunt's bad taste could not be shaken off easily; colloquialisms, vulgarisms, and a soft lusciousness of style and sentiment mar *Endymion,* particularly in the amorous passages; but on the other hand there are exquisite felicities, single lines of terse grandeur, and (memorably in the "Song of Sorrow") a prodigal wealth of imagery drawn from poetry, mythology, and the fine arts. The too abundant use of run-on couplets, imitated not so much from Hunt as from Drayton, William Browne, and other poets of the English Renaissance, gives a slipshod effect that is due not to carelessness but to faulty taste. The reviewers who noted that the rimes often seem to dictate the sense rather than the sense the rimes made a valid criticism. Keats took the story of the love of Endymion and Diana from Drayton's *The Man in the Moon* and perhaps from the same poet's *Endimion and Phoebe*. Some suggestions seem to have come from Lyly's court-satire, *Endimion,* and others from allusions to the myth in other Renaissance poets. Lemprière's *Classical Dictionary* and other books of reference were at hand. The interwoven episodes of Venus and Adonis, Glaucus and Scylla, and Alpheus and

---

[10] S. A. Larrabee, *English Bards and Grecian Marbles* (1943), ch. ix.
[11] *Poems of 1817*, Noel Douglas Replica (1927).
[12] Published 1818. Type-facsimile, ed. H. C. Notcutt (1927). See Leonard Brown, "The Genesis, Growth, and Meaning of *Endymion*," *SP*, xxx (1933). 618 653.
[13] See C. F. E. Spurgeon, *Keats's Shakespeare, a Descriptive Study Based on New Material* (1928).

Arethusa came from like sources. Drayton had used the moon as a symbol of Ideal Beauty; but Keats's central idea, the Platonic theme of the quest of a unity transcending the flux of the phenomenal world, came in the main from Spenser's *Four Hymns,* with suggestions from Shelley's *Alastor.*[14] The thread of this theme, though never broken, is often lost to sight in the luxuriant decorative detail. Endymion passes through four stages of experience, to each of which one of the four books of the poem is devoted. On his progress towards the attainment of "fellowship with Essence" he experiences the beauty of Nature; of Art (and more especially of Poetry); of Friendship; and of Love. The Renaissance concept of friendship as the love of man for man Keats converted, under the influence of Wordsworth, into philanthropy or universal humanitarianism. Unlike the Platonists of the Renaissance, he placed love higher than friendship; but, as he afterwards recognized, he failed to mark the distinction between the Uranian and Pandemian Aphrodite and fused and confused spiritual and physical love. Keats was dissatisfied with *Endymion* and even before its completion he had passed beyond it into another stage. This being the case, it might have been wiser, and certainly would have served his prospects better, had he left the poem unpublished. For the manners of the malignant reviewers there is neither excuse nor forgiveness; but the magnanimity with which Keats faced ridicule was due in part to his recognition that in some of their strictures there was justice.

Frequent personal contact with Wordsworth disillusioned Keats, because of the elder poet's complacency, egotism, and didacticism; and as a consequence there was during the winter of 1817-1818 a drift away from humanitarianism. The counterbalance was an ever-deepening appreciation of the impartiality and impersonality of Shakespeare. This antithesis may have been sharpened for Keats by Hazlitt's comment upon the "intense intellectual egotism" of Wordsworth and his observation that Shakespeare enters so completely into his various characters as "scarcely to have an individual existence of his own." [15] It may have been with this distinction between objective and subjective genius in his memory that Keats evolved his famous doctrine of "Negative Capability." [16] By this not very happily chosen term he meant, he said, "when a man is capable of being in uncertainties, mysteries, doubts, without any irritable reaching after fact and reason." As examples by contrariety he chose Wordsworth, who imparted a direct philosophical view of life, and Coleridge, who was "incapable of remaining content with half-knowledge." The poetic ideal after which Keats was here reaching is that of imaginative insight and suspended judgment, "a selfless sympathy" not only with other human beings but

*"Negative Capability"*

[14] Keats's indebtedness to Shelley, in *Endymion* and elsewhere, is demonstrated (and exaggerated) in L. J. Thompson, *More Magic Dethroned* (1925). The desire to retain his "unfettered scope" kept Keats from responding to Shelley's advances in 1817; and in 1820 he was too ill to respond.

[15] Hazlitt, "On Mr. Wordsworth's *Excursion*" and "On Posthumous Fame," *The Round Table; Works,* ed. Waller and Glover, I. 113 and 23.

[16] Keats, *Letters,* I. 77 (December 28, 1817).

with all life. Of himself he said that he could enter into a sparrow's personality and "pick about the gravel."

While seeing *Endymion* through the press, Keats planned with John Hamilton Reynolds [17] a series of narrative poems based upon stories from the *Decameron*. Since this project was an outgrowth from Hunt's recommendations of Italian literature as affording subjects for poetry, it is not surprising to note in *Isabella, or The Pot of Basil* [18] a reversion to the cloying diction of Hunt. Yet there is an increased firmness of style, and the handling of *ottava rima* is masterly. The digressions, such as the invocation of Boccaccio and the complaint to Melancholy, are in imitation of old conventions. The touches of the macabre anticipate a taste of the eighteen-twenties.

Shortly after the publication of *Endymion* (April, 1818) Keats was separated from his brother George, who with his bride set sail for America. The illness of his second brother, Tom, who was now stricken with tuberculosis, proved to be a severe test of the ideal of suspended judgment, and we find Keats expressing his longing for a fixed philosophy based upon reason.[19] It may be, however, that students of Keats have taken these fluctuations of opinion too seriously, for Keats's nature was of a chameleon-like sensitiveness to his surroundings. How strong the influence of Wordsworth was upon him still is shown in the famous letter in which he likened *"The* life to "a mansion of many apartments." [20] Of these, two only were as yet *Chambers* open to him: "the infant or thoughtless chamber" and "the chamber of *of Life"* Maiden-Thought." In the latter "we see nothing but pleasant wonders, and think of delaying there for ever with delight." At his present point of growth he was conscious of passing thence, of being "in a mist," unable to balance good and evil but aware of the "burden of the mystery." Keats expressly drew the analogy to Wordsworth's case (as recorded in *Tintern Abbey*) and believed that the elder poet had explored those further chambers, those "dark passages" which were as yet closed to himself.

A strong vein of humanitarianism continued to manifest itself in Keats's letters during the walking-tour with Charles Armitage Brown in the summer of 1818. The friends visited the Lowlands of Scotland, the Lake District, and, for a fleeting moment, Ireland. By overtaxing his physical powers this tour hastened Keats's decline. The vicious attacks on *Endymion* in the *Quarterly* and *Blackwood's* were accepted with the nobly philosophic re-

[17] On Reynolds see below, ch. XIV.

[18] For his material Keats went not directly to Boccaccio but to an English version first published in 1620. See H. G. Wright, "Keats's *Isabella*," *LTLS*, April 17, 1943, p. 192.

[19] *Letters*, I. 132. This was in March, 1818. Three months earlier Keats had expressed the oft-quoted aspiration "O for a Life of Sensations rather than of Thoughts!" (*ibid.*, I. 73). Professor Finney (*op. cit.*, I. 301) argues that Keats has here in mind Wordsworthian or Hazlittian empiricism. "The sensations which a man receives from natural objects, he [Keats] believed, produce strong passions or emotions in him and induce a state of ecstasy in which his imagination, stimulated by his passions, apprehends or intuits truth in the form of being." The context of the letter hardly supports the weight of this interpretation. Contrast H. N. Fairchild's matter-of-fact interpretation of Keats's use of "sensation" (*The Romantic Quest*, p. 414).

[20] *Letters*, I, 156.

mark: "I was never afraid of failure, for I would sooner fail than not be among the greatest." [21] But later these hostile reviews undermined his confidence, as he came to realize that by warning the public away from him they had deprived him of the hope of winning a livelihood from poetry.

In the late summer of 1818 Keats began work on *Hyperion*.[22] The theory that *The Fall of Hyperion,* the "dream" version commonly regarded as an attempt to recast the original poem, is really a preliminary draft [23] has met with no acceptance; but the alternative view which accepts the traditional chronological order probably over-simplifies the problem. The view which, though it rests upon internal evidence, best meets the case is that Keats began *Hyperion* under the influence of Wordsworth, composing the introductory colloquy with Moneta in which the goddess upbraids him for having been "a dreaming thing, a fever of thyself" and declares that none can usurp the heights of poetic power save those "to whom the miseries of the world are misery." [24] In revulsion from this humanitarian sentiment he may have set aside this introduction and made a new beginning with the objective and Miltonic version of which he had completed two books and begun a third by the spring of 1819. The sensuousness, subjectivism, and exuberant beauty of the fragmentary third book reflect the heightening of Keats's personal emotion consequent upon his meeting with Fanny Brawne, with whom he had fallen passionately in love.[25] This ardent feeling, which for a time conquered the despondency caused by his brother's death in December, 1818, burns brightly in the theme of *Hyperion*. From allusions in Renaissance poetry and from works of reference Keats took the story of the fall of the Titans and triumph of the Olympians. The celestial warfare is reminiscent of *Paradise Lost,* of which there are many echoes in the diction; and such stylistic features as repetition, inversion, elliptical construction, and elaborate simile come from close study of Milton.[26] The landscape and imagery owe something to Keats's recent impressions of rugged mountain scenery; and the marmoreal quality of certain passages (notably the opening scene) are suggestive of his contemplation of Greek sculpture. To all this he gave a modern coloring. Whether or not the history of the French Revolution was in the back of his mind as he wrote, his theme is progressive evolution. Up the Scale of Being evolution must move, towards the ideal. Each generation of the gods is supplanted by another more beautiful, for "the first in beauty should be first in might."

The change in tone in Book III is a modulation from *Hyperion* to the

Hyperion

---

[21] *Ibid.,* I. 243.

[22] Facsimile of Keats's autograph manuscript of *Hyperion*, ed. E. de Selincourt (1905).

[23] Amy Lowell, *The Life of John Keats,* II. 339-348.

[24] *The Fall of Hyperion,* I. 148-149; 168-169. — The theory here outlined is that of C. L. Finney, *The Evolution of Keats's Poetry,* II, ch. v.

[25] Whether or not Fanny Brawne appreciated the greatness of her lover's genius is a hotly disputed problem. Over against the notorious letter in which she expressed the wish that his memory might be permitted to die must be set the evidence in the *Letters of Fanny Brawne to Fanny Keats,* ed. Fred Edgecumbe (1936).

[26] On Keats's indebtedness to Milton see in general R. D. Havens, *The Influence of Milton on English Poetry* (1922), ch. x.

poem which occupied Keats early in 1819. In *The Eve of St. Agnes* youthful romantic love is set against a background of family feud, coarse carousing, storm, and bitter cold. Memories of *Romeo and Juliet* and *Cymbeline* and of the Gothic romances [27] are here combined with quaint superstitions and folk-rites about which Keats had read in Ben Jonson, Burton, and Brand's *Popular Antiquities*. Keats's creative art was at its happiest and most spontaneous in this poem. The diction is of a flawless purity. Though the Spenserian stanza is employed and the sensuous imagery and lavish adornment of the narrative are suggestive of Spenser, there is nothing that is merely imitative. The reliance upon elaborate and vivid presentation rather than upon suggestion differentiates the quality of Keats's romanticism from Coleridge's.

But alarming symptoms of tuberculosis were developing, among which are to be numbered the torments of jealousy expressed in the first ode *To Fanny*. It is likely, as Rossetti suggested long ago, that there is a connection of thought and mood between this ode and the fragmentary *Eve of St. Mark*.[28] According to the old belief, those who watch in the porch of the parish church on this eve will see shadowy forms pass into the portal. The forms that do not pass out again are of those who are doomed to die within the succeeding year. Is it Fanny who watches by the church-door? Is Keats the lover who passes in, not to reappear? In April, 1819, he wrote *Bright Star* (miscalled his "Last Sonnet"), and shortly afterwards the agonizing second ode *To* —— [Fanny] and *La Belle Dame Sans Merci*, that miraculously weird evocation of the *femme fatale* which exalts to the highest imaginative plane the fatal thraldom in which Keats found himself.

He was now discontented with the sonnet form which he had used with such mastery, and while expressing his dissatisfaction in the irregular sonnet, "If by dull rhymes our English must be chain'd," he experimented with three new patterns which proved to be unsuccessful. Keats's music tends to move in stanza lengths. His "continuous verse" is either diffusive or else falls into such well defined paragraphs as the opening movement of *Hyperion*, which is precisely the length of a sonnet. The theory is acceptable

*The Odes*

that these experiments in new sonnet forms led directly to the series of odes composed in the late spring and early summer of 1819.[29] The scanty external evidence as to their order of composition may be supplemented by study of the links of thought between the odes and the growth and decline of mastery of the form. The *Ode to Psyche* was probably written first. It is more in the tradition of the pseudo-Pindaric than are the other odes; a

---

[27] M. H. Shackford, *"The Eve of St. Agnes* and *The Mysteries of Udolpho," PMLA*, XXXVI (1921). 104-118.

[28] In an undated letter (August, 1820 ?) to Fanny Brawne (*Letters*, II. 548) Keats refers to a poem which he has in mind but which his health does not permit him to write. Rossetti believed that the reference was to the unfinished *Eve of St. Mark*. The overlapping of ideas between this poem and *The Cap and Bells* may also be significant. See C. L. Finney, *The Evolution of Keats's Poetry*, II. 566-567; and, more specifically on this poem, W. E. Houghton, "The Meaning of Keats's *Eve of St. Mark*," *ELH*, XIII (1946). 64-78.

[29] This theory was first advanced by H. W. Garrod, *Keats* (1926).

formal pattern has not yet been established. The Wordsworthian theme that the poet is the myth-maker provides a link, not present in the other odes, between the *Psyche* and Keats's earlier thought. The *Ode to a Nightingale,* in which the happy world of natural loveliness is contrasted with the human world of pain, is flawless in design and expression and almost perfect in the development of its theme.[30] It seems likely that it preceded the *Ode on a Grecian Urn* where another contrast is developed, that of the permanence of art with the fleetingness of human passion. For all its beauty this ode is not quite flawless,[31] and the oft-quoted conclusion is open to the charge of ambiguity.[32] The *Ode to Indolence* is on a lower level of achievement, and both in subject and treatment reflects the poet's spiritual apathy after a period of intense creation. A study of the sources in literature, art, and personal experience of Keats's imagery in the odes, of their varying stanzaic patterns or approximations to pattern, and of the beautiful, tenuous links among them (as of the night-moth, the Grecian vase, Lethe, and drowsiness) is one of the most rewarding of literary investigations.

By midsummer of 1819 Keats's health was failing and he was living under the pressure of dire poverty. While staying in Winchester he and his friend Charles Brown collaborated upon a tragedy with the hope that they might dispose of it to the theatre and that Edmund Kean would assume the title-rôle. This drama, *Otho the Great,* is on a historical theme of the tenth century and involves the rivalry of two brothers and a conflict between father and son. The tradition is that Brown supplied the characters and action, scene by scene, and that Keats wrote the dialogue from this outline; but it is probable that Keats shared the responsibility for the general plan and concept. The question is of no great importance, for though there are a few passages of fine poetry in the play,[33] as a whole it must be adjudged a failure.

Another attempt to win attention with something in a popular vein is **Lamia** of much more consequence. This is *Lamia,* composed in the late summer. The story of the serpent-woman who fell in love with a youth of Corinth and was detected and exorcised by Apollonius, the philosopher, Keats drew from Burton's *Anatomy of Melancholy.* Dryden's verse was the model for the firmly wrought couplets with well-spaced triplets and alexandrines in which it is composed; and the astringent style of the latter part of the poem is also suggestive of Dryden. The contrast between the romantic beauty and mystery of Part I and the intrusive cynicism in Part II is, indeed, remarkable. It is probably explicable on biographical grounds. A little earlier Keats had written what he described as the "flint-worded" letters to Fanny Brawne—hysterical, passionate outcries of agony in the face of consuming

---

[30] "Almost perfect"—the description of the nightingale's song as a "plaintive anthem" in the final stanza contradicts, and jars ever so slightly upon, the earlier indications of its happiness and ecstasy. What had been purely objective becomes subjective.

[31] The flaw is in stanza v; the ugly repetition of sound in "O Attic shape! Fair attitude!"

[32] The best discussion of "Beauty is Truth, Truth Beauty" is in J. M. Murry, *Studies in Keats* (ed. 1930), pp. 71-92.

[33] For example, Ludolph's speech at IV, ii. 18.

love and jealousy, encroaching disease, and the ever-more-certain threat of death with work unfinished and ambitions unrealized. In these letters he affirmed his dedication to poetry and resolve to reject the distractions of love.[34] About the same time he wrote in a mood of desperate cynicism three stanzas expanding the narrative of the meeting of the lovers in *The Eve of St. Agnes*. These were ruinously out of keeping with the rest of the poem, and Keats afterwards wisely let himself be persuaded to suppress them. But they help to account for the satiric element in *Lamia*. Is there autobiographical symbolism in the story of Lycius and the serpent-woman?[35] Is "the tender-personed lamia"—who is beautiful, mysterious, and *not* malign—the Poetic Imagination? Is her lover, Lycius, the poet Keats? Does the feast at Corinth symbolize the publication of his poems? Are the guests the reading-public? If this interpretation holds, then Apollonius symbolizes the reviewers who destroyed the Imagination and—tragic prescience on Keats's part!—brought about the poet's death.[36]

What remains to tell is a story of decline. The ode *To Autumn*, for all its gorgeous sensuousness, shows no intellectual advance. *The Fall of Hyperion* is (if the view here adopted be generally accepted) an attempt to dovetail the original Wordsworthian opening into the second, Miltonic fragment, with other revisions under the influence of Dante's *Purgatorio*. There was a passionate revulsion of feeling expressed in a letter to Fanny Brawne on October 10, 1819, and in the moving but languorous sonnet *The Day is Gone*. An effort to write a chronicle play, *King Stephen*, was beyond Keats's strength, and the opening scenes remain a fragment of high but uncertain promise. *The Cap and Bells*, patterned upon Ariosto and *Don Juan* and combining fairy-lore and topical allusion in a satire on the Prince Regent with side-glances at Lord Byron, was tragically alien from Keats's genius and was set aside. At the close of the manuscript of this fantasy are found the beautiful and terrible lines beginning "This living hand," without title but undoubtedly addressed to Fanny Brawne.

During 1820, which he called his "posthumous year," Keats wrote no poetry. In February came the first hemorrhage from the lungs. He was watched over by Brown, then by the Hunts, and then by Mrs. Brawne and Fanny. In the spring he prepared his last volume for the press, and in July was published *Lamia, Isabella, The Eve of St. Agnes, and Other Poems*,[37] the greatest single volume of English poetry of the nineteenth century. In September, with his faithful friend Joseph Severn, he sailed for Italy in search of health. The quest was hopeless. He died in Rome on February 23, 1821, and was buried in the old Protestant Cemetery, close to the pyramid of Caius Cestius which serves as a beacon for pilgrims to his grave.

*Death*

---

[34] *Letters*, II. 400-403 (August 17, 1819).
[35] C. L. Finney, *The Evolution of Keats's Poetry*, II. 696-702.
[36] This interpretation accounts for the denunciation of "cold Philosophy" and meets Robert Bridges's objection, *Collected Essays* (1929), IV. 127, that the poem should not have ended with the death of Lycius.
[37] *Poems of 1820*, Noel Douglas Replicas (1927).

The evidence of Shelley's letters supplements the impression from *Adonais* that Shelley was not aware of the greatness of Keats's accomplishment. The elegy is a chivalrous protest against Keats's detractors; but together with Byron's pitying scorn of one who had let himself "be snuffed out by an article" it helped to keep alive the false tradition that Keats was a weakling. The loyal friends who preserved Keats's letters and assembled a vast quantity of records of his life provided for posterity the means to refute this conception. But even the temporary prevalence of this opinion and the association of his name with the "Cockney School" did not long retard his fame and influence. That influence is visible in the poetry of Darley and Hood, Tennyson and the youthful Browning. After 1848, the year when R. M. Milnes's biography of the poet with his letters and literary remains appeared, the poetry of Keats became the greatest single influence upon the poetry and painting of the Victorian generation.[38] Emphasis upon the value of Keats's thought is a phenomenon of the criticism of our own day.

[38] See G. H. Ford, *Keats and the Victorians. A Study of his Influence and Rise to Fame* (New Haven, 1944).

# XIV

## Thomas Hood, Thomas Lovell Beddoes, and Other Poets

In the eighteen-twenties a number of poets appeared of whom some died early and some, discouraged, subsided into silence, while others continued to write for many years. There was abundant talent in most of them and two possessed powers beyond their actual achievement; but none was a poet of anywhere near the first order. They do not divide the Romantic Period, narrowly so called, from the Victorian, but illustrate the continuity of the romantic tradition. They are not a very homogeneous group, but several among them are near allied and there are loose links among the rest.

*The Grotesque and the Macabre*

Of these points of connection the most conspicuous is the taste for the extravagant, the weird, and the horrible which they acquired from Gothic romance. The popular art of the period catered to the same liking for the "horrid." The grotesque and the macabre are dominant motifs in the designs of Thomas Rowlandson and George Cruikshank.[1] Pater's doctrine, that in romantic art strangeness is allied to beauty and that if the strangeness is exaggerated the beauty tends to disappear and we have the grotesque, is of dubious validity as a generalization; but it is applicable here. Only a poet of austere soul can invest the terrors of the charnel-house with an aura of beauty. The Italian Leopardi had done so; but few of these English poets possess, even momentarily, the austerity of a Leopardi. Generally they do not take their horrors quite seriously. Like their French *confrères* they seek to provoke a "new shudder"; but they smile or even chuckle when their readers are horrified. Some of their poems are weirdly romantic and others wittily satirical, and the one kind shades off into the other. An expert technique with surprising effects of rimes, curious stanzaic forms, and startling juxtapositions of images is employed for either purpose. Yet beneath the surface of grim or merry wit there is, in almost every case, an underlying sadness. Sometimes this contracts to a point of personal introspection where all that is expressed is a sense of the aimlessness and futility of life; but at other times it broadens from the characteristic romantic sympathy with the unfortunate into a bold and not uninfluential poetry of social protest dealing with substantial wrongs.

---

[1] Noteworthy is the reappearance of the "Dance of Death" theme in art. Rowlandson's *English Dance of Death* (1816) and Dagley's *Death's Doings* (1826) are examples. The material in Francis Douce's *Dissertation on the Dance of Death* (1833) had been collected much earlier.

# I

The entire gamut, from romantic loveliness, through weirdness and horror, *Hood*
and wit and humor, to satiric protest and the championship of the oppressed,
is sounded in the poetry of Thomas Hood [2] (1799-1845). It is not apparent
that the quality and range of his writings were conditioned by the circumstances of his career, for though amid disappointments, poverty, drudgery,
and sickness he was, as he said, "a lively Hood for his livelihood," it is
improbable that health and affluence would have altered his congenital disposition. His humor was that of his time and milieu. He was a friend
of Charles Lamb, the master of the art of punning, and a contemporary of
Theodore Hook, the master of the craft of "high jinks." The use of verbal
play for serious poetic effects has the warrant of long lineage, and in Hood's
day not all the good puns had been perpetrated. Nevertheless, this part of
Hood's work in verse and prose—work it often was rather than play—is
now sadly faded.

But the sparkle which has vanished from these things still plays upon
the seas of old romance which Hood viewed from the magic casements
thrown open for him by Keats. He was the earliest and closest disciple of
that master.[3] His *Hero and Leander* is "Elizabethan" in a sense but with
a difference; and the difference is due to Keats. *The Two Swans,* though a
poem in the Spenserian tradition, is closer to *Isabella* than to *The Faerie
Queene*; and its heavy, sultry imagery and slow-moving cadences anticipate
effects with which Tennyson, likewise taught by Keats, was soon to be
experimenting. *The Plea of the Midsummer Fairies* (1827), Hood's most
extended effort in the romantic line, can still charm those who have the
abundant time needed for its perusal, provided they are not offended by the
passages of light quaintness and grotesquerie which do not quite harmonize
with the context. The influence of Keats, evident in these longer things, is
still more apparent in various short pieces; in *Ruth* and *Autumn,* especially,
one is brought up abruptly with the consciousness of having heard the
same thing before. But the echoes are so beautiful that Hood may claim
them for his own.

An undertone of horror is audible in some of these poems. Horror is
clangorous in *The Dream of Eugene Aram.* Though in metrical effects and
turns of phrase it owes much to *The Ancient Mariner,* this narrative resembles the popular broadside ballads of the seventeenth century, even in
such particulars as the edifying emphasis upon the murderer's remorse and
the crude woodcuts with which the original edition was adorned. Quieter,
more subtle, and more allusive are *The Elm-Tree* and *The Haunted House*

[2] *Works* (11v, n.d. [1882?]); *Poetical Works,* ed. Walter Jerrold (1906). — Mrs. F. F.
Broderip (Hood's daughter), *Memorials of Thomas Hood* (2v, 1860); Walter Jerrold, *Thomas
Hood: His Life and Times* (1907); Emil Oswald, *Thomas Hood und die Soziale Tendenz-
dichtung seiner Zeit* (Vienna, 1904); George Saintsbury, "Thomas Hood," *Essays and Papers,*
II. 132-150.
[3] Shelley's influence is visible in a few pieces, notably *Lycus the Centaur.*

in which Hood gains his effects by means of indirection and understatement. Through other horror-pieces we are led into the region of the humorous-grotesque, where Hood is in line of descent from Southey and in proximity to *The Ingoldsby Legends*.[4] On occasion he can use his peculiar technique for serious purposes; and this he does in *Miss Kilmansegg and her Precious Leg*. The froth of fun has long since evaporated from this extravaganza, but a precipitate of serious intent remains—the intent to satirize the tragic absurdity of man's pursuit of gold.

Hood's touch is in general too light and his nature too kindly to admit him to the company of formidable satirists; but he first attracted attention by the *Odes and Addresses to Great People* (1825) in which he collaborated with some other writers. His manner here is suggestive of a better-bred "Peter Pindar"; and the ingenious rimes owe something to *Don Juan*. Topical poetry of this kind does not last well; but the humorous sympathy of the address to Mrs. Fry (the worker among the prisoners of Newgate) is still attractive, and there is sharp and effective indignation in the *Ode to Rae Wilson, Esquire*, in which Hood castigates a hypocrite. The indignation which is buoyed up with humor in some pieces is entirely serious in others of later date. The aims of the social reformers who worked to remedy conditions among the poor during the "Hungry Forties" were expressed by Hood in such poems as *The Lay of the Labourer, The Workhouse Clock*, and—on a higher level of workmanship and celebrity—*The Bridge of Sighs* and *The Song of the Shirt*. Distilling into a few stanzas the awareness of social wrongs which Dickens scattered through many volumes, Hood proved himself to be as influential as Dickens in aiding the reformers who were driving through Parliament the factory, mining, and sanitation acts. A problem which the modern sociologist faces in a different though not less sympathetic spirit is faced by Hood in *The Bridge of Sighs* with a pathos redeemed from mawkishness by its sincerity. The over-ingenious rimes are sustained upon the emotion of the poem, with its picture of the black-flowing river, the dark arch, and the unfortunate victim of man's inhumanity to woman. There is less beauty but more energy in the companion-piece on the misery of the sweat-shop worker. This *Song of the Shirt* rang through England as did Mrs. Browning's *Cry of the Children*. Its publication in *Punch* was the foundation of the popularity of that hitherto not very successful periodical. Appropriately and at his own request there was inscribed upon Hood's tombstone: "He Sang *The Song of the Shirt*."

---

[4] Richard Harris Barham (1788-1845), who used the pen-name "Thomas Ingoldsby," began to publish legends in prose and verse, whimsical and grotesque but stuffed with sound antiquarianism, in 1837. A First Series of these pieces was collected as *The Ingoldsby Legends* (1840); Second and Third Series (1847). The complete edition (1870; Oxford, 1926) contains a memoir of the author by his son, R. H. D. Barham. "Ingoldsby" descends from Southey's grotesques, is immediately contemporary with "Bon Gaultier" (see ch. XIV, n. 29, below), and points forward to some of the *Bab Ballads* of W. S. Gilbert (see ch. XXXVIII). — More completely fantastical than Barham's inventions (some critics now say surrealist) are *The Book of Nonsense* (1848) and its successors by Edward Lear (1812-1888). In Lear's "limericks" and other pieces there are elements which give promise of the work of "Lewis Carroll" (see below, ch. XXI).

Near Hood may be grouped several lesser men. Ebenezer Elliott [5] (1781- *Ebenezer*
1849) is best remembered as a poet of social protest. A Yorkshire laborer *Elliott*
who rose to be an iron-manufacturer in Sheffield, he knew well the hardships of the lives of industrial workers and rustics. He was closest to poetry
when closest to the soil. In the very early poem *A Vernal Walk* (1801) he
obviously chose Thomson for his guide. But when after many years he
returned to verse his masters were Campbell and Byron, who had taught
him a fierce rhetoric. In *The Ranter* (1827) and *Corn-Law Rhymes* (1828)
he exposed the horrors of factories and slums and the injustice to workingmen of the law against the importation of foreign cereals. In such fiery
poems as *Child, Is Thy Father Dead?* and *Day, like our Souls, is fiercely
Dark*, commonplace but easily comprehended words are set to commonplace but memorable cadences. The "Corn-Law Rhymer" helped to mold
sentiment which led two decades later to repeal. He was an excellent propagandist and occasionally a true poet, albeit more often inflated than inspired. The tales in *The Village Patriarch* (1829) in which he depicts with
stern clarity the lives of humble folk show him to be a disciple of Crabbe.

On the other side of Hood are two poets who have little in common with *J. H.*
Elliott's reforming spirit but much with Hood's facile romanticism and *Reynolds*
satiric wit. John Hamilton Reynolds [6] (1794-1852) is remembered as the
friend of Keats, but his poems show the influence of almost all the greater
poets of the time. *The Eden of the Imagination* (1814) is an introspective
analysis of his own emotional and imaginative development. *Safie* (1814) is
an Oriental tale in the manner of Byron. The Elizabethan influence is obvious in some fairy poems which foreshadow Hood and Darley; the
"Cockney" influence is apparent in the imperfections of his style. Reynolds
is nearest to Keats in *The Garden of Florence* (1821) which is a story from
the *Decameron* (and hence is like *Isabella*) in couplets on Dryden's model
(and hence is like *Lamia*). The romantic vein presently ran out, and most
of Reynolds' energy went thereafter into the practice of law and what
remained for literature into satire. His *Peter Bell* [7] is a parody not of
Wordsworth's poem in particular but of the general spirit and manner of
the *Lyrical Ballads*. It is fairly amusing, but pert rather than really clever.

Romance and satiric wit are allied in the verses of Winthrop Mackworth *Praed*
Praed [8] (1802-1839) with the added factor of an intimate knowledge of
well-bred English society. Praed's narratives of King Arthur owe something,
metrically, to Coleridge and more, for their manner, to Scott, while from
Frere he seems to have taken the hint to season his romantic tales with a
dash of topical satire. Abandoning romance, Praed came to specialize in the

[5] *Poems* (2v, 1876). — January Searle, *Memoirs of Ebenezer Elliott* (1852).
[6] *Prose and Poetry* (selections), ed. G. L. Marsh (1928).
[7] This preceded Shelley's satire, which is why Shelley called his poem *Peter Bell the Third*.
See G. L. Marsh, "The *Peter Bell* Parodies of 1819," *MP*, XL (1943). 267-274.
[8] *Select Poems*, ed. W. M. Praed, with introduction by A. D. Godley (1909). — Derek
Hudson, *A Poet in Parliament: The Life of William Mackworth Praed* (1939); Mathilde
Kraupa, *W. M. Praed, sein Leben und seine Werke* (Vienna, 1910); George Saintsbury,
"Praed," *Essays and Papers*, II. 31-52.

grotesque. Of his poems in this kind *The Red Fisherman* is the best and best known; its grim humor and facility anticipate Barham's characteristic effects. On a smaller scale Praed used the technique of surprising rimes and ingenious stanzaic schemes in a large amount of *vers de société*, touched with light malice but essentially kindly. Some of these things, such as *The Belle of the Ball* and *The Letter of Advice,* still possess a winning freshness and grace. Related to them but more serious in purpose and untouched with sentiment are his political pieces. These squibs and skits, which he wrote from experience, for he sat in Parliament and supported the movement for reform,[9] have lost most of their interest with the fading from memory of the persons and events which prompted them; but the best, such as *Stanzas on Seeing the Speaker Asleep,* retain some residue of their pungency. Praed's manner was often too light for the seriousness of his subjects, and his good-nature generally restrained him from penetrating to his victim's quick; but in a few poems, notably the *Counsels of a Father to his Son,* the stiletto reached vital parts.

## II

*Beddoes*

The most memorable figure of these transitional years is Thomas Lovell Beddoes [10] (1803-1849). Just before his death he wrote: "I ought to have been—among other things—a good poet." The fact is, he was a "good" poet and "ought to have been" a great one. The failure to realize his potentialities is attributable to various causes—to distracted aims, for he was a physician and anatomist and, in later years in Germany and Switzerland, something of a political agitator; to discouragement, for *The Improvisatore* (1821) and *The Bride's Tragedy* (1822), which he published while an Oxford undergraduate, met with no success; to isolation, for he got out of touch with English literary society and came to feel that his native English was being supplanted by his acquired German; and to a profound melancholy and lethargic eccentricity which made him skeptical of the value of effort. After the two volumes just named he published no more. His most famous work, *Death's Jest-Book,* was begun about 1825 and for a quarter of a century he tinkered with it, revising, deleting, and expanding. He

[9] Yet not without misgivings; see Praed's *The New Order of Things* (1830). In his last years he was shifting towards the Tories.
[10] A selection from the mass of Beddoes' writings was published posthumously in 1851 by a devoted friend, Thomas Kelsall. *Death's Jest-Book,* as it then appeared, was a patchwork of several different versions left in manuscript. Beddoes' manuscripts were bequeathed by Kelsall to Robert Browning, who intended to "do something" with them but procrastinated. After his death the box of papers passed to Browning's son, and after *his* death it was reported as lost beyond recovery. Years later it became known that the elder Browning had permitted J. Dykes Campbell to make copies of the entire contents of the box; and from these transcripts it has been possible to publish at long last a definitive edition of the poetry and prose. This is *Works,* ed. H. W. Donner (1935), superseding all earlier editions. Supplementing this is *The Browning Box, or the Life and Work of T. L. Beddoes as reflected in Letters by his Friends and Admirers,* ed. H. W. Donner (1935). — H. W. Donner, *Thomas Lovell Beddoes: The Making of a Poet* (1935); R. H. Snow, *Thomas Lovell Beddoes, Eccentric and Poet* (1928); Lytton Strachey, "The Last Elizabethan," *Books and Characters* (1922), pp. 235-265.

wrote the massive fragments in dramatic form, *Torrismond* and *The Second Brother;* began but made little headway with a strange visionary romance, in mixed verse and prose; and composed a quantity of lyrics and lyrical fragments, some of ethereal loveliness and others harsh and grotesquely humorous. Friends in England received occasional letters and verse epistles in which he commented with engaging and often caustic candor upon the stage and theatrical criticism, upon the state of literature in England and Germany, and upon his own shortcomings as a poet. The more self-revealing of these letters suggest that his eccentricity was at times close to madness. At Zurich, in circumstances of eerie lugubriousness he committed suicide.

In youth Beddoes was one of the earliest admirers of Shelley. It is easy to detect Shelley's influence upon him, but it is equally easy to over-empha-size it. The dozen perfect lyrics—*Dream-Pedlary, If Thou Wilt Ease Thine Heart,* and the rest—are worthy of Shelley, but the rarified atmosphere in which the music sounds, the Debussy-like delicacy of the fingering, the pure, thin tone—these are Beddoes' own peculiar qualities. Equally individual are the repulsively grotesque ditty, *Lord Alcohol,* and the uncanny song of which the refrain is "In the ghosts' moonshine." Beddoes' fondness for sinister and spectral imagery probably owes something to Shelley; but both poets were influenced by tales of terror and Jacobean tragedies.

Beddoes was, indeed, at the very center of the Elizabethan revival. It is not a matter of imitation of the gnomic Webster, the dour Tourneur, the acrid Marston; rather it is a spiritual kinship or, more accurately, an identity of imaginative processes. To this Jacobeanism were added ingredients from German romanticism. That Beddoes had read Tieck we know; and some-thing of tender sentiment (like that in *Undine*) and of ghostly and diabolic horror (like that in *Sintram*) probably came from De la Motte Fouqué. Bal-lads of the "Spectre Bridegroom" type stirred his imagination. How often must he have contemplated old German paintings and engravings in which the figure of Death appears among the living! [11] Through his anatomical studies in textbooks and the laboratory he became familiar with, and hence, as he said, contemptuous of, the horrors of mortality. To this exotic and sinister amalgam was added an awareness of new scientific speculation and experiment in dim regions of physiology and psychology. First among English poets he used as material for poetry the discoveries of the paleon-tologists. "The mighty thought of an old world," where amid the fern wildernesses titanic reptilian forms glistened, troubled his somber fantasy.[12] There are passages in his poetry which suggest that he believed in the evo-lution of species.[13]

[11] Particularly the numerous engravings of Death and the Maiden, and Death and the Lovers. The analogy to *Death's Jest-Book* is startling in the case of Hans Sebald Beham's exquisite little engraving of Death and the Woman (1541). Here the skeleton wears a fool's cap and carries a fool's bauble.

[12] Beddoes, *Song by Thanatos; Works,* ed. Donner, p. 142.

[13] G. R. Potter, "Did Beddoes Believe in the Evolution of Species?" *MP,* xxi (1923). 89-100.

Death's
Jest-Book

The two fragmentary dramas are not carried far enough to permit us to guess their intended course. The plot of *Death's Jest-Book* in summary reads like a parody of Jacobean tragedies of revenge: a duke who commits a murder; an avenger who disguises himself as a court-jester; the victim who rises from the tomb and at the close conducts his murderer into the world of the dead. Beddoes' imagery is powerful, condensed, aphoristic, disturbing. Earth is "this grave-paved star"; ivy, a "creeping darkness"; Time is a cataract falling into Eternity over ruined worlds. Death lurks always very near. So close are tombs together that those of latest date lie just beneath the surface of life in "the garrets of Death's town." "Death is old and half worn out; are there no chinks in it?" a character asks; and the reply takes the form of the numerous dead who rise, not furtive and wraith-like but social and substantial, and hobnob with the living, warning, counseling, mocking them; who chat and sing and dance, as they do in Holbein or Rowlandson; but who can be tender as well as terrible. In Beddoes' drama there is much of madness and more of sin; but horror is not the soul of the plot. There is a weird glee not only in some of the interspersed lyrics but in the antic prose; there is subtlety of thought and fancy; and over all there is cast a veil of shimmering loveliness. Beddoes did not possess the strength of character and structural skill to carry to completion a greatly conceived design. To ask of him significance of plot or profundity of psychology is to ask for what he cannot give. He is memorable for scattered lines and passages, cadences of haunting beauty, and images of arresting grandeur.

# III

Of the other poets who belong to the Elizabethan revival those who won any considerable success in the theatre are noticed in the next chapter. The rest may be considered here. Of these the least in merit but personally closest to Beddoes was Bryan Waller Procter [14] (1787-1874), who wrote under the pen-name of "Barry Cornwall." He is a link between Shelley's generation [15] and the Victorians, for he was a friend of Browning and a recipient of Swinburne's homage. Procter began with *Dramatic Scenes* (1819), limpid little pieces, one of which is on the story in the *Decameron* which Tennyson afterwards dramatized in *The Falcon*. A tragedy, *Mirandola* (1821), was a success at Covent Garden rather because of its striking theme—the marriage of a father to his son's betrothed—than for any distinction of style or technique. It is obviously patterned upon Massinger, but in it the wine of the old drama is diluted to a feeble draught. Procter's contemporary fame rested upon his *English Songs* (1832)—of the sea and of love and of the jolly life. Some of them are faintly Shelleyan, others obviously Tom-Moorish.

"Barry
Cornwall"

---

[14] *Poetical Works* (3v, 1822). There is no modern edition. — Franz Becker, *B. W. Procter* (Vienna, 1911).
[15] He and Beddoes helped to bear the cost of printing Shelley's *Posthumous Poems*.

Charles Jeremiah Wells [16] (1800-1879), another link between the genera- *Wells*
tions, was in youth a friend of Keats and in old age a protégé of the Pre-
Raphaelites. His *Stories after Nature* (1822), from the *Decameron,* are one
more instance of the influence of Boccaccio at this time. The sprawling and
grandiloquent dramatic poem, *Joseph and His Brethren* (1824), is in its
prosody and more than life-size characterizations sufficiently like Marlowe's
plays to resemble more nearly the plays of Marlowe's imitators. Wells could
catch the large utterance of the early gods; but he could not catch the attention of the public. *Joseph* passed promptly into oblivion and its author, being
possessed of a competence, to an aimless existence in France. Both were
rediscovered half a century later by Rossetti and Swinburne, who persuaded
the old man to permit the republication of his play. For a while *Joseph* was
a touchstone of taste in Rossetti's circle. Today it is sinking into a second
obscurity which it does not altogether deserve, for in it there are passages
of torrential poetry, a richly laden Oriental atmosphere, and keen glimpses
into human character. But it is better to dip into than to read entire; the
monotony of its rhetorical splendor soon becomes a burden on the spirit.[17]

More versatile and persevering than Wells was the Irishman George *Darley*
Darley [18] (1795-1846). His first volume, *The Errors of Ecstasie* [19] (1822),
was neglected and is negligible save as a precursor of the "spasmodic" poetry
of the mid-century. But the dramatic criticism and prose tales [20] which he
contributed to *The London Magazine* attracted attention. One of his tales,
*Lillian of the Vale,* he reshaped into *Sylvia, or the May Queen* (1827), a
resuscitation of the fairy-lore of Shakespeare, Drayton, and Fletcher. The
Lilliputian warfare of fairies and fiends over Sylvia is pleasant, but this
delicate fretwork in a complicated pattern is marred by incongruous
clownish jocosity. The play is scarcely more than a vehicle for some lovely
songs. Darley could sing an individual melody.[21] From light Fletcherian
grace he passed on to a graver style. *Nepenthe* (1836) is incoherent in its
rush of words, but the tragedies, *Thomas à Becket* (1840) and *Ethelstan*
(1841), have something of the sober dignity of Massinger.

Grave, high-minded, labored, and slow-moving are the "closet" dramas of

[16] *Joseph and His Brethren,* introduction by A. C. Swinburne (1876; World's Classics,
1908); *Stories after Nature,* ed. W. J. Linton (1891).
[17] Another "Elizabethan" of even slenderer renown is Thomas Wade (1805-1875). His
drama on the Griselda-theme, *Woman's Love, or the Triumph of Patience* (1828), was a
success at Covent Garden, but *The Jew of Arragon* (1830), reminiscent of Marlowe, failed.
Before and after these plays Wade published volumes of lyrics and sonnets, the former
Shelleyan in manner, the latter curiously Shakespearean.
[18] *Complete Poetical Works,* ed. Ramsay Colles (The Muses' Library, n.d.) — C. C. Abbott,
*The Life and Letters of George Darley, Poet and Critic* (1928).
[19] This contains a strange dialogue between a Mystic and the Moon in which the Moon
argues for the Golden Mean between metaphysical speculation and sensuous enjoyment.
[20] Gathered into *The Labours of Idleness* (1826). These are mainly sketches in the manner
of Washington Irving.
[21] He could also recapture the tune of cavalier lyric, as he did in *It is not Beauty I Demand*
which F. T. Palgrave mistook for genuine seventeenth-century work. From another of Darley's
songs George Meredith seems to have taken the stanza of *Love in the Valley.*

*Taylor*

Sir Henry Taylor [22] (1800-1886). *Philip Van Artevelde* [23] (1834) is not a stage-play but a historical romance cast in dramatic form. Its theme is the contrast between the *vita contemplativa* and the *vita activa*. For his people's sake Artevelde dedicates himself to soul-destroying service, moving from the life of thought to that of political power, and from power to personal ambition. There is noble poetry in this work and it was for long admired by thoughtful readers. Taylor's other plays—*Isaac Comnenus* (1827), *Edwin the Fair* (1842)—are of less interest. Richard Henry Horne [24] (1803-1884) is remembered for *Orion* (1843), a poem which he called an epic but which is rather a symbolic romance, a work of overwrought and clouded imagination, not without passages of splendor. Much of Horne's intense activity went into poetic drama. *Cosmo de' Medici* (1837) is another example of the attraction of Italian themes. *The Death of Marlowe* [25] (1837) is violent and vivid. The social and literary studies in Horne's *New Spirit of the Age* [26] (1844) are written with forceful conviction and are interesting for their indications of changing taste.

*Horne*

*Scotch Poets*

Allan Cunningham [27] (1784-1842), a Scot, tried his hand at sensational drama in *Sir Marmaduke Maxwell* (1822) and other plays, but he is remembered today for the sea-chantey *A Wet Sheet and a Flowing Sea,* and for a few other lyrics. With him may be grouped two older minor poets of Scotland, Hector MacNeill (1746-1818), whose serious verse is forgotten but whose whimsical humor touched with sentiment (as in *Saw Ye My Wee Thing?*) possesses a lasting charm, and Carolina, Lady Nairne (1766-1845), whose *Land o' the Leal* was often mistakenly ascribed to Burns. Through these and other writers [28] the tradition of Scottish humor, sentiment, and loyalty to the Jacobite cause was passed down to William Edmonstoune Aytoun (1813-1865), in whose *Lays of the Scottish Cavaliers* (1848) Jacobitism received almost its last poetic expression.[29]

[22] *Works* (5v, 1883); *Autobiography* (2v, 1885); *Correspondence,* ed. Edward Dowden (1888).

[23] The preface to *Artevelde,* a defense of Wordsworth and an attack upon Byronism, arguing that reason should dominate imagination in poetry and reflection should dominate emotion, is a document of importance in the history of taste.

[24] Or Richard Hengist Horne, as he called himself. Horne had an early life of adventure in America and in Australia. In England he was a civil commissioner engaged on the problem of child labor, and in that capacity inspired Elizabeth Barrett to write *The Cry of the Children.* His correspondence with her (1839-1846) was published in 1877. She was one of his collaborators in *The New Spirit of the Age.* Horne's works range from *Judas Iscariot,* a miracle play, to *The South Sea Sisters,* a masque. He also wrote novels, travel narratives, biographies, and books for children. — E. J. Shumaker, *Bibliography* (Granville, Ohio, 1943) and a forthcoming biography.

[25] Reprinted in Marlowe's *Works,* ed. A. H. Bullen (1885), III, Appendix.

[26] In the World's Classics, introduction by Walter Jerrold (1907).

[27] Cunningham, who began life as a mason, was for many years manager of the studio of F. L. Chantrey, the sculptor. Of his prose work the *Lives of Eminent British Painters, Sculptors, and Architects* (1829-1833) is entertaining and still worth consulting. He edited Burns and *Songs of Scotland* and palmed off as genuine antiques some dialect ballads of his own composition.

[28] For example, Mrs. Anne Grant (1755-1838), the author of *O Where, Tell Me, Where Has My Highland Laddie Gone?*

[29] *Poems* (1921). Aytoun, though of a younger generation, may be noticed here. The *Lays* include the moving *Execution of Montrose* and the plangent, martial *Burial March of Dundee.* An appendix in which Aytoun crosses swords valiantly with Lord Macaulay is note-

## IV

Enduring popularity for other than strictly literary reasons is assured to *The Hym-*
some of the writings of the hymnodists. There is necessarily a rhetorical *nodists*
rather than strictly poetical quality in the impassioned, up-surging, eminently singable, and movingly devout hymns of Reginald Heber [30] (1783-
1826). *From Greenland's Icy Mountains, The Son of God Goes Forth to
War,* and *Holy, Holy, Holy* are in the great tradition of dignified Anglicanism inherited from the eighteenth century. They are of slightly earlier date
than most of the work mentioned in this chapter. A note of more personal devotion is heard in the equally popular hymns of James Montgomery [31] (1771-
1854), such as *For Ever with the Lord* and *Hail to the Lord's Annointed.*
Montgomery's reforming spirit expressed itself also in secular verse, a little
in the manner of Cowper, as in his poems of protest against the employment
of tiny boys as chimney-sweeps. His longer poems are forgotten. Comment
upon John Keble's *The Christian Year* (1827) belongs to our account of
the Oxford Movement,[32] but here it may be noted that some stanzas of the
*Evening Hymn* in that collection form one of the best loved of all hymns,
*Sun of my Soul, Thou Saviour Dear.* Through Heber, Montgomery, and
Keble the tradition of devotional song descended from Watts, Toplady,
and Cowper to the greatest of Victorian hymnodists, John Mason Neale.[33]

Connected with the Oxford Movement by personal ties was the Hispano- *Blanco*
Irish poet Blanco White (1775-1841), whose reputation rests upon one great *White*
sonnet, *On Night* (1829), praised by Coleridge and expressing the devout
but uncertain speculations of an inquiring spirit.

The sonnet was the favorite medium of expression used by Hartley *Hartley*
Coleridge [34] (1796-1849). He wrote in other forms: the idyll, the meditative *Coleridge*
lyric, even the heroic couplet (in which he praised various English poets of
former times); but he found his true voice—humble, penitent, and devout—
within the sonnet's narrow limits. He seldom rises above a level of quiet

worthy. In *Firmilian . . . a Spasmodic Tragedy* (1854) Aytoun parodied and satirized tellingly
Alexander Smith and Sidney Dobell at the moment when Tennyson, in *Maud,* was under the
influence of these poets. See below, ch. XXVI, n. 12. The rollicking and robust fun at *Ta Fhairson*
is still enjoyable. This is one of the *Ballads by Bon Gaultier* which Aytoun wrote with Theodore
Martin. They were collected in 1845.

[30] *Poetical Works* (1841).

[31] *Poetical Works* (4v, 1850). — John Holland and James Everett, *Memoirs of the Life
and Writings of James Montgomery* (2v, 1854).

[32] See below, ch. XVIII.

[33] J. M. Neale (1818-1866) belongs to the next generation but it is appropriate to notice
him in this connection. He wrote fiction, theological works, and books for young people, but
is best remembered for his hymns. *Art Thou Weary?* is exceptionally beautiful and *Christian,
Dost Thou See Them?* exceptionally vigorous; but the best known are *Jerusalem the Golden*
and its three companion excerpts from his translation of *The Rhythm of Bernard of Morlaix
on the Celestial City* (1859). According to *DNB* one-eighth of the entire contents of the
original edition of *Hymns Ancient and Modern* was by Neale, original or translated. — See
Eleanor A. Towle, *John Mason Neale, D. D., a Memoir* (1906).

[34] *Poems,* with a Memoir by Derwent Coleridge (2v, 1851); *Poems,* ed. Ramsay Colles
(2v, 1908); *New Poems,* ed. E. L. Griggs (1942); *Letters,* ed. G. E. and E. L. Griggs (1936).
— E. L. Griggs, *Hartley Coleridge. His Life and Work* (1929); Herbert Hartman, *Hartley
Coleridge: Poet's Son and Poet* (1931).

competence, but on rare occasions he can be magnificent, as in the self-revelatory *Let Me Not Deem that I Was Made in Vain* and in the profoundly religious *Multum Dilexit*. His prose criticism, ranging from the early Tudors to the eighteenth century, is not unworthy of the great tradition in which he was reared. The story of the bright promise of his youth and the tragic failure of his young manhood is today better known than his poetry or criticism.

*Clare*　　Another pathetic figure is that of John Clare [35] (1793-1864), the Northamptonshire peasant-poet, who, because of the affinity of his nature poetry to that of William H. Davies and Edward Thomas, has of late been overpraised for his sensitive descriptions of the small sights and sounds of the natural world. After an obscure youth as a ploughboy in such circumstances as the romanticists, with their confidence in the virtues of primitive man, loved to contemplate as the natural nursery of genius, Clare won sudden fame with his *Poems Descriptive of Rural Life* (1820). Other volumes—*The Village Minstrel* (1821) and *The Rural Muse* (1834)—were less well received. Clare was as "uneducated" (in Southey's phrase) [36] as Robert Bloomfield,[37] but he had in him more of the genuine poetic quality, a quality like that of the brook which in "the leafy month of June" hums "a quiet tune" to itself. As the observer of nature he descends from Thomson, Cowper, and Wordsworth; as the special poet of a particular corner of England he points forward to later regionalists. But he was ill content with the sequestered way of life of which he sang; Melancholy marked him for her own; and in later life he passed into the twilight of lunacy. The verses which he wrote in an asylum have a childlike charm for those who ignore the circumstances in which they were written and a painful interest for those who remember them. His *Last Lines* are in a different key from that characteristic of him; and their poignancy is somewhat rhetorical.

*Mrs.*　　Women writers, very active in the field of popular fiction, produced little
*Hemans*　poetry at this time. Two only are of any consequence. The lofty intentions, moral purity, and generous nature of Felicia Dorothea Hemans [38] (1793-1835) attracted the large contemporary audience who praised her innumerable and exuberant poems, lyrical, narrative, dramatic, and meditative. Only once or twice, however, as in *England's Dead*, did she discipline her redundance into noble form. It has been the misfortune of this "holy spirit" (as Wordsworth called her, mourning her death) to be chiefly remembered —and then with a disdainful smile—for *Casabianca*. Even more popular

---

[35] *Poems*, ed. Arthur Symons (1908); *Poems*, ed. J. W. Tibble (2v, 1935); *Poems chiefly from Manuscript*, ed. Edmund Blunden and Alan Porter (1920); *Sketches in the Life of John Clare Written by Himself*, ed. Edmund Blunden (1931). — J. W. and Anne Tibble, *John Clare, a Life* (1932); M. Chaning-Pearce, "John Clare," *Hibbert Journal*, xxxix (1941). 291-298.
[36] See Southey's *Lives and Works of the Uneducated Poets*, ed. J. S. Childers (1925). This was originally the introduction to *Attempts in Verse, by John Jones, an Old Servant* (1831).
[37] The career of Robert Bloomfield (1766-1823) overlaps that of Clare, for Bloomfield's *Mayday with the Muses* appeared so late as 1823.
[38] *Poetical Works* (1914).

was Letitia Elizabeth Landon, "L.E.L.," [39] (1802-1838). Her life—gay in *"L.E.L."* its promise, tragic in its ending—has an abiding interest not found in her poetry. She supplied her public with sentiment and prettiness in the manner of the "annuals" to which she was a contributor.[40]

[39] D. E. Enfield, *L. E. L., a Mystery of the Thirties* (1928); M. M. H. Thrall, *Rebellious Fraser's* (1934), ch. IX.

[40] From the above survey many minor poets have necessarily been excluded. There is room here to mention three more. Bernard Barton (1789-1849), the Quaker poet, is better remembered as the friend and correspondent of Charles Lamb and Edward FitzGerald than as the author of feeble and ineffectual verse. Robert Pollok (1798-1827) achieved among the devout a high reputation which now seems almost inexplicable, with his pretentious apocalyptic poem in blank verse, *The Course of Time* (1827). See David Pollok, *The Life of Robert Pollok* (1843). The same public found edification and consolation in *The Omnipresence of Deity* (1828) and *Satan* (1830) by Robert Montgomery—or Gomery (1807-1855), who is now remembered as the subject of an excoriating review (1830) by Macaulay.

# XV

## The Drama in Decline[1]

Of the nine theatres in regular use in London at the beginning of the nineteenth century the two principal houses were soon destroyed by fire, Covent Garden in 1808 and Drury Lane in 1809. They were rebuilt. Most of the others underwent drastic alterations. The enormous growth of the city during the next four decades created a demand for places of amusement which was met by the construction of new theatres in and around London. These were more receptive to innovations than the two great houses. Forbidden to offer "legitimate" drama,[2] their managers were ingenious in providing substitutes—melodramas, burlettas, extravaganzas, farces, operettas, and other sorts of entertainment that were within the law. Machinery was elaborate; ghosts and demons rose through traps of various device; goblins and fairies floated on wires through the air. Some theatres, notably Sadler's Wells (because of its proximity to the New River), made a specialty of water-spectacles with practicable ships; the Olympic Pavilion was licensed for pantomime and equestrian acts; other houses catered to the taste for performing animals—not only dogs and horses but sometimes larger and wilder beasts. Under a thin veneer of drama these variety entertainments were often little more, and no better, than circuses.

Certain technical innovations wrought great changes. The apron, which had formerly jutted far out into the pit, continued to shrink; and as the actors retreated behind the proscenium arch, the "picture-frame" stage assumed almost its modern form. The removal of the old proscenium doors and stage-boxes widened the gap between actors and spectators. The introduction of illumination by gas afforded opportunities for effects hitherto undreamed of. Scenery was elaborate, and talented decorators and skillful machinists were employed; but because of the great cost of mounting, large numbers of sets were kept in stock, and scenes made for one play often did service in another, with a resulting incongruity which amused discriminating

*The New Theatres*

---

[1] *Representative British Dramas, Victorian and Modern,* ed. M. J. Moses (1937), with introductions and bibliographies; Allardyce Nicoll, *A History of Late Eighteenth Century Drama, 1750-1800* (1927) and *A History of Early Nineteenth Century Drama, 1800-1850* (2v, 1930); John Genest, *Some Account of the English Stage* (10v, Bath, 1832); E. B. Watson, *Sheridan to Robertson: A Study of the Nineteenth-Century London Stage* (Cambridge, Mass., 1926); N. W. Sawyer, *The Comedy of Manners from Sheridan to Maugham* (Philadelphia, 1931); U. C. Nag, "The English Theatre of the Romantic Revival," *Nineteenth Century and After,* CIV (1928). 384-398; A. E. DuBois, "Shakespeare and Nineteenth-Century Drama," *ELH,* I (1934). 163-196.

[2] This prohibition was lifted from the Haymarket during the two summer months when Drury Lane and Covent Garden were closed. The Licensing Act was repealed in 1843.

patrons. Antiquarian research and the vogue of the historical novel encouraged a relative accuracy of costume and setting in plays on subjects from times past; and in such plays a reliance upon pageantry enabled Covent Garden and Drury Lane to compete with those minor theatres that were noted for spectacular performances. The immense size of the two licensed houses made for a robust style of acting, loudly rhetorical and dependent upon large, conventional gestures, and dictated the choice of grandiose and spectacular pieces, since quiet, austere drama was unsuited to these vast spaces.

Under the pressure of Evangelical opinion most sober and godly people *The* avoided the theatres. Patronage came from rough and disreputable elements: *Audience* the well-to-do fast set occupying the boxes; their footmen crowding the galleries; and the bullies and prostitutes disgracing the side-boxes and the lobbies. The turbulence of audiences is suggested by the obsequious requests for order found in many prologues. In the face of this unruliness the aristocracy deserted the theatres almost altogether and frequented the opera instead. Yet long before the Victorian era the decorousness of moral tone and respect for the proprieties of language in the plays offered often amounted to prudishness. The Lord Chamberlain's censorship was vigilant in condemning anything indecent or tending to bring religion into disrespect or seeming to countenance sedition. Allusions hostile to government were forbidden; but contemporary events might be dramatized provided they appealed to the emotion of patriotism.

Some of the minor theatres were run at a profit, but the two patent houses were constantly in financial difficulties. The salaries of leading actors rose steadily during the first half of the century; the pay-rolls were very large, since separate stock companies were maintained for tragedy, comedy, opera, and pantomime and were on salary even when idle; the scenery and machinery cost a great deal. The management never solved the dilemma that if they raised prices the mob raised riots [3] and if they lowered them expenses could not be met. They resorted to versions of French plays for which they paid next to nothing; since copyright was insecure there was much piracy; and the native playwrights received starvation wages. Notwithstanding these and other economies the history of Covent Garden and Drury Lane is a succession of bankruptcies and consequent changes in management.

The Romantic Period was an age of great actors. Yet the genius and *The* prestige of Kemble, Kean, and Macready were partly responsible for the *Actors* drama's decline, for the star sacrificed the other actors to his own glory, brought his own part too prominently into the limelight, and made a proper coördination of effects difficult or impossible. Old texts were often mangled to bring the principal rôle into still greater prominence. When

---

[3] The most notorious disturbance occurred in 1809 when Kemble reopened Covent Garden at advanced rates and the "O. P. riots" lasted nearly seventy nights till the old prices were restored, save for the boxes.

playwrights wrote with particular stars in view, the setting of the luminaries was apt to carry the plays into oblivion. A further consequence of the star-system was the small demand for new plays. The star's desire was to challenge comparison with his predecessors in famous rôles. A like situation obtains in opera today. In comedy and farce the talents of a remarkable line of actors (Liston, Munden, Johnstone, and others) popularized contemptible pieces which, less well acted, would have been hissed off the stage.

In general the plays produced had the least pretensions to literary merit, while those deserving the respect of people of refined taste were as a rule shut out from the theatres. Actable plays came almost entirely from ready writers with little or no artistic conscience, working for a pittance and subservient to imperious managers and stars. Yet from Gifford's *Maeviad* to Byron's prefaces to his plays there was a succession of pleas for the reform of the stage; and all the distinguished poets tried their hands at drama. Not one of them succeeded perfectly and most of them failed altogether. The dramas written by the great romanticists have therefore been noticed in connection with their other work. They never grasped the basic principle that "those who live to please must please to live." They did not cater to the public taste. Their subjects were mostly remote from contemporary interests and their style was derivative. Mistakenly, they laid their stress upon poetry at the expense of action. Naturally exuberant (not to say long-winded), they made no attempt to master the condensation and restraint required for effective drama. The self-centeredness of most of them was ill-suited to the playwright's art. It may also be that they shrank from the rude ordeal of facing the disapproval of ill-mannered audiences.

The French Revolution made no break in the continuity of English drama. Some writers, notably Thomas Holcroft, injected cautious hints of radical opinions into their plays, and others, notably Mrs. Inchbald, used their plays as vehicles for social criticism. But in general the stage was not alive to the great political issues of the age. Types of drama inherited from the previous era underwent slow change or disappeared.[4] In the last years of the century, coinciding with the vogue of German romance, there was a phenomenal demand for German plays. The democratic sentiments in the plays of the Austrian dramatist August von Kotzebue were in harmony with current sentiment, and his technical cleverness (as in *The Stranger*) went well in the theatre. Sheridan's *Pizarro* (1799) is a feeble version of Kotzebue's *Die Spanier in Peru*; and there were translations of other plays of his. Gothic romance influenced the melodramas which were in vogue before a name for them was imported from France.[5] These were spectacular

*The German Vogue*

[4] The few belated examples of neo-classical tragedy are of no account. George Lillo's plays failed to establish domestic tragedy as a popular genre. Parallel with the beginnings of the historical novel came plays on subjects from English history but none are of consequence. Cumberland invaded the historical field once with *The Days of Yore* (1796), a drama laid in Anglo-Saxon times.

[5] The first English play to be announced as a "melo-drama" was Holcroft's *Tale of Mystery* (Covent Garden, 1802), a free version of *Coeline, ou l'enfant du mystère* by Guilbert de Pixérécourt, the chief French writer of *melodrame*. The incidental music which the etymology of the word *melodrama* implies gradually ceased to be an essential feature of the genre.

productions, gloomy and mysterious, sometimes introducing the supernatural, infused strongly with sentimental morality, and ending in accordance with "poetic justice." Typical and among the most successful of
this kind are *The Castle Spectre* (1798) by "Monk" Lewis and *The Iron
Chest* (1796) by George Colman the Younger.

Sentimental comedy continued to be popular. The veteran Richard
Cumberland (1732-1811) was active in this and in other kinds of drama.
*The Wheel of Fortune* (1795), one of his best plays, provided John Kemble
with the famous part of the misanthropist who cannot forget his wrongs
but learns to forgive. In the social comedies of Mrs. Elizabeth Inchbald [6]
(1753-1821)—*I'll Tell You What* (1785) and later plays—the sentimentalism
is lightened by wit and technical expertness which make her a not altogether
unworthy successor of Goldsmith and Sheridan. Sentimentalism is but one
ingredient in the plays of Thomas Holcroft [7] (1745-1809), the most considerable dramatist at the turn of the century. Holcroft owed his outstand- *Holcroft*
ing success to the practical knowledge of the theatre which he acquired
as a prompter in Dublin and member of a strolling company. In Paris
shortly before the Revolution he attended performances of Beaumarchais'
*Le Mariage de Figaro* [8] and absorbed the new political and social ideas.
These he expressed in guardedly general terms in his famous sensational
and sentimental drama, *The Road to Ruin* (1792), in which are shown the
inevitable disasters attendant upon gambling. Holcroft's mastery of stage
technique is demonstrated by the fact that at so late a date as 1873 a revival
of this play ran for more than a hundred nights. Other playwrights at this
time were Frederick Reynolds, author of *The Dramatist* (1793), and Thomas
Morton, author of *Speed the Plough* (1800).

Between 1800 and 1830 there was a long series of adaptations and imitations of Guilbert de Pixérécourt, followed from about 1825 till the mid-
century by versions of Eugène Scribe. From native sources came numerous
adaptations of novels, particularly those of Scott and at a later date of
Cooper, Bulwer, Ainsworth, Egan, and Dickens. Burlettas (comic pieces
with accompanying music) were sometimes founded upon Shakespeare's
plays; and how confidently the theatres could count upon familiarity with
Shakespeare is shown by the number of travesties. Farces and extravaganzas, flimsy in plot, loose in construction, and dependent upon humorous
types such as the "stage Irishman," were poured out by the hundreds down
to the mid-century. Among writers of these things may be mentioned
Edward Fitzball [9] (1792-1873), J. R. Planché (1796-1880), and Douglas
Jerrold [10] (1803-1857). In *Black-eyed Susan* (1829) Jerrold turned his early

[6] S. R. Littlewood, *Elizabeth Inchbald and her Circle* (1921), and see above, ch. VIII.

[7] V. R. Stallbaumer, "Thomas Holcroft: a Satirist in the Stream of Sentimentalism," *ELH*,
III (1936). 31-62.

[8] Holcroft's version of this was produced as *The Follies of the Day* (Drury Lane, 1784).

[9] Fitzball was successful in many genres. He specialized in nautical dramas such as *The
Floating Beacon* (1824), which ran for 140 nights, and *The Pilot* (1825), which ran for two
hundred. Among his many melodramas is *Jonathan Bradford, or the Murder at the Roadside
Inn* (1833). He also wrote opera librettos.

[10] On Jerrold's nondramatic work see ch. XVI, below.

nautical experiences to good account and won an enormous and long-lived success. Dion Boucicault [11] (1822-1890) belongs in the main to the post-Robertson period, but his first success, *London Assurance* (1841), held out, in its attempt at realism of dialogue and situation, accompanied by a more naturalistic style of acting, some promise of better things to come.

Midway between the successful plays of little or no literary value and the closet dramas by the great romanticists which were either not aimed at the theatres or else missed their mark are certain tragedies and tragi-comedies written with more literary taste than the former and more know-ledge of stagecraft than the latter. In this category belong the plays of

*Joanna Baillie*

Joanna Baillie [12] (1762-1851), who, having been vastly overrated by Sir Walter Scott, has been somewhat underrated ever since. Her *Plays on the Passions* appeared in four series between 1798 and 1836.[13] She believed that of late the stage, in concentrating upon grand vicissitudes of fortune and startling dramatic situations, had neglected its true mission, and she would recall it to "the boundless variety of nature" by portraying in each of her plays a single ruling passion. Reducing action to a minimum and concentrating upon the exposition of motive by means of dialogue, she foreshadowed Byron's tragedies (as he recognized) and even Browning's. Her aim was a high one; but the faulty psychology inherent in her theory is ineradicable, and Hazlitt hit the mark when he said that she was "a Unitarian in poetry. With her passions are, like the French Republic, one and indivisible; they are not so in nature, or in Shakespeare." [14]

*Poetic Tragedy*

The triumphs of the great tragedians—the Kembles, Kean, and Miss O'Neil—encouraged in the years after 1810 the writing of poetic tragedies. Coleridge's *Remorse* was produced at Drury Lane in 1813. The large bor-rowings from Shakespeare in his second play, *Zapolya,* which the Drury Lane committee rejected, show how heavily the dead hand of Elizabethan-ism lay upon the talent of the time. Of the five tragedies by Henry Hart Milman (1791-1868) the best is *Fazio* (Covent Garden, 1816), an Italianate-Elizabethan drama of jealousy and crime. Milman's interest in biblical studies is reflected in three other plays; and his last is on the story of Anne Boleyn (1826). Richard L. Sheil [15] (1791-1851) wrote half a dozen plays, of which *The Apostate* (1817) and *Evadne* [16] (1819) are the best. James Sheridan Knowles [17] (1784-1862) had the advantage of practical experience as an actor before he won his first success with *Leo* (1810). *Virginius* (1820) provided Macready with one of his most famous parts. Other plays by Knowles are *William Tell* (1825) and *The Hunchback* (1832), which re-

[11] Townsend Walsh, *The Career of Dion Boucicault* (1915).

[12] *Dramatic and Poetical Works* (1851). — M. S. Carhart, *The Life and Work of Joanna Baillie* (New Haven, 1923).

[13] See the discourse prefixed to *Plays on the Passions,* Series I. Favorable specimens of her plays are *De Montfort* (hate) and *Ethwald* (ambition).

[14] Hazlitt, *Lectures on the English Poets; Works,* ed. Waller and Glover, V. 147.

[15] W. T. M'Cullagh, *Memoirs of Richard Lalor Sheil* (2v, 1855).

[16] *Evadne* is an amalgam of motifs from James Shirley's *The Traitor* and Massinger and Field's *The Fatal Dowry.*

[17] L. H. Meeks, *Sheridan Knowles and the Theatre of his Time* (Bloomington, Ind., 1933).

mained for a long time in the theatrical repertory. Among several plays by Mary Russell Mitford [18] (1787-1855) may be mentioned *Foscari* (1826), which challenged comparison with Byron, and *Rienzi* (1828), which had a considerable run. On a higher level are two tragedies on classical themes by Sir Thomas Noon Talfourd (1795-1854). In *Ion* (1836) and in *The Athenian Captive* (1838) there is grave dignity; but these and Talfourd's other plays did not long maintain themselves upon the stage. Brilliant and eminently actable was Edward Bulwer's [19] *Richelieu* (1839), which kept its place in the repertory down to the time of Irving. His comedy, *The Lady of Lyons* (1838), with its romantic plot won immediate and prolonged popularity. In *Money* (1840) Bulwer dealt seriously with contemporary questions and showed himself definitely a precursor not only of Robertson but of later dramatists. Most of the plays of John Westland Marston (1819-1890) are merely derivative, but in *The Patrician's Daughter* (1841) he accomplished the noteworthy feat of adapting the Elizabethan form to a modern subject.

Glancing back over the poetic drama of the first half of the century, we observe that the closer the dramatists adhered to Elizabethan models in subject, style, and technique, the further were they from the modern stage. At one end of the line are such poets as Beddoes and Wells who wrote only to be read; at the other end are Bulwer and Marston, who almost freed themselves from traditionalism. Beddoes in one of his letters passes judgment upon himself and his fellow-poets:

These reanimations are vampire-cold. Such ghosts as Marlowe, Webster &c are better dramatists, better poets, I dare say, than any contemporary of ours—but they are ghosts—the worm is in their pages.... With the greatest reverence for all the antiquities of the drama, I still think that we had better beget than revive—attempt to give the literature of this age an idiosyncrasy and spirit of its own and only raise a ghost to gaze on, not to live with—just now the drama is a haunted ruin.[20]

[18] Miss Mitford is better remembered for *Our Village* (1819), sketches of rural life, character, and scenery, suggestive of Crabbe in their wealth of homely "Dutch" detail, but genial and without Crabbe's censoriousness.

[19] On Bulwer's novels and other nondramatic work see below, ch. xxv.

[20] *Works*. ed. H. W. Donner, p. 595. The letter is of January, 1825.

# XVI
## The Novel Between Scott and Dickens

*A Period of Transition*

The *terminus a quo* of this chapter is 1814, the year of *Waverley*, but there is no precise *terminus ad quem*, for much of the fiction to be considered here appeared later than 1837, the year of *Pickwick Papers*.[1] Bulwer and Disraeli are not included, because though they began to publish before Dickens and exhibit certain characteristics of this period of transition, their activities extended over so many years and their books are so intimate a part of the Victorian scene that to treat of them at this point would be an anachronism. Peacock will be taken up first and in isolation, for his idiosyncrasies are marked, and he cannot be forced into a category. Among the other novelists of this time certain groups and lines of development are discernible. Hope, Morier, Trelawny, and Marryat have this in common, that they all draw upon their own experiences in distant lands. The historical material in Hope's and Marryat's fiction relates them to the novelists who followed the path blazed by Scott. Sir Walter's Scottish followers and successors include two men—Lockhart and Hogg—who, though active in other fields of literature besides fiction, are most conveniently disposed of here; and among the Scottish writers are two other novelists—John Galt and Susan Ferrier—who depart widely from the pattern laid down by Scott. From them we shall pass to the English writers of historical fiction, with the reminder that a part of Bulwer's work might be studied in this connection but for the reasons already given. The Irish novelists are also deeply indebted to Scott, whether they deal with the historic past of their country or apply something of his technique to their treatment of the contemporary state of Irish politics and society. But there was in them a vein of broad humor and low farce like that in the English novelists of sporting life. This group of Englishmen and the artists whose designs in color or black-and-white accompanied their "letter-press" portrayed "life in London" in a manner foretelling the advent of "Boz." In summary fashion we have thus set up a series of sign-posts along the way which we are now to travel.

[1] Only the specialists, and not all of them, have read all the novels of all the novelists of this period of transition. The present chapter is largely indebted to Baker, VII, chs. I-IV, and to George Saintsbury, *The English Novel* (1913), chs. VI-VII. The subject is well treated in Oliver Elton, *Survey of English Literature, 1830-1880* (1920), II, ch. XX, though Professor Elton admits that some of his facts and opinions are taken from the writings of the specialists.

# I

After trying his hand at poetry and after years of indecision, Thomas *Peacock*
Love Peacock[2] (1785-1866) found a comfortable berth as an official of the
East India Company. The friendship of this classically-minded and sophisticated man with Shelley may have awakened in him his critical and
satiric talent, for though he is not precisely an anti-romantic (as sometimes
rated) and though his poems are in the current mode,[3] he was alert to the
excesses and vagaries of the romantic pose. Yet two of his little novels—
*Maid Marian* (1822) and *The Misfortunes of Elphin* [4] (1829)—are steeped
in fantasy and in them the satire is almost mute. He is more famous for,
and his peculiar flavor may be more pungently tasted in, his five other tales:
*Headlong Hall* (1815), *Melincourt* (1817), *Nightmare Abbey* (1818), *Cro-
chet Castle* (1831), and *Gryll Grange* (1860). In each of these the setting is
romantic; the plot is so simple as to be almost non-existent; and the characters and their conversations are all-important. In a slightly ambiguous
tribute Shelley said that Peacock's "fine wit makes such a wound, the knife
is lost in it." [5] This wit is directed against fanatics and bigots, the frenetic
enemies of classical serenity and the pretentious purveyors of panaceas for
the ills of humanity, "perfectibilitarians, deteriorationists, statusquo-ites,
phrenologists, transcendentalists, political economists, theorists in all sciences,
projectors in all arts, morbid visionaries, romantic enthusiasts," and any and
every sort of humbug. Peacock's method is to bring a company of such
eccentrics together and let them talk. Their conversation is their undoing.
Many great figures are recognizable among them: Wordsworth, Coleridge,
and Southey; Byron and Shelley. The twist given to their sentiments and
opinions is seldom so violent as to be mere caricature, but rather, just sufficient to make them ridiculous. The portraits of Wordsworth and Coleridge
are unkind; but the song which Mr. Cypress (Byron) sings [6] is better than
parody—it is triple-distilled Byronism; and Shelley was not offended by the
portraits of himself. Peacock does not direct the "silvery arrows of the Comic
Spirit" only against individuals; he shoots Folly wherever it flies, mocking
at theories of political economy, at the newspapers, at the Gothic revival
in architecture, at the movement for popular education, at reform—but also

[2] *Works,* Halliford Edition, ed. H. F. B. Brett-Smith and C. E. Jones (10v, 1924-1934),
with a biography in Vol. I; *Novels,* ed. R. B. Johnson (2v, n.d.). — Carl Van Doren, *The
Life of Thomas Love Peacock* (1911); J. B. Priestley, *Thomas Love Peacock* (EML Series,
1927); Jean-Jacques Mayoux, *Un Epicurien anglais: T. L. Peacock* (Paris, 1932); George
Saintsbury, "Peacock," *Essays and Papers,* II. 82-109.
[3] *Poems,* ed. R. B. Johnson (n.d.). Peacock's chief poems are *Palmyra* (1806), *The Genius
of the Thames* (1810), and *Rhododaphne* (1818). *The Four Ages of Poetry* (1820) is his
only important prose work outside the novel. In this paradoxical piece of whimsicality Peacock
argued that poetry moves through the iron or "bardic" ages to the golden ages (represented
by Homer and Shakespeare), thence to the silver ages (Virgil and the period of Dryden and
Pope), and ultimately to the brazen age (his own). The essay is memorable chiefly for having
called forth Shelley's *Defence of Poetry.*
[4] On the setting of *Elphin* see Herbert Wright, "The Associations of T. L. Peacock with
Wales," *E&S,* XII (1926). 24-46.
[5] For Shelley's tribute to Peacock see the *Letter to Maria Gisborne,* lines 232-247.
[6] "There is a fever of the spirit," in *Nightmare Abbey,* ch. XI.

at the Tory enemies of reform. In his last book there is more urbanity, and the wit has been diluted by old age. Yet Peacock remained a singularly homogeneous writer, an epicurean humanist impatient of pretense. Something of his temper was transmitted to his son-in-law, George Meredith, and his books admirably illustrate Meredith's doctrine of "thoughtful laughter" and saving common sense.[7] Of recent years there have been signs of Peacock's influence upon contemporary novelists who portray groups of argumentative intellectuals and who use the novel-form as a vehicle for criticism and satire.[8]

## II

A parallel to the historical novel was fiction dealing not with past times but with remote parts of the world. The eighteenth-century roots of Oriental exoticism were kept alive during the Romantic period by the Byronic vogue, the popularity of travel literature, and interest in the Greek War of Independence. Thomas Hope (c. 1770-1831), a wealthy art collector and connoisseur who had traveled extensively in the Near East, was the author of *Anastasius, or Memoirs of a Greek* [9] (1819). This is a cross between historical and picaresque romance. Hope's failure to correlate the incidents in his tale betrays his dependence upon the note-books of his own travels, and the amount of attention paid to authentic but obscure history does not make for liveliness. The hero, a puzzling compound of profligacy and sentiment, generosity and greed, becomes involved in the Russo-Turkish war which Byron, who admired *Anastasius,* afterwards introduced into *Don Juan.*[10] There are exciting episodes and vigorous descriptions in Hope's book, but the interest is not well sustained.

*Hope*

*Morier*

Far more entertaining are two books by James Morier (1780-1849): *Hajji Baba of Ispahan* (1824) and its sequel, *Hajji Baba in London* [11] (1828). Morier, an explorer, linguist, and diplomat, made two wide journeys through the Near and Middle East.[12] Among the Persians he had close friends. He knew intimately the court etiquette, the domestic life, the bazaars, the religious beliefs, and the manners of Persia. With sympathetic understanding but with an eye for absurdities he turned this knowledge to the purposes of fiction in the two delightful books which carry on the tradition of the pseudo-Oriental *conte.* When he brings his exotic hero to London he happily combines the old literary convention of the "Foreign Visitor" with his own

---

[7] Meredith, however, never mentions Peacock in the *Essay on Comedy.*

[8] For example, in the novels of Aldous Huxley and, in lighter vein, in J. B. Priestley's *Adam in Moonshine.*

[9] There is no biography of Thomas Hope and no modern edition of *Anastasius.* Scott praised it along with Morier's *Hajji Baba* in the introduction to *The Talisman* (ed. 1832).

[10] See Anton Pfeiffer, *Thomas Hope's "Anastasius" und Lord Byron's "Don Juan"* (Munich, 1913).

[11] *Hajji Baba of Ispahan,* with an introduction by E. G. Browne (Blue Jade Library, n.d.); with an introduction by C. W. Stewart (World's Classics, 1923); *Hajji Baba in London* (World's Classics, 1925).

[12] Morier's *Journey through Persia* (1816) and *Second Journey* (1818) are as brightly informative as his novels.

experiences as an English official attached to the retinue of a Persian envoy to England. In later novels Morier failed to repeat the success of *Hajji Baba*.

The life of Edward John Trelawny [13] (1793-1881) bridges the long in- *Trelawny* terval between Byron and Swinburne. His *Adventures of a Younger Son* (1831) resembles Hope's and Morier's stories in its exotic scenes and its foundation in personal experience. How much there is of autobiography in it is a disputed problem. That the author was a pretty ruffianly buc- caneer is certain, and the "primitive" hatred of civilization expressed in the book is in keeping with the man; but the adventurous and amorous exploits and even the brutality are probably greatly exaggerated. It is safest to describe it as an autobiography heightened in color, with some incidents invented and many others "arranged."

Captain Frederick Marryat [14] (1792-1848) worked autobiography into *Marryat* fiction, but he was also in a sense a historical novelist, for he drew largely upon his experiences in the Mediterranean and the West Indies where he served as a naval officer from 1806 till the close of the Napoleonic Wars. He crosses history with other strains, following Smollett as a chronicler of adventures at sea, with touches of his master's Gothicism. Though he yields occasionally to the lure of the supernatural, as in *The Phantom Ship* (1839), on the theme of the Flying Dutchman, his proper vein is more realistic and there is more of comedy than of terror. Marryat draws blackguards admir- ably; he can be both coarse and gruesome; but he possessed a genuine feel- ing for the hardships and heroisms of the sailor's lot, and he used his talent effectively for the reform of naval administration and discipline. The best remembered of his books are *Midshipman Easy* (1836), a mixture of ad- venture, humor, and naval history, and *Masterman Ready* (1841), which has points of resemblance to *Robinson Crusoe*. Having descended the scale of literary values till they became "standard juveniles," these books held that place till the close of the nineteenth century when they were ousted by Stevenson's stories of adventure.

## III

Of the Scottish novelists two might have been considered elsewhere in this *Lockhart* history because of the miscellaneous character of their writings. The learned, arrogant, and fastidious John Gibson Lockhart [15] (1794-1854) is known to everybody as the biographer of his father-in-law. After his early career on

[13] *The Adventures of a Younger Son*, with an introduction by Ethel C. Mayne (World's Classics, 1925); *Letters*, ed. H. B. Forman (1910); *Recollections of the Last Days of Byron and Shelley* (1858). — H. J. Massingham, *The Friend of Shelley. A Memoir of Edward John Trelawny* (1930); Margaret Armstrong, *Trelawny: a Man's Life* (1940).

[14] *Novels*, ed. R. B. Johnson (26v, 1929-1930). — Florence Marryat, *The Life and Letters of Captain Marryat* (2v, 1872); Christopher Lloyd, *Captain Marryat and the Old Navy* (1939); Michael Sadleir, "Captain Marryat, a Portrait," *London Mercury*, x (1924). 495-510.

[15] Andrew Lang, *The Life and Letters of John Gibson Lockhart* (1897); Gilbert Macbeth, *John Gibson Lockhart, a Critical Study* (Urbana, 1935); George Saintsbury, "Lockhart," *Essays and Papers*, ii. 1-30; Donald Carswell, *Scott and his Circle* (1930), pp. 216-270. For the many short contributions on Lockhart and his circle by A. L. Strout see the annual bibliographies in *PMLA*.

the staff of *Blackwood's,* where his malicious satire and cruel reviews earned for him the sobriquet of "the Scorpion," he was for long editor of *The Quarterly Review* and an influence in criticism and scholarship.[16] His original verse and translations are nearly forgotten.[17] The deft characterizations of Edinburgh types in *Peter's Letters to his Kinfolk* (1819) exhibited some of the talents of a novelist; but his *Valerius* (1821), in which he tried to use Scott's technique in a romance of ancient Rome, is a failure. The short novel *Adam Blair* (1822), the story of a Calvinistic minister who is guilty of adultery, is memorable for its anticipation of the theme of Hawthorne's *Scarlet Letter.*[18] *Matthew Wald* (1824), a powerful study of mental and moral degradation, owes something to William Godwin's fiction and resembles Hogg's *Justified Sinner* which appeared in the same year.

**Hogg**

James Hogg, "the Ettrick Shepherd" [19] (1770-1835), had published much verse before he made his name with *The Queen's Wake* (1813), a collection of narrative poems supposedly sung before Mary Stuart by rival poets in whom are recognizably mirrored Hogg himself and his contemporaries. The charming "frame," the ballad of *The Witch of Fife,* and the lovely other-worldliness of *Kilmeny* compensate for the poor quality of the other pieces. In *The Poetic Mirror* [20] (1816) Hogg imitated and parodied the "Living Bards of Britain," but succeeded in revealing his own vanity more clearly than his victims' shortcomings. Hogg is better in the lyric than in poems of ambitious length; his *Skylark* and *When the Kye Comes Hame* live in the anthologies. His efforts to rival Scott in the field of historical fiction need not be mentioned; but *The Private Memoirs and Confessions of a Justified Sinner* [21] (1824) is still not only readable but read. It is at once a satire on the unco guid, a powerful example of the macabre fiction with which the *Blackwood's* group supplied their public, and a strange re-creation of the Faust story in an Edinburgh setting in a period not long after that of *Old Mortality.* The fact that it has more coherence than most of Hogg's writings led George Saintsbury to suspect that Lockhart had a hand in it; [22] but Saintsbury's arguments have not carried conviction.

**Galt**

John Galt [23] (1779-1839), a man widely experienced in business and travel, success and failure, was scarcely at all influenced by Scott and much by Smollett. *The Ayrshire Legatee* (1820) is a satiric sketch in letter-form

[16] As a critic Lockhart wrote much on modern foreign literatures and paid special attention to Spanish culture and antiquities.

[17] Some of Lockhart's original verse is serious and sentimental, but his best piece is *The Mad Banker of Amsterdam* (1818-1819), a serio-comic poem in *ottava rima,* following Tennant and Frere and immediately contemporary with Byron's *Beppo.*

[18] See Henry James's comparison of the two in his *Hawthorne* (EML Series), pp. 114-117.

[19] Edith C. Batho, *The Ettrick Shepherd* (1927); Donald Carswell, *Scott and his Circle* (1930), pp. 171-215; A. L. Strout, "The *Noctes Ambrosianae* and James Hogg," RES, XIII (1937). 46-63; 177-189; A. L. Strout, *The Life and Letters of James Hogg* (Vol. 1, Lubbock, Texas, 1947).

[20] Ed. T. Earle Welby (1929).

[21] Ed. T. Earle Welby (1924).

[22] George Saintsbury, "Hogg," *Essays and Papers,* I. 49-51.

[23] *Works,* ed. D. S. Medrum and William Roughhead (10v, Edinburgh, 1936). — J. W. Aberdein, *John Galt* (1936); F. H. Lyell, *A Study of the Novels of John Galt* (Princeton, 1942).

closely modeled upon *Humphry Clinker. Annals of the Parish* (1821) displays powerfully though coarsely drawn types of the new industrialists; *The Provost* (1822) is the story of a self-made man in the period of the industrial revolution; and *The Entail* (1823) covers the fortunes of a family through three generations. These are all of value to the social historian and are precursors of an important kind of Victorian fiction. Later Galt wrote too much and sometimes condescended to Gothic supernaturalism which was uncongenial to his broad comedy and hard realism. His biography of Byron (1830) is the shrewdest of all early portraits of the poet; and his *Autobiography* (1833) is also noteworthy. Another descendant from Smollett was Michael Scott (1789-1835) whose *Tom Cringle's Log* (1833) and *The Cruise of the Midge* (1834), based on personal experiences in the West Indies, contain nautical adventures, sensational incidents, and grotesque characterizations in the manner of *Roderick Random*. Susan Edmonstone Ferrier [24] (1782-1854) is in the line from Fanny Burney on a much lower level than Jane Austen. The best of her three novels is *Marriage* (1818) in which the union of an English girl and a Highlander brings out the contrast between two modes of life. *The Inheritance* (1824) is on the old theme of the changeling who turns out to be the rightful heir. Miss Ferrier's good-natured satire tends toward caricature. The identifiable pen-portraits of real people in her books were a factor in their success. *Michael Scott*

In the generation after Scott two English writers shared with Bulwer the field of historical fiction. G. P. R. James [25] (1801-1860), who began under Sir Walter's auspices and was finished by Thackeray's satire,[26] was a prolific writer in this kind. Among his subjects are Cardinal Richelieu, Henry of Navarre, and Monmouth's rebellion. Till the middle of the century he was enormously popular, a rival of both Dickens and Thackeray. He remains an interesting figure but his books are no longer read. In style he is pompous and frigid; he has no humor or talent for characterization; his conventional characters are involved in webs of intrigue every strand of which James painstakingly disentangles, leaving no smallest knot for the reader's intelligence to untie. The works of William Harrison Ainsworth [27] (1805-1882) are of more lasting interest. Beginning with old-fashioned Gothic stories, he turned out a long series of pseudo-historical romances of which *The Tower of London* (1840), *Old Saint Paul's* (1841), *Windsor Castle* (1843), and *The Lancashire Witches* (1849) are the best. On a ground of solid *G. P. R. James* *Ainsworth*

[24] *Novels,* ed. R. B. Johnson (6v, 1894); *Memoirs and Correspondence,* ed. J. A. Doyle (1898).
[25] S. M. Ellis, *The Solitary Horseman: G. P. R. James* (1927). Many of James's stories open with a solitary horseman crossing a dark and desolate landscape; hence the title of this biography. On James, Lever, and Marryat see Lionel Stevenson, "The Novelist as Fortune-Hunter," *Virginia Quar. Rev.,* XIII (1937). 376-390. — On the historical novel after Scott there is material in H. Butterfield, *The Historical Novel* (1924) and A. T. Sheppard, *The Art and Practice of Historical Fiction* (1930).
[26] The tricks of James's manner are caught in *Barbazure,* the cleverest of Thackeray's *Novels by Eminent Hands.*
[27] S. M. Ellis, *William Harrison Ainsworth and his Friends* (2v, 1911); Harold Locke, *Bibliographical Catalogue of ... Ainsworth* (1925).

antiquarianism Ainsworth applied "local color" thickly, touching it off with sentiment, rhetoric, and horror. The horrific has proved to be his most memorable note; and with the help of Cruikshank's illustrations there are episodes in *The Tower of London* which may still provoke a shudder.

## IV

*Irish Novelists*

Only the most important of the Irish novelists can be brought within our survey.[28] They followed not the lead of Miss Edgeworth but that of Scott, finding in the struggles of Ireland with England and of Catholic Ireland with the Protestant North, and in the relationship of landlord with tenant, materials which could be treated in a fashion analogous to that which Scott used in his stories of border warfare. After the Act of Union (1798) fiction was employed in Ireland as an instrument of political agitation. The "stage Irishman" of the English tradition appears in some novels, but in general there was an honest effort to picture the land, the people, and the problems realistically. As a part of the regional atmosphere much of this fiction introduces Celtic superstitions of fairies, leprechauns, and similar sprites.[29] Social themes are generally treated in a bitterly controversial and polemical spirit. The brothers Banim—Michael (1796-1874) and John (1798-1842)—

*Michael and John Banim*

proposed to "insinuate through fiction the causes of discontent" and to show how discontent leads to crime. Often they point the contrast between the lives of the gentry and the lives of the peasants. But they wasted their talents upon melodrama and ghastly criminality. The three series of their *Tales by the O'Hara Family* (1825-1829) have to do with outlawry, the cruel suppression of sedition, and Celtic superstitions. John Banim's *The Boyne Water* (1826) challenges Scott directly. In this story of William III's suppression of the Irish supporters of James II there is so much careful history that much of the narrative is not fictitious at all. The most powerful

*Carleton*

of the Irish writers was William Carleton [30] (1794-1869). His many stories of peasant life are too long drawn out and have in them a superfluity of coarse humor, rollicking, and buffoonery. But he had a gift for lively dialogue, intimate knowledge of Irish folk-beliefs, and an awareness of the various causes and expressions of discontent—the miseries of famine and typhus, the cruelties of eviction, the callousness of absentee landlords, the

[28] H. S. Krans, *Irish Life in Irish Fiction* (1903); Father S. J. Brown, *Ireland in Fiction* (1916); and for the further background Fritz Mezger, *Der Ire in der englischen Literatur bis zum Angang des 19. Jahrhunderts* (Leipzig, 1929). — Three lesser Irish novelists may be mentioned. Sydney, Lady Morgan (1775-1859) won her greatest success with *The Wild Irish Girl* (1806). William Hamilton Maxwell (1792-1850), parson and sportsman, wrote many sketches and untidy tales of a kind better represented by the work of Lever. Gerald Griffin (1803-1840), poet, dramatist, and folklorist, as well as novelist, dealt with the lives of fishermen and smugglers, with feuds, and with the clash of peasantry and gentlefolk. From his novel, *The Collegians* (1828), Dion Boucicault made his famous melodrama, *The Colleen Bawn*. On these and other Irish novelists see Baker, VII (1936), ch. I.

[29] This element brings Irish fiction close to the records of the folklorists, and consequently at this point may be mentioned Thomas Crofton Croker (1798-1834) whose *Fairy Legends of the South of Ireland* (1825) was the precursor of a large literature on such subjects.

[30] *Stories of Irish Life* (new ed., 1936). — D. J. Donoghue, *The Life of William Carleton* (2v, 1896); Rose Shaw, *Carleton's Country* (1930).

secret societies, the "Peep o' Day Boys," and the ruffians bred by social distress. Samuel Lover (1797-1868), who, like his friend Tom Moore, wrote *Lover* songs and sang them sweetly, is a more trivial figure than Carleton. *Handy Andy* (1842) and his other books are in the main farcical and burlesque, depending too much upon high jinks and broad jokes to retain lasting esteem. Charles Lever [31] (1806-1872) had a more varied talent. Belonging *Lever* to the gentry and of half-English blood, he looked at the peasantry from outside and from above. He began with *The Confessions of Harry Lorrequer* [32] (1839) and other farragoes of military and sporting life, wenching and drinking, in the tradition of the old jest-books and the picaresque; but in *Charles O'Malley, the Irish Dragoon* (1841), along with realistic or farcical pictures of high and low society in Ireland, there is a good deal of history, for the hero goes through the Peninsular and Waterloo campaigns. In later books Lever became more serious, facing the problems of poverty, the decline of great estates, and the misery of the peasants.

The noisy farce of Lover and Lever and their scenes of sporting life con- *Egan* nect them with a contemporary group in England. Pierce Egan (1772-1849) is now remembered chiefly for the color-plates which illustrate his *Life in London* (1821-1828), vivid evocations of the rough vitality of the Regency and reign of George IV. With buffoonery in the manner of the jest-books and coney-catching pamphlets of an earlier age he mixed scandalous gossip and libelous caricatures of actual people of the day. He held up the well-to-do, flashy sporting set to the mingled admiration, envy, and emulation of the masses. Theodore Hook [33] (1788-1841) lies on the borderland between *Hook* literature and journalism. His scandalous newspaper, *John Bull,* was conducted with much vigor and an entire lack of principle. His novels mixed practical jocosity with libelous gossip and were dangerous at the time but are unreadable today save by historians who discover in their coarse realism a presage of Dickens without Dickens' humanity. Robert S. Surtees [34] (1803- *Surtees* 1864) has retained a specialized renown as the annalist of the hunting field which he depicted in *Handley Cross* (1843), *Mr. Sponge's Sporting Tour* (1853), and many other books. But Surtees' view is broader than that of his fox-hunters; he chronicled all sorts of amusements, not always without satiric intent. Samuel Warren (1807-1877) contributed to *Blackwood's* a *Warren* series of powerful short stories which he gathered together as *Passages from the Diary of a Late Physician* (1838). The ghoulish horrors of these pieces are in "Maga's" tradition but they are combined with realistic pictures of degraded life. Warren's *Ten Thousand a Year* (1841) is rough satire, farcical

[31] *Novels* (37v, 1897-1899). — W. J. Fitzpatrick, *The Life of Charles Lever* (1884); Edmund Downey, *Charles Lever: His Life in his Letters* (2v, 1906); Lionel Stevenson, *Dr. Quicksilver: the Life of Charles Lever* (1939).

[32] Reprinted in the Nelson Classics (1937).

[33] M. F. Brightfield, *Theodore Hook and his Novels* (Cambridge, Mass., 1928).

[34] E. D. Cummings, *Robert Smith Surtees, Creator of Jorrocks* (1924); A. Steel, *Jorrocks' England* (1932); Frederick Watson, *The Life of R. S. Surtees* (1933) and *R. S. Surtees, a Critical Study* (1933). One of the most typical of Surtees' books, *Hillingdon Hall,* has been reprinted with an introduction by Siegfried Sassoon (1931). — On the novel of hunting and sporting life see Harvey Darton, *From Surtees to Sassoon* (1931).

humor, and squalid melodrama, a portrayal of dishonesty, greed, and imposture. It was one of the most popular novels of the period, and for those who can stomach its crude pathos, too obvious moralizing, and other extravagances it is readable for the sake of its swiftly moving plot. Lastly, the tradition that Douglas Jerrold [35] (1803-1857) was a great humorist is still alive, though most of his jokes are forgotten. His *Mrs. Caudle's Curtain Lectures* (1846) helped to establish the popularity of *Punch*.[36]

*Jerrold*

[35] *Works,* with an introductory memoir by Jerrold's son (4v, n.d.).
[36] Two women-novelists wrote on fashionable life: Mrs. Catherine Gore (1799-1861) and Mrs. Frances Trollope (1780-1863). On the latter see below, ch. XXIV, n. 8. On the "fashionable novel" of the period see M. W. Rosa, *The Silver Fork School* (1936).

# XVII
## The Background: 1832-1868
## The Progress of Reform

The precisian may limit the Victorian period to the years between the Queen's accession in 1837 and her death in 1901, but a new era really began with the passage of the Reform Bill in 1832 and closed at the end of the Boer War in 1902. The seven decades between these two dates are often divided into three phases of national life, what is called the "Mid-Victorian" period being considered as embracing the years 1855 to 1879 from the ascendency of Palmerston to the great economic depression. For our purposes, however, it is more convenient to recognize but two divisions—"Early" and "Late"—of almost exactly equal length. According to this scheme the Early Victorian period extends from the Reform Bill of 1832, which coincides with the death of Scott, the definite emergence of Carlyle, and the publication of Tennyson's first significant volume, to the formation of Gladstone's first administration in 1868, the year which saw the climax of Browning's career with the appearance of *The Ring and the Book* and of Morris's with *The Earthly Paradise*. Of the thirty-six years to be surveyed in this chapter the first fourteen were filled with unrest, alarm, and misery, and they contrast with the growing prosperity and general good feeling of the succeeding twenty-two years when England, having committed herself to industrialism and free trade, became for a time "the workshop of the world." [1]

Of purely political history little more than a reminder is needed here. The rearrangement of the old Whig and Tory groups which resulted in the modern Liberal and Conservative parties is of small significance for the student of literature. Party intrigues provided material for such writers of

[1] E. L. Woodward, *The Age of Reform 1815-1870* (1938); G. M. Trevelyan, *History of England* (1926), Book VI, ch. II, and *English Social History* (1942), ch. XVII; Gilbert Slater, *The Making of Modern England* (rev. ed., 1915), chs. VII-XVII; Elie Halévy, *Histoire du peuple anglais au dix-neuvième siècle* (1923; English trans., 1924-1927) had reached the year 1841 before the author's death; H. W. C. Davis, *The Age of Grey and Peel* (1929); F. E. Gillespie, *Labor and Politics in England, 1850-1867* (1927); S. Maccoby, *English Radicalism 1832-1852* (1935); M. Hovell, *The Chartist Movement* (1918); J. L. and B. Hammond, *The Age of the Chartists* (1930); G. D. H. Cole, *Chartist Portraits* (1941); R. J. Conklin, *Thomas Cooper the Chartist* (1935); C. R. Fay, *Life and Labor in the Nineteenth Century* (1920) and *The Corn Laws and Social England* (1932). An elaborate survey of many phases of the life and activities and tastes of the period, by a corps of experts, is *Early Victorian England*, ed. G. M. Young (2v, 1934). The final chapter, by the editor, is reprinted, expanded to cover the entire period to 1901, in *Victorian England: Portrait of an Age* (1936). A. L. Hayward, *The Days of Dickens: a Glance at Some Aspects of Victorian Life in London* (1926) is in popular vein but informative and supplied with an abundance of illustrations.

memoirs as Creevey [2] and Greville [3] and for a kind of fiction revived by Disraeli and carried on by Trollope—the political novel. But Carlyle, Ruskin, and other writers who were concerned with the pressing social problems of the time viewed with scornful impatience the parliamentary see-saw of "Ins" and "Outs." Postponing to the next two chapters the subject of the religious revival and the repercussions of evolutionary speculation, we shall here summarize the history of the progress of reform. The awakened social conscience is, it is safe to say, the predominant theme in Early Victorian literature. But first we must have in mind the most important changes in administrations.

*Whigs* vs. *Conservatives*
The Whigs under Melbourne kept office till 1841 when they were succeeded by Sir Robert Peel's Conservative ministry. Peel, who in the "manifesto" to his constituents at Tamworth (1834) had accepted parliamentary reform as a *fait accompli,* had amalgamated the *disjecta membra* of the old Tory party with certain of the Whig oligarchs into the new Conservative party. His conversion to the principle of free trade, of which the sweeping reduction in tariffs in 1842 was a sign, was completed with the repeal of the Corn Laws in 1846. This act, with which the history of "modern" England is sometimes considered to begin, split the Conservatives into protectionists and Peelites. The former group found a nominal leader in the Earl of Derby [4] but their real new leader was Benjamin Disraeli. The cynical opportunism which was part of Disraeli's character as a politician was evinced when within a short time of his denunciation of Peel as a betrayer of party principles he admitted that the issue of protection was "dead and damned." The Peelites, of whom Gladstone was the greatest, presently coöperated with the Whigs and ultimately formed the core of the modern Liberal party. Peel's downfall and the division in the ranks of the Conservatives led to the administration (1846-1852) of the arch-Whig, Lord John Russell,[5] which, after a brief interim under Derby, was succeeded by Aberdeen's coalition of Whigs and Peelites. The inefficient conduct of the Crimean War (1854-1855) forced Aberdeen's resignation and the Palmerstonian era began, to continue, with the short interruption of Derby's second ministry, till Palmerston's death in 1865. Russell then became prime minister again and brought in a bill for the further extension of the franchise. The defection of some of his Whig supporters ("the Adullamites") led to the rejection of this measure and Russell resigned. Derby's third administration was formed,

[2] Thomas Creevey (1768-1838) belongs in the main to an earlier period, but many of his most vivid impressions are of the eighteen-thirties. See *The Creevey Papers: a Selection from the Correspondence and Diaries of the late Thomas Creevey,* ed. Sir Herbert Maxwell (2v, 1903).

[3] Charles Cavendish Fulke Greville (1794-1865) belonged to the world of high society, fashion, and sport. As secretary of the Privy Council he had unrivaled opportunities for many years to possess himself of information and gossip. His diaries, parts of them in short-hand, cover the years 1815-1860. — *The Greville Memoirs,* ed. Lytton Strachey and Roger Fulford (8v, 1938). *The Greville Diary, Including Passages Hitherto Withheld from Publication,* ed. P. W. Wilson (2v, 1927), is a selection only.

[4] As a scholarly poet Derby is remembered for his translation of the *Iliad* (1864).

[5] Lord John Russell (1792-1878), afterwards first Earl Russell, wrote, besides stories and essays which are now forgotten, a biography of Charles James Fox (1859-1866).

and Disraeli, as leader of the House of Commons, introduced a suffrage act in some respects more far-reaching than that which had just been defeated. Thus the Conservatives "dished the Whigs" with the Reform Bill of 1867 which Disraeli in a famous phrase called "the leap in the dark" and which Carlyle called "shooting Niagara." After Derby's resignation in 1868 Disraeli was prime minister for a few months, but in the general election of that year the Conservatives were driven from office—largely by the votes of the very classes whom they had just enfranchised—and Gladstone's first ministry, the high tide of English Liberalism, began.

With this brief outline in mind, we may now turn back to the eighteen-thirties to consider the progress of social reform. For want of firm leadership and a sound financial policy the large Whig majority under Melbourne gradually disintegrated. It bought the unreliable support of the Irish members of Parliament (led by Daniel O'Connell) with palliative measures which did not meet the chronic distress in Ireland. Consequently the dismal round of concession and coercion continued in the government of that country. The most important immediate legislative accomplishment of the reformed Parliament was the emancipation of slaves in British dominions. This triumph (1833) of the long struggle of the abolitionists (about which something more will be said in the next chapter) was not won without *Abolition* recalcitrance on the part of the slave-owners, especially in Jamaica, notwith- *of* standing the fact that they were compensated for their losses. The dis- *Slavery* turbance in Jamaica coincided with turbulence in Canada where the clash between the English and French races and between the dominant families and the new settlers reached the proportions almost of an insurrection. The pacific settlement of the Canadian disputes embodied in Lord Durham's famous Report (1838) became the basis of the new system of English colonial administration and of the relations between the dominions and the mother country.

The impetus of reform had other progressive results. The admission of Quakers to Parliament, with the substitution of an affirmation for the oath, was a notable advance in toleration. Steps towards the abolition of various cruel forms of sport were signs of increasing refinement and compassion. The first effective act regulating child labor in factories was passed in 1833. *Child* From the beginning of the century there had been measures to protect *Labor* orphan apprentices from merciless exploitation, but these had been easily evaded because the responsibility for inspection and enforcement had been left to the local justices of the peace. After several years of agitation in Lancashire and the West Riding of Yorkshire, a Royal Commission was appointed in 1833 which took testimony from the victims of industrial oppression and made recommendations embodied in the Factory Act of that year. This act, which applied to all the textile industries but only to them, limited the hours and kinds of child labor and provided for inspectors to enforce its provisions. Its passage was largely due to the efforts of Lord

Ashley (afterwards Earl of Shaftesbury), one of the most energetic and enlightened philanthropists of the age.

Under pressure of the Benthamite radicals in and out of Parliament the government faced the problem of pauperism. The old method of out-door relief with parochial responsibility for the indigent was often corrupt and almost always inefficient in administration. The reckoning of the amount of relief on the basis of the number of children, legitimate or illegitimate, put a premium upon improvident marriages and even upon immorality. The general tendency was to pass responsibility from parish to parish. The

*The New Poor Law*

Poor-Law-Amendment Act of 1834 abolished out-door relief and parochial responsibility. The system of workhouses which already obtained in London was applied to the whole country, contiguous parishes being amalgamated into a "union" and central control over the entire system of unions being vested in three commissioners. In lieu of the compulsory, unpaid services of citizens in the different localities, full-time salaried civil servants were employed in each workhouse. The ignorance, incapacity, and heartlessness of many of these employees moved Dickens and other writers to bitter satire; but the new policy was a change in the right direction. More broadly, the policy underlying the New Poor Law was not to help the deserving unfortunate who might be in temporary difficulties owing to illness or unemployment but to give food and shelter in the workhouses only to the absolutely destitute who would be driven to apply for it only when they had exhausted all possible means of self-support. Life in the workhouse was deliberately standardized below the meanest obtainable at the lowest wage of the independent laborer. Not until the Lancashire cotton famine during the American Civil War did it come to be realized that another criterion than mere destitution must guide relief work among the deserving poor. The failure to search out, and attempt to deal with, the causes of indigence was the fundamental fault with the legislation of 1834. Honest workmen in distress were not carried over bad times but left to shift for themselves till it was too late for anything but the workhouse. A stigma attached to poverty as such, irrespective of its causes, because of the acceptance by the governing class of the Malthusian doctrine attributing social misery to the tendency of population to increase faster than the means of subsistence. The "lower orders" were themselves to blame for breeding too abundantly. The new law, though an advance upon the old methods of dealing with pauperism, was enforced with a grim Benthamite rigidity and impersonality which caused needless suffering and humiliation. The later policy of segregating children from adults, the healthy from the diseased, and the innocent from the morally corrupt greatly improved conditions among these unfortunates. The picture in *Oliver Twist* (1838) is of the typical workhouse in the years before experience and protests introduced ameliorating modifications in the administration of the law. Hatred of the workhouse, a threat constantly hanging over the head of the laboring man, was one cause of the social unrest of the time.

The Chartist Movement sprang from "the social degradation produced by the unregulated growth of industry and by the subordination of human to commercial interests." [6] Unrestricted private enterprise, which found theoretical justification in the doctrine of laissez faire advanced by David Ricardo and the political economists of the so-called "Manchester School," made for intolerable relations between labor and capital. Until Peel reintroduced the income-tax in 1842 as a compensation for the loss of revenue from tariffs, indirect taxation bore down heavily upon the working classes. Laborers without reserve funds for hard times lived from hand to mouth at the mercy of the fluctuations in trade. The rapidly increasing population which was concentrated in London, Liverpool, Glasgow, and the new manufacturing *Social* towns of the Midlands [7] lived in circumstances of physical and moral wretch- *Conditions* edness. The "rookeries" of London and Westminster were pestiferous dens of iniquity, and a large fraction of the populations of Liverpool, Manchester, and other towns lived in crowded cellars. The lack of sanitation of even the most rudimentary kinds was scandalous—the water-supply costly, inadequate, and often contaminated; proper means for the disposal of sewage and refuse non-existent; noisome graveyards in immediate proximity to the living. The pictures of the London slums in *Oliver Twist* and of the cemetery in *Bleak House* are not the romantic exaggerations of a Gothic imagination but transcripts from actuality that can be verified. The demand for new houses was met by jerry-builders, under no control of government and guided by no city-planning, who ran up cheap and flimsy dwellings which soon fell into disrepair and became new slums. The efforts of social workers to improve sanitation were impeded by the "vested interests" of undertakers, the private water companies, the "dustmen" such as figure in *Our Mutual Friend,* and other vultures who preyed upon the public. The visitations of cholera, a pestilence closely associated with filth, in 1831, 1848, and 1853-54, at length taught the necessity of remedial action to secure pure and abundant water, proper drainage, and the closing of the old graveyards. The activities of Edwin Chadwick [8] in this field of social reform are worthy of honorable remembrance. In the next generation there were many to heed Disraeli's counsel: *Sanitas sanitatum, omnia sanitas!*

Between 1832 and 1836 a greater confidence, born of good harvests, brisk *Chartism* trade, railway building,[9] and higher wages, led to increased activity in the trade-unions. In 1836 the "London Workingmen's Association" determined to embark upon a campaign of political propaganda and drew up a

---

[6] Gilbert Slater, *The Making of Modern England* (ed. 1915), p. 214.

[7] Manchester and Birmingham were without representation till 1832 and were not incorporated till 1838. The Municipal Reform Act (1835) established a uniform system of town government throughout England. It did not, however, include London, which had its own system.

[8] Charles Kingsley drew Chadwick's portrait as Tom Thurnall in *Two Years Ago* (1857).

[9] The railway boom of 1835-1836 collapsed in 1837. There was a revival of construction in 1840 which led on to the "railway mania" of 1845. Acts of Parliament regulated the new companies. These enormous enterprises withdrew capital from other businesses but created a huge demand for labor and before long were a great source of new wealth. Armies of "navvies" (construction gangs) were familiar sights in Early Victorian times both along the rights of way and in the city terminals.

"Charter" which embodied and enlarged upon the demands in the petition of 1819. Of the six "points" in the Chartists' program, four—manhood suffrage, the removal of property qualifications for membership in the House of Commons, the payment of members, and the secret ballot—have long since become part of English law; while the two others—annual Parliaments and equal electoral districts—remain to this day unrealized. Though this program was on the face of it political, the basic purpose of the Chartists was the redress of social grievances which could, they held, be accomplished only when workingmen had representation in Parliament. There were two conflicting elements in Chartism—the men who relied upon moral suasion and those who advocated the use of threats and force. For want of possessing votes with which alone pressure could be brought upon their governors, and also for want of wise leadership, a unified purpose, and funds with which to propagandize, the movement fizzled out. A national convention of workingmen held in London to present a petition and overawe Parliament failed; the moderate men withdrew timidly, and the physical force party was easily dispersed by the authorities. This failure had much to do with Carlyle's increasing conviction that in democracy there lay no hope for radical reform. Yet Carlyle recognized in Chartism a symptom of a diseased society.[10] During the "Hungry Forties" it hung over England like a threatening cloud, while in the minds of the prosperous classes two fears were ever present—terror of pestilence and terror of a rising of the "mob." Tennyson discerned this omen of conflict between the laboring and governing classes:

> Slowly comes a hungry people, as a lion creeping nigher
> Glares at one that nods and winks behind a slowly-dying fire.[11]

The revival of Chartism in 1846-1848, when a "monster petition" of nearly two million signatures was presented to Parliament, was the last flicker of what had once threatened to become a conflagration.

*The Anti-Corn Law League*

Meanwhile, in contrast to the ill-managed fanaticism of this movement, had been the efficient and well-directed purposefulness of the Anti-Corn-Law League. The League had the advantages of ample funds and of guidance by Richard Cobden.[12] The repeal of the Corn Laws was only part of their larger program of freedom of trade. Even after 1832 the landed interests controlled four-fifths of the votes in the House of Commons while the industrial and commercial classes controlled but one-fifth; but the ability and influence of the latter group was out of all proportion to its numerical membership. The free traders had the further advantage that they adhered to the classical doctrine of Adam Smith and had the support of the Manchester economists. Commerce and industry opposed the tariff on cereals on grounds of self-interest because cheap bread would mean

---

[10] See especially Carlyle's *Chartism* (1839).
[11] *Locksley Hall* (published 1842 but probably written some years earlier), lines 135-136.
[12] John Morley, *The Life of Richard Cobden* (2v, 1881).

lower wages and an English market for foreign food-stuffs would enable foreign countries to pay for English manufactured goods. But these employers, among whom were multitudes whom Ruskin would have described as "thoroughly honest merchants" and who possessed stout nonconformist consciences, were actuated by other considerations, disinterested and patriotic. They were convinced that peace and friendliness among nations would be secured by freedom of trade. The League was supported not only by the mercantile class and urban labor but by many landless rural workers who were without security. It was opposed by the landed interests, both gentry and freehold farmers. An indirect result of the clash between the protectionists and the advocates of free trade was the further advance of social reform, for when the industrialists upbraided the land-owners for the low wages paid rural labor the land-owners countered with reproaches against the conditions of labor in factories and mines.[13]

As early as 1842 Peel reduced the tariff on a large number of articles. The failure of the potato crop and the consequent famine in Ireland in 1845 convinced him of the necessity of repeal. In 1846 an act provided that the "sliding scale" of duties on cereals should be reduced gradually till after three years a uniform duty of one shilling a bushel was to be reached. The dire consequences of repeal predicted by the protectionists did not eventuate —at least immediately. Trade expansion and higher wages, which came in part from the new markets for English manufactured goods in food-selling countries, and in part were the result of the discovery of gold in California and Australia, enabled the working classes to eat more bread, so that foreign cereals supplemented the home-grown crops and did not drive them off the market. But in the long run the revolutionary change in British fiscal policy ruined the native agriculture, especially after the building of railways in the United States opened the vast granary of the Middle West. England, predominantly industrial, found herself dependent upon supplies of food from abroad. The complacent confidence and ostentatious prosperity of the "Mid-Victorian" period show how blind the newly powerful English middle class was to the future. The European nationalistic conflicts of 1856-1870 retarded the industrial development of the Continent, and with her favorable position in advance of her neighbors England did not see that she could remain "the workshop of the world" only so long as other nations did not industrialize themselves in imitation of her. For the time prosperity brought an era of good feeling, making it possible to widen the franchise

*Repeal of the Corn Laws*

---

[13] In briefest summary here are some of the most important steps in advance. In 1842 an act prohibited the employment of women and children in underground places, and this was followed in 1847-1850 by more measures of protection. In 1862 it was required that ventilation and safety devices be installed in mines. Imprisonment for debt was abolished in 1843. In 1848 came the first Public Health Act. The first society for the suppression of the liquor traffic was organized in 1853. The great Education Act of 1870 belongs to the next period, but it had tentative forerunners. These and many other measures, such as the "Baths and Wash-Houses Act," the "Housing of the Working Classes Act," and the "Free Libraries Act" were expressions of the social conscience which had been roused by philanthropists, enlightened officials, the sociological novelists, and clergymen who preached "the social implications of the Gospel."

in 1867 with but few of those forebodings of disaster which had preceded the earlier Reform Bill.

A few words only need be added on foreign affairs. Between 1832 and 1848 England, preoccupied with domestic problems, kept herself pretty much aloof from the Continent; but as one result of increasing prosperity and confidence and also of the rising tide of liberal sentiment, this attitude changed in the mid-century. Four decades of peace and the rise of a generation which remembered nothing of the horrors of the Napoleonic Wars account for the blitheness with which England plunged into the needless

*The*
*Crimean*
*War*

conflict with Russia in the Crimea (1854-1855). The unthinking emotionality of the time is reflected in Tennyson's *Maud* (1855) and in the writings of the "Spasmodic" poets. Tennyson went so far as to preach a doctrine, as incomprehensible as it is atrocious, of the purifying influence of war. It is difficult to see why he expected a struggle by a professional army in a remote Russian province to remedy social abuses at home. The course of the conflict brought England to her senses. Mismanagement in strategy, sanitation, and the organization of supply taught valuable lessons. Though the necessary reforms in army administration had to wait for the coming of Cardwell in Gladstone's ministry, the inefficiency of government was brought to light, since war is an activity which even the most extreme supporter of laissez faire cannot leave to private enterprise. The work of Florence Nightingale in the hospitals of Scutari raised permanently the public estimation of the capacity of women for professional work. The alliance with France helped to ward off a long-threatening war with that country.

England gave nothing but ineffectual moral support and sympathy—and even that only from private individuals and not officially from her government—to the Continental revolutionists of 1848. But during the Palmerston era (1855-1865) English diplomacy was exerted with such skill by playing off France and Austria against each other that without active intervention an important part was taken in the later course of the Italian Risorgimento which led to the liberation and unification of Italy. This sympathy with the aspirations of peoples struggling for national independence was eloquently expressed by Mrs. Browning, Meredith, and Swinburne. But this period of interference in Continental affairs was brought to a close with England's failure when, after threatening military intervention, she found herself unable to make good her threat to stop Prussia's raid upon Denmark in 1864. She stood meekly aside when Prussia defeated Austria in 1866 and France in 1870. Over Germany the clouds were darkening, but in England there were few to discern what the future held in store.

# XVIII

## The Religious Revival
## and Its Expression in Literature

### I

The influx of revolutionary ideas from France had the negative result *The Evan-* of strengthening the Evangelical party in the Church of England and *gelical* gradually rousing the High Church party from its long somnolence.[1] The *Party* Evangelicals were descendants of those followers of John Wesley who did not pass with the Methodists into schism but aimed to regenerate the Establishment from within. By the close of the eighteenth century they had mostly fused with the old Low Church party, whose rationalistic tendencies declined and pietism increased under the impact of Jacobinism. The Evangelicals rejected the doctrine of the Apostolic Succession, regarded the sacraments as mere "forms," and emphasized the "Protestant" position of the Church. For them personal conversion to Christ was the center of religion. Their creed rested upon the infallibility and inerrancy of the Bible as the very Word of God. Its three chief articles were the total depravity of man, the substitutionary atonement of Christ, and justification by faith. But a concern for the reform of manners had the consequence among many Evangelicals of a softening of the Calvinistic elements in their theology, so that both faith and works were recognized as essential to salvation. Their reliance upon the emotional element in religion—their "enthusiasm"—was distrusted by moderate men, but their hold upon the masses of the people was firm. By the time we reach the Victorian era Evangelical morality affected not only the great majority of middle-class people but most of the great leaders as well, whatever their doctrinal beliefs.

At the beginning of the nineteenth century the Evangelicals were an organized party within the Establishment, with a clerical center at Cam-

[1] F. W. Warre Cornish, *History of the English Church in the Nineteenth Century* (1910); H. O. Wakeman, *History of the Church of England* (6ed., 1899), chs. xix and xx; V. F. Storr, *The Development of English Theology in the Nineteenth Century* (1913) and *Freedom and Tradition: a Study of Liberal Evangelicalism* (1940); R. W. Church, *The Oxford Movement* (1891); S. L. Ollard, *A Short History of the Oxford Movement* (1915); P. M. P. Thureau-Dangin, *The English Catholic Revival in the Nineteenth Century,* trans. by Wilfred Wilberforce (2v, 1915); W. J. Warner, *The Wesleyan Movement in the Industrial Revolution* (1930); A. W. Benn, *History of English Rationalism in the Nineteenth Century* (2v, 1906); H. N. Fairchild, "Romanticism and the Religious Revival in England," *JHI,* ii (1941). 330-338; and the relevant chapters in general histories of the period. There is much material in biographies and memoirs. See also W. E. Gladstone, *Correspondence on Church and Religion,* ed. D. C. Lathbury (2v, 1910), and Lord Acton, *Letters to Mary Gladstone,* ed. Herbert Paul (1904).

*Wilber-*
*force*

bridge and another center, made up mainly of laymen, at Clapham near London—the so-called "Clapham Sect." Several of this group were members of Parliament, and through their connections with the country gentry they were able to bring pressure upon the politicians and to win the adherence of men of education, wealth, and social prestige. A leader of the community at Clapham was William Wilberforce [2] (1759-1833), the author of *A Practical View of the Prevailing Religious System of Professed Christians in the Higher and Middle Classes in this Country Contrasted with Real Christianity* (1797), which is a foundation-stone of the Religious Revival of the following half-century. Wilberforce denounced the silence of the Anglican pulpit on points of doctrine and its inculcation of mere morality. Looking upon the self-assertion of the individual (a cardinal tenet of revolutionary thought) as an offence against the Divine Unity, he was convinced of the corruption of human nature and the need for redemption through Christ. His teaching foreshadows the Tractarian Movement, for Newman, who was reared in the Evangelical milieu, did not so much alter this theology as enrich it with elements rescued from the past. The *Practical View* sets forth a rigid code of behavior in which may be detected germs of Victorian sabbatarianism. Along with Thomas Clarkson, Wilberforce conducted the campaign for the abolition of the slave trade.[3] In other fields of endeavor [4] he was close to Hannah More.

*Hannah*
*More*

Hannah More [5] (1745-1833), who in youth had moved in the circles of Johnson and Garrick and later won some reputation as a dramatist,[6] turned her vivacious common sense to the services of practical piety. Her *Estimate of the Religion of the Fashionable World* (1790) anticipates in lighter vein the conclusions of Wilberforce's *Practical View*. She assailed Jacobinism, and in a long series of ethical tracts, including the enormously popular *Coelebs in Search of a Wife* (1809), which is in the form of fiction, exposed the corrupting influences of Regency "high life." Her enthusiasm brought against her the charge of "Methodism," and she was subjected to clerical abuse; but she did not waver in her philanthropic work. Her favorite field was among the children of the poor, especially in the mining districts.

*The High*
*Church*
*Party*

There were no such shining lights of energy and devotion in the old High Church party. The characteristic feature of this group was a feeble loyalty to the historic claims of the Church, to the Prayer Book, and to the sacraments. Amid social distractions their conduct of the services of the Church

---

[2] R. I. and Samuel Wilberforce, *The Life of William Wilberforce* (5v, 1838).

[3] The Society for the Abolition of the Slave Trade was founded in 1787. See E. L. Griggs, *Thomas Clarkson, the Friend of Slaves* (1936) and for the background of the movement Wylie Sypher, *Guinea's Captive Kings: British Anti-Slavery Literature in the Eighteenth Century* (Chapel Hill, 1942). — *The Christian Observer,* the organ of the abolitionists, was edited by Zachary Macaulay, father of the historian.

[4] Wilberforce was an advocate of educational reform, a champion of the cause of the poor curates against the greed of the higher clergy, and one of the founders of the London Missionary Society (1795) and of the British and Foreign Bible Society (1804).

[5] Charlotte M. Yonge, *Hannah More* (1888); "Marion Harland" (pseudonym), *Hannah More* (1900).

[6] *Percy,* a tragedy (Covent Garden, 1779); *Sacred Dramas* (1782).

had degenerated into a lifeless routine. During the Whig supremacy of the Walpole era they had commanded little influence, but with the Tory dominance of the Revolutionary and Napoleonic period their authority increased. The ecclesiastical constitution of England harmonized with the political, in that power was in the control of the landed proprietors. The episcopal bench presented a solid phalanx of Tories. Church emoluments were controlled and enjoyed by aristocratic families. As in the civil administration so in the ecclesiastical, a profitable appointment was regarded as a sinecure, its duties being deputized to an underling. During the wars other careers were open to talents; but after 1815 the younger sons of great families crowded into the Church. With no sense of vocation or dedication, they regarded the ministry as they did any other profession in which they might make their way.[7] The evils of pluralities and of non-residence were scandalous. While a small privileged group of clerics were very wealthy,[8] the hard-working curates without influence lived—or starved—on pittances. The shift of populations from old centers to the new industrial towns left many of the cathedrals over-staffed and largely empty of worshipers, while in the new communities there were too few churches. Though some beneficed divines feared for their own emoluments should the ecclesiastical revenue be reapportioned to meet this need, the more disinterested clergy contemplated with alarm the free field left to the proselytizers of dissent; and defenders of political stability and the established order recognized the danger of leaving the "masses" exposed to Jacobin propaganda (as indeed they were). These considerations led to the organization of the Church Building Society (1818) and the passage of an act granting a million pounds for new churches in populous districts.[9]

Neither the Evangelicals nor the High Church party paid much heed to theological studies. There was no examination in theology for candidates for holy orders at the universities, though at Cambridge the beginnings of reform in this matter date from 1809. Only the vaguest notion existed of the biblical scholarship of Germany, where, following the earliest disintegrating analysis of the Pentateuch, the theory of a lost proto-gospel had already been advanced. The standard textbook of ethics was William *Paley* Paley's *Principles of Moral and Political Philosophy* (1785) which formulated the teaching of Christ in purely utilitarian terms. The same author's *View of the Evidences of Christianity* (1794) is a notorious specimen of Low Church rationalizing. In his *Natural Theology* (1802) Paley elaborated in the light of scientific observations the argument from design which had long been prevalent, instancing the adjustments of organ to function and of organism to environment as proofs of the existence and providence of

[7] What seems to be cynicism in Jane Austen on the choice of the ministry as a profession (*Sense and Sensibility*, ch. xix; *Pride and Prejudice*, ch. xvi) merely reflects the ordinary contemporary state of mind.

[8] For examples of the abuse of the ecclesiastical revenues see E. L. Woodward, *The Age of Reform*, pp. 489-492.

[9] On the so-called "commissioners' churches" see Kenneth Clark, *The Gothic Revival* (1928), pp. 116-119.

God. The effort of lecturers at the universities was to minimize the miraculous and sacramental elements in Christianity, while moralizing and rationalizing the contents of the Creeds.

*The Broad Church Group*

As yet the Broad Church group, which was more scholarly than the other two and better informed of the new criticism that was fermenting in Germany, had scarcely emerged as a separate party. Later it was to provide the leaders of the attack upon the Tractarians. Conspicuous in this group were Richard Whately [10] (1787-1863), the logician, and Thomas Arnold [11] (1795-1842), the historian. To both men the mystical element in Tractarian thought and the emotional element in Evangelicalism were alike incomprehensible. Both tended to reduce the content of Christianity to the absolute minimum of belief in the divinity of Christ; all else was, they held, a matter not of faith but of "order." To the historic claims of the Church they were indifferent. Arnold's point of view was Erastian, that is, he desired to subordinate the ecclesiastical to the secular power.

## II

*Ecclesiastical Reform*

Three measures of reform roused the opposition of the Establishment. In 1828 the Tory ministry under Wellington, under compulsion of the Whigs, repealed the Test and Corporation Act. For many years annual acts of indemnity had rendered this oppressive law inoperative, but now dissenters were placed on a basis of legal equality with members of the Church of England. The opponents of this just and salutary reform argued that the House of Commons as the representative assembly of the Church of England could not manage ecclesiastical affairs if it were opened to nonconformists. The logical reply was disestablishment; but though this would have made the Church of England autonomous it was a remedy which most of the clergy rejected because it would entail the sacrifice of revenue and prestige. The final triumph in 1829 of the long struggle for Catholic Emancipation in Ireland was a second blow to the Establishment. Partisans, blind to the inherent justice of this act, argued that it had been forced upon England under duress. This was to a degree true, for Emancipation was intended to pacify Irish discontent which under O'Connell's leadership had threatened open war. When the Reform Parliament met in 1833 a bill was introduced for the suppression of ten Anglican bishoprics in Ireland. The measure was reasonable and just, for the number of such sees was out

---

[10] Whately is still remembered for his *Historic Doubts relative to Napoleon Bonaparte* (1819), a brilliant parody of the skeptical methods of critics of the Gospel history. His *Christian Evidences* (1837) was influential, widely used, and translated into many tongues. He became Archbishop of Dublin. See his *Life and Correspondence*, edited by his daughter (1864).

[11] Arnold was headmaster of Rugby (1827-1841) and professor of modern history at Oxford (1841-1842). His chief works, besides volumes of sermons, are his edition of Thucydides and his *History of Rome* (3v, 1838-1843). The influence of his character and thought upon younger men, notably his own son, Matthew Arnold, was profound. See A. P. Stanley, *The Life and Correspondence of Thomas Arnold* (1844), and for modern estimates the clever but distorted portrait in Lytton Strachey, *Eminent Victorians* (1918), pp. 205-242, and the sympathetic and just characterization in Lionel Trilling, *Matthew Arnold* (1939), pp. 39-76.

of all proportion to the non-Catholic population. But Lord Grey's frankly Erastian purpose—and Erastianism was anathema to the High Church party—was to reapportion the diocesan revenues so that they might be used in place of certain hated taxes which it was determined to abolish. In the minds of a number of devout clergymen, consulting together in the common-room of Oriel College at Oxford, the affair of the Irish bishoprics brought matters to a crisis. The "crisis," save in so far as the Irish Church Bill was an assault upon ecclesiastical property and inferentially upon the principle of Establishment, was a figment of their cloistered imagination. But it initiated the Tractarian Movement at Oxford.[12]

The initiator of the Movement was John Keble [13] (1792-1866) who had *Keble* lately returned to Oxford from a curacy in Gloucestershire. In 1827 he had published anonymously *The Christian Year*, a cycle of devotional poems which combine simple piety with a mildly Wordsworthian love of nature. In these pieces the Anglican prerogative is assumed and the emotionalism of the Evangelicals is raised to a higher and drier level. Today their senti-mental piety seems to be charged with the religiosity they were designed to combat. Keble's reputation as a poet and scholar led to his appointment as professor of poetry at Oxford in 1831. His part in the Movement will appear presently. His later life was passed in a parish near Winchester, whence his sanctity shed its influence upon a younger generation. A second member of the group was Richard Hurrell Froude (1803-1836), a brother *R. H.* of the historian. The impression of great ability made upon his friends is *Froude* scarcely substantiated by his posthumous *Remains* (1836). He was the con-necting link between Keble and John Henry Newman [14] (1801-1890). Friendship with Keble and Froude led Newman away from the Calvinistic *Newman* Evangelicanism in which he had been brought up. In 1828 he was appointed vicar of St. Mary's in Oxford, whose pulpit he was to make famous.[15] Dur-ing a sojourn for his health in Italy in 1832 he was impressed with what he termed "the polytheistic, degrading, and idolatrous Roman Catholic religion." On his voyage home he wrote *The Pillar of the Cloud*, better known as the hymn *Lead, Kindly Light*. The fourth leader of the Move-ment (which, however, he did not join actively till 1835) was Edward Bouverie Pusey [16] (1800-1882). Pusey had studied Oriental languages and *Pusey*

---

[12] On the environment of the Movement and of the later, liberal reaction see W. S. Knickerbocker, *Creative Oxford: Its Influence on Victorian Literature* (1925).
[13] *The Christian Year, Lyra Innocentium, and other Poems. Together with* [Keble's] *Sermon on "National Apostasy"* (1914); *Lectures on Poetry*, translated by E. K. Francis (2v, 1912). The lectures were delivered in Latin and so published (1844). — Sir John Taylor Coleridge, *A Memoir of John Keble* (1869).
[14] *The Life and Correspondence of John Henry Newman*, ed. Anne Mozley (1892); Wilfrid Ward, *The Life of John Henry Cardinal Newman* (2v, 1912); William Barry, *Newman* (1904); C. F. Harrold, *John Henry Newman* (1945); J. J. Reilly, *Newman as a Man of Letters* (1925); T. B. Kittredge, *The Influence of Newman on the Oxford Movement* (Berkeley, 1914).
[15] *Parochial and Plain Sermons*, ed. W. J. Copeland (8v, 1868), originally published in various volumes between 1834 and 1843.
[16] H. P. Liddon, J. C. Johnston, and R. J. Wilson, *The Life of Edward B. Pusey* (5v, 1893-1899). — The popular name "Puseyism" came to be attached to the Movement because the first of the *Tracts for the Times* (No. XVIII) not published anonymously was from his pen.

theology at Göttingen, was in advance of most English scholars in mastery of the new biblical criticism, and was professor of Hebrew at Oxford. Like Keble, he never wavered in his allegiance to the Church of England, and after the Movement at Oxford had disintegrated he was for many years a leader of the Anglo-Catholics.

At the opening of the Oxford Assize in July, 1833, Keble preached a sermon on "National Apostasy" in which he attacked the Whig government as traitors to the Church. The passionate intolerance of this utterance created a sensation which reverberated beyond the university, and Newman and his associates, looking beyond the ephemeral political "crisis" and desiring to awaken the Church of England to a consciousness of her Catholicity, at once planned to enlarge upon Keble's appeal. The result was the

*Tracts for the Times*

initiation of the *Tracts for the Times* [17] (as they came later to be called). The early Tracts were generally brief notes on doctrinal, historical, liturgical, and disciplinary subjects. Later, especially when Pusey's heavy hand contributed to them, they became less personal and direct in appeal and more elaborate treatises upon theological tradition and documents. [18] From the start they were Catholic in teaching, but there was no defiant severance from the Protestant party in the Church of England till the publication of Tracts xxxviii and xli in the summer of 1834, in which Newman expounded the doctrine of the *Via Media*. Concurrently with the series were the beautiful and persuasive sermons at St. Mary's in which Newman exploited the charm of his eloquence and personality. Opposition was soon vocal and the charge of "Romanizing" was raised. In 1836 the publication of Froude's posthumous writings seemed to confirm these accusations; and in the same year the appointment of R. D. Hampden to a professorship of divinity was bitterly but unsuccessfully opposed by the Tractarians on the ground of his Arianism. Prejudice was enhanced by Newman's lectures on *The Prophetical Office of the Church, Viewed Relatively to Romanism and Popular Protestantism* [19] (1837), in which, developing further the doctrine

*The "Via Media"*

of the *Via Media,* he claimed for the Church of England a position midway between absolute submission to infallible authority and entire freedom of private judgment, a firm middle ground traceable unbroken back to apostolic times, free alike from the errors which had accumulated in the Church of Rome and those which owed their inception to the Reformation. In later life Newman repudiated this as a "paper theory" irreducible to practice, where, as he said, he could find no sure footing between Roman Catholicism and agnosticism. The term *Via Media* was widely misapprehended, suggesting as it did not the Golden Mean but a compromise for the sake of gaining adherents.

[17] *The Oxford Movement. Being a Selection from the Tracts for the Times,* ed. W. G. Hutchinson (1906), eighteen *Tracts,* including Nos. xxxviii and xc.

[18] As a supplement to the later Tracts, designed to make original sources available to readers who knew no Greek or Latin, Pusey, Newman, and Keble began in 1838 *The Library of the Fathers,* which, extending to forty-five volumes, was not completed till 1885.

[19] Reprinted in *The Via Media of the Anglican Church* (1877), where it occupies the whole of Vol. I.

In the next years several Tracts that were markedly Catholic in tone [20] led to the climax of the Movement. Newman argued that the two signs of Catholicity were world-wide extension and the preservation of the primitive faith intact; on the score of universality Rome could support her claim; but in view of certain of her dogmas how could she pretend to hold unaltered the Faith once for all delivered? Much later, Newman found in his "doctrine of development" the answer to this question; but in 1838 it seemed to him an irrefutable argument against the Roman position. Early in 1841 Newman issued Tract xc. He undertook to demonstrate that the Thirty-Nine Arti- *Tract XC* cles of Religion in *The Book of Common Prayer,* popularly regarded as a stronghold of Protestantism, were, though hostile to Rome, not hostile to Catholic principles; that they condemned not uses but abuses; and that they were susceptible of Catholic interpretations which would remove from the path of his disciples the stumbling-block of obligatory subscription.[21] To accomplish this it was necessary in some cases to resort to a non-natural meaning in order to wring a reluctant Catholicity from Protestant doctrines. This laid Newman open to the charge of sophistry, a charge from which he is not entirely relieved by the fact that, whether or not the Anglican divines who framed the Articles in 1563 were deliberately ambiguous,[22] long experience has shown that they can be conscientiously signed by men who hold different opinions. Tract xc occasioned a great scandal; many men who had till now favored the Movement withdrew their support; the Bishop of Oxford requested Newman to discontinue the series; and the *Tracts for the Times* came to an end.

To recount briefly the story of Newman's alienation from the Church of England is to over-simplify what he has told with incomparably subtle self-analysis.[23] Studying certain heresies of the early Church, he was struck by the fact that though possessing valid orders they were separated from the Church of Rome. Consequently valid orders, which he believed that the Anglican communion possessed, did not constitute a proof of Catholicity. The proud words of St. Augustine—*Securus judicat orbis terrarum* [24]—rang in his ears as a death knell of his loyalty to Anglicanism. Then the arrangement between England and Prussia whereby each government should alternately appoint a bishop of Jerusalem seemed to Newman an official recognition of the practical identity of Lutheranism and Anglicanism. This was a repudiation of all he stood for. He retired into lay communion, yet still hesitated upon the brink, for certain "errors" of the Roman Church

[20] Especially *On Reserve in Religious Teaching,* by Isaac Williams, Newman's curate, and *On the Catholicity of the English Church,* by Newman himself.

[21] The line of argument was not original; it had been followed by Laudian controversialists.

[22] F. D. Maitland held that the charge of deliberate ambiguity could not fairly be brought against the sixteenth-century divines. Maitland's chapter, "The Anglican Settlement," *Cambridge Modern History,* II. 550-598, should be read in connection with Tract xc.

[23] *Apologia pro Vita Sua,* Parts v and vi.

[24] "The slightest reflection would have told [Newman] that the Catholic Church of St. Augustine's time was but a small fraction of the earth's population, and was controlled by a small minority of its own members" (A. W. Benn, *English Rationalism,* I. 17-18).

*The
Doctrine
of Devel-
opment*

seemed to him insurmountable. But in his "doctrine of development" he found a satisfying solution.[25] He did not argue, as is sometimes said, that new religious truths gradually develop but that men slowly grasp the complete implications of the Truth "once for all delivered to the saints." He was, in fact, opposed to the liberal Protestant conception of religion as developmental or evolutionary. His doctrine is more truly analogous to the "preformationism" of the naturalist Charles Bonnet. "The original world-plan was like a photographic roll which had been exposed but not developed. The pictures were already there potentially, so pour on the 'developer' of time and circumstance and they will come out."[26] This theory enabled Newman to accept Roman dogmas which, as he now came to hold, were implicit but not explicit in primitive Christianity. Thus his sole remaining doubt was swept away, and in October, 1845, he was received into the Roman Catholic Church.

For a long while Newman lived in loneliness, isolated from old friends and not altogether trusted by new. In 1848 he received permission to found a house of the Oratorians at Birmingham, which was his home thereafter. In 1851 he helped to organize the Catholic University of Dublin of which he was appointed Rector.[27] The Achilli trial[28] (1851-1853) helped to re-establish his prestige and public confidence in his integrity. But he was still living under a cloud when in 1864 Charles Kingsley accused him slanderously of having informed the world that "truth for its own sake" need not be, and on the whole ought not to be, "a virtue with the Roman clergy."[29]

*Apologia
pro Vita
Sua*

Newman's publication of the inconclusive exchange of letters which followed inspired Kingsley's boisterous and unconvincing attempt at a refutation, *What, then, does Dr. Newman Mean?* in reply to which Newman wrote the *Apologia pro Vita Sua*[30] (1864).

Newman's style was normally suave and urbane,[31] but at Oxford, by his own admission, he had delighted in logical fence and in the use of irony

[25] *An Essay on the Development of Christian Doctrine* (1845). — For the part played by the impetuous logician W. G. Ward, a follower of Newman who led his chief Romeward, see Ward's *Ideal of a Christian Church* (1844) and Wilfrid Ward, *William George Ward and the Oxford Movement* (1889).

[26] Woodbridge Riley, *From Myth to Reason* (1926), p. 260. — There is some irony in the fact that Newman opposed the promulgation of the dogmas of the Immaculate Conception (1854) and of Papal Infallibility (1869).

[27] The discourses which Newman delivered at Dublin, collected in *The Idea of a University* (new edition, 1903), combat the opinion that theology is not a science and therefore has no part in the curriculum and discuss the relation of theology to physical science and literature. Newman declares that science and faith inhabit separate spheres. In his novel *Callista* there is a witch who symbolizes physical science and her son is modern liberalism.

[28] On this notorious case see Wilfrid Ward, *Life of John Henry Cardinal Newman*, I, ch. x.

[29] This statement appeared in a review of J. A. Froude's *History of England* in *Macmillan's Magazine*, January, 1864.

[30] The reissue of 1865 with the passages on Kingsley omitted bore the title *History of My Religious Opinions*. The original title was afterwards restored. The edition by Wilfrid Ward (1913) contains the texts of 1864 and 1865 with the pamphlets which led up to the *Apologia* and other supplementary material.

[31] As seen not only in his sermons but in his attempts at fiction: *Loss and Gain: the Story of a Convert* (1848) and *Callista: a Sketch of the Third Century* (1856). The former contains some sharply polemical passages, but in general the suavity in these two books is a little soft and there is a strained emotionalism.

to disconcert opponents, and years of controversy had sharpened a weapon of formidable temper. But when once by means of the finest irony he had disposed of his blustering antagonist, he resumed his accustomed urbanity. His purpose in the *Apologia* was not to proselytize but to justify himself. He knew that to remove prejudice he must exhibit himself as he really was; as in the pulpit so here he relied upon his personality. *Cor ad cor loquitur.* He employed persuasion rather than syllogistic reasoning. The emotional stress under which this spiritual autobiography was composed did not distract his attention from the subtlest influences upon his long and at times almost imperceptible progress towards Rome. At the risk of wearying his readers every particle of the truth must be revealed. Candor, quiet humor, psychological insight, understatement, sudden, piercing irony—these are the qualities of a style which represents the classical tradition of confidence and repose as contrasted with the stormy romanticism of Carlyle and Ruskin. Yet at the heart of the *Apologia,* as in his most characteristic sermons, there is a sense of the mystery of existence which allies him with the romanticists.[32] Newman shows himself, as in the sermons, to be a great though quiet rhetorician; but rhetoric is never employed for its own sake. The irony is not merely destructive but has a positive argumentative value. Even those who were not convinced of the validity of his opinions were convinced of his sincerity. His reputation was henceforth secure.

With the subsidence of turmoil Newman turned to the composition of poetry of which he had written little since about 1836.[33] Warned by a physician of his precarious state of health and under a vivid apprehension of approaching death, he wrote *The Dream of Gerontius* [34] (1866), a semi-dramatic poem in which the Soul passes from the body, is borne by the Guardian Angel through the abyss, and having come to the Judgment Seat, is carried thence to Purgatory. The death bed with which the poem opens, the passing of the Soul into silence and solitude, the consciousness of the angelic presence, and the colloquy between the Soul and the Angel are rendered with a solemn dignity which makes the *Dream* one of the most moving of religious poems. *(margin: The Dream of Gerontius)*

The last decades of Newman's life were of ever-widening recognition.[35] In 1879 he was created a cardinal, with special permission (rarely granted to non-diocesans) not to reside in Rome. He died in Birmingham in 1890. On his tomb are the words: *Ex umbris et imaginibus in veritatem.*

[32] The sense of mystery is never of mystic intensity. P. E. More (*The Drift of Romanticism,* p. 65) remarks that Newman was unable to understand the position of the pure mystic, dependent as he was upon revelation through the Church.

[33] Newman contributed more than a hundred poems to *The British Magazine.* These, with contributions by Keble, Froude, and others, were gathered together in *Lyra Apostolica* (1836), ed. H. S. Holland and H. C. Beeching (1899). Of Newman's short pieces only a few are of great merit: *The Pillar of the Cloud, Refrigerium,* and *A Voice from Afar.*

[34] Ed. M. F. Egan (1919). Sir Edward Elgar's oratorio (1900) has maintained the fame of Newman's poem. It is likely that Newman, who was a musician and who loved every association with St. Philip Neri, had the oratorio form in mind.

[35] The last of Newman's major works is *The Grammar of Assent* (1870), an examination of the grounds of religious belief.

## III

*Tractarianism*

Broadly speaking, the Oxford Movement was part of the Romantic Revival. Newman himself recognized the influence of Sir Walter Scott in turning men's minds back to the Middle Ages and thus making them sympathetically receptive to Catholic dogma. The revival of Gothic architecture antedated the Tractarians and was independent of them, but Pugin was a romantic medievalist whose theory and practice were in harmony with their teaching; and as the clergy came to lay more emphasis upon proper ritualistic observance they were able to correct the technical errors of the earlier Gothicizers.[36] The Tractarians' insistence upon the principle of authority resembles the conservative reaction of the early nineteenth century from the intellectual emancipation of eighteenth-century radicalism. Their pessimistic view of this present world was a like reaction from the unlimited confidence of the perfectibilitarians. Their rejection of Reason as a guide is characteristic of romanticism; Truth for them as for the transcendentalists is above Logic. The use in Newman's sermons and in Tractarian poetry of symbols drawn from the natural world to suggest the supernatural is thoroughly romantic.

Apart from Newman's writings few of the polemical and exegetical works produced by the Tractarians are remembered today. Newman's poetry, Keble's *Christian Year,* and the hymns of John Mason Neale,[37] with three or four by Isaac Williams and F. W. Faber, make up their contribution to English poetry, though their beliefs strongly influenced Christina Rossetti, a poet of genius. More broadly, the Movement colored Tennyson's conception of the religious life of the Middle Ages and helped to shape the mood of the early poetry and painting of the Pre-Raphaelites. Of the many religious novels emanating from Tractarianism or combatting it scarcely any are readable today, though the stories of Charlotte M. Yonge once enjoyed a great vogue.[38] Less definitely it contributed something to the writings of Joseph Henry Shorthouse; and the ritualistic or ceremonial expression of High Anglicanism appealed strongly to Walter Pater. Mingled with other streams of thought and emotion the influence of Anglo-Catholicism is discernible in many other places and has been perpetuated to the present time.[39]

To Evangelicalism the Tractarians contributed little save a more reverent regard for the visible Church as the Body of Christ and a new feeling for

[36] On the architectural work of A. W. N. Pugin see Kenneth Clark, *The Gothic Revival,* ch. VII, and on the influence of ecclesiology upon architecture, *ibid.,* ch. VIII.

[37] On Neale see above, ch. XIV, n. 33.

[38] On Anglo-Catholic novels, Evangelical attacks on the Tractarians in the guise of fiction, and so forth see J. E. Baker, *The Novel and the Oxford Movement* (Princeton, 1932). See also Amy Cruse, *The Victorians and their Reading* (1935), chs. II and III.

[39] The student who is neither a theologian nor a liturgist may obtain an idea of the questions still at issue from A. H. T. Clarke, "The Passing of the Oxford Movement," *The Nineteenth Century and After,* LXXI (1912). 133-147, 341-346; and the rejoinder by E. G. Selwyn, "The Future of the Oxford Movement," *ibid.,* 532-546. See also H. L. Stewart, *A Century of Anglo-Catholicism* (1929). The vitality of these issues is further shown by the preoccupation with them in the writings of T. S. Eliot.

the dignity of worship. In both respects the Evangelicalism of the mid-century was different from what it had been fifty years earlier, and the difference was due to the Oxford men.

Yet there is a measure of truth in Mrs. Browning's remark that the *Tracts* *Liberal* were not "for" but "against" the times. The direction in which the winds *Theology* of doctrine were blowing is shown by the growth of the Broad Church party. This group was profoundly affected by romantic philosophy, especially as interpreted by Coleridge, and was well informed on the new discoveries of science and biblical scholarship. In the eighteen-fifties the influence of F. C. Bauer and the "Tübingen School" of biblical studies began to make itself seriously felt in England. Their recognition of a primitive Judaistic form of Christianity; the distinction which they drew between the teaching of Jesus and that of Paul; and especially their arguments against the traditional authorship of the Fourth Gospel (which they regarded as an allegorical work of the second century)—these and similar opinions permeated the thought of the Broad Churchmen. This influence is well illustrated by the career of Carlyle's friend, John Sterling; [40] but it is more significant in that it was a chief force in alienating men from the Oxford Movement. Two men are of special note because each was a brother of a leading Tractarian. Francis W. Newman [41] (1805-1897) has suffered in *F. W.* reputation from Arnold's incisive criticism of his translation of Homer; but *Newman* his spiritual history makes him a representative of the spirit of the age. The course of his renunciation of supernatural Christianity, while retaining a vague belief in a vague Divinity, is set forth in his autobiography, *Phases of Faith* (1850). James Anthony Froude (1818-1904) chose the form of semi- *J. A.* autobiographical fiction—*Shadows of the Clouds* (1847); *The Nemesis of* *Froude* *Faith* (1849)—in which to trace the stages of the disintegration of his beliefs. He had been a Tractarian and had taken orders; his final revulsion from what he regarded as the superstitions of the Anglo-Catholic revival was experienced while translating one of the Tractarian series of *The Lives of the Saints*. The reaction from childish legends diverted Froude's attention to the English Reformation, with consequences for historiography which will engage our attention in a later chapter.[42] Other latitudinarians who were conspicuous figures in the Victorian scene were F. D. Maurice [43] and H. L. Mansel.[44]

[40] See Anne K. Tuell, *John Sterling, a Representative Victorian* (1941); A. W. Benn, *English Rationalism*, I. 385-390.
[41] The account of F. W. Newman in Lionel Trilling, *Matthew Arnold* (1939), pp. 168-178, is witty but biased. His importance is stressed by Benn, *op. cit.*, II. 17-36.
[42] See below, ch. xxi.
[43] Frederick Denison Maurice (1805-1872) commanded a great personal following because of his piety and social-service work. He exerted a strong influence upon Charles Kingsley in the field of Christian Socialism.
[44] Henry L. Mansel (1820-1871), professor of philosophy at Oxford and afterwards Dean of St. Paul's, was a follower of Sir William Hamilton. His most famous work is *The Limits of Religious Thought* (1858) in which Christian apologetic is based upon agnosticism. God, in His essence, and "absolute morality" are alike beyond the reach of human knowledge. Therefore, Mansel argues, since knowledge is only relative, theological doctrines based upon human conceptions of good and evil may be accepted. Mansel was a notable stylist, combining

*Essays and Reviews*     Timidity and a reluctance to challenge accepted beliefs kept some scholars silent and others but semi-articulate, but notwithstanding bitter hostility the "higher criticism" continued to gather force. In 1860 a group of seven writers, among whom were Benjamin Jowett, afterwards Master of Balliol, and Frederick Temple, afterwards Archbishop of Canterbury, spoke out in a manifesto entitled *Essays and Reviews*. The counsel communicated to Christians in this eloquent and courageous book was that the new discoveries in natural science and biblical scholarship should be accepted as not threatening but reinvigorating faith. One writer went so far as to commend Darwin's *Origin of Species* as "a masterly book" which would revolutionize opinion "in favor of the grand principle of the self-evolving powers of Nature." The volume made a great stir. Frederick Harrison, the Positivist, and Arthur P. Stanley, afterwards Dean of Westminster, were among its defenders; but Pusey attacked it with acrimony and circulated a declaration of belief in biblical infallibility to which no less than eleven thousand clerical signatures were obtained. The seven authors were prosecuted and condemned in the ecclesiastical court. Two years later controversy broke out afresh, when Bishop J. W. Colenso,[45] who by arithmetical methods had demonstrated "the unhistorical character of very considerable portions of the Mosaic narrative," was tried for heresy. Colenso's reputation has suffered from Matthew Arnold's supercilious ridicule. Other phases of the warfare between orthodox Christianity and science will be touched on in the next chapter.

*Bishop Colenso*

---

effects obviously derived from the seventeenth-century divines with others echoing Newman. See George Saintsbury, *A History of English Prose Rhythm* (1912), pp. 416-420.

[45] *A Critical Examination of the Pentateuch and the Book of Joshua* (1862). See Benn, *op. cit.*, II. 135-145.

# XIX

## The Theory of Evolution and Its Repercussions

The concept of the Scale of Being or Ladder of Life, widely disseminated *"The Scale* in the eighteenth century,[1] influenced the speculations of evolutionists, *of Being"* though in itself it was creationist rather than evolutionary.[2] What was envisaged was not a series of events in chronological order but a sequence of hierarchies extending upwards through the stages of organized life to its culmination in man. The metaphysical implications of this concept were worked out by Schelling and other German thinkers and attracted the attention of Coleridge.[3] Buffon, Diderot, and Kant had conjectured that species have not remained unalterable through all time but that "higher" forms have been derived by natural means from "lower" forms. But for definite statements of the idea of the mutability of species we must turn to the poet-naturalist Erasmus Darwin[4] (1731-1802). The faults of Dr. Darwin's *Erasmus* poetic style are of no moment in this connection; his fame as a pioneer in *Darwin* scientific speculation is secure. His theories are set forth in the medico-

[1] A. O. Lovejoy, *The Great Chain of Being* (1936); J. W. Beach, *The Concept of Nature,* pp. 172-176. Famous allusions to the concept are in Pope, *Essay on Man,* I. 233-240; Akenside, *The Pleasures of Imagination,* first version, II. 323-350; and Thomson, *The Seasons, Summer,* lines 333-337.

[2] The present writer does not claim to speak with authority in this chapter nor to have controlled more than a fraction of the enormous literature of the subject. Works which he has found of special value are: H. F. Osborn, *From the Greeks to Darwin* (2ed., 1898), which, however, needs correction at many points; J. W. Judd, *The Coming of Evolution* (1912); S. C. Schmucker, *The Meaning of Evolution* (1916), a popular account; A. F. Shull, *Evolution* (1936), especially ch. XI; L. T. More, *The Dogma of Evolution* (1925), an impressive corrective to overconfidence; Douglas Dewar, *Difficulties of the Evolution Theory* (1931); A. M. Davies, *Evolution and its Modern Critics* (1937), in part a reply to Dewar; Julian Huxley, *Evolution: The Modern Synthesis* (1942); J. A. Thomson, *Darwinism and Human Life* (1910; 1946). See also L. J. Henkin, *Darwinism in the English Novel, 1860-1910* (1940).

[3] As Professor Beach has pointed out, Coleridge's phraseology is so ambiguous that when he writes of the efforts of "lower natures" to ascend (*Aids to Reflection; Complete Works* (ed. 1868-1871), I. 181), he might seem to be enunciating evolutionary doctrine did we not know that elsewhere he repudiated the hypothesis, branding as "absurd" the notion "of man's having progressed from an ourang-outang state—so contrary to all history, to all religion, nay, to all possibility" (*Letters,* ed. E. H. Coleridge, II. 648). — Lord Monboddo (1714-1799), in *The Origin and Progress of Language* (1773), classified man and the ourang-outang as species of the *genus Homo.* But Monboddo was a creationist; he made no suggestion of transmutation, but merely drew the line below, not above, the highest apes; and the line demarking species from species remained impassable. Thomas Love Peacock's satire in *Melincourt* (1817) keeps Monboddo in remembrance.

[4] Hesketh Pearson, *Doctor Darwin* (1930). On Darwin's *The Loves of the Plants* (1789) and *The Botanic Garden* (1791) see W. J. Courthope, *History of English poetry,* VI (1910). 33-40. See also Ernst Krause, *Erasmus Darwin und seine Stellung in der Geschichte der Descendenz-theorie* (Leipzig, 1887; translated by W. S. Dallas, 1889); and monographs by Leopold Brandl on *The Temple of Nature* and *The Botanic Garden* (Vienna, 1902 and 1909). On Darwin the poet see J. V. Logan, *The Poetry and Aesthetics of Erasmus Darwin* (Princeton, 1937).

philosophical work, *Zoönomia* (1794-1796), and in the posthumously published poem, *The Temple of Nature* (1803). From Greek and later theorists
he derived his belief in the spontaneous origin of life in minute forms in the
ocean. Thence came fishes, and from fishes amphibians, and finally ter-
restrial animals. Discerning the significance of accidental variations which
are of value to the organism acquiring them, he believed that transforma-
tions were produced by the exertions of the organisms themselves, in response to pleasures and pains. These acquired forms and propensities are
transmitted to posterity—a clear anticipation of the doctrine of Lamarck.
Darwin described what later came to be called "the struggle for existence"
but saw in it merely a check upon overcrowding, thus missing the connection between this struggle and the principle of the survival of the fittest.

*Lamarck*        Whether the Chevalier de Lamarck (1744-1829) knew Darwin's writings
is not demonstrable but appears probable. The fame of Lamarck's work,
based upon wide knowledge of botany and zoology and upon precise powers
of description, obscured the speculations of his predecessor. Altered wants
(*besoins*) through changes in environment lead, Lamarck holds, to altered
habits, and hence to the formation of new organs and the modification or
disappearance of those already existing. Organs do not give rise to habits,
but habits give rise to organs. Living beings have not been created for a
certain mode of life; it is the mode of life which has created the beings.
Within the organism there is a "will" to adapt itself. This is the theory of
appetency or of variation "definitely directed" from within. The desire for
any action on the part of an animal leads to efforts to accomplish that desire;
environment furnishes the stimuli for these adaptive changes; and the
resultant organ and its functions can be transmitted to future generations.
The crux of the conflict between the Lamarckians and the Darwinians is
in this theory, for Charles Darwin held that variation is indefinite and in all
directions and that with change in environment a *chance* variation may prove
advantageous to the organism and is then continuously and increasingly
selected. The question at issue is crisply summarized in the title of one of
Samuel Butler's books: *Luck or Cunning?*

*Cuvier*         Lamarck, who was ridiculed for the extravagances of his illustrative ex-
*and Catas-*   amples (as in his discussion of the way in which the snake lost its legs),
*trophism*     was further discredited by the opposition of the great naturalist, George
Cuvier [5] (1769-1832). Cuvier, a Catholic and creationist, opposed transmu-
tationism. Yet his creationism, which was supposed to harmonize the evi-

---

[5] Cuvier adumbrated his theory in various earlier works before he presented it in its most
extravagant form in the third edition of his *Discours sur les révolutions sur la surface du globe*
(1825).Though the *Discours* was not translated into English until 1829, his views were
accessible in English in his *Essay on the Theory of the Earth,* translated by Robert Kerr (1813)
and stirred the imagination of Byron, who combined catastrophism with the "poetical fiction"
of the pre-Adamites which he took from Beckford's *Vathek.* See *Cain,* II. ii. 130-147; *Don
Juan,* IX. xxxvii-xxxviii; *Heaven and Earth,* I. iii. 40-46; and *Letters and Journals,* ed. R. E.
Prothero, v. 368. — On catastrophism see further Charles Singer, *The Story of Living Things*
(1931), pp. 231-232, and Erik Nordenskiöld, *The History of Biology* (1928), pp. 338-339.

dence of science with the narrative in Genesis, differed widely from the old orthodoxy. He inherited and enlarged upon the "Theory of Catastrophes" or doctrine of discontinuity, that is, of cataclysmic changes in the earth's history necessitating supernatural intervention. On the evidence of the stratification of the rocks and of the abrupt extinction of organisms as evinced by fossils it was argued that the earth had undergone a series of convulsive changes alternating with periods of calm. Cuvier himself held that after each catastrophe "such few beings as escaped have spread and propagated their kind"; but as popularized by some of his followers the theory took the extreme form that in each cataclysm all life had been destroyed and a new series of creations by God had followed. The view that at different moments in the past God interfered with natural processes, repairing the damage which He was, it would seem, unwilling or power-less to prevent, is the ignoble doctrine of "special creation" which for many years satisfied the orthodox. The advance of evolutionary theory is partly due to the quest for a tenable alternative hypothesis.

Materials for the refutation of catastrophism had been patiently assembled *Lyell and* by the English geologists, James Hutton, John Playfair, and William Smith,[6] *Uniformi-* and the *coup de grâce* was delivered by Sir Charles Lyell (1797-1875), whose *tarianism* monumental *Principles of Geology* (1830) overthrew the doctrine of discontinuity and, inferentially, of special creation. Moreover, by showing that natural causation is competent to account for the inorganic portion of our globe, Lyell raised the question why it should not also account for the living part. Thus, his uniformitarianism prepared the way for Charles Darwin; and it is significant that one of the works which Darwin studied during the voyage of the *Beagle* was Lyell's *Geology*. Lyell did not seek to explain the origin of life, but he demonstrated that geological history is one of gradual development and that the evidence of fossils supports the belief that living organisms, since their first appearance on earth, have continued to exist thereon.[7] Lyell was not a transmutationist; but his chronological sequence from lower to higher forms tended, like the hierarchic sequence of the Scale of Being, to over-emphasize progress and the idea of betterment. The Victorian evolutionists who adhered to the idealistic notion of a steady and inevitable progress towards a state of perfection were as much influenced by Lyell as by the philosophic perfectibilitarians.

During the three decades intervening between *The Principles of Geology* and *The Origin of Species* a number of convergent lines of argument were

---

[6] James Hutton, *Theory of the Earth* (1785; expanded, 1795); John Playfair, *Illustrations of the Huttonian Theory of the Earth* (1802); William Smith, *Order of the Strata and their embedded Organic Remains, in the Neighborhood of Bath* (1799) and *A Geological Map of England and Wales* (1815).

[7] It is now generally held that Lyell overstated his case. The modern view is that at the close of each geological era there were large redistributions of land and water which caused changes of climate with which multitudes of species were unable to cope. Some geologists now calculate that in the intense cold of the Permian period with which the Palaeozoic era closed twenty-nine out of every thirty species perished. Lyell did not make sufficient allowance for the effect of these perturbations. Moreover, he did not recognize the importance of degeneration, that is, of reversion to earlier modes of life.

*The Evo-
lutionary
Hypothesis*

assembled in support of the evolutionary hypothesis.[8] The general presumption of science was against "supernatural" explanations of phenomena. If astronomical and geological phenomena are shown to be the result of the operation of natural "laws," [9] why not biological? Are we to believe that organisms fossilized in strata which have come about through natural means are themselves the result of special acts of creation? Cuvier had argued, with reservations which destroyed the validity of his contention, that no fossil species had analogues among living species. The proof to the contrary was emphasized by Chambers in 1844 and this argument from the persistence of types was a telling blow to the special creationists. The argument from homologies in vertebrates had been recognized by eighteenth-century naturalists and much new evidence along this line had been gathered by the comparative anatomists. The theory of recapitulation in stages of embryo life was pressed for as much as it was worth—or more. The existence of vestigial organs was taken as evidence of ancestral forms of independent species. The argument from the variability of existing species was advanced; but one of the most telling arguments of the anti-evolutionists (afterwards candidly recognized by Darwin) was the lack of evidence of variations so wide as to produce varieties sterile *inter se*. Such sterility is a mark of distinct species. Finally, there was the argument from the sequence of types in paleontology. The abrupt extinction of multitudes of species as we pass from one geological stratum to the next was an argument for catastrophism and special creationism. In fossils there was very little evidence of continuity. The negative argument of course does not hold, for the chances of fossilization are small and the opportunities for destruction immense. The evolutionists searched for "missing links" with the result that in later years several convincing "form-series" were discovered.[10]

Despite the force of these arguments the opinion of the majority of scientists remained creationist. Some may have believed in evolution *in petto* but they were either ambiguous in statement or else kept silent. The difficulties confronting the pious geologist who sought to reconcile the chronology deduced from the biblical narrative with the testimony of the rocks

*Buckland*

are illustrated in the writings of William Buckland (1784-1856): *Reliquiae Diluvianae* (1823) and *Geology and Mineralogy* (1836), the latter one of the famous *Bridgewater Treatises* which were designed to exhibit "the power, wisdom, and goodness of God, as manifested in the creation." When a human skeleton was discovered in strata containing the bones of "antediluvian" animals, Buckland would not accept the evidence before his eyes but argued that the skeleton was of recent date and had by accident in-

[8] The summary which follows is condensed from A. O. Lovejoy, "The Argument for Organic Evolution before *The Origin of Species*," *Popular Science Monthly*, LXXV (1909). 499-514, 537-549.
[9] The Nebular Hypothesis of Laplace was widely accepted at this time. The dynamic difficulties which disposed of it in its original form were not demonstrated till 1859.
[10] The example most familiar to every visitor to our museums of natural history is that of the *Equidae*. Huxley made much of the ancestry of the horse in his address to the Geological Society in 1870.

truded into the lower level of stratification. This resort to sophistry by a scientist of repute is significant of the spiritual unease of the time. A more curious case is that of the naturalist Philip Henry Gosse, the author of *P. H. Omphalos: an Attempt to Untie the Geological Knot* (1857). This book's *Gosse* quaint title is taken from the problem, which had vexed Sir Thomas Browne, as to whether painters err who depict Adam and Eve with navels. Just as God—so runs Gosse's argument—actualized his *idea* of Adam and Eve when they had reached maturity but included in their forms characters from earlier stages of growth through which they had passed only in His mind, so the earth was created at the moment when, though its earlier phases had had only an ideal existence, it had reached that stage in the mind of God which is recorded in the geological evidence. "We might still speak of the inconceivably long duration of the processes in question," Gosse concedes, "provided we understand *ideal* instead of actual time—that the duration was projected in the mind of God and not really existent." [11] Gosse, who hoped to satisfy alike the believers in revelation and in scientific induction, was mortified when, far from ingratiating himself with either party, he was upbraided for picturing God as a manufacturer of false evidence.[12]

While the professional scientists temporized and the pious retreated to *Chambers* one or another untenable position, some of the poets evinced an awareness of the startling new speculations,[13] and a brilliant amateur of science spoke out boldly. In 1844 Robert Chambers (1802-1871) published anonymously *Vestiges of the Natural History of Creation.* The outcries which greeted this book are indicative of the general state of mind.[14] Though some scien-

[11] *Omphalos,* p. 369.

[12] For the entire episode see Edmund Gosse, *Father and Son* (1907), ch. v.

[13] Lionel Stevenson, *Darwin among the Poets* (Chicago, 1932); J. W. Beach, *The Concept of Nature,* chs. xv and xvi. — As an undergraduate at Cambridge Tennyson discerned in the Nebular Hypothesis the implications for geology and biology and advanced the theory that "the development of the human body might possibly be traced from the radiated, vermicular, molluscous, and vertebrate organisms" (*Alfred Lord Tennyson: a Memoir by his Son,* I. 44). *In Memoriam* (1850) has as its groundwork the idea of the steady upward progress of organized life; and in the memorable section cxviii the poet sketches the hypothesis that the earth began "in tracks of fluent heat," implies that man rose from "brutish forms," and expresses the belief that man is "the herald of a higher race." Yet in no poem is there a clear indication that Tennyson believed in transmutation and he certainly did not account for the presence of mind in man as due to natural evolution—as Meredith did later. In later life he held, cautiously, that "evolution in a modified form was partially true" (*Memoir,* II. 167). See W. R. Rutland, "Tennyson and the Theory of Evolution," *E&S,* xxvi (1941). 7-29. On the evolutionary passages in Browning's *Paracelsus* and *Cleon* and on his tentative admission, in *Prince Hohenstiel-Schwangau* (1871), of the theory of the genesis of the human being from lower forms, see J. W. Beach, *op. cit.,* pp. 437-447. The new ending which in 1869 Arnold supplied to *In Utrumque Paratus* (1849 or earlier) presents the view that man has grown out of the "stuff" of inorganic matter. Arnold later deleted this stanza and reverted to the original ending. See C. B. Tinker and H. F. Lowry, *The Poetry of Matthew Arnold: A Commentary* (1940), p. 55. On Beddoes and evolution see above, ch. xiv.

[14] Among various attempted refutations of Chambers—e.g., S. R. Bosanquet, *Vestiges ... the Arguments Examined and Exposed* (1845) and T. M. Mason, *Creation by the Immediate Agency of God, as opposed to Creation by Natural Law* (1845)—the most popular and influential was Hugh Miller's *Footprints of the Creator* (1849). Here much is made of the negative evidence from the discontinuity of organisms between geological periods. Hugh Miller (1802-1856) was an enormously popular and thoroughly devout writer on geology, to which subject he had been drawn from work as a stone-mason. His careful and abundant observations won the respect of Agassiz and other scientists; the charm of his descriptions won the public. His chief books, besides the *Footprints,* are *The Old Red Sandstone* (1841) and *The*

tists were scornful of the *Vestiges* and made much of its errors of detail, Chambers had grasped firmly and stated clearly nearly all the arguments which, after 1859, were adopted by Huxley, one of his severest critics. Darwin and Spencer were more tolerant of the small mistakes for which the force of the general argument afforded ample compensation. Chambers denied that he intended to advance a system "independent or exclusive of Deity." Natural laws are "only the instruments in working out and realizing" "the original Divine conception of all the forms of being." The impulse imparted by God advances all forms of life, from lower to higher and from simpler to more complex. The consequent gap at the bottom of the scale is, Chambers seems to think, filled by continuous spontaneous generation. To the objection that the idea of man's descent from lower animals is degrading Chambers replies that this impression may be due simply to human prejudice and that in any case "it is our part to admire and to submit." [15]

*Spencer*     The *Vestiges* influenced the early thought of Herbert Spencer (1820-1903), who by 1850 had realized that in the absence of any third reasonable hypothesis it was necessary to choose between that of a series of special acts of creation and that of the production of species through the gradual modification of simpler forms.[16] In *The Development Hypothesis* (1852) he opposed the theory of special creation, though he offered no explanation of how development has come about. In *Progress: Its Law and Cause* (1857) he stressed the influence of changes in climate and environment upon life and argued for the development of the heterogeneous from the homogeneous. These books, like the *Vestiges,* are precursors of Darwin's *Origin of Species,* though Spencer's vast attempt to synthesize all knowledge by means of the evolutionary concept did not begin until 1862.[17]

*Charles Darwin*     Charles Darwin [18] (1809-1882), the grandson of Erasmus Darwin, had an early training in biology and geology which led to his appointment as Naturalist on the scientific expedition of the *Beagle* round South America (1831-1836). His observation of the near resemblance, but not identity, between animals of neighboring latitudes and between existing species and fossils of recent date illuminated the theories of Lamarck as discussed in Lyell's *Geology,* which Darwin studied on the voyage. After his return to England, while publishing the scientific results of the expedition,[19] he

---

*Testimony of the Rocks* (posthumous, 1857). — Chambers replied to his critics and amplified, clarified, and corrected his book in *Explanations: a Sequel to "Vestiges of the Natural History of Creation"* (1845). On the reception of *Vestiges* see Amy Cruse, *The Victorians and Their Reading*, pp. 84-90. See also Disraeli's witty satire on "The Revelations of Chaos" (i.e., the *Vestiges*) in *Tancred* (1847), Book II, ch. VIII.

[15] *Vestiges* (ed. New York, 1845), pp. 177-178.

[16] See D. Duncan, *Life and Letters of Herbert Spencer* (1908), II. 317.

[17] See below, ch. XXI.

[18] Francis Darwin, *The Life and Letters of Charles Darwin* (3v, 1887); Geoffrey West, *Charles Darwin, the Fragmentary Man* (1937).

[19] The first edition of Darwin's Diary of the voyage forms Vol. III of the official *Voyages of H. M.'s Ships Adventure and Beagle*, ed. Robert Fitzroy (1839). It was issued separately later in the same year. The definitive edition is *Charles Darwin's Diary of the Voyage of H. M. S. "Beagle,"* ed. Nora Barlow (Cambridge, 1934). The zoology and botany of the expedition were published by Darwin and assistants (8v, 1840-1846).

began an intensive study of artificial selection by breeders of domestic animals. (It needs to be remembered that much of his material was not scientifically controlled, having been derived at second-hand from pigeon-fanciers, stud-breeders, and kennel-men.) By selective breeding the fancier can produce the fan-tail or the pouter. How can nature apply such methods? That was Darwin's problem. In 1838 he read Malthus' *Essay on the Principle of Population* in which it was argued that since the food supply increases by arithmetical progression while the population increases by geometrical progression, starvation must ensue unless the population is kept down by war, vice, disease, and misery. Upon this ground of the struggle for existence Darwin erected the hypothesis that variations (however originating), if favorable to the struggle, would become emphasized; if unfavorable would lead to the extinction of the individual or type retaining them.[20] Darwin's later claim that he worked in strict accord with the Baconian method of induction is not admissible, for he had arrived at his hypothesis long before all his evidence was assembled. His method was really that of inverse deduction. Though he was as careful to note evidence against his theory as for it, there must have been some bias in favor of the hypothesis. His hesitations and modifications show that he was not absolutely satisfied. By 1844 he had advanced far enough to compose a preliminary summary. Another summary followed, and then in 1858 came the dramatic communication from Alfred Russell Wallace [21] (1823-1913) suggesting almost the same hypothesis (with minor technical differences). By a strange coincidence Wallace's hypothesis, like Darwin's, had been suggested to him by a reading of Malthus. He was also influenced by Chambers. Darwin had already confided his theory to Lyell and other friends; there was therefore no possibility of any charge of non-independence. The two men displayed the finest reciprocal magnanimity, and Wallace's essay and Darwin's summary were published together in *The Journal of the Linnean Society,* in June, 1858. *Wallace*

In 1859 appeared the epoch-making volume *On the Origin of Species by Means of Natural Selection, or the Preservation of Favoured Races in the Struggle for Life.* The arguments supporting the fact of evolution were already, as we have seen, assembled; what was lacking was a convincing explanation of the means whereby it was brought about.[22] Darwin denied the Lamarckian principle that there is a "necessary progression" or "prin- *On the Origin of Species*

---

[20] In 1813 W. C. Wells had advanced the theory that species originated by means of natural selection; and in 1831 Patrick Matthew arrived independently at the same opinion. But of their writings Darwin knew nothing till after the publication of his book. He then acknowledged their priority in handsome terms—terms beyond their claims since their views were based on little evidence or research.

[21] Author of *Darwinism: an Exposition of the Theory of Natural Selection* (1889); *Man's Place in the Universe* (1903); *My Life: a Record of Events and Opinions* (1905); and other works. — James Marchant, *Alfred Russell Wallace: Letters and Reminiscences* (1916).

[22] Darwin's case would have been stronger had he known of the experiments conducted by Mendel at this very time. Mendel's report on his researches was not delivered till 1865, but there is no reason why Darwin should not have known of them while they were in progress. Yet even in later editions of the *Origin of Species* no reference to them was introduced.

ciple of improvement" within organisms. His search had been for something natural to supplant the breeder as a selective agent. This he found in the usefulness or harmfulness of the qualities of the organisms themselves. How the original minute variations which are subsequently developed occur he did not attempt to explain, but took them for granted. His emphasis upon "natural selection" was due in part to his inheritance from Paley of the idea that all characters in an organism are useful; actually it is often difficult to find a utilitarian explanation of the differences which mark distinct species. He did not sufficiently perceive that "natural selection" is generally a destructive agency, acting not on the "fit" but on the unfit or less fit. He and his first disciples did not realize how small is the fraction of extinct forms of life ancestral to existing forms; how incomplete is the evidence; how dependent upon chance the investigator is to fill the gaps.[23] The vastness of geological time and the multitude of steps in the process of evolution have become more apparent to his successors than these factors were to him. In later years he somewhat modified his views, and in his final position he recognized a three-fold causation—natural selection, the inheritance of the effects of use and disuse, and the direct action of the environment. Sexual selection, upon which at first he set considerable store, he later minimized. He was silent with regard to the problem of the origin of life, and in 1859 he had little to say about the ancestry of man save by inference in the famous promise that his theory would throw light upon "the origin of man and his history."

The great book did not immediately excite opposition. That the first small edition was exhausted on the day of publication was probably due to the interest of theologians and scientists who were already aware of evolutionary speculation. Many older scientists were reluctant to accept Darwin's conclusions. Agassiz remained a stubborn creationist; Lyell hesitated and temporized; Richard Owen never accepted the Darwinian explanation, though he recognized a progressive or ascending course of evolution. But younger men rallied to Darwin's side. With some reservations [24] Huxley accepted the theory, and, since his master was by temperament ill-suited to controversy, constituted himself, as he said, Darwin's "bull-dog." Quickly mounting clerical hostility reached its climax at the meeting of the British Association at Oxford in 1860 when Huxley made his famous, crushing rejoinder to the sarcastic remarks of Bishop Samuel Wilberforce.[25] But the Broad Church party, expressing itself in *Essays and Reviews,* was, as we

[23] On the extreme imperfection of the paleontological record see A. M. Davies, *Evolution and its Modern Critics,* pp. 105-106.

[24] Huxley's reservations were partly due to his previous acceptance of Cuvier's doctrine of four *embranchements,* corresponding to archetypal "ideas" in the mind of the Creator. Within each of these four groups are variations which are, however, subordinate to conformity in essentials to the archetype. — Huxley never accepted Darwin's theory of pangenesis, put forward in *The Variations of Animals and Plants under Domestication* (1868). This is the theory that every separate unit or cell of an organism reproduces itself by contributing its share to the germ or bud of the future offspring.

[25] The several versions of this famous story are identical in essentials. See Leonard Huxley, *Life and Letters of Thomas Henry Huxley,* I. 196-203.

have seen, willing to face the implications of new truths. In succeeding years the storm rumbled on. Huxley's *Man's Place in Nature* (1863), in which the theory was explicitly applied to "the human animal" (an expression which was now, significantly, becoming current), occasioned a new outcry. But when Darwin published *The Descent of Man* [26] (1871), though Pusey and Gladstone attacked it, there was no general excitement. The public was becoming accustomed to the new ideas, and the Church was retreating to new lines of defense. When Darwin died in 1882 he was buried in Westminster Abbey.

In contrast to Darwin, Thomas Henry Huxley [27] (1825-1895) possessed gifts of style which could popularize science by lucid and readily intelligible presentation, as in the renowned lecture *On a Piece of Chalk*. His discoveries as a scientist lie beyond the horizon of the historian of literature. He did useful work in advancing the cause of popular education, though, as Arnold argued, he laid too much emphasis upon the value of the natural sciences as a discipline at the expense of the older humane curriculum. Unlike Darwin, he was not content with the task of merely assembling facts and drawing inferences from them but regarded this as the preliminary spadework for philosophy. Beyond Darwin's range but characteristic of Huxley is, for example, the profound suggestion, with its social implications, that the organism can adapt itself to environment not by modifying itself but by altering the environment. Endowed as he was with a self-assurance that invited controversy, he attacked orthodox theology harshly,[28] even while evincing sympathy with ethical aspects of Christian doctrine. Though his championship of freedom of thought, unfettered by tradition, dogma, or prejudice, is memorable and honorable, it cannot be held, in the light of the

*T. H. Huxley*

[26] Here Wallace parted company with Darwin, arguing that natural selection could have endowed a savage with a brain only a little superior to that of the ape. To which the thorough-going Darwinian replies that the great difference between ape and man is easier to account for than would be the sudden substitution of a new law for one which operates everywhere else through nature. — In these years the public became aware of the quest for types intermediate between man and the anthropoid apes, and the term "missing link" was on everybody's lips. The fossil evidence was still extremely scanty, consisting of but two anthropoids and two skulls of *Homo neanderthalensis*.

[27] *Collected Essays* (9v, 1893). — Leonard Huxley, *Life and Letters of Thomas Henry Huxley* (2v, 1900); P. C. Mitchell, *Thomas Henry Huxley* (1900); Clarence Ayres, *Huxley* (1932). — Huxley's famous Edinburgh address, *The Physical Basis of Life* (1868), is included in *Lay Sermons* (1870). His little volume on *Hume* (1879), in the *EML Series*, is important for the background of Huxley's "agnosticism" (a word of his invention). The Romanes lecture *Ethics and Evolution* (1893) is based upon his dualistic belief that the cosmic process has no sort of relation to moral ends, man's moral nature being a striving against the stream.

[28] See the controversy with Gladstone on the reliability of the narrative of the creation in Genesis, in the *Nineteenth Century*, November and December, 1885, January and February, 1886; and the satiric attack on Gladstone in "The Keepers of the Herd of Swine," *ibid.*, December, 1890 (reprinted in *Collected Essays*, v). Controversial papers by Huxley, Gladstone, and others are gathered together in *The Order of Creation: The Conflict between Genesis and Geology* (n.d., 1890 ?). In 1888-1889 a lively discussion went on between Huxley and the Rev. Henry Wace, Principal of King's College, London, in the pages of the *Nineteenth Century*. In this Mrs. Humphry Ward and W. G. Magee (the Bishop of Peterborough) took part; and W. H. Mallock intervened in the *Fortnightly Review*. These important papers are assembled in *Christianity and Agnosticism: a Controversy* (1889).

evidence, that his claim to be regarded as the uncompromising disciple of Truth is invulnerable.[29]

Any discussion of the present state of evolutionary theory, requiring as it would a mastery of genetics, embryology, and other disciplines, is beyond our province and the writer's competence; but a few remarks may be offered by way of postscript to this chapter. In contrast to those Victorians who thought that they discerned "one increasing purpose" running through the cosmic process, the modern evolutionist is likely to hold to the view that this apparent purpose is but a product of blind forces. The old common conception that evolution implies "an intrinsic tendency in everything to become something higher"[30] cannot survive the evidence that, while there are dominant types which have acquired a greater and greater independence of environment, there are, equally, other dominant types which have been forced by their very control over environment into lines of specialization from which there is no escape. Moreover, the misconception, when the argument was by an insecure analogy transferred from the biological to the social sphere, has resulted in bitter disappointment. The doctrine of the survival of the fittest had dangerous points of connection with the doctrine of the dominant race, implicit in Carlyle's teaching. Popular thought seized upon natural selection to the exclusion of other factors which Darwin had taken into account. "As applied to human society," says Professor Whitehead, "this theory is a challenge to the whole humanitarian movement.... Instead of dwelling on the brotherhood of man, we are now directed to procure the extermination of the unfit."[31]

[29] See the devastating exposure of Huxley's claim in L. T. More, *The Dogma of Evolution,* pp. 256-267.
[30] F. H. Collins, *An Epitome of the Synthetic Philosophy of Herbert Spencer* (1889), p. 351.
[31] A. N. Whitehead, *Adventures of Ideas* (1933), pp. 44-45.

# XX

## Thomas Carlyle

### I

Born at Ecclefechan in the Scottish Lowlands, Thomas Carlyle [1] (1795-1881) was the eldest child of pious and intelligent peasants. From the Annan Grammar School he proceeded to the University of Edinburgh, where, while making fair progress in the classics, he showed an aptitude for mathematics. In 1814 he began to teach at Annan, and two years later transferred to a school at Kirkcaldy, where he became intimate with Edward Irving, a somewhat older man of brilliant promise, and fell in love with Margaret Gordon, the original of Blumine in *Sartor Resartus*.[2] Hating teaching, he abandoned it at the end of 1818 and returned to Edinburgh. Already he had read widely. Mme de Staël's *De l'Allemagne* had opened to him the treasures of German thought and fixed his romantic conception of German literature. Gibbon, Hume, and Voltaire were leading him into the paths of history. His study of Newtonian physics and eighteenth-century rationalism had undermined his inherited Calvinistic creed. Religious doubts, the mech-

*Youth and Education*

---

[1] *Works*, Centenary Edition, ed. H. D. Traill (30v, 1897-1901); *Reminiscences*, ed. J. A. Froude (1881), ed. C. E. Norton (2v, 1887); *Two Notebooks*, ed. Norton (1898); *Early Letters*, ed. Norton (1887); *Letters, 1826-1836* (2v, 1888); *Correspondence between Goethe and Carlyle*, ed. Norton (1887); *Correspondence of Carlyle and Emerson*, ed. Norton (1886); *Letters to his Youngest Sister*, ed. C. T. Copeland (1899); *New Letters*, ed. Alexander Carlyle (2v, 1904); *Early Letters of Jane Welsh Carlyle, with some of Thomas Carlyle* (1889); *Love Letters of Thomas Carlyle and Jane Welsh*, ed. A. Carlyle (2v, 1909); *Letters to John Stuart Mill, John Sterling, and Robert Browning*, ed. A. Carlyle (1923); *Briefwechsel mit Varnhagen von Ense*, ed. R. Preuss (Berlin, 1892); *Last Words of Thomas Carlyle* (1892); *Letters and Memorials of Jane Welsh Carlyle, Prepared for Publication by Thomas Carlyle*, ed. J. A. Froude (3v, 1883); *New Letters and Memorials of Jane Welsh Carlyle, Annotated by Thomas Carlyle*, ed. A. Carlyle (2v, 1903); *Jane Welsh Carlyle: Letters to Her Family, 1839-1863*, ed. Leonard Huxley (1924). — I. W. Dyer, *Bibliography* (Portland, Maine, 1928). — James Anthony Froude, *Thomas Carlyle: History of the First Forty Years of his Life* (2v, 1882) and *Thomas Carlyle: History of his Life in London* (2v, 1884). On the "Froude Controversy" see David Masson, *Carlyle Personally and in his Writings* (1885); D. A. Wilson, *Froude and Carlyle* (1898) and *The Truth about Carlyle* (1913); J. A. Froude, *My Relations with Carlyle* (posthumous, 1903); J. Crichton-Browne, *Froude and Carlyle* (1903); J. Crichton-Browne and Alexander Carlyle, *The Nemesis of Froude* (1903). The case is reviewed and a verdict rendered generally favorable to Froude in Waldo Dunn, *Froude and Carlyle* (1930). — D. A. Wilson, *Life of Carlyle* (6v, each with individual title; Vol. VI finished by D. W. MacArthur, 1923-1934); R. S. Craig, *The Making of Carlyle* (1908); Louis Cazamian, *Carlyle* (Paris, 1913), English translation by E. K. Brown (1932); Bliss Perry, *Carlyle: How to Know Him* (Indianapolis, 1915); Emery Neff, *Carlyle* (1932); Norwood Young, *Carlyle: His Rise and Fall* (n.d., 1936 ?); W. S. Johnson, *Thomas Carlyle: a Study of his Literary Apprenticeship, 1814-1831* (New Haven, 1911); Osbert Burdett, *The Two Carlyles* (1931); Elizabeth Drew, *Jane Welsh and Jane Carlyle* (1928).

[2] R. C. Archibald, *Carlyle's First Love: Margaret Gordon, Lady Bannerman* (1910). — Blumine has also been identified, less plausibly, with a Miss Kirkpatrick whom Carlyle knew in 1824.

anistic materialism which was the current philosophy, the selfish individualism which passed for ethics, disappointment in love, poverty, and an ailing
stomach (for already he was afflicted with the dyspepsia which was to be
a lifelong complaint) combined with a consciousness of the possession of
powers which had as yet found no outlet and produced misery. He was in
the clutches of "the Everlasting No," the Spirit that denies.

To me the Universe was all void of Life, of Purpose, of Volition, even of Hostility: it was one huge, dead, immeasurable Steam-engine, rolling on, in its dead
indifference, to grind me limb from limb. O, the vast gloomy, solitary Golgotha
and Mill of Death!

But he met the devil of despair and defied him, asserting: "I am not thine,
but Free, and forever hate thee!" Thus, having repudiated the evidence that
no moral order sustains the world, he accepted "the Everlasting Yea," faith
in the Divine Fatherhood and adherence to the gospel of self-renunciation
and duty.[3]

*Jane
Baillie
Welsh*

To this stage Carlyle had progressed by 1821 when he fell in love with
Jane Baillie Welsh, a girl of brilliant intellect and charm, his superior in
social status. She recognized his genius and force of character, and her
admiration soon deepened into love. He had obtained commissions to write
some articles for *The Edinburgh Encyclopaedia* [4] and to translate Legendre's
*Geometry*; and in 1822 he got the tutorship of the two sons of wealthy people
named Buller, in whose company he saw something of the world of fashion
—and despised it. Studies in German literature provided him with literary
material and shaped his philosophy.[5] His biography of Schiller appeared in
*The London Magazine* [6] (1823-1824), and in 1824 he published a translation
of the first part of Goethe's *Wilhelm Meister*. The book trade was flourish-
ing; there was a special demand for works on German culture; and encouraged by the situation and by Goethe's commendation, Carlyle committed
himself to a life of letters.

Visiting London in 1824, he met Coleridge and was probably more impressed with him than he permitted to appear when years later he composed
his famous pen-portrait of the sage of Highgate.[7] Other men of letters
seemed to him of small account; both at the time and in old age he expressed contemptuous pity for Lamb, De Quincey, and Campbell. In a
fortnight's visit to Paris he saw much that remained vividly in memory. In
1825, despite misgivings on both sides, he and Jane Welsh became engaged.

---

[3] *Sartor Resartus*, Book II, chs. VII-IX. — On this "conversion" and related aspects of
Carlyle's life and ideas see C. F. Harrold. "The Mystical Element in Carlyle," *MP*, XXIX (1932).
459-475.
   [4] These articles were first collected in *Montaigne and other Essays*, ed. S. R. Crockett (1897).
   [5] C. F. Harrold, *Carlyle and German Thought* (New Haven, 1934); C. E. Vaughan,
"Carlyle and his German Masters," *E&S*, I (1910). 168-196; Margaret Storrs, *The Relation
of Carlyle to Kant and Fichte* (Bryn Mawr, 1929); Susanna Howe, *Wilhelm Meister and his
English Kinsmen* (1930); J. A. S. Barrett, "Carlyle's Debt to Goethe," *Hibbert Journal*, XXX
(1931). 61-75; F. Kuchler, "Carlyle und Schiller," *Anglia*, XXVI (1903). 1-93, 393-446.
   [6] In book form, enlarged, 1825.
   [7] *The Life of John Sterling* (1851), Book I, ch. VIII.

Carlyle's plan for living at Craigenputtock, her ancestral farm near Dumfries, she rejected, for she dreaded its rude isolation; and having decided upon a house on the outskirts of Edinburgh, they were married in October, *Marriage* 1826. Meanwhile, the financial crash of 1825 had caused the bottom to drop out of the book market and Carlyle's situation was precarious. He was at work upon a philosophic novel, *Wotton Reinfred*,[8] but this was abandoned, for the creative imagination which was soon to mold the facts of history to Carlyle's purposes was impeded by the necessity to invent incident, just as his genius, master of a thousand effects in prose, was fettered when he tried to write in verse.

A meeting with Francis Jeffrey was happily fruitful, for the editor of *The* *First* *Edinburgh Review* was in search of fresh talent and recognized Carlyle's *Essays* promise. He commissioned him to write an article on Jean Paul Richter (1827), the first of the *Miscellaneous and Critical Essays*.[9] This was followed by a more important essay, *The Present State of German Literature*. An attempt to meet Scott came to nothing, for Scott, in the midst of distracting anxieties, did not reply to a letter from Carlyle. This discourtesy, as he thought it, colored Carlyle's later estimate of Sir Walter.[10] Contact with John Wilson was not congenial, though Carlyle attended a session of the Ambrosian Nights. He translated and published four volumes of *German Romances*[11] (1827); but the market was glutted with such things and the work did not sell. At this juncture the launching of *The Foreign Review* provided him with a new medium, and before this periodical stopped in 1830 he had written for it eight essays, including *Goethe's Helena, Goethe, Voltaire,* and the second *Richter*. In the *Edinburgh* appeared the *Burns* (1828) and *Signs of the Times* (1829), the first of the articles on contemporary social problems. Most of these essays were written at Craigenputtock, whither, for economy's sake, the Carlyles had gone in 1828. Loneliness was a hardship to Mrs. Carlyle, who loved society; but the domestic jars of this period, though they existed, are exaggerated in Froude's biography. New commissions were not forthcoming and financial anxieties increased. Jeffrey, who had been forbearance itself, found Carlyle's radicalism increasingly out of harmony with the opinions of the *Edinburgh*; and after his retirement from the editorship his successor, Macvey Napier, employed his irascible contributor but seldom and then upon non-controversial literary topics.

In 1830 Carlyle began a history of German literature (which survives, however, only in fragments sold to periodicals), formed a friendship with John Stuart Mill which opened to him the pages of *The Westminster Re-*

---

[8] First published in *Last Words of Thomas Carlyle* (1892). *Wotton Reinfred* underlies the biographical portion of *Sartor Resartus*.
[9] This general title was first used by Carlyle in the collected edition of 1839.
[10] H. J. C. Grierson, "Scott and Carlyle," *E&S*, XIII (1928). 88-111.
[11] In selecting these romances Carlyle sought the advice of Henry Crabb Robinson. To placate the popular taste he translated folk-tales by Musäus and Tieck, a fantasy by Hoffmann, and Fouqué's *Aslauga's Knight;* but he went on to Richter (very difficult to translate and hitherto accessible in English only in fragments) and to the second part of *Wilhelm Meister*.

*view*, and established contact with the newly founded *Fraser's Magazine*. In October he noted in his diary: "Written a strange piece 'On Clothes.' Know not what will come of it." What came of it was *Sartor Resartus*, for when the "strange piece" was rejected by London editors, Carlyle, instead of setting it aside, enlarged it into a book. This was rejected by Murray and Longman and at length appeared serially in *Fraser's* (1833-1834). Meanwhile the magnificent essay, *Characteristics*, designed to prepare the public for the vagaries of style and strangeness of thought in *Sartor*, came out in the *Edinburgh* (1831). Goethe's death in 1832 was the occasion for the solemnly elegiac *Death of Goethe* and the *Goethe's Works*. In the latter, as in the *Johnson* (also 1832), Carlyle's concern is not for the "work" but for the author's personality as revealed in the work. Carlyle's drift towards revolutionary France as the theme of a book, already apparent in the *Voltaire*, became more marked in the *Diderot* (1833). He was confirmed in his choice of subject when Mill, abandoning a similar design, turned over his materials to him. He had formed his conviction that history is a revelation of the "Divine Idea" and had determined the manner in which his should be composed. A first experiment in the "poetico-historical" kind was the article on Count Cagliostro (1833), the "arch-quack" whose career, as Carlyle viewed it, was symptomatic of the rottenness of the *ancien régime*. A companion-piece, *The Diamond Necklace*, did not reach publication till 1837.

In 1834 the Carlyles moved to London and settled permanently in Cheyne Row, Chelsea. For the next three years he published nothing save an obituary article on Irving. The labor upon his history was increased when the manuscript of the first volume, entrusted to Mill, was accidently destroyed by fire. At length financial need forced him to raise money by an article on Mirabeau (1837). *The Diamond Necklace* was also published. By the time when the great work was completed Carlyle was in distress for want of funds, and friends arranged for a series of lectures on German Literature, a subject on which he could discourse with little or no fresh preparation.[12] Immediately afterwards *The French Revolution: A History* was published,[13] and Carlyle's position in the top rank of living writers was secure.

## II

*Lectures*

For a while he rested, lying fallow. The only noteworthy essay of 1838 is the *Sir Walter Scott*, which distressed the admirers of the critic and his subject alike. A course of lectures on the history of literature was carefully prepared and enthusiastically received.[14] A third series, on the revolutions

---

[12] No report of this course is extant.
[13] Ed. C. R. L. Fletcher (3v, 1902); ed. J. Holland Rose (2v, 1909).
[14] Leigh Hunt reported this course in somewhat disputatious vein in *The Examiner*. The reporter for *The Times*, almost certainly Thackeray, was very eulogistic. T. C. Anstey, an admirer of Carlyle, took stenographic notes which he afterwards amplified from a "lecture-book" borrowed from Mrs. Carlyle. This amalgam was eventually published as *Lectures on the History of Literature*, ed. J. R. Greene (1892).

*(Margin notes:)* Sartor Resartus · Revolutionary France · Lectures

of modern Europe, was given in 1839; [15] and in 1840 a fourth and final series, the famous lectures *On Heroes, Hero-Worship, and the Heroic in History*.[16] A misunderstanding broke off work on an essay on Cromwell which Mill had suggested for the *Westminster*; but the labor was not wasted as this was the start of his second great historical work. Carlyle was now reaching an ever widening audience. Through Emerson came an invitation to visit America, which was declined. In 1839 the sales of the collected edition of the miscellaneous essays, of the first English edition of *Sartor,* of the second edition of *The French Revolution,* and of *Chartism* [17] brought in sufficient funds to enable Carlyle to devote himself to research. His original intention to write the history of the Puritan revolution was narrowed to a collection of Cromwell's letters and speeches with interspersed narrative, character-portraits, and comment. This rehabilitation of the Puritan "hero" was his principal work during the next four years. In 1843 he turned aside to write *Past and Present*,[18] a remarkable exercise of the historical imagina- Past and tion in which twelfth-century leadership in the person of Abbot Samson [19] Present is contrasted with the chaos of modern individualism. An article (1844) on Dr. Francia, the dictator of Paraguay, was the first alarming indication of the extreme to which he was later to push his doctrine of leadership. *Oliver Cromwell's Letters and Speeches. With Elucidations* appeared in 1845.[20] Cromwell

For several years Carlyle remained comparatively idle, much sought after in society. In his gruff fashion he enjoyed this lionizing; but it was a sad time for Mrs. Carlyle, who was jealous of the attentions lavished on her husband by the wealthy Lady Harriet Baring (later Lady Ashburton). Froude made too much of the resultant partial estrangement, but some later biographers have made too little. The neglect of his wife was the chief cause of Carlyle's poignant remorse after her death.

Impressions of Ireland, gained hurriedly in 1846, brought home to him vividly the Irish troubles of 1847-1848. He talked about writing a book on the subject, but the intention was never fulfilled. Watching Continental *Anti-* events during the Year of Revolutions, he predicted that the French Re- *democratic* public could not endure, and though ties of friendship bound him to Maz- *Views* zini he was convinced that that leader's triumph in Rome was but temporary. The failure of the European revolutionists and the second Chartist fiasco in London confirmed him in his negation of the democratic principle. His

---

[15] Very few notes on this course survive; Hunt's reports were meager and irregular.

[16] Published, with emendations and additions, in 1841.

[17] Lockhart had regretfully rejected *Chartism* as too extreme in its opinions for *The Quarterly Review*, and it was consequently published as a book.

[18] Ed. Oliphant Smeaton (1902).

[19] To the subject Carlyle was attracted by Jocelin of Brakelond's *Chronicle* of the reforms of Abbot Samson in the monastery of St. Edmundsbury, which had just been published by the Camden Society (1840).

[20] Ed. Mrs. S. C. Lomas (3v, 1904). — Among additions to the second edition of the *Cromwell* (1846) were the so-called "Squire forgeries" whose acceptance by Carlyle as authentic has occasioned ironic comment upon the ease with which the arch-foe of sham was taken in by documents obviously spurious. See C. H. Firth's introduction to *Cromwell,* ed. Lomas, I. xlii-xiv; and the less judicious consideration of the subject in Norwood Young, *Carlyle: His Rise and Fall,* pp. 214-224.

first violently anti-democratic pamphlet was *The Nigger Question* (1849), to which Mill replied vigorously, thus terminating a friendship which had hitherto stood the strain of opposed opinions.[21] During 1850 the vituperative and declamatory *Latter-Day Pamphlets* were issued in eight monthly parts. The extreme violence with which Carlyle's views on modern society were here displayed roused the opposition of every supporter of laissez faire, alienated the doubtful, and bewildered many of Carlyle's disciples; and in consequence his reputation suffered an abrupt decline. To recover serenity and to pay personal homage to a dead friend he wrote the quietly beautiful *Life of John Sterling* (1851).

Frederick
the Great

He considered and rejected the career of the Cid as the subject of a book. The mists of distance and the incrustations of legend round the Spanish hero would have presented great difficulties; yet the theme might have been a happier choice than that actually selected—the career of Frederick the Great.[22] He plunged into thirteen years of research, not without ceaseless lamentations on the stupidity of "Dryasdust" and the hardness of his own lot. The toil was interrupted by two visits to Germany (1852 and 1858) to survey Frederick's battlefields.[23] The moral problem whether the evidence really supported his interpretation of Frederick's character troubled him; but he suppressed these scruples and persevered. The huge work appeared in three installments, the last in 1865.[24] Now at the summit of his fame, Carlyle was elected rector of the University of Edinburgh and was received with great acclaim when he delivered his inaugural address in April, 1866.

Death
of Mrs.
Carlyle

Immediately afterwards came the news of his wife's sudden death; and he passed into his grief-stricken and desolate old age.

He arranged and annotated the *Letters and Memorials* of his wife.[25] In 1867 he published *Shooting Niagara: and After?* in protest against the second Reform Bill. His championship of Governor Eyre, brought to trial for the cruelty with which he had suppressed an uprising of the Negroes in Jamaica, is another indication of the extreme to which the doctrine of leadership had now advanced. In 1871, in a letter to the *Times,* he defended Prussia's annexation of Alsace-Lorraine and contrasted "noble, patient, deep, pious, and solid Germany" with "vapouring, vainglorious, gesticulating, quarrelsome, restless, and over-sensitive France."[26] Once more, in 1876, he intervened in public affairs, warning his countrymen of the danger that

[21] Emery Neff, *Carlyle and Mill, Mystic and Utilitarian* (1924).

[22] On earlier and contemporary English interest in this subject see Hans Marcus, *Friedrich der Grosse in der englischen Literatur* (Leipzig, 1930).

[23] See Carlyle's diary, *Journey to Germany: Autumn 1858,* ed. R. A. E. Brooks (New Haven, 1940).

[24] Abridgement by E. Sanderson (1909); *The Battles of Frederick the Great, abstracted from Carlyle's Biography,* ed. C. Ransome (1892).

[25] Carlyle turned these papers over to Froude with the injunction that they be not published without editorial excisions. In 1883 Froude published them with no deletions, and when the storm of controversy burst round him pleaded that Carlyle had rescinded verbally his previous directions.

[26] The *Times* refuted editorially Carlyle's arguments and rejected his conclusions. — As much for his services in 1871 as for his tribute to Prussia in *Frederick the Great* Bismarck bestowed on Carlyle the Order of Merit.

Disraeli might involve them on the side of Turkey against Russia in the Eastern Crisis.[27] In so doing he was consistent, for in 1854, despising Napoleon III and favoring the Russian method of despotic rule, he had opposed the Crimean War.

After losing the use of his right hand he resorted to dictation, but the only *Last* results were the two essays, *Norse Kings* and *Portraits of John Knox* (both *Years* 1875). In his increasing feebleness devoted disciples—Froude, Ruskin, Huxley, Tyndall, and others—ministered to him, harkening to the prophecies of woe to fall upon a world which, heedless of his warnings, was moving towards catastrophe. The death of his brother John (1878) severed almost the last link with the far past. He lingered three years longer, dying in February, 1881. Burial was offered in Westminster Abbey, but by his directions his body was committed to the ground at Ecclefechan.

## III

In temperament, manner, and intensity of conviction Carlyle was more closely akin to the Hebrew prophets than to any counselor of the people of his own day. His concern was to rescue society from materialism, greed, irresponsibility, uncontrolled competition, and industrial chaos. The value of history, in his estimate, lay in the lessons of the past which are applicable to the present; and he believed that a right interpretation of the contemporary situation would throw a beam of light into the darkness of the future. Thus he combined the functions of the historian, social reformer, and *Transcen-* prophet; and he based them upon a transcendental metaphysic. Dissatisfied, *dentalism* like his fellow romanticists, with the science of Newton, the epistemology of Locke, the skepticism of Hume, and the ethics of the Utilitarians, he turned to his own intuitions, finding sustenance for them in German romantic philosophy. From his superficial knowledge of Kant he derived the distinction between the Reason and the Understanding and the concept of the ideality of Space and Time. His debt to Fichte was far greater—to Fichte's popular expositions of his philosophy rather than to his earlier, more technical writings. Fichte taught Carlyle to respect the outward world and scientific law as revelations of Divine power and idea. From him, rather than from a mere phrase in Hume, came the doctrine of heroes and hero-worship. Fichte's teaching that in the struggle between the Self and the Non-Self each individual must by means of justice, love, and sympathetic understanding spiritualize the world of matter was translated into the practical terms of aiding the work of scientific progress and social amelioration. These ideas came to Carlyle largely through the imaginative interpretations of Novalis and especially Goethe. In Goethe to a greater degree than in any other modern man Carlyle discerned the inward experiences which gave meaning

---

[27] This second letter to the *Times* prompted Swinburne's eloquent and bitter attack on Carlyle and the pro-Russian party: *Notes of an English Republican on the Muscovite Crusade* (1876).

to life. He recognized Goethe's tolerance (though he himself rarely imitated it) and the submission to the inevitable upon which that tolerance was founded. He imagined that Goethe taught a philosophy of self-renunciation. Actually Goethe's ideal was to subordinate the "lower" elements in human nature in order to gain a harmonious development of the whole, a line of thought to which Carlyle gave a puritanically ascetic twist which owes more to Geneva than to Weimar.

*Sartor Resartus* [28] is the most eloquent and elaborate statement of Carlyle's transcendental philosophy. There was nothing that was novel in its essence, for the illusioned romanticists should have accustomed readers to the ideas set forth in the "Clothes Philosophy"—that Language is the clothing of Thought, the Body the vestment of the Soul, the entire Universe the "living Garment of God" woven upon the roaring loom of Time. Moreover, Carlyle had prepared the way for *Sartor* in earlier writings in which he adumbrated his concepts of "the greatness of great men" and of the Divine Idea underlying the world of phenomena. But the fantastic style in which these ideas were conveyed—the Germanic locutions, the vast range of allusions, the bold colloquialisms, the rhetorical flights, the proximity of the ridiculous and the sublime, and the heterogeneous mixture of autobiography, romance, satire, ethics, metaphysics, and humor—bewildered the English public.

"*Hero-Worship*"   Elements from many sources had sunk into Carlyle's memory to come forth fused by his fiery imagination into the doctrine of "hero-worship." [29] The Hebraic concept of the divinely appointed Messiah, the Platonic concept of the philosopher-king, and the Plutarchian concept of the law-giver were combined with eighteenth-century speculations upon genius and with the romanticists' idea of the "great man." [30] In Fichte Carlyle thought he discovered a philosophic support for the idea. Liberty is the reign of law; compulsion must be applied to rebellious individuals for whom is secured thereby their only true freedom, which is found in the fostering, not thwarting, of the general will. Within each soul burns, more brightly or more dimly, an awareness of the Divine Idea of the World. The hero is distinguished from the common throng by his possession of this consciousness to an extraordinary degree. His shape is Protean; he may be a man of action or of thought—god, prophet, priest, poet, king, man of letters (or other manifestation, for Carlyle's categories in *Heroes and Hero-Worship* are limited only by the number of his lectures). The leader's shape is conditioned by the exigencies of the time in which he appears. There are ages in which

[28] Ed. Archibald MacMechan (Boston, 1896); ed. P. C. Parr (1913).
[29] B. H. Lehman, *Carlyle's Theory of the Hero: Its Sources, Development, History, and Influence on Carlyle's Work* (Durham, N. C., 1928). — *On Heroes and Hero-Worship*, ed. A. MacMechan (Boston, 1901); ed. P. C. Parr (1910).
[30] Wordsworth turns often to the idea of the leader. See, for instance, *The Prelude*, xiv, 112: "Such minds are truly from the Deity," and the sonnet "Great men have been among us." Coleridge's view of the statesman as a "Coadjutor with God" is set forth in *The Friend*, *The Statesman's Manual*, and elsewhere. Shelley shows the Liberator failing in *The Revolt of Islam* but triumphant in *Prometheus Unbound*. Compare also Keats's sonnet "Great spirits now on earth are sojourning." Lehman detects something of the idea even in the Byronic rebel; but this is doubtful.

no hero comes forth; but when he does so he responds to the needs of his time. He has the right and the duty to compel mankind, representing the *Staatslehre* in which is the compulsive power ordained by God. Carlyle was not unmindful of the problem, noted by Mill in his review of *The French Revolution,* of the means by which the hero is to be discovered. Burke had held that men instinctively subordinate themselves to declared authority; but Carlyle found an answer to Mill's question in the Goethean doctrine of "reverence," the faculty natural to men of recognizing and becoming obedient to the heaven-sent leader. With Emerson's later effort, in *Representative Men,* to reconcile the idea of leadership with the democratic principle of free choice Carlyle had no sympathy. His anti-democratic social radicalism was a reversion to the feudal concept of obedience to the lord who in return vouchsafes protection to his followers. How ominous an anticipation it was of the modern *Führerprinzip* is obvious.[31]

The development of this doctrine may be traced through Carlyle's literary *Criticism* essays.[32] He conceived the critic's function to be the interpretation of the poet's revelation of the Divine Idea.[33] The poet—and within this term Carlyle includes the historian, the man of letters, the philosopher—puts this revelation into a form apprehensible by the senses. More than this, the poet is himself, as is every man to a greater or less degree, a revelation. Thus Carlyle shifts the emphasis from the work of art to the man who made the work. From the first his approach was biographical. "What manner of man was this?" is his question. The *Burns* (1828) attempts to answer it rather than to solve any problem in literary history. The *Johnson* (1832), written during the agitation for reform, takes Boswell's *Life* as a text for a sermon on hero-worship and an excuse for a tract for the times. *Goethe's Works* (1832) tells us little about the "works" and rhapsodizes on Goethe. In the *Scott* (1838) Carlyle touched lightly upon the novels and passed upon the man a judgment which scandalized contemporaries but is now seen to be almost uncannily shrewd. The same increasing emphasis upon biography is seen in the essays on French subjects as we pass from the *Voltaire* through the *Diderot* to the *Mirabeau.* These, like *Cagliostro* and *The Diamond Necklace,* prepare the way for *The French Revolution.*

Eighteenth-century rationalism, in line with the Cartesian principle of *History* immutable natural laws, held that history must reveal the uniformity and regularity of recurring phenomena. As a historian [34] Carlyle opposed this rationalistic historiography, finding for this opposition support in various elements of romantic thought and practice. Burke had regarded history as a reservoir of the accumulated wisdom of the past. Coleridge affirmed that the philosopher must reinterpret to each generation the Idea underlying

[31] Sir H. J. C. Grierson, *Carlyle and Hitler* (1930).
[32] F. W. Roe, *Thomas Carlyle as a Critic of Literature* (1910).
[33] K. E. Gilbert and Helmut Kuhn, *A History of Esthetics* (1939), pp. 407-409.
[34] Louise M. Young, *Thomas Carlyle and the Art of History* (Philadelphia, 1939), to which the discussion which follows is much indebted. See also G. P. Gooch, *History and Historians in the Nineteenth Century* (1913), pp. 323-332; René Wellek, "Carlyle and the Philosophy of History," *PQ*, XXIII (1944). 55-76.

human institutions. Scott supplied an example of the blend of a wide observation of the manners of the present with an imaginative apprehension of the life of the past. Herder and other German romanticists, rejecting the notion of universally valid "laws," showed Carlyle how the destiny of every nation is conditioned by its "Folk-Spirit" and taught him the importance of the irrational and individualistic elements in history. Schiller helped to form his concept of the historian as the artist who selects those facts which are related to the present constitution of society and molds them into form.

The Divine Idea is revealed in man, in institutions, and in universal history. History is the indubitable proof of a purposeful Deity shaping the destiny of man. The loftiest visible emblem of the Idea is poetry; and of poetry history is the highest order. Thus religion, poetry, and history are fused.[35] Carlyle repudiates the theory of the contractual basis of society. Institutional and social origins lie deep in the primal chaos, the unconscious having been informed with the law of order and righteousness. Carlyle adheres to the evolutionary concept of a slow, upward-moving spiral, as opposed to the Platonic concept of recurring historic cycles; but he is more interested in the process of progress than in its goal. There is a periodicity or rhythm; successive ages are critical or creative, characterized by faith or skepticism. From the mutability which is a primary quality of the social organism comes Carlyle's concentration upon periods of revolution in which the process of change is speeded up. Not that he considered revolution the inevitable mode of change; on the contrary, he held that institutions and states grow more steadily when they grow calmly. Upheavals are the penalty for stagnant disobedience to the laws of normal development. Revolution to be justified must spring from the profound instinctual level of a people's consciousness. The mandate to revolt against outworn institutions is communicated to society through the hero. Carlyle's interest in what he called "the Revolution Prodigy" accounts for the limitations which he imposed upon his treatment of the French Revolution, his concern being neither for causes nor for aftermath but for the phenomenon in itself. In similar fashion he concentrated upon Cromwell as the embodiment of the Puritan Revolution, which collapsed after the leader's death. The achievements of Frederick were revolutionary because in his age Prussia emerged from the dominance of decadent France and the anachronistic Holy Roman Empire.

Carlyle's perennial interest was in Man, in the motives which underlie human behavior. History, in his famous phrase, "is the essence of innumerable biographies"; and through it we may hope to gain "some acquaintance with our fellow creatures, though dead and vanished." [36] The artist's effort is to identify himself with his subject, to "blow his living breath between dead lips," to abolish by his own life the death in things. Carlyle therefore

[35] Hill Shine, *Carlyle's Fusion of Poetry, History and Religion by 1834* (Chapel Hill, 1938) and *Carlyle and the Saint-Simonians: The Concept of Historical Periodicity* (Baltimore, 1941).
[36] *On History* (1830); *Works,* Centenary Edition, xxvii. 86. See Godfrey Davies, "Biography and History," *MLQ,* 1 (1940). 79-94.

distinguishes between the archivist—the "simple husbandman" who labors mechanically and for whom, as "Dryasdust" or "Smelfungus," he expressed an unwarranted contempt—and the artist-historian who has the right to exercise judgment in his choice of emphasis and whose duty it is to select and condense, since under the pressure of contractions and epitomes untruths and trivialities disappear.[37] "The two pinions on which History soars," he wrote, "are stern Accuracy in inquiring, bold Imagination in expounding and filling-up." [38] His method (which entailed greater risks of error than "Dryasdust" was ready to run) was to depend not upon notes but on the upsurging stores of memory. His plastic imagination molded into artistic form the visual and the concrete, presenting with unequaled vividness the appearances of people, their clothes and complexions and mannerisms, and the sounds of individual voices and of the uproar of the mob or the hurly-burly of battle. When engaged upon the last volume of *The French Revolution* he wrote to his wife:

It all stands pretty fair in my head, nor do I mean to investigate much more about it, but to splash down what I know in large masses of colours, that it may look like a smoke-and-flame conflagration in the distance, which it is.[39]

Critics have done him wrong who have taken this to mean that he had not "investigated" thoroughly. To the materials assembled by laborious research he applied his power of revivifying the past, of probing into motive, and of sociological analysis.

The unanswerable charge against Carlyle is that he made history serve the ends of his transcendental philosophy. The spectral effects of his great dioramas are achieved with superb literary art; but as history they are not trustworthy. For the validity of the doctrine that history is a revelation of the Divine Idea he can offer his vehemently affirmed convictions but not an atom of proof. Was he not a victim of romantic illusionism? And even as an artist his technique is uncertain and fumbling. The story of Abbot Samson in *Past and Present* is told not only forcefully but with exquisite clarity; but in the sequel the presentation of the contemporary situation as a chaos is as much due to Carlyle's confused vision as to the confusions of modern life. He abandoned the plan to tell the story of the Puritan Revolution because he could not mold it into shape. The *Frederick*, with its dull reversion to the far past and its alternately narrowing and expanding perspectives, is badly designed, admirable in scattered passages of narrative and analysis, unreadable as a whole.[40] As a work of art *The French Revolution*,

[37] *On History Again* (1833); *Works*, xxviii. 172.
[38] *Count Cagliostro* (1833); *Works*, xxviii. 259-260. Carlyle attributes the aphorism to his imaginary friend "Sauerteig" and admits that in the particular case of Cagliostro he is committing himself in the main to the "pinion" of Imagination.
[39] J. A. Froude, *Thomas Carlyle: Life in London*, i. 65.
[40] The charges of inaccuracy brought against the magnificent narratives of Frederick's battles (see, e.g., Norwood Young, *Carlyle: His Rise and Fall*, p. 291) have been convincingly disproved by R. A. E. Brooks in his edition of Carlyle's *Journey to Germany*, appendices I-XII. More serious is the evidence that Carlyle was deliberately reticent when, as his investigations progressed, he realized that his original conception of Frederick's character was a mistaken one.

The
French
Revolution

with its beautiful trifold structure—the destruction of the old; the purging by terror; the beginnings of the new—stands alone among his historical writings. To echo a judgment which has been delivered of Gibbon's *History* —it has been superseded but has not been surpassed. He studied the Revolution as a sociological phenomenon and thus earned the disapproval of the "scientific" historians who were more intent to note his errors and omissions than to comprehend his intentions. The lack of any thorough treatment of constitutional and economic problems, of events in the provinces, and of foreign relations and wars is due to the concentration upon his chosen aspect. The episodic treatment came naturally from Carlyle's epic imagination, but it is also due to the limitations of the source-material at his command.[41] There are no more preconceptions than in other narratives of the Revolution written before the criterion of dispassionate objectivity was established by historians of a later school. In this respect Carlyle's book, with its emphasis upon retributive justice, is no more biased than Michelet's interpretation of the Revolution as the "birth-throes" of democracy, or Guizot's prejudice in favor of the English form of government, or the socialism of Louis Blanc, or the narrow constitutionalism of Thiers, or the anti-French position of Sybel and Treitschke.

Carlyle's reputation as a historian did not pass unchallenged in his own day and suffered a decline after his death. The influence of Henry Thomas Buckle's *History of Civilization* (1857) was adverse, for Buckle reduced the process of history to laws based upon man's physical environment. The historical materialism of Karl Marx, with its emphasis upon economic forces, was opposed to Carlyle's transcendentalism. The critical methodology of the "scientific" school, represented by William Stubbs, E. A. Freeman, and J. R. Green, relied upon archivistic research with a corresponding distrust of the recreative imagination.

The lessons of history Carlyle sought to apply to the problems of his own day. He taught, and would fain have believed, that the world was God's; but beneath his loudly proclaimed trust there were gloomy doubts. The *Ewige Nein* was never completely exorcised. While blind to the signs of progress in his own day, he was ruthless in his exposure of the shortcomings of modern society—the widening gap between rich and poor; the callous indifference of the "ruling classes"; the failure of the promises held out by the advocates of parliamentary reform; the bewildered gropings of the Demos. But he offered no counsel of value for the reconstruction of a democratic society. He had no trust in collective humanity or in the organic unity

---

[41] Of about 1700 paragraphs in *The French Revolution* about 1200 are narrative and descriptive, the rest Carlyle's reflections. An examination of Carlyle's sources (some 83) confirms his general soundness and good faith. Concrete detail is sometimes exaggerated and there are a very few violations of chronological order. See C. F. Harrold, "Carlyle's General Method in *The French Revolution*," PMLA, XLIII (1928). 1150-1169. The great French authority, Aulard, has testified that Carlyle used nearly everything available at the time he wrote, and, moreover, used it with discriminating judgment. Contrast the extremely unfavorable verdict passed upon Carlyle by Lord Acton, *Letters to Mary Gladstone,* ed. Herbert Paul (1904), pp. 170-171, and *Lectures on the French Revolution* (1910), pp. 358-359.

of the race. The one popular right, he held, is to be well governed. He is nearer to Gobineau, with his theory of the dominant race, than to Marx, with his theory of the class-conflict; and nearest to Nietzsche, with his division of humanity into Supermen and Helots. His views he expounded with somber vehemence and in later life with violent extravagance. To their exposition he brought all the resources of his genius as a writer: pathos and gloom; humor, ridicule, and sarcasm; an intense earnestness; and a style completely individualized.[42] After Carlyle's death George Meredith wrote of him:

He was the greatest of the Britons of his time—and after the British fashion of not coming near perfection; Titanic, not Olympian; a heaver of rocks, not a shaper.[43]

[42] The range of Carlyle's style is best displayed in *Sartor*. Verbal coinages, elaborate metaphors, apostrophes; rhetorical questions, compounds of various kinds, and the use of nicknames are among its chief characteristics. The style seems to owe something to Richter but more came from Carlyle's native Annandale than from any literary model. It is constantly suggestive of spoken—or shouted—words; and there is testimony that Carlyle talked almost as he wrote.

[43] George Meredith, *Letters*, II. 333.

# XXI

## Philosophy, History, and Miscellaneous Prose

### I

It is difficult to determine the boundary beyond which the historian of literature need not, or may not, pass into the various fields of specialized and technical writing. The choice, which to some extent must be arbitrary, should be based in part upon a writer's greatness of stature but chiefly upon the qualities of style and breadth of popular appeal which entitle him to a place in the history of literature as well as of thought. When marginal cases are discarded,[1] there remain among English philosophers Mill and Spencer.

*Mill*　　John Stuart Mill[2] (1806-1873), the last great figure in the history of British empiricism, was like most English thinkers no recluse but rather a man active in the world of affairs—editor of *The Westminister Review,* an official at India House, a worker for practical reform, and in his later years a member of Parliament. The remorselessly rigorous education to which, in accordance with Benthamite principles, he was subjected by his father would have turned into a hopeless prig the boy who at the age of fifteen had formed a little society of "Utilitarians" had not his character contained hidden elements of greatness. At the age of twenty he passed through a "spiritual crisis" from which he emerged with an awareness of reaches of experience beyond the comprehension of the strict Benthamites. Though, like all members of the philosophical sect in which he was reared, he would continue to "calculate," henceforth the influence of poetry and the fine arts was to enter into Mill's calculations. The poetry of Wordsworth and the speculations of Coleridge helped to shape his new ideas. The struggle in his mind was between the old "enlightenment" and the new "romanticism," or, as he displayed it antithetically in two great essays published

---

[1] Among the philosophers more or less reluctantly set aside are Sir William Hamilton, James Mill, Alexander Bain, James Martineau, and J. F. Ferrier.

[2] *Autobiography* (1873), ed. J. J. Coss (1924); ed. H. J. Laski (1944); *Principles of Political Economy,* ed. W. J. Ashley (1909); *On Liberty; Representative Government; On the Subjection of Women,* ed. M. C. Fawcett (World's Classics, 1912); *Letters,* ed H. S. R. Elliot (2v, 1910). — W. L. Courtney, *Life of John Stuart Mill* (1889); Leslie Stephen, *The English Utilitarians* (3v, 1900), III; H. K. Garnier, *John Stuart Mill and the Philosophy of Mediation* (1919); Emery Neff, *Carlyle and Mill* (1924); C. L. Street, *Individualism and Individuality in the Philosophy of John Stuart Mill* (Philadelphia, 1926); A. W. Levi, *A Study in the Social Philosophy of John Stuart Mill* (Chicago, 1940); James Seth, *English Philosophers and Schools of Philosophy* (1912), pp. 246-278; Rudolf Metz, *A Hundred Years of British Philosophy* (1938), pp. 62-74; J. S. Schapiro, "John Stuart Mill, Pioneer of Democratic Liberalism in England," *JHI,* IV (1943). 127-160.

in *The Westminster Review,* between Bentham (1838) and Coleridge (1840). The opposition was essentially this, that "Coleridge's doctrine is ontological, conservative, religious, concrete, historical, and poetic, while Bentham's is experimental, innovative, infidel, abstract, matter-of-fact, and essentially prosaic." [3] Mill made the attempt to master the premises and combine the methods of these two thinkers. Later there was a reaction in the direction of Bentham; but Mill's ethics, as set forth in *Utilitarianism* (1863), differed from the system which he had learned from his father and his father's master, in that by distinguishing between the qualities of various pleasures he introduced a criterion above that of ethical hedonism. Mill's *System of Logic* (1843) followed Whately in reviving interest in a subject which had been long neglected in England. Denying intuitive knowledge, he studied the inductive process, dealt with the problem of causation, and theorized on the formation of scientific concepts and the conduct of exact inquiry by means of induction, ratiocination, and verification. But the *Logic,* like the *Principles of Political Economy* (1848), in which he followed Adam Smith and simplified David Ricardo, scarcely belongs, by any stretching of the terms of definition, to literature. Long used as standard textbooks, both these works have now been superseded.

Mill's lasting fame rests, so far as the general reader is concerned, upon the three long essays or short books, *On Liberty* (1859), *Considerations on Representative Government* (1861), and *On the Subjection of Women* (1869). The ringing assertions that "genius can only breathe freely in an atmosphere of freedom," that to silence the expression of opinion is to rob the human race, that "the despotism of custom is everywhere the standing hindrance of human advancement," and that "society has now fairly got the better of individuality; and the danger which threatens human nature is not the excess but the deficiency of personal impulses and preferences" serve to show why *On Liberty* is regarded as one of the finest expressions of nineteenth-century liberalism. Like Herbert Spencer, Mill insisted that "the individual is not accountable to society for his actions, in so far as these concern the interests of no person but himself." He deplored the world's loss in promising intellects combined with timid characters who refrain from following out a train of thought for fear lest "it land them into something considered irreligious or immoral." In *Representative Government* he demonstrated the superiority of free institutions to even the best of despotisms, discussed the provision of checks upon the power of government, and argued for a system of proportional representation. In his third treatise he showed that the principles of liberty and representation were as applicable to women as to men, and he provided what was one of the greatest impelling forces of the movement for the political emancipation of women.

The posthumous publication of *Three Essays on Religion* (1874) came as a surprise to those who had regarded Mill as a "saint of rationalism." In them he went beyond his basis in empiricism to a discussion of transcen-

On Liberty

---

[3] Thus condensed by Metz, *op. cit.,* p. 65.

dental problems. They show how much there was latent in him which did not find a place in his inherited system. In harmony with the moral and religious experience of mankind he found the idea of a morally perfect God whose power is not infinite and who, needing the active coöperation of man in the struggle against the negative world-principle, leads the cosmic process upward.[4]

## II

*Spencer*

Today the dust lies thick upon the work and reputation of Herbert Spencer.[5] The *Synthetic Philosophy* was so exact an expression of Victorian liberalism that with the passing of the age which produced it, it, too, has become discredited. The pioneering originality of a great mind has been obscured by the fact that many of the theories which were fructifying in their originality sixty or seventy years ago have been absorbed into the general body of ideas, while many of the other theories which were poured forth so lavishly have been falsified by events. Science in an age of specialization was from the first suspicious of one who took all knowledge as his province and who had the super-Baconian energy not only to envisage a new Organon but to design and construct it in almost all its parts. The trend towards socialism and state-control was hostile to the fundamental Spencerian argument for the free development of the individual, and the mounting armaments of the age into which the philosopher unhappily lived seemed a mockery of his devotion to the cause of peace. Spencer himself recognized the eternal "flux"—devolution following evolution and evolution devolution—but it is unlikely that with another turn of the cosmic wheel his ideas will reappear.

In youth as throughout his life Herbert Spencer (1820-1903) was not amenable to intellectual discipline save in so far as it was self-imposed. There were as great gaps in his education as in what he afterwards claimed to be his philosophic synthesis. Intellectually, as in his celibate life, he was very largely independent. This tended to make him arrogant and censorious, but it provided him with the immense self-confidence and the will to persevere which in spite of poverty and ill health enabled him, through thirty-six years (1860-1896) of arduous work, to carry to completion his vast design, a synthesis of all knowledge under the universal law of evolution.

---

[4] Rudolf Metz, *A Hundred Years of British Philosophy*, p. 74.

[5] Herbert Spencer, *Autobiography* (2v, 1904); David Duncan, *Life and Letters of Herbert Spencer* (1908); William Henry Hudson, *Introduction to the Philosophy of Herbert Spencer* (1894) and *Herbert Spencer* (1908); J. Arthur Thomson, *Herbert Spencer* (1906); Hugh Elliot, *Herbert Spencer* (1917); J. Rumney, *Herbert Spencer's Sociology* (1934); James Seth, *English Philosophers and Schools of Philosophy* (1912), pp. 284-297; Rudolf Metz, *A Hundred Years of British Philosophy* (1938), pp. 98-110. For the opposition in this country to Spencer's competitive individualism see Richard Hofstadter, *Social Darwinism in American Thought, 1860-1915* (Philadelphia, 1944). — The range of Spencer's interests is well illustrated for the ordinary reader in his miscellany entitled *Facts and Comments* (1902), in which he treats of law and justice, imperialism, militarism, slavery, education, gymnastics, music, sanitation, and much else.

In the essay on *Progress, its Law and Cause* (1857) Spencer offered an exposition of the universality of the evolutionary process, founded upon his study of the nebular hypothesis and of the Lamarckian theory of the inheritance of acquired characters. In the next year he chanced in his reading upon the observation that organisms tend to develop from homogeneity to heterogeneity, and wrote to his father that his "ideas on various matters have suddenly crystallized into a complete whole." [6] That "whole," that basic law, he afterwards condensed into his famous definition of evolution as "an integration of matter and concomitant dissipation of motion, during which the matter passes from an indefinite incoherent homogeneity to a definite coherent heterogeneity and during which the retained motion undergoes a parallel transformation." In 1859 Darwin provided him with another explanation of the phenomenon of organic evolution, and without entirely discarding the theory of the inheritance of acquired characters Spencer at once absorbed natural selection into his system. His life work was now laid out for him. In *First Principles* (1862) he adumbrated his plan to present a genetic history of the universe in terms of matter, motion, and force. From the first his object was fundamentally ethical, to provide "a basis for a right rule of life, individual and social." [7] The bibliography of the successive installments of the *Synthetic Philosophy* is too complicated to be presented here, for there were overlappings, revisions, enlargements, and confusing changes of titles; but broadly speaking the chronology is as follows: *The Principles of Biology* (1864-1867), *The Principles of Psychology* (1855-1872), *The Principles of Sociology* (1876-1896), and *The Principles of Ethics* (1879-1893). Of the subsidiary works may be mentioned *Education* (1861), of which the argument runs counter to the modern claim to equal education for all but which strongly influenced modern theory and practice; *The Man versus the State* (1884), the most thoroughgoing exposition of Spencer's individualism; the suppressed volume on *The Nature and Reality of Religion* (1885); and the posthumously published *Autobiography* (1904). *The Synthetic Philosophy*

The synthesis was incomplete from the very start, for Spencer never included save by implication and in the early essay on the nebular hypothesis, the realm of inorganic matter, and by not considering "the step preceding the evolution of living forms" failed to force into his scheme the all-important problem of the origin of life. There is another unbridged gap between his *Biology* and *Psychology,* that is, between matter and mind. The phenomena of social life no less than of organic nature were shown to conform to law, for as in organisms so in society (the "super-organic") there is a tendency to the increased specialization of interdependent elements. In Spencer's *Sociology* state-control is reduced to the minimum needed for the coöperative life (protection against external enemies and the maintenance of internal order), and individual liberty is expanded to the maximum possible in the state. Competition is the condition of progress. He would *The Individual and Society*

[6] *Autobiography,* II. 19.
[7] *Ibid,* II. 314.

turn over to private competing companies not only such affairs as the postal service but sanitation and the measures necessary for public health. Spencer's ethics were an outgrowth from utilitarianism. The end of conduct is the complete life. Holding that morality becomes instinctive (an "acquired character"), he foresaw the day when there would be an "approximately complete balance" between the desires of the individual and the needs of society. When this adjustment is effected, all sense of compulsion will disappear, and with it the need to exercise a moral choice.

Notwithstanding the immense and imposing accumulation of facts, Spencer's process of reasoning is essentially deductive, not inductive. He admitted that his mind was "ready to receive" material which could be taken into his system, while "ideas and sentiments of alien kinds, or unorganizable kinds" were either rejected "or soon dropped away." [8] A Spencerian theory has been likened to a magnet; as it is passed over particles of different metals, the iron facts cling to it; the rest are left behind.

Spencer attempted a reconciliation of science and religion in the common meeting-ground of reverent contemplation of the Unknowable and Absolute First Cause which he found to be behind both religious beliefs and scientific observation and experiment. But in this cold abstraction the religious-minded found no substitute for faith in a Divine Father; and science refused to be turned from its task of enlarging the boundaries of the known to pay homage to what was beyond the reach of knowledge.

Spencer's style is dry, technical, cumbrous, and pedantic, but it is always precise, sometimes fervent, and on occasion of a lofty dignity. A panoramic view of the *Synthetic Philosophy* inspires admiration for the patient ingenuity which fitted the interdependent parts into the vast, definite, and coherent heterogeneity.

# III

*Historians*

With the exception of Carlyle (to whom some would deny the title altogether), no historian of high rank as a figure in English literature appeared between the death of Gibbon and the advent of Macaulay.[9] The authority of many works has declined because their writers did not submit themselves to the discipline of the new science of the analysis of evidence which, initiated in Germany, made its way slowly in England. Moreover, such works as William Mitford's *History of Greece* (1784-1810) and Sir Archibald Alison's *History of Europe* (1833-1842) were colored by their authors' intense anti-Jacobin prejudices. Connop Thirlwall's *History of Greece* (1835-1847) is, however, dispassionate in its massive intellectual power, and George Grote's *History of Greece* (1846-1856) is still a recognized authority. The Roman histories of Thomas Arnold and Charles Merivale have been quite

---

[8] *Autobiography*, I. 242.

[9] On writers in the fields of European and English history see G. P. Gooch, *History and Historians in the Nineteenth Century* (1913), pp. 282-294, and in the field of ancient history, *ibid.*, pp. 308-322. See also T. P. Peardon, *The Transition in English Historical Writing, 1760-1830* (1933); E. L. Woodward, *British Historians* (1943).

superseded. The works of Henry Hart Milman (1791-1868) have a special claim upon our attention because of their connection with liberal theology and biblical criticism. His *History of the Jews* (1829) was denounced by the High Church party for its semi-rationalistic outlook. In the *History of Christianity* (1840) Milman adopted the theory of "accommodation" which holds that a belief in miracles has suited certain stages of religious progress and that this belief, though not the miracles themselves, is the work of God— an uncomfortable, not to say blasphemous, compromise. The liberal reaction had set in by the time his *History of Latin Christianity* appeared (1855).

Sharon Turner's *History of the Anglo-Saxons* (1799-1805), a pioneer effort to reconstruct a culture and civilization, supplied a demand for information about the national past in which the literary antiquarians were rousing interest. Henry Hallam (1777-1859), on the other hand, lacked the sympathetic imagination to re-create a past epoch, and in his *Europe in the Middle Ages* (1818) he was not so much a narrator as a moralist, drawing from the past lessons applicable to his own age. His *Constitutional History of England* (1827) broke with the tradition of Tory history, inherited from Hume, and thus led directly to Macaulay. The *Introduction to the Literature of Europe in the Fifteenth, Sixteenth, and Seventeenth Centuries* (1838-1839) surveys a vast number of books and hazards many broad generalizations of varying degrees of validity. Among Hallam's works it retains perhaps most interest for the general reader.

## IV

The precocious childhood of Thomas Babington Macaulay [10] (1800-1859) *Macaulay* was passed among the Evangelicals of Clapham. After a brilliant career at Cambridge he published his first essays in *Knight's Quarterly Review* (1823-1824). The first of his contributions to *The Edinburgh Review* was the essay on Milton (1825) which owed its success in part to qualities of style but also to the author's prestige in Whig society where his powers as a conversationalist were already famous. In 1829 he was elected to Parliament. His five speeches in advocacy of the Reform Bill were an invaluable aid to Lord Grey's government. Between 1834 and 1838 he was in India as a member of the Supreme Council. His labors there resulted in educational reforms which lasted almost to our own day. On his return to England Macaulay was a member of Melbourne's ministry. In 1847 he lost his seat in Parliament, retired from public life, and devoted himself entirely

[10] *Works,* ed. Lady Trevelyan (8v, 1866); *Critical and Historical Essays,* ed. F. C. Montague (3v, 1903); *Miscellaneous Writings,* ed. T. F. Ellis (2v, 1860); *History of England,* ed. Sir Charles Firth (6v, 1913-1915). — Sir G. O. Trevelyan, *Life and Letters of Lord Macaulay* (2v, 1876); Arthur Bryant, *Macaulay* (1932); R. C. Beatty, *Lord Macaulay, Victorian Liberal* (Norman, Oklahoma, 1938); Sir Charles Firth, *A Commentary on Macaulay's History of England* (1938); G. P. Gooch, *op. cit.,* ch. xv; John Morley, "Macaulay," *Critical Miscellanies* (1908), I. 253-291. — Macaulay was raised to the peerage as Baron Macaulay of Rothley in 1857.

to the *History of England,* which appeared in three installments (1848, 1855, and 1861), the last unfinished and posthumous.

*The Essays*    In later years Macaulay was ashamed of the superficial glitter of the *Milton*; but the essay exhibits many of the characteristics of his mature style.[11] The opinions expressed may be unreliable, but they are set forth with perfect clarity in pure English. The marked intellectual arrogance probably came from associations in boyhood with the high-minded but opinionated men of Clapham. The rough give-and-take of parliamentary debate presently increased the brutality of his style. Inexcusably severe is the attack on Southey (1830) who had argued in the *Colloquies* that all was not well with plutocratic England. The Whig essayist rages at the suggestion that the doctrine of a "stake in the country" was open to question and that the prosperity of the moneyed classes was perhaps not essential to the well-being of the "lower orders." Still worse is Macaulay's onslaught (1830) on the pathetic poetaster Robert Montgomery, where he seems to delight in invective for its own sake. A quarrel with the Tory John Wilson Croker culminated in a savage attack upon Croker's edition of Boswell's *Johnson* (1831), in which Macaulay outdid the current vituperative manner of the reviewers. The party animus is here so flagrant that Macaulay's intellectual integrity may well be questioned.[12] For the quarrel with Henry Brougham there was even less excuse, for Brougham had been his father's friend, was of Macaulay's own party, and had helped to give the young man his first step up the political ladder. That Macaulay could, however, estimate justly the achievement of a great man is evident from the article on Clive (1841), and that when his prejudices were not excited he could be both courteous and respectful is shown by the review of Ranke's *History of the Popes* (1841), where, for once, he seems almost humble in the presence of a historian greater than himself. The essay on Warren Hastings (1841) established the celebrity of his subject but is one of the least accurate of Macaulay's historical portraits. That on Frederick the Great (1842), though inaccurate and incomplete, is more penetrating than usual. The essays on men of letters are generally unreliable; Macaulay was himself dissatisfied with most of them. The *Dryden* (1828) is a study of the status of a man of letters in an uncongenial age when science was the center of interest. In the *Byron* (1830) there is not much more than shallow shrewdness. The portraits of Johnson and Boswell are notoriously flagrant caricatures. The *Walpole* (1834) is distorted by the writer's lack of sympathy with his subject's tastes and temperament. The *Lord Bacon* (1837) exposes Macaulay's incompetence to write on philosophical subjects. The account therein of Platonic doctrine is of a superficiality to shame Macaulay's own proverbial "school-boy"; and Bacon's achievement in inductive science is magnified beyond all reason, as is, antithetically, his moral turpitude. Only in the

---

[11] That it owed a good deal in ideas and style to Hazlitt is shown by P. L. Carver, "The Sources of Macaulay's *Essay on Milton*," *RES,* VI (1930). 49-62.

[12] R. C. Beatty, *Lord Macaulay,* p. 143.

*Addison* (1843) have we a thoroughly trustworthy piece of literary criticism.

The *Lays of Ancient Rome* (1842) are vigorous narratives from Livy, lacking shade and subtlety of diction and cadence but written with a forthright clarity which made them immediately popular. *Horatius* is still recitable; the other *Lays* are now neglected. They are the work of a historian interested in the problem of the transmission of traditions. Reversing the process whereby Livy composed his narrative, Macaulay attempted to reconstruct something like the lost ballad sources which the Roman historian had used.[13]

Lays of Ancient Rome

In the essay entitled *History* (1828) Macaulay set forth the ideal which he was himself to follow. "By judicious selection, rejection, and arrangement" the perfect historian, he says, "gives to truth those attractions which have been usurped by fiction." Macaulay would, then, redeem for history the provinces too frequently abandoned to the novelist: those small and vivid incidents and circumstances which restore life to the past; the rich cultural and social background without which the great figures of history have no perspective; the vast and variegated assortment of facts which earlier historians in England had rejected as beneath the dignity of their calling. He had ample precedent for employing history to maintain or refute opinions currently debated. The choice of his subject was determined by his devotion to the principles upon which the compromise of 1689 was founded; and this choice was confirmed when Sir James Mackintosh's fragmentary and posthumous *History of the Revolution in England in 1688* appeared (1834). Macaulay's criticism of his immediate predecessors was that they "miserably neglected the art of narrative." His own *History* is at its best when a great episode distracts him momentarily from his prejudices and he is content to be a literary artist working in a field not far removed from that of the historical novelist. In the narrative of Jeffrey's "Bloody Assizes" and of the last interview of the condemned Monmouth with King James the novelists were challenged and beaten on their own ground. In sweep and grasp nothing comparable to the great third chapter, surveying England in 1685, had appeared since Gibbon's prologuizing panorama of Rome in the age of the Antonines. There is, of course, perpetual overvehemence; and, in contrast to Gibbon, Macaulay never realized the value of condensation. His points are made, not by packing them into single sharp sentences, but by expanding them into paragraphs. The prolixity of parts of the narrative cannot be denied; but they are forgotten in the excited and impetuous flow at dramatic moments. The parade of historical parallels is occasionally tiresome; but by parallels of another sort—modern analogies—interest is sustained and the reader is made to understand the importance of the past for a comprehension of the present.

The History of England

Macaulay collected his material with astonishing energy and rapidity. He

---

[13] On a level higher than Macaulay elsewhere reached in verse is the *Epitaph on a Jacobite* (strange and moving theme for the arch-Whig to choose!) which has a deserved place in several anthologies.

went about England visiting the scenes which he intended to describe; he read (though he did not always inwardly digest) innumerable pamphlets and manuscript sources; and having accumulated these impressions in his miraculous memory he composed a draft with great swiftness, afterwards expending much toil upon the process of revision. The opinion of Brougham that Macaulay was never in search of truth but aimed only to produce "an effect of glitter and paint" is in harshness worthy of Macaulay himself, but it is not without warrant. The dazzling style is without shade; neither the whites (generally the Whigs) nor the blacks (generally the Tories) admit of any adulteration of gray. There is not even an appearance of impartiality. For the reliability of evidence he cared less than for its usefulness for the purposes of his argument.[14] "He marches," says John Morley, "through the intricacies of fact with a blaze of certainty." Yet recognition is due to the intellectual power which wrests the evidence to the support of a thesis. Those aspects of his subject which did not enlist his interest or did not lend themselves to his thesis he tended to neglect; there is, for example, little about England's relations with her colonies and with the Continental powers; the *History* is as insular as Macaulay himself.[15] The basic opinions maintained throughout are that all the blessings of England have flowed from the settlement of 1689 and that the present era in England is the most prosperous and enlightened age in the history of mankind. The gospel of material wealth is promulgated in a tone of infallibility. The moral complacency is extreme.[16]

## V

*Froude*

When James Anthony Froude [17] (1818-1894) had broken with the Tractarians,[18] he turned to historical research. From the mid-century, date the earliest of the essays, published in the *Westminster Review, Fraser's Magazine,* and elsewhere, which were later gathered into the four series of *Short Studies on Great Subjects* (1867-1883). Among these papers that on *The Oxford Counter-Reformation* presents most interestingly the Protestant obverse of the Catholic picture drawn in Newman's *Apologia.* With it may

*Short Studies*

---

[14] Various parts of the *History* provoked refutations. Of these the most penetrating is a series of papers, dealing chiefly with Macaulay's estimate of Marlborough, contributed by John Paget to *Blackwood's* in 1859. These have been reprinted with an introduction by Winston S. Churchill as *The New Examen* (1934).

[15] Macaulay admitted as much: "The book is quite insular in spirit. There is nothing cosmopolitan about it" (Trevelyan, *Life,* II. 390).

[16] A word must be added on Macaulay's private Journals. Trevelyan made some use of them and Professor Beatty much more, but as a whole they are still unpublished. Scholars who have read the manuscripts at Cambridge have brought away a disquieting impression of the self-portrait they contain. The censoriousness which Macaulay inherited from the Clapham group became even more extreme in his later life. An attitude of hatred and contempt towards nearly all contemporaries who were not in precise accord with his opinions was uniformly maintained. Disparagement was his almost unvarying position not only towards open foes but towards many who considered themselves his friends. The consciousness of his own rectitude was unfaltering.

[17] Herbert Paul, *Life of Froude* (1905); Algernon Cecil, *Six Oxford Thinkers* (1909), pp. 156-213; G. P. Gooch, *op. cit.,* pp. 332-339. On the Froude-Carlyle controversy see above, ch. xx, n. 1.

[18] See above, ch. XVIII.

be associated the coldly analytical review of Newman's *Grammar of Assent*. *England's Forgotten Worthies* is a spirited tribute to those Elizabethan adventurers whose exploits are brought into the forefront of Froude's *History*. The sketches of travel reveal an interest in colonial problems and point forward to Froude's *Oceana, or England and her Colonies* (1886) which was an influence upon the growing imperialistic sentiment of the time. *The Scientific Method applied to History* is in part an exposition of Froude's opinion that history is an art, not a science; it contains the startling pronouncement that "the most perfect English history which exists is to be found, in my opinion, in the historical plays of Shakespeare." [19] The remark casts a flood of light upon Froude's own methods and standard of accuracy, and it reveals the gulf fixed between him and his opponents. The biography of Carlyle (1882-1884) and the controversy which sprang from it have already been touched on. The biographical studies of Caesar and Luther and some other minor works have not proved to be of lasting value.

In revulsion from Anglo-Catholicism Froude, as we have seen, was attracted to the subject of the Protestant Reformation in England, which preserved English liberties from the temporal ascendency of the Papacy. **The History of England** This dominant theme accounts for the modification of Froude's original plan, which was to narrate the history of the reign of Elizabeth. But on the one hand he worked back to the reign of Henry VIII and on the other he brought his story to a close with the artistic and historical climax of the Battle of the Armada. The first installment of his *History of England,* which at once rivaled Macaulay's *History* in popularity, appeared in 1856; the last in 1870. In the choice both of theme and emphasis Froude was influenced and encouraged by his master, Carlyle, though his pure English style is quite uncontaminated with "Carlylese." Froude made much use of documentary material hitherto unexplored, but with gross carelessness, much misinterpretation of evidence, and a complete inability to maintain a judicial impartiality. The anti-Catholic bias which pervades the whole work is as notorious in the bitter blackening of the character of Mary Stuart as in the "white-washing" of Henry VIII. The celebration of the triumph of Protestantism perhaps necessitated a glorification of the instrument which made that triumph possible; but the special pleading in the matter of the King's marriages, the denial that he was a despot, the misinterpretation of the position and power of Parliament, the defense of the execution of More and Fisher, the condoning of atrocities provided they were committed on the Protestant side, and the eagerness to let ends justify the most revolting means, all are characteristics of the *History* which have led modern historians to declare bluntly that Froude's work must be done over again. Even those who recognize his splendid pictorial gift (as in the famous opening chapter which is comparable to the analogous panoramas in Gibbon and Macaulay) and equally admirable gift of narrative (as in the death-scene of Henry VIII or Mary's flight from Scotland or the scene at Fother-

[19] *Short Studies on Great Subjects* (ed. 1910), II. 471.

ingay) repudiate Froude's authority as a historian. Freeman's attacks were of such unmeasured violence as to do as much harm to himself as to Froude; but the more calmly pronounced strictures of Stubbs are in substance as condemnatory; and a representative modern opinion is that "Froude closes the age of the amateurs, whose brilliant writings belong as much to literature as to history." [20] The worship of force, which Froude learned from Carlyle, is displayed most repulsively in the narrative of Elizabethan rule in Ireland; and this part of the subject is carried in a later work, *The English in Ireland* (1872-1874), down to the Act of Union. Froude's argument that a policy of conciliation was useless was his unhappy contribution to contemporary discussions of the Irish problem; and the opinion expressed that the right of a small people to self-government depends upon their power to defend themselves was, like Carlyle's doctrines, ominous of the appalling disasters which were later to fall upon the little nations.

Like Carlyle, Froude emphasized the influence of great men—a Henry VIII or a Burleigh—in shaping the course of history. Opposed to this view and probably a reaction from the exaggerations of Carlyle was the doctrine of impersonal laws determining the progress of mankind which was set forth by Henry Thomas Buckle (1821-1862) in his unfinished *History of Civilization in England* (1857-1861). The less speculative inquiries of W. E. H. Lecky (1838-1903) [21] furthered the growth of toleration. Of the so-called

*The Oxford School*

"Oxford School" of historians [22] only John Richard Green (1837-1883) won the attention of a large public. Into his *Short History of the English People* (1874) he introduced the cultural and scientific aspects of the nation's life and thus satisfied readers who wished for something else than constitutional, military, and diplomatic history. The prestige of William Stubbs (1825-1901) on account of his impartiality and intellectual grasp has proved lasting among professional historians, but his *Constitutional History of England* (1873-1878) and many monographs scarcely belong to literature. Unlike Stubbs, Edward Augustus Freeman (1823-1892) refused to divorce the chronicle of fact from a moral judgment of the fact. His studies in Ottoman history (1877) helped to stimulate anti-Turkish opinion during

*Other Historians*

the Near East Crisis. His best-known work is the *History of the Norman Conquest* (1867-1879). To his influence is in part attributable the concept, popular at the end of the century, of the superiority of the Anglo-Saxons to the "lesser breeds." At Cambridge the massive erudition of J. E. E. D. Acton, Baron Acton (1834-1902) failed to bear fruit in books of great scope. He never wrote the "History of Liberty" which he planned as his life-work. [23] The royalist and parliamentary causes in seventeenth-century

[20] G. P. Gooch, *op. cit.*, p. 339.
[21] *A History of the Rise and Influence of Rationalism in Europe* (1865); *A History of European Morals from Augustus to Charlemagne* (1869).
[22] G. P. Gooch, *op. cit.*, ch. XVIII.
[23] Three volumes of Acton's historical studies were issued posthumously, ed. J. N. Figgis and R. V. Laurence (1907-1910). See F. A. Gasquet, *Lord Acton and his Circle* (1906).

England were interpreted with equal insight and impartiality by Samuel R. Gardiner (1829-1902); his *History* has yet to be superseded.[24] Justin McCarthy (1830-1912) wrote in more popular vein a *History of the Four Georges and of William IV* (1884-1901). Goldwin Smith (1828-1910), vigorous and voluminous controversialist, colored his interpretation of history with his anti-imperialist opinions; in *The Empire* (1863) he urged that the colonies should separate from England. Sir John R. Seeley (1834-1895), on the other hand, sensed the inevitable process of empire-building and in *The Expansion of England* (1883) and other writings was influential in impressing upon his countrymen the idea of "the White Man's Burden." [25]

Walter Bagehot [26] (1826-1877), a writer whom it is difficult to classify, was *Bagehot* a man of business, publicist, economist, historian, and literary critic. In *The English Constitution* (1867) he argued against the separation of the legislative and executive functions and commended their practical fusion through the cabinet in the English system. *Physics and Politics* (1869), one of the first attempts to apply to the study of politics the methods of psychology, developed the implications of Darwinism by describing the evolution of communities of men. Among Bagehot's *Literary Studies* (collected in 1879 but written much earlier) may be mentioned that on Wordsworth, Tennyson, and Browning as examples of pure, ornate, and grotesque art, and that on Shakespeare with its illuminating discussion of "experiencing nature" and its effort to discover the personality of the man behind the poet and dramatist.

## VI

In the mid-nineteenth century a series of narratives of travel in the Near *Travel* and Middle East points forward to the great books by Doughty and Colonel Lawrence. Alexander William Kinglake (1809-1891) followed in *Eothen* [27] (1844) the English tradition of treating "Oriental encounters" in the spirit of comedy. The little book still retains its fresh charm. On an ampler scale but without Kinglake's touch of genius Eliot Warburton (1810-1852) wrote *The Crescent and the Cross* (1844). Robert Curzon (1810-1873) told of the quest of ancient manuscripts in his *Monasteries of the Levant* [28] (1849), and Sir Austen Henry Layard (1817-1894) reported vividly upon some of the most notable archaeological achievements of the age in *Discoveries at Nineveh* (1851) and later books. The life of Sir Richard Francis Burton [29]

[24] *History of England, 1603-1642* (1863-1882); *The Great Civil War* (1886-1891); *Commonwealth and Protectorate* (1895-1901).

[25] Seeley's early work, *Ecce Homo* (published anonymously, 1866), a study of the life of Christ, occasioned wide discussion.

[26] William Irvine, *Walter Bagehot* (1939).

[27] Ed. David G. Hogarth and V. H. Collins (1906); also in Everyman's Library.

[28] Ed. David G. Hogarth (1916).

[29] N. M. Penzer, *Bibliography* (1923); Thomas Wright, *The Life of Sir Richard Francis Burton* (2v, 1906); Fairfax Downey, *Sir Richard Burton: Arabian Nights Adventurer* (1931); Seton Dearden, *The Arabian Knight: a Study of Sir Richard Burton* (1936); H. J. Schonfield, *Richard Burton, Explorer* (1936); Sir Arnold Wilson, *Richard Burton* (1937). — For the student, though not for the general reader, Burton's translation of *The Thousand Nights and a Night* (1885-1888) superseded the expurgated and condensed version which Edward William

(1821-1890) belongs to the history of heroism rather than of literature. *A Pilgrimage to Al-Medinah and Meccah* [30] (1855) is the record of his most famous achievement; but the style is both random and braggart, the color laid on too thick, and the sardonic humor overdone. These strictures hold for Burton's other narratives of exploration. [31] Other explorers in Hither Asia and Africa who gave accounts of their accomplishments were W. G. Palgrave (1826-1888), David Livingston (1813-1893), Sir Henry Morton Stanley (1841-1904), and John Hanning Speke (1827-1864), the discoverer of the sources of the Nile.

*Borrow*

George Borrow [32] (1803-1881) was a wanderer over Europe, and his best books are the records of his wanderings. The amount of fiction that he mixed with autobiography cannot be estimated precisely. His versatility as a linguist was extraordinary, though his pretentions as a philologist rest on slender foundations. The strident anti-popery to which he gave voice was genuine, but the piety which won him his job as an agent of the Bible Society in Russia and Spain was of a dubious sort. His associations with rough characters lost nothing in the telling, but he did know gypsy life intimately. Humor, sentiment, graphic observation, satire, erudition, and romance mingle in the books of this eccentric individualist. The basic ingredient is a love of the open road and "the wind on the heath." *The Bible in Spain* (1843), *Lavengro* (1851), *The Romany Rye* (1857), and *Wild Wales* (1862) are episodic, inchoate, and inconsequential; but these strange, untidy, racy books still appeal not only to "the Borrovians" but to all lovers of the picaresque.

## VII

*"Lewis Carroll"*

From such exotic lands as Russia and Arabia we may pass to the authentic wonderlands down the rabbit-hole and behind the mirror. The transition is sufficiently logical to satisfy "Lewis Carroll" [33] (Charles L. Dodgson, 1832-1898), the author of *Alice in Wonderland* (1865) and *Through the Looking-Glass* (1871). Written by an eccentric Oxford don to amuse his little girl-friends, these two world-famous books have proved to be enduringly delightful and are the best of all memorials of the Victorian love of nonsense. In them are elements of satire and parody which connect them with a long tradition, but they are shot through with a quaintly distorted

Lane (1801-1876) had published in 1838-1840. Burton's version has been praised by Arabists for its fidelity to the tone and idiom of the original, but it lacks the literary quality of John Payne's translation.

[30] Ed. Isabel, Lady Burton and S. Lane Poole (2v, 1906).

[31] Among which the best are *First Footsteps in East Africa* (1856), *Unexplored Syria* (1872) *The Land of Midian* (1879), and the books on Brazil (1869) and Paraguay (1870).

[32] *Works*, ed. Clement K. Shorter (16v, 1923-1924). — W. I. Knapp, *Life, Writings and Correspondence of George Borrow* (2v, 1899); R. A. J. Walling, *George Borrow, the Man and his Work* (1909); C. K. Shorter, *George Borrow and his Circle* (1913); R. T. Hopkins, *George Borrow, Lord of the Open Road* (1922); S. M. Elam, *George Borrow* (1929).

[33] S. H. Williams, *Bibliography* (1924; rev. ed., 1931); S. D. Collingwood, *Life and Letters of Lewis Carroll* (1898); *Selection from Letters of Lewis Carroll to his Child-Friends*, ed. E. M. Hatch (1933); Langford Reed, *Life of Lewis Carroll* (1932); Walter de la Mare, *Lewis Carroll* (1932); F. B. Lennon, *Victoria through the Looking-Glass* (1945).

logic (for their author was a professional mathematician and logician) which is inimitable and unique. It is a misfortune that of late years Dodgson and his charming books have been somewhat besmirched by the prying hands of the psychologists. "Lewis Carroll's" other writings (apart from professional papers) include *The Hunting of the Snark* (1876), a fantastical narrative poem, and the much less successful *Sylvie and Bruno* (1889-1893). Sir John Tenniel's illustrations to the *Alice* books share the fame of the text.

# XXII

## John Ruskin

Before 1860 Ruskin [1] was primarily an aesthetician and historian of art; afterwards he was primarily a social economist and reformer. But there was no interruption of continuity; the course of evolution from his first dominant interest to his second was consistent.

It is now known that John Ruskin (1819-1900) was a mental invalid; the attacks of insanity in his old age were the culmination of manic disturbances which manifested themselves, with periods of remission and exacerbation, from early life. The evidence for this is overwhelming. [2] What concerns us is the effect upon his work—the arrogance, dogmatism, capriciousness, self-contradictions, petulance, discursiveness, and alternations from depression to elation, from furious activity to gloomy indolence. His greatness is undeniable; but the thin partitions which divide great wits from madness were in his case distressingly insecure.

The education given him by fond and wealthy parents was neither normal nor wise. An only child, he had no companions of his own age, little regular instruction, and strict religious discipline. His tastes were indulged and it was assumed that he was a genius. He accompanied his father on his travels, and *The Iteriad*, a memorial of a visit to the Lake Country in 1830, [3] is one

---

[1] *Works*, Library Edition, ed. E. T. Cook and Alexander Wedderburn (39v, 1903-1912); Vols. xxxvi-xxxvii contain a selection from Ruskin's vast correspondence but many letters are still unprinted or scattered through various publications; Vol. xxxviii contains a bibliography exhaustive down to 1910. — E. T. Cook, *The Life of John Ruskin* (2v, 1911); R. H. Wilenski, *John Ruskin: an Introduction to further Study of his Life and Work* (1933); Alice Meynell, *John Ruskin* (1900); Frederick Harrison, *John Ruskin* (EML Series, 1902); A. C. Benson, *John Ruskin, a Study in Personality* (1911); Amabel Williams-Ellis, *The Exquisite Tragedy: an Intimate Life of John Ruskin* (1929). Older books still useful are E. T. Cook, *Studies in Ruskin* (1891); Charles Waldstein, *The Work of John Ruskin: its Influence on Modern Thought* (1894); J. A. Hobson, *John Ruskin, Social Reformer* (1898); J. Bardoux, *Le mouvement idéaliste et social dans la littérature anglaise au XIX⁰ siècle: John Ruskin* (Paris, 1900). On Ruskin's aesthetic see Robert de la Sizeranne, *Ruskin et la religion de la beauté* (Paris, 1909); H. A. Ladd, *The Victorian Morality of Art: an Analysis of Ruskin's Esthetic* (1932); Bernard Bosanquet, *History of Aesthetics* (ed. 1934), pp. 447-454; Katharine E. Gilbert and Helmut Kuhn, *History of Esthetics* (1939), pp. 412-422; K. E. Gilbert, "Ruskin's Relation to Aristotle," *Philosophic Rev.*, xlix (1940). 52-62. See also F. W. Roe, *The Social Philosophy of Carlyle and Ruskin* (1921); E. B. Hagstotz, *Educational Theories of John Ruskin* (Lincoln, Neb., 1942). Various estimates are collected in *Ruskin the Prophet and other Centenary Studies*, by John Masefield, Laurence Binyon, and other writers, ed. J. H. Whitehouse (1920).

[2] R. H. Wilenski, *John Ruskin*, pp. 27-181, and the "synoptic tables," pp. 15-24.

[3] *On Skiddaw and Derwent Water*, a poem written at the age of nine, was Ruskin's first published piece; *The Spiritual Times*, February, 1830 (*Works*, ii. 265-266). Other poems appeared in *Friendship's Offering* in 1835 and 1836. At Oxford, after two unsuccessful attempts, Ruskin won the Newdigate Prize with *Salsette and Elephanta* (1839). Ruskin's father privately printed *Poems. By J. R.* (1850). In this were collected almost all the poems already in print with a few others published for the first time. The poems are gathered together in *Works*, ii.

of many poems composed and illustrated by the young prodigy. In 1832 Samuel Rogers' *Italy* with Turner's vignettes opened to him two worlds at once; in 1833 he first saw Chamounix and in 1835 Venice, his "two homes on earth." Three articles which appeared in 1834 [4] manifest the interest in natural science which was one of the bases of his art criticism. In 1836 the impudent strictures of *Blackwood's* upon Turner's recent paintings moved Ruskin to write a reply [5] which he afterwards described as a "first chapter" of *Modern Painters*; but the germs of his principles are more clearly discernible in the articles on *The Poetry of Architecture* [6] (1837-1838). Illness cut short his career at Oxford, and after a period of desultory activity he was in Italy in 1840-1841. New attacks on Turner provoked him to another defense (1842); and then, in 1843, appeared the book whose long original title accurately indicated its contents: *Modern Painters: Their Superiority in the Art of Landscape Painting to all the Ancient Masters proved by Examples of the True, the Beautiful, and the Intellectual, from the Works of Modern Artists, especially those of J. M. W. Turner. By a Graduate of Oxford.* [7] The notion that Turner was "unknown" till Ruskin came to his rescue is, of course, baseless. He was famous, but his later manner was not intelligently appreciated. Ruskin held him up to admiration at the expense of Claude and Salvator Rosa who for a century had been in English estimation touchstones of artistic achievement. An Evangelical zeal, both moral and religious, permeates the book and biases the critic's judgment. Art being, as he held, "a noble and expressive language," it follows that "the greatest picture is that which conveys to the mind of the spectator the greatest number of the greatest ideas." [8] What, then, are the ideas conveyed by art? In answer Ruskin formulated the five categories of Power, Imitation, Truth, Beauty, and Relation. Thus, he, the least systematic of writers, involved himself from the outset in a show of system. Actually his attention was concentrated, as was proper in a treatise on aesthetic, upon the idea of Beauty; but his definitions were so broad that his discursive mind could range as widely as it would.

From sojourns abroad (1844-1845) he returned with impressions of Venetian and Florentine art which provided the material—displayed in descriptive passages of gorgeous coloring and elaborate cadence, yet with minute fidelity in verbal renderings of paintings and natural scenery—for a second volume (1846). Because of the Protestant bigotry of its outlook Ruskin came later to dislike this book; but it is one of his most significant. Religion is the basis of the aesthetic which he expounds. The "theoretic faculty" is

*(marginal notes: J.M.W. Turner; Modern Painters)*

[4] In *Loudon's Magazine of Natural History*, on the causes of the color of the water of the Rhine, on the perforation of a leaden pipe, and on the strata of Mont Blanc—remarkable topics for discussion by a boy of fifteen. See *Works*, I. 190-196.

[5] This, though submitted to Turner at the time, was first published in *Works*, III. 635-640.

[6] In *The Architectural Magazine*. The full title almost constitutes a program of Ruskin's art criticism: *Introduction to the Poetry of Architecture; or, the Architecture of the Nations of Europe considered in its Association with Natural Scenery and National Character.* The papers were signed "Kataphusin" (i.e., "According to Nature"). Reprinted in *Works*, I. 5-188.

[7] The authorship, soon known in Ruskin's circle, was first publicly acknowledged in 1849.

[8] *Modern Painters*, I. i. 2; *Works*, III. 92.

*The "Theoretic Faculty"*

opposed to the merely aesthetic, that is, the moral perception of beauty is contrasted with the sensuous. The mind must confront Beauty with reverent contemplation (*theoria*) because through Beauty the attributes of God are revealed. It is plain how close this is to Carlyle's teaching that the visible universe is "the living Garment of God." With faulty logic Ruskin went on to develop his theme that "all Art being the formative action of a Spirit, the character of the Deed must necessarily depend upon that of the Doer, and according to that character the Deed is bad or good." [9] In other words, no "bad" man can be a great imaginative painter. Hence the first essentials for good art are true faith, sound morality, right education, and proper social conditions. This thought was to lead through the two treatises on architecture to Ruskin's social economics. The latter part of *Modern Painters*, II, is devoted to the three forms of the imagination: the associative, the penetrative, and the contemplative.

Work on *Modern Painters* was interrupted for a decade during which a vast growth in knowledge, necessitating some modification of his views, was accompanied by an illusory conviction of rightness upon every matter upon which he elected to speak. In 1848 Ruskin married [10] and passed his honeymoon in Normandy studying the cathedrals. Something of the excitement of French politics went into *The Seven Lamps of Architecture* (1849) in which the object was to show "that certain right states of temper and moral feeling were the magic powers by which all good architecture had been produced." [11] The line of thought which led him from the Venetian School of painting to the most communal of the arts was his realization of the historic importance of architecture as the record of the life of a people. Since, as he held, great art depends upon nobleness of life, it is the visible sign of a nation's virtue, and debased art is a sign of national decadence. Where it ministers only to luxury and pride it contributes to that decadence and itself degenerates. In this way of looking at architecture there was nothing new. A. W. N. Pugin and his fellow Gothicizers had already "tried to gauge the merit of a building by the virtue of its builders." [12] But Ruskin's eloquence forced a hearing where Pugin was unheeded. The "lamps" burning before God's altar are Sacrifice, Truth, Power, Beauty, Life, Memory, and Obedience. Discussions of such technical problems as the proportions of color, light, and shade and the use of honest materials are interrupted by passages of impassioned exhortation. The book offended architects because an amateur had intruded into their professional preserve with attacks upon the tastelessness and ignorance of contemporary design, the deceptions prac-

The Seven Lamps

---

[9] *Ibid.*

[10] The marriage to Euphemia Chalmers Gray ended in an annulment in 1854. For the circumstances see the letters in "Ruskin and the Women," ed. Peter Quennell, *Atl. Mo.*, CLXXIX (1947), Feb., pp. 37-45.

[11] *The Crown of Wild Olive*, II; *Works*, XVIII. 443.

[12] Kenneth Clark, *The Gothic Revival* (1928), p. 253. Pugin's delightful and ingenious *Contrasts; or a Parallel between the Architecture of the Fifteenth and Nineteenth Centuries* (1836) is essential to an understanding of the aesthetic "atmosphere" in which Ruskin's taste and theory developed.

tised in materials and workmanship, and the gross errors of the self-styled "restorers" of ancient buildings. But the resonant voice raised in the "Age of the Ugly" was gradually heeded, and to this noble book, with its bold attack upon conventions, its background of social concern, its plea for a dignified and truly representative national style, its practical lessons, and its moral fervor, is largely due the regeneration of English taste.

Living in Venice, Ruskin now dedicated himself to the "hard, dry, *The* mechanical toil" of assembling material for *The Stones of Venice* (1851- *Stones of* 1853), a particular exemplification of the general principles of *The Seven* *Venice* *Lamps*. Of all his major works this is the most orderly in design, the three volumes being devoted to the periods, respectively, of origins and growth, of full flowering in the Byzantine and Gothic buildings of the city, and of decline in morals, life, and art. He found it difficult to adjust history to his theory because of the paradox that Venetian art reached its apogee amidst Renaissance pride and worldliness when the religious faith of the Republic had declined. The heights of his flamboyant, romantic prose (into which the rhythms of blank verse persistently force themselves) are attained in the description of St. Mark's; [13] and the central chapter on "The Nature of Gothic," [14] which became the bible of the new aesthetic school, contains the quintessence of his teaching. Since all art is for the glory of God, the concept is of more significance than the execution—or, as Browning was putting it at just this time, "a man's reach should exceed his grasp." Moreover, since a man is not a mere tool and true workmanship is imaginative creation, every workman must design for himself and not be a mere copyist.

So complex are the wheels within wheels of Ruskin's mobile energy that *Many* it is difficult to compress into short space an indication of his activities during *Activities* the eighteen-fifties. In 1851 he championed the Pre-Raphaelites, in whose paintings he detected, as he thought, some of the results of his own teaching.[15] Turner's death involved him in the long toil of cataloguing the paintings and drawings bequeathed to the nation.[16] In 1853 he lectured publicly for the first time; thereafter such appearances were frequent and this mode of communication enhanced his tendency to dogmatize. In 1854 he was one of the founders of the Working Men's College, where he gave drawing lessons and lectured. For his pupils he wrote the very popular

[13] *The Stones of Venice*, II, ch. IV, section 14; *Works*, x. 82-83. See George Saintsbury, *A History of English Prose Rhythm* (1912), pp. 395-396.

[14] *The Stones of Venice*, II. ch. VI, sections 1-78; *Works*, x. 180-245. These sections deal with the "mental expression" of Gothic architecture; the remainder of the chapter is concerned with technical problems of "material form."

[15] Two letters on the Pre-Raphaelites appeared in the *Times* in 1851; two more in 1854; all four were reprinted in *Arrows of the Chace* (1880); *Works*, XII. 317-335. A longer defense is *Pre-Raphaelitism* (1851); *Works*, XII. 337-393. Ruskin's association with Rossetti as patron and self-appointed mentor is one of the most interesting episodes in his life. In the end Rossetti could no longer tolerate Ruskin's arrogance and the friendship was ruptured.

[16] On the dispute in Chancery about Turner's will, Ruskin's renunciation of the executorship, and his subsequent work on the bequest see E. T. Cook, *The Life of John Ruskin*, I. 411-417. Ruskin issued various letters, notes, and catalogues dealing with the collection. All this material on Turner is gathered together in *Works*, XIII.

*Elements of Drawing* (1857) and the more technical *Elements of Perspective* (1859), both admirable pieces of exposition. The courageous address on *The Political Economy of Art*,[17] delivered at Manchester in 1857, expounds the relationship between employers and workmen and between government and industry; it is the bridge between Ruskin's earlier and later career. Annually, in his self-assigned rôle of arbiter of taste, he issued his *Academy Notes* (1855-1859). The third and fourth volumes of *Modern Painters* appeared in 1856 and the final volume in 1860.

The best-known chapters in Volume III are those on the "Grand Style" and on the "Pathetic Fallacy"; but the most coherent and characteristic are those contrasting classical, medieval, and modern landscape. From the formalism of Renaissance architecture studied in *The Stones of Venice* Ruskin had turned with enthusiasm and evident relief to the study of natural beauty. A moving epilogue, for which the reader is quite unprepared, is on the Crimean War. Volume IV was planned to be an analysis of the beauty of mountains, trees, and clouds; but love of the Alps won the mastery and the book became "a hymn to the mountains." It is the most clearly designed of all the five. The first seven chapters deal quite strictly with Turner's technique in mountain landscape; the next four, written with intense imaginative power controlling a mass of scientific detail, analyze the materials of the mountains and give an account of the geological changes from which they have resulted. Chapters XIV-XVIII are laboriously technical discussions of the resultant forms. Then, in chapters XIX and XX—"The Mountain Gloom" and "The Mountain Glory"—comes the response to the question: "What actual effect upon the human race has been produced by the generosity, or the instruction of the hills?" The splendid rhetoric of Ruskin's reply does not conceal a stubborn disregard of fact. Without thought of the great painters of the Low Countries he asserts that the fountain-heads of art are in the mountains, and argues from the lack of any great poet in Antwerp and Amsterdam without asking himself whether Switzerland has produced any such. The volume closes with the peroration recounting three scriptural mountain scenes: the death of Aaron, the death of Moses, and the Transfiguration. Volume V, in portions of which the incoherence is pronounced, is chiefly notable for the elaborate contrasts of the attitudes towards death displayed by various artists. This survey leads up to "The Two Boyhoods," one of Ruskin's most famous chapters, in which he points the contrast in the upbringing of Giorgione and Turner by rhapsodizing on Venice and then grimly describing modern London.

*Social Economy*

*Unto This Last,* the "truest, rightest, most serviceable" of all his books (as Ruskin afterwards described it), appeared in *The Cornhill Magazine* in 1860. This series of papers on political economy was to be longer, but Thackeray, the editor, alarmed by the hostility of reviewers and defections among his subscribers, brought the work to an abrupt close. The same fate

---

[17] Renamed, when republished in expanded form in 1880, *"A Joy For Ever"; (and its Price in the Market); Works,* XVI. 3-169.

overtook four *Essays on Political Economy* [18] published in *Fraser's* in 1862-1863. In letters to the newspapers, gathered together in *Time and Tide* (1867), Ruskin defended and elaborated his opinions. For them he did not claim originality, for he was one of a group who, following Owen and Carlyle, revolted against the classical school of mercantile economics which postulated "economic man" without the social and moral elements in human nature and by deductive reasoning arrived at absolute "laws" that were vitiated by application to concrete cases into which the social and moral elements always entered. Without denying men opportunities for self-development Ruskin urged that government should regulate and limit freedom of competition. From the analogies of the household, the professions, and the army Ruskin argued that in commerce and industry unselfish treatment of employees would give employers the best return. His appeal to the honor of manufacturers is reminiscent of Carlyle's hope for a "Working Aristocracy." The vigor of the protests against these views (which today seem old-fashioned in their mildness) is a measure of the strength of individualism, social irresponsibility, and belief in unrestricted competition in the mid-century. For long ridiculed or ignored, *Unto This Last* gradually made its way and was a telling influence upon the labor movement of the last decades of the century. *Time and Tide* contains scattered suggestions for an ideal commonwealth which passed into the program of William Morris and later Socialists.[19] Ruskin's more technical theories—his definition of wealth; his view that there is no profit in exchange; his conviction that all interest is usury—must be left to the economic historians. What concerns us is the burning sense of wrong and the militant social conscience which he evinced.

The years 1861-1863 were unhappy. Ruskin's religious views were unsettled and his incursion into the economic field had displeased his father. More alarming was the growth of a morbid attachment to the child Rose La Touche in whom his thoughts were henceforth centered and whom he later desired to marry. The story of this obsession, as of his over-emotional friendships with other girls of tender age, is a painful one. All this was a premonition of his later mental collapse. The death of Ruskin's father in 1864 may have caused a subconscious relief; at any rate a new period of intense activity began in that year. He could not find repose. The dogmatism and irritability increased and sought release in frequent lecturing, his audiences ranging from boarding-school girls to the Institute of British Architects. *The Cestus of Aglaia* (1865-1866), a series of papers on the laws of art, exhibits an eccentric discursiveness. To 1865 belongs the most widely popular of all his books: *Sesame and Lilies,* that is, in Ruskin's symbolism, the

---

[18] Reissued as *Munera Pulveris* (1872).

[19] Ruskin argued that the form of government is of no consequence; its efficiency in promoting social welfare is all-important. It must regulate marriage and provide compulsory schools. Occupations will be adapted to the tastes and talents of the workmen. The so-called "law" of supply and demand will prevail no longer, having been rooted in injustice. The rate of wages will depend not upon the supply of labor but upon the quality of the work. The working day will be eight hours. Menial tasks will be imposed upon a slave-caste, drawn perhaps from the criminal element. The suffrage will be limited by intelligence.

magic of right reading which opens the treasuries of human thought, and the purity which is the scepter with which women rule. Today the book seems as tritely Victorian as *The Princess*; but once upon a time it pointed towards the future when girls would have an education equal to that for boys, and there would be free public libraries, and better sanitation. Included in the volume was the beautiful and somber lecture on *The Mystery of Life and its Arts* which Ruskin later suppressed temporarily because of the evidence in it of religious unrest. It leads on to the eloquent discourses in *The Crown of Wild Olive* (1866), Ruskin's closest approximation to the agnosticism of the period.

The amazing versatility which came from the urge to be always active and the inability to concentrate upon one occupation is seen in the lectures on Greek mythology published as *The Queen of the Air* (1869); the consultations with Miss Octavia Hill, the social worker, on housing schemes for the poor; the visits to Switzerland and Italy; the botanizing and geologizing; the grandiose design to curb the Alpine torrents and conserve the waterfall; and yet other expressions of extreme mobility of interests. When in 1869 Ruskin was appointed Slade Professor of Fine Arts at Oxford, he undertook his new duties with feverish enthusiasm, publishing six volumes of lectures, writing guides for art-lovers, teaching drawing, trying to turn his doctrines to practical account, giving generously to museums of art, and exerting his influence upon younger men. Between 1871 and 1878 he was also much occupied with St. George's Guild and with *Fors Clavigera*. The Guild was a coöperative agricultural and manufacturing organization which he endowed with a tithe of his fortune. Essentially it was an attempt to revert to an irrevocable past, to establish a sort of neo-feudalism in industry. In plan it was in some respects practical, in others hopelessly utopian. Profits were to be shared; but there were no profits to share. The fortunes of the Guild were entangled with Ruskin's conviction that all interest upon capital is usury. The communistic basis led to disagreements and disappointments. The long series of letters addressed to the "Workmen of England" which Ruskin cryptically entitled *Fors Clavigera* [20] express many of his interests; but those critics who consider *Fors* the finest of Ruskin's works are misled by the richness of the medley. The style, in its relative simplicity, is far removed from the gorgeous periods of *Modern Painters*; but it is so flexible that Ruskin can bend it to any purpose. Inconsistent and pugnacious, sometimes blatantly boastful, often bitterly satiric, and always garrulous, these letters range over countless topics. Ruskin was, as it were, thinking on paper, following the train of thought wherever it led him. Often the drift is hard to follow and the rambling discontinuity painfully pronounced. But the mind is not everywhere unstable, and of its nobility there can be no question. The serenest portions are the "readings" in history, mythology, and literature. Other papers are on social economics, education, and the creed and

*St. George's Guild*

*Fors Clavigera*

---

[20] Nos. 1-87 appeared regularly in monthly installments, 1871-1878; Nos. 88-96 at irregular intervals, 1880-1884. The title is based upon Horace, *Odes*, I, 35.

rule of life of the Guild. Throughout the series runs a kind of diary of the author's activities, and in the occasional reminiscences of his early years are the germs of *Praeterita*.

Obsessions multiplied [21] and the relationship with Rose La Touche became more distressing till her death in 1875. In 1876-1877 Ruskin was in Venice, occupied with *St. Mark's Rest,* a history of the city. After his return home came the first complete breakdown, and he had to resign his professorship.[22] The story of the onslaught upon J. M. Whistler and the suit for libel which went against Ruskin is amusing only to those who are not aware of his malady.[23] In 1880 he recovered sufficiently to write the brilliant but erratic essays entitled *Fiction, Fair and Foul*. On a visit to France he began *The Bible of Amiens* (published 1885). In the lectures on *The Art of England* (1883) and *The Pleasures of England* (1884) insight flashes from tenebrous mists of eccentricity. The evidence of mental aberration is even more apparent in *The Storm-Cloud of the Nineteenth Century* (1884). *Mental* Repeated attacks of delirium now led to his permanent retirement to Brant- *Breakdown* wood, the home on Lake Coniston which he had purchased in 1871. There, in periods of temporary recovery between 1885 and 1889, he wrote *Praeterita,* the touching and delightful memories of his youth. The last decade—when by a tragic irony his prestige and influence were at their height—was, save for rare lucid intervals, a living death in which periods of violent excitement alternated with periods of gloomy silence. When he died in 1900 the age against whose cruel individualism and social apathy he had waged valiant warfare was passing and a new age which he had attempted to direct towards the light was at hand. At his funeral a wreath sent by one of his disciples bore the inscription: "There was a man sent from God whose name was John."

[21] The obsession with roses is of obvious origin. The obsession with young girls was expressed in his extravagant admiration for Kate Greenaway's pictures and even in his interpretation of Carpaccio's St. Ursula. The obsession with fireflies and lights against darkness has a direct bearing upon his violent criticism of Whistler's painting of fireworks in Cremorne Gardens.

[22] 1878; resumed for a short time in 1882.

[23] See J. M. Whistler, *Whistler v. Ruskin* (1878); reprinted in *The Gentle Art of Making Enemies* (ed. 1912), pp. 1-34. See also E. R. and J. Pennell, *The Life of James McNeill Whistler* (5ed, 1911), ch. XIX.

# XXIII

## Charles Dickens,
## Wilkie Collins, and Charles Reade

### I

Some recent writers on Dickens blame him unfairly for faults that he had in common with his age and social class. But without accepting all the conclusions of the psychoanalysts one may recognize that certain defects in his character help to explain the shortcomings in his achievement. There is evidence in his novels and his life that a troubled childhood left its mark upon the man and his work. The sense of power and the self-assertion, combined with an incapacity for self-criticism, were perhaps compensations for the frustrations of his early years.

*Early Years*  Charles Dickens [1] (1812-1870) came of a family of the lower middle-class which regarded itself as genteel, yet tended to decline in the scale of consequence. Though born on the South coast, he was so young when brought by his parents to the outskirts of London that it is to the Kentish background of *Great Expectations* we must look for his earliest memories. His father, an ineffectual person destined to be caricatured as Mr. Micawber, went up and down in the world; and it was during one of his periods of degradation in a debtor's prison that Charles, then nine years old, was apprenticed in a blacking warehouse, a humiliating experience to the sensitive boy. After two years, better family fortunes enabled him to continue schooling; but his real education came from his reading and from wanderings in

---

[1] *Works*, Gadshill Edition, with introductions by Andrew Lang and B. W. Matz (36v, 1897-1908); Nonesuch Edition (23v, 1937-1938), with the largest collection of Dickens' letters. — John Forster, *The Life of Charles Dickens* (3v, 1872-1874), ed. B. W. Matz (2v, 1911), ed. J. W. T. Ley (1928), abridged by George Gissing (1898); G. K. Chesterton, *Charles Dickens* (1906) and *Appreciations and Criticisms of the Works of Charles Dickens* (1911); George Gissing, *Dickens, a Critical Study* (1898); A. W. Ward, *Charles Dickens* (EML Series, 1902); A. C. Swinburne, *Charles Dickens* (1913); J. W. T. Ley, *The Dickens Circle* (1918); Edward Wagenknecht, *The Man, Charles Dickens* (1929); A. S. G. Canning, *Dickens and Thackeray* (1911); Bernard Darwin, *Dickens* (1933); Stephen Leacock, *Charles Dickens: His Life and Work* (1933); Thomas Wright, *The Life of Charles Dickens* (1935); T. A. Jackson, *Dickens: The Progress of a Radical* (1938); Gladys Storey, *Dickens and His Daughter* (1939); Humphry House, *The Dickens World* (1941); Una Pope-Hennessy, *Charles Dickens* (1945); W. C. Phillips, *Dickens, Reade and Collins, Sensation Novelists* (1919); Pearl S. Buck, "My Debt to Dickens," *English Review*, LXII (1936). 408-412; E. R. Davis, "Dickens and the Evolution of Caricature," *PMLA*, LV (1940). 231-240; Lord David Cecil, "Dickens," *Early Victorian Novelists* (1935), pp. 37-74; Sir Arthur Quiller-Couch, *Charles Dickens and Other Victorians* (1925), pp. 3-99; George Santayana, "Dickens," *Soliloquies in England* (1924), pp. 58-73; Edmund Wilson, "Dickens: The Two Scrooges," *The Wound and the Bow* (1941), pp. 1-104. — *The Dickensian* (1905—in progress), the publication of the Dickens Fellowship. contains stores of information. — At this point a general reference may be made to Cornelius Weygandt, *A Century of the English Novel* (1925).

London and beside the Thames estuary. In 1827 he was articled to a solicitor, meanwhile mastering shorthand and attending sessions of the courts. He became parliamentary reporter for ·a small newspaper and then for *The Morning Chronicle*. By 1833, when the first of his sketches of London life appeared, he had had his share of hardships and humiliations, but also of small triumphs; he knew the metropolis and its infinite variety of human types; and he possessed abounding energy and self-assurance. Henceforth the story of his life is, for us, in the main the story of his books; but before turning to them let us glance ahead along his course. The success of his first volume enabled Dickens to marry Catherine Hogarth in 1836, though it was to her sister Mary that he was romantically attached. Mary is idealized in more than one of the novels, while poor Mrs. Dickens, who bore her husband many children, became the butt of the crude jocosity at the expense of over-fecund females that crops up persistently in the novels. The marriage ended in a separation in 1856. Dickens pressed the advantage of immediate success for all that it was worth—perhaps for more, for in the not very long run the burden of commitments was greater than even his tremendous *An* vitality could sustain. The widening of literacy was opening a vast market *Exhausting* to enterprising publishers who, to meet the new demand, purveyed fiction *Burden* in cheap form in monthly parts or serially in magazines. The need to swell a novel to proportions that could be spread over a year or eighteen months explains the unconscionable padding characteristic of this fiction; and the need to hold interest from month to month forced the novelist to close each installment with an unsolved mystery or on a note of interrogation. These requirements of his trade left their stigmata upon Dickens' art; and they kept his imagination upon a strain, for often he foresaw no more than his readers what was to happen next. More than once he began a fresh novel before he had completed its predecessor. Then there were his burdens as editor of *Bentley's Miscellany* (1837-1839), of *Household Words* (1850-1859), and later of *All the Year Round*. His many friendships brought a delightful but wearying round of social distractions of which we have the record in his letters and in Forster's *Life*. Responsibility for a large establishment and family often involved him in debt and necessitated the constant pursuit of profits. Amateur and semi-professional theatricals were emotionally exhausting, and towards the end there were the yet more exacting public "readings" from his books. Small wonder that he died, worn out, at the age of fifty-eight.[2]

Dickens' impressions of the world around him began to appear in periodi- Sketches cals in 1833, and in 1836 were gathered together as *Sketches by Boz, Illustra-* by Boz *tive of Every-Day Life, and Every-Day People,* with plates by George

---

[2] Hugh Kingsmill, *The Sentimental Journey* (1935), applies the methods of psycho-analysis in a cynical and exaggerated fashion to the interpretation of Dickens' character and writings. Bernard Darwin (*Dickens*, p. 114) and Baker (VII. 306) protest against Thomas Wright's disclosure of Dickens' relations with the actress Ellen Lawless Ternan, insisting that the "proof" advanced is mere hearsay. But Kingsmill and Edmund Wilson. among other recent writers, accept the story as true.

Cruikshank. A second series followed in 1837 and a complete edition in 1839. These evocations and episodes of London life, which contain the germs of much that is characteristic of his later work, spring partly from the ancient tradition of "character-writing," partly from Leigh Hunt's impressionistic essays and Washington Irving's *Sketch-Book* (1819), but in the main from the author's own talent as a keen observer of the superficialities of the human comedy. The success of the *Sketches* brought an invitation to contribute the "letter-press" to a series of jocular prints to be designed by Robert Seymour portraying the adventures of a club of amateur sportsmen. Thus, in *The Posthumous Papers of the Pickwick Club* (1836-1837), Dickens came to rival and immediately outstrip Hook, Egan, and Surtees in the field of episodical, anecdotal, facetious fiction concentrating upon sporting life.[3] Obligated to make his cockney clubmen merely ridiculous, Dickens got off to something of a false start. Seymour's suicide might have brought the plan to disaster, but in H. K. Browne ("Phiz") an ideal collaborator was found, and Dickens, no longer the minor partner, took the reins into his own hands. The character of Mr. Pickwick developed quickly from a mere figure of fun into something more attractive and substantial, and after Sam Weller appeared, these two—simple, kindly idealism supported by homely common sense—became as inseparable as Don Quixote and Sancho Panza. A note of richer humor was struck in the characterization of the elder Weller. Gradually a panoramic view of English life unfolded. The element of farce was never entirely abandoned, but there were hints of tragic implications, an awareness of injustice, an admiration of moral courage. The scenes in the Fleet prison point forward to Dickens' later advocacy of penal reforms. What seemed to be inexhaustible material encouraged the author to depend upon improvisation. *Pickwick* is loosely put together with the formlessness of life itself. The scene shifts from the London streets to rural leisure, from the world of sport to the tumult of an election, from the public-house to the prison and the law-courts. A romantic love affair, humorously treated, leads on to the thrilling narrative of a wild pursuit with coach-and-horses through the night. Ladies and gentlemen, politicians, lawyers and journalists, jailers and jail-birds, humbugs, eccentrics, snobs and charlatans, with a mixture of undifferentiated humanity, jostle one another in these crowded pages. *Pickwick,* the first fruit of Dickens' genius, remains in the opinion of many readers the most delightful of all his books.

From this humorous extravaganza Dickens turned in *Oliver Twist* (1837-

Pickwick
Papers

---

[3] The picaresque element owes much to Smollett. In the character of Mr. Pickwick there are close resemblances to the comic protagonist of William Combe's *Dr. Syntax* (1812, 1820, and 1821). See William Dibelius, "Zu den *Pickwick Papers*," *Anglia*, xxxv (1912). 101-110. — William Combe (1741-1823) had already written many ephemeralities before *The Tour of Dr. Syntax in Search of the Picturesque* made him famous when it appeared serially in 1809-1811. The subsequent *Tours* are *in Search of Consolation* and *in Search of a Wife*. They owed their popularity as much to Thomas Rowlandson's coarsely vigorous illustrations as to Combe's pseudo-Hudibrastic verse, which is not much above the level of doggerel. *The English Dance of Death* and *The Dance of Life* are also more memorable for Rowlandson's designs than for Combe's "letter-press."

1838) to the novel of crime and terror, following where Bulwer and Ains- Oliver
worth had led the way but refusing to idealize criminals as they had done. Twist
Some of the effects are modernizations and urbanizations of Gothic devices
and others are borrowed from the melodrama of the popular stage. Some
characters are drawn with humorous realism, but for the most part humor
is dimmed by gloomy memories of the author's own neglected childhood,
and sensational scenes are shrouded in an atmosphere genuinely eerie and
sinister. The few pleasant people heighten by contrast the brutality of Bill
Sykes and Fagin the Jew, which is very little relieved by the squalidly
pathetic figure of Nancy. That Dickens shared with his contemporaries
the conviction that the novel should be an instrument of social reform is
evident in *Oliver Twist*.

At this time disquieting rumors were current about the mismanagement Nicholas
of certain private schools in Yorkshire. The outcome of a journey to investi- Nickleby
gate the conditions said to prevail in these institutions was the picture in
*Nicholas Nickleby* (1838-1839) of Mr. Squeers and his academy, a caricature so much exaggerated as to spoil its effect as an indictment though not
as a series of coarsely humorous episodes. The plot of this novel is more
complex than in the earlier books. To sustain the interest of his subscribers
Dickens provided a series of climaxes, but between them are long level
stretches where the interest sometimes flags. Attention is often distracted
from the nominally principal figures to the subordinate. Nicholas himself
is colorless in comparison with his mother, Mr. Squeers and his daughter,
Mr. and Mrs. Mantalini, and Crummles. The Cheeryble brothers are among
the earliest of those "good" characters for whom Dickens bespoke more
affection than the modern reader is inclined to give them.

Master Humphrey's Clock* was designed as a "frame" in which are set The Old
*The Old Curiosity Shop* and *Barnaby Rudge* (1840-1841). The clumsy Curiosity
"clock" matter was afterwards discarded and the two main stories issued Shop
independently. In *The Old Curiosity Shop* Dickens pulled out the *vox
humana* and *tremolo* stops upon his organ. In *Oliver Twist* indignation
had held pathos in restraint, but in the story of Little Nell no curb was put
upon emotion. A more cynical age than his is inclined to question the
sincerity of Dickens' pathos; but the fact that it is overwrought and that
Dickens, knowing that his readers enjoyed a "good cry," made it his practice
to wring the last possible tear from a situation does not prove that his
sentiments were feigned. He was as much moved as were his readers; he
and they were alike inheritors of the romantic conception of childhood
surviving into an industrial civilization which tolerated the employment of
little children in mines and workshops. Not all the Victorians were blind
to this contrast between their ideal and the actuality; that is one reason
why they wept. Little Nell and her Grandfather move through a crowd of
secondary figures, among them Dick Swiveller and the Marchioness and
Mrs. Jarley and that monstrous but effective embodiment of evil, the dwarf

Quilp. The earlier horror-romancers had devised nothing so memorably gruesome as Quilp's death in the slimy waters.

**Barnaby Rudge**

Scott's exalted example made it incumbent upon every ambitious novelist to try his hand at historical fiction, and this Dickens essayed in *Barnaby Rudge*. How closely he followed Scott appears from a comparison of his scenes of the Gordon riots with the Porteous riots in *The Heart of Midlothian*. The narrative of the outrages committed by the London mob is thrilling, but it would have gained in power from more restraint in style. In the episodes of ordinary life there is little attempt to differentiate the eighteenth-century scene from that of Dickens' own day. The absurd misrepresentation of the character of Lord Chesterfield in the figure of Sir John Chester shows that Dickens possessed nothing of Scott's ability to breathe life into people of the real past. With all this more or less authentic history a love story and an intrigue of crime and mystery are interwoven. A faded charm still lingers about Dolly Varden; and her lover is a not unattractive lad. But the mystery of the crime no longer rouses interest, for Dickens was both inept and stingy in providing clues. The poor simpleton Barnaby is a painful rather than pathetic figure; and Dennis the hangman is drawn in Ainsworth's Gothic style. On the whole this experiment in historical fiction was an aberration from Dickens' appropriate path.

**Martin Chuzzlewit**

After a visit to the United States [4] Dickens published *American Notes* (1842), by no means altogether hostile but a foretaste of what followed in *Martin Chuzzlewit* (1843-1844). The picture here painted of American vulgarity, boastfulness, and dishonesty wounded and offended Dickens' admirers over here, and the long, dreary episode is in inartistic contrast to the English scenes. The latter are rich in fantastic creations—Mr. Pecksniff, the quintessence of hypocrisy; Mrs. Gamp and Betsy Prig and that immortal shadow, Mrs. Harris; Todgers, sprung from the heart of cockney London; Tom Pinch, the most appealing of Dickens' pathetic figures; and Jonas Chuzzlewit, perhaps the most terrible of his villains.

**Dombey and Son**

The small sales of this novel indicated a decline in popularity, and Dickens, apparently realizing that his original vein was exhausted, struck out on new lines. Absence from familiar scenes while he lived on the Continent may explain his choice as the setting of *Dombey and Son* (1847-1848) of a higher social stratum than he had hitherto done more than glance at. But a sympathy with the aristocracy, new to him, is visible in the portrait of Cousin Feenix, who, though drawn humorously, behaves in a crisis as a gentleman should. Unusual care was devoted to the style and construction of this book. Yet the shift of interest after Little Paul's death to his sister might have been better prepared for and is accomplished not without some break in continuity. Mr. Carker is a vestige of theatrical melodrama, but his last journey and terrible death are narrated with great power. The serious

---

[4] W. G. Wilkins, *Charles Dickens in America* (1911). — *A Christmas Carol* (1843) is the first of the *Christmas Books,* short stories of a fantastic or fairy-tale kind which included, among other things, *The Chimes* (1845), *The Cricket on the Hearth* (1846), and *The Haunted Man* (1848).

story is lightened by the humorous characters, Major Bagstock (who is tiresome), Susan Nipper, and the delightful Captain Cuttle, who belongs to the tribe of Smollett's sea-faring folk. In general tone and atmosphere *Dombey and Son* is closer to actuality than Dickens had come hitherto; but this may be due as much to a decline in vitality as to deliberation.

Dickens' preference for *David Copperfield* (1849-1850) among all his books has been shared by the great majority of his readers. The early, more closely autobiographical chapters contain the most vivid and moving pages in all the novels; when purely fictitious incidents take the place of elaborated memories the later portions show some falling off. The comparative vagueness in the character of David himself, by some critics considered a weakness, is really part of the story's charm. David's are the eyes through which the other characters are seen; and what an array they are!—the Murdstones and Aunt Betsie Trotwood; the Peggottys; the Micawbers; Dora and her family; Uriah Heep. Mr. Dick is the least offensive of the simpletons and crazy folk whom Dickens, following an old tradition, turned to purposes of comedy. Mr. Micawber is perhaps the best of all his comic creations. There are both melodrama and false sentiment in the story of Steerforth's seduction of Little Em'ly; but in general this novel stays within the bounds of probability and truth to life.

When Dickens founded *Household Words* in 1850, he enlisted as contributors a group of younger authors, chief among them Wilkie Collins. The influence of this master of the technique of fiction dependent upon sensation, mystery, and intrigue is apparent in the more firmly knit plot of *Bleak House* (1853), where the story of the endless Chancery suit is ingeniously intertwined with that of Lady Dedlock's sin and retribution. An immense number of characters are wonderfully differentiated. The satire on the law's delays was of practical value in exposing the need of reforms. Never before or after did Dickens picture more vividly the London streets, the quiet of the precincts of the law-courts, the horror of the city graveyards, the gruesome and degraded atmosphere of old houses tainted with old crimes. Death broods over the somber story. The pathos of the end of poor Joe, the crossing-sweeper, still moves the sensitive reader; and there is real spiritual terror in the narrative of the death of Mr. Tulkinghorn.

The shift of interest in *Hard Times* (1854) was strangely sudden. The intention to use fiction for purposes of social protest, already apparent in the earlier books, now became the principal motive of an entire novel. The story, appropriately dedicated to Carlyle, was based on Dickens' own observations of industrial conditions in Manchester. The bitter sincerity of Dickens' social indignation, which before now had led him to sacrifice artistic refinement and reticence in order to bring home the wrongs of society to the consciences of his readers, lessens the value of this book as a work of art. His passion makes him unfair, for though employers like Bounderby may have existed they did not represent their entire class, nor was the almost saintly patience of Dickens' workingman and working-girl

*David Copper-field*

*Bleak House*

*Hard Times*

typical of theirs.[5] Dickens was within his rights in using the novel as a medium for agitation, and while he had no other solution of the problem of industrial relations than an emphasis upon benevolence, as an artist he was justified in declining to discuss practical remedies.

**Little Dorrit**

*Little Dorrit* (1857) shows a serious falling off in power. The stagy scenes in the Clennam residence are so many remnants of Gothic romance. The dreary business of the "Circumlocution Office" is topical satire on bureaucratic inefficiency. In the foreign episodes Dickens went far beyond the range within which he was master. The scenes in the Marshalsea are somberly autobiographic, and the distressing delineation of Flora Finching almost justifies the conclusions drawn from it by the psychoanalytical critics. On the whole, *Little Dorrit* is, of all Dickens' books, that which has worn least well.

**A Tale of Two Cities**

*A Tale of Two Cities* (1859), inspired by Carlyle's *French Revolution* and planned with an intricate artifice suggestive of Wilkie Collins, is a second effort in the field of historical fiction. About it there is a pretentious grandiosity, as though Dickens had set himself to a task on lines to which his admirers were unaccustomed. There is too much of mystery and melodrama; but the opening scene in the stagecoach, the pictures of the bloodthirsty women of the Parisian proletariat, and the death of Sydney Carton have secured places in the memory of three generations of readers.

**Great Expectations**

After the comparative failure of the three preceding books Dickens made a recovery in *Great Expectations* (1861), where loose capaciousness gives place to clear-cut condensation in plot, and the usual slipshod style is brought into order and beauty. The famous opening in the dismal Kentish lowlands is an evocation of Dickens' early memories. Pip, the hero, is less of a lay-figure than Copperfield had been, not only an observer of other people but an actor in his own drama who is not the less alive for being far from faultless. There is much stirring adventure, but it seldom goes beyond the bounds of plausibility, though Miss Havisham and her strange household are one more reminiscence of Gothic grotesquerie. The convict and Joe Gargery and Mrs. Joe are among Dickens' less extravagant creations, neither the grimness of the one nor the humors of the other two being overdone. Of Estella's rôle there are two opinions, some holding that Dickens should have retained his original conception of her as the evil principle in Pip's life, while others welcome the sacrifice of that conception for the sake of the romantically happy ending. This vivid, simply contrived and compellingly interesting story was the last expression of Dickens' full power.

**Our Mutual Friend**

The decline in *Our Mutual Friend* (1865) is obvious to most readers. The plot, with its absurdity of the supposed dead man who slinks through the story in disguise, is a tissue of crossed motives scarce worth the unraveling. The character of Riah, the pious old Jew, is too obviously an atonement for

---

[5] Ruskin (*Unto This Last*, I, 10; *Works*, XVII. 31) commended *Hard Times* but thought that its usefulness was diminished by the error of making Bounderby "a dramatic monster" and Stephen Blackpool "a dramatic perfection."

the prejudices revealed in the early portrait of the malignant Fagin. The satire on snobbery and social ambitions is even more heavy-handed than it had been in *Little Dorrit*. The mingling of comedy and pathos in the character of the doll-dressmaker is laborious, as are the futile humor-studies of the Golden Dustman and Silas Wegg. The book is partially redeemed by the powerful, though overwrought, delineation of Headstone's tragic passion for Lizzie Hexam and by the magnificent opening scene on the Thames and other episodes along the water-front.

The scale upon which Dickens lived kept him burdened with debt. He worked the gold mine of public readings and in 1867 made a second tour of the United States. Avoiding the strain of original composition, he underwent the severer strain of these readings into which he threw himself with all the force of his emotional temperament. He returned home exhausted, but heedless of advice continued his public appearances till 1870. In that year he began the publication of *The Mystery of Edwin Drood,* which was inter- *The* rupted, with the mystery unsolved, by his death. Many attempts have been *Mystery* made to construct the probable ending. No solution is satisfactory, though *of Edwin* the most nearly convincing relates the plot to Dickens' interest in the secret *Drood* society of Thugs in India.[6]

## II

Adapting with many reservations Dryden's characterization of Shake- *"A Com-* speare, one may say of Dickens that he was of all the Victorian novelists *prehensive* the man of most comprehensive soul. He saw life, as no earlier novelist had *Soul"* seen it, from the point of view of the poor of a great city. Possessed of a buoyant temperament, it is the more remarkable that he was not deceived by the blatant assurances of industrialism, but sought to mitigate its evils. He worked for practical reforms without advocating any change in the system of society because he believed that when institutions and their administration were remedied the fundamental goodness of human nature would make the reform of individuals an easy matter. Nearly all his bad characters are capable of conversion, and many are converted. Through most of his life he addressed his appeals for reform to the middle classes, and though towards the end there are signs that he was turning from hope in them to hope in the aristocracy, his pictures of the upper classes are almost always prejudiced and exaggerated, generally inaccurate, seldom kindly. His basic belief in the primary benevolent impulses of man—affection, charity, gaiety, fun, kindliness, spontaneity—brought within the compass of his sympathy any man or woman in whom he discerned the working of these impulses.

But he had not a Shakespearean understanding of evil. His unconverted *Characters*

---

[6] For a list of solutions of the problem of *Edwin Drood* see Thomas Wright, *The Life of Charles Dickens,* Appendix IV, to which add Howard Duffield, "John Jasper—Strangler," *The Bookman,* LXX (1930). 581-588.

"bad" people are saved from absolute condemnation only if, like Silas Wegg or Mrs. Gamp, they can be delineated grotesquely. The characters therefore tend to fall into two classes, almost as sharply differentiated as are the Virtues and Vices of the old moralities. But Dickens was not a creator of types; his figures are seldom truly representative of humanity at large. When he draws from observation of real people, as in his portraits of Landor and Leigh Hunt, the result is caricature. He is at his best when, peopling a world of his own devising with creatures of his own imagination, he fashions individuals who are beyond caricature because they are not distorted reflections of someone else but are themselves. No one has ever encountered a Mrs. Gamp or a Silas Wegg; but they are alive in their own right. To object that Dickens exaggerates is to question the very basis of his art. "It would be as sensible," says an excellent critic, "to criticize a gargoyle on the ground that it is an exaggerated representation of the human face" as to criticize Pecksniff because he is an exaggerated representation of a hypocrite.[7] This creative imagination is exercised upon literally hundreds of characters, each unlike all the rest, so that individual traits distinguish one charlatan from another, one shabby old woman from another, one villain from another, even one good man or "hero" from another. This intense individualization is accomplished by emphasizing the innumerable external qualities which are present in different combinations and permutations in every man and woman, marking the distinction of each from other. Dickens is far less alert to the underlying traits in which all human beings share and share alike. The colonel's lady and Judy O'Grady may be sisters under the skin, but since Dickens does not look beneath the surface he is not struck by the family resemblance. His is essentially a grotesque art, the art of the caricaturist, even when the result is not, properly speaking, caricature. But though to secure an effect a weakness is overemphasized, there is unerring insight in detecting the weakness. He sees the outward man rather than the inward motive; there is little effort to trace the development of character; and when once the idiosyncrasy or "humor" is established, the person either remains what he is to the end of the story or else undergoes a violent and unconvincing change at the close for the sake of the plot. A disconcerting feature of Dickens' work is the juxtaposition of the fantastic and the real. Creatures who live only in his imagination, though there with unexampled vitality, jostle with people drawn from actuality. Similarly, melodramatic incident protrudes with startling suddenness from a context which is real. Limelight and daylight play upon the scene at the same time.[8] Like Scott and unlike Jane Austen, Dickens focuses the interest upon characters and episodes irrelevant to the main story. The structural center is seldom the center of interest. For long stretches of narrative the principal plot—often a tangle of intrigue so elaborate that the reader follows it with difficulty or is quite indifferent to it—

*Plot and Setting*

---

[7] Lord David Cecil, *Early Victorian Novelists*, p. 44.
[8] *Ibid.*, p. 39.

is neglected, while the vital, though nominally subordinate, figures live and move before us. For plots Dickens relied with cheerful brazenness upon the shoddy and paltry devices of romance—the disguised lover, the long-lost heir, mistaken identity, the supposed dead who turn up in the nick of time, and other such tricks of the trade. But though Dickens' craftmanship and taste are alike defective, reflecting as they do the vulgarity and false sentiment of his age and class, the setting of these plots is almost always admirable. From the Gothic romancers he inherited a love of the fantastic in places, houses, objects, and names. He rendered marvelously the sights and sounds and smells of London—the fog, the drizzle, the slime, the dust, the crowded streets, picturing with equal authenticity the river, the water-side, the City, the law-courts, the West End, the suburbs. At further removes he was equally successful only when equally at home, as in the scenes beyond London in *David Copperfield* and *Great Expectations*. When he ranged beyond his own intimate experience, as in the Italy of *Little Dorrit* or the America of *Martin Chuzzlewit,* he was not at ease.

## III

Wilkie Collins [9] (1824-1889) served under Dickens on the staff of *Household Words* and, later, *All the Year Round*. Dickens' shift from novels of humorous character to novels of sensational intrigue was partly due to Collins' precepts and example. But there are differences. Whereas Dickens conceived his characters and then invented a plot to set them in motion, Collins invented his plot and then fitted characters into it. Far more than Dickens, Collins depended upon the technique of the popular sensational theatre; how closely is shown by the ease with which he adapted several of his novels to the stage. His tales contain almost invariably three ingredients: an intricate plot; humor in not very good imitation of Dickens; and a love-story. He often tells his story through the mouths of different characters, sacrificing continuity for the sake of startling effects. His three best books are *The Woman in White* (1860), the story of a crime based upon the resemblance of two women of whom one turns out to be the illegitimate sister of the other; *Armadale* (1866), where an ingenious plot is unfolded in an atmosphere of sinister eerieness; and *The Moonstone* (1868), on the theme (which Collins passed on to many imitators) of a jewel stolen from an Indian idol and retrieved by Brahmin conspirators. Collins was a master of climax and suspense, but the men and women in his tales are scarcely

*Wilkie Collins*

---

[9] S. M. Ellis, *Wilkie Collins, Le Fanu and Others* (1931); Baker, VIII. 191-201. — Other sensation novelists of the mid-century were Joseph Sheridan Le Fanu (1814-1873), an Irishman with a mastery of the occult, the uncanny, and the ominous; Mary Elizabeth Braddon (1837-1914), whose *Lady Audley's Secret* (1862) won for her a devoted public, though her realistic and historical novels are now forgotten; Mrs. Henry Wood (1814-1887), whose *East Lynne* (1861) is still remembered and who depended less upon sensationalism than realism; and Marie Louise de la Ramée, "Ouida" (1840-1908), whose love of the gorgeous and stupendous endeared her to a public blind to her meretriciousness. *Under Two Flags* (1867) is her best-known book. See Yvonne ffrench, *Ouida, a Study in Ostentation* (1938).

*Charles Reade*

characterized at all, being but pawns upon his chessboard of intrigue. He was in some ways an ancestor of modern writers of detective fiction.

Charles Reade [10] (1814-1884) was not so close to Dickens. Before turning to fiction he had been a successful dramatist, and his novels, with their crudity and violence and large dependence upon dialogue and dramatic presentation, have an affinity to the stage. *Peg Woffington* (1853), the first of them, was made over from his comedy, *Masks and Faces*. Like Dickens he used the novel to expose abuses and advocate reforms. *It's Never Too Late to Mend* (1856) has to do with the management of prisons and the mistreatment of criminals; *Hard Cash* (1863) with the scandals of private lunatic asylums. In *Put Yourself in His Place* (1870) Reade attacked the trade-unions. His other books are not to the same degree novels with a purpose. Several, of which the powerful but too vehement *Griffith Gaunt* (1866) is the best, are studies in character. Like Emile Zola, whose *L'Assommoir* he dramatized as *Drink* (1879), Reade accumulated and classified in huge ledgers and notebooks immense amounts of material for his studies of the human situation, drawing it from personal observation, newspapers, reports of commissions of inquiry, and other sources. Generally his imagination was stifled rather than vitalized by all this information. He followed the same method in the composition of *The Cloister and the Hearth* (1861), putting into that great and still widely read historical novel material from Erasmus, Froissart, Luther, the chronicles, the old jest-books and beggar-books, and quantities of miscellaneous erudition. The remoteness of the scene and period imparted geniality to a style made coarse and brutal by sincere but too vociferous indignation in the propaganda novels. The resultant picture of Europe at the dawn of the Renaissance—its every level of life from palace and monastery to tavern and highroad; its every type of character from bishop and burgomaster to beggar and freebooter—is at once spacious and dignified and beautiful and wonderfully informed with life. *The Cloister and the Hearth* was an entire departure, and a welcome one, from Reade's predictable line of development. Its interest and value have proved lasting; and Reade is likely to be remembered as *homo unius libri*.

[10] C. L. Reade and Compton Reade, *Charles Reade, a Memoir* (2v, 1887); Malcolm Elwin, *Charles Reade, a Biography* (1931); Léonie Rives, *Charles Reade: sa vie, ses romans* (Toulouse, 1940); A. C. Swinburne, "Charles Reade," *Miscellanies* (1886), pp. 271-302; Baker, VIII. 202-213; A. M. Turner, *The Making of the Cloister and the Hearth* (1938). Important articles on Reade by E. G. Sutcliffe are in *SP*, XXVII (1930). 64-109; 654-688; *ibid.*, XXXVIII (1941). 521-542; *PMLA*, XLVI (1931). 1260-1279; *ibid.*, XLVII (1932). 834-863.

# XXIV

## Thackeray and Trollope

### I

Thackeray's injunction to his daughters, "Mind, no biography!" was prompted not by fear of discreditable disclosures but by distrust of cant and insincerity. In default of an "official" *Life,* scholars have ransacked his writings for autobiographical allusions. Something has been detected and more has been surmised; there are few untouched transcripts from actuality but many portraits of real people "worked up" into imaginative creations. This search for "originals" has, however, been carried too far.

William Makepeace Thackeray [1] (1811-1863) was born in Calcutta of a *Early* family of Anglo-Indian officials. After his father's death his mother sent *Years* him as a child back to England. School-days at Charterhouse were not a happy time, though memory softened asperities and what he had once called "Slaughter House" became the kindly "Grey Friars" where Colonel Newcome died a pensioner. In 1829 he entered Trinity College, Cambridge, where he and Edward FitzGerald became intimate friends. Between them there was a spiritual kinship; each found in his own breast an echo of the words *Vanitas Vanitatum, omnia Vanitas!* Leaving Cambridge without a degree and with but a smattering of classical education, Thackeray traveled in Germany, visited Paris, and returning to London entered the Middle Temple. From the study of law he derived little save memories afterwards used in *Pendennis.* The loss of a small legacy in speculation and gaming was also turned later to good account in fiction. Like Clive Newcome, he had a talent for caricature and hoped to be an artist. This, in the severest technical sense, he never was; but only a very crotchety aesthetician can fail to enjoy his illustrations to many of his own writings. The date of his first contact with *Fraser's Magazine* is uncertain; few contributions from his pen have been identified with certainty of an earlier date than 1835, when he

1 *Works,* Centenary Biographical Edition, introductions by Anne, Lady Ritchie (26v, 1910-1926); Oxford Edition, introductions by George Saintsbury (17v, 1908); *Letters and Private Papers,* ed. G. N. Ray (4v, Cambridge, Mass., 1945-1946); *Letters to an American Family* (1904); other letters by Thackeray are in *Letters of Anne Thackeray Ritchie,* ed. Hester Ritchie (1924). — Lewis Melville, *The Life of William Makepeace Thackeray* (2v, 1899), which contains a bibliography (II, 133-376); Charles Whibley, *Thackeray* (1993); G. K. Chesterton, *Thackeray* (1909); A. J. Romilly, *Thackeray Studies* (1912); Raymond Las Vergnas, *Thackeray: l'homme, le penseur, le romancier* (Paris, 1932); Malcolm Elwin, *Thackeray, a Personality* (1932); H. N. Wethered, *On the Art of Thackeray* (1938); J. W. Dodds, *Thackeray: a Critical Portrait* (1941); J. C. Bailey, "Thackeray and the English Novel," *The Continuity of Letters* (1923), pp. 193-217; Lord David Cecil, *Early Victorian Novelists* (1935), ch. III; Baker, VII, ch. VII; J. W. Dodds, "Thackeray as a Satirist before *Vanity Fair,*" MLQ, II (1941). 163-178; Lionel Stevenson, *The Showman of Vanity Fair* (1947).

figures in Maclise's drawing of the "Fraserians." [2] He began as a trenchant critic and an imitator of Maginn's burlesques. In 1836 he married. His wife's insanity, after a few years of marriage, is the tragedy of Thackeray's life. Round his two daughters his affections clung, and in his later years he made a home for them. Solaces of different kinds were provided by the friendship with Mrs. Brookfield and by an ever increasing habit of "dining out."

*Early Writings*

The miscellaneous writings that appeared before his great year, 1847-1848, are not to be enumerated exhaustively here. The majority were published in *Fraser's,* but after 1841 Thackeray was on the staff of *Punch* [3] and connected also with other publications. After his home was broken up he lived in London clubs or at Brighton or Paris, or wandered from place to place. *The Paris Sketch Book* (1840) is a miscellany of small, uncomfortable episodes of travel, ephemeral and not very well considered chat on French politics and history, and comment on the art, literature, and theatres of contemporary Paris. Rather incongruous intrusions are two stories in the grotesque vein, *The Painter's Bargain* and *The Devil's Wager. The Irish Sketch Book* (1843) has an abundance of anecdote and local color but evinces little sympathetic understanding of Ireland and its problems; it was as a disillusioned tourist that Thackeray remembered the discomforts of journeys more vividly than the sights he went to see. In 1845 he undertook the tour of the Levant recounted in *Notes of a Journey from Cornhill to Grand Cairo* (1846) where the excellent writing does not conceal the fact that when contemplating the wonders of antiquity he was as much of a Philistine as Mark Twain.

*Yellow-plush*

Meanwhile he had been progressing towards the novel. *The Memoirs of Mr. C. J. Yellowplush* and *The Diary of C. Jeames de la Pluche* (1837-1838) have to do with a footman who makes a fortune by gambling in railway shares. Fashionable life is viewed from the servants' hall, and the satiric thrusts at what Mr. Yellowplush calls—or rather spells—"fashnabble novvles" are directed at Bulwer. The ingenuities of Jeames's phonetic spelling are still amusing, though this device has been staled by imitators. Bulwer and Ainsworth, as novelists of crime, are assailed in *Catherine* (1839-1840), the detestable story of a woman who murdered her husband and was burned at Tyburn, founded upon an actual case of 1726. Thackeray's intention was to deflate the pretensions of the criminal-as-hero; but as in other early work in lighter vein his footing is unsteady. To the novel of crime he returned with more assurance in *Barry Lyndon* (1844), recounting with ironic detachment a rascal's actual exploits. *Jonathan Wild* was his model, but Thackeray could not, or at any rate did not, sustain his irony throughout and obscured his effect by endowing Lyndon with genuinely attractive qualities. In the *Novels by Eminent Hands,* originally called *Punch's Prize*

[2] On Thackeray's connection with, and contributions to, *Fraser's* see M. M. H. Thrall, *Rebellious Fraser's* (1934), pp. 55-80, 295-298. See also H. S. Gulliver, *Thackeray's Literary Apprenticeship* (1924).

[3] M. H. Spielmann, *The Hitherto Unidentified Contributions of W. M. Thackeray to "Punch." With a . . . Bibliography from 1843 to 1848* (1900).

*Novelists* (1847), Thackeray parodied more directly his favorite victim, Bulwer, along with Disraeli, G. P. R. James, and other popular writers of fiction. During these years some very amusing things, along with others that have not worn so well, appeared in *Punch* and annuals and "Christmas Books." The fantastic romance, *A Legend of the Rhine,* is still attractive; *Mrs. Perkins's Ball* is a lively succession of social caricatures; *Rebecca and Rowena* is good sense and sound criticism as well as enjoyable parody; and *The Rose and the Ring* (published so late as 1855) is Thackeray's master-piece in this minor kind, unforgettable for its illustrations, its rimed page-headings, its speeches in inflated verse embedded in the prose, its sense and nonsense, parody and romance.

Reverting to an earlier date, we remark that in its opening chapters *A Shabby-Genteel Story* (1840) gives promise of the serious realism lightened with ironical comedy of which Thackeray was afterwards a master. But at this time he was distracted and distressed by his wife's breakdown, and after some fumbling he fell into mere burlesque where the note is patheti-cally forced. Much later Thackeray attached to this story *The Adventures of Philip,* but the sequence of events is not made clear. A new tenderness and delicacy of treatment, probably not unconnected with the author's personal sadness, is apparent in *The History of Samuel Titmarsh and the* Titmarsh *Great Hoggarty Diamond* (1841), the story of the morally innocent but foolishly gullible employee in a swindling company who is involved in the crash in its affairs and goes to prison. There is a recovery of spirits and a significant change in spirit in *The Snobs of England. By One of Them-selves (Punch,* 1846-1847), better known by its later title, *The Book of Snobs.* Thackeray had formerly known the word *snob* as Cambridge slang, but he now used it with serious intent. Snobbery is "toad-eating," "climbing," and vulgar humbug. In his definition the snob is one who, seeking to emu-late his social superiors, "meanly admires mean things."

Up to this time Thackeray's writings, for all their variety and brilliance, Vanity had not been commensurate with his powers. The failure to establish him- Fair self on an equality with Dickens and above other contemporary novelists had weighed upon his spirits. But when *Vanity Fair* appeared in twenty serial numbers in 1847-1848, it was not long in making its way to the summit of contemporary fiction. In setting the events back a generation and thus not criticizing his own period too directly Thackeray perhaps dis-played a little timidity; but essentially this is a novel of contemporary life. He had often mocked at sensational romances and historical novels. Now he picked up the thread of the novel of manners where Jane Austen had let it fall, and wove his pattern upon a vastly larger loom than hers. He em-ploys no romantic machinery, no intrigue to be unraveled, no secrets to be disclosed. Apart from the episode of Waterloo (where the battle reverberates in the distance), he is concerned with the commonplaces in the life of people who, as he says, have "no reverence except for prosperity, and no eye for anything beyond success," "a set of people living without God in the world."

His anxiety lest he be taken in by such men and women is responsible for the tendency to associate cleverness with evil and goodness with foolishness, and this was the basis for the charge that he was cynical. Conventional categories of human types were disregarded in favor of an individualization so complete that we know the characters better than we know our friends. The very fact that a few inconsistencies can be detected is evidence of the fullness of our knowledge. To this day the debate continues as to whether Becky Sharp killed Joseph Sedley. Thackeray, when asked, said that he did not know; and when readers give reasons for this verdict or that, they are transferring the problem from the domain of fiction to actuality. This is the very triumph of art. A triumph of another kind is the portrayal of Becky in all her wicked worldliness yet with revealing touches that explain her attractiveness.

Pendennis

*Pendennis* (1849-1850) has had its enthusiastic admirers but is little read today. In its scenes in town and country and university there is the plotlessness of life itself, and, as in life, there are stretches of tedium. The surface is broad, but the deeps are seldom plumbed. Thackeray drew upon his own experiences of school and university and the world of journalism; but Pen, though a "portrait of the artist as a young man," is so with variations which make him no mere copy from memory. Major Pendennis has been thought in some respects a portrait of the novelist in his maturity. Rather he is what Thackeray might have been but for the grace of his genius.

Henry Esmond

The hero of *Henry Esmond* (1852) is another self-portrait, such a man as Thackeray might have been had he lived a century and a half earlier. The grave detachment and serene melancholy in Esmond's bearing are suggestive of the novelist, as is the awareness of all-pervading futility and vanity. The political, social, and cultural background of the reign of Queen Anne is painted with a masterly confidence grounded upon long familiarity and lately refreshed by the lectures on *The English Humorists of the Eighteenth Century* which Thackeray had delivered in 1851.[4] Breathing, as it were, the very atmosphere of Augustan England, Thackeray attempted to write *Esmond* in the style of the period. The archaism is an appropriate artifice, but the pastiche is far from convincing. The supreme creation is the character of Beatrix in her fascinating and imperious beauty, her calculating worldliness, and her tragedy. Thackeray was justified in his daring when he portrayed her in her old age in *The Virginians,* for the Baroness de Bernstein is the person whom Beatrix was fated to become.

With the lectures on the *Humorists* as his wares to sell, Thackeray, who needed money, visited the United States in 1852-1853, and with another series on *The Four Georges* made a second tour in 1855-1856.[5] Whether because he was forewarned by Dickens' experiences or because he was more disillusioned and therefore more tolerant, he had on the whole a happy

[4] The word *humorist* is used not in the loose modern sense but with the old meaning of one who displays the *humors* of mankind.
[5] J. G. Wilson, *Thackeray in the United States* (2v, 1904).

time on both visits. He was willing, as Dickens had not been, to see the greatness of the country and recognize that the promise of the future atoned for the shortcomings of the present. His American connections were pleasant and the tours profitable. Impressions of the second tour were worked into *The Virginians* (1857-1859), a rambling novel with characters connected by ties of blood with those in *Esmond* but in a period two generations later. It suffers, as does Dickens' *Chuzzlewit,* from the shifting of scenes between England and America. Between his first transatlantic journey and the second came *The Newcomes* (1853-1855), in the opinion of many readers his most beautiful book. But such readers are swayed by memories of the closing pages and by the character of Ethel Newcome, Thackeray's warmest tribute to the noble qualities of womanhood; and they forget the bitter insistence upon the follies and infirmities and depravities of life. For all the beauty of his nature Colonel Newcome is both fond and foolish; and the portraits of Barnes Newcome, the meanly successful worldly man, and of Clive's mother-in-law, "the Old Campaigner," are terrible in their uncompromising clarity.

*The Virginians*

*The Newcomes*

In 1859 Thackeray accepted the editorship of the newly founded *Cornhill Magazine.* The duties irked him and he soon resigned; but the last two novels and the fragment of a third appeared in its pages. In *Lovel the Widower* (1860) comic power is wasted upon dull and disagreeable people. *The Adventures of Philip* (1861-1862) has its defenders but betrays to most people flagging invention. There was promise of recovery in *Denis Duval* (posthumous, 1864), a historical romance of the late eighteenth century, but Thackeray's death left this unfinished. It has roused no controversy like that which has raged round *Edwin Drood* because the plan of what was to follow is known. The little that was written has a vigor and expansive charm making the loss the more regrettable.[6]

*Last Novels*

## II

Did Thackeray spend so much time parodying and satirizing romantic sentiment because he recognized and distrusted sentimentality in himself and subjected himself to his own satiric scrutiny? *The Book of Snobs,* it will be recalled, was written "by one of themselves." He possessed a terrible power to detect and expose men's self-deceptions, shams, pretenses, and unworthy aspirations. Disillusionment was dominant in his temperament from early life, and the tragedy which shattered his home fixed the mood upon him. He can show anger and indignation, but his usual manner is urbane. He was, as has often been remarked, a spectator of the battle of life, not a com-

*Point of View*

---

[6] Thackeray's poetry has been overshadowed by the novels. He belongs in the company of Victorian writers of light verse touched with sentiment. As in his early prose burlesques, so in his early verse-parodies his footing is not quite certain and the effects aimed at are not always hit—at any rate from our modern angle of vision. But the best of his *vers de société* are of a finesse beyond the reach of his master, Maginn, and comparable to those of Praed. *The Willow Tree* is a unique thing, a double parody; the first part takes off romance with such delicacy that, as in some things by Peacock, almost one is persuaded of the seriousness of the poet's intentions; and then a second part broadly, but with equal cunning, burlesques the first. *The Ballad of Bouillabaisse* combines sad and tender memories of the past with the gourmet's enjoyment of the immediate present; and the incongruous combination is made

batant therein. For this detachment he has incurred the charge of cynicism, because the Victorians expected of their novelists that they would crusade for good causes, and Thackeray, unlike Dickens, was no crusader. Comparisons with Dickens have always been as inevitable as those of Tennyson with Browning; and most of them are inept. But two points of contrast are as important as they are obvious. One is that whereas we are interested in the creatures of Dickens' imagination because they are unlike anyone we have ever known, our interest in Thackeray's is due to their resemblance to people within the experience of most of us. The other is that while Dickens depended for his best effects upon externalities of setting, in Thackeray a moral atmosphere is created.

Thackeray suffered, and complained of suffering, from the prudish inhibitions of his time. Many modern critics have held against him that he ignored or at most hinted at "the sins of the flesh"; but had he defied convention he would not have gained an audience. In the tendency to divide his characters into good and bad he reflects an age which was uncompromising on moral issues; yet here he struggles against convention, insinuating mitigating circumstances into "wicked" natures and showing how often "good" people are weak and foolish.

*Technique*    The technical and structural defects of the novels are obvious—the habit, inherited from Fielding, of stepping down to the footlights and discoursing in his own person; the occasional inconsistencies and lapses of memory; the garrulity and repetitiousness for which he now pays dearly in the loss of readers; the slack and patternless structure. But in his hands the novel advanced in several ways, upon only two of which there is space here to remark. In *Vanity Fair* events are seen not from the point of view of any one character, and there is no one with whom the reader is expected especially to sympathize. Yet the reader does not survey the scene precisely from the author's angle of vision. A double emotion is imparted: that of the actors in the events and that of the author who records them. There is alternately a withdrawal for the sake of a wider view and an approximation for the sake of minute scrutiny. In all the novels the reader is made aware of the flight of time, of renewal and decay, of the generations trodden down by their successors. This effect of time's remorseless flow, associated with such later novelists as Bennett and Galsworthy, Thackeray first introduced into English fiction.

## III

Anthony Trollope [7] (1815-1882) came naturally by the novelist's trade

---

touching and beautiful. The half-humorous, half-pathetic is the kind in which Thackeray worked most successfully, but some of his extravaganzas are still amusing and once at least, in *The Chronicle of the Drum,* he was wholly serious with success. The translations from Béranger are worth mentioning, for as a poet Thackeray exhibits some affinity with the French song-writer and satirist.

[7] There is no definitive edition of Trollope's writings. The Shakespeare Head Edition was designed to fill this want, but since the publication of the *Autobiography* and the *Barchester Novels,* ed. Michael Sadleir (14v, 1929) has proceeded no further. Of some novels there are

(the term is used advisedly), for his mother was a prolific writer.[8] After a *Anthony* boyhood which, as he admits in his candid *Autobiography,* had been un- *Trollope* promising, he obtained a position in the Post Office administration which, with a brief but memorable interim, kept him busy in Ireland from 1841 to 1859. A ramble among the ruins of an Irish mansion gave him the idea for his first novel (1847) which, with its immediate successor, is in the tradition of Carleton and Lever. These books are no longer esteemed even by Trollope's devotees. When he held temporarily an inspectorship in the west of England, the cathedral close of Salisbury opened his imagination to the little world of clerical society. The result was *The Warden* (1855), followed by *Barchester Towers* (1857) and *Doctor Thorne* (1858). *Framley* *The* *Parsonage* appeared in *Cornhill* (1859-1860) and, as Thackeray generously *Barchester* acknowledged, was responsible for the immediate success of the new maga- *Novels* zine. *The Small House at Allington* (1864) followed, and the series of *Barchester Novels* was closed with *The Last Chronicle of Barset* (1867). Trollope's attention was not limited to the region he knew so intimately; *Can You Forgive Her?* (1864), *The Claverings* (1865), *The Belton Estate* (1866), and other books show a wider outlook. Moreover, he visited many countries and recorded his observations in travel books. In 1867 he resigned from the Post Office and in 1868 stood unsuccessfully as a Liberal candidate for Parliament. The disappointment of defeat could not have been great, for he had neither an aptitude for a public career nor stoutly held political convictions. His candidacy merely shows that as a novelist his interest was veering to the political scene. Among the novels on public life are *Phineas* *Other* *Finn* (1869) and *The Prime Minister* (1876).[9] With the systematic industry *Novels* of which he has given an account in the *Autobiography* he turned out novel after novel almost faster than admirers could devour them. The specialists have classified them,[10] and only the specialists have read them all. In addition to the Barchester series and the political novels, there are novels of "manners, convention, and the social dilemma"; half a dozen social satires; four Irish and two Australian novels; four historical and romantic novels; six "psychological analyses and stories of single incident"; four collections of short stories; and (in a class by itself) *The Fixed Period* (1882), one of those glimpses into futurity of which the late nineteenth century produced

many reprints, in Everyman's Library, the World's Classics, and elsewhere. *The Warden,* ed. R. M. Gay (1935) is of special value. — Michael Sadleir, *Bibliography* (1928) and *Anthony Trollope, a Commentary* (1927; rev. ed., 1945); T. H. S. Escott, *Anthony Trollope, his Works, Associates, and Literary Originals* (1913); S. van B. Nichols, *The Significance of Anthony Trollope* (1925); Hugh Walpole, *Anthony Trollope* (EML Series, 1928); L. P. and R. P. Stebbins, *The Trollopes: the Chronicle of a Writing Family* (1945); J. H. Wildman, *Anthony Trollope's England* (Providence, 1940); Baker, VIII, ch. IV; George Saintsbury, "Trollope Revisited," *Essays and Papers* (1923), II. 312-343. See also *The Trollopian* (1945-    ).

[8] Mrs. Frances Trollope (1780-1863), author of the *Domestic Manners of the Americans* (1832), which gave great offense in the United States; *The Vicar of Wrexall* (1837), an anti-clerical novel; and forty-odd other books. The recent vogue of Anthony Trollope has resulted in some overestimates of her worth as a novelist. See Michael Sadleir, *Anthony Trollope,* pp. 29-97. — Anthony's elder brother, Thomas Adolphus Trollope (1810-1892), lived long in Italy and wrote popular history, miscellaneous fiction, and stories of Italian society.

[9] M. E. Speare, *The Political Novel* (1924), ch. VII.

[10] Michael Sadleir, *Anthony Trollope,* pp. 415-419.

many examples. It is a very unconvincing forecast of life in 1980; Trollope was no visionary. All told, these categories embrace some fifty titles.

When it is remembered that he was forty when *The Warden* appeared and over fifty when the Barchester series was closed, it is not surprising that many of the later books are of little value and the best of them uneven in quality. The general line of his development was from the familiar to the exceptional and abnormal. There were early raids into strange countries but he did not attempt to occupy them till he was too old to become acclimated. "His great, his inestimable merit," said Henry James, "was a complete appreciation of the usual" [11]—an opinion which George Moore repeated in a less bland fashion when he said that Trollope "carried commonplace further than anyone dreamed it could be carried." [12] In the parsonage or bishop's palace or cathedral stall or close he observed the immemorial round of English custom. It chanced that he selected for his freshest scrutiny "scenes of clerical life," but that other representatives of the "governing classes" served his purposes almost as well is shown by the glimpses of the political world that appear in his pictures of the ecclesiastical and by the ease with which he turned from the latter to the former. His clergymen are Englishmen first and divines only a long way after. Such a book as Mrs. Humphry Ward's *Robert Elsmere* was beyond his intellectual range and beside his artistic purpose. With the problems of faith and doubt, religious meditation, and the theological issues that were dividing the churches he evinces no concern, just as in the political novels he is not interested (as was Disraeli) in the great questions of the day but in the party game. The little world of a diocese is a stage broad enough for him. Whole classes of society that live in the sociological fiction of the period never appear in his pages. In his microcosm the lesser faults and foibles of human nature are displayed—the heart-burnings of social aspirants; the distinctions of caste and class; the gossip and scandal, jealousy and arrogance of petty people. Serious moral obliquity is rarely his theme, save in *The Eustace Diamonds* (1873) and in *The Way We Live Now* (1875). The latter, openly but unsuccessfully challenging comparison with *Vanity Fair,* is one long piece of satiric invective against modern life, surprising as coming from a writer usually so genial and tolerant. Because his intention is generally to "sport with human follies, not with crimes," Trollope's natural manner suggests indulgent amusement. When derisive or censorious he generally fails, for his laughter, unlike Meredith's, is not "corrective." He did not use the novel as a vehicle for a "philosophy of life" which he did not claim to possess.

Henry James observed that of the two kinds of literary taste, "the taste for the emotion of surprise and the taste for the emotion of recognition," Trollope gratified the latter.[13] Here he resembled his master, Thackeray.

*"The Usual"*

11 Henry James, *Partial Portraits* (ed. 1919), p. 100.
12 George Moore, *Avowals* (1919), p. 89.
13 *Partial Portraits.* p. 133.

Excluding from his best work the exceptional and minimizing the improbable, he was truthworthy in his reading of life. He knew men and women not in those isolated examples of moral grandeur which make us proud of our human nature nor in those of turpitude which horrify and shame, but on the average level where contemplation makes us tolerant and a little humble. His method as an artist was to begin with a group of such characters and *Method* having set them in relation to one another, to depend upon the logic of circumstances for the "plot" which was bound to result from the clash of opposing egotisms. Knowing intimately the people of his imaginary world, very rarely could he bring himself to violate the probabilities of motive and action for the sake of the "story." A technical device, used rarely but always with startling effectiveness, is his sudden intrusion in his own person (though he has no part in the story) to record an encounter with this character or that. The reappearance of people in novel after novel, sometimes in principal, sometimes subordinate capacities, enhances this sense of intimacy. All this coming and going produces an impression of an actual world like that of the *Comédie Humaine*. A realism less sincere would have been hopelessly deformed by Trollope's adherence to the old convention of bestowing upon his characters such fantastic names as Mr. Quiverful, Mr. Stickatit, or Dr. Fillgrave. This was all very well so long as people so encumbered remained in the background behind Archdeacon Grantly or Mrs. Proudie; but when in later novels men with names suggestive of *Pilgrim's Progress* are promoted (as is Mr. Quiverful) to a principal rôle the blemish is serious and the reader does not without effort suspend disbelief. Faith is put to a severer test by Trollope's unnecessary and persistent habit of reminding us that the story he tells is, after all, only make-believe.[14] In the long run his meticulousness in detail, his insistence upon explanation, his inability to let suggestion do the work of statement, his too faithful record of tedious conversation, his prolixity, his undistinguished style (a heavy-footed amble for which George Moore found the wittily apt epithet "Trollopy")—all this will tell against his reputation.

Trollope's posthumous revelation of his calculated, scheduled, daily stint *Post-* was responsible for the conception of him as a mere industrious journeyman- *humous* of-letters. Obviously, without methodical habits he could not have accom- *Vogue* plished his immense amount of work. Obviously, had he written less he would probably have written better. In the period between the World Wars his reputation rose to new heights. This revival of interest was initiated by the recommendations of a few authoritative critics who, however, would not have been heeded had not Trollope appealed to a disillusioned and anxious generation, skeptical of the heroic virtues and amused by a candid and psychologically convincing picture of average humanity.

---

14 James, who remarks upon this habit, calls it "suicidal" (*ibid.*, p. 116).

# XXV

## Other Novelists of the Mid-Century

To complete a survey of Victorian fiction before the appearance of Meredith and Hardy we must revert to the eighteen-twenties when Bulwer and Disraeli published their first novels.

### I

*Edward Bulwer*

The life of Edward Lytton Bulwer [1] (1803-1873) as politician and "dandy" cannot be recounted here, and there is space to touch on only the most significant of his novels. [2] The earliest of these are tainted with Gothic and Godwinian insincerities. The first that is memorable is *Pelham* (1828), a picture of fashionable society whose satiric intent was not apprehended by Carlyle. [3] With *Paul Clifford* (1830) Bulwer started the vogue of romances of crime and social injustice, and continued this vein in *Eugene Aram* (1833), inventing a motive for the murder, with which motive the reader is asked to sympathize. In a series of historical novels he followed Scott with

*Historical Novels*

much careful and self-conscious documentation. *The Last Days of Pompeii* (1834) presents the contrast of pagan brutality, sensuality, and superstition with the simplicity and piety of primitive Christianity. *Rienzi* (1835), on the medieval Roman "tribune," *Leila* (1838), on the Conquest of Granada, *The Last of the Barons* (1843), on the Wars of the Roses, and *Harold* (1848), on the Norman Conquest, followed. All display the same qualities of careful, scholarly preparation, smoothness of construction, over-facility of style, and a bookishness which makes for an effect of low vitality. Romance and history are conjoined in them, and though in places the romance is heavily laid on, for long stretches it is quite subordinated to history. Questions of relative merit apart, a point of contrast with Scott is that Bulwer built his stories round some great personage of authentic history,

---

[1] On inheriting Knebworth Bulwer took the additional surname of Lytton; he was knighted; and in 1866 was created Baron Lytton. — *Novels*, New Knebworth Edition (29v, 1895-1898). — The Earl of Lytton, *The Life of Edward Bulwer, First Lord Lytton* (2v, 1913); Michael Sadleir, *Bulwer, a Panorama: I: Edward and Rosina* (1931). When the projected "panorama" was abandoned, Mr. Sadleir renamed this book *Bulwer and his Wife* (1933). Material for the intended second part went, with a shift of emphasis, into *The Strange Life of Lady Blessington* (1935). See also E. B. Burgum, *The Literary Career of Edward Bulwer, Lord Lytton* (1924).

[2] On Bulwer's plays see above, ch. xv. On his pretentious poem *King Arthur* (1848), of interest only as a precursor of Tennyson's *Idylls of the King*, see Howard Maynadier, *The Arthur of the English Poets* (1907), pp. 351-352. His other poems are forgotten. Still of some value as a document is *England and the English* (1833), a shrewd and lively survey of contemporary society and culture, with an emphasis upon snobbery and class-consciousness.

[3] *Sartor Resartus*, Book III, ch. x.

whereas Scott relegated illustrious figures to the middle distance or the background, reserving the foreground for characters of his own creation.

Bulwer did not limit himself to historical fiction. *Zanoni* (1842) is a fantastic romance of terror, supernaturalism, and occultism. The protagonist is granted immortality on the condition that he never yield to the dictates of human sympathy; but after five thousand years he sacrifices himself during the French Revolution, for the sake of the woman he loves. Bulwer returned more than once to supernatural themes, and in *A Strange Story* (1862) he almost succeeded in creating a masterpiece of weird terror. What he called "Varieties of English Life" (though there is not much variety) he depicted in a succession of realistic stories of which the best are *The Caxtons* (1849) and *My Novel* (1853). *The Coming Race* (1871) is a utopian fantasy of a lost subterranean people. In *Kenelm Chillingly* (1873) Bulwer's sociological speculations came down—or up—to earth. The wealthy hero is a "muscular Christian" who lives in the slums and works as a laborer. *Other Novels*

Bulwer was a writer whose restless and versatile talent took color from some fashions and helped to shape others. An opportunist alike in his parliamentary and literary career, and driven on by need of money, he wrote too much and too fast in too many genres of literature. It is only as a novelist that he is remembered—and even as such he is in peril of oblivion.

The crowded life of Benjamin Disraeli [4] (1804-1881) belongs to political rather than literary history, and a survey of his novels may be undertaken with little reference to his career. In *Vivian Grey* (1826) the young author's limited experiences and unlimited aspirations are attached to a story of political intrigue enlivened with witty dialogue in the manner of Peacock. Dialogue is the main ingredient in the Lucianic fantasies, *The Voyage of Popanilla* (1828) and *Ixion in Heaven* (1833). *The Young Duke* (1831) is so much encumbered with ephemeral politics as to be today unreadable. *Contarini Fleming* (1832) is chiefly interesting for what is obviously a self-portrait set against the background of the Levant where Disraeli had traveled in 1828-1831. The political theme is abandoned in *Henrietta Temple* (1836) in favor of a love story. The hero is loved by two women, to one of whom he is betrothed while with the other he is infatuated. Disraeli was always unable to render passion convincingly; the effort to remedy this defect merely heightened the affectations of his style. *Venetia* (1837) has been kept in remembrance because two of the characters share between them, with a curious redistribution, the traits and circumstances of Byron and Shelley, about whom Disraeli, through his father [5] and John Murray, *Benjamin Disraeli*

[4] *Novels and Tales,* Bradenham Edition, introduction by Philip Guedalla (12v, 1926-1927). — W. F. Monypenny and G. E. Buckle, *The Life of Benjamin Disraeli, Earl of Beaconsfield* (6v, 1910-1920) in which the following parts are important for Disraeli as a writer: I, chs. VI, X, XV; II, chs. VII, IX; III, ch. II; V, chs. IV and Appendix; VI, ch. XV. See also M. E. Speare, *The Political Novel* (1924), chs. II-VI; F. T. Russell, *Satire in the Victorian Novel* (1920).

[5] Isaac Disraeli (1766-1848), author of *The Curiosities of Literature* (five series, 1791-1834), *The Calamities of Authors* (1812-1813), *The Quarrels of Authors* (1814), and other works.

possessed somewhat more information than was then known to the public.

When Disraeli became a member of the parliamentary group of "Tory Democrats" known as "Young England," he promulgated their theories and program in a trilogy of novels dealing, respectively, with the political, social, and religious problems of the day. *Coningsby* (1844) pictures the English governing classes. The slender plot unfolds the development of the political ideas of the hero, a young aristocrat with a sense of social responsibility. Contrasted with him is his grandfather, a man of immense wealth and immovable conservatism. Disraeli's fondness for the pseudo-occult finds an outlet in the theatrical character of the Jew, Sidonia, through whom the wisdom of the East is brought to bear upon the problems of the West. "Comic relief" is provided by the figures of the political agents; there is a variety of swiftly moving scenes; and a great deal of discussion reminiscent of Peacock but without Peacock's brilliant brevity. *Sybil* (1845) has for its theme the "Two Nations," that is, the rich and the poor of England. Disraeli had supported the Chartists' petition to Parliament, had visited Manchester, and had studied the reports of Shaftesbury's committee on mines and factories. There is consequently real feeling springing from first-hand observation in his portrayal of industrial squalor and agricultural misery, the cruelty to children, and the brutalization of the poor. The contrast between the two divisions of society is epitomized in the splendor of Mobray Castle and the wretchedness of the town of Mobray near by. Disraeli's indictment of Whigs and Tories alike is that for all their public protestations they are indifferent to social wrongs. The hero, a "Tory Democrat," who falls in love with the daughter of one of the Chartists, argues that the people are too weak to right these wrongs themselves; hope lies in the awakening of the aristocracy to a sense of their responsibilities as hereditary leaders. There is thus a close connection between *Sybil* and Carlyle's *Chartism* and *Past and Present,* though Carlyle, without faith in the degenerate aristocracy, sought to arouse the new "Captains of Industry," and though Disraeli was without Carlyle's moral fervor. *Tancred* (1847) centers attention upon religious issues and contains some of Disraeli's strongest satire and absurdest occultism. The wisdom of the East is again summoned to the aid of occidental bewilderment; but the consequence is merely more bewilderment; there is no revelation of saving truth, and though the hero's journey to Jerusalem provides the occasion for some fine descriptions of landscape, the dabbling in supernaturalism is but so much clap-trap and the famous "Great Asian Mystery" remains unexplained and inexplicable.

Not till the close of his first ministry did Disraeli again occupy himself with fiction. The central figure in *Lothair* (1870) is a young man of wealth and title who is in quest of the true path. A number of recent conspicuous conversions to Roman Catholicism suggested the admirable narrative of Catholic intrigue and the recognizably real people engaged therein. The rival claims of Canterbury and Rome are argued in Peacockian style. The theme of the three women who influence the hero is a fanciful variation

*"The Two Nations"*

upon the part played by female friendships in the author's own career. Lothair goes to Italy during the Risorgimento and is wounded at the battle of Mentana. But here Disraeli touches only the fringes of a great subject and his treatment of Italian politics and aspirations cannot bear comparison with Meredith's in *Vittoria*. Before the end we have once more the appeal to the wisdom of the East, for Disraeli, though a Christian, was in mind and temperament an Oriental Semite; the ancient East, for romantic Englishmen a way of escape, was his racial and spiritual home. *Endymion* (1880), written after Disraeli's second and final retirement from the premiership, proved not so intimately autobiographical as the public had hoped, but is a backward glance over the author's triumphant career. Again there is the romantic fantasy of the influence of feminine friendships upon the hero; but more interesting are the vivid pictures of Whig and Tory politics, of the Tractarian Movement, the railway mania and collapse, and many other events and affairs, all set against the opulent background of high society.

This taste for opulence is the conspicuous weakness of Disraeli as a novelist *Character-* of social reform. As in Bulwer so in Disraeli, a genuine sympathy with the *istics* poor and outcast is vitiated by a delight in luxury and display and a fondness for "great" people. Another and more fundamental weakness is the want of a creative imagination. Disraeli is not a Protean artist, able to assume many shapes. He can manage skilfully not only events but characters and thoughts so long as they are within the range of his own experiences, hopes, and dreams; but when he attempts to create a character with whom he has nothing in common, his power fails and he can draw only conventional figures or caricatures. The flamboyance of his style, the inconclusiveness of his arguments, and the ephemerality of many of his themes are severe handicaps upon his books. They are no longer widely read, but it is likely that the lasting fascination of Disraeli's personality and career will keep them long in remembrance.

## II

Charles Kingsley [6] (1819-1875), clergyman, naturalist, sportsman, and *Charles* something of a poet,[7] employed fiction for purposes of propaganda more *Kingsley* effectively than Bulwer and Disraeli because his sympathies were more sincerely engaged than theirs in the task of social reform. He began to write

[6] *Life and Works* (19v, 1901-1903), Vols. I-IV being a reprint of *Charles Kingsley. His Letters and Memories of his Life*, ed. by his wife (1877). — S. E. Baldwin, *Charles Kingsley* (Ithaca, 1934); M. F. Thorp, *Charles Kingsley* (Princeton, 1937); L. Cazamian, *Le Roman social en Angleterre* (Paris, 1903), pp. 436-531; L. Cazamian, *Kingsley: le socialisme chretien* (Paris, 1904); Ella Juhnke, "Charles Kingsley als sozialreformatorischer Schriftsteller," *Anglia*, n.f., XXXVII (1925). 32-79; M. W. Hanavalt, "Charles Kingsley and Science," *SP*, XXXIV (1937). 589-611; Baker, VIII. 166-176; Karl Brunner, "Charles Kingsley als christlich-sozialer Dichter," *Anglia*, XLVI (1922). 289-322; XLVII (1923). 1-33.

[7] *Andromeda* (1858), in hexameters, is Kingsley's most ambitious poem; *The Sands of Dee* his best known. *The Saint's Tragedy* (1848), a closet-drama on St. Elizabeth of Hungary, is in blank verse with passages in prose. — Kingsley published lectures on history and science, sermons, and social and theological tracts. *The Water-Babies* (1863) has slipped from the high place it formerly occupied among children's books.

novels under the inspiration of the eloquent theorizing of Carlyle and the practical Christian Socialism of F. D. Maurice. Along with faint echoes of Carlyle's style there are repetitions, rather than mere echoes, of his doctrines of work and duty, leadership and silent strength. Kingsley's books express the stirring social conscience of the mid-century, and it is not without significance that his first novel appeared in 1848, the Year of Revolutions. This was *Yeast,* followed by *Alton Locke* (1850). The title of the former is symbolic of the ferment of new ideas. Both are as much sociological tracts as works of fiction, with little plot and a great deal of discussion (in which there are reminiscences of Disraeli's *Sybil*). In *Alton Locke* an old Chartist, after the failure of the movement, renounces force as an instrument of reform in favor of moral suasion; and in both books there is offered in place of discredited Chartism that Christian philanthropy which is a form of benevolent individualism. Trade-unionism is attacked, but the horrors of insanitation and slum-dwellings are exposed and there is an ardent advocacy of free schools, country life, and hygiene.

Kingsley dared greatly and did not quite succeed when he used the historical novel for the purpose indicated in the title *Hypatia: New Foes with an Old Face* (1853). Accepting the principle that human nature does not change, he transplanted modern moral and intellectual types to ancient Alexandria, implying parallels between nineteenth-century controversies and the old antagonisms of Jews, Christians, heretics, and pagans. The analogies are forced, but they may be disregarded while we watch the turbulence of the cosmopolitan city which is depicted with considerable brilliance and archaeological accuracy. *Westward Ho!* (1855) was written with the intention to brace English nerves in wartime by means of a recital of the Elizabethan adventurers' heroic deeds. But to fasten upon these grand old sea-rovers a code of morals characteristic of mid-Victorian England was a gross anachronism, and the Protestant bias is as extreme as Froude's. The high spirits and martial fervor of the tale made it enormously popular, and the genuinely tragic close is still moving.

From antiquity and the Elizabethan age Kingsley returned to his own time in *Two Years Ago* (1857), the title pointing back to the year of the Crimean War. Here Kingsley preached the gospel of strength and self-sacrifice and the ennobling virtues of war. More appealing to us is the narrative of bravery shown amid the ravages of the cholera. The transformation which various characters undergo under the stress of war is not explained psychologically but merely stated sentimentally. The same compound of manly virtues which Kingsley celebrated in earlier books appears for the last time in *Hereward the Wake* (1866) where, turning back to a heroic age, Kingsley captures at least suggestions of the tragic grandeur of the Norse sagas, the self-reliance and dauntless courage of brutal and passionate primitive heroes.

The declamatory verve with which Kingsley expressed an admiration for strength and courage combined with his genuine high-mindedness to win him an enormous following in his own generation. The Victorians found satisfaction in seeing young men exchange ledgers for swords. We have become more doubtful of the benefit, and our doubts overshadow Kingsley's reputation today.[8]

## III

As the wife of a Unitarian minister in Manchester, Elizabeth Cleghorn Gaskell [9] (1810-1865) worked among the poor, knew at first-hand the misery of the industrial areas, and was in the midst of the Chartist agitation. As the champion of the mill-hands she first appeared as a novelist with *Mary Barton, a Tale of Manchester Life* (1848). The melodramatic plot is of no consequence in a book which, exposing the callousness of employers to the sufferings of the operatives, is memorable as a specific, if perhaps not entirely impartial, illustration of the social wrongs against which Carlyle was fulminating in more general terms. *Ruth* (1853) is for its date a bold, if over-emotional, plea for a "single standard" of sexual morality; it points forward to *Tess of the d'Urbervilles*. When invited by Dickens to contribute to *Household Words,* Mrs. Gaskell turned from these sociological problems to the memories of her own childhood in Cheshire. *Cranford* (1853) is not precisely a novel, but rather a series of sketches of simple, often humble, provincial people. There is little satire but an abundance of quiet humor and sympathy (reminiscent of Goldsmith) in the narration of the little incidents that make up their lives. Mrs. Gaskell worked the same vein but with less simplicity and success in later books. In *North and South* (1855) she reverted to the serious theme of the struggle between capital and labor. As the title promises, there is presented a contrast between the old agricultural gentry of the South of England who with their wealth have inherited a feudal sense of responsibility, and the new moneyed industrialists of the North. Mrs. Gaskell's endeavor to be fair is seen in her portrayal of a philanthropic manufacturer. Types of importance for understanding the period are the clergyman who relinquishes his living because he cannot still

*Elizabeth Gaskell*

---

[8] Henry Kingsley (1830-1876) possessed a subtler and at the same time less effective mind than his brother Charles. With no great gift for narrative he displays considerable psychological insight. Having lived in the Antipodes, he made use of his experiences in *Geoffrey Hamlyn* (1859). *Ravenshoe* (1862; World's Classics, 1925) is his best book, hopelessly confused in narrative but with some fine episodes and appealing characters which are drawn from the author's benevolent view of human nature. — See S. M. Ellis, *Henry Kingsley: Towards a Vindication* (1931). — Charles Kingsley's insistent preaching of the gospel of health and the out-of-doors connects his books with the enormously popular *Tom Brown's School Days* (1856) by Thomas Hughes (1823-1897) which spread the doctrines of "Muscular Christianity" and pictured young men with, as was said, "the souls of saints and the bodies of vikings." Another novelist who glorified the saga-spirit was G. A. Lawrence (1827-1876), the author of *Guy Livingston* (1857) and other tales depicting heroes of magnificent courage and physique. This "physical force" school of fiction was of practical benefit in promoting interest in games and athletics.

[9] *Works,* Knutsford Edition, introduction by A. W. Ward (8v, 1906); *Letters of Mrs. Gaskell and C. E. Norton,* ed. Jane Whitehill (1932). — A. S. Whitfield, *Mrs. Gaskell: Her Life and Work* (1929); G. De W. Sanders, *Elizabeth Gaskell* (New Haven, 1929), with bibliography by C. S. Northup; Elizabeth Haldane, *Mrs. Gaskell and her Friends* (1930).

his spiritual doubts and the trade-unionist official who combines social radicalism with militant atheism. This book has obvious connections with Dickens' *Hard Times* and Charlotte Brontë's *Shirley*. Mrs. Gaskell's last novel, *Wives and Daughters* [10] (1866), delineates two daughters of contrasting temperaments, who are further contrasted with their foolish mother, Mrs. Gibson. The mother is a memorable creation because though humorously drawn she is kept within the bounds of truth. The satire on snobbishness, though more gentle in manner than Thackeray's, is none the less penetrating.

Mrs. Gaskell has points of connection with George Eliot as a woman who turned fiction to the purposes of morality, though she carried the burden of her mission more lightly than George Eliot did hers. As a shrewd observer of the provincial scene she is allied to Trollope and as a novelist of social reform to Charles Kingsley. There are echoes of Charlotte Brontë in her books, and as a compensation for the lack of the passion which her friend possessed abundantly, she shows a humorous aloofness which is wanting in the novels of that greater woman of genius. Mrs. Gaskell's *Life of Charlotte Brontë* (1857) is a masterpiece of biography.[11]

## IV

The
Brontës

The three Brontë sisters [12] have been overlaid with so much biography, criticism, and conjecture that in reading about them there is danger lest their own books be left unread. Theory and surmise, taking their start from the indubitably autobiographic character of parts of Charlotte's novels, have

---

[10] Posthumous; completed all but a few pages at the time of Mrs. Gaskell's death.

[11] Other women novelists who were interested in social reform used fiction for moral and uplifting purposes. Harriet Martineau (1802-1876), the daughter of James Martineau the philosopher and Unitarian divine, besides writing copiously on public affairs, travel, history, Positivism, and economics, resorted to fiction in her *Illustrations of Political Economy* (1831) and *Illustrations of Taxation* (1834). Frankly didactic, these tales were immediately popular and very influential. She also published two novels less directly tendentious. See Theodora Bosanquet, *Harriet Martineau* (1927). — Dinah Maria Mulock, Mrs. Craik (1826-1887), was the author of *John Halifax, Gentleman* (1856), one of the most famous of Victorian "bestsellers." In it the hero rises from poverty to wealth without sacrificing his integrity. Mrs. Craik's other novels are forgotten. — Charlotte Mary Yonge (1823-1901) commanded a wide audience. *The Heir of Redclyffe* (1853), another "best-seller," develops with characteristic earnestness the theme of wrong and expiation. *The Daisy Chain* (1856) shows Miss Yonge's intimate connection with High Anglicanism. *The Dove in the Eagle's Nest* (1866) is the best example of her historical novels; she ranged widely through history and took great liberties with it. Among her stories for children *The Little Duke* (1854) is still attractive. She also specialized in chronicles of family life. — The two Jane Austen-like novels of Emily Eden (1797-1869), *The Semi-attached Couple* and *The Semi-detached House* (both 1860), were rescued from oblivion by reprints in 1928 when their light irony made a special sophisticated appeal.

[12] *The Shakespeare Head Brontë*, ed. T. J. Wise and J. A. Symington (20v, 1931-1940), contains, besides the novels, poems and juvenilia, the correspondence, some unpublished material, and a biography; *Life and Works of Charlotte Brontë and her Sisters*, Haworth Edition, with introductions to the novels by Mrs. Humphry Ward and to Mrs. Gaskell's *Life* (see below) by C. K. Shorter (7v, 1899; many reprints); Emily Brontë, *Complete Poems*, ed. C. W. Hatfield (1941); Charlotte Brontë, *The Twelve Adventurers*, ed. C. W. Hatfield (1925) and *The Spell: an Extravaganza*, ed. G. E. MacLean (1931); *Brontë Poems: Selections*, ed. A. C. Benson (1915). — Laura L. Hinkley, *Charlotte and Emily: The Brontës* (1945); Mrs. E. C. Gaskell, *The Life of Charlotte Brontë* (2v, 1857), ed. May Sinclair (1908); C. K.

played fantastic tricks with probability. *Wuthering Heights* has been assigned in part to their brother, Branwell, or, taken wholly from Emily, has
been attributed to Charlotte.[13] The origins of their genius have been traced
to such diverse stimuli as their Celtic ancestry [14] or their unfortunate wastrel
of a brother [15] or their reading of Methodist magazines.[16] The novels have
been interpreted as *romans à clef* (which to some extent they are), and there
is scarcely a character or scene that has not been identified with actuality.[17]
The postponed publication and slow release of materials kept from psychologists information that might have modified their conclusions.[18]

The Rev. Patrick Brontë [19] was an Irishman; his wife came from Cornwall. To this pair were born six children: two elder daughters, then
Charlotte (1816-1855), Patrick Branwell (1817-1848), Emily Jane (1818-1848),
and Anne (1820-1849). Shortly after Anne's birth the family came to
Haworth parsonage in Yorkshire, and there in 1821 the mother died. Mr.
Brontë invited his sister-in-law, Elizabeth Branwell, to live with him and
share the responsibility for the rearing of his children. In 1824 all the girls

Shorter, *The Brontës and their Circle* (1896) and *The Brontës: Life and Letters* (2v, 1908);
Ernest Dimnet, *Les Soeurs Brontë* (Paris, 1910), translated by Louise M. Sill (1927); May
Sinclair, *The Three Brontës* (1914) Mrs. E. H. Chadwick, *In the Footsteps of the Brontës*
(1914); J. C. Wright, *The Story of the Brontës* (1925); Romer Wilson [Mrs. F. R. M. O'Brien],
*All Alone: The Life and Private History of Emily Jane Brontë* (1928); K. A. R. Sugden,
*A Short History of the Brontës* (1928); Emile and Georges Romieu, *La Vie des soeurs Brontë*
(Paris, 1930), English translation, *Three Virgins of Haworth* (1931); E. M. Delafield, *The
Brontës* (1935); E. F. Benson, *Charlotte Brontë,* (1932); I. C. Willis, *The Brontës* (1933);
W. B. White, *The Miracle of Haworth: a Brontë Study* (1937); F. E. Ratchford, *The Brontës'
Web of Childhood* (1941), of first importance; *The Transactions of the Brontë Society* (Brad-
ford, 1895—in progress); Baker, VIII chs. I and II; J. C. Smith, "Emily Brontë," *E&S*, v
(1914). 132-152; Janet Spens, "Charlotte Brontë" *E&S*, XIV (1929). 54-70.

13 Some critics believe that Branwell wrote the first two chapters. He claimed to be joint-
author, but his word is not to be trusted. Emily may have talked over her plans with him,
but at the time the book was written he was too far gone in drink to have contributed much
to it. For the theory of Charlotte's authorship see J. M. Dembley, *The Key to the Brontë
Works* (1911); I. C. Willis, *The Authorship of Wuthering Heights* (1936).

14 C. O'Bryne, *The Gaelic Source of the Brontë Genius* (1933). See also William Wright,
*The Brontës in Ireland* (1894) and A. M. MacKay's reply, *The Brontës: Fact and Fiction*
(1897), which also reviews other Brontë "myths."

15 E. E. Kinsley, *Pattern for Genius: a Story of Branwell Brontë and his Three Sisters* (1939).
See also F. A. Leyland, *The Brontë Family with Special Reference to Patrick Branwell Brontë*
(2v, 1886).

16 Mrs. G. E. Harrison, *Methodist Good Companions* (1935), ch. v: "Reactions in Haworth
Parsonage." It is here shown that these magazines, with their accounts of revivalist meetings,
fanaticism, hysteria, and preternatural manifestations, had some influence upon the sisters. For
their effect upon Emily see Baker, VIII. 72. note I.

17 *Sources of Charlotte Brontë's Novels, Persons and Places; Publications of the Brontë
Society*, VIII, Part IV (1935). Isabel Clarke, *Haworth Parsonage* (1927), introduces into her
narrative a conjectured love affair between Emily and her father's curate Weightman for which
there is not a shred of evidence. On the basis of an incorrectly deciphered manuscript annotation Emily has been given a lover who never existed; see Virginia Moore, *The Life and Eager
Death of Emily Brontë* (1936), and C. W. Hatfield's letter in *LTLS*, August 29, 1936, showing
that Miss Moore misread Charlotte Brontë's annotation "Love's Farewell" as "Louis Parensell"
and thus created the lover. On the basis of Emily's occult experiences she has also been given
a kind of demon-lover in whom (if one understands the theory) the features of Lord Byron
are faintly discernible. There are of course Byronic and "Satanic" elements in Emily's thought.
See Helen Brown, "The Influence of Byron on Emily Brontë," *MLR*, XXXIV (1939). 374-381.

18 Rosamond Langbridge, *Charlotte Brontë: a Psychological Study* (1929); Lucile Dooley,
"Psycho-Analysis of Charlotte Brontë as a Type of the Woman of Genius," *American Journal
of Psychology*, XXXI (1920). 221-273.

19 On Patrick Brontë's earlier career see W. W. Yates, *The Father of the Brontës: His Life
and Work at Dewsbury and Hartshead* (1897).

but Anne were put into a school for clergymen's daughters, where the two eldest died—of under-nourishment and harsh discipline, as Charlotte thought,[20] but more likely of tuberculosis. Charlotte and Emily were brought back to Haworth, where, though their father guided them in unmethodical study, they were left largely to their own devices, to play among the graves in the churchyard, roam over the moors, and build a world of their own imagining. At this time they began those strange, famous little books, generally written in microscopic hands, wherein Charlotte, with some bungling help from Branwell, recorded the adventurous, passionate lives of the people of "Angria,"[21] while Emily composed the *Gondal Chronicle*[22] on the wars and intrigues of Royalists and Republicans in a mysterious kingdom of the North.[23] In Charlotte's childish and adolescent fantasies have been discovered anticipations, in characters and situations, of her mature work. Emily continued to make the *Gondal Chronicle* a receptacle for her poems and was working on it as late as 1845; but the prose cycle was destroyed. When her poems were published the links with Gondal were as far as possible obliterated.

In 1831 Charlotte was sent to a boarding-school where she made friends with Mary Taylor and Ellen Nussey to whom in later years many of her most interesting letters were addressed. Once more at Haworth, she helped in the education of her younger sisters, and four years later returned to the same school, this time as a governess, while Emily and then Anne were pupils for a short time. After filling two other posts as governess, she planned with Emily to open a school of their own; and to gain proficiency in French and other polite accomplishments the two sisters went to Brussels, with funds provided by their aunt, and became pupils in the Pensionnat Héger. Eight months of 1842 were passed there till they were called home by the death of their aunt. For Charlotte there was a second, longer sojourn in Brussels in 1843-1844, this time as a teacher in the same establishment. Her loneliness and despondency and what most biographers have interpreted as her passion for Constantin Heger enter into *Villette*. When she rejoined Emily at Haworth, the sisters advertised for pupils—but none came. In the following years they watched with sorrow and shame the moral degradation of their brother whose talents were wasted long before he went to a drunkard's grave in 1848. In 1845 Charlotte made the accidental discovery of Emily's poems in manuscript; Anne had also been writing verse; and

---

[20] Mrs. Gaskell made it clear that the Clergy Daughters School at Cowan Bridge, of which the Rev. W. C. Wilson was the principal, is the "Lowood" of *Jane Eyre*. See Henry Shepheard, *A Vindication of the Clergy Daughters School and the Rev. W. Carus Wilson from the Remarks in the Life of Charlotte Brontë* (1857).

[21] F. E. Ratchford, "Charlotte Brontë's Angrian Cycle of Stories," *PMLA*, XLII (1928). 494-501.

[22] Emily Brontë, *Gondal Poems*, ed. Helen Brown and Joan Mott (1938); M. H. Dodds, "Gondaliand," *MLR*, XVIII (1923). 9-21, and "A Second Visit to Gondaliand," *ibid.*, XXI (1926). 373-379; F. E. Ratchford, *Two Poems by Emily Brontë: with the Gondal Background of her Poems and Novel* (Austin, 1934).

[23] Anne, though in Emily's confidence, never entered so deeply into these imaginary countries as did her elder sisters.

Charlotte herself had composed many poems. The result of this discovery was *Poems by Currer, Ellis and Acton Bell* (1846); it attracted no attention whatsoever. All three were now busy writing novels. *The Professor,* Charlotte's first novel, a determined effort to escape from the romantic dream-world of Angria into actuality, went the round of the publishers; but Smith, Elder and Company, in rejecting it, intimated that they would be glad to consider another story of "more varied interest." *Jane Eyre* was submitted immediately and on its publication (1847) achieved a sensational success.[24] Another publisher brought out together Emily's *Wuthering Heights* and Anne's *Agnes Grey*, and taking advantage of the popularity of *Jane Eyre,* accepted Anne's *The Tenant of Wildfell Hall* (1848), letting a rumor get about that the pseudonyms Currer and Acton Bell concealed the same individual. To prove the contrary Charlotte and Anne visited London and showed themselves to the former's publisher. They had not long been home when Branwell died; and in December Emily died. An attempt to arrest the course of Anne's disease by seeking a change of air proved unavailing, and she died at Scarborough in May, 1849. Charlotte was left alone, to continue her writing and care for her father, now going blind.

*Shirley,* begun in confidence, was resumed in distress; the transition occurs in the chapter entitled "The Valley of the Shadow of Death." In sorrowful loneliness Charlotte could not bring herself to adhere to what was apparently her original intention, to bring the story to a tragic ending, and wrenching probabilities, she closed it in happiness. It was published in the autumn of 1849. The years of social lionizing followed when in London and elsewhere she met Thackeray, Matthew Arnold, Mrs. Gaskell, Harriet Martineau, and other famous people. *Villette* appeared in 1853. Having already rejected three suitors, Charlotte married her father's curate, the Rev. Arthur Bell Nichols, who long outlived her. Less than a year afterwards she died in March, 1855. *The Professor,* her first novel, was published posthumously in 1857, and *Emma,* a short fragment, in 1860.

The pathos and nobility of the story of the Brontës must be read between the lines of the above brief summary of these lives which were almost as circumscribed as Haworth churchyard, almost as illimitable as the sky above the Yorkshire moorland.

## V

Charlotte Brontë's four novels have generally been regarded as variations upon her own story of frustrated passion. While her great predecessor, Jane Austen (to whom she never did justice), had looked deep into the human heart, she had been reticent about what she saw there and had kept her own heart veiled from public view. Charlotte Brontë, in her subjectivism, her dwelling in the world of the inner life, her reliance upon her own experi-

*Charlotte Brontë*

---

[24] Upon the chorus of acclaim broke belatedly the hostile voice of Elizabeth Rigby (afterwards Lady Eastlake) in the *Quarterly Review,* December, 1848; reprinted in *Notorious Literary Attacks,* ed. Albert Mordell (1926), pp. 101-121. On the reception of *Jane Eyre* see further Amy Cruse, *The Victorians and their Reading* (1935), pp. 263-265.

ences, was an innovator in bringing English fiction into the domain of the writer's own emotional consciousness. The demonstration of the close parallels between the novels and the Angrian stories, while it reduces the element of autobiography, does not altogether invalidate the traditional view that directly or indirectly she wrote of her love for Héger, the accomplished Belgian scholar, married to another, who was her friend and mentor. *The Professor,* her first tedious and clumsy effort, thinly disguises autobiography by a curious inversion of the principal rôles, Crimsworth, the professor, being Charlotte. There is much reliance upon actuality, all the chief characters being identifiable. The provinciality of tone, the stylistic uncertainties, the artificiality of the dialogue (defects that Charlotte never rid herself of, though she was overcoming them at the time of her death) are at their worst in this story, which is now unreadable save for the light it casts upon the author and her later works. The sudden change that is seen in *Jane Eyre* is most plausibly accounted for by a liberation from inhibitions effected by the power and passion of her sister's *Wuthering Heights* and a consequent reversion to the romantic wonderland of Angria. Yet the faults are still evident—the unsophistication which would provoke a smile were it not pathetic; the prim and stilted dialogue when she tries to imitate the chit-chat of society folk of whom she knew next to nothing; the unmodulated alterations of style from homely colloquialism to the most turgid rhetoric; the distressing attempts at humor and the heavy satire; the blunders in depicting social conventions; the inability to be tolerant or nonchalant; and all the rest of the familiar indictment. Though the love of Jane Eyre for Rochester, the married man, parallels the love of Charlotte for Héger, Rochester is not a portrait from actuality but an ideal of strong and ruthless masculinity painted by a woman who knew very little of men but had for years dreamed of the supermen of Angria. The setting of the central episodes recalls the *mise-en-scène* of the Gothic romances, and none of the Gothicizers invented an incident more sensational than that of the mad wife kept in the husband's house.[25] Melodrama is the stuff of the plot, but though it held readers to breathless attention and can still hold them, such greatness as *Jane Eyre* possesses lies not in the story but in the fiery imagination and poetic passion with which characters and situations are realized. Anxious dread of the developing situation with Branwell at Haworth threw a shadow over the narrative; but apart from this, the wildness, the sense of tremendous issues involved in humble scenes, and the illimitable passions of people outwardly insignificant, the atmosphere of sinister gloom, the suggestions of the occult and mysterious, all qualities that we associate rather with poetry than with fiction and that remove the book utterly from the field of the novel of man-

Jane
Eyre

---

[25] Despite the anticipations discovered by Miss Ratchford in the Angrian cycle, there remain resemblances so close as to indicate unconscious borrowing from J. S. Le Fanu's *A Chapter in the History of a Tyrone Family* (1839), reprinted in *The Watcher and other Weird Stories* (1894). The story is summarized in *CHEL,* XIII. 460-463. — The qualities in *Jane Eyre* that "date" may be indicated by the fact that Ainsworth was inclined to attribute the authorship to G. P. R. James.

ners, are of the essence of the Brontë genius. Romance, which in its profounder sense had till now shunned prose fiction, took to itself this new domain.[26] With an emotional tension hitherto unknown in the novel and foreshadowing the work of George Meredith, Charlotte Brontë portrayed the ecstasies of love, as in the unforgettable scene when Rochester meets Jane in the garden while the nightingales sing. The human story is set against a background so intimately realized that nature seems to have her part in it; the constantly recurring "pathetic fallacy" seems not fallacious because it is so intense.

For *Shirley* Charlotte chose a setting foreign to her own experience, the industrial troubles between mill-owners and operatives in Yorkshire in 1807-1812.[27] Nevertheless, the unrequited love of Caroline for Robert Moore has been thought to be another reflection of the Brussels episode. The book contains what are probably portraits from real life, chief among them the splendid, clear-sighted Shirley, drawn, not with entire convincingness, from Emily. The somewhat wearisome discussions of the rights of women are reflections of contemporary opinion. The distrust of beauty and honest joy, the censoriousness, the sternness of moral commendation or condemnation which makes the clashing characters almost symbols of the warfare between sin and virtue, come from a nature that was grand and formidable but neither easy-going nor lightly tolerant. The harshness of judgment becomes positively repellent in the savage, rasping satire on the curates, who labor under the disadvantage of belonging to the only class of men whom Charlotte had had the opportunity to observe with coldly analytical disapproval. *Shirley*

*Villette* is usually described as a reversion to direct autobiography. The transcription from real life, with a multitude of betraying details, was considered so close that protests were later forthcoming from Brussels. The portrait of Lucy Snowe in her love-sick longing reflects, according to the traditional view, Charlotte's hopeless passion; and Paul Emanuel, with his insight and power to dominate, is Héger. Yet there is more of Angria in *Villette* than in any of the other novels, and before committing ourselves to the autobiographical theory we must weigh in the balance the parallels from Charlotte's dream-world of a date before she had visited Brussels. The plot relies upon gross improbabilities and various incredible coincidences, yet the story holds the reader's attention for its own sake, and to those who accept it as autobiography its stark self-revelation is almost painful. *Villette*

## VI

To turn from Charlotte's novels [28] to *Wuthering Heights* is to turn from schools and parsonages, governesses and curates, to the wild moorlands and *Emily Brontë*

---

26 See Baker, VIII. 11-25.
27 In a newspaper file she "read up" conscientiously the Luddite riots; but there had been industrial troubles in Angria!
28 And Anne's. No injustice is done to Anne Brontë's reputation by limiting remarks upon her novels to a footnote, for only her connection with her sisters has kept them in remem-

the free air of heaven, and from faulty works redolent of genius to the masterpiece of a greater genius. Emily's life, so far as we know, was almost without outer event. From the age of seven till sixteen she was never away from Haworth, and in the last seven years of her brief life only once and then for but a few days. Little is to be gathered of her personality, though much of her opinions, from Charlotte's portrait of her as Shirley. The virginal passion, the strength of soul, the maintenance of complete integrity of thought and expression are revealed in her one novel—call it rather her prose-poem—and in the best of her poems. Perpetually conscious of two planes of life, she manifested that conjunction of transcendentalism and descendentalism which marks the Romantic Movement in its deepest implications. Like Wordsworth, she was "true to the kindred points of heaven and home." Yet she was not so near to Wordsworth as to Blake, of whom she probably never so much as heard. Like Blake, she was "beyond Good and Evil," repudiating restraint and law, relying upon freedom and passion and the unfettered imagination. Blake had said that "no bird soars too high if it soars with its own wings"; and Emily rose to the empyrean upon her own strength. That to put it this way is not mere rhetoric will be acknowledged by anyone who has read such poems as *The Prisoner, Remembrance, The Old Stoic, The Visionary,* and *No Coward Soul is Mine.*[29]

*A Mystic*

What is fragmentary and only partially expressed in the poems is fused into a consistent whole in *Wuthering Heights.*[30] There is no evidence that she was deeply read in the literature of mysticism, but there is equally no doubt that she was a mystic.[31] Unlike Blake, however, who was constantly "under the direction of messengers from heaven," it seems from the testimony of her poems that Emily had attained the mystical experience in its entirety only in early youth, possibly only once. Later it returned fitfully and more dimly. The memory of that early union with the Divine is the "rapturous pain," the "divinest anguish," of which she sings in one of her grandest poems; no human lover has lain for "fifteen wild Decembers" "cold in the earth" (*Remembrance*). In another poem she exclaims:

---

brance. *Agnes Grey,* a plain, honest, dull narrative, without satire, passion, or romantic illusion, possesses autobiographic value for its picture of the trials of a governess in an unamiable family. *The Tenant of Wildfell Hall* goes beyond the range of Anne's experience into fast society which she knew only from reading fiction. Arthur Huntingdon has been thought to be a portrait of the degraded Branwell but the differences between the imaginary figure and the real are greater than the resemblances. See W. T. Hale, *Anne Brontë: Her Life and Writings* (Bloomington, Indiana, 1929).

[29] Generally but inaccurately known (from Charlotte's statement) as *Last Lines*; but probably written about three years before Emily's death.

[30] K. W. Maurer, "The Poetry of Emily Brontë," *Anglia,* LXI (1937). 443-448.

[31] See J. C. Smith, "Emily Brontë: a Reconsideration," *E&S,* V (1914). 132-152; Charles Morgan, "Emily Brontë," in *The Great Victorians,* ed. H. J. and Hugh Massingham (1932), pp. 63-79; C. F. E. Spurgeon, *Mysticism in English Literature* (1913), pp. 80-84. Charlotte Brontë refers to Shirley's (i.e., Emily's) visions and trances and "genii-life." On the ground that the poems are part of the lost Gondal cycle in prose and are therefore dramatic and not self-revelatory, Miss Ratchford denies that Emily was a mystic. But it is not obvious why poems put into the mouths or minds of imaginary characters should not have been inspired by personal experience.

> Speak, God of visions, plead for me,
> And tell me why I have chosen thee!

This "God of visions" is the "strange Power" for whose return she looks at twilight and whose might she trusts as she bids him trust her constancy (*The Visionary*).[32] In *The Prisoner* the crude Gondalian Gothicism is merely the frame for the central description of the ecstatic vision. As in the case of Blake, so in her case there is neither room nor need to discuss here the explanations of the mystical phenomena. All that requires insistence is that in her case as in his there can be no question of the sincerity of the passionate conviction of their authenticity.

*Wuthering Heights* must be read in the light of this fact. To seek in this wonderful book a successor to the Gothic romances to which, superficially, it owes something, is to misapprehend it quite. It is of an altogether different kind. The attempts to connect it with the lost Gondal stories do not carry us very far. Though firmly based upon the moorlands, with peasant characters as realistic as Hardy's, it is not to be judged by standards of realism and probability. *Wuthering Heights* is not merely an allegory of the intersecting relationship between the earthly and the divine plane of being but a vision of their interpenetration.[33] The cosmic vision is of two contending principles, the one dynamic, the other passive. Both principles are good. But dynamism, diverted from its proper course, becomes a power of destruction; and this is the tragedy of Heathcliff. Like will to like; Heathcliff and Catherine Earnshaw are affinities. When Catherine marries Edgar Linton storm and calm are mismated and disaster follows. In the second generation the union of the dynamic characters is renewed upon the spiritual plane and the passive characters find happiness on earth. The pattern is much more complex than can be indicated briefly here, and the best interpreters have shown that it accounts triumphantly for the construction of the story, which, on grounds applicable to any ordinary novel, has been criticized as awkward and uncouth. When the book opens, the first Catherine is already dead; her pale ghost flutters at the window, imploring admission to Wuthering Heights. To plunge, as Emily did, not merely into the midst of the action but into the very conclusion of the whole matter (for Heathcliff is near his death) was to challenge the laws of narrative. But Emily knew that it was impossible to lead the reader by degrees into the occult realm of her story; the fortress of incredulity must be taken at once and by storm. From this beginning at the end, the tale folds back, first in the narration by Nelly Deans, afterwards in part by Lockwood, the intruder from the outside world to whom are allotted the immortal concluding words of the story.

[marginal note] *Wuthering Heights*

---

[32] The last eight lines of this poem were added by Charlotte to the Gondalian opening twelve lines; but the present writer finds it impossible to believe they are not by Emily. Charlotte probably transcribed them from another copy.

[33] The construction as well as the thought of the book Lord David Cecil discusses admirably in *Early Victorian Novelists* (1935), ch. v. See also "C. P. S.," *The Structure of Wuthering Heights* (1926).

Much might be—much has been—said of the intensity and solidity of Emily's imagination, of her strong apprehension of character, situation, and underlying theme. Too much cannot be said in praise of the style of the book, at once subtle and colloquial, imparting new vitality to conventional idiom, as exhilarating as the moorland winds, evoking the beauty of the world, capable of candid ferocities. Its rhythms, piercingly sad or exultantly joyous, invigorate even those readers who have no sympathy with occultism and mysticism. When Catherine tells of her vision the voice is Emily's own:

I see a repose which neither earth nor hell can break, and I feel an assurance of the endless and shadowless hereafter, . . . where life is boundless in its duration, and love in its sympathy, and joy in its fullness.


# VII

George
Eliot

Not without effort is the mind adjusted to a new point of view as one turns from a novel which has proved to be of enduring vitality to the writings of George Eliot.[34] No other Victorian novelist of major rank is so little read today. The effort to lift fiction to a higher plane than that upon which her predecessors and contemporaries were satisfied to work, though it brought her immense temporary prestige, has ultimately been responsible for this decline. Whereas Dickens, Kingsley, and Mrs. Gaskell, when they used the novel as an instrument for social agitation, did not forget to mix pleasure with edification, in George Eliot's hands the novel was not primarily for entertainment but for the serious discussion of moral issues. If these issues are no longer felt to be vital, as the Victorians felt them, and if the solutions proposed now seem unsatisfactory, the *raison d'être* of the stories which are but vehicles for these ideas is enfeebled, if, indeed, it does not vanish altogether. Moreover, George Eliot's own uneasiness as to the honesty of invention in fiction was from the beginning a hazard in the way of lasting success. "Have I any time," she asked herself, "to spend on things that never existed?"[35] Such a question, which would never disturb a born novelist, might have given her pause. To teach was, she held, the paramount purpose in authorship. What, then, did she aim to teach? "My artistic bent," she told her publisher, "is directed not at all to the presentation of eminently

[34] *Works*, Warwickshire Edition (25v, 1908); *George Eliot's Life as Related in her Letters and Journals,* ed. J. W. Cross (2v, 1885); *George Eliot's Family Life and Letters,* ed. Arthur Paterson (1938); *Letters,* ed. R. B. Johnson (1926); G. S. Haight, *George Eliot and John Chapman* (1940), contains hitherto unpublished correspondence. — Leslie Stephen, *George Eliot* (EML Series, 1902); E. S. Haldane, *George Eliot and her Times* (1927); J. Lewis May, *George Eliot; a Study* (1930); E. and G. Romieu, *La Vie de George Eliot* (Paris, 1930), trans. by B. W. Downes (1932); A. T. Kitchel, *George Lewes and George Eliot: a Review of Records* (1933); P. Bourl'honne, *George Eliot: Essai de biographie intellectuelle et morale, 1819-1854* (Paris, 1933); Blanche C. Williams, *George Eliot: a Biography* (1936); M. C. Wade, "George Eliot's Philosophy of Sin," *English Journal,* xiv (1925). 269-277; J. J. Bassett, "The Purpose in George Eliot's Art," *Anglia,* liv (1930). 338-350; Helene Richter, "Die Frauenfrage bei George Eliot," *Anglia,* xxvii (1903-1904). 333-380; Lord David Cecil, *Early Victorian Novelists,* pp. 291-336; Baker, viii, ch. vi.
[35] *Letters and Journals,* i. 38.

irreproachable characters, but to the presentation of mixed human beings in such a way as to call forth tolerant judgment, pity, and sympathy." She exhibits men and women in relation to an ideal based on certain principles of truth and goodness. She inculcates the importance of being earnest; but the virtues so earnestly striven after—industry, self-restraint, conscientiousness—are very drab; "school-teachers' virtues," they have been unkindly called.[36]

Mary Anne (or Marian) Evans (1819-1880), who after 1857 was known to the world as George Eliot, began to write fiction when on the verge of middle age. Behind her were memories of girlhood in Warwickshire and of the spiritual conflict of the severance from her father's religion. Under the influence of friends in Coventry, Charles Bray and Charles Hennell, she had been drawn to the "advanced" biblical and theological scholarship of Germany, and this led to her translation (1846) of D. F. Strauss's *Leben Jesu*. Her father, whom she had distressed by her skepticism, died in 1849. After a sojourn on the Continent Marian Evans was brought into touch with a group of rationalists in London of whom the chief figure was John Chapman. Chapman, who was engaged in resuscitating *The Westminster Review*, took her on as assistant editor, a post which she occupied from 1851 to 1854. In the set in which she moved there were men of brilliant gifts and others of decidedly "bohemian" standards of morality. Herbert Spencer became a close friend, and through him she met George Henry Lewes.[37] Lewes was separated from his wife but could not obtain a divorce. In 1854 Miss Evans took the defiant step of entering into an irregular union with him which lasted till his death in 1878. The moral conflict of this situation is part of her background as a novelist. In all but the law they regarded each other as man and wife and were accepted as such by their friends. For a time they lived in Germany, occupied with philosophical and psychological studies.

In 1857 George Eliot (the pseudonym which she now assumed) published in *Blackwood's* her first works of fiction—*Amos Barton, Mr. Gilfil's Love-Story,* and *Janet's Repentance,* three short stories which were gathered together in the same year as *Scenes of Clerical Life. Adam Bede,* the first full-length novel, followed quickly (1857), and then *The Mill on the Floss* and *Silas Marner* (both 1860). A visit to Florence roused her interest in the Italian Renaissance and after laborious studies and with elaborate documentation she produced *Romola* (1863). From this not completely successful excursion to the realm of the historical novel she returned to modern England in *Felix Holt, the Radical* (1866) and *Middlemarch* (1871-1872), the longest and most crowded of her books. The last work, *Daniel Deronda* (1876), is an illustration of her moral philosophy in which the characters

---

36 Lord David Cecil, *Early Victorian Novelists,* p. 327.
37 G. H. Lewes (1817-1878) was the author of many works on philosophy, natural science, and literary history, including a *Life of Goethe* (1855). He was instrumental in introducing knowledge of Comte's Positivism into England. On the foundation of *The Fortnightly Review* he was its first editor (1865-1867).

are but so many examples of the theory she expounds. After Lewes's death she married J. W. Cross (1880). She died in the same year.

*The Novels*

Memories of Warwickshire furnish the background of the novels of modern England, though not all are actually laid in that county. George Eliot's world is that of town folk and peasantry. Her concern is for absolutely commonplace people, and this concern is without a trace of patronage. The quiet humor is often of the sort we associate with Thomas Hardy. It is limited in range by her avoidance of any trace of unkindness and her stern discrimination between subjects that may be treated humorously and those that may not. Mrs. Poyser, in *Adam Bede,* is a humorous character in the mode of Dickens; more representative of George Eliot's own peculiar quality are some of the lesser figures in *Silas Marner.* But no matter how attractive a subsidiary character may be, she never lets him run away with her imagination. In the ability to concentrate attention upon the chief figures in her story she differs markedly from most of her predecessors in the novel. These principal persons are very unlike the conventional run of heroes and heroines, for she discarded the standardized formula of plot-construction in which the tale is built round an attractive young pair who are to be married in the last chapter. Along with this conventional couple the old convention of the "happy ending" sometimes goes into the discard. Wrenching probability, she did close *Adam Bede* with the marriage of Adam and Dinah; [38] but *The Mill on the Floss* ends distressfully; and all the others more or less somberly. In *Middlemarch* there is no central figure at all, interest being divided among several groups of people whose fates are entangled with much ingenuity though not without some bewilderment to the reader. In this book some fifty characters are not only drawn but analyzed. Nowhere else is George Eliot's peculiar power of describing how character develops more fully exhibited. An entire world, albeit a little world, which she knew intimately is here depicted, on a scale and with a thoroughness unexampled elsewhere in Victorian fiction. When, however, she attempted in *Romola* to portray in similar detail the crowded and tempestuous scene of the Italian Renaissance she passed beyond her range. She endows the men and women of fifteenth-century Italy with the moral sense and standard of her own age and milieu. They are transplanted Victorians. Leslie Stephen says roundly that Romola and Tito Melema did not really live in old Florence. "They were only masquerading there, and getting the necessary properties from the history-shops at which such things are provided for the diligent student." [39] The labor with which George Eliot "got up" her history resembles that with which she amassed from her memories and wide reading the material for the novels of modern England. This thoroughness of preparation has naturally suggested comparisons with the method of Flaubert, and George Eliot has frequently been described as the first English writer of the *roman expérimental.* But the resemblances

[38] J. S. Diekhoff, "The Happy Ending of *Adam Bede,*" ELH, III (1936). 221-227.
[39] Leslie Stephen, *George Eliot,* p. 136.

to Flaubert are not so obvious as the dissimilarities, and in particular her humane feeling for her men and women, commonplace as they almost always are and often both unattractive and futile, contrasts with the French novelist's feelings of lofty and bitter contempt as displayed in *Madame Bovary* and *L'Education sentimentale*.

Aware though she was of the influence of environment upon character, George Eliot never showed environment determining character. In each novel there is a moral clash, generally involving the need for a woman to choose between two men or a man between two women. She maintained firmly her belief in the freedom of the will. The moral choice is everything. "Our deeds," she says in *Adam Bede*, "determine us as much as we determine our deeds." With stern, sad firmness, with a massive implacability that is at once impressive and depressing, she insisted upon the importance and irrevocability of actions. Moral degeneration follows acts committed from selfish motives; moral regeneration is accomplished by acts of love unregardful of self. Consequently, we have on the one hand such selfish characters as Tito or Hetty or Arthur Donnithorne, and on the other such grand figures as Romola or Dinah Morris or Daniel Deronda. But George Eliot's moral theories often interfere with the spontaneity of her imagination. More than once what she exhibits as the working of immutable moral law—"the wages of sin"—turns out to be the working of crass "poetic justice," a mere literary device which is something quite different. In homely phrase, the punishment does not invariably fit the crime. Nor is she content to let the reader draw for himself the required lesson from the narrative but must constantly intersperse philosophic remarks to serve her didactic purpose.[40]   *The Moral Basis*

Close to George Eliot in one department of her work was the popular and enormously prolific novelist Margaret Oliphant (1828-1897). The resemblance is particularly marked when, as in *Salem Chapel* (1863), she pictures the world of dissent. The accuracy of her delineation of Scottish life has been commended by no less an authority than Sir James Barrie. Mrs. Oliphant also wrote stories of the occult, among which *A Beleaguered City* (1880) is memorable. Her miscellaneous writings include biographies and historical studies.   *Mrs. Oliphant*

[40] It was not for want of industry and determination that George Eliot did not succeed in becoming a poet. There is too much sententiousness and too little spontaneity in her verse. Her best-known poem is a sort of Positivist hymn, beginning "O may I join that choir invisible." There is genuine charm in *How Lisa Loved the King* (1869) on a story in the *Decameron* which suggested to Swinburne his *Complaint of Lisa*. *The Legend of Jubal* (1869; published 1874) tells the old story of the return of the aged inventor of the art of music to his old home, to find that he is himself forgotten but also to find consolation in the honor in which his art is held. George Eliot's most ambitious poem, *The Spanish Gypsy* (1868), is an amalgam of narrative, dramatic scenes, lyrics, and choral commentary. The theme is the conflict of the rival loyalties of love and race. This piece, to which she devoted only too much labor and learning, has sunk out of sight under its own weight.

# XXVI

## Alfred Tennyson

Alfred Tennyson [1] (1809-1892) came of a family of scholarly tastes and some literary accomplishments. His father, a clergyman at Somersby in Lincolnshire, could turn "a copy of verses," and two of his brothers, Frederick and Charles,[2] possessed in slight measure the poetic gift. Alfred passed quickly through an imitative phase of discipleship to Thomson in descriptive poetry and to Scott in narrative. A clever little play, *The Devil and the Lady* (published posthumously), exhibits boyish fun, a taste for the grotesque, and the beginnings of a tendency to speculate upon the mystery of existence. A collective venture of the three brothers was in deference to Frederick's modesty entitled *Poems by Two Brothers* (1827). A rather winning self-conscious pride in wide-ranging erudition both classical and modern, an attraction to Oriental themes, and a prevalent Byronism are the chief characteristics of a volume which contains little

Poems
by Two
Brothers

[1] *Life and Works* (12v, 1898-1899), includes the *Memoir* (see below); *Works*, ed. Hallam Lord Tennyson (6v, 1908); *Poetic and Dramatic Works*, ed. W. J. Rolfe (1898); *The Devil and the Lady*, ed. Charles Tennyson (1931); *Unpublished Early Poems*, ed. Charles Tennyson (1931); *Tennyson and William Kirby: Unpublished Correspondence*, ed. L. A. Pierce (1929); *Selections*, ed. W. C. and M. P. DeVane (1940); *Representative Poems*, ed. S. C. Chew (1941); *A Selection*, introduction by W. H. Auden (1944). — T. J. Wise, *Bibliography* (1908), to be used with caution because it includes the forgeries exposed by John Carter and Graham Pollard in *An Enquiry into the Nature of Certain Nineteenth Century Pamphlets* (1934); T. G. Ehrsam, R. H. Deily, and R. M. Smith, "Tennyson," *Bibliographies of Twelve Victorian Authors* (1936), pp. 299-362 (hereinafter referred to as Ehrsam, *Bibliographies*); Hallam Lord Tennyson, *Alfred Lord Tennyson, a Memoir* (2v, 1897) and *Tennyson and his Friends* (1911); Andrew Lang, *Tennyson* (1901); R. M. Alden, *Tennyson: How to Know Him* (1917); A. C. Benson, *Tennyson* (1907); H. I'A. Fausset, *Tennyson: a Modern Portrait* (1923); Sir A. C. Lyall, *Tennyson* (*EML Series*, 1902); Harold Nicolson, *Tennyson: Aspects of his Life, Character and Poetry* (1923); T. R. Lounsbury, *The Life and Times of Tennyson* (1915), an account of the critical reception of Tennyson's earlier work; Morton Luce, *A Handbook to the Works of Alfred Lord Tennyson* (1906); J. F. A. Pyre, *The Formation of Tennyson's Style* (Madison, 1921); W. P. Mustard, *Classical Echoes in Tennyson* (1904); A. E. Baker, *Concordance* (1914) and *A Tennyson Dictionary* (1916); Sir T. Herbert Warren, *The Centenary of Tennyson* (1909), a lecture; A. C. Bradley, *The Reaction against Tennyson*, English Association Pamphlets, No. 39 (1917); Alfred Noyes, "Tennyson and Some Recent Critics," *Some Aspects of Modern Poetry* (1924), pp. 133-176; Lascelles Abercrombie, "Tennyson," *Revaluations: Studies in Biography* (1931), pp. 60-76; G. N. G. Orsini, *La Poesia di Alfred Tennyson* (Bari, 1928); Cornelius Weygandt, *The Time of Tennyson* (1936). — Passages in this chapter are taken, by permission of the Odyssey Press, from the writer's introduction to *Representative Poems*. — In 1884 Tennyson was raised to the peerage as Baron Tennyson of Aldworth.

[2] Frederick Tennyson (1807-1898) published four volumes of verse, of which *Days and Hours* (1854) is the best. Charles Tennyson-Turner (1808-1879) published his *Sonnets* in 1830 and added to them in successive editions till the final *Collected Sonnets, Old and New* (posthumous, 1880), with an appreciative essay by James Spedding. There is a quality of wildness in Frederick's poetry, as in his strange personal life, that is characteristic of the Tennysons. The Wordsworthian influence is strong in Charles. Examples of their work are included in *Representative Poems*, ed. S. C. Chew, Appendix III.

promise of what was soon to come. When Tennyson went to Cambridge and made friends with several brilliant young men—Arthur Henry Hallam,[3] Edward FitzGerald, James Spedding, and Richard Monckton Milnes (afterwards Lord Houghton)—the Byronic influence waned and he was soon aware of the two rising stars of English poetry, Shelley and Keats, posthumously renowned. The effect of Shelley upon him was intermittent and slight; but that of Keats was profound, as is seen in the luxuriant texture and rich coloring of some of the *Poems, Chiefly Lyrical* (1830), such as *Recollections of the Arabian Nights* and *Mariana,* which are connecting links between Keats and the Pre-Raphaelites. The imaginary portraits of fair women in this collection of 1830 show that Tennyson was not unaffected by the vogue of prettiness exemplified in the immediately contemporary gift-books and annuals. Tennyson never quite rid himself of the feminine ideal they are intended to suggest. There is real passion, bolder and less characteristic, in the *Ballad of Oriana.* Other poems sound a morbid note and in yet others the young poet luxuriates in stately melancholy. Experiments in novel metrical combinations, though the fingering was as yet uncertain, gave promise of a fresh music in English poetry.

Poems,<br>Chiefly<br>Lyrical

Without denying that the expansion of Tennyson's emotional and intellectual horizon and his mastery of style and technique were slow processes covering many years, one may recognize the next two years as the most remarkable period of growth. This was a happy time of close association with Hallam. The two young men went to Spain together with the quixotic intent to aid the insurgents; and Tennyson returned with memories of Pyrenean landscape which he worked into his poetry. Hallam, betrothed to the poet's sister, was a regular visitor at Somersby where Tennyson lived with his widowed mother, devoting himself to the cultivation of his art. The imagery and accessories of *A Dream of Fair Women* show the affinity to Keats. *The Hesperides,* which Tennyson afterwards suppressed, reveals that wildness in his nature which was too often subdued to Victorian sobriety. In *Œnone* a moral purpose is infused into old myth; the colors are radiant, but the Judgment of Paris is told from the point of view of the forsaken wife and the speech of Pallas is the central incident. In this poem, as in *The Lotos-Eaters,* Tennyson was feeling his way towards the dramatic monologue. *Œnone* is, however, an idyll in which a story is related, not a monologue in which the situation is implied; and *The Lotos-Eaters,* after the introductory narrative in Spenserian stanzas, is a choric song which the sailors chant in unison. The conflict between Wisdom and Beauty, the theme of *The Palace of Art,* suggests a deliberate effort at self-discipline as though the poet were rejecting the aestheticism to which he had been devoting his gift. At Cambridge he had thought of writing a poem or drama on the Arthurian legend upon which he would impose an allegorical inter-

---

[3] Contemporary testimony is unanimous as to the brilliant promise of A. H. Hallam (1811-1833), son of the historian. *Remains in Verse and Prose* (1834); *Writings,* ed. T. H. V. Motter (1943).

pretation (Arthur representing "Religious Faith" and the Round Table "Religious Institutions") with the intent to enrich its meaning for the modern world. But of this purpose there is no sign in *The Lady of Shalott* or in *Sir Launcelot and Queen Guinevere*. The pieces named in this paragraph form the principal contents of *Poems* published at the close of 1832.

*Death of A. H. Hallam*

So far, life had been full of happy promise; but in the autumn of 1833 came the crushing blow of Hallam's sudden death. This loss combined with symptoms of failing eyesight and the contemptuous reception accorded his poems by hostile critics [4] to weigh him ·down. *The Two Voices* (originally entitled *Thoughts on Suicide*) discloses his state of mind in the dark days when *In Memoriam* was begun. Tennyson became betrothed to Emily Sellwood, but the uncertainty of his prospects put marriage out of the question for a long while. The next years were passed mainly at Somersby till 1837 when the family were turned out of the rectory.[5]

Little verse was written till about two years after Hallam's death. In lyric elegy the poet recalled "the tender grace of a day that is dead"; but in the magnificent dramatic monologue *Ulysses* he looked to the future, albeit without the "old strength." The determination to follow knowledge wherever it may lead is characteristic of the period which was becoming aware of the perilous seas of scientific speculation. Thus Tennyson poured the new wine of modern thought into the old wine-skins of mythology. *Tithonus*,[6] though lacking the immediacy of application obvious in *Ulysses,* is perhaps an even finer poem. The art with which the shimmering lights and cool airs of the Palace of the Dawn are suggested by words and cadences is as wonderful as are the full-voiced vowels of the companion piece, suggesting the ocean beating upon a rocky coast; and as in *Ulysses* the ancient theme is brought home to the modern reader by means of the emphasis upon knowledge and unyieldingness, so the situation in *Tithonus,* beyond all human experience, is yet humanized by the speaker's longing to share the common lot of mortality. During an entire decade Tennyson published nothing [7] save *O that 'twere possible,* out of which *Maud* afterwards developed, and *St. Agnes' Eve,* the first of his evocations of the asceticism of the Middle Ages. Both poems belong to 1837. In the following five years he was active in the revision of old work and the composition of new. In 1842 he emerged from the long twilight with *Poems in Two Volumes.* To contrast the earlier and later versions of famous poems is to learn much about the development and refinement of his art. Thus, in *Œnone* the central episode of Pallas was expanded and the landscape background redrawn in closer

*Poems, 1842*

[4] See E. F. Shannon, Jr., "Tennyson and the Reviewers, 1830-1842," *PMLA*, LVIII (1943). 181-194. The most notorious of these attacks was in the *Quarterly Review*, XLIX (1833). 81-96. This, long attributed to Lockhart, was written by J. W. Croker.

[5] There were several changes of residence before Tennyson settled at Farringford in the Isle of Wight in 1853. Subsequently he built himself another home, Aldworth, in Surrey.

[6] *Tithonus,* though not published till 1860, belongs to about the same date as *Ulysses.* On Tennyson's treatment of classical themes see Bush, ch. VI; W. P. Mustard, *Classical Echoes in Tennyson* (1904).

[7] *The Lover's Tale* was printed in 1833 but immediately suppressed and not published till 1879.

resemblance to the Troad; and in *The Lotos-Eaters* the Lucretian picture of the careless gods was added and the conclusion altered into its final superb form. In these and other cases, though there may be some sacrifice of beauty of detail, the new version, whether in the precision of the rendering of mental states or in the delicacy of the visualization of outward objects, is better than the old.

The new poems which made up the second volume of the collection of 1842 show a large expansion of interests and sympathies. Besides *Ulysses*, another dramatic monologue is *St. Simeon Stylites*, a study in religious psychopathology which impinges upon Browning's province. The "Matter of Arthur" is represented by *Sir Galahad*, which is off the road leading to epical narrative, and the *Morte d'Arthur*, which points forward to the *Idylls of the King*. Tennyson sets the narrative of Arthur's last battle within a "frame" of modern life. A young poet (recognizably a self-portrait) reads to his friends the fragment of an epic. The inference is plain that Tennyson had already in mind a poem of epical proportions. The homely realism of this "frame" has something in common with the poems of "domestic" life which bulk large in this collection. *Dora* and *The Gardener's Daughter* still possess a quiet prettiness, and their lovely passages descriptive of "haunts of ancient peace" show Tennyson's kinship to the English school of landscape painters. But there is little vitality in the men and women who people this tranquil world, and no conceivable retrogression of taste is likely to reverse the modern repudiation of Tennysonian sentiment. The Queen of the May has suffered the fate of Little Nell. Fashioned out of more substantial stuff is *Locksley Hall*, the first of Tennyson's poems of social protest and very moving to those of his contemporaries who were active in reform. The "rowdy or bullying element" in Tennyson's poetry which William Morris found distasteful [8] is audible here. Was he as angry as he appeared to be? At heart he was content with his time, on the side of the Church in religion and of the middle classes in economics, less boastful than Macaulay but none the less complacent in his assurance that the "Anglo-Norman race" is "the noblest breed of men." To many readers the rhetorical denunciations of the pursuit of gain do not ring true. The assumption that a poet must be "a leader of thought" led him too often to the choice of subjects unsuited to his temperament and artistry.

*The Princess* (1847), while a disappointment to the judicious, suited the general taste because of its mild liberalism and "gentlemanly" support of the cause of female education. The theme of this versified novelette is one which might have been handled entertainingly as an intellectual comedy; but wit was not among Tennyson's gifts. There are amusing episodic passages, but the reasoning was inconclusive at the time and is negligible today. Only the two lyrics in blank verse (*Tears, Idle Tears* and *Come down, O Maid*) and the intercalary songs are of perennial loveliness.[9]

[8] J. W. Mackail, *The Life of William Morris* (Pocket Edition, 1912), I. 47-48.
[9] The six songs were added in the third edition (1850).

In
Memoriam

Tennyson's structural skill was not sufficiently robust to build a poem of more than medium length. *In Memoriam* [10] (1850) is no exception to this statement. Periods of intermittent composition extended over seventeen years, and the task of welding the disparate parts into something approximating a unified whole was accomplished in the later eighteen-forties. Many sections were then written to clarify the connections of thought and progress of emotion. The links are often weak, but the use of the same stanzaic form throughout imposes an outward semblance of unity.[11] Such inner harmony as *In Memoriam* possesses comes from the drift of spiritual experience rather than from the too laborious artistic effort. The tradition of the English elegy is followed, in that the note of mourning modulates into a hymn of faith; as in *Lycidas* and *Adonais,* the turning point is discernible, but the looser structure involves a recurrence of earlier moods, so that the pattern is less precise. For this reason, among others, the poem is poignantly convincing as an expression of personal loss, the alternate subsidence and upwelling of grief, and the outcome in renewed happiness. Seeking to impose upon the original simple "elegies" a vague hint of allegorical intent, Tennyson spoke of *In Memoriam* as "a Way of the Soul." The value of the poem, however, is not in this philosophic afterthought but in its lyrical and meditative record of changing moods. There is the gradual healing of grief with the continuance and widening of a love so spiritualized that it can exist without the presence of the beloved.

In some sections Tennyson sought to reconcile traditional faith with the new ideas of evolutionary science; but in others faith and reason are opposed. From both the poetical and psychological points of view this dichotomy is part of the lasting attractiveness of *In Memoriam*. The concessions to the scientific spirit have been derided as feeble attempts to rescue something from the wreck of creeds; they express a characteristic Victorian state of mind. The contrasting mood comes and goes, as do all mystical experiences, with the breath of the spirit; it is revealed in passages of profound feeling and haunting beauty, especially in the incomparable ninety-fifth section, perhaps Tennyson's supreme utterance. These passages are founded upon certain trance-like experiences in which the poet seemed to be, like St. Paul, caught up into a region beyond earth. They are equally beyond the region of argument in which much of the poem moves. The course of speculation passes through doubt to an affirmation of belief in personal immortality. The future life is contemplated as a continuation of the evolutionary process ever nearer and nearer to God.

*In Memoriam* was received with approbation by leaders of the most diverse schools of thought. The imagery drawn from recent discoveries in astronomy and geology attracted the attention of the scientists, who also marked the poem's underlying evolutionary assumptions. The liberals wel-

[10] A. C. Bradley, *A Commentary on Tennyson's "In Memoriam"* (1901).
[11] Tennyson thought he had invented the tetrameter quatrain with inner rimes (*abba*); but it had been used by Lord Herbert of Cherbury and other poets.

comed its attempted compromise between science and religion. The orthodox recognized the effort to save faith from the grip of conquering
materialism. Modern readers, brushing aside these old claims upon their
attention, are still won by its sustained beauty, its deep feeling, its wealth
of imagery, now tender and intimate, now gorgeous and elaborate, and its
revelation of the poet's personality. It is easier today to sympathize with
Tennyson's wistful yearning after certainty than with arrogant dogmatism.
The fused tremulousness of doubt and faith makes the poem the more
moving.

In 1850, the year of his marriage, Tennyson succeeded Wordsworth as *Poet*
poet laureate. The seriousness with which he undertook the duties of an *Laureate*
office which had hitherto been little more than a sinecure is shown by the
dignity of the "poems on affairs of state" produced in his official capacity,
such as the gravely eloquent *Ode on the Death of the Duke of Wellington*
(1852), the *Welcome* to Princess Alexandra (1863), and various poems for
special occasions and elegies on public men. But his position gradually
committed him to an increasingly complacent acceptance of English institutions and virtues.

There is, however, no complacency in *Maud* (1853), which reflects the *Maud*
irresolution and uncertainty to which Arnold and Clough were giving expression at the same time, and which voices this mood in the manner of
the poets of the "Spasmodic School," then in the midst of their brief vogue.[12]
That Tennyson was influenced by these poets is evident from the discontinuity of the thought and the extravagances of the style.[13] *Maud* is a
"monodrama," that is, an extension of the form of the dramatic monologue
through a succession of episodes wherein the story is unfolded in soliloquies.
Those who identified the speaker with the poet were to this degree correct,
that the moody side of Tennyson's nature is mirrored in the character of
the hero. The plot, with its poor but proud lover pitted against the heroine's
wealthy family and his haughty rival, and leading to death and madness, is
quite commonplace. The self-revelations of a speaker of abnormal mentality
owe something to the scenes of madness in prose fiction. The hysterical tone,

---

[12] The "Spasmodic" poets were Sydney Dobell (1824-1874) and Alexander Smith (1830-
1867). Dobell wrote *The Roman* (1850), *Balder* (1854), *England in Time of War* (1856),
and other poems. See his *Poetical Works* (2v, 1875); *Life and Letters* (2v, 1878). His finest
piece is the weird ballad, *Keith of Ravelston*. The dominant note in his verse is the struggle
of free men against autocracy. His style is over-excited, often to the point of incoherence; and
from passages of power he lapses into banality. Some of his poems on the Crimean War
were written in collaboration with Alexander Smith, author of *A Life-Drama and other
Poems* (1855), *City Poems* (1857), and the charming volume of essays, *Dreamthorp* (1863).
The best estimate of the poetry of Dobell and Smith is in Hugh Walker, *The Literature of the
Victorian Era* (1910), pp. 513-526. They were satirized in W. E. Aytoun's parody, *Firmilian:
a Spasmodic Tragedy* (1854). Walker writes: "What Aytoun condemned in them was the
confusion and inequality and extravagance of their work, its passion piled on passion, its
thought disjointed from thought, the rant and fustian of the style, the lavishly sprinkled and
overwrought metaphors."

[13] Walker, *op. cit.*, p. 514, says that *Maud* "is just a very fine example of many of the
faults and of more than all the merits" of the "School." Aytoun reviewed *Maud* savagely as
"an ill-conceived and worse-expressed screed of bombast," in *Blackwood's Magazine*, September, 1855; reprinted in *Notorious Literary Attacks*, ed. Albert Mordell (1926), pp. 138-161.

dubiously appropriate, to a madman, is close to fustian when used to denounce the evils of modern society; and the advocacy of war as a remedy for these ills is both unreasonable and shocking. *Maud* presents the paradox of worthlessness as a story, as a psychopathological study, and as a contribution to social criticism, and yet of enduring readability beyond most of Tennyson's poetry. The form has kept the matter alive; the prosody is a triumph of the adaptation of various metres to varying moods.

**Idylls of the King**

Tennyson now devoted himself to his long-meditated great task. The Tractarian Movement, the historical novel, the Gothic revival in architecture, and the writings of Pugin and Ruskin had all served to intensify interest in the Middle Ages, and the Arthurian theme was in the air of the mid-century. Bulwer had published his epic, *King Arthur* (1848); Arnold, his *Tristram and Iseult* (1853); the young painters of Rossetti's circle had chosen subjects from the legend for their murals at Oxford (1857); Morris had published *The Defence of Guenevere* (1858); and Tennyson's friend Robert Stephen Hawker was writing *The Quest of the Sangraal* (not published till 1864). Tennyson's *Idylls of the King* appeared in 1859.[14] These original four *Idylls* display a symmetry that is lacking in the completed twelve parts of the poem. Almost, if not quite, devoid of allegorical implication, they are studies in contrasted types of womanhood, "the True and the False." Judged as metrical tales, they are not very different from the domestic "Idyls" on modern subjects. Though there is little of the authentic medieval flavor, it is but fair to insist that Tennyson, in subjecting the legends to modern treatment, was following the same procedure successfully used in his renderings of classical myths. Disregarding for the moment his other poems, we may look ahead to consider the *Idylls* as a whole. *The Holy Grail and other Poems* (1869) contained, beside the title poem and two other idylls, an expanded version of the old *Morte d'Arthur* with a new title, *The Passing of Arthur*. *The Last Tournament* and *Gareth and Lynette* were published together in 1872. In that year the *Enid* of 1859 was split into two idylls, *The Marriage of Geraint* and *Geraint and Enid*. *Balin and Balan,* though written about 1870, was not published till 1885, when it rounded out the cycle to twelve.

*The Coming of Arthur,* the opening idyll, shows the imperfect success with which Tennyson wrestled with the difficulty of making clear the various motives intended to bind together a series of narratives composed dispersedly over many years. He never welded into a jointless whole the medieval, supernatural stories, their modern application, and the allegorical significance he attached to them. The difficulty is not that there is too much allegory but that there is too little and that little too vague. Tennyson expects his readers to rise to the allegorical plane, but he does not hold them there

---

[14] Two "trial issues," privately printed, preceded the published volume. These are, *Enid and Nimuë; or, the True and the False* (1856) and *The True and the False: Four Idylls of the King* (1857). — See in general M. W. MacCallum, *Tennyson's Idylls of the King and Arthurian Story from the Sixteenth Century* (Glasgow, 1904); Howard Maynadier, *The Arthur of the English Poets* (1907), ch. XXII.

securely. Arthur, who is "Faith," is constantly becoming Arthur the deceived husband. In the former capacity he acts in character; in the latter he is both self-righteous and ungentlemanly. Trouble of another sort was encountered when, as in the cases of the legends of Tristram and Balin, Tennyson, in order to fit them into the allegorical conception of the corruption of society, was forced to degrade noble material. Only when allegory was practically in abeyance, as in the tales of Enid and Lynette, or when, as in *The Holy Grail,* the theme was precisely congenial to the poet's purpose, is the result satisfactory. In the tales of the two "true" women the narrative flows as gently as the limpid brooks which Tennyson loved; and the story of the quest of the Grail is shrouded in mystery through which the lights shine as they do through the mist when Guinevere sees Arthur for the last time.

While the *Idylls* were expanding, Tennyson produced some of the most characteristic poems of his middle period. *Enoch Arden* (1864) was one of the most popular of all his poems, but with the exception of the "inset" of gorgeous tropical description it is flat and commonplace. *The Northern Farmer, Old Style,* and its companion piece, *New Style,* are vigorous monologues in Lincolnshire dialect, contrasting the type of tenant farmer, who was disappearing with the new freeholders. *Lucretius* (1868), the longest of the poems on classical subjects, is both eloquent and erudite, and so unwontedly bold in its treatment of an erotic subject as to make critics suspect that, consciously or unconsciously, Tennyson was challenging comparison with Swinburne.

About 1870 a reaction began to set in against Tennyson's position of unquestioned supremacy among the poets of the period. It was expressed privately by George Meredith [15] and publicly by Swinburne in *Under the Microscope* [16] (1872), where there is a savage onslaught on Tennyson's treatment of the Arthurian story. There were other signs that the laureate's reputation was under a cloud. He had to compete with Browning, who had won belated popular recognition with *The Ring and the Book*; with Swinburne, whose *Poems and Ballads* had taken the world by storm; with Morris, whose *Earthly Paradise* had just appeared; and with Rossetti, whose *Poems* of 1870 brought the "new poetry" to a climax. The progress of his fame was, moreover, impeded by the imitators who trailed behind him.[17] Within

*Reaction Against Tennyson*

[15] Meredith, *Letters* (1912), I. 197.
[16] *Under the Microscope* (ed. 1872), pp. 36-45; *Works,* Bonchurch Edition (1925-1927), XVI. 377-444.
[17] Echoes of Tennyson's style are audible in much late Victorian poetry, particularly in the work of writers not susceptible to the influence of Rossetti and Swinburne. The Earl of Lytton (1831-1891), diplomat and Viceroy of India, published a dozen volumes of verse under the pen-name of "Owen Meredith." Of these the best remembered are *Tannhäuser* (1861), which is of some slight Wagnerian interest because of its date, and *Lucile* (1860), a novel in verse, both romantic and witty. Lytton's poetry is fluent and facile, lax and slovenly. Tennyson was but one of many poets whom he imitated, sometimes so closely that the charge of plagiarism can in some cases be sustained. See *Personal and Literary Letters of Robert First Earl of Lytton,* ed. Lady Betty Balfour (2v, 1906); A. B. Harlan, *Owen Meredith* (1945). — Sir Edwin Arnold (1832-1904), who passed much of his life in the East, is remembered for *The Light of Asia* (1879), a poem on the life and teaching of the Buddha. Half a dozen other volumes of poetry deal in the main with Oriental themes. In subject Arnold's work has little in common with Tennyson's, but his blank verse is closely imitative. See his *Poetical*

*The
Dramas*

a shadow of comparative indifference he remained for a decade. These years were devoted in the main to the three tragedies—*Queen Mary* (1875), *Harold* (1877), and *Becket* (1879)—in which he sought to dramatize the story of "the Making of England." Unremitting toil was expended upon these earnest, bulky, and stagnant things, but Tennyson had neither the practical experience of the theatre nor the gift of delineating characters and making them interact upon one another without which plays cannot live. These tragedies and four other plays—*The Falcon* (1879), *The Cup* (1881), *The Promise of May* (1892) and *The Foresters* (1892)—have shared the fate of almost all the poetic dramas of the nineteenth century. Several of them reached the boards, but only *Becket* had a successful run and that only after it had been much revised by Sir Henry Irving.

After this unprofitable decade Tennyson returned to the kinds of poetry of which he was a master. The abandonment of the historical drama may have brought a relief which accounts for the recovery of genius in his seventieth year. There was also a noticeable withdrawal from the position of *vates* or counselor to his countrymen which he had assumed in middle life. Save in a few pieces such as the ranting, ineffectual *Locksley Hall, Sixty Years After,* he was content in this final period to resume once more the manner and matter native to his genius as a poet of solemn, introspective, and melancholy moods, of romantic atmosphere and lovely landscape, and as an elegist and the contemplator of the mysteries of life and death. In 1878 appeared the spirited ballad of *The Revenge. Ballads and other Poems* (1880) ushered in the final decade of his glory in which his reputation in England and America eclipsed all competitors. This volume was followed by four other collections of miscellaneous lyrical, narrative, and meditative verse: *Tiresias and other Poems* (1885), *Locksley Hall, Sixty Years After, Etc.* (1886), *Demeter and other Poems* (1889), and *The Death of Œnone, Akbar's Dream, and other Poems* (posthumous, 1892). That the old laureate possessed a wonderful reserve of power is proved by the admirable *Rizpah*, the address *To Virgil*, the symbolic narrative, *The Voyage*, the allegorical autobiography, *Merlin and the Gleam,* and the last poems on

*The
Last
Decade*

---

Works (8v, 1888). — Sir Lewis Morris (1833-1907), after publishing *Songs of Two Worlds* (1871), established a fame that has proved ephemeral with *The Epic of Hades* (1876-1877), a series of monologues by characters in Greek mythology whom the poet meets in the other world. *A Vision of Saints* (1890), on Christian themes, is similar in design. In these and numerous other volumes Morris wrote smoothly and cheerfully in the style Tennyson had made popular. — Alfred Austin (1835-1913), whom Lord Salisbury rewarded with the laureateship for services rendered to Tory journalism, was Byronic rather than Tennysonian, so far as he was anything. His two score volumes of worse than mediocre verse include satires, dramas, lyrics, the pretentious narrative poem, *The Human Tragedy* (1862; revised 1876) and *England's Darling* (1896), a play on Alfred the Great. *The Poetry of the Period* (1870) is a piece of impudently cocksure criticism of some interest for its connection with Browning. *The Garden that I Love* (1894) is a pleasant piece of prose, once quite popular. Austin's *Autobiography* (2v, 1911) is a curious revelation of overweening self-esteem.— On an even lower level than Austin was an older poetaster, Martin Tupper (1810-1889), whose enormous popularity in the mid-century is a phenomenon in the history of taste. His innumerable poems and ballads on public affairs, emigration, the Crimean War, and so forth are patriotic in feeling and shot through with complacent Whiggery. His once-famous and still proverbially bad *Proverbial Philosophy* (four series, 1838-1867) expresses in unrimed verse a facile and pretentious but doubtless sincere morality.

classical themes (though these incorporate some work of early years).[18] In meditative pieces Tennyson sought again and again to epitomize his thoughts on life. Many poems are in memory of departed friends. The purely lyrical note is seldom sounded, perhaps most clearly in *The Silent Voices,* for *Crossing the Bar* does not belong in the category of song. He was engaged upon his latest poems till shortly before his death (October 4, 1892).[19]

Tennyson's posthumous reputation passed through a period of more *After-*
violent denigration than that suffered by any of his great contemporaries. *fame*
Of this there had been anticipations in the strictures passed upon the *Idylls of the King* by Meredith and Swinburne. It reached its most forceful expression in *Tennyson as a Thinker* (1893) by Henry S. Salt, the rationalist, and survived to color critical pronouncements of the nineteen-twenties. The gravamen of adverse criticism has been concerned with the disproportion between the manner and the matter of Tennyson's poetry. Subjects either outmoded or essentially insignificant are made to bear too heavy a weight of ornament, and this ornamentation is designed in accordance with a formula of imagery and cadence which, once devised, is repeated again and again. The elaborate surface covers a paucity of ideas; and such thought as exists is timid, complacent, conventional when critical of society, and fundamentally conservative. His wide-mindedness made him aware of contemporary issues and tendencies, but he was a follower, a popularizer, not an originator. His poetry is therefore of little consequence as a "criticism of life." Such was the indictment. The wind of extreme disfavor, which has carried his dramas, his "domestic" pieces, and his poetry of social protest into something like oblivion, has now passed by; and recent criticism has readjusted the balance which sank too far against him. The meditative poems, often touched with the majestic Virgilian melancholy; the poems on classical subjects and a few other dramatic monologues, such as the magnificent *Rizpah;* some of the shorter narrative pieces and some episodes in the *Idylls of the King;* the poems of moods and places far withdrawn; the all too few lyrics; *Maud,* not for its subject but for its mastery and range of prosody; and *In Memoriam,* in which faith and doubt contend for the possession of a soul—these parts of Tennyson's work belong in the enduring heritage of English poetry.

---

18 In *Tiresias* it is easy to discriminate between the early work (the prophet on the mountain; the vision of Pallas; the forecast of the prophet's death) and the later.

19 For a list of a score of elegies inspired by Tennyson's death, mostly by writers of note, see *Representative Poems,* ed. S. C. Chew, pp. lv-lvi. By far the finest of these is Sir William Watson's *Lachrymae Musarum,* published in the *Illustrated London News,* October 15, 1892; *Poems* (2v, 1905), I. 3-8.

# XXVII

## The Brownings

### I

Part of the heritage of Robert Browning [1] (1812-1889) from his well-to-do parents was a love of books, pictures, and music. Their home was near Dulwich, and the gallery there was one of the boy's favorite haunts. His father shared with his son a passion for old tales of intrigue and violence, and the two followed together the latest crime-stories in the newspapers. In the light of Browning's subsequent predilection for criminal types and morally warped characters this early shaping influence upon his imagination requires emphasis. For the austere atmosphere of worship in the religion of Evangelical dissent in which his mother instructed him he retained a reverence which long afterwards he expressed in his poetry. Of his childhood there are the usual stories of precocity; his father was proud of his juvenile verses. After the age of fourteen he had no regular education, but in the library at home he read widely and acquired the taste for out-of-the-way books which was to furnish him with his vast but undisciplined erudition. "Ossian" and Byron were his first masters, but in 1826 he met with the poems of Shelley and became an avowed disciple of the "Sun-treader." [2] Attendance at the theatres roused his ambition to be a "maker of plays";

[1] *Works,* Centenary Edition, ed. Sir F. G. Kenyon (10v, 1912); *New Poems,* ed. Kenyon (1914); *Works,* ed. H. E. Scudder (1895); *Works,* ed. C. Porter and H. A. Clarke (12v, 1910). No edition is absolutely complete. *Shorter Poems,* ed. W. C. DeVane (1934). *Letters of Robert Browning and Elizabeth Barrett Barrett, 1845-1846* (2v, 1899); *Robert Browning and Alfred Domett,* ed. Kenyon (1906), a collection of letters; *Letters of Robert Browning to Miss Isa Blagden,* ed. A. J. Armstrong (1923); *Letters of Robert Browning, Collected by T. J. Wise,* ed. T. L. Hood (1933); *Robert Browning and Julia Wedgwood. A Broken Friendship as Revealed by Their Letters,* ed. Richard Curle (1937); *Letters of Elizabeth Barrett Browning,* ed. Kenyon (2v, 1897); E. B. Browning, *Letters to her Sister, 1846-1859,* ed. Leonard Huxley (1929). — T. J. Wise, *Bibliography* (1897); H. W. Griffin and H. C. Minchin, *Life of Robert Browning* (1910; rev. ed. 1938); W. C. DeVane, *A Browning Handbook* (1935), an invaluable reference-guide; Mrs. Sutherland Orr, *Life and Letters of Robert Browning* (1891), ed. Kenyon (1908); G. K. Chesterton, *Robert Browning* (EML Series, 1903); C. H. Herford, *Robert Browning* (1905); Pierre Berger, *Robert Browning* (Paris, 1912); L. Whiting, *The Brownings: Their Life and Art* (1917); Osbert Burdett, *The Brownings* (1929); H. L. Hovelaque, *La Jeunesse de Robert Browning* (Paris, 1932); J. P. McCormick, *As a Flame Springs* (1940); Mrs. Sutherland Orr, *Handbook to the Works of Robert Browning* (1886), still important because authorized by Browning; W. L. Phelps, *Browning: How to Know Him* (1931); F. G. R. Duckworth, *Browning: Background and Conflict* (1931); Edward Berdoe, *The Browning Cyclopaedia* (1897); L. N. Broughton and B. F. Stelter, *Concordance* (2v, 1924-1925); George Santayana, "The Poetry of Barbarism," *Interpretations of Poetry and Religion* (1900), pp. 166-216, relates Browning to Walt Whitman and is hostile to both. — Baylor University, Waco, Texas, has been made an important center of Browning studies under the direction of A. J. Armstrong, who has published there various monographs and brochures.
[2] F. A. Pottle, *Shelley and Browning, a Myth and Some Facts* (Chicago, 1923).

but first he conceived the idea of writing a poem, an opera, and a novel, each to appear under a different pseudonym. Nothing more is heard of the opera and novel, but the poem was *Pauline* which came out anonymously in 1833.[3] The heroine of this has no function save to listen to the confidences of the young poet (an Alastor-like creation) who lays bare his soul. Scattered lines and passages give promise of a greatness which *Pauline,* in its incoherent entirety, does not display. A copy of it with manuscript comments by John Stuart Mill got back to Browning. Some of Mill's remarks were beside the point, but his reproof of the writer's self-centeredness and morbidness was salutary. Browning shifted his point of view with swift determination and henceforth regarded *Pauline* as a false start which he preferred to have forgotten. {.Pauline}

In 1834 he made a journey to St. Petersburg in company with a Russian consul. Not till late in life did he make poetic use of impressions gathered there. On his return home he applied for a post in a mission to Persia but failed of appointment. His interest in the wiles and casuistry of diplomatic dealings may have been fed by the Russian experience; and the Persian dream may have been transmuted long afterwards into *Ferishtah's Fancies.* But travel and plans for a career did not turn him from his vocation. He had written as wonderful a poem as ever came from a youth of genius: *Paracelsus*[4] (1835). It had little success with the public, but recognition by Wordsworth, Landor, and other men of influence started Browning on the road to the renown which he might have reached soon had he courted readers instead of alienating them. Macready asked him to write a tragedy[5] and the poet's response was *Strafford* (1837) which ran feebly for five performances.[6] He had now for long been wrestling with the subject of his next poem, and to acquire a first-hand knowledge of its setting and atmosphere he went to Italy in 1838. He brought back not only the impressions immediately needed but a love of the country that was lifelong. *Sordello* (1840) did almost irreparable harm to his reputation, for it became promptly a byword for wilful and impenetrable obscurity in subject, treatment, and style. To this day, even after a century of interpretation, its difficulties remain well-nigh insuperable and, for most people, not worth the trouble of surmounting. The tangled political situation in medieval Italy with which it deals had called for clarity of treatment, and the young poet, blindly confident that matters plain to him would be plain to his readers, had not responded. During seven years of composition there had been successive

*(marginal notes: Pauline; Paracelsus; Sordello)*

---

[3] *Pauline,* ed. N. H. Wallis (1931).

[4] On the reception of *Paracelsus* see T. R. Lounsbury, *The Early Literary Career of Robert Browning* (1911), pp. 29-44. This book carries the story of the reception of Browning's work by the reviewers down to 1846.

[5] *Diaries of William Charles Macready,* ed. William Toynbee (2v, 1912), contains much information on the relations between the actor and the poet.

[6] Browning helped John Forster with the biography of Strafford contributed to Lardner's *Cyclopaedia* (1836); but F. J. Furnivall exaggerated when he reprinted this as *Robert Browning's Prose Life of Strafford* (Browning Society, 1892). — On Browning's misinterpretations of history in the play but essential truth of characterization see S. R. Gardiner's preface to *Strafford,* ed. E. H. Hicksey (1884).

stages of incubation, involving radical alterations in the theme, and vestiges of earlier concepts remain in the later strata.[7] When Sordellists expound the theme ultimately chosen, the candid reader is inclined to repeat Lowell's judgment: "It was a fine poem before the author wrote it."

**Bells and Pomegranates**

Between 1841 and 1846 Browning published eight little pamphlets entitled *Bells and Pomegranates*.[8] The first of these was *Pippa Passes* which, had not *Sordello* frightened readers away, might have been at once what it ultimately became, one of Browning's most popular poems. Five of the *Bells* contained six dramas. *A Blot on the 'Scutcheon*[9] was the cause of a bitter quarrel with Macready. After writing *A Soul's Tragedy* Browning abandoned his long effort to write for the stage. He had found in the dramatic monologue the medium ideally suited to his genius. Of poems in this form *Dramatic Lyrics* contained, among other things, *My Last Duchess* and *Soliloquy in a Spanish Cloister*. The perfection of these famous pieces is of a narrower order than that of some of the more elaborate monologues of later date. *Dramatic Romances and Lyrics* included, with much else on a somewhat lower level, the lastingly popular *How They Brought the Good News from Ghent to Aix, The Flight of the Duchess,* the first nine sections of *Saul,* and that masterpiece of psychological and historical insight, *The Tomb at St. Praxed's*.[10] Here, too, was *The Lost Leader,* the attack on Wordsworth (which Browning afterwards regretted), written under the impetus of the sympathy with liberalism which had permeated *Strafford* and *King Victor and King Charles.*

Meanwhile Browning had visited Italy for a second time in 1844. In that year Elizabeth Barrett published her *Poems* in one of which Browning read a commendation of himself. He and the poetess already had friends in common, and now he addressed her a letter of admiration which led at once to friendship and soon (impetuously on his part and timidly on hers) to love. The earliest of her *Sonnets from the Portuguese* date from this time. Browning's virile confidence triumphed over paternal despotism[11] and Elizabeth's ill-health, and on September 12, 1846, the lovers eloped. Mr. Barrett never forgave his daughter.

**Marriage and Italy**

They went to Italy, and after a short stay at Pisa settled in Florence at Casa Guidi which was their home from 1847 till Mrs. Browning's death in 1861. For years their financial situation was precarious till a munificent

[7] W. C. DeVane, "Sordello's Story Retold," *SP*, xxvii (1930). 1-24.

[8] i: *Pippa Passes* (1841); ii: *King Victor and King Charles* (1842); iii: *Dramatic Lyrics* (1842); iv: *The Return of the Druses* (1843); v: *A Blot on the 'Scutcheon* (1843); vi: *Colombe's Birthday* (1844); vii: *Dramatic Romances and Lyrics* (1845); viii: *Luria* and *A Soul's Tragedy* (1846).

[9] The plot—a melodramatic quarrel between two noble houses in the eighteenth century—is of Browning's invention, but it has points of resemblance to *Romeo and Juliet,* just as in *Luria,* on a quarrel between Florence and Pisa in the fifteenth century, there are similarities to *Othello.* For a general discussion see G. R. Elliot, "Shakespeare's Significance for Browning," *Anglia,* xxxii (1909). 90-162.

[10] Renamed in 1849 *The Bishop Orders His Tomb at St. Praxed's Church.*

[11] For the view of Mr. Barrett's feelings for his daughter spread abroad in Rudolf Besier's successful play *The Barretts of Wimpole Street* (1931) there is **no valid evidence** whatsoever.

bequest from John Kenyon in 1856 put them beyond anxiety. In 1849 their son was born. Mrs. Browning, impressionable and emotional, was no sooner established in Italy than she became an enthusiastic partisan of the Italian patriots struggling for freedom. Browning, though he shared her sympathies, remained cool and more detached. To her Italy meant mainly contemporary politics; to him, painting, music, history, landscape, and the complex temperament of a fascinating people. He observed disapprovingly the elaborate ritual of Catholic worship, contrasted it with the simple piety of English dissent, and from his reading of Strauss's *Leben Jesu* [12] drew out the further contrast between faith and rationalism. Such was the trifold subject of *Christmas-Eve and Easter-Day* (1850). A critique of Shelley, attached to a collection of Shelley letters that turned out to be forgeries (1852), is Browning's only work in prose and is important for an understanding of his conception of poetry. The Brownings visited London in 1855. *Men and Women,* a collection of fifty poems, was now published. The enthusiasm of Rossetti and his circle furthered the immediate sales of the new work, but these soon dropped off and though reviews were generally favorable few readers seem to have discerned the surpassing excellence of many of these poems. Among the few, however, were some of the foremost men of the time. Carlyle had long been Browning's admirer; Landor ranked him with Chaucer; Ruskin praised him in *Modern Painters,* IV.

*Men and Women*

At the time of their return to Florence in 1856 a shadow of difference had come between husband and wife, for Mrs. Browning had been taken in by D. D. Home, the American medium, while Browning was completely skeptical about spiritualistic phenomena. *Mr. Sludge, "the Medium,"* in which he satirized Home, was not published till after Mrs. Browning's death. In 1860 Browning discovered on a Florentine bookstall an "Old Yellow Book" containing a collection of records of a murder trial at Rome and the execution of the murderer in 1698. Only gradually did the poet come to realize that this was material precisely, almost providentially, suited to his interest in psychology, in casuistry, in the criminal mind, and in Italian social history, and to the technique of the dramatic monologue. Meanwhile his wife's health was declining; she was overwrought when Italian hopes languished after the Peace of Villafranca; and she died in 1861. Life in Florence was henceforth impossible for Browning; he left the city, never to return; and with his son made his home in London with occasional sojourns in France. [13] *Dramatis Personae* (1864) shows a shift of interest from Italian to English themes and an alert attention to such vital issues of the day as the Darwinian hypothesis (*Caliban upon Setebos*) and the "higher criticism" (*A Death in the Desert*). An increased ruggedness of manner and a

*The "Old Yellow Book"*

*Death of Mrs. Browning*

[12] K. Goritz, "Robert Browning's *Christmas-Eve and Easter-Day* und *Das Leben Jesu* von D. F. Strauss," *Archiv,* CXLVII (1924). 197-211; W. O. Raymond, "Browning and Higher Criticism," *PMLA,* XLIV (1929). 590-621.

[13] On his return to London Browning began the correspondence with Isa Blagden which is a chief source of information for the next decade. The letters in Armstrong's edition (1923) are supplemented by others in the Wise collection, ed. T. L. Hood (1933).

**The Ring and the Book**

greater emphasis upon the grotesque presage the work of his last two decades. The next years were devoted to *The Ring and the Book,* which was published in four installments, 1868-1869. This masterpiece was received with almost universal acclaim; in popular estimation Browning was henceforth second only to Tennyson among living poets and by many he was accorded the first place.

In 1871 came the affair of his proposal of marriage to Lady Ashburton, which was made with such tactless, albeit touching, loyalty to the memory of his wife that the lady had no choice but to refuse his hand. Browning bitterly regretted not that he had been rejected but that he had made the offer. Covert allusions to the unhappy incident occur in later poems. *Balaustion's Adventure* (1871) is his first extended incursion into the field of classical mythology which he was now for some years to cultivate diligently.[14] The choice of the theme of Alcestis is a tribute to his dead wife. Bewilderingly unlike this offshoot from Euripides is the intricate and crabbed *Prince Hohenstiel-Schwangau* (1871). The speaker of this long monologue is, as was clear to all readers, Napoleon III. The inception of the poem and possibly parts of it date from 1859; it was resumed after the fall of the French Empire. The harshness of style and fine-drawn psychologizing, with the many no longer easily comprehensible allusions to contemporary affairs, make it one of the least readable of Browning's poems.

**Fifine at the Fair**

To 1872 belongs *Fifine at the Fair.* This involved but to some tastes fascinating study in erotic psychology is connected only by the names of the husband and wife with the legend of Don Juan and Elvire; but it has an immediate contemporary reference in that it is a commentary by indirection upon the Rossetti-Buchanan quarrel and is inferentially a partial condemnation of Rossetti's poetry.[15] Even while strengthening the admiration of devotees who now clustered round the poet, the two volumes just named alienated many readers; for they justified the old charge of harsh obscurity which had been less vocal during his middle years. The fascination which crime and the mentality of criminals had for Browning now led him into the dark thickets of *Red Cotton Night-Cap Country* (1873). The uncouth title [16] is as repellent as the sordid narrative. It concerns an actual con-

---

[14] The short and beautiful *Artemis Prologuizes* is of earlier date. — On the relation of Browning's Alcestis to other modern versions of the myth see E. M. Butler, "Alkestis in Modern Dress," *Jour. of the Warburg Institute,* I (1937-1938). 46-60. On Browning's poems on classical subjects see Bush, pp. 358-385; T. L. Hood, "Browning's Ancient Classical Sources," *Harvard Studies in Classical Philology,* XXXIII (1922). 79-180. On the relation of *Cleon* (a study of dying paganism as *A Death in the Desert* is of dawning Christianity) to Arnold's *Empedocles on Etna* see A. W. Crawford, "Browning's *Cleon,*" *JEGP,* XXVI (1927). 485-490.

[15] On the autobiographical element in *Fifine* (Browning's proposal of marriage to Lady Ashburton) see W. O. Raymond, "Browning's Dark Mood," *SP,* XXXI (1934). 578-599. On the relation of the poem to Rossetti's *Jenny* see W. C. DeVane, "The Harlot and the Thoughtful Young Man," *SP,* XXIX (1932). 463-484. Rossetti detected the allusions to himself in *Fifine* and broke off his long friendship with Browning.

[16] Not to vindicate but to explain the title it may be noted that a friend of Browning's called the Calvados country of Normandy "White Cotton Night-Cap Country" with reference to the head-dresses worn by women there. Browning changed the color to "red" in allusion to the bloody tragedy narrated in his poem.

temporary French trial involving a contested will and a suspected suicide. Another psychological study of villainy is *The Inn-Album* (1875) founded upon the case of a card-sharper in *The Greville Memoirs,* with material inserted from the case of the Tichborne Claimant, which had just been engaging public attention. To 1875 belongs also *Aristophanes' Apology,* a sequel to *Balaustion's Adventure* and a defense at once of Euripides against current detraction and of Browning's own poetic faith and practice.[17]

In tone different from all Browning's other books is the curious volume *Of Pacchiarotto and How He Worked in Distemper* (1876). Alfred Austin, a journalist and poetaster, had criticized Browning in impudent fashion in *The Poetry of the Period* (1870) and for years had been sniping at him in the newspapers. Browning now turned on him savagely but not very effectively, for his invective is overloaded with erudition and the grotesque rimes employed as a weapon of satire are not handled with the requisite light Byronic touch. That Austin had held up Byron as a model for contemporary poets to copy accounts for Browning's mockery of *Childe Harold,* which, beginning in *Fifine,* had been continued in *The Inn-Album* and reappeared in *Pacchiarotto.*[18] Two other poems in the same volume are of personal interest: *House* is apparently an indirect reproof of Rossetti, a remonstrance against the intimate revelations of *The House of Life; St. Martin's Summer,* in which the ghost of an old love intervenes in a belated love affair, is obviously an atonement to the memory of his wife for the proposal of marriage made to Lady Ashburton.

Browning's version of *The Agamemnon of Aeschylus* (1877) is the most unattractive of all his books. He seems deliberately to have reproduced as closely as possible, and with clumsy literalness, the harshness and obscurity of the Greek, doing this as a vindication of his beloved Euripides from those who exalted Aeschylus at the expense of the younger dramatist. Thus to load the dice against the author to whose text he devoted so much toil was a curiously perverse occupation.

In 1877 a newly founded periodical, *The Nineteenth Century,* attracted wide attention by publishing under the general title *A Modern Symposium* a series of articles by a distinguished group of intellectuals, Sir James Stephen, W. G. Ward, Frederick Harrison, and others. Among the problems discussed were the influence of morality upon religious beliefs and "The Soul and Future Life."[19] Browning followed these essays with eager attention, and *La Saisiaz* (1878), a poem inspired by the death of a friend, is in

---

[17] F. M. Tisdel, "Browning's *Aristophanes' Apology,*" *University of Missouri Studies,* II (1927). 1-46; Donald Smalley, "A Parleying with Aristophanes," *PMLA,* LV (1940). 823-838.

[18] See *Letters of Robert Browning,* ed. T. L. Hood, pp. 358-363; W. L. Phelps, "Robert Browning and Alfred Austin," *Yale Review,* n.s. VII (1918). 580-591; and on Browning's earlier and later opinions of Byron, S. C. Chew, *Byron in England* (1924), p. 237 and pp. 285-287.

[19] This was the title of an article by Frederick Harrison, *The Nineteenth Century,* I (1877). 623-636 and 832-842. To it Lord Selborne and others replied, and Harrison was permitted the last word, *ibid.,* pp. 497-536. To these articles Browning alludes by title in *La Saisiaz.*

a way an intervention in the debate. The uncharacteristic gloom of this poem culminates in an emphatic and disturbing asseveration:

> I must say—or choke in silence—"Howsoever came my fate,
> Sorrow did and joy did nowise—life well weighed—preponderate." [20]

This solemn statement is not always taken into account by those who speak of the "facile optimism" of Browning. *La Saisiaz* shows that he did not easily come by his assurance of God's Love. *The Two Poets of Croisic* in the same volume is, however, in lighter mood; and in the first series of

*Dramatic Idyls* (1878) there are a vigor of narrative, a freshness, and an interest that, despite the verbosity and the mannerisms, are fairly well sustained. This group of stories is the most readable of the later books. *Dramatic Idyls, Second Series* (1880) shows a sudden and pathetic loss of spontaneity: the fantastic rimes are but so much misapplied ingenuity; the grotesquerie is wearisome; the tales are obscure and dull, fit exercise only for the minds of the Browning Society, which began its activities in the following year. *Jocoseria* (1883) is, as the title promises, a miscellany in light vein; the most interesting of its contents are the renderings of rabbinical legends, and of these the best is *Solomon and Balkis*.[21] *Ixion,* almost the last fruit of Browning's love of Greek myth, interprets the familiar story in a novel fashion; by softening Ixion's guilt Browning is able to fulminate against tyrannical omnipotence in a manner reminiscent of Shelley. *Ferishtah's Fancies* (1884) is a group of little tales that are with one exception of Browning's own invention. There is a thin veneer of Eastern coloring, but the Persian sage is transparently the poet himself. *Parleyings with Certain People of Importance in Their Day* (1887) is a stumbling-block in the path of even the most devoted admirers of the poet. These pieces are desperately crabbed, obscure, verbose, and dull; nowhere else is the subtlety more intricate and tedious. It has been shown that the seven men with whom the "parleyings" are carried on were not chosen at random but represent the seven major interests in Browning's life: philosophy, history, poetry, painting, politics, Greek, and music.[22] Lacking this autobiographical key, reviewers of the day were bewildered; and it may be questioned whether, possessing it, many modern readers find pleasure in unlocking the mystery.

In the summer of 1889, turning over the pages of the newly published *Letters* of Edward FitzGerald, Browning came across a passage in which FitzGerald wrote: "Mrs. Browning's death is rather a relief to me, I must say: no more Aurora Leighs, thank God!" This was addressed to a private correspondent and should not have been published; at worst the writer is to be blamed only for tasteless facetiousness. But, agitated and furious,

---

[20] *La Saisiaz,* lines 332-333. Compare the bitter doubts expressed in the *Epilogue* to *Ferishtah's Fancies.*

[21] Solomon confesses to his royal visitor that his vanity is stronger than his wisdom. W. C. DeVane, *A Browning Handbook,* p. 416, compares FitzGerald's version of Jami's *Sálamán and Absál* where the king confesses that his basic emotion is avarice, not love of wisdom.

[22] W. C. DeVane, *Browning's Parleyings: the Autobiography of a Mind* (New Haven, 1927).

Browning wrote the vituperative sonnet *To Edward FitzGerald who Thanked God My Wife was Dead*.[23] The painful episode is of biographical importance because it shows the passionate tenderness of the poet's memories and because the shock probably hastened his end. In the autumn he visited his beloved Asolo and then became a guest in his son's home in Venice, where he died on December 12, 1889. On the morning of that day he found *Death* pleasure in the telegraphed word of the favorable reception of his last volume, *Asolando: Fancies and Facts*. This is a sheaf of love lyrics, versified anecdotes, and philosophical pronouncements. It closes with the *Epilogue* in which Browning described himself as

> One who never turned his back but marched breast forward,
>    Never doubted clouds would break,
> Never dreamed, though right were worsted, wrong would triumph,
> Held we fall to rise, are baffled to fight better,
>    Sleep to wake.

## II

Life meant "intensely" to Browning, and meant "good." His confidence in *Love* the final triumph of the right was based upon a belief in the Divine Love which he found manifested through power in nature and through intellect in mind. The antithesis which he intended to make plain in *Paracelsus* is not only between one who would know and one who would love, but between two conceptions of love. The dying Paracelsus realizes that love is not a passion for human perfection but a divine condescension to human frailty.[24] The alterations in the theme of *Sordello* show successive stages in the young Browning's thought. Directly from Dante he had taken the conception of his hero as a poet whose high visions had failed. This had shifted to the theme of martial glory versus human love; and in the final concept Sordello becomes the champion of the poor against the powerful. The poem thus expresses the same humanitarianism which in *Strafford, King Victor and King Charles,* and *Colombe's Birthday* is a championship of popular rights. The disillusioned tone of *A Soul's Tragedy* is an indication that Browning became dissatisfied with political liberalism. In *Christmas-Eve and Easter-* *Faith* *Day* he searched for a secure ground for modern faith and found it neither in nature nor intelligence but in love. How did he arrive at this principle? Quite empirically; love underlay the facts of life as he experienced them; love in the human heart was for him the best evidence of God's providential Love. In the face of intellectual incertitude he asserted with forcible iteration the ultimate validity of his own emotions and intuitions. Critics contemptuous of Browning's sentimental optimism—both those who are complete

[23] On second thoughts Browning attempted to recall the lines, but it was too late; they were published in *The Athenaeum*, July 13, 1889. In the next issue W. A. Wright, the editor of FitzGerald's *Letters*, apologized for the oversight in printing the offensive passage.

[24] W. O. Raymond, "Browning's Conception of Love as represented in *Paracelsus*," *Papers of the Michigan Academy of Science, Arts and Letters*, IV (1924). 443-463.

skeptics and those who rely on dogma—have pointed out that such asseveration are not argument. But the tenuousness of the analogy between human love which could be tested by experience and the Divine Love which could only be inferred therefrom was plain to Browning himself. In general he was convinced of the superiority of the intuitive faculties over the intellectual in giving man a knowledge of God. But there were moments when he was not convinced; there was the heart-rending moment when he questioned whether the parallel between human love and the Divine was not a deceit—

> Only, at heart's utmost joy and triumph, terror
> Sudden turns the blood to ice: a chill wind disencharms
> All the late enchantment: What if all be error—
> If the halo irised round my head were, Love, thine arms? [25]

*Doubt*    What, indeed! Fortunately for his robust confidence, for the boisterous joy in life which has discredited him with many readers of a later day, the question does not often arise. When it does, Browning seeks assurance in an illogical and paradoxical attainment of faith through doubt; St. Michael stands the more secure just because he feels the serpent writhe beneath his feet.[26] Doubt is a spiritual Purgatorio and cleanses the soul; the error is to turn it into a guiding principle instead of regarding it as a stage through which to pass.

*Evil*    But if there is an overruling providential Love, what of evil in the world? Browning is constantly preoccupied with the problem. Evil and falsehood have no real existence in themselves but are manifestations by contrariety of love and truth. Care and pain are pledges of the divine regard. Strength comes from an obstructed road; assurance would breed torpor, but difficulty increases power. The thought is in line with German idealism which taught that the imagination creates evil in order that by combatting it the moral will may be strengthened. Hence "the paradox that comforts while it mocks," the doctrine of the spiritual value of failure. This doctrine, which the poet's contemporaries found of inestimable worth, our generation has contemptuously rejected, perhaps because our failures have been incalculably disastrous and our values have gone awry. Aspiration, the poet taught, should exceed man's grasp; achievement is not evidence of greatness but of an easy objective. Ruskin counseled his readers "not to set the meaner thing, in its narrower accomplishment, above the nobler thing, in its mighty progress." [27] Browning shared the Victorian belief in progress; Time, he declared,

> means amelioration, tardily enough displayed,
> Yet a mainly onward moving, never wholly retrograde.[28]

[25] *Epilogue* to *Ferishtah's Fancies.*
[26] *Bishop Blougram's Apology.*
[27] *The Stones of Venice,* II, ch. VI.
[28] *La Saisiaz.*

But the mighty progress of the nobler thing is beyond the possibility of *Immor-*
fulfillment in this life. Thus failure is used as an argument for belief in *tality*
immortality; the disappointments of this world are so great that in another
there must be reparation. Virtue and happiness will ultimately be brought
into harmony with one another through the agency of God. No shadow of
proof is offered for this assertion.[29] That most people seem to be made
less rather than more fitted for the things of the spirit by their experience
of the world does not trouble Browning overmuch. In the case of most of
his villains he seeks to show that they have become wicked through the
perversion of good; and though Guido Franceschini's very element seems,
like Iago's, to be wickedness, yet Browning leaves it an open question
whether Guido's last cry to Pompilia was not a recognition of the truth and
consequently a sign of salvation; and even if the cry was of despair his soul
went not to hell but to the "sad sequestered place" where God remakes it.

If for the sake of the artist we ignore Browning's pontifical didacticism,    *Characters*
we see that his acceptance of the world as he finds it makes him the great
creator of character that he is. Sense as well as spirit has its value; human
life, full and vigorous, of the past and the present,[30] but always grounded
upon reality, is his theme. He is like Shakespeare in the absolute centering
of his interest in humanity, and Shakespearean in his understanding of the
weak, the erring, and the self-deceived. His theatre is the human spirit, his
great subject the soul's development. The regular dramas are failures because
the interest in the plot is sacrificed to inquiry into motive. What men aspire
to be and are not is a proper subject for discussion; but the stage demands
action. Consequently he found his medium in the dramatic monologue, *The*
where the subject's case could be presented from the inside. The "Old Yel-    *Dramatic*
low Book"[31] provided him with a perfect theme since the recorded testi-    *Monologue*

[29] In an early satire which he did not publish Swinburne, while echoing Arnold's *Empedocles,*
mocks at Browning:

> Thus runs our wise men's song:
> Being dark it must be light;
> And most things are so wrong
> That all things must be right;
> God must mean well, he works so ill by all men's laws.

[30] Browning's antiquarian enthusiasms which made him so lavish with historical detail
obscure the fact that though he used subjects from the past as frequently as from the present
his emphasis is upon those aspects of human nature which do not change. His concern, between
1870 and 1882, with subjects from classical antiquity was probably a revulsion from stories of
sordid crime. But a notable characteristic of the classical pieces is the realistic treatment of
persons and setting. In *Gerard de Lairesse* (*Parleyings*) he insists, as Mrs. Browning had done
in *Aurora Leigh*, upon the need to choose modern subjects. Poets must not "push back reality,
repeople earth with vanished shapes." It is thought that he had Morris's *The Earthly Paradise*
in mind as an example of what the poet should *not* do.

[31] The literature of *The Ring and the Book* is extensive. See especially A. K. Cook, *Commentary upon Browning's The Ring and the Book* (1920), indispensable; C. W. Hodell, *The
Old Yellow Book with Translation, Essay and Notes* (Washington, 1908), a photo-reproduction
of the original now at Oxford; the translation is reprinted in Everyman's Library (1911); J. M.
Gest, *The Old Yellow Book* (1925), which corrects Hodell's translation at important points
and shows that Browning altered the characters in the story more profoundly than had hitherto
been thought; W. O. Raymond, "New Light on the Genesis of *The Ring and the Book*,"
*MLN*, XLIII (1928). 357-368 and cf. *ibid.*, 445-450; Sir Frederick Treves, *The Country of
the Ring and the Book* (1913); F. T. Russell, *One Word More on Browning* (1927), which
argues that Browning deliberately misrepresented Pompilia and Caponsacchi. That in drawing

mony of the murder trial suggested that the character of the several speakers would alter their presentation of the facts and their presentation of the facts would shed light upon the character of the speakers. The conclusion we are to draw, however, is not that truth is relative but that somewhere in the maze of casuistry and deceit it can be found and is absolute.

The number and variety of the men and women whom he created make for the illusion that Browning possessed a wide range of ideas; but the fact is that he illustrated by innumerable case-histories a small recurring group of themes. He seeks to understand people of the most varied sorts; and because the "good" people present fewer problems he is fascinated by the "bad." His poems of most lasting appeal are psychological stories. The intricacies of motive are disentangled and light is thrown upon the self-deceiver even as he seeks to justify himself. Browning's rich though amateurish scholarship attracted him to subjects from authentic history. His assertion that in *The Ring and the Book* he made no alteration in fact is not supported by the documents; but essentially he aimed at a psychological interpretation of actual fact. The subtlety of this interpretation, necessitating, as he thought (often mistakenly), expansive treatment, makes his poems almost always too long. Moreover, though he wrote very little "nature poetry," he set an elaborate background for his spiritual dramas. His antiquarian enthusiasm spares no detail of architecture and ornament; his quick-darting mind can resist no temptation to digress. This wealth of interests finds appropriate expression in the labyrinthine Gothicism of his verse, the range of effects in his blank verse, the almost unrivaled variety of his stanzaic *Style*   forms. The illusion of breadth is enhanced by the confused energy of his style, the reposelessness, the persistent allusiveness, and the quality that an unsympathetic critic has described as "garrulous pedantry" and "lumpy and gritty erudition." [32] On occasion the exuberant vitality offended or even scandalized contemporary admirers, as in the notorious case of *The Statue and the Bust* where, censuring the lovers who had not the courage to fulfill their destiny, he seemed to advocate adultery. To many modern readers his dynamism is an offense. [33] Yet he will certainly outlive the detraction from which his fame has suffered since about 1910. Much of his work is dead— but of what poet of vast productivity cannot this be said? At every stage in his career he wrote too much and at too great length and too often sank the poet in the teacher. But the residue is large and very vital and very grand;

---

Pompilia the poet had in mind his own wife and that Caponsacchi's rescue of her is reminiscent of the Brownings' elopement has long been suspected. The idealization of Pompilia as a tribute to Mrs. Browning in the manner of Dante's idealization of Beatrice is studied by J. E. Shaw, "The 'Donna Angelicata' in *The Ring and the Book*," *PMLA*, XLI (1926). 55-81.

[32] Bush, p. 373.

[33] F. R. G. Duckworth, *Browning, Background and Conflict* (1932), contains a survey of Browning's reputation in the eighteen-fifties, in the decade following his death, and in the nineteen-twenties. See also D. C. Somervell, "The Reputation of Robert Browning," *E&S*, XV (1929). 122-138.

and there are few good judges who will reject the opinion that *The Ring and the Book* is the greatest English poem of the Victorian Period.[34]

## III

When Robert Browning had not yet emerged from the shadow of *Sordello* and his wife was the most highly esteemed poetess of England, there were few to foresee the day when an estimate of her achievement would properly be a short appendage to an extended account of his; but the authoress of the *Sonnets from the Portuguese* realized what would be the comparative opinions of posterity.

*Mrs. Browning*

The story of Elizabeth Barrett Browning [35] (1806-1861) is familiar to thousands of people who never read her poems.[36] She began to write under the influence of Byron (*The Seraphim*, 1838) and passed thence to the company of the "Spasmodic" poets (*A Drama of Exile*, 1845). She was too emotional and overstrained to receive either influence without disaster. Of the generosity of her enthusiasms—for Greek literature (she translated the *Prometheus* twice); for social reform (*The Cry of the Children*, 1843); for the lower classes and the rights of women (*Aurora Leigh*, 1857); for the cause of Italian freedom (*Casa Guidi Windows*, 1851; *Poems before Congress*, 1860); and for other noble causes—there can be no question; but much of what she had to say might have been better said in prose, and more succinctly. Her intensity of feeling was rarely controlled by the discipline of form. The verse is too fluent and too facile, and the fact that the many false rimes and approximations to rime were introduced in accordance with a theory that she herself expounded is an explanation of their presence rather than an excuse for it. She depended upon large and loose effects, and rarely sought or found the perfect cadence or the inevitable word. The poems of social protest connect her with the movement for reform; the poems dealing with the Risorgimento contain vivid descriptions of the Florentine scene during the eventful year 1848, and though (as she later realized) she backed the wrong horse when she praised Napoleon III, these pieces form a not unworthy link between Byron and Shelley before her and Swinburne and Meredith after. But only in the sonnets addressed to her husband did she fashion her feeling into the form of art. It would seem that her profounder emotions were the more controlled, for in the *Sonnets from the Portuguese* (1850) there is little of the "confused impetuosity" [37] of *Aurora Leigh*. Though written over a period of several years, the sonnets form a homo-

[34] The "modern" view of the poem discounts the religious and ethical aspects and finds interest in the "novel" element—the complications, the suspense, the entanglements of motive, the conflicts of testimony, the bustle and excitement; while objecting to the arguments, casuistries, doubts, and aspirations. See V. S. Pritchett in *The New Statesman*, xx (1940). 66.

[35] On Elizabeth Barrett's forebears in Jamaica and on her "health-history" see Jeannette Marks, *The Family of the Barrett* (1938).

[36] Familiar from Rudolf Besier's play mentioned above and from Virginia Woolf's *Flush, a Biography* (1933).

[37] The phrase is Virginia Woolf's, who has said all that can be said, and more than most critics would say, for *Aurora Leigh*. See *The Second Common Reader* (1932), pp. 218-231.

geneous sequence. In tone they are almost uniform; occasional attempts at lightness of touch are not very successful, but on other occasions (as in the magnificent twenty-second sonnet) she rises to a height she nowhere else attains. There was abundant fire in Mrs. Browning's spirit, but generally it burned with more smoke and heat than light. In some of the *Sonnets* it is pure flame.

# XXVIII

## Matthew Arnold and Arthur Hugh Clough;
## Edward FitzGerald and James Thomson ("B.V.")

### I

The story of Clough's spiritual conflict is important for an understanding *Clough* of Arnold and therefore we begin this chapter with the less famous of the two Oxford poets. The early promise of Arthur Hugh Clough [1] (1819-1861) failed of fulfillment because of indecisiveness. At Rugby the influence of Dr. Arnold induced in him an excessive introspectiveness, and at Oxford the Tractarians drew him one way and the liberal theologians another with the consequence that he wandered between two worlds, a perplexed spirit, hesitating almost to the point of paralysis, yet maintaining a receptive open-mindedness. He was one of those who retained for the word *skepticism,* which for many contemporaries had become the polite term for the rejection *Skepticism* of religious beliefs, its proper meaning of suspension of judgment. Clough's skepticism was due to the destructive conclusions of the new biblical criticism. Not without poignant misgivings did he relinquish his faith in orthodox Christianity, and he continued to recognize that to submit to reason was as blind a course as to adhere to dogma. *The New Sinai,* a satiric poem, expresses his distrust in science. Several poems reveal the effect of the "higher criticism" upon his hypersensibility. When (in *The Shadow*) men repeat the arguments for the Resurrection, the ghost of Jesus knows no such arguments. In *Easter-Day* the evidence for the Resurrection is rejected; but the poem goes on to a second part in which it is affirmed that in an ideal sense Christ has indeed risen. [2] Clough tries to accept the Carlylean counsel to "do the duty that lies nearest thee." Only—by what criterion can duty be recognized? That question gives him pause. He said of Carlyle that "he led us out into the wilderness and left us there."

The poet soon passed into the wilderness of the world. He recanted his *Principal* subscription to the Thirty-nine Articles and resigned his Oriel fellowship. *Poems*

---

[1] *Poetical Works,* ed. Charles Whibley (1913); *The Emerson-Clough Letters,* ed. H. F. Lowry and R. L. Rusk (Cleveland, 1934). — Ehrsam, *Bibliographies,* pp. 67-75; Goldy Levy, *Arthur Hugh Clough* (1938); Laura Lutonsky, *Arthur Hugh Clough* (Vienna, 1912); J. I. Osborne, *Arthur Hugh Clough* (1920); Stopford A. Brooke, *A Study of Clough, Arnold, Rossetti and Morris* (1908), pp. 26-48; H. W. Garrod, *Poetry and the Criticism of Life* (1931), pp. 109-127.

[2] A. W. Benn, *English Rationalism,* II. 48, emphasizes the significance of these two poems. Other short pieces recording Clough's spiritual struggles are *Qui Laborat Orat, Blank Misgivings, A Song of Autumn, Qua Cursum Ventus, Sic Itur,* and *Parting.* The most popular of his poems, *Say Not the Struggle Nought Availeth,* is not quite typical.

In the next years (1848-1850) he wrote his three principal poems. *The Bothie of Tober-na-Vuolich*, a novelette in hexameters [3] with amusing Scarron-like echoes and burlesques of Virgilian effects, tells of the love of a radical young Oxonian for a Highland girl who rejects him on the ground of the differences in their stations in life. But when he suggests that they emigrate to New Zealand she accepts him.[4] The grace and charm of the love scenes, the clever argumentation, and the zestful cheerfulness of the poem reflect Clough's temporary buoyancy after his escape from entanglements at Oxford. A second story in hexameters, *Amours de Voyage*, was written in Rome in 1849 during the short-lived Republic. In mood, if not in incident, it is autobiographical. The desire for action with doubts as to its efficacy is thoroughly characteristic. The overintellectualized art student who is the hero is representative of "feeble and restless youth born to inglorious days." His languid love affair with an English girl ends in separation. The emotional situations are subtly analyzed; the episodes are entertainingly developed; and the background of great events is sketched with a vividness due to the poet's own presence upon the scene whereof he wrote. The despondent and wayward ending of the *Amours* points forward to *Dipsychus*, which Clough began and left unfinished at Venice in 1850. This has been called "a little Victorian *Faust*." The debt to Goethe and Byron is obvious, and Clough had also in mind a poem then widely read though unreadable today, the *Festus* of Philip James Bailey.[5] The Spirit with whom Dipsychus holds converse is not "a fallen and hateful fiend" but his own worldly common sense. In the end he submits to the standards of the world, with a consequent coarsening of his moral fiber and with regret for forsaken ideals.

In his last years Clough wrote little. The voice of doubt and despondency was not suited to the contentment he at length won. He made a happy marriage, found work in the Education Office, and assisted Florence Nightingale in her philanthropic activities. He and Arnold, close friends at Oxford and for several years thereafter, drifted apart, estranged by Arnold's impatience with Clough's indecisiveness. In failing health he went to live in

---

[3] In 1847 Longfellow, in *Evangeline,* had revived the English hexameter. For Arnold's defense of its use see *On Translating Homer*, pp. 210-216.

[4] Emigration was in the air of the mid-century. Tennyson thought of going to Australia; Thomas Woolner, the sculptor, went there. Samuel Butler farmed sheep in New Zealand. Compare the concluding pages of *David Copperfield* and Ford Madox Brown's popular picture "The Last of England."

[5] Philip James Bailey (1816-1902) published *Festus* in 1839 and enlarged it in subsequent editions to some forty thousand lines. In scope the poem is cosmic; in style occasionally noble, more often inflated and absurd; in form it is semi-dramatic, a succession of fifty-two scenes in which Festus, Lucifer, and other characters engage in colloquies. Bailey does not fear to challenge comparison with Milton, Byron, and Goethe; he comes off the worse from these encounters. Two English versions of Goethe's *Faust*, Part I, were current (Hayward's, 1832; Anster's, 1835); but Bailey, though he did not know much German, borrows also from Part II, which was not translated till much later. See G. A. Black, "Bailey's Debt to Goethe's Faust," *MLR*, xxviii (1933). 166-175. The contemporary popularity of *Festus* was due to its theme of universal salvation. See Emil Goldschmidt, "Der Gedankengehalt von Baileys *Festus*," *ESt*, lxvii (1932). 228-237. For an estimate with favorable specimens of its style see Hugh Walker, *The Literature of the Victorian Era* (1910), pp. 346-349.

Florence and died there in 1861. Not till three years later did Arnold write *Thyrsis* in which the greater poet, not without hints of his own superior moral strength which led him to share in the intellectual warfare of the age, sang of his dead friend's choice of an easier road. Thyrsis could not wait the passing of the storm that raged. "It irk'd him to be here; he could not rest."

## II

In his essay on George Sand, Arnold outlined unconsciously the pattern *Arnold* of his own development, the "grand elements" which he distinguished in the mind of the French novelist being discernible in his own. Each inherited from the French Revolution "the cry of agony and revolt" and "the aspiration towards a purged and renewed human society," and each possessed a trust in nature as "a vast power of healing and delight for all." [6] The cry of revolt sounds in the poetry of Arnold's earlier life; the aspiration towards a new society in the prose writings of his later years.

Matthew Arnold [7] (1822-1888), the son of Arnold of Rugby, passed much of his boyhood in the Lake Country, and the beauty of Westmorland, "where mountains make majestical man's lowliest fate," [8] impressed upon him forever a sense of the healing power of nature. The heritage from Dr. Arnold was of utmost importance in shaping the son's ideas on religion and society—religion conceived not in terms of dogma and ritual but of an organization to be remolded on nationally comprehensive lines for social and ethical betterment; society conceived in terms of the state strong enough to exert authority over warring factions and classes. In his historical studies Dr. Arnold had emphasized the need to understand the development of institutions; and the obligation to adjust the mind to social and political change became part of the son's message to his countrymen. Of the many

[6] Matthew Arnold, "George Sand," *Mixed Essays* (ed. 1904), p. 241.
[7] There is no complete edition. *Works* (15v, 1903-4); *Poems* (3v, 1889; often reprinted); *Poems (1840-1867)*, introduction by Sir A. T. Quiller-Couch (1930); *Arnold: Prose and Poetry*, ed. Sir E. K. Chambers (1939); *Culture and Anarchy*, ed. J. Dover Wilson (1932); *Thoughts on Education Chosen from the Writings of Matthew Arnold*, ed. Leonard Huxley (1912); *Note-Books* (1902); *Essays in Criticism, Third Series*, ed. E. J. O'Brien (Boston, 1910), hitherto uncollected essays; *Letters, 1848-1888*, ed. G. W. E. Russell (2v, 1895); *Unpublished Letters*, ed. Arnold Whitridge (New Haven, 1923); *Letters to Arthur Hugh Clough*, ed. H. F. Lowry (1932). — T. B. Smart, *Bibliography* (1892); Ehrsam, *Bibliographies*, pp. 14-45. George Saintsbury, *Matthew Arnold* (1899); Herbert W. Paul, *Matthew Arnold* (EML Series, 1902); Stuart Sherman, *Matthew Arnold: How to Know Him* (Indianapolis, 1917); Hugh Kingsmill, *Matthew Arnold* (1928); Lionel Trilling, *Matthew Arnold* (1939); C. B. Tinker and H. F. Lowry, *The Poetry of Matthew Arnold, a Commentary* (1940); J. B. Orrick, *Matthew Arnold and Goethe* (1928); Otto Elias, *Matthew Arnolds Politische Grundanschauung* (Leipzig, 1931); Iris E. Sells, *Matthew Arnold and France: The Poet* (1935); F. L. Wickelgren, "Arnold's Literary Relations with France," *MLR*, XXXIII (1938). 200-214; L. Bonnerot, "La Jeunesse de Matthew Arnold," *Revue Anglo-Américaine*, VII (1930). 520-537; John Drinkwater, "Some Letters from Matthew Arnold to Robert Browning," *Cornhill Mag.*, n.s. LV (1923). 654-664; W. S. Knickerbocker, "Matthew Arnold at Oxford," *Sewanee Rev.*, XXXV (1927). 399-418; C. B. Tinker, "Arnold's Poetic Plans," *Yale Rev.*, n.s. XXII (1933). 782-793; Margaret Woods, "Matthew Arnold," *E&S*, xv (1929). 7-19; T. Sturge Moore, "Matthew Arnold" *E&S*, XXIV (1938). 7-27; H. W. Garrod, *Poetry and the Criticism of Life* (1931), pp. 3-84.
[8] Sir William Watson, *In Laleham Churchyard* (an elegy on Arnold).

men whom the elder Arnold prepared for life none bore his impress more deeply than his son.

The prize-poems *Alaric at Rome* (1840) and *Cromwell* (1843) are more or less derivative, but the austerity and restraint are characteristic of Arnold's mature poetry. Yet the young man who entered Balliol in 1841 was distinguished rather for a protectively ironical manner than for "high seriousness." Something of this manner he retained throughout life and his persiflage was at times offensive to his opponents. At Oxford he appeared gay and self-assured, but the restless play of his mind as he sought in the welter of modern thought for a criterion of conduct is reflected in the letters to Clough.

*"Marguerite"*

In Switzerland in 1848 Arnold fell in love with a French girl, the "Marguerite" of the cycle of poems from which some biographers have tried to reconstruct the course of the fascination, the passion, and the parting.[9] All that can safely be conjectured is that, distrusting impulse and aware of unbridgeable differences of "race" and breeding, Arnold rejected the dictates of his heart and reluctantly withdrew. The poems written in retrospect show that the experience left its scar; but in 1851 he married an English woman. Appointed to an inspectorship of schools, he threw himself into the arduous work of a post which he did not relinquish till near the close of his life. The reports written for the Education Department [10] are, with the possible exception of *A French Eton* (1864), of no moment as literature, but they have their place among the records of educational reform.

*Poetry*

Almost all Arnold's poetry was written during his young manhood. The few pieces of later date are for the most part resuscitations of earlier moods. The poems are generally variations upon the themes of youthful anguish and aspirations. When Arnold described them as recording a "main movement of mind" of his generation he did not mean that they reflected the confident, expanding world of Whig commercialism but that they expressed the thoughts of the intellectuals who, disturbed by new, subversive ideas, found themselves adrift from old moorings upon a wide, uncharted sea. This poetry is contained in five slender collections: *The Strayed Reveller and other Poems. By A.* (1849); *Empedocles on Etna and other Poems. By A.* (1852); *Poems* (two volumes, 1853), where Arnold's name first appeared upon a title-page; *Poems, Second Series* (1855); and *New Poems* (1867). There was a good deal of suppression, reprinting, and rearrangement from volume to volume;[11] *Empedocles* disappeared till, at Browning's solicita-

---

[9] The "Marguerite Cycle" is contained in two groups of poems, *Switzerland* and *Faded Leaves*; it is possible, however, that one or two in the latter group may have been addressed to Frances Lucy Wightman, whom Arnold married. For a highly dubious psychoanalytical interpretation see Hugh Kingsmill, *Matthew Arnold* (1928). A more sympathetic, not to say sentimental, view is set forth in I. E. Sells, *Matthew Arnold and France* (1935), chs. VIII and IX. See also Tinker and Lowry, *Commentary*, pp. 153-157.

[10] *Reports on Elementary Schools, 1852-1882*, ed. Sir Francis Sanford (1889); new edition with additional material and an introduction by F. S. Marvin (1908).

[11] For details see Tinker and Lowry, *Commentary, passim*.

tion, it was republished in the *New Poems* of 1867. Save for that belated volume and the drama *Merope* (1858), most of Arnold's verse had been written by 1855. To the volume of 1853 he attached a preface in which he deprecated "timeliness" as a requisite in poetry, urged the importance of the choice of subject, and counseled poets not to waste their art upon random verbal felicities but, mindful of "total effect," to strive for a unified and consistent impression.

The half-dozen poems of considerable length support the opinion that Arnold's genius was not quite equal to the task of such sustained efforts in poetry and was at ease only within narrow compass. *Tristram and Iseult* (1852), the first modern version of the legend,[12] betrays in its imperfectly coördinated metrical experiments the characteristics of the transition period between Tennyson and the Pre-Raphaelites. The prominence accorded to the Second Iseult—Tristram's wife—is perhaps not without personal significance, as is the brooding regret for the brevity of passionate youth. *Empedocles on Etna,* though semi-dramatic in form,· is meditative in tone. The reminiscences of *Paracelsus* pleased Browning but may account for Arnold's dissatisfaction with the poem. The theme is the contrast of the life of the reason, in the character of Empedocles, with that of the imagination, in the character of Callicles. The long discourse in which Empedocles recommends compromise and submission to the limitations of life concludes with the philosopher's suicide because he cannot bring himself to follow his own counsel—an end which Arnold intended to be moving but which, despite the grave sonority of the verse, is faintly ridiculous.[13] *Sohrab and Rustum* (1853) displays an effort towards complete "objectivity"; the choice of a story from Firdawsí's *Shah Nameh*[14] is an illustration of Arnold's contention that poetry should be remote from contemporary issues; but the theme of the son slain by the mightier father is susceptible of a personal interpretation.[15] In *The Church of Brou* (1853) the simple, Scott-like opening narrative and the quiet Wordsworthian description in the second part enhance by contrast the superb concluding section in which the poet imagines the awakening of the lovers from their tomb.[16] Is it fanciful to discern a personal application in this dream of reunion? *Merope* (1858), a drama classical in

*The Longer Poems*

[12] Howard Maynadier, *The Arthur of the English Poets* (1907), pp. 382-389. — The tentative beginnings of Richard Wagner's *Tristan und Isolde* date from 1852, but the opera was composed in the main between 1857 and 1859. It is probable that Wagner knew, and took some hints from, Arnold's version.

[13] George Meredith laughed at it, as he did at *Manfred* and *Hernani*. See his impish but wise little poem, *Empedocles; Poetical Works,* ed. G. M. Trevelyan (1912), pp. 411-412.

[14] Arnold took his story not directly from Firdawsí but from Sainte-Beuve's review of Jules Mohl's translation of the *Shah Nameh*. He borrowed details of Oriental atmosphere and color from Sir John Malcolm's *History of Persia* and Sir Alexander Burnes's *Travels into Bokhara*. See Tinker and Lowry, *Commentary,* pp. 75-85.

[15] Lionel Trilling, *Matthew Arnold*, pp. 134-135.

[16] For the indebtedness of this final section to Edgar Quinet's essay on the Church of Brou in his *Mélanges* (1839) see Charles Cestre, "*The Church of Brou* de Matthew Arnold," *Revue Germanique*, IV (1908). 526-538; I. E. Sells, *Matthew Arnold and France*, pp. 202-207. The topographical errors in the poem were soon commented on and were the cause of Arnold's dissatisfaction with it. See Tinker and Lowry, *Commentary,* pp. 38-41.

form, is on a subject [17] hardly worthy of the austere dignity of the style and is so flat a failure that we may pass it by. Arnold's laborious effort to be impersonal and remote from modernity was wasted; *Merope* has no particle of life in it.

*Doubt*

The cornerstone of Arnold's meditative and elegiac verse is doubt. This comes as much from the *Zeitgeist* as from his own temperament. Though he could not as yet share the confidence of the rationalists, the tradition of skepticism reasserted itself in a mind uninfluenced by transcendentalism. He is consistent in his denial of revelation, but a feeling for the grandeur of the Christian tradition and for the influence of the historic Jesus (he was never much concerned with Strauss's "Christ-mythus") acts as a check upon

*Conduct*

his agnosticism. He shares the tendency of the mid-century to subordinate faith to conduct. "Has man no second life? Pitch this one high!" [18] The categorical imperative is accepted with a realization of the formidable responsibility it places upon the individual. How is the standard to be maintained? Arnold's answer is: through self-trust. Meditations upon the

*The Self-contained Soul*

self-contained soul provide one of the most persistent motives in his poetry.[19] Goethe is the type and exemplar of this ideal. The need for self-sufficiency strengthens, at the same time that it is intensified by, the sense of estrangement from one's fellows. Images of the castaway, of wreckage, and of the sea which isolates man from man recur frequently. The calm, confident unity of the Middle Ages is gone forever; the French Revolution was a great watershed of history dividing the present from the past. The poet and his generation wander between a dead world and a world "powerless to be born." In this bewildering turmoil the need is for a fixed ideal; and those great figures whom Arnold holds up to admiration—Sophocles, Shakespeare, Wellington, his own father—possessed a "vision of the general law," chose a "path to a clear-purposed goal," and "saw life steadily." [20] So long as Arnold was primarily a poet, he yearned to set his feet upon the secure path; his verse records the quest and the disappointment.

There can be but partial substitutes for lost faith in supernatural religion. What are these substitutes? Mere "natural" life is not an ultimate resource and guide; Arnold rejects that illusion of the romanticists.

[17] A son, returning home in disguise, barely escapes being murdered by his mother. The situation is uncomfortably close to that in George Lillo's *Fatal Curiosity.*
[18] *The Better Part, Poems* (ed. 1889), I. 260. Compare Rossetti's early sonnets, *The Choice,* in *The House of Life,* lxxi-lxxiii. Similar sentiments, nobly expressed, are in the Preface to Ruskin's *Crown of Wild Olive* and in a famous letter by Huxley on the death of his son (Leonard Huxley, *Life and Letters of Thomas Henry Huxley,* I. 237).
[19] See, for examples, the close of *Mycerinus*; the salutation to Emily Brontë as "the spirit which dared trust its own thoughts" (*Haworth Churchyard*); the lament that we modern men "never once possess our soul" (*A Southern Night*); the poet's desire to withdraw from the world "till I possess my soul again" (*Stanzas from the Grande Chartreuse*).
[20] *To a Friend; Shakespeare; To the Duke of Wellington; Rugby Chapel.* The famous line "Who saw life steadily and saw it whole" is often misunderstood. Arnold does not make for Sophocles the extravagant claim that he saw the whole of life. What came within the range of his vision he saw integrally.

> Know, man hath all which Nature hath, and more,
> And in that *more* lie all his hopes of good. . . .
> Man must begin, know this, where Nature ends.[21]

Nor is there ever a suggestion of a sensual anodyne; Omar's solace is to Arnold nothing else than abhorrent "lubricity." To follow the counsel of the Spirit in Clough's *Dipsychus* and feign an outward conformity is a solution which Arnold spurns. May one, then, fly from the fevered conflict of modern civilization? The temptation to do so is well-nigh overwhelming. Arnold feels an affinity to souls who have fled from life,[22] finding in Nature, "calm soul of all things," [23] the promise of spiritual restoration. But he inherited too impelling a consciousness of moral responsibility to rest content in such a solution. Is action, then, the remedy? Is the Carlylean Gospel of Work the outlet from the Everlasting No? In the practical sphere, despite intellectual doubts, Arnold resolutely followed this counsel; but it did not satisfy him as a poet. What remains? A Stoic resignation. Man, *in utrumque paratus,*  *Stoicism* must "waive all claim to bliss and try to bear," [24] recognizing that the secret of life is "not joy but peace." [25] But this attitude of serene acquiescence, characteristic of Arnold at his noblest, he does not always maintain. In the poem which the modern reader (not without cause) has taken to his heart  *Despair* as he has no other of Arnold's there is a despair as desolating as James Thomson's:

> The world, which seems
> To lie before us like a land of dreams,
> So various, so beautiful, so new,
> Hath really neither joy, nor love, nor light,
> Nor certitude, nor peace, nor help for pain;
> And we are here as on a darkling plain
> Swept with confused alarms of struggle and flight,
> Where ignorant armies clash by night.[26]

Arnold's finest poems are reveries, profoundly personal and introspective. In verse he rarely assumes the function of the teacher and guide. He feels the need for a new social order but is powerless to suggest the way. This critical and melancholy ineffectuality reveals his spiritual kinship to Clough. In harmony with this prevailing mood is the chill aloofness of his treatment of subjects which have given other poets the opportunity for passionate expression. Marguerite is a fading memory; the lovers in the Church of Brou

---

[21] *In Harmony with Nature.* In Arnold's use the word *Nature* means the "world of things" as opposed to the moral world of man. This is in contradistinction to the use to designate "the natural order" which includes both worlds, material and moral. See J. W. Beach, *The Concept of Nature,* pp. 397-405.

[22] For example, Senancour, Amiel, Wordsworth (as Arnold interpreted him), the Scholar-Gipsy.

[23] *Lines written in Kensington Gardens.*

[24] *The Scholar-Gipsy.*

[25] *Resignation.*

[26] *Dover Beach.* See Tinker and Lowry, *Commentary,* pp. 172-178.

lie in their tombs; even the story of Tristram focuses sympathy **not upon** the lovers but upon the widow and her children. This austere **control of** emotion has its counterpart in Arnold's technique. Save for his **experiments** in cadenced rimeless verse, he was content to write in a few traditional metres and stanzaic forms. His imagery is remarkable for a few oft-recurring figures drawn from his love of flowers and streams and mountains. In contrast to the Venetian richness of Tennyson's color-sense, his poetry is in *grisaille*; the impression it imparts is of grays and cold moonlight.

## III

*The Criticism of Life*
The spiritual void of modern life had been the theme of Arnold's poetry. In prose his effort was to give shape to his "aspiration towards a purged and renewed human society." On his election (1857) to the professorship of poetry at Oxford he chose for his inaugural theme *The Modern Element in Literature*.[27] He lectured in English, not Latin as his predecessors had done, and thus underscored his conviction that literary studies must be pursued not in aesthetic isolation but in intimate relation with the largest issues of social life. Later he delivered two formal series of lectures. In those *On Translating Homer* (1861-1862), with a discriminating insight which has won the praise of so exacting a scholar as A. E. Housman, he discussed the Homeric poems with the object of analyzing the constituent elements of the "grand style," showing to what extent and with what shortcomings each English translator has succeeded in rendering the qualities of the original. The problem has the widest social significance, for the "grand style" is an expression of the nobility of the human spirit and Arnold felt that the conditions of contemporary life had diminished the stature of that spirit.[28] The lectures *On the Study of Celtic Literature* (1867) are in part vitiated by Arnold's acceptance of the prevalent theory of "race" which enabled him with a confidence hardly justified by the disputable evidence to isolate those elements in the English temper that spring, respectively, from Celtic, Saxon, and Norman ancestors. Once more the emphasis is upon the social importance of literary studies.

*Essays in Criticism*
Meanwhile the first series of *Essays in Criticism* had appeared (1865). This famous volume represents a reaction from romanticism and from earlier, insular standards of English literary criticism. By the term *criticism* Arnold intends something much broader than literary scholarship. It embraces all branches of knowledge with the object of making "the best" prevail. The critic, drawing upon all the resources of cosmopolitan culture,

[27] Published in *Macmillan's Magazine*, February, 1869; never reprinted by Arnold; first gathered into his works in *Essays by Matthew Arnold* (Oxford, 1914), pp. 454-472. — Arnold's pamphlet *England and the Italian Question* (1859) is an early example of his cosmopolitan outlook. Rising above the immediate issues of Napoleon III's campaign and the policy of Lord Derby's ministry, Arnold relates the problem to the larger one of the need for the English aristocracy to adapt itself to democratic change.

[28] Lionel Trilling, *Matthew Arnold*, p. 174; T. S. Omond, "Arnold and Homer," *E&S*, III (1912). 71-91.

seeks to supply what is lacking in the English character and thus to remedy the defects in English society. The endeavor is towards an integration of the individual and the social order. Arnold dwells upon the virtue born of the submission of individual genius to general law. Taking as his illustration the great tradition cherished by the French Academy, he urges the need to impregnate the English genius with that flexibility of intelligence and "regard for the whole" which are the marks of the classic spirit. In the English poetry of the romantic era there had been a lack of what T. S. Eliot was later to call "the objective correlative"; too much energy had been expended to too little purpose. On the same grounds Arnold deprecates Carlyle's exaltation of the German romanticists and turns to Heine, the intellectual liberator. The intense, preoccupied individualism of the English poets finds its parallel on a lower level among those people who believe that the greatness of England depends upon her material prosperity and who are indifferent to the things of the spirit. These people are the "Philistines," enemies of the "Children of Light." They are characterized by their concern for their own interests at the expense of society as a whole. Criticism rises above this "practical view of things" to a universality of outlook grounded upon disinterestedness. The emphasis laid upon poetry in these discussions comes from Arnold's conviction that since the great problem of modern life is the disunity which has been brought about by the decline of faith, poetry must assume the function of a religion to bind life afresh into a whole. For the poet sees life steadily and in its entirety. In this sense "Poetry is a Criticism of Life."

These lines of thought were extended and their practical application clarified in *Culture and Anarchy* (1869). Robust people (Walt Whitman among them) derided the term *culture* for its supposed connotation of snobbish, academic fastidiousness. For this misunderstanding Arnold's own self-deprecation was in part to blame. Actually the term embraces the complete realization of the potentialities of the human spirit under the guidance of reason. The argument (obviously directed against Mill's essay *On Liberty,* though Arnold does not refer to it directly) is for an authority strong enough to discipline the individual's claim to liberty of action. The English tradition of unrestrained individualism encourages that "dissidence of dissent" which is characteristic of the Protestant mind and which, if unchecked, inevitably breeds anarchy. It must be combatted by the disinterested objectivity which regards society as a whole. To the three classes of society—aristocracy, the middle class, and the lower classes—which are opposed in interests to one another Arnold attaches the famous nicknames of Barbarians, Philistines, and Populace; but to bestow such names is not argument. He makes great play with "the God-given right of every Englishman to do as he likes" and with light irony exposes the pettiness of the self-styled "practical" men, who, blind to universal issues, expend their energies upon the passage of an act permitting a widower to marry his sister-in-law. (This satiric method of argument was continued in *Friendship's Garland,* 1871). But the irritating

*Culture and Anarchy*

*Hellenism and Hebraism*

flippancy does not conceal the serious intent. Necessary to the argument is the antithesis between Hellenism and Hebraism, the illuminated mind which sees things as they are and the moral conscience which is obsessed with thoughts of sin. Admitting that "Conduct is three-fourths of Life," Arnold contends that Puritanism has expanded it yet further, thus affording another illustration of that regard for the parts which is inimical to the well-being of the whole. But Culture opens the mind to the possibilities of perfection. "Not a having and a resting but a growing and a becoming, is the character of perfection as culture conceives it." In this respect "it coincides with religion." The individual self must become part of the "best self," the "national right reason" upon which the State must be founded. "Individual perfection is impossible so long as the rest of mankind are not perfected along with us." It was of this doctrine of a disciplined community whose members rise above self-interest that H. G. Wells was thinking when in the midst of a great crisis he affirmed roundly in *Mr. Britling Sees It Through* (1916) that "the trouble with England is that she did not listen to Arnold."

*Biblical and Theological Essays*

The space devoted in *Essays in Criticism* to religious problems (especially in the two papers on the Guérins) was indicative of the direction in which Arnold's thought was soon to move. With *St. Paul and Protestantism* (1870) he entered upon a decade dedicated largely to biblical and theological controversy. With his favorite technique of antithesis he contrasted the spirit of contentiousness which informs Protestantism with the "sweet reasonableness" of St. Paul. But he refashioned St. Paul in his own image and wrested his meaning to his own purposes. In his quest for a concept of God that would satisfy the rationalist and scientist he resorted to a method of interpretation entirely without warrant in the text of the Epistles. Thus, while wounding the orthodox, his attempt to effect a compromise alienated the secularists. His rash amateurishness shocked biblical scholars who had devoted their lives to the textual and historical problems which he handled so lightly. The shakiness of his reasoning, as when he defined religion as "morality touched with emotion," exposed him to a devastating onslaught by F. H. Bradley, the great logician.[29] Furthermore, serious-minded people were offended by his levity of manner in dealing with sacred things.[30] In *Literature and Dogma* (1873) the attempted demonstration that the ancient Hebraic concept of God was identical with the idea of Righteousness led on to his own definitions of God as "a stream of tendency," "a something not ourselves that makes for righteousness." Once more he laid himself bare

[29] Lionel Trilling, *Matthew Arnold*, pp. 357-359 and index. — Francis Herbert Bradley (1846-1924), who lived to become the most influential English philosopher of his time, first revealed his critical power in *Ethical Studies* (1876). His *Principles of Logic* (1883) broke with, and advanced beyond, the accepted empirical logic of the time. *Appearance and Reality* (1893) is his most famous book and is the representative exposition of Bradley's idealism. *Essays on Truth and Reality* (1914) appeared when his influence was waning. Almost alone among modern British philosophers Bradley had at his command a prose style of a grace and beauty that won him readers beyond the boundaries of the schools.

[30] Arnold defended his levity; see *Letters*, ed. Russell, II. 120.

to the logician's scourge. *God and the Bible* (1875) is a defense of his position and an interpretation of details in the two earlier books. Later he became conscious of a revulsion of public feeling from the hard and narrow rationalism of the past two decades and expressed a belief that he might end his days "in the tail of a return current of popular religion, both ritual and dogmatic." [31]

Gradually Arnold forsook religious controversy. He wrote on the Irish question and in an eloquent estimate of George Sand returned to literary criticism.[32] In 1883 he retired from professional work and visited the United States, where he lectured on *Democracy,* on *Literature and Science* (here crossing swords with Huxley), and on *Emerson.*[33] His latest manner, in the essays on Wordsworth, Byron, Shelley, and Keats in *Essays in Criticism, Second Series* (1888), is more intimate and winning than that of former books; the levity and the superciliousness have almost disappeared. The mixture of biography and critical comment in these essays approximates to the method and style of Sainte-Beuve.[34] The purity and refinement of Arnold's prose (traits which he generously attributed to the influence of Newman), the qualities of grace and repose and calm clarity are here exhibited at their most persuasive. On occasion he is master of a restrained eloquence with no false or forced note. The fastidiousness which was displeasing when he dealt with social problems, suggesting as it did that he was more offended with the hideousness of poverty and crime than moved to deep moral indignation, was a useful instrument for the analysis of literary values. Yet Arnold's values have not been universally accepted. The interpretation of Wordsworth is curiously one-sided. The generous estimate of Byron is colored by mid-century liberalism. The opinion of Shelley's "ineffectuality" has been hotly contested. The concept of Keats is warped and limited. But for their suggestiveness, their sureness of touch, their display of wide horizons of culture, their cosmopolitan outlook, these final essays remain the part of Arnold's prose writings which posterity has valued most highly.

*Last Essays*

Arnold died suddenly in 1888. Sir William Watson's *In Laleham Churchyard* is not a mere conventional elegiac tribute but an analysis of the strength and grace and lucidity of Arnold's genius, of that element of the "worldling" that mingled with "the bard and sage," that shunning of "the common touch" which was his weakness, and that preservation of "the fortress of his 'stablished soul" which was his strength.[35]

[31] Arnold to Grant Duff, August 22, 1879, *Letters,* ed. Russell, II. 187.
[32] *Mixed Essays* (1879); *Irish Essays* (1882).
[33] *Discourses in America* (1885).
[34] Arnold wrote the article on Sainte-Beuve in *Encyclopaedia Britannica,* ninth edition. His obituary notice of Sainte-Beuve (*Academy,* November 13, 1869) is reprinted in *Essays by Matthew Arnold* (Oxford, 1914), pp. 482-487. See Paul Furrer, *Die Einfluss Sainte-Beuve auy die Kritik Matthew Arnolds* (Zurich, 1920).
[35] Sir William Watson, *Poems* (2v, 1905), I. 27-30.

## IV

*FitzGerald*    Of all poems written during the Victorian period that which is best known today came from the pen of a scholarly recluse whose other writings never reached many readers. The intellectual powers of Edward FitzGerald [36] (1809-1881) were highly prized by contemporaries at Cambridge. But temperament and a small competence led him into a pleasant rural life where an uncongenial marriage, followed by a separation, scarcely ruffled the surface of his placid existence. *Dolce far niente.* Actually, FitzGerald found it sweet to do not precisely nothing but only what he wished to do. This was to read, visit London for the sake of music and the theatre, acquire a knowledge of exotic tongues, and correspond with his friends. His letters are among the most charming in English literature. They lack the wide social horizon of Walpole's, the homely humor and pathos of Cowper's, the tempestuous wit of Byron's; but their intimacy and whimsicality picture for us a personality of singular charm. As the century moved towards its self-confident middle years, FitzGerald, like the recluse he was, found himself out of sympathy with the new tendencies. Yet his thought and feeling were in the very vortex of one of the principal currents of the age. So passed a harmlessly selfish, gently hedonistic life. He set down his meditations in a prose dialogue, *Euphranor* (1851), whose delicacy of style befits the insignificance of its contents. He made paraphrases from the Greek and Spanish.[37] He cultivated his garden.

*The*    And then the study of Persian led him, after two preliminary experiments
*Rubáiyát*    in translation,[38] to Omar Khayyám. In the *Rubáiyát* or quatrains of the twelfth-century poet he found the revelation of a kindred heart. He rendered into English the quintessence of their thought and emotion. Persian scholars who have compared the version with the original tell us that much has been omitted but little added; that quatrains separated in the alphabetical sequence of the Persian have been brought together for the sake of coherence; that what is loose and lax has been tightened and what is coarse has been refined away.[39] The metrical pattern lent itself admirably to English adapta-

---

[36] *Poetical and Prose Writings*, ed. George Bentham (7v, 1902); *Letters and Literary Remains*, ed. W. A. Wright (7v, 1902-1903). The four versions of *The Rubáiyát of Omar Khayyám* (1859, 1868, 1872, 1879) were reprinted together with the original prefaces and notes in 1890; the first and fourth versions, with variants from the other two, are in the Golden Treasury Series (1899). Facsimile of ed. 1859 (1939). — Ehrsam, *Bibliographies*, pp. 78-90; John Glyde, *Life of Edward FitzGerald* (1900); A. C. Benson, *Edward FitzGerald* (*EML Series*, 1905); Thomas Wright, *The Life of Edward FitzGerald* (2v, 1904); N. C. Hannay, *A FitzGerald Friendship* (1932), with hitherto unpublished letters to W. B. Donne; A. M. Terhune, *The Life of Edward FitzGerald* (1947), with many hitherto unpublished letters.

[37] The best of these is *Such Stuff as Dreams Are Made Of*, from Calderón's *La Vida es Sueño* (*Six Dramas of Calderón*, 1853).

[38] The *Sálamán and Absál* of Jamí and *The Bird Parliament* (or *The Language of Birds*) of Attar. On FitzGerald's version of Jamí see E. G. Browne, *Literary History of Persia*, III (1928). 523-526. Browne does not mention the version of Attar.

[39] E. H. Allen, *Edward FitzGerald's Rubáiyyát of 'Omar Khayyám with their Original Persian Sources* (1898). The statistical results of Allen's investigation are interesting: 49 of the quatrains are from 49 originals; 44 are condensations of more than one original quatrain,

tion. FitzGerald wisely discarded the scheme with four like rimes and re-tained the alternative design in which the rimeless third line has the effect of a thought hovering or fluttering before finding repose, an effect either of lyrical delicacy or of witty sharpness. Other poets have since used the form,[40] but in the history of English prosody it remains the "FitzGerald stanza."

The *Rubáiyát* (1859) attracted no attention till Rossetti came across it and introduced it to his friends. Very soon the little book "caught on." On the whole it is proper that the fourth version should be the definitive text; yet there is an occasional Oriental boldness of imagery in the version of 1859 which we see sacrificed with regret.[41]

Two modes of thought and feeling are intertwined in the poem. One is *Hedonism* the desire to snatch the utmost of pleasurable sensation from the irretriev-able passing moment, for (as Pater was soon to be warning the young Oxonians who were among the first readers of the *Rubáiyát*) "we have an interval and then our place knows us no more." The nightingale and the harkening poet alike vanish from the garden, and the moon looks down upon other pleasure-lovers who will vanish in their turn. It is as obvious as are all the eternally repeated forms of human experience; but it is ex-pressed with a freshness and beauty comparable to Ecclesiastes and with the same burden: "Rejoice, O young man, in thy youth," for "there is no work, nor device, nor knowledge, nor wisdom in the grave, whither thou goest." Time's wingéd chariot hovers near, and audible is the noise of greedy Acheron.

But with this desire to enjoy while it is day the fleeting loveliness of the light mingle more somber thoughts of the Power that has created beauty and in man a capacity to appreciate beauty but has cursed him with transi-ence and holds him responsible for the actions of a nature not determined by himself. But should the pots blame the potter for fashioning this one ugly and that one fragile? Wherefore not, if the potter attaches to the pots blame for ugliness or fragility not of their choosing? Is justice conceivable in the scheme of things?[42] Had the thought of the *Rubáiyát* been expressed in the terms of modern occidental philosophy it would have won adherents

---

2 are found in only one text of Omar; 2 reflect the spirit of the whole but are not direct translations; 4 are from other Persian poets; 3 (which appeared in the first and second versions but were afterwards suppressed) are not attributable to any Persian poet. — In Persian poetry a quatrain is invariably a complete and isolated unit; there is no such thing as a poem com-posed of a number of quatrains. The units are assembled in mere alphabetical order according to the rime-word.

[40] Swinburne used the form with ingenious variations. In *Laus Veneris* each pair of quatrains is linked together by riming the third lines. In the elegy on Gautier the FitzGerald stanza is crossed with *terza rima* to produce a new form, *quarta rima*.

[41] See, for example, the very opening. In the fourth version the Sun "strikes the Sultan's Turret with a Shaft of Light," but in the first "the Hunter of the East" has caught "the Sultan's Turret in a Noose of Light."

[42] FitzGerald wrote but, anxious lest he give offense (and probably conscious that anger was out of keeping with the prevailing calm of the poem), suppressed this quatrain:

> Nay, but for terror of His wrathful face,
> I swear I will not call Injustice Grace;
>    Not one good fellow of the tavern but
> Would kick so poor a coward from the place.

but not devotees and lovers. Not in the garb of harsh, repellent materialism, but voluptuous, genial, courteous, ceremonious, and sadly smiling, cloaked in gorgeous and elaborate imagery, came forward into the Victorian world the figure of the astronomer-poet of Persia.[43] He spoke with the authority of age-long experience and with the wisdom of the East. *Ex oriente lux!* "But if thy light be darkness, how great is that darkness!" In words and cadences of haunting loveliness a desolating message was communicated to numberless hearts. The *Rubáiyát* helped to shape the melancholy hedonism and moral incertitude of late nineteenth-century England.

## V

*James Thomson ("B.V.")*

In social standing and way of life the translator of Omar and the author of *The City of Dreadful Night* were worlds apart; but money might have made of Thomson another such hedonistic recluse as FitzGerald, and poverty might have driven FitzGerald to drink and despair as it did Thomson. The depths of their natures were much alike, though FitzGerald kept them hid and Thomson exposed them bleakly to the world.

The most formidable and uncompromising use of the speculations of the mechanistic materialists for the purposes of poetry is in *The City of Dreadful Night* by James Thomson [44] (1834-1882). It is difficult to imagine "this poetical offense of dark monotonousness" (in Meredith's phrase) being written at any other time or by any other poet. By heredity, poverty, ill fortune, bad habits, and intense conviction Thomson was prepared for his gloomy task. From personal experience he drew his material, and he had "the largeness of utterance" (as George Eliot said of him) and the sense of form to shape his nightmare into a work of art. His father was a drunken sailor; his mother a woman of sensitiveness and refinement; both died when he was a child, leaving to him the heritage of an addiction to alcohol and a love of poetry. With little regular education, the orphan boy read widely. The initials "B. V." over which he published much of his verse memorialize two of his early passions, "B" standing for "Bysshe" (that is, Shelley) and "V" for "Vanolis" (an anagram of Novalis, the German romanticist). From 1854 till 1862 he was a schoolmaster to soldiers' children at an army-post in Ireland. There he fell in love with the daughter of the regimental ser-

The denunciation is as audacious as that of the speaker in Thomson's dark City who would not, even were he rewarded with God's power and glory, assume His "ignominious guilt." Compare also the famous middle chorus in Swinburne's *Atalanta in Calydon*. On the "cosmic irony" or "ironic reproach" which FitzGerald added to Omar and which is heard also in Thomson's poem see David Worcester's suggestive study, *The Art of Satire* (1940), pp. 132-135.

[43] A. C. Benson, *Edward FitzGerald*, p. 97.

[44] *Poetical Works* (2v, 1895); *The City of Dreadful Night and Other Poems*, ed. Bertram Dobell (1910); ed. G. H. Gerould (1927); ed. Edmund Blunden (1932). — H. S. Salt, *James Thomson* (1889); Josefine Weissel, *James Thomson der Jüngere, sein Leben und seine Werke* (Vienna, 1906); Bertram Dobell, *James Thomson* (1910); J. E. Meeker, *The Life and Poetry of James Thomson* (1917); B. I. Evans, *English Poetry in the Later Nineteenth Century* (1933), ch. IX.

geant. She died; and without sentimentality it may be said that from the shadow of her loss his soul was never henceforth lifted.

Thomson was dismissed from his post on an unspecified charge (perhaps *Early* drunkenness) and through friendship with Charles Bradlaugh, the atheistic *Poems* radical, obtained work on *The National Reformer*. From 1862 till 1874 he contributed to the secularist press. He had already written some verse, including a long poem, *The Doom of a City* (1857). The descriptive passages foreshadow some of the imagery in Thomson's masterpiece, and there is an evident trend towards pessimism, but the basic contrast is more striking than the superficial resemblance, for in this early poem there is still a recognition of Divine Providence.

*Sunday at Hampstead* (1863) and *Sunday up the River* (1865), transcripts of cockney life, show inherent capacities for humor and realism which in happier circumstances the poet might have developed further. *The Naked Goddess* (1866) has a Shelleyan element of vague allegory combined, not very successfully, with satiric passages. *Weddah and Om-el-Bonain* (1868) shows a romantic yearning for beauty which, when we remember Thomson's circumstances, is pathetic. But it is not by these poems that he is remembered.

The line of development from *The Doom of a City* brings us to *A Festival of Life* (1859), describing a dance where the masquers are startled by the appearance ever and anon of two hooded strangers who conduct away now one and now another of the guests. The resemblance to Poe's *Masque of the Red Death* is apparent, and the two aspects of Death, as a gracious deliverer and a malignant demon, suggest that Thomson knew Alfred Rethel's engravings of "Death the Avenger" and "Death the Friend." To the same year belongs *Mater Tenebrarum,* a poem of agonizing sensibility which is suggestive of De Quincey. In *Our Ladies of Death* (1861) the three-fold concept of Death as Beatitude, Annihilation, and Oblivion is reminiscent of De Quincey's *Levana and Our Ladies of Sorrow*. Then came the prose phantasmagoria, *A Lady of Sorrow* (1862). Sorrow appears to the poet in three guises: first as an Angel in the form of the lost Beloved; then as a Siren, symbolizing the effort to forget the past in sensuality; lastly as a constantly attending Shadow. There are striking anticipations of the imagery of *The City of Dreadful Night*; indeed, the value of this feverish little piece is that it enables us to watch Thomson's conceptions taking their final form.

*The City of Dreadful Night* [45] appeared in *The National Reformer,* The City March-May, 1874. The keynote of the poem is the motto from Leopardi: of Dread-"In thee, O Death, our naked nature finds repose; not joyful, but safe from ful Night the old sadness." Prologuizing, the poet asks why he should write, and answers that to express his woe in words imparts a sense of power and passion.[46] The structure of the poem, hard, obvious, and unsubtle, is massively impressive in its clarity. In alternate sections there are descriptions of

[45] See L. A. Cotten, "Leopardi and *The City of Dreadful Night*," *SP*, XLII (1945). 675-689.
[46] Compare Tennyson's *Lucretius*, lines 223-225: "Shutting reasons up in rhythm . . . To make a truth less harsh."

the City and a series of episodes recounting the death-in-life therein. The general sections are in a seven-line stanza riming *ababccb,* with double endings in the fifth and sixth lines whose effect of weighty, mournful iteration suits the mood.[47] The episodic sections are in a variety of stanzaic forms, with one in blank verse. The topography of the City—the river, the embankment, the tenebrous streets, the enormous cathedral, the suburbs rising to the North—is drawn from London. Only three or four of the most memorable episodes can be noticed here. In the famous "As I came through the desert" (the desert of life) the traveler is the poet as he now is, while the figure seen mourning by the dead is the poet as he had been in the far past when the loss of his beloved was fresh upon him. This motif is repeated in the central scene in the vision of the young man who kneels beside a bier in the *chapelle ardente.* In the tremendous dialogue between a demonist and a determinist, the poet is to be identified not with the former, who in hysterical fashion seeks to fix the blame for circumstance upon some malevolent divinity, but with the latter, who with grim-eyed resolution expounds the same mechanistic materialism that is later the subject of the sermon to which the brotherhood of sorrow listen in the cathedral. The poem rises at its close almost to sublimity in the description of the great statue of Melancholia (drawn in every particular from Dürer's engraving) which broods over the City as the emblem of despair.

The impact of the poem upon a sensitive reader is so soul-shaking that there is danger lest it be appraised too highly. Guidance to a sounder judgment may be had from Arnold's remark (in his Preface of 1853) that there is one kind of situation unsuitable for poetry because it cannot give that joy which great art imparts, namely, a situation "in which a continuous state of mental distress is prolonged, unrelieved by incident, hope, or resistance, in which there is everything to be endured, nothing to be done."

During his last decade Thomson made some notable translations from Leopardi and wrote some not very distinguished critical papers. Friends were loyal to him and he won the attention of influential people.[48] By 1880 he had gained sufficient fame to warrant the publication of two volumes of poetry.[49] But it was too late. Sleeplessness, whose horrors are described in the impressive poem *Insomnia,* was added to his afflictions, and his drunkenness increased to dipsomania. He died in distressing circumstances in 1882, leaving a few friends to cherish his reputation till the coming of a later generation which has sensed his genius and his tragedy.

[47] The rime-scheme, but without the double-endings in the fifth and sixth lines, had been employed in *Our Ladies of Death.* Thomson is said to have taken the stanza from Browning's *The Guardian Angel;* but it is also the stanza of Vigny's *La Maison du Berger* where there are striking anticipations of Thomson's thought and manner.

[48] Notably George Meredith. See Meredith's *Letters* (1912), II. 302, 307, 413, and 437 for some illuminating comments upon Thomson and his work. The blind poet P. B. Marston and the poetical bookseller Bertram Dobell were close friends of his last years.

[49] *The City of Dreadful Night and other Poems* and *Vane's Story, Weddah and Om-el-Bonain and other Poems* (both 1880). *Essays and Phantasies* (1881) is a collection of prose. *A Voice from the Nile and other Poems* appeared posthumously (1884).

# XXIX
## Rossetti and His Circle

### I

Dante Gabriel Rossetti [1] (1828-1882) was the son of Gabrielle Rossetti, a political exile from Italy, poet, opera librettist, and student of Dante.[2] The future poet-painter passed his youth in the Italian colony in London, but his father was a constitutional royalist and saw little of Mazzini and the other exiled republicans.[3] A characteristic indifference to politics dates probably from Rossetti's boyhood. His education was irregular and mostly at home. He and his brother and two sisters [4] were brought up under "the shadow of Dante," who remained one of the great influences upon his imagination.[5] To the later poets of Italy he was never much attracted, nor did he ever visit the land of his ancestors. He was a child of precocious promise, writing a drama at the age of four, imitating in early drawings the style of contemporary German illustrators, and, when he was twelve, composing a ballad, *Sir Hugh the Heron,* in the manner of Scott. A few

[1] *Works,* ed. W. M. Rossetti (4v, 1911); *Poems,* ed. W. M. Rossetti (2v, 1904), valuable for the illustrations; *Poems,* ed. P. F. Baum (1937), including also a selection from the prose; *Family Letters,* ed. W. M. Rossetti (2v, 1895); *Letters to William Allingham,* ed. G. B. Hill (1897); *Letters to F. S. Ellis,* ed. Oswald Doughty (1928); *Three Rossettis: Unpublished Letters,* ed. J. C. Troxell (Cambridge, Mass., 1937); *Letters to Fanny Cornforth,* ed. P. F. Baum (Baltimore, 1940). — Ehrsam, *Bibliographies,* pp. 201-225; W. M. Rossetti (ed.), *Ruskin, Rossetti, Preraphaelitism* (1899) and *Preraphaelite Diaries* (1900); A. C. Benson, *Rossetti* (EML Series, 1904); Henri Dupré, *Un Italien d'Angleterre, le poète-peintre Dante Gabriel Rossetti* (Paris, 1921); Frances Winwar, *Poor Splendid Wings: the Rossettis and their Circle* (1933); William Gaunt, *The Pre-Raphaelite Tragedy* (1942); Evelyn Waugh, *Rossetti: His Life and Works* (1928); R. L. Mégroz, *Dante Gabriel Rossetti: Painter-Poet of Heaven in Earth* (1929); R. D. Waller, *The Rossetti Family, 1824-1854* (Manchester, 1932). There is much information in memoirs and biographies; see especially, G. Burne-Jones, *Memorials of Edward Burne-Jones* (2v, 1912); W. Holman Hunt, *Pre-Raphaelitism and the Pre-Raphaelite Brotherhood* (2v, 1905); J. W. Mackail, *The Life of William Morris* (2v, 1899); William Bell Scott, *Autobiographical Notes,* ed. William Minto (2v, 1892). The superb caricatures in Max Beerbohm, *Rossetti and his Circle* (1922) are valuable as criticism and literary history.

[2] Gabrielle Rossetti's autobiography in Italian verse was translated by W. M. Rossetti. His theory, based upon a symbolic interpretation of *The Divine Comedy,* that Dante was a precursor of the Reformation is expounded in *Disquisitions on the Antipapal Spirit which produced the Reformation: its Secret Influence on the Literature of Europe,* translated by Caroline Ward (1834). See E. R. P. Vincent, *Gabrielle Rossetti in England* (1936).

[3] For the Italian exiles, their British connections, and their influence on English literature see H. W. Rudman, *Italian Nationalism and English Letters: Figures of the Risorgimento and Victorian Men of Letters* (1940).

[4] William Michael Rossetti (1829-1919) became the prosy but indispensable chronicler of the Pre-Raphaelite movement and of his family. Maria Francesca Rossetti (1827-1876) wrote, among other things, *The Shadow of Dante,* a commentary. On Christina Rossetti see further on in this chapter.

[5] B. J. Morse, "Rossetti and Dante Alighieri," *ESt,* LXVIII (1933-1934). 227-248; R. D. Waller, "The Blessed Damozel," *MLR,* XXVI (1931). 129-141, on the debt to Dante and to the *dolce stil nuovo.*

years later he made versions of Bürger's *Lenore* and of portions of the *Nibelungenlied*. His interests were always divided evenly between poetry and painting,[6] and while he studied at the Royal Academy and afterwards as a pupil of Ford Madox Brown,[7] he began a translation of the *Vita Nuova*. The poetry of Keats [8] and Browning, the tales and poems of Edgar A. Poe, and the Gothic romances were among the formative influences; and after he made the lucky purchase of a manuscript volume of unpublished poems by Blake, that poet, then practically unknown, also influenced him.[9] During 1847-1848 he composed the first versions of *The Blessed Damozel, The Portrait,* and other poems which, circulating in manuscript, established his reputation in a privileged circle as a new force in poetry long before he became known to the public. In 1848 he and six friends [10] formed the Pre-Raphaelite Brotherhood.

*The*
*"P.R.B."*            The "P.R.B." aimed to reclaim for the artist the freedom in manner and choice of subject which he was supposed to have exercised before Raphael's example and prestige became dominant. The movement was also a protest against the influence of Sir Joshua Reynolds and the tradition of the "grand style." These young men would paint what they saw, not what the artists of the past who were held up to them as models had seen. They rejected various established principles of technique. Their special preoccupation was with problems of light. They altered the conventional proportions and distribution of light which academic theorists had legislated from the practice of Rembrandt. They discarded the use of bitumen as a groundwork, and instead of building up their lights from shade they built up their shades from light. They were thus feeling their way along the same line as that of the young Impressionists of France. But unlike the French group, so great was their devotion to religious, medieval, and romantic themes that their art was often subservient to literature. Moreover, while the French school, reacting against the newly invented art of photography, moved away from representation, the "P.R.B.", influenced by photography, became entangled in minute representationalism. Their meticulous attention to detail often involved the sacrifice of central emphasis; and when they first exhibited in 1849 this fidelity to fact was thought to be unworthy of religious art and Millais was even accused of blasphemy. In 1850 Rossetti and some

*The*
*Germ*              of his colleagues initiated a little periodical, *The Germ,* as a medium for the promulgation of their doctrines and a vehicle for their poems; but it died after four numbers. In later years the movement disintegrated, some of the brethren compromising with the general taste, and Rossetti going his

---

[6] Eva Tietz, "Das Malerische in Rossettis Dichtung," *Anglia*, LI (1927). 278-306.

[7] F. M. Brown (1821-1893), associated with the "P. R. B." but not a member, later became a member of Morris's firm of decorators. A few poems which he wrote to accompany his paintings show Rossetti's influence.

[8] Hill Shine, "The Influence of Keats upon Rossetti," *ESt,* LXI (1926-1927). 183-210.

[9] Preston Kerrison, *Blake and Rossetti* (1944); B. J. Morse, "D. G. Rossetti and William Blake," *ESt,* LXVI (1931-1932). 364-372.

[10] This Pléiade was composed of Rossetti, W. Holman Hunt, John Millais, Thomas Woolner the sculptor, Walter Deverell who died young, James Collinson, and W. M. Rossetti.

own way. Analogies drawn between one art and another are seldom secure, and in the case of the Pre-Raphaelites they are tenuous and difficult to discern. There is a certain naïveté, not without some affectation, in their early poems and paintings; in both arts there is painstaking representationalism; in both there is religiosity rather than deep religious feeling; in both a love of romantic subject-matter; and the use of color words in their poems corresponds to the brilliant coloring of their canvases. But in the poems of Rossetti's maturity there is little to remind one of the theories of the Brotherhood.

In 1857 Rossetti collaborated with Morris and Burne-Jones upon the now vanished murals of the Oxford Union and at this time he met Swinburne. The impact of Rossetti's powerful personality is apparent in the early poetry of Morris and Swinburne. To 1857 belongs the famous volume of Tennyson's poems illustrated by the brethren. Many of Rossetti's finest paintings date from 1850 to 1860 before the morbid mannerisms of his later style had mastered him. To these years belongs also the friendship with Ruskin to which, as to the subsequent estrangement, reference has been made in an earlier chapter. In 1860 Rossetti married Elizabeth Siddal, one of his models.[11] Fragile in beauty and in health, she was loved by Rossetti after his fashion, though he was unfaithful to her. She pined and, in peculiarly distressing circumstances, died in 1862. As a token of penitence he placed the manuscripts of his poems in her coffin.

In 1861 he had published *The Early Italian Poets*,[12] a series of translations. Rallying after a while from the despondency into which he sank after his wife's death, he set up house in Cheyne Walk. In the luxuriant paintings of the following years may be traced chronologically the growth of mannerism and obsession. Symptoms of eye-strain led him to renew his activities as a poet in 1868, and in 1869, acting upon the counsel of friends, he consented to the opening of his wife's grave that his manuscripts might be retrieved. The way for the reception of his *Poems* (1870) had been for so long prepared by volumes from other members of his circle that the degree to which he was the master and impelling force of the new movement was not so apparent to the public of the day as it is now. Nevertheless the book was well received till in the following year Robert Buchanan perpetrated his cruel and foolish attack, *The Fleshly School of Poetry*.[13] Without considering the personal issues involved in the celebrated quarrel that followed,[14] we may note that the effect upon Rossetti was to increase his gloom and isolation. The last decade is the story of chloral and its conse-

*Poems, 1870*

[11] Violet Hunt, *The Wife of Rossetti* (1932).
[12] Revised as *Dante and his Circle* (1874).
[13] Reprinted in *Notorious Literary Attacks*, ed. Albert Mordell (1926), pp. 185-213. — Robert Buchanan (1841-1901), a Scot, published *London Poems* (1866) and many later volumes, including plays and novels. That he had genuine power is shown by *Judas Iscariot* and a few other things, but his talent was dissipated over too many fields and his nature was corroded by jealousy of his betters. — See A. S. Walker, *Robert Buchanan, the Poet of Modern Revolt* (1901).
[14] For a succinct account of the quarrel, in which Swinburne became involved, see S. C. Chew, *Swinburne* (1929), pp. 242-243.

quences. A friend, ignorant of the dangers of the newly discovered drug, had recommended it as a cure for insomnia. An attempt at suicide by an overdose was barely averted in 1872. A mental disorder took the form of suspicion of hidden enemies and the conviction that his friends were treacherous. Morris did what he could for Rossetti, bearing the discomfort of his presence at Kelmscott House. Despite the ravages of disease, there were periods of intellectual vigor in both the arts. The paintings of this last phase show mannerisms pathologically exaggerated, but there are still power and splendor in them. In poetry Rossetti wrote *The White Ship* and *The King's Tragedy* in 1880 and so late as 1881 published the volume of *Ballads and Sonnets*. Two new young friends, Hall Caine and William Sharp,[15] were much with him towards the end. He died in 1882.

Rossetti's personality dominated all who knew him; and upon posterity he makes the impression of a genius greater than anything that he accomplished. Whatever the judgment of his accomplishments as a painter, there can be no question of the integrity and consistency of his work as a poet. He became grasping in his negotiations with clients and often the merely salable was his aim in the atelier; but no such commercialism mars his poetry. At times an overelaboration of detail obscures the central effect. The thronging images, balanced between decoration and symbol, blur the concept. Yet, generally speaking, the luxuriance is but the covering of a fundamental austerity and a sense is imparted of intellectual control over the exuberant sensuousness. So careful were successive recensions that earlier and later versions of many of the poems might well serve as illustrations of a treatise upon the poetic process. Thus, *The House of Life*,[16] which is the connecting link between his early and late poetry, was not a coherent sequence when parts of it, intermingled with lyrics, were published in 1870; but in subsequent years, while expanding it greatly, he molded it into form. Rossetti seems never to have improvised, but brooded long over his poems. Through intellectual contemplation he disciplined sensuous feeling. Everywhere there is a syntactical tightness, and there is little unnecessary dilation of figures of speech. This discipline he had in mind when he insisted upon the "fundamental brain-work" requisite for the production of poetry. Consequently, almost alone among poets of the nineteenth century, he does not require of the critic that the work of high excellence be separated from the mediocre. He wrote comparatively little and his poems are almost all on a singularly even level of accomplishment.

Italian and "Gothic" strands are interwoven in the rich fabric of his verse. The influence of Dante was, though limited, profound. The exacting task of the translations from the poets of the *dolce stil nuovo* helped to give

*"Funda-
mental
Brain-
work"*

---

[15] Caine's *Recollections of D. G. Rossetti* (1882) is still of some value; Sharp's *D. G. Rossetti: a Record and a Study* (1882) was a hasty supply for the market and is of no importance.

[16] *The House of Life*, ed. P. F. Baum (Cambridge, Mass., 1928); R. C. Wallerstein, "Personal Experience in Rossetti's *House of Life*," *PMLA*, XLII (1927). 492-504.

his own style firmness, though it probably confirmed him in certain technical mannerisms (such as the employment of imperfect rimes and of rimes upon unaccented syllables) which he later exaggerated into defects. But apart from a conception of love—half personified, half spiritualized, never wholly apprehended—he took less from Dante and his contemporaries than from the somber superstitions of the North.[17] From boyhood, when he read *Melmoth the Wanderer* and translated *Lenore,* Rossetti was fascinated by the weird, the occult, the supernatural, the unknown. He read Hoffmann and Chamisso and other German exploiters of terror and wonder. The theme of the Doppelgänger troubled his imagination as it had Shelley's. The visionary instinct also found sustenance in medieval dream-literature and in the ritual and symbols of the faith of his forefathers.

In tracing Rossetti's development it must be kept in mind that the dates of his two volumes of original poetry are misleading both because many pieces in them were written long before publication and because he subjected them to repeated revisions. A few memorable poems are not characteristic. *Jenny,* with its pathos and delicate irony, stands as much apart from the rest of his verse as does *Found* from his other pictures. *A Last Confession* is Browningesque pastiche. Such poems as *On the Sunrise of 1848* and the tribute to Wellington are quite uncharacteristic. Along his true path he moved from the realistic Pre-Raphaelitism of some of the early poems ever deeper into the world of dreams. The conflict of the realistic and the visionary is wonderfully resolved in *The Blessed Damozel* in which elements from the atelier combine with motives inspired by Dante. *The Burden of Nineveh* and *Dante at Verona* are sustained midway between the outer and the inner world. In both these poems the corridors of time past are seen in strange perspective. Rossetti never wrote purely descriptive poetry, but for the purpose of simile natural imagery is beautifully employed. In *The House of Life* nature is representative of every mood, changing as the mood changes. In many poems the human situation has its harmonizing background—the wind in *Sister Helen*; the thunder and dull rain-drops in *The Portrait*. Rossetti penetrates far into the twilit recesses of life: forests with dim waters where silence and shadow reign, fit abodes of a spirit oppressed with "sick fervor" and vain longing. In such places he is aware of mystery: there ghosts walk and the phantom double. His imagination broods upon ancient magical lore: the beryl-stone and the waxen image; and upon non-human beings or women with thaumaturgic powers: Lilith or Sister Helen. The extant prose fragments (most of them synopses of poems never written) are variations upon themes that are somberly ominous. The dream-world was for him no mere piece of poetic decoration derived from old literary traditions; in his mind the barriers between the conscious and the subconscious were thin. From some of the sonnets in *The House of Life* it is difficult or impossible to wrest a logical meaning; but it is not to be

*The World of Dreams*

---

[17] L. A. Willoughby, *Dante Gabriel Rossetti and German Literature* (1912).

inferred that this is due to confusion of thought; the obscure inapprehensibility is deliberately contrived to convey a sense of the stress of an unresolved emotional conflict. It is the more impressive because he retained command of another and simpler style, rich in recondite archaisms and steeped in eerie atmosphere but more direct and objective than are the introspective poems. To this style belong such early pieces as *The Staff and Scrip* (1851-1852) and *Sister Helen* (of which the first version dates from 1851-1854); such poems of his middle years as *Eden Bower* and *Troy Town;* and the two narrative pieces, *The White Ship* and *The King's Tragedy,* which were written in intervals of comparative calm shortly before the end. From first to last the impression of concentrated thought and constricted energy dominates the effects of sensuousness.

## II

*Christina Rossetti*

Not the leader of the Pre-Raphaelites but his almost cloistered sister, Christina Georgina Rossetti [18] (1830-1894), first attracted attention to the new movement in poetry. Her *Goblin Market* (1862) offered something very different from the conventional Tennysonian diffuseness and sentimentality, something strange and fantastic and resolute. She presents points of resemblance and contrast to her brother. They are alike in the intensity and concentration of their work; but he is generally elaborate and ornate while she is simple and spontaneous. The sensuality of his nature is opposed to the asceticism of hers. Both were drawn to Catholicism, but he by its aesthetic charm and she by its devotional appeal. Yet it was the unbelieving brother who often hovered on the verge of mystical experience from which the devout sister was shut off. She longed for the visionary ecstasy but was too honest and humble to lay claim to what she did not possess. Within the Anglican communion she found her spiritual home; but though her opinions are those of the Tractarians and though there are similarities between her poetry and Keble's,[19] a closer affinity is with the devotional poetry of Herbert and Vaughan. She found contentment in the family circle and in friendships with people of talent or genius; but she refused to marry James Collinson, the man she loved, because of differences on matters of faith. This renunciation is the subject of the sonnet-sequence *Monna Innominata,* the shorter sequence *By Way of Remembrance,* and various individual poems. Apart from this her life is the record of her books.[20] In the devo-

[18] *Poetical Works,* ed. W. M. Rossetti (1904). — Ehrsam, *Bibliographies,* pp. 189-199; Dorothy M. Stuart, *Christina Rossetti (EML Series,* 1930); Fredegond Shove, *Christina Rossetti: a Study* (1931); Eleanor W. Thomas, *Christina Georgina Rossetti* (1931); M. A. Sandars, *The Life of Christina Rossetti* (n.d.).

[19] The poems in *Some Feasts and Fasts,* a section of her work written at long intervals between 1853 and 1893, follow the Church Calendar in the manner of Keble's *The Christian Year.*

[20] She published seven poems in *The Germ* (1850). Her volumes of poetry are: *Goblin Market* (1862); *The Prince's Progress* (1866); *Sing-Song* (1872); *A Pageant, and other Poems* (1881); *Verses* (1893); and *New Poems* (posthumous, 1896).

tional works in prose,[21] which contain a good deal of verse subsequently assembled with her other poetry, she places much emphasis upon the symbols lying, or supposed to lie, beneath the literal surface of the Bible.

Like all her family, she enjoyed the eerie fantasies of German romanticism. In several poems [22] she played variations upon the theme of the spectre bride or bridegroom, imparting to it a Christian interpretation. *Goblin Market*,[23] for all its lightly tripping measures, is not gay or trivial but sinister, for the creatures of the other world are malignant, not frolicsome, sprites. For those who could "catch the clues" there is a warning against the spiritual wickedness with which the soul must wrestle. When, expanding the lyric dirge *Too late for Love, too late for Joy,* she turned the tale of the Sleeping Beauty into the romantic narrative of *The Prince's Quest,* it is as much a parable as a fairy tale, for the lover who lets himself be tempted by the pleasures of the way arrives too late and finds the bride dead who had long awaited him. Who will may disregard the symbolism; but it is there. Other, shorter poems are simple allegories of the Way of the Soul—the Choice of the Paths, the distractions of the World, the frustrations of Love, the journey of Life towards Death. Of such pieces the most impressive is *Up-Hill.* But Christina Rossetti has lighter moments, and when the allegory is ignored some of these pieces are almost as childlike as the nursery rimes which she gathered in *Sing-Song.* The lilt and jingle of these tiny ditties show the lightness of her fingering and her command of rime. Something of their simplicity reappears in her lovely carols, of which an example is *In the Bleak Mid-Winter.*[24] In another direction the nursery rimes point towards the pageant of *The Months.* All these things modulate by almost imperceptible shades and almost inaudible overtones into her austere religious verse. Many of the latter bear the general title *Songs for Strangers and Pilgrims.* She moved through this life conscious of its transitoriness and desirous of a better country. This desire is expressed perfectly in *Marvel of Marvels* and *Passing away, saith the World.* Both these are built upon monorime. The danger of this metrical form is that it may seem a mere *tour de force*; but from this Christina Rossetti escapes through the energy and intensity of her desire. Of a quieter beauty is the little poem for Whitsunday, "We know not the voice of that River," in which is quintessentialized that mood of longing which does not attain to the immediacy of the mystic vision.

*Goblin Market*

*Religious Poetry*

---

[21] *Seek and Find* (1879); *Called to be Saints* (1881); *Letter and Spirit* (1883); *Time Flies* (1885), which is semi-autobiographic; and *The Face of the Deep* (1892), a commentary on the Apocalypse. All were published by the S. P. C. K.

[22] *The Hour and the Ghost; The Poor Ghost; The Ghost's Petition.*

[23] B. I. Evans, "The Sources of Christina Rossetti's *Goblin Market*," MLR, xxviii (1933). 156-165.

[24] Widely popular today in the beautiful setting by Gustav Holst.

## III

A number of lesser poets moved in Rossetti's circle. Among them were William Bell Scott [25] (1812-1892), the painter, and Thomas Woolner [26] (1825-1892), the sculptor. Many of Rossetti's best letters are addressed to the Anglo-Irish poet William Allingham [27] (1824-1889). Another Anglo-Irish poet in the same group was Arthur O'Shaughnessy [28] (1844-1881). The misfortunes of the blind poet Philip Bourke Marston [29] (1850-1887) evoked tender responses from the Pre-Raphaelites. John Payne [30] (1842-1916), who won renown as a translator, was a more independent figure moving in the same circle. William Sharp [31] (1855-1905) regarded Rossetti as his master and shows his influence in the poetry published under his own name; but his fame was due to the verse and prose published under the pseudonym "Fiona Macleod" which are in the most exaggerated manner of the writers of the "Celtic Twilight" school. At a further remove from Rossetti but influenced by his work in translation were the writers of *vers de société*, a genre fashionable in the eighteen-seventies.[32] Impeccably moral itself, this light verse preluded the "Decadence" by its emphasis upon form. The early poems of Andrew Lang [33] (1844-1912) stem directly from Rossetti's versions

[25] Scott's long poems, *Hades* (1838) and *The Year of the World* (1846) are pseudo-Shelleyan in style and thought and were written before he felt Rossetti's influence. *Poems* (1854) and later volumes show his new orientation.
[26] Woolner published four volumes of verse. His once popular *My Beautiful Lady*, a soft and silly thing which reads almost like a parody of the Pre-Raphaelite manner, he later expanded (1863) under the influence of Patmore's *The Angel in the House*.
[27] Between 1850 and 1887 Allingham published a dozen volumes of verse. See also his *Diary*, ed. H. Allingham and D. Radford (1907). Allingham's place in the Irish Literary Revival is as a poet who sensed the *genius loci* rather than as a nationalist. He had a pleasant fancy for witches and leprechauns and an ear for light lyric. He exercised a considerable influence upon the young Yeats.
[28] *Poems*, ed. W. A. Percy (1923). O'Shaughnessy's first book, *An Epic of Women* (1870), is in an ironic manner afterwards abandoned. *Music and Moonlight* (1874) is more characteristic. *The Fountain of Tears* and *We Are the Music Makers* are his best-known poems.
[29] Marston's four volumes of verse were collected together in 1892. His poems are shot through with Pre-Raphaelite imagery and mannerisms, but in their mood of resignation mingled with revolt there is an individual note.
[30] *Poetical Works* (2v, 1902). There are Pre-Raphaelite elements in such pieces as *The Rhyme of Redemption* and evidence of indebtedness to Swinburne elsewhere. The marsh-lights which play over *Lautrec* are the product of the decomposition of romanticism. Payne translated Villon, Boccaccio, Omar, Hafiz, Heine, and *The Thousand Nights and a Night*. — See Thomas Wright, *The Life of John Payne* (1919); C. R. H. Williams, *John Payne* (Paris, 1926).
[31] *Earth's Voices* (1884); *Romantic Ballads* (1888). Among the "Fiona Macleod" volumes *From the Hills of Dream* (1897) is the best. The problem of Sharp's "dual personality" concerns the psychologist rather than the literary historian. See *The Writings of "Fiona Macleod,"* ed. Elizabeth A. Sharp (7v, 1909-1910); E. A. Sharp, *William Sharp (Fiona Macleod), a Memoir* (1910); P. E. More, "Fiona Macleod," *The Drift of Romanticism* (1913), pp. 119-143.
[32] The vogue began with *Lyra Elegantiarum* (1867), edited by Frederick Locker-Lampson (1821-1895) who was in the line of descent from Prior through Praed. Elegance, sparkle, light irony, and perfect finish are the effects aimed at in this genre.
[33] *Ballads and Lyrics of Old France* (1872); *Ballads in Blue China* (1880-1881). Lang's *Helen of Troy* (1882), a narrative poem reminiscent in manner of William Morris, is related to his Homeric studies and to his translations, done in collaboration, of the *Odyssey* (1879) and the *Iliad* (1883). A sonnet on the *Odyssey* is his best-known poem. — *Poetical Works* (2v, 1923). On Lang's prose work see below, ch. XLII.

of Villon. Austin Dobson [34] (1840-1921) and Edmund Gosse [35] (1849-1928) were accomplished practitioners of these dainty forms, and the parodies and witty verses of Charles Stuart Calverley [36] (1831-1884) and James Kenneth Stephen [37] (1859-1892) display something of the same manner.

[34] *Vignettes in Rhyme* (1873); *Proverbs in Porcelain* (1877); *Old-World Idylls* (1883); *Complete Poetical Works* (1923). Dobson shaped his fragile material exquisitely and in his hands the rondeau and the triolet attained their trivial perfection. His besetting fault was sentimentality. On his prose see ch. XLII, below.

[35] *On Viol and Flute* (1873). See also Gosse's "Plea for Certain Exotic Forms of Verse," *Cornhill Mag.*, XXXVI (1877). 53-71, which makes apparent the indebtedness of this school to the French poet Théodore de Banville. *Firdausi in Exile* (1885) is Gosse's most substantial poem. *Collected Poems* (1911). On Gosse's prose see ch. XLII, below.

[36] *Fly Leaves* (1872); *Complete Works* (1901). See also P. L. Babington, *Browning and Calverley* (1925), where *The Cock and the Bull* is reprinted with the relevant passages from *The Ring and the Book*; and R. B. Ince, *Calverley and Some Cambridge Wits* (1929).

[37] *Lapsus Calami* (1891).

# XXX

## William Morris

### I

The career of William Morris [1] (1834-1896) falls into two well-defined periods: till 1877 he was primarily concerned with poetry and the fine arts; thereafter with the ills and problems of modern society.

*The
Middle
Ages*

A boyish love of everything medieval led him to the study of architecture, armor, heraldry, romance, and Chaucer. At Oxford he was attracted to Anglo-Catholicism, and he and his closest friend, Edward Burne-Jones (1833-1898), planned to take orders and establish a monastery. Ruskin was their master; the famous chapter on "The Nature of Gothic" their inspiration.[2] His teaching and the activities of the "Christian Socialists" directed their attention to actual conditions in England. Meanwhile, drawing and architectural design were the first outlets for their creative enthusiasm. By 1855 Morris was composing poems and prose romances; and some of these things were printed in 1856 in *The Oxford and Cambridge Magazine*. From the manner of his early verse Morris afterwards made a wide departure; but the tales in prose foreshadow in their languorous rendering of action that is often violent the style of his latest romances.

The strong personality of Rossetti, whom these two young men now met, confirmed the decision to devote themselves to art, and they began to put into practice the aesthetic doctrines which Ruskin preached. In London in 1857 they set up house in Red Lion Square in what they called their "Palace of Art." The same year saw the decoration of the Oxford Union. Morris's share in this joint enterprise was an episode from the legend of Tristram

*The
Defence of
Guenevere*

and Iseult. *The Defence of Guenevere and other Poems* (1858) was the first public indication that a new movement in poetry was under way. Morris had in mind a cycle of Arthurian stories, in style and treatment unlike

---

[1] *Collected Works*, introductions by May Morris (24v, 1910-1915), supplemented by May Morris, *William Morris: Artist, Writer, Socialist* (2v, 1936), which contains hitherto unpublished material, an index to the *Works*, and an essay by George Bernard Shaw; *Prose and Poetry, 1856-1870* (1913). — Ehrsam, *Bibliographies*, pp. 161-187; J. W. Mackail, *The Life of William Morris* (2v, 1899), Pocket Edition (2v, 1912); Elizabeth L. Cary, *William Morris: Poet, Craftsman, Socialist* (1902); A. Clutton-Brock, *William Morris: His Work and Influence* (1914); John Drinkwater, *William Morris* (1912); Alfred Noyes, *William Morris* (EML Series, 1908); Holbrook Jackson, *William Morris* (1908; revised edition, 1926); B. I. Evans, *William Morris and His Poetry* (1925); *Some Appreciations of William Morris*, ed. G. E. Roebuck (Walthamstow, 1934), essays by Lascelles Abercrombie, J. W. Mackail, G. B. Shaw, and others; L. W. Eshleman, *A Victorian Rebel* (1940); Oliver Elton, *Poetic Romance after 1850* (1914); J. Middleton Murry, *Heroes of Thought* (1938), ch. xxvii; Karl Litzenberg, "William Morris and the Reviews: A Study in the Fame of the Poet," *RES*, XII (1936). 413-428.

[2] They were also influenced by Henry Kenelm Digby's *The Broad Stone of Honour* (1829).

Tennyson's *Morte d'Arthur* though owing something to *The Lady of Shalott,* in intensity of phrase stimulated by *Maud,* and in technique reminiscent of Browning's dramatic monologues. The mystic coloring of *The Chapel in Lyoness* is foreign to Morris's temperament and probably due to Rossetti's influence. The obscurity of some pieces comes not from profundity of thought but from an as yet incomplete mastery of expression; yet the roughness of rhythms is not to be ascribed to an inadequate prosodic technique but to a deliberate avoidance of the patterns of mid-Victorian metrics as long since fixed by Tennyson. The niceties of character are seldom delineated, but there is a genuine realization of tragic moments. How astonishing is the abrupt opening of the *Guenevere,* without scene-setting or explanation, the poet driving impetuously into the central situation! The Middle Ages are conceived not in the guise of Victorian sentiment, but as rough, hard, and barbarous. Thus, these early Arthurian pieces point forward to Morris's interpretations of the heroic sagas of Iceland. *Sir Galahad* marks his revulsion from his youthful ascetic ideal. The "gramarye" of *Rapunzel* points back to Coleridge rather than forward along the course he was to take. *Sir Peter Harpdon's End* is a tragic incident from Froissart dramatized with conspicuous, though not precisely dramatic, power. In one respect Morris never fulfilled the poetic promise of this first book. Save in brief infrequent passages, the later poetry does not possesss the force, the passion, the concentrated energy of these poems of his early manhood. Perhaps it was because, as he became active in many affairs, he came to look upon poetry as a recreation and relaxation. Certainly the poetic fiber was relaxed.

In 1859 Morris married the beautiful Jane Burden. The failure to find satisfactory furniture for their home in Kent led to the establishment in 1861 of the firm of "Morris, Marshall, Faulkner and Co., Fine Art Workmen in Painting, Carving, Furniture, and the Metals." [3] For some time Morris had little opportunity to write, but by 1865, when he returned to London to live, his business was prospering along several lines, he was freed from the necessity of immediate supervision, and time was released for literary work. He planned a cycle of poems on the Fall of Troy, but of these only two parts were written.[4] Plans for *The Earthly Paradise* were now taking shape, but one of the stories intended for it outgrew the space provided and was published separately. This was *The Life and Death of Jason* [5] (1867). His intention was to tell the old story as a troubadour would have told it, with sources freely adapted, with no striving for archaeological accuracy, with, indeed, a flavor that was deliberately medieval rather than classical. The

Jason

---

[3] See the Prospectus in J. W. Mackail, *The Life of William Morris,* Pocket Edition, I. 154-156. Among the craftsmen employed by Morris was William F. De Morgan (1839-1917) who in old age came before the public, like an apparition from another world, as the writer of sprawling, long-winded novels: *Alice-for-Short* (1907), *Somehow Good* (1908), and others with more faults and fewer merits. In them De Morgan combined elements from Dickens and Trollope. Their great vogue proved to be temporary.

[4] *Scenes from the Fall of Troy; Collected Works,* XXIV. 3-51. See Bush, pp. 298-303.

[5] Ed. E. Maxwell (1914). Morris drew his material from Ovid, Apollodorus, and Apollonius of Rhodes, with details from Lemprière. See Bush, pp. 303-313.

pictorial style, the subdued coloring, and the modulation from episode to episode without any abrupt discontinuity have been likened to the effects of tapestry, and the comparison is apt, for Morris loved old tapestries. The exquisite interspersed lyrics make scarcely a ripple on the surface of a narrative which flows with leisurely amplitude, its strength consisting not in isolated passages but in the cumulative impression till in the final book the pace quickens with the vengeful meditations of the abandoned Medea. No longer, as in the early poems, is there any obscurity or hesitation; but with the gain in clarity and confidence there is loss in intensity. Morris's besetting fault of over-fluency becomes apparent and the passion, though genuine, is watered down with words. There is no conscious intention to pour the new wine of modern thought into the old wine-skins of myth, but the recurrent motives of the beauty and brevity of life, the inevitability of death, and the dark uncertainty of any future existence color the poem's elemental pathos with modern skepticism.

The Earthly Paradise

Morris now hastened through the composition of the forty-two thousand lines of *The Earthly Paradise*. It was published in four volumes in two installments (1868 and 1870).[6] The tales are set in an ingenious "frame": to escape a visitation of the Black Death a company of Germanic, Norse, and Celtic folk of the Middle Ages sail westward and come to an island inhabited by descendants of the ancient Greeks who, cut off from the world, have kept their traditions and culture unalloyed. This artifice affords an opportunity for contrasts which Morris, who was no subtle psychologist, did not fully realize. The story-tellers, Greek and medieval, are old men, wistfully looking back to their lost youth. The situation enabled the poet to juxtapose tales in which the clear beauty of classic myth contrasts with the somber fantasies of barbaric ages and climes.[7] There are twenty-four stories, two for each month of the year, linked by lovely descriptive interludes. As the calendar moves round, the temper of the stories changes, becoming stronger and darker, and at the end the tone is sinister. Thus, the full effect can be gained only by continuous and consecutive reading—but this is a heavy task. The interludes are personal utterances, glimpses into the poet's mind, for though Morris disapproved of introspective poetry he did not altogether avoid it. They repeat with variations the keynote of the Prologue in which he declares that he, "the idle singer of an empty day," has no power to sing of heaven or hell or to make death durable. This characterization of himself as "idle" and his day as "empty" has been thought an affectation, but it is not; by an idle song he intended one which

---

[6] A plan to issue the poem in folio with five hundred illustrations by Burne-Jones was abandoned for want of trained wood-engravers.

[7] E. C. Kuster, *Mittelalter und Antike bei William Morris* (Berlin, 1928). The twelve stories of classical antiquity are from Homer, Herodotus, Apollodorus, Ovid, and other obvious sources. Some of the eleven western medieval tales come from the *Gesta Romanorum*, the *Legenda Aurea*, William of Malmesbury, and Mandeville. *The Hill of Venus* is from Tieck's *Erzählen. The Lovers of Gudrun*, from the *Laxdaela Saga*, is the first heir (other than translations) of Morris's Icelandic studies. *The Man who Never Laughed Again*, the only Oriental tale, is from the *Arabian Nights*. For stories which Morris discarded see *Collected Works*, xxiv. 87-316.

would afford distraction from everyday cares; and he was ever conscious of a spiritual emptiness. The general design—the outer "frame," the linking "months," and the balanced pairs of stories—is beautifully symmetrical. The deepening of tone, partly a matter of conscious art, is due also to the change from the romantic to the epic manner as Morris became more influenced by Norse myths. Through the whole there runs a note of doubt and despondency, a mild skepticism in harmony with the poet's ingenuous pity for humanity. There is an elemental vigor, a sense of the glory of youth and power and possessions and love; but these things that make life worth while are envisioned in the memories of aged men. The narrative, even though the action be swift and strong, is generally slow-moving; the diffuseness of the poem stands between us and it. There is little attempt to individualize the characters, either the tale-tellers or the actors in the tales. Once more we are reminded of figures on tapestries.[8]

In 1871 came the removal to Kelmscott on the upper Thames and the first visit to Iceland; in 1872 the "morality play" *Love is Enough*. The tenuous connection of this semi-dramatic poem with the old moralities is just sufficient to alienate it from most modern sympathies. There is too much comment and didacticism at the expense of action; and the metre used for the central theme (an adaptation of the old alliterative verse) encouraged diffuseness. Yet the poem is of singular loveliness. The intricate structure involves five concentric "layers" of the action. On the periphery are two peasants, sweethearts, who comment upon the morality and upon the Emperor and Empress, who, somewhat removed from ordinary humanity, watch the performance given in celebration of their wedding-day. Then, there is the figure of Love, who, bearing emblems which change from episode to episode, acts as the Expositor. The play shows the quest of Pharamond for Azalais. At the center of the design, and its essence, is the Music. All these motives are interwoven in a kind of poetic counterpoint and at the climax they combine in full harmony. The Music, Morris's most wonderful achievement in prosody, modulates on each of its soundings from mood to mood till it reaches a triumphant tone in the famous "Love is enough: ho ye who seek saving." This "morality" is not so remote from modern issues as it seems; indeed in one passage it looks forward to the social revolution: Love proclaims that he will be the leader at Armageddon. *Love is Enough*

In the next years Morris's activities were multifarious. He visited Italy and was disappointed. He went to Iceland for a second time. To his earlier translations from the Icelandic he added *Three Northern Love Stories* (1875). He translated the *Aeneid* (1876), not very satisfactorily. A disagreement with his partners forced him to reconstruct his business. Yet he had time to write his greatest narrative poem, *Sigurd the Volsung*[9] (1876), *Sigurd the Volsung*

---

[8] See Bush, pp. 313-327, on Morris' medievalizing treatment of classical myth in *The Earthly Paradise*.

[9] The story is from the *Volsunga Saga* which Morris had already translated (1870) in collaboration with Eirikr Magnússon, his teacher of Icelandic. See D. M. Hoare, *The Works of Morris and Yeats in relation to Early Saga Literature* (1937).

a strong and massive evocation of the passion and heroism of the North. In it he reveals his deepest thoughts upon human destiny. There is a lowering sense of doom; the Norns are heavy and hard and determine man's fate regardless of his efforts. There may be truth in the suggestion that the stimulus of the rugged North helped to turn Morris's thoughts towards Socialism. How acute was his discontent with modern civilization is apparent from various passages in *Sigurd*. At all events the following year is a turning point in his life.

## II

The part Morris now played in two undertakings enlarged his sense of social responsibility. He organized the Society for the Protection of Ancient Buildings; and during the crisis of 1877-1878 he was an active member of the Eastern Question Association which supported Gladstone in his pro-Russian attacks upon Disraeli's pro-Turkish policy. These activities brought Morris into contact with the leading radicals.

*Socialism*        His Socialism [10] was founded upon the teaching of Ruskin, but that teaching was tested by his practical and experienced intelligence. Everywhere he saw round him vulgarity, debased Gothic, machine-made ornament, ugliness, and squalor. His disgust was enhanced by his experiences in trying to procure first-rate material from which to manufacture his furniture, wall-papers, fabrics, and other articles. He raised the condition of life of his own workmen and later shared profits with them; but he could not, without action, contribute to any general amelioration of the conditions in which laborers lived. His knowledge of the Middle Ages confirmed Ruskin's doctrine that only in a society in which the need to work was not divorced from happiness would it be possible to produce a truly popular art of sound design and craftsmanship. He repudiated, however, Ruskin's neo-feudalism with its acceptance of social inequality; and though he was strongly affected by the medieval institution of the craft-guilds, he advocated no archaistic "return to the Middle Ages." Abandoning hope in the propertied classes as agents of reform, he came to believe not only that the advent of revolution would be speedy but that it was desirable. Only after a catharsis could the classless society be established. He studied *Capital,* and while admitting that he did not understand Marx's theory of surplus value he was deeply impressed with the historical parts of the book, drawn as they were in large measure from social and economic conditions in England. The lethargy and caution of the Liberal government in the enactment of social legislation and their coercive policy towards Ireland were factors in Morris's decision to join the Socialist Party. In 1881 H. M. Hyndman had founded the Demo-

[10] A. A. Helmholtz-Phelan, *The Social Philosophy of William Morris* (Durham, N. C., 1927); Granville Hicks, *Figures of Transition* (1939), ch. II (to which the present account is especially indebted); M. R. Grennan, *William Morris, Medievalist and Revolutionary* (1945); William Sinclair, "Socialism according to William Morris," *The Fortnightly Review,* n.s., LXXXVIII (1910). 722-735; J. B. Glasier, *William Morris and the Early Days of the Socialist Movement* (1921), of value as the narrative of a fellow-worker with Morris.

cratic Federation, the first modern English Socialist body. This Morris joined in 1883, but, distrusting Hyndman, he left it in 1884 to found the Socialist League. Early in 1885 he brought out the first number of *The Commonweal,* a periodical designed to spread the doctrine of the League.

Morris's views are simplifications of Marxian doctrine for popular consumption. They are familiar to everyone today, but because they are basic to an understanding of Morris they must be summarized. There are two classes of society, the wealth-possessing and the wealth-producing, the former controlling the instruments for making wealth—lands, machinery, capital; the latter using these instruments only by permission of, and for the benefit of, the former. Capital lives on the efforts of labor; labor strives to better itself at the expense of capital. The aim in work is to obtain a profit. The workers must sell their labor on terms imposed by the capitalists. Hence comes the competition among workers for a share in wages and among employers for a division of profits. The result is the hideous squalor in the lives of the proletariat. Morris's positive program was equally simple in its essentials. All means of production are to be held in common for all by the state. The motive of production and distribution is to be a decent livelihood for all, not the profit of the few. Duty to the commonweal is to be substituted for obedience to any system of private ethics. Education shall fit the tastes and talents of each individual. Hard, distasteful, but necessary work shall be apportioned equably among all the able-bodied. In his own labor the workman will find joy. Morris believed that under Socialism art, now the possession of the few and unknown to, and unenjoyed by, the many, would flourish.

These propositions and corollaries he enunciated in *The Commonweal* and from the lecture-platform. They are implicit in *The Day is Coming* and *All for the Cause* and other pieces in *Poems by the Way* (1891). At Oxford, at a meeting presided over by Ruskin, he announced them boldly, causing a considerable furore. So late as 1893 he wrote with E. Belford Bax *Socialism, its Growth and Outcome.* Bax was probably chiefly responsible for the theoretical portions of this treatise, but Morris certainly subscribed to them and he illuminated the whole with his imagination and his minute knowledge of the Middle Ages. Long before this, in 1885, he had been arrested for joining in a demonstration. However, after witnessing the riots in Trafalgar Square on "Bloody Sunday" in November, 1887, he deplored mere scuffling with the police and argued that education must precede any revolutionary action that could hope to succeed. Consequently he came to believe that the way advocated by Sidney Webb and the other Fabians was the only right way; but feeling that his talents were not adapted to the Fabian organization he retired after 1889 into "passive Socialism," keeping the communistic cause alive in the group gathered round him at Kelmscott.

The essays and lectures on Socialism which bulk so large in the *Collected Works* are not "literature" in the narrow sense of the word. They were part of a program of action: to instruct, controvert, convert, encourage, and

The
Dream of
John Ball

agitate. But two books which supplement this propaganda are parts of Morris's literary work of lasting beauty and value. *The Dream of John Ball* (1888) is not a treatise but an imaginative romance, not a connected system of sociology but a reverie. The narrator returns in a dream to fourteenth-century England and finds himself in the midst of the Peasants' Revolt. He hears a fiery speech by John Ball and afterwards talks long and earnestly with the peasant leader. He tells him all the woes which must come to pass before the fulfillment of Ball's ideal; yet the preacher dies for that ideal. Awaking, the narrator hears the factory whistles of modern industrialism calling the people to work. There is thus a projection from the fourteenth century into the nineteenth. The lesson is that change, even with advancement, means new problems. The ideal will not be quickly or easily attained.

News
from
Nowhere

Unlike Marx and Engels, who discouraged the planning of Utopias and declined to predict the form which the classless society would take, Morris gave free play to his imagination. Stimulated by Edward Bellamy's *Looking Backward* (1887) but disagreeing radically with it, he wrote *News from Nowhere* (1890). Bellamy predicted that when capitalism had become all-embracing it would be taken over by the state without the necessity of any violence. Morris held that monopoly would never become co-terminal with society but that there would be disintegrations and rearrangements, accompanied by competition and wars, till the revolution destroyed the entire system. Bellamy held out the promise of a reduction of labor to a minimum; Morris the promise of a reduction of the pains of labor. In *News from Nowhere* we have again a dreamer, who this time finds himself in the classless future. Surroundings are beautiful and healthy; the profit motive has vanished and men are happy in their work. The sanction of morality rests upon active endeavor for the common good. Details of this Utopia which are discussed at tedious length we must pass over, to note the burning emotion with which the book is brought to a close and which has made it a classic in the literature of Socialism.

Refusing to postpone activities in the arts till the cause had triumphed, Morris did not limit himself to revolutionary propaganda in his later years. He helped to organize the Guild of Arts and Crafts whose first exhibition was held in 1888. He began to issue books from the Kelmscott Press in 1891. The Kelmscott *Chaucer* (1894) was the crown of his lifework in the arts. He composed a series of prose stories based upon medieval themes.[11]

Prose
Romances

As in *The Earthly Paradise* there had been a movement from romance to epic, so in this sequence there is a withdrawal from epic to romance. We move from a tale of the Roman conflict with the heroic North to a tale laid in a soft and lovely fairyland. In these romances Morris had no motive save to entertain; he aimed to provide solace as the reward of work well done. Yet there are connections with his writings on Socialism, for the dream-

[11] *The House of the Wolfings* (1889); *The Roots of the Mountains* (1890); *The Story of the Glittering Plain* (1891); *The Wood beyond the World* (1894); *The Water of the Wondrous Isles* (1897); and *The Sundering Flood* (1897), the last two posthumous.

world or fairyland of these books has much in common with the world of the future which he envisaged. A seemingly simple style only half conceals the artifice. In *The Wolfings* there is much archaism of idiom and vocabulary; [12] this is gradually reduced in subsequent tales to the point where it is but a beautifully appropriate coloring.

When Morris died in 1896 Swinburne sang his praises as the "warrior and dreamer" who strove to redeem the world "by sword and by song." [13] In a better ordered society Morris would not have concerned himself with the problems which even the ideal commonwealth will have to face. Like all good workmen he would have dedicated himself to the work for which his talents suited him. He would have remained in his shops and library. But faced with society as it is and being what he was, and therefore unable to "escape" with the archaistic dreamers into the past, he was compelled to practical effort. He could not remain within the shelter of art. With Ruskin he might have written:

For my own part I will put up with this state of things, passively, not an hour longer. . . . I simply cannot paint, nor read, . . . nor do anything else that I like . . . because of the misery that I know of, and see signs of, where I know it not, which no imagination can interpret too bitterly.[14]

*Narrative Gift*

Poetry was for Morris what he intended it to be for his readers—a recreation and a delight. It was at once a picture and a tale. He did not see things in generalizations or symbols or abstractions but as concrete pictures, dream-like, tapestry-like, but clearly realized. As the world was to Shakespeare a drama, so to Morris it was a tale. He wrote lovely lyrics but primarily he was a narrative poet. Without Chaucer's genius for characterization, he lacked also Chaucer's humor. He was not a subtle artist (though not so naïve as he wished his readers to think) and he depended upon broad effects, not upon the inevitable and ultimate phrase. He did not load every rift of his subject with ore but spread the gold-leaf over as large a surface as possible.

*Melancholy*

For all his almost miraculous accomplishments in so many arts,[15] for all his enthusiasm and renown, there is a vein of sadness in his poetry, wistful, never plangent, but the more poignant because restrained. Why this undercurrent of melancholy? He could not avoid his age and environment. The

[12] The paraphrase of *Beowulf* which Morris made with A. J. Wyatt (1895) is so archaic as to be disconcerting to the reader who knows no Old English.
[13] Swinburne, *A Channel Passage and Other Poems* (1904), *Dedication* to the memory of Morris and Burne-Jones.
[14] Ruskin, *Fors Clavigera*, I (1871); *Works*, XXVII. 13.
[15] Morris's firm began with ecclesiastical work, wall-papers, and furniture. After 1875 he was sole proprietor and manager and in that year began to print and weave fabrics. In 1877 tapestry-weaving commenced and in 1879 carpets and rugs. In 1881 larger and better equipped works were opened at Merton Abbey. Morris never supplied a large part of the general market, but gradually his example was followed by other firms with consequent improvements in design. In particular he undermined the Victorian confidence in machine-made ornament. In addition to these arts and crafts and his typography Morris illuminated manuscripts, bound books, carved in wood and stone, made architectural designs, and worked in metal, jewelry, and stamped leather. He was an expert cook. He said he avoided music because he was afraid that if he devoted himself to it he would be distracted from his other work.

heavy and weary weight of an unintelligible world pressed upon him. At times he must have felt acutely the odds against any individual at war with capitalistic society. But there was something deeper yet. Like all Cyrenaics, he was possessed with a heart-stabbing sense of the brevity of life and the swift approach of death. He insisted on the duty of each individual to labor for the happiness of the community, but he knew that each moment of that temporal happiness is lost as soon as it is gained. He who filled each day to the full longed for that immortality in which he could not believe. The central fires of his spirit shine in *The Story of the Glittering Plain* where he pictures the "Acre of the Undying," the Norse Elysium, where youth is renewed forever and men live without the fear of death.

# XXXI

## Algernon Charles Swinburne

### I

At the moment when, in 1879, Swinburne was entering upon a new life *"Thalas-* in which he was to become gradually reconciled to colorless respectability he *sius"* looked back with wistful detachment to his experiences in past years and composed the allegorized autobiography, *Thalassius*. He was the child of the Sun (Reason and Art and Song) and the Sea (Liberty). A foster-father (Landor or, rather, Landor's writings) reared this child, teaching him to love truth and hate tyranny. Love, first, and then Lust, led Thalassius astray into disillusionment, satiety, and skepticism; and escaping thence he reverted to his first ideals. The poem is as significant for its reticences as for its candor. In particular, there is no direct allusion to the influence of Mazzini and the Italian Risorgimento upon the poet's thought. The renunciation of sensuality must be regarded as an aspiration rather than an accomplished fact.

Although born in London, Algernon Charles Swinburne [1] (1837-1909) was of North-Country blood with a tradition of rebelliousness as part of his heritage. At Eton his frail physique and peculiarities of temperament isolated him from other boys. He arrived at Oxford with a budding reputation as a poet, tastes formed from reading "Dodsley's grand old plays," sub- *Oxford* versive opinions that derived from Landor, Shelley, and Hugo, and the manuscripts of his first experiments in tragedies of lust and violence modeled on those of the Jacobeans. At Balliol he became intimate with John Nichol, a dour and forceful Scot, who strengthened him in his dangerous views. In politics the two young men were republican and in religion nihilistic. Nichol was an ardent disciple of Mazzini and under this influence Swinburne composed a perfervid *Ode* to the exiled Italian patriot. [2] His mind was a receptacle for those mid-century streams of tendency which we

[1] *Complete Works,* Bonchurch Edition, ed. Sir Edmund Gosse and T. J. Wise (20v, 1925-1927). This, despite its title, is not complete. Among other things omitted are letters in Thomas Hake and Arthur Compton-Rickett, *Letters of Swinburne. With Some Personal Recollections* (1918) and in Coulson Kernahan, *Swinburne as I Knew Him* (1919). — T. J. Wise, *Bibliography,* (2v, 1919-1920), rev. ed. in Bonchurch Edition, xx; Ehrsam, *Bibliographies,* pp. 263-297; Sir Edmund Gosse, *The Life of Swinburne* (1917), rev. ed. in Bonchurch Edition, xix; Georges Lafourcade, *La Jeunesse de Swinburne, 1837-1867* (2v, 1928) and *Swinburne: a Literary Biography* (1932); Edward Thomas, *Swinburne* (1912); John Drinkwater, *Swinburne: an Estimate* (1913); W. B. D. Henderson, *Swinburne and Landor* (1918); T. E. Welby, *A Study of Swinburne* (1926); Harold Nicolson, *Swinburne* (EML Series, 1926); S. C. Chew, *Swinburne* (1929); Paul de Reul, *L'œuvre de Swinburne* (Brussels, 1922); W. R. Rutland, *Swinburne, a Nineteenth Century Hellene* (1931); C. K. Hyder, *Swinburne's Literary Career and Fame* (Durham, N. C., 1933); Ludwig Richter, *Swinburnes Verhältnis zu Frankreich und Italien* (Leipzig, 1911).

[2] The fullest study of the influence of Mazzini on Swinburne is in H. W. Rudman, *Italian Nationalism and English Letters* (1940).

have already observed elsewhere. He was, as Tennyson said later, "a reed through which all things blow into music." A sense of dedication to the cause of liberty was counterbalanced by a conviction that art was of value for its own sake, and a confidence in progress by an underlying feeling of disillusionment and despair. From republican politics and Jacobean pastiche he was diverted in 1857 when he met Rossetti and Morris. Under the influence of the one he composed poems of aesthetic religiosity, and of the other a never finished narrative poem on Tristram and Iseult.[3] Indiscretions in behavior alarmed the authorities (among whom was Benjamin Jowett who recognized his pupil's genius), and to escape being expelled Swinburne withdrew from the university.

The "demoniac youth" (as Ruskin called him) published together two little plays in 1860: *The Queen-Mother* and *Rosamond*. The latter has an attractive Pre-Raphaelite, thin freshness. The former, a more substantial work, shows a variety of influences, among them that of Beddoes. Its darkly passionate theme, set against the background of the Massacre of St. Bartholomew, makes it, as it were, an antechamber to the later trilogy on Mary Queen of Scots. The failure to attract attention by these two dramas may account for a waste of time during the next two years, which are notable only for a visit to Italy in 1861. To 1862 belongs *Laus Veneris* on the theme of Tannhäuser; and in that year disappointment in his only serious love affair inspired one of the greatest of his poems, *The Triumph of Time*. Swinburne contributed several articles to *The Spectator,* among them a review of Baudelaire's *Les Fleurs du Mal* and a defense of Meredith's *Modern Love*; but presently R. H. Hutton, the editor, severed relations with him. In 1863 he visited Paris and met Manet and Whistler. That summer he

**Atalanta in Calydon**

began the composition of *Atalanta in Calydon*. On a second visit to Italy [4] (1864) occurred the famous meeting with Landor when England's "youngest singer" offered to her oldest the dedication of his Greek tragedy. *Atalanta* appeared in 1865, winning the applause of the critics but attracting no wide attention; and later in the same year came *Chastelard,* for the moment an independent play but destined to be the first part of a dramatic trilogy. It is written with a passionate *brio* suggestive of the libretto of some Italian opera. Through these years Swinburne had been writing the lyrical and meditative poems, narratives, and dramatic monologues which in the sum-

**Poems and Ballads**

mer of 1866 burst upon the world as the first series of *Poems and Ballads*. The resultant scandal, when the reviewers, led by John Morley,[5] pursued the poet as the laureate of libidinousness and the apostle of despair, is one

---

[3] The first canto appeared in *Undergraduate Papers* (December, 1857); five more were privately printed by T. J. Wise (1918); the six (all written of an intended ten) are assembled in *Complete Works*, i.

[4] *Notes on Designs of the Old Masters at Florence,* written at this time, is an essay which anticipates the method and manner of Pater's art criticism. Pater acknowledged his indebtedness to Swinburne.

[5] Morley's anonymous onslaught in the *Saturday Review,* August 4, 1866, is reprinted in *Notorious Literary Attacks,* ed. Albert Mordell (1926), pp. 171-184. W. M. Rossetti defended Swinburne, with qualifications, in *Swinburne's Poems and Ballads: a Criticism* (1866).

of the most familiar episodes in the history of English taste and morals. Swinburne stood his ground and struck back in the eloquent though overwrought Notes on Poems and Reviews in which he proclaimed the doctrine of Art

his elegiac poems and near the summit of English elegiac poetry. In its grave, elaborate beauty it suggests a closer affinity between Swinburne and the author of Les Fleurs du Mal than actually existed. William Blake (1868),

cataract of fervent lyricism. A Song of Italy (1867), it was not personal

not with the flush of dawn but with the drab twilight of the Sabaudean

accounts for the poet's rapid withdrawal from the field of political poetry.

Much too much research was undertaken in preparation for Bothwell

that are dramatic in their intensity, the monotony of sustained eloquence

criticism. His exuberance, verbosity, inflated style, and tendency to exag-

Violent in controversy and not suffering pedants gladly, he was an unsafe guide when he assumed a hostile position; but if the rhetoric be overlooked and the exaggerations reduced to a normal scale of values, there is matter of permanent worth in his appreciations. The study of Blake was, as we have noted, a trail blazer. The Study of Shakespeare (1880), in some re-

his London lodgings, and nursed him back to health at his home in Putney. The famous tragicomedy of life at "The Pines" had begun.

There was an immediate recovery of energy and productiveness. *Songs of the Springtides* and *Studies in Song* both appeared in 1880. Swinburne resumed and pushed to completion the dramatic trilogy which closed with *Mary Stuart* (1881), and *Tristram of Lyonesse* (1882). Much later *Tristram* was followed by a second Arthurian poem, *The Tale of Balen* (1896). With waning power and ever-increasing reliance upon self-imitations, a succession of volumes of miscellaneous poetry marked the passage of the years: *A Century of Roundels* (1883); *Poems and Ballads, Third Series* (1889), to which a misleading impression of freshness was imparted by the inclusion of a group of ballads in northern dialect written long since at Oxford; *Astrophel* (1894), largely literary and elegiac in themes; and *A Channel Passage* (1904), a most heterogeneous collection. During these years Swinburne was encouraged by Watts to expend much effort upon poetry of nature description to which his gifts were not suited. There are, however, gorgeous passages in *By the North Sea* and *A Swimmer's Dream*; and in *The Garden of Cymodoce* and *A Nympholept* suggestions of experiences of almost mystical intensity. Watts also undertook to mold Swinburne's political opinions with the consequence that the poet composed a number of rash anti-Gladstonian tirades against Home Rule. A nobler patriotism informs *Athens: an Ode,* where the parallel is drawn between Greece and England; the less formal ode on *The Armada*; and *The Commonweal,* Swinburne's contribution to the celebration of Victoria's Golden Jubilee (1887). In yet other poems there is a wistful groping after belief in personal immortality, which comes strangely from the once vociferous nihilist.

A continuing interest in the drama was evinced in *Marino Faliero* (1885), the last expression of Swinburne's Mazzinean ideals; *Locrine* (1887), the reworking of an Elizabethan theme interesting for its metrical experiments; *The Sisters* (1892), a tragedy of modern life barely redeemed from failure by passages of autobiographic interest; *Rosamund, Queen of the Lombards* (1899), on the ghastly, barbaric story of the queen forced by her husband to drink from her father's skull; and *The Duke of Gandia* (1908), a brief dramatic episode which is almost all that took form from an early plan to

*The Tragedies*

---

counselor of Rossetti. See H. W. Wright, "Unpublished Letters from Theodore Watts-Dunton to Swinburne," *RES,* x (1934). 129-155 (on Swinburne's tangled financial affairs in 1872 and showing Watts already in his capacity as a literary adviser). Watts nourished literary ambitions beyond his talents but had a considerable critical faculty and a flair for personalia which he exercised for many years in *The Athenaeum.* Some of his essays are reprinted in *Old Familiar Faces* (1916). *Poetry and the Renaissance of Wonder* (1916) consists of a reprint of the article on "Poetry" in *The Encyclopaedia Britannica,* ninth edition, and the introduction to the third volume of *Chambers' Cyclopaedia of English Literature* (1904). *Aylwin* (1898), a romance, was a momentary sensation because of the recognizable portraits of Rossetti and other celebrities it contained. Its gypsy-lore connects it with George Borrow. But the romanticism is thin and it is no longer readable. Watts-Dunton's poetry was collected in *The Coming of Love* (1897). There is some personal interest in a few pieces, and an intimate knowledge of gypsy life supplies an individual note; but on the whole his verse is of little moment. The problem of his influence on Swinburne has been much debated; for the present writer's view see S. C. Chew, *Swinburne,* pp. 273-278.

write a tragedy on the Borgias.[9] Swinburne's tragedies are to be numbered among the closet dramas which were mostly still-born of romanticism. The unpublished juvenile imitations of the Jacobeans are mere curiosities. *Chaste-lard* is informed with beauty and passion, but in the two later parts of the Scots trilogy Swinburne became bogged in a morass of complex historical intrigue. That he weighed carefully the conflicting evidence may be seen from his article on Mary Stuart in *The Encyclopaedia Britannica*; but the conscientiousness of the historian was no substitute for the technique of the dramatist which he did not possess. The characterization of Knox is admirable and the scene of Darnley's murder really well handled; but the general impression that remains after reading the trilogy is of mere torrential eloquence. *Marino Faliero* is of interest for the improvements in design and dramatic technique and the more convincing interpretations of motive as compared with Byron's play on the same subject. The later tragedies have little to commend them.

The long seclusion at Putney, while transforming the apostle of liberty into an opponent of Home Rule, an imperialist, and a champion of England against the Boers, changed also the disquieting phenomenon of the eighteen-sixties into a respectable little old man of letters; the "crimson mackaw among owls" (of Gosse's metaphor) had himself, through the agency of time and Watts, become owlish. To regret the transformation is an affectation. But for Watts, Swinburne would have died in 1879; and, besides, the Putney period provides the antithesis which is essential to the Swinburne legend. In 1904 the first collected edition of his poems and tragedies was published, prefaced by a remarkable survey and estimate of his achievement.[10] Swinburne died in April, 1909; and by his express direction the burial service was not read over his grave at Bonchurch on the Isle of Wight.

## II

*Style*

The Word is omnipotent in Swinburne's poetry; language breaks through all structural barriers. The stanzaic patterns (of which he invented a large number while adapting to new effects many that were traditional) are invariably impeccable and often marvels of complex ingenuity. But in a larger sense his poems are often formless. When once the verbal music has begun there is no logical reason why it should ever cease; the only end is the end of exhaustion. The fact can easily be put to experimental test, that almost any stanza or scattered groups of stanzas may be omitted without loss of any, save a quantitative, effect. No developing sequence of emotions and ideas is interrupted by such excisions. The music—whether the bright,

---

[9] See also the fragmentary, posthumous prose "chronicle," *Lucretia Borgia*, ed. Randolph Hughes (1943).

[10] Unaccountably omitted from the Bonchurch Edition of Swinburne's *Works*. — About 1900 Swinburne wrote but did not publish a vigorous and vitriolic reply to those who accused him of having abandoned the political opinions and literary tastes of his earlier life. See C. K. Hyder, "Swinburne: *Changes of Aspect* and *Short Notes*," *PMLA*, LVIII (1943). 223-244.

swift melody of the Spring Chorus in *Atalanta,* or the convolutions of *Dolores,* or the muted notes of *The Garden of Proserpine,* or the sultry monotone of *Laus Veneris,* or the plangent passion of *The Triumph of Time,* or the elaborate harmonies of *Ave atque Vale,* or the trumpet-call of *Mater Triumphalis,* or the full orchestration of the *Prelude* to *Tristram* and *The Last Oracle,* or such dexterous counterpointing as *At a Month's End*— sings itself in the memory; but it is immaterial which stanzas are got by heart. No other poet of equal rank has implanted fewer individual lines of verse in the general memory. The too luxuriant alliteration is mere arabesque, not (as in Gerard Hopkins) a series of hammer-blows to rivet an image upon the mind. The flower-soft spilth of fluent verbiage leaves behind it but a thin precipitate of imagery. The virtuoso plays innumerable variations upon a few themes—the sea and the sun, flowers and foam and blood. A concordance to Swinburne's poetry (did one exist) would reveal the meagerness of his vocabulary and the constant repetition of a few characteristic epithets in new stanzaic patterns. His color sense was weak; there is no such variety and gradation of tone as is observed in Keats's and Tennyson's poetry; and to a degree greater even than Shelley Swinburne depended upon effects of light.

This is not to reaffirm the old charge that Swinburne "lacked thought," *Fatalism* that he was, as Browning said, "a fuzz of words." On the contrary, till his *and* retirement to Putney he was sensitively responsive to contemporary ideas. *Satiety* In *Atalanta in Calydon* the pseudo-Hellenism [11] made for a sense of detachment from modern issues; but the bitter fatalism of the tragedy—the essential nobility of helpless man in the presence of malignant fate—was a direct challenge to the religious ideas of Victorian England. The philosophy of despair enunciated in the second Chorus and culminating in the tremendous indictment of "the supreme evil, God," relates *Atalanta* to the *Rubáiyát* and *The City of Dreadful Night.* The shimmering beauty of the verse, the metrical artifices, the far-off idealized landscape, and the seeming remoteness of the theme obscured to many contemporaries the implications of the play; but they are clear to us. The Chorus beginning "We have seen thee, O Love, thou art fair" associates love with pain and bitterness and death and connects *Atalanta* with *Chastelard.* In that drama Mary Stuart is the *femme fatale* of the romantic imagination and her lover is the victim of a *belle dame sans merci.* Thus *Chastelard* points forward to those pieces in *Poems and Ballads* which electrified the English imagination—*Laus Veneris, Dolores, Anactoria, Faustine,* and the rest. To our taste these may seem a little tawdry and obvious both in sentiments and rhythms; but to Swinburne's contemporaries, accustomed to the ideal of domestic love set before them by Tennyson, they were "a wind of liberation," at once destroying and invigorating. The positive motif of *Poems and Ballads* was hedonistic, anticipating the doctrine which Pater was presently to impose upon

---

[11] For opposing views of *Atalanta* and of *Erechtheus* see W. R. Rutland, *Swinburne, a Nineteenth Century Hellene* (1931), and Bush, ch. x.

the "aesthetic" generation. The negative note was that of satiety, disillusion, and despair. Thus was the range of poetry extended beyond the limitations erected by the poet laureate. It is not surprising that young men and women, chanting this new music that seemed to them miraculous, hailed Swinburne as a portent.

Liberty may relax into license; and license brings satiety; satiety leads to perversity; and perversity breeds despondency and despair. Bitter is the fruit of these flowers of evil. Love is associated with Death, as cause with consequence. The sequence closes with somber probings into the ultimate mystery; and upon that dark quest Swinburne, in *Ave atque Vale,* led his readers far into "that low land" where the "sun is silent." To this theme he returned in later poems, in a mood of elegiac wistfulness (as in *A Vision of Spring in Winter*), or of passionate regret for the "perfume" of lost days (as in *At a Month's End*), or of almost exultant recognition of Time's power over all things (as in *A Forsaken Garden*). The retrospective mood dominated his poetry from a period of life when normal persons are still living in the full tide of the present.

*The "Life-Force"*   But liberty need not degenerate into license; it may be a stern and exacting discipline. As such it is celebrated in many of Swinburne's noblest poems. He was not, as he is sometimes described, the prophet merely of a federated republic of Europe or a "Parliament of Man." He proclaimed himself the herald and "trumpet" of Mater Triumphalis, Hertha, the Life-Force working not only in each individual but in the social order. Society cannot progress save through the exertion of conscience and reason; and it is this action, thus working, that Swinburne contemplated when, in *A Song of Italy* and in the more visionary and less topical of the *Songs before Sunrise,* he hailed the Republic which is to be. For that ideal the individual must be glad to die. This sacrifice is the theme of *Super Flumina Babylonis, The Pilgrims,* and *Teresias.* It is implicit in *Erechtheus,* which is more nearly related to Mazzinean doctrine than to Greek thought. In the thick darkness of the cosmos which seemed to envelop him when Mazzini's dream vanished, Swinburne found no star to guide him "save his own soul." This thought, which enters his poetry in the *Prelude* to *Songs before Sunrise,* is the motive of many poems of his middle years and the burden of *The Altar of Righteousness,* his final testament to the world. The thought is positivist and secularist. A confidence in man's ability to conquer evil leads the poet to the conclusion of his *Hymn of Man:* "Glory to Man in the highest, for Man is the master of things!" [12] That such an assertion would be ridiculous were it not pathetic is obvious to us who have lived amid the disasters of the twentieth century. But it reflected the confidence of a time which John Morley described as "an epoch of hearts uplifted with hope, and brains

[12] The *Hymn of Man* was composed for recitation at the anti-Catholic Council which met at Naples in 1869 during the sitting of the Oecumenical Council in Rome. This meeting adjourned, however, before the poem was completed. See Lafourcade, *Swinburne, a Literary Biography,* pp. 172-175.

made active with sober and manly reason for the common good." [13] More-over, Swinburne does not say that this mastery over "things" is yet attained; it is to be realized when the sun has risen, and before that glad confident morning there must be toil and sacrifice. Hard tasks are imposed upon the individual for the benefit of the race.

[13] Lord Morley, *Recollections* (1917), II. 365.

# XXXII

## The Background: The Victorian Decline (1868-1901) and the Aftermath (1901-1939)

The Late Victorian Period,[1] three decades of waning confidence, commercial and industrial rivalries, imperial expansion, and increasing political, economic, social, and spiritual anxieties, extends from the beginning of Gladstone's first administration in 1868 to the death of Queen Victoria in 1901 and the close of the Boer War in 1902. In literary history it extends from the beginning of the Aesthetic Revival with Pater's first essays (1867-1868) to the death of Ruskin in 1900 and of Spencer in 1903. The activities of many of the writers already surveyed continued, but with few exceptions they are more characteristic of an earlier era. Thus, Herbert Spencer's huge project unfolded, but its inception dates from the mid-century; Ruskin had still to publish many volumes, but his work of most value had been done by 1868; Morris's career as a Socialist was yet to come, but his best poetry had been written; and though Rossetti and Swinburne overlap the dividing line (the latter by many years), Rossetti is obviously a mid-century figure and Swinburne's later poetry is in the main derivative from his earlier. On the other hand, though Meredith published his first noteworthy book as early as 1859, he seems to belong beyond the watershed; and Hardy's first published novel dates from 1871.

*The High-tide of Liberalism*    The extension of the franchise (1867) brought the Liberals into power on a tide of confidence in 1868. Among the writers who gave expression to the rationalistic liberalism and radicalism characteristic of the time were Frederic Harrison [2] (1831-1923) and Sir Leslie Stephen [3] (1832-1904). On

---

[1] R. C. K. Ensor, *England, 1870-1914* (1936); G. M. Trevelyan, *British History in the Nineteenth Century* (1922) and *English Social History* (1942), chap. xviii; Elie Halévy, *Histoire du peuple anglais: Epilogue I: 1895-1905* (1926); G. P. Gooch, *History of Modern Europe, 1878-1919* (1923); J. H. Clapham, *Economic History of Great Britain*, II (1933), for the period before 1886; R. E. Prothero (Lord Ernle), *English Farming, Past and Present* (1927); Sidney and Beatrice Webb, *The History of Trade Unionism* (rev. ed., 1920); and the biographies of Disraeli, Gladstone, Parnell, Salisbury, Chamberlain, and other leaders.

[2] A leader of the Positivists and active in political reform, working-class legislation, and jurisprudence. Harrison's writings, often trenchantly controversial, represent but a fraction of his accomplishment. *The Choice of Books* (1886), the studies assembled in *Early Victorian Literature* (1896), and the life of Ruskin (1902)—an act of homage by a disciple to his master—are on a level of serenity above the battles in which he engaged in public life. See also his *Collected Essays* (4v, 1907-1908) and *Selected Essays* (1925).

[3] Stephen applied the principles of rationalism to the interpretation of the history of ideas. The world of the "Enlightenment" was his intellectual home; and *English Thought in the Eighteenth Century* (1876-1881) his most massive work. His other principal book is *The English Utilitarians* (1900). Relatively lighter fare is to be had in *Hours in a Library* (1892). *An Agnostic's Apology* (1893) is characteristic not only of Stephen (who had renounced holy

taking office Gladstone put through three great measures of reform: the Irish Church Disestablishment Act; the first Irish Land Act (a half-way measure but a step toward the solution of the problem of landlords, tenants, and eviction for non-payment of rent)·; and the Education Act, which established primary education upon a national basis, practically abolished illiteracy, and disciplined the hitherto uncared-for hordes of slum children. Army reform and the beginnings of naval expansion were signs that England read correctly the omens drawn from the victory of Prussia over France in 1870-1871. The effect of German predominance on the Continent was to dampen in England the cosmopolitan liberal spirit. A wave of pessimism and materialism, spreading across the Channel from defeated France, swept many men of letters into an aesthetic isolation from practical life and was one cause of the "Art for Art's Sake" movement. But there were other writers who remained in close touch with political and social events and were strongly affected by the Irish Question, imperial expansion, and the economic decline. In retrospect the growing German peril, while the struggle for colonies, raw materials, and markets developed, is seen as the most significant current of the time. Sir George Chesney's sensational pamphlet, *The Battle of Dorking* (1871), brought home a realization of the German threat and the possibility of invasion, but the alarm it created soon subsided. The traditional enmity with France loomed larger in the contemporary consciousness because of the intense rivalry with England in Africa.

The election of 1874 showed that the Liberal impetus of the past six years had spent its force; Gladstone's ministry had become, in Disraeli's famous phrase, "a row of extinct volcanoes." A new personality now came to the fore. By 1870 Ireland had recovered from the prostration which followed the great famine, and the movement for the repeal of the Act of Union was again under way. The Home Rule party, an outgrowth from the older Fenian Movement, emerged in 1874, and in the following year Charles Stewart Parnell began his obstructionist tactics in the House of Commons. The Irish Land League, a strong influence upon the Irish Literary Revival, was formed in 1879. Ireland was now governed by coercion, and the problem of a settlement of the Irish Question was a legacy from the Conservatives to Gladstone in 1880. *Parnell and Home Rule*

During his second administration (1874-1880) Disraeli was anxious to demonstrate the connection between Conservatism and social reform. New sanitary measures were initiated, but before much could be accomplished the economic depression of 1876-1881 set in and the problem of the unemployed came to the fore. Disraeli's interest centered in foreign affairs and the expansion of the British Empire. The day was long past when he had described the colonies as "millstones" around England's neck. After the

orders) but of his time. Much of his energy was expended upon the *DNB* of which he was the first chief editor. In all his writings there is much light but little warmth. See his *Collected Essays* (10v, 1907); F. W. Maitland, *Life and Letters of Sir Leslie Stephen* (1906); Desmond MacCarthy, *Leslie Stephen* (1937). Stephen was the brother of Sir James Fitzjames Stephen the philosopher, and the father of Virginia Woolf the novelist.

Mutiny the government of India had been transferred from the old East India Company to the Crown; and in 1876, following the purchase of the shares in the Suez Canal (1875) which made England more conscious of her destiny in the East, Victoria was proclaimed Empress of India. The Near East Crisis of 1875-1878, temporarily composed at the Congress of Berlin (1878), was provoked in part by dread of Russian expansion, in part by generous indignation against the Ottoman treatment of subject Christian populations in the Balkans. This indignation was fanned by Gladstone in the most eloquent of Victorian political pamphlets, *The Bulgarian Horrors and the Question of the East* (1876). In South Africa Zulu barbarities were suppressed and the Transvaal was annexed for the first time (1877). On the Northwest frontier of India the Afghan War led to Lord Roberts' triumph at Kandahar (1879).

How far-flung were England's powers and responsibilities was made manifest by these and other events. But in reaction from Tory "jingoism" the Liberals were reinstated in 1880. The chief successes of Gladstone's second ministry were the new Land Act for Ireland (1881), which gave greater security of tenure and an assurance of equitable rent; and the ex-
*Economic* tension of the franchise to miners and agricultural laborers. The long-
*Depression* predicted decline in agriculture now moved downward precipitously, hastened by the importation of frozen meat and the increased consumption of American wheat. The position of England as "the workshop of the world" was imperiled in the Continental countries, which were becoming indus-trialized and were erecting tariff walls against English goods. The early eighteen-eighties saw the rise of Socialism and of the new Birmingham radicalism of which Joseph Chamberlain was spokesman. Attacks upon irresponsible wealth divorced from association with the land helped to stimulate class hatred. The famous "unauthorized program" of Chamber-lain and Dilke was one expression of radical sentiment.

The problem of the relations of the English and the Cape Dutch was another legacy from Disraeli to Gladstone, who after the defeat at Majuba decided to cut England's losses and recognize the independence of the Transvaal. This proved to be but a temporary palliative, for the grievances of the "Uitlanders" remained to plague England in the closing years of the century. Turkish misrule of Egypt and the mismanagement of the Khedive's
*Egypt* finances led to the British occupation of that country in 1882, with the sup-pression of Arabi's revolt. A premature effort to conquer the Sudan resulted in the death of General Gordon at Khartoum (1885), a blow from which Gladstone's prestige never entirely recovered. Only after England's predomi-nant position in Egypt had been established by Cromer was she able to extend her power permanently in the South (1898). The immediate con-sequence of the disaster of 1885 was the defeat of Gladstone at the polls. Lord Salisbury's first Conservative government proved to be of short dura-tion and little consequence, for the Home Rule Party under Parnell held the balance of power between the two English parties. Gladstone came to

an agreement with Parnell with the result that Salisbury was defeated and Gladstone's third ministry was formed. Conspicuous among his lieutenants were two prominent men of letters, John Morley [4] (1838-1923) and James Bryce [5] (1838-1922). The First Home Rule Bill, embracing Protestant Ulster in its scope, was introduced (1886). In the general election consequent upon the defeat of this measure in Parliament the Conservatives with the Liberal Unionists who had seceded from the Gladstonian Liberals obtained a majority over the latter party and the Irish Home Rulers combined. The new ministry resorted to the strictest coercion in governing Ireland, with Arthur James Balfour [6] (1848-1930) as Irish Secretary. The attempt to discredit Parnell by means of the forged letters published in *The Times* roused intense feelings which made a rational settlement impossible; and in 1890 the O'Shea divorce case in which Parnell was cited as co-respondent shattered the leader's prestige with the tragic consequence that the solution of the Irish Question was postponed for a generation. *The First Home Rule Bill*

Meanwhile, during Salisbury's second ministry (1886-1892), there was social unrest but also social progress. The theories of Henry George set forth in *Progress and Poverty* (1877) were of widening influence. *Fabian Essays* (1889) by Sidney Webb and other advanced thinkers was followed by William Booth's powerful exposure of the social question, *In Darkest England and the Way Out* (1890). Robert Blatchford's *Merrie England* (1894) was another stimulus to practical action. Statistical research exposed conditions in the slums of London and other great cities; great strides were made in municipal reform; and volunteer "settlements" such as Toynbee Hall sprang up in various localities. Symptomatic of the changed balance of *Social Progress*

---

[4] Afterwards Viscount Morley. His career as a statesman, which does not concern us here, overshadows his claim to notice as a writer. He had already acquired a reputation for aggressive radicalism and agnosticism and for his forceful literary criticism when he became editor of *The Fortnightly Review* in 1867. (See E. M. Everett, *The Party of Humanity*, Chapel Hill, 1939). In 1878 he initiated as editor the EML series of biographies. His own writings have largely but not exclusively to do with the "Enlightenment" and the Utilitarians. Of both these movements he was the Late Victorian heir and representative. His Stoicism and uncompromising moral integrity, wide intellectuality, and weight of style made him one of the great forces of the dying Liberalism of the late century. His literary judgments, expressed with a restrained eloquence, moral fervor, and on occasion grave irony, are often founded upon values not strictly literary. His principal books are *Voltaire* (1872); *Rousseau* (1873); *Diderot* (1878); *Burke* (1879); *Walpole* (1889); *Studies in Literature* (1890); *The Life of W. E. Gladstone* (1903); *Literary Essays* (1906); *Recollections* (1917). The last, a noble *apologia* not so much for himself as for Victorian Liberalism, will perhaps be remembered longest. — *Works* (15v, 1921). F. W. Hirst, *Early Life and Letters of John Morley* (2v, 1927); G. M. Harper, *Lord Morley and Other Essays* (1920); J. D. MacCallum, *Lord Morley's Criticism of English Poetry and Prose* (Princeton, 1921); F. M. Knickerbocker, *Free Minds: John Morley and His Friends* (1943); Warren Staebler, *The Liberal Mind of John Morley* (1943); Algernon Cecil, *Six Oxford Thinkers* (1909), pp. 252-301.

[5] Afterwards Viscount Bryce. He made an early reputation with the brilliant historical sketch, *The Holy Roman Empire* (1864). *The American Commonwealth* (1888), a study of institutions in the United States, is a classic in its field. From wide experiences of travel he made several books, notably *Transcaucasia and Ararat* (1877). — H. A. L. Fisher, *James Bryce* (2v, 1927).

[6] Afterwards prime minister and Earl of Balfour. The claim of Balfour to be taken quite seriously as a philosopher was hindered by a reputation for dilettantism and flippancy, but his *Defence of Philosophic Doubt* (1879), *Foundations of Belief* (1895), and later studies in theism reveal a critical mind of considerable power, though Balfour contributed little to the philosophic currents of his time.

political power was the popular press, led by Harmsworth's *Daily Mail,* which reached an enormous semi-educated public and exerted a dangerous influence. In foreign affairs Salisbury's second ministry is memorable for the policy of "splendid isolation" which kept England without an ally while the Continental powers were forming the rival groups of the Triple Alliance (Germany, Austro-Hungary, and Italy.) and the Dual Alliance (France and Russia). Till the close of the century English policy was on the whole Germanophile, a deterioration in relations not setting in till the Kaiser embarked upon his program of naval expansion. French relations remained precarious because of disputes over spheres of influence in Africa. The Fashoda incident of 1898 was the culmination of a series of misunderstandings and brought the two countries to the verge of war. Not for several years thereafter did the growing danger of Germany lead to a reorientation of policy resulting in the Entente Cordiale. But this is to look ahead.

*The Second Home Rule Bill*

By 1892 the Unionists [7] had fulfilled their mandate and in the general election Gladstone was returned to office, though not to power because he was dependent for a majority upon the support of the Irish members. By this association he was committed to a Second Home Rule Bill, which met defeat in the House of Lords. On Gladstone's resignation in 1894 the Earl of Rosebery [8] (1847-1929) became prime minister. The Liberal interlude of 1892-1895 is notable for the formation of the Independent Labor Party under Keir Hardie and for the development of imperialistic thought, expressed in the political world by Chamberlain, in South Africa by Cecil Rhodes, and in the world of letters by Rudyard Kipling. In the election of 1895 the Unionists swept the country but were forced to share power with the radical Chamberlain who had allied himself with the Unionists on the Irish issue. Chamberlain, though never prime minister, was as potent as Salisbury and more potent than A. J. Balfour, who succeeded Salisbury in 1902. He chose the cabinet post of Colonial Secretary which had hitherto been held in small estimation. In so choosing he rode the crest of the wave

*Imperialism*

of Imperialism. This reached its climax of grandiose display at the Queen's Diamond Jubilee of 1897; and though Kipling sounded an impressive warning in the *Recessional,* the country drifted confidently towards war in South Africa. The steps towards war were, briefly, these: the intensification of the

*The Boer War*

hostility between the old Boer farmers of the Transvaal and the new British diamond-miners and gold-miners; the increasing power of Rhodes's Chartered Company; the settlement of Rhodesia; the haste to push northward in order to check German expansion east and west which threatened to block the British dream of an empire extending from the Cape to Cairo; the impatience of Rhodes with the Boer President, Paul Kruger, which

---

[7] The coalition of Conservatives and anti-Home-Rule Liberals and radicals called themselves Unionists because the maintenance of the Act of Union of Ireland and Great Britain was their basic principle.

[8] In literature as in political life Rosebery failed to fulfill his early promise, but his brief monographs on Pitt (1891) and Peel (1899) and the more famous *Napoleon, the Last Phase* (1900) are historical miniatures revealing a gift for characterization.

culminated in Dr. Jameson's Raid (1895); and the decision of Chamberlain and Sir Alfred Milner to settle the question at issue by war. English men of letters were as sharply divided as statesmen as to the justification of the conflict which began in 1899. Public confidence was rudely shaken by the stupidity of English strategy, bad organization, and underestimation of the Boers' powers of resistance. Victoria's reign ended (1901) during the final, terrible phase of the Boers' guerilla warfare and Kitchener's concentration camps. The treaty of peace (1902) led on to the wise and magnanimous pacification accomplished by Sir Henry Campbell-Bannerman after the Liberal triumph of 1905.

It is customary today to look back upon the reign of Edward VII (1901-1910) as a period of opulent ease and blind complacency. For this notion there is no foundation in the facts. At no time in English history has the strife of parties been more bitter. The differences between Balfour and Chamberlain over fiscal policy led to the Unionist defeat and the return of the Liberals to office, but the outstanding features of the election of 1905 were the appearance of Labor as a separate party in the house of commons and the power exercised by John Redmond, the Irish leader. A contentious Unionist minority, a series of industrial strikes, and the militant activities of the advocates of woman suffrage embittered public life. During the pre-war years of the reign of George V these and other disturbing movements were intensified, but they were already apparent in his father's reign. Europe moved through a series of crises—over German claims in Morocco in 1905 and 1911; over Austria's annexation of Bosnia in 1908; and a chain of events links the first of these to the outbreak of the Italo-Turkish war in Tripoli (1911) and the two Balkan wars (1912-1913) which were preludes to the catastrophe of 1914. Germany's intransigence in the matter of the limitation of naval armaments led to the Entente Cordiale with France (1904) and the later understanding with Russia which produced the Triple Entente as a counterpoise to the Triple Alliance. For England's military preparedness—such as it was—the chief credit attaches to the War Secretary, Lord Haldane.[9] The increased naval appropriations forced upon England were the main cause of Lloyd George's sensational budget of 1909, which in turn caused the bitter quarrel between the two houses of Parliament. After two general elections the Lords' veto-power was abolished by the Parliament Act of 1911. The Liberal government under Asquith (who had succeeded Campbell-Bannerman as prime minister in 1908) attempted a new solution of the Irish Question, but racial and religious antagonisms were even stronger than they had been in 1886 and the plan to include Ulster in a scheme satisfactory to the Roman Catholic majority of Irishmen met with an opposition which under the leadership of Sir Edward Carson had almost

*The Reign of Edward VII*

[9] Richard B. Haldane (1856-1928), later Viscount Haldane, brought from Germany, his "spiritual home" (his own famous phrase which temporarily ruined his career in 1914), the knowledge of Schopenhauer whose *World as Will and Idea* he translated (1883-1886). Haldane's weightiest philosophic writings—*The Reign of Relativity* (1921) and *The Philosophy of Humanism* (1922)—belong to his closing years.

reached the point of open rebellion in the summer of 1914. These were some of the principal factors making for a pervasive sense of social disintegration which, though more fully expressed in the post-war years, was already a "note" in modern literature before the outbreak of the Great War.

Beyond August, 1914, it is unnecessary to carry this sketch of the political and social background. Any indication of the underlying and immediate causes of the war would take us beyond our space and beside our purpose. It is impossible to generalize as to the mood in which the English people entered the conflict. There were those who, like Rupert Brooke, welcomed it as a relief from domestic controversy and the feeling of personal frustration. Others felt the pity and tragedy of the breakdown of western civilization, and to this feeling John Masefield gave expression in his poem *August, 1914.* Yet others, looking beyond the dark present, discerned a brighter future, as did H. G. Wells in his pamphlet, *The War that Will End War,* and in other utopian visions. The contrast between the hope of a better world and the actuality of the Peace of Versailles; between the politicians' promise of "a land fit for heroes to live in" and the actuality of unemployment, distressed areas, strikes, the long-drawn agony of the struggle in Ireland before the establishment of the Free State, the rise of the Continental dictatorships, the economic depression, and the waning prestige of the League of Nations—these and other contrasts between the vision of desire and the desolating reality confirmed in many thoughtful minds the sense that old moorings had been cast off, that humanity was adrift upon a chartless sea, that inherited criteria of conduct no longer possessed authority, and that all values had been discredited. True, there were still some voices bidding men hope, but the prevailing mood was one of futility and frustration. During the Long Armistice those able to interpret the signs of the times were uttering warnings of a worse disaster to follow in a world where, as Yeats said,

*Between Two Wars*

> The best lack all conviction, while the worst
> Are full of passionate intensity.

# XXXIII

## George Meredith

### I

George Meredith [1] (1828-1909) declared that he would "most horribly haunt" anyone who should write his biography. After his death it became known that there were facts about his origin he wished to conceal. They are trivial, but their concealment is significant. Did he hope to dictate the estimate of himself to be held by posterity? Were we to see in him something of proud, elaborate, Olympian indifference, with much of the clear-sightedness, touched with light malignancy, of the Comic Spirit? Admit a suspicion of "the taint of personality" and he is seen, not seated overhead with this Spirit, but himself the target of its volleys of silvery laughter. The poet who described the distempered devil of Self was caught in the snares of that "scaly Dragon-fowl." His proud declaration that "station is nought, nor footways laurel-strewn" consorts ill with evident restiveness under by no means total popular indifference to his work.

But though he did not take the world into his confidence, there was no *Birth and* self-deception. Evan Harrington, who was ashamed of his low birth and *Breeding* "would be a gentleman," is a piercing satire upon Meredith's own mortification because of his socially inferior connections. Of Welsh and Irish descent, he was the son and grandson of naval outfitters at Portsmouth. His mother died when he was a child; he was estranged from his father; and two impressionable years (1842-1844) were spent at a Moravian school at Neuwied on the Rhine. Here a wise and gentle education encouraged a tolerant and cosmopolitan outlook upon life. Here also he acquired a love

[1] *Works*, Memorial Edition (29v, 1909-1912); *Poetical Works;* ed. G. M. Trevelyan (1912); *Letters*, ed. W. M. Meredith (2v, 1912); *Letters to Edward Clodd and C. K. Shorter*, ed. T. J. Wise (privately printed, 1913); *Letters to Alice Meynell* (1923). — M. B. Forman, *Bibliography*, (1922) and *Meredithiana* (1924); S. M. Ellis, *George Meredith: his Life and Friends in Relation to his Work* (1919); J. B. Priestley, *George Meredith* (EML Series, 1926); René Galland, *George Meredith: les cinquante premières années* (Paris, 1923); M. S. Gretton, *The Writings and Life of George Meredith* (1926); R. E. Sencourt, *The Life of George Meredith* (1929); J. H. E. Crees, *George Meredith: A Study of his Works and Personality* (1918); E. J. Bailey, *The Novels of George Meredith* (1907); James Moffatt, *George Meredith: A Primer to the Novels* (1909); J. W. Beach, *The Comic Spirit in George Meredith* (1911); Constantin Photiades, *George Meredith: sa vie, son imagination, son art, sa doctrine* (Paris, 1910; trans. by A. Price, 1913); H. B. Forman, *George Meredith: Some Early Appreciations* (1909); J. A. Hammerton, *George Meredith in Anecdote and Criticism* (1909); G. M. Trevelyan, *The Poetry and Philosophy of George Meredith* (1907); Robert Peel, *The Creed of a Victorian Pagan* (Cambridge, Mass., 1931); M. E. Mackay, *Meredith et la France* (Paris, 1937); J. W. Beach, *The Concept of Nature*, ch. XVIII; Baker, VIII (1937). chs. VII-IX; O. J. Campbell, "Some Influences of Meredith's Philosophy upon his Fiction," *Univ. of Wisconsin Stud. in Lang. and Lit.*, II (1919). 323-339; C. D. Locock, "Notes on the Technique of Meredith's Poetry," *ESt*, XLVI (1912-1913). 86-97.

for the extravagances of German romanticism. Features of his style that suggest Carlyle are in part imitations of Jean Paul Richter. Meredith had not long returned to England when the generous liberalism of 1848, sweeping from a Continent in revolt, helped to mold his political opinions. He now met Thomas Love Peacock and fell in love with his daughter, a widow nine years his elder. After their marriage (1849) they lived with or near Peacock, whose influence was strong upon him.[2] Peacock had drawn cranks and eccentrics; he had attacked sentimentality and egoism; he had affirmed the intellectual equality of women; he believed in the corrective power of laughter. There is no sign of this influence in Meredith's first book, *Poems* (1851), which contained the first version of *Love in the Valley* and won Tennyson's commendation; but the Peacockian strain of fantasy, mockery, and grace is present in *The Shaving of Shagpat* (1855), an oriental extravaganza hovering on the brink of allegory, in which are the germs of Meredith's later advocacy of the active life in accord with nature. Different ingredients are mixed in *Farina: a Legend of Cologne* (1857): romantic supernaturalism purposely reduced to absurdity, sentimentality half-serious and half-mocking, and bits of picaresque that give promise of *Harry Richmond*. Meredith was still experimenting.

Meanwhile his marriage had proved disastrous and in 1858 his wife left him, going to the Continent with a lover. She died in 1861. Something of his own experience went into the tragic-ironic narrative poem, *Modern Love* (1862), and it influenced the choice of unsuccessful marriage as the subject of several of the novels. A run-away wife and the problem of a father left to educate his son form the autobiographical background of *The Ordeal of Richard Feverel* (1859). Though not his greatest book, this is one of the most memorable, for its freshness and the plenitude of joy and pity. Already the defects of Meredith's qualities are apparent: the tendency towards too elaborate characterization; the overplus of shadowy minor figures; the aphorisms which flash too frequently, though as yet they are not dark with excessive light. The greatness of the book does not lie in the entire conception, which is incoherent, but in certain scenes—the idyllic raptures of first love; the news of his son's marriage brought to Sir Austin Feverel; the "Enchantress" chapter (though this is overwrought); the parting of Richard and Lucy; and Richard's walk in the forest after hearing of his son's birth. Whether the final catastrophe of Lucy's death is properly prepared for or whether Meredith forces the issue has always been disputed. The basic irony is in the antithesis between romance and reality; and the satire is expended upon a system of education through which human nature insists upon breaking. There are reminiscences of Sterne, Dickens, and Bulwer; but the novel breaks new ground. Beneath the brilliant satire and lyrical romanticism there is an idea that is fundamental to all Meredith's thought: Richard should have worked to-

*Richard*
*Feverel*

[2] A. H. Able, *George Meredith and Thomas Love Peacock: A Study in Literary Influences* (Philadelphia, 1933).

wards brain and spirit through the blood; but this natural development was thwarted; and when one part of the Meredithian Triad is sundered from the rest, disaster follows.

*Evan Harrington* [3] (1860) showed no advance. It concerns the conflict of Evan's love for Rose Jocelyn with his duty to pay his dead father's debts and maintain the business which he had inherited and of which he was ashamed. In the end he is ashamed of his shame. The theme is not rich enough for a long novel and it is expanded by the story of Evan's three beautiful sisters who storm society by making advantageous marriages. In this study of snobbery there is thus a conflict of different social strata. The portraits from real life are of Meredith himself and his three aunts. The book wounded his father, as well it might, for the "great Mel," the dead tailor, is drawn from family reminiscences of Meredith's grandfather. *Evan Harring-ton*

*Modern Love and Poems of the English Roadside* appeared in 1862. The title poem, though founded upon Meredith's own marital unhappiness, presents a more complex situation than that of his own experience. [4] In intensity and beauty of phrase, variety of styles to suit the different situations, incisiveness of psychological analysis, dramatic power, and grasp of character it stands alone among Meredith's poems. Among other things in this volume, *Juggling Jerry* and *The Old Chartist* are monologues somewhat reminiscent of Browning's manner, and the *Ode to the Spirit of Earth in Autumn* [5] is the first of Meredith's important nature poems written under the influence of the evolutionary concept. *Modern Love*

In 1864 Meredith married again. The union was a happy one. [6] In the same year he published *Sandra Belloni* (originally called *Emilia in England*). In the character of Wilfrid Pole he offered his most elaborate analysis of sentimentalism, and in the characters of Pole's sisters, of social affectation. Opposed to Wilfrid is the exquisite figure of Sandra, as yet an immature girl but already adumbrating that "ideal of the heroical feminine type" to which she would approximate in the sequel. The course of Pole's degeneration as the sentimental egoist is traced downward to the point where his story would later be resumed. But before that sequel appeared, Meredith turned aside to a rural theme and in *Rhoda Fleming* (1865) challenged comparison with George Eliot. Dahlia Fleming, a girl of the yeoman class, has been seduced by Edward Blancove, the squire's son. His nefarious design to marry her off to a bribed ruffian and the reappearance of the latter's wife *Sandra Belloni*

*Rhoda Fleming*

---

[3] In 1860 Meredith became literary adviser to the firm of Chapman and Hall. He rejected Mrs. Henry Wood's *East Lynne* (1861), which became a best-seller, Butler's *Erewhon*, which became famous, and early work of G. B. Shaw. On the other hand, he gave encouragement to Hardy and Gissing. See B. W. Matz, "George Meredith as Publisher's Reader," *Fortnightly Review*, n.s., LXXXVI (1909). 282-298.

[4] The story is told in fifty sixteen-line sonnet-like stanzas. Having a definite plot, involving four characters, it resembles the Victorian sonnet-sequences, such as Mrs. Browning's and Rossetti's, less than it does William Ellery Leonard's *Two Lives*.

[5] This is a reworking of *South-West Wind in the Woodland* (1851).

[6] Meredith's sorrow and quest of consolation at the time of his wife's death (1885) are recorded in *A Faith on Trial*, the *Hymn to Colour*, and other poems included in *A Reading of Earth* (1888).

at the moment to prevent this iniquity are of the stuff of melodrama, as is Edward's sudden change of heart. The story centers in the efforts of the strong-minded sister, Rhoda, to right her sister's name. Dahlia, far from belonging to the Victorian type of "fallen" woman, develops, as do all Meredith's women, under adversity. Rustic characters providing a lighter vein are well drawn but without that affectionate intimacy of understanding which George Eliot and Hardy display and with a not altogether agreeable "superior" tolerance. This novel is strangely off the line of Meredith's predictable development.

**Vittoria**    Sandra's story is continued in *Vittoria* (1866), Meredith's only historical novel. It deals with the outbreak of 1848 in Milan against the Austrians and the Italian defeat at Novara.[7] Political and military events are, however, impressionisticly related or hinted at, and though there are recognizable historical portraits (memorably of "the Chief," who, though not named, is Mazzini), and though the scene is crowded with soldiers, politicians, and conspirators, the heroine is the central figure and her growth in dignity and personality from the promise of her girlhood is the central theme. There are superb episodes, such as the meeting of the plotters on the mountain behind Stresa, the performance at La Scala when Vittoria sings the patriotic song which initiates the revolt, and the duel in the mountain pass; but much of the story is obscurely told by indirection. Wilfrid Pole reappears among the minor figures, but his sentimentalism is of small consequence amid great events. Meredith's concept of the Risorgimento was strongly influenced by Swinburne, contact with whom affected not only his political ideas but his naturalistic philosophy.

**Harry Richmond**    In *The Adventures of Harry Richmond* (1871) Meredith mingled realism and fantasy in the strangest fashion, bringing together characters taken directly from English life and others that are the creation of his poetic humor. Though told from the point of view of the son, Harry, this is really the story of the father, the magnificent and, in the end, disgraced charlatan, Richmond Roy. The general tone is of comic and romantic extravagance, but there is tragedy in Harry's gradual disillusionment. To the boy his father had been all that was wonderful; the shock is the greater as he is revealed in his true character. The revelation culminates in the famous scene of Squire Beltham's denunciation of the rogue. The women in the story are among the most attractive in all the Meredithian gallery of radiant female portraits. The exuberance of Meredith's fancy made the story far too long, but the vitality never flags. He seems, for once, to have written solely for the pleasure of creating and without thought of imparting any doctrine.

**Beauchamp's Career**    *Beauchamp's Career* (1875) is a love story combined with politics. The love story is more intelligible than are the affairs of state, for the distinctions among grades and shades of political opinion are tenuous and are obscured

---

[7] Meredith was special correspondent of *The Morning Post* during the Austro-Italian War of 1866. — Between 1860 and 1866 he had been on the staff of *The Ipswich Journal* and later wrote leaders for the *Post*. He seems to have quieted his own conscience, but the spectacle of a leading radical writing in the Conservative interest has troubled many of his admirers.

by the artifices of a style more epigrammatic and tortuous than in any earlier book. The hero was drawn from one of Meredith's friends, and the program of state control, universal suffrage, limitation of private wealth, and provision for future generations is that of the radicals of the period. Beauchamp's mentor, the philosophical Dr. Shrapnel, though the mouthpiece for Meredith's own views, seems to be drawn in part from Carlyle. Less even than in the case of Lucy Feverel is the reader prepared for the death with which the story ends. Beauchamp's drowning in saving a boy demonstrates the tragic irony of the accidental.

In 1877 came the lecture on *The Idea of Comedy and the Uses of the Comic Spirit*.[8] After a brilliant survey of writers of comedy, Meredith contrasts comedy with irony, farce, and satire, and develops themes already touched on in the novels: that comedy is the sword of common sense, the corrective of vanity, egoism, and sentimentality, and that under the aegis of the Comic Spirit women attain equality—and more than equality—with men. But comedy is not mere castigating; it is "the sacred chain of man to man," binding together the members of an intelligent, forward-looking society.[9] A most complex example of the corrective power of thoughtful laughter is supplied in *The Egoist*[10] (1879). In this story of the mortification of the jilted lover, Sir Willoughby Patterne, Meredith pushed the analytical method to such an extreme that the narrative takes far longer than the events narrated. It is overlaid with digressions and confused with a crowd of supernumerary people. The tendency becomes marked to make characters the vehicles of the novelist's doctrines; and persons in fiction do not easily stay alive when such a burden is imposed upon them. The brilliant manner has become a brilliant mannerism. The reader is blinded with the blaze and sputter of aphoristic pyrotechnics. Subtlety of thought is refined to the point of extinction, elliptical expression has become mercilessly obscure, spontaneity is no longer the quality of the dialogue, and matters essentially trivial are anatomized microscopically. Humiliation at his failure to win wide popular recognition was at the bottom of the stubborn exaggeration of the defects of Meredith's style and mode of narrative.

Having read the story of the love affair of Ferdinand Lassalle and Helene von Dönniges and of the death of the famous Jewish Socialist in a duel with the man who became Helene's husband,[11] Meredith wrote in impassioned haste *The Tragic Comedians* (1880) which is of little interest today save as an experiment in a hybrid literary form that came into vogue forty years later—the "fictionized" biography. *Poems and Lyrics of the Joy of Earth* (1883), Meredith's finest volume of verse, contains the enlarged version of

*The Comic Spirit*

*The Egoist*

---

[8] Ed. Lane Cooper (1918).

[9] See G. F. Reynolds's study of the *Ode to the Comic Spirit* in "Two Notes on the Poetry of George Meredith," *Univ. of Colorado Stud.*, xv (1925). 1-12.

[10] To 1879 belongs also the finest of Meredith's three short stories, the tragic *Tale of Chloe*, an episode of Bath society in the eighteenth century.

[11] Meredith took his material from Helene von Dönniges' *Meine Beziehungen zu Ferdinand Lassalle* (Breslau, 1879).

*Love in the Valley; The Day of the Daughter of Hades,* the most notable of his renderings of classical myth;[12] and the two most important statements of his philosophy of naturalism: *The Woods of Westermain* and *Earth and Man.*

**Diana of the Cross- ways**

The popular success of *Diana of the Crossways* (1885) was due in part to the influence of such admirers as Stevenson and Henley upon the general taste and in part to the faint aroma of scandal which emanated from the book. It was founded on the career of Sheridan's granddaughter, Mrs. Caroline Norton, against whom the false charge had been brought that she had given to Delane of *The Times* confidential news of Peel's conversion to free trade.[13] Meredith afterwards added a cryptic foreword to the effect that the accusation was unfounded and that the story was to be "read as fiction." The real difficulty is that he fails to make Diana's action plausible; nothing in her character leads us to expect her to be guilty of such disloyalty—or stupidity. In a few episodes (notably Dacier's denunciation of Diana for her betrayal of the secret of state) Meredith surpassed himself in brilliance; but the old vice of narrative by indirection is more pronounced than ever, the epigrams are of too studied a polish, and the metaphors at once too laborious and too quick-darting.

Two volumes of verse now intervened before fiction was resumed. *Ballads and Poems of Tragic Life* (1887) contains much that is harsh and clangorous in style and desperately obscure in subject. *A Reading of Earth* (1888) is more varied in manner and substance, from the simple melodiousness of the *Dirge in Woods* to the condensed thought of the *Hymn to Colour* and the repellent turgidity of the *Ode to the Comic Spirit.* Admirers of Meredith who fancied that in *Diana* they had caught up with him were deceived, for he escaped from them into yet more tangled jungles of language. *One of*

**Later Novels**

*Our Conquerors* (1891) is the most ruthless of all his assaults upon the loyalty of readers. Syntax, diction, and allusion are alike obscure; there are constant irrelevancies; and the narrative is carried on in so indirect a fashion that the situation is often lost to sight. This is the greater pity because the story of the tragic Nataly and her illegitimate daughter is a moving one, and there is wonderful delicacy in the analysis of the young girl's feelings when the secret of her parents' irregular relations becomes known to her. *Lord Ormont and his Aminta* (1894) presents another matrimonial entanglement in a more lucid and vivacious style; but the fantastic plot overtaxes credulity. *The Amazing Marriage* (1895) is a better story, albeit tortuously told. Moved by sudden impulse, the hero, a sort of Byronic type, proposes marriage to the heroine, a simple child of nature. He regrets his impulse, but is forced into marriage by the girl's uncle. He leaves his wife, only to realize her worth when it is too late. But Meredith's vein was now

---

12 On Meredith's classical poems see Bush, pp. 385-395.

13 Lord Aberdeen, not Mrs. Norton, was the guilty party. — Mrs. Norton, having been sued by her husband for her earnings from writing, published *English Laws for Women in the Nineteenth Century* (1853), a pamphlet which led eventually to the passing of the Married Women's Property Act. Her part in this needed reform certainly attracted Meredith's sympathy.

running thin, and the story is supplemented with persistent disquisition.[14]

Of the four *Odes in Contribution to the Song of French History* (1898) *France*
the finest, *France: 1870,* had been published at the time of the Prussian
victory. The others—*The French Revolution, Napoleon,* and *Alsace-Lorraine*
—belong to the eighteen-nineties. The connecting theme is the faithfulness and unfaithfulness of France to her true lover, Liberty, "the young
Angelical." To this union France has aspired constantly and has been as
constantly distracted from her path. During the earlier stages of the Revolution she was clasped in this lover's embrace; her first disloyalty was during
the Terror. Victory over external foes raised in her the lust for glory. She
abandoned her heavenly lover and turned to Napoleon, the demoniac chief,
"earth's chosen, crowned, unchallengeable upstart." The Emperor's triumphs
and ultimate overthrow are narrated in verse which reverberates as with
cannon-shot. Then, amidst the gross materialism of the Bourbon reaction,
Napoleon's legend shapes itself

> like some rare treasure-galleon,
> Hull down, with masts against the Western hues.

*France: 1870* has for its theme retributive justice, a vindication of the moral
order. The mother of pride and luxury is overthrown; but being also the
mother of reason, France must herself justify the blow. She who under
Napoleon had sown in blood must reap in blood. The Napoleonic conquests
are the cause of her present shame. The final ode, *Alsace-Lòrraine,* traces
the regeneration of France after 1870. In harsh and puzzling metaphors the
course of French history during the next three decades is traced, with the
legitimist conspiracies, the sporadic revival of Napoleonism, and the gradual
decline of the spirit of *revanche.* In the light of subsequent history Meredith's
belief that France was abandoning her claim to the lost provinces is now
seen to have been tragically impercipient.[15]

Meredith's last volume of poems, *A Reading of Life* (1901), broke no
fresh ground. In his last two decades he was the recipient of many honors,
succeeding Tennyson as President of the Society of British Authors and
made one of the original members of the Order of Merit. He died in 1909,
and was buried near his home at Box Hill in Surrey. On his grave is the
inscription, from the song in *Vittoria:*

> Life is but a little holding, lent
> To do a mighty labour.

## II

It is likely that Meredith's poems, though temporarily somewhat discredited, will prove to be of more lasting value than his novels. Truths

[14] After Meredith's death the fragment of another novel, *Celt and Saxon,* was published
(1910). The date of its composition is unknown. It appears to be fairly early work overlaid
with later highly mannered revision. It is a conversation-piece breaking off with no indication
of the course events were to take. — *The Sentimentalists* is Meredith's only attempt at drama.

[15] In another poem, *England before the Storm,* Meredith showed himself as tragically per-
cipient; he pictured an ill-prepared England confronting the peril of invasion by Germany.

applicable to all humanity shine in his prose and reënforce the teaching of the poems; but there is a limitation of time and nationality and social stratum that already "dates" this fiction; too much of the nineteenth century, of Victorian England, and of the manners and motives of a self-styled "upper class." Meredith's satire was salutary and is still invigorating; but already the point of many of his shafts is blunted. He is concerned with artificial people —the landed aristocracy, the ruling classes. When he descends to the "lower levels" the tendency to caricature, inherited from Dickens, becomes pronounced. In *Rhoda Fleming,* notwithstanding a deep feeling for social injustice, he depicted a world whose intimate history remained closed to him Though some parts of Meredith's political and social gospel are in advance of the position we have yet reached, the general trend has been along other lines than he predicted and his radicalism will not necessarily keep him in remembrance. His championship of women represents a great advance from the conventional adoration combined with secret patronage which Tennyson offered them; he protested against this "charity of chivalry." The novels of his last phase helped to shape opinion in favor of women who, suffering from the injustice of the marriage laws, had no redress. He looked forward to the time when the minds of women, nourished by "light," would no longer need to flatter "a tyrant's pride," but with equal economic opportunities based upon equal educational advantages would meet men as equals in a marriage of true minds. But the reformer of yesterday enunciates the commonplace of today. Meredith realized this when he said that another generation reaps that which we speak in protest.[16]

The great and memorable theme of all Meredith's writings, in verse and prose, is the frank and joyous acceptance of the idea of evolution, of life as a process of becoming. The troubled generation that preceded him had faced this idea with anxiety and alarm. Although Tennyson, superficially considered, had seemed to meet the scientists half-way, he was at bottom suspicious and hostile towards the new order. But Meredith hymns gladly that "Philosophy of Change" which teaches that progress is the law of all being.

> Sameness locks no scurfy pond
> Here for Custom crazy-fond:
> Change is on the wing to bud
> Rose in brain from rose in blood.[17]

Men have "come out of brutishness," "not forfeiting the beast with which they are crossed" but moving upward towards the "stature of the Gods." [18] As the race has emerged from savagery and is passing through supernaturalism (which is grounded in egoism) to a faith in the natural order, so the individual, avoiding alike the ascetic rocks and the sensual whirlpool, must

*Meredith's "World"*

*Women*

*Evolution*

---

[16] *The Empty Purse.* — For a brilliant "modern" estimate of Meredith's novels, on the whole adverse, see Virginia Woolf, *The Second Common Reader* (1932), pp. 245-256.
[17] *The Woods of Westermain.*
[18] *Hymn to Colour.*

achieve a harmony of blood, brain, and spirit, the Triad in whose union "*The* true felicity is attained. Meredith's use of the word *spirit,* to which old *Triad*" religious meanings that he discards are traditionally attached, presents some difficulty; but it appears to be the equivalent of the social sense, the sense of society and the moral order, rising above egoism. Men must cease to question Whence? and Whither? and must learn from nature to live in their offspring. A true marriage—"the senses running their live sap, and the minds companioned, and the spirits made one by the whole-natured conjunction"—is "more than happiness"; it is "the speeding of us ... to the creation of certain nobler races, now very dimly discerned." [19] In *The World's Advance* this progress is likened to a reeling spiral with many backslidings yet upward moving. The soul is "wind-beaten but ascending." Struggle is of the essence of life, and in the course of that struggle consciousness and a moral sense have been evolved. Meredith does not feel, as does Hardy, "the intolerable antilogy" of this birth of consciousness and morality in men and women who are the creatures of impercipience. He is an empiricist; he cannot explain the "Why" of evolution but rejoices in the fact, loving nature "too well to ask." He counsels submission to "those firm laws which we name gods," that unalterable reign of law evidenced in the steadfast course of the stars at the sight of which Lucifer sank back reproved.[20] This confidence in the moral order sustained his faith in severest trials.[21] Throughout his life he faced the prospect of personal dissolution with serenity. The "Daughter of Hades" was content with her day of life in the sunlight. The stars are not "frosty lamps illumining dead space," mere cogs in the great machine which grinds out good and ill indifferently, but spirits, sisters of the earth, fellow-workers that still sojourning still move onward in silent joy. Here and there these ideas are touched with a transcendentalism inherited from the romantic generation, but in the main there is a firm refusal of illusion, and what seems to be of religious and even mystical intent is due to the use of traditional figurative language without the traditional connotations. Man must not appeal with "wailful prayers" from nature to the Invisible, nor search mystically for "symbol-clues" in the facts of life. Life for those who hold the freedom of the Woods of Westermain is "a little holding, lent to do a mighty labor." Accepting this privilege and responsibility, man craves no further goal than to live in his offspring and bequeath the young generation no broken house; [22] and when his hour arrives he can fall without shuddering "into the breast that gives the rose."

[19] *Diana of the Crossways.*
[20] *Lucifer in Starlight.*
[21] *A Faith on Trial.*
[22] *The Empty Purse.* — See James Moffat, "*The Empty Purse,* a Meredithian Study for the Times," *Hibbert Journal,* xiv (1916). 612-626.

# XXXIV
## Thomas Hardy

### I

The ideas and emotions which Hardy cautiously termed his "tentative metaphysic" took shape so gradually that no point in his career can be indicated where the fatalism of his youth gave way to the determinism of his old age. There are anticipations of his final convictions in his earliest writings and vestiges of early speculation in his latest. Nor does the publication of his first volume of poems in 1898 mark a clear division, since Hardy wrote poetry in his youth, turned to prose only when he could not find an audience for his verse, never renounced his intention to be a poet during the quarter of a century of novel-writing, and, abandoning fiction, reverted to poetry at last. It is impossible, therefore, to divide his career into "periods," and perhaps the question had best be left where he left it in the contrasting titles of the two volumes of his memoirs—titles (as their muted despondency makes evident) indubitably suggested by himself: "The Early Life" and "The Later Years."

*The Past*    Born in a small hamlet close to the wild stretch of upland in Dorsetshire which he called Egdon Heath, Thomas Hardy [1] (1840-1928) came of old

[1] *Works,* Wessex Edition (22v, 1912-1922); *Works,* Mellstock Edition (37v, 1921-1922); *Collected Poems* (1919); *The Dynasts,* one-vol. ed. (1919); *Poems,* Golden Treasury Series (1920); *Selected Poems,* ed. G. M. Young (1940). Hardy never reprinted his occasional essays and letters to the press, but there is a convenient, albeit unauthorized, collection, *Life and Art,* ed. Ernest Brennecke (1925). — A. P. Webb, *Bibliography* (1916); R. L. Purdy, *Thomas Hardy: Catalogue of Memorial Exhibition* (New Haven, 1928); Professor Purdy has in preparation a definitive *Bibliography* of Hardy's writings; C. J. Weber, *The First Hundred Years of Thomas Hardy, 1840-1940: a Centenary Bibliography of Hardiana* (Waterville, Me., 1942); Ehrsam, *Bibliographies,* pp. 91-125; Florence Emily Hardy, *The Early Life of Thomas Hardy, 1840-1891* (1928) and *The Later Years of Thomas Hardy, 1892-1928* (1930), of which Mrs. Hardy was rather the compiler than author, for to a large extent the writing, as well as the work of assembling material from letters, diaries, note-books, etc., was Hardy's own; Lionel Johnson, *The Art of Thomas Hardy* (1894; ed. with a chapter on the poetry by J. E. Barton, 1923); F. A. Hedgcock, *Thomas Hardy: Penseur et artiste* (Paris, 1910); Lascelles Abercrombie, *Thomas Hardy: A Critical Study* (1912); S. C. Chew, *Thomas Hardy: Poet and Novelist* (1921; rev. ed., 1928), from which are drawn some parts of the present chapter; J. W. Beach, *The Technique of Thomas Hardy* (1922); Ernest Brennecke, *Thomas Hardy's Universe* (1924); H. B. Grimsditch, *Character and Environment in the Novels of Thomas Hardy* (1925); Pierre d'Exideuil, *Le Couple humain dans l'œuvre de Thomas Hardy* (Paris, 1928; translated by F. W. Crosse, 1929); H. M. Tomlinson, *Thomas Hardy* (privately printed, 1929); Federico Olivero, *An Introduction to Thomas Hardy* (Turin, 1930); Arthur McDowall, *Thomas Hardy* (1931); Louise de Ridder-Barzin, *Le Pessimisme de Thomas Hardy* (Paris, 1932); A. P. Elliott, *Fatalism in the Works of Thomas Hardy* (Philadelphia, 1935); H. C. Duffin, *Thomas Hardy: A Study of the Wessex Novels, the Poems, and The Dynasts* (Manchester, 1937); W. R. Rutland, *Thomas Hardy: A Study of his Writings and their Background* (1938); C. J. Weber, *Hardy of Wessex: His Life and Literary Career* (1940) and *Hardy in America* (1946); for Professor Weber's smaller, but valuable, contributions to Hardy-

yeoman stock. From childhood the impressions of the past—Celtic, Roman, Saxon, medieval, Georgian—were strong upon him. Vestiges of primitive ideas and superstitions, folkways and folklore, thrust themselves through the more superficial modern and sophisticated strata of his writings.[2] Though under the impact of scientific speculation he discarded old beliefs, he was always attentive to the uncanny and preternatural. Peasant song and dance and old church music never ceased to fascinate him. His father's trade of master-builder helped to dictate the choice of architecture as a profession, and at the time when the movement for church-restoration was in full swing he was articled to a local practitioner. Later he pursued this vocation in London; but his natural bent was towards literature. He was at the center of intellectual ferment during the critical eighteen-sixties; and reading Spencer's *First Principles* he meditated upon the unknown First Cause and upon the incalculable element of "Casualty" in human destinies. At this *Early* time he wrote a good deal of verse. Many of these pieces were afterwards *Poems* destroyed, but some remain and others are probably imbedded or reworked in poems of much later date. The freaks and pranks of the purblind "Doomsters" who mismanage man's life are the themes of some poems, and in a few there are hints of the contrast between the "unweening" First Cause and the human consciousness which by some unaccountable cosmic irony has evolved from that Cause. Chance is sometimes personified as a malignant deity who deliberately "sports" with human misery. For this angry fatalism Hardy found support in Swinburne's upbraiding of "the gods"; and in fact Swinburne was a strong influence upon him. Sensitive to the intellectual and emotional atmosphere of the time, he thus shaped his thoughts towards that "twilight view of life" which Meredith was later to deprecate. This despondency was lightened by his rustic humor and at other times darkened with resentment against the social distinctions of which he was more conscious in London than in his native Dorset. Something of the spiritual conflict of these early years is certainly recorded in the narrative of Angel Clare's renunciation of the Christian ministry in *Tess,* and something of the social conflict in Jude Fawley's thwarted aspirations in *Jude the Obscure.*[3]

But there was probably little of metaphysical speculation though much *The First* social radicalism in Hardy's first novel, *The Poor Man and the Lady* (1867- *Novel* 1868), which mingled scenes of rural life with satire directed against the metropolitan "upper classes." This book was rejected by three publishers. Portions of it were incorporated in later novels; one section survives as the novelette, *An Indiscretion in the Life of an Heiress* (1878); the remainder

study, too numerous to list here, see the annual bibliographies in *PMLA*; Edmund Blunden, *Thomas Hardy (EML Series,* 1942); Lord David Cecil, *Hardy, the Novelist* (1943). Of many books on the Hardy country the best is Herman Lea, *Thomas Hardy's Wessex* (1913). The *Southern Rev.,* VI (Summer, 1940), is a "Thomas Hardy Centennial Issue" devoted to articles on Hardy by W. H. Auden, Allen Tate, Bonamy Dobrée, and others. Baker, IX (1938), chs. I and II; D. H. Lawrence, "A Study of Thomas Hardy," in *Phoenix: The Posthumous Papers of D. H. Lawrence* (1936), pp. 398-516.

[2] Ruth A. Firor, *Folkways in Thomas Hardy* (Philadelphia, 1931).

[3] In old age Hardy denied the existence of any autobiographical substratum in his novels; it is there nonetheless, though not to be interpreted too literally.

was ultimately destroyed. But it is possible to reconstruct the original with some plausibility.[4] Both John Morley and George Meredith, who were then publishers' readers, recognized the promise of the book; and Meredith advised Hardy to try again, this time avoiding social satire and contriving an intricate plot. The result was *Desperate Remedies* (1871), a highly improbable tale of mystery and murder which in its sensational incidents and complex concatenation of circumstances reveals the influence of Wilkie Collins. *Under the Greenwood Tree* (1872) is a slight tale of rural courtship and feminine wiles mingled with episodes of rich rustic humor. *A Pair of Blue Eyes* (1873) combines sensational intrigue and incredible coincidences in the swiftly moving narrative of a romantic tragedy. The yokels in the humorous or gruesome episodes are drawn with a more intimate art than are their social superiors in the main plot. The success of this romance brought an invitation from Leslie Stephen to contribute to *Cornhill,* where in 1874 appeared Hardy's first masterpiece, *Far from the Madding Crowd.*[5] Its anonymity provoked widespread speculation as to its authorship; its success was enormous; and Hardy, now securely launched upon his career, was able to marry. His bride was Emma Lavinia Gifford to whom he had become betrothed four years earlier when engaged upon church-restoration work in Cornwall. After a honeymoon in France and Belgium, the Hardys lived either in London or in one or another southern town till 1885, when they settled at Max Gate on the outskirts of Dorchester, Hardy's home for the long remainder of his life.

*Popular Success*

Resenting the attribution of *Far from the Madding Crowd* to George Eliot, which he interpreted as a charge of imitation, Hardy essayed in his next book, *The Hand of Ethelberta* (1876), something wholly different and achieved only a negligible piece of frivolity. But this was followed by the book which in its balance and control is his greatest work of fiction, *The Return of the Native* (1878). It was rejected by Leslie Stephen on the ground that a tale of tragic passion would displease *Cornhill's* clientèle and was accepted by *Belgravia* only when Hardy had consented to bring the secondary plot of Venn and Thomasin to the "happy ending" which was *de rigueur* in current fiction.[6] *The Trumpet-Major* (1880), the most genial of the Wessex Novels, was the first considerable sign of Hardy's interest in Napoleonic traditions. Criticism of *A Laodicean* (1881) is disarmed by the fact that, having been contracted for, it was composed during convalescence from a severe illness. It is quite worthless. *Two on a Tower* (1882), though fragile in theme and almost dream-like in tone, is memorable for its projection of human passion against the background of starry distances. Hardy's

---

[4] See *An Indiscretion in the Life of an Heiress*, ed. C. J. Weber (Baltimore, 1935).

[5] Here Hardy first revived the ancient name of Wessex for the southern and southwestern counties and fixed imaginary names to many identifiable actual places. In later editions of the first three novels he revised the nomenclature to conform to this scheme. See *Far from the Madding Crowd*, ed. C. J. Weber (1937).

[6] On the alterations in the various novels to conform to the requirements of editors see Mary E. Chase, *Thomas Hardy from Serial to Novel* (Minneapolis, 1927). Professor Weber also has made valuable contributions to the history of Hardy's texts.

outspokenness in this book on the subject of the sexual relation did not conform to contemporary standards of literary propriety and "rumblings of British prudery" were audible. Apart from the pretty novelette, *The Romantic Adventures of a Milkmaid* (1883), nothing more was published for four years. The resultant reserve of energy was expended upon *The Mayor of Casterbridge* (1886). Here the interest is not divided among four or five main characters as in the earlier books but is concentrated upon the figure of Michael Henchard; and though external circumstance and crass coincidence continue to play their part, there is a new emphasis upon faults in Henchard's character which the directing Force of the universe uses to bring him to destruction. The book is firmly constructed and austere in tone almost to brutality. What it lacks as compared with the earlier novels is charm and sweetness and poetry. Two of these qualities and something of bitter-sweet as well are abundantly present in *The Woodlanders* (1887), the tenderest of Hardy's stories, thrilling in its narrative power and memorable both for the nobility of its two central figures and for its exquisitely observed scenes and customs of the woodland folk.

A first set of short stories, assembled as *Wessex Tales* (1888), was followed by *A Group of Noble Dames* (1891), *Life's Little Ironies* (1894), and *A Changed Man and Other Stories* (1913). Disregarding chronology for a moment, we may notice these together. Hardy was not a great short-story-teller, though he wrote a few fine short stories. *The Three Strangers, The Withered Arm, The Distracted Preacher, On the Western Circuit, For Conscience' Sake,* and *A Tragedy of Two Ambitions* are little masterpieces, exhibiting a wide range of power—ironic, humorous, grim, sardonic, or eerie. But too frequently Hardy's tales are either trivial or extravagant local anecdotes cast in literary form or else give the impression of being sketches or drafts for full-length novels. The tone of many is bitter or sinister, though they do not afford scope for much explicit comment upon the human quandary. *[margin: Short Stories]*

Hardy needed a larger canvas for an exposition of the view of life he now held. The first notes for *Jude the Obscure* were jotted down in 1887 and the composition of *Tess* was begun not much later. For these books he attempted to prepare the public by two articles in the nature of manifestoes: *The Profitable Reading of Fiction* (1888) and *Candor in English Fiction* (1890).[7] In these he asked for the novelist the right to treat controversial topics with the same sincerity as is permitted in private intercourse, to discuss candidly the sexual relation, the problems of religious belief, and the position of man in the universe. Notwithstanding this urgent argument, he was forced, for the sake of his livelihood, to bowdlerize and dismember *Tess of the d'Urbervilles* when he published it serially in 1891;[8] and this, the most famous of his novels, was bitterly denounced when its integrity was restored in the book form. The two-fold polemic—against social prejudice and against *[margin: Tess]*

[7] Reprinted in *Life and Art,* pp. 56-74; 75-84.
[8] C. J. Weber, "On the Dismemberment of *Tess,*" *Sat. Rev. of Lit.,* XI (1934). 308-309.

*Jude*

"the President of the Immortals"—roused a storm of protest. *The Well-Beloved* (1892),[9] a semi-allegorical Platonic fantasy, shows a temporary exhaustion after the profound emotional effort called forth by *Tess*; nor did Hardy entirely recover his artistic control in the last novel, *Jude the Obscure* (1895), a powerful but overwrought story of "the derision and disaster that follow in the wake of the strongest passion known to humanity." That a book of such formidable candor could achieve publication shows that Victorian prudery was waning; that it caused a great scandal shows that that prudery was not extinct. The experience "cured" Hardy, as he wrote afterwards, of any desire to write more novels. As a matter of fact, he had had his say in a medium which, for all his mastery, was never entirely congenial to him and was ready to turn again to poetry, the native country of his mind.

*Return to Poetry*

*Wessex Poems* (1898) and *Poems of the Past and the Present* (1902) preceded the epic-drama, *The Dynasts* (1903-1906-1908), the stupendous result of his life-long interest in the Napoleonic Wars, and, more than this, an exposition upon the amplest scale of his mechanistic determinism. Subsequent collections of short poems were *Time's Laughing-Stocks* (1909), *Satires of Circumstance* (1914), *Moments of Vision* (1917), *Late Lyrics and Earlier* (1922), *Human Shows* (1925), and *Winter Words* (posthumous, 1928). *The Queen of Cornwall* (1923), a short drama on the legend of Iseult, is an attempt, more ingenious than convincing, to harmonize the two conflicting versions of the story. In his later years Hardy also occupied himself with the memoirs which appeared after his death as a biography professedly by his widow. When his first wife died in 1912, his thoughts turned to their romance of long ago and he wrote a series of poignant little elegies. Differences of temperament and opinion had come between the pair, but there had never been an entire estrangement.[10] In a second marriage (1914), to Florence Emily Dugdale, he found congeniality and happiness. During the last two decades his fame widened enormously. He bore his honors with deprecating modesty, yet was curiously sensitive to the few voices of dissent.[11] He died in January, 1928, and his ashes were placed in Westminster Abbey among England's poets.[12]

[9] Not published in book form till 1897.

[10] Distorted rumors of scandalous estrangement form the basis of Somerset Maugham's *roman à clef, Cakes and Ale*. For a clear and candid statement of the matter see C. J. Weber, *Hardy of Wessex* (1940), ch. xv.

[11] The present writer knew of the anxiety at Max Gate when report came of George Moore's intention to attack Hardy. Moore's violent but not altogether unwarranted onslaught, prompted by jealousy, was published in *Conversations in Ebury Street* (1924), ch. vi. Moore attached to Hardy the blame for some of the extravagant expressions of praise on the part of Hardy's admirers—which was scarcely fair. J. Middleton Murry replied to Moore in a hysterically abusive brochure, *Wrap Me Up in My Aubusson Carpet* (1925). A campaign of denigration against Hardy of another sort made way under the leadership of T. S. Eliot. The most arrogant statement of this critic's disapproval is in *After Strange Gods* (1934), pp. 59-62. Mr. Eliot has criticized Hardy with the acerbity of a spiritual pride which, the Christian may hold, gives greater offense to God than Hardy's irremediable impercipience.

[12] Hardy had expressed the wish to be buried in Stinsford churchyard, near Max Gate. The universal opinion that burial must be in the Abbey resulted in a compromise: the heart was cut out and buried at Stinsford; the ashes after cremation were taken to the Abbey. The almost pagan primitiveness of this proceeding was not out of keeping with the man.

## II

As a regionalist Hardy had forerunners of a kind in Maria Edgeworth *Region-*
and other Irish novelists and in John Galt and other Scots; but those writers *alism*
had not confined themselves to a small, well-defined area and were nationalistic rather than regionalist. In a modest way the claim to be Hardy's
predecessor belongs to the Dorset poet, William Barnes.[13] But though, like
Barnes, he was steeped in the traditions of his countryside, Hardy was not
primarily "folkloristic." His yokels do not form a class entirely apart from
the other characters in the Wessex Novels, but by almost imperceptible
gradations, through persons of middle rank, are connected with the characters who are higher in the social scale. From the latter the rustics are
distinguishable by their use of dialect and by the serenity with which they
hold their place in the world. Hardy laid no stress upon their poverty and
insisted that their misery had been much overestimated.[14] They have discovered the secret of happiness, which, as is said in *The Woodlanders,* lies
in limiting one's aspirations. Many are shrewd, some witty, nearly all unconsciously humorous. They are at once a part of the Wessex background
and a sort of chorus commenting upon the actions in which their superiors
are engaged. Apart from the villains, who are almost always sophisticated
intruders from the outside world, the leading characters are of Wessex
blood. When, as in some of the minor novels, Hardy ventured beyond
Wessex he was beyond his range. On his chosen, restricted stage as high
drama could be enacted as in parts of the world seemingly more significant,
for, like Wordsworth, he believed that in rustic life "the essential passions of
the heart find a better soil" and are "less under restraint" than in urban
society. The closer man lives to nature in humility and ignorance the likelier *Nature*
he is to be happy, for knowledge is sorrow. But nature[15] is full of cruelty,
and Hardy stresses those aspects of the natural world that are hostile to
man. Yet with faulty logic he is on the side of natural impulse (as in *Tess*
or *Jude*) in opposition to social law, convention, and restrictions. Nature is
not a setting for his stories but an integral part of them. Man is a plaything
in the grip of vast forces. The dominant theme is the ineffectual struggle
of the individual against the obscure power which moves the universe. Since
love accentuates individuality, it is in love that the conflict of humanity
with destiny is at its most intense. In such earlier masterpieces as *The Return
of the Native* and *The Mayor of Casterbridge* the blows of fate are to some

13 William Barnes (1801-1886), clergyman, poet, and local antiquary, author of three series
of *Poems of Rural Life in the Dorset Dialect* (1854, 1859, 1862; collected ed., 1879). These
are little eclogues, love poems, nature pieces, bits of folklore and superstition, and the like.
See his *Select Poems,* chosen by Thomas Hardy (1908). — Another "regionalist" poet was
Thomas Edward Brown (1830-1897) who wrote narrative and lyrical verse, some in standard
English, much in the Manx dialect. *Collected Poems,* ed. W. E. Henley (1901); *Letters,* ed. S. T.
Irwin (2v, 1900).
14 See Hardy's article on "The Dorsetshire Labourer," *Longman's Mag.,* July, 1879, and his
letter "On the Use of Dialect," *Spectator,* October 15, 1881. Both are reprinted in *Life and
Art,* pp. 20-47; 114-115.
15 See J. W. Beach, *The Concept of Nature,* pp. 503-521.

extent consequent upon weaknesses of character, so that one may speak of "blame" and "retribution"; but in *Tess* and *Jude* culpability is of no consequence because blind destiny strikes the innocent and the guilty with stupid impartiality. Hardy came to view man and nature as fellow-sufferers from the cosmic imbecility. His myth-making imagination gave "a kind of rationality to the hoary old superstitions of hostile or capricious powers which he cherished and half-believed." [16] But he was really a scientific determinist, and by "Fate" or "Chance" or "Casualty" meant human life as determined by all antecedent circumstances in a chain of causality.[17] Groping for a name for this concept, he abandoned such terms as "Nature," "Hap," or "God" and finally—whether or not after reading Schopenhauer [18]—chose to call the unintelligent and unconscious urge or impulse in things the Immanent Will. But this term is nothing more than a "metaphysical convenience" to express the unity and pattern of existing things.[19] Critics have deplored the sacrifice of tragic grandeur which this concept requires, for since human protagonists are reduced to automata so that even in their struggles against destiny they are merely pulled to and fro by the "halyards" of the Will, there is no room for that internal conflict which is the essence of tragedy. Hardy would have agreed; the root of his indictment against life was "the intolerable antilogy of making figments feel." "The emotions," he remarked, "have no place in a world of defect, and it is a cruel injustice that they should have developed in it." [20] Yet in the inexplicable evolution of human consciousness from the Unconscious and of intelligence from the Unknowing lay Hardy's strange, dim hope that "in some day unguessed of us" the Will may "lift its blinding incubus" and, becoming informed by consciousness, "fashion all things fair." [21]

In personal relations Hardy was jovial, but his temperament was fundamentally saturnine and he found this "twilight view of life" congenial to him. A rich fund of sympathy with suffering often made him angry and indignant and (again with a want of logic) he indicted Circumstance and the miseries of man's own contriving alike. He was not a sociological novelist, but he was happy to recognize that reforms often begin in sentiment and sentiment sometimes begins in a novel.[22] As a professional man of letters it was

*"The Immanent Will"*

---

[16] Baker, IX. 81.

[17] J. W. Beach, *op. cit.*, p. 511.

[18] Agnes Steinbach, *Thomas Hardy und Schopenhauer* (Leipzig, 1925), pp. 434-474; H. Garwood, *Thomas Hardy: An Illustration of the Philosophy of Schopenhauer* (Philadelphia, 1912).

[19] J. W. Beach, *op. cit.*, p. 518.

[20] Florence E. Hardy, *The Early Life of Thomas Hardy*, p. 192.

[21] *The Blow*; and the final Chorus of the Pities in *The Dynasts*. Professor Beach repudiates this "mitigating concession" as not a serious element in Hardy's philosophy; but the idea, that just as man has attained consciousness through some evolutionary process so conceivably may the Immanent Will, recurs constantly in Hardy's poetry. In the practical, unspeculative sphere Hardy described himself as a meliorist, and in a poem addressed to "the Unknown God" he hymned the praise of the Divinity because he saw here and there "old wrongs dying as of self-slaughter." But he said to the present writer and to others that had he written *The Dynasts* after the Treaty of Versailles he could not have closed it upon a note of hope.

[22] Final preface to *Tess*. Compare George Moore's satisfaction when *Esther Waters* was efficacious in suggesting practical philanthropies.

his business to entertain, and only gradually, when he had made his way, did he come to use fiction openly for polemic. But what finally became explicit had always been implicit. In "loading the dice" against his characters and in relying to an extravagant degree upon coincidence he was at once following the sensational fashion in fiction and hinting at his indictment of life. It has been held that in the end—that is, in *Jude*—the bitterness of his indignation overreached itself; but even those who do not feel the spiritual terror of that book see that the element of realism is subordinated to something like allegory—the old allegory of the Choice of the Two Paths. The suicide of Jude's son, whether or not suggested by Hartman's *Philosophy of the Unconscious,* is an omen of humanity's escape from life; the Will-Not-to-Live is to triumph ultimately over the Life-Urge.

With his architect's training in design Hardy found satisfaction in the symmetry of his plots. Today, when mere plot is at a discount in fiction, the almost diagrammatic regularity of his plans is severely criticized. "Slices of life" do not fall into such symmetrical segments. The even tenor of life attracted neither his interest nor that of the readers for whose suffrages he first bid. But he held, when inventing sensational incident, that "the uncommonness must be in the events, not in the characters." Of the melodramatic quality of many of his "events" it is unnecessary to speak; some are merely preposterous. His characters fall into a few recurrent types which reveal his prepossessions in favor of honest worth and his prejudices against sophistication. A master of narrative, he was less successful in dialogue, where, save in the peasant scenes, there is almost always more than a touch of the artificial and declamatory. In the decades when the doctrine of impersonality in art was gaining ground he continued to avail himself of the privilege of the Victorian novelist to intrude his own opinions into his stories. Whatever the value as propaganda for the reform of sentiment and convention, the savage satire with which he attacked the Church, the universities, marriage, and various social prejudices marred his last two novels as works of art.[23]

*Structure of the Novels*

---

[23] The influence of the Wessex Novels is apparent to a greater or less degree in the writings of various regionalists; and others, though perhaps not directly affected by Hardy's example, show affinities to him.

Richard D. Blackmore (1825-1900) won a single great success with *Lorna Doone* (1869), a historical novel in the line of descent from Scott but with elements of mystery and melodrama imitated from Wilkie Collins. It is permeated with a love and knowledge of Exmoor. In later novels, now forgotten, Blackmore imitated Hardy. See Q. G. Burris, *R. D. Blackmore, His Life and Novels* (Urbana, 1930).

Sabine Baring-Gould (1834-1924) exploited the antiquities and folklore of Devon and Cornwall in stories ranging from antiquity to the very recent past.

William Black (1841-1898) specialized in the regionalism of the Highlands and the Hebrides with elaborate landscapes and seascapes and with the traditional contrast between remote simplicities and modern sophistication.

Samuel R. Crockett (1860-1914) told tales of his native Galloway with so lavish a use of dialect that a glossary was compiled for his readers. See M. M. Harper, *Crockett and Grey Galloway: The Novelist and his Works* (1907).

Closer in mood though not in form to Hardy is Richard Jefferies (1848-1887), the author of *The Story of My Heart* (1883) and of novels and fantasies many of which are set in Wiltshire. There is a passionate "paganism" in his celebration of love, and his philosophic determinism is characteristic of his time. See *Selections,* ed. H. Williamson (1937); *Jefferies'*

## III

Besides *The Dynasts* Hardy wrote about nine hundred short poems.[24] No other considerable poet exhibits a like contrast between a single work of ample scope and a multitude of little things; but the sheer bulk of the miscellaneous poetry is a counterbalance to the epic-drama and an essential supplement to it. A good deal of this minor verse must go into the discard. Such idiosyncrasies of style as violent inversions of word-order, uncouth neologisms, the wrenching of words from their familiar meanings, the revival of half-intelligible archaisms, and the drastic clipping of words to force them into a metrical pattern, though by such means as these he sometimes achieved his best effects, impose a strain upon the reader which is not tolerable when his theme is trivial or cynical or would-be humorous. On the other hand, a great deal remains. Returning to poetry when his position was assured, he was under obligations to no school (though he betrays stylistic affinities to Browning and was himself conscious of an indebtedness to Donne) and could experiment as he liked. Some of his innovations are analogous to those of Hopkins and Doughty, but in the main his poetry stands apart from that of his time. There is an avoidance of the decoration and embroidery of decadent romantic verse. The trained storyteller is seen in the vigorous ballads (such as *A Tramp-Woman's Tragedy,* which was his own favorite among his poems), the ironic "satires of circumstance," and the little incidents told with sardonic humor. His poems, he said, were "explorations of reality." There is a ruthless insight, a precision that needs no over-emphasis, a lovely quietness, and an ability to achieve his purposes without resort to merely verbal imagery. A gruesome humor in many pieces was not, he insisted to friends, to be taken too seriously; some of his many graveyard poems show a sort of cheerful ghoulishness; but others are cynical, sardonic, melancholy, tender, eerie, or wonderfully spectral. In many poems he exposed the disenchantments and incompatabilities of love; but he was convinced that in the marriage of true minds men and women find the best that life has to offer. The most beautiful of his short poems was ad-

*England: Nature Essays,* ed. S. J. Looker (1937); Edward Thomas, *Richard Jefferies* (1909); C. J. Masseck, *Richard Jefferies* (Paris, 1913).

Eden Phillpotts (1862-1960) was Hardy's closest disciple, though the influence is less marked in his late books. The setting of his best novels, of which *The River* (1902) is a good example, is generally in the western country beyond Wessex. The congenital wisdom of Phillpotts' yokels is precisely in the manner of the master. Phillpotts has also written plays, several volumes of poems, and a number of mere "thrillers."

The novels of Mary Webb (1885-1927) have wider affiliations, but her emphasis upon her native region (the Welsh marches) owes much to Hardy. Her literary ancestry is, however, complex. Characteristic books are *The House in Dormer Forest* (1920) and *Precious Bane* (1924). *Novels,* Sarn Edition (7v, 1942); *A Mary Webb Anthology,* ed. H. B. L. Webb (1940); Thomas Moult, *Mary Webb: Her Life and Work* (1932).

[24] On Hardy's verse technique see E. C. Hickson, *The Versification of Thomas Hardy* (Philadelphia, 1931); G. R. Elliott, "Spectral Etching in the Poetry of Thomas Hardy," *PMLA,* XLIII (1928). 1185-1195; and several of the articles in "Hardy Centennial Issue" of the *Southern Review.* See also Amiya Chakravarty, *The Dynasts and the Post-War Age in Poetry* (1938).

dressed to the woman who became his second wife. He has the ability to cast an unfamiliar light upon familiar things, to contrast the fugitive and the permanent, and (in Tennyson's words) to give "a sense of the abiding in the transient." Occasionally but less characteristically he was master of the grand style, as in the lines written in Gibbon's garden or in the sonnet *At a Lunar Eclipse*. There is no room to say more, though much more might be said, save to indicate his range by naming a few poems in addition to those to which attention has been directed already. These are: *Heiress and Architect, The Impercipient, The Oxen, The Darkling Thrush, Let Me Enjoy, The Blow, Jubilate, A Singer Asleep, Quid hic agis?, The Clock-Winder*, and *Afterwards*. The list might be greatly extended; but every reader can make his own anthology. Today, after a shorter period of denigration than usually follows the death of a famous writer, critics are again studying in minutest detail his technique and style, and the opinion prevalent in the nineteen-twenties is once more expressed that even if Hardy was not a great poet he wrote great poetry.

Concerning *The Dynasts* opinion has not yet crystallized. The general tendency is to assert that a partial failure is redeemed by the greatness of the conception. As the appropriateness of the poetic style to the structure and theme becomes more apparent it is likely that this half-heartedness will give way to less qualified admiration. Upon a scale of cosmic proportions Hardy undertook to exhibit the Immanent Will, which "like a knitter drowsed" weaves "with absent heed," entangling in its web human automata. It was not Hardy's purpose to contribute anything new to the analysis of Napoleon's character or that of any other figure in the tragedy of the "Clash of Peoples." The conduct of the action upon two planes—Europe and the Over-World where dwell "the great intelligences . . . which range above our mortal state" —is an extraordinary feat of the creative imagination. In the group of overseeing spirits the poet succeeded in rendering in dramatic form abstractions of human emotion and experience. Parts of the material assembled with the conscientiousness of a historian proved intractable to verse; but almost invariably the poetry rises to greatness upon great occasions. Some of the choruses are of tragic grandeur and others are beautiful and tender or bluff and hearty or of sinister humor. The "stage-directions" in prose are of a wonderful imaginative clarity, whether the scene is viewed near at hand or is a vast panorama spread before spirit-eyes from celestial heights. With such palpitating excitement yet historical accuracy are the battles dramatized that these scenes have been likened to those in Tolstoy's *War and Peace*. The rustic episodes are beyond compare with anything of the kind save those in Shakespeare and in some of Hardy's own romances. The glimpse of the mad King George III is as convincing in its pathos as is that of the rakish Prince Regent in its satiric realism. The death of Nelson; the burial of Sir John Moore; the deserters skulking in a Spanish cellar; the retreat from Moscow; the return from Elba; and the entire Waterloo campaign—

The Dynasts

these are a few of the high points in a drama which sometimes sinks, as does life itself, to lower levels, but rises majestically upon fit occasion. To read it is to have implanted in the memory forever the august and tragic spectacle of humanity entangled in the web of "the all-urging Will, raptly magnipotent."

# XXXV
## Aestheticism and "Decadence"

### I

The origins of the Aesthetic Movement [1] are found in various streams of speculation. At Oxford in the eighteen-sixties the Hegelian evaluation of the various kinds of human experience was expounded by Thomas Hill Green (1836-1882) and was of primary importance for the determination of Walter Pater's point of view.[2] At just this time Swinburne, following Gautier and Baudelaire, was controverting the Utilitarian criticism which demanded of art a moral emphasis and declaring that art should serve no religious, moral, or social end, nor any end save itself. Rossetti, while avoiding precept and controversy, was a strong and disturbing example of the artist dedicated wholly to his art. By seeking to make the social order comely, Ruskin, even while insisting upon moral values in art, prepared the way for Pater's doctrine of the comeliness of the individual life as a criterion of right conduct. Behind these and other expressions of dissatisfaction with the dominant Utilitarian creed was the pessimism of the mid-century which was a further stimulus towards hedonism. After the French defeat of 1870 the withdrawal of French artists and men of letters from the political and social arena into aesthetic isolation was a gesture imitated in England.

For want of an authoritative biography it is difficult to determine the *Pater* degree to which early influences of family and environment shaped the temperament of Walter Horatio Pater [3] (1839-1894), the somewhat reluctant leader of the Aesthetic Movement. *The Child in the House* is indubitably an evocation of his own early years; but here, as in his accounts of the boyhood of Marius, Gaston, and Emerald Uthwart, it is impossible to draw a precise line between the imaginary and the autobiographical. Throughout his books there are obscure personal allusions. Florian Deleal, the child who

---

[1] A. J. Farmer, *Le Mouvement esthétique et "décadent" en Angleterre, 1873-1900* (Paris, 1931); Louise Rosenblatt, *L'Idée de l'art pour l'art dans la littérature anglaise pendant la periode victorienne* (Paris, 1931); William Gaunt, *The Aesthetic Adventure* (1944); Albert Cassagne, *La Théorie de l'art pour l'art en France* (Paris, 1906).

[2] B. Fehr, "Walter Pater und Hegel," *ESt*, L (1916). 300-308.

[3] *Works*, Library Edition (10v, 1910); *Selected Essays*, ed. H. G. Rawlinson (1927). — Thomas Wright, *The Life of Walter Pater* (2v, 1907); A. C. Benson, *Walter Pater* (*EML Series*, 1906); Edward Thomas, *Walter Pater, a Critical Study* (1913); A. J. Farmer, *Walter Pater as a Critic of English Literature* (Grenoble, 1931); H. H. Young, *The Writings of Walter Pater, a Reflection of British Philosophical Opinion from 1860 to 1890* (Bryn Mawr, 1933); J. G. Eaker, *Walter Pater, a Study in Methods and Effects* (Iowa City, 1933); R. C. Child, *The Aesthetic of Walter Pater* (1940); Algernon Cecil, "Walter Pater," *Six Oxford Thinkers* (1909), pp. 214-251.

possessed "a positive genius for tranquility," [4] suggests the actual man who at Oxford passed a life of almost quietistic seclusion and who emerged but rarely, and then shyly, into London society. Save for a few visits to the Continent Pater's career was almost eventless. At Oxford he assembled round him a small company of disciples, meanwhile publishing in periodicals a series of essays of which most, with some new material, were collected as *Studies in the History of the Renaissance* [5] (1873). Other essays in philosophy, literature, and the fine arts followed, with a little group of highly characteristic "portraits," some purely fictitious, others with some historical foundation. Much of this miscellaneous work was assembled in *Imaginary Portraits* (1887), *Appreciations* (1889), and *Plato and Platonism* (1893), while much else was first gathered together or first published in posthumous volumes.[6] Though, like his own Marius, "essentially but a spectator" even in "his most enthusiastic participation" in the ways of the restricted world in which he moved,[7] Pater came to feel a responsibility towards those of the younger generation who, following his leadership, evinced a misunderstanding of his teaching; and after the appearance of W. H. Mallock's *The New Republic* (1877), in which his doctrines were cruelly caricatured,[8] he undertook an elaborate *apologia* which resulted in his masterpiece, *Marius the Epicurean* (1885). A second effort along similar lines, *Gaston de Latour,* was abandoned after five chapters had been published in 1888. Pater was at work upon an essay on Pascal when he died suddenly at the height of his powers and prestige.

In an age of doctrinal controversies often productive of bitter personalities Pater held himself aloof from quarrels; and equally he had no share in the humanitarian movement of the time. Even though his mature thought found a place for compassion, it is not on record that this sympathy was ever expressed in any positive, remedial social action. He virtually never sounded any other note than that of appreciation, keeping silent on his antipathies. Of two dominant traits of temperament which helped to shape his thought, one was his extraordinary keenness of sensitivity: of Florian he wrote that he "seemed to experience a passionateness in his relation to fair outward objects," and of Gaston, that he tended towards "a new religion, or at least a new worship, maintaining and visibly setting forth a single overpowering apprehension." [9] With this hypersensuousness was

---

[4] See *The Child in the House,* in *Miscellaneous Studies.*

[5] Renamed *The Renaissance. Studies in Art and Poetry.*

[6] *Miscellaneous Studies* and *Greek Studies* (both 1895); *Gaston de Latour* (1896); *Essays from "The Guardian"* (1896); *Sketches and Reviews* (1919).

[7] *Marius the Epicurean,* I. 46.

[8] William H. Mallock (1849-1923) voiced in a succession of volumes his hostility to the tendencies of his time, his opposition to advancing democracy and Socialism receiving final expression in *Memories of Life and Literature* (1920). But he never repeated the success of *The New Republic.* In this pseudo-Peacockian satire most of the characters, identifiable as Ruskin, Tyndall, and other eminent Victorians, are drawn sympathetically. Not so "Mr. Rose," i.e., Pater, in whose portrait there is deliberate malice. In contemporary keys "Mr. Rose" is identified with Rossetti, an error showing how little Pater was known to the general public, which associated Rossetti with the movement of "Art for Art's Sake."

[9] *The Child in the House, Miscellaneous Studies,* p. 186; *Gaston de Latour,* p. 70.

combined a poignant awareness of the brevity of life which directed his *Cyrenai-* thought towards Cyrenaicism, that philosophy which has "no basis of un- *cism* verified hypothesis" and relies upon the security of the present moment "set between two hypothetical eternities." [10] To fill each passing moment with intense experience, "to maintain this ecstasy," is success in life. Yet this passionate apprehension of beauty and the sense of its fleetingness do not bring happiness. Not only in Pater's early writings but in the works of his maturity there is a troubling unwholesomeness. The famous "medita-tion" upon the Mona Lisa, the exquisite penultimate paragraph of *The Poetry of Michelangelo,* the narrative of Flavian's death in *Marius,* the appearance of Denys from the tomb, and the gruesome episode of the extraction of the bullet from the dead heart of Emerald Uthwart are ex-amples of this morbidity, this unhealthy curiosity. The attraction exerted by mysterious iniquity is expressed with greatest power in *Apollo in Picardy,* one of the "portraits" of latest date (1893). The fascination which the theme of the pagan gods who have "grown diabolic among ages that would not accept [them] as divine" exercised upon Pater is one expression of this re-current mood.[11] This aspect of his work is premonitory of the coming "Decadence." But it must not be overemphasized, for there was a develop-ment in Pater's thought. In *Diaphanéité,* his earliest extant essay (1864), and even so late as *Marius* the counsel is that life should be lived in the spirit of art; but almost from the first there was the realization that though pursued for its own sake, art does contribute to the ethical nature of man; and towards the end there was an increasing emphasis upon the beauty of order and upon the need to discipline the soul. At times there is an am-biguity, a suggestion of transcendental possibilities, an open-minded recogni-tion of the *grand peut-être.*

When Pater began to write, Ruskin's exaltation of the Middle Ages and denigration of the Renaissance had given the latter period the attraction of a fresh subject.[12] In approach and in critical theory Pater was quite un-Ruskinian. He is nearer to Arnold in his fastidiousness, though without

---

[10] *Marius the Epicurean,* i. 149; *Conclusion* to *The Renaissance.*

[11] See J. S. Harrison, "Pater, Heine, and the Old Gods of Greece," *PMLA,* xxxix (1924). 655-686.

[12] This field of research was intensively cultivated by John Addington Symonds (1840-1893). *The Renaissance in Italy* (7v, 1875-1886) is desultory in design, flamboyant in style, and not altogether trustworthy; but a fine descriptive talent displays the rich coloring, violent movement, and strong personalities of the Renaissance. Symonds also wrote *Sketches in Italy and Greece* (1874), *Studies of the Greek Poets* (1873 and 1876), biographies of Michelangelo, Sidney, and Shelley, and critical studies of Dante, Whitman, and Shakespeare's predecessors in the English drama. *In the Key of Blue* (1893) is a significant volume of essays. The qualities conspicuous in his critical and historical work—the scholarship, the love of art and the classics, the sensitiveness to the genius of places, the febrile response to the loveliness of Italian and Alpine scenery—are present also in Symonds' verse: *Many Moods* (1878); *New and Old* (1880). Occasionally he gives expression to the mood of late-century dejection and suggests the quandary into which mechanistic materialism has led thoughtful men. — With Pater may also be associated Violet Paget (1856-1935), whose pen-name was "Vernon Lee." Among her studies in art, literature, and aesthetics are *Euphorion* (2v, 1884) and *Genius Loci* (1899). *Ariadne in Mantua* (1903) is a delicately graceful "dramatic romance." Her novels are of little moment, but later books, such as *Gospels of Anarchy* (1908) and *Vital Lies* (1912), show that she kept abreast of the age, refusing to be a mere belated voice of aestheticism.

Arnold's superciliousness.[13] But he accepted as the function of criticism the duty to "see the object as it really is"; and his modification of this rule introduced by the question "What is it to *me?*" has been misunderstood by those who have disregarded the context in the preface to *The Renaissance.* Nevertheless it cannot be convincingly denied that his subjective impressionism led to a confusion between the critical and creative processes which involved him in falsifications of history and contributed to the distortion of his theory in Oscar Wilde's *The Critic as Artist.*[14] At times this subjectivity reduces criticism to Anatole France's oft-quoted definition: "the adventures of a sensitive soul among masterpieces." (But though there are resemblances between Pater and France, the English writer is less profoundly sensual and has austere depths beneath his suave and polished surface.)[15] In some of the studies in *The Renaissance,* notably that on Leonardo da Vinci, the method is that of the *Imaginary Portraits,* and this method betrayed Pater into misinterpretations of evidence even in the *Plato and Platonism,* a work of his latest years.[16]

But from the beginning he advocated, though he did not always follow, another conception of the aesthetic function—to discover and analyze each particular manifestation of beauty, the "active principle" of the mind of each individual artist. This quest of the "formula" (which he may have learned from Baudelaire's criticism) led him, for example, to construct his essays on Leonardo and Sir Thomas Browne around the word "curiosity," the study of Wordsworth on the importance of contemplation in the conduct of life, the essay on Lamb on his subject's dainty epicureanism, and so forth. Of the suggestiveness of the method there can be no question, but every resultant portrait is to some degree distorted and "imaginary," and when we note that in each case the quality selected for emphasis is one possessed by Pater himself, we find it difficult to refute the charge that his subjects are projections of his own personality.

*Marius the Epicurean* and the unfinished *Gaston de Latour* are projections of Pater's inner life into other epochs, transitional as was his own. The former book, a body of doctrine rather than a novel,[17] was undertaken to clarify, or rather to modify, the "dangerously" misleading Cyrenaicism of the *Conclusion* to *The Renaissance.*[18] Though it is admitted that "the

---

[13] Contrasts rather than resemblances are brought out in T. S. Eliot, "Arnold and Pater," *Selected Essays* (1932), pp. 346-357.

[14] The meditation on the Mona Lisa, which carries to its zenith the romantic cult of the *femme fatale,* Wilde described as "criticism of the highest kind. It treats the work of art simply as a starting point for a new creation." The beholder "lends the beautiful thing its myriad meanings." See E. J. Bock, *Walter Paters Einfluss auf Oscar Wilde* (Bonn, 1913).

[15] See Irving Babbitt, *Masters of Modern French Criticism* (1912), p. 322.

[16] A special kind of unwarranted manipulation of literary material is exposed in S. C. Chew, "Pater's Quotations," *Nation* (N. Y.), xcix (1914). 404-405.

[17] Ed. Sir J. C. Squire (2v, 1929); Joseph Sagmaster (1935). For what can be said of *Marius* as fiction, as of Pater's related minor works, see Baker, ix (1938). 209-213. See also Louise Rosenblatt, "*Marius l'Epicurien* de Walter Pater et ses points de départ français," *RLC,* xv (1935). 97-106.

[18] The *Conclusion* was suppressed in the second edition, to reappear, with the addition of one quiet but all-important concessive clause, in the third edition, where there is a footnote directing the reader's attention to *Marius.*

burden of positive moral obligation" rested lightly upon Marius, Pater fashioned of "the New Cyrenaicism" a philosophy not of pleasure but of "fullness of life" which embraced, or might embrace, disinterested activity, kindness, compassion, and self-sacrifice. Passing from his ancestral religion through stages of Epicureanism and Stoicism, Marius is brought to the threshold of Christianity and in the end meets a death approximating to martyrdom. But the picture drawn of the Church in the age of the Antonines is as false to history as is Pater's delineation of Sparta in *Plato and Platonism*. In *The Renaissance* he had implied a valuation of all religions for their beauty, strangeness, and passion, and in *Marius* a lively sympathy with ecclesiastical tradition and a delight in the aesthetic charm of ritual are all that are offered as a substitute for faith. There is a report that towards the end of his life Pater was contemplating the resumption of a youthful intention to take holy orders. It is as well for his reputation that he did not do so, for he remained always a fastidious pragmatist.[19] It is not surprising that in the minds of young men who sought in *Marius* not fiction but a rule of life the evolution of Marius towards Christianity went unnoticed while the cult of Beauty gained new adherents. Nor is it without significance that Pater, dissatisfied, abandoned work on *Gaston* in which he had made a further effort to reconcile "the exigence of his sensibility with the needs of his conscience." [20]

Notwithstanding the subtlety and austerity of his thought, the impression *Style* will not down that in Pater's writings the manner is more important than the matter. In the infinitely patient discrimination of his own impressions, the elaborate artistry displayed in the precise expression of every shade of idea and sentiment with a constant introduction of hair-splitting qualifications seems often to be undertaken as much for the sake of the musical cadence of the sentences as for the ideas expounded in them. To most readers the verbal virtuoso appears more memorable than the humanist. In the judgment of the greatest of his disciples (and the adjective is employed relatively, for Pater influenced no mind of absolutely first rank), he was "all-powerful in written word, impotent in life." [21]

## II

Not the greatest but certainly the most famous of the followers of Walter *Oscar* Pater was Oscar Wilde [22] (1856-1900). The story of his rise to the dizzy *Wilde*

[19] Compare James Huneker, *The Pathos of Distance* (1913), p. 280: "In the Aristippean flux and reflux of his ideas we discern a strong family likeness to the theories of William James and Henri Bergson, a pragmatism poetically transfigured."

[20] A. J. Farmer, *Le mouvement esthétique*, p. 64.

[21] George Moore, *Avowals* (1919), p. 215.

[22] *Works* (14v, 1908); *Complete Works* (4v, Paris, 1936); *Selected Works*, ed. Richard Aldington (1946). — Frances Winwar, *Oscar Wilde and the Yellow 'Nineties* (1940), with bibliography; Lord Alfred Douglas, *My Friendship with Oscar Wilde* (1932), an *apologia*, notwithstanding the same writer's *Without Apology* (1938); Frank Harris, *Oscar Wilde: His Life and Confessions* (2v, 1918), to be used with caution; R. H. Sherard, *Life of Oscar Wilde* (1906; 1928) and *The Real Oscar Wilde* (1917), by a loyal friend; W. W. Kenilworth,

summit of fame and of his catastrophic fall will be remembered when oblivion, the penalty for their fundamental insincerity, overtakes most of his writings. To the historian he is already the symbol of a period.

Inheriting artistic tastes from his clever mother, Wilde came to Oxford in 1874. There he attended Ruskin's lectures and, while differing radically on the question of the function of art in society, he caught from the master a sympathy with the poor and outcast that helps explain his views on Socialism. But a stronger influence was that of Pater whose favorite disciple he became. Adopting a pose of extravagant aestheticism, he dressed exotically, paraded his love of "blue china" and other objects of virtu, and discoursed upon the complete indifference of art to morality or to anything save itself. Having won the Newdigate prize with *Ravenna* (1878), a negligible piece of Swinburnian pastiche, he left Oxford in 1878, traveled in Greece, and by 1881 had achieved in London sufficient celebrity to give point to Gilbert and Sullivan's *Patience* and to a long series of satiric thrusts by Du Maurier in *Punch*. Only popular curiosity about Wilde can account for the success of *Poems* (1881) which went through five editions within the year. The poems are imitations of Rossetti and Swinburne discordantly juxtaposed to borrowings from Milton, Wordsworth, Tennyson, and Arnold. The sympathy expressed at once with radicalism and Catholicism is specious, and the adaptation of so many styles and moods to the purposes of artifice reveals at once Wilde's facility and his want of truth. From the first he was a literary opportunist.[23]

A lecture-tour of the United States [24] (1882) during which Wilde carried the gospel of aestheticism to the Philistines was followed by several comparatively barren years of less eccentricity but probably not less depravity. He edited *The Woman's World,* published essays, including *The Decay of Lying* and *The Critic as Artist* which elaborated his theory of the complete indifference of art to subject-matter, and then, somewhat unexpectedly, *The Happy Prince and Other Tales* (1888), a collection of graceful fairy stories with wittily satiric allusions to contemporary topics and (in some of them) an expression of his humanitarian sentiments and sympathy with the sufferings of the poor. It is in the light of this latter motive that must be read the more pretentious essay, *The Soul of Man under Socialism* (1891), in which are ideas borrowed from Morris and G. B. Shaw and which indicates that Wilde's way of life was in part at least due to dissatisfaction with the contemporary state of society. *Lord Arthur Savile's Crime and Other Stories,*

Poems

A *Study of Oscar Wilde* (1912); Arthur Ransome, *Oscar Wilde, a Critical Study* (1912); O. T. Hopkins, *Oscar Wilde, a Study of the Man and His Work* (1916); Arthur Symons, *A Study of Oscar Wilde* (1930); G. J. Renier, *Oscar Wilde* (1933); Vincent O'Sullivan, *Aspects of Wilde* (1936); Boris Brasol, *Oscar Wilde, the Man, Artist, and Martyr* (1938); Hesketh Pearson, *Oscar Wilde, His Life and Wit* (1946). — On the background of the period see Holbrook Jackson, *The Eighteen Nineties* (1913); Richard Le Gallienne, *The Romantic Nineties* (1925); Thomas Beer, *The Mauve Decade* (1926); Joseph and E. R. Pennell, *The Life of James McNeill Whistler* (1908); Sir William Rothenstein, *Men and Memories* (2v, 1931-1932); W. B. Yeats, *The Trembling of the Veil* (1916).
23 See further B. I. Evans, *English Poetry in the Later Nineteenth Century* (1933), ch. XIV.
24 Lloyd Lewis and H. J. Smith, *Oscar Wilde Discovers America* (1936).

*Intentions* (a collection of essays chiefly memorable for the further develop-ment of the implications underlying his theory of the uselessness of art), and *The Duchess of Padua,* a tragedy in verse, all followed in 1891; and in the same year came *The Picture of Dorian Gray,* a novel which is the most typical product of the "Decadence." The "unwholesome" overtones audible in this book and in the earlier *Portrait of Mr. W. H.* (a theory of Shake-speare's Sonnets couched in the form of fiction) increased Wilde's notoriety.

A series of successful comedies now carried Wilde to the zenith of his *Plays* career. *Lady Windermere's Fan* (produced 1892; published 1893), *A Woman of No Importance* (1893; 1894), and *The Ideal Husband* (1895; 1899) have much in common with one another. The presence of a "problem" shows that Wilde, always the opportunist, was conscious of the influence of Ibsen, probably through the medium of Pinero's plays; but the substance is thin and out of accord with the coruscating epigrams and paradoxes. In 1893 a license was refused ˙for the performance of *Salomé.* It was written in French [25] and was produced in Paris by Sarah Bernhardt in 1894. To that year belongs *The Sphinx,* a revery upon the lusts of ancient times closing upon the note of renunciation and acceptance of religion which is sug-gestive of Joris-Karl Huysmans and very typical of the eighteen-nineties.[26] In 1895 came Wilde's masterpiece of comedy, *The Importance of Being Earnest,* in which, for once, he achieved a perfect combination of theme and style in airily insolent and witty paradox.

This play and *The Ideal Husband* were both running at London theatres when Wilde's world crashed round him. The Marquis of Queensberry (the father of Lord Alfred Douglas) accused him of homosexual practices. Wilde brought suit for libel; lost it; was at once arrested and put on trial; and having been convicted was sentenced to two years' imprisonment. Before his release in 1897 he had written *De Profundis,*[27] an *apologia* that is an expres-sion of self-pity and wounded pride rather than of contrition. Even in the depths of mortification he found satisfaction in his pose. *The Ballad of Reading Gaol* (1898), written, as Wilde's letters show, under the impulse of intense emotion, is moving in its expression of sympathy with outcasts from society; but the rhetorical exaggeration and the inappropriate echoes from other poets smack of artifice, and the basic theme, that "all men kill the thing they love," is an absurd generalization from Wilde's personal ex-perience. Two years followed of squalid life in exile upon the Continent from which he was relieved by death in Paris in 1900. Upon his grave Jacob Epstein's gigantic sphinx presses down.

---

[25] The English version was made by Lord Alfred Douglas (1870-1945). Douglas's original verse of later years has had its admirers. His best work is in the sonnet form. *Complete Poems* (1928). See W. Sorley Brown, *Lord Alfred Douglas: The Man and the Poet* (1918); Patrick Braybrook, *Lord Alfred Douglas: His Life and Work* (1931).

[26] Even the stanzaic form betrays the insincerity and artifice of this poem. The interior rimes were commended for their ingenuity; but the stanza is simply that of *In Memoriam* printed as two long lines instead of four short lines. — Another poem of this period is *The Harlot's House,* a rhetorical but not unimpressive allegory of the degeneration of love.

[27] Published posthumously, with excisions, in 1905; complete text, 1949.

Wilde struck in various directions, but not at random, against contemporary standards of taste and morality, and more fundamentally at contemporary society.[28] In his social criticism he was probably as sincere as it was in his nature to be; but one feels that he desired a free society rather for the sake of the freedom it would give him than for the general good. His "Socialism," like his aestheticism, was a rationalization of his own sensual impulses. The real Wilde, so far as he is discoverable at all, is to be found not in *De Profundis* but in *The Picture of Dorian Gray*. The analysis of the search for rare sensations clarifies the logical consequences of the acceptance of Pater's doctrines without the moralistic concessions which Pater had suggested; and in so far as the novel is an apologue of divided personality it is prophetic of the ruin into which its author was soon to fall.

## III

The
Yellow
Book

Though the most conspicuous figure of the "mauve decade," Wilde was not the leader of the group of writers and artists who formed the "Rhymers' Club," published jointly slim volumes of verse, and in 1894 were associated together in John Lane's quarterly, *The Yellow Book*.[29] The real leader of the "Decadence" was the artist Aubrey Beardsley[30] (1872-1898) whose drawings of exquisite, sinuous line and startling contrasts of light and shade quintessentialize in their morbidity and perversity the audacities of the movement. As art-editor of *The Yellow Book* Beardsley coöperated with Henry Harland (1861-1905), the literary editor, afterwards author of *The Cardinal's Snuff-Box* (1900) and other short novels notable for a dainty wit that does not conceal their lack of substance. John Lane, the publisher, anxious not to offend, included among his contributors Henry James, Richard Garnett, Edmund Gosse, and other writers, and Leighton and other artists; and the respectable tone given by them to the quarterly was intended to offset the impression made by the more troubling minority. Even so, the tone set by Beardsley's drawings was dominant and after several numbers had appeared during 1894-1895, William Watson, according to the well-known story, issued an ultimatum to Lane that either Beardsley's work must be suppressed or else he, Watson, would sever his connection with the periodical. As a consequence Beardsley left *The Yellow Book* (which with dwindling brilliance continued for another two years) and launched

The
Savoy

*The Savoy* (1896) with Arthur Symons as editor. Among its contributors

[28] See Granville Hicks, *Figures of Transition* (1939), ch. VI.

[29] One of the contributors to *The Yellow Book* was Frederick William Rolfe (1860-1913) who called himself "Baron Corvo." An isolated figure, shabby and sinister, Rolfe was utterly *fin de siècle*. "Caviare to the general" best describes his work, but, as D. H. Lawrence said, "if caviare, at any rate it came from the belly of a live fish." Six *Stories Toto Told Me* (1898), published in *The Yellow Book*, were expanded as *In His Own Image* (1900; ed. Shane Leslie, 1925). *Chronicles of the House of Borgia* (1901) is a learned, highly colored, and extravagant history. Rolfe is best remembered for *Hadrian the Seventh* (1904), a romance heavily charged with autobiography, and a "compensation" for the writer's failures and disrepute. *Don Tarquinio* (1905) and later books are of less interest. — See A. J. A. Symons, *The Quest for Corvo* (1934).

[30] H. Macfall, *Aubrey Beardsley, the Man and his Work* (1928).

were G. B. Shaw, Max Beerbohm, W. B. Yeats, Ernest Dowson, and the artists Charles Conder and William Rothenstein. *The Savoy* was decidedly more "advanced" than its predecessor, in fact so far ahead or to one side of the public taste that after running for a year it failed for lack of support. Wilde's downfall had discredited aestheticism; and with England rapidly approaching a crisis in her old quarrel with the Boers the strident voices of the imperialists drowned out the delicate music of decadent literature.

The exquisite grace and urbane artificiality of decadent prose at its best is seen in the essays of Max Beerbohm [31] (1872-1956). More characteristic, however, is the work in verse and prose of Arthur Symons [32] (1865-1945). *Arthur* In his poetry there is a remoteness from contemporary society that expresses *Symons* the point of view of the entire group of "Decadents." The substitution of suggestion for statement; the effects of "correspondences" of words and music and color; the dim sadness and misty unwholesomeness; the profound sensuality; and the reliance upon symbols—these are characteristics which Symons shares with his French masters, Verlaine and Mallarmé. His critical study, *The Symbolist Movement in Literature* (1899), though inadequate from the historian's point of view, is of historical importance as a sort of belated manifesto. Richard Le Gallienne (1866-1947), though ranging more widely and vigorously than most of the writers considered in this chapter, displays *fin de siècle* traits in much of his work. The two series of *Prose Fancies* (1894-1896) are typical of the time and the man. The many essays and impressionistic sketches cannot be enumerated here. The novels, which do not fall into any simple category, are, like Le Gallienne's verse, mostly forgotten, though *The Quest of the Golden Girl* (1896) still has the interest of a period-piece.

Many writers on the periphery of the "Decadence" will be considered *Ernest* later. We may conclude this chapter with the typical figure of Ernest Dow- *Dowson* son [33] (1867-1900). His febrile, sordid and lonely, pathetic and tragically short life was in strictest harmony with *fin de siècle* aestheticism. Influences from Swinburne, Verlaine, Catullus, and Propertius are intertwined in his poetry with others from the Catholic liturgy and hymnology. An exquisite technician within a narrow range, he sang of chaste and tender love, of uncontrolled passion resulting in remorse, of renunciation of the world, and of the fleetingness of mortality. His prose is of little moment and his play,

---

[31] *Works* (1896); *More* (1889); *And Even Now* (1920); and other volumes of essays; and in fiction: *The Happy Hypocrite* (1897) and *Zuleika Dobson* (1911). Sir Max Beerbohm was the most brilliant caricaturist of his time. The student of literature must know his two volumes, *The Poet's Corner* (1904) and *Rossetti and His Circle* (1922).

[32] *London Nights* (1895); *Images of Good and Evil* (1899); *Poems* (2v, 1902), a severely sifted collected edition; and later volumes. In prose, besides impressionistic studies of men and places, Symons wrote more elaborately on Blake, Hardy, Rossetti, Swinburne, and the Elizabethan dramatists. — See his autobiographical *Confessions* (1930) and T. E. Welby, *Arthur Symons, a Critical Study* (1925).

[33] Contributions to *The Book of the Rhymers' Club* (1892) and their *Second Book* (1894); *Verses* (1896); *Decorations* (1899); *Poetical Works*, ed. Desmond Flower (1934); *Stories*, ed. Mark Longaker (Philadelphia, 1947). The most extended study is Mark Longaker, *Ernest Dowson* (Philadelphia, 1944).

*The Pierrot of the Minute* (1897), a slight thing; but the best poems in *Verses* (1896)—such poems as *Nuns of the Perpetual Adoration, Amor Umbratilis,* and the famous *Non sum qualis eram bonae sub regno Cynarae* —possess a quality of permanence because of their sincerity of passion and their individuality of style that sets them apart from the ephemeral sensualities and sadnesses of the other "Decadents."

# XXXVI
## The Novel: Naturalism and Romance

### I

To include Samuel Butler among the novelists is perhaps to suggest a *Samuel* false emphasis, since this man of versatile talents wrote but one novel; but *Butler* *The Way of All Flesh* is substantial enough to validate the claim, and the element of fiction is considerable in three of his other books.

Samuel Butler [1] (1835-1902) was the son of a clergyman and grandson of Bishop Samuel Butler whose biography he wrote (1902). In boyhood he suffered from the extremes to which parental control was then generally carried, and in *The Way of All Flesh* he later took vengeance upon his father.[2] The gradual process of escape from the strict educational discipline and sanctimonious priggishness imposed upon him is narrated ironically but with scarcely any embroidery upon the facts. Butler was destined for the ministry, but after graduation from Cambridge religious doubts led to the abandonment of an intention that had been his family's rather than his own. In 1859 he emigrated to New Zealand [3] where he accumulated a small fortune through sheep-farming. Here began the friendship with C. P. Pauli which was to cost him much money and more pain, for, by an arch-irony, Butler, the ironist, was hoodwinked by this handsome, fascinating man who sponged shamelessly upon his benefactor. The relationship is central to an understanding of Butler's character. He could satirize his father and family, his enemies and some of his friends; but the wound made by Pauli's unfaithfulness was too deep to be cauterized by satire.

An interest roused by *The Origin of Species* was expressed in articles con-

---

[1] *Works*, Shrewsbury Edition, ed. H. F. Jones and A. T. Bartholomew (20v, 1923-1926); *Erewhon*, ed. Aldous Huxley (1934); *The Way of All Flesh*, ed. G. B. Shaw (World's Classics, 1936). — A. J. Hoppé, *Bibliography* (1925); H. Festing Jones, *Samuel Butler, a Memoir* (2v, 1919); Gilbert Cannan, *Samuel Butler, a Critical Study* (1915); J. F. Harris, *Samuel Butler, the Man and His Work* (1916); C. E. M. Joad, *Samuel Butler* (1924); Mrs. R. S. Garnett, *Samuel Butler and His Family Relations* (1929); C. G. Stillman, *Samuel Butler: A Mid-Victorian Modern* (1932); J. B. Fort, *Samuel Butler. Etude d'un caractère et d'une intelligence* (Bordeaux, 1924) and *Samuel Butler. Etude d'un style* (Bordeaux, 1925); R. F. Rattray, *Samuel Butler, a Chronicle and an Introduction* (1935); Malcolm Muggeridge, *The Earnest Atheist: A Study of Samuel Butler* (1936); Madeleine L. Cazamian, *Le Roman et les idées en Angleterre*, 1 (Strassburg, 1923), ch. III; Baker, x. 244-270.

[2] The letters from Theobald Pontifex to Ernest are almost exact transcripts from the letters of Canon Butler to his son.

[3] Butler's letters home were put together by his father as *A Year in Canterbury Settlement* (1863). — See Donald Cowie, "Samuel Butler in New Zealand," *London Mercury*, xxxv (1937). 480-488.

tributed to a New Zealand newspaper.[4] Here began Butler's speculations upon evolution. After his return to England in 1864 he devoted himself to painting, exhibiting regularly at the Royal Academy between 1868 and 1876.[5] At art school he met Eliza M. A. Savage, a clever spinster of homely appearance and tart disposition with whom he corresponded for many years.[6] Quantities of her witty observations he borrowed for his own books. Art did not distract him from the problems of religion and science. In *The Evidence for the Resurrection of Jesus Christ* (privately printed, 1865) he subjected the Gospel narratives to an ironical analysis. This pamphlet was afterwards incorporated in *The Fair Haven* (1873) with the pretense that it had been written by a certain John Pickard Owen, lately deceased, whose biography, purporting to be written by a surviving brother, serves as an introduction. In this ruthlessly clever skit the irony is maintained with such quiet skill that more than one Evangelical reviewer was misled into commending *The Fair Haven* as a serious defense of Christian doctrine.

**Erewhon**     Meanwhile Butler had published *Erewhon, or Over the Range* (1872), his only book to win fame among his contemporaries. Mr. Higgs, the hero (if he may be so called), traverses the mountains of New Zealand and finds himself in a hitherto undiscovered country among strange people. Butler's imaginary commonwealth is not an ideal state, though some of its characteristics—gracious living, prosperity, physical health—reflect Butler's ideal. But in other respects—the worship of the goddess Ydgrun ("Mrs. Grundy," i.e., respectability) and the institution of the Musical Banks (conventional religion based upon pharisaic smugness)—the story is a satiric and ironic mirror of English society, resembling parts of *Gulliver's Travels* but described with a cool amusement in which there is nothing of Swift's *saeva indignatio*. Fallacies are exposed by means of ingenious paradox, and with infinite cleverness cogent reasoning is conducted from designedly unsound premises. The theory that machines are extensions of human organs is a parody of popular Darwinism but not without tragic implications for the future of mankind. Butler's modernity is also evinced in his doctrines of the rectifiability of moral error and the criminality of disease as an offense against the race.

On a visit to Canada in 1875 Butler composed a little masterpiece in verse, *A Psalm of Montreal,* in which the contrast between the virile beauty of the neglected Discobolus and the repulsive drabness of the taxidermist symbolizes the contrast between pagan grace and nineteenth-century respectability.

*Evolution*     During the following decade much of his energy went into the exposition of his biological theories in a series of volumes: *Life and Habit* (1877), *Evolution, Old and New* (1879), *Unconscious Memory* (1880), and *Luck or*

---

[4] *The Press,* Christchurch. *Darwin among the Machines* was afterwards incorporated in *Erewhon. Darwin on the Origin of Species, a Philosophical Dialogue* (1862) was reprinted at Christchurch in 1912.
[5] Butler's best-known painting, "Mr. Heatherley's Holiday," is now in the National Gallery of British Art. His "Family Prayers" recalls the atmosphere of Ernest Pontifex's boyhood.
[6] *Letters between Samuel Butler and Miss E. M. A. Savage* (1935).

*Cunning?* (1887).[7] Butler was at first not unsympathetic with Darwin and had been in personal touch with him in 1872. It is needless to retell the story of their quarrel. [8] Apart from the personal disagreement involved, Butler deceived himself in believing that the professional scientists had organized "a conspiracy of silence" against him. Patient experimenters are justified in ignoring the guesswork of a brilliant amateur. It helped Butler's fame immensely that the progress of research brought evolutionary doctrine in some particulars into harmony with his theories; but the same position would have been reached had he never lived. As an amateur he accepted the data collected by the professionals; but questioning their lines of reasoning and their conclusions, he repudiated the purposelessness inherent in Darwin's theory, and in place of "small fortuitous variations" he argued for purposive evolution. Without altogether eliminating the part played by "luck" in the evolutionary process, he held that needs, intelligence, and memory are implied in any acceptable theory. There is a deliberate intention in the individual cell which so acts upon its chance environment as best to serve its own ends. Butler thus restored, with a difference, the teleological argument of the pre-Darwinian evolutionists. Moreover, he found evidence of an unconscious racial memory in which serviceable habits are stored up. This memory asserts itself through the "identity" of parents and offspring. From this he deduced the doctrine of "vicarious immortality" which is the subject of the sermon in *Erewhon Revisited* and of the sonnet *Not on Sad Stygian Shore,* and also the doctrine of "the omnipresence of mind and intelligence throughout the universe to which no name can be so fittingly applied as God." [9]

The shaping influence of inherited habits is illustrated in the long account of Ernest Pontifex's ancestors which opens *The Way of All Flesh* so unpromisingly. This largely autobiographical novel was written between 1873 and 1885.[10] Butler himself appears in two characters, the hero and the hero's counselor and friend. He put into the book his parents, Pauli, Miss Savage, and other people he had known. Irony is employed for a serious and legitimate purpose, and though the candor is unreticent and unrelenting there is a sincere effort to avoid exaggeration. Realism is made a vehicle for a philosophy of wordly wisdom, the advocacy of a *via media* that is not golden but commonplace, with a recognition of the world's frauds and fallacies and with a confidence reposing upon sound physical health, the practice of the "comely virtues," and the possession of a sufficient income. The satiric picture of family life in mid-Victorian England is so vivid that the story

The Way of All Flesh

---

[7] See also parts of *God the Known and God the Unknown,* a series of articles in *The Examiner* (1879); in book form posthumously (1909). Many of the memoranda posthumously published in *The Note-Books* (1912) have to do with the subject of evolution.

[8] The conclusion reached by impartial inquiry is that Butler, not having been informed of the accident whereby Darwin cut out of the proofs of the preface to Krause's volume on evolution his acknowledgement of the use of Butler's *Life and Habit,* was justified in believing that a slight was intended. Much bad feeling might have been avoided if Darwin had followed his family's advice to offer an explanation instead of Huxley's, that Butler be ignored.

[9] H. Festing Jones, *Samuel Butler,* II. 41.

[10] Published posthumously, 1903.

is a document as well as an indictment. With all its wit and wisdom *The Way of All Flesh* is a sad and bitter book. Satire was the cloak with which Butler covered a brooding, suspicious, and disappointed nature.

*Italy; Handel; Homer*

Yet he had his compensations, chief among them Italy and the music of Handel. The fruit of many visits to the land he loved are the two travel books, *Alps and Sanctuaries* (1881) and *Ex-Voto* (1888), in which he recounted his wanderings in Piedmont and his appreciation of the votive chapels on the Sacro Monte at Varallo. The composition of an oratorio, *Ulysses,* in imitation of Handel, turned his thoughts to Homeric problems. After a visit to Asia Minor he evolved the theory that the *Iliad* was written by a Greek of the Troad secretly in sympathy with the Trojans. But he was convinced that the *Odyssey* had been written at Trapani in Sicily and by a woman. Upon *The Authoress of the Odyssey* (1897) he wasted elaborate pains. Butler's reputation as an ironist led many to take this for a hoax, but he was as serious as he was perverse, and the annoyance of the bigwigs of scholarship was merely a by-product of his work.[11] An equal amount of energy was expended upon *Shakespeare's Sonnets Reconsidered* (1899) in exposition of a theory that has not even the merit of being original. In his later years he spent much time arranging and docketing his correspondence and other papers against the day when a biography might be called for.

*Erewhon Revisited* (1901) is as closely related to *The Fair Haven* as to the original *Erewhon,* for, occupying his mind with the problem of the origins of religious beliefs, Butler hit upon the notion that the escape of Mr. Higgs had been interpreted by the Erewhonians as a miracle, had taken on legendary accretions, and had given rise to "Sunchildism," a new religion. The story, written with much spontaneity, is the most artistic of Butler's creations; there is pathos and gentleness in it as well as wit and humor; but these qualities do not conceal the fierceness of the caricature of revealed religion. George Bernard Shaw, who had a hand in its publication, did much to enhance Butler's posthumous fame, declaring that he was, in his own special department of satire, the greatest English author of the second half of the nineteenth century.

## II

*William Hale White*

If the semi-autobiographical novels of William Hale White (1831-1913), who wrote under the pen-name of "Mark Rutherford," [12] are kept in remembrance, it will be rather as documents in the history of certain phases of Victorian thought than as works of imaginative literature. A few short

---

[11] B. Farrington, *Samuel Butler and the Odyssey* (1939). — Butler published translations of the *Iliad* (1898) and the *Odyssey* (1900), rendering the Greek into what he called "Tottenham Court Road English." See also his pleasant lecture, *The Humor of Homer* (1892).

[12] The three series of "Mark Rutherford's" *Pages from a Journal* (1900; 1910; 1915) are important supplements to his novels. — Sir W. R. Nicoll, *Introduction to the Novels of Mark Rutherford* (1924); H. W. Massingham, "Memorial Introduction" to *The Autobiography of Mark Rutherford* (ed. 1923); A. E. Taylor, "The Novels of Mark Rutherford," *E&S,* v (1914). 51-74; Baker, ix (1938). 97-115.

stories apart, White showed in his loosely woven, inconsequential books little evidence of structural capacity. He pictures with sympathy rather than disgust the nonconformist world of small shopkeepers and laborers who live in the borderland between indigence and ignoble decency. His special province is that of the religious-minded fundamentalists who are shaken in their faith by the new ideas of science and the new criticism of the Bible. Much of White's own experience went into *The Autobiography of Mark Rutherford* (1881) and *Mark Rutherford's Deliverance* (1885), the former dealing with his emancipation from Calvinism, the latter with the nether world of London. *The Revolution in Tanner's Lane* (1887), set in the period of industrial unrest following Waterloo, tells of the emancipation of a mind brought up in nonconformity and obtaining glimpses in the poetry of Wordsworth and Byron of a larger world of thought and emotion. Characteristic of White as of his time is the close association of religious doubt with sociological discussion and social reform. He had little humor but commanded a quiet kind of satire.

Immediately contemporary with White's narratives of the doubts and deliverance of Rutherford is *The Story of an African Farm* (1883) by Olive Schreiner [13] (1855-1920). Because of its passionate intensity and also because of the relationship of the two principal characters by affinity of temperament this story reminded its first readers of *Wuthering Heights*; but though the descriptions of the African veldt are not altogether unworthy of comparison with Emily Brontë's descriptions of the Yorkshire moors, the story does not really bear comparison with that masterpiece. The clumsy narrative concerns the efforts of certain sensitive souls to find a philosophy of life after abandoning the religion of childhood. The characterization of the heroine is one of the earliest expressions of the "new" femininism which was to gain ground during the last years of the century. *Olive Schreiner*

The conflict of faith and doubt is the motive running through the novels of Mrs. Humphry Ward (1851-1920). *Robert Elsmere* (1888), which made a great stir and troubled Mr. Gladstone, is the story of a clergyman in whom skepticism triumphs over faith with a consequent estrangement from his wife. Mrs. Ward, who was a niece of Matthew Arnold, reflected in her books the controversial issues of her youth long after the world had passed them by. Consequently her later novels seemed to be "dated" even at the time of their appearance. Today they are chiefly interesting for their recognizable portraits of actual people. *Mrs. Humphry Ward*

An unceasing attention to religious problems connects these writers with Joseph Henry Shorthouse [14] (1834-1903), though in his case the problem is that of reconciling mystical insight with orthodoxy and Roman Catholicism *Shorthouse*

[13] S. C. Cronwright, *The Life of Olive Schreiner* (1924).
[14] *Life, Letters and Literary Remains*, ed. Sarah Shorthouse (2v, 1905); M. Polak, *The Historical, Philosophical and Religious Aspects of John Inglesant* (1934); P. E. More, "Shorthouse," *Shelburne Essays*, III (1905). 213-243; W. K. Fleming, "Some Truths about *John Inglesant*," *Quarterly Rev.*, CCXLV (1925). 130-148. — Shorthouse's five other novels are nearly negligible, but *The Countess Eve* is notable for its spiritual feeling and delicate morbidity.

with Anglicanism. In *John Inglesant* (1880) Shorthouse transferred the questions at issue in the Tractarian Movement to an appropriate seventeenth-century setting. The hero, a mystic misled for a time into worldliness, is a courtier of Charles I, comes under the influence of Little Gidding, is present at a Papal consistory, and is in Naples during a visitation of the plague. His private story, which involves an avenging quest of his brother's murderer, is interwoven with public affairs in a panorama of European life which remains impressive even after Shorthouse's inaccuracies have been exposed. With infinite pains Shorthouse put together in a sort of mosaic countless passages from seventeenth-century books, but though no acknowledgment is made, the result is not plagiarism but something highly original. When Pater's *Marius the Epicurean* appeared readers were quick to notice an unlike likeness between the two books.

## III

Gissing

George Gissing [15] (1857-1903) is the most significant figure in the period of transition from the Victorian to the modern novel. Tastes and scholarship fitted him for an academic career; but while a student at Manchester an infatuation with a girl of the streets whom he desired to "rescue" involved him in thefts for which he served a short prison term. Thus his hopes were ruined. On his release he attempted a new start in life in the United States, where he underwent the great hardships afterwards turned to the account of fiction in *New Grub Street*. He sold to the Chicago *Tribune* a few short stories [16] (1877). On his return to England he quixotically married the woman who had been the occasion of his misfortunes. The union was a wretched failure, endured in direst poverty and ending in a separation. Kept from starvation by tutoring and clerical jobs, he wrote a first novel which did not find a publisher and has disappeared. A small legacy carried him over the writing of *Workers in the Dawn* [17] (1880), which was published at his own expense. Though commercially a failure, it attracted the attention of Frederick Harrison, who gave Gissing employment as tutor to his sons and proved a valuable friend. For the next twenty years Gissing published on the average one novel a year, and though he was subjected

[15] There is no collected edition of Gissing's works; some of the novels are out of print. *Letters of George Gissing to Members of his Family,* ed. A. and E. Gissing (1927) is indispensable for want of anything better, but passages in the letters are suppressed with no indication of lacunae and towards the end of the book allusions to "Mrs. Gissing" are deliberately misleading. Other correspondence has been privately printed. *Selections, Autobiographical and Imaginative,* introduction by Virginia Woolf (1929). — A definitive biography is needed. Morley Roberts, *The Private Life of Henry Maitland* (1912), a biography thinly disguised as fiction, must serve till superseded, but it is a disservice to Gissing's memory by one of his oldest friends. Frank Swinnerton, *George Gissing, a Critical Study* (1912); see R. C. McKay, *George Gissing and his Critic Frank Swinnerton* (Philadelphia, 1933). May Yates, *George Gissing, an Appreciation* (Manchester, 1923); Anton Weber, *George Gissing und die Soziale Frage* (Leipzig, 1932); S. V. Gapp, *George Gissing, Classicist* (Philadelphia, 1936); Baker, IX, ch. IV.
[16] Eleven stories are reprinted in *Sins of the Fathers and Other Tales,* ed. Vincent Starrett (Chicago, 1924) and *Brownie,* ed. G. E. Hastings, Vincent Starrett, and T. O. Mabbott (1931).
[17] Ed. Robert Shafer (1935), with introduction and bibliography.

to incessant drudgery, never becoming a popular author and often reduced to despair, he won the esteem of so discriminating a judge as Henry James [18] and the friendship of various men of letters, notably H. G. Wells.[19] After the death of his first wife he repeated the mistake of his youth by making a second ill-fated marriage. With the years of abject poverty behind him, he was able, by practising severest economies, to gratify his scholarly longing to see the lands of classical antiquity, visiting Greece once and Italy three times. From his wanderings in Calabria in 1897 he drew the material for a travel book, *By the Ionian Sea* [20] (1901). Unable to obtain a divorce from his second wife, Gissing in his last years found solace in an irregular union with a French woman of refined tastes with whom he lived in the Pyrenees. The quiet pessimism of his final phase is expressed in *The Private Papers of Henry Ryecroft* (1903), a beautifully composed series of *pensées* which has often, but mistakenly, been taken as autobiographical. Into this book he put many of his ripest, but not all his deepest, thoughts on human experience. Before his death he brought almost to completion *Veranilda*,[21] a historical novel on the struggle of the dying Roman Empire with the Goths. With this he had been occupied for many years, and upon it he lavished an erudition comparable in richness though not in imaginative intensity to that of Flaubert's *Salammbô*. Apart from his novels the tale of his books is rounded out with two inconsiderable collections of short stories [22] and a monograph on Dickens (1898) which illuminates not only the subject but the mind of the critic.[23] Dickens was Gissing's first master and remained a paramount influence upon him.

In Gissing's novels the continuity of English fiction is preserved yet at the same time deflected from its former course by the attraction of French and Russian writers and by the doctrine of *l'art pour l'art*. In his studies of environment he follows Dickens, but he probes deeper and does not gloss over with humor and sentiment the appalling conditions of the life of the poor. Nor does he often offer human kindliness as a compensation or remedy for this state of affairs. It is sometimes said that he cherished the ambition to write an English *Comédie Humaine;* but he lacked Balzac's energy and wide-ranging curiosity and variety of social experience. There *Natur-* is a closer analogy to Zola, the Goncourts, and the French naturalistic move- *alism* ment in general.[24] But Gissing, though his "saturation" in his subject won the commendation of Henry James, did not rely upon "scientific" documentation, and, unlike Zola, he was not involved by his concern with the

[18] Henry James, *Notes on Novelists* (1914), pp. 437-443.
[19] H. G. Wells, *Experiment in Autobiography* (1934), pp. 481-493.
[20] New ed., with introduction by Virginia Woolf (1933).
[21] Posthumous, 1904, with preface by Frederick Harrison.
[22] *Human Odds and Ends* (1898); *The House of Cobwebs* (posthumous, 1906), with a "Survey" of Gissing's work by Thomas Seccombe.
[23] Supplementing this formal study is a series of prefaces written for the never completed Rochester Edition of Dickens' works and gathered together as *Critical Studies of the Works of Charles Dickens*, ed. Temple Scott (1924).
[24] See W. C. Frierson, *L'Influence du naturalisme français sur les romanciers anglais de 1885 à 1900* (Paris, 1925), especially pp. 205-218.

problem of environment in the related problem of heredity. Save perhaps in *Demos* (1886), where he demonstrates the failure of Socialism, and in *Born in Exile* (1892), in which he narrates the efforts of a young man to rise above his own social class, there is little in these novels to remind one of Zola's characteristic stress upon a central theme or thesis. Moreover, though there is a conscientious effort to be "objective," Gissing does not succeed in being impersonal; his own tastes, prejudices, and opinions persistently intrude. Nevertheless the emphasis upon the brutalized poor, upon pestiferous crowds, and upon squalid amorousness is suggestive of Zola, albeit a Zola restrained by English reticences. The connection with Flaubert is more remote, though there are resemblances between *Madame Bovary* and *The Whirlpool* (1897). The Russians Gissing knew in French or German translations; there is something of Turgenev in his outlook, but, save in *Isabel Clarendon* (1886), where the imitation may have been deliberate, little of Dostoëvsky in his art.[25] Basically he remained in the native tradition. Till his later books Gissing was committed to the old "three-decker" Victorian novel, with its elaborate and often melodramatic plot, its crowd of supernumerary characters, its different groups of people, its tendency to argue about them instead of making them self-revealing, and its tidy ending. In his studies in abnormal temperaments he was in advance of his time, but he subjected them to the caprice of old-fashioned intrigue. Yet in his experiments with a purely dramatic method and his attempts, albeit never completely successful, to stand, as an artist, outside his work, he points the way towards a more modern technique.

*Studies in Environment and Psychology*
    The two categories into which these novels (apart from *Veranilda*) fall are suggested by the contrasted aims of the two authors who are principal characters in *New Grub Street* (1891). Biffen's object was to secure "absolute realism in the sphere of the ignobly decent," while Reardon was "a psychological realist for the more cultivated." The keynote of many of the studies in environment is the ignobility of poverty. In some, notably *The Nether World* (1889), the lowest classes of slum life are portrayed with intense realism and from personal experience—but experience, as it were, from the outside, for Gissing, even in the worst days of his youth, was never a part of the life he was compelled to lead and viewed it with a horror and loathing which left no room for any comprehension of the mitigating circumstances of habit and insensitivity that perhaps dull the miseries of the very poor. In other novels he rises to a slightly higher social stratum of suburban or provincial life, but a life still under the burden of a poverty perhaps all the more intolerable because not so degraded. *New Grub Street*, the finest of the novels dealing with the lower middle class, makes use of Gissing's own bitterly familiar acquaintance with the life of writers who, having once aspired to literary renown, have sunk to the ranks of literary hacks. Of the many authors packed into this book one dies of starvation and another commits suicide. Apart from the novels of environment are the

[25] Helen Muchnic, *Dostoëvsky's English Reputation* (Northampton, Mass., 1939).

studies in psychological analysis. Of these the most elaborate is *Thyrza* (1887) in which the character of the heroine, torn between her low-born fiancé and her high-born lover, is portrayed with elaborate, loving, and sentimental care. Here it may be remarked that in almost all his books Gissing's grim realism is softened by the charm and tenderness with which at least one woman in each story is idealized. In *A Life's Morning* (1888), where he evidently imitated *Richard Feverel,* and in *The Crown of Life* (1899) the influence of Meredith is apparent; but Gissing was not fortified with that master's comic spirit and poetry and confidence in life.

Longing for the "retired leisure" of which *Ryecroft* is the dream and compelled to drudge without rest and without hope yet with an artistic conscience that permitted no compromise with the popular taste of the day, Gissing viewed life with humorless disgust. He had no trust in the processes of democracy. He was skeptical of the promises held out by the Socialists. No other writer of the period foresaw more clearly the catastrophe towards which the world was heading and no other prophesied so forcefully and repeatedly the coming of "a time of vast conflicts which will pale into insignificance the thousand wars of old." [26]

Several lesser novelists have points of connection with Gissing. Sir Walter Besant (1836-1901) used fiction in advocacy of social reforms. *All Sorts and Conditions of Men* (1882) portrays life in the East End of London, and later novels expose the miseries of urban labor. In fiction of another sort Besant, who was an authority on the antiquities of London, re-created the life of the metropolis in the eighteenth century. Resembling Gissing in that they wrote novels about the lives of the lowly are Richard Whiteing (1840-1928), author of *No. 5 John Street* (1889), and Arthur Morrison (1863-1945), author of *Tales of Mean Streets* (1894) and *A Child of the Jago* (1896). Israel Zangwill (1864-1926) pictured humble Jewish life in *Children of the Ghetto* (1892) and later stories and plays. Closer to Maupassant in technique but related to Gissing by virtue of his unflinching realism was Leonard Merrick (1864-1938), author of *Conrad in Quest of His Youth* (1903) and other novels much admired by his fellow-craftsmen.[27] The debt to Gissing both in subjects and technique is apparent in the work of several younger novelists whose achievement will be noticed in a later chapter.

## IV

The career of George Moore [28] (1852-1933) seems to be as sinuous and unaccountable as his personality, but for all its diversity it is unified by *George Moore*

[26] *The Private Papers of Henry Ryecroft,* "Winter," XVIII.

[27] See the introductory tributes by H. G. Wells, Maurice Hewlett, and other writers in Merrick's *Works* (12v, 1918-1919).

[28] *Works,* Carra Edition (21v, 1922-1924); Ebury Edition (20v, 1936-1938). There is no complete edition of Moore's works, and so long as his testamentary directions are in force there may not be. He suppressed some of his books altogether and ruled others out of the "canon" without prohibiting their publication. *Letters,* introduction by John Eglinton (1942). — I. A. Williams, *Bibliography* (1921), needing revision and amplification: Joseph Hone, *The Life of*

unfailing signs of his dedication to art. After an undisciplined boyhood at Moore Hall in Ireland, where he learned more from stablemen and book-makers than at school, he went to Paris to study painting, consort with artists and men of letters, and live the *vie de Bohème*. His nature was, he said, as receptive to impressions as a sheet of wax. In the milieu of Médan he assimilated the doctrines of the *roman expérimental*—naturalism and "scientific" impersonality in fiction. But he also absorbed much from Balzac and Flaubert, and in French translation he read Turgenev. Agrarian troubles in Ireland reduced his income and forced him to return to London in 1880. A volume of verses, *Flowers of Passion,* had appeared in 1878 and was fol-lowed by *Pagan Poems* in 1881. These bits of Baudelairian pastiche are pre-cursors of the "decadent" poetry of the eighteen-nineties.

Moore's first phase as a novelist (1883-1894) began with an adherence to strict Zolaesque naturalism and moved towards a freer and sincerer realism upon which the greatest influence was Balzac's. *A Modern Lover* [29] (1883), written with a challenging candor that provoked protests, closely resembles Maupassant's *Bel-Ami* but preceded that story by two years. *A Mummer's Wife* (1884) is naturalistic in its painstakingly detailed portrayal of the life of a squalid troupe of actors. The emphasis upon the forces of heredity and environment derives from Zola, but the narrative of Kate Ede's degradation through drink is suggestive of Flaubert and there is a striking likeness to the work Gissing was doing at just this time. The outcry against *A Mum-mer's Wife* and the prosecution of the publisher of translations of Zola's novels for which Moore was partly responsible occasioned his forceful pamphlet, *Literature at Nurse* (1885), an attack upon the circulating li-braries which by means of financial pressure imposed strait-laced moral standards upon English literature. From the drab seriousness of Kate's story Moore turned, in *A Drama in Muslin* (1886), to a frivolous picture of well-to-do Irish society. Here the new naturalism is strangely crossed with a manner reminiscent of Jane Austen. That Moore had been studying Huysmans is shown by the close parallels in *A Mere Accident* (1887) to *À Rebours*; a more poetic quality now informed a style that had hitherto been as commonplace as the subject-matter. The *Confessions of a Young Man* (1888), which attracted the somewhat condescending attention of Walter Pater who doubtless recognized in it the evidence of his influence,[30] reveals Moore as definitely a precursor along lines that were to lead to the "Decadence." Noteworthy are the sensuality and fastidiousness, the attacks on materialism and Philistinism, and the modish and probably insincere

*George Moore* (1936); John Freeman, *A Portrait of George Moore in a Study of his Work* (1922); Charles Morgan, *Epitaph on George Moore* (1935); A. J. Farmer, *Le Mouvement esthetique et "décadent" en Angleterre* (Paris, 1931), Part I, ch. III; W. C. Frierson, *L'Influence du naturalisme français sur les romanciers anglais* (Paris, 1925), pp. 83-120; Baker, IX, ch. v. For a personal impression of Moore and his opinions by the present writer see *Readings from the American Mercury*, ed. G. C. Knight (1926), pp. 61-81.

[29] Rewritten as *Lewis Seymour and Some Women* (1917) and ultimately ruled out of the "canon."

[30] R. P. Sechler, *George Moore, a Disciple of Walter Pater* (Philadelphia, 1931).

expressions of admiration for the Roman liturgy and for the literature of the late Roman Empire. With the *Confessions* may be grouped *Impressions and Opinions* (1891) and *Modern Painting* (1893), the latter influential in spreading knowledge of the French Impressionists. Passing over a couple of novels and a play, we reach the fine book with which Moore's first phase closed.

This is *Esther Waters* (1894). That the influence of Zola was now no longer paramount is evident from the fact that the cardinal tenet of "scientific" naturalism—the crushing power of heredity and environment over the individual—is disregarded in this history of a girl who struggles against adversity and social prejudice and in the end triumphs. The novel has something in common with *Germinie Lacerteux,* but whereas the lowly heroine of the Goncourts is merely pathetic, Esther possesses courage and strength of character. The resemblance to Hardy's *Tess* is the more striking because of the nearness in dates of publication of the two books; but in Moore's realism there is nothing of Hardy's coloring of romance and no indictment of malignant Fate. The story, which is told with an artistic impersonality so complete that the author's genuine feeling must be read between the lines, is of the seduction of a young girl; her valiant and successful efforts to rear her son to sturdy manhood; and her life with her husband, the race-track bookmaker and public-house keeper. The style is serious, honest, humane, and restrained. There are no digressions into the facetious, the grotesque, or the romantic. The Victorian principle of alternation, with the interest shifting from one group of characters to another, is discarded in favor of a restricted point of view, so that every chapter is mainly about Esther.[31] This technique Moore learned from Flaubert, Turgenev, and Henry James.

The next seven years form a somewhat unfruitful intermediate phase. *Celibates* [32] (1895) is a group of short stories of more or less abnormal and neurotic people. *Evelyn Innes* (1898) and *Sister Teresa* (1901) are really one novel in two parts. Again the point of view is restricted, attention being concentrated upon the aesthetic, emotional, and intellectual life of the heroine. In the analysis of the conflicting claims of the world and of religion the influence of Huysmans has been detected; but there is more of difference than of resemblance. Ultimately Moore came to condemn these books as insincere and ruled them out of the "canon." Whether faked or not, they are undeniably dull and "dated," memorable, if at all, for the appreciations of Wagner's music.

The shock of the Boer War and especially the cruelty of Kitchener's concentration camps alienated Moore from English life and in 1901 he returned to Ireland. During the ten years of his "Irish" phase he associated with Yeats, Synge, Lady Gregory, Edward Martyn, A. E., and other writers who were active in the Irish Literary Renaissance. For a time he was an

*Esther Waters* (margin note)

*Ireland* (margin note)

---

[31] J. W. Beach, *The Twentieth Century Novel* (1932), pp. 135-138.
[32] Revised as *In Single Strictness* (1922) and again as *Celibate Lives* (1927).

enthusiastic supporter of the Abbey Theatre and as enthusiastic an amateur of folk-tales. The story of these years he afterwards told with infinite zest and unscrupulousness in *Hail and Farewell,* manipulating the characters of actual people for the purposes of something that is close to fiction. He had brought to Ireland the ripe experience of a novelist who had at last found himself—or one of his many selves. Trained to observe the human scene and to analyze the human heart, he was able to store up a multitude of impressions to which he gave literary form. *Memoirs of my Dead Life* (1906) looks backward to former times and is largely devoted to amatory episodes which lose nothing in the telling. *The Untilled Field* (1903) is a collection of stories of Irish life, intended for translation into Irish [33] and deeply marked with the impress of Turgenev. The racy idiom may well, as Moore claimed, have influenced Synge's dialogue style. In general the tales are straightforward, but in some there is a suggestive, latent symbolism which shows how sensitive Moore was to contemporary currents in literary theory and practice. Symbolism is again apparent beneath the surface of *The Lake* (1905), in purity of English and clarity of design one of the most beautiful of Moore's books. This story of the escape of a young priest from the "prison-house of Catholicism" is an outgrowth from the earlier analysis of the spiritual misgivings of Evelyn Innes; but its searching into the roots of religious belief indicates the direction in which Moore's thoughts were moving. He described this novel as "an uninterrupted flow of narrative." The author's ideas are never permitted to intrude; and with an art reminiscent of Henry James the action is witnessed entirely from the point of view of Father Gogarty.

In 1911 Moore returned to England. His relations with the Irish writers, his enthusiasm, and his disillusionment form the principal subject of the autobiographical trilogy, *Hail and Farewell* (1911, 1912, 1914) in which wit, malice, perversity, impishness, and insinuation are inextricably intertwined, and fact and fancy so cleverly fused that it is difficult to determine just where truth yields place to something very like mendacity. His former associates (most of whom, not unnaturally, never forgave him) are caricatured in a manner which Moore himself likened to that of Max Beerbohm. There is a keen sense of the comedy of enthusiasm, and even more remarkable is the self-revelation—call it rather self-creation. The zestful and challenging critical ideas point forward to *Avowals* (1919) and *Conversations in Ebury Street* (1924).

**The Brook Kerith** Concurrently with the autobiography Moore began work on *The Brook Kerith* (1916), the germ of which is in *The Apostle* (1911), a drama on the character of Saint Paul. Adopting the rationalistic theory that Jesus did not die on the cross but was taken down by Joseph and secretly nursed back to health, Moore led the story to a tremendous climax when the fanatical missionary Paul comes face to face with the man whose resurrection and divinity he had proclaimed. Moore's prejudices are visible only in his portrayal of the apostles as stupid men; and his unseemly desire to

[33] The versions in Irish appeared (1902) before the English originals.

shock for the sake of shocking is suppressed save in the lubricity of one comic episode. The narrative is conducted without the irony which Anatole France would have employed and with no such complacent delight in exposing a fraudulent fable as Butler exhibited in *The Fair Haven*. The Syrian landscape is beautifully delineated from actual observation, for Moore, who could sacrifice himself for his art if for nothing else, made a toilsome journey to Palestine for the purpose. Serene or lively pastoral incidents fill the background without distracting attention from the theme. The narrative flows smoothly on with no interruption for comment or philosophic digression. The influence of Landor and Pater is apparent and was proudly acknowledged by the author; but he is more humane than Landor and more cosmopolitan than Pater. Everywhere there is the effect, as it were, of the speaking voice.

This method of "oral narrative," deriving from Irish folk-tale and polished by Moore's practice of dictating to a secretary, reached perfection in *Heloïse and Abelard* (1921) in which he re-created the twelfth century as an exotic dream world despite his display of antiquarian detail and philosophic background. A multitude of clerics and scholars, trouvères and gleemen, lords and ladies, monks and nuns move to and fro through perilous woods or flowery fields or beside pleasant rivers or through the streets of Paris and Blois. The landscape often suggests some mural by Puvis de Chavannes, and there are exquisite little genre scenes in the manner of Pater's *Imaginary Portraits*. With perfect judgment Moore brings the story to a close when the lovers, separated forever, are about to begin to write the famous *Letters*. All the pulsing life of the time is seen through the eyes of Heloïse to whom Moore devotes his most sympathetic knowledge of the depths and wanderings of the human heart. The sinuous prose, seemingly artless but the result of numberless revisions, has been likened to that of Morris's romances; but Moore is less luxuriant than Morris and more restrained. The resemblance is closer to Pater.

*Heloïse and Abelard*

The same style, suggestive as ever of the human voice, is heard again in *Ulrick and Soracha* (1926), a tale of medieval Ireland; in *A Story-Teller's Holiday* (1928), a group of Irish stories; and in *Aphrodite in Aulis* (1930), where the manner has become almost a parody of itself. In its intimacy this style is perfectly appropriate to the two volumes of literary dialogues. Various books of earlier date were heavily revised to bring them into conformity with this latest manner. At the time of his death Moore was working upon *A Communication to My Friends,* telling once again the oft-told, much-loved story of his life and opinions.

To peruse in sequence all Moore's books is to receive the impression of an extreme mobility and sensitivity of mind. He led the way along naturalistic and "decadent" lines only to turn from them to new sources of inspiration in Ireland, classical and biblical antiquity, and the Middle Ages. In his earlier work he aimed at a critical interpretation of life (implicit rather than explicit, because his objective method did not permit the intrusion of per-

*Characteristics*

sonal opinion save in the avowedly autobiographical books). With as little dependence as possible upon imagination and with a contempt for the old intrigues of outmoded fiction he presented contemporary people confronted with actual problems. His naturalism was informed with bold candor and clarity of purpose. The psychological insight laboriously attained he afterwards applied to his resuscitations of the life of former ages, for, as he often insisted, human nature has not changed. Often he wasted time and talent upon trivial literary gossip and the satisfaction of that jealousy of distinguished contemporaries which was the worst defect in his character. Often he seemed to be playing upon the mere surface of men and things. He could be insincere and factitious, but he could also be tender and grave and deeply moved and moving. He had at his command a variety of styles, from the robust, straightforward English of *Esther Waters* and the impassioned, poetic prose of *The Lake* to the witty malice of *Hail and Farewell* and the slippered ease of *Avowals*. The famous final manner, with its trailing sentences in which coördinate clauses so rarely make way for the subordinate, has a unique beauty at its best, but it is often languid and it can be tedious. Moore set an example to all artists of absolute devotion to his art. A consciousness of widening experience and increasing expertness and a sense of the contrast between conception and execution led to his unremitting rearrangements and rewritings of his books, and to the peremptory rejection of many of them. His achievement, it has been said, was a series of experiments; and dissatisfaction with anything that fell short of his ideal in style and design was a characteristic of his genius.

## V

*Stevenson*

The tradition of the personal charm of Robert Louis Stevenson [34] (1850-1894) still colors most estimates of his work. It is difficult to deal dispassionately with a man whose life was a ceaseless and gallant search for health. The quest took him from his native Scotland to Switzerland, to southern Europe, to the Far West, to Saranac, and ultimately to the South Seas. He was sustained by the zest of adventure, and from every part of the world that he visited he derived material for his essays. The charm of personality permeates his radiant letters, mingling with impressions of people, places, and books. It is significant that he was an essayist and writer of short stories before he attempted the novel form, and to the end he was more successful in briefer than in more expanded fiction. The record of his

[34] *Works,* Pentland Edition, ed. Edmund Gosse (20v, 1906-1907); Vailima Edition, ed. Lloyd Osbourne and F. Van de G. Stevenson (26v, 1922-1923); *Letters,* ed. Sidney Colvin (2v, 1899). — W. F. Prideaux, *Bibliography* (rev. ed., 1917); Ehrsam, *Bibliographies,* pp. 227-261; Graham Balfour, *The Life of Robert Louis Stevenson* (2v, 1901; new ed., 1912); John A. Steuart, *Robert Louis Stevenson, a Critical Biography* (2v, 1924); L. C. Cornford, *R. L. Stevenson* (1899); Frank Swinnerton, *R. L. Stevenson, a Critical Study* (1914); R. O. Masson, *The Life of Robert Louis Stevenson* (1923); Lloyd Osbourne, *An Intimate Portrait of R. L. S.* (1924); G. S. Hellman, *The True Stevenson: a Study in Clarification* (1925); D. N. Dalglish, *Presbyterian Pirate: a Portrait of Stevenson* (1937); Janet A. Smith, *Robert Louis Stevenson* (1937); Baker, IX. 296-327.

early wanderings on the Continent is in *An Inland Voyage* (1878), about a trip by canoe in Belgium and France, and in *Travels with a Donkey in the Cevennes* (1879). In both there is evident the incipient romancer alert to discern and exploit the picturesque in incident and locale. A first visit to the United States (1879), whither he was drawn by love of the woman whom he married in California, is memorable for his experience of life in a rough mining-camp. Many years later he recalled this pioneer life in *The Silverado Squatters* (1893). On his return to Europe tuberculosis drove him to Davos Plaz. There he composed some of his essays which, with others of earlier date, form *Virginibus Puerisque* (1881), an intimate and self-revelatory book. More critical in tone but still informal and personal is the set of papers entitled *Familiar Studies of Men and Books* (1882). Though he had not yet attracted wide attention, he had published various short stories which were now assembled in *New Arabian Nights* (1882), a collection memorable for the little masterpiece of sinister scene-painting, *The Pavilion on the Links*. Fame and fortune arrived with the publication of *Treasure Island* (1883), a swashbuckling tale of the quest for Captain Kidd's hidden loot, the rivalry of two parties on the search, and the triumph of the hero. This was intended for young readers who, reading it for its adventurous story, were doubtless indifferent to the care with which it was stylized and psychologized.

Encouraged by this success, Stevenson brought out *A Child's Garden of Verses* (1885), followed by *Underwoods* (1887), a second volume of poems, addressed for the most part to readers of maturity. In these years Stevenson collaborated with William Ernest Henley upon a few plays, but both men were without experience in the theatre and they did not achieve success. *Prince Otto* (1885) is a story of ultra-romantic kind, redeemed from being no more than an anticipation of *The Prisoner of Zenda* type of tale by the delicacy of Stevenson's psychological analysis. *Kidnapped* (1886), another tale of adventure, is primarily for a juvenile audience; its sequel, *Catriona*, did not appear till 1893. *Dr. Jekyll and Mr. Hyde* (1886), immediately and lastingly Stevenson's most famous story, is a moral apologue of divided personality. A collection of short stories, *The Merry Men* (1887), included the very powerful tales, *Markheim* and *Thrawn Janet*. While all this work was in progress Stevenson was ceaselessly and unsuccessfully in search of health. During 1887-1888 he lived at Lake Saranac where he wrote *The Master of Ballantrae* (1889) and many essays. His last wanderings were in the Antipodes. From 1890 till his death he lived in Samoa where his feverish energy involved him actively in native politics. He collaborated with his stepson, Lloyd Osbourne, on *The Wrong Box* (1889), *The Wrecker* (1892), and *The Ebb-Tide* (1894). The fragment that remains of *Weir of Hermiston* [35] shows that in the months before his death Stevenson had attained a power

---

[35] Published posthumously, 1896. The central motive is the old one of the father, a judge, who condemns his son to death; but the fragment breaks off before the two great scenes which we know Stevenson had planned—the trial and the subsequent rescue of the hero from prison. — Another fragment, *St. Ives* (1897), was completed by Sir Arthur Quiller-Couch ("Q").

of character analysis and a strength of style beyond the promise of any of his earlier books. His grave, "under the wide and starry sky," is on the summit of a mountain overlooking the Pacific.

*Art and Morality*

Stevenson's work was conditioned on the one side by his theological and ethical heritage and on the other by his literary environment. While, like many of his contemporaries, repudiating the opinion that art has a direct ethical function, he confessed that morality was always his "veiled mistress." It is characteristic of a spirit which along some lines was ready to compromise that he concealed his agnosticism.[36] Yet the Calvinism from which he could not wholly escape forced the intrusion of moral issues into his fiction. The essay form, where the discussion of such issues is appropriate, he practised throughout his life with grace and vigor. It colors not only the short moral apologues but some of the longer works of fiction. He was inclined to blame the restrictions imposed by British reticence for turning him from the novel of real life to romance. It is sometimes said that he would not risk the loss of public approbation by a resolute adoption of the principles of naturalism. But his mastery of horror, his suggestions of supernaturalism, and his pleasure in the ingenuity of his own inventions support the suspicion that, for all his obsession with moral issues and all his awareness of the direction in which the novel was moving, he was a romancer not through compulsion but free choice. He sought to give psychological depth to the characters of romance. This is apparent even in *Treasure Island.* Scott's influence is at its most effective in *Weir of Hermiston,* but in the character of the father-judge Stevenson surpasses all but the greatest of Scott's portraits. Again Scott's influence is discernible in *The Master of Ballantrae* but combined with fantastic and somber motives from other sources and even with overtones that suggest Meredith. The Meredithian influence is even more apparent in *Prince Otto.* Stevenson is often suspected

*Style*

of attitudinizing in style as in personal pose. There is some foundation for both accusations, yet neither is entirely just. What he imitated he made his own, whether it was the elaborate, periodic sentence of Sir Thomas Browne or De Quincey, or the confidential familiarity of Lamb, or the subtle character-analysis of Meredith. He was strongly affected by current discussions of *l'art pour l'art.* He insisted upon skill in handling material, both in the largest structural sense and also in finesse of detail, rather than upon the value of ideas. The extreme labor and sedulous attention to the great masters with which he cultivated his style often resulted in a manner disproportionate in elaborateness to the matter of his books. It is significant that his influence was effective not upon the psychological novelists or the naturalists or the experimenters in new forms of fiction but upon a group of writers of romance.

---

[36] Stevenson's first biographers did his memory a disservice by concealing the fact of his agnosticism. Moreover, the history of his various youthful amatory indiscretions did not become known till long after his death. He was entitled to his own reticences, but the something other than candor of the early biographers has in some recent estimates been transferred to Stevenson himself.

In some of his "regional" stories Stevenson invaded the province of the so-called "Kailyard School." Sir James Barrie's novels have connections with this group. The typical "Kailyarder" was John Watson (1850-1907) who under the pen-name of "Ian Maclaren" wrote *Beside the Bonnie Briar Bush* (1894) and *The Days of Auld Lang Syne* (1895). Their wide contemporary popularity has not proved lasting and today the sentiment seems forced and the regionalism factitious. Stronger, and truer to actualities, is *The House with the Green Shutters* (1901) by George Douglas Brown ("George Douglas," 1869-1902) which was intended in part as a corrective of false notions of Scottish life. S. R. Crockett, who has already been noticed as a regionalist, was a "Kailyarder." *The "Kailyard School"*

Sir Henry Rider Haggard (1856-1925) had an immense following for his ultra-romantic stories, *King Solomon's Mines* (1885), *She* (1887), and *Allan Quatermain* (1887). Less extravagant were the semi-historical romances of Stanley J. Weyman (1855-1928), of which *A Gentleman of France* (1893) is the best. Here belong the adventure stories of Sir Arthur Quiller-Couch, "Q" (1863-1944), of which *The Splendid Spur* (1889) and *The Ship of Stars* (1899) are among the best. Many of these tales have a Cornish background. "Q" was a genial professor, prolific critic, and the most influential anthologist of our day. Sir Arthur Conan Doyle (1859-1930) wrote *The White Company* (1891), *Rodney Stone* (1896), and other romances, some of them based on history, but it is as the creator of the most famous character in all English fiction that he is known to everybody. Sherlock Holmes [37] made his first appearance in *A Study in Scarlet* (1887). Presently millions of readers were watching him applying his "methods" in *The Adventures of Sherlock Holmes* (1892), *The Hound of the Baskervilles* (1902), and other books. The dashing tales of Sir Anthony Hope Hawkins [38] ("Anthony Hope," 1863-1933), *The Prisoner of Zenda* (1894) and *Rupert of Hentzau* (1898), contrast strangely with the witty social sophistication of his *Dolly Dialogues* (1894). Of all the romancers Neil Munro (1864-1930) was nearest to Stevenson. His *John Splendid* (1898) owes much to Scott, but the analysis of character and motive is in Stevenson's manner. The resounding success of these and other purveyors of romance proves that decadent aestheticism and stern naturalism were by no means the only currents in literature at the end of the century. *Romance*

Maurice Hewlett [39] (1861-1923) offered in his early books an unusual

[37] H. W. Bell, *Sherlock Holmes and Dr. Watson* (1932); Vincent Starrett, *The Private Life of Sherlock Holmes* (1933), with bibliography. For the development of the detective story from the days of Poe and of Dickens' Inspector Buckett, through Wilkie Collins and Emile Gaboriau, to Doyle and beyond see H. D. Thomson, *Masters of Mystery: A Study of the Detective Story* (1931); Howard Haycraft, *Murder for Pleasure: The Life and Times of the Detective Story* (1942); F. W. Chandler, *The Literature of Roguery* (2v, 1907), II, ch. XIII; and the introductions to *The Great Detective Stories*, ed. W. H. Wright (1927); *Crime and Detection*, ed. E. M. Wrong (World's Classics, 1926); and *Great Short Stories of Detection, Mystery, and Horror*, ed. Dorothy L. Sayers (1928).

[38] Sir Charles Mallet, *Anthony Hope and His Books* (1936).

[39] *Letters*, ed. Laurence Binyon (1926). Milton Bronner, *Maurice Hewlett* (1910); A. B. Sutherland, *Maurice Hewlett: Historical Romancer* (Philadelphia, 1938); H. W. Graham, "Maurice Hewlett," *Fortnightly Rev.* LXXIV (1925). 47-63.

combination of romance, erudition, artifice, and modernism. *The Forest Lovers* (1898) is a medieval tale avowedly modeled on Malory but too softly voluptuous to remind many readers of its prototype. *Little Novels of Italy* (1899) have some resemblance to Pater's *Imaginary Portraits*. *Richard Yea-and-Nay* (1900) and *The Queen's Quair* (1904) in which something of Meredith's manner and technique are applied to the elucidation of the characters, respectively, of Richard Coeur de Lion and Mary Queen of Scots, are the most substantial re-creations of history in the form of fiction produced in the period. Stylistic artificialities and a naturalistic philosophy alike reminiscent of Meredith are combined in *Halfway House* (1908), *Open Country* (1909), and *Rest Harrow* (1910), the trilogy on John Senhouse, lover of flowers and enemy of marriage.[40]

# VI

*Kipling*        Rudyard Kipling [41] (1865-1936) was born in India, where his father, the accomplished John Lockwood Kipling, had been appointed to a chair of sculpture in the University of Bombay. A multitude of impressions of the East were already stored in memory when at the age of six the child was sent to England. There he led at first a lonely and unhappy life with relatives. These experiences he afterwards turned to literary use in *Baa-baa, Black Sheep* and in the opening chapters of *The Light that Failed*. Presently he was put into the school for the sons of army and navy men of which he afterwards drew a picture in *Stalky and Co.,* a boisterous and rowdy tale of the pranks and adventures of boys who fancied themselves outlaws.[42] But the young Kipling did other things besides cut up. Verses which he sent home to his family in India his proud father had privately printed as *Schoolboy Lyrics* (1881). Here, among much that is, naturally enough, merely imitative, there is one piece, *Ave Imperatrix,* that strikes for the first time the authentic Kipling note of service to the British Empire.

[40] Hewlett's *Song of the Plough* (1916), an "epic" (or rather a series of episodes) of the life of Hodge (the typical English agricultural laborer) from the Norman Conquest to modern times, evinces sincere feeling and intimate knowledge (for Hewlett, though urbane in literary tastes, lived close to the soil), but it fails as a poem for want of profundity, freshness of imagery, and any novelty of technique.

[41] *Writings in Prose and Verse* (36v, 1898-1937); Burwash Edition (28v, 1941); and many other collected editions; *A Choice of Kipling's Verse*, introduction by T. S. Eliot (1941). — There is as yet no definitive "Life and Letters." Mrs. F. V. Livingston, *Bibliography* (1927); Ehrsam, *Bibliographies*, pp. 127-160; Edward Shanks, *Rudyard Kipling, a Study in Literature and Political Ideas* (1940), an excellent corrective to the denigrations of recent criticism; Hilton Brown, *Rudyard Kipling* (1945); Sir George MacMunn, *Rudyard Kipling, Craftsman* (1938); Cyril Falls, *Rudyard Kipling, a Critical Study* (1915); W. M. Hart, *Kipling, the Story-Writer* (Berkeley, 1918); A. M. Weygandt, *Kipling's Reading and its Influence upon his Poetry* (1939); R. A. Durand, *A Handbook to the Poetry of Rudyard Kipling* (1914); W. A. Young, *A Dictionary of the Characters and Scenes of the Stories and Poems of Rudyard Kipling, 1886-1911* (1911); André Chevrillon, *Three Studies in English Literature* (1923), 1: "Rudyard Kipling's Poetry"; Baker, x (1939), ch. III; Edmund Wilson, "The Kipling that Nobody Read," in *The Wound and the Bow* (1941), pp. 105-181.

[42] G. C. Beresford, the original of M'Turk, gives a picture of these boys' doings and of the school somewhat at variance with Kipling's. See his *Schooldays with Kipling* (1936). See also General L. C. Dunsterville's *Stalky's Reminiscences* (1928) and Kipling's own memoirs, *Something about Myself* (posthumous, 1937).

Returning to India at the age of seventeen, Kipling became sub-editor of *India* the Lahore *Gazette,* thus serving an apprenticeship in journalism which taught him to observe sharply, judge quickly, and report tersely. To the paper he contributed with precocious virtuosity the verses and tales that were collected, respectively, in *Departmental Ditties* (1886) and *Plain Tales from the Hills* (1888). The latter were followed by others of the same kind, among them *Soldiers Three* and *The Phantom 'Rickshaw,* in separate, pamphlet form for reading on railway journeys. The last-named story shows the attraction which the occult had for Kipling, and others are colored by somewhat cruel humor and a love of the gruesome. In many of these juvenilia Kipling displayed a cynicism, crude jocularity, coarse flippancy, and brutality that were expressed with a slick assurance of style that merited and won the epithet "brassy." Style and pattern owed something to Bret Harte and perhaps to Maupassant, but the themes were Kipling's own— the comic or tragic scandals of Anglo-Indian society, the hardships and courage of common soldiers, the patient efficiency of the Civil Servants, and the misery and mystery of the teeming native life. The reappearances of various characters (especially the famous "soldiers three," Mulvaney, Ortheris, and Learoyd) helped to bind this heterogeneous mass of verse and fiction into a whole which, as it grew enormously in later years, remained coherent in manner and atmosphere.

A shipment of the *Ditties* and *Plain Tales* to England revealed Anglo-Indian life to stay-at-homes with the consequence that Kipling's fame preceded his own return. A leisurely journey home took him through China and Japan and across the United States. To the Allahabad *Pioneer* he sent back impressions which were later collected in *From Sea to Sea* (1899), a volume now obscured by the fame of his other work but which is not negligible journalism because in it may be found his characteristically forcible criticism of inefficiency, his distrust of democracy, his belief in authority, and his advocacy of war as a necessary instrument of good government.

The vigor, snap, vividness, self-assurance, and even the vulgarity of the early tales won Kipling an immediate audience and on his arrival in England he found himself *persona grata* with publishers. Stories published in *Macmillan's Magazine* were collected in *Life's Handicap* (1891). *The Light that Failed* [43] (1891), Kipling's first attempt at full-length fiction, cannot be judged an entire success, though the character of Maizie Duncan is finely drawn. W. E. Henley published in *The National Observer* the poems which, Barrack-when collected as *Barrack-Room Ballads* (1892), enormously widened Kip-Room ling's fame. Many a pithy phrase and many a resonant line were soon on Ballads everybody's lips. With suggestions from Burns for the use of dialect and

[43] As an example of publishers' exigencies (compare the case of Hardy's *Tess*) it may be noted that in the magazine version this novel ended "happily." In book form Kipling reverted to the original tragic ending. — *The Maulakha* (1891), a novel written in collaboration with Wolcott Balestier, an American whose sister Kipling married in 1892, must be judged a failure.

with a gift for mating Swinburnian measures to the style of music-hall lyric he had evolved a poetry all his own. In other pieces there are reminiscences of Browning's manner which read almost like parody but are not. Greatly daring, he had seen the possibilities for music, pathos, and humor in the speech of the cockney, a dialect hitherto despised as low and sub-literary. If some of the results were vulgar, brash, and blatant, in others he created things of beauty such as *The Road to Mandalay*. Association with Henley fortified Kipling's imperialism [44] and encouraged the didacticism which grew upon him with the years.

*Many Inventions* (1893)—far too many, indeed, to be recorded by title here—is another collection of stories, among them such little masterpieces as *His Private Honor* and *Love o' Women*. The famous but overpraised *Man Who Was* gives expression to the jingoism which Kipling both echoed from the crowd and further stimulated. Even more noteworthy is *In the Rukh,* in the same volume, for here Mowgli, though grown-up, makes his first appearance.[45] Kipling saw that in this human companion of the beasts there was the making of a myth, and altering his conception just sufficiently,

**The Jungle Books**

he wrote, at the top of his inspiration, *The Jungle Book* (1894) and *The Second Jungle Book* (1895). These are beast-fables, not of the old kind which attributed human qualities to animals but of a new which attempted to see into the very depths of animal natures (granting the convention of endowing them with speech). With a like sympathetic selflessness Kipling in other stories laid bare the "souls" of ships and locomotives and other inanimate things. He was now at the height of a fame that was maintained, if not enlarged, by the poems in *The Seven Seas* (1896); by *Captains Courageous* (1897), a novel-length yarn of the redemption of a spoilt child of the rich who, falling overboard from a liner, learns courage and self-sacrifice among the fishermen of Newfoundland; and by *The Day's Work* (1898), another batch of stories.

**The Boer War**

In July, 1897, the English-speaking world was electrified by the publication of the *Recessional*. This, as Kipling afterwards said, was written to "avert the evil eye" directed against England because of the *hubris* of the Diamond Jubilee. The rôle of counselor of the people sat well upon him, and in 1899 he spoke again, in *The White Man's Burden,* this time on the duties of the imperial races towards "the lesser breeds." During the South African War he voiced no vindictiveness against the Boers but only an anxiety for the welfare of Tommy Atkins and an insistence that lessons for the future be drawn from the inefficient management of the campaign. In the midst of the war appeared *Kim* (1901), a picaresque yarn on the largest scale, evoking life in India. The inaccuracies in the interpretation of native character are redeemed by wisdom, geniality, and humor. Notwithstanding his brutal

---

[44] On the origins and development of the "imperial theme" in English literature see Friedrich Brie, *Imperialistische Strömungen in der englischen Literatur* (Freiburg, 1928).

[45] For this greatest creation of his imagination Kipling probably owed something to remarks upon legends and rumors of children suckled by wolves in his father's undeservedly neglected book, *Man and Beast in India* (1891).

common sense the mysterious East always fascinated Kipling; he could not share its visions but he could suggest their infinitude.[46] In the charming *Just-So Stories* (1902) his humor, often an uncertain quality, is at its best.

With the close of the Boer War the mood of England to which Kipling had given such vigorous expression changed. Though his popularity with the masses did not wane, he was, not altogether fairly, identified with the blatant, jingoistic imperialism of the preceding decade, and his reputation began to decline. A mellower Kipling drew for his countrymen the lesson from the late struggle that if civilization was to be guarded, order, authority, and discipline must be enforced. In these years he was living in Sussex, where the consciousness of an age-long civilization [47] inspired *Puck of Pook's Hill* (1906) and its sequel, *Rewards and Fairies* (1910). These stories are grounded upon England's past and illustrate the continuity of tradition. On the outbreak of the Great War he bade his countrymen in stern and measured rhetoric protect the ramparts of civilization against the barbarians at the gate. In a sense he had foreseen what was coming, though in former years he had held, as was natural from the point of view of an Anglo-Indian, that the arch-foe was not Germany but Russia. Against the "Hun" he wrote with a fierce hatred that contrasts with his earlier attitude towards the Boers. They were the betrayers of Western Civilization, disloyal to "the Law." [48] He lived long enough to be vigilant against the renewal of the German menace. Within our limits it is impossible to record all his later publications. He had little that was new to say in verse, and the last two series of prose stories, though written with the old mastery of technique, contain little that is fresh in substance.

It being impossible to divorce the two departments of Kipling's achieve- *Poetry* ment, something further must be said here of his poetry. As a virtuoso in verse he had more than one style at his command. The swagger and swash-buckling are often detestable, but he could give expression alike to Tommy Atkins' hopes for loot and to his weariness when upon the march. The cockney dialect is sometimes used for mere music-hall vulgarities but again for lovely verbal music. Of a different order are the surging rhythms of *The Last Chantey* and *The Long Trail*. Alone among poets his ear caught the cadences of clanking machinery and pulsating ships. There is a solemn rhetoric in the prophetic tones of counsel and warning to England, though in some pieces the gnomic style is so terse that the meaning is with difficulty interpreted. No other writer was capable of uttering such a *sursum corda* in time of national peril. There was always something of the journalist in the absorbed attention he gave to public affairs. As the unofficial laureate of his people he could express their feelings on great occasions of state, as in *The Dead King,* where the impressiveness lies in the very contrast be-

[46] See A. Rumson, *Kipling's India* (1915).
[47] See R. T. Hopkins, *Kipling's Sussex* (1921).
[48] Realizing that England had not learned the lessons of the Boer War, Kipling was forced in 1914-1918 to bring renewed charges of inefficiency against those responsible for operations, especially in the Mesopotamian campaign.

tween the poet's estimate of Edward VII and the actuality. More rarely he was master of a subtler music, as in the beautiful *Epitaph,* "Call me not false, beloved."

**"The Law"**

Implicit in all his writings, explicit in the *Jungle Books,* and first emphasized in *The Day's Work* is the central theme of obedience to "the Law"— the law whereby civilized society is so ordered that every man can obtain from life the fruits thereof within the limits of his obligations to his fellowmen. Kipling was not an "authoritarian" in the modern "totalitarian" sense. Men are not the servants of the state, but trained experts are the servants of the community. Tools to the hands of those who can use them! His criticism of democracy [49] was that ill-informed people choose representatives who legislate upon subjects about which they know nothing. With such he contrasts the efficiency of the specially trained, whether the Roman soldier guarding the Wall, or the Sussex farmhand inheriting an age-long technique, or the Civil Servant organizing famine-relief in India, or the proconsul directing the restoration of order in the chaotic Sudan. The praise of machinery, the delight in engineering technicalities displayed in the story *The Bridge-Builders,* in *M'Andrew's Hymn,* and in a hundred other places, is due to Kipling's admiration of the coördination of functions of which the machine is not only a symbol but the perfect example. He seems to have had no foresight of the perils to a civilization that had become "the Machine Age."

[49] This criticism deeply wounded many of Kipling's American admirers. Kipling lived for several years in Vermont, having married an American. His attitude towards the United States, in the worst tradition of British superciliousness, is partly to be explained by a bitter quarrel with his brother-in-law. See F. F. Van de Water, *Rudyard Kipling's Vermont Feud* (1937).

# XXXVII

## The Irish Literary Renaissance

The Irish political leaders who, abandoning their efforts to effect reforms within the British Parliament, gradually roused the national enthusiasm which prepared the way for Home Rule have a stronger claim than the regionalists in Irish fiction to be regarded as the precursors of the Irish Literary Renaissance.[1] From about 1830 Trinity College, Dublin, became a center of political and literary activity, and in 1833 *The Dublin University Magazine* was founded. Among its contributors was James Clarence Mangan [2] *Mangan* (1803-1849) who because of his personal history has been called "a sort of Irish Poe." Besides such self-revelatory poems as *The Nameless One,* Mangan wrote verse paraphrases of Gaelic songs from prose translations supplied (for he knew no Gaelic) by his friends. Among these is the fervently patriotic address to Ireland, *My Dark Rosaleen.* Mangan contributed also to *The Nation,* of which the founders (1842) were Charles Gavan Duffy [3] (1816-1903) and Thomas O. Davis [4] (1814-1845). These men and their collaborators, impatient of the cautious policy of Daniel O'Connell, seceded from his following to form the group known as "Young Ireland." It had little immediate *"Young* practical effect and after 1848 seemed to dwindle away. But part of the *Ireland"* program was to stimulate patriotism by rousing interest and pride in the national past, and of that past legend, lore, and literature were the chief glories. Thus it came about that (with no separation from the men active in contemporary politics) antiquarians, philologists, and historians advanced to the foreground of the Irish picture. Sir Samuel Ferguson [5] (1810-1886), who, unlike Mangan, was a Gaelic scholar, was the first to make known to *Ferguson* Englishmen and to Irishmen lacking knowledge of their ancestral language, *and* in anything like their original form and fullness the cycle of epic legends *O'Grady* of the deeds of Cuchulain and the loves of Deirdre. With no claim to rank

[1] E. A. Boyd, *Ireland's Literary Renaissance* (1916); N. J. O'Conor, *Changing Ireland: Literary Background of the Irish Free State, 1889-1922* (1924); David Morton, *The Renaissance of Irish Poetry* (1929); Cornelius Weygandt, *Irish Plays and Playwrights* (1913) and *The Time of Yeats* (1937); A. E. Malone, *The Irish Drama* (1929); Una Ellis-Fermor, *The Irish Dramatic Movement* (1939). There is much material in the more or less autobiographical writings of the leading figures in the movement. See especially W. B. Yeats, *Autobiographies* (1926) and "The Irish Dramatic Movement," in *Plays and Controversies* (1923); Lady Gregory, *Our Irish Theatre* (1914); George Moore, *Hail and Farewell* (1911-1914); Lady Gregory, *Diaries* (1946).
[2] *Poems* (Dublin, 1903). — D. J. O'Donoghue, *The Life of James Clarence Mangan* (1897).
[3] Sir C. G. Duffy, *My Life in Two Hemispheres* (1898). Duffy's *Ballad Poetry of Ireland* (1843) is noteworthy.
[4] *Poems* (1846); *Selections* (1915). — Sir C. G. Duffy, *The Life of Thomas Davis* (1890).
[5] Lady Ferguson, *The Life of Sir Samuel Ferguson* (2v, 1896).

as an original poet Ferguson performed as an antiquarian, through his *Lays of the Western Gael* (1865), *Congal*[6] (1872), and *Deirdre* (1880), an inestimable service to Ireland in restoring to the general consciousness these monuments of the heroic past. Work equally necessary as a preliminary to a cultural renaissance was done by Standish James O'Grady (1846-1915) in his *History of Ireland: Heroic Period*[7] (1878-1880). In surging, eloquent prose O'Grady vitalized the ancient stories of the Gael. The original materials for work of this kind were now being made available by archaeological and philological societies. During the ascendency of Parnell, Irish energies were mostly diverted from literature to politics; but after the recuperation from the shock of his downfall the claims of Irish culture were reasserted. In 1892 there was organized at Dublin the Irish Literary Society, of which the first president was George Sigerson (1839-1925), a productive scholar. Of the Gaelic League (1893) the first president was Douglas Hyde (1860-    ) who has lived to become President of the Irish Free State. Hyde was influential as a folklorist, editor, translator, and writer of original poetry in Gaelic. His *Literary History of Ireland* (1899) did much to advance the claims of Irish letters to be judged independently of English literature.

Meanwhile there had appeared an anthology of *Poems and Ballads of Young Ireland* (1888). Among the poets here represented was John Todhunter (1839-1916) who, after several earlier volumes of verse, had turned his attention to the bardic legends in *The Banshee and Other Poems* (1888). Despite the sincerity of his sympathies Todhunter belonged among the expatriated Anglo-Irish writers of London.[8] Another poet in the anthology was Katharine Tynan, afterwards Mrs. Hinkson[9] (1861-1931). She had been influenced in her early work by the Pre-Raphaelites, and her devotional poetry connects her with the group of Roman Catholic poets.[10] But this association links her poetry also to the tradition of the Irish religious lyric. Gaelic themes are dominant in her *Shamrocks* (1887) and *Ballads and Lyrics* (1891), and much later she published *Irish Poems* (1913). Her talent was sweet but fragile and her popularity has now declined.

*Yeats*    The editor of this anthology was William Butler Yeats[11] (1865-1939),

[6] Founded on the bardic romance, *The Battle of Moyra*.

[7] O'Grady later attached to the *History* an essay on *Early Bardic Literature* (1879). His more conventional *History of Ireland* (1881) remains a fragment. Of his historical romances the best are *Red Hugh's Captivity* (1889) and *The Flight of the Eagle* (1897). *The Bog of Stars* (1893) is a collection of short stories.

[8] An Anglo-Irish poet of the previous generation was Aubrey de Vere (1814-1902). His mild Wordsworthian verse covers many subjects, classical, medieval, hagiological, political, and religious. *Inisfail* (1862) and various other poems are Irish in subject; but in general he was apart from the Movement. — For two other Anglo-Irish poets, Allingham and O'Shaughnessy, see above, ch. xxix, notes 27 and 28.

[9] *Collected Poems* (1930).

[10] See below, ch. xxxix.

[11] *Collected Works* (8v, 1908); *Collected Poems* (1933; expanded edition, 1950); *Collected Plays* (1935); *New Poems* (1938); *Letters on Poetry to Dorothy Wellesley* (1940). — A. J. A. Symons, *Bibliography* (1924); Joseph Hone, *W. B. Yeats* (1943), the authorized biography; Forrest Reid, *William Butler Yeats, a Critical Study* (1915); C. L. Wrenn, *William Butler Yeats, a Literary Study* (1920); J. H. Pollock, *William Butler Yeats* (Dublin, 1935);

then at the outset of his career. Sprung from Irish Protestantism and the son of an Irish painter, Yeats was born in Dublin, but his childhood was passed in London save for vacations in the west of Ireland. Some early attempts at poetic drama were in the nature of a false start. The first poem that matters was *The Wanderings of Oisin* [12] (1889), the volume with which the Irish Literary Revival attained complete self-consciousness. No intrusion of modern political ideas sullies the other-worldly atmosphere, but the Gaelic theme of the pagan who relates to St. Patrick his adventures in fairyland is overlaid with stylistic ornament reminiscent of Spenser, Shelley, and William Morris, [13] and the design of the poem owes something to *Endymion*. Though in succeeding years Yeats was a member of the coterie of poets and aesthetes in London, he was already in quest of a fresh tradition and an individual style. There is little that is derivative from English sources in the poetic plays, *The Countess Cathleen* (1892) and *The Land of Heart's Desire* (1894), or in the lyrics and ballad-pieces that accompanied the former. The delicate light rimes (frequently "off-rimes" and assonances), the insubstantial rhythms, and the vague outlines are characteristics of Yeats's first manner. The aesthetic theory of the separation of art from life, which Yeats was later to repudiate, is implicit; and the exploitation of the strange and the intense and of spiritual weariness ("the soul with all its maladies") is characteristic of the time and milieu rather than of the poet himself. His *Poems* were collected in 1895, but for several years he was chiefly occupied with prose. The contrast between the simple fairy-lore of *The Celtic Twilight* (1893) and the difficult occultism of *The Secret Rose* (1897) is a measure of his advance during these years. The studies which *Symbolism* had resulted in his edition of Blake's *Works* (1893) strengthened his interest in symbols, and at a later date a meeting with Mallarmé and association with Arthur Symons confirmed his acceptance of the doctrines of the Symbolists. The influence of the French school and of Maeterlinck is apparent in *The Wind among the Reeds* (1899), a new collection of verse. Some of the early symbols, particularly those drawn from the natural world, are simple enough; the moon stands for weariness (as often in Shelley),

---

J. P. O'Donnell, *Sailing to Byzantium, a Study in the Development of the later Style and Symbolism of W. B. Yeats* (Cambridge, Mass., 1939); Louis MacNeice, *The Poetry of W. B. Yeats* (1941); V. K. N. Menon, *The Development of William Butler Yeats* (1942); Edmund Wilson, *Axel's Castle* (1931), ch. II; David Daiches, *Poetry and the Modern World* (1940), chs. VII-VIII; *The Southern Review*, VII (Winter, 1941-1942), "William Butler Yeats Memorial Issue," essays by T. S. Eliot, J. C. Ransom, and other poets and critics; *Scattering Branches*, ed. Stephen Gwynn (1940), memorial articles by Maud Gonne MacBride, Lennox Robinson, and others.

[12] On turning to Ireland Yeats was influenced by Sigerson's *Poets and Poetry of Munster* (1860) and later by Hyde's *Love Songs of Connacht* (1893) where the syntax is partly Gaelic and the vocabulary partly Elizabethan. Yeats, who did not know Gaelic, occasionally used the Anglo-Irish of the peasantry, but most of his poetry is written in standard English, refreshed from new sources in imagery rather than vocabulary. Space is lacking here to record the heavy revisions and significant modifications to which Yeats afterwards subjected much of his early work. — Yeats's indebtedness to the eighteenth-century Irish poet Michael Comys and to other sources acknowledged and unacknowledged is demonstrated by R. K. Alspach, "Some Sources of Yeats's *The Wanderings of Oisin*," *PMLA*, LVIII (1943). 849-866.

[13] Morris said to Yeats: "You write my sort of poetry" (Yeats, *Autobiographies*, p. 181).

water for the fleetingness of beauty, and the rose, over and over again, for the principle of Eternal Beauty. The life of ecstatic reverie, hidden from the world, is suggested by the image of the veil. But in Irish mythology Yeats had found a treasury of symbols hitherto unused in English poetry. The clues to these are not always readily accessible and the precise significance of some figures is often difficult to apprehend. Fairyland itself—the country of the Sidhe, the Irish fairy-folk—is itself a symbol of the imagination. Over against the world of the imagination is set the naturalistic, scientific world, sometimes symbolized by Yeats in hostile allusions to Huxley or Tyndall.

Yet gradually there was a drift towards actuality. The influence of Ibsen's problem plays has been discerned. And notwithstanding Yeats's aloofness, there was the influence of Irish politics. He could not escape from his environment—the less so because he was in love with the fiery Nationalist, Maud Gonne. In 1899 he and Lady Gregory founded the Irish National Theatre Society which was presently housed in the Abbey Theatre in Dublin.[14] Isabella Augusta, Lady Gregory (1859-1932) was a forceful influence upon the entire Irish movement. Of her many translations *Gods and Fighting Men* (1904) is typical. Her explorations of folklore and legend are recorded in various volumes. But her principal work was in the drama. She collaborated with Yeats in *The Unicorn from the Stars* (1908) and other plays. Of her own comedies some are in one act, others full-length. Not all are of much literary value, but they display an insight into peasant character and are full of humor. *The Rising of the Moon* and *The Workhouse Ward* are perhaps her best, showing as they do her deft craftsmanship and economy of means. Her tours of the United States with the Abbey company in 1911-1913 are memorable for her difficulties and triumphs. In Dublin the company maintained their enthusiasm despite discouragements and they persisted in the face of violent and occasionally riotous opposition provoked by their supposed "blasphemy" in some cases and their supposedly discreditable portrayal of Irish character in others.

Yeats's energetic activity during the formative, combative period of the Abbey Theatre had a profound effect upon him as a poet, but the theatre was not a perfectly appropriate medium for his imagination. Notwithstanding his practical experience, he did not always grasp either its opportunities or its limitations. Of sturdier texture than the dramatic fairy fantasies of his youth are the *Plays for an Irish Theatre* (1904), and of these the finest is *Cathleen ni Houlihan* (performed 1902) in which beneath the dramatiza-

*Lady Gregory*

14 With Yeats and Lady Gregory was associated Edward Martyn (1859-1923), author of *The Heather Field* (1899) and *The Tale of a Town* (1902), the latter adapted by George Moore as *The Bending of the Bough*. The maliciously witty portrait of Martyn in Moore's *Hail and Farewell* requires a corrective. See Denis Gwynn, *Edward Martyn and the Irish Literary Revival* (1930). — Yeats and Lady Gregory had the good fortune to secure the services of the talented actors, Frank and William Fay. See W. G. Fay and Catherine Carswell, *The Fays of the Abbey Theatre* (1935). See also in addition to authorities already cited, Dawson Byrne, *The Story of Ireland's National Theatre* (1929); Camillo Pellizzi, *English Drama: the Last Great Phase*, trans. by Rowan Williams (1935), ch. VI; Lennox Robinson (ed.), *The Irish Theatre* (1939), lectures by Robinson, T. C. Murray, and others.

tion of a story of 1798 there is discernible a symbolic nationalism. In other plays subjects are taken from the heroic sagas, as in the tragic *Deirdre* (1907). At a later date Yeats was occupied with obscure and difficult abstractions in which he made use of dancers, musicians, and masked actors. These pieces, for which he derived suggestions from the Nōh plays of Japan, were collected as *Four Plays for Dancers* (1921).

For a time during his middle years Yeats seemed to be less dependent upon symbolism. *In the Seven Woods* (1904) and *The Green Helmet* (1910), the latter a reworking in ballad metre of an earlier play in prose, are hard and dry in manner. Yet concurrently with his substitution of lively, homely detail for the dreamy vagueness of background in his renderings of Irish myths, his studies were becoming increasingly esoteric. The symbolism which he evolved is extremely difficult. It is true that he sometimes drew upon traditional and hence easily intelligible sources (such as Plato), but he inquired also into astrology, theosophy, the phenomena of clairvoyance, oriental speculation, and various "hermetic" writings. At the time when he was engaged upon *Reveries over Childhood and Youth* (1915) and *The Trembling of the Veil* (1922)—afterwards printed together as *Autobiographies* [15] (1926)—he came to use events in his own life as symbols for his poetry that are often "private" and obscure to the verge of incommunicability. Increasingly he had to rely upon prose comments appended to the poems. In later work there are often multiple connotations which are not successfully communicable. A few (such as the cat-headed figures) are utterly uncouth. Yeats was profoundly interested in, and disturbed by, reports of mystic experiences; but though he would have liked to be, he never was a genuine mystic. The theory of the "Earth Memory" which he held in common with his friend A. E. (who, however, held it with sincere conviction) is in Yeats little other than a literary device; and in all the ingenuity and complexity of the theory elaborated in *A Vision* (privately printed, 1926), with its exposition of the phases of human experience symbolized by the Hunchback, the Saint, and the Fool, and with its great show of secret *gnosis,* in this pseudo-mystic erudition, one detects something of sham. Did not Yeats himself admit that it might be no more than metaphors for poetry, "a painted scene"? There was a core of rationalism in Yeats's nature. Nevertheless, though at bottom he remained unconvinced, these speculations provided for him the wonderful contrasts conveyed in his verse between the pagan world and the Catholic, between the natural and the supernatural, between the transient and the abiding. The sense of the conflict between soul and sense, between Being and Becoming, is suggested with greatest depth and splendor in *Sailing to Byzantium,* one of the finest of his later poems.

*Later Poems*

[15] In various collections of essays Yeats expounded his views on poetry, symbolism, the theatre, and other subjects. The principal volumes are *Ideas of Good and Evil* (1903); *Discoveries* (1907); *The Cutting of an Agate* (1912); and *Per Amica Silentia Lunae* (1918). Yeats's reception of the Nobel Prize for Literature in 1923 inspired the tribute, *The Bounty of Sweden* (1925). See also *Dramatis Personae* (1936).

A reaction from what he considered the weak sentiment of his earlier poetry was sometimes pushed to the extreme of sheer brutality. It took the form of substituting for the old suggestiveness the precise, hard-hitting word. He was dissatisfied because formerly he had separated his imagination from life; yet he was dissatisfied with life itself—"this pragmatical pig of a world." This is expressed with terrible and prophetic force in various poems, notably *The Second Coming* where some readers have detected a prediction of the world catastrophe which came about in the year of his death. Yeats seemed to abandon the effort to give, through his art, order to a chaotic world. From *The Tower* (1928) onward, humor, sarcasm, scorn, audacity, and a most unexpected sensuality mark his final phase. He resisted and resented the on-coming of old age. In his latest poems there is at once a passionate regret for the passing of the passionate experiences of youth and at the same time an indignant remoteness from the world. The gyre, the spiral, and the winding stair are constantly recurring symbols of the cyclic philosophy which he had evolved from reading and from life.

"*A. E.*"    The mysticism which in Yeats is no more than the expression of a poetic mood is accepted, experienced, and revealed as profoundest truth by A. E., George W. Russell [16] (1867-1935), artist, poet, philosopher, journalist, economic theorist, and practical worker for agricultural reform in Ireland. The immense services which A. E. rendered to Ireland do not all belong to a history of literature; a considerable portion of his prose was ephemeral in subject. The insight and foresight which he applied to public affairs are also found in those poems in which he urges upon his fellow-countrymen a new outlook: "the first-born of the coming race" rather than "the last splendors of the Gael." But in most of his poems and in the beautiful fragment of autobiography entitled *The Candle of Vision* (1918) he is concerned with the varying manifestations of the one and eternal Truth of which intimations had come to him through his mystic experiences. There is a special devotion to evening, night, and dawn, when the soul is at furthest remove from the care and turmoil of the day. A quietism of Oriental intensity is combined with a devotion to the Earth, the Earth Memory, and the divinity of Earth. These ideas were expressed in *Homeward: Songs by the Way* (1894), in *The Earth Breath and other Poems* (1897), and in several volumes of later verse. There is necessarily a certain monotony of subject-matter but it is more than atoned for by the exquisite beauty with which A. E. plays his gentle and profound variations upon the theme of vision. How intensely, nevertheless, this visionary felt the charm of the world of phenomena is revealed in *The Symbol Seduces,* one of his loveliest poems.

Yeats made one of his most memorable contributions to the Irish Theatre

---

[16] *Collected Poems* (1913); the volumes of later date have not yet been collected; *The Living Torch,* ed. Monk Gibbon (1937), a selection from A. E.'s writings in *The Irish States-man,* of which he was editor. — John Eglinton (pseudonym for W. K. Magee), *A Memoir of A. E.* (1937).

when he persuaded John Millington Synge [17] (1871-1909) to return from *Synge*
Paris in 1898 to his native land. Synge brought back with him a tinge of
Maeterlinck's nature mysticism and an acquaintance with Pierre Loti's
stories and studies of the Breton peasantry; but he owed little to these
Continental influences. In the Aran Islands [18] he absorbed the rich dialect
of a people quite uncontaminated with modern sophistication. Observing
the precepts and practice of Lady Gregory and Douglas Hyde, which were
strengthened by his own sense of style, he elevated and purified the peasant
idiom till it became the singularly vigorous and poetic medium of his plays.
Synge kept apart from Irish politics, and he indulged neither in didacticism
nor in metaphysical implications. He was concerned with the motivating
ideas and emotions of small groups of isolated men and women. (In his
hands even the traditional grandiosity of the Deirdre story is simplified).
He was aware of the savagery in human nature and he loved wildness in
nature and in men. Occasionally, especially in farcical situations, his plays
are brutal. He depicted a hard, coarse life and the unrestrained feelings,
alike in joy and sorrow, of simple people, close to earth. The background
of mist and mountain is essential to the effect of *The Shadow of the Glen,*
and the ocean, though never personified in the dialogue, seems to be one
of the dramatis personae in *Riders to the Sea.* There was an elemental quality
in his imagination which gave something of universality to the comedy and
tragedy of humble folk.

Setting aside a negligible farce, a few undistinguished poems and translations, and his accounts of the Aran Islanders and the people of West Kerry,
we are concerned with five plays, all work of his last decade. *The Shadow
of the Glen* (1903), a one-act piece about a miser who by pretending to
be dead entraps his wife (a theme as old as the story of the Widow of
Ephesus), is no more than a sketch, too abrupt in its brevity and puzzlingly
poised between farce and melancholy. Far finer (partly because the subject lent itself to condensation in a single act) is *Riders to the Sea* (1904), *Riders*
on the struggles of the fisher-folk with the element which is at once their *to the*
livelihood and their doom. In swift cumulativeness of effect and in piercing *Sea*
sweetness and direct incisiveness of speech Synge never surpassed this little
play. *The Well of the Saints* (1905), a full-length play, is set in a vague
period of the past; very wonderful is the effect throughout of strange remoteness from modernity. The theme, which is suggestive of old French
fabliaux, is bitter, melancholy, and sardonic. A man and woman, beggars
old and blind, have their sight restored with consequences other than had
been hoped for. Synge's instinct for theatrical effectiveness is at its best in

---

[17] *Complete Works* (1935) and other collected editions. — Maurice Bourgeois, *John Millington Synge and the Irish Theatre* (1913); P. P. Howe, *John Millington Synge, a Critical Study*
(1912); Daniel Corkery, *Synge and Anglo-Irish Literature* (1931); A. D. Estill, *The Sources
of Synge* (Philadelphia, 1939); John Masefield, *J. M. Synge. A Few Personal Recollections
with Biographical Notes.* (1921).

[18] For Synge's informal impressions of the peasantry of the west of Ireland see *The Aran
Islands* (Dublin, 1907), with drawings by Jack B. Yeats. Supplementary to this are the prose
sketches, *In Wicklow, In West Kerry,* and *In the Congested Districts.*

the postponed entry of the Saint who accomplishes the miracle. The uses to which Martin Doul puts his recovered sight gave offense in Dublin as a supposed reflection upon the national character. But the affront to Irish sensibilities on both religious and nationalistic grounds was more serious when Synge's most famous play, *The Playboy of the Western World* (1907), was produced. The protests and disturbances it occasioned in Dublin and later in the United States are part of Irish literary history. It was suggested by an actual case of parricide, but by substituting for the crime Christy Mahon's mistaken notion that he had killed his father, Synge, while retaining tragic overtones, turned the subject into vigorous, brilliant, and extravagant comedy—a comedy too exceptional in its subject, however, to claim the place among masterpieces which some admirers have assigned it. At the time of his death Synge was at work upon *Deirdre of the Sorrows* (posthumous, 1910), on the legendary theme of Beauty doomed to early death. In its bleak and tragic intensity of style *Deirdre,* unfinished though it is, is Synge's greatest work.

*Padraic Colum*

The intentions and the earlier accomplishments of the Irish playwrights had been poetic and folkloristic; but the study of actual peasant types, the adoption of the living idiom, the proximity of social and political agitation, and the impact of the English problem play opened the door to realism. The pioneering examples of realistic drama are the plays of Padraic Colum (1881-    ): *Broken Soil* (1903), later rewritten as *The Fiddler's House; The Land* (1905); and *Thomas Muskerry* (1910). A finer and more experienced craftsman was Lennox Robinson (1886-1958), director, actor, and producer, whose plays have been among the mainstays of the Abbey Theatre in recent years. In them there is scarcely a trace of the old folklore and in mood and technique they are not far apart from the work of Galsworthy and Granville-Barker. *The Whiteheaded Boy* (1916) is one of Robinson's liveliest comedies. He sometimes drew his subjects from recent Irish history, most notably in *The Lost Leader* (1918), which is founded on the popular report that Parnell had not died but was still alive under an assumed name. In his later plays Robinson tended to touch comedy with sentiment. There is room here but to name other contemporary realistic dramatists who have portrayed the changing conditions of Irish life—T. C. Murray, J. B. MacCarthy, George Shiels, and Brinsley MacNamara.

*Lennox Robinson*

*Sean O'Casey*

Towering above these writers was Sean O'Casey (1884-1965), who in three masterpieces dramatized the tragic events in which he took part. Born among the poor of Dublin, he passed his youth in humble labor, and in 1916 participated in the Easter Rebellion.[19] His first play, *The Shadow of a Gunman,* was produced at the Abbey Theatre in 1923. It is on the struggle between the Sinn Feiners and the English soldiery in 1920; the violence of

---

[19] See O'Casey's prose narrative of the Rebellion, *The Story of the Irish Citizen Army* (1919). — The three volumes of O'Casey's as yet unfinished autobiography—*I Knock at the Door* (1939), *Pictures in the Hallway* (1942), and *Drums under the Windows* (1946)—possess vivid intensity and brutal power.

conflict in the streets of Dublin forms effectively the background for scenes in the life of poor people in a tenement. In *Juno and the Paycock* (1924) the civil war of 1922 between the new-born Free State and the bitter-end Republicans is the setting of the story of a poor family's expectation of an inheritance and their subsequent disappointment. Bitter comedy and stark tragedy clash in violent contrast with no softening by means of such glamorous poetic style as Synge would have introduced. *The Plough and the Stars* (1926), on the Easter Rebellion, reaches in the final act a climax of horror in which national and private tragedy intermingle. In *The Silver Tassie* (1928) O'Casey turned to the larger subject of the Great War, making use of an "expressionistic" technique to bring a theme so huge within the boundaries of the theatre. The rejection of this play by the Abbey Theatre occasioned a notorious exchange of letters between O'Casey and Yeats in which the former had the better of the argument. *Within the Gates* (1933) deals, with an even freer technique, with the subject of the unemployed; the scene is Hyde Park. It shows how deeply O'Casey was moved by the plight of the poor. His torrential and often virulent power of language; the moral integrity which refuses to devise for the sake of aesthetic satisfaction a technical unity of fundamentally discordant elements; and the ability to show the impact of mighty events upon humble people, thus universalizing the tragedy of the life of the poor—these gifts mark him as one of the greatest writers of the Irish Literary Renaissance.[20]

[20] The writings of James Stephens (1882-1950) are almost entirely apart from the Irish theatre. In fiction and poetry he has delineated peasant life and made use of Irish folklore and supernaturalism. His charm and fantasy are at times contaminated with the merely whimsical. *The Crock of Gold* (1912) and *The Demi-Gods* (1914) are his best-known books. Several volumes of his verse were collected in 1926, and he wrote much in later years.—The talent of Daniel Corkery (1878-    ) is of a kind less popular but more distinguished and of probably more lasting quality. Dramatist, scholar, and author of one novel, Corkery is best known for the short stories collected in *A Munster Twilight* (1917), *The Hounds of Banba* (1920), and *Earth out of Earth* (1939). In them there are tragedy and pathos, an effect of remoteness, and often a strange poetic quality.

# XXXVIII

## Modern Drama

### I

In the mid-nineteenth century, well before the "renovation" of the theatre associated with the names of T. W. Robertson and Sir Squire and Lady Bancroft, there was a vital and developing stagecraft, albeit unaccompanied by any literary drama worthy of the name.[1] Since evasions of the old monopolies had been permitted, or at any rate winked at, the repeal of the Licensing Act (1843) caused little or no immediately perceptible change, though in the long run the effect was wholesome. The minor theatres were already coming into prominence. Reforms for which Robertson has often been given credit were, it is now recognized, under way before he appeared. Apart from technical innovations in the structure of the theatres and the mounting of plays, there was evidence of progress in various kinds of drama. In melodrama the development was from vulgar staginess to a considerable degree of dignity and fidelity to reality, and in naturalistic burlesque, as performed by Mme Vestris and Charles Mathews, a piquant contrast between the extravagances of sentiment and situation and the quietness of acting and deportment. Before 1865 a decidedly realistic kind of acting had appeared in the London theatres. What was lacking was a playwright to provide dramas giving scope to the actors of the new school.

*Boucicault*

*Tom Taylor*

Neither Dion Boucicault [2] (1820?-1890) nor Tom Taylor [3] (1817-1880) could satisfy this requirement. Boucicault, whose first successes were in the eighteen-forties, fixed the type of Victorian melodrama, adapted plots from Dumas *fils* and other foreign writers, and in *The Colleen Bawn* (1860) and later plays exploited Irish subjects. Taylor's talent was facile and prolific. In *Our American Cousin* (1858) the "character-part" of Lord Dundreary points the way towards individualization as opposed to reliance upon con-

[1] For antecedents of the modern period see E. B. Watson, *Sheridan to Robertson* (1926) and Ernest Reynolds, *Early Victorian Drama: 1830-1870* (1936). William Archer, *The Theatrical World* (5v, 1894-1898), contemporary surveys of the crucial years 1893-1897; F. W. Chandler, *Aspects of Modern Drama* (1914); P. P. Howe, *Dramatic Portraits* (1913); Graham Sutton, *Some Contemporary Dramatists* (1924); Frank Vernon, *The Twentieth Century Theatre* (1924); J. W. Cunliffe, *Modern English Playwrights* (1927); Ramsden Balmforth, *The Problem-Play and its Influence on Modern Thought and Life* (1928); B. H. Clark, *A Study of the Modern Drama* (1928); W. P. Eaton, *The Drama in English* (1930); T. H. Dickinson, *The Contemporary Drama in England* (1931); Camillo Pellizzi, *Il Teatro Inglese* (Milan, 1934), trans. by Rowan Williams as *English Drama: The Last Great Phase* (1935); Allardyce Nicoll, *A History of Late Nineteenth Century Drama, 1850-1900* (2v, Cambridge, 1946).

[2] See above, ch. xv.

[3] Journalist, wit, critic, and editor (1874-1880) of *Punch*. — See Winton Tolles, *Tom Taylor and the Victorian Drama* (1940).

ventional stage types. *The Fool's Revenge* (1859), adapted from Hugo, is the best of Taylor's pseudo-historical plays, and *The Ticket-of-Leave Man* (1863) is the best of his melodramas.

The effort of Thomas William Robertson [4] (1829-1871) was towards *Robertson* naturalism in dialogue, feeling, and situation and the creation of the atmosphere of modern life with no artificialities of plot or violence of passion. In Marie Wilton (afterwards Lady Bancroft) he found an actress-manager in sympathy with his views, and in her small, intimate theatre a place where he could put into practice his ideal of restrained acting and contemporaneousness of effect. When *Society* was produced (1865) some critics sneered at the new "cup-and-saucer" comedy, but London flocked to see it. Robertson followed this success with *Ours* (1866), *Caste* (1867), and three other plays. To us his technique seems elementary, his dialogue flat or stilted, his fidelity to actuality questionable; and the literary value of his plays is of the slightest. But in the history of modern drama he has a secure place as a pioneer.

Sir William S. Gilbert [5] (1836-1911) wrote many farces and pantomimes *Gilbert* and in several comedies combined something of Robertson's technique with *and* a cynicism that was all his own. There are motives in his "fairy comedies" *Sullivan* as well as in his *Bab Ballads* (1867-1869) that reappear in the "Savoy Operas" [6] (1875-1889) which he wrote for Sir Arthur Sullivan's music. These operettas are unique among librettos in that they are enjoyable even apart from the music. Lyric charm and lightly parodied romantic themes are joined to a cynicism that is often quietly ruthless and to mordant satire upon contemporary fads and humbugs. The formula requires a humorous topsy-turviness of situation and reasoning; and over all there is a dainty, shimmering grace.

## II

The French ideal of the *pièce bien faite*—exposition; situation; "great scene"; disentanglement—lived on till the close of the century, but in the eighteen-eighties the tide of Ibsenism began to flow.[7] The "discoverer" of *Ibsenism*

---

[4] *Principal Dramatic Works* (2v, 1889); *Caste* and *Society,* ed. T. E. Pemberton (1905). —·T. E. Pemberton, *Life and Writings of T. W. Robertson* (1893); Sir Squire and Lady Bancroft, *Recollections of Sixty Years* (1909); Sir Arthur W. Pinero, "The Theatre of the 'Seventies," in *The Eighteen-Seventies,* ed. H. Granville-Barker (1929), pp. 135-163.

[5] *The Savoy Operas* (1926); *The Bab Ballads* [and] *Songs of a Savoyard* (1919). — Isaac Goldberg, *Sir William S. Gilbert: a Study in Modern Satire* (1913) and *The Story of Gilbert and Sullivan* (1929); Hesketh Pearson, *Gilbert and Sullivan: A Biography* (1935); G. K. Chesterton, "Gilbert and Sullivan," in *The Eighteen-Eighties,* ed. Walter de la Mare (1930), pp. 136-158.

[6] *Trial by Jury* (1875); *H. M. S. Pinafore* (1878); *The Pirates of Penzance* (1880); *Patience* (1881); *Iolanthe* (1882); *The Mikado* (1885); *Ruddigore* (1887); *The Yeoman of the Guard* (1888); *The Gondoliers* (1889). Gilbert and Sullivan quarreled in 1889. After their reconciliation they collaborated again but without their former success.

[7] Miriam A. Franc, *Ibsen in England* (1919); Elizabeth Robins, *Ibsen and the Actress* (*Hogarth Essays,* Series II, xv, 1928); Harley Granville-Barker, "The Coming of Ibsen," in *The Eighteen-Eighties* (1930), pp. 159-196; Halvdan Koht, *The Life of Ibsen* (English translation, 1931), II. 114-115 and 266-270; and the table of dates, based on Koht, in Una Ellis-Fermor, *The Irish Dramatic Movement* (1939), Appendix 3.

the Norwegian dramatist had been Edmund Gosse, who since 1871 had written several critiques bringing him to notice [8] and in 1876 had translated *Emperor and Galilean*. In 1880 William Archer's [9] translation of *Pillars of Society* appeared, and in 1884 Henry Arthur Jones collaborated on a bowdlerized perversion of *A Doll's House*. With the production in 1889 of Archer's faithful rendering of that play the storm began to rise, Clement Scott, the dramatic critic, being the leader of the opposition, and Sir Henry Irving, the foremost actor of the period, setting his face against the "new" drama. When in 1891 the Lord Chamberlain refused to license *Ghosts*, the controversy became acute. To this year belongs G. Bernard Shaw's *The Quintessence of Ibsenism*, the expansion of a lecture of the previous year. The organization of the Independent Theatre in London (1891), following the lead of the Théâtre Libre in Paris (1887), provided an outlet for serious realistic drama. With Elizabeth Robins' production of *Hedda Gabler* in 1892 the status of Ibsen began to be accepted and controversy gradually subsided. That the English theatre preferred the social plays of Ibsen's middle period to his earlier poetic plays and continued to prefer them to his later symbolic dramas was not the fault of the pioneer Ibsenites but due rather to the prominence of the contemporary "problem novel" and to current sociological speculation. The "bleak Norwegian" furnished weighty support to English criticism of middle-class society. Fearlessly confronting subjects hitherto proscribed, he was as fearless in driving forward from ominous situations to their logical conclusions. His emphasis upon heredity and the marital relation brought sexual problems into startling prominence, and the tendency towards pessimism was pronounced. Ibsen's English disciples imitated for the most part no more than his external audacities without penetrating to the revolutionary foundations; but at least they advanced the cause of the theatre's claim to deal seriously and purposefully with "the whole of life."

*Jones*     Yet the two most successful playwrights of the period were anti-Ibsenite or at most pseudo-Ibsenite. Henry Arthur Jones [10] (1851-1929), having scored a great hit with *The Silver King* (1882), a melodrama which won Matthew Arnold's commendation, did prudish violence, as we have noted, to *A Doll's House* in *Breaking a Butterfly* (1884). At that time he knew, as he afterwards said, "nothing of Ibsen, but a great deal of Robertson." Thereafter he moved away from the old allegiance without ever unreservedly accepting the new. He had nothing of Ibsen's ability to universalize the characters and situations of a particular time and place, but he had some-

[8] Gosse's principal papers on Ibsen (1873 and 1889) are reprinted in *Northern Studies* (1890), pp. 38-104.
[9] 1856-1924. — See Charles Archer, *William Archer: Life, Work and Friendships* (1931).
[10] Of Jones's hundred plays a good many were never published. *Representative Plays of Henry Arthur Jones*, ed. Clayton Hamilton (4v, 1926). Of Jones's writings on the drama the most important are collected in *The Renascence of the English Drama* (1895) and *Foundations of a National Theatre* (1912). — See Doris Arthur Jones [Mrs. Thorne], *Life and Letters of Henry Arthur Jones* (1930); R. A. Cordell, *Henry Arthur Jones and the Modern Drama* (1932); Marjorie Northend, "Henry Arthur Jones and the Development of Modern English Drama," *RES*, XVIII (1942). 448-463. — The dates given are of stage production.

thing of the master's polemic fervor in his effort to reclaim for the drama the lost provinces of religion and morality. He was influenced by the ideas of Ruskin and Morris, but with a social conscience never greatly troubled he did not enlist in the cause of any thorough-going rebellion against "things as they are," for he remained involved in the prejudices of the age and, like Tennyson, criticized a social system with which he was at heart content. Writing and lecturing ceaselessly on the dramatist's function and opportunity in society, on the play-reading public, in advocacy of a subsidized National Theatre, and on similar topics, he constituted himself a propagandist for the stage, insisting that the art of the drama was not merely a matter of cleverly devised situations and effective "curtains" but the portrayal of life as a whole. But he never really freed himself from the demands of the commercial theatre. To write with one eye on the actor-manager and the other on the box-office is not to write at liberty. The fact is that Jones's position as a critic was always in advance of that which he assumed as a playwright. How narrowly he was content to circumscribe the freedom he professed is shown by the contrast between the claims advanced in the preface to *Saints and Sinners* (1884) and the timid sentimentality of the play itself. *Michael and His Lost Angel* (1896), the story of an erring Anglican clergyman, concludes with a scene of false theatricality. (Jones turned in other plays to the provincial nonconformist world from which he sprang, hating it but bearing the scars of cast-off chains.) In this play, as in others, the satiric exposure of social corruption is but incidental to this basic sentimentality. The theme of marital infidelity in *The Case of Rebellious Susan* (1894) and the problem of divorce as adumbrated in *The Liars* (1897)—the latter a technically admirable example of the "well-made play" against which Shaw fulminated—are handled in a manner that now seems old-fashioned. Jones continued to exploit social problems in *Mrs. Dane's Defense* (1900), but in *Dolly Reforming Herself* (1908) there is genuine high comedy and a mellow art instead of the old hard vehemence. From about 1897, coincident with Kipling and the Boer War, an "imperialistic" note had sounded in some of his plays. This grew in volume and fervor after 1914, and it was over differences of opinion regarding England's policy in war and peace that Jones quarreled bitterly with Shaw and H. G. Wells.[11]

Sir Arthur Wing Pinero [12] (1855-1934) learned his craftsmanship in the school of Scribe and Sardou and never discarded completely the conventions of the *pièce bien faite* with its over-ingenious plotting, its "great scene," its conversational exposition, and its use of "asides." From 1877 he put out a succession of comedies and farces, light in substance and noteworthy only for the expertness with which comic entanglements are devised and resolved.    **Pinero**

[11] See especially Jones's *My Dear Wells* (1921), ch. XIX. Cf. Archibald Henderson, *Bernard Shaw, Playboy and Prophet* (1932), pp. 648-655.

[12] *Social Plays*, ed. Clayton Hamilton (4v, 1917-1922). — Hamilton Fyfe, *Sir Arthur Wing Pinero's Plays and Players* (1930); W. Stocker, "Pinero's Dramen," *Anglia*, XXXV (1912). 1-79. The account of Pinero in P. P. Howe, *Dramatic Portraits*, is exquisitely cruel. Pinero's *Stevenson the Dramatist* (*Publications of the Dramatic Museum of Columbia University*, 1914) is illuminating on his own ideals and limitations. — The dates given are of stage production.

Overtones of melancholy and hints of serious purpose gradually became audible. For *The Profligate* (1889) he wrote alternative dénouements—a suicide or a technically happy ending; the theatre-folk chose the latter but Pinero published the play with the tragic close. *The Second Mrs. Tanqueray* (1893), the tragedy of a "woman with a past," must be judged not only in relation to Ibsen (at the height of whose notoriety it was produced) but to several immediately contemporary novels such as *Tess, Esther Waters,* and Grant Allen's *The Woman Who Did.* Pinero's skill is displayed in the admirable exposition and in the tense critical scenes; but the tragic conclusion is melodramatic, and Shaw's indictment of the play—that the tragedy does not develop from character but from an exceptional and improbable chain of events—is justified. From a situation which would have provided Ibsen with crushing accusations against society Pinero extracted good "theatre." In subsequent plays he continued to exploit "delicate"—or, as Shaw wittily called them, "Pinerotic"—subjects. *The Gay Lord Quex* (1899) is notable for its wit, its ingenious stage-setting, and its deft adjustment of the audience's sympathies whereby the "villain" becomes the "hero." Pinero's technique in tragedy can be best studied in *Iris* (1901), old-fashioned though it now is. *Mid-Channel* (1909), Pinero's most powerful play, is a study in neurasthenia leading to a wrecked marriage. Pinero continued to write till about 1930; but his post-war plays are, like Jones's, of little consequence.

Whatever the shortcomings of their plays as literature, Jones and Pinero are significant transitional figures in the revival of the theatre, for they set examples of formal excellence. As expert craftsmen they claim more attention than the bare mention usually vouchsafed them in histories of English literature.

## III

*Shaw*

George Bernard Shaw [13] (1856-1950), Irish in birth but of Yorkshire blood, commanded for his campaign of ideas the position of vantage of a man without a country. After his childhood in Dublin, his youth was a period of poverty and struggle in London. He became attached to the Socialist movement and a member of the Fabian Society (1884) for which he wrote the *Manifesto.* Later he collaborated with Sidney and Beatrice Webb on the *Fabian Essays* (1889). With a natural forensic gift he developed into an alert and hard-hitting debater and public speaker. Meanwhile, between 1879 and 1883, he had written five novels. *Cashel Byron's Profession* (1882;

[13] *Collected Works* (30v, 1930-1931); *Complete Plays* (1931); *Prefaces* (1934). — G. H. Wells, *Bibliography* (1925-1929); C. L. and V. M. Broad, *Dictionary to the Plays and Novels of Bernard Shaw, with a Bibliography* (1929); Archibald Henderson, *George Bernard Shaw: His Life and Work* (1911) and *Bernard Shaw, Playboy and Prophet* (1932); *Table Talk of G. B. S. Conversations . . . between Bernard Shaw and His Biographer* [Henderson] (1925); H. L. Mencken, *G. B. Shaw: His Plays* (1905); G. K. Chesterton, *George Bernard Shaw* (1909); Charles Cestre, *Bernard Shaw et son œuvre* (Paris, 1912); P. P. Howe, *Bernard Shaw: A Critical Study* (1915); E. C. Wagenknecht, *A Guide to Bernard Shaw* (1929); R. F. Rattray, *Bernard Shaw: A Chronicle and an Introduction* (1934); Sen Gupta, *The Art of Bernard Shaw* (1936); T. A. Knowlton, *The Economic Theory of George Bernard Shaw* (1936); H. C. Duffin, *The Quintessence of Bernard Shaw* (1939); Hesketh Pearson, *G. B. S.: A Full-Length Portrait* (1942).

published 1885-1886), the best of them, was later dramatized as *The Admirable Bashville* (1901). *Love among the Artists* (1881; published 1886) is concerned largely with music. Wagner had been one of the shaping influences on Shaw's youth; and it was as a musical critic for *The Star* (1889) and art critic for *The World* (1890-1894) that he first attracted attention.[14] The keen and forthright dramatic criticisms in *The Saturday Review* (1895-1898) made the initials "G. B. S." famous.[15]

Long before that time this immensely energetic journalist, critic, publicist, and reformer had found in the drama the congenial medium for the dissemination of his ideas. In 1885 he and William Archer had attempted to collaborate on a play. It did not come off; but in 1892, with Ibsen as an incentive rather than a model, Shaw drastically altered the play into *Widowers' Houses,* which was produced by the Independent Theatre group. This grotesque and ironical exposure of slum landlordism and municipal graft is crude enough, but the rapid interchange of ideas gives life to the characters. *The Philanderer* (1893), which did not achieve production, is a disagreeable piece no longer vitalized by its ephemeral topicalities on the Ibsenites, the vivisectionists, and the "new women." *Mrs. Warren's Profession* (1894) ran afoul of a censorship which could not stomach a serious treatment of the "social evil." In it Shaw broadens an attack upon the problem of the prostitute and the procuress into an apologue of the iniquities of industrialism. By this time Shaw had probably derived suggestions from the sparkling dialogue and impudent paradoxes of Wilde's comedies,[16] but independently of Wilde he possessed from the first a sense of style which distinguishes his dialogue from the usual commonplaces of Jones and Pinero. The gay and witty comedy *Arms and the Man* (1894), which under the patronage of Emily Horniman (later the financial "backer" of the Irish Players) had a limited success with an intellectual coterie but failed to win the larger public, satirizes romantic notions of military glory and false ideals of heroism.

If people would not attend performances of his plays, perhaps he could persuade them to read them. *Plays Pleasant and Unpleasant* (1898) collect in the latter category Shaw's first three pieces and in the former *Arms and the Man, Candida, The Man of Destiny,* and *You Never Can Tell.* In *Candida* the contrast is developed between the large, unpractical vision of a poet and the narrow but boldly benevolent opinions of a Christian Socialist clergyman. Candida, the parson's wife, is the most charming of Shaw's heroines (he designed the rôle for Ellen Terry [17]) and in no other play till

*Plays Pleasant and Unpleasant*

---

[14] Reprinted as *London Music in 1888-9* (1937) and *Music in London, 1890-1894* (1932). Shaw's most important contribution to musical criticism, *The Perfect Wagnerite* (1898), expounds the revolutionary thought in *The Ring of the Nibelungs* with a characteristic neglect of the emotional content.

[15] Assembled as *Our Theatres in the Nineties; Collected Works,* XXIII-XXV.

[16] See above, ch. XXXV.

[17] What has been called the struggle of Shaw and Irving for the possession of the soul of Ellen Terry (too complex a story to be related here) typifies the conflict between the modern and the traditional-classic view of the function of the stage. See *Ellen Terry and Bernard Shaw: A Correspondence* (1931).

*Saint Joan* did this dramatist who is so nearly pure intelligence approach so closely to an understanding of emotion. *The Man of Destiny* carries on the attack upon the falsity of martial glory by contrasting the historic Bonaparte with the Napoleon of legend. *You Never Can Tell* is an irresponsible farce-comedy almost wholly devoid of social theses save what may be read into the contrast between the kindly wisdom and lowly social status of William the Waiter. He is one of the most memorable creations of the English Comic Muse.

Of *Three Plays for Puritans* (1901) *The Devil's Disciple* is a melodrama of the American Revolution, *Captain Brassbound's Conversion* a comedy, and *Caesar and Cleopatra* the delineation of a supremely famous man who, true to his own nature, does not need the pedestal of legend for the recognition of his genius. The amusing anachronistic topical allusions are part of Shaw's method of bringing history home to the modern spectator. But after the admirable opening episode of Caesar's first encounter with Cleopatra,

**Man and Superman**

action and characterization are blurred by too much sheer talk. *Man and Superman* (1903) presages the philosophy to be elaborated later; but lacking Act III (the Dream of Hell), which is almost always omitted on the stage, this is a disconcerting comedy of a woman's pursuit and capture of a reluctant male. Marriage is "a man-trap baited with ... delusive idealizations." What is implied in the comedy is made explicit in John Tanner's dream of Don Juan Tenorio and still more so in the Preface to the play. Woman is the agent of the "Life-Force" which directs her more strongly than it does man towards procreation, the supreme end of the species. With suggestions of Bergson's doctrine of creative evolution (the *élan vital*) and hints from Schopenhauer, Nietzsche, and Samuel Butler are combined "advanced" views on eugenics and selective breeding. Shaw the philosopher dominates Shaw the dramatist.

Till 1904 Shaw had had but a limited theatrical success and had been almost wholly dependent upon provincial audiences and the coterie acclaim of the semi-private Stage Society, but now came fame and financial success. Harley Granville-Barker and J. E. Vedrenne began their brilliant management of the Court Theatre where by 1907 there were several hundred productions of nearly a dozen of Shaw's plays. At the summit of renown, he was also at the top of his form. *John Bull's Other Island,* a wise and witty

**Major Barbara**

comedy on Irish character and politics, was rejected by the Abbey Theatre for which it was written, produced in London, and published with *Major Barbara* (1907). In power of thought and brilliance of style Shaw never surpassed the latter play, and when the prestige of some of his later dramas has declined it may come to be considered his masterpiece. In the munitions business he found a peculiarly hateful example of the evils of industrialism and in Undershaft, the war-profiteer, an illustration of man's following of self-interest disguised as duty. The Salvation Army provides the other side of the picture and affords an occasion for the development of the theme, taken directly from Samuel Butler, that "poverty is the worst of crimes" and the lack of money the root of all evil.

There was now some evidence of decline in power. *The Shewing-up of Blanco Posnet* (1909), refused a license but acted in Dublin beyond the Lord Chamberlain's jurisdiction, evinces some understanding of crude religiosity but is not worth the pother about it in Shaw's preface. *Misalliance* (1910) is scarcely more than a specific illustration of the matters discussed in the appended "Treatise on Parents and Children." *Getting Married* (1908), is really not a play at all but a dialogue, much of it tedious. *The Doctor's Dilemma* (1911), written, according to the report, to meet Archer's challenge that Shaw had never attempted a death scene, does not meet it successfully. The incidental attacks upon the medical profession as an organization preying upon the public spill over into a huge preface. *Fanny's First Play* (1911), which on the stage scored one of Shaw's greatest hits, uses the old device of the play-within-the-play and reminiscences of *The Rehearsal* and *The Critic* to satirize the dramatic critics. *Androcles and the Lion* (1913) afforded much mirth to those who were not shocked by the mingling of buffoonery with the serious presentation of different types of Christian faith. The play is not wanting in passages of solemn beauty, and the lion is really funny. *The Dark Lady of the Sonnets* (1910) is amusing, if unconvincing, as a comedy of the court of Queen Elizabeth, and more serious as an argument for a National Theatre. In reply to Frank Harris's accusation that Shaw had pilfered the "Mary Fitton" theory of Shakespeare's *Sonnets* from him, Shaw in his preface gave an account of Thomas Tyler, the originator of that theory. *Pygmalion* (1913) is a satire on snobbery and a contribution of no great value to educational theory. That the normalization of Judy O'Grady's use of the aspirates will make her the equal of the Colonel's lady does not carry us very far.

Shaw's expression of opinions during the War of 1914-1918 cost him temporarily his popularity. Actually he directed his attack not against England's participation in the war but against the official justification of her entrance into the conflict. But as his arguments were nearly identical with those in German propaganda he was accused, not without reason, of giving aid and comfort to the enemy. Certainly his levity of tone was ill-timed and seemed heartless. Shaw's far-sighted proposals for the peace may have had some influence upon Woodrow Wilson. The "playlets of the war" (as he called a few dramatic sketches) are negligible topicalities. *Heartbreak House* (1917), attacking the ruling classes held responsible for the crash of civilization, is an inartistic amalgam of discussion and farce, making use of parable and symbol and anticipating the mood of disillusioned futility which was to prevail in the literature of the nineteen-twenties. The cycle of five plays entitled *Back to Methuselah* (1921), beginning with the Garden of Eden and peering into the future "as far as thought can reach," develops with unrestrained garrulity the theme of creative evolution. Death is a mere device of natural selection and if prolongation of life is ever found necessary for the preservation of the race it will be prolonged. "The power that produced Man when the monkey was not up to the mark, can produce a higher creature than Man if Man does not come up to the mark." Yet the pallid and sexless "vortices of thought" towards which humanity is held to be evolving seem singularly dispiriting. Shaw's anti-Neo-Darwinism and his arguments for a restatement of religious mythology in modern terms are more convincingly presented in his preface (a hundred pages of his finest prose) than in the plays themselves. *Saint Joan* (1923) was a great success in the theatre, partly because the circumstance of the former self-proclaimed atheist offering his homage to a heroine of religion seemed piquant. But the characterization of Joan of Arc is regarded as a purely intellectual problem; the emotional content of religion, though not ignored, is misunderstood. The great trial-scene gave Shaw an opportunity to dramatize a clash of opposites wherein Joan's enemies are permitted to have the better of the arguments. This satisfies logic at the expense of intuition; but a "vortex of pure thought" cannot be expected to comprehend the character of a saint. Shaw's plays after *Saint Joan,* such as *The Apple Cart* (1930) and *Geneva* (1939) were either topicalities or "tomfooleries" (his own term) and may be passed over without comment.

*Saint*
*Joan*

"In all my plays," Shaw remarked to his authorized biographer, "my economic studies have played as important a part as a knowledge of anatomy does in the works of Michael Angelo." These studies led to his rejection of the Marxian theory of value, while practical experience with workingmen and revolutionists led to a denial of the existence of the "class-conflict." Revolutionists, he found, were generally intelligent, and therefore dissatisfied, members of the bourgeoisie, at war with their own class, while self-interest attached the proletariat to the capitalistic system which exploited it. From revolutionary Marxism Shaw passed to the conviction that public ownership would come gradually. Not till late in his career did he bring together his ideas on society in *The Intelligent Woman's Guide to Capitalism and Socialism* (1928), but from the beginning his effort was, as he said, "to force the public to reconsider its morals," especially current morality as to economic and sexual relations. To this end (and not merely for self-advertisement) he used every resource of a nature that was never loath to clown, to shock, and to parade, but also to fight hard and generously against cruelty and hypocrisy. The ardor of his convictions made for the volubility and repetitiousness which are his greatest weaknesses as a writer and for the persistent confusion of art and ethics which turned so many of his plays into pieces of propaganda. There is little or nothing that is original in his thought. His gift was for the vigorous enunciation and brilliant illustration of the ideas of other men. His satire ranged over the church, the law, penology, medicine ("organized" medicine and the vivisectionists), science (especially Neo-Darwinism which he opposed as cruel, mindless, and futile), and numberless other subjects. A distrust of emotional values led

*The*
*Drama of*
*Ideas*

to his derision of romantic notions of love; love he regarded as a biological mechanism for the propagation of the race. War he exposed as futile folly, but he argued that at the present stage of evolution man is naturally destructive though he invents such excuses as justice and patriotism. This is a particular example of Shaw's exposure of the contrast between the public profession of ideals of conduct and society and the secret evasion of those ideals. Men search for high-sounding excuses for following the path of desire. What is wrong with civilization? is his ever-recurring question. Consequently his basic concern was not with individual characterization but with problems in character and conduct of universal import, with the further consequence that in the later plays there is a tendency towards the symbolic which accounts for the resemblance that has been found between his plays and the Jonsonian Comedy of Humors. There are no real villains in the plays, or rather, Society as it exists is the villain, for, as Shaw asserted, "until Society is reformed, no man can reform himself except in the most insignificant small ways." His aim was not to tell a story but to convey ideas. In this there is the danger to Shaw's future reputation that these ideas will be absorbed into, or rejected by, the general consciousness. Putting it more hopefully, not the ideas but the entertaining way in which they are illuminated will keep the comedies in remembrance. In some plays he does not entirely discard the *raisonneur* or disinterested *tertium quid* of whom Jones and Pinero made so much use; but more frequently, seeking a perpetual display of contrary arguments, Shaw permits the characters, who are sometimes mere burlesques, to illustrate and comment upon the author's theses. Often they are no more than his mouthpieces. "Debated drama," Shaw called this kind of play; that is, the discussion of the mental and spiritual states and changes in the characters of men and women who are involved in a situation rather than an action.[18]

## IV

The dramatist most closely associated with Shaw was Harley Granville-Barker (1877-1946). Early experience as an actor and producer contributed to his success as a playwright. At the Court Theatre he created several of Shaw's most famous rôles. In the years shortly before the First World War he was responsible for Shakespearean productions which are famous in stage history for their beauty and intelligence. With Gordon Craig he was an innovator in methods of mounting and illumination. His three important

*Granville-Barker*

[18] St. John Hankin (1860-1909) was another contributor to the "drama of ideas," but in a sense other than that in which the phrase is applied to Shaw. The dramatist's business, Hankin said, is to "represent life, not argue about it." The life he represents affords the spectator the satisfaction of recognition rather than of surprise. Instead of making his plays vehicles of ideas, as did Shaw, he used a clear-cut idea, apt for comedy and touched with cynicism, as the central motive in each. Hankin avoided cheap theatrical effects, sudden "curtains," and the like. A feeling for style makes his plays more readable today than are most of the period. *The Cassilis Engagement* (1905) is probably his best play, and *The Last of the De Mullins* (1908) his most serious. — *Plays,* introduction by John Drinkwater (2v, 1923).

plays all belong to the first decade of the century. These varied experiences as actor, manager, producer, playwright, translator, adapter and experimenter lie behind the brilliant Shakespearean and other dramatic criticism of his later years, in which the emphasis is upon the practical problems of the theatre.[19]

*The Marrying of Ann Leete* (1901), Granville-Barker's first significant play, deals with the problem of *mésalliances* into which the heroine and her brother are driven by the "Life-Force." Ideas suggestive of Shaw and George Meredith[20] are combined with elements of fantasy and symbolism faintly resembling Barrie's work. *Prunella* (1904) is a light and charming thing written in collaboration with Laurence Housman. *The Voysey Inheritance* (1905) presents the conflict between the older generation, represented by an energetic, dishonest father, and the younger, represented by the sensitive son who must face a heritage of debt and dishonor. The conflicting counsel given him by his sister and his betrothed provides a clash of opposites, and at the close the situation is left in dramatic suspense. *Waste* (1907), which the censor refused to license, is a somber "domestic" tragedy of a young politician who when his mistress dies as the result of an operation to escape child-bearing is left without the son he longed for and the woman he loved and, faced with a scandal ruinous to his career, kills himself. *The Madras House* (1910) is another study of the conflicting generations and reflects also the "feminist" agitation of the pre-war years. *The Secret Life* (1923) reflects the moral and spiritual desolation of the post-war world, mooting questions to which no answer is forthcoming. Characteristic of this small body of work of high distinction are an extreme precision in dialogue, an intimate sympathy with the characters he has created, a most effective employment of understatement, an ability to make details contribute to the mood of an entire play, and a sensitiveness to the subtle relationships existing between small things and great.

*Houghton*    The theatre at Manchester supported by Miss Horniman afforded an outlet for several dramatists of whom William Stanley Houghton (1881-1913) was the most distinguished. A direct, frank realism in which there is nothing of the doctrinaire is characteristic of his best play, *Hindle Wakes* (1912). This is an austere and genuinely modern treatment of the problem of the "double standard." Fanny passes a holiday at the seaside with Alan; facing a scandal the parents try to force marriage upon them. The weak Alan is brought to the point of proposing marriage, but it is Fanny who refuses; she does not love him and declines to let a passing affair enmesh her for life. The play ends without any attempt to solve the underlying problem.

It seems likely that John Galsworthy[21] will be longer remembered for

[19] *Prefaces to Shakespeare* (4v, 1927-1945); *On Dramatic Method* (1931); *Associating with Shakespeare* (1932); and other works.

[20] Compare Granville-Barker's discussion of *The Sentimentalists* in "Tennyson, Swinburne, and Meredith—and the Theatre," in *The Eighteen-Seventies* (1929), pp. 187-193.

[21] For the novels and for general bibliographical references see ch. XL, below. Galsworthy's plays are collected in seven series (1909-1930). See also his *Representative Plays*, ed. G. P. Baker (1924). The correspondence with Edward Garnett in H. V. Marrot, *The Life and Letters*

one work of fiction than for his plays. He had already published several *Galsworthy* novels and begun *The Forsyte Saga* when his first play, *The Silver Box,* was produced by Granville-Barker (1906). Standing as always within the confines of the privileged class, Galsworthy here indicts society for its contrasting treatment of two men, the one rich the other poor, who are guilty of the same crime. *Strife* (1909) presents the conflict of extremes as represented by capital and labor, the lock-out, and the strike. In the end and after much misery, both parties repudiate their recalcitrant leaders and accept a compromise ready at hand from the beginning of the dispute. The fact that *Justice* (1910) led to reforms in prison-administration is more to Galsworthy's credit as a humanitarian than as a dramatist. Falder, the protagonist, is neither innocent nor an incorrigible criminal; but when after the theatrically effective trial scene and the harrowing episode of the solitary confinement Falder, now a ticket-of-leave man, forges references in order to find employment, is again arrested, and in the act of escape meets his death, no solution of the problem of the ex-prisoner has been offered; the dramatist has merely put before us an extreme case. *The Pigeon* (1913) contrasts the treatment of social outcasts by a charitable sentimentalist with the treatment accorded by three types of social workers. *The Skin-Game* (1920) presents yet another contrast, this time between the "county families" and the newly rich. In *Loyalties* (1922) sympathy is extended to a vulgar young Jew from whom a "gentleman" has stolen money to buy off his former mistress. Facing discovery, the thief shoots himself. *Old English* (1924), which in mood is nearest of the plays to *The Forsyte Saga,* studies the vanishing type of ruggedly individualistic man of affairs. From this rapid survey a dozen lesser plays, no longer acted or read, have been omitted. The charge brought against Galsworthy at the beginning of his career that he was cold and "inhuman" in his impartiality yielded later to the criticism that he was sentimental, that his sympathy was not untouched with aristocratic patronage of the unfortunate, and that his pity often sinks into the lachrymose. He applied an anxious seriousness, unalleviated by wit or humor, as much to the effective theatrical arrangement of his material as to his exposure of defects in modern society. The desire to be fair to both sides carries in later plays the consequence not only of over-symmetry of design but also of seeming to refuse to take a firm stand. His lucid and all too facile compassion was expended rather upon social groups than upon individuals, and his hostility, like Shaw's, was to institutions rather than to men and women. He is the perpetual pleader of those extenuating circumstances which society must often brush aside if it is to protect itself. The criticism that while demonstrating the need for reform he was not a reformer is true of the plays but not of the man, as his correspondence with Winston Churchill and other public officials shows. His hope was in social evolution, not revolution; but in his desire to be just to the under-dog he did less than justice to society itself.

---

of John Galsworthy (1936) is illuminating for his intentions and techniques. See also his essay, *Some Platitudes concerning the Drama,* in *The Inn of Tranquility* (1912), pp. 189-202.

*Maugham*      William Somerset Maugham [22] (1874-    ) is destined to be remembered rather for his novels (or one of them) than for his numerous plays. Like Galsworthy, he was already a writer of fiction when the Stage Society produced his first play, *A Man of Honor,* in 1903. This tragedy of mismating gave promise of profounder things, but Maugham chose to expend his polished technique for many years upon already well-worn themes. The literary grace of such an essentially trivial play as *The Land of Promise* (1909) marks its descent from Oscar Wilde and its cynicism is suggestive of Restoration comedy. The same manner survives in some of his post-war plays, *The Constant Wife* (1926), for example. More substantial and on the highest level of his craftsmanship is *The Circle* (1921). Often he satirized the self-assured pose of the "Bright Young Things" of the post-war generation, and his somewhat supercilious sophistication sometimes anticipates the tone of Noel Coward. But in his final phase as a dramatist Maugham, writing not "what the public wants" but what he wished to write, rose to a high level of sincerity and power. *The Breadwinner* (1930), deft in craftsmanship and sardonic in humor, is suggestive of Maugham's novel, *The Moon and Sixpence. For Services Rendered* (1932) is a grim commentary upon the politicians' promise of "a land fit for heroes to live in." In the last act of *Sheppey* (1933) the action shifts most impressively from the realistic to the symbolic plane, with the introduction of the old morality motive of the Coming of Death. Maugham had for long followed the melodramatic or farcical path of least resistance, but from it he turned to express his cynical contempt for the world in which he has been forced to live.

*Barrie*      While some of the novels of Galsworthy and Maugham are more likely to survive than their plays, the converse is true of Sir James Matthew Barrie [23] (1860-1937). Like them he was practised in other literary forms before he turned to the drama. In his early writings he sketched with humor and pathos the life of Kirriemuir: *Auld Licht Idylls* (1888) and *A Window in Thrums* (1889) are Scottish regionalism of the "Kailyard School." The sketches in *My Lady Nicotine* (1890) are somewhat broader in scope. *The Little Minister* (1891), humorous and unabashedly sentimental, won success as a novel and far more success when it was dramatized (1897). The humorous types in *The Professor's Love Story* (1894) are steeped in cloying sentiment. But that there was a hard core beneath Barrie's surface softness was shown in the two novels, *Sentimental Tommy* (1896) and its sequel *Tommy and Grizel* (1900). The costume-play *Quality Street* (1902) treats with genuinely moving tenderness the old theme of lovers meeting after

[22] *Collected Plays* (6v, 1931-1934). For the novels and for bibliographical references see below, ch. XL.

[23] *Works,* Kirriemuir Edition (10v, 1922), Peter Pan Edition (18v, 1929-1941); *Plays,* Uniform Edition (10v, 1918-1938); *Plays,* Definitive Edition, ed. A. E. Wilson (1942); *Letters,* ed. Viola Meynell (1942). — Herbert Garland, *Bibliography* (1928); Denis Mackail, *Barrie* (1941); J. A. Hammerton, *Barrie: The Story of a Genius* (1929); H. M. Walbrook, *J. M. Barrie and the Theatre* (1922); J. A. Roy, *J. M. Barrie* (1937); W. A. Darlington, *J. M. Barrie* (1938). — Barrie's plays were generally printed several years after their appearance on the stage; the dates here given are those of production.

long separation. *The Admirable Crichton* (1902) is sturdier stuff. With perfect mastery of his art Barrie presents the imperturbable, sagacious butler who when the fashionable people by whom he is employed are wrecked on a desert island assumes the leadership for which his nature fits him. He becomes arrogant and plans to marry his master's daughter. But the party is rescued and with the return to Mayfair he returns to his menial rank. The sound social criticism in all this came appropriately from a countryman of Burns, but it is kept implicit and does not clash with the comedy of the situation. *Peter Pan* (1904) developed from the somewhat shadowy elfin-child in the volume of fantasies called *The Little White Bird* (1902). The boy who, dwelling in the "Never-Never Land," refused to grow up and carried Wendy and his companions to the fairy world, to the pirate ship, and to his home in the tree tops, has assumed the proportions of a myth in the imagination of modern England. Certainly the merging of reality and dream is accomplished with most delicate art; but, whatever may be the case with juvenile readers and spectators, to most adult minds there is something a little distasteful in the combination of humor and adventure with sentimentality. Passing over a number of not very substantial pieces, we come to Barrie's masterpiece, *Dear Brutus* (1917). Here once more, reality fades into dream and dream into reality. In the magic wood just outside old Lob's house each character in a mixed company of guests has his or her "second chance" at life. The awakening in the third act, which in other hands might have been grim or tragic, is kept perfectly within the region of comedy, and the moral—that "the fault, dear Brutus, is not in our stars, but in ourselves"—is as clear as it is unobtrusive. Barrie's short war-plays are of no lasting interest. In *Mary Rose* (1920) a dramatized ghost-story is touched with symbolism. *Shall We Join the Ladies?* (1921) is a murder play beginning with a startling interest that is scarcely sustained. *The Boy David* (1936) depended upon Barrie's renown for such success as it achieved.

There is altogether too much *larmoyante* sensibility and pathos in Barrie's writings, especially when he expends his sympathy upon women and children, but there is also mockery, slyness, and, for all his apparent want of robustness, a disillusioned, quietly ironical view of life, not without hints of cruelty. He skirts round tragedy only by constantly availing himself of the by-path of fantasy. His plays are consequently nearer to the poetic drama than to the drama of social reform.

That poetic tragedy might be reinstated in the theatre was the promise held out by the brief, brilliant success of Stephen Phillips (1868-1915) during the first years of this century.[24] But this flash in the pan was quickly extinguished. *Paolo and Francesca* (1899; acted 1902), his first and best play, has an operatic kind of theatricality which imposed itself upon audiences for a while. Thereafter there was a decline through the lyricism of *Herod*

---

[24] Phillips first attracted attention with his nondramatic poem *Christ in Hades* (1896). The contemporary evaluation of Phillips is shown by the space allotted to him in F. W. Chandler, *Aspects of Modern Drama* (1914), pp. 382-394.

(1901) and the episodic pageantry of *Ulysses* (1904) to later plays that need not be listed. The large, unsubtle rhetoric of these plays, easily mouthed and easily comprehended, with their dependence upon panoramic spectacle, exotic costumes, and theatrical emotionality, provided the public with refreshment from the staple fare of the problem play.

*Bottomley*    Gordon Bottomley[25] (1874-1948) applied the large utterance of his non-dramatic poetry to his strenuous and closely-knit plays in which there is a brutal force and directness that is not mere theatricality nor pseudo-Jacobean pastiche but springs from something primitive in the poet's own nature. After three one-act pieces he wrote *The Riding to Lithend* (1909), *King Lear's Wife* (1915), and his two finest dramas, *Gruach* and *Britain's Daughter* (both 1921). It remains to be seen whether posterity will make to these strong, sincere, and highly individual creations reparation for the neglect from which they have suffered.

*Dunsany*    Edward J. M. D. Plunkett, Lord Dunsany[26] (1878-1957) was an Irishman and was briefly associated with the Abbey Theatre; but instead of availing himself of Celtic legends for his stories and plays he invented a mythology of his own. Of the volumes in which Dunsany shaped his fantasies into narrative form the best are *Time and the Gods* (1906), *The Book of Wonder* (1912), *Tales of Wonder* (1916), and the exquisite little masterpiece, *The Charwoman's Shadow* (1926). In other books of more recent date he drew upon his own experiences of war and far travel. In the within narrow limits and not without repetition he achieved effects of sometimes a little suggestive of Blake. A more clearly discernible influence is that of Maeterlinck. The symbolism underlying his stormy gods and helpless mortals is apprehensible, if at all, only with difficulty; yet working within narrow limits and not without repetition he has achieved effects of weird, romantic beauty. *The Gods of the Mountain* (1914) and *A Night at an Inn* (1917) are among his best plays.

*Masefield*    As poet laureate John Masefield requires consideration in a later chapter.[27] In his first play, *The Tragedy of Nan* (1909), which was produced at Manchester, the influence of Synge is apparent. But a manner natural to the west of Ireland is less appropriate to the west of England. A grim story, culminating in a moment of sheer horror, is played out against the background of the Severn river and its mighty tides. A dignified prose style is employed to better purpose in *The Tragedy of Pompey the Great* (1910). *Good Friday* (1915) pointed forward to *A King's Daughter* (1923) —the story of Jezebel, *The Trial of Jesus* (1925), *The Coming of Christ* (1928), and *Easter* (1928). *Tristan and Isolt* (1927) and *End and Beginning* (1933), on Mary Queen of Scots, are, like the plays on biblical themes, noble if not entirely successful experiments in interweaving verse and prose,

[25] Bottomley's first five plays were collected in 1920; the later plays have not yet appeared in a collected edition. For his nondramatic poetry see below, ch. XLI.
[26] *Five Plays* (1914); *Plays of Gods and Men* (1917); *Seven Modern Comedies* (1928); and other dramas. — See E. H. Bierstadt, *Dunsany the Dramatist* (1917).
[27] See ch. XLI, below.

dialogue and choruses. The quest for freedom from modern conventionalities of form and diction led Masefield back to something like the medieval mystery plays.

Experience as an actor and as author of several now forgotten plays was *Drink-* behind John Drinkwater [28] (1882-1937) when *Abraham Lincoln* (1918) *water* made him famous. The great theme of the captain slain at the moment of the safe arrival of the victor ship evoked an immediate response at a time when the forward-looking, with malice towards none and charity to all, were seeking to bind up the wounds of a broken world. The play, though of late unjustly denigrated, is memorable not only for nobility of sentiment and dignity of versification but for the occasional deliberate manipulations of history which raise mere fact to the level of the artistic sense of fact. Later plays, *Mary Stuart* (1921), *Oliver Cromwell* (1921), and *Robert E. Lee* (1923), though equally competent, did not equally engage public attention.

[28] *Collected Plays* (2v, 1925). On Drinkwater's nondramatic poetry see ch. XLI, below. He wrote also critical studies of Morris and Swinburne and biographies of Byron, Charles James Fox, and Pepys.

# XXXIX

## Other Late-Victorian Poets[1]

### I

*Patmore*

Coventry Patmore[2] (1823-1896) inherited from an eccentric father[3] a marked individuality of temperament, but his strength of purpose was his own. His *Poems* (1844), of which the best reappeared with new pieces in *Tamerton Church Tower* (1853), introduced him to the Pre-Raphaelite circle, and he contributed to *The Germ*. To the Pre-Raphaelites and Browning his wife's beauty was an inspiration, as it was to himself. Wedded love is the theme of *The Angel in the House* (1854) with its sequels, *The Espousals* (1856) and *Faithful Forever* (1860), as it is of *The Victories of Love* (1863).[4] In 1862 Mrs. Patmore died. In 1864 Patmore became a Roman Catholic and married again. The *Odes* (1868) are in a new, elaborate, irregular style which is fully developed in *The Unknown Eros* (1877). In later life there was little poetry, but Patmore wrote a treatise on English metrics, some rather eccentric literary criticism, and several essays in mystical speculation, among them the lost *Sponsa Dei* the manuscript of which he destroyed at the behest of his spiritual advisers.

*The Two Styles*

Patmore believed that the poet possesses a supersensual knowledge which he imparts by means of symbols and parables drawn from sensible things.[5] This is the unifying principle binding together his earlier and later work. There was no real breach of continuity when, about 1862, his first manner, simple and sentimental to the point of insipidity, modulated into his second style, heightened, ornate, and occasionally sublime. The figure of him drawn

---

[1] Brief estimates of certain lesser poets of the late nineteenth century have been introduced, as seemed appropriate, in earlier chapters. The rest, now to be passed in review, are so grouped that points of contact of either a common faith or a common skepticism are emphasized. This chapter is limited, with two exceptions, to writers who had obtained recognition or had at any rate done their best work by the beginning of the present century. The exceptions are Hopkins, who was unknown to the general public till long after his death, and Doughty, who though self-dedicated to poetry from his early years, published his first poem of consequence in 1906.

[2] *Poems* (4v, 1879); *Selected Poems,* ed. Derek Patmore (1931). Patmore's prose works include: *Principle in Art* (1889); *Religio Poetae* (1893); *The Rod, the Root, and the Flower* (1895). — Basil Champneys, *Memoirs and Correspondence of Coventry Patmore* (2v, 1900); Edmund Gosse, *Coventry Patmore* (1905); Osbert Burdett, *The Idea of Coventry Patmore* (1921); Frederick Page, *Patmore: A Study in Poetry* (1933). See also G. N. Shuster, *The Catholic Spirit in Modern English Literature* (1922).

[3] Peter George Patmore, a friend of Hazlitt and author of *My Friends and Acquaintances* (1854), the indiscretions in which occasioned much scandal.

[4] In the final version of *The Angel in the House* the three installments were amalgamated into two books. *The Victories of Love,* though a sequel, is an independent poem, telling with more "plot" the story of another wedded pair.

[5] *Religio Poetae* (ed. 1898), p. 3.

by Francis Thompson is of one who held in one hand "a cup of milk and honey" and in the other "a lightning-bolt." [6] In *The Angel in the House* the husband tells of the courtship and marital happiness over which the Angel (spiritual love) keeps watch and ward. The art of sinking in poetry has seldom been exemplified more candidly than in the smooth-flowing quatrains of these "idyls of the dining-room and the deanery." [7] But if the poem sinks it can also rise, as it does in the "preludes" and other passages *The Odes* of symbolic interpretation. Needing a grander style for his symbolism, Patmore resorted to the irregular ode, made up of longer and shorter lines with rimes falling capriciously, which had its precursors in Cowley and Crashaw and in the *Canzoniere* of Petrarch. Verbal and metrical splendor support themes so simple as to seem inappropriate to the style; yet in this very contrast are found Patmore's finest effects, for from the lowliest experiences of domestic life (as in *The Toys*) he drew analogies of eternal significance. The prevailing symbols are parental and marital love. For the analogy of the sexual relationship to the relationship of God and the soul Patmore had the sanction of traditional interpretations of The Song of Songs and the ecstasies of the love-mystics. This symbolism was developed in *The Unknown Eros* and was, it seems, carried from resemblance to identification in the destroyed *Sponsa Dei*. In the nature of married love Patmore found a clue to the problems of life. Man, the rational soul, is wedded to woman, the sensitive soul. Only in marriage can humanity's natural goodness and nobility find their scope. Thus an ideal—both a philosophy and a creed—is founded upon commonplace experience. With this love, death is associated in Petrarchan or Pre-Raphaelite fashion, as in the memorials to his wife (*The Azalea, Departure,* and *A Farewell*) which are among Patmore's finest odes.

Francis Thompson [8] (1859-1907), weak in will but strong in faith, pre- *Thompson* served his spiritual integrity in circumstances of poverty and degradation. The Roman Catholic college into which he was put could do little for the slovenly and shiftless boy. Drifting to London (1885), he plumbed the depths, selling matches on the street. Forlorn and faint, he outwatched the inquisitive stars, and in the extremity of illness was given shelter by a girl of the streets who shared with him her "scant pittance," asked no reward, and was afterwards sought for in vain. [9] The resemblance of this episode to the story of Ann in De Quincey's *Confessions* is no reason for questioning

[6] Francis Thompson, *Ode for the Diamond Jubilee; Works,* II. 139.

[7] Swinburne, *Notes on Poems and Reviews* (1866), p. 22. Swinburne's cruel but amusing parody, *The Person of the House,* written in 1859, was published in *The Heptalogia* (1880).

[8] *Works* (3v, 1913); *Poems,* ed. T. L. Connolly (1941); *Selected Poems,* ed. Wilfrid Meynell (1912). — Everard Meynell, *The Life of Francis Thompson* (1913); R. L. Mégroz, *Francis Thompson: The Poet of Earth in Heaven* (1927); T. H. Wright, *Francis Thompson and His Poetry* (1927); Agnès de la Gorce, *Francis Thompson et les poètes catholiques d'Angleterre* (Paris, 1932); Federico Olivero, *Francis Thompson* (Turin, 1938); Katherine Tynan, "Francis Thompson," *Fortnightly Rev.,* n.s. LXXXVII (1910). 349-360; Cornelius Weygandt, *Tuesdays at Ten* (Philadelphia, 1928). ch. XI; F. B. Tolles, "The Praetorian Cohorts: a Study of the Language of Francis Thompson's Poetry," *English Studies* (Amsterdam), XXII (1940). 49-64.

[9] *A Child's Kiss,* from *Sister Songs.*

its authenticity. Poems submitted to *Merry England,* a magazine edited by Wilfrid Meynell, were accepted, and in its pages appeared *The Hound of Heaven* in 1891 and other pieces earlier or later. Thompson's worst days were now over. He was taken up by the genial circle of the Meynells, and in 1893 a volume of *Poems* appeared. That here was a new poet of power and promise was evident, though conservative critics could not comprehend this new idiom with its elaborate rhythms, exotic vocabulary, and startling and strained imagery. *Sister Songs* (1895) and *New Poems* (1897) followed; but in his last years Thompson declined into journalism, producing little that was not ephemeral save the rhapsodic essay on Shelley. Consumption and laudanum hastened his end. Among poems published posthumously the greatest is *The Kingdom of God.*

For all its individuality the poetry of Thompson is steeped in tradition. His immediate master was Patmore—the later Patmore of the *Odes.* The use of archaic and exotic words is reminiscent of Rossetti and the rhapsodic passages sometimes echo Shelley. But the searcher after influences must look further back, for Thompson was one of the first to reintroduce a strain of "metaphysical" conceit into English poetry. That he had pondered upon Donne is evident, but Crashaw's amorous mysticism had a more profound effect upon him. Dantesque elements are also present, and the sonorous Latinisms are often drawn from the liturgy. Hypersensitive, withdrawn, a recluse by temperament and (in later years) by addiction to opium, Thompson is one of the most introspective of poets. He fashioned his poetry from his memories, weaknesses, gratitudes, spiritual fears, even from his art itself. The "objective" poems have often a false and heavy pomp, but only let him write of himself and there is nothing of the meretricious in his splendor. When commissioned to write an elegy on Cardinal Manning he does not "perturbate the paradisal state" of the dead by needless praise but takes the "holy soul" apart "to press a private business"—has the poet's devotion to his art been to the detriment of his immortal soul? This catechizing of a released spirit might, had it been managed less subtly, have been absurd; in Thompson's hands it is profoundly moving. So with *The Hound of Heaven.* The conception of Christ, the Lover, pursuing the Soul, the Beloved, was one to appeal to a baroque Spanish mystic; but there were modern Englishmen who, forgetting the ancient symbols of Lamb and Fish and Pelican and Phoenix, were shocked by the symbol of the Hound. The poem is charged with extravagant imagery. The Soul flees down the labyrinthine ways of the mind. The casements of the heart are blown to with the gust of the divine approach. God chars the wood before he can limn with it. Other poems contain metaphors of like bold magnificence: Time "shoots his barbed minutes"; Death flushes "the cumbered gutters of humanity." The Body is a house at whose "clay-shuttered doors" the pinions of the angels beat. Thompson's imagery is often merely thick and clotted. His vocabulary of almost unequaled gorgeousness is often turgid. He falls into far-fetched

The
Hound
of
Heaven

conceit when inspiration fails. But he rises to majestic heights when impassioned fervor fuses thought and style.

The poetry of Alice Meynell [10] (1847-1922), though spread through nine *Alice* volumes from *Preludes* (1875) to *Last Poems* (1923), is small in quantity. *Meynell* Her spiritual reticence, her inhibitions, and her exacting standards of craftsmanship limited her output; nor did she have a great deal to say. Her faculty, when she looked out upon the world, was for the exquisite rendering of little things, and when she looked inward, for the analysis of her own religious and emotional experiences. Whether this still, small voice will continue to be heard is doubtful, but her two best-known poems, the *Letter from a Girl to Her Own Old Age* and the sonnet *Renouncement,* should remain in the anthologies.[11]

Lionel Pigot Johnson [12] (1867-1902), who became a Roman Catholic *Lionel* by conversion in early life, was a contributor to the *Book of the Rhymers' Johnson Club* and in touch with the Irish Literary Renaissance. Apart from his fine study, *The Art of Thomas Hardy* (1894), and the literary essays collected posthumously in *Post Liminium* (1911), his writings are found in *Poems* (1895) and *Ireland and Other Poems* (1897). He shared with Thompson a cloistered medievalism of outlook, but there is nothing of Thompson's grandiloquence in his spare and chiseled verse. He derived inspiration from his classical scholarship, and, as became a son of Oxford, he attached himself to "lost causes and impossible loyalties," as in his finest poem, *By the Statue of King Charles at Charing Cross.* Drink undermined his delicate health; but the motive of contrition which in some writers seems a "decadent" pose was in his case indubitably sincere. The faith that gave him assurance despite the bleak tragedy of his life is expressed with stern grandeur in *The Dark Angel.*

With all the foregoing may be associated two men of the older generation *Roden* who were not Roman Catholics but in whose verse the religious element *Noel* predominates. Roden B. W. Noel [13] (1834-1894) expresses the reaction from pessimistic realism to religious faith. *A Little Child's Monument* (1881) is a series of elegies illuminated with Christian hope. From experiences of oriental travel he derived the subjects of various poems. Others show his sympathy with the workers for social betterment, and yet others his prescience of the disaster towards which militarism was driving the world. Frederick W. H. Myers [14] (1843-1901) is best remembered for his long dra- *Myers*

[10] *Poems,* Complete Edition (1940); *Selected Poems* (1930); *Selected Essays* (1926). — Viola Meynell, *Alice Meynell* (1929); A. K. Tuell, *Mrs. Meynell and her Literary Generation* (1925).
[11] Mrs. Meynell wrote a good deal of literary criticism, distinguished for its subtlety and note of calm authority, but not without its limitations (seen, for example, in her attack on Gibbon).
[12] *Poetical Works,* introduction by Ezra Pound (1915); *Selections* (1908); *A New Selection,* ed. H. V. Marrot (1927); *Reviews and Critical Papers* (1921). — Cornelius Weygandt, *Tuesdays at Ten* (Philadelphia, 1928), ch. III.
[13] *Behind the Veil* (1863); *Songs of the Heights and Deeps* (1885); and many other volumes of verse; *Poems,* introduction by Robert Buchanan (1890); *Collected Poems* (1902).
[14] *Collected Poems,* ed. E. Myers (1921); *Saint Paul,* ed. E. J. Watson (1916); *Wordsworth* (EML Series, 1880); *Science and a Future Life* (1893); and other books.

matic monologue *Saint Paul* (1867), fervent in feeling for the character of the militant apostle and composed in a clarion-like metre which Swinburne borrowed for *Mater Triumphalis*. Myers' literary criticism is Arnoldian in substance and in manner too close an imitation of Pater.

## II

*Dixon*    The oldest member of the group of which Robert Bridges was the center was Richard Watson Dixon [15] (1833-1900). He was a friend of William Morris, and in *The Wizard's Funeral* and other early poems are a sense of "wonder" and love of the supernatural characteristic of the circle he frequented. His first volume, *Christ's Company* (1861), carries to excess the Pre-Raphaelite quaintness and search for curious words and rimes. The poems on Wellington and Marlborough which gave the title to *Historical Odes and Other Poems* (1864) reflect Dixon's scholarly interests. *Mano* (1883) is a long poem in harsh *terza rima* on an obscure tenth-century theme. In later years he accomplished some of his best work, dealing often with the thoughts and moods provoked by consciousness of advancing age. His range is narrow and his monotonous somberness, though not without moments of real greatness, expresses a religious faith without religious joy. In practically all his work there is a technical roughness and uncouthness, especially in the matter of faulty rimes. His friendship with Father Hopkins resulted in a noteworthy correspondence and the friendship with Bridges bore fruit in the volume of selections from his poems by which Bridges made him better known. Another poet who owed such reputation as he won to

*Dolben*    Bridges' influence is Digby Mackworth Dolben [16] (1848-1867) in whom a religious ardor which, had he lived, might have carried him, like Hopkins, to Rome, is blended with a love of pagan beauty. Dolben is best when he is

*Mary Coleridge*    simplest, as in the tender little poem *Homo Factus Est*. Mary Elizabeth Coleridge [17] (1861-1907), the friend of Dixon and Bridges, occasionally suggests Christina Rossetti, but there are also signs in her work of the influence of Blake and the "metaphysical" poets, and there are reminiscences of a greater Coleridge in the fantasy of such pieces as *The Witch* and *Wilderspin*. In general her poems record the varying moods of a steadfast religious experience.

*Hopkins*    Unknown to the public but in close touch with Patmore, Dixon, and Bridges, Gerard Manley Hopkins [18] (1844-1889) wrote the poems which

---

[15] *Poems, a Selection*, with memoir by Robert Bridges (1909). Dixon was a Canon of Carlisle Cathedral and author of a voluminous *History of the Church of England* (1870-1902).

[16] *Poems*, ed. Robert Bridges (1911).

[17] *Poems*, ed. Sir Henry Newbolt (1908); *Gathered Leaves*, with a memoir by Edith Sichel (1910).

[18] *Poems*, ed. Robert Bridges (1918); revised and enlarged with introduction by Charles Williams (1931); *Correspondence with Richard Watson Dixon* (1935); *Letters to Robert Bridges* (1935); *Further Letters* (1938), all ed. C. C. Abbott; *Note-Books and Papers*, ed. Humphry House (1937).—G. F. Lahey, *Gerard Manley Hopkins* (1930); E. E. Phare, *The Poetry of Gerard Manley Hopkins: A Survey and a Commentary* (1933); John Pick, *Gerard Manley Hopkins: Priest and Poet* (1942); W. H. Gardner, *Gerard Manley Hopkins* (1944);

were published posthumously in 1918. As a student at Oxford he was interested in stylistic and prosodic theory, though what little survives of his early
verse shows no radical departure from tradition. He destroyed nearly all
his manuscripts when, in 1868, he became a Jesuit. His career as teacher and
preacher does not concern us. Hopkins' superiors in the Society encouraged
him to resume the writing of poetry, and when he did so (1875) it was with
a change of manner for which his speculations had prepared him but for
which little in the previous course of English poetry prepares the reader who
comes for the first time upon *The Wreck of the Deutschland*. The drowning
of some nuns in a disaster at sea moved the devout priest to this passionate,
ejaculatory mingling of prayer and amazement. Bridges likened the poem
to a great dragon coiled at the entrance to the cavern which is Hopkins'
poetry. To this day, despite the panegyrics and the interpretations, the dragon
remains frightening to many would-be explorers of the cave.[19] Hopkins'
letters, note-books, and other papers contain unorganized critical and theoretical discussion and *dicta* which illuminate his practice and aims. Yet
obscurities remain, partly because he trusted to the insecure analogies of
musical terminology, partly because he used technical terms of his own
devising to describe metrical and stylistic phenomena which were innovations only in the extremes to which he carried them, thus persuading himself
(and many of his admirers) that he had invented something when he was
really calling an old thing by a new name. His "sprung rhythm" is a principle which poets have had ready at hand since Anglo-Saxon times—the
employment of a fixed number of stressed syllables and a varying number of
unstressed in each line. What he called "counterpoint" is much the same as
resolved stress or what Saintsbury called "equivalence"—the occasional substitution of a different foot for the foot that is the norm of the metrical pattern. The stylistic quality which he tried to secure in his own poetry he called
"inscape." This term has provoked much discussion of pattern, texture, and
what not, but essentially a poem possesses "inscape" when the design is
perfectly adapted to the theme; it is "the suiting of the unique experience
to a unique form." Hopkins outran Browning in his search of far-fetched
rimes (for example, "boon he on"—"Communion"); but whereas Browning
aimed generally at the grotesque, Hopkins, even in his worst offences, was
intensely serious. Moreover, he revived from the seventeenth century the
ugly device of the "run-over" rime.[20] For the use of alliteration he had vener-

---

Eleanor Ruggles, *Gerard Manley Hopkins* (1944); B. I. Evans, *English Poetry in the Late Nine-
teenth Century* (1933), pp. 210-218; F. R. Leavis, *New Bearings in English Poetry* (1938), pp.
159-193; David Daiches, *Poetry and the Modern World* (1940), pp. 24-34; J. G. Southworth,
*Sowing the Spring: Studies in British Poets from Hopkins to MacNeice* (1940), pp. 15-32;
Herbert Read, *In Defence of Shelley and other Essays* (1936), pp. 111-144; four articles in the
*Kenyon Rev.* (Summer, 1944), occasioned by the Hopkins centenary.

[19] See W. H. Gardner, "The Wreck of the Deutschland," *E&S*, XXI (1936). 124-152, an
elaborate study illustrating the lengths to which Hopkins' devotees have gone; useful also,
perhaps, as a counterbalance to the present writer's distaste for Hopkins.

[20] Thus in *The Windhover*, one of the poems most extravagantly admired, Hopkins uses a
"run-over" rime at the end of the first line, so that the first syllable of "kingdom" rimes with
"wing" in line four.

able precedent and many of his best effects of detonating impetuousness are gained by this device. He tried to eliminate every colorless, passive, merely connective word (especially the relative pronouns) so that only the poetic vocables should remain—every substantive a picture, every verb a deed. This "passionate condensation" is, at best, a sort of poetical shorthand, at worst, an intolerably licentious violation of every law of syntax. That his ardor, which instead of finding an outlet in luxuriant verbosity sought an extreme condensation, could impart new life and color to over-worn words is not to be denied; but generally condensation was purchased at too high a cost. The stylistic rebelliousness may have come from his isolation as a Jesuit, and the delight in oddness and incoherence may have been a reaction from ascetic discipline and an ordered philosophy. The sympathetic student recognizes that Hopkins' "altogether unusual problem of personal adjustment sought expression in an altogether unusual style." That he wrestled in spiritual anguish the moving sonnets, *No worse, there is none* and *Thou art indeed just, Lord,* make manifest. His eager apprehension of natural loveliness, as in *Inversnaid* and *The Starlight Night* and *The Windhover,* is one expression of his worship. Probing, as in *The Loss of the Eurydice,* into the mystery of God's ways, he possessed "a passionate sense of the terror of the nearness of God." Spiritual grief, not spiritual joy, is his theme. But even when the mystery was darkest he rejected the "carrion comfort," despair. Not Hopkins' religion, however, but his poetic style attracted the admiration of the post-war generation. This poetry, completely independent of the Victorian tradition, has appealed to those who fail to recognize that imagery is a good servant but a bad master; who are in quest of "something craggy to break the mind upon"; and who do not distinguish between the thought that is obscure because it is difficult and the thought that is difficult because it is obscurely expressed. Interesting experiment has been mistaken for accomplishment.

*Robert Bridges*

Robert Bridges[21] (1844-1930) emerged slowly into prominence. While a practising physician he wrote verse, and in 1882 he abandoned medicine to dedicate himself wholly to his art. Between 1873 and 1896 came eight little pamphlets of verse, afterwards brought together in the *Shorter Poems. The Growth of Love* (1876), a sonnet-sequence later much expanded, expresses the resolve to remain faithful to the poet's calling even though it goes against the scientific tendencies of the age. Love gives new values to life and new spurs to the searcher after beauty. *Prometheus the Firegiver* (1883) is composed in austere blank verse with choric interludes. Bridges called it "a Mask in the Greek Manner." He seems to have hesitated between a mere

[21] *Poetical Works* (6v, 1898-1905); *Poetical Works* (1912), excluding the eight dramas; *Collected Essays, Papers, etc.* (10v, 1927-1936). — There is as yet no full biography. G. L. McKay, *Bibliography* (1933); Sir T. Herbert Warren, *Robert Bridges, Poet Laureate* (1913); L. P. Smith, *Robert Bridges,* S. P. E. Tract, xxxv (1931); F. E. Brett Young, *Robert Bridges: A Critical Study* (1914); G. S. Gordon, *Robert Bridges* (1932); Albert Guérard, Jr., *Robert Bridges: A Study of Traditionalism* (1941); Edward Thompson, *Robert Bridges* (1944); B. I. Evans, *English Poetry in the Late Nineteenth Century* (1933), pp. 219-243; Ernest de Selincourt, "Robert Bridges," *Oxford Lectures on Poetry* (1934), pp. 233-256.

"reconstruction" of the lost first part of the Aeschylean trilogy and a fresh, individual interpretation of the myth, and as a consequence the piece is neither the one nor the other; nor is it a true masque. *Eros and Psyche* (1885), which appeared in the same year with Pater's *Marius* with its beautiful prose version of Apuleius' tale, implicitly challenged comparison with the version in *The Earthly Paradise,* for Bridges was antagonistic to Morris's loose and facile manner of story-telling. It was perhaps to suggest this challenge that Bridges divided his poem into the twelve months of the year (as *The Earthly Paradise* is planned), going Morris one better by assigning to each month as many stanzas as it contains days. Beneath these surface artifices Bridges' interpretation of the myth (so far as he suggests any) connects it with Keats's ode *To Psyche.* Beauty allied to love permits man to "gather an enchantment" from life which would otherwise pass unregarded. While these longer poems were being written, Bridges' lyrical, meditative, and elegiac faculty was developing from the first blossoms to the fairest fruit. How soon he attained the simplicity that is the very refinement of art is shown by *Long are the Hours the Sun is above,* a perfect poem and of very early date. The delicate cadences of the lyrics sometimes echo the Elizabethan song-writers, and those of richer texture Edmund Spenser; but though traditional they are not merely imitative. The more elaborate nature-pieces, such as *London Snow,* come later, as do the grander harmonies of *Whither, O Splendid Ship,* the elegy *On a Dead Child,* and the great *Elegy on a Lady.* These and countless other "shorter poems" convey that sense of the wide variety of experiences and intellectual interests to be found in the world which at the end of Bridges' life was to make *The Testament of Beauty* so rich a store of wisdom and erudition. But Bridges was no mere "intellectual.'" He knows that beauty fades and he is capable on rare occasions of a poignant expression of grief, but "the best of his art is gay" and he is the votary of that beauty which liberates the human spirit from the tyranny of circumstance and of that deep but untumultuous love which the gods approve. *The Shorter Poems*

Between 1885 and 1905 Bridges wasted much labor upon poetic dramas. The uncongenial subject of *Nero* (two parts, 1885 and 1894) did not permit him to grasp firmly his own purpose. *The Return of Ulysses* (1890) might have been handled acceptably in episodic narrative but it proved recalcitrant to the dramatic form. To imitate Terence displayed Bridges' scholarship but not any gift for comedy. The adaptations from Calderon took him into a world of "cloak-and-sword" intrigue where he was not at home. *Demeter* (1905) is a lovely but slight thing. *The Dramas*

Close study of the principles of English metrics led to the treatise on *Milton's Prosody* (1893; final revision, 1921) and later to the unattractive experiments in quantitative metres. Gradually Bridges worked out the form which in *New Verses* (1921) he called "Neo-Miltonic syllabics" and in *The Testament of Beauty* "loose alexandrines" based on "the secure bedrock of Milton's prosody." In the explorations of metrical law and the experiments

The Testa-
ment of
Beauty

in new rhythms Bridges followed the lead of Father Hopkins but with less waywardness and a more disciplined taste. Hopkins' example is behind his use of "counterpoint" and internal rime. The final manner is fully displayed in *The Testament of Beauty* (1929). Bridges had made no effort to secure a large audience. Forty years earlier he had had the recognition of such authoritative critics as Dowden and Lang, but his emergence had proceeded so slowly that when, in 1913, he had been appointed poet laureate he was still generally unknown. The subsequent absorption in prosodic experimentation did not broaden his reputation. Consequently he was as much surprised as gratified when *The Testament of Beauty*,[22] appearing on his eighty-fifth birthday, became a popular success. Circumstances extraneous to the poem's intrinsic merit account for this—the great age of the poet and his dignity, and the phenomenon, not to have been expected in the cynical nineteen-twenties, of a poem exalted in theme, of ample scope, containing the wisdom and learning of a long life, and representative of the great tradition of English poetry. The genitive case of the title is both objective and subjective. This is the poet's testament concerning Beauty but it is also Beauty's testimony, her "witness." The theme is that which runs through all Bridges' poetry, that in the life of man

> Beauty is the prime motiv of all his excellence,
> his aim and peaceful purpose.

"Self" and "Breed" (by which Bridges intends the instinct of propagation which by slow degrees rises into the most exalted love) draw man up the "ladder of joy" to his "peace with God." There is an elaborate attempt to fuse this Platonic concept with modern evolutionary thought. The poem is, indeed, overburdened with scientific theory. In speculations upon the future course of society Bridges opposes Socialism and champions "individual worth." He put into his *Testament* anything and everything that came within his wide intellectual horizon, from the dawn of the inventive faculty to the airplane and the radio, from the excavations at Ur and Kish to "far Pasadena's roseland." At first the poem was rated too highly and there has since been time for second thoughts. Difficulties of phrase, idiom, and allusion which immediately inspired commentaries are not to be held against it; and objections to the superficial eccentricities of "reformed" spelling and elocutionary punctuation may be set aside. Of the nobility of certain parts (especially the opening and the close) there can be no question. Yet doubts remain. Obviously here was the material out of which a great poem might have been molded, but to many critics it is equally obvious that a truly great poem has not been molded out of this material. Bridges' fame rests more securely upon his lyrical poetry.

[22] N. C. Smith, *Notes on The Testament of Beauty* (1931); H. W. Garrod, "The Testament of Beauty," *Poetry and the Criticism of Life* (1931), pp. 129-147; Ernest de Selincourt, "The Testament of Beauty," *Oxford Lectures on Poetry* (1934), pp. 233-256.

# III

By a hard irony the fame of Charles Montagu Doughty [23] (1843-1926)  *Doughty*
rests upon "the secure bedrock" of the *Travels in Arabia Deserta* while his
poetry remains almost unknown. Yet the Arabian adventure (1876-1878)
and the following decade employed in writing the narrative of it were but
interludes in a life dedicated to the cultivation of "the Muse of Britain."
There was a massive, primitive simplicity about Doughty's character which
perhaps explains the early choice of geological and philological studies; and
these studies in turn help to explain the qualities of his poetry. The heavy
beat of the accents, the abundant alliteration, the clashing epithets, and the
harsh yet majestic march of the rhythm have their far-descended historical
justification. Self-taught and self-secure, he was the disciple of Chaucer,
Langland, and Spenser; and passionately patriotic, he would redeem his
native tongue from modern feebleness and vulgarity. Having completed his
prose masterpiece in 1888, he spent a decade and a half in writing *The
Dawn in Britain* (1906), an epic in six volumes.[24] Space is lacking here to
discuss the word-lore that filled, and the verbal experimentation that issued
from, his vigorous but undisciplined mind. The epic [25] moves ponderously
through the vast period of British history from the taking of Rome by
Brennus to the revolt of Bonduca. There is a vague underlying allegorical
intent suggesting the conflict between the forces of darkness and light in
the contrast between the woad-stained pagans and the meek Christian
missionaries who come to Britain. Defective in the large matters of composition and exasperatingly humorless, the poem contains passages of stately
narrative, gentle pastoral episodes, and an abounding spiritual joy. But
there are few readers to be found willing to overcome the difficulties of the
way for the sake of the occasional rewards. *Adam Cast Forth* (1908) is as
rugged as the stony desert through which our First Parents wandered, but
it is shorter and simpler than the epic and not without a grave gentleness.
It is the best introduction to Doughty's poetry; few readers will go further.
*The Cliffs* (1909) and *The Clouds* (1912) were intended to arouse England
to an awareness of the imminent peril of war with Germany. In them
Doughty's wisdom attained to "something like prophetic strain," for there
are few stranger episodes in literary history than the fulfillment of his vision,
not merely of the actualities of submarine and aerial warfare but in his
clairvoyant sense of the spirit of a people threatened with the horrors of
invasion. Both poems contain interludes, not very well integrated with the

---

[23] D. G. Hogarth, *The Life of Charles M. Doughty* (1928); Barker Fairley, *Charles M.
Doughty: A Critical Study* (1927); Anne Treneer, *Charles M. Doughty: A Study of his Prose
and Verse* (1935), with bibliography; Walt Taylor, *Doughty's English*, S. P. E. Tract, LI
(1939); Barker Fairley, "The Modern Consciousness in English Literature," *E&S*, IX (1923).
127-144. Some sentences in the present discussion are taken from S. C. Chew, "The Poetry of
Charles Montagu Doughty," *No. Amer. Rev.*, CCII (1925-1926). 287-298. — On the *Arabia
Deserta* see ch. XLII, below.
[24] Centenary Edition in one volume (1943), with introduction by Ruth C. Robbins.
[25] See Friedrich Brie, "Charles Doughty und sein Epos *The Dawn in Britain*," *Anglia*,
LXIV (1940). 256-295.

context, in which, by night while the human actors sleep, gnomes and dapper elves disport themselves and play their part in the protection of Britain. *The Titans* (1916) is an obscure allegory of man's gradual conquest of the forces of nature. In Arabia, when the Bedouin inquired of him "Who art thou?" Doughty's answer had been: "God's wanderer, who, not looking back to his worldly interest, betakes himself to the contemplative life's pilgrimage." *Mansoul, or the Riddle of the World* (1920) is the record, under the medieval convention of the poet's dream, of the life-long effort to discover

> What were indeed right paths of a man's feet,
> That lacking light wont stumble in World's murk?

The poet (who is not clearly differentiated from his companion Minimus) is guided by Mansoul into the world of the dead where he confronts the prophets and sages with this persistent question. At the close the words "that abide, a perfume in our hearts" are those of Jesus: "Fear ye not, little flock; God is Love." Doughty's poetry has its advocates, few but ardent; but it must be said that had he deliberately set out to do so, he could not have erected between himself and all but the most intrepid reader more effective barriers than those of his archaistic vocabulary, dialect words, eccentricities of syntax and style, harsh and monotonous prosody, and massive and uncouth mythology. Those who force their way into his fastness will discover flowers of poetry growing amid the rocks.

## IV

The poets now to be considered all express the pessimism and skepticism of the period, though the expression ranges from a serene "paganism" to an iron-shod despair.

*Lord de Tabley*  John B. Leicester Warren, Lord de Tabley [26] (1835-1895) obtained belated recognition when at the end of his life he gathered the best work of many volumes into *Poems Dramatic and Lyrical* (1893 and 1895). In the sad dignity of his bearing he typifies a late Victorianism untouched by the "Decadence." Of all the lesser poets of the period he missed greatness by the narrowest margin. Those who would know him at his lofty best must read his *Napoleon the Great* and the three odes: *To Astarte, To Aphrodite,* and *Sire of the Rising Day.*

*Blunt*  For Wilfrid Scawen Blunt [27] (1840-1922) poetry was a by-product of a life of travel and political agitation. Of the poems written for purposes of propaganda we need notice only *Satan Absolved* (1899), a *Faust*-like "Mystery" satirizing imperialistic expansion and the current cant of "the White Man's

---

[26] *Collected Poems* (1903); *Select Poems,* ed. John Drinkwater (1924). — Robert Bridges, "Lord de Tabley's Poems," *Collected Essays, Papers, etc.,* VII (1931).

[27] *Poetical Works* (2v, 1914); *Poems,* ed. Floyd Dell (1923). The six volumes of Blunt's memoirs or "Secret History" deal with public affairs in England, Ireland, Egypt, and India, together with much matter of social and literary interest. They are a mine of not absolutely trustworthy material on the period. — Edith Finch, *Wilfrid Scawen Blunt* (1938); Sister Mary Joan Reinehr, *The Writings of W. S. Blunt* (Milwaukee, 1940).

Burden." But Blunt is remembered as a "love poet." Sincerity of passion and self-revelation is the characteristic of *The Love-Sonnets of Proteus* [28] (1881). "Sad child of doubt and passionate desires," he describes himself. The happy moments of triumphant love are set against a background of dark fatalism, and the course of passion is traced to satiety and estrangement. There are resemblances to Meredith's *Modern Love,* but the moods are more fluctuating and the art is less well sustained. The sonnet's laws are infringed by irregular rime-schemes and by the extension of members of the sequence, when the thought refuses to be compressed, to eighteen or twenty lines. *Proteus* is less memorable as a whole than for such splendid individual sonnets as *Lost Opportunity* and *Sibylline Books.* A second sequence, *Esther* (1882), is a narrative of the fascination exerted upon a young man by a beautiful woman, older and more experienced than he.

Eugene Lee-Hamilton [29] (1845-1907) has been undeservedly neglected. *Lee-* His first noteworthy volume is *Imaginary Sonnets* (1891), each a tiny *Hamilton* dramatic monologue on themes from the German and Italian Renaissance. His fragile art attained maturity in *Sonnets of the Wingless Hours* (1894), written during years of illness. In some of these a puckish fancy plays, but others are macabre and most are burdened with the pessimism of the epoch. The beautiful sonnet-sequence *Mimma Bella* (1909), in memory of his little daughter, expresses "the burden of the mystery" with a despair that is restrained by perfect artistry.

The poetry of Sir William Watson [30] (1858-1935) is often dismissed as *Watson* "derivative," but it is at any rate in a great tradition going back through Arnold to Wordsworth and Landor. In it there is a revulsion from Swinburne's flamboyance to austerity. In *Wordsworth's Grave* (1890), in *Lachrymae Musarum,* an elegy on Tennyson (1892), and in poems on Burns, Shelley, and Arnold, Watson used verse for laudatory estimates of fellow poets. Notable is his mastery of *rime couée* (the "Burns stanza") in *A Child's Hair* and elsewhere. There is sometimes passion held in severe control (as in *The Glimpse* and *Lux Perdita*); but generally, as he asserts in his *Apologia,* his art is dedicated to other emotions than that of love. The splendid, fervent *Ode in May* is on the highest level of his achievement. In *The Hope of the World* and *The Dream of Man* the agnosticism and the evolutionary meliorism show the influence of Herbert Spencer. Watson's courageous opposition to the Boer War placed him beside Blunt and against Kipling and Henley.[31] He could command the trenchant phrase, but this faculty easily degenerates into rhetoric. The poetic gift, though genuine, was soon exhausted and the long remainder of his life was pathetically ineffectual.

[28] Expanded from *Songs and Sonnets by Proteus* (1875) with the omission of the songs, and further expanded after 1881.

[29] There is no collected edition or biography. See the brief biographical preface by his widow in *Mimma Bella* (1909).

[30] *Poems,* with an introduction by J. A. Spender (2v, 1904); *Poems: 1878-1935* (1936). No biography has yet appeared.

[31] *For England: Poems written during Estrangement* (1903).

*Henley*

William Ernest Henley [32] (1849-1903) wrote verse in various modes and moods. His best-known poem exhibits him as braggartly superior to the blows of fortune; but to keep in mind that he was a cripple is to forgive— perhaps to admire—this posturing. In the poems on his own illness entitled *In Hospital* he experimented in unrimed, irregularly cadenced forms and in harshly realistic subject-matter; and in *London Voluntaries* (1893) he sketched the streets and squares of his city. Henley, who was in close touch with Kipling, sounded the imperialistic note in *England, My England, The Song of the Sword,* and *For England's Sake* (1900). He was skilled in the use of the "old French forms," but employed them for other purposes than Dobson's or Gosse's, often producing new effects by crossing these artifices with intense realism. Like Kipling, he sometimes had recourse to slang and "low" dialect. Rarely, he commanded a more delicate style, as in the elegy on his child and in *Some Twilit Garden Grey with Dew*. With him may

*Newbolt*

be grouped Sir Henry Newbolt [33] (1862-1937) to whom came temporary fame when he expressed the inarticulate feelings of a people deeply moved by the approach of the Boer War. The titles of his two principal volumes of verse—*Admirals All* (1897) and *The Island Race* (1898)—suggest his dominant themes and his limitations. "The strength and splendor of England's war" is a recurring motive.

*Davidson*

Imperialism is one note in the poetry of John Davidson [34] (1857-1909) who came to London from a Scotch Calvinistic milieu "where savage faith works woe." In his *Ballad in Blank Verse of the Making of a Poet* he tells how he revolted from this upbringing and adopted a militant atheism. After several false starts the real Davidson began to emerge in *Smith, a Tragic Farce* (1888), with its hints of autobiography, its description of society as "the mud wherein we stand up to the eyes," and its counsel: "Obey your nature, not authority." *Scaramouch in Naxos* (1888) is an extravaganza on the theme of "the gods in exile." *In a Music-Hall* (1891) and *Fleet Street Eclogues* (1893; second series, 1896) turn urban modernity to the uses of poetry somewhat as Henley was doing. Then followed Davidson's best work, in *Ballads and Songs* (1894), *New Ballads* (1897), and *The Last Ballad and Other Poems* (1899). One of the first Englishmen to be influenced by Nietzsche, Davidson gave a new turn to romantic subjects by introducing vigorous modern ideas of self-expression and the fulfillment of desire. Thus, in *A New Ballad of Tannhäuser* the knight is not contrite but exultant when he returns to Venus, and in *The Ballad of a Nun* the Blessed Virgin takes

---

[32] *Poems* (1912); *Works* (7v, 1908; 5v, 1921). — L. C. Cornford, *William Ernest Henley* (1913); Kennedy Williamson, *William Ernest Henley, a Memoir* (1930); J. H. Buckley, *William Ernest Henley* (Princeton, 1945). — On Henley's criticism see ch. XLII, below.

[33] *Collected Poems* (1910). — Newbolt wrote several historical works, popular and patriotic. *Modred* (1895) is a rather conventional Arthurian tragedy.

[34] There is no collected edition or full-length biography. *Selected Poems* (1905). — Davidson wrote novels, including the satiric *Earl Lavender* (1895); essays, notably those in *A Random Itinerary* (1894); and literary criticism. — H. Fineman, *John Davidson: A Study of the Relation of his Ideas to his Poetry* (Philadelphia, 1916); Gertrud von Petzold, *John Davidson und sein geistiges Werden unter dem Einfluss Nietzsches* (Leipzig, 1928); B. I. Evans, *English Poetry in the Later Nineteenth Century* (1933), ch. XIII.

the place of Sister Beatrice in the convent because she sympathizes with her desire to escape and experience life to the full.[35] There is a like exaltation of egoism in the tremendously forceful *Ballad of Hell*. But this note, over-driven, modulated into morbidly subjective poems, fiercely indignant against the hardships of life, in which Davidson wrote of his own disappointments and distresses. In some poems he fused the current imperialism with the philosophic concept of the superman. When he turned again to the dramatic form the most notable results were *Self's the Man* (1901) and the unfinished trilogy *God and Mammon* (1907-1908). Lack of wide recognition and constant poverty preyed upon him; the morbidity and bitter satire of his later work gradually approached the borders of the psychopathic; and there were hints of contemplated suicide. A confused and violent "Satanic" philosophy sought to identify the Self with the God which is Energy. This is the theme dominating the series of strange, ill-organized, repellent *Testaments: Of a Vivisector* (1901), *Of a Man Forbid* (1901), *Of an Empire-Builder* (1902), *Of a Prime Minister* (1904), and *Of John Davidson* (1908). In these there are passages of power and passion, such as the vision of hell in *The Empire-Builder*; but as a whole they are unrewarding. There is much that is crude and something that is vulgar in Davidson's verse, but in the best work of his middle years, there are also energy and vitality, and occasionally a true lyric gift. In *The Man Forbid* a materialist banished by the orthodox finds comfort in the springtime on the sea-bordered hills. Davidson disappeared near Penzance in March, 1909; months later his body was found in the sea. There was no proof of suicide, but it is believed that he threw himself from the cliffs.

The enigmatic personality of Alfred Edward Housman [36] (1859-1936) *Housman* contrasts so strangely with the crystal clarity of his poetry that critical inquiry has been directed less towards *A Shropshire Lad* (1896) than towards its author. How explain that "continuous excitement" in the spring of 1895 under which, as he told long afterwards, most of the poems were written? How did it come about that what is evidently his own pessimism was projected into the figure of the "lad"? Is this pessimism to be traced to a lasting melancholy caused by the early death of an adored mother? Or is it to be ascribed to disappointment and wounded pride when he failed in "Greats" at Oxford? Was there a tragic love affair of which the secret has been kept? Or (remembering that the poems have far more to do with "lads" than "lassies") was there some friendship whose rupture left a lasting wound? To what degree did thwarted ambition and a consciousness of intellectual

[35] The thirteenth-century story (an *exemplum* of the boundless range of divine forgiveness to the penitent however late) had been retold by Adelaide Proctor in *A Legend of Provence*. There are other modern English versions. Compare also Maeterlinck's *Sœur Beatrice* and Humperdinck's opera.

[36] *Collected Poems* (1940). — T. G. Ehrsam, *Bibliography* (1941); R. W. Stallman, "Annotated Bibliography," *PMLA*, LX (1945). 463-502; A. S. F. Gow, *A. E. Housman: A Sketch together with a List of his Writings* (1936); Laurence Housman, *My Brother, A. E. Housman: Personal Recollections* (1938); Percy Withers, *A Buried Life: Personal Recollections of A. E. Housman* (1940); *A. E. Housman* (1937), recollections by A. W. Pollard, R. W. Chambers, and others.

superiority mold his temperament? Does the explanation lie in Housman's consciousness that accepted standards were crumbling, that with the disappearance of old values reliance must be placed in stoic pride and personal integrity? Or was his despair due not to experience of life but to a preconception of life's futility? There may be some truth in an affirmative answer to each of these questions. It is obvious that Housman's nature, like Hardy's, was one that became "vocal to tragedy," that saw the frustrations of life more clearly than its satisfactions, though his bitter pity has in it little of Hardy's all-embracing compassion. With laconic brevity, forceful directness, and exquisite simplicity a dark fatalism was expressed. Carouse and make love, lad, and enjoy youth and the loveliness of the spring while you can, for death comes quickly—and it may come violently or shamefully. This grim counsel was set to the music of familiar metres, with cadences from ballads and well-loved hymns and with echoes, never too recondite, from Latin poetry. After 1895 the impulse to write verse subsided as suddenly as it had swelled, to reappear fitfully thereafter. Housman was determined to leave a lasting monument in English verse, and his standards of excellence were as rigorous in original composition as in his professional classical studies, where, as the arrogant prefaces to his edition of Manilius show, he was always willing to wound and never afraid to strike. The *Last Poems* (1922) and the posthumous *More Poems* (1936) contain, along with other things of less excellence, some as perfect in their kind as anything in *A Shropshire Lad*. This poetry, so narrow in range of thought and emotion and so slender in quantity, bids fair to survive current efforts at detraction. It may be read in the light of the sardonic and deliberately disillusioning lecture on *The Name and Nature of Poetry* (1933) which is Housman's only prose work apart from his classical papers.[37]

---

[37] The exquisitely refined style of William Johnson Cory (1823-1889), author of *Ionica* (1858, and later, expanded editions), was certainly an influence upon Housman. Cory aimed at the effects of the Greek Anthology. *Mimnermus in Church,* a beautifully restrained expression of "pagan" agnosticism, and *Heraclitus,* a version of a Greek epigram, are his best known poems. He expressed a pensive wistfulness very different from the "horror and scorn and hate and fear and indignation" of the *Shropshire Lad.*

# XL

## The Modern Novel [1]

### I

The task of making an estimate of the achievement of Henry James [2] (1843-1916) proportionate in scale to its significance may be renounced on *James* the ground that though he became an Englishman shortly before his death his writings belong to the history of American Literature. But because he was, by temperament and taste, long residence, and passionate devotion to the country of his adoption, an Englishman, and also because his work occupies "a pivotal position in the development of the twentieth-century novel," [3] he must be included within this survey.

James came of the well-to-do, erudite, and highly individualistic family of which he wrote long afterwards in *A Small Boy and Others* (1913) and *Notes of a Son and Brother* (1914). Visits to England, France, and Italy roused in his "famished" American soul a yearning to become part of an old culture, richer in tradition and associations than his native land could provide. While engaged upon his first reviews, travel sketches, and attempts in fiction, he alternated wanderings abroad with sojourns in the United States. He did not quickly reach a decision, but the desire to regain the lost heritage of the past led him in 1880 to settle permanently in England. He never married, took no part in public affairs, and never evinced any genuine

---

[1] Percy Lubbock, *The Craft of Fiction* (1921); E. M. Forster, *Aspects of the Novel* (1928); Edwin Muir, *The Structure of the Novel* (1928); C. H. Grabo, *The Technique of the Novel* (1928); J. W. Beach, *The Twentieth Century Novel: Studies in Technique* (1932), henceforth referred to as Beach; David Daiches, *The Novel and the Modern World* (1939); W. C. Frierson, *The English Novel in Transition, 1885-1940* (Norman, Okla., 1942); Philip Henderson, *The Novel Today* (1936); Abel Chavelley, *Le Roman anglais de notre temps* (1921); Agnes C. Hansen, *Twentieth Century Forces in European Fiction* (1934); Herbert Muller, *Modern Fiction: A Study in Values* (1937); Helen E. Haines, *What's in a Novel* (1942); Elbert Lenrow, *Reader's Guide to Prose Fiction* (1940).

[2] *Novels and Tales,* New York Edition (26v, 1907-1917). James excluded some novels and many short stories from the canon of his collected works. Some of the omitted items are accessible in recent reprints. *Short Stories,* ed. Clifton Fadiman (1945). The Prefaces are assembled in *The Art of the Novel: Critical Prefaces,* ed. R. P. Blackmur (1934). James's theories may also be studied in *Notes on Novelists* (1914) and *Notes and Reviews* (1921). There is no definitive biography but much material for one may be found in James's *Letters,* ed. Percy Lubbock (2v, 1920). — F. M. Hueffer, *Henry James, a Critical Study* (1913); Rebecca West, *Henry James* (1916); J. W. Beach, *The Method of Henry James* (1918); Van Wyck Brooks, *The Pilgrimage of Henry James* (1925); H. L. Hughes, *Theory and Practice in Henry James* (1926); Pelham Edgar, *Henry James, Man and Author* (1927); Theodora Bosanquet, *Henry James at Work* (1927); Morris Roberts, *Henry James's Criticism* (1929); C. P. Kelley, *The Early Development of Henry James* (1930); Leon Edel, *The Prefaces of Henry James* (Paris, 1931); C. H. Grattan, *The Three Jameses, a Family of Minds: Henry James, Sr., William James, Henry James* (1932); F. O. Matthiessen, *Henry James: The Major Phase* (1944).

[3] Beach, p. 186.

understanding of the economic and social changes that were shaking the foundations of his world. Even of that world of international society whose centers were London, Paris, and Rome (with New York and Boston hull-down upon the horizon) he remained a spectator. From the beginning his department of fiction was a restricted section of the novel of manners—the manners of wealthy, leisurely, sophisticated people, steeped in tradition, trained in a code, so subtle in their reactions one to another that they appear to belong not in the rough work-a-day world but in a world of James's imagining, where motives are more complex and the discrimination of values more microscopic than in what we call reality. In James's absorbed attention to the ultimate refinements of sensibility and of moral and social scruple, in his reliance upon exquisite taste, tact, and fineness of perception, and in his increasingly tortuous and abstruse exploration of mental states there is a resemblance to Pater's critical theories and practice. For James, as for Pater, life was a fine art.

*The International Scene*

The typical character in such outstanding novels of James's first phase as *Roderick Hudson* (1875) and *The American* (1877) is the American abroad, and the typical theme is the clash between transatlantic Puritanism and European tolerance.[4] The comic aspects of situations developing from these antagonistic traditions James very rarely explored; he was more interested in serious social contrasts. During his first years in Europe he was a fascinated observer of Mayfair and the Quartier St. Germain, the world of privilege and prestige. There was a gradual diminution of emphasis upon the theme of the expatriated American, and by the time we reach *The Portrait of a Lady* (1881), the masterpiece of this first period, the fact that Isabel Archer is an American is an almost immaterial consideration in her story.

*The First Phase*

As the original glamour faded, there crept in a note of disillusion which is characteristic of James's middle years. In *The Princess Casamassima* (1886) he showed himself dimly and disturbingly aware of restlessness beyond the boundaries of his world. It is significant that in *The Tragic Muse* (1890) he quite obviously champions the cause of the artist against aristocratic society. This change in tone is accounted for by his somewhat bewildered resentment of the fact that he had failed to win any popular success.[5] For some years after 1890 he neglected fiction, other than the short story, in favor of the drama, but though two of his plays were performed there was no genuine success. These experiments, however, were not unprofitable since they helped him to solve problems of craftsmanship in fiction: the approximation to the dramatic form; the selection of those aspects of experience to be presented; the complete separation of the author from his work.

*The Second Phase*

The gradual assumption of a stoical indifference to popular neglect led

[4] The few novels, such as *Washington Square* (1881), in which the scene is laid in America did not call for the exercise of James's full powers because he never "saturated" himself in material which he regarded as thin.

[5] Save in the early, unimportant novel, *Daisy Miller* (1877), which was widely read and provoked much discussion because its heroine was declared to be "a libel on young American womanhood."

James to the determination to write only to please himself and his limited *The* clientèle. This state of mind is characteristic of his third period. There was *Third* increasingly a limitation of the field of vision with a correspondingly en- *Phase* riched saturation in the social and psychological situation and an intense preoccupation with the problems of selection, approach, arrangement, and emphasis. Broad and comparatively superficial evocations of the social scene were abjured in favor of an intimate concentration upon situations composed out of innumerable touches of finesse in a kind of literary *pointillisme*. There were vibrations of sensibility almost beyond the human auditory range. To many readers the subjects of the later books seem to be crushed by the weight of the technique. *The Spoils of Poynton* (1897) is, in comparison with James's former novels, restricted in scope, but what is lost in range is gained in profundity and insight. *What Maisie Knew* (1897) is a display of technical virtuosity, the lives of corrupt worldlings being seen exclusively through the eyes of an innocent little girl. *The Awkward Age* (1899) is an attempt to apply the dramatist's technique to fiction, the action being conducted almost entirely in dialogue.[6] These comparatively slight books lead to the massive novels of James's last years. In *The Wings of the Dove* (1902) the faint suggestions of an underlying symbolism reveal James's sensitiveness to at least one contemporary tendency; and there is also an obscure obsession with evil which had already betrayed itself in earlier books and is most manifest in the famous short story, *The Turn of the Screw*. That problems of moral obliquity fascinated James is evident, but there is little to be said for the theory that this fascination was due to a "guilt-complex" arising from his failure, as a young man, to take part, as his brothers had done, in the War between the States. Rather it was a special product of his interest in any and every variety of mental experience. The same explanation holds for his stories of the occult, whether of the supernatural, as in the story just named, or the supernormal, as in *The Altar of the Dead*. He worked this ground only in short stories, though in *The Sense of the Past* (posthumous, 1917) the uncanny experiences of the young American who tries to live into the past approximate the occult in their effect upon the reader. In his last books James reverted to his old interest in international social relations. *The Ambassadors* (1903), in which an American is brought into contact with French traditions of the richest texture, is a delight to those for whom the enjoyment of a novel consists in observing and analyzing technical skill, for the chief protagonist is at once the "reflector" of the situation and the leading actor therein. In the international complication here set forth with what most readers deem wearisome elaboration, American Philistinism comes off the worse from the encounter. But in *The Golden Bowl* (1905), which many devotees of James consider the crown of his life's work, the most mellow and exquisitely sensitive of his books, that same Philistinism, in its finer guise of Puritanism, is vindicated in its struggle with moral turpitude.

[6] The approximation to the form of drama is carried even further in *The Outcry* (1911).

The change from the Victorian to the modern novel has been accounted for as due to the weakening of traditional values, with the consequence that the novelist, no longer able to rely upon truth as viewed in terms of the conventions and assumptions of a stable civilization, came to depend more and more upon his own individual experiences.[7] To all outward seeming James was confident in the stability and enduring value of his world. Yet we remark in him, as in his successors, that "the personal sense of truth replaces the formulas of a civilization." [8] He set the example of attempting to make the mind of the artist "a clear glass through which objective truth can pass undisturbed," [9] but since the choice of persons and things to be represented depends upon the artist's personal estimate of their value, this quest of entire objectivity, in James as, again, in his successors, ends in complete subjectivity. He is present in every page of every book from which he sought so assiduously to eliminate himself. In the prefaces to the New York Edition of his collected works [10] and, less directly, in various studies of other novelists, James expounded the principles of the art of fiction. These principles have been as influential as his practice upon such successors as Conrad, Galsworthy, Katherine Mansfield, Virginia Woolf, and Dorothy Richardson. The reader is required to focus his attention not upon the mere "fable" but, increasingly, upon the manner of presentation, the point of view—which is not the simplest and clearest but deliberately the most arduous, the richest in overtones of meaning. To an extent differing in different books James employed the dramatic method—the projection of the mind of a character without comment or explanation. The effort is to have the author, as a separate individuality, cease to exist, and to impart to the reader the illusion of being present at the moment of the action. For the old formal, descriptive introductions of the persons in a story James substituted a gradual unfolding of characters by means of a multitude of fine touches. This was intended to impart that "solidity of specification" upon which he set supreme value. The data, once selected, must be composed, arranged, and set in the appropriate lights. In the effort to hide behind his work he made much use of persons in whose minds actions, characters, and situations are mirrored. He remarked upon his preference "for dealing with [his] subject-matter . . . through the opportunity and the sensibility of some more or less detached, some not strictly involved, though thoroughly intelligent, witness or reporter." Occasionally he preferred the fitting together of parts of a tale known fragmentarily to various witnesses—a mode of narration which he passed on to Conrad. But is there an honest reader who can affirm that in absorbed attention to James's creations he forgets James himself? Though ever so artfully hidden, is not the puppeteer pulling the strings? Does not

*The
Point
of View*

---

[7] This is the central thesis of David Daiches' book, *The Novel and the Modern World* (henceforth, in this chapter, referred to as Daiches). Professor Daiches does not include James within his survey.

[8] Daiches, p. 78.

[9] *Ibid.*, p. 72, and compare Katherine Mansfield's *Journals, passim.*

[10] Gathered together as *The Art of the Novel*, ed. R. P. Blackmur (1934).

James seem always to be demanding of his reader not that he listen to what is being told but that he observe with unflagging attention how it is being told? And does not this demand divert attention from the work of art to the artist? An affirmative answer to these questions does not cast doubt upon the significance of James's experiments in craftsmanship. He turned the course of the novel into new directions (though some of these directions, as is beginning to be apparent, were blind alleys). He might have applied his method to material of a different kind, but his technical dexterity was ideally suited to the subject-matter of his choice. The lessons in craftsmanship, taught and exemplified, remain fruitful. But with the disappearance of his "world" the books in which the theories were given practical application are likely to become, save in the estimation of a small and diminishing band of devotees, mere documents in the history of a phase of European sensibility almost as remote from today's actualities as is the *Carte du Tendre*.

## II

The unique position of Joseph Conrad [11] in English literary history is due *Conrad* not only to the fact that he wrote in a language not native to him but to his isolation from the main movement of the novel. In some respects his work resembles that of Henry James and in other more superficial respects the work of Kipling and Stevenson. But he made no contribution either to the novel of manners or to sociological fiction, and even in the few stories having a European setting the subjects are remote from typical western experience.

Jozef Teodor Konrad Nałęcz Korzeniowski (1857-1924)—the name afterwards so nobly simplified—came by inheritance to his chivalrous and romantic temperament and outlook upon life. Resenting the undifferentiated designation as a Slav, he insisted upon his Polish blood. As a Pole his cultural connections were with the West. From childhood he knew French and to the end of his life would resort to it when at a moment's loss for an English word. But his father was a student of English literature, and in translation the boy read Shakespeare and Dickens. In his veins ran the blood of martyrs for freedom, and it is not too fanciful to suppose that the

[11] *Collected Works*, Memorial Edition (21v, 1925); there are several other collected editions. *Letters, 1895-1924* [to Edward Garnett] (1928); *Letters to a Friend* [Richard Curle] (1928); *Lettres françaises*, ed. G. Jean-Aubry (Paris, 1929); *Letters to Marguerite Poradowska*, translated from the French, ed. J. A. Gee and P. J. Sturn (1940); parts of Conrad's correspondence are still unpublished. — T. J. Wise, *Bibliography* (1921); G. T. Keating, *A Conrad Memorial Library* (1929); G. Jean-Aubry, *Joseph Conrad: Life and Letters* (2v, 1927); Gustav Morf, *The Polish Heritage of Joseph Conrad* (1930); Ford Madox Ford, *Joseph Conrad, a Personal Remembrance* (1924); Richard Curle, *Joseph Conrad, the History of His Books* (n.d.) and *The Last Twelve Years of Joseph Conrad* (1928); Jessie Conrad, *Joseph Conrad and His Circle* (1935); W. W. Bancroft, *Joseph Conrad, His Philosophy of Life* (Boston, 1933); R. L. Mégroz, *Joseph Conrad's Mind and Method* (1931); Edward Crankshaw, *Joseph Conrad: Some Aspects of the Art of the Novel* (1936); Raymond Las Vergnas, *Joseph Conrad* (Paris, 1938); J. D. Gordan, *Joseph Conrad, the Making of a Novelist* (1940); M. C. Bradbrook, *Joseph Conrad, England's Polish Genius* (1941); J. H. Retinger, *Conrad and His Contemporaries* (1943); F. M. Stawell, "Conrad," *E&S*, VI (1920). 88-111; W. L. Cross, *Four Contemporary Novelists* (1930), ch. II; Baker, x (1939), chs. I and II; Beach, pp. 337-365 and *passim*.

*Poland*

sense of man's conflict with terrific powers, which was afterwards heightened by Conrad's experiences at sea, derived ultimately from the Polish dread and hatred of Russia. In this scion of a land-locked race rose strangely the desire to follow a sailor's life. In overingenious detail the theory has been developed that throughout Conrad's books there is evidence of an obsession, a "guilt-complex," originating in his abandonment of Poland. Certainly the cases are very numerous of disloyalty, infidelity, sullied honor, and hidden shame, as also of retribution or the restoration of self-respect through self-immolation.

Not without opposition from his family was the lad able to fulfill his desire. In 1874 he made his way to Marseilles, where he was involved in gun-running adventures for the Spanish Carlists and in the conspiratorial and emotional experiences afterwards recalled in *The Arrow of Gold*. He soon joined the English merchant service and was at sea for the next twenty years, rising gradually from a common sailor to mate and master. He learned English (though he always spoke it with an accent), and so strong a hold did the idiom, the cadences, and the rich vocabulary of the language have upon him that, as he afterwards said, when he began to write he did not adopt English but it adopted him. To beguile the hours of calm weather all sailors spin yarns; and it was in part from "tales of hearsay" in fo'c'sle

*Hearsay*

and master's cabin that Conrad shaped his technique as a novelist. His themes were drawn from people he had known or heard of, places he had visited or coasted past, and the storms and calms of the ocean. He had tried his hand at one or two short things before he began, while still at sea, to write the story of a Dutchman whose moral nature had been degraded through long years among aliens in the tropics. From the first, Conrad's imagination exercised itself not in the invention of incident and character but in the shaping and interpretation of reality. The circumstances in which this first novel was written are a principal subject of *A Personal Record*, his autobiographical recollections. *Almayer's Folly* was published in 1895, at a time when the first successes of Kipling, a long series of travel books, and the British consciousness of world-wide responsibilities had stimulated interest in distant parts of the world and in people and things remote from occidental experience. It is noteworthy that W. H. Hudson's and Cunninghame Graham's books, on the borderland of fiction and travel literature, began to appear about the same time. The personality of Almayer remains shadowy notwithstanding the patient probing into character and motive, and the style is lush and over-written, but there was promise in the gorgeous descriptions of the tropical environment and in the portrayal of the natives of the Malay peninsula. Into a second novel, *An Outcast of the Islands* (1896), Conrad brought many of the characters of his first book, reverting, however, to an earlier period of this Dutch-Malayan history.

In both these novels there is a leisurely and elaborate scrutiny of the consequences of the impact of events upon character. In other books—short stories or narratives that are expansions of the short-story technique—

Conrad's aim was to give the effect of immediate contact with events. The change from the one to the other method and style is apparent in *The Nig-* ***Experience*** *ger of the "Narcissus"* (1897) where in place of events observed or surmised Conrad offers something from his own experience. This same firm foundation underlies his greatest short pieces, *Youth* (1902), *Heart of Darkness* (1902), and *Typhoon* (1903). These do not have the amplitude, movement, and pattern of novels, each being the elaboration of a single episode. As *Youth* was, by Conrad's own admission, "a feat of memory," so in *Heart of Darkness* he carried the situation only a little beyond his own experience of a journey to the Congo in order, as he said, to add to it "a sinister resonance." We are to note that Conrad leaves unexplained the remorse which weighs upon the dying Kurtz and, further, that there is a symbolic darkness in Kurtz's own heart. Conrad admitted the presence of overtones of symbolism in many of his books. In *Youth* Marlow first makes his appearance. This narrator (who in the very long run became tiresome and pretended to an oracular wisdom and psychological insight not convincingly in the character of a ship's officer) obviously found his original among yarn-spinning seamen. Marlow was a means of bringing stories close to the reader by avoiding the old convention of the omniscient author. He pieced them together from scraps of hearsay and observation. This, subtilized almost beyond recognition, was the way in which Conrad had heard sailors tell their tales. It was also a device to maintain the artist's attitude of aloofness, as though the irony and compassion expressed were not Conrad's but Marlow's. The objection is that the effect of corroborative testimony which Conrad sought is often marred by complexities. The reader does not always suspend his disbelief in Marlow's phenomenal memory for the *ipsissima verba* of lengthy dialogues and for the subtle minutiae of appearance, gesture, and changing countenance.

Upon a notorious actual case of a pilgrim-ship which was abandoned by ***Lord*** her officers in a supposedly sinking condition but which nevertheless got ***Jim*** to port [12] Conrad based *Lord Jim* (1900). It is a story of betrayal of trust, shame, and the redemption of character and the regaining of self-respect. Lord Jim becomes the trusted counselor of the natives and dies in the performance of a deed of chivalrous generosity. In none of the earlier stories had Conrad made use of so complex a method of indirect narration.[13] But this pattern is simple in comparison with the intricacies of *Nostromo* (1904). The South American people and environment Conrad had to divine from very little experience of his own. The confusing and overopulent story of revolution and the theft of a cargo of silver is told from various points of view and by the most obscure indirection. It cost Conrad agonizing efforts

[12] See the discussion of the incident of the *Jeddah* (which took place in 1880) in J. D. Gordan, *Joseph Conrad: The Making of a Novelist*, pp. 60-63, and the nearly contemporary allusion to this scandal in Wilfrid Scawen Blunt, *The Future of Islam* (1882), p. 30.
[13] Conrad wrote *The Inheritors* (1901) and *Romance* (1902) in collaboration with Ford Madox Hueffer (Ford) (1873-1939). Of Ford's many novels four on the First World War, *Some Do Not* and its sequels (1924-1928), are the most noteworthy; but his fiction has failed to take a lasting place. His critical studies in art and literature are intensely personal.

in the composition and it imposes a heavy burden upon the reader. Perhaps it was an association of ideas which led Conrad from a story of revolution in South America to narratives of European revolutionists. *The Secret Agent* (1907) is founded upon the fact that a Russian *agent provocateur* had attempted in 1894 to blow up the Greenwich Observatory as a means of rousing British indignation against the Nihilists. Conrad's Russophobia is apparent in the sinister atmosphere of the underworld of terrorists. A circle of international conspirators in Geneva forms the setting of *Under Western Eyes* (1911), the most Slavic of his books. Razumov, the conspirator turned informer, is one of the most memorable of Conrad's creations. Much in his motives is left unexplained, for, piecing together fragments of impression and rumor, Conrad gains his effects in part by his professed inability to understand his characters completely.

*Later Novels*     He now returned to stories of the sea. *Chance* (1913) is a not altogether successful blend of a love story with a tale of sordid wickedness, drifting or sinking towards the close into mere melodrama. The irony of haphazard works not only in the chances that keep the lovers apart but in the chance that unites them at the end. Marlow tells the story. He had had a part in the events, but much of his knowledge consists of deductions from what he had been told by another actor in them. *Victory* (1915), grounded upon personal acquaintance with Heyst and Mr. Jones (the latter the most repulsive of all Conrad's villains), is in tone much like *Chance;* and to an even greater degree the mingling of sensationalism, hideous crime, and idealized love is unconvincing. *The Shadow-Line* (1919) conveys strange hints of the occult. The reader is left to 'guess whether the spirit of the wicked dead captain is responsible for the criminal substitution of salt for quinine with the consequence that the sailors are fever-stricken. This touch of supernaturalism is quite uncharacteristic of Conrad, for whom there were mysteries enough in nature without exploring beyond the boundaries of the natural world. The Carlist adventures of his youth which he had related succinctly in *The Mirror of the Sea* (1906) are reworked elaborately in *The Arrow of Gold* (1919), in which obscure rumors are pieced together into a story of which the reader may make as much as he can. *The Rescue* (1920) is too long, intolerably repetitious, and dull. *The Rover* (1923) is Napoleonic in theme, and *Suspense* (posthumous, 1925), long meditated, obviously planned on a large scale, and left unfinished when Conrad died,[14] has as its basis the return of Napoleon from Elba. These last half-dozen novels, appearing in the years when Conrad's long delayed but at length immense reputation was at its height, were over-praised by contemporary critics. His fame rests more securely upon his earlier work.[15]

---

[14] There has been a good deal of discussion of Conrad's probable design in *Suspense*. For the present writer's suggested solution see *Sat. Rev. of Lit.,* II (November 14, 1925).

[15] Five collections of short stories are to be noted: *Tales of Unrest* (1898), of which some are of lyrical intensity and others labored; *A Set of Six* (1908), a Napoleonic, nautical, and terroristic miscellany; *'Twixt Land and Sea* (1912), memorable for the romantic story of Freya and for *The Secret Sharer*, a little masterpiece; *Within the Tides* (1915), of less note; and *Tales of Hearsay* (posthumous, 1925), another miscellany covering the years from 1884

Life, Conrad was wont to say, is a spectacle of terror and pity, yet also of *Conrad's* beauty. His reason is baffled by the mystery of a world whose beauty holds *World* him in thrall. His most characteristic situation shows the conflict of the primitive and the civilized. Europeans who in their own environment might have led normal lives are set in alien circumstances which bring to the surface the best or the worst qualities in human nature. Puny and courageous man struggles with natural forces but also with forces within his own nature. Conrad's interest is not in the typical human being but in the exceptional, whether in moral heroism or moral degradation. Cautious mediocrity provokes his contempt. In his ability to draw inferences from minute externalities of appearance, gesture, and behavior he is like Henry James. He described James as "the historian of fine consciences," and he was such a historian himself. Cases of puzzling mental pathology, studies in hopeless degeneration, fascinated him, but though he sometimes contemplated them with sardonic detachment he was pitiful, not cruel. In particular he sought to trace the weakening of character through environment. Action is of secondary importance, despite the violence of many crucial episodes. Those critics are mistaken who hold that his "psychology" is merely one ingredient of his atmosphere. Rather the sensitive subtleties of atmosphere are part of the psychology. His gorgeous word-painting, especially in the earlier books before he pruned his luxuriance, won him more readers than did his probings into the human heart. He conveyed the spell · of eastern islands lying "clothed in their dark garments of leaves, in a great hush of silver and azure, where the sea without murmur meets the sky in a ring of magic stillness." But all this was only the setting for the tragedy of man. The loneliness of an alien environment is often the symbol of the soul's loneliness.

### III

A meeting with John Galsworthy on shipboard was the chance that gave *Gals-* Conrad the first step up the ladder to fame as a writer; but though the *worthy* two men became close friends there is an utter dissimilarity in their novels both in form and subject-matter. John Galsworthy [16] (1867-1933) viewed English society from within the pale of the well-bred and well-to-do upper bourgeoisie. He possessed little real understanding of the great world beyond and beneath his class, and though, as in his plays, he expressed a sense of "injustice" and a troubled compassion, he was unaware of the full extent of the social disintegration going on around him. Late-Victorian and post-

---

to post-war England. *The Mirror of the Sea* (1906) supplements both the autobiographical *Personal Record* and the novels and tales.

[16] *Novels, Tales and Plays,* Devon Edition (22v, 1926-1929); Manaton Edition (30v, 1922-1933); *Autobiographical Letters* [to Frank Harris] (1933); *Letters* [to Edward Garnett] (1934). — H. V. Marrot, *Bibliography* (1928) and *The Life and Letters of John Galsworthy* (1936); Joseph Conrad, *John Galsworthy, an Appreciation* (1922); L. M. Schalit, *John Galsworthy, a Survey* (1929); Edouard Guyot, *John Galsworthy* (Paris, 1933); Natalie Croman, *John Galsworthy, a Study in Continuity and Contrast* (1933); Hermon Ould, *John Galsworthy* (1934); Baker, x (1939). 319-344; Beach, ch. xxi; Daiches, ch. iii. — On Galsworthy's plays see ch. xxxviii, above.

Victorian life is criticized in his novels by exposing not the miseries of the poor but the complacency of the propertied class, acquisitive and possessive. Galsworthy neither offers any profound diagnosis of social ills nor suggests any drastic remedy. His characteristic combination of gentility, fastidiousness, and pity often degenerates into sentimentality. There is always something ineffectual about his indignation, a lack of emotional force, though there is no reason for questioning his sincerity. His later books betray a wistful fondness for the very society which he began by satirizing.

His first four novels, published between 1897 and 1901 under the pseudonym "John Sinjohn," must be disregarded here. *The Man of Property* (1906) was not conceived as the first part of a trilogy; it is a well-made and well-rounded novel, complete in itself. From this first chronicle of the Forsyte family Galsworthy turned to other subjects. In *Fraternity* (1909) he looked from the world of property into the world of poverty which he did not understand. *The Dark Flower* (1913) recounts with genuine but soft and overwrought emotion a man's three love affairs, in the spring, summer, and autumn of his life. Other novels of these middle years are *The Patrician* (1911), *The Freelands* (1915), and *Saint's Progress* (1919).[17] Galsworthy then resumed the Forsyte series. From the opulent Victorianism of *The Man of Property, In Chancery* (1920) brings us to the period of the Boer War and *To Let* (1921) to the years immediately following the Armistice of 1918. With the addition of short connecting links these three books were brought together as *The Forsyte Saga* (1922). The chronicle was carried into the age of the "bright young people" of the nineteen-twenties in *The White Monkey* (1924), *The Silver Spoon* (1926), and *Swan Song* (1928) which together form a second trilogy, *A Modern Comedy* (1929). Even then Galsworthy was not done with his Forsytes; further episodes appeared between 1931 and 1933 and were assembled as *End of the Chapter* (posthumous, 1934). The half-dozen later installments of this huge "novel in sequence" carry the story into the post-war world of which Galsworthy, a disapproving and bewildered spectator, knew little. They are scarcely more than bi-annual journalistic records, thrown into the form of fiction, and they are on a much lower level than the original trilogy.

**The Forsyte Saga**

Galsworthy's fame rests upon *The Forsyte Saga* and even there somewhat precariously. The *Saga* is not a *Comédie Humaine,* broad-based as society itself; nor does it concentrate narrowly upon a few individuals. Galsworthy "expatiates free" over an entire class whose types are represented by the different members of a large family. The Forsytes belong to what seems a stable and secure stratum of society whose roots are money. Soames Forsyte is "the man of property" whose claims extend even to a reluctant wife. Irene's first effort towards emancipation ends with the accidental death of the artist who loves her. In the second part of the trilogy the ill-mated pair are divorced and each marries again. The third part centers in the love that

---

[17] Fifty short stories, an ample selection from five original collections, were gathered together in *Caravan* (1925).

springs up between the children of these second marriages, Soames's daughter and Irene's son. Throughout, Irene stands outside the circle of the Forsytes and is seen only through the eyes of members of the family—a device of technique to which Galsworthy himself called attention. To her, as to Old Jolyon Forsyte and to various inanimate objects, Galsworthy attaches a symbolic value, but this value is lessened by the persistent sentimentality. Galsworthy's greatest accomplishment from the point of view of the craftsman in fiction is the presentation of the flow of time. This sense of the tragic passage of the years is concentrated in the character of Soames Forsyte, Galsworthy's greatest creation. Beginning by detesting him, the novelist gradually grows fond and understanding of Soames as he survives, almost the last vestige of Victorian stability, into the restless, rootless postwar world. On the whole, however, the *Saga* offers little of interest to the student of technique. The perpetual shifting of the point of view is distracting and is in keeping with the clear but shallow delineation of character. Since the world which Galsworthy knew widely and intimately, though scarcely with psychological profundity, has disappeared, the question arises in his case, as in the case of Henry James, whether the reflection in the mirror of Galsworthy's art possesses sufficient vitality of its own to endure now that the thing mirrored is gone.

Arnold Bennett [18] (1867-1931), Galsworthy's exact contemporary, came *Bennett* from one of the "Five Towns" of Staffordshire, the district known as "the Potteries." Many of his books, including his two masterpieces, are set wholly or in part in this grimy and unlovely locality, and his affectionate knowledge of it made him one of the foremost of the regionalists. After a start in journalism he began to write fiction in 1898 and evinced serious promise in *Anna of the Five Towns* (1902). *The Old Wives' Tale* (1908) put him in the forefront of contemporary novelists. *Clayhanger* (1910) is the first part of a trilogy which would have been his greatest work had not the sequels, *Hilda Lessways* (1911) and *These Twain* (1915), showed a decline in power which was still more evident in subsequent books. There was some recovery in *Riceyman Steps* (1923), though Bennett here seems overwhelmed in detailed documentation of his own accumulation; and the immense expenditure of effort upon *Imperial Palace* (1930) turned out to be not worth while. Much of Bennett's work was ephemeral, and even of the large portion that has not lost its vitality we must here pass over a good deal: shorter novels, farcical tales, "thrillers," plays, criticism, impressions of art and travel, popular counsel, and autobiographical notes, including *Things That Have Interested Me* (three series, 1906-1925) and the posthumous *Journals*.

Bennett's candor on the subject of his financial success has obscured to

[18] There is no collected uniform edition of Bennett's works. In addition to the novels, plays, and miscellaneous more or less journalistic productions the posthumous *Journals* (3v, 1932-1933) and the *Letters to his Nephew* (1936) are illuminating. — There is as yet no definitive biography. Dorothy C. Bennett, *Arnold Bennett* (1935); Rebecca West, *Arnold Bennett* (1931); Geoffrey West, *The Problem of Arnold Bennett* (1932); J. B. Simons, *Arnold Bennett and His Novels* (1936); Georges Lafourcade, *Arnold Bennett* (1939); Baker, x (1939). 288-319; Beach, pp. 238-245.

some critics the fact that though he made much money by his art he was first and foremost an artist. He was fascinated by vast enterprises and by the processes of wealth and luxury, as symbolized, for example, in the complex organization of a modern hotel. But there was no sycophancy in the attention he paid to such large affairs. It was part of his intense interest in life itself, an interest lavished even more abundantly upon the poor and humble. His province is not the "nether world" of Gissing's most despairing books but the urban lower-middle class which he depicted not with fastidious distaste but with affectionate sympathy. Unlike the naturalists who preceded him, he was not in quest of ugliness for the sake of "documented" art or for less valid reasons—in fact, not in quest of ugliness at all. In unlikely places he perceived a homely beauty or at any rate the beauty of homeliness. He is concerned with small lives, but in narrowly circumscribed environment the souls of his people are not small. He conveyed the excitement and significance of commonplace experiences in the unromantic, normal give-and-take of family life. A rich knowledge of his characters is imparted not through ever deeper probing and analysis but by enabling the reader to live with them, as it were, through the long lapse of time. There is pathos rather than tragedy in his books. No other novelist has narrated with such intensity and precision the circumstances of non-violent, natural death; and few have rendered more impressively than Bennett, in the history of Constance and Sophia, the sense of the relentless passage of the years. But Bennett's was a nature which became vocal to comedy rather than to tragedy. He was no crusader, no reformer; and if a teacher, the lesson he taught was "how to get the best out of life." An expert craftsman, he was content in general with the older forms of the novel and made no innovation of consequence. From the point of view of technique, both *The Old Wives' Tale* and the *Clayhanger* trilogy repay study for the alternation of sections in which the lives of the chief characters are concurrently narrated with other sections in which they are told separately, either because the characters have not yet met (as with Clayhanger and Hilda Lessways) or because they have drifted apart (as with Constance and Sophia in *The Old Wives' Tale*).

*Wells*    Herbert George Wells [19] (1866-1946), journalist, propagandist, and reformer, used fiction as a vehicle for his criticism of existing society and for his utopian visions of the future. His early training in biology (which he studied under Huxley) accounts for his confidence that scientific progress will bring about the social millennium, his basic error in underestimating the force of irrational impulses in man, and his persistent denigration of the arts.

[19] *Works*, Atlantic Edition (28v, 1925-1927); the books since 1927 have not yet been collected together. — F. A. Chappell, *Bibliography* (1924); Van Wyck Brooks, *The World of H. G. Wells* (1915); Edouard Guyot, *H. G. Wells* (1920); J. S. Price, *The World in the Wellsian Era* (1923); Sidney Dark, *Outline of Wells* (1924); Geoffrey West, *The Works of H. G. Wells: A Bibliography, Dictionary and Subject-Index* (1926) and *H. G. Wells, a Sketch for a Portrait* (1930); F. H. Doughty, *H. G. Wells, Educationist* (1926); George Connes, *Etude sur la pensée de Wells* (Paris, 1926) and *A Dictionary of the Characters and Scenes in the Novels, Romances and Short Stories of H. G. Wells* (1926).

To the opinion that artistic considerations were always secondary with him certain exceptions must, however, be made. The early "scientific" fantasies such as *The Time Machine* (1895), *The Stolen Bacillus* (1895), *The Island of Dr. Moreau* (1896), and *The Invisible Man* (1897) are beautifully written with a clarity of design and economy of means that put them on an altogether higher level than that of their prototypes in Jules Verne. Criticism of society is delicately handled in *The Wonderful Visit* (1895)—the visit of an angel to the earth. In *The War of the Worlds* (1898) an invasion of the Martians is made wonderfully convincing by means of touches of minute realism. Wells was least the reformer and most nearly the artist in fiction of sustained length in such comedies of middle-class life as *Love and Mr. Lewisham* (1900), *Kipps* (1905), and *The History of Mr. Polly* (1910). *When the Sleeper Wakes* (1899) began the series of utopian novels that was carried on in *In the Days of the Comet* (1906), *The Dream* (1924), *The Autocracy of Mr. Parham* (1930), and other books. In *Ann Veronica* (1909) the balance is sustained between form and substance, plot and thesis. This was the first of various books—among them *Joan and Peter* (1918) and *Christina Alberta's Father* (1925)—having as their theme sexual disharmony and advocating utopian schemes for the relationship of the sexes which it is often difficult to distinguish from libertinage. In the earlier books, even those that were most argumentative, Wells displayed a rich inventive faculty and, when depicting commonplace people, kindly humor and pathos. But he did not possess the born novelist's interest in individual human beings; he was more concerned with ideas. The tendency to overweigh the thesis at the expense of the story is apparent in *Tono-Bungay* (1909), amusing as it is in its exposure of crafty business practices barely within the law; and even more so in *The New Machiavelli* (1911) which deals with the world of politics. *Mr. Britling Sees It Through* (1916) is a piece of war-propaganda which was very effective in its day. *The Undying Fire* (1919) proclaimed Wells's "discovery" of a finite God who in his struggle with evil needs the aid of man. In some of these books and in others not named it is at times difficult to discern the point where the novel form gives place to the sociological treatise. In *The World of William Clissold* (1926) the protagonist's experiences, amatory and otherwise, are thinly imagined and the narrative is constantly being interrupted by massive blocks of discussion of one or another of Wells's many interests. From such a novel, so-called, as this it is but a step to treatises from which the needless element of story has been eliminated, such as *The Work, Wealth, and Happiness of Mankind* (1931) and *The Shape of Things to Come* (1933). Since from the past, if from anywhere, man must draw lessons for the future, it was to be expected that Wells, whom no task could daunt, should tell the story of mankind. Discarding nationalistic history in favor of a world-view and interpreting that story in terms of evolutionary speculation, he wrote *The Outline of History* (1920), a more remarkable achievement than most professional historians have been willing to admit.

*The Novel of Ideas*

From the above brief survey many volumes have perforce been omitted. The task of selection from Wells's eighty-odd books has indeed already been accomplished in large measure by the lapse of time, for in much of his writing there is too little of artistic value to give enduring life to subject-matter that was of transitory interest. Wells moved with the times, leaving quantities of his books and pamphlets behind him and behind the times. Repetitiveness, long-windedness, and an inability to distinguish between the trivial and the significant impose an insuperable barrier between his work as a whole and any reader too young to have read his Wells in installments from year to year—almost, like his newspaper, from day to day. His novels offer little of interest to students of craftsmanship, for far from introducing innovations in the art of fiction, they generally exhibit a reversion to Victorian formlessness. In his use of fiction to convey ideas he followed the Victorian sociological novelists, while carrying further than they had done the custom of making plot and characterization mere pegs upon which to hang disquisitions on every sort of topic. For the future historian of the political, economic, social, moral, and religious unrest and aspirations of the first forty years of our century his books provide a mountain of evidence of varying degrees of value and reliability, to be sifted, assorted, and condensed. The number and variety of his Utopias have often been derided; but actually they testify to the alertness and fecundity of an imagination ready to discard an old, and embrace a new, idea in accord with social change. The buoyant optimism of this writer who held that we fall to rise and are baffled to fight better was a tonic through years of skepticism, lassitude, and despair.

## IV

*Joyce*

James Joyce [20] (1882-1941) is reported to have declared that to understand him the reader must devote his life to the study of his books. The readjustment of values that is sure to come will spare future lovers of literature this self-immolation, and meanwhile the commentators supply short cuts. Already it is apparent that startling innovations in technique are not in themselves evidence of artistic success, and even among Joyce's admirers there are those who admit that one of his two massive books is but partially successful and the other a failure. Joyce's contemporary renown was in part due to factors extraneous to literary excellence. These are so notorious as to call for no comment here. Of his mastery of language—indeed, his tyranny over it—there can be no question, nor of the beauty, profundity, strength, and significance of parts of his achievement. But the separation of the author from any considerable body of readers, already apparent in his early books,

---

[20] Herbert Gorman, *James Joyce* (1940), the authorized biography, complete to within a year of the subject's death; Frank Budgen, *James Joyce and the Making of Ulysses* (1934); Stuart Gilbert, *James Joyce's Ulysses, a Study* (1931); Harry Levin, *James Joyce, a Critical Introduction* (1941); Edouard Dujardin, *Le Monologue intérieur, son apparition, ses origines, sa place dans l'œuvre de James Joyce* (Paris, 1931); R. M. Kain, *Fabulous Voyager* (1947); Edmund Wilson, *Axel's Castle* (1931), ch. VI; Beach, ch. XXXII; Daiches, chs. VI-IX.

became a chasm only to be bridged by the erudite in *Ulysses* and a great gulf of incommunicability in *Finnegans Wake*.

A Dubliner educated by the Jesuits for the priesthood, Joyce rebelled against the inhibiting forces of family, church, and native country. Despite the encouragement given him by Yeats, he stood completely apart from the Irish Literary Revival. Yet in a sense he could no more escape from the Ireland of his youth than from his education. Few readers possess the intimate knowledge of Irish history and politics and of Dublin life and topography requisite for a thorough understanding of his local and topical allusions. *Dublin* The main fact about his life—his self-imposed Continental exile from 1904 till his death—is also the main fact about his art: he was absolutely aloof from the society which with his phenomenal memory he depicted in such detail. Using for defense, as he said, the weapons of "silence, exile, and cunning," he lived at first in Paris and later in Trieste, Rome, and Zurich, supporting himself as a bank-clerk and as a teacher in the Berlitz schools, while with single-minded determination he pursued his path. His poetry is over-valued by the enthusiasts. *Chamber Music* (1907) attracted almost no attention, and Joyce returned only once to verse (apart from *jeux d'esprit*) when he published *Pomes Penyeach* (1927). *Dubliners* (1914), a collection of short stories including one, *The Dead,* that is a little masterpiece, showed him to be not only a keen observer of the squalid life of his native city but also an exquisite artist in language and in the delicate patterning of apparently casual accumulations of seemingly unrelated detail. *A Portrait of the Artist as a Young Man* (1916), of which the posthumously published *Stephen Hero* (1944) is all that remains of a first draft, is autobiographical; Stephen Dedalus, who purges himself of racial and religious inhibitions, is obviously Joyce himself. The book is, further, a necessary prologue to the *Ulysses* greater work which followed. *Ulysses* (1922), published in Paris, was suppressed in England and the United States. The blasphemy and obscenity which gained it immediate notoriety insured its success as a commercial venture but were of little moment to those who recognized the book's significance as an ambitious experiment in creative literature along new lines. The correspondence between the experiences of Leopold Bloom on a single day in Dublin and the adventures of Ulysses is not, as some critics have declared, a mere scholarly jest or *tour de force* but is fundamental to the design. Joyce held that Ulysses, far more than Hamlet or Faust, was the "complete" or representative man—son, husband, father; wise, courageous, shrewd; subject to many trials. Each episode in *Ulysses* has its parallel in the *Odyssey*, as when Dedalus finds himself between the Scylla of Aristotelian realism and the Charybdis of Platonic mysticism. For the detection of many of these parallels the reader needs the guidance of the commentators. The episodes are, moreover, associated each with an hour of the day and an organ of the body, and each may be connected with one of the arts and may have its peculiar color and symbol and "technique." There are innumerable reticulations and decussations of recurrent motives, many of them so tenuous as to be discernible only after the closest scrutiny. Not every reader finds the effort always rewarding. Joyce had an astonishing command of the resources of the English language, and when conventional vocabulary and syntax failed to meet his requirements he had recourse to neologisms, truncated and telescoped words, and a sort of counterpoint derived from his knowledge of music. In one chapter the development of the embryo from conception to birth is symbolized by a chronological succession of English prose styles imitated with dazzling virtuosity. The technical expertness often overreaches itself, for though there are passages of lucid beauty more often there is an orgiastic tumult of vocables. Joyce plumbed the depths of the subconscious to draw thence half-formed thoughts and unspeakable desires. These are interlaced with description, narrative, and dialogue. The *monologue intérieur* is carried beyond the limit of candor and length in the famous reverie of Molly Bloom with which *Ulysses* concludes. Though the end is a magnificent glorification of the "life-urge," the prevailing tone of the book is of a desolating irony; and though there is abundant humor it is a mistake to describe it as Rabelaisian, unless we apply to Joyce Coleridge's characterization of Swift as an *anima rabelaisiana habitans in sicco*. The book succeeds best where it communicates most, as when we follow Bloom's thoughts in the cemetery or when Dedalus develops his theory of *Hamlet* in the library. When it fails, the failure is in communication; contact between author and reader can be established, if at all, only through the mediation of the commentators.

This fundamental objection to *Ulysses* applies *a fortiori* to *Finnegans Wake*[21] (1939). From Giambattista Vico's theory of the three phases of civilizations Joyce here built up a vast phantasmagoria of the stream of time. The thoughts and activities are those of the world of dreams. Though Joyce never makes clear how the mind of the Dublin public-house keeper, H. C. Earwicker, became charged with such a wealth of knowledge and associations, this extraordinary phenomenon is evidently suggested by Jung's theory of the "collective consciousness." The distortions and convolutions of language transcend the extreme limits of intelligibility. Single sentences are brilliant, ingenious, amusing, or profound.[22] The extraordinary linguistic acrobatics may hold the reader's attention for a while. But before long, light dies before Joyce's "uncreating word" "and universal Darkness buries All." Joyce has retired so far within himself as to be beyond reach.

The modern cultural phenomenon of the artist who, amid the disruption of society, withdraws into the stronghold of his own personality is illustrated

[21] The clearest exposition is Edmund Wilson, "The Dream of H. C. Earwicker," in *The Wound and the Bow* (1941), pp. 243-271. But the light provided by Mr. Wilson is quickly extinguished in the phantasmagoric darkness of the text. — See also J. Campbell and H. M. Robinson, *A Skeleton Key to Finnegans Wake* (1946).

[22] Here is a relatively simple example (cited by Mr. Wilson): "Nobirdy aviar soar anywing to eagle it" which is a *Jabberwocky* distortion of: "Nobody ever saw anything to equal it."

in another way in the case of David Herbert Lawrence [23] (1885-1930). Liter- *D. H.* ary criticism cannot disengage itself from the record of the neuroses, fixa- *Lawrence* tions, and complexes, originating in his social and psychological maladjustment, which is found in the autobiographical stratum of his books and in the frequently conflicting testimony of his friends and biographers. Lawrence, the son of a Nottinghamshire miner, was encouraged by the forceful mother to whom he was excessively attached, to get himself some education and become a schoolteacher. Brooding resentment of his social inferiority found expression in suspiciousness, and compensation in arrogance. For the obsession with sex which tormented him throughout his career there was perhaps a physiological or psychic explanation. His earliest poems, published by F. M. Ford in *The English Review* in 1908, show that already he aimed to interpret all life in terms of his own personal experience. Two novels—*The White Peacock* (1911), which is faintly Hardy-esque, and *The Trespassers* (1912), the romanticized record of a trivial love affair —preceded *Sons and Lovers* (1913), which remains his greatest book. The story is composed out of the "passionate experience" of the conflict between Lawrence's mother and the woman to whom he was attached (the "Miriam" of the novel and the "E. T." of actuality). At this time, when psychoanalysis was directing attention to the Unconscious but apparently before he had read Freud, Lawrence began in this book his probings into the "underground roots," "the dark founts of creative life." It needs to be noted, however, that despite his sexual obsession, he never accepted Freud's theory as to the predominance of the sexual instinct but subordinated it to the "male passion of collective purpose." In *The Rainbow* (1915) he explored the problem of successful mating in the cases of three pairs of lovers. This book brought him into conflict with the police. Its suppression enraged and humiliated him, for not only was he sincere in the assertion of his high moral purpose but he knew that the prosecution was actuated in part by his anti-militaristic opinions and the fact that he had married a German woman. Henceforth he ate his heart out in bitterness. *Women in Love,*

[23] There is no collected edition. In addition to the books mentioned in the text the following may be noted. *Love Poems* (1913); *Amores* (1916); *Birds, Beasts and Flowers* (1923) and other volumes of verse were collected in 1928, after which five other volumes appeared, including *Last Poems,* ed. Richard Aldington (1932). Much of Lawrence's most beautiful writing is in the travel books, *Twilight in Italy* (1916), *Sea and Sardinia* (1921), and *Mornings in Mexico* (1927). *Fantasia of the Unconscious* (1922) is important for its criticism of Freud. *Studies in Classic American Literature* (1923) contains some first-rate criticism mixed with eccentricities. *Letters,* ed. Aldous Huxley (1932), are of more value for Lawrence's life than the biographies. *Apocalypse* (1932) is a posthumous "revelation" of his view of life. *Phoenix,* ed. E. D. McDonald (1936), contains the posthumous papers. — E. D. McDonald, *Bibliography* (1925), with *Supplement* (1931); J. Middleton Murry, *Son of Woman: The Story of D. H. Lawrence* (1931) and *Reminiscences of D. H. Lawrence* (1933); Stephen Potter, *D. H. Lawrence* (1930); Catherine Carswell, *The Savage Pilgrimage, a Narrative of D. H. Lawrence* (1932); Ada Lawrence and G. S. Gelder, *Young Lorenzo, the Early Life of D. H. Lawrence* (1931); Dorothy Brett, *Lawrence and Brett: A Friendship* (1933); Horace Gregory, *Pilgrim of the Apocalypse, a Critical Study of D. H. Lawrence* (1933); Frieda Lawrence, *Not I but the Wind* (1934); E. T. ["Miriam"], *D. H. Lawrence, a Personal Record* (1935); Paul de Reul, *L'Œuvre de D. H. Lawrence* (1938); Knud Merrill, *A Poet and Two Painters: A Memoir of D. H. Lawrence* (1938); Hugh Kingsmill, *D. H. Lawrence* (1938); W. Y. Tindall, *D. H. Lawrence and Susan His Cow* (1939); Baker, x (1939), ch. VIII; Beach, ch. xxx.

a sequel to *The Rainbow,* did not find a publisher till 1921. Meanwhile, in 1919, Lawrence had left England, and for the remainder of his life he was a wanderer, impelled by his sense of the post-war chaos to try to construct a social group round himself but taking with him wherever he went his resentments and his fears. In Italy he wrote *The Lost Girl* (1920), in which he compromised with, or rather concealed, his convictions in order to re-establish a besmirched reputation. *Aaron's Rod* (1922), partly Italian in setting, contains hints of his sympathy with the incipient Fascist movement. Lawrence then lived for a time in Australia. There he wrote *Kangaroo* (1923), an interminable discussion-novel in which the advocacy of the principle of "leadership" is downright and there are violent and obscure expatiations upon a darkly "mystical" concept of God. *The Boy in the Bush* (1924) is a work of collaboration. There followed the sojourn in Taos, New Mexico, of which members of Lawrence's coterie have given contra-dictory accounts. In Mexico he wrote *The Plumed Serpent* (1926), an occult and macabre, exotic and hysterical book, which contains the fullest and most fantastic expression of his awareness of "old life-modes," his sense of modern man's heritage from primitive ancestors. It is, however, impossible to take quite seriously the narrative of the upsurging of the old soul of Mexico through the crust of Spanish civilization and its triumph in a new Fascist order which would revive the brutal horrors of the old Mexican religion. Yet there is here something premonitory of the Nazi cult of the old Ger-manic pantheon. Lawrence's defiant repudiation of modern society now goaded him to write the notorious novel, *Lady Chatterley's Lover* (1929). The bitter indictment of the hypocrisies of civilization shows Lawrence at his strongest; the calculated improprieties are forcibly-feeble and the phallic obsession which led alike to the book's suppression and its surreptitious success is of a naked shamelessness which would be ridiculous were it not a painful symptom of exacerbated nerves. *The Virgin and the Gipsy* (1930) repeats the theme of the woman of higher social rank who finds emotional satisfaction in the embraces of a man of brutish primitiveness. Lawrence published many short stories. The requirements of magazine publication kept a rein upon his tendency to divagate and his urge to shock, and many of these tales have a raciness and even a humor that the full-length novels do not display. Over these things, as over his poems and travel books, we must pass without comment. The last journey was to the French Riviera where he died of tuberculosis.

*The "Life-Urge"*

The testimony of those who knew Lawrence confirms the impression made by his books of a powerful, ruthlessly dominating personality. He was a genius, albeit an ill-directed genius. He attempted to harmonize the intellectual and emotional forces in human nature, yet in exasperated revolt against intellectualism he overvalued the significance of the primitive and instinctive. "The body is the soul," he said, without ever making clear what he intended by this paradox. Again, he was wont to declare that the flesh is wiser than the intellect—an assertion which students of his own case **may** be inclined to call in question. He was primarily concerned not with individual characterization or even with broad human types but with the "life-urge" common to all humanity and pulsing throughout the cosmos. With this all-pervading force he sought obscurely to identify himself. In the exposition of his erotic psychology he could descend to vulgar self-exhibitionism, but he could also ascend to the heights of vision. He carried extraordinarily far the analysis of the complexities of modern emotional reactions and responses. The strained metaphors, the violences and incoherencies are due to the effort to achieve an idiom suitable for the exploration of the Unconscious. The chaos of Freudian depths is illuminated by flashes from whirling thunderheads of words. Lawrence's mastery of style is best displayed not in the expositions of his cloudy "mysticism" but in his descriptions of desert and mountain landscape.

Like Lawrence, Aldous Huxley[24] (1894-1963) repudiated contempo- *Aldous* rary society, in terms, however, not of fury and hatred but of cynical *Huxley* disgust.[25] Earth seemed to him a sterile promontory and the air a foul and pestilent congregation of vapors. This grandson of a great Victorian scientist found the old belief in scientific progress a vain deceit. Life, standardized and mechanized, has been bereft of joy. Endeavor, disinterested or otherwise, leads to frustration. Sensual satisfactions turn to dust and ashes. There is a nostalgic envy of the happy few who hold sincerely to the ancient ways of faith, but religion is mostly a pretense. That aesthetic values are still vital Huxley's essays on the arts prove, but in his novels art, too, is sterile. A Swiftian obsession with stench and filth comes from an indignant realization that romance is an illusion. This bitterly jesting Pilate's pursuit of truth carried him, in his attempt to isolate himself from a society which appalled him, into a sort of pseudo-Hindu quietism. Huxley, as he acknowledged in drawing his own portrait in the character of Philip Quarles in *Point Counter Point,* was not "a congenital novelist" but a thinker using fiction as the vehicle for his ideas. His are "discussion-novels" in which the plot is negligible or non-existent and the action consists in the clash of contrary opinions.[26] As in Peacock's books, the setting is chosen merely

[24] See Daiches, ch. xi; Beach, ch. xxxvi. There is no satisfactory full-length criticism of Huxley's work. — Much of Huxley's best writing is in his essays and travel books. Among the former are *Essays New and Old* (1926), *Proper Studies* (1927), and *Holy Face* (1929); and among the latter *Along the Road* (1925), *Jesting Pilate* (1926), and *Beyond the Mexique Bay* (1934). Earlier biographical studies led the way to *Grey Eminence* (1941), a biography of Richelieu's counselor Father Joseph. Into this Huxley introduces his own despairing repudiation of the active life and his advocacy of withdrawal into a *vita negativa*.

[25] The cynical, urbane wit of Hector H. Munro ("Saki," 1870-1916) was anticipatory of a dominant mood of the nineteen-twenties. He satirized society from the point of view of aristocratic Toryism in short stories (collected posthumously from half a dozen volumes in 1930). His deft competence has in the long run failed to conceal his shallowness.

[26] A significant discussion-novel of slightly earlier date than Huxley's is *South Wind* (1916) by Norman Douglas (1868-1952). The boldness of Douglas's assault upon conventional moral standards is indicative of that disintegration of values of which the period affords so many other signs. Equally indicative is his inability to supply any positive convictions (other than a delight in scholarship and exotic landscape) to take the place of those he ruthlessly discards. Douglas recorded life in southern Italy in *Old Calabria* (1931) and a series of books on Capri (collected in 1930). He also wrote essays, literary criticism, and technical monographs. See H. M. Tomlinson. *Norman Douglas* (1931).

to account for the presence together of a group of intellectual eccentrics, each representative of a point of view. The character of each person is implied in the ideas of which he is the mouthpiece. Huxley's early novels— *Crome Yellow* (1921), *Antic Hay* (1923), and *Those Barren Leaves* (1925), and the short stories in *Limbo* (1920), *Two or Three Graces* (1926), and other volumes have something of Peacock's concise wit; but in the later books, though he retains his method, there is a ponderous elaboration of ideas. *Point Counter Point* (1928) is his best balanced and most representative book. *Brave New World* (1932) is a utopian nightmare of the futility of scientific "progress." If the cynical skepticism of *Eyeless in Gaza* (1936) and the contemptuous satire directed in *After Many a Summer* (1939) against the waste land of materialism and sensuality are fair pictures of the *vita activa,* small wonder that Huxley sought to withdraw into the *vita contemplativa.* The burden of topicality bodes ill for the lasting popularity of these novels, but they will remain valuable as records of a prevailing mood in the dark transition period between the two wars.

*Dorothy M. Richardson*

Both Lawrence and Huxley are off the path trodden by the experimenters in technique. On that path, parallel with rather than stemming from Joyce, are several women-novelists. Between 1915 and 1938 Dorothy M. Richardson[27] issued *Pilgrimage* in a dozen installments, each with its individual title. When she began this novel Marcel Proust was engaged on his task of reconstructing experience from within the mind of a single individual. Miss Richardson was not influenced by him but was, as it were, aware of his proximity. Henry James had already often depended upon the eye of a single observer of the human conflict. But while James had permitted himself to interpret and explain, Miss Richardson, seeking to identify herself completely with her heroine, does not intrude *in propria persona.* There is never a lapse from the technique of the stream of consciousness—the succession of fleeting images of the external world mingled with thoughts and half-thoughts and shadows of thought attached to the immediate present or moving back and forth in memory. There is the variety, but also the insignificance, of ordinary experience, and the effect is of garrulous, meandering, and objectless fluidity. It is a pity that Miriam, the heroine, is so dull and commonplace a person. Men who doubt whether the record of so much that is tedious and trivial is worth while must leave to women the decision as to whether this study in feminine psychology rings true. *Pilgrimage* has not been widely read, but as an experimenter Miss Richardson has influenced other novelists. One who helped to gain her a hearing was May Sinclair (1879-1946). After winning a success with *The Divine Fire* (1904), a novel traditional in form, Miss Sinclair turned to Freudianism and the stream of consciousness in *Mary Olivier* (1919) and other books. Her touch is lighter than Miss Richardson's and she does not discard the element of plot or detach her subjects wholly from the external world.

*May Sinclair*

[27] *Pilgrimage* (4v, 1938), with a foreword by the author. — J. C. Powys, *Dorothy M. Richardson* (1931); Beach, ch. xxxi. Professor Beach relates Miss Richardson's work to the poetry of the Imagists.

Virginia Woolf [28] (1882-1941) owed a good deal to the example of *Ulysses*   *Virginia*
and *Pilgrimage,* but she was without Joyce's amplitude and creative vitality   *Woolf*
and her range of experimentation, though wider, was on a smaller scale
than Miss Richardson's. A first novel, *The Voyage Out* (1915), is fairly
conventional in pattern, and the impressive climax is too long in preparation.
The short stories or sketches in *Monday and Tuesday* (1921) show her feeling her way towards one of her methods—the method of impressionism.
*Jacob's Room* (1922) is not concerned with Jacob's view of the world but
with the world's view of Jacob, the hero's portrait being built up from the
hinted testimony of friends and strangers. In *Mrs. Dalloway* (1925) the
limit of time to a single day and of place to a single city is suggestive of
*Ulysses*. The stream of consciousness technique is employed, with this difference that we pass from mind to mind through transitional impressions of
environment. When within a personality the movement is back and forth
through time, and during the meticulously indicated pauses in time the
movement is from one personality to another. The aim is to convey a sense
of immediacy, but the effect upon some readers is of a refined remoteness
from actuality, a pale, stylized intellectuality. A setting far withdrawn from
the busy stir of life is best suited to Mrs. Woolf's method, and for this reason
*To the Lighthouse* (1927) is the most successful of her novels. The inter-
related problems of time and personality are turned to fantastic account in
*Orlando* (1929) which, despite its brilliant evocation of periods of the past,
is an unconvincing *tour de force. The Waves* (1931), with its incredibly
elaborate soliloquies, *The Years* (1933), and *Between the Acts* (1941) are
further experiments in pattern and method. The attempt is to rarify life to
its quintessence and then enrich that refined distillation with all the resources of elaborately intellectual metaphor. There was an ever-increasing
remoteness till at length Mrs. Woolf of her own volition withdrew from
life. She had once compared life to "a luminous halo, a semi-transparent
envelope surrounding us" and she had conceived it to be the novelist's task
to impart to the reader a sense of this "unknown and uncircumscribed
spirit." But is not this luminous halo a mist that slips between Mrs. Woolf's
fingers as she attempts to apprehend it? [29]

[28] Daughter of Sir Leslie Stephen; married Leonard Woolf (1880-    ), sociologist and
journalist. In addition to books mentioned in the text Mrs. Woolf's work includes the critical
essays in *The Common Reader* (two series, 1925 and 1932) and in *The Death of the Moth*
(1942), and *Flush* (1933), the story of the Brownings from the point of view of Mrs. Browning's pet dog. — E. M. Forster, *Virginia Woolf* (1942); David Daiches, *Virginia Woolf* (1942);
Joan Bennett, *Virginia Woolf* (1945); Beach, pp. 428-432, 490-493; Daiches, ch. x.
[29] If promise and not performance were the historian's criterion, Katherine Mansfield
(pseudonym for Kathleen Beauchamp) (1888-1923) would be a major figure. She wrote no
full-length novel. *In a German Pension* (1911), *Bliss* (1920), and *The Garden Party* contain
short stories in the impressionistic manner of Chekhov. Plot counts for very little. Delicate
observation is recorded with exquisite precision of phrase and the subtlest choice of detail. The
tensity of emotion and clarity of insight into character are remarkable. On her art and intentions see her *Journal* (1927) and *Letters* (2v, 1928), both edited by her husband, J.
Middleton Murry. See also R. E. Mantz and J. M. Murry, *The Life of Katherine Mansfield*
(1933)

V

E. F.
Benson

Montague

Tomlinson

Beresford

Maugham

Several novelists of distinguished talent stand apart from the experimenters in technique who have attracted most critical attention. As these writers do not fall into obvious categories it is best to consider them in chronological order. Edward Frederick Benson (1867-1940) created a sensation with his first novel, *Dodo* (1893), which was followed by many other lightly satirical novels of different strata of society. Among them the "Lucia" books and *Paying Guests* (1929) may be mentioned. Benson also wrote stories of the supernatural. Charles Edward Montague (1867-1928), a first-rate journalist, was a novelist rather by taking thought than by native endowment. From his experiences in the First World War he drew the material for *Disenchantment* (1922) and *Rough Justice* (1926), the latter containing an unforgettable account of a soldier's cowardice. In these books there is little of the bitter revulsion from warfare which was a dominant note of many "war novels." Some of these, written by poets, receive notice in the next chapter. Montague's *Right Off the Map* (1927) is a disillusioned liberal's satiric fantasy of international relations. His literary criticism is of value, especially *A Writer's Notes on His Trade* (1930). Henry Major Tomlinson (1873-1958), journalist, critic, and author of books of travel of which *The Sea and the Jungle* (1912) is the best known, won a place among novelists with his *Galleon's Reach* (1927), a romance of the Far East which calls Conrad to mind, and *All Our Yesterdays* (1930), a story notable for its indictment of the civilization which culminated in catastrophe. An admirable stylist, Tomlinson was as individualistic in his choice of imagery as in his love of obscure, exotic, far-off places. Often he blended fiction with personal experience, especially in the world of docks and ships; *London River* (1921) and similar books are filled with the *genius loci*. The social disintegration which Gissing had predicted is mirrored in the novels of John Davys Beresford (1873-1947). His realism and gift for psychological analysis have fullest scope in the *Jacob Stahl* trilogy (1911-1915). A second novel in sequence is made up of *The Old People* (1931), *The Middle Generation* (1932), and *The Young People* (1933). Beresford also wrote novels and short stories in lighter vein. There is said to be much autobiography in his fiction.

William Somerset Maugham [30] (1874-1965) began his career as a conscious or unconscious disciple of Gissing. *Liza of Lambeth* (1897) and other early books offered a promise that was impressively fulfilled in the powerful, partly autobiographical novel, *Of Human Bondage* (1915), which in the opinion of many good judges remains his best book. *The Moon and Sixpence* (1919) is based upon the career of the painter Gauguin, and *Cakes and Ale* (1930) upon gossip about Hardy's private life. Other novels, earlier

[30] C. S. McIver, *William Somerset Maugham, a Study of Technique and Literary Sources* (Philadelphia, 1936); R. H. Ward, *William Somerset Maugham* (1937); R. A. Cordell. *W. Somerset Maugham* (1937). On Maugham's plays see above, ch. xxxviii.

and later in date, must be passed over without mention. Half a dozen volumes of short stories are reprinted in *Altogether* (1934). In parts of his work the influence of Maupassant is paramount and there is often a strain of exoticism. A favorite setting is the tropics, as in the famous short story, *Rain*. In general Maugham's tales exhibit technical expertness rather than depth of feeling; in fact, the restraint imposed upon his own emotions sometimes gives the effect of callousness. He likewise wrote volumes of impressions, opinions, and recollections of art, letters, peoples, and countries. *The Summing Up* (1938) contains illuminating accounts of his intentions and ideals in fiction and the drama.

The most widely read novel of Edward Morgan Forster [31] (1879-    ) is *A Passage to India* (1924); its fame is in part due to considerations adventitious to its high merits in style, pattern, characterization, and atmosphere. Of his four other novels, all of earlier date, *A Room with a View* (1908), which is set in part in Italy, and *Howards End* (1910), which is on an ampler scale, may be mentioned. Veins of quietism and symbolism run through Forster's books with a constantly recurring contrast between the inner and the outer life. A peculiar characteristic is the sudden interruption of delicate psychological analysis with episodes of melodramatic violence. A debt to Henry James is apparent, but also, curiously crossed with it, a debt to Gissing. Resemblances to the novels of D. H. Lawrence have often been remarked upon, and it is indeed likely that Forster influenced Lawrence. The subtlety but also the limitations of his opinions on the art of fiction are shown in his *Aspects of the Novel* (1927). His essays and a few short stories afford small compensation for the abrupt and as yet unexplained cessation of novel-writing in early middle life.

*Forster*

Of younger writers only a few can be singled out for mention. Compton Mackenzie (1883-    ) never fulfilled the promise of his first success, *Sinister Street* (1913-1914), though he wrote a vast number of other novels. The book just named is memorable for its descriptions of life at Oxford and its narrative of a conversion to Roman Catholicism. Ralph Hale Mottram (1883-    ) is the author of *The Spanish Farm Trilogy* (1924-1926) which is of lasting value for its rendering of the spiritual atmosphere of Europe at the close of the First World War. Frank Swinnerton (1884-    ), a disciple of Gissing, has dealt in the main with lower middle-class urban society. *Nocturne* (1917), *Young Felix* (1923), *The Georgian House* (1932), and a dozen other novels have generally to do with the seamy side of city life, viewed, however, with more of Arnold Bennett's cheerfulness than of Gissing's gloom. Swinnerton's candid and amusing impressions, *The Georgian Literary Scene* (1934), may be recommended to students of the period. The contemporary popularity of the novels of Sir Hugh Walpole (1884-1941) does not seem likely to endure. Out of his experiences of war in Russia came *The Dark Forest* (1916) and *The Secret City* (1919) in

*Compton Mackenzie*

*Mottram*

*Swinnerton*

*Hugh Walpole*

[31] Rose Macaulay, *The Writings of E. M. Forster* (1938); Lionel Trilling, *E. M. Forster* (1943).

which are strains of "mysticism" obviously foreign to his temperament. Equally foreign, though deftly accomplished, are the stories of mystery and horror,[32] *Portrait of a Man with Red Hair* (1925) and *Above the Dark Circus* (1931). Walpole was more sincere in tales of ecclesiastical society suggestive of Trollope and in romances that owe something to Scott. His most ambitious, not to say pretentious, efforts went into the "Herries" series: *Rogue Herries* (1930), *Judith Paris* (1931), *The Fortress* (1932), and *Vanessa* (1933). He was a master of smoothly flowing narrative, but he carried to great lengths analyses of character which give the effect of being somewhat beyond his intellectual capacity. Much more likely to be permanently remembered though for the time being neglected by critics who are obsessed with problems of technique are the best novels of Francis Brett Young (1884-1954). Among these some readers give their suffrage to *Cold Harbour* (1924), others to *Portrait of Clare* (1927). The grim terror of the one contrasts with the graciousness of the other. Young always ranged widely in settings, themes, and moods. Many of his stories take place in the border-country between England and Wales; others in ports; others at sea or in countries oversea. A devotion to beauty expressed in his early novels and in his study of Robert Bridges (1914) later yielded place to attacks upon "progress," sometimes angry or complaining, sometimes lightly satirical. The prediction may be ventured that when the reappraisal of this accomplished stylist and incisive commentator upon society is made—it is long overdue—Young will be accorded a high rank among the novelists of his generation.

*F. B. Young*

With two women we close this chronological survey. Rose Macaulay (who seems to have kept secret the date of her birth) portrayed the generation between the wars with an acidulous wit and an alert intellectualism which cover but do not conceal her profound pessimism. Among her many novels, *Potterism* (1920), a satire on middle-class values, *Dangerous Ages* (1921), analysing the motives and standards of the modern "career-woman," and *Told by an Idiot* (1923) are still the best. Others books are in the field of the historical novel, or are exotic in setting, or are merely topical. She also wrote literary criticism and verse. The most impressive work of Rebecca West (1892-    ) has been done outside fiction, though she rates as a considerable novelist by virtue especially of *The Judge* (1922). Her hard, clear intelligence, of the sort which men like to call "masculine," has been largely directed to the elucidation of political and social problems;

*Rose Macaulay*

*Rebecca West*

---

[32] For really excellent tales of mystery and the supernatural we must turn to three older writers. The best ghost-stories of the period were written by the great scholar Montague Rhodes James (1862-1936); he published three series of them (1904, 1911, 1919). William W. Jacobs (1863-1943) specialized in the humors and human oddities of London dock-land in short stories collected in three "omnibus" volumes (1931-1934); but his most powerful work has been done in tales on the borderland of the supernatural, as in the truly horrifying story, *The Monkey's Paw*. Algernon Blackwood (1869-1951) explored the same borderland and beyond, achieving effects of genuine spiritual terror in *The Empty House* (1906), *The Listener* (1907), and other stories of the occult and the supernatural of which the best are collected in *The Willows and Other Queer Tales* (1932).

and in her comments upon events and personalities she is by turns bantering, satiric, serious, and impassioned. *Black Lamb and Gray Falcon* (1942), an account of a visit to Jugoslavia, with divagations anthropological, cultural, literary, philosophical, and emotional, is her most massive work and is likely to be long remembered.

# XLI

## Poetry in the Twentieth Century

*Tradition
and
Innovation*

In essaying a sketch of the progress of English poetry from the beginning
of the present century to the outbreak of the Second World War, the
historian must select from among the almost innumerable poets of the
period.[1] A catalogue of names would be unprofitable, and a mere chronological survey would bring together writers who have nothing but birth-
years in common with one another. This chapter begins with poets in whom
the Victorian tradition was still alive, and proceeds through the era of experimentation that became apparent about 1910 to the innovators who
captured critical attention during the period between the two wars. The
rough classifications "traditionalists" and "experimenters" are employed
without prejudice. The poet who works within the frame of a great tradition is entitled to consideration provided he has something to say. On the
other hand, it is possible to overestimate the significance of innovations.

There was no abrupt break in the continuity of English poetry during,
or immediately after, the war of 1914-1918. The war did not initiate change,
though it probably hastened it. Actually, one of the most remarkable of the
innovators, Father Hopkins, had died as long ago as 1889, though the delay
in publishing his *Poems* (1918) postponed the impact of his experiments
in style, syntax, prosody, and imagery. Of other poets already noticed in this
history several who lived far down into this century endeavored, each in his
own way, to liberate poetry from late-Victorian debasement, reinvigorating
the idiom and enlarging and refreshing the vocabulary. The great variety
of readers, receptive, as usual, to the familiar rather than to the strange,
supported the traditionalists, while the innovators only gradually roused
interest. Even so, that interest has been generally limited to circles of "intellectuals." A remarkable phenomenon in English literary history between
1918 and 1939 is the alienation of poets who have been competent masters of
their art from the large public consciousness.

[1] H. P. Collins, *Modern Poetry* (1925); E. L. Davison, *Some Modern Poets* (1928); Charles
Williams, *Poetry at Present* (1930); R. L. Mégroz, *Modern English Poetry, 1882-1932* (1933);
Geoffrey Bullough, *The Trend of Modern Poetry* (1934); Cornelius Weygandt, *The Time of
Yeats* (1937); F. R. Leavis, *New Bearings in English Poetry* (1938); Cleanth Brooks, *Modern
Poetry and the Tradition* (1939); H. W. Wells, *New Poets from Old: A Study in Literary
Genetics* (1940); David Daiches, *Poetry and the Modern World* (1940); J. G. Southworth,
*Sowing the Spring: Studies in British Poets from Hopkins to MacNeice* (1940); H. V. Routh,
*English Literature and Ideas in the Twentieth Century* (1945).

# I

The typical traditionalist of the period was Alfred Noyes [2] (1880-1958) whose poetry was never touched by the theories and experiments of his *Noyes* contemporaries. His fluently melodious *Poems* (1904), in which were echoes of Tennyson, Swinburne, Kipling, and the old ballads, won him a large audience and some of his pieces found their way promptly into the repertories for school recitations. This is no reason for despising them provided they are good of their kind; and *The Barrel-Organ* and *The Highwayman* are good of their kind. But there was something factitious about Noyes's Orientalism in *The Flower of Old Japan* (1903), his "gramerye" in *The Forest of Wild Thyme* (1905), his medievalism in the drama *Robin Hood* (1911), and his Elizabethanism in the epic poem *Drake* (1906-1908) and in *Tales of the Mermaid Tavern* (1913). The trilogy of *The Torch-Bearers* (1922-1930), a poem of epical proportions on man's achievements in invention and discovery, exhibits Noyes beyond his depth though not beyond an audience that liked poetry to be instructive. Another poet carrying on the late romantic mood and idiom was Herbert Trench [3] (1865-1923) who *Trench* was attracted to classical and Celtic themes, retained the Victorian love of Italy, and even in his war poems, such as the *Requiem of Archangels for the World,* relied upon a derivative style. Richard Middleton [4] (1889-1911), *Middleton* whose death by his own hand seems a pathetically belated *fin de siècle* gesture, carried into the pre-war years a pseudo-Swinburnian floridness of style and a passionately "pagan" outlook upon life not unlike the early work of Rupert Brooke. The longevity of established modes is further *Wolfe* illustrated in the poetry of Humbert Wolfe (1885-1940). He, too, depended upon a Swinburnian facility and intricacy of rhythm and rime. In *Kensington Gardens* (1924), *The Unknown Goddess* (1925), and other volumes this virtuoso accomplished a semblance of freshness by the skill with which he played variations upon old themes. There is an elaborate patterning in his formerly much-praised *Requiem* (1927) on the "Losers" and "Winners" of the world. That he was not wholly out of accord with the temper of post-war England is shown by *Lampoons* (1925) and *News of the Devil* (1926), and it is a pity that he did not exercise more freely his gift for satire.

Robert Laurence Binyon [5] (1869-1943) made no radical break with tra- *Binyon* ditional forms, but he experimented in elaborate stanzas and played individualized variations upon inherited melodies. His poetry bears the impress of a cosmopolitan culture. The narratives and dramas are less likely to be remembered than some of his lyrical and elegiac poetry. Representative volumes are *London Visions* (1896), *Porphyrion* (1898), *Odes* (1901), *The*

[2] *Collected Poems* (2v, 1928) and later volumes; also various volumes of prose, chiefly critical.
[3] *Collected Poems* (3v, 1924); *Selected Poems*, ed. H. Williams (1924).
[4] Middleton published only in periodicals; his verse was collected posthumously in *Poems and Songs*, two series (1912 and 1913).
[5] *Collected Poems* (2v, 1931); *Selected Poems* (1922). The best study of Binyon's poetry is in J. G. Southworth, *Sowing the Spring*, pp. 46-63.

*Secret* (1920), and *The Sirens* (1924). Binyon always evinced an awareness of contemporary sentiment, even when, as often, he did not share it.
*For the Fallen,* the best-known of his war poems collected in *The Four
Years* (1919), though it went to the heart of England as did few poems of
the time, is not really typical of Binyon's response to the world calamity.
The note usually struck is that war must be accepted as a temporary deflec-
tion from the main current of life. In an age of discouragement he offered
the bracing doctrine of regeneration through contact with the common life
of man. In a restrained style he advocated "excess"—but an excess of kindness, mercy, and courage. The heart, he declared, should "overbrim."

*De la Mare* — The poetry of Walter de la Mare [6] (1873-1956) shows how a strong
individuality, intensity of feeling, and an exquisite sense of style may
revitalize old romantic themes without recourse to any novelty of technique.
De la Mare was accused of being an "escapist" from real life—but
what is called "reality" was never his home; and it has been said that
his poetry can be appreciated by the half-awake intelligence—but that is
precisely the mental state he required for its reception. The familiar touched
with mystery has been a note often sounded since the onset of romanticism;
in De la Mare, from his earliest work to *Alone* (1927) and *The Fleeting*
(1933), it was dominant. While cautioning himself against the instinct to
"lure his fantasy to its utmost scope," he was always "amorous of the
far" and his conscience indicted his mind less "for idle days than
of which he wrote in *Songs for Children* (1902) and *Peacock-Pie* (1913);
are close to one another, children are at home in those parts of his world
of which he writes in *Songs for Children* (1902) and *Peacock-Pie* (1913);
but other parts, where ghosts and demons walk beneath a waning moon,
are morbid, terrible, and dreadful. *The Listeners* (1912), one of his most
famous poems, cannot be read without a shudder; and there is a sense of
awe imparted by the Ozymandias-like poem, *The Image,* De la Mare could
be genial, as in *Jenny Wren* or *Titmouse*; but generally he suggests the
instability of the world, and there is an underlying pessimism as he gropes
his way through the cosmic mystery. Sometimes the theme is so vague that
the reader is left in doubt as to the poet's intentions—a state of mind which
it was his intention to induce. Of De la Mare's prose stories *Henry Brocken*
(1904) is a literary fantasy that does not quite succeed, and *Memoirs of a
Midget* (1921), apart from the implicit symbolism, is morbid to excess. His
delight in curious lore is shown in *Desert Islands and Robinson Crusoe*
(1930) and he threw more light upon his strange and fascinating
mind in *Pleasures and Speculations* (1940).

*T. Sturge Moore* — Thomas Sturge Moore [7] (1870-1944), engraver, art critic, and aesthetician,
was one of the first modern poets to attempt to reform poetic diction. This
independence in style is a curious feature of the work of one who was

---

[6] *Collected Poems* (1942); *Poems for Children* (1930). — R. L. Mégroz, *Walter de la Mare,
a Biographical and Critical Study* (1924); Forrest Reid, *Walter de la Mare, a Critical Study*
(1929).
[7] *Poems,* collected edition (4v, 1931-1933); *Selected Poems* (1934).

peculiarly faithful to classical and mythological themes, as in *Danaë* (1903), and later poems on Pan, Theseus and Medea, the Centaurs, and the Amazons. Of his dramas *Aphrodite against Artemis* (1901) and *Tragic Mothers* (1920) are the most impressive; but the dramatic form seems not really congenial to him. His thought is often recalcitrant to expression, as in the obscurely powerful *Judas* (1923). There is an austerity and rugged grandeur about Sturge Moore's best work that is suggestive of Doughty, though the stylistic eccentricities are less extreme. He expounded his aesthetic in various prose works, notably *Life and Art* (1910) and *Armour for Aphrodite* (1929). Gordon Bottomley [8] (1874-1948) likewise sought to redeem the language of poetry from sweetness and sentimentality. How far he had to go before he mastered his mature style is shown by the lavish sensuousness of his early *Poems at White Nights* (1899). The contrast is extreme in the two series of *Chambers of Imagery* (1907 and 1912), *A Vision of Giorgione* (1910), and *Poems of Thirty Years* (1925). Here, as in the dramatic poems mentioned in an earlier chapter, there is a strength of utterance suggestive of, and perhaps imitated from, the Jacobean dramatists. There is a closely knit texture of thought and rhythm and an exploitation of themes of weirdness and horror with a violence that sometimes stuns and sometimes merely deafens the reader. Like other contemporary poets Bottomley often wrote on rural subjects, and these pieces are occasionally meditations upon those "nameless men" of the far past who fashioned what are now prehistoric antiquities. Bottomley led a secluded life, but that he was not unaware of contemporary stirrings in the social order is evident from various poems, notably *To Iron-Founders and Others*. Somewhat resembling Bottomley's is the poetry of Lascelles Abercrombie [9] (1881-1938), but though often gnarled and contorted, its stern thoughtfulness is without Bottomley's violence. Abercrombie did not attempt to sever himself completely from the Victorian tradition; there are, in fact, many signs of Browning's influence upon him. But he offers yet another example of the effort to rescue style from the languor of the "Decadents." He made frequent use of the dialogue form; and *Emblems of Love* (1912), "designed in several discourses," connect closely with his verse-plays. Of the latter *The Sale of Saint Thomas* (published in part in 1911 but not entire till 1930) is the most memorable. Remarkable, too, is *The End of the World*—one of *Four Short Plays* (1922)—where there is comedy as well as grimness in the portrayal of the superstition-ridden yokels. Abercrombie, however, was seldom attracted to comic situations. He was a master of horror and dread, though he sometimes descended to the lurid and condescended to the supernatural. His reputation was academic rather than popular, and his hold upon the intellectuals was strengthened by his work in criticism and aesthetics. *An Essay towards a Theory of Art* (1922), *The Idea of Great Poetry* (1925), *Romanticism* (1926), and *Principles of Literary Criticism* (1932) are weighty professorial pronouncements.

*Bottomley*

*Abercrombie*

[8] On Bottomley's plays see ch. xxxviii, above.
[9] *Poems*, Oxford Edition (1930).

*Gibson*

Wilfred Wilson Gibson[10] (1878-1962) passed a long apprenticeship to Tennysonian sweetness and Swinburnian passion before discovering his proper subjects in the lives of poor and humble folk—fishermen, track-walkers, charwomen, industrial workers, a drover lost in the snow, a miner lost underground. These people are often of his native Northumberland, and occasionally he employed dialect. To this extent he was a regionalist, and he was obviously close to the naturalists in prose fiction. In reading his poetry George Crabbe comes to mind, though the resemblance has been denied on the ground that whereas Crabbe is diffuse Gibson's best effects are of an energetic condensation. In his use of the dramatic monologue he is suggestive of Browning. His most powerful poems are in *Daily Bread* (1910), a series of dramatized incidents; *Fires* (1912); *Thoroughfares* (1914); and *Livelihood* (1917), a series of what he called "dramatic reveries" or interior monologues. From narratives such as *The Blind Rower* and dialogues such as *The Operation* he moved on to the plays, *Krindlesyke* (1922) and *Kestrel Edge and Other Plays* (1928). Here, however, he over-extended himself, for he was most effective in incidents lending themselves to restricted treatment. Like various contemporaries, he enlarged the boundaries of poetry by bringing within its purview modern industrial life. His grim realism informs the controlled, ironic bitterness of poems on the war. Gibson was no innovator in technique; his diction is quite commonplace and his versification frequently crude; but these are qualities in keeping with his themes.

*Masefield*

The rough, stark life of the poor was the subject of the poem that made John Masefield[11] (1878-    ) famous. He had had his own experiences of hardship. Before he came of age there had been three years at sea in the merchant service and two more years of earning a living at odd jobs in and around New York. On his return to England he published *Salt-Water Ballads* (1902). That most of these derive from Kipling, with sailors' chanteys substituted for barrack-room ditties, is plain enough, but in *Sea-Fever* and a few other pieces there is a fresh note. In the proem to this collection Masefield "consecrated" himself to themes of the lowly, the burdened, and the forlorn. Then came *The Everlasting Mercy* (1911), being the confessions of a drunken poacher who is converted to gentleness. The tough subject, set forth in tough language, stood out against the idyllic background of the nature poetry that was the mode of the moment, and the poem made a sensation. Less violent than *The Everlasting Mercy* is *The Widow in the Bye Street* (1912) about a mother who loses her reason after her son is hanged for murder. *The Daffodil Fields* (1913) is another piece of stern realism. The comment of the sociological critics that Masefield is moved not by indignation against the condition of outcasts but by a sense of its picturesqueness is unfair to a poet who is manifestly burdened with the pitiful-

[10] *Collected Poems, 1905-1925* (1926); *Sixty-three Poems* (1926); and later volumes.
[11] *Collected Poems* (1932); *Selected Poems* (1938); and later volumes. — C. H. Simmons, *Bibliography* (1930); W. H. Hamilton, *John Masefield, a Critical Study* (1922); Cecil Biggane, *John Masefield, a Study* (1924); Gilbert Thomas, *John Masefield* (1933). — On Masefield's plays see ch. xxxviii, above.

ñess of life, but it is to this extent justified, that the devotee of Beauty, as Masefield declares himself, can face ugliness only by showing how it can be transmuted into the beautiful. Later narrative pieces are less depressing in tone. *Dauber* (1913) contains Masefield's memories of the sea in calm and storm. *Reynard the Fox* (1919) has a prologue describing in a manner intended to resemble Chaucer's the characters who assemble at a meet. The story of the hunt which follows is not important enough to bear the weight of this introduction. *Right Royal* (1920) is about horse-racing; *Enslaved* is a bit of melodramatic orientalism; and *The Wanderer of Liverpool* (1930) is a medley of verse and prose. Only in this last is there a suggestion of some symbolic intent below the surface of the narrative. The crudities and violences (though often deliberate), the lack of insight into character, the colors too thickly laid on, and all the noise and glare of these pieces have deafened and blinded many readers who have consequently missed the quieter tones and subtler shades of Masefield's lyrical and meditative poetry, in *Lollingdon Downs* (1917) and elsewhere. His appointment as poet laureate in 1930 did not meet with the approval of the intellectuals, but it was a deserved recognition of the only poet of the period who had won a nation-wide audience; and to a traditional office it was proper to appoint a traditionalist. Masefield's plays have been considered in an earlier chapter, and space is lacking to do more than mention by title the best of his novels, *Sard Harker* (1924) and *Bird of Dawning* (1933), and the best of his criticism, *Shakespeare* (1911), *Ruskin* (1920), and *Chaucer* (1931). Two other works are in a special category as narratives of tragic heroism: *Gallipoli* (1916) and *The Nine Days' Wonder* (1941), the latter on the evacuation of Dunkirk.

William Henry Davies [12] (1871-1940), peddler, mendicant, and "super- *Davies* tramp," knew what it was to be poor. After rough experiences in the United States he became a poet at the age of thirty-four, and presently a picturesque and patronized figure in London society. Among a score of volumes of poems *Songs of Joy* (1911) and *Raptures* (1918) may be named because their titles convey his peculiar quality. He could be odd or grim, but he had found the secret of happiness in a fresh contact with the natural world of fields and woodlands, flowers, birds, and small four-footed creatures. He jogged merrily along the footpath way of life, a sort of modern improvisatore whose facility often betrayed him into doggerel but whose joy was like Blake's and whose content was like Dekker's. The resemblances were not coincidental, for Davies was steeped in English lyric poetry. His apparent artlessness was in harmony with the more self-conscious simplicities of other poets of the pre-war years, and he became one of them. Like him, but with less fecundity, Ralph Hodgson (1871-1962) sang of his delight in creatures *Hodgson* and the creation. *The Bull* is the best of many poems about animals written at just this time because it does not assimilate animal and human nature

---

[12] *Collected Poems* (1929) and later volumes, including *Poems* (1934). — Thomas Moult, *William H. Davies* (1931).

*Thomas*

but recognizes the barriers between. *A Song of Honour* is rapturous in a manner a little too like Christopher Smart's *Song to David*. These poems are both of 1913; in later years Hodgson failed to fulfill their promise. Edward Thomas [13] (1878-1917) is as close to nature as Davies or Hodgson but in a different way. His early essays show an affinity to Richard Jefferies and his attempts at fiction to Hardy. Towards the end of his life he turned to poetry, adopting the pen-name of "Edward Eastaway." He was killed in the battle of Arras. *Poems* (1917) and *Last Poems* (1918) show in their delicately precise observation the influence of contemporary theory and experiment and in their predominantly rural themes the prevailing mood of pre-war poetry; but the peculiar angle of his approach individualizes his subjects in a way that is more easily felt than described. Thomas's literary

*Freeman*

scholarship was a bond between him and three other poets. John Freeman [14] (1880-1929), an accomplished critic, published about ten volumes of verse between 1909 and 1926, the high point of his reputation being reached in *Poems New and Old* (1920). Sound in craftsmanship and sincere in thought,

*Drink-*
*water*

he was not very original in either. John Drinkwater [15] (1882-1937) profited by his reputation as a dramatist, critic, and biographer to gain a hearing for his nondramatic verse, the bulk of which is much larger than his present fame. Occasionally he tried to be stark and strong in the manner of his friends Gibson and Abercrombie, but generally his poetry is nearer to that

*Squire*

of Edward Thomas in its quietness and love of nature. Sir John C. Squire [16] (1884-1958) managed to save from his life as a journalist time enough for a dozen volumes of polished but not very significant serious verse. *Steps to Parnassus* (1913) and *Tricks of the Trade* (1917) are of more lasting interest, for they show, as only good parody can show, the response of a conservative taste to innovation.

James Elroy Flecker [17] (1884-1915), who passed the fruitful years of his life in the Near East, was not so remote from his contemporaries as this geographical factor might indicate, for many of them were "amorous of the

*Flecker*

far," whether it were Babylon or Cotopaxi. In *The Golden Journey to Samarkand* (1913) and in the formerly overpraised poetic drama *Hassan* (posthumous, 1922) Flecker's object was to evoke the splendor and color of the Orient in a style stript of romantic excess and a mood purged of romantic subjectivity. His masters were the French Parnassians with their

---

[13] Robert Eckert, *Edward Thomas* (1937).

[14] *Collected Poems* (1928); *Last Poems*, ed. Sir J. C. Squire (1930). Freeman's critical studies include *A Portrait of George Moore* (1922) and *Herman Melville* (1926).

[15] *Collected Poems* (1923); *Summer Harvest: Poems, 1924-1933* (1933). — On Drinkwater's plays see ch. xxxviii, above.

[16] *Poems*, collected edition (1926); *Collected Parodies* (1921). Squire's critical articles, written under the pen-name of "Solomon Eagle," are collected in *Books in General*, three series (1918, 1920, 1921). His play, *Berkeley Square* (1928), written in collaboration with J. L. Balderston, was a success on stage and screen. Squire's monthly journal, *The London Mercury* (1919-1934), patronized new writers provided they were not too radical, but its cautious modernity disguised basic conservatism.

[17] *Collected Poems* (1923); *Collected Prose* (1920); *Letters* (1926); *Letters from Abroad* (1930). — Douglas Goldring, *James Elroy Flecker, an Appreciation* (1922); Geraldine E. Hodgson, *The Life of James Elroy Flecker* (1925).

doctrines of cool objectivity and the statuesque. Today Flecker is a faded figure, yet of interest for his attempt to escape from Victorianism.

## II

The half-decade before the First World War was enlivened with new movements in poetry and the other arts. The famous "Futurist" Manifesto issued by the Italian Filippo Tomaso Marinetti dates from 1909; Cubism was a sensation in New York in 1911; Richard Strauss was at the top of his fame; and the Russian Ballet was the rage. That the yeast was working in the post-Victorian dough is evident in much of the poetry we have passed in review; and some of the younger poets were attempting to design new bottles for their new wine. That the period-adjective "Georgian" became current within a year or two of the accession (1910) of George V is an indication of the self-consciousness of the time. *Georgian Poetry,* an an-   **Georgian** thology edited by Edward Marsh, appeared in 1912; sequels with the same   **Poetry** title in 1915, 1917, 1919, and 1922. De la Mare, Davies, and Gibson were represented in the first four of these compilations; other poets appeared less often; a few soon drifted away; and fresh talent was recruited for the later volumes. A few contributors, notably Chesterton on the extreme "right" and D. H. Lawrence on the extreme "left," were strangely out of place in this company. With such a variety of tastes, talents, and points of view, the limits of the group of "Georgian" poets were ill-defined and it is difficult to generalize. In so far as these poets shared a common program, it was an unexcited protest against the meretricious passion of the "Decadents" and against the stylistic flaccidity and lassitude of late-nineteenth-century verse. There was a revulsion from urban life into a sentimentalized rusticity. The prevailing mood was of quiet decorum. The "Georgians" did not extend the boundaries of poetry, and it is obvious today that theirs was not a revolution but a retreat. These generalizations do not apply to some of the contributors to Marsh's anthologies, but they are true of the movement as a whole. One   *Harold* of the poets repeatedly represented in these volumes was Harold Munro [18]   *Munro* (1879-1932). Munro's own verse is of less importance than his management of the "Poetry Bookshop" where poets forgathered to read and discuss their writings, and whence were issued the short-lived *Poetry Review* (1912) and later *The Chapbook* (1919-1921). These were but two of various "little magazines" whose aim was to stimulate interest in poetry and the other arts. Another outlet for new poets was the periodical *Rhythm* (1911-1912), edited by J. Middleton Murry and Katherine Mansfield. Binyon, Gibson, and Davies were among the poets who appeared in its pages. *New Numbers* (1914) was edited, and largely written, by Gibson, Abercrombie, Drinkwater, and Rupert Brooke. Much more radical than any of these publications was *Wheels* of which six annual issues appeared between 1916 and   *Wheels* 1921. The moving spirits of *Wheels* were Edith Sitwell and her two brothers,

---

[18] *Collected Poems* (1933), with memoir by F. S. Flint and introduction by T. S. Eliot.

Sacheverell and Osbert. Their object was to rouse public interest by deliberate eccentricity and aggressive self-advertisement; and in tone and technique their poetry was premonitory of tendencies of the nineteen-twenties. For this reason "the Sitwells" can best be considered when we reach the post-war years.

*Imagism*    Contemporaneous with these magazines and annuals were certain publications in the United States. This it is necessary to note because the Imagist movement of the same years was not limited to English poets but was Anglo-American.[19] As in the case of the "Georgians," the boundaries of the Imagist group were vague, for some writers seceded, others joined up, some were always on the periphery, and in later years most of them found the form with which they had experimented too constricted for their purposes. In the end they went their several ways. Within the limits of the form nothing was accomplished commensurate with the amount of discussion of theories and intentions. In its use of *vers libre* with cadences governed by breath-pauses instead of regular metres following the beat of the metronome, Imagism owed something to Whitman and Henley and much to the French Symbolists; it was also much influenced by tiny poetic forms from Japan. But (though there was some confusion on this point) Imagism was not a matter of prosody; an Imagist poem might have been written in regular metres or even in rime. It aimed at a "hard and dry" clarity and precision in the rendering of natural objects and of ideas, and it was opposed to exuberance, sentiment, and cloudily romantic lushness. The "tree of language" was, as Osbert Sitwell put it, to be pruned of its "dead fruit." The anti-

*Hulme*    romantic opinions of Thomas Ernest Hulme[20] (1883-1917) provided a theoretical basis for Imagism, and the scanty sheaf of what now seem to be his quite insignificant poems exemplified the practice. Five of these (thirty-three lines in all) were first published in 1912 by the American poet Ezra Pound. In the same year some early Imagist poetry was published in America. In 1914 Pound issued *Des Imagistes: An Anthology;* and after he had withdrawn from the movement another American poet, Amy Lowell, brought out three more Imagist anthologies (1915, 1916, 1917). Among the

*Flint*    English members of the group was Frank Stewart Flint[21] (1885-1960) whose one significant volume is *Cadences* (1915). After 1920 Flint aban-

*Aldington*    doned poetry in favor of work as a translator. Richard Aldington[22] (1892-1962) and his wife, the American poet "H. D." (Hilda Doolittle), were the most expert of the Imagists. The exquisite purity, clarity, and restraint of some of "H. D.'s" poems inspired by Greek subjects show Imagism at its finest. Aldington's *Images* (1915), *Images of War* (1919), and *Images of Desire* (1919) are the fruits of his search for new cadences in *vers libre* with precise attention to the exclusion of every word that does not contribute to the presentation of the subject. Later on, Aldington loosened his ties with

[19] Glenn Hughes, *Imagism and the Imagists* (1931).
[20] Michael Roberts, *T. E. Hulme* (1938). Appendix 1 contains Hulme's eight poems.
[21] *In the Net of Stars* (1909); *Cadences* (1915); *Otherworld, Cadences* (1920).
[22] *Collected Poems* (1928); *Poems* (1934).

Imagist theory, developed a talent for satire, and made odd but effective use of colloquialisms in verse. Turning to prose, he wrote short stories and novels. One of the latter, *Death of a Hero* (1929), is a bitter indictment of war. The Imagists did not hold together long; but while the movement lasted it helped to cleanse and discipline poetic diction and cadence, and its indirect influence both on later poets such as T. S. Eliot and upon the impressionistic technique of the stream of consciousness novelists was considerable.

## III

The First World War produced little poetry of a high order of excellence. Such poems as *The Spires of Oxford* by Winifred Letts and *In Flanders Fields* by John McCrae were of poignant significance at the time because the poets were experiencing that of which they wrote and their readers that of which they read. After August, 1914, every living poet was to a greater or less extent a "war poet." There were, however, a few young men who formed a more or less homogeneous group; and of these Rupert Brooke [23] (1887-1915) remains in the general memory as the typical poet of the war, because of his radiant personality and his Byronic death in one of "the isles of Greece." The five war sonnets called *1914* are the best known of all poetic utterances inspired by the conflict. In the nineteen-twenties the reaction following Brooke's tremendous posthumous renown took the form of sneering at the mood in which he had welcomed the coming of war. Had he lived, it is likely that he would have had his own second thoughts on that subject. In fact, in some of his pre-war pieces there is an incipient cynicism which might have developed into something congenial to the mood of post-war disillusionment. Other early poems, such as the still charming *Grantchester,* show the characteristically "Georgian" love of "haunts of ancient peace." Probably a much greater poet was lost when Wilfred Owen [24] (1893-1918) was killed in battle a week before the Armistice. In his poetry Owen moved rapidly from indignant renderings of the horrors of battle (as in *The Disabled* and *Dulce et Decorum*) to elegiac meditations upon the tragedy of youth sacrificed. In the preface to a projected volume which he did not live to publish he wrote: "My subject is War and the Pity of War. The Poetry is in the Pity." His *Anthem for Doomed Youth* and *Strange Meeting* are of lasting value not merely as records of a dominant mood of 1918 but as poetry. Owen's experiments in imagery, half-rime, and consonance suggest that, had he lived, he would have been a leader of the innovators of the nineteen-twenties. Another young poet slain in battle was Francis Led-

*The "War Poets"*

*Brooke*

*Owen*

---

[23] *Collected Poems* (1915); *Complete Poems* (1932); *Letters from America* (1916), with a preface by Henry James. Brooke's *John Webster and the Elizabethan Drama* (1916), an undergraduate essay, is of interest as anticipating the taste for Jacobean drama evinced by poets after the war. — E. H. Marsh, *Rupert Brooke, a Memoir* (1918); Walter de la Mare, *Rupert Brooke and the Intellectual Imagination* (1919); Maurice Browne, *Recollections of Rupert Brooke* (1927).

[24] *Poems,* ed. with "notices of his life and work" by Edmund Blunden (1931).

*Ledwidge*  widge [25] (1891-1917). This Irish peasant was torn from the fairies and folklore of which he had written, and he visualized the war as a bad dream against the reality of the rustic Ireland of happier days. In the war poems of

*Blunden*  Edmund Blunden [26] (1896-    ) there is pity, not anger or disgust; the futile strife is contrasted with memories of times of peace. Blunden carried into the war something of the pastoral mood of the "Georgians" and he carried over something of this mood into his poetry of the post-war years. Contrasting with Blunden's quiet pity are the horror and hate and scorn of

*Sassoon*  Siegfried Sassoon [27] (1886-    ). Sassoon's early poems, from about 1906, are acrid satires and parodies that stand out against the decorous "Edwardian" background. In the war his was one of the earliest and most influential expressions of satiric revulsion from the elation of Rupert Brooke. From his own experiences he wrote the brief and bitter poems in *The Old Huntsman* (1917) and *Counter-Attack* (1918) against profiteers and place-hunting politicians and the obscene fiction of military "glory." It is easy to deplore the crude violence of such pieces as *The General* or *Suicide in the Trenches*, but it is also heartless, for Sassoon wrote these aggressive poems with his heart's blood. After the war he continued to publish verse, often under assumed names, generally satiric. His two autobiographies in the guise of semi-fiction, *Memoirs of a Fox-Hunting Man* (1928) and *Memoirs of an Infantry Officer* (1930), the one picturing the old country life of hunting, racing, and cricket, the other a grim narrative of war, present the contrast between what was gone forever and what had taken its place.[28]

*Graves*  His friend Robert Graves [29] (1895-    ) opposed British policy and leadership with equal aggressiveness but less art. After the war Graves satirized and parodied most of his poetic contemporaries in somewhat indiscriminate fashion, and in a dozen volumes published his own abstruse and increasingly "metaphysical" verse. His autobiography, *Good-bye to All That* (1929), which was suppressed in its original form, had a success of notoriety. Two novels re-creating the Rome of the Emperor Claudius were much esteemed in 1934, and later novels are set in seventeenth-century England and prehistoric Greece.

## IV

*Poetry*  During the period between the two wars the significance of a poet could
*Between*  not be measured on the scale of popularity. It is a question whether poetry
*the Two*  became esoteric because the public had abandoned it or whether the public
*Wars*  abandoned it because it had become esoteric. Conscious of the political and social chaos caused by the war and its aftermath and of the moral chaos

[25] *Complete Poems* (1926). — Another casualty of the war was Charles Hamilton Sorley (1895-1915). His posthumously published *Marlborough and Other Poems* (1916) and *Letters* (1919) give evidence of his bright promise.

[26] *Poems, 1914-1930* (1930); *Undertones of War* (1928). Blunden has done notable work as a critic and biographer especially attached to the Romantic Period.

[27] *War Poems* (1919); *Selected Poems* (1925).

[28] See also *The Weald of Youth* (1942).

[29] *Poems, 1914-1926* (1927) and later volumes.

consequent upon the widespread acceptance of Freudian psychology; repudiating this chaotic world yet reflecting in his work the chaos which disgusted him, the post-war poet claimed to be the voice of "a generation for whom the dissolution of value had in itself a positive value." [30] By the larger public the voice was unheeded, not because there was not sympathy with the point of view but because contemporary novelists such as Aldous Huxley mirrored the scene of moral desolation more clearly. The poet came to feel that he was living in a world hostile to the artist, and realizing that he was no longer popular he had "no incentive to gild his poetry with the stuff of entertainment." [31] "Communication" was enfeebled and often completely interrupted. Poetry became obscure, experimental, irregular, antagonistic to didacticism, indifferent to any social value, the private language of small coteries, with much dependence upon verbal subtleties and patterns of association so complex, unstable, and fleeting as sometimes to become presently incomprehensible to the writers themselves. For some of the critics the interpretation of poetry became a sort of game; one of them has acknowledged the "thrill" experienced in "decoding" modernistic verse. The need was to fashion a new technique in diction and prosody to meet the requirements of the new subject-matter of a changing world. How much of the effort was the exploration of blind alleys and how much the blazing of a highway into the future of English poetry only time can tell. We are still too close to the brilliant and bewildering phenomena to judge dispassionately. Critical pronouncements were, however, clear. An arrogant assumption of authority in matters of taste was a characteristic of the period; personal predilections were mistaken for dogma. From judgments enunciated *ex cathedra* there could be, it was implied, no appeal. The poets and critics of poetry encouraged the widespread skepticism with regard to inherited ideals and established reputations. The great names and achievements in literature were subjected to a fresh valuation. Milton was dethroned in favor of Donne, in whose poetry was found a satisfying and imitable fusion of sensibility and intellectuality. The romantic poets were excommunicated and Dryden and Pope canonized. Into limbo went all the Victorian poets save Hopkins—who was not really Victorian. These "moderns" went in quest of strange gods—John Skelton and Thomas Middleton; Laudian divines; baroque and rococo artists. There was a great display of abstruse learning—in Sanskrit or Provençal or Japanese or what not, ostentation overreaching itself in the Sitwells' poems, and the *Cantos* of the American Ezra Pound, and the notes to T. S. Eliot's *The Waste Land*. The capriciousness of taste during these unstable years was astonishing. Thus, T. S. Eliot placed a vulgar little ditty in one of Dryden's plays on a par with the final chorus in Shelley's *Hellas,* and pronouncing *Hamlet* "a failure as a work of art" declared that *Coriolanus* was Shakespeare's greatest play. Another arbiter of taste said that Father Hopkins' *The Windhover* was the

[30] T. S. Eliot, writing of Marcel Proust, in *The Criterion,* IV (1926). 752-753.
[31] C. Day Lewis, *Revolution in Writing* (1934), p. 34.

greatest of all English poems. Such absurdities had no effect upon sound literary scholarship, but scholarship must notice them because they are symptomatic of the time. Adrift from old moorings, there were sensitive spirits who sought safe anchorages in some strong principle of authority. In this quest of "a help and stay secure" there was something touching; and equally touching at this distance of time seems the cynical repudiation of all standards, which was another expression of the *Zeitgeist.*

*Satire* Satiric poetry, dormant since Byron's time, expressed the prevailing sense of the fatuousness and futility of post-war life. We have already glanced at the satiric elements in the later poetry of Aldington, Sassoon, and Wolfe. But scorn and anger whose roots were very deep generally wasted itself *Roy* upon the agreeable task of breaking butterflies. Roy Campbell (1902- ), *Campbell* who had exhibited an exuberance of imagery in *The Flaming Terrapin* (1924) and other volumes of verse, chastised in *The Georgiad* (1931) the pre-war poets and the social basis of their point of view, while Osbert Sitwell, in *The Jolly Old Squire* (1922), expended a lot of ammunition upon *The London Mercury,* its editor, and its group of poets. Little of this satiric verse is likely to survive, but that it was produced is of interest to the historian because it helps to explain the early poetry of T. S. Eliot and the writings and attitudes of the Sitwells.

*The*  The Sitwell trio—Edith (1887-1964), Sir Osbert (1892- ), and Sacheverell *Sitwells* (1897- )—have their different individual qualities, Edith being the most caustic, Osbert the most robust, and Sacheverell the most learned; but they have worked harmoniously and may be considered together.[32] Reared in an aristocratic tradition of wealth, leisure, and culture, they have delighted to bait the reviewers and *épater la bourgeoisie* with a showy clowning and self-exhibitionism that disguise a fundamental seriousness and sadness. From the Philistinism they abhor they have sought an escape into the past. Their eclecticism is wide-ranging, but their favorite period has been that of the baroque and the rococo. Their poetry draws imagery and allusion from the refined artificiality of the *commedia dell' arte,* the opera, and the ballet; from Claude and Poussin; from periwigs and lacquers and chinoiserie and all the pleasing extravagances of Augustanism. Allusions remote in origin from one another are patterned into strange mosaics; but all this museum bric-à-brac is assimilated into modern idioms and themes, and Edith's verse in particular was influenced by the new rhythms of contemporary music. With her brother Osbert she published *Twentieth Century Harlequinade and Other Poems* (1916), and afterwards, singly, *Façade* (1922), *Elegy on Dead Fashion* (1926), *Five Variations on a Theme* (1933), and other and later volumes. Beneath the glitter and artificiality of her verse there is the pathos of the fleetingness of youth and a haunting fear of old age and death. Osbert Sitwell's poetry is generally satiric. He is less learnedly allusive than

---

[32] Edith Sitwell, *Collected Poems* (1930) and later volumes; Osbert Sitwell, *Collected Satires and Poems* (1931). There is no collected edition of Sacheverell Sitwell's poems. See Sir Osbert Sitwell, *Left Hand, Right Hand!* (1944) for the family background. This autobiography is continued in *The Scarlet Tree* (1946), and three later volumes.

she, and, unlike her, he does not hold the modern world at arm's length, for he wants to hit it hard. More notable than his poetry is his novel, *Miracle on Sinai* (1933), a *roman à clef*. Sacheverell Sitwell's most memorable poem is the as yet unfinished *Doctor Donne and Gargantua* (1921-1930), which, beginning with the statement of a moral problem, modulates into a pastoral ballet. The best introduction to the poetry of this remarkable trio is their critical work in literature and the fine arts. Edith's biography of Alexander Pope (1930) is, notwithstanding its extravagance, a valuable corrective to Victorian denigration of that master. Her three anthologies—Augustan, Romantic, and Victorian—entitled *The Pleasures of Poetry* (1930-1932) illuminate her tastes. *The English Eccentrics* (1933) is a witty piece of literary and antiquarian research. Osbert Sitwell's *Discursions on Travel, Art, and Life* (1925) and *Winters of Content* (1932) have opened the eyes of many tourists to the charms and glories of South Italian baroque art. Sacheverell Sitwell's prose is more voluminous and even more learned. Besides lesser travel books, there are the three influential studies of the baroque—Southern (1924), German (1927), and Spanish (1931); the study of medieval life, art, and thought entitled *The Gothick North* (1929); and the intricately erudite phantasmagoria, *Splendours and Miseries* (1943). A reading of their prose confirms the impression made by their poetry, that their delight in a sophisticated culture, their fastidious eclecticism, and their frivolousness are grounded upon despair of the modern world. The curtain of their persiflage muffles this note but does not render it inaudible.

The most famous and influential poet of the post-war period was *T. S.* Thomas Stearns Eliot [33] (1888-1965), who, born in America, embraced *Eliot* English citizenship in 1927. The story of his progress from disdainful desperation to spiritual peace within the Anglican fold can be traced with such precision in his poetry that almost it appears to have been patterned beforehand. There may seem to be nothing in common between the creator of Prufrock, Burbank, Bleistein, and Sweeney and the theologian who was a mainstay of the Malvern Conference, but it is possible to follow each step along this pilgrim road. The journey starts with the poems collected in *Prufrock and Other Observations* (1917), *Ara Vos Prec* (1919), and *Poems* (1920). In many of these the barrenness of the present is contrasted with the fruitfulness of the past. There is an apparent casualness in weaving together banal modern allusions and literary references which widen the vista and embrace tradition. With a boldness that at once attracted attention, imagery was drawn from things hitherto regarded as "unpoetic"—coffee-spoons, and trouser-cuffs, and an etherized patient; but recourse was also had to allusive quotations that demanded for their comprehension a certain amount of specialized scholarship. In style the modern and the traditional were fused into a new synthesis: on the one hand, there is an indebtedness

[33] *Collected Poems, 1909-1935* (1936) and later volumes; *Selected Essays* (1932); *Essays Ancient and Modern* (1936). — H. R. Williamson, *The Poetry of T. S. Eliot* (1932); F. O. Matthiessen, *The Achievement of T. S. Eliot* (1935); G. W. Foster, "The Archetypal Imagery of T. S. Eliot," *PMLA*, LX (1945). 567-585.

to Ezra Pound and the Imagists and to certain French poets, particularly Tristan Corbière and Jules Laforgue; and on the other, there is the use of simple, inherited verse forms, especially the quatrain, and blank verse modeled upon that of Webster and Middleton. The contemporary is set in the frame of a long tradition, for Eliot's is the head upon which all the ends of the world are come, and his eyelids are a little weary. In a bare, dry, satiric tone he makes his statements without qualification, expressing with seeming flippancy his contempt for vulgarity. Modern types are characterized, or rather caricatured, in such poems as the *Portrait of a Lady;* and the vulgarity of *l'homme sensuel moyen* is exposed in the poems on Prufrock, Sweeney, and the tourists in Venice. Eliot's early success was not the reward of his occasional profundities but of his witty and blasé unmasking of shallowness. His essential qualities of austerity and precision in the use of words, of novelty in rhythms and cadences, and of intensity of observation were present in these first poems. But already there was an attempt to generalize about life on the basis of a narrow, academic, almost cloistered existence.

The Waste Land

The poem *Gerontion*—"thoughts of a dry brain in a dry season"—is the connecting link between the early poems and *The Waste Land* (1922). This most famous of modern poems is not merely, as is sometimes said, a picture of the spiritual and moral vacuity of the post-war period. It had, indeed, its contemporary significance, but as always in Eliot's writings, the contemporary is bound to the past in a thousand ways. The present fades into the past and the past into the present. The remote is near. The "Waste Land" is the fallen nature of humanity. The rôle of the prophet Tiresias as the focus of the present and the past is central to an understanding of the poem. Alternately the horizon expands and contracts in a phantasmagoria resembling some of the effects accomplished by James Joyce. Everyone knows that the poem is based upon Jessie L. Weston's *From Ritual to Romance,* a monograph relating the Grail legend to the fertility cults of Tammuz and Adonis. There is consequently much sexual symbolism. Other images are taken from *The Golden Bough*. But this anthropological lumber is incompletely assimilated, and chips and splinters strew the footnotes. With all this are interwoven allusions to Dante, Buddhism, the Jacobean dramatists, and much else. Cleopatra and Dido, Tristan and Isolde, Queen Elizabeth and Leicester, Spenser, Goldsmith, Saint Augustine, and the Buddha —these and other figures loom dimly through the chaos. The figure of the Vegetation God is dominant, ranging in his Protean manifestations from the Crucified Jesus to the Hanged Man of the Tarot cards. Eliot realized that "communication" with the reader was incomplete and he attached notes which leave most matters unexplained. *The Waste Land* is not an artistic entity since even the attempt to grasp its meaning leads us to something outside itself. It has been held that this is not merely a poem of despair of the present but of hope and promise for the future, since at the close the thunder speaks, foretelling the coming of the life-giving rain. But no rain falls. The same mood is continued in *The Hollow Men* (1925), a picture of the "inert resignation" of those who breathe the small, dry air of modern spiritual emptiness. The change came in *Ash-Wednesday* (1930) of which the theme is the search for peace found in humble and quiet submission to God's Will. This is a poem not of Easter joy but of the beginning of the penitential season. The mystic vision is not attained, but there is the record of the steps along the mystic way. Depending upon a great tradition of Dantesque and liturgical imagery, *Ash-Wednesday* is comparatively easy to understand and loses nothing for being comprehensible. "Intellect," as Eliot says of Donne, "is at the tip of the senses"; and the most beautiful part of the poem is found in the sensuous loveliness of the evocation of the New England coast. But the impression that remains is of an intellectual effort to find faith rather than of a spiritual conviction surging from within. *Ash-Wednesday*

The poems of the following decade show for the most part an increasing hardness and thinness of manner, with rhythms often scarcely distinguishable from prose. *Sweeney Agonistes* (1932) marks a reversion to the early mood of satiric revulsion from modern vulgarity. In *The Rock* (1934) the words only are Eliot's, the scenario of this ecclesiastical pageant having been supplied by someone else. It contains interesting experiments in rhythms and the characteristic juxtaposition of the exalted and the commonplace. *Murder in the Cathedral* (1935), a drama on Thomas à Becket, has as much significance for the dogmatist and moralist as for the student of drama. The sequence collectively entitled *Four Quartets,* beginning with *Burnt Norton* (written in 1935 though not published till 1939) and continuing through *East Coker* (1940) and *The Dry Salvages* (1941) to its culmination in *Little Gidding* (1942), brings together the intricacies of modern technique and imagery and the simplicities of traditional lyric measures. In the austere asceticism and confident dogmatism of these poems there is an impressive restatement of Christian belief in terms of contemporary poetic idiom and contemporary speculations about time.

Space is lacking for a full estimate of Eliot's work as a critic. The six volumes from *The Sacred Wood* (1920) to *Elizabethan Essays* (1934) contain the richest collection of critical pronouncements our age has to show. To be sure, they contain eccentricities of judgment sufficient to illustrate a primer of modern critical heresy. Often mistaking personal predilections for principles of universal validity, Eliot, by the pontifical self-assurance of his manner, imposed his tastes and opinions upon his following. But no other modern critic has so thoroughly ploughed the old fields of literature, bringing forth new fruit by forcing even his opponents to subject inherited values to new scrutiny. *Homage to John Dryden* (1924) and *For Lancelot Andrewes* (1928) exhibit characteristic lines of thought and feeling. *Dante* (1929) is Eliot's profoundest piece of criticism and *After Strange Gods* (1931) his most arrogant. Occasional essays of recent date have often been on theological subjects. *Eliot's Criticism*

The poets born in the present century are still young and in full productivity and some of them, one assumes, still immature. Their point of view *Younger Poets* was conditioned not by the immediate aftermath of the First World War, for at that time they were still schoolboys, but by the problems of unemployment and the distressed areas, by ideological discussion, communist and anti-communist, by the economic depression, and by the encroaching menace of Fascism. In their early verse they made so much use of cryptic symbolism comprehensible only to the initiated that, when published, these poems, as one of the group expressed it, were "private faces in public places." But the extremes of esotericism of the years 1925-1935 provoked a reaction, and these younger poets have of late retreated from snobbish and sophisticated exclusiveness and have attempted, by employing an idiom more widely intelligible, to come to terms with a larger body of readers than the coteries could supply. Running the gamut from wrath to pity, they have attacked the privileged classes and denounced social conditions calling for radical change, and they have intermingled these politico-sociological motives with sympathetic analyses of abnormal sexual psychology. In style they have *Auden* ranged from spluttering incoherence to forceful clarity. The most conspicuous of these poets is Wystan Hugh Auden (1907-    ) who first challenged attention with *The Orators* (1932), a loud and confused piece of rhetoric from which the reader was expected to gather that nought was well with England. Much of Auden's work has been done in collaboration with other writers. His finest verse is in *The Ascent of F. 6* and in *Look, Stranger* (both 1936). In *Letters from Iceland* (1936) and *The Double Man* (1941) he has simplified his technique, not, however, without a descent to levels close to ephemeral journalism. Of finer quality is *For the Time Being* (1944) which contains some remarkable prose. His *Selected Poems* (1940) show the range of his modes, moods, and themes. Stephen Spender (1909-    ) is subtler, more pitiful, and less violent than Auden (with whom he is closely associated in the public consciousness). The titles of his volumes—*Forward from Liberalism* (1937), *Poems for Spain* (1939), and *Ruins and Visions* (1941)—suggest the history of recent tragic years. Other poets of this group are Cecil Day Lewis (1904-    ) and Louis MacNeice (1907-1963). Apart from them stands F. J. Ronald Bottrall (1906-    ) whose *Festivals of Fire* (1934) and *The Turning Path* (1939) may one day win him more renown than has yet come to him.[34]

[34] From this summary final paragraph many names have necessarily been omitted. Here may be added Hugh MacDiarmid, the Scots communist (*Selected Poems,* 1940), and Dylan Thomas, (1914-1953), *Collected Poems* (1952).

# XLII
## Anthropology; Travel; History; Criticism

### I

Two writers of the closing years of the nineteenth century helped to lib- *Carpenter* eralize thought and in particular to extricate the study of problems of sex from prurient obscurantism. Edward Carpenter [1] (1844-1929), who was active in Socialist agitation, proclaimed his vision of a pure and primitivistic democratic society, expressing emotionally in his poems *Towards Democracy* (1883-1902) and *Chants for Labour* (1888) the ideals for which he argued in *Civilization: Its Cause and Cure* (1889) and other prose works. *Love's Coming of Age* (1896) and other books gave him a special reputation, but his thought ranged widely over literature, aesthetics, sociology, ethics, and religion. Carpenter was much influenced by Walt Whitman (whom he visited twice) and by Thoreau and Tolstoy; and a journey to India left the impress of Oriental mysticism upon his thought. The charm of his personality is revealed in his autobiography, *My Days and Dreams* (1916). The emotional exuberance of his style alienates many even of those readers who are in entire accord with his objectives, but the influence of his nobly ardent nature will not quickly disappear. Another courageous pioneer was Havelock Ellis [2] (1859-1939) whose *Studies in the Psychology* *Ellis* *of Sex* (1897-1928) brought him an un-sought-for notoriety. For long these monographs could be procured only surreptitiously in England, and by the time they became easily accessible Ellis's researches had been absorbed into those of his successors. Ellis explored in many other directions, being a literary critic, traveler, essayist, philosophic exponent of the art of living, and counselor-at-large to the English people. *The New Spirit* (1890) is still of value for the appreciations of Whitman, Ibsen, and Tolstoy. *The Soul of Spain* (1908) reveals a remarkable insight into the spirit of a people alien from most Englishmen. *The Dance of Life* (1923), advocating grace, pattern, and rhythm in the conduct of life, contains much of Ellis's ripest wisdom, and a like sagacious serenity informs the three series of his *Impressions and Comments* (1914, 1921, and 1924).

[1] Edward Lewis, *Edward Carpenter: An Exposition and an Appreciation* (1915); A. H. M. Sime, *Edward Carpenter: His Ideas and Ideals* (1916); G. Lowes Dickinson, Havelock Ellis, and others, *Edward Carpenter: In Appreciation* (1931).
[2] Isaac Goldberg, *Havelock Ellis, a Biographical and Critical Survey* (1926); Houston Peterson, *Havelock Ellis, Philosopher of Love* (1928), with bibliography; Bertrand Russell, H. L. Mencken, and others, *Havelock Ellis: In Appreciation* (1929).

Tylor

Winwood
Reade

William
Robertson
Smith

Frazer

Sir G.
Elliot
Smith

The assault upon Victorian reticence was prosecuted vigorously upon the battleground of religious beliefs, where inquiry extended beyond biblical criticism into the wider problems of the origins of religion and the different levels of belief and ritual. Sir Edward B. Tylor (1832-1917) helped to re-shape ideas and to awaken the modern interest in prehistory. *Primitive Culture* (1871), the most influential of his works, deals with the beginnings and early stages of development of mythology, philosophy, religion, art, and culture. A more impassioned but less scientific book is *The Martyrdom of Man* [3] (1872) by Winwood Reade (1838-1875), a survey of human history divided and recomposed under the heads of War, Religion, Liberty, and Intellect. Reade's indignant agnosticism is expressed with a "fine gloom" for which he was commended by H. G. Wells.[4] William Robertson Smith (1846-1894), the chief editor of the ninth edition of *The Encyclopaedia Britannica* (to which he contributed articles of great pith and moment on biblical subjects), was one of the last victims of the Victorian heresy-hunters, being deprived of his professorship at Aberdeen. His chief works are *The Prophets of Israel* (1882) and *The Religion of the Semites* (1889), the latter an outstanding example of the methods and results of comparative criticism. Smith was the revered master of Sir James George Frazer [5] (1854-1941), classical scholar, translator of Pausanias (1898), anthropologist, historian of various forms of religious beliefs, and author of *The Golden Bough* (1896; third edition, greatly expanded, 1912), from which have branched out sub-sidiary studies of totemism, the worship of the dead, the religion of nature, Old Testament folklore, and related problems. *The Golden Bough* did more than any other single book to reorient men's minds towards fundamental questions of custom and belief. Many of Frazer's theories are now dis-credited; the evidence upon which he drew is of varying degrees of reli-ability; the pseudo-scientific "laws" which he detected at work beneath savage custom emphasize the logical at the expense of the emotional element in the savage mind; and since Frazer's day the methods of anthropology have changed. But however much it has been discredited as science, *The Golden Bough* endures as literature, an immense and fascinating repository of curious and far-fetched lore, arranged according to a vast design, and set forth in a prose style of pellucid grace touched with an irony suggestive of Anatole France. Of anthropologists of a younger generation there is room to mention only Sir G. Elliot Smith (1871-1937), who was the center of con-troversy as the leader of the "diffusionist" school of prehistorians. *The Ancient Egyptians and the Origins of Civilization* (1923) argued the thesis that civilization originated in the Valley of the Nile and spread thence to

[3] New edition, in the Travellers' Library, with an introduction by J. M. Robertson (1927).
[4] See the preface to *The Outline of History,* where Wells acknowledges his indebtedness to Reade. — Reade's *African Sketch-Book* (1873) is a vivid narrative of exploration.
[5] R. A. Downie, *James George Frazer: A Portrait of a Scholar* (1940). For a more extended estimate by the present writer than is here possible see "Nemi and the Golden Bough," *No. Amer. Rev.,* ccxviii (1923). 814-824. — Andrew Lang, an expert in controversy, was among the first to show how insecure was Frazer's "high-piled castle of hypotheses." See Lang's *Magic and Religion* (1901), which is largely concerned with *The Golden Bough.*

the uttermost parts of the planet. This theory, much discussed without evoking much credence, is opposed to that of Tylor and Frazer who did not
derive àll cultural elements from any single source but accounted for resemblances on the ground that at any given stage of social development the
human mind reacts to similar circumstances in similar ways.

## II

The anthropologists who, like Frazer, were not themselves field-workers *Travel*
depended largely upon the reports of travelers. To the literature of travel
there have been notable additions since the mid-nineteenth century. The
temptation must be resisted to review the narratives of exploration in the
Arctic and Antarctic, in Central Asia and Tibet, in the Australian desert,
and in many other perilous and remote portions of the globe. The modern *Mountain*
sport of mountaineering has produced a literature of its own. Of this, *Hours* *eering*
*of Exercise in the Alps* (1871) by the scientist John Tyndall (1820-1893),
*Peaks, Passes and Glaciers* (1859-62), and Sir Leslie Stephen's *The Playground
of Europe* (1871) are popular examples.[6] Sir Martin Conway (1856-1937)
went farther afield, writing narratives of adventure in the Himalayas and
the Andes. The recent attempts upon the summits of Mt. Everest and
other Himalayan peaks have been recorded in narratives distinguished for
nobility of spirit. The Far East was productive of no great travel book. That
strange exotic, Lafcadio Hearn (1850-1904), who became a citizen of Japan *Lafcadio*
and married a native, made his adopted country the subject of *Glimpses of* *Hearn*
*Unfamiliar Japan* (1894) and other impressionistic volumes.

From experiences in the Near and Middle East have been shaped those
travel books that have best claims upon our attention, for since the days of
Burton, Palgrave, and Warburton,[7] Englishmen have been irresistibly attracted to the rock-strewn wilderness of Arabia and have given us a series
of narratives unequaled elsewhere in the literature of man's wanderings "on
sands and shores and desert wildernesses." Edwin Henry Palmer (1840-1882),
a distinguished Arabist, wrote *The Desert of the Exodus* (1871), which was *Palmer*
long afterwards Colonel Lawrence's authority for the topography of Sinai.
Its vivid accuracy is lightened with a humor that now seems old-fashioned. *Lady*
Lady Anne Blunt (1837-1917) accompanied her husband, Wilfrid Scawen *Anne*
Blunt, on journeys recorded in her *Bedouin Tribes of the Euphrates* (1879) *Blunt*
and *Pilgrimage to Nejd* (1881). Topographically to one side of the explorers
of Arabia stands Edward G. Browne (1862-1925), the historian of Persian *Browne*
literature. His exquisitely written book, *A Year among the Persians* [8] (1893),
is touched with the mystery and mysticism of Babism. *Persian Pictures*

---

[6] *The Englishman in the Alps*, ed. Arnold Lunn (1927), is an excellent anthology.
[7] See ch. XXI, above. — There is excellent literary criticism in D. G. Hogarth, *The Pene-
tration of Arabia* (1904).
[8] New edition, with a memoir by Sir E. Denison Ross (1926). — Without the charm
of Browne's book but a work of broader scope distinguished for its authoritativeness is *Persia
and the Persian Question* (1892) by George Nathaniel Curzon, Marquis Curzon (1859-1925).

*Gertrude Bell*

*Hogarth*

*Other Arabists*

*Doughty*

(1894) by Gertrude Bell [9] (1868-1926) is a slighter work than Browne's, but her account of Syria, *The Desert and the Sown* (1907), is a classic in its field. During the First World War she was associated with David G. Hogarth (1862-1927) in the Arab Bureau in Cairo. Hogarth's reminiscences of archaeological experiences, *A Wandering Scholar in the Levant* (1896) and *Accidents of an Antiquary's Life* [10] (1910), won, and still hold, admiration. Of Arabists still living mention must be made of Eldon Rutter, whose *Holy Cities of Arabia* (1928) received Colonel Lawrence's praise; Bertram Thomas, whose superb feat in crossing the Rub'-al-Khāli is narrated in *Arabia Felix* (1932); and St. John Philby, an English Moslem, whose later accomplishment of the same arduous journey is the subject of *The Empty Quarter* (1933). [11] The books in which Miss Freya Stark has recorded her explorations and adventures in Arabia are of even more recent date. These were all men and women of high courage and renown; there remain to be noted two men of genius associated with Arabia.

The famous adventure of Charles Montagu Doughty [12] was, as has been noted in an earlier chapter, but an interlude in a life dedicated to poetry. After his return from Arabia Doughty devoted a decade to the composition of *Travels in Arabia Deserta* [13] (1888) which won the admiration of William Morris, Wilfrid Blunt, and other good judges but remained unknown to the general public for many years and at length, partly through the support of Colonel Lawrence, received acclaim as a masterpiece of English prose and a work of first magnitude in the history of travel. It is a surpassingly sincere, sure, and sensitive record of Arabian life both among the Bedouin and in the oasis towns. But it is more than that. With dim suggestions of allegorical intent, it shows the solitary man upon some exalted spiritual journey, groping for light through "the moral desolation of the world." Doughty was drawn to the barren peninsula (1876-1878) by his philological, geological, and antiquarian studies and his feeling for the primitive and the near to earth. Throughout his wanderings and afterwards while composing his masterpiece he remained true to his vocation as a poet. The prime consideration was that his language should be "right English of the best period." The *Arabia Deserta* is a supreme experiment in style, the result of an effort to refresh and invigorate the mother tongue, redeeming it from modern venality and flaccidity by a return in idiom and vocabulary to the larger utterance of an earlier and nobler time. The archaisms, neologisms, and absolute constructions; the effects of the spoken word; the use of Arabic terms and turns of phrase; and the other elements of Doughty's

---

[9] *The Letters of Gertrude Bell,* ed. Lady Bell (2v, 1927). — Ronald Bodley and Lorna Hearst, *Gertrude Bell* (1940), an inadequate biographical sketch which must serve for the present for want of anything better.

[10] The best parts of both these books have been combined to form *The Wandering Scholar* (1925).

[11] Both Thomas and Philby have written other books on Arabia.

[12] For Doughty's poetry see ch. xxxix, above, where will also be found a bibliography.

[13] New edition, with introduction by T. E. Lawrence (2v, 1921); *Wanderings in Arabia* (1908), an abridgment made by Edward Garnett; *Passages from the Arabia Deserta,* selected by Edward Garnett (1931).

style are matters for special study. It must be granted that he "writ no language" and that mastery of the great book is not won without toil; but this extraordinary archaistic revival in style is magnificently in keeping with Doughty's noble simplicity of personality and with the primitive society in which he lived through two memorable years.

Among the younger English Arabists for whom the *Arabia Deserta* was *T. E.* the bible of their profession was Thomas Edward Lawrence [14] (1888-1935). *Lawrence* Lawrence went to Syria to pursue studies in military architecture of which the fruit was a monograph, *Crusader Castles,* published posthumously (1936). On the outbreak of war in 1914 he was attached to the Arab Bureau in Cairo where Hogarth was his chief and Gertrude Bell a colleague. There followed the celebrated mission which resulted in the rising of the Arab tribes against their Ottoman overlords. In conjunction with Allenby's advance through Palestine, Lawrence directed the desert campaign which terminated in the Turkish defeat and the occupation of Damascus. Lawrence, though always (as is not always remembered) subordinate to Allenby, proved himself a master of the strategy of open warfare. For a time he was a prisoner in the hands of the Turks and endured shameful experiences that left a sense of defilement upon him. Moreover, he found that he had been made the medium for conveying to the Arabs promises which were incompatible with English commitments to the French. It was therefore in a mood of disillusionment and mortification that he pleaded unavailingly the cause of Pan-Arabism at Versailles. Afterwards he assisted Winston Churchill in securing a reasonably equitable settlement in the Near East. But he had lost faith, and, changing his name first to "Ross" and then to "Shaw", he sought seclusion from the world, ultimately finding in the R. A. F. a sort of modern equivalent to medieval monastic life. Yet he never escaped from his enormous celebrity, nor can it be said that he really desired to do so. The manuscript of the first draft of his narrative of the Arab revolt was lost and never recovered. In its second version, *Seven Pillars of Wisdom* was privately printed in 1922 and in definitive form in a limited, costly edition in 1926.[15] For anything like a final judgment of this book the needed perspective is as yet lacking, and criticism is of many minds. Lawrence's romantic and baffling personality, in which, if there was not (as is sometimes held) something of the charlatan, there was certainly much of the showman, but to whose extraordinary greatness there is ample testimony, stands between us and his book. The extent and significance of his contribution to Allenby's

[14] *Secret Despatches from Arabia* (1938); *Oriental Assembly* (1938); *Men in Print* (1940); *Letters,* ed. David Garnett (1939); *Letters to his Biographers Liddell Hart and Robert Graves* (2v, 1938); *Letters to H. S. Ede* (1942). — Liddell Hart, *Colonel Lawrence: The Man behind the Legend* (1934); Robert Graves, *Lawrence and the Arabian Adventure* (1928); *T. E. Lawrence by his Friends,* ed. A. W. Lawrence (1937). For more extended estimates by the present writer than are here possible see *New York Herald Tribune Books,* April 8, 1934; July 4, 1937; January 8, 1939.

[15] Lawrence would not permit the publication of an ordinary edition in his lifetime; consequently *Seven Pillars of Wisdom* was first published in regular fashion in 1935. *Revolt in the Desert* (1927), a so-called abridgment, is really a hasty affair of scissors-and-paste, published to defray the costs of the limited edition of the complete work.

plan of campaign, his mastery of strategy, his gullibility as a diplomat—these are not problems for the literary critic, but for the moment they confuse critical judgment. Certainly, in clarity of execution *Seven Pillars of Wisdom* does not match the desert campaign. Though overlong and overwritten, it is yet so incomplete that to be fully understood the narrative must be supplemented from other sources. Its levities seem mistimed, its touches of malice misplaced. Parts are greater than the whole; and these parts include the analysis of the character of the Semite, the story of the approach to Arabia, the assembling of the tribes, the destruction of the Meccan railway, the battle in the narrow defile, and the final scenes in Damascus. There are magnificent descriptions of desert landscape and vigorous characterizations of Arab personalities. At times (as in the *Arabia Deserta*) there are hints that the story is moving upon two planes—Lawrence journeyed upon a spiritual as well as a military road to Damascus. The monotony and incoherence of parts of the narrative suggest the chaotic monotony of war. In later years, when new perils lowered over England, there were those who hoped that Colonel Lawrence would emerge from his seclusion to become a leader of his people. It was not to be. He was killed when thrown from his motor-cycle while riding at reckless speed.[16]

*Cunning-hame Graham*

Life among the Moslems formed only part of the far-flung adventures of Robert B. Cunninghame Graham [17] (1852-1936)—"Don Roberto," "Hidalgo," "Modern Conquistador," as he was called. He never won in the United States the fame that was his due, perhaps because he included all Americans within his stormy, aristocratic scorn of comfort-loving, lethargic Philistinism. Nor has he yet achieved the legendary reputation of a Burton or a Lawrence, though with both he may be compared. Scottish but of partly Spanish descent, bold, generous, emancipated, and vehement, Cunninghame Graham had adventures and opinions and learning and prejudices enough to fill many volumes—and he did, in fact, fill three dozen. In youth he was a gaucho in the Argentine, a farmer in Mexico, and a soldier in Uruguay. Like his friend W. H. Hudson, he loved the wild men, wild animals, and wild vegetation of the pampas. Many of his reminiscences and semi-fictitious sketches and most of his historical and biographical works have a South American setting. But, unlike Hudson's, no years of his life were sedentary. His finest book, *Mogreb-el-Acksa* (1898), tells of his journey in the disguise of a Turkish physician beyond the Atlas mountains where he was arrested and held captive. Another time he joined the Meccan *haj*. At home he threw himself into the Labor movement and sat for a while in Parliament. "Don Roberto" had as rich and full a life as ever falls to the lot of man; it offers alluring material to the biographer. That material will be quarried

---

[16] Lawrence made a prose translation of the *Odyssey* (1932; reissued in paperback ed., Oxford, 1956). A long and candid account of life in the Royal Air Force, entitled *The Mint*, finally appeared in 1955.

[17] There is no collected edition. *Thirty Tales and Sketches*, ed. Edward Garnett (1929) and *Rodeo: a Collection of Tales and Sketches*, ed. A. F. Tschiffely (1936) offer characteristic examples of Cunninghame Graham's work. — See H. F. West, *A Modern Conquistador: Robert Bontine Cunninghame Graham: His Life and Works* (1932).

from his books, but probably they will themselves never be widely read. In theme they are often too remote from ordinary English interests, and they are too allusive, caustic, and ironical. Writing was one of Graham's ample, magnificent gestures. He waved the pen as he did the sword and made as few concessions to his reader as to an opponent in a quarrel. The pride that ruled his years was not so becoming in his books as in his noble and picturesque personality. Life was to him more than letters; he lacked the patience which is part of genius in the arts.

William Henry Hudson [18] (1841-1922) is sometimes numbered among *Hudson* writers of fiction, but this is to suggest a false emphasis, for he was a novelist only sporadically and inexpertly. His own preference would have been for a place among adventurers who tell of wild and lawless lands. Of English stock but American parentage, he was born in the Argentine and remained in South America till 1874 when he went to live in England. "My life ended when I left the pampas," he said; rather, it became a *recherche du temps perdu.* Hudson hated the drab, urban civilization in which, matched with an uncongenial wife, he was fated to live in poverty; and though he loved the intimate English countryside and instilled a quiet charm into such books as *Birds in London* (1898), *Afoot in England* (1909), and *A Hind in Richmond Park* (1922), his dreams were of the solitary grandeur of the Patagonian desert, the Argentine plains silent under the stars, the impetuous, fantastic gauchos, and the turbulent, revolutionary life of South America in the days of his youth. *The Purple Land* [19] (1885), a tale of revolution in Uruguay, is of little moment as fiction, but the rich incidental descriptive passages are exquisite evocations of memories of long ago. *Green Mansions* (1904), the only other "novel" that counts, is set in the tropical jungles of Venezuela where Hudson had never been, so that this romantic creation is an ideal contemplated in compensation for the ugly realities of Bayswater. The character of Rima in this story is intended to suggest natural beauty as opposed to nature's cruelties. But the transcendental and human elements in the tale are not well harmonized. *El Ombú* (1912) is a collection of sketches, rather than of short stories, of the gauchos, full of violence and anguish, poverty and cruelty. In all these the mode of tale-telling is quite artless, dependent upon Hudson's own experiences or upon hearsay. His material was not unlike Conrad's, but though he was that master's admiring friend, he was without Conrad's subtleties in "arranging" the data stored in memory. But how astonishing was the memory of this "traveller in little things"! Gilbert White's *Selborne* was one of his favorite books; he resembles White in his patient observation and faithfulness in description of minute objects. But his approach to nature was not "scientific"; in his books there are a latent symbolism (especially when he wrote of birds—

[18] *Collected Works* (24v, 1922-1923); *Letters to Edward Garnett* (1925). — G. F. Wilson, *Bibliography* (1922); Morley Roberts, *W. H. Hudson: A Portrait* (1924); R. H. Charles, "The Writings of W. H. Hudson," *E&S,* xx (1935). 135-151; Baker, x (1939). 86-94.
[19] Originally entitled *The Purple Land that England Lost*—that is, by her failure to seize and colonize Uruguay in the early nineteenth century.

Rima chirps like a bird) and a pantheistic fervor that put him in the line of Thoreau and the other transcendentalists. The passionate love of wild nature, animate and inanimate, and the intensity of his fellow-feeling with animals show his affinity to D. H. Lawrence, as does his hatred of the urban middle-class. In old age he wrote *Far Away and Long Ago* (1918), the history of his early life, recalling in it the animistic sense which he possessed in youth and which, he held, is at the root of all nature-worship. Rejecting Darwin's explanation of the evolutionary process, he responded to the Lamarckian theory because it made room for intelligence and desire.

## III

*The Cambridge Histories*

Much of the historical research accomplished in an era of minute specialization is beyond the horizon of the historian of literature. The most imposing monuments of recent English historical scholarship are the three series, *The Cambridge Ancient History* (12 volumes, 1923-1939), *The Cambridge Medieval History* (8 volumes, 1911-1936), and *The Cambridge Modern History* (12 volumes, 1902-1910).[20] Lord Acton, laying down the plan of the *Modern History,* had defined as his object a work which should be "not a rope of sand but a continuous development, . . . not a burden on the memory but an illumination of the soul."[21] This aspiration and ideal cannot be accepted as a summary of accomplishment except with more reservations than can be considered here. Professor Toynbee, drawing an analogy from the industrialist's search for raw materials, exploitation of sources, and division of labor, has described the *Cambridge Histories* as "monuments of the laboriousness, the factual knowledge, the mechanical skill, and the organizing power of our society."[22] The analogy is acceptable with qualifications, but it fails in appreciation of the highly individualized excellence of many of the contributions to the Cambridge volumes. In the *Ancient History,* more particularly, there are chapters worthy of the finest tradition of English historiography.

*"The Hammonds"*

The specialized work of two pairs of scholars must be mentioned for its bearing upon the growth of Socialism and consequently upon a main movement in modern creative literature. John L. Hammond (1872-1949) and his wife Lucy B. Hammond (1873-    ) investigated the social conditions of the working-classes during the Industrial Revolution. Their three volumes covering the period from 1760 to 1832 on *The Village Labourer* (1911), *The Town Labourer* (1917), and *The Skilled Labourer* (1919), with the two sequels, *The Rise of Modern Industry* (1925) and *The Age of the Chartists* (1930), are outstanding examples of contemporary economic history. Sidney Webb (1859-1947) and his wife Beatrice Potter Webb (1858-1943), later Lord and Lady Passfield, collected evidence and disseminated humane ideas

*"The Webbs'*

[20] Specialists of many nations were among the contributors, but the great majority were English historians.
[21] Lord Acton, *Lectures on Modern History* (1907), p. 317.
[22] Arnold J. Toynbee, *A Study of History,* 1 (1934). 4.

in their *History of Trade Unionism* (1894), *Industrial Democracy* (1897), *Problems of Modern Industry* (1898), and later books. As one of the original Fabians, Webb was closely associated with George Bernard Shaw. The writings of "the Webbs" can scarcely be judged as literature, but every creative writer who has touched on the field of sociology has, directly or indirectly, been influenced by them.

For all its devotion to the task of assembling and organizing masses of fact, the period has not lacked historians capable of brilliant synthesis and popular exposition. John B. Bury (1861-1927) made a special reputation as *Bury* an authority on the Byzantine Empire, but he may be longer remembered for a by-product of his original research, his indispensable edition of Gibbon (1896-1900). As Acton's successor at Cambridge, it was appropriate that Bury should write a *History of Freedom of Thought* (1913), albeit on a scale too small for the greatness of the theme and with a liberal-minded hopefulness that has been refuted by subsequent events. Bury's successor at Cambridge was George Macaulay Trevelyan (1876-1962), great-nephew of *Trevelyan* Lord Macaulay and most widely known for his brilliantly presented brief *History of England* (1926). On an ampler scale and in a style that has won him deserved popularity Trevelyan wrote two historical trilogies, one on Garibaldi's part in the Risorgimento—*Garibaldi's Defence of the Roman Republic* (1907), *Garibaldi and the Thousand* (1909), and *Garibaldi and the Making of Italy* (1911); the other on the reign of Queen Anne—*Blenheim* (1930), *Ramelies and the Union with Scotland* (1932), and *The Peace and the Protestant Succession* (1934). With the latter trilogy may be associated the chief historical work of Winston Spencer Churchill (1874-1965), *Marlborough: His Life and Times* (4v, 1933-1938), which presents the *Churchill* writer's ancestor against the background of the age of which he was the greatest figure. Churchill had already displayed his narrative talent in volumes on the Boer War and on Kitchener's conquest of the Sudan; in these history is mingled with personal reminiscence. Vaster conflicts, *quorum magna pars fuit,* form the subject of Churchill's *The World Crisis* (4v, 1923-1929), with its supplementary volume on the Eastern Front entitled *The Unknown War* (1931). In this massive work, part history, part *apologia,* there surges and thunders the grand rhetoric which since the retreat from Dunkirk has become familiar to all the world. Churchill's war-speeches have been collected in several volumes. Upon his mastery of the tradition of parliamentary oratory it is needless to comment.

The Oxford tradition of historiography was ably maintained by Herbert *Fisher* A. L. Fisher (1865-1940). His *Napoleon* (1913) is a little masterpiece of condensation. In his *History of Europe* (1935) he evinced remarkable powers of organization and clarification. Oxford-trained is the most interesting historian of our time, Arnold Joseph Toynbee (1889-    ). Only a provisional opinion can be offered of his *Study of History* (6v, 1934-1939) *Toynbee* for it is still unfinished. Moved by "the deep impulse to attempt to envisage and comprehend the whole of life" and taking all historical knowledge (and much else) as his province, Toynbee has undertaken to define the political, social, economic, and cultural characteristics whereby a civilization or "great society" can be distinguished; to isolate for examination such portions of each society as the "dominant minority" and the "internal" and "external" proletariat; to formulate such general principles as those of "apparentation and affiliation," "challenge and response," and "withdrawal and return"; and, in a word, to discover the "laws" governing the rise, florescence, and decline of civilizations. The general course of the argument is overlaid with much erudite detail, not all of it obviously pertinent. Till the remaining portions of the *Study* appear, judgment cannot be passed upon the validity of this vast interpretation of human experience; but it is already evident that in scale, organization, and profundity of both thought and feeling this is a work of major importance. Its great theme has a solemn significance for our time. By a tragic coincidence, the point in the discussion reached at the outbreak of the Second World War was the problem of the breakdown and disintegration of civilizations.

## IV

*Lang*

From these professional historians we turn to men of letters who combined the writing of history with activity in other departments of literature. Andrew Lang [23] (1844-1912) with immense industry touched and adorned many subjects. The eclecticism of his interests led to a dissipation of his talents with the consequence that he accomplished absolutely first-rate work in no one field. *Myth, Ritual and Religion* (1887), his best-known book, connects him with Tylor and other inquirers into the origins of religious beliefs. The popular series of vari-colored *Fairy Books* were by-products of his investigations into folklore. To problems of occult phenomena, forgeries, and other debatable subjects he applied a shrewdly analytical and argumentative intelligence. He was most stimulating, though not always most reliable, when discussing such matters as the significance of totemism, or ballad origins, or the Homeric problem, or the authenticity of the Casket Letters, or what you will. Of Lang's historical works the best is *The History of Scotland* (1890-1897). Among his minor books may be mentioned the witty and attractive *Letters to Dead Authors* (1886)—some of which are in verse.

*Belloc*

Joseph Hilaire Pierre Belloc [24] (1870-1953), while all too productive in many departments of literature, was primarily a historian. Born in Paris and of French blood with a dash of Irish, Belloc was Roman Catholic by birth and conviction and Continental in his outlook upon English history and institutions. He began as a humorist—often a savage humorist—with *The Bad Child's Book of Beasts* (1896), a volume that had several sequels. In

---

[23] R. L. Green, *Andrew Lang: A Critical Biography* (1946), with bibliography. On Lang's poetry see ch. xxix, n. 33, above.

[24] C. C. Mandell and Edward Shanks, *Hilaire Belloc, the Man and his Works* (1916), needs to be supplemented by a survey of Belloc's later writings.

verse he was an effective satirist, though not always a fair one. His small amount of serious poetry is deft and delicate, and there is reticent good taste in his poems on religious subjects. Of a score of collections of essays, often trivial though generally amusing, it is unnecessary to give the titles here. Particularly noteworthy among many impressions of travel are *The Path to Rome* (1902) and *The Old Road* (1904). Belloc was an expert in combining with history something of the qualities of an informal guide-book, as in *The River of London* (1912) and *The Stane Street* (1913). He wrote several novels, but it is evident that he did not take them quite seriously, nor is the historian of literature obligated to do so. Of numerous historico-biographical monographs his *Wolsey* (1930), *Cranmer* (1931), and *Cromwell* (1934) are representative. As a historian he was controversial, partisan, and tendentious, most trustworthy, though not always most effective, when his sectarian prejudices were least engaged. His *History of England* (1925-1931) is so strongly Roman Catholic in bias as to be illuminating rather of his mind than of his subject. Its inaccuracies have been severely criticized. A controversy with H. G. Wells which began with Belloc's *Companion to Mr. Wells' "Outline of History"* (1926) is worth mentioning. *The Servile State* (1912), Belloc's most influential book, is an attack at once upon capitalistic industrialism and upon the socialistic Utopias of the opponents of capitalism.

Gilbert Keith Chesterton [25] (1874-1936), who was not a historian though he took large liberties with history, may be introduced at this point as Belloc's co-religionist, ally, and sharer in his opinions and prejudices. His innumerable books are known *in toto* today only to those old enough to have read them as they appeared. His *Browning* (1903) and *Dickens* (1903) reveal him as an acutely analytical, if often wayward, critic. These two exuberant writers were congenial to his temperament. Sometimes he resorted to fiction of a fantastic sort to convey his ideas, as in *The Napoleon of Notting Hill* (1904), *The Man Who Was Thursday* (1908), *The Flying Inn* (1914), and the series of detective-stories (with a strong distillation of religiosity) which began with *The Innocence of Father Brown* (1911). *The Ballad of the White Horse* and *Lepanto* (both 1911) have a fine swashbuckling rhetoric, but Chesterton was not a poet as Belloc, within narrow limits, was. Like his partner, Chesterton tried to lead men away from capitalism towards a kind of neo-medievalism of craft guilds. Both men fashioned out of their dreams and fantasies a medieval England that had never existed—a "Merrie England" of hearty faith and brotherhood.[26] Chesterton

*Chesterton*

---

[25] Patrick Braybrooke, *Gilbert Keith Chesterton* (1922); G. W. Bullett, *The Innocence of G. K. Chesterton* (1923); G. N. Shuster, *The Catholic Spirit in Modern English Literature* (1922).

[26] The most formidable opponent of Belloc and Chesterton in exposing the inaccuracies in their conception of the Middle Ages was George Gordon Coulton (1858-1947). His case, based on wide knowledge of first-hand evidence, is not demolished by Belloc's wittily insolent satire beginning:

> Remote and ineffectual don
> Who dares attack my Chesterton.

did not enter the Church of Rome till 1922, but the direction in which he was moving was obvious as early as 1909 when he published *Orthodoxy*. Of the miscellaneous controversial works of his later years, apologetical and polemic, *The Everlasting Man* (1925) is representative. Chesterton was primarily a journalist and consequently wasted much talent on ephemeral subjects. His best work was accomplished before his mannerisms became fixed upon him. The perpetual effort to be clever was often misdirected into mere silliness, and the reliance upon the see-saw of antithesis and the whimsicalities of paradox became tiresome. Yet he forced readers to think, though they often thought the worse of Chesterton. It would be unsafe to predict confidently of any of his books that they will be long remembered. Yet this pillar of conservatism and reaction was in his day a significant figure of protest against the current winds of doctrine and streams of tendency.

*Strachey*

Blown by those winds and floating on those streams was Giles Lytton Strachey (1880-1932), the most brilliant representative in the field of historico-biographical studies of the cynical skepticism towards established reputations which we have noted as characteristic of the nineteen-twenties. Having attracted some attention with his *Landmarks of French Literature* (1912), a little book that remains the best balanced of his works, Strachey turned in the last and most disillusioned year of the First World War to the agreeable task of "de-pedestalizing" popular idols. Discarding reverence and reticence, he relied upon ironic wit, urbanity, and ultra-sophistication. "Psychography," as it was called, would discover by a facile use of what was believed to be the Freudian method the hidden weakness and lay bare the "damaged soul." By means of the disillusioning anecdote and caricaturing detail Strachey aimed to strip the great of their false trappings and expose the hollowness of their pretentions. He did not realize that greatness is not dependent upon externalities. The four subjects of *Eminent Victorians* (1918), dissimilar in other respects, possessed in common religious convictions and moral fervor. Strachey and his readers had no understanding of religious experience and no sympathy with moral fervor. By emphasizing Dr. Arnold's pompousness, Florence Nightingale's bustling activity, General Gordon's addiction to brandy (a malicious calumny), and Cardinal Manning's worldly ambitions he would "deflate" these eminent reputations. When, however, in *Queen Victoria* (1921), he attempted to apply the formula again, he had enough of fairness to capitulate to the evidence of genuine greatness, and having come to scoff he remained to praise. *Elizabeth and Essex* (1928) displays a minimum of research and a maximum of manner. He had always used something of the method of the novelist, with the telling episode, the

Coulton dared attack, and attacked successfully, other partisan, sectarian historians. He was the guiding spirit of a Cambridge school of medievalists who have not permitted romantic idealizations to hide from them "the spotted actuality." Coulton's *Chaucer and his England* (1909) is an admirable introduction to the subject. The *Five Centuries of Religion* (3v, 1923-1926, in progress) is his most massive work. *A Medieval Panorama* (1938), an excellent synthesis, is the ripest fruit of a fine scholarship. — See his *Four Score Years* (1944), an autobiography memorable for the account in the last two chapters of one of the fiercest controversies in which he was engaged.

avoidance of the tedious even where it is relevant, and an unwarranted employment of the "interior monologue"; and in this last book he approximated to the hybrid type of "fictionized biography" for whose florescence in the nineteen-twenties his example was in part responsible. With Strachey it is natural to group Philip Guedalla (1889-1944), though this is unfair to *Guedalla* a historian whose solid research and serious intent are hidden from the eyes of most readers by the too unremitting brilliance of his style. *The Second Empire* (1922), *Palmerston* (1926), and *Wellington* (1931) are Guedalla's finest books.[27]

V

A number of miscellaneous writers—scholars, journalists, publicists, and *Nevinson* essayists—cannot be forced into a category. Henry W. Nevinson (1856-1941), for long on the staff of *The Manchester Guardian,* was a war-correspondent in many parts of the world between 1897 and 1918. His outspoken *Essays in Freedom and Rebellion* (1921) are still of value for the light they cast upon Liberal sentiment and policy in the first post-war years. *In the Dark Backward* (1934) is on the borderland of the essay, travel book, history, and fiction. Goldsworthy Lowes Dickinson [28] (1862-1932), historian, sociologist, *G. Lowes* internationalist, and "Good European," was representative of much that is *Dickinson* finest in the Liberal tradition. *The Greek View of Life* (1896) established his reputation. His impartial and lucid intelligence enabled him to assume other points of view than his own, as in the anonymous *Letters from a Chinese Official* (1903) which certain people accepted as genuinely Oriental, and in *A Modern Symposium* (1905). Other important books are *Religion, a Criticism and a Forecast* (1905) and *War: Its Nature, Cause and Cure* (1923). The Platonic dialogue was a form ideally adapted to the purposes of this admirably fructifying mind, and Dickinson's last book was appropriately *Plato and His Dialogues* (1931). Gilbert Murray (1866-1957), classical *Gilbert* scholar, philosopher, and publicist, is famous for his verse-translations from *Murray* Euripides and Aeschylus. These have been criticized as too unliteral paraphrases, but they have the great merit of being fine poetry and alive in their own right. Among Murray's classical studies are *The Rise of the Greek Epic* (1907) and *Euripides and His Age* (1913). In later years Murray devoted much of his energy to supporting the League of Nations and to the furtherance of international coöperation. *The Problem of Foreign Policy* (1921) advances ideas and suggestions of which the fault is that they are too good for an evil world. Both in his life and writings Murray was representative of the best hopes that struggled to keep alive during the Long Armistice. Maurice Baring (1874-1945), a widely traveled connoisseur of the art of *Baring* living, was a poet whose verse leaves an impression of graceful talent rather than of any creative urge. His best work was in prose. Novels, such as *Cat's*

---

[27] On Strachey and Guedalla see Mark Longaker, *Contemporary Biography* (Philadelphia, 1934), chs. II and VI.
[28] E. M. Forster, *Goldsworthy Lowes Dickinson* (1934).

*Cradle* (1925) and *Tinker's Leave* (1927), are easy to read and easy to forget. His *Dead Letters* (1910) and *Unreliable History* (1934) show a gift for burlesque and not too unkindly satire. As a critic Baring wrote with special authority on Russian life and literature. *The Puppet Show of Memory*
*Percy* (1922) tells the story of his life. Percy Lubbock (1879-1965), friend and
*Lubbock* disciple of Henry James, wrote several biographies, something like an autobiography in *Earlham* (1922), something approximating to fiction in *Roman Pictures* (1923), and an extremely subtle study, *The Craft of Fiction*
*Art* (1921). The most notable art critics of the period have been the poet
*Critics* Laurence Binyon (1869-1943), Roger Fry (1866-1934), and Clive Bell (1881-1964). Binyon spoke with special authority on the art of the Far East. Fry was influential as an interpreter of contemporary French painters. Bell, in addition to his criticisms of modern painting, wrote an excellent study of Proust (1928) and in *Civilization* (1928) ventured into the arena of social
*A. C.* problems. Arthur Christopher Benson (1862-1925) wrote verse and fiction
*Benson* of little consequence and won the esteem of a wide, gentle public with *The House of Quiet* (1904) and other volumes of semi-autobiographic meditations which were "comforting," mildly pietistic, and not too profound; but
*E. V.* his most sensitive writing is in his studies of Tennyson, Ruskin, FitzGerald,
*Lucas* Rossetti, and Pater. Edward Verrall Lucas (1868-1938), disciple, biographer (1908), and editor of Charles Lamb, was a voluminous essayist, critic, novelist, gentle satirist, and "wanderer" in famous cities. For many years he was on the staff of *Punch.* Another essayist, less widely ranging than
*Lynd* Lucas, was Robert Lynd (1879-1949), who combined experiences of travel and a love of books and animals in pleasing and witty fashion.

## VI

*Literary*      Of the great company of literary critics of the late Victorian period and
*Critics* after, only the most prominent can be mentioned here. To obviate invidiousness, they are considered in chronological order. Stopford Augustus Brooke (1832-1916), an influential nonconformist divine, was the author of a widely used manual of English Literature and of many popular studies of the poets. His most distinctive interest is displayed in *English Literature from the Beginning to the Norman Conquest* (1898). Richard Garnett (1835-1906) was engaged in history, biography, and criticism. With Edmund Gosse he collaborated on the well-known *Illustrated Record* of English Literature (1903-1904). Garnett's poems are now lost to sight, but still attractive is *The Twilight of the Gods* [29] (1888; enlarged edition, 1903), a series of learned, witty, and sardonic tales and apologues. Henry Austin Dobson [30] (1840-1921) took the eighteenth century as his province, writing biographies of Hogarth, Horace Walpole, Goldsmith, and Fanny Burney, and many

[29] New edition, with introduction by T. E. Lawrence (1926).
[30] See Cornelius Weygandt, *Tuesdays at Ten* (Philadelphia, 1928), ch. XIII: "Austin Dobson, Augustan." — On Dobson's poetry see ch. XXIX, n. 34, above.

critical papers. The grace and lightness of his verse are characteristics also of his prose, but there is more substance in the prose. William John Court-hope (1842-1917), assuming the task which Thomas Gray had projected and Thomas Warton had left unfinished, wrote a *History of English Poetry* (6v, 1895-1910), ample in design and philosophical in temper but in use-fulness marred by a too strict adherence to the thesis that there is a close connection between literary fashions, tastes, and values and contemporary social and political opinions and conditions. Edward Dowden [31] (1843-1913) made a great reputation with his *Shakespeare: His Mind and Art* (1873), the most influential "subjective" treatment of the subject till the appearance of Bradley's work. Dowden was the most famous of the critics who professed an ability to discern in the plays evidence of Shakespeare's own intellectual, moral, and spiritual experiences. For a *Life of Shelley* (1886) the family documents were made available to Dowden, but the biography was too partisan and too emotional in tone to remain definitive. Miscellaneous critical essays show this scholar to greater advantage than these two ambitious works. Andrew Cecil Bradley (1845-1933) brought to a climax in his *Shakespearean Tragedy* (1904) the Coleridgian tradition of philosophic and subjective criticism. In the Shakespearean world, it is safe to say, his was the dominant voice for thirty years, and it is still harkened to. His *Oxford Lectures on Poetry* (1909) ·are partly on Shakespeare, partly on the Romantic and Victorian poets. George Edward Bateman Saints-bury [32] (1845-1933) was an omnivorous, genial, zestful, and indefatigable critic and historian of literature. Of his vast and varied work there is room to note only the *Short History of French Literature* (1882), the *Short History of English Literature* (1898), the *History of Criticism* (1900-1904), the *History of English Prosody* (1906-1910), the *History of English Prose Rhythm* (1912), and the *History of the French Novel* (1917-1919). The *Collected Essays and Papers* (4v, 1923) contain the best of his innumerable lesser studies. The tonic quality of Saintsbury's criticism is found in his undeviating loyalty to values that were strictly literary and strictly his own. Neither his clear-sightedness nor occasional wrong-headedness was borrowed from other men. His style—informal, circumlocutory, and allusive, with parenthetical qualifications and concessions—was often the despair of the precisian, but it reflected the man. Sir Edmund Gosse [33] (1849-1928) ranged through English literature, was influential in introducing modern Scandi-navian culture to English readers, and has claims to be regarded as the initia-tor of the modern vogue of John Donne, whose *Life and Letters* (1899) is his most substantial work. Gosse was an adept in the *causerie* and literary portrait, deft, sly, and often lightly malicious, hinting faults and hesitating dislikes. His reticences and innuendoes are abundant in his biography of Swinburne (1917). His scholarship, though wide, was often inaccurate. In *Father and*

*Dowden*

*A. C. Bradley*

*Saintsbury*

*Gosse*

[31] *Letters of Edward Dowden,* ed. E. D. and H. M. Dowden (1914).
[32] A. B. Webster, *George Saintsbury* (Edinburgh, 1934).
[33] *Collected Essays* (12v, 1912-1927). — Evan Charteris, *The Life and Letters of Sir Edmund Gosse* (1931). On Gosse's poetry see ch. XXIX, n. 35, above.

*Son* (1907), a document in the history of the mid-nineteenth century con-flict between the older and younger generations, there are subtleties and profundities to which Gosse's other writings afford no parallel and which support the opinion (for which there is other evidence) that he was aided in its composition by George Moore. William Ernest Henley [34] (1849-1903), poet, critic, and reviewer, was editor of *The National Observer,* which boasted of a brilliant company of contributors, and of *The New Review,* where Conrad and Wells got their start. With T. F. Henderson, Henley edited the works of Burns, his special contribution being the forceful and candid estimate of the poet's genius and achievement. As a critic Henley was often truculent, especially when attacking the "Aesthetes" and the Socialists, and his strength was lessened rather than enhanced by an affecta-tion of bravado; but he had the hard-hitting courage of convictions that were not notably original. Augustine Birrell [35] (1850-1933) wrote biographies of Marvell and Hazlitt, but is better known for the essays on life and letters in *Obiter Dicta* (1884, 1887, and 1924) and in *Res Judicatae* (1896). Birrell was a master of the essay form, graceful, easy, and sincere, with a wit that never condescended to facetiousness. The literary studies of William Paton Ker [36] (1855-1923) covered English literature from the Middle Ages to the nineteenth century and reached into foreign fields. His *Epic and Romance* (1896) has a weight impressively in contrast to its slight mass. Sir Walter Raleigh [37] (1861-1922) possessed a style happily compounded of grace and vigor. He first won attention with a compact monograph on *The English Novel* (1894), continued with studies of Milton (1900) and Wordsworth (1909), and proved worthy of the responsibility and honor when he was chosen to supply the long-missing volume on Shakespeare (1907) for the *English Men of Letters Series.* For condensed suggestiveness, regard for basic principles, and conscientious avoidance of personal eccentricities in theory and judgment this small book remains without a rival among intro-ductions to Shakespeare. An admirable essay on *The English Voyagers* appended to a reprint of Hakluyt (1905) shows that Raleigh yearned for a life of action, and at the close of his life he was engaged upon a *History of the Royal Air Force.* Charles Whibley (1862-1930) has claims on our gratitude as editor of the series of *Tudor Translations.* His *Literary Por-traits* (1904) and *Literary Studies* (1919), though marred by the intrusion of his Tory prejudices, display a wide culture and a distinguished style. This paragraph would have to be greatly extended if it were to include critics and historians in the fields of foreign literatures.

*Henley*

*Birrell*

*Ker*

*Raleigh*

*Whibley*

----

[34] *Works* (5v, 1921); *Views and Reviews* (1890). On Henley's poetry, and for bibliography, see ch. XXXIX, and n. 32, above.
[35] *Collected Essays and Addresses* (3v, 1922). Birrell was in public life and was Secretary of State for Ireland in Asquith's cabinet.
[36] *Collected Essays,* ed. Charles Whibley (2v, 1925).
[37] *Letters,* ed. Lady Raleigh (2v, 1928).

Here, with homage offered to the memory of this last group of writers, representative of the much larger company who have devoted their learning and insight to the history and interpretation of English literature, and with the wish that "what we have written may be read by their light," we bring this history to a close. New names and new talents appear each year, and of these some will doubtless claim places of honor in chapters that cannot yet be written. As the historian of English literature turns his face from the past to look into the future, he feels that he is standing upon a shore

> where a confident sea
> Is ever breaking, never spent.

# BOOK IV:
# THE NINETEENTH CENTURY
# AND AFTER (1789-1939)

## I. The Background of Revolution, Repression, and Reform:
### 1789-1832

**1111** On England in the period of the French Revolution: J. Steven Watson, *The Reign of George III, 1760-1815* (Oxford, 1960); Asa Briggs, *The Age of Improvement 1783-1867* (1959); Muriel Jaeger, *Before Victoria* (1956); S. Maccoby, *English Radicalism, 1786-1832: From Paine to Cobbett* (1955); R. K. Webb, *The British Working-Class Reader, 1790-1848: Literacy and Social Tension* (1955); *The British Political Tradition*, Vol. II: *The Debate on the French Revolution, 1789-1800*, ed. Alfred Cobban (1950); *English Historical Documents*, Vol. XI, 1783-1832, ed. A. Aspinall and E. A. Smith (1959).

**1112** Ralph M. Wardle, *Mary Wollstonecraft: A Critical Biography* (Lawrence, Kan., 1951). On Mackintosh, Samuel Parr, Joseph Fawcett, and other English sympathizers with the French Revolution, including disciples of Godwin and apostles of Pantisocracy, see M. Ray Adams, *Studies in the Literary Backgrounds of English Radicalism* (Lancaster, Pa., 1947).—Paine: *Complete Writings*, ed. Philip S. Foner (1945); *Selected Works*, ed. Howard Fast (1945). Alfred O. Aldridge, *Man of Reason: The Life of Thomas Paine* (Philadelphia, 1959); James T. Boulton, "Tom Paine and the Vulgar Style," *EIC*, XII (1962). 18-33.

**1113** Godwin: *Enquiry Concerning Political Justice*, ed. F. E. L. Priestley (3v, Toronto, 1946), important for variant texts. Rosalie Glynn Grylls, *William Godwin and His World* (1953); D. H. Monro, *Godwin's Moral Philosophy* (1953); *Godwin and the Age of Transition*, ed. A. E. Rodway (1952); Doris Fleisher, *William Godwin: A Study in Liberalism* (1951); Burton Ralph Pollin, *Education and Enlightenment in the Works of William Godwin* (1962).

**1117** On the period from Waterloo to the First Reform Bill, see, in addition to the works cited above (suppl. to p. 1111): Arthur Bryant, *The Age of Elegance, 1812-1822* (1950); R. J. White, *Waterloo to Peterloo* (1957); T. S. Ashton, *The Industrial Revolution, 1760-1830* (1948); David Thomson, *England in the Nineteenth Century, 1815-1914* (1950), chs. I-III; E. P. Thompson, *The Making of the English Working Class* (1963); Arthur Aspinall, *Politics and the Press, 1780-1850* (1949), important for the journalistic activities of most of the romantic writers. Halévy's *History of the English People in the Nineteenth Century* has appeared in a complete English translation (7v, 1952).

**1119**  Cobbett: *Rural Rides,* ed. S. E. Buckley (1949), an abridgment; ed. E. W. Martin (1959), text of 1830, with Gillray cartoons. M. L. Pearl, *William Cobbett: A Bibliographical Account of His Life and Times* (1953); W. Baring Pemberton, *William Cobbett* (1949).—Herschel M. Sikes, "William Hone: Regency Patriot, Parodist, and Pamphleteer," *Newberry Library Bull.,* v (1961). 281-294.

**1120**  Bentham: *A Fragment on Government,* ed. Wilfred Harrison (Oxford, 1948); *Handbook of Political Fallacies,* ed. H. A. Larrabee (Baltimore, 1952). Mary Mack, *Jeremy Bentham: An Odyssey of Ideas, 1748-92* (1962); David Baumgardt, *Bentham and the Ethics of Today* (Princeton, 1952); Robert Preyer, *Bentham, Coleridge, and the Science of History* (Bochum-Langendreer, 1958).

# II. Romanticism

**1122**  A revised edition of Bernbaum's *Guide through the Romantic Movement* was published in 1949. Valuable bibliographical reviews of scholarship and criticism on all the major English romantic authors and on the romantic movement in general are available in *The English Romantic Poets: A Review of Research,* ed. Thomas M. Raysor (1950, rev. 1956)—hereafter cited as Raysor —and *The English Romantic Poets and Essayists: A Review of Research and Criticism,* ed. C. W. Houtchens and L. H. Houtchens (1957, rev. 1966)—hereafter cited as Houtchens. The annual bibliography of current writings on the romantic movement, published in *ELH* from 1937 to 1949 and in *PQ* from 1950 to 1964, is now found in *English Language Notes.* Two volumes of the *Oxford History of English Literature* are devoted to the period: W. L. Renwick, *English Literature, 1789-1815* (Oxford, 1963), a sketchy and erratic survey, and Ian Jack, *English Literature, 1815-1832* (Oxford, 1963), notably readable and well informed, with excellent bibliographies. See also *The [Pelican] Guide to English Literature,* ed. Boris Ford: Vol. v, *From Blake to Byron* (1957, rev. 1962). Other general studies include D. G. James, *The Romantic Comedy* (1948); Graham Hough, *The Romantic Poets* (1953); Edward E. Bostetter, *The Romantic Ventriloquists* (Seattle, 1963); and Allan Rodway, *The Romantic Conflict* (1963). Walter J. Bate, *From Classic to Romantic* (Cambridge, Mass., 1946) deals with the transition to the romantic age. On the romantic spirit as it affected later generations: John Heath-Stubbs, *The Darkling Plain* (1950); John Bayley, *The Romantic Survival* (1957); Morse Peckham, *Beyond the Tragic Vision: The Quest for Identity in the Nineteenth Century* (1962). On romantic criticism: M. H. Abrams, *The Mirror and the Lamp* (1953); René Wellek, *History of Modern Criticism, 1750-1950* (New Haven, 1955-  ), Vol. II; *Contemporary Reviews of Romantic Poetry,* ed. John Wain (1953); *The Poets and Their Critics,* ed. Hugh Sykes Davies (1962), Vol. II. On various other aspects of the romantic movement: Hoxie N. Fairchild, *Religious Trends in English Poetry,* Vol. III: *1780-1830, Romantic Faith* (1949); John Middleton Murry, *Katherine Mansfield and Other Literary Portraits* (1949), essays on five writers; W. H. Auden, *The Enchafèd Flood* (1950); Mario Praz, *The Romantic Agony* (rev. 1951); Donald Davie, *Purity of Diction in English Verse* (1952), Part II; Herbert Read, *The True Voice of Feeling* (1953); Albert Gérard, *L'Idée romanti-*

*que de la poésie en Angleterre* (Paris, 1955); Josephine Miles, *Eras and Modes in English Poetry* (Berkeley, 1957), chs. IV-VIII; *The Major English Romantic Poets: A Symposium in Reappraisal,* ed. C. D. Thorpe *et al.* (Carbondale, Ill., 1957); C. P. Brand, *Italy and the English Romantics* (Cambridge, 1957); R. A. Foakes, *The Romantic Assertion: A Study in the Language of Nineteenth-Century Poetry* (New Haven, 1958); Eudo C. Mason, *Deutsche und englische Romantik* (Göttingen, 1959); Karl Kroeber, *Romantic Narrative Art* (Madison, Wis., 1960); Harold Bloom, *The Visionary Company* (1961); Upali Amarasinghe, *Dryden and Pope in the Early Nineteenth Century* (Cambridge, 1962); James Benziger, *Images of Eternity: Studies in the Poetry of Religious Vision from Wordsworth to T. S. Eliot* (Carbondale, Ill., 1962); Bernard Blackstone, *The Lost Travellers: A Romantic Theme with Variations* (1962); H. W. Piper, *The Active Universe: Pantheism and the Concept of Imagination in the English Romantic Poets* (1962); *Romanticism Reconsidered (English Institute Essays 1962),* ed. Northrop Frye (1963); *From Sensibility to Romanticism: Essays Presented to Frederick A. Pottle,* ed. F. W. Hilles and Harold Bloom (1965), mainly on the early phase of the movement; Murray Roston, *Prophet and Poet: The Bible and the Growth of Romanticism* (Evanston, Ill., 1965); F. E. L. Priestley, "Newton and the Romantic Concept of Nature," *UTQ,* XVII (1948). 323-336; William K. Wimsatt, Jr., "The Structure of Romantic Nature Imagery," *The Age of Johnson: Essays Presented to Chauncey Brewster Tinker* (New Haven, 1949), pp. 291-303; Wellek, "The Concept of 'Romanticism' in Literary History," *CL,* I (1949). 1-23, 147-172; Raymond D. Havens, "Discontinuity in Literary Development: The Case of English Romanticism," *SP,* XLVII (1950). 102-111; Peckham, "Toward a Theory of Romanticism," *PMLA,* LXVI (1951). 5-23, continued in *Stud. in Romanticism,* I (1961). 1-8; A. S. P. Woodhouse, "Romanticism and the History of Ideas," *English Studies Today,* I (1951). 120-140; C. G. Hoffman, "Whitehead's Philosophy of Nature and Romantic Poetry," *JAAC,* X (1952). 258-263; Georges Poulet, "Timelessness and Romanticism," *JHI,* XV (1954). 3-22; Gérard, "On the Logic of Romanticism," *EIC,* VII (1957). 262-273; Raymond Williams, *Culture and Society 1780-1950* (1958), pp. 3-70; Herbert M. Schueller, "Romanticism Reconsidered," *JAAC,* XX (1962). 359-368; Earl R. Wasserman, "The English Romantics: The Grounds of Knowledge," *Stud. in Romanticism,* IV (1964). 17-34. Collections of reprinted critical essays: *English Romantic Poets: Modern Essays in Criticism,* ed. Abrams (1960); *Romanticism: Points of View,* ed. R. F. Gleckner and G. E. Enscoe (1963).

# III. William Blake

**1128**   *Complete Writings, with All the Variant Readings,* ed. Geoffrey Keynes (1957); *Poetry and Prose,* ed. David V. Erdman (1965), two admirable editions; *The Portable Blake,* ed. Alfred Kazin (1946); *Selected Poetry and Prose,* ed. Northrop Frye (1953); *A Selection of Poems and Letters,* ed. J. Bronowski (1958); *Poems* (selections), ed. Ruthven Todd (1949), F. W. Bateson (1957), Stanley Gardner (1962); *Letters,* ed. Keynes (1956).—G. E. Bentley, Jr., and Martin K. Nurmi, *A Blake Bibliography: Annotated Lists of Works, Studies, and Blakeana* (Minneapolis, 1965); Keynes and E. Wolf, *Blake's Illuminated*

*Books: A Census* (1953); bibliography of scholarly and critical work in Houtchens, ch. 1. Mona Wilson's *Life,* rev. 1948, remains standard. W. P. Witcutt, *Blake: A Psychological Study* (1946); Northrop Frye, *Fearful Symmetry* (Princeton, 1947); J. G. Davies, *The Theology of William Blake* (Oxford, 1948); Keynes, *Blake Studies* (1949); Bernard Blackstone, *English Blake* (1949); Margaret Bottrall, *The Divine Image: A Study of Blake's Interpretation of Christianity* (Rome, 1950); H. M. Margoliouth, *William Blake* (1951); Margaret Rudd, *Divided Image* (1953) and *Organiz'd Innocence: The Story of Blake's Prophetic Books* (1956); David V. Erdman, *Blake: Prophet Against Empire* (Princeton, 1954); Stanley Gardner, *Infinity on the Anvil* (Oxford, 1954); Hazard Adams, *Blake and Yeats: The Contrary Vision* (Ithaca, 1955) and *William Blake: A Reading of the Shorter Poems* (Seattle, 1963); George W. Digby, *Symbol and Image in William Blake* (Oxford, 1957); *The Divine Vision: Studies in the Poetry and Art of Blake,* ed. Vivian de Sola Pinto (1957); Anthony Blunt, *The Art of William Blake* (1959); Robert F. Gleckner, *The Piper and the Bard* (Detroit, 1959); Peter F. Fisher, *The Valley of Vision: Blake as Prophet and Revolutionary* (Toronto, 1961); George M. Harper, *The Neoplatonism of William Blake* (Chapel Hill, 1961); Harold Bloom, *Blake's Apocalypse: A Study in Poetic Argument* (1963); Jean H. Hagstrum, *William Blake, Poet and Painter: An Introduction to the Illuminated Verse* (Chicago, 1964); Alicia Ostriker, *Vision and Verse in William Blake* (Madison, Wis., 1965); Frye, "Poetry and Design in William Blake," *JAAC,* x (1951). 35-42, and "Blake After Two Centuries," *UTQ,* xxvii (1957). 10-21; Karl Kiralis, "A Guide to the Intellectual Symbolism of William Blake's Later Prophetic Writings," *Criticism,* i (1959). 190-210; E. D. Hirsch, Jr., "The Two Blakes," *RES,* n.s. xii (1961). 373-390; Kathleen Raine, "Blake's Debt to Antiquity," *Sewanee Rev.,* lxxi (1963). 352-450; essays by Josephine Miles, Frye, and Erdman in *English Institute Essays 1950,* ed. Alan S. Downer (1951); *Discussions of William Blake,* ed. John E. Grant (Boston, 1961).—S. Foster Damon, *A Blake Dictionary* (Providence, R.I., 1965).

**1130**   C. M. Bowra, *"Songs of Innocence and Experience," The Romantic Imagination* (Cambridge, Mass., 1949), ch. ii. The single poem in *Songs of Experience* which has received most critical attention has been *The Tyger.* See Kathleen Raine, "Who Made the Tyger?", *Encounter,* ii, no. 6 (1954). 43-50; Martin K. Nurmi, "Blake's Revisions of *The Tyger," PMLA,* lxxi (1956). 669-685; Hazard Adams, "Reading Blake's Lyrics: *The Tyger," Texas Stud. in Lit. and Lang.,* ii (1960). 18-37; John E. Grant, "The Art and Argument of *The Tyger," ibid.,* ii (1960). 38-60; Paul Miner, *"The Tyger:* Genesis and Evolution in the Poetry of William Blake," *Criticism,* iv (1962). 59-73.—Martin K. Nurmi, *Blake's "Marriage of Heaven and Hell": A Critical Study* (Kent, Ohio, 1957).

**1131**   *Vala, or The Four Zoas,* ed. H. M. Margoliouth (Oxford, 1956) and Gerald E. Bentley, Jr. (Oxford, 1963). Bentley, "The Failure of Blake's *Four Zoas," Texas Stud. in English,* xxxvii (1958). 102-113.

**1132**   Karl Kiralis, "The Theme and Structure of William Blake's *Jerusalem," ELH,* xxiii (1956). 127-143; W. H. Stevenson, "Blake's *Jerusalem," EIC,* ix (1959). 245-264.—Morchard Bishop [pseudonym of Oliver Stoner], *Blake's Hayley* (1951).

# IV. William Wordsworth

**1136**  De Selincourt's and Helen Darbishire's edition of the *Poetical Works* was completed with the publication of Vol. v in 1949. The de Selincourt edition of *The Prelude* was revised by Miss Darbishire, 1959. *Poems,* ed. Philip Wayne (1955); *Poetry and Prose,* ed. W. M. Merchant (1955); *"The Prelude" with a Selection from the Shorter Poems and Sonnets,* ed. Carlos Baker (1948); *Selected Poetry,* ed. Mark Van Doren (1950); *Selected Poems,* ed. G. W. Meyer (1964); *Selected Poems and Prefaces,* ed. Jack Stillinger (Boston, 1965); *Critical Opinions,* ed. M. L. Peacock, Jr. (Baltimore, 1950); *Political Tracts of Wordsworth, Coleridge, and Shelley,* ed. R. J. White (Cambridge, 1953); *Letters,* ed. Wayne (1954), a selection.—James V. Logan, *Wordsworthian Criticism, A Guide and Bibliography* (Columbus, Ohio, 1947), supplemented by Elton F. Henley and David H. Stam, *Wordsworthian Criticism 1945-1964* (1965); Raysor, ch. II. Mary Moorman, *William Wordsworth* (2v, Oxford, 1957-1965), the most authoritative biography; F. W. Bateson, *Wordsworth: A Re-Interpretation* (1954, rev. 1956), a Freudian speculation; Newton P. Stallknecht, *Strange Seas of Thought* (Durham, N. C., 1945); Jane Worthington, *Wordsworth's Reading of Roman Prose* (New Haven, 1946); de Selincourt, *Wordsworthian and Other Studies* (Oxford, 1947), chs. I-II; Norman Lacey, *Wordsworth's View of Nature* (Cambridge, 1948); Darbishire, *The Poet Wordsworth* (Oxford, 1950); Kenneth MacLean, *Agrarian Age: A Background for Wordsworth* (New Haven, 1950); *Tribute to Wordsworth: A Miscellany of Opinion for the Centenary of the Poet's Death,* ed. Muriel Spark and Derek Stanford (1950); *Wordsworth: Centenary Studies,* ed. G. T. Dunklin (Princeton, 1951); Lascelles Abercrombie, *The Art of Wordsworth* (1952); Florence Marsh, *Wordsworth's Imagery* (New Haven, 1952); C. N. Coe, *Wordsworth and the Literature of Travel* (1953); Geoffrey Hartman, *The Unmediated Vision* (New Haven, 1954), and *Wordsworth's Poetry, 1787-1814* (New Haven, 1964); John Jones, *The Egotistical Sublime: A History of Wordsworth's Imagination* (1954); J. C. Smith, *A Study of Wordsworth* (1955); F. M. Todd, *Politics and the Poet: A Study of Wordsworth* (1957); David Ferry, *The Limits of Mortality* (Middletown, Conn., 1959); David Perkins, *The Quest for Permanence: The Symbolism of Wordsworth, Shelley, and Keats* (Cambridge, Mass., 1959), and *Wordsworth and the Poetry of Sincerity* (Cambridge, Mass., 1964); E. D. Hirsch, Jr., *Wordsworth and Schelling: A Typological Study of Romanticism* (New Haven, 1960); John F. Danby, *The Simple Wordsworth: Studies in the Poems, 1797-1807* (1960); C. C. Clarke, *Romantic Paradox: An Essay on the Poetry of Wordsworth* (1962); Karl Kroeber, *The Artifice of Reality: Poetic Style in Wordsworth, Foscolo, Keats, and Leopardi* (Madison, Wis., 1964); Carl R. Woodring, *Wordsworth* (Boston, 1965); Christopher Salvesen, *The Landscape of Memory: A Study of Wordsworth's Poetry* (1965); Darbishire, "Wordsworth's Belief in the Doctrine of Necessity," *RES,* xxiv (1948). 121-125, and "Wordsworth and the Weather," *REL,* I, no. 3 (1960), 39-49; R. H. Bowers, "Wordsworthian Solitude," *MLQ,* x (1949). 389-399; Herbert Read, "Wordsworth's Philosophical Faith," *Sewanee Rev.,* LVIII (1950). 563-585; Kenneth Muir, "Centenary Eclogue: A Conversation About Wordsworth," *EIC,* I (1951). 17-37; Roger Sharrock, "Wordsworth's Revolt Against Literature," *EIC,* III (1953).

396-412; James R. Baird, "Wordsworth's 'Inscrutable Workmanship' and the Emblems of Reality," *PMLA*, LXVIII (1953). 444-457; Charles J. Smith, "The Contrarieties: Wordsworth's Dualistic Imagery," *PMLA*, LXIX (1954). 1181-1199; Kathleen Coburn, "Coleridge and Wordsworth and 'the Supernatural,' " *UTQ*, XXV (1956). 121-130; Patrick Cruttwell, "Wordsworth, the Public and the People," *Sewanee Rev.*, LXIV (1956). 71-80; Stallknecht, "On Poetry and Geometric Truth," *Kenyon Rev.*, XVIII (1956). 1-20; John Wain, "The Liberation of Wordsworth," *Preliminary Essays* (1957), pp. 78-92; Carl R. Sonn, "An Approach to Wordsworth's Earlier Imagery," *ELH*, XXVII (1960). 208-222; Bennett Weaver, "Wordsworth: Poet of the Unconquerable Mind," *PMLA*, LXXV (1960). 231-237; Paul de Man, "Symbolic Landscape in Wordsworth and Yeats," *In Defense of Reading*, ed. R. A. Brower and W. R. Poirier (1962), pp. 22-37; Lionel Stevenson, "The Unfinished Gothic Cathedral: A Study of the Organic Unity of Wordsworth's Poetry," *UTQ*, XXXII (1963). 170-183; Michael Irwin, "Wordsworth's 'Dependency Sublime,' " *EIC*, XIV (1964). 352-362; Alex Swerdling, "Wordsworth and Greek Myth," *UTQ*, XXXIII (1964). 341-354; Seymour Lainoff, "Wordsworth's Final Phase: Glimpses of Eternity," *SEL*, I, no. 4 (1961). 63-79; essays by Josephine Miles, Stallknecht, and Darbishire in *The Major English Romantic Poets*, ed. Thorpe *et al.*, chs. IV-VI; *Discussions of William Wordsworth*, ed. Jack Davis (Boston, 1964).

**1138** Ben Ross Schneider, Jr., *Wordsworth's Cambridge Education* (Cambridge, 1957); Christopher Wordsworth, *The Early Wordsworthian Milieu*, ed. Z. S. Fink (Oxford, 1958).

**1139** Z. S. Fink, "Wordsworth and the English Republican Tradition," *JEGP*, XLVII (1948). 107-126.

**1140** D. E. Hayden, "Toward an Understanding of Wordsworth's *The Borderers*," *MLN*, LXVI (1951). 1-6; Geoffrey H. Hartman, "Wordsworth, *The Borderers*, and 'Intellectual Murder,' " *JEGP*, LXII (1963). 761-768.—H. M. Margoliouth, *Wordsworth and Coleridge, 1795-1834* (1953).

**1142** *Lyrical Ballads . . . The Text of the 1798 Edition with the Additional 1800 Poems and the Prefaces*, ed. R. L. Brett and A. R. Jones (1963); W. J. B. Owen, *Wordsworth's Preface to the "Lyrical Ballads"* (Copenhagen, 1957); Robert Mayo, "The Contemporaneity of the *Lyrical Ballads*," *PMLA*, LXIX (1954). 486-522; Stephen M. Parrish, "Dramatic Technique in the *Lyrical Ballads*," *PMLA*, LXXIV (1959). 85-97; John E. Jordan, "De Quincey on Wordsworth's Theory of Diction," *PMLA*, LXVIII (1953). 764-778; M. H. Abrams, "Wordsworth and Coleridge on Diction and Figures," *English Institute Essays 1952*, ed. Alan S. Downer (1954), pp. 171-201; George Whalley, "Preface to *Lyrical Ballads:* A Portent," *UTQ*, XXV (1956). 467-483; Roger Sharrock, "Wordsworth on Science and Poetry," *REL*, III, no. 4 (1962). 42-50; Mark L. Reed, "Wordsworth, Coleridge, and the 'Plan' of the *Lyrical Ballads*," *UTQ*, XXXIV (1965). 238-253; Max F. Schulz, "Coleridge, Wordsworth, and the 1800 Preface to *Lyrical Ballads*," *SEL*, V (1965). 619-639.—James Benziger, "*Tintern Abbey* Revisited," *PMLA*, LXV (1950). 154-162; Albert S. Gérard, "Dark Passages: Exploring *Tintern Abbey*," *Stud. in Romanticism*, III (1963). 10-23. Abbie F. Potts, *Wordsworth's "Prelude": A Study of Its Literary Form* (Ithaca, 1953); Herbert Lindenberger, *On Wordsworth's "Prelude"* (Princeton, 1963); Francis Christensen, "Creative Sensibility in Wordsworth," *JEGP*, XLV (1946).

361-368; Kenneth MacLean, "The Water Symbol in *The Prelude*," *UTQ*, XVII (1948). 372-389; C. Clarke, "Nature's Education of Man," *Philosophy*, XXIII (1948). 302-316; Ellen D. Leyburn, "Recurrent Words in *The Prelude*," *ELH*, XVI (1949). 284-298; George W. Meyer, "The Early History of *The Prelude*," *Tulane Stud. in English*, I (1949). 119-156; William Empson, "Sense in *The Prelude*," *Kenyon Rev.*, XIII (1951). 285-302; Edwin Morgan, "A Prelude to *The Prelude*," *EIC*, V (1955). 341-353; Barbara Everett, *"The Prelude," Critical Quar.*, I (1959). 338-350; Jonathan Bishop, "Wordsworth and the 'Spots of Time'," *ELH*, XXVI (1959). 45-65; J. R. MacGillivray, "The Three Forms of *The Prelude*, 1798-1805," *Essays in English Literature . . . Presented to A. S. P. Woodhouse* (Toronto, 1964), pp. 229-244; Francis Christensen, "Intellectual Love: the Second Theme of *The Prelude*," *PMLA*, LXXX (1965). 69-75.

**1143**  George W. Meyer, *"Resolution and Independence:* Wordsworth's Answer to Coleridge's *Dejection: An Ode*," *Tulane Stud. in English*, II (1950). 49-74; W. W. Robson, *"Resolution and Independence," Interpretations*, ed. John Wain (1955), pp. 117-128; Anthony E. M. Conran, "The Dialectic of Experience: A Study of Wordsworth's *Resolution and Independence*," *PMLA*, LXXV (1960). 66-74; Alan Grob, "Process and Permanence in *Resolution and Independence*," *ELH*, XXVIII (1961). 89-100.—Cleanth Brooks, "Wordsworth and the Paradox of the Imagination," *The Well-Wrought Urn* (1947), pp. 114-138; John K. Mathison, "Wordsworth's *Ode: Intimations of Immortality*," *SP*, XLVI (1949). 419-439; Bowra, *The Romantic Imagination*, ch. IV; George W. Meyer, "A Note on the Sources and Symbolism of the *Intimations Ode*," *Tulane Stud. in English*, III (1952). 33-45; Thomas M. Raysor, "The Themes of Immortality and Natural Piety in Wordsworth's *Immortality Ode*," *PMLA*, LXIX (1954). 861-875; Robert L. Schneider, "The Failure of Solitude: Wordsworth's *Immortality Ode*," *JEGP*, LIV (1955). 625-633; Alan Grob, "Wordsworth's *Immortality Ode* and the Search for Identity," *ELH*, XXXII (1965). 32-61.

**1144**  Note 40: See also Peter Coveney, *Poor Monkey: The Child in Literature* (1957), ch. III.

**1145**  Judson S. Lyon, *"The Excursion": A Study* (New Haven, 1950).

**1147**  Ellen D. Leyburn, "Radiance in *The White Doe of Rylstone*," *SP*, XLVII (1950). 629-633; Martin Price, "Imagination in *The White Doe of Rylstone*," *PQ*, XXXIII (1954). 189-199.—Stewart C. Wilcox, "Wordsworth's River Duddon Sonnets," *PMLA*, LXIX (1954). 131-141.—Melvin R. Watson, "The Redemption of *Peter Bell*," *SEL*, IV (1964). 519-530.—Note 52: *Diary of Benjamin Robert Haydon*, ed. Willard Bissell Pope (5v, Cambridge, Mass., 1960-1963); *Autobiography and Journals*, ed. Malcolm Elwin (1950). Eric George, *The Life and Death of Benjamin Robert Haydon, 1786-1846* (1948); Clark Olney, *Benjamin Robert Haydon: Historical Painter* (Athens, Ga., 1952); Varley Long, "Benjamin Robert Haydon," *PQ*, XXVI (1947). 235-247.

# V. Samuel Taylor Coleridge

**1149**  *Philosophical Lectures* (1949); *Notebooks* (11v, 1957-    ); *Inquiring Spirit* (1951), selections from "his published and unpublished prose writings"

—all ed. Kathleen Coburn; *Coleridge on the Seventeenth Century*, ed. Roberta F. Brinkley (Durham, N. C., 1955); *Political Tracts of Wordsworth, Coleridge, and Shelley*, ed. R. J. White (Cambridge, 1953); *Writings on Shakespeare*, ed. Terence Hawkes (1959); *Shakespearean Criticism*, ed. T. M. Raysor (1960); *The Portable Coleridge*, ed. I. A. Richards (1950); *Selected Poetry and Prose*, ed. Elisabeth Schneider (1951); *Poems and Prose*, ed. Kathleen Raine (1957); *Poems*, ed. Geoffrey Grigson (1951), Morchard Bishop (1954); *Selected Poems*, ed. James Reeves (1959); *Collected Letters*, ed. Earl L. Griggs (6v, Oxford, 1956-    ).—Bibliography in Raysor, ch. III. Malcolm Elwin, *The First Romantics* (1947); Wilma Kennedy, *The English Heritage of Coleridge of Bristol, 1798* (New Haven, 1947); H. M. Margoliouth, *Wordsworth and Coleridge, 1795-1834* (1953); D. G. James, *The Romantic Comedy* (1948), Part III; Humphry House, *Coleridge* (1953); Elio Chinol, *Il Pensiero di S. T. Coleridge* (Venice, 1953); James V. Baker, *The Sacred River: Coleridge's Theory of the Imagination* (Baton Rouge, 1957); J. B. Beer, *Coleridge the Visionary* (1959); John A. Colmer, *Coleridge: Critic of Society* (Oxford, 1959); James D. Boulger, *Coleridge as Religious Thinker* (New Haven, 1961); Carl R. Woodring, *Politics in the Poetry of Coleridge* (Madison, Wis., 1961); Richard H. Fogle, *The Idea of Coleridge's Criticism* (Berkeley, 1962); Werner W. Beyer, *The Enchanted Forest* (1963), on the influence of Wieland's *Oberon;* Max F. Schulz, *The Poetic Voices of Coleridge* (Detroit, 1963); Paul Deschamps, *La Formation de la pensée de Coleridge, 1772-1804* (Paris, 1964); Herbert Read, "Coleridge as Critic," *Sewanee Rev.*, LVI (1948). 597-624; W. J. Bate, "Coleridge on the Function of Art," *Perspectives of Criticism*, ed. Harry Levin (Cambridge, Mass., 1950), pp. 125-159; Albert Gérard, "Coleridge, Keats and the Modern Mind," *EIC*, I (1951). 249-261; Barbara Hardy, "Distinction Without Difference: Coleridge's Fancy and Imagination," *EIC*, I (1951). 336-344, and " 'I Have a Smack of Hamlet': Coleridge and Shakespeare's Characters," *EIC*, VIII (1958). 238-255; Margaret L. Wiley, "Coleridge and the Wheels of Intellect," *PMLA*, LXVII (1952). 101-112; George Watson, "Contributions to a Dictionary of Critical Terms: *Imagination* and *Fancy*," *EIC*, III (1953). 201-214; Howard H. Creed, "Coleridge's Metacriticism," *PMLA*, LXIX (1954). 1160-1180; Frederick B. Rainsberry, "Coleridge and the Paradox of the Poetic Imperative," *ELH*, XXI (1954). 114-145; D. B. Lang, "Point Counterpoint: The Emergence of Fancy and Imagination in Coleridge," *JAAC*, XVI (1958). 384-397; Richard Haven, "Coleridge, Hartley, and the Mystics," *JHI*, XX (1959). 477-494; Emerson R. Marks, "Means and Ends in Coleridge's Critical Method," *ELH*, XXVI (1959). 387-401; Herbert Piper, "The Pantheistic Sources of Coleridge's Early Poetry," *JHI*, XX (1959). 47-59; Lucyle Werkmeister, "Coleridge on Science, Philosophy, and Poetry," *Harvard Theological Rev.*, LII (1959). 85-118, and "The Early Coleridge: His 'Rage for Metaphysics,' " *ibid.*, LIV (1961). 99-123; M. M. Badawi, "Coleridge's Formal Criticism of Shakespeare's Plays," *EIC*, X (1960). 148-162; Leonard W. Deen, "Coleridge and the Radicalism of Religious Dissent," *JEGP*, LXI (1962). 496-510; Craig W. Miller, "Coleridge's Concept of Nature," *JHI*, XXV (1964). 77-96; essays by Herbert M. McLuhan, D. G. James, and Kathleen Coburn in *The Major English Romantic Poets*, ed. Thorpe *et al.*, chs. VII-IX; Basil Willey, *Nineteenth Century Studies* (1949), ch. I; Wellek, *History of Modern Criticism*, II. ch. VI.

**1153** *The Rime of the Ancient Mariner* has attracted much critical attention in recent years, some of it owing to the provocative introduction Robert Penn Warren wrote for an edition of the poem (1946). Bernard Martin, *"The Ancient Mariner" and the "Authentic Narrative"* (1949) and C. S. Wilkinson, *The Wake of the "Bounty"* (1953)—both on additional sources of the poem; George Whalley, "The Mariner and the Albatross," *UTQ*, xvi (1947). 381-398; E. E. Stoll, "Symbolism in Coleridge," *PMLA*, LxIII (1948). 214-233; E. M. W. Tillyard, *"The Rime of the Ancient Mariner," Five Poems 1470-1870* (1948), pp. 66-86; Bowra, *The Romantic Imagination*, ch. III; Lionel Stevenson, *"The Ancient Mariner* as a Dramatic Monologue," *Personalist*, xxx (1949). 34-44; Coleman O. Parsons, "The Mariner and the Albatross," *Virginia Quar. Rev.*, xxvi (1950). 102-123; Tristram P. Coffin, "Coleridge's Use of the Ballad Stanza in *The Rime of the Ancient Mariner*," *MLQ*, xII (1951). 437-445; J. W. R. Purser, "Interpretation of *The Ancient Mariner*," *RES*, n.s. vIII (1957). 249-256; Richard H. Fogle, "The Genre of *The Ancient Mariner*," *Tulane Stud. in English*, vII (1957). 111-124; Elliott B. Gose, Jr., "Coleridge and the Luminous Gloom: An Analysis of the 'Symbolic Language' in *The Rime of the Ancient Mariner*," *PMLA*, LxxV (1960). 238-244; R. L. Brett, "Coleridge's *The Rime of the Ancient Mariner*," *Reason and Imagination* (1960), pp. 78-107; Ward Pafford, "Coleridge's Wedding Guest," *SP*, Lx (1963). 618-626; Gayle S. Smith, "A Reappraisal of the Moral Stanzas in *The Rime of the Ancient Mariner*," *Stud. in Romanticism*, III (1963). 42-52; A. M. Buchan, "The Sad Wisdom of the Mariner," *SP*, LxI (1964). 669-688; Daniel McDonald, "Too Much Reality: A Discussion of *The Rime of the Ancient Mariner*," *SEL*, Iv (1964). 543-554; *"The Rime of the Ancient Mariner," A Handbook*, ed. Royal A. Gettmann (San Francisco, 1961).

**1154** Edgar Jones, "A New Reading of *Christabel*," *Cambridge Jour.*, v (1951). 97-110; Charles Tomlinson, *"Christabel," Interpretations*, ed. John Wain (1956), pp. 103-112; Virginia L. Radley, "*Christabel*: Directions Old and New," *SEL*, Iv (1964). 531-541.

**1155** Marshall Suther, *Visions of Xanadu* (1965); Dorothy F. Mercer, "The Symbolism of *Kubla Khan*," *JAAC*, xII (1953). 44-66; Carl R. Woodring, "Coleridge and The Khan," *EIC*, Ix (1959). 361-368; Warren U. Ober, "Southey, Coleridge and *Kubla Khan*," *JEGP*, LvIII (1959). 414-422; R. H. Fogle, "The Romantic Unity of *Kubla Khan*," *College English*, xxII (1960). 112-116; S. K. Heninger, Jr., "A Jungian Reading of *Kubla Khan*," *JAAC*, xvIII (1960). 358-367; George Watson, "The Meaning of *Kubla Khan*," *REL*, II, no. 1 (1961). 21-29; Alan C. Purves, "Formal Structure in *Kubla Khan*," *Stud. in Romanticism*, I (1962). 187-191; Richard Gerber, "Keys to *Kubla Khan*," *ES*, xLIv (1963). 321-341.—On the group of "conversation poems" to which *Frost at Midnight* belongs, see Richard H. Fogle, "Coleridge's Conversation Poems," *Tulane Stud. in English*, v (1955). 103-110; Albert Gérard, "The Systolic Rhythm: The Structure of Coleridge's Conversation Poems," *EIC*, x (1960). 307-319.—Note 24: Miss Schneider's article is superseded by her book, *Coleridge, Opium, and "Kubla Khan"* (Chicago, 1953).

**1156** Richard H. Fogle, "The Dejection of Coleridge's Ode," *ELH*, xvII (1950). 71-77; Stephen F. Fogle, "The Design of Coleridge's *Dejection*," *SP*, xLvIII (1951). 49-55; Charles S. Bouslog, "Structure and Theme in Coleridge's

*Dejection: An Ode,*" *MLQ,* xxiv (1963). 42-52.—Note 27. See George Whalley, *Coleridge and Sara Hutchinson and the Asra Poems* (Toronto, 1955).

**1157** *Biographia Literaria,* ed. George Watson (1956), with useful apparatus.

# VI. Robert Southey, Walter Savage Landor, and Other Poets

**1159** Southey: *New Letters,* ed. Kenneth Curry (2v, 1965); *Letters from England by Don Manuel Esprielle,* ed. Jack Simmons (1952); *Journals of a Residence in Portugal 1800-1801 and a Visit to France 1838,* ed. Adolfo Cabral (Oxford, 1960); *Life of Nelson,* ed. E. R. H. Harvey (1953).—Bibliography in Houtchens, ch. v. Geoffrey Carnall, *Robert Southey and His Age* (Oxford, 1960); Rose Macaulay, "A Romantic Among Philistines," *They Went to Portugal* (1946), pp. 143-165; Malcolm Elwin, *The First Romantics* (1947); George Whalley, "Coleridge and Southey in Bristol, 1795," *RES,* n.s. 1 (1950). 324-340; Kenneth Hopkins, *The Poets Laureate* (1954), ch. xi.

**1162** Landor: *Poetry and Prose,* ed. E. K. Chambers (Oxford, 1946); *Poems,* ed. Geoffrey Grigson (1964), a selection.—Bibliography in Houtchens, ch. viii; Robert H. Super, *The Publication of Landor's Works* (1954). Super, *Walter Savage Landor: A Biography* (1954); Malcolm Elwin, *Landor: A Replevin* (1958), not the same book as his *Savage Landor* (1941); Pierre Vitoux, *L'Oeuvre de Walter Savage Landor* (Paris, 1964).

**1164** Ernest de Selincourt, "Landor's Prose," *Wordsworthian and Other Studies* (Oxford, 1947), ch. iv.

**1166** *The Shorter Poems,* ed. J. B. Sidgwick (Cambridge, 1946). Donald A. Davie, "The Shorter Poems of Walter Savage Landor," *EIC,* i (1951). 345-355 (cf. discussion, *ibid.,* ii [1952]. 214-219).

**1167** Crabbe: *New Poems,* ed. Arthur Pollard (Liverpool, 1960). The biography by Crabbe's son was reprinted, with an introduction by Edmund Blunden, in 1947. Lilian Haddakin, *The Poetry of Crabbe* (1955); Oliver F. Sigworth, *Nature's Sternest Painter: Five Essays on the Poetry of George Crabbe* (Tucson, 1964); R. L. Chamberlain, *George Crabbe* (1965); Ian Gregor, "The Last Augustan," *Dublin Rev.,* ccxxix (1955). 37-50; W. K. Thomas, "The Flavour of Crabbe," *Dalhousie Rev.,* xl (1961). 489-504; Walter E. Broman, "Factors in Crabbe's Eminence in the Early Nineteenth Century," *MP,* li (1953). 42-49.

**1169** *Recollections of the Table-Talk of Samuel Rogers,* ed. Morchard Bishop (1952); *Italian Journal,* ed. J. R. Hale (1956), first publication. Carl P. Barbier, *Samuel Rogers and William Gilpin: Their Friendship and Correspondence* (1959); Donald Weeks, "Samuel Rogers: Man of Taste," *PMLA,* lxii (1947). 472-486.

**1170** Virtually no significant scholarly or critical work has been published on Campbell in recent decades. There is a bibliography in Houtchens, ch. vi.

**1171** Moore: *Letters,* ed. Wilfred Dowden (2v, Oxford, 1965). Bibliography in Houtchens, ch. VII. Robert Birley, "Thomas Moore: *Lalla Rookh,*" *Sunk Without Trace: Some Forgotten Masterpieces Reconsidered* (1962), ch. V; Hoover H. Jordan, "Thomas Moore: Artistry in the Song Lyric," *SEL,* II (1962). 403-440.

**1172** Leigh Hunt: *Dramatic Criticism, 1808-1831* (1949), *Literary Criticism* (1956), *Political and Occasional Essays* (1962)—all ed. L. H. and C. W. Houtchens.—Bibliography in Houtchens, ch. IX. Clarence D. Thorpe, "Leigh Hunt as Man of Letters," *Literary Criticism,* just cited, pp. 3-73; Carl R. Woodring, "Leigh Hunt as a Political Essayist," *Political and Occasional Essays,* just cited, pp. 3-71; George D. Stout, *The Political History of Leigh Hunt's "Examiner"* (St. Louis, 1949); Jeffrey Fleece, "Leigh Hunt's Shakespearean Criticism," *Essays in Honor of Walter Clyde Curry* (Nashville, 1954), pp. 181-195; Stout, "Leigh Hunt's Shakespeare: A 'Romantic' Concept," *Studies in Memory of Frank Martindale Webster* (St. Louis, 1951), pp. 14-33; Alba H. Warren, *English Poetic Theory, 1825-1865* (Princeton, 1950), ch. VI; Wellek, *History of Modern Criticism,* III. 120-125.

**1173** Note 48: A. Lytton Sells, *The Italian Influence in English Poetry* (Bloomington, Ind., 1955); Oswald Doughty, "Dante and the English Romantic Poets," *English Miscellany,* II (1951). 125-169.

**1174** William H. Marshall, *Byron, Shelley, Hunt, and "The Liberal"* (Philadelphia, 1960). *Autobiography,* ed. J. E. Morpurgo (1949), well annotated; *Leigh Hunt's Autobiography: The Earliest Sketches,* ed. Stephen F. Fogle (Gainesville, Fla., 1959).

# VII. Reviews and Magazines: 1802-1830; The Essayists

**1176** John Clive, *Scotch Reviewers: The Edinburgh Review, 1802-1815* (Cambridge, Mass., 1957); Irwin Griggs, John D. Kern, and Elisabeth Schneider, "Early *Edinburgh* Reviewers: A New List," *MP,* XLIII (1946). 192-210; Frank W. Fetter, "The Authorship of Economic Articles in the *Edinburgh Review,* 1802-47," *Jour. of Political Economy,* LXI (1953). 232-259; Thomas Crawford, "The *Edinburgh Review* and Romantic Poetry (1802-29)," *Auckland Univ. College Bull.,* No. 47 (1955).

**1177** James A. Greig, *Francis Jeffrey of the Edinburgh Review* (Edinburgh, 1948); J. R. Derby, "The Paradox of Francis Jeffrey: Reason Versus Sensibility," *MLQ,* VII (1946). 489-500; Byron Guyer, "Francis Jeffrey's *Essay on Beauty,*" *HLQ,* XIII (1949). 71-85, and "The Philosophy of Francis Jeffrey," *MLQ,* XI (1950). 17-26.—Frances Hawes, *Henry Brougham* (1957); Chester W. New, *The Life of Henry Brougham to 1830* (Oxford, 1961); Elisabeth Schneider, Irwin Griggs, and John D. Kern, "Brougham's Early Contributions to the *Edinburgh Review*: A New List," *MP,* XLII (1945). 152-173.

**1178** *Letters of Sydney Smith,* ed. Norwell C. Smith (2v, Oxford, 1953); *Selected Writings,* ed. W. H. Auden (1956). Gerald Bullett, *Sydney Smith: A Biography and a Selection* (1951).—Hill Shine and Helen C. Shine, *The Quarterly Review under Gifford: Identification of Contributors, 1809-1824* (Chapel

Hill, 1949).—F. O. Tredreÿ, *The House of Blackwood, 1804-1954* (Edinburgh, 1954); A. L. Strout, *A Bibliography of Articles in Blackwood's Magazine, 1817-1825* (Lubbock, Tex., 1959).

**1180**  Josephine Bauer, *The London Magazine, 1820-29* (Copenhagen, 1953). —Note 13: On Mahony, see Ethel Mannin, *Two Studies in Integrity* (1954).— Note 14: Studies of Victorian periodicals: *A Century of Punch Cartoons*, ed. R. E. Williams (1955); R. G. G. Price, *A History of Punch* (1957); Diderik Roll-Hansen, *The Academy: 1869-1879* (Copenhagen, 1957); Cyprian Blagden, "Longman's Magazine," *REL*, IV, no. 2 (1963). 9-22; A. J. Gurr, "Macmillan's Magazine," *REL*, VI, no. 1 (1965). 39-55.

**1180-1181**  *The Portable Charles Lamb*, ed. John Mason Brown (1949); *Essays of Elia*, ed. Malcolm Elwin (1952), both with useful introductions; *Selected Essays, Letters, Poems*, ed. J. L. May (1953); *Letters*, ed. G. Woodcock (1950), a selection; *Selected Letters*, ed. T. S. Matthews (1956). On the deficiencies of Lucas' still unsuperseded edition of the Lambs' letters, see George L. Barnett in *MLQ*, IX (1948). 303-314, and *HLQ*, XVIII (1955). 147-158.—Bibliography in Houtchens, ch. II. J. E. Morpurgo, *Charles Lamb and Elia* (1948); Barnett, *Charles Lamb: The Evolution of Elia* (Bloomington, Ind., 1964); Charles I. Patterson, "Charles Lamb's Insight into the Nature of the Novel," *PMLA*, LXVII (1952). 375-382; Bertram Jessup, "The Mind of Elia," *JHI*, XV (1954). 246-259; Sylvan Barnet, "Charles Lamb's Contributions to the Theory of Dramatic Illusion," *PMLA*, LXIX (1954). 1150-1159; Richard Haven, "The Romantic Art of Charles Lamb," *ELH*, XXX (1963). 137-146; Daniel J. Mulcahy, "Charles Lamb: The Antithetical Manner and the Two Planes," *SEL*, III (1963). 517-542; René Fréchet, "Lamb's 'Artificial Comedy,'" *REL*, V, no. 3 (1964). 27-41; Donald H. Reiman, "Thematic Unity in Lamb's Familiar Essays," *JEGP*, LXIV (1965). 470-476. On the genre to which Hunt and Hazlitt, as well as Lamb, contributed, see Melvin R. Watson, "The *Spectator* Tradition and the Development of the Familiar Essay," *ELH*, XIII (1946). 189-215.

**1185**  Hazlitt: *Essays*, ed. Catherine M. Maclean (1949), a selection; Maclean, *Hazlitt Painted by Himself* (1948), a synthetic autobiography.—Bibliography in Houtchens, ch. III. Herschel Baker, *William Hazlitt* (Cambridge, Mass., 1962), especially valuable for Hazlitt's intellectual milieu; William P. Albrecht, *William Hazlitt and the Malthusian Controversy* (Albuquerque, 1950) and *Hazlitt and the Creative Imagination* (Lawrence, Kan., 1965); John W. Bullitt, "Hazlitt and the Romantic Conception of the Imagination," *PQ*, XXIV (1945). 343-361; Clarence D. Thorpe, "Keats and Hazlitt," *PMLA*, LXII (1947). 487-502; Charles I. Patterson, "William Hazlitt as a Critic of Prose Fiction," *PMLA*, LXVIII (1953). 1001-1016; Alvin Whitley, "Hazlitt and the Theater," *Univ. of Texas Stud. in English*, XXXIV (1955). 67-100; Albrecht, "Hazlitt's Preference for Tragedy," *PMLA*, LXXI (1956). 1042-1051, and "Hazlitt on the Poetry of Wit," *PMLA*, LXXV (1960). 245-249; G. D. Klingopulos, "Hazlitt as Critic," *EIC*, VI (1956). 386-403; Wellek, *History of Modern Criticism*, II. 188-212; Joseph W. Donohue, Jr., "Hazlitt's Sense of the Dramatic Actor as Tragic Character," *SEL*, V (1965). 705-721.

**1187**  *Liber Amoris and Dramatic Criticisms*, ed. Charles Morgan (1948), with a long introduction; *Conversations of James Northcote*, ed. Frank Swinnerton (1949).—Robert E. Robinson, *William Hazlitt's Life of Napoleon Buonaparte: Its Sources and Characteristics* (Geneva, 1959).

**1188** DeQuincey: *Recollections of the Lake Poets,* ed. E. Sackville-West (1948), John E. Jordan (1961, as *Reminiscences of the English Lake Poets*); *Confessions of an English Opium Eater,* ed. Sackville-West (1950), Malcolm Elwin (1956), Jordan (1960); *The English Mail Coach and Other Essays,* ed. Jordan (1961). (The volumes by Jordan, in Everyman's Library, are noteworthy for the authority of their editing.) *Selected Writings,* ed. Philip Van Doren Stern (1949). —Bibliography in Houtchens, ch. x. Jordan, *Thomas DeQuincey: Literary Critic* (Berkeley, 1952) and *DeQuincey to Wordsworth: A Biography of a Relationship* (Berkeley, 1962); Albert Goldman, *The Mine and the Mint* (Carbondale, Ill., 1965), on De Quincey's sources; Jordan, "DeQuincey's Dramaturgic Criticism," *ELH,* xviii (1951). 32-49; Charles I. Patterson, "DeQuincey's Conception of the Novel as Literature of Power," *PMLA,* lxx (1955). 375-389; Clifford Leech, "DeQuincey as Literary Critic," *REL,* ii, no. 1 (1961). 38-48; Geoffrey Carnall, "DeQuincey on the Knocking at the Gate," *ibid.,* pp. 49-57; J. Hillis Miller, *The Disappearance of God* (Cambridge, Mass., 1963), ch. ii.

**1190** Note 33: See also Elisabeth Schneider, *Coleridge, Opium, and "Kubla Khan"* (Chicago, 1953), pp. 72-80.

**1191** Shozo Kobayashi, *Rhythm in the Prose of Thomas DeQuincey* (Tokyo, 1956); Ian Jack, "DeQuincey Revises His *Confessions,*" *PMLA,* lxxii (1957). 122-146; Richard H. Byrns, "DeQuincey's Revisions in the *Dream-Fugue,*" *PMLA,* lxxvii (1962). 97-101.

# VIII. Gothic Romance and the Novel of Doctrine

**1192** On fiction in general during the romantic period, see Walter Allen, *The English Novel* (1954), ch. iii; Lionel Stevenson, *The English Novel* (Boston, 1960), chs. vii-viii.—Devendra P. Varma, *The Gothic Flame, Being a History of the Gothic Novel in England* (1957); Lowry Nelson, Jr., "Night Thoughts on the Gothic Novel," *Yale Rev.,* lii (1962). 236-257.

**1193** Alan D. McKillop, "Charlotte Smith's Letters," *HLQ,* xv (1952). 237-255.

**1194** Aline Grant, *Ann Radcliffe* (Denver, 1951); R. D. Havens, "Ann Radcliffe's Nature Descriptions," *MLN,* lxvi (1951). 251-255; William Ruff, "Ann Radcliffe, or the Hand of Taste," *The Age of Johnson: Essays Presented to C. B. Tinker* (New Haven, 1949), pp. 183-193.
Note 7: William Powell Jones, "New Light on Sir Egerton Brydges," *Harvard Library Bull.,* xi (1957). 102-116.

**1195** *The Monk,* original text ed. Louis F. Peck (1952); Karl S. Guthke, "M. G. Lewis' *The Twins,*" *HLQ,* xxv (1962). 189-223, first printing of a farce. Peck, *A Life of Matthew G. Lewis* (Cambridge, Mass., 1961).—Note 13: *Singular Travels,.Campaigns and Adventures of Baron Münchhausen,* ed. John Carswell (1948). Carswell, *The Prospector: Being the Life and Times of Rudolf Erich Raspe* (1950).

**1196** Mary Shelley: *Mathilda,* ed. Elizabeth Nitchie (Chapel Hill, 1959);

*Journal,* ed. Frederick L. Jones (Norman, Okla., 1947); *My Best Mary: The Selected Letters,* ed. Muriel Spark and Derek Stanford (1953).—Spark, *Child of Light* (1952); Nitchie, *Mary Shelley* (New Brunswick, 1953); Ernest J. Lovell, Jr., "Byron and the Byronic Hero in the Novels of Mary Shelley," *Univ. of Texas Stud. in English,* xxx (1951). 158-183, and "Byron and Mary Shelley," *KSJ,* ii (1953). 35-49; Burton R. Pollin, "Philosophical and Literary Sources of *Franken-stein,*" *CL,* xvii (1965). 97-108.

Maturin: *Melmoth the Wanderer,* ed. W. F. Axton (Lincoln, Neb., 1961). H. W. Piper and A. Norman Jeffares, "Maturin the Innovator," *HLQ,* xxi (1958). 261-284.

**1197** Godwin: *Imogen: A Pastoral Romance from the Ancient British,* ed. Jack Marken *et al.* (1963), reprinted from the 1784 edition.—P. N. Furbank, "Godwin's Novels," *EIC,* v (1955). 214-228; Patrick Cruttwell, "On *Caleb Williams,*" *Hudson Rev.,* xi (1958). 87-95; Harvey Gross, "The Pursuer and the Pursued: A Study of *Caleb Williams,*" *Texas Stud. in Lit. and Lang.,* i (1959). 401-411; George Sherburn, "Godwin's Later Novels," *Stud. in Romanticism,* i (1962). 65-82.—Note 23: Rodney M. Baine, *Thomas Holcroft and the Revolutionary Novel* (Athens, Ga., 1965); V. R. Stallbaumer, "Thomas Holcroft as a Novelist," *ELH,* xv (1948). 194-218.

**1198** Maria Edgeworth: *Castle Rackrent,* ed. George Watson (1964), scholarly text.—Isabel C. Clarke, *Maria Edgeworth* (1950); P. H. Newby, *Maria Edgeworth* (1950); Elisabeth Inglis-Jones, *The Great Maria* (1959); W. H. G. Armytage, "Little Woman," *Queen's Quar.,* lvi (1949). 248-257.

# IX. Jane Austen

**1200** The definitive Oxford Edition of Jane Austen's works, ed. R. W. Chapman, was completed in 1954 with the publication of Vol. vi, *Minor Works,* incorporating *Volume the First* (first published 1933), *Love and Freindship* (1922, retitled *Volume the Second* when edited from manuscript by B. C. Southam, 1963), and *Volume the Third* (1951). Chawton Edition (6v, 1948); *The Watsons,* a fragment "continued and completed" by John Coates (1958); *Letters to Her Sister Cassandra and Others,* ed. Chapman (rev. 1952), *Letters 1796-1817,* ed. Chapman (1955), a selection.—Chapman, *Jane Austen: A Critical Bibliography* (Oxford, 1953, rev. 1955). Chapman, *Jane Austen: Facts and Problems* (Oxford, 1948); Elizabeth Jenkins, *Jane Austen* (1949); Marvin Mudrick, *Jane Austen: Irony as Defense and Discovery* (Princeton, 1952); Andrew Wright, *Jane Austen's Novels: A Study in Structure* (1953); Howard S. Babb, *Jane Austen's Novels: The Fabric of Dialogue* (Columbus, Ohio, 1962); Robert Liddell, *The Novels of Jane Austen* (1963); Southam, *Jane Austen's Literary Manuscripts* (1964); W. A. Craik, *Jane Austen: The Six Novels* (1965); A. Walton Litz, *Jane Austen: A Study of Her Artistic Development* (1965); Louise D. Cohen, "Insight, the Essence of Jane Austen's Artistry," *NCF,* viii (1953). 213-224; Frank O'Connor, "Jane Austen and the Flight from Fancy," *The Mirror in the Roadway* (1956), pp. 17-41; Frank W. Bradbrook, "The Letters of Jane Austen," *Cambridge Jour.,* vii (1954). 259-276; Langdon Elsbree, "Jane Austen and the Dance of Fidelity and Complaisance," *NCF,* xv (1960). 113-136; Cynthia

Griffin, "The Development of Realism in Jane Austen's Early Novels," *ELH*, xxx (1963). 36-52; Frederick R. Karl, "Jane Austen: The Necessity of Wit," *An Age of Fiction: The Nineteenth Century British Novel* (1964), pp. 27-62; *Discussions of Jane Austen*, ed. William Heath (Boston, 1961); *Jane Austen: A Collection of Critical Essays*, ed. Ian Watt (1963).

*Sense and Sensibility*, ed. David Daiches (1950), Lord David Cecil (1957).—Christopher Gillie, "*Sense and Sensibility*: An Assessment," *EIC*, ix (1959). 1-9.

*Pride and Prejudice*, ed. David Daiches (1950), Mark Schorer (Boston, 1956), Robert Daniel (1960), Bradford A. Booth (1963), the last-named with excerpts from the criticism.—Samuel Kliger, "Jane Austen's *Pride and Prejudice* in the Eighteenth Century Mode," *UTQ*, xvi (1947). 357-370; Mark Schorer, "Pride Unprejudiced," *Kenyon Rev.*, xviii (1956). 72-91; Howard S. Babb, "Dialogue with Feeling: A Note on *Pride and Prejudice*," *Kenyon Rev.*, xx (1958). 203-216; E. M. Halliday, "Narrative Perspective in *Pride and Prejudice*," *NCF*, xv (1960). 65-71; Charles J. McCann, "Setting and Character in *Pride and Prejudice*," *NCF*, xix (1964). 65-75; Dorothy Van Ghent, *The English Novel: Form and Function* (1953), pp. 99-111—hereafter cited as Van Ghent.

*Mansfield Park*, ed. Mark Schorer (1959), R. A. Brower (Boston, 1965).—Lionel Trilling, "*Mansfield Park*," *Partisan Rev.*, xxi (1954). 492-511; Joseph M. Duffy, Jr., "Moral Integrity and Moral Anarchy in *Mansfield Park*," *ELH*, xxiii (1956). 71-91; Charles Murrah, "The Background of *Mansfield Park*," *From Jane Austen to Joseph Conrad: Essays Collected in Memory of James T. Hillhouse*, ed. Robert C. Rathburn and Martin Steinmann (Minneapolis, 1958), pp. 23-34 (this collection is cited hereafter by title alone); David Lodge, "A Question of Judgment: The Theatricals as Mansfield Park," *NCF*, xvii (1962). 275-282; Thomas R. Edwards, Jr., "The Difficult Beauty of *Mansfield Park*," *NCF*, xx (1965). 51-67; Joseph W. Donohue, Jr., "Ordination and the Divided House at Mansfield Park," *ELH*, xxxii (1965). 169-178.

*Emma*, ed. Trilling (Boston, 1957).—F. W. Bradbrook, *Jane Austen: "Emma"* (1961); E. N. Hayes, "*Emma*: A Dissenting Opinion," *NCF*, iv (1949). 1-20; Joseph M. Duffy, Jr., "*Emma*: The Awakening from Innocence," *ELH*, xxi (1954). 39-53; Edgar F. Shannon, Jr., "*Emma*: Character and Construction," *PMLA*, lxxi (1956). 637-650; Wayne C. Booth, "Point of View and Control of Distance in *Emma*," *NCF*, xvi (1961). 95-116; R. E. Hughes, "The Education of Emma Woodhouse," *NCF*, xvi (1961). 69-74; G. Armour Craig, "Jane Austen's *Emma*: The Truths and Disguises of Human Disclosure," *In Defense of Reading*, ed. R. A. Brower and W. R. Poirier (1962), pp. 235-255; Malcolm Bradbury, "Jane Austen's *Emma*," *Critical Quar.*, iv (1962). 335-346; Edward M. White, "*Emma* and the Parodic Point of View," *NCF*, xviii (1963). 55-63; Ward Hellstrom, "Francophobia in *Emma*," *SEL*, v (1965). 607-617; Arnold Kettle, "*Emma*," *An Introduction to the English Novel* (2v, 1951), i. 90-104—hereafter cited as Kettle.

John K. Mathison, "*Northanger Abbey* and Jane Austen's Conception of the Value of Fiction," *ELH*, xxiv (1957). 138-152; Alan D. McKillop, "Critical Realism in *Northanger Abbey*," *From Jane Austen to Joseph Conrad*, pp. 35-45.

*Persuasion*, ed. David Daiches (1958), Andrew Wright (1965), D .W. Harding (1965).—Joseph M. Duffy, Jr., "Structure and Idea in Jane Austen's *Persuasion*," *NCF*, viii (1954). 272-289; Paul N. Zietlow, "Luck and Fortuitous Circumstance in *Persuasion*: Two Interpretations," *ELH*, xxxii (1965). 179-195.

# X. Sir Walter Scott

**1207**  Scott's *Private Letters of the Seventeenth Century* was first published in full, ed. Douglas Grant (Oxford, 1947). *Selections from the Prose,* ed. J. C. Trewin (1952). Tait's edition of Scott's *Journal* was completed with the publication of Vol. III (Edinburgh, 1946).—Bibliography in Houtchens, ch. IV. Una Pope-Hennessy, *Sir Walter Scott* (1948); Hesketh Pearson, *Walter Scott: His Life and Personality* (1954); *Sir William Gell's Reminiscences of Sir Walter Scott's Residence in Italy,* ed. G. H. Needler (Toronto, 1953; rev. J. C. Corson, 1957), first publication from the manuscript; Needler, *Goethe and Scott* (Toronto, 1950); *Sir Walter Scott Lectures, 1940-1948* (Edinburgh, 1950), by Sir Herbert Grierson, Edwin Muir, G. M. Young, and S. C. Roberts; George Lukács, *The Historical Novel* (English trans., 1962), Part I; Alexander Welsh, *The Hero of the Waverley Novels* (New Haven, 1963); Coleman O. Parsons, *Witchcraft and Demonology in Scott's Fiction* (1964); Christina Keith, *The Author of Waverley: A Study in the Personality of Sir Walter Scott* (1964); David Daiches, "Scott's Achievement as a Novelist," *Literary Essays* (Edinburgh, 1956), pp. 88-121; John Lauber, "Scott on the Art of Fiction," *SEL,* III (1963). 543-554; Duncan Forbes, "The Rationalism of Sir Walter Scott," *Cambridge Jour.,* VII (1953). 20-35; Paul Roberts, "Sir Walter Scott's Contributions to the English Vocabulary," *PMLA,* LXVIII (1953). 189-210; Richard French, "The Religion of Sir Walter Scott," *Stud. in Scottish Lit.,* II (1964). 32-44; Alice Chandler, "Sir Walter Scott and the Medieval Revival," *NCF,* XIX (1965). 315-332.

**1208**  William Montgomerie, "Sir Walter Scott as Ballad Editor," *RES,* n.s. VII (1956). 158-163.

**1210**  On *Harold the Dauntless* see J. T. Hillhouse, "Sir Walter's Last Long Poem," *HLQ,* XVI (1952). 53-73.

**1211**  S. Stewart Gordon, "*Waverley* and the 'Unified Design,'" *ELH,* XVIII (1951). 107-122; Nelson S. Bushnell, "Walter Scott's Advent as a Novelist of Manners," *Stud. in Scottish Lit.,* I (1963). 15-34.—*Rob Roy,* ed. Edgar Johnson (Boston, 1956).—Note 14: This theory was finally disposed of by Robert D. Mayo, "The Chronology of the Waverley Novels: The Evidence of the Manuscripts," *PMLA,* LXIII (1948). 935-949.

**1212**  *The Heart of Midlothian,* ed. David Daiches (1948).—P. F. Fisher, "Providence, Fate, and the Historical Imagination in Scott's *The Heart of Midlothian,*" *NCF,* X (1955). 99-114; Robin Mayhead, "*The Heart of Midlothian:* Scott as Artist," *EIC,* VI (1956). 266-277 (cf. David Craig, *ibid.,* VIII [1958]. 217-255); Winifred Lynskey, "The Drama of the Elect and the Reprobate in Scott's *Heart of Midlothian,*" *Boston Univ. Stud. in English,* IV (1960). 39-48; William H. Marshall, "Point of View and Structure in *The Heart of Midlothian,*" *NCF,* XVI (1961). 257-262; Van Ghent, pp. 113-124.—Robert C. Gordon, "*The Bride of Lammermoor:* A Novel of Tory Pessimism," *NCF,* XII (1957). 110-124.— Joseph E. Duncan, "The Anti-Romantic in *Ivanhoe,*" *NCF,* IX (1955). 293-300.

**1213**  David Daiches, "Scott's *Redgauntlet,*" *From Jane Austen to Joseph Conrad,* pp. 46-59; D. D. Devlin, "Scott and *Redgauntlet,*" *REL,* IV, no. 1 (1963). 91-103.

**1218** Donald Davie, *The Heyday of Sir Walter Scott* (1961); John Henry Raleigh, "What Scott Meant to the Victorians," *VS*, VII (1963). 7-34; Francis R. Hart, "*The Fair Maid*, Manzoni's *Betrothed*, and the Grounds of Waverley Criticism," *NCF*, XVIII (1963). 103-118.

# XI. Lord Byron

**1219** *Poems*, ed. Guy Pocock (3v, 1948); *Selections*, ed. Peter Quennell (1949); *Selected Poetry*, ed. Leslie A. Marchand (1951); *Selected Poetry and Letters*, ed. E. E. Bostetter (1951); *Byron: A Self-Portrait*, ed. Quennell (2v, 1950), a selection from the letters and journals; *His Very Self and Voice: Collected Conversations*, ed. Ernest J. Lovell, Jr. (1954); *Selected Letters*, ed. Jacques Barzun (1953).—Bibliography in Raysor, ch. IV, and annually in *KSJ*. Marchand, *Byron: A Biography* (3v, 1957), the standard life; Lovell, *Byron: The Record of a Quest* (Austin, Tex., 1949); G. Wilson Knight, *Lord Byron: Christian Virtues* (1952); Paul West, *Byron and the Spoiler's Art* (1960); Andrew Rutherford, *Byron: A Critical Study* (Edinburgh, 1961); William H. Marshall, *The Structure of Byron's Major Poems* (Philadelphia, 1962); Peter L. Thorslev, Jr., *The Byronic Hero: Types and Prototypes* (Minneapolis, 1962); M. K. Joseph, *Byron the Poet* (1964); Marchand, *Byron's Poetry: A Critical Introduction* (1965); Marius Bewley, "The Colloquial Mode of Byron," *Scrutiny*, XVI (1949). 8-23; Carl Lefevre, "Lord Byron's Fiery Convert of Revenge," *SP*, XLIX (1952). 468-487; W. W. Robson, "Byron as Poet," *Proc. Brit. Acad.*, XLIII (1957). 25-62; West, "Byronic Romance and Nature's Frailty," *Dalhousie Rev.*, XXXIX (1959). 219-229, and "Byron's Farce with Language," *Twentieth Century*, CLXV (1959). 138-151; Bernard Blackstone, "Guilt and Retribution in Byron's Sea Poems," *REL*, II, no. 1 (1961). 58-69; David V. Erdman, "Byron and 'the New Force of the People,'" *KSJ*, XI (1962). 47-64; Frederick L. Beaty, "Byron's Concept of Ideal Love," *KSJ*, XII (1963). 37-54; essays by W. W. Pratt and Marchand in *The Major English Romantic Poets*, ed. Thorpe *et al.*, chs. XI-XII; *Byron: A Collection of Critical Essays*, ed. West (1963).

**1220** William A. Borst, *Lord Byron's First Pilgrimage* (New Haven, 1948). —Note 5: Michael Joyce, *My Friend H* (1948); E. R. Vincent, *Byron, Hobhouse, and Foscolo* (Cambridge, 1949); Andrew Rutherford, "The Influence of Hobhouse on *Childe Harold's Pilgrimage*, Canto IV," *RES*, n.s. XII (1961). 391-397.

**1222** See G. Wilson Knight, *Lord Byron's Marriage: The Evidence of the Asterisks* (1957), a highly controversial treatment.

**1223** Bertrand Evans, "Manfred's Remorse and Dramatic Tradition," *PMLA*, LXII (1947). 752-773; Maurice J. Quinlan, "Byron's *Manfred* and Zoroastrianism," *JEGP*, LVII (1958). 726-738; Ward Pafford, "Byron and the Mind of Man: *Childe Harold III-IV* and *Manfred*," *Stud. in Romanticism*, I (1962). 105-127.

**1224** *Don Juan*, ed. T. G. Steffan and W. W. Pratt (4v, Austin, Tex., 1957), Vols. II-IV providing a variorum text of the poem and full notes; ed. Peter Quennell (1949), Louis Kronenberger (1949), L. A. Marchand (Boston, 1958), with valuable apparatus.—Steffan, *The Making of a Masterpiece* (Vol. I of the edition first cited), describes in detail Byron's composing and revising of *Don Juan;* see also his articles in *MP*, XLIV (1947). 141-164, and XLVI (1949). 217-241; *Texas Stud. in English*, XXVI (1947). 108-168; and *SP*, XLVI (1949). 440-452. Andràs Horn, *Byron's "Don Juan" and the Eighteenth Century English Novel* (Bern, 1962); George M. Ridenour, *The Style of "Don Juan"* (New Haven, 1960), and "The Mode of Byron's *Don Juan*," *PMLA*, LXXIX (1964). 442-446; W. H. Auden, *"Don Juan," The Dyer's Hand* (1962), pp. 386-406; C. N. Stavrou, "Religion in Byron's *Don Juan*," *SEL*, III (1963). 567-594; Bowra, *The Romantic Imagination*, ch. VII; Lovell, "Irony and Image in Byron's *Don Juan*," *The Major English Romantic Poets*, ed. Thorpe *et al.*, ch. X.

**1226**  Much new light is thrown on Byron's liaison with the Countess Guiccioli in Iris Origo, *The Last Attachment* (1949). See also Leslie A. Marchand, "Lord Byron and Count Alborghetti," *PMLA*, LXIV (1949). 976-1007.

**1228**  See C. L. Cline, *Byron, Shelley, and Their Pisan Circle* (Cambridge, Mass., 1952).—The acrimonious aftermath of Byron's death is described in detail in Doris Langley Moore, *The Late Lord Byron* (1961).

# XII. Percy Bysshe Shelley

**1230**  *Shelley's Prose, or The Trumpet of a Prophecy*, ed. David Lee Clark (Albuquerque, 1954), important for texts; *The Esdaile Notebook: A Volume of Early Poems*, ed. Kenneth N. Cameron (1964); *The Esdaile Poems*, ed. Neville Rogers (1966). Volumes of selections by H. J. Stenning (1948), Morchard Bishop (1949), Richard Church (1949), John Heath-Stubbs (1949), A. S. B. Glover (1951), Carlos Baker (1951), Cameron (1951), Edmund Blunden (1954), John Holloway (1960), G. M. Matthews (1964). *Letters*, ed. Frederick L. Jones (2v, Oxford, 1964), replacing the Ingpen edition; *Shelley and His Circle, 1773-1822*, ed. Cameron (8v, Cambridge, Mass., 1961-     ), an important assemblage of documents.—Bibliography in Raysor, ch. v, and annually in *KSJ*. Cameron, *The Young Shelley: Genesis of a Radical* (1950); *Mary Shelley's Journal*, ed. Jones (Norman, Okla., 1947); Joseph Barrell, *Shelley and the Thought of His Time* (New Haven, 1947); A. M. D. Hughes, *The Nascent Mind of Shelley* (Oxford, 1947); Baker, *Shelley's Major Poetry: The Fabric of a Vision* (Princeton, 1948); D. G. James, *The Romantic Comedy* (1948), Part II; Anthony Durand, *Shelley on the Nature of Poetry* (Quebec, 1948); James A. Notopoulos, *The Platonism of Shelley* (Durham, N.C., 1949); Richard H. Fogle, *The Imagery of Keats and Shelley* (Chapel Hill, 1949); Sylva Norman, *Flight of the Skylark: The Development of Shelley's Reputation* (Norman, Okla., 1954); Peter Butter, *Shelley's Idols of the Cave* (Edinburgh, 1954); C. E. Pulos, *The Deep Truth: A Study of Shelley's Skepticism* (Lincoln, Neb., 1954); Bice Chiappelli, *Il Pensiero religioso di Shelley* (Rome, 1956); Neville Rogers, *Shelley at Work: A Critical Inquiry* (Oxford, 1956); David Perkins, *The Quest for Permanence: The Symbolism of Wordsworth, Shelley, and Keats* (Cambridge, Mass., 1959); Desmond King-Hele, *Shelley: His Thought and Work* (1960); Hélène Lemaître, *Shelley, Poète des éléments* (Paris, 1962)—these two important for scientific matters; Glenn O'Malley, *Shelley and Synesthesia* (Evanston, Ill., 1964); Raymond D. Havens, "Structure and Prosodic Pattern in Shelley's Lyrics," *PMLA*, LXV (1950). 1076-1087; Frederick A. Pottle, "The Case of

Shelley," *PMLA*, LXVII (1952). 589-608; Matthews, "A Volcano's Voice in Shelley," *ELH*, XXIV (1957). 191-228; three articles by Newell F. Ford, "Paradox and Irony in Shelley's Poetry," *SP*, LVII (1960). 648-662, "The Wit in Shelley's Poetry," *SEL*, I, no. 4 (1961). 1-22, and "The Symbolism of Shelley's Swans," *Stud. in Romanticism*, I (1962). 175-183; Ross G. Woodman, "Shelley's Changing Attitude to Plato," *JHI*, XXI (1960). 497-510; Daniel Hughes, "Kindling and Dwindling: The Poetic Process in Shelley," *KSJ*, XIII (1964). 13-28; essays by Havens, Baker, S. C. Wilcox, and Herbert Read in *The Major English Romantic Poets*, ed. Thorpe *et al.*, chs. XIII-XVI; *Shelley: A Collection of Critical Essays*, ed. George M. Ridenour (1965).

**1231** Winifred Scott, *Jefferson Hogg* (1951).

**1232** The life and character of Harriet Westbrook Shelley are sympathetically studied in Louise S. Boas, *Harriet Shelley: Five Long Years* (1962).

**1234** Frederick L. Jones, "The Inconsistency of Shelley's *Alastor*," *ELH*, XIII (1946). 291-298, and "The Vision Theme in Shelley's *Alastor* and Related Works," *SP*, XLIV (1947). 108-125; Evan K. Gibson, "*Alastor*: A Reinterpretation," *PMLA*, LXII (1947). 1022-1045; A. M. D. Hughes, "*Alastor, or the Spirit of Solitude*," *MLR*, XLIII (1948). 465-470; Albert Gérard, "*Alastor*, or the Spirit of Solipsism," *PQ*, XXXIII (1954). 164-177.

**1235** Note 19: W. M. Parker, "The Stockbroker Author," *Quarterly Rev.*, CCXC (1952). 121-134.

**1236** Carlos Baker, "Shelley's Ferrarese Maniac," *English Institute Essays 1946* (1947), pp. 41-73; G. M. Matthews, "*Julian and Maddalo*: the Draft and the Meaning," *Studia Neophil.*, XXXV (1963). 57-84, the best text.

*Prometheus Unbound: A Variorum Edition*, ed. Lawrence J. Zillman (Seattle, 1959).—Bennett Weaver, "*Prometheus Unbound*" (Ann Arbor, 1957), "Pre-Promethean Thought in the Prose of Shelley," *PQ*, XXVII (1948). 193-208, and "*Prometheus Bound* and *Prometheus Unbound*," *PMLA*, LXIV (1949). 115-133; Earl R. Wasserman, *Shelley's "Prometheus Unbound": A Critical Reading* (Baltimore, 1965); Bowra, *The Romantic Imagination*, ch. V; Richard H. Fogle, "Image and Imagelessness: A Limited Reading of *Prometheus Unbound*," *KSJ*, I (1952). 23-36; D. J. Hughes, "Potentiality in *Prometheus Unbound*," *Stud. in Romanticism*, II (1963). 107-126.

**1238** Richard H. Fogle, "The Imaginal Design of Shelley's *Ode to the West Wind*," *ELH*, XV (1948). 219-226; Stewart C. Wilcox, "Imagery, Ideas, and Design in Shelley's *Ode to the West Wind*," *SP*, XLVII (1950). 634-649; W. Schrickx, "Shelley's *Ode to the West Wind*: An Analysis," *Revue des langues vivantes*, XIX (1953). 396-404; Neville Rogers, "Shelley and the West Wind," *London Mag.*, III, no. 6 (1956). 56-68.—Stewart C. Wilcox, "The Sources, Symbolism, and Unity of Shelley's *Skylark*," *SP*, XLVI (1949). 560-576.—On Shelley's last years see Ivan Roe, *Shelley: The Last Phase* (1953) and Milton Wilson, *Shelley's Later Poetry: A Study of His Prophetic Imagination* (1959).

**1239** Kenneth N. Cameron, "The Planet-Tempest Passage in *Epipsychidion*," *PMLA*, LXIII (1948). 950-972; D. J. Hughes, "Coherence and Collapse in Shelley, with Particular Reference to *Epipsychidion*," *ELH*, XXVIII (1961). 260-283.—Melvin R. Watson, "The Thematic Unity of *Adonais*," *KSJ*, I (1952). 41-46; Earl R. Wasserman, "*Adonais*: Progressive Revelation as a Poetic Mode," *ELH*, XXI (1954). 274-326; Patrick J. Mahony, "An Analysis of Shelley's Craftsmanship in

*Adonais," SEL,* IV (1964). 555-568.—Donald H. Reiman, *Shelley's "The Triumph of Life": A Critical Study* (Urbana, Ill., 1965), including variorum text; G. M. Mathews, *"The Triumph of Life:* A New Text," *Studia Neophil.,* XXXII (1960). 271-309; P. H. Butter, "Sun and Shape in Shelley's *The Triumph of Life,"* RES, n.s. XIII (1962). 40-51.

**1240** The many inconsistencies and inaccuracies in Trelawny's successive narratives of Shelley's death and cremation are pointed out by L. A. Marchand, "Trelawny on the Death of Shelley," *Keats-Shelley Memorial Bull.,* IV (1952). 9-34.

# XIII. John Keats

**1241** Garrod's definitive ed. of Keats's *Poetical Works* was revised in 1958. There are numerous convenient editions of the poems, most of them selections: John Middleton Murry (1948), Richard Church (1948), Lawrence Whistler (1950), George H. Ford (1950), R. Vallance and B. Ifor Evans (1950), Richard H. Fogle (1951), Harold E. Briggs (1951), J. E. Morpurgo (1953), J. H. Walsh (1954), J. R. Caldwell (1954), Douglas Bush (Boston, 1959). *Letters,* ed. Hyder E. Rollins (2v, Cambridge, Mass., 1958), superseding the Buxton Forman edition; *Selected Letters,* ed. Lionel Trilling (1951, rev. 1956); *Letters,* ed. Frederick Page (1954), another selection.—James R. MacGillivray, *John Keats: A Bibliography and Reference Guide* (Toronto, 1949); Raysor, ch. VI; annual bibliography in *KSJ.* Walter J. Bate, *John Keats* (Cambridge, Mass., 1963); Aileen Ward, *John Keats: The Making of a Poet* (1963)—the two best biographical studies; Dorothy Hewlett, *Adonais, A Life of John Keats* (rev. 1949); three books by Rollins, *The Keats Circle* (2v, Cambridge, Mass., 1948), *More Letters and Poems of the Keats Circle* (Cambridge, Mass., 1955)—reissued together (2v, Cambridge, Mass., 1965)—and *Keats's Reputation in America to 1848* (Cambridge, Mass., 1946); Robert Gittings, *John Keats: The Living Year* (1954) and *The Mask of Keats: A Study of Problems* (1956), both controversial but often stimulating and illuminating; J. R. Caldwell, *John Keats' Fancy* (Ithaca, 1945); Lord Gorell, *John Keats: The Principle of Beauty* (1948); D. G. James, *The Romantic Comedy* (1948), Part II; Murry, *The Mystery of Keats* (1949) and *Keats* (1955), two more revisions of his *Studies in Keats;* Richard H. Fogle, *The Imagery of Keats and Shelley* (Chapel Hill, 1949); Newell F. Ford, *The Prefigurative Imagination of Keats* (Stanford, 1951); Earl Wasserman, *The Finer Tone* (Baltimore, 1953), highly sophisticated readings of five poems; Guy Murchie, *The Spirit of Place in Keats* (1955); Michele Renzulli, *John Keats: L'Uomo e il poeta* (Rome, 1956); E. C. Pettet, *On the Poetry of Keats* (Cambridge, 1957); Bernice Slote, *Keats and the Dramatic Principle* (Lincoln, Neb., 1958); *John Keats: A Reassessment,* ed. Kenneth Muir (Liverpool, 1958), essays by various writers; David Perkins, *The Quest for Permanence: The Symbolism of Wordsworth, Shelley, and Keats* (Cambridge, Mass., 1959); Bernard Blackstone, *The Consecrated Urn: An Interpretation of Keats in Terms of Growth and Form* (1959); Walter H. Evert, *Aesthetic and Myth in the Poetry of Keats* (Princeton, 1965); Robert W. Stallman, "Keats the Apollinian: The Time-and-Space Logic of His Poems as Paintings," *UTQ,* XVI (1947). 143-156; Ford, "Keats, Empathy, and 'the Poetical Character,'" *SP,* XLV (1948). 477-490; R. D. Havens, "Of Beauty and Reality in Keats," *ELH*, xvII (1950). 206-213; Albert Gérard, "Coleridge, Keats, and the Modern Mind," *EIC*, I (1951). 249-261, and "Keats and the Romantic *Sehnsucht*," *UTQ*, xxvIII (1959). 160-175; Jacob D. Wigod, "Negative Capability and Wise Passiveness," *PMLA*, lxvII (1952). 383-390; Dorothy Van Ghent, "Keats's Myth of the Hero," *KSJ*, III (1954). 7-25; Roberta D. Cornelius, "Keats as a Humanist," *KSJ*, v (1956). 87-96; James D. Boulger, "Keats's Symbolism," *ELH*, xxvIII (1961). 244-259; John Bayley, "Keats and Reality," *Proc. Brit. Acad.*, xLvIII (1962). 91-125; essays by Bate, Bush, Cleanth Brooks, and Murry in *The Major English Romantic Poets*, ed. Thorpe *et al.*, chs. xvII-xx; *Keats: A Collection of Critical Essays*, ed. Bate (1964).

**1244** Newell F. Ford, "*Endymion*—a Neo-Platonic Allegory?", *ELH*, xIV (1947). 64-76, and "The Meaning of 'Fellowship with Essence' in *Endymion*," *PMLA*, lxII (1947). 1061-1076; Jacob I. Wigod, "The Meaning of *Endymion*," *PMLA*, lxvIII (1953). 779-790; Carroll Arnett, "Thematic Structure in Keats's *Endymion*," *Texas Stud. in English*, xxxvI (1957). 100-109; Glen O. Allen, "The Fall of Endymion: A Study in Keats's Intellectual Growth," *KSJ*, vI (1957). 37-57; Robert Harrison, "Symbolism of the Cyclical Myth in *Endymion*," *Texas Stud. in Lit. and Lang.*, I (1960). 538-554; Paul Haeffner, "Keats and the Faery Myth of Seduction," *REL*, III, no. 2 (1962). 20-31; Stuart M. Sperry, Jr., "The Allegory of *Endymion*," *Stud. in Romanticism*, II (1962). 38-53; Bruce E. Miller, "On the Meaning of Keats's *Endymion*," *KSJ*, xIV (1965). 33-54.

**1247** Kenneth Muir, "The Meaning of *Hyperion*," *EIC*, II (1952). 54-75; Bernard Blackstone, "*Poetical Sketches* and *Hyperion*," *Cambridge Jour.*, vI (1952). 160-168; Barbara Garlitz, "Egypt and *Hyperion*," *PQ*, xxxIV (1955). 189-196; Stuart M. Sperry, Jr., "Keats, Milton, and *The Fall of Hyperion*," *PMLA*, lxxvII (1962). 77-84.

**1248** Arthur Carr, "Keats's Other Urn," *Univ. of Kansas City Rev.*, xx (1954). 237-242.

**1248-1249** On Keats's odes generally: John Holloway, "The Odes of Keats," *Cambridge Jour.*, v (1952). 416-425; David Perkins, "Keats's Odes and Letters: Recurrent Diction and Imagery," *KSJ*, II (1953). 51-60; Edmund Blunden, "Keats's Odes: Further Notes," *KSJ*, III (1954). 39-46.—Kenneth Allott, "Keats's *Ode to Psyche*," *EIC*, vI (1956). 278-301; Max F. Schulz, "Keats's Timeless Order of Things: A Modern Reading of the *Ode to Psyche*," *Criticism*, II (1960). 55-65. —Richard H. Fogle, "Keats's *Ode to a Nightingale*," *PMLA*, lxvIII (1953). 211-222; Janet Spens, "A Study of Keats's *Ode to a Nightingale*," *RES*, n.s. III (1952). 234-243.—Harvey T. Lyon, *Keats's Well-Read Urn* (1958), eighty-six critics quoted on the *Ode on a Grecian Urn*; Cleanth Brooks, "Keats's Sylvan Historian," *The Well-Wrought Urn* (1947), ch. vIII; Bowra, *The Romantic Imagination*, ch. vI; Robert Daniel, "Odes to Dejection," *Kenyon Rev.*, xv (1953). 129-140; Charles I. Patterson, "Passion and Permanence in Keats's *Ode on a Grecian Urn*," *ELH*, xxI (1954). 208-220; Martha Hale Shackford, "The *Ode on a Grecian Urn*," *KSJ*, Iv (1955). 7-13; Jacob D. Wigod, "Keats's Ideal in the *Ode on a Grecian Urn*," *PMLA*, lxxII (1957). 113-121; Albert Gérard, "Romance and Reality: Continuity and Growth in Keats's View of Art," *KSJ*, xI (1962). 17-29.—Ernest J. Lovell, Jr., "The Genesis of Keats's Ode *To Autumn*," *Univ. of Texas Stud. in English*, xxix (1950). 204-221; B. C. Southam, "The Ode *To Autumn*," *KSJ*, ix (1960). 91-98.

O. B. Hardison, Jr., "The Decorum of *Lamia*," *MLQ*, xix (1958). 33-42.

# XIV. Thomas Hood, Thomas Lovell Beddoes, and Other Poets

**1253**  Hood: *Poems*, ed. C. Dyment (1948), a selection.—John C. Reid, *Thomas Hood* (1963); N. Hardy Wallis, "Thomas Hood," *Essays by Divers Hands* (Royal Soc. of Lit.), n.s. xxiii (1946). 103-115; Alvin Whitley, "Thomas Hood as a Dramatist," *Univ. of Texas Stud. in English*, xxx (1951). 184-201; "Thomas Hood: The Language of Poetry," *LTLS*, Sept. 19, 1952, pp. 605-606; Edmund Blunden, "The Poet Hood," *REL*, i, no. 1 (1960). 26-34; William G. Lane, "A Chord in Melancholy: Hood's Last Years," *KSJ*, xiii (1964). 43-60; Heath-Stubbs, *The Darkling Plain*, pp. 49-59.

**1254**  Note 4: *The Ingoldsby Legends, Selected*, ed. J. Tanfield and G. Boas (1951). William G. Lane, "The Primitive Muse of Thomas Ingoldsby," *Harvard Library Bull.*, xii (1958). 47-83, 220-241.—*Complete Nonsense of Edward Lear*, ed. Holbrook Jackson (1947); *Teapots and Quails, and Other New Nonsenses*, ed. Angus Davidson and Philip Hofer (Cambridge, Mass., 1953); *Indian Journal*, ed. Ray Murphy (1953); *Edward Lear in Southern Italy*, ed. Peter Quennell (1964); *Edward Lear in Greece* (1965); *Journals*, ed. Herbert van Thal (1952), a selection. Elizabeth Sewell, *The Field of Nonsense* (1952).

**1255**  Elliott: "Corn Law Rhymer," *LTLS*, Dec. 2, 1949, p. 794; Asa Briggs, "Ebenezer Elliott, the Corn Law Rhymer," *Cambridge Jour.*, iii (1950). 686-695. Praed: *Selected Poems*, ed. Kenneth Allott (1953).

**1256**  Beddoes: *Plays and Poems*, ed. H. W. Donner (1950). Geoffrey Wagner, "Centennial of a Suicide: Thomas Lovell Beddoes," *Horizon*, xix (1949). 417-435; Louis O. Coxe, "Beddoes: The Mask of Parody," *Hudson Rev.*, vi (1953). 252-265; Donner, "Echoes of Beddoesian Rambles: Edgeworthstown to Zürich," *Studia Neophil.*, xxxiii (1961). 219-264, including new facts; Charles A. Hoyt, "Theme and Imagery in the Poetry of T. L. Beddoes," *ibid.*, xxxv (1963). 85-103; Heath-Stubbs, *The Darkling Plain*, pp. 37-49.

**1259**  George C. Haddow, "George Darley: A Centenary Sketch," *Queen's Quar.*, liii (1946). 491-501; "The Poet of Solitude," *LTLS*, Nov. 23, 19.. , p. 580; Graham Greene, "George Darley," *The Lost Childhood and Other Essays* (1951), pp. 143-152; Heath-Stubbs, *The Darkling Plain*, pp. 22-37.

**1260**  Cyril Pearl, *Always Morning: The Life of Richard Henry "Orion" Horne* (Melbourne, 1960).

Aytoun: *Stories and Verse*, ed. W. L. Renwick (Chicago, 1964). Erik Frykman, *W. E. Aytoun, Pioneer Professor of English at Edinburgh* (Stockholm, 1963).

**1261**  W. J. A. M. Beek, *John Keble's Literary and Religious Contribution to the Oxford Movement* (Nijmegen, 1959); Georgina Battiscombe, *John Keble: A Study in Limitations* (1963); Warren, *English Poetic Theory*, ch. iii.

Arthur G. Lough, *The Influence of John Mason Neale* (1962). On nineteenth-century hymnody in general, see the relevant chapters in Fairchild, *Religious Trends in English Poetry*, Vols. III-IV.

**1262** *Poems of John Clare's Madness*, ed. Geoffrey Grigson (1949); *The Shepherd's Calendar* (1964) and *The Later Poems of John Clare* (Manchester, 1964), pieces hitherto unpublished, both ed. Eric Robinson and Geoffrey Summerfield; *Selected Poems*, ed. Grigson (1950), James Reeves (1954); *Prose*, ed. J. W. and Anne Tibble (1951); *Letters*, ed. J. W. and Anne Tibble (1951).—June Wilson, *Green Shadows* (1951); J. W. and Anne Tibble, *John Clare: His Life and Poetry* (1956), revision of their 1932 biography; Frederick Martin, *The Life of John Clare* (1964); John Middleton Murry, *John Clare and Other Studies* (1950), pp. 7-24, and "Clare Revisited," *Unprofessional Essays* (1956), pp. 53-111; Rayner Unwin, *The Rural Muse* (1954), pp. 121-142; Heath-Stubbs, *The Darkling Plain*, pp. 65-75.

**1263** Helen Ashton, *Letty Landon* (1951); Lionel Stevenson, "Miss Landon, 'the Milk-and-Watery Moon of our Darkness,' 1824-30," *MLQ*, VIII (1947). 355-363.—Note 40: On Montgomery, see Kenneth Hopkins, "Reflections on Satan Montgomery," *Texas Stud. in Lit. and Lang.*, IV (1962). 351-366.

# XV. The Drama in Decline

**1264** *Nineteenth Century Plays*, ed. George Rowell (1953); Allardyce Nicoll, *A History of English Drama* (6v, Cambridge, 1952-59), Vols. IV-V; Rowell, *The Victorian Theatre: A Survey* (1956); Bertrand Evans, *Gothic Drama from Walpole to Shelley* (Berkeley, 1947); M. Wilson Disher, *Blood and Thunder: Mid-Victorian Melodrama and Its Origins* (1949).

**1268** Richard D. Altick, "Dion Boucicault Stages *Mary Barton*," *NCF*, XIV (1959). 129-141.—M. Norton, "The Plays of Joanna Baillie," *RES*, XXIII (1947). 131-143.

**1269** Vera Watson, *Mary Russell Mitford* (1949); Jack, pp. 338-344.—*Bulwer and Macready: A Chronicle of the Early Victorian Theater*, ed. Charles H. Shattuck (Urbana, Ill., 1958).

# XVI. The Novel Between Scott and Dickens

**1271** Peacock: *Novels*, ed. David Garnett (1948); *The Pleasures of Peacock*, ed. Ben Ray Redman (1947); *Nightmare Abbey* and *Crotchet Castle*, introduction by J. B. Priestley (1948).—Bill Read, "Thomas Love Peacock: An Enumerative Bibliography," *Bull. of Bibliography*, XXIV (1963-64). 32-34, 70-72, 88-91. Olwen W. Campbell, *Thomas Love Peacock* (1953); Sidney J. Black, "The Peacockian Essence," *Boston Univ. Stud. in English*, III (1957). 231-242.

**1272** Sandor Baumgarten, *Le Crépuscule néo-classique: Thomas Hope* (Paris, 1958).—Morier: *Hajji Baba in Ispahan*, ed. Richard D. Altick (1954).

**1273** *The Last Days of Shelley and Byron: Being the Complete Text of Trelawny's "Recollections,"* ed. "with additions from contemporary sources" by J. E.

Morpurgo (1952).—R. Glynn Grylls, *Trelawny* (1950); Lady Anne Hill, "Tre-lawny's Family Background and Naval Career," *KSJ*, v (1956). 11-32.

Marryat: *Diary in America,* ed. Jules Zanger (Bloomington, Ind., 1960). Oliver Warner, *Captain Marryat: A Rediscovery* (1953).

Lockhart: *John Bull's Letter to Lord Byron,* ed. A. L. Strout (Norman, Okla., 1947). Marion Lochhead, *John Gibson Lockhart* (1954).

**1274** Hogg: *Private Memoirs and Confessions of a Justified Sinner,* with introduction by André Gide (1947). Louis Simpson, *James Hogg* (Edinburgh, 1962); Alan L. Strout, "James Hogg's *Chaldee Manuscript,*" *PMLA*, lxv (1950). 695-718.

**1276** Thomas J. B. Flanagan, *The Irish Novelists, 1800-1850* (1959). On Carleton: Benedict Kiely, *Poor Scholar* (1947).—Marcel Ian Moraud, *Une Irlandaise libérale en France sous la Restauration, Lady Morgan* (Paris, 1954).—On Gerald Griffin: Ethel Mannin, *Two Studies in Integrity* (1954).

**1277** Leonard Cooper, *R. S. Surtees* (1952); Robert L. Collison, *A Jorrocks Handbook* (1964). (Inadvertently omitted from the text is mention of Surtees' most famous novel, *Jorrocks' Jaunts and Jollities* [serialized 1831-1834, book publication 1838].)

**1278** Note 36: See also Friedrich Schubel, *Die "Fashionable Novels"* (Uppsala, 1952).

# XVII. The Background: 1832-1868
## The Progress of Reform

**1279** Woodward's *The Age of Reform* appeared in a revised ed. (Oxford, 1962). One further volume of Halévy's *Histoire du peuple anglais au XIX<sup>e</sup> siècle* appeared after the author's death: *The Age of Peel and Cobden* (1947). David Thomson, *England in the Nineteenth Century* (1950); *English Historical Documents*, Vol. xii (1), 1833-1874, ed. G. M. Young and W. D. Handcock (1956); Asa Briggs, *The Age of Improvement, 1783-1867* (1959); Anthony Wood, *Nineteenth Century Britain, 1815-1914* (1960); W. L. Burn, *The Age of Equipoise: A Study of the Mid-Victorian Generation* (1964).—General studies of the intellectual, cultural, and social background: Bernard N. Schilling, *Human Dignity and the Great Victorians* (1946); *Ideas and Beliefs of the Victorians*, ed. Harman Grisewood (1949); Basil Willey, *Nineteenth Century Studies* (1949) and *More Nineteenth Century Studies* (1956); Jerome H. Buckley, *The Victorian Temper* (Cambridge, Mass., 1951); John W. Dodds, *The Age of Paradox: A Biography of England, 1841-1851* (1952); L. E. Elliott-Binns, *English Thought, 1860-1900* (1956); Walter E. Houghton, *The Victorian Frame of Mind* (New Haven, 1957); Raymond Williams, *Culture and Society, 1780-1950* (1958), Part i; G. M. Young, *Victorian Essays*, ed. Handcock (1962); G. Kitson Clark, *The Making of Victorian England* (1962).—General works on Victorian literature: There is an annual bibliography of books and articles in *MP* (to 1957) and *VS* (1958-    ). Issues for 1932-1944 were gathered into one volume, ed. W. D. Templeman, and those for 1945-1954 into another, ed. Austin Wright (Urbana, Ill., 1945, 1956). Two convenient reviews of scholarship and criticism are *The Victorian Poets: A Guide to Research,* ed. Frederic E. Faverty (Cambridge,

Mass., 1956)—hereafter cited as Faverty—and *Victorian Fiction: A Guide to Research*, ed. Lionel Stevenson (Cambridge, Mass., 1964)—hereafter cited as Stevenson. *The [Pelican] Guide to English Literature*, ed. Boris Ford: Vol. VI, *From Dickens to Hardy* (1958, rev. 1963); *The Reinterpretation of Victorian Literature*, ed. Joseph E. Baker (Princeton, 1950); Sherard Vines, *100 Years of English Literature* [1830-1940] (1950); Clarence R. Decker, *The Victorian Conscience* (1952), on the reaction to realism; Richard D. Altick, *The English Common Reader: A Social History of the Mass Reading Public, 1800-1900* (Chicago, 1957); Geoffrey Tillotson, *Criticism and the Nineteenth Century* (1951), essays on various topics; *Victorian Literature: Modern Essays in Criticism*, ed. Austin Wright (1961).

# XVIII. The Religious Revival and Its Expression in Literature

**1288**  L. E. Elliott-Binns, *The Early Evangelicals* (1953); Ford K. Brown, *Fathers of the Victorians: The Age of Wilberforce* (Cambridge, 1961); Oliver Warner, *William Wilberforce and His Times* (1962); E. M. Forster, *Marianne Thornton* (1956), a biography of a leading member of the Clapham sect; David Spring, "The Clapham Sect: Some Social and Political Aspects," *VS*, v (1961). 35-48.—M. G. Jones, *Hannah More* (Cambridge, 1952), the definitive life; Mary Alden Hopkins, *Hannah More and Her Circle* (1947).

**1290**  Thomas Arnold: *Principles of Church Reform*, with introduction by M. J. Jackson and J. Rogan (1962).—Norman Wymer, *Dr. Arnold of Rugby* (1953); Frances J. Woodward, *The Doctor's Disciples* (1954); T. W. Bamford, *Thomas Arnold* (1960); David Newsome, *Godliness and Good Learning* (1961); Eugene L. Williamson, *The Liberalism of Thomas Arnold* (University, Ala., 1964); Willey, *Nineteenth Century Studies*, ch. II.

**1291**  A projected definitive edition of Newman's works was left incomplete at the death of the editor, Charles Frederick Harrold. The volumes published (1947-1949) were: *Apologia pro Vita Sua, An Essay in Aid of a Grammar of Assent, The Idea of a University, Sermons and Discourses* (2v), *Essays and Sketches* (3v) and *An Essay on the Development of Christian Doctrine*. A number of volumes have presented Newman's previously unpublished or uncollected writings: *University Sketches*, ed. Michael Tierney (Dublin, 1952); *Faith and Prejudice, and Other Unpublished Sermons* (1956); *Catholic Sermons* (1957); *The Argument from Conscience to the Existence of God*, ed. Adrian J. Boekraad and Henry Tristram (Louvain, 1961); *Realizations: Newman's Selection of His Parochial and Plain Sermons*, ed. Vincent F. Blehl (1964). *A Newman Anthology*, ed. W. S. Lilly (1949); *Prose and Poetry*, ed. Geoffrey Tillotson (1957), a selection; *A Newman Reader*, ed. Francis X. Connolly (1964); *Autobiographical Writings*, ed. Tristram (1956); *Letters and Diaries*, ed. Charles S. Dessain and others (1961-    ), a monumental editorial project; *Letters, a Selection*, ed. Derek Stanford and Muriel Spark (1957); Meriol Trevor, *Newman: The Pillar of the Cloud* and *Newman: Light in Winter* (both 1962), the best biography; Eleanor Ruggles, *Journey into Faith* (1948); Maisie Ward, *Young Mr. Newman*

(1948); Seán O'Faoláin, *Newman's Way: The Odyssey of John Henry Newman* (1952); *John Henry Newman: Centenary Essays* (1945); Robert D. Middleton, *Newman and Bloxam: An Oxford Friendship* (1947) and *Newman at Oxford: His Religious Development* (1950); *American Essays for the Newman Centennial,* ed. J. K. Ryan and E. D. Benard (Washington, 1947); Boekraad, *The Personal Conquest of Truth According to Newman* (Louvain, 1955); Owen Chadwick, *From Bossuet to Newman: The Idea of Doctrinal Development* (Cambridge, 1957); Terence Kenney, *The Political Thought of John Henry Newman* (1957); J. H. Walgrave, *Newman the Theologian* (Tournai, 1957, as *Newman: le Développement du dogme;* English trans. 1960); Louis Bouyer, *Newman: His Life and Spirituality* (1958); Ernest E. Reynolds, *Three Cardinals: Newman-Wiseman-Manning* (1958); Thomas S. Bokenkotter, *Cardinal Newman as an Historian* (Louvain, 1959); Tillotson, "Newman's *Essay on Poetry:* an Exposition and Comment," *Perspectives of Criticism,* ed. Harry Levin (Cambridge, Mass., 1950), pp. 161-195 (on the same topic, see also Warren, *English Poetic Theory,* ch. 11); Russell Kirk, "The Conservative Mind of Newman," *Sewanee Rev.,* LX (1952). 659-676; Merritt E. Lawlis, "Newman on the Imagination," *MLN,* LXVIII (1953). 73-80; J. M. Cameron, "The Night Battle: Newman and Empiricism," *VS,* IV (1960). 99-117; John Holloway, *The Victorian Sage* (1953), ch. VI.

**1294** Note 27: Newman's *Idea of a University,* considerably more important than is implied by its relegation to a note, was edited by George N. Shuster (1959) and Martin J. Svaglic (1960). See A. Dwight Culler, *The Imperial Intellect: A Study of Newman's Educational Ideal* (New Haven, 1955) and Fergal McGrath, *Newman's University: Idea and Reality* (1951).

**1295** *Apologia pro Vita Sua,* ed. A. Dwight Culler (Boston, 1956), Philip Hughes (1956), Basil Willey (1964).—As a work of literary art, the *Apologia* has been perhaps more intensively studied than any other example of Victorian non-fictional prose. See Walter E. Houghton, *The Art of Newman's "Apologia"* (New Haven, 1945), and articles by Martin J. Svaglic in *PMLA,* LXVI (1951). 138-148, and *MP,* L (1952). 43-49; by Robert A. Colby in *Jour. of Religion,* XXXIII (1953). 47-57, and *Dublin Rev.,* CCXXVII (1953). 140-156; and by Leonard W. Deen, *ELH,* XXIX (1962). 224-238. On the ideas of the *Apologia,* see *Newman's "Apologia": A Classic Reconsidered,* ed. Vincent F. Blehl and Francis X. Connolly (1964).

**1296** *The Mind of the Oxford Movement,* ed. Owen Chadwick (1960); Willey, *Nineteenth Century Studies,* ch. III.—Note 38: See also Margaret M. Maison, *The Victorian Vision: Studies in the Religious Novel* (1962; English title, *Search Your Soul, Eustace*).

**1297** On F. W. Newman: Willey, *More Nineteenth Century Studies,* ch. I.— Kingsbury Badger, "The Ordeal of Anthony Froude, Protestant Historian," *MLQ,* XIII (1952). 41-55; Willey, *More Nineteenth Century Studies,* ch. III.—Florence M. G. Higham, *Frederick Denison Maurice* (1947); Herbert G. Wood, *Frederick Denison Maurice* (Cambridge, 1950); A. M. Ramsey, *F. D. Maurice and the Conflicts of Modern Theology* (Cambridge, 1951); W. Merlin Davies, *An Introduction to F. D. Maurice's Theology* (1964); Olive Brose, "F. D. Maurice and the Victorian Crisis of Belief," *VS,* III (1960). 227-248.

# XIX. The Theory of Evolution and Its Repercussions

**1299** Douglas Bush, *Science and English Poetry, A Historical Sketch, 1590-1950* (1950), ch. v; Charles C. Gillispie, *Genesis and Geology* (Cambridge, Mass., 1951); Ruth E. Moore, *Man, Time, and Fossils* (1953); Georg Roppen, *Evolution and Poetic Belief* (Oslo, 1956); Loren Eiseley, *Darwin's Century: Evolution and the Men Who Discovered It* (1957); *Forerunners of Darwin, 1745-1859*, ed. Bentley Glass, Owsei Temkin, and William L. Straus, Jr. (Baltimore, 1959).

**1303** Milton Millhauser, *Just Before Darwin: Robert Chambers and "Vestiges"* (Middletown, Conn., 1959).

**1305** *The Origin of Species: A Variorum Text*, ed. Morse Peckham (Philadelphia, 1959); *Charles Darwin and the Voyage of The Beagle*, ed. Nora Barlow (1945), the first full publication of his letters and notebooks from the expedition; *Autobiography*, ed. Sir Francis Darwin (1949) and Barlow (1958), the latter "with original omissions restored"; *The Darwin Reader*, ed. Marston Bates and Philip S. Humphrey (1956); *Darwin for Today: The Essence of His Works*, ed. Stanley E. Hyman (1963).—William Irvine, *Apes, Angels, and Victorians* (1955), a dual biography of Darwin and Huxley; Paul Bigelow Sears, *Charles Darwin: The Naturalist as a Cultural Force* (1950); Ruth E. Moore, *Charles Darwin* (1955); Sir Arthur Keith, *Darwin Revalued* (1955); *A Century of Darwin*, ed. Samuel A. Barnett (Cambridge, Mass., 1958), a collection of fifteen essays; Alvar Ellegård, *Darwin and the General Reader* (Göteborg, 1958), on Darwin's reception in the Victorian press; Gertrude Himmelfarb, *Darwin and the Darwinian Revolution* (1959); Darwin centenary issues of *Antioch Rev.*, xix (Spring, 1959) and *VS*, iii (Sept., 1959); *Evolution After Darwin: the University of Chicago Centennial*, ed. Sol Tax (3v, Chicago, 1960); Hyman, *The Tangled Bank: Darwin, Marx, Frazer and Freud as Imaginative Writers* (1962); Irvine, "The Influence of Darwin on Literature," *Proc. Amer. Philos. Soc.*, ciii (1959). 616-628; James Collins, "Darwin's Impact on Philosophy," *Thought*, xxxiv (1959). 185-248; Lionel Stevenson, "Darwin and the Novel," *NCF*, xv (1960). 29-38; Donald Fleming, "Charles Darwin, the Anesthetic Man," *VS*, iv (1961). 219-236.

**1307** Huxley: *Touchstone for Ethics 1893-1943* (1947), Romanes Lectures by T. H. Huxley and Julian Huxley.—Cyril Bibby, *T. H. Huxley: Scientist, Humanist, and Educator* (1959), and three articles by Bibby: "Thomas Henry Huxley's Idea of a University," *Universities Quar.*, x (1956). 377-389, "The Prince of Controversialists," *Twentieth Century*, clxi (1957). 268-276, and "Huxley and the Reception of the *Origin*," *VS*, iii (1959). 76-86; William Irvine, "Carlyle and T. H. Huxley," *Booker Memorial Studies* (Chapel Hill, 1950), ch. v; Walter E. Houghton, "The Rhetoric of Huxley," *UTQ*, xviii (1949). 159-175; three articles by Charles S. Blinderman: "Thomas Henry Huxley," *Scientific Mo.*, lxxxiv (1957). 171-182, with new material; "Semantic Aspects of T. H. Huxley's Literary Style," *Jour. of Communication*, xii (1962). 171-178; "T. H. Huxley's Theory of Aesthetics: Unity in Diversity," *JAAC*, xxi (1962). 49-55; Sydney Eisen, "Huxley and the Positivists," *VS*, vii (1964). 337-358.

# XX. Thomas Carlyle

**1309** *Carlyle's Unfinished History of German Literature*, ed. Hill Shine (Lexington, Ky., 1951); *Letters to William Graham*, ed. John Graham, Jr. (Princeton, 1950); *Letters to His Wife*, ed. Trudy Bliss (1953); *The Correspondence of Emerson and Carlyle*, ed. Joseph Slater (1964); *Jane Welsh Carlyle: A New Selection of Her Letters*, ed. Bliss (1950). A complete edition of the Carlyle correspondence is being prepared by Charles Richard Sanders. *Carlyle: An Anthology*, ed. G. M. Trevelyan (1953); *Selected Works, Reminiscences, and Letters*, ed. Julian Symons (1956).—Symons, *Thomas Carlyle: The Life and Ideas of a Prophet* (1952), the best modern life; Lawrence and Elisabeth Hanson, *Necessary Evil* (1952), a life of Jane Carlyle; Hill Shine, *Carlyle's Early Reading, to 1834* (Lexington, Ky., 1953); Richard Pankhurst, *The Saint Simonians, Mill, and Carlyle* (1957); Raymond Williams, *Culture and Society* (1958), pp. 77-93; Robert M. Estrich and Hans Sperber, *Three Keys to Language* (1952), pp. 108-125, on Carlyle's influence on contemporary language; Sanders, "Carlyle, Poetry, and the Music of Humanity," *Western Humanities Rev.*, XVI (1962). 53-66; G. B. Tennyson, "Carlyle's Poetry to 1840: A Checklist and Discussion," *VP*, I (1963). 161-181; Willey, *Nineteenth Century Studies*, ch. IV; Warren, *English Poetic Theory*, ch. V, on "The Hero as Poet"; Holloway, *The Victorian Sage*, chs. II-III; Gaylord LeRoy, *Perplexed Prophets* (Philadelphia, 1953), ch. II; Wellek, *History of Modern Criticism*, III. 92-100.

**1310** Hill Shine, "Carlyle's Early Writings and Herder's *Ideen:* The Concept of History," *Booker Memorial Studies* (Chapel Hill, 1950), ch. I; J. W. Smeed, "Thomas Carlyle and Jean Paul Richter," *CL*, XVI (1964). 226-253.

**1313** *Past and Present*, ed. Richard D. Altick (Boston, 1965). Grace Calder, *The Making of "Past and Present"* (New Haven, 1949), a valuable study of Carlyle's habits of composition.

**1316** Study of Carlyle's literary artistry has recently centered on *Sartor Resartus* and the works that led up to it. See Marjorie P. King, "*Illudo Chartis:* An Initial Study in Carlyle's Mode of Composition," *MLR*, XLIX (1954). 164-175; Francis X. Roellinger, Jr., "The Early Development of Carlyle's Style," *PMLA*, LXXII (1957). 936-951; articles by Daniel P. Deneau and John Lindberg in *Victorian Newsletter*, No. 17 (Spring, 1960), pp. 17-23; Leonard W. Deen, "Irrational Form in *Sartor Resartus*," *Texas Stud. in Lit. and Lang.*, V (1963). 438-451; George Levine, "*Sartor Resartus* and the Balance of Fiction," *VS*, VIII (1964). 131-160; G. B. Tennyson, *Sartor Called Resartus* (Princeton, 1965). Other aspects of *Sartor* are studied in Carlisle Moore, "*Sartor Resartus* and the Problem of Carlyle's 'Conversion,'" *PMLA*, LXX (1955). 662-681, and C. R. Sanders, "The Byron Closed in *Sartor Resartus*," *Stud. in Romanticism*, III (1964). 77-108. (Inadvertently omitted from note 28 is C. F. Harrold's edition of *Sartor* [1937], with a long and indispensable introduction to its ideas.)

**1320** H. Ben-Israel, "Carlyle and the French Revolution," *Historical Jour.*,

I (1958). 115-135; Alfred Cobban, "Carlyle's *French Revolution,*" *History,* n.s. XLVIII (1963). 306-316.

## XXI. Philosophy, History, and Miscellaneous Prose

**1322**  Mill: *Prefaces to Liberty: Selected Writings,* ed. Bernard Wisby (Boston, 1959); *Essays on Politics and Culture,* ed. Gertrude Himmelfarb (1962); *Mill on Bentham and Coleridge,* ed. F. R. Leavis (1950); *The Early Draft of John Stuart Mill's Autobiography,* ed. Jack Stillinger (Urbana, Ill., 1961); *Earlier Letters, 1812-1848,* ed. Francis E. Mineka (2v, Toronto, 1963), the first volumes of a projected complete edition of the works; *John Mill's Boyhood Visit to France,* ed. Anna Jean Mill (Toronto, 1960).—Ney MacMinn, J. R. Hainds, and James McN. McCrimmon, *Bibliography of the Published Writings of John Stuart Mill* (Evanston, 1945); Michael St. John Packe, *The Life of John Stuart Mill* (1954), an outstanding biography; F. A. Hayek, *John Stuart Mill and Harriet Taylor: Their Correspondence and Subsequent Marriage* (Chicago, 1951); R. P. Anschutz, *The Philosophy of J. S. Mill* (Oxford, 1953); Karl Britton, *John Stuart Mill* (1953); Iris W. Mueller, *John Stuart Mill and French Thought* (Urbana, Ill., 1956); Richard Pankhurst, *The Saint Simonians, Mill, and Carlyle* (1957); Dorothea Krook, *Three Traditions of Moral Thought* (Cambridge, 1959); Maurice Cowling, *Mill and Liberalism* (Cambridge, 1963); John B. Ellery, *John Stuart Mill* (1964); Britton, "John Stuart Mill: the Ordeal of an Intellectual," *Cambridge Jour.,* II (1948). 96-105; Hainds, "John Stuart Mill's *Examiner* Articles on Art," *JHI,* XI (1950). 215-234; Walter J. Ong, "J. S. Mill's Pariah Poet," *PQ,* XXIX (1950). 333-344; R. V. Sampson, "J. S. Mill: An Interpretation," *Cambridge Jour.,* III (1950). 232-239; R. J. White, "John Stuart Mill," *ibid.,* V (1951). 86-96; Robert Preyer, "The Utilitarian Poetics: John Stuart Mill," *Univ. of Kansas City Rev.,* XIX (1952). 131-136; Keith Rinehart, "John Stuart Mill's *Autobiography:* Its Art and Appeal," *ibid.,* XIX (1953). 265-273; Bertrand Russell, "John Stuart Mill," *Proc. Brit. Acad.,* XLI (1955). 43-59; John M. Robson, "J. S. Mill's Theory of Poetry," *UTQ,* XXIX (1960). 420-438; Robert Carr, "The Religious Thought of John Stuart Mill," *JHI,* XXIII (1962). 475-495; Willey, *Nineteenth Century Studies,* ch. VI; Warren, *English Poetic Theory,* ch. IV.

**1327**  Macaulay: *Prose and Poetry,* ed. G. M. Young (Cambridge, Mass., 1952; *Essays,* ed. Hugh Trevor-Roper (1965).—Robert L. Schuyler, "Macaulay and His *History*—a Hundred Years After," *Political Science Quar.,* LXIII (1948). 161-193; J. H. Plumb, "Thomas Babington Macaulay," *UTQ,* XXVI (1956). 17-31; Andrew Browning, "Lord Macaulay, 1800-59," *Historical Jour.,* II (1959). 149-160; John Clive, "Macaulay, History, and the Historians," *History Today,* IX (1959). 830-836; Edwin M. Yoder, Jr., "Macaulay Revisited," *So. Atl. Quar.,* LXIII (1964). 542-551. The special Macaulay number of *REL,* I, no. 4 (Oct., 1960) contains several useful articles.

**1330**  Waldo H. Dunn, *James Anthony Froude: A Biography* (2v, Oxford, 1961-1963).

**1332** Giles St. Aubyn, *A Victorian Eminence: The Life and Works of Henry Thomas Buckle* (1958).—Lecky: *A Victorian Historian: Private Letters, 1859-1878*, ed. H. M. Hyde (1947); J. J. Auchmuty, *Lecky: A Biographical and Critical Essay* (1946).—W. G. Addison, *J. R. Green* (1946); Robert L. Schuyler, "John Richard Green and his *Short History*," *Political Science Quar.*, LXIV (1949). 321-354; L. M. Angus-Butterworth, "John Richard Green," *So. Atl. Quar.*, XLVI (1947). 109-118.—Acton: *Essays on Freedom and Power*, ed. Gertrude Himmelfarb (Boston, 1948); *Essays on Church and State*, ed. Douglas Woodruff (1952); David Mathew, *Acton: the Formative Years* (1946); George E. Fasnacht, *Acton's Political Philosophy* (1952); Himmelfarb, *Lord Acton: A Study in Conscience and Politics* (Chicago, 1952); Lionel Kochan, *Acton on History* (1954); W. Watkin Davies, "The Politics of Lord Acton," *Hibbert Jour.*, XLV (1946). 21-30; Harold Acton, "Lord Acton," *Chicago Rev.*, XV (1961). 31-44; E. D. Watt, "Ethics and Politics: The Example of Lord Acton," *UTQ*, XXXIII (1964). 279-290.

**1333** Bagehot: *Complete Works*, ed. Norman St. John-Stevas (8v, 1965-    ); *Physics and Politics*, ed. Jacques Barzun (1948); *The English Constitution*, ed. with a long introduction by R. H. S. Crossman (1963).— Alastair Buchan, *The Spare Chancellor* (1959); St. John-Stevas, *Walter Bagehot: A Study of His Life and Thought* (Bloomington, Ind., 1959); St. John-Stevas, "Walter Bagehot as a Writer," *Wiseman Rev.*, CCXXXVII (1963). 38-65; Wellek, *History of Modern Criticism*, IV. 180-185.

Kinglake: *Eothen*, ed. Robin Fedden (1948), P. H. Newby (1949).—Gordon Waterfield, *Layard of Nineveh* (1963); Nora B. Kubie, *Road to Nineveh: The Adventures and Excavations of Sir Austen Henry Layard* (1964); Robert Silverberg, *The Man Who Found Nineveh* (1964).—Burton: *The Perfumed Garden of the Shaykh Nefzawi* (1963); *The City of the Saints*, ed. Fawn M. Brodie (1963). Byron Farwell, *Burton* (1963); Allen Edwardes, *Death Rides a Camel: A Biography of Sir Richard Burton* (1963); Thomas J. Assad, *Three Victorian Travellers: Burton, Blunt, Doughty* (1964); Jonathan Bishop, "The Identities of Sir Richard Burton: The Explorer as Actor," *VS*, I (1957). 119-135.

**1334** Borrow: *Lavengro* and *The Romany Rye*, both ed. Walter Starkie (1948); *The Bible in Spain*, ed. Peter Quennell (1959).—Martin Armstrong, *George Borrow* (1950); Eileen Bigland, *In the Steps of George Borrow* (1951); Brian Vesey-Fitzgerald, *Gypsy Borrow* (1953); René Fréchet, *George Borrow* (Paris, 1956); John E. Tilford, Jr., "The Critical Approach to *Lavengro-Romany Rye*," *SP*, XLVI (1949). 79-96, and "The Formal Artistry of *Lavengro-Romany Rye*," *PMLA*, LXIV (1949). 369-384; Andrew Boyle, "Portraiture in *Lavengro*," *N&Q*, various issues, 1951-1952; Fréchet, "George Borrow devant la critique," *Études anglaises*, VII (1954). 257-270.

Carroll: *The Annotated Alice*, ed. Martin Gardner (1960, rev. 1964); *The Annotated Snark*, ed. Gardner (1962); *Useful and Instructive Poetry*, ed. Derek Hudson (1954); *Diaries*, ed. Roger Lancelyn Green (2v, 1954).—Sidney H. Williams and Falconer Madan, *The Lewis Carroll Handbook* (1962), a revision by R. L. Green of a volume first published in 1931; Alexander Taylor, *The White Knight* (Edinburgh, 1952); Derek Hudson, *Lewis Carroll* (1954); Phyllis Greenacre, *Swift and Carroll* (1955), a psychoanalytic study; Elizabeth Sewell, *The Field of Nonsense* (1952); Green, "The Real Lewis Carroll," *Quarterly Rev.*, CCXCII (1954). 85-97.

# XXII. John Ruskin

**1336**  *Selected Writings,* ed. Peter Quennell (1952); *The Lamp of Beauty: Writings on Art,* ed. Joan Evans (1959); *The Genius of John Ruskin: Selections,* ed. John D. Rosenberg (1963); *Ruskin Today,* ed. Sir Kenneth Clark (1963); *Diaries,* ed. Joan Evans and J. H. Whitehouse (3v, Oxford, 1956-1959); *The Gulf of Years: Letters from John Ruskin to Kathleen Olander,* ed. Rayner Unwin (1953); *Ruskin's Letters from Venice, 1851-52,* ed. John L. Bradley (New Haven, 1955); *Letters to Lord and Lady Mount-Temple,* ed. Bradley (Columbus, Ohio, 1964).—Quennell, *John Ruskin: The Portrait of a Prophet* (1949); Derrick Leon, *Ruskin: The Great Victorian* (1949); Evans, *John Ruskin* (1954); Helen G. Viljoen, *Ruskin's Scottish Heritage* (Urbana, Ill., 1956); Francis G. Townsend, *Ruskin and the Landscape Feeling* (Urbana, Ill., 1951); John T. Fain, *Ruskin and the Economists* (Nashville, 1956); Rosenberg, *The Darkening Glass* (1961); Quentin Bell, *Ruskin* (Edinburgh, 1963); Buckley, *The Victorian Temper,* ch. VIII; Robert Kimbrough, "Calm Between Crises: Pattern and Direction in Ruskin's Mature Thought," *Trans. Wisconsin Acad.,* XLIX (1960). 219-227; LeRoy, *Perplexed Prophets,* ch. IV; Graham Hough, *The Last Romantics* (1947), ch. I; Wellek, *History of Modern Criticism,* III. 136-149.

**1337**  On *Modern Painters,* see Warren, *English Poetic Theory,* ch. X, and the following articles by Van Akin Burd: "Another Light on the Writing of *Modern Painters,*" *PMLA,* LXVIII (1953). 755-763; "Ruskin's Quest for a Theory of Imagination," *MLQ,* XVII (1956). 60-72; "Ruskin's Defense of Turner: The Imitative Phase," *PQ,* XXXVII (1958). 465-483; and "Background to *Modern Painters:* The Tradition and the Turner Controversy," *PMLA,* LXXIV (1959). 254-267.

**1338**  Note 10: The circumstances of the annulment are controversially dealt with in Admiral Sir William James, *John Ruskin and Effie Gray* (1947; English title, *The Order of Release*) and J. H. Whitehouse, *Vindication of Ruskin* (1950).

# XXIII. Charles Dickens, Wilkie Collins, and Charles Reade

**1344**  On Victorian fiction generally: Michael Sadleir, *XIX Century Fiction: A Bibliographical Record Based on His Own Collection* (2v, 1951); *Victorian Fiction: A Guide to Research,* ed. Lionel Stevenson (Cambridge, Mass., 1964); Lucien Leclaire, *A General Analytical Bibliography of the Regional Novelists of the British Isles (1800-1950)* (Clermont-Ferrand, 1954); Leo J. Henkin, "Problems and Digressions in the Victorian Novel (1860-1900)," *Bull. of Bibliography,* XVIII (1943)-XX (1950). Walter Allen, *The English Novel* (1954), chs. IV-V; Lionel Stevenson, *The English Novel: A Panorama* (Boston, 1960), chs. IX-XV; Frederick R. Karl, *An Age of Fiction: The Nineteenth Century British Novel* (1964). Richard Stang, *The Theory of the Novel in England, 1850-1870* (1959);

Kenneth Graham, *English Criticism of the Novel, 1865-1900* (1965); Irène Simon, *Formes du roman anglais de Dickens à Joyce* (Liége, 1949); Frank O'Connor, *The Mirror in the Roadway: A Study of the Modern Novel* (1956); V. S. Pritchett, *The Living Novel* (1946); *From Jane Austen to Joseph Conrad,* ed. R. C. Rathburn and Martin Steinmann (Minneapolis, 1958), a large collection of critical essays; Leclaire, *Le Roman régionaliste dans les Iles Britanniques (1800-1950)* (Clermont-Ferrand, 1954); Margaret Dalziel, *Popular Fiction 100 Years Ago* (1957); Louis James, *Fiction for the Working Man 1830-1850* (1963); Patricia Thomson, *The Victorian Heroine: A Changing Ideal, 1837-1873* (1956); Mario Praz, *The Hero in Eclipse in Victorian Fiction* (1956); Mortimer R. Proctor, *The English University Novel* (Berkeley, 1957); Margaret M. Maison, *The Victorian Vision: Studies in the Religious Novel* (1962); Kathleen Tillotson, *Novels of the Eighteen-Forties* (1954), especially Part 1, on the authors, publishers, and readers of fiction in the period; Gilbert Phelps, *The Russian Novel in English Fiction* (1956); Stevenson, "The Intellectual Novel in the Nineteenth Century," *Personalist,* XXXI (1950). 42-57, 157-166; G. Armour Craig, "The Unpoetic Compromise: On the Relation between Private Vision and Social Order in Nineteenth-Century English Fiction," *Society and Self in the Novel (English Institute Essays 1955),* ed. Mark Schorer (1956), pp. 26-50, and "Victims and Spokesmen: The Image of Society in the Novel," *1859: Entering an Age of Crisis,* ed. Philip Appleman *et al.* (Bloomington, Ind., 1959), pp. 229-246.

New Oxford Illustrated Dickens (21v, 1947-1958). A long-needed edition with textual authority and scholarly apparatus is being published by the Clarendon Press. *Speeches,* ed. K. J. Fielding (Oxford, 1960); Pilgrim edition of *Letters,* ed. Madeline House and Graham Storey (11v, Oxford, 1965-    ); *The Heart of Charles Dickens,* ed. Edgar Johnson (1952; English title, *Letters from Charles Dickens to Angela Burdett-Coutts); Selected Letters,* ed. F. W. Dupee (1960).—William Miller, *The Dickens Student and Collector: A List of Writings Relating to Charles Dickens and His Works, 1836-1945* (Cambridge, Mass., 1946), the fullest bibliography but very inaccurate; cf. severe review in *Papers of the Bibl. Soc. of America,* XLI (1947). 293-320. Extensive bibliography of recent criticism in Stevenson, ch. III. Edgar Johnson, *Charles Dickens, His Tragedy and Triumph* (2v, 1952), the standard modern biography; Hesketh Pearson, *Dickens: His Character, Comedy, and Career* (1949); Jack Lindsay, *Charles Dickens: A Biographical and Critical Study* (1950); Julian Symons, *Charles Dickens* (1951); Sylvère Monod, *Dickens Romancier* (Paris, 1953); George H. Ford, *Dickens and His Readers: Aspects of Novel-Criticism Since 1836* (Princeton, 1955); John Butt and Kathleen Tillotson, *Dickens at Work* (1957), an illuminating study of Dickens' manuscripts and work sheets; K. J. Fielding, *Charles Dickens: A Critical Introduction* (1958, rev. Boston, 1964); J. Hillis Miller, *Charles Dickens: The World of His Novels* (Cambridge, Mass., 1958); Monroe Engel, *The Maturity of Dickens* (Cambridge, Mass., 1959); John Manning, *Dickens and Education* (Toronto, 1959); A. O. J. Cockshut, *The Imagination of Charles Dickens* (1961); P. W. Collins, *Dickens and Crime* (1962) and *Dickens and Education* (1963); J. C. Reid, *The Hidden World of Charles Dickens (Univ. of Auckland Bulletin,* LXI [1962]); *Dickens and the Twentieth Century,* ed. John Gross and Gabriel Pearson (1962), a collection of original essays on all of the novels; Steven Marcus, *Dickens from Pickwick to Dombey* (1965); Robert Garis, *The Dickens Theatre: A Reassessment of the Novels* (Oxford, 1965); Taylor Stoehr, *Dickens: The Dreamer's Stance* (Ithaca, 1965). A small selection of essays and chapters on various topics: Richard Aldington, "The Underworld of Young Dickens," *Four English Portraits* (1948), pp. 147-189; Warrington Winters, "Dickens and the Psychology of Dreams," *PMLA*, LXIII (1948). 984-1006; Dorothy Van Ghent, "The Dickens World: A View from Todgers's," *Sewanee Rev.*, LVIII (1950). 419-438; Graham Greene, "The Young Dickens," *The Lost Childhood and Other Essays* (1951), pp. 51-57; Frank O'Connor, "Dickens: The Intrusion of the Audience," *The Mirror in the Roadway* (1956), pp. 70-82; Peter Coveney, "The Child in Dickens," *Poor Monkey* (1957), ch. v; Douglas Bush, "A Note on Dickens' Humor," *From Jane Austen to Joseph Conrad*, pp. 82-91; Lauriat Lane, Jr., "Dickens' Archetypal Jew," *PMLA*, LXXIII (1958). 94-100 (cf. Harry Stone, "Dickens and the Jews," *VS*, II [1959]. 223-253); R. D. McMaster, "Dickens and the Horrific," *Dalhousie Rev.*, XXXVIII (1958). 18-28; John Henry Raleigh, "Dickens and the Sense of Time," *NCF*, XIII (1958). 127-137; Stone, "Dickens and Interior Monologue," *PQ*, XXXVIII (1959). 52-65; Ellen Moers, *The Dandy* (1960), ch. x; Barbara Hardy, "The Change of Heart in Dickens' Novels," *VS*, v (1961). 49-67; Randolph Quirk, "Some Observations on the Language of Dickens," *REL*, II, no. 3 (1961). 19-28; *The Dickens Critics*, ed. Ford and Lane (Ithaca, 1961); *Discussions of Charles Dickens*, ed. William Ross Clark (Boston, 1961).

**1345**  Note 2: Ada Nisbet, *Dickens and Ellen Ternan* (Berkeley, 1952), confirms the story of the liaison beyond reasonable doubt. Felix Aylmer, *Dickens Incognito* (1959) adds more evidence, although his most sensational "discovery" —that of the birth of a child to Ellen Ternan—has since been disproved.

**1346**  General treatments of *The Pickwick Papers* in the perspective of Dickens' subsequent career are found in Miller, *Charles Dickens: The World of His Novels*, ch. 1; Marcus, *Dickens from Pickwick to Dombey*, ch. 1. Special aspects of the book are examined in H. N. MacLean, "Mr. Pickwick and the Seven Deadly Sins," *NCF*, VIII (1953). 198-212; David M. Bevington, "Seasonal Relevance in *The Pickwick Papers*," *NCF*, XVI (1961). 219-230; William Axton, "Unity and Coherence in *The Pickwick Papers*," *SEL*, v (1965). 663-676.

**1347**  *Oliver Twist*, ed. J. Hillis Miller (1962). V. S. Pritchett, "*Oliver Twist*," *Books in General* (1953), pp. 191-196; Kathleen Tillotson, "*Oliver Twist*," *E&S*, n.s. XII (1959). 87-105; Alec Lucas, "*Oliver Twist* and the Newgate Novel," *Dalhousie Rev.*, XXXIV (1955). 381-387; Keith Hollingsworth, *The Newgate Novel* (Detroit, 1963), pp. 111-130; Kettle, I. 123-138.

**1348**  James K. Gottshall, "Devils Abroad: The Unity and Significance of *Barnaby Rudge*," *NCF*, XVI (1961). 133-146; Harold F. Folland, "The Doer and the Deed: Theme and Pattern in *Barnaby Rudge*," *PMLA*, LXXIV (1959). 406-417.—Edwin B. Benjamin, "The Structure of *Martin Chuzzlewit*," *PQ*, XXXIV (1955). 39-47.—*Dombey and Son*, ed. Edgar Johnson (1963). Kathleen Tillotson, "*Dombey and Son*," *Novels of the Eighteen-Forties*, pp. 157-201; William Axton, "Tonal Unity in *Dombey and Son*," *PMLA*, LXXVIII (1963). 341-348; F. R. Leavis, "*Dombey and Son*," *Sewanee Rev.*, LXX (1962). 177-201.

**1349**  *David Copperfield*, ed. E. K. Brown (1950), George H. Ford (Boston,

1958), Edgar Johnson (1962). Brown, *"David Copperfield," Yale Rev.*, xxxvii (1948). 651-666; Gwendolyn B. Needham, "The Undisciplined Heart of David Copperfield," *NCF*, ix (1954). 81-107; Arnold Kettle, "Thoughts on *David Copperfield*," *REL*, ii, no. 3 (1961). 65-74; Roger Gard, *"David Copperfield," EIC*, xv (1965). 313-325.—*Bleak House*, ed. Morton D. Zabel (1956). George H. Ford, "Self-Help and the Helpless in *Bleak House," From Jane Austen to Joseph Conrad*, pp. 92-105; Norman Friedman, "The Shadow and the Sun: Notes Toward a Reading of *Bleak House*," *Boston Univ. Stud. in English*, iii (1957). 147-166; Louis Crompton, "Satire and Symbolism in *Bleak House*," *NCF*, xii (1958). 284-303; James H. Broderick and John E. Grant, "The Identity of Esther Summerson," *MP*, lv (1958). 252-258; Robert A. Donovan, "Structure and Idea in *Bleak House*," *ELH*, xxix (1962). 175-201; articles by Trevor Blount on the novel's topicality, in *RES*, n.s. xiv (1963). 370-378; *MLQ*, xxv (1964). 295-307; *MP*, lxii (1965). 325-339; *MLR*, lx (1965). 340-351; and *EIC*, xv (1965). 414-427.—*Hard Times*, ed. W. W. Watt (1958). F. R. Leavis, *"Hard Times:* An Analytic Note," *The Great Tradition* (1948), pp. 227-248 (cf. reply by David H. Hirsch, *Criticism*, vi [1964]. 1-16).

**1350** Lionel Trilling, *"Little Dorrit," Kenyon Rev.*, xv (1953). 577-590; Edmund Bergler, "*Little Dorrit* and Dickens' Intuitive Knowledge of Psychic Masochism," *American Imago*, xiv (1957). 371-388; John Butt, "The Topicality of *Little Dorrit*," *UTQ*, xxix (1959). 1-10; R. D. McMaster, *"Little Dorrit:* Experience and Design," *Queen's Quar.*, lxvii (1961). 530-538.—*A Tale of Two Cities*, ed. Edward Wagenknecht (1950), Morton D. Zabel (1958).—*Great Expectations*, ed. Earle Davis (1948), Louis Crompton (Indianapolis, 1964), Angus Calder (1965). Van Ghent, pp. 125-138 (cf. Ruth M. Vande Kieft, "Patterns of Communication in *Great Expectations*," *NCF*, xv [1961]. 325-334, and George Levine, "Communication in *Great Expectations*," *NCF*, xviii [1963]. 175-181); G. Robert Stange, "Expectations Well Lost: Dickens' Fable for His Time," *College English*, xvi (1954). 9-17; Julian Moynahan, "The Hero's Guilt: The Case of *Great Expectations*," *EIC*, x (1960). 60-79; John H. Hagan, Jr., "The Poor Labyrinth: The Theme of Social Injustice in Dickens's *Great Expectations*," *NCF*, ix (1954). 169-178, and "Structural Patterns in Dickens's *Great Expectations*," *ELH*, xxi (1954). 54-66; Howard Mumford Jones, "On Rereading *Great Expectations*," *Southwest Rev.*, xxxix (1954). 328-335; Thomas E. Connolly, "Technique in *Great Expectations*," *PQ*, xxxiv (1955). 48-55; Arnold P. Drew, "Structure in *Great Expectations*," *Dickensian*, lii (1956). 123-127; K. J. Fielding, "The Critical Autonomy of *Great Expectations*," *REL*, ii, no. 3 (1961). 75-88; Charles R. Forker, "The Language of Hands in *Great Expectations*," *Texas Stud. in Lit. and Lang.*, iii (1961). 280-293; Barbara Hardy, "Food and Ceremony in *Great Expectations*," *EIC*, xiii (1963). 351-363; Harry Stone, "Fire, Hand, and Gate: Dickens' *Great Expectations*," *Kenyon Rev.*, xxiv (1962). 662-691; Joseph A. Hynes, "Image and Symbol in *Great Expectations*," *ELH*, xxx (1963). 258-292. A number of these articles are reprinted in *Assessing "Great Expectations*," ed. Richard Lettis and William E. Morris (San Francisco, 1960).—Robert Morse, *"Our Mutual Friend," Partisan Rev.*, xvi (1949). 277-289; Sylvère Monod, "L'Expression dans *Our Mutual Friend:* manière ou maniérisme?", *Études anglaises*, x (1957). 37-48; R. D. McMaster, "Birds of Prey: A Study of *Our Mutual Friend*," *Dalhousie Rev.*, xl (1960). 372-381; Robert Barnard, "The Choral Symphony: *Our Mutual Friend*," *REL*, ii, no. 3 (1961). 89-99; Sister M. Corona Sharp, "The Archetypal

Feminine: *Our Mutual Friend,*" *Univ. of Kansas City Rev.,* xxvii (1961). 307-311, xxviii (1961). 74-80.

**1351** *The Mystery of Edwin Drood,* ed. "Michael Innes" [J. I. M. Stewart] (1950), C. Day Lewis (1956). Richard M. Baker, *The Drood Murder Case* (Berkeley, 1951); Felix Aylmer, *The Drood Case* (1964).

**1353** Collins: Bibliography in Stevenson, pp. 277-284. Kenneth Robinson, *Wilkie Collins* (1951), the best biography; Robert Ashley, *Wilkie Collins* (1952); Nuel P. Davis, *The Life of Wilkie Collins* (Urbana, Ill., 1956); Bradford A. Booth, "Wilkie Collins and the Art of Fiction," *NCF,* vi (1951). 131-143.—Le Fanu: *In a Glass Darkly,* ed. V. S. Pritchett (1947); *A Strange Adventure in the Life of Miss Laura Mildmay* (1947); *Uncle Silas,* ed. Elizabeth Bowen (1948); *The Diabolical Genius,* ed. Michael Eenhoorn (1959), a collection of his writings. Nelson Browne, *Sheridan Le Fanu* (1951).—Eileen Bigland, *Ouida: The Passionate Victorian* (1950).

**1354** Reade: Bibliography in Stevenson, pp. 284-293. Wayne Burns, *Charles Reade: A Study in Victorian Authorship* (1961); Royal A. Gettmann, "The Serialization of Reade's *A Good Fight,*" *NCF,* vi (1951). 21-32; J. B. Price, "Charles Reade and Charles Kingsley," *Contemporary Rev.,* clxxxiii (1953). 161-166; Sheila M. Smith, "Propaganda and Hard Facts in Charles Reade's Didactic Novels," *Renaissance and Mod. Stud.,* iv (1960). 135-149.

# XXIV. Thackeray and Trollope

**1355** Thackeray: Bibliography in Stevenson, ch. iv. Gordon N. Ray, *Thackeray: The Uses of Adversity, 1811-1846* (1955) and *Thackeray: The Age of Wisdom, 1847-1863* (1958), the standard biography; Ray, *The Buried Life: A Study of the Relation between Thackeray's Fiction and His Personal History* (Cambridge, Mass., 1952); J. Y. T. Greig, *Thackeray: A Reconsideration* (1950); Lambert Ennis, *Thackeray, the Sentimental Cynic* (Evanston, Ill., 1950); Geoffrey Tillotson, *Thackeray the Novelist* (Cambridge, 1954); John Loofbourow, *Thackeray and the Form of Fiction* (Princeton, 1964); Eva B. Touster, "The Literary Relationship of Thackeray and Fielding," *JEGP,* xlvi (1947). 383-394; John A. Lester, Jr., "Thackeray's Narrative Technique," *PMLA,* lxix (1954). 392-409; Ralph W. Rader, "Thackeray's Injustice to Fielding," *JEGP,* lvi (1957). 203-212; Greig, "Thackeray, a Novelist by Accident," *From Jane Austen to Joseph Conrad,* pp. 72-81; Myron Taube, "Thackeray and the Reminiscential Vision," *NCF,* xviii (1963). 247-259.

**1356** *Contributions to the "Morning Chronicle,"* ed. Gordon N. Ray (Urbana, Ill., 1955).—On the background of *Catherine,* and Thackeray's intentions, see Keith Hollingsworth, *The Newgate Novel* (Detroit, 1963), pp. 148-165, and Robert A. Colby, "*Catherine:* Thackeray's Credo," *RES,* n.s. xv (1965). 381-396. —Note 3: The list is extended by Gordon N. Ray, "Thackeray and *Punch:* Forty-Four Newly Identified Contributions," *LTLS,* Jan. 1, 1939, p. 16.

**1357** *The Rose and the Ring,* ed. G. N. Ray (1947), a facsimile reproduction of the manuscript.—*Vanity Fair,* ed. Joseph Warren Beach (1950), John W. Dodds (1955), Lionel Stevenson (1958), Geoffrey and Kathleen Tillotson (1963), the last-named important for text. Kathleen Tillotson, "*Vanity Fair,*" *Novels of* *the Eighteen-Forties,* pp. 224-256; Russell A. Fraser, "Pernicious Casuistry: A Study of Character in *Vanity Fair,*" *NCF,* xii (1957). 137-147; G. Armour Craig, "On the Style of *Vanity Fair,*" *Style in Prose Fiction (English Institute Essays 1958),* ed. H. C. Martin (1959), pp. 87-113; E. D. H. Johnson, "*Vanity Fair* and *Amelia:* Thackeray in the Perspective of the Eighteenth Century," *MP,* lix (1961). 100-113; Myron Taube, "Contrast as a Principle of Structure in *Vanity Fair,*" *NCF,* xviii (1963). 119-135; A. E. Dyson, "*Vanity Fair:* an Irony against Heroes," *Critical Quar.,* vi (1964). 11-32; Joan Stevens, "Thackeray's *Vanity Fair,*" *REL,* vi, no. 1 (1965). 19-38; Ann Y. Wilkinson, "The Tomeavesian Way of Knowing the World: Technique and Meaning in *Vanity Fair,*" *ELH,* xxxii (1965). 370-387; Edgar F. Harden, "The Field of Mars in *Vanity Fair,*" *Tennessee Stud. in Lit.,* x (1965). 123-132; Van Ghent, pp. 139-152.

**1358** Martin Fido, "*The History of Pendennis:* A Reconsideration," *EIC,* xiv (1964). 363-379.—*Henry Esmond,* ed. Gordon N. Ray (1950), G. Robert Stange (1962). Howard O. Brogan, "Rachel Esmond and the Dilemma of the Victorian Ideal of Womanhood," *ELH,* xiii (1946). 223-232; John E. Tilford, Jr., "The Love Theme of *Henry Esmond,*" *PMLA,* lxvii (1952). 684-701; William H. Marshall, "Dramatic Irony in *Henry Esmond,*" *Revue des langues vivantes,* xxvii (1961). 35-42; George J. Worth, "The Unity of *Henry Esmond,*" *NCF,* xv (1961). 345-353; Henri-A. Talon, "Time and Memory in Thackeray's *Henry Esmond,*" *RES,* n.s. xiii (1962). 147-156.

**1359** Russell A. Fraser, "Sentimentality in Thackeray's *The Newcomes,*" *NCF,* iv (1949). 187-196.

**1361** Oxford Illustrated Trollope, ed. Michael Sadleir and Frederick Page (1948-1954), abandoned after the publication of only eight volumes. Crown Edition of the political novels, also ed. Sadleir and Page (15v, 1948-1954); *North America,* ed. Donald Smalley and Bradford Booth (1951); *Hunting Sketches,* ed. L. Edwards (1952); *Did He Steal It?,* ed. R. H. Taylor (Princeton, 1952); *The Two Heroines of Plumplington* (1953); *The Trollope Reader,* ed. Esther C. Dunn and M. E. Dodd (1947); *Letters,* ed. Booth (1951).—Bibliography in Stevenson, ch. v. Elizabeth Bowen, *Anthony Trollope: A New Judgement* (1946); Beatrice C. Brown, *Anthony Trollope* (1950); A. O. J. Cockshut, *Anthony Trollope: A Critical Study* (1955); Rafael Helling, *A Century of Trollope Criticism* (Helsingfors, 1956); Booth, *Anthony Trollope: Aspects of His Life and Art* (Bloomington, Ind., 1958); Chauncey B. Tinker, "Trollope," *Yale Rev.,* xxxvi (1947). 424-434; W. L. Burn, "Anthony Trollope's Politics," *Nineteenth Century and After,* cxliii (1948). 161-171; Mario Praz, "Anthony Trollope," *English Miscellany,* i (1950). 93-143; Asa Briggs, "Trollope, Bagehot, and *The English Constitution,*" *Cambridge Jour.,* v (1952). 327-338; John Hagan, "The Divided Mind of Anthony Trollope," *NCF,* xiv (1959). 1-26; Hugh Sykes Davies, "Trollope and His Style," *REL,* i, no. 4 (1960). 73-85; Jerome Thale, "The Problem of Structure in Trollope," *NCF,* xv (1960). 147-157; Audrey L. Laski, "Myths of Character: An Aspect of the Novel," *NCF,* xiv (1960). 333-343; Gerald Warner Brace, "The World of Trollope," *Texas Quar.,* iv, no. 3 (1961). 180-189; John E. Dustin, "Thematic Alternation in Trollope," *PMLA,* lxxvii (1962). 280-287; William Cadbury, "Shape and Theme: Determinants of Trollope's Forms," *PMLA,* lxxviii (1963). 326-332; Winifred G. Gerould and James T. Gerould, *A*

*Guide to Trollope* (Princeton, 1948).—Of the Barchester novels, *The Warden*
has been edited by Booth (1962), *Barchester Towers* by Booth (1949) and
Sadleir (1956), the two together by Harlan Hatcher (1950), *Dr. Thorne* by
Elizabeth Bowen (Boston, 1959), and *The Last Chronicles of Barset* by Gerald
Warner Brace (1964) and Arthur Mizener (Boston, 1964). Sherman Hawkins,
"Mr. Harding's Church Music," *ELH*, XXIX (1962). 202-223; M. A. Goldberg,
"Trollope's *The Warden:* A Commentary on the 'Age of Equipoise,' " *NCF*,
XVII (1963). 381-390; William Cadbury, "Character and the Mock Heroic in
*Barchester Towers*," *Texas Stud. in Lit. and Lang.*, v (1964). 509-519. The con-
temporary scandals utilized in *The Warden* are discussed by G. F. A. Best, "The
Road to Hiram's Hospital," *VS*, v (1961). 135-150; Ralph Arnold, *The Whiston
Matter* (1961); and R. B. Martin, *Enter Rumour* (1962), ch. III.—*Autobiography*,
ed. Booth (Berkeley, 1947) and Page (1950: part of the Oxford Illustrated
Trollope).—Note 8: *Domestic Manners of the Americans*, ed. Donald Smalley
(1949). W. H. Chaloner, "Mrs. Trollope and the Early Factory System," *VS*, IV
(1960). 159-166.

## XXV. Other Novelists of the Mid-Century

**1364** Bulwer-Lytton: *The Last Days of Pompeii*, ed. Edgar Johnson (1957).—
Bibliography in Stevenson, pp. 35-43. The Earl of Lytton, *Bulwer-Lytton* (1948);
Curtis Dahl, "Bulwer-Lytton and the School of Catastrophe," *PQ*, XXXII (1953).
428-442, and "History on the Hustings: Bulwer-Lytton's Historical Novels of
Politics," *From Jane Austen to Joseph Conrad*, pp. 72-81; Michael Lloyd, "Bulwer-
Lytton and the Idealizing Principle," *English Miscellany*, VII (1956). 25-39;
Joseph I. Fradin, " 'The Absorbing Tyranny of Every-day Life': Bulwer-Lytton's
*A Strange Story*," *NCF*, XVI (1961). 1-16; Geoffrey Wagner, "A Forgotten Satire:
Bulwer-Lytton's *The Coming Race*," *NCF*, XIX (1965). 379-385; Ellen Moers,
*The Dandy* (1960), ch. III; Keith Hollingsworth, *The Newgate Novel* (Detroit,
1963), ch. IV.

**1365** Disraeli: Bibliography in Stevenson, pp. 22-35. Hesketh Pearson, *Dizzy*
(1951); Cecil Roth, *Benjamin Disraeli* (1952); Bernard R. Jerman, *The Young
Disraeli* (Princeton, 1960); Muriel Masefield, *Peacocks and Primroses: A Survey
of Disraeli's Novels* (1953); Robert Hamilton, "Disraeli and the Two Nations,"
*Quarterly Rev.*, CCLXXXVIII (1950). 102-115, on *Sybil;* Eric Forbes-Boyd, "Disraeli,
the Novelist," *E&S*, n.s. III (1950). 100-117; Maurice Edelman, "A Political Novel
[*Coningsby*]," *LTLS*, Aug. 7, 1959, pp. x-xi; Holloway, *The Victorian Sage*, ch.
IV; Ellen Moers, *The Dandy* (1960), ch. IV.

**1367** Kingsley: *Westward Ho!* (1953) and *Hereward the Wake* (1955), both
ed. L. A. G. Strong; *American Notes: Letters from a Lecture Tour*, ed. Robert
B. Martin (Princeton, 1958).—Bibliography in Stevenson, pp. 263-276. Guy
Kendall, *Charles Kingsley and His Ideas* (1947); Una Pope-Hennessy, *Canon
Charles Kingsley* (1948); Martin, *The Dust of Combat* (1960); Gillian Beer,
"Charles Kingsley and the Literary Image of the Countryside," *VS*, VIII (1965).
243-254.

**1369** Gaskell: *Cranford* and *Cousin Phillis*, ed. Elizabeth Jenkins (1947);

*Mary Barton,* ed. Lettice Cooper (1947) and Myron F. Brightfield (1958); *Wives and Daughters,* ed. Rosamond Lehmann (1948); *North and South,* ed. Elizabeth Bowen (1952); *Letters,* ed. J. A. V. Chapple and Arthur Pollard (Manchester, 1965).—Bibliography in Stevenson, pp. 245-263. Yvonne ffrench, *Mrs. Gaskell* (1949); Annette B. Hopkins, *Elizabeth Gaskell* (1952); Edgar Wright, *Mrs. Gaskell: The Basis for Reassessment* (1965); Pollard, *Mrs. Gaskell* (Manchester, 1965); John G. Sharps, *Mrs. Gaskell's Observation and Invention* (Fontwell, Sussex, 1965); H. P. Collins, "The Naked Sensibility: Elizabeth Gaskell," *EIC,* III (1953). 60-72; Tillotson, *Novels of the Eighteen-Forties,* pp. 202-223, on *Mary Barton;* Pollard, "The Novels of Mrs. Gaskell," *Bulletin of the John Rylands Lib.,* XLIII (1961). 403-425; Martin Dodsworth, "Women Without Men at Cranford," *EIC,* XIII (1963). 132-145.

Note 8: Angela Thirkell, "Henry Kingsley, 1830-1876," *NCF,* V (1950). 175-187, and "The Works of Henry Kingsley," *NCF,* V (1951). 273-293; Robert Lee Wolff, "Henry Kingsley," *Harvard Library Bull.,* XIII (1959). 195-226.—Edward C. Mack and W. H. G. Armytage, *Thomas Hughes* (1953).

**1370**   Note 11: Joseph B. Rivlin, *Harriet Martineau: A Bibliography of Her Separately Printed Books* (1947); Vera Wheatley, *The Life and Work of Harriet Martineau* (1957); Robert K. Webb, *Harriet Martineau: A Radical Victorian* (1960).—Margaret Mare and Alicia C. Percival, *Victorian Best-Seller: The World of Charlotte Mary Yonge* (1948).

**1370-1371**   Heather Edition of the Brontës' novels, ed. Phyllis Bentley (6v, 1949); Charlotte Brontë's novels, ed. Margaret Lane (4v, 1953-1957). Emily's *Complete Poems,* ed. Philip Henderson (1951); *Gondal's Queen,* ed. Fannie E. Ratchford (Austin, Tex., 1955), eighty-four of Emily's poems rearranged into a coherent narrative; *Letters of the Brontës,* ed. Muriel Spark (Norman, Okla., 1954), a selection.—Bibliography in Stevenson, ch. VI. Bentley, *The Brontës* (1947); Lawrence and Elisabeth Hanson, *The Four Brontës* (1949); Muriel Spark and Derek Stanford, *Emily Brontë: Her Life and Work* (1953); C. Day Lewis, "Emily Brontë and Freedom," *Notable Images of Virtue* (Toronto, 1954), ch. 1; Jacques Blondel, *Emily Brontë: Expérience spirituelle et création poétique* (Paris, 1955); Ada Harrison and Derek Stanford, *Anne Brontë: Her Life and Work* (1959); Winifred Gérin, *Anne Brontë* (1959); Margaret Lane, *The Brontë Story: A Reconsideration of Mrs. Gaskell's "Life of Charlotte Brontë"* (1953); Richard Chase, "The Brontës: A Centennial Observance," *Kenyon Rev.,* IX (1947). 487-506; Melvin R. Watson, "Form and Substance in the Brontë Novels," *From Jane Austen to Joseph Conrad,* pp. 106-117; Robert B. Heilman, "Charlotte Brontë's 'New' Gothic," *ibid.,* pp. 118-132, and "Charlotte Brontë, Reason, and the Moon," *NCF,* XIV (1960). 283-302; J. Hillis Miller, *The Disappearance of God,* ch. IV (on Emily); Philip Momberger, "Self and the World in the Works of Charlotte Brontë," *ELH,* XXXII (1965). 349-369.

**1371**   Note 15: Daphne du Maurier, *The Infernal World of Branwell Brontë* (1960); Winifred Gérin, *Branwell Brontë* (1961)—neither very satisfactory.—Note 16: See also Mrs. Harrison's *The Clue to the Brontës* (1948), on the influence of Evangelicalism.—Note 19: Annette B. Hopkins, *The Father of the Brontës* (Baltimore, 1958); John Lock and W. T. Dixon, *A Man of Sorrow* (1965).

**1374**   *Jane Eyre,* ed. Joe Lee Davis (1950), William Peden (1950), Mark

Schorer (Boston, 1959). Kathleen Tillotson, *"Jane Eyre," Novels of the Eighteen-Forties,* pp. 257-313; M. H. Scargill, " 'All Passion Spent': A Revaluation of *Jane Eyre," UTQ,* XIX (1950). 120-125; Edgar F. Shannon, Jr., "The Present Tense in *Jane Eyre," NCF,* X (1955). 141-145; William H. Marshall, "The Self, the World, and the Structure of *Jane Eyre," Revue des langues vivantes,* XXVII (1961). 416-425; R. E. Hughes, *"Jane Eyre:* The Unbaptized Dionysos," *NCF,* XVIII (1964). 347-364.

**1375**   Jacob Korg, "The Problem of Unity in *Shirley," NCF,* XII (1957). 125-136; Asa Briggs, "Private and Social Themes in *Shirley," Brontë Soc. Trans.,* XIII (1958). 203-219; J. M. S. Tompkins, "Caroline Helstone's Eyes," *ibid.,* XIV (1961). 18-28.—Robert A. Colby, *"Villette* and the Life of the Mind," *PMLA,* LXXV (1960). 410-419.

**1377**   *Wuthering Heights,* ed. Bruce McCullough (1950), Mark Schorer (1950), Royal A. Gettmann (1950), Bonamy Dobrée (1955), V. S. Pritchett (Boston, 1956), Thomas Moser (1962), T. Crehan (1962), William Sale (1963), David Daiches (1965).—Mary Visick, *The Genesis of "Wuthering Heights"* (1958); D. G. Klingopulos, "The Novel as Dramatic Poem: *Wuthering Heights," Scrutiny,* XIV (1947). 269-286; Derek Traversi, *"Wuthering Heights* After a Hundred Years," *Dublin Rev.,* CCXXII (1949). 154-168; Melvin R. Watson, "Tempest in the Soul: The Theme and Structure of *Wuthering Heights," NCF,* IV (1949). 87-100; Schorer, "Fiction and the 'Matrix of Analogy,' " *Kenyon Rev.,* XI (1949). 539-560; B. H. Lehman, "Of Material, Subject, and Form: *Wuthering Heights," The Image of the Work* (Berkeley, 1955), pp. 3-17; John K. Mathison, "Nelly Dean and the Power of *Wuthering Heights," NCF,* XI (1956). 106-129; Carl R. Woodring, "The Narrators of *Wuthering Heights," NCF,* XI (1957). 298-305; James Hafley, "The Villain in *Wuthering Heights," NCF,* XIII (1958). 199-215; Miriam Allott, *"Wuthering Heights:* The Rejection of Heathcliff?", *EIC,* VIII (1958). 27-47; Edgar F. Shannon, Jr., "Lockwood's Dreams and the Exegesis of *Wuthering Heights," NCF,* XIV (1959). 95-109; Robert C. McKibben, "The Image of the Book in *Wuthering Heights," NCF,* XV (1960). 159-169; Moser, "What is the Matter with Emily Jane? Conflicting Impulses in *Wuthering Heights," NCF,* XVII (1962). 1-19; Wade Thompson, "Infanticide and Sadism in *Wuthering Heights," PMLA,* LXXVIII (1963). 69-74; Philip Drew, "Charlotte Brontë as a Critic of *Wuthering Heights," NCF,* XVIII (1964). 365-381; John E. Jordan, "The Ironic Vision of Emily Brontë," *NCF,* XX (1965). 1-18; F. H. Langman, *"Wuthering Heights," EIC,* XV (1965). 294-312; Van Ghent, pp. 153-170.

**1378**   Eliot: *Essays,* ed. Thomas Pinney (1963); *Letters,* ed. Gordon S. Haight (7v, New Haven, 1954-1955).—Bibliography in Stevenson, ch. IX. Gerald Bullett, *George Eliot: Her Life and Books* (1947); Lawrence and Elisabeth Hanson, *Marian Evans and George Eliot* (1952); Joan Bennett, *George Eliot: Her Mind and Her Art* (Cambridge, 1948; rev. 1962); Robert Speaight, *George Eliot* (1954); Barbara Hardy, *The Novels of George Eliot* (1959); Reva Stump, *Movement and Vision in George Eliot's Novels* (Seattle, 1959); Jerome Thale, *The Novels of George Eliot* (1959); Charles B. Cox, *The Free Spirit: A Study of Liberal Humanism in the Novels of George Eliot* [and others] (1963); Walter Allen, *George Eliot* (1964); U. C. Knoepflmacher, *Religious Humanism and the Victorian Novel* (Princeton, 1965), chs. II-III; Bernard J. Paris, *Experiments in*

*Life: George Eliot's Quest for Values* (Detroit, 1965); F. R. Leavis, "George Eliot," *The Great Tradition* (1948), pp. 28-125; Walter Naumann, "The Architecture of George Eliot's Novels," *MLQ*, ix (1948). 37-50; Graham Hough, "Novelist-Philosophers: George Eliot," *Horizon*, xvii (1948). 50-62; Claude T. Bissell, "Social Analysis in the Novels of George Eliot," *ELH*, xviii (1951). 221-239; Martin J. Svaglic, "Religion in the Novels of George Eliot," *JEGP*, liii (1954). 145-159; Alice R. Kaminsky, "George Eliot, George Henry Lewes, and the Novel," *PMLA*, lxx (1955). 997-1013; James D. Rust, "The Art of Fiction in George Eliot's Reviews," *RES*, n.s. vii (1956). 164-172; William J. Hyde, "George Eliot and the Climate of Realism," *PMLA*, lxxii (1957). 147-164; Haight, "George Eliot's Originals," *From Jane Austen to Joseph Conrad*, pp. 177-193; Alexander Welsh, "George Eliot and the Romance," *NCF*, xiv (1959). 241-254; Miriam Allott, "George Eliot in the 1860's," *VS*, v (1961). 94-108; George Levine, "Determinism and Responsibility in the Works of George Eliot," *PMLA*, lxxvii (1962). 268-279; N. N. Feltes, "George Eliot and the Unified Sensibility," *PMLA*, lxxix (1964). 130-136; Darrel Mansell, Jr., "George Eliot's Conception of 'Form,'" *SEL*, v (1965). 651-662; Ian Adam, "Character and Destiny in George Eliot's Fiction," *NCF*, xx (1965). 127-143; Willey, *Nineteenth Century Studies*, chs. viii-ix; Holloway, *The Victorian Sage*, ch. v; *Discussions of George Eliot*, ed. Richard Stang (Boston, 1960); *A Century of George Eliot Criticism*, ed. Haight (Boston, 1965).

**1379**   Thomas S. Noble, *George Eliot's "Scenes of Clerical Life"* (New Haven, 1965).—*Adam Bede*, ed. Gordon S. Haight (1948), Maxwell Goldberg (1956). Maurice Hussey, "Structure and Imagery in *Adam Bede*," *NCF*, x (1955). 115-129; George R. Creeger, "An Interpretation of *Adam Bede*," *ELH*, xxiii (1956). 218-238; Ian Gregor, "The Two Worlds of *Adam Bede*," *The Moral and the Story* (1962), pp. 13-32; Van Ghent, pp. 171-181.—*The Mill on the Floss*, ed. Haight (Boston, 1961). W. R. Steinhoff, "Intent and Fulfillment in the Ending of *The Mill on the Floss*," *The Image of the Work* (Berkeley, 1955), pp. 231-251; Bernard J. Paris, "Toward a Revaluation of George Eliot's *The Mill on the Floss*," *NCF*, xi (1956). 18-31.—*Silas Marner*, ed. Jerome Thale (1962). Robert B. Heilman, "Return to Raveloe," *English Jour.*, xlvi (1957). 1-10; Fred C. Thomson, "The Theme of Alienation in *Silas Marner*," *NCF*, xx (1965). 69-84.—M. Tosello, *Le Fonti italiane della "Romola" di George Eliot* (Turin, 1956); Carole Robinson, "*Romola*: A Reading of the Novel," *VS*, vi (1962). 29-42.—*Felix Holt*: Raymond Williams, *Culture and Society* (1958), pp. 102-109; Fred C. Thomson, "The Genesis of *Felix Holt*," *PMLA*, lxxiv (1959). 576-584, and "*Felix Holt* as Classic Tragedy," *NCF*, xvi (1961). 47-58; David R. Carroll, "Felix Holt: Society as Protagonist," *NCF*, xvii (1962). 237-252.—*Middlemarch*, ed. Haight (1956), W. J. Harvey (1965). *Quarry for "Middlemarch,"* ed. Anna T. Kitchel (Berkeley, 1950); Jerome Beaty, *"Middlemarch" from Notebook to Novel* (Urbana, Ill., 1960); David Daiches, *George Eliot: "Middlemarch"* (1963); Mark Schorer, "Fiction and the 'Matrix of Analogy,'" *Kenyon Rev.*, xi (1949). 539-560; F. George Steiner, "A Preface to *Middlemarch*," *NCF*, ix (1955). 262-279; Beaty, "History by Indirection: The Era of Reform in *Middlemarch*," *VS*, i (1957). 173-179; Sumner J. Ferris, "*Middlemarch*: George Eliot's Masterpiece," *From Jane Austen to Joseph Conrad*, pp. 194-207; David R. Carroll, "Unity Through Analogy: An Interpretation of *Middlemarch*," *VS*, ii (1959). 305-316; Sylvère

Monod, "George Eliot et les personnages de *Middlemarch*," *Études anglaises*, XII (1959). 306-314; Newton P. Stallknecht, "Resolution and Independence: A Reading of *Middlemarch*," *Twelve Original Essays on Great English Novels*, ed. Charles Shapiro (Detroit, 1960), pp. 125-152; John Hagan, "*Middlemarch:* Narrative Unity in the Story of Dorothea Brooke," *NCF*, XVI (1961). 17-31; Lloyd Fernando, "George Eliot, Feminism and Dorothea Brooke," *REL*, IV, no. 1 (1963). 76-90; Neil D. Isaacs, "*Middlemarch:* Crescendo of Obligatory Drama," *NCF*, XVIII (1963). 21-34; Kettle, I. 170-190.—*Daniel Deronda*, ed. F. R. Leavis (1961). Maurice Beebe, " 'Visions Are Creators': The Unity of *Daniel Deronda*," *Boston Univ. Stud. in English*, I (1955). 166-177; D. R. Carroll, "The Unity of *Daniel Deronda*," *EIC*, IX (1959). 369-380; Jerome Beaty, "*Daniel Deronda* and the Question of Unity in Fiction," *Victorian Newsletter*, No. 15 (1959), pp. 16-19; Robert Preyer, "Beyond the Liberal Imagination: Vision and Unreality in *Daniel Deronda*," *VS*, IV (1960). 33-54; Carole Robinson, "The Severe Angel: A Study of *Daniel Deronda*," *ELH*, XXXI (1964). 278-300.—Note 37: *Literary Criticism*, ed. Alice R. Kaminsky (Lincoln, Neb., 1965); three articles by Morris Greenhut, "George Henry Lewes and the Classical Tradition in English Criticism," *RES*, XXIV (1948). 126-137; "George Henry Lewes as a Critic of the Novel," *SP*, XLV (1948). 491-511; "G. H. Lewes's Criticism of the Drama," *PMLA*, LXIV (1949). 350-368; Jack Kaminsky, "The Empirical Metaphysics of George Henry Lewes," *JHI*, XIII (1952). 314-332; R. L. Brett, "George Henry Lewes: Dramatist, Novelist and Critic," *E&S*, n.s. XI (1958). 101-120.

**1381** Mrs. Oliphant: Katharine Moore, "A Valiant Victorian," *Blackwood's Mag.*, CCLXXXIII (1958). 231-243; Robert and Vineta Colby, "*A Beleaguered City:* A Fable for the Victorian Age," *NCF*, XVI (1962). 283-301.

# XXVI. Alfred Tennyson

**1382** *Poems and Plays* (Oxford, 1953); selections by F. L. Lucas (1947), Sir John Squire (1947), John Heath-Stubbs (1949), Stephen Gwynn (1950), Douglas Bush (1951), Herbert M. McLuhan (1956), Jerome H. Buckley (Boston, 1958); *Poems, 1832-1842*, ed. J. H. Fowler (1950).—Bibliography in Faverty, ch. II. Charles Tennyson, *Alfred Tennyson* (1949), the best biography, and *Six Tennyson Essays* (1954); Ralph W. Rader, *Tennyson's "Maud": The Biographical Genesis* (Berkeley, 1963), important biographical information for the period 1833-1854; George O. Marshall, *A Tennyson Handbook* (1963), to be used with caution; Paull F. Baum, *Tennyson Sixty Years After* (Chapel Hill, 1948), unsympathetic; Edgar F. Shannon, Jr., *Tennyson and the Reviewers* [1830-1850] (Cambridge, Mass., 1952); Buckley, *Tennyson: the Growth of a Poet* (Cambridge, Mass., 1960); Valerie Pitt, *Tennyson Laureate* (Toronto, 1962); Elton E. Smith, *The Two Voices: A Tennyson Study* (Lincoln, Neb., 1964); McLuhan, "Tennyson and Picturesque Poetry," *EIC*, I (1951). 262-282; E. D. H. Johnson, *The Alien Vision of Victorian Poetry* (Princeton, 1952), pp. 3-68; Milton Millhauser, "Tennyson: Artifice and Image," *JAAC*, XIV (1956). 333-338; Allan Danzig, "The Contraries: A Central Concept in Tennyson's Poetry," *PMLA*, LXXVII (1962). 577-585; James Kissane, "Tennyson: the Passion of the Past and the Curse of Time," *ELH*, XXXII (1965). 85-109; *Critical Essays on the Poetry of*

*Tennyson*, ed. John Killham (1960); Willey, *More Nineteenth Century Studies*, ch.ii.—Note 2: Charles Tennyson-Turner: *A Hundred Sonnets*, ed. John Betjeman and Charles Tennyson (1960). Harold Nicolson, *Tennyson's Two Brothers* (Cambridge, 1947); Charles Tennyson, "The Vicar of Grasby," *English*, viii (1950). 117-120, and "The Somersby Tennysons," *VS* (Christmas Supplement, 1963), pp. 14-16.

**1383-1385** Tennyson's earlier poems are studied in Lionel Stevenson, "The 'High-born Maiden' Symbol in Tennyson," *PMLA*, lxiii (1948). 234-243; Robert Preyer, "Tennyson as an Oracular Poet," *MP*, lv (1958). 239-251; Carl R. Sonn, "Poetic Vision and Religious Certainty in Tennyson's Earlier Poetry," *MP*, lvii (1959). 83-93; G. Robert Stange, "Tennyson's Garden of Art: A Study of *The Hesperides*," *PMLA*, lxvii (1952). 732-743; Alan Grob, "Tennyson's *The Lotos-Eaters:* Two Versions of Art," *MP*, lxii (1964). 118-129.

**1385** John Killham, *Tennyson and "The Princess": Reflections of an Age* (1958); Milton Millhauser, "Tennyson's *Princess* and *Vestiges*," *PMLA*, lxix (1954). 337-343; Ryals, "The 'Weird Seizures' in *The Princess*," *Texas Stud. in Lit. and Lang.*, iv (1962). 268-275.

**1386** Eleanor B. Mattes, *"In Memoriam": The Way of a Soul* (1951); Graham Hough, "The Natural Theology of *In Memoriam*," *RES*, xxiii (1947). 244-256; E. D. H. Johnson, "*In Memoriam:* The Way of a Poet," *VS*, ii (1958). 139-148; John D. Rosenberg, "The Two Kingdoms of *In Memoriam*," *JEGP*, lviii (1959). 228-240; Jonathan Bishop, "The Unity of *In Memoriam*," *Victorian Newsletter*, No. 21 (1962). 9-14; Stephen Allen Grant, "The Mystical Implications of *In Memoriam*," *SEL*, ii (1962). 481-495; Carlisle Moore, "Faith, Doubt, and Mystical Experience in *In Memoriam*," *VS*, vii (1963). 155-169; J. C. C. Mays, "*In Memoriam:* An Aspect of Form," *UTQ*, xxxv (1965). 22-46.

**1387** Edgar F. Shannon, "The History of a Poem: Tennyson's *Ode on the Death of the Duke of Wellington*," *Stud. in Bibliography*, xiii (1960). 149-177.— Roy P. Basler, "Tennyson's *Maud*," *Sex, Symbolism, and Psychology in Literature* (New Brunswick, N.J., 1948), pp. 73-93; E. D. H. Johnson, "The Lily and the Rose: Symbolic Meaning in Tennyson's *Maud*," *PMLA*, lxiv (1949). 1222-1227. —Note 12: Jerome Thale, "Sydney Dobell's *Roman:* The Poet's Experience and His Work," *American Imago*, xii (1955). 87-113; Robert Preyer, "Sidney Dobell and the Victorian Epic," *UTQ*, xxx (1961). 163-179. There is a good treatment of the Spasmodics in Buckley, *The Victorian Temper*, ch. iii.

**1388** F. E. L. Priestley, "Tennyson's *Idylls*," *UTQ*, xix (1949). 35-49; Samuel C. Burchell, "Tennyson's 'Allegory in the Distance,'" *PMLA*, lxviii (1953). 418-424; Edward Engelberg, "The Beast Image in Tennyson's *Idylls of the King*," *ELH*, xxii (1955). 287-292; Charles Tennyson, "*The Idylls of the King*," *Twentieth Century*, clxi (1957). 277-286; Ryals, "The Moral Paradox of the Hero in *The Idylls of the King*," *ELH*, xxx (1963). 53-69.

**1389-1390** Note 17: Brooks Wright, *Interpreter of Buddhism to the West: Sir Edwin Arnold* (1957).—Norton B. Crowell, *Alfred Austin: Victorian* (Albuquerque, 1953).—Derek Hudson, *Martin Tupper: His Rise and Fall* (1949).

**1390** On the style of *The Revenge*, see Robert M. Estrich and Hans Sperber, *Three Keys to Language* (1952), ch. xiv.

# XXVII. The Brownings

**1392** Robert Browning: Selected poems, ed. Humphrey Milford (Oxford, 1949), Simon Nowell-Smith (1950), Kenneth L. Knickerbocker (1951), Horace Gregory (1956), Donald Smalley (Boston, 1956); *New Letters,* ed. William C. DeVane and Knickerbocker (New Haven, 1950); *Dearest Isa,* ed. Edward C. McAleer (Austin, Tex., 1951), replacing Armstrong's edition of *Letters to Isa Blagden; Letters of the Brownings to George Barrett,* ed. Paul Landis and Ronald E. Freeman (Urbana, Ill., 1958); *Browning to His American Friends: Letters Between the Brownings, the Storys and James Russell Lowell, 1841-1890,* ed. Gertrude R. Hudson (1965).—L. N. Broughton, C. S. Northup, and Robert Pearsall, *Robert Browning: A Bibliography, 1830-1950* (Ithaca, 1953); Faverty, ch. III. DeVane's *Browning Handbook* appeared in a revised ed., 1955. There is no really satisfactory life of Browning; until one appears, Betty Miller, *Robert Browning: A Portrait* (1952) will serve despite its Freudian bias. W. O. Raymond, *The Infinite Moment and Other Essays in Browning* (Toronto, 1950; rev. 1965); J. M. Cohen, *Robert Browning* (1952); Roma J. King, Jr., *The Bow and the Lyre* (Ann Arbor, 1957), "new critical" readings of five poems; Park Honan, *Browning's Characters: A Study in Poetic Technique* (New Haven, 1961); Norton B. Crowell, *The Triple Soul: Browning's Theory of Knowledge* (Albuquerque, 1963); DeVane, "The Virgin and the Dragon," *Yale Rev.,* XXXVII (1947). 33-46; "A Version of Browning," *LTLS,* Dec. 30, 1949, p. 856; Hoxie N. Fairchild, "Browning the Simple-Hearted Casuist," *UTQ,* XVIII (1949). 234-240; E. D. H. Johnson, *The Alien Vision of Victorian Poetry,* pp. 71-143; Richard D. Altick, "The Private Life of Robert Browning," *Yale Rev.,* XLI (1952). 247-262; "The Browning Puzzle," *LTLS,* Nov. 14, 1952, p. 742; J. A. Boulton, "Browning—a Potential Revolutionary," *EIC,* III (1953). 165-176; Joseph E. Duncan, "The Intellectual Kinship of John Donne and Robert Browning," *SP,* L (1953). 81-100; G. Robert Stange, "Browning and Modern Poetry," *Pacific Spectator,* VIII (1954). 218-228; J. Hillis Miller, *The Disappearance of God* (Cambridge, Mass., 1963), ch. III; William Cadbury, "Lyric and Anti-Lyric Form: A Method for Judging Browning," *UTQ,* XXXIV (1964). 49-67; Robert Preyer, "Two Styles in the Verse of Robert Browning," *ELH,* XXXII (1965). 62-84; *The Browning Critics,* ed. Boyd Litzinger and Knickerbocker (Lexington, Ky., 1965); *Robert Browning: A Collection of Critical Essays,* ed. Philip Drew (1966).

**1393** Robert Preyer, "Robert Browning: A Reading of the Early Narratives," *ELH,* XXVI (1959). 531-548.—F. E. L. Priestley, "The Ironic Pattern of Browning's *Paracelsus,*" *UTQ,* XXXIV (1964). 68-81.—Earl Hilton, "Browning's *Sordello* as a Study of the Will," *PMLA,* LXIX (1954). 1127-1134; Daniel Stempel, "Browning's *Sordello*: the Art of the Makers-See," *PMLA,* LXXX (1965). 554-561.

**1394** James P. McCormick, "Browning and the Experimental Drama," *PMLA,* LXVIII (1953). 982-991.—Robert Langbaum, *The Poetry of Experience: The Dramatic Monologue in Modern Literary Tradition* (1957), important not only for Browning; Benjamin W. Fuson, "Browning and His English

Predecessors in the Dramatic Monolog," *State Univ. of Iowa Humanistic Stud.,* viii (1948).

**1395** The so-called "Essay on Shelley" is not Browning's "only work in prose": see the *Essay on Chatterton,* ed. Donald Smalley (Cambridge, Mass., 1948)—first published in the *Foreign Quar. Rev.,* 1842. On the critique of Shelley, see Warren, *English Poetic Theory,* ch. vii; Philip Drew, "Browning's *Essay on Shelley*," *VP,* i (1963). 1-6 (cf. reply by Thomas J. Collins, *VP,* ii [1964]. 119-124).—Note 13: As noted above, Armstrong's edition of the letters to Isa Blagden is superseded by *Dearest Isa,* ed. McAleer.

**1396** Charlotte C. Watkins, "The 'Abstruser Themes' of Browning's *Fifine at the Fair*," *PMLA,* lxxiv (1959). 426-437, and "Browning's *Red Cotton Night-Cap Country* and Carlyle," *VS,* vii (1964). 359-374.

**1397** Note 19: See also Hoxie N. Fairchild, *"La Saisiaz* and *The Nineteenth Century*," *MP,* xlviii (1950). 104-111.

**1399-1401** William Whitla, *The Central Truth: The Incarnation in Robert Browning's Poetry* (Toronto, 1963); Kingsbury Badger, " 'See the Christ Stand!': Browning's Religion," *Boston Univ. Stud. in English,* i (1955). 53-73; Joseph E. Baker, "Religious Implications in Browning's Poetry," *PQ,* xxxvi (1957). 436-452; H. N. Fairchild, "Browning's Heaven," *Rev. of Religion,* xiv (1949). 30-37.

**1401** Note 31: *The Ring and the Book,* with introduction by Wylie Sypher (1961). Beatrice Corrigan, *Curious Annals: New Documents Relating to Browning's Roman Murder Story* (Toronto, 1956); Paul A. Cundiff, "The Clarity of Browning's Ring Metaphor," *PMLA,* lxiii (1948). 1276-1282 (cf. the discussion of this metaphor in *Victorian Newsletter,* Nos. 16-17 [1959-1960], and George R. Wasserman, "The Meaning of Browning's Ring-Figure," *MLN,* lxxvi [1961]. 420-426).

**1403** Elizabeth Barrett Browning: *Sonnets from the Portuguese: Centennial Variorum Edition,* ed. Fannie Ratchford (1950), important for text; *Elizabeth Barrett to Miss Mitford,* ed. Betty Miller (1954); *Elizabeth Barrett to Mr. [Hugh Stuart] Boyd,* ed. Barbara P. McCarthy (New Haven, 1955).—Bibliography in Faverty, pp. 84-92. Dorothy Hewlett, *Elizabeth Barrett Browning* (1952); Gardner B. Taplin, *Life of Elizabeth Barrett Browning* (New Haven, 1957); Alethea Hayter, *Mrs. Browning: A Poet's Work and Its Setting* (1962).

# XXVIII. Matthew Arnold and Arthur Hugh Clough; Edward FitzGerald and James Thomson ("B. V.")

**1405** Clough: *Poems,* ed. H. F. Lowry, A. L. P. Norrington, and F. L. Mulhauser (Oxford, 1951)—cf. criticism by Richard M. Gollin, *MP,* lx (1962). 120-127; *Correspondence,* ed. Mulhauser (2v, Oxford, 1957).—Bibliography in Faverty, pp. 104-110; Walter E. Houghton, "The Prose Works of Arthur Hugh Clough: A Checklist and Calendar," *Bull. N.Y. Library,* lxiv (1960) 377-394. Katherine Chorley, *Arthur Hugh Clough: The Uncommitted Mind* (Oxford, 1962); Houghton, *The Poetry of Clough* (New Haven, 1963); Paul

Veyriras, *Arthur Hugh Clough* (Paris, 1965); Kingsbury Badger, "Arthur Hugh Clough as Dipsychus," *MLQ*, XII (1951). 39-56; Doris N. Dalglish, "Arthur Hugh Clough: the Shorter Poems," *EIC*, II (1952). 38-53; three articles by Michael Timko, "The 'True Creed' of Arthur Hugh Clough," *MLQ*, XXI (1960). 208-222, "The Poetic Theory of Arthur Hugh Clough," *ES*, XLIII (1962). 240-247, and "The Satiric Poetry of Arthur Hugh Clough," *VP*, I (1963). 104-114; Clyde de L. Ryals, "An Interpretation of Clough's *Dipsychus*," *VP*, I (1963). 182-188; Masao Miyoshi, "Clough's Poems of Self-Irony," *SEL*, V (1965). 691-704.

**1406** Note 5: Robert Birley, "Philip James Bailey: *Festus*," *Sunk Without Trace* (1962), ch. VI.

**1407** Arnold: *Complete Prose Works*, ed. Robert H. Super (Ann Arbor, 1960-    ); *Poetical Works*, ed. C. B. Tinker and Howard F. Lowry (1950); *Poems*, ed. Kenneth Allott (1965); *The Portable Matthew Arnold*, ed. Lionel Trilling (1949); *Poetry and Criticism*, ed. A. Dwight Culler (Boston, 1961); *Selected Poetry and Prose*, ed. Frederick W. Mulhauser (1953); *Poetry and Prose*, ed. John Bryson (Cambridge, Mass., 1954); *Matthew Arnold: an Introduction and a Selection* (1948) and *Poems* (1949), both ed. C. Dyment; *Selected Essays*, ed. Noel Annan (1964); *Five Uncollected Essays*, ed. Allott (Liverpool, 1953); *Essays, Letters, and Reviews*, ed. Fraser Neiman (Cambridge, Mass., 1960), pieces hitherto unreprinted; *England and the Italian Question*, ed. Merle M. Bevington (Durham, N.C., 1953); *Notebooks*, ed. Lowry, Karl Young, and Waldo H. Dunn (1952).—Bibliography, mainly on Arnold the poet, in Faverty, ch. v. Louis Bonnerot, *Matthew Arnold, Poète: Essai de biographie psychologique* (Paris, 1947); Edmund Chambers, *Matthew Arnold* (Oxford, 1947); E. K. Brown, *Matthew Arnold: A Study in Conflict* (Chicago, 1948); W. F. Connell, *The Educational Thought and Influence of Matthew Arnold* (1950); J. D. Jump, *Matthew Arnold* (1955); John Henry Raleigh, *Matthew Arnold and American Culture* (Berkeley, 1957); William A. Jamison, *Arnold and the Romantics* (Copenhagen, 1958); Paull F. Baum, *Ten Studies in the Poetry of Matthew Arnold* (Durham, N.C., 1958); William Robbins, *The Ethical Idealism of Matthew Arnold* (Toronto, 1959); David G. James, *Matthew Arnold and the Decline of English Romanticism* (Oxford, 1961); Wendell S. Johnson, *The Voices of Matthew Arnold* (New Haven, 1961); H. C. Duffin, *Arnold the Poet* (1962); Leon Gottfried, *Matthew Arnold and the Romantics* (1963); Patrick J. McCarthy, *Matthew Arnold and the Three Classes* (1964); Edward Alexander, *Matthew Arnold and John Stuart Mill* (1965); Warren D. Anderson, *Matthew Arnold and the Classical Tradition* (Ann Arbor, 1965); Harold Nicolson, "On Re-reading Matthew Arnold," *Essays by Divers Hands* (Royal Soc. of Lit.), n.s. XXIV (1948). 124-134; John Holloway, "Matthew Arnold and the Modern Dilemma," *EIC*, I (1951). 1-16; E. D. H. Johnson, *The Alien Vision of Victorian Poetry*, pp. 147-213; Kathleen Tillotson, "Matthew Arnold and Carlyle," *Proc. Brit. Acad.*, XLII (1956). 133-153; Neiman, "The Zeitgeist of Matthew Arnold," *PMLA*, LXXII (1957). 977-996; E. N. Greenwood, "Matthew Arnold: Thoughts on a Centenary," *Twentieth Century*, CLXII (1957). 469-479; W. S. Johnson, "Matthew Arnold's Dialogue," *Univ. of Kansas City Rev.*, XXVII (1960). 109-116; Albert J. Lubell, "Matthew Arnold: Between Two Worlds," *MLQ*, XXII (1961). 248-263; Walter J. Hipple, Jr., "Matthew Arnold, Dialectician," *UTQ*,

XXXII (1962). 1-26; N. N. Feltes, "Matthew Arnold and the Modern Spirit: A Reassessment," *ibid.*, pp. 27-36; J. Hillis Miller, *The Disappearance of God*, ch. v; Willey, *Nineteenth Century Studies*, ch. x; Holloway, *The Victorian Sage*, ch. vii; LeRoy, *Perplexed Prophets*, ch. iii.—*Concordance to the Poems*, ed. Stephen M. Parrish (Ithaca, 1959).

**1408** W. S. Johnson, "Matthew Arnold's Sea of Life," *PQ*, xxxi (1952). 195-207; Allan Brick, "Equilibrium in the Poetry of Matthew Arnold," *UTQ*, xxx (1960). 45-56; John M. Wallace, "Landscape and 'The General Law': The Poetry of Matthew Arnold," *Boston Univ. Stud. in English*, v (1961). 91-106; Alan H. Roper, "The Moral Landscape of Arnold's Poetry," *PMLA*, lxxvii (1962). 289-296; U. C. Knoepflmacher, "Dover Revisited: The Wordsworthian Matrix in the Poetry of Matthew Arnold," *VP*, i (1963). 17-26; Herbert R. Coursen, Jr., "'The Moon Lies Fair': The Poetry of Matthew Arnold," *SEL*, iv (1964). 569-581.

On specific poems: Leon A. Gottfried, "Matthew Arnold's *The Strayed Reveller*," *RES*, n.s. xi (1960). 403-409; Howard W. Fulweiler, "Matthew Arnold: The Metamorphosis of a Merman," *VP*, i (1963). 208-222, on *The Forsaken Merman* and *The Neckan*; M. G. Sundell, "The Intellectual Background and Structure of Arnold's *Tristram and Iseult*," *VP*, i (1963). 272-283; Louis Bonnerot, introduction to his translation of *Empedocles on Etna* (Paris, 1947); Walter E. Houghton, "Arnold's *Empedocles on Etna*," *VS*, i (1958). 311-336; S. Nagarajan, "Arnold and the *Bhagavad Gita*: A Reinterpretation of *Empedocles on Etna*," *CL*, xii (1960). 335-347; Fred L. Burwick, "Hölderlin and Arnold: *Empedocles on Etna*," *CL*, xvii (1965). 24-42; Kathleen Tillotson, "'Yes: in the Sea of Life,'" *RES*, n.s. iii (1952). 346-364; G. Wilson Knight, "*The Scholar Gypsy*: An Interpretation," *RES*, n.s. vi (1955). 53-62 (cf. reply by A. E. Dyson, "The Last Enchantments," *RES*, n.s. viii [1957]. 257-265); Murray Krieger, "*Dover Beach* and the Tragic Sense of Eternal Recurrence," *Univ. of Kansas City Rev.*, xxiii (1956). 73-79; Norman N. Holland, "Psychological Depths and *Dover Beach*," *VS*, ix (1965), supplement, pp. 5-28; Harvey Kerpneck, "The Road to *Rugby Chapel*," *UTQ*, xxxiv (1965). 178-196.

**1409** Sidney M. B. Coulling, "Matthew Arnold's 1853 Preface: Its Origin and Aftermath," *VS*, vii (1964). 233-263; Warren, *English Poetic Theory*, ch. ix.

**1412-1413** Frederic E. Faverty, *Matthew Arnold, the Ethnologist* (Evanston, Ill., 1951); John V. Kelleher, "Matthew Arnold and the Celtic Revival," *Perspectives of Criticism*, ed. Harry Levin (Cambridge, Mass., 1950), pp. 197-221.

John S. Eels, *The Touchstones of Matthew Arnold* (1955); F. J. W. Harding, *Matthew Arnold, The Critic and France* (Geneva, 1964); David Perkins, "Arnold and the Function of Literature," *ELH*, xviii (1951). 287-309; Wayne Shumaker, "Matthew Arnold's Humanism: Literature as a Criticism of Life," *SEL*, ii (1962). 387-402; Wellek, *History of Modern Criticism*, iv. 155-180.

Robert A. Donovan, "The Method of Arnold's *Essays in Criticism*," *PMLA*, lxxi (1956). 922-931; Sidney M. B. Coulling, "The Background of *The Function of Criticism at the Present Time*," *PQ*, xlii (1963). 36-54.

**1413** Geoffrey Carnall, "Matthew Arnold's 'Great Critical Effort'," *EIC*, viii

(1958). 256-268; Sidney M. B. Coulling, "The Evolution of *Culture and Anarchy*," *SP*, LX (1963). 637-668.

**1414** On *Literature and Dogma:* Dorothea Krook, *Three Traditions of Moral Thought* (Cambridge, 1959), pp. 202-225.

**1416** FitzGerald: *Selected Works,* ed. Joanna Richardson (1962); *FitzGerald's Rubáiyát: Centennial Edition,* ed. Carl J. Weber (Waterville, Maine, 1959), and A. J. Arberry, *The Romance of the Rubáiyát* (1959), both with the text of the first edition; Arberry, *FitzGerald's Salámán and Absál* (Cambridge, 1956), the texts of 1856 and 1879; *Letters,* ed. J. M. Cohen (Carbondale, Ill., 1960), a selection. The definitive edition of FitzGerald's correspondence is being prepared by A. McKinley Terhune.—Bibliography in Faverty, pp. 92-103. Terhune, *Life of Edward FitzGerald* (New Haven, 1947); Arberry, *Omar Khayyám* (New Haven, 1952), translation of a manuscript from 1207.

**1418** Thomson: *Poems and Some Letters,* ed. Anne Ridler (Carbondale, Ill., 1963).—Imogene B. Walker, *James Thomson (B. V.): A Critical Study* (Ithaca, 1950); William D. Schaefer, *James Thomson (B. V.)* (Berkeley, 1965); R. A. Forsyth, "Evolutionism and the Pessimism of James Thomson," *EIC,* XII (1962). 148-166; Jerome J. McGann, "James Thomson (B. V.): The Woven Hymns of Night and Day," *SEL,* III (1963). 493-507; Heath-Stubbs, *The Darkling Plain,* pp. 111-121; LeRoy, *Perplexed Prophets,* ch. v.

**1419** George M. Harper, "Blake's *Nebuchadnezzar* in *The City of Dreadful Night*," *SP,* L (1953). 68-80.

# XXIX. Rossetti and His Circle

**1421** Rossetti: *Poems,* ed. Oswald Doughty (1957); *Jan Van Hunks,* ed. John Robert Wahl (1952), the only scholarly text; *Letters,* ed. Doughty and Wahl (4v, 1965-      ); *The Rossetti-Macmillan Letters* (written by Dante Gabriel, William Michael, and Christina), ed. Lona Mosk Packer (Berkeley, 1963).—The bibliographical treatment of Rossetti in Faverty, ch. VII, is unsystematic; but much Rossetti material is listed in Fredeman, *Pre-Raphaelitism,* cited below. Doughty, *Dante Gabriel Rossetti* (1949, new ed. 1960), the standard biography; Helen R. Angeli, *Dante Gabriel Rossetti: His Friends and Enemies* (1949); Jacques Savarit, *Tendences mystiques et ésotériques chez Dante Gabriel Rossetti* (Paris, 1961), a psychological treatment; Doughty, "Rossetti's Conception of the 'Poetic' in Poetry and Painting," *Essays by Divers Hands* (Royal Soc. of Lit.), n.s. XXVI (1953). 89-102; Clyde K. Hyder, "Rossetti's *Rose Mary*: A Study in the Occult," *VP,* I (1963). 197-207; Harold L. Weatherby, "Problems of Form and Content in the Poetry of Dante Gabriel Rossetti," *VP,* II (1964). 11-19; LeRoy, *Perplexed Prophets,* ch. VI; Hough, *The Last Romantics,* ch. II.

Note 4: On William Michael Rossetti, see Jerome Thale, "The Third Rossetti," *Western Humanities Rev.,* X (1956). 277-284.

**1422** William E. Fredeman, *Pre-Raphaelitism: A Bibliocritical Study* (Cambridge, Mass., 1965), is comprehensive and valuable. *The Pre-Raphaelites in Literature and Art,* ed. D. S. R. Welland (1953); Rayner Unwin, "Keats and Pre-Raphaelitism," *English,* VIII (1951). 229-235; Humphry House, "Pre-Raphaelite Poetry," *All in Due Time* (1955), pp. 151-158.

**1423** Note 13: John A. Cassidy, "Robert Buchanan and the Fleshly Controversy," *PMLA,* LXVII (1952). 65-93 (cf. reply by George G. Storey, "Robert Buchanan's Critical Principles," *PMLA,* LXVIII [1953]. 1228-1232).

**1424** On Hall Caine: Samuel Norris, *Two Men of Manxland* (Douglas, I.o.M., 1947).—On *The House of Life:* W. E. Fredeman, "Rossetti's 'In Memoriam': An Elegiac Reading of *The House of Life,*" *Bull. John Rylands Library,* XLVII (1965). 298-341; Bowra, *The Romantic Imagination,* ch. IX.

**1426** Marya Zaturenska, *Christina Rossetti* (1949); Lona Mosk Packer, *Christina Rossetti* (Berkeley, 1963); Barbara Garlitz, "Christina Rossetti's *Sing-Song* and Nineteenth-Century Children's Poetry," *PMLA,* LXX (1955). 539-543; Packer, "Symbol and Reality in Christina Rossetti's *Goblin Market,*" *PMLA,* LXXIII (1958). 375-385; Bowra, *The Romantic Imagination,* ch. XI.

**1428** Note 32: Madison C. Bates, "'That Delightful Man': A Study of Frederick Locker," *Harvard Library Bull.,* XIII (1959). 92-113, 265-291, 444-470.

**1429** James K. Robinson, "Austin Dobson and the Rondeliers," *MLQ,* XIV (1953). 31-42.—Anthony W. Preston, "Calverley of Cambridge," *Queen's Quar.,* LIV (1947). 47-60.

# XXX. William Morris

**1430** *Selected Writings and Designs,* ed. Asa Briggs (1963); *On Art and Socialism,* ed. Holbrook Jackson (1947); *Letters to His Family and Friends,* ed. Philip Henderson (1950).—Esther Meynell, *Portrait of William Morris* (1947); Lloyd Eric Grey, *William Morris, Prophet of England's New Order* (1949), identical with L. W. Eshelman, *A Victorian Rebel* (1940); Robert P. Arnot, *William Morris: the Man and the Myth* (1964); Hough, *The Last Romantics,* ch. III.

**1430-1431** Laurence Perrine, "Morris' *Guenevere:* An Interpretation," *PQ,* XXXIX (1960). 234-241; Curtis Dahl, "Morris's *The Chapel in Lyoness:* An Interpretation," *SP,* LI (1954). 482-491.

**1432** Oscar Maurer, "Morris's Treatment of Greek Legend in *The Earthly Paradise,*" *Univ. of Texas Stud. in English,* XXXIII (1954). 103-118.

**1434** Edward P. Thompson, *William Morris: Romantic to Revolutionary* (1955); Margaret Cole, "The Fellowship of William Morris," *Virginia Quar. Rev.,* XXIV (1948). 260-277.

**1436** Charles H. Kegel, "William Morris's *A Dream of John Ball:* A Study in Reactionary Liberalism," *Papers of the Michigan Acad.,* XL (1954). 303-312.

# XXXI. Algernon Charles Swinburne

**1439** *Novels,* with introduction by Edmund Wilson (1962); selections, ed. H. Treece (1948), Humphrey Hare (1950), Edward Shanks (1950), Kenelm

Foss (1955), Edith Sitwell (1960), Bonamy Dobrée (1961); *Lesbia Brandon,* ed. Randolph Hughes (1952), first publication; *New Writings,* ed. Cecil Y. Lang (Syracuse, N.Y., 1964); *Letters,* ed. Lang (6v, New Haven, 1959-1962). —Bibliography in Faverty, ch. vi. Hare, *Swinburne: A Biographical Approach* (1949); John A. Cassidy, *Algernon C. Swinburne* (1964); Robert L. Peters, *The Crowns of Apollo: Swinburne's Principles of Literature and Art* (Detroit, 1965); Thomas E. Connolly, *Swinburne's Theory of Poetry* (Yellow Springs, Ohio, 1965); Wellek, *History of Modern Criticism,* iv. 371-381.

**1440**   The story of the origin of *The Triumph of Time* has been entirely discredited. See John S. Mayfield, *Swinburne's Boo* (privately printed, 1954), and Cecil Y. Lang, "Swinburne's Lost Love," *PMLA,* lxxiv (1959). 123-130.— On *Atalanta in Calydon,* see Bowra, *The Romantic Imagination,* ch. x.

# XXXII. The Background: The Victorian Decline (1868-1901) and the Aftermath (1901-1939)

**1448**   The history of the period is traced in J. A. R. Marriott, *Modern England, 1885-1945* (1948); Herman Ausubel, *The Late Victorians: A Short History* (1955); Henry M. Pelling, *Modern Britain, 1885-1955* (Edinburgh, 1960); Thomas L. Jarman, *A Short History of Twentieth-Century England* (1963); and A. J. P. Taylor, *England, 1914-1945* (Oxford, 1965). See also *Edwardian England,* ed. Simon Nowell-Smith (1964) and Raymond Williams, *Culture and Society* (1958), Part ii ("Interregnum").—General studies of the literature of the era include William Y. Tindall, *Forces in Modern British Literature* (1947, rev. 1956), Vivian de Sola Pinto, *Crisis in English Poetry, 1880-1940* (1951), and H. N. Fairchild, *Religious Trends in English Poetry,* Vol. v: *Gods of a Changing Poetry, 1880-1920* (1962). The persistence and revival of "romantic" elements in the literature of the time are discussed, from differing points of view, in Graham Hough, *The Last Romantics* (1949), John Heath-Stubbs, *The Darkling Plain* (1950), Frank Kermode, *Romantic Image* (1957), and John Bayley, *The Romantic Survival* (1957). *Edwardians and Late Victorians (English Institute Essays 1959),* ed. Richard Ellmann (1960) contains seven essays on "the literature written shortly before or shortly after 1900."

S. Marandon, "Frederic Harrison (1831-1923)," *Études anglaises,* xiii (1960). 415-426; Martha S. Vogeler, "Matthew Arnold and Frederic Harrison: The Prophet of Culture and the Prophet of Positivism," *SEL,* ii (1962). 441-462.

Stephen: *Men, Books, and Mountains,* ed. S. O. A. Ullmann (Minneapolis, 1956), previously uncollected essays.—Noel Annan, *Leslie Stephen: His Thought and Character in Relation to His Time* (1951); Gertrude Himmelfarb, "Mr. Stephen and Mr. Ramsay: the Victorian as Intellectual," *Partisan Rev.,* xix (1952). 664-679; Oscar Maurer, "Leslie Stephen and the *Cornhill Magazine,* 1871-82," *Univ. of Texas Stud. in English,* xxxii (1953). 67-95; John W. Bicknell, "Leslie Stephen's *English Thought in the Eighteenth Century:* A Tract for the Times," *VS,* vi (1962). 103-120.

**1449**  I. F. Clarke, "*The Battle of Dorking*, 1871-1914," *VS*, VIII (1965). 309-328.

**1451**  On John Morley: Willey, *More Nineteenth Century Studies*, ch. VI.

# XXXIII. George Meredith

**1455**  *Selected Poems*, ed. Graham Hough (1962).—Bibliography in Stevenson, ch. x, and Faverty, pp. 232-236. Siegfried Sassoon, *Meredith* (1948); Lionel Stevenson, *The Ordeal of George Meredith* (1953); Walter F. Wright, *Art and Substance in Meredith* (Lincoln, Neb., 1953); Jack Lindsay, *George Meredith: His Life and Work* (1956), a strongly Marxist interpretation; Norman Kelvin, *A Troubled Eden: Nature and Society in the Works of George Meredith* (Stanford, 1961); J. Gordon Eaker, "Meredith's Human Comedy," *NCF*, v (1951). 253-272; Joseph C. Landis, "George Meredith's Comedy," *Boston Univ. Stud. in English*, II (1956). 17-35; Deborah S. Austin, "Meredith on the Nature of Metaphor," *UTQ*, XXVII (1957). 96-102; Stevenson, "Meredith and the Problem of Style in the Novel," *Zeitschrift für Anglistik und Amerikanistik*, VI (1958). 181-189; Phyllis Bartlett, "The Novels of George Meredith," *REL*, III, no. 2 (1962). 31-46; Donald Fanger, "Meredith as Novelist," *NCF*, XVI (1962). 317-328; Jean Sudrann, " 'The Linked Eye and Mind': A Concept of Action in the Novels of Meredith," *SEL*, IV (1964). 617-635.

**1456**  *The Ordeal of Richard Feverel*, ed. Lionel Stevenson (1950), Norman Kelvin (1961), Charles J. Hill (1964).—William R. Mueller, "Theological Dualism and the 'System' in *Richard Feverel*," *ELH*, XVIII (1951). 138-154; Frank D. Curtin, "Adrian Harley: The Limits of Meredith's Comedy," *NCF*, VII (1953). 272-282; Phyllis Bartlett, "Richard Feverel, Knight-Errant," *Bull. N.Y. Public Library*, LXIII (1959). 329-340; Irving H. Buchen, "The Importance of the Minor Characters in *The Ordeal of Richard Feverel*," *Boston Univ. Stud. in English*, v (1961). 154-166; John W. Morris, "Inherent Principles of Order in *Richard Feverel*," *PMLA*, LXXVIII (1963). 333-340; Henri-A. Talon, "Le Comique, le tragique, et le romanesque dans *The Ordeal of Richard Feverel*," *Études anglaises*, XVII (1964). 241-261.

**1457**  Royal A. Gettmann, "Serialization and *Evan Harrington*," *PMLA*, LXIV (1949). 963-975.—*Modern Love*, ed. C. Day Lewis (1948). Lewis, "George Meredith and Responsibility," *Notable Images of Virtue* (Toronto, 1954), ch. II; Norman Friedman, "The Jangled Harp: Symbolic Structure in *Modern Love*," *MLQ*, XVII (1957). 9-26; Elizabeth Cox Wright, "The Significance of the Image Patterns in Meredith's *Modern Love*," *Victorian Newsletter*, No. 13 (1958). 1-9.—On *Rhoda Fleming*: Charles J. Hill, "Meredith's 'Plain Story,' " *NCF*, VII (1952). 90-102; Lionel Stevenson, "Meredith's Atypical Novel," *The Image of the Work* (Berkeley, 1955), pp. 89-109.

Note 3: Royal A. Gettmann, "Meredith as Publisher's Reader," *JEGP*, XLVIII (1949). 45-56.

**1458**  Barbara Hardy, " 'A Way to Your Hearts through Fire or Water': The Structure of Imagery in *Harry Richmond*," *EIC*, x (1960). 163-180; L. T. Hergenhan, "Meredith's Revisions of *Harry Richmond*," *RES*, n.s. XIV (1963).

24-32.—*Beauchamp's Career,* ed. G. M. Young (1950). Charles J. Hill, "The Portrait of the Author in *Beauchamp's Career,*" *JEGP,* LII (1953). 332-339.

**1459** *The Egoist,* ed. Lord Dunsany (1947), Lionel Stevenson (Boston, 1958). Richard B. Hudson, "The Meaning of Egoism in George Meredith's *The Egoist,*" *Trollopian,* III (1948). 163-176; C. J. Hill, "Theme and Image in *The Egoist,*" *Univ. of Kansas City Rev.,* XX (1954). 281-285; Irving H. Buchen, "The Egoists in *The Egoist:* The Sensualists and the Ascetics," *NCF,* XIX (1964). 255-269; Van Ghent, pp. 183-194.—Gillian Beer, "Meredith's Revisions of *The Tragic Comedians,*" *RES,* n.s. XIV (1963). 33-53, and "Meredith's Idea of Comedy: 1876-1880," *NCF,* XX (1965). 165-176.

**1460** On Mrs. Norton, see Alice Acland, *Caroline Norton* (1948).—Joseph E. Kruppa, "Meredith's Late Novels: Suggestions for a Critical Approach," *NCF,* XIX (1964). 271-286.—Fabian Gudas, "George Meredith's *One of Our Conquerors,*" *From Jane Austen to Joseph Conrad,* pp. 222-233; Fred C. Thomson, "The Design of *One of Our Conquerors,*" *SEL,* II (1962). 463-480.—Bernard A. Brunner, "Meredith's Symbolism: *Lord Ormont and His Aminta,*" *NCF,* VIII (1953). 124-133.

# XXXIV. Thomas Hardy

**1464** *Selected Poems,* ed. John Crowe Ransom (1961); *Our Exploits at West Poley,* ed. Richard L. Purdy (1952), first published in *The Household,* 1892-1893; *Love Poems,* ed. Carl J. Weber (1964); *Letters,* ed. Weber (Waterville, Maine, 1954), limited to the letters at Colby College; *"Dearest Emmie":* *Hardy's Letters to His First Wife,* ed. Weber (1963); *Notebooks,* ed. Evelyn Hardy (1955).—Purdy, *Thomas Hardy: A Bibliographical Study* (1954); bibliographies of Hardy criticism in Stevenson, ch. XI, Faverty, pp. 238-241, and Maurice Beebe *et al.,* "Criticism of Thomas Hardy: A Selected Checklist," *Mod. Fiction Stud.,* VI (1960). 258-279. Weber's *Hardy of Wessex* had been revised, 1965. Evelyn Hardy, *Thomas Hardy: A Critical Biography* (1954); Emma Lavinia Hardy, *Some Recollections,* ed. Evelyn Hardy and Robert Gittings (1961); James G. Southworth, *The Poetry of Thomas Hardy* (1947); Harvey C. Webster, *On a Darkling Plain* (Chicago, 1947); Albert Guerard, *Thomas Hardy: the Novels and Stories* (Cambridge, Mass., 1949); Desmond Hawkins, *Thomas Hardy* (1951); Douglas Brown, *Thomas Hardy* (1954, rev. 1961); Thomas Hardy number of *Mod. Fiction Stud.,* VI (Autumn, 1960); Samuel Hynes, *The Pattern of Hardy's Poetry* (Chapel Hill, 1961); George Douglas Wing, *Thomas Hardy* (1963); three articles by James O. Bailey, "Hardy's 'Mephistophelian Visitants,'" *PMLA,* LXI (1946). 1146-1184, "Hardy's Visions of the Self," *SP,* LVI (1959). 74-101, and "Evolutionary Meliorism in the Poetry of Thomas Hardy," *SP,* LX (1963). 569-587; J. I. M. Stewart, "The Integrity of Hardy," *English Stud.* (*E&S,* n.s.), I (1948). 1-27; C. Day Lewis, "The Lyrical Poetry of Thomas Hardy," *Proc. Brit. Acad.,* XXXVII (1951). 155-174; Carol R. Andersen, "Time, Space and Perspective in Thomas Hardy," *NCF,* IX (1954). 192-208; C. M. Bowra, "The Lyrical Poetry of Thomas Hardy," *Inspiration and Poetry* (1955), pp. 220-241; Eugene Goodheart, "Thomas Hardy and the Lyrical Novel," *NCF,* XII (1957). 215-225; John Holloway, "Hardy's Major

Fiction," *From Jane Austen to Joseph Conrad*, pp. 234-245; William J. Hyde, "Hardy's View of Realism: A Key to the Rustic Characters," *VS*, II (1958). 45-59; David Perkins, "Hardy and the Poetry of Isolation," *ELH*, XXVI (1959). 253-270; Roy Morrell, "Hardy in the Tropics: Some Implications of Hardy's Attitude towards Nature," *REL*, III, no. 1 (1962). 7-30; James F. Scott, "Thomas Hardy's Use of the Gothic: An Examination of Five Representative Works," *NCF*, XVII (1962). 363-380; Richard Beckman, "A Character Typology for Hardy's Novels," *ELH*, XXX (1963). 70-87; Guerard, "The Illusion of Simplicity: The Shorter Poems of Thomas Hardy," *Sewanee Rev.*, LXXII (1964). 363-388; Holloway, *The Victorian Sage*, ch. VIII; Stewart, *Eight Modern Writers* (Oxford, 1963), ch. II; *Hardy: A Collection of Critical Essays*, ed. Guerard (1963).

**1466** Lawrence O. Jones, "*Desperate Remedies* and the Victorian Sensation Novel," *NCF*, XX (1965). 35-50.—John F. Danby, "*Under the Greenwood Tree*," *Critical Quar.*, I (1959). 5-13; Harold E. Toliver, "The Dance under the Greenwood Tree: Hardy's Bucolics," *NCF*, XVII (1962). 57-68.—*Far from the Madding Crowd*, ed. Carl J. Weber (1959), Richard L. Purdy (Boston, 1957). Richard C. Carpenter, "The Mirror and the Sword: Imagery in *Far from the Madding Crowd*," *NCF*, XVIII (1964). 331-345; Howard Babb, "Setting and Theme in *Far from the Madding Crowd*," *ELH*, XXX (1963). 147-161.—Clarice Short, "In Defense of *Ethelberta*," *NCF*, XIII (1958). 48-57.—*The Return of the Native*, ed. Albert Guerard (1950). John Paterson, *The Making of "The Return of the Native"* (Berkeley, 1960); Robert W. Stallman, "Hardy's Hour-Glass Novel," *Sewanee Rev.*, LV (1947). 283-296; M. A. Goldberg, "Hardy's Double-Visioned Universe," *EIC*, VII (1957). 374-382; S. F. Johnson, "Hardy and Burke's 'Sublime,'" *Style in Prose Fiction (English Institute Essays 1958)*, ed. H. C. Martin (1959), pp. 55-86; Paterson, "*The Return of the Native* as Antichristian Document," *NCF*, XIV (1959). 111-127; Otis B. Wheeler, "Four Versions of *The Return of the Native*," *NCF*, XIV (1959). 27-44; Leonard W. Deen, "Heroism and Pathos in Hardy's *Return of the Native*," *NCF*, XV (1960). 207-219; Louis Crompton, "The Sunburnt God: Ritual and Tragic Myth in *The Return of the Native*," *Boston Univ. Stud. in English*, IV (1960). 229-240; Charles C. Walcutt, "Character and Coincidence in *The Return of the Native*," *Twelve Original Essays on Great English Novels*, ed. C. Shapiro (Detroit, 1960), pp. 153-173; John Hagan, "A Note on the Significance of Diggory Venn," *NCF*, XVI (1961). 147-155; Robert C. Schweik, "Theme, Character, and Perspective in Hardy's *The Return of the Native*," *PQ*, XLI (1962). 757-767.—George H. Thomson, "The *Trumpet-Major* Chronicle," *NCF*, XVII (1962). 45-56.

**1467** *The Mayor of Casterbridge*, ed. Harvey C. Webster (1948), S. C. Chew (1950), Albert Guerard (1956), Robert B. Heilman (1962). Douglas Brown, *Thomas Hardy: "The Mayor of Casterbridge"* (1961); Howard O. Brogan, "'Visible Essences' in *The Mayor of Casterbridge*," *ELH*, XVII (1950). 307-323; D. A. Dike, "A Modern Oedipus: *The Mayor of Casterbridge*," *EIC*, II (1952). 169-179; John Paterson, "*The Mayor of Casterbridge* as Tragedy," *VS*, III (1959). 151-172; Heilman, "Hardy's *Mayor* and the Problem of Intention," *Criticism*, V (1963). 199-213, and "Hardy's *Mayor*: Notes on Style," *NCF*, XVIII (1964). 307-329.—William H. Matchett, "*The Woodlanders*, or Realism in Sheep's Clothing," *NCF*, IX (1955). 241-261; George S. Fayen, Jr., "*The Woodlanders*: Inwardness and Memory," *SEL*, I, no. 4 (1961). 81-100.—*Tess of the d'Urber-*

*villes,* ed. Carl J. Weber (1951), William E. Buckler (Boston, 1960), Scott Elledge (1965). Allan Brick, "Paradise and Consciousness in Hardy's *Tess,*" *NCF,* XVII (1962). 115-134; Ian Gregor, "The Novel as Moral Protest: *Tess of the d'Urbervilles,*" *The Moral and the Story* (1962), pp. 135-150; Philip M. Griffith, "The Image of the Trapped Animal in Hardy's *Tess of the d'Urbervilles,*" *Tulane Stud. in English,* XIII (1963). 85-94; Elliott B. Gose, Jr., "Psychic Evolution: Darwinism and Initiation in *Tess of the d'Urbervilles,*" *NCF,* XVIII (1963). 261-272; Van Ghent, pp. 195-209.

**1468** *Jude the Obscure,* ed. William E. Buckler (1959), Irving Howe (Boston, 1965). Emma Clifford, "The Child: the Circus: and *Jude the Obscure,*" *Cambridge Jour.,* VII (1954). 531-546; Norman Holland, Jr., "*Jude the Obscure:* Hardy's Symbolic Indictment of Christianity," *NCF,* IX (1954). 50-60; Ted R. Spivey, "Thomas Hardy's Tragic Hero," *NCF,* IX (1954). 179-191; John Paterson, "The Genesis of *Jude the Obscure,*" *SP,* LVII (1960). 87-98; Arthur Mizener, "The Novel of Doctrine in the Nineteenth Century: Hardy's *Jude the Obscure,*" *The Sense of Life in the Modern Novel* (Boston, 1964), pp. 55-77; Lewis B. Horne, "Fawley's Quests: A Reading of *Jude the Obscure,*" *Tennessee Stud. in Lit.,* IX (1964). 117-127; William J. Hyde, "Theoretic and Practical Unconventionality in *Jude the Obscure,*" *NCF,* XX (1965). 155-164.

**1469** Note 13: Barnes: *Poems,* ed. Bernard Jones (2v, 1962), the first collected edition; *Poems Grave and Gay,* ed. Giles Dugdale (Dorchester, 1949); *Selected Poems,* ed. Geoffrey Grigson (1950).—Willis D. Jacobs, *William Barnes, Linguist* (Albuquerque, 1952); Dugdale, *William Barnes of Dorset* (1953); William Turner Levy, *William Barnes: The Man and the Poems* (1960); Rayner Unwin, *The Rural Muse* (1954), pp. 150-164; R. A. Forsyth, "The Conserving Myth of William Barnes," *VS,* VI (1963). 325-354.—On T. E. Brown, see Samuel Norris, *Two Men of Manxland* (Douglas, I. o. M., 1947).— Note 14: See G. W. Sherman, "Thomas Hardy and the Agricultural Laborer," *NCF,* VII (1952). 111-118.

**1471-1472** Note 23: Waldo H. Dunn, *Richard D. Blackmore, the Author of "Lorna Doone"* (1956); Kenneth Budd, *The Last Victorian* (1960).—W. E. Purcell, *Onward Christian Soldier: A Life of Sabine Baring-Gould* (1957); William J. Hyde, "The Stature of Baring-Gould as a Novelist," *NCF,* XV (1960). 1-16.—Jefferies: *The Story of My Heart,* ed. Samuel J. Looker (1947); *The Gamekeeper at Home,* ed. C. Henry Warren (1948); *The Essential Richard Jefferies,* ed. Malcolm Elwin (1948); *The Jefferies Companion* and *The Nature Diaries and Notebooks,* both ed. Looker (1948). A number of additional volumes of Jefferies' writings have been edited by Looker and others.—Reginald Arkell, *Richard Jefferies and His Countryside* (1947); W. J. Keith, *Richard Jefferies: A Critical Study* (1965); Samuel J. Looker and Crichton Porteous, *Richard Jefferies, Man of the Fields* (1965); J. W. Blench, "The Novels of Richard Jefferies," *Cambridge Jour.,* VII (1954). 361-377; William J. Hyde, "Richard Jefferies and the Naturalistic Peasant," *NCF,* XI (1956). 207-217.—*Eden Phillpotts: An Assessment and a Tribute,* ed. Waverly Girvan (1953).

**1473** James O. Bailey, *Hardy and the Cosmic Mind: A New Reading of "The Dynasts"* (Chapel Hill, 1956); Harold Orel, *Thomas Hardy's Epic-Drama* (Lawrence, Kan., 1963); Emma Clifford, "The '*Trumpet-Major* Notebook' and

*The Dynasts*," *RES*, n.s. VIII (1957). 149-161, and "The Impressionistic View of History in *The Dynasts*," *MLQ*, XXII (1961). 21-31; Roy Morrell, "*The Dynasts* Reconsidered," *MLR*, LVIII (1963). 161-171.

# XXXV. Aestheticism and "Decadence"

**1475**  *The Religion of Beauty: Selections from the Aesthetes*, ed. Richard Aldington (1950). Ruth Z. Temple, *The Critic's Alchemy: A Study of the Introduction of French Symbolism into England* (1953); Barbara Charlesworth, *Dark Passages: The Decadent Consciousness in Victorian Literature* (Madison, Wis., 1965); James K. Robinson, "A Neglected Phase of the Aesthetic Movement: English Parnassianism," *PMLA*, LXVIII (1953). 733-754; John Wilcox, "The Beginning of *l'art pour l'art*," *JAAC*, XI (1953). 360-377; Clyde de L. Ryals, "Toward a Definition of *Decadent* as Applied to British Literature of the Nineteenth Century," *JAAC*, XVII (1958). 85-92 (cf. Robert L. Peters, *JAAC*, XVIII [1959]. 258-264, and Russell M. Goldfarb, *ibid.*, XX [1962]. 369-373); Temple, "The Ivory Tower as Lighthouse," *Edwardians and Late Victorians* (1960), pp. 28-49; Buckley, *The Victorian Temper*, chs. IX, XI-XII; Hough, *The Last Romantics*, ch. V.

Pater: *Selected Works*, ed. Richard Aldington (1948); *Selected Writings*, ed. Derek Patmore (1949); *The Renaissance*, ed. Kenneth Clark (1961); *Imaginary Portraits: A New Collection*, ed. Eugene Brzenk (1964).—Germain d'Hangest, *Walter Pater: l'Homme et l'oeuvre* (2v, Paris, 1961); Edmund Chandler, *Pater on Style* (Copenhagen, 1958); Wolfgang Iser, *Walter Pater: die Autonomie des ästhetischen* (Tübingen, 1960); R. V. Johnson, *Walter Pater: A Study of His Critical Outlook and Achievement* (Cambridge, 1961); Bernard F. Huppé, "Walter Pater on Plato's Aesthetics," *MLQ*, IX (1948). 315-321; C. M. Bowra, "Walter Pater," *Sewanee Rev.*, LVII (1949). 378-400; Geoffrey Tillotson, "Arnold and Pater: Critics Historical, Aesthetic and Otherwise," *E&S*, n.s. III (1950). 47-68; Milton Millhauser, "Walter Pater and the Flux," *JAAC*, XI (1953). 214-223; Derek Stanford, "Pater's Ideal Aesthetic Type," *Cambridge Jour.*, VII (1954). 488-494; Lord David Cecil, *Walter Pater: the Scholar-Artist* (Cambridge, 1955); Angelo P. Bertocci, "French Criticism and the Pater Problem," *Boston Univ. Stud. in English*, I (1955). 178-194; Paul West, "Pater and the Tribulations of Taste," *UTQ*, XXVII (1958). 424-432; R. T. Lenaghan, "Pattern in Walter Pater's Fiction," *SP*, LVIII (1961). 69-91; Wendell V. Harris, "Pater as Prophet," *Criticism*, VI (1964). 349-360; U. C. Knoepflmacher, *Religion and Humanism in the Victorian Novel*, chs. V-VI; Hough, *The Last Romantics*, ch. IV; Wellek, *History of Modern Criticism*, IV. 381-399.

**1476**  R. V. Osbourn, "*Marius the Epicurean*," *EIC*, I (1951). 387-403; Jean Sudrann, "Victorian Compromise and Modern Revolution," *ELH*, XXVI (1959). 425-444; Bernard Duffey, "The Religion of Pater's *Marius*," *Texas Stud. in Lit. and Lang.*, II (1960). 103-114; Billie A. Inman, "The Organic Structure of *Marius the Epicurean*," *PQ*, XLI (1962). 475-491; Louise M. Rosenblatt, "The Genesis of Pater's *Marius the Epicurean*," *CL*, XIV (1962). 242-260; Martha S. Vogeler, "The Religious Meaning of *Marius the Epicurean*," *NCF*, XIX (1964). 287-299.

Note 8: *The New Republic*, ed. J. Max Patrick (Gainesville, Fla., 1950).— Charles C. Nickerson, "The Novels of W. H. Mallock: Notes toward a Bibliography" and "A Bibliography of the Novels of W. H. Mallock," *English Lit. in Transition*, VI, no. 4 (1963). 182-198. Carl R. Woodring, "William H. Mallock: A Neglected Wit," *More Books*, XXII (1947). 243-256; P. M. Yarker, "Voltaire among the Positivists: A Study of W. H. Mallock's *The New Paul and Virginia*," *E&S*, n.s. VIII (1955). 21-39, and "W. H. Mallock's Other Novels," *NCF*, XIV (1959). 189-205; Patrick, "The Portrait of Huxley in Mallock's *New Republic*," *NCF*, XI (1956). 61-69; Albert V. Turner, "W. H. Mallock and Late Victorian Conservatism," *UTQ*, XXXI (1962). 223-241.

**1477** Note 12: Phyllis Grosskurth, *John Addington Symonds* (1964); Robert L. Peters, "Athens and Troy: Notes on John Addington Symonds' Aestheticism," *English Fiction in Transition*, V, no. 5 (1962). 14-26; Grosskurth, "The Genesis of Symonds's Elizabethan Criticism," *MLR*, LIX (1964). 183-193.—Paget: *The Snake Lady and Other Stories*, ed. Horace Gregory (1954). Peter Gunn, *Vernon Lee: Violet Paget, 1856-1935* (1964).

**1479-1480** Wilde: *Works*, ed. G. F. Maine (1948); *Essays*, ed. Hesketh Pearson (1950); *The Portable Oscar Wilde*, ed. Richard Aldington (1946); *Plays, Prose Writings, and Poems*, ed. Pearson (1955); *Selected Writings*, ed. Richard Ellmann (1961); *Letters*, ed. Rupert Hart-Davis (1962).—Edouard Roditi, *Oscar Wilde* (Norfolk, Conn., 1947); Robert Merle, *Oscar Wilde* (Paris, 1948); *The Trials of Oscar Wilde*, ed. H. Montgomery Hyde (1948); George Woodcock, *The Paradox of Oscar Wilde* (1949); St. John Ervine, *Oscar Wilde* (1951); Vyvyan Holland, *Son of Oscar Wilde* (1954); Aatos Ojala, *Aestheticism and Oscar Wilde* (2v, Helsinki, 1954-55); Hyde, *Oscar Wilde: The Aftermath* (1963); "Oscar Wilde After Fifty Years," *LTLS*, Nov. 24, 1950, pp. 737-739; Alan Harris, "Oscar Wilde as Playwright: A Centenary Review," *Adelphi*, XXX (1954). 212-240; Arthur Ganz, "The Divided Self in the Society Comedies of Oscar Wilde," *Modern Drama*, III (1960). 16-23; Ted R. Spivey, "Damnation and Salvation in *The Picture of Dorian Gray*," *Boston Univ. Stud. in English*, IV (1960). 162-170; Ellmann, "Romantic Pantomime in Oscar Wilde," *Partisan Rev.*, XXX (1963). 342-355; LeRoy, *Perplexed Prophets*, ch. VII.

**1481** *The Importance of Being Earnest*, ed. Sarah A. Dickson (2v, 1956), the texts of the original manuscript and the corrected typescript.— Note 25: William Freeman, *The Life of Lord Alfred Douglas: Spoilt Child of Genius* (1948); Marie C. Stopes, *Lord Alfred Douglas: His Poetry and Personality* (1949); Rupert Croft-Cooke, *Bosie: The Story of Lord Alfred Douglas, His Friends and Enemies* (1963).—Note 27: The first full edition of the text of *De Profundis* was published in 1950, ed. Vyvyan Holland.

**1482** *The Yellow Book: A Selection*, ed. Norman Denny (1949); Katherine L. Mix, *A Study in Yellow: the Yellow Book and Its Contributors* (Lawrence, Kan., 1960).—*The Savoy: Nineties Experiment*, ed. Stanley Weintraub (University Park, Pa., 1966), an anthology. Wendell Harris, "Innocent Decadence: the Poetry of the *Savoy*," *PMLA*, LXXVII (1962). 629-636.—*The Best of Beardsley* (1948) and *A Beardsley Miscellany* (1949), both ed. R. A. Walker. Robin Ironside, "Aubrey Beardsley," *Horizon*, XIV (1946). 190-202; "Pierrot of the Minute," *LTLS*, March 19, 1949, p. 184.—Note 29: Cecil Woolf has edited Baron Corvo's *The Cardinal Prefect of Propaganda and Other Stories* (1957), *Nicholas Crabbe* (1958), *Don Renato* (1963), *Letters* (1959-    , various titles); as well as *A*

*Bibliography of Frederick Rolfe, Baron Corvo* (1957) and, with Brocard Sewell, *Corvo, 1860-1960* (Aylesford, 1961), a collection of eleven essays.

**1483**  Beerbohm: *Mainly on the Air* (1946; enlarged ed. 1957); *Max in Verse: Rhymes and Parodies*, ed. J. G. Riewald (Brattleboro, Vt., 1963); *The Incomparable Max*, ed. S. C. Roberts (1962), an anthology; *Letters to Reggie Turner*, ed. Rupert Hart-Davis (1964).—A. E. Gallatin and L. M. Oliver, *A Bibliography of the Works of Sir Max Beerbohm* (Cambridge, Mass., 1952). Riewald, *Sir Max Beerbohm* (The Hague, 1953); S. N. Behrman, *Portrait of Max* (1960; English title, *Conversation with Max*); Lord David Cecil, *Max: A Biography* (1964); Derek Stanford, "The Writings of Sir Max Beerbohm," *The Month*, XIII (1955). 325-365; Ellen Moers, *The Dandy* (1960), ch. XIV.

Roger Lhombreaud, *Arthur Symons: A Critical Biography* (1963); Arnold B. Sklare, "Arthur Symons: An Appreciation of the Critic of Literature," *JAAC*, IX (1951). 316-322; Ian Fletcher, "Symons, Yeats and the Demonic Dance," *London Mag.*, VII, no. 6 (1960). 46-60; John M. Munro, "Arthur Symons as Poet: Theory and Practice," *English Lit. in Transition*, VI (1963). 212-222; Edward Baugh, "Arthur Symons, Poet: A Centenary Tribute," *REL*, VI, no. 3 (1965). 70-80.

Richard Whittington-Egan and Geoffrey Smerdon, *The Quest of the Golden Boy: The Life and Letters of Richard LeGallienne* (1960).

Dowson: *Stories* (Philadelphia, 1947) and *Poems* (Philadelphia, 1963), both ed. Mark Longaker. Thomas B. Swann, *Ernest Dowson* (1964).

# XXXVI. The Novel: Naturalism and Romance

**1485**  On the fiction of this period and later see, in addition to some of the books cited above (suppl. to p. 1344), Madeleine M. Cazamian, *Le Roman et les idées en Angleterre, 1860-1914*, Vol. III: *Les Doctrines d'action et d'aventure, 1880-1914* (Paris, 1955). Earlier volumes of this work were published at Strasbourg in 1923 and 1935.

Butler: *Notebooks*, ed. Geoffrey Keynes and Brian Hill (1951), selections; *The Essential Samuel Butler*, ed. G. D. H. Cole (1950); *Correspondence of Samuel Butler with his Sister Mary*, ed. Daniel F. Howard (Berkeley, 1962); *The Family Letters of Samuel Butler*, ed. Arnold Silver (Stanford, 1962).—Stanley B. Harkness, *The Career of Samuel Butler (1835-1902): A Bibliography* (1955). P. N. Furbank, *Samuel Butler* (Cambridge, 1948); Philip Henderson, *Samuel Butler, the Incarnate Bachelor* (1953); Lee Holt, *Samuel Butler* (1964); Basil Willey, *Darwin and Butler: Two Versions of Evolution* (1960); Angus Wilson, "The Revolt of Samuel Butler," *Atl. Mo.*, CC (Nov., 1957). 190-198; Robert E. Shoenberg, "The Literal-Mindedness of Samuel Butler," *SEL*, IV (1964). 601-616; U. C. Knoepflmacher, *Religious Humanism and the Victorian Novel* (Princeton, 1965), chs. VII-VIII.

**1486**  Joseph J. Jones, *The Cradle of "Erewhon": Samuel Butler in New Zealand* (Austin, Tex., 1959).

**1487**  *The Way of All Flesh*, ed. William Y. Tindall (1950), Royal A. Gettmann (1948), Morton D. Zabel (1950), A. J. Hoppé (1954), Daniel F. Howard (Boston, 1964), the last-named printing Butler's original, uncut text. G. D. H. Cole, *Samuel Butler and "The Way of All Flesh"* (1947); Kettle, II. 35-48.

**1488**  Wilfred H. Stone, *Religion and the Art of William Hale White* (Stanford, 1954); Catherine M. Maclean, *Mark Rutherford: A Biography of William Hale White* (1955); Irvin Stock, *William Hale White* (1956); E. S. Merton, "The Autobiographical Novels of Mark Rutherford," *NCF*, v (1950). 189-207 and "The Personality of Mark Rutherford," *NCF*, vi (1951). 1-20; Patricia Thomson, "The Novels of Mark Rutherford," *EIC*, xiv (1964). 256-267; Willey, *More Nineteenth Century Studies*, ch. v.

**1489**  Vera Buchanan-Gould, *Not Without Honour: the Life and Writings of Olive Schreiner* (1949); D. L. Hobman, *Olive Schreiner: Her Friends and Times* (1955); Lyndall Gregg, *Memories of Olive Schreiner* (1957).

On Mrs. Humphry Ward: Basil Willey, "How *Robert Elsmere* Struck Some Contemporaries," *E&S*, n.s. x (1957). 53-68; Clara Lederer, "Mary Arnold Ward and the Victorian Ideal," *NCF*, vi (1951). 201-208.

On Shorthouse: Morchard Bishop, "*John Inglesant* and Its Author," *Essays by Divers Hands* (Royal Soc. of Lit.), n.s. xxix (1958). 73-86.

**1490**  Gissing: *Commonplace Book*, ed. Jacob Korg (1962); *Letters to Eduard Bertz, 1887-1903*, ed. Arthur C. Young (New Brunswick, N.J., 1961); *George Gissing and H. G. Wells: Their Friendship and Correspondence*, ed. Royal A. Gettmann (Urbana, Ill., 1961); *Letters to Gabrielle Fleury*, ed. Pierre Coustillas (1964).—Bibliography in Stevenson, pp. 401-413, and Joseph J. Wolff, "George Gissing: An Annotated Bibliography of Writings about Him," *English Fiction in Transition*, iii, no. 2 (1960). 3-33. Morley Roberts, *The Private Life of Henry Maitland* was reissued in 1958 with extensive annotations by Morchard Bishop. Mabel C. Donnelly, *George Gissing: Grave Comedian* (Cambridge, Mass., 1954); Korg, *George Gissing* (Seattle, 1963); "The Permanent Stranger," *LTLS*, Feb. 14, 1948, p. 92; Russell Kirk, "Who Knows George Gissing?", *Western Humanities Rev.*, iv (1950). 213-222; Korg, "George Gissing's Outcast Intellectuals," *Amer. Scholar*, xix (1950). 194-202, and "Division of Purpose in George Gissing," *PMLA*, lxx (1955). 323-336; Jackson I. Cope, "Definition as Structure in Gissing's *Ryecroft Papers*," *Modern Fiction Studies*, iii (1957). 127-140; John Middleton Murry, "George Gissing," *Katherine Mansfield and Other Literary Studies* (1959), pp. 3-68; C. J. Francis, "Gissing and Schopenhauer," *NCF*, xv (1960). 53-63.

**1492**  Jacob Korg, "The Spiritual Theme of George Gissing's *Born in Exile*," *From Jane Austen to Joseph Conrad*, pp. 246-256.—*New Grub Street*, ed. Irving Howe (Boston, 1962).

**1493**  Fred W. Boege, "Sir Walter Besant: Novelist," *NCF*, x (1956). 249-280, xi (1956). 32-60; Ernest Boll, "Walter Besant on the Art of the Novel," *English Fiction in Transition*, ii, no. 1 (1959). 28-35.

**1493-1494**  *Letters to Lady Cunard, 1895-1933*, ed. Rupert Hart-Davis (1957). —Bibliography in Stevenson, pp. 389-401, and Helmut E. Gerber, "George Moore: An Annotated Bibliography of Writings about Him," *English Fiction in Transition*, ii, no. 2 (1959). 1-91; iii, no. 2 (1960). 34-46; iv, no. 2 (1961). 30-42. Nancy Cunard, *GM: Memories of George Moore* (1956); Sonja Nejdefors-Frisk, *George Moore's Naturalistic Prose* (Uppsala, 1952); Malcolm Brown, *George Moore: A Reconsideration* (Seattle, 1955); Georges-Paul Collet, *George Moore et la France* (Geneva, 1957); Max Beerbohm, "George Moore," *Atl. Mo.*, clxxxvi

(Dec., 1950). 34-39; J[oseph] H[one], "George Moore: The Making of a Writer," *LTLS*, Feb. 29, 1952, pp. 149-150; Wayne Shumaker, "The Autobiographer as Artist: George Moore's *Hail and Farewell*," *The Image of the Work* (Berkeley, 1955), pp. 159-185; Graham Hough, "George Moore and the Nineties," *Edwardians and Late Victorians* (1960), pp. 1-27, and "George Moore and the Novel," *REL*, I, no. 1 (1960). 35-44.

**1495**  *Esther Waters*, ed. Malcolm Brown (1958), Lionel Stevenson (Boston, 1963).

**1498**  Stevenson: *Collected Poems*, ed. Janet Adam Smith (1950), authoritative texts; *Novels and Stories*, ed. V. S. Pritchett (1945); *Selected Writings*, ed. Saxe Commins (1947); *The Stevenson Companion*, ed. John Hampden (1950); *Essays*, ed. Malcolm Elwin (1950); *Tales and Essays*, ed. G. B. Stern (1950); *Selected Essays*, ed. George Scott-Moncrieff (1959); *The Mind of Robert Louis Stevenson: Selected Essays, Letters and Prayers*, ed. Roger Ricklefs (1963); *Edinburgh: Picturesque Notes*, ed. Smith (1954); *Henry James and Robert Louis Stevenson: A Record of Friendship and Criticism*, ed. Smith (1948); *RLS: Stevenson's Letters to Charles Baxter*, ed. DeLancey Ferguson and Marshall Waingrow (New Haven, 1956). A comprehensive edition of Stevenson's letters is being prepared by Bradford A. Booth.—George L. McKay, *A Stevenson Library . . . Formed by Edwin J. Beinecke* (6v, New Haven, 1951-1964). J. C. Furnas, *Voyage to Windward* (1951), the best biography; Lettice Cooper, *Robert Louis Stevenson* (1947); Malcolm Elwin, *The Strange Case of Robert Louis Stevenson* (1950); Laura L. Hinkley, *The Stevensons: Louis and Fanny* (1950); Richard Aldington, *Portrait of a Rebel* (1957). Additional biographical material is in Anne B. Fisher, *No More a Stranger* (Stanford, 1946); A. R. Issler, *Happier for His Presence* (Stanford, 1949) and *Our Mountain Heritage* (Stanford, 1950); Joseph W. Ellison, *Tusitala of the South Seas* (1953); *Our Samoan Adventure*, ed. Charles Neider (1955), Mrs. Stevenson's diary; and Elsie N. Caldwell, *Last Witness for Robert Louis Stevenson* (Norman, Okla., 1960). David Daiches, *Robert Louis Stevenson* (Norfolk, Conn., 1947); Robert Kiely, *Robert Louis Stevenson and the Fiction of Adventure* (Cambridge, Mass., 1964); H. W. Garrod, "The Poetry of R. L. Stevenson," *Essays, Mainly on the Nineteenth Century, Presented to Sir Humphrey Milford* (1948), pp. 42-57.

**1501**  George Blake, *Barrie and the Kailyard School* (1951).
J. E. Scott, *A Bibliography of the Works of Sir Henry Rider Haggard* (1947). Lilias Rider Haggard, *The Cloak That I Left* (1951); Morton Cohen, *Rider Haggard: His Life and Works* (1960).
"*Q*" *Anthology*, ed. F. Brittain (1948). Brittain, *Arthur Quiller-Couch: A Biographical Study* (Cambridge, 1947).
John Dickson Carr, *The Life of Sir Arthur Conan Doyle* (1949); Pierre Nardon, *Sir Arthur Conan Doyle* (Paris, 1965); Hugh Kenner, "Baker Street to Eccles Street: the Odyssey of a Myth," *Hudson Rev.*, I (1949). 481-499, on the Holmes "myth" and its analogues in Joyce. See also the files of the *Baker Street Journal* (1946-    ) and the numerous books and brochures issued by Holmesian enthusiasts.
S. Gorley Putt, "The Prisoner of *The Prisoner of Zenda*: Anthony Hope and the Novel of Society," *EIC*, VI (1956). 38-59.—Note 37: "Ellery Queen," *Queen's Quorum: A History of the Detective Crime Short Story* (Boston, 1951); Suther-

land Scott, *Blood in Their Ink: the March of the Modern Mystery Novel* (1953); special issue of *LTLS*, Feb. 25, 1955; A. E. Murch, *The Development of the Detective Novel* (1958).

**1502** *A Choice of Kipling's Prose*, with introd. by W. Somerset Maugham (1952). *The Best Short Stories of Rudyard Kipling*, with introd. by Randall Jarrell (1961).—James McG. Stewart, *Rudyard Kipling: A Bibliographical Catalogue* (Toronto, 1959); Helmut E. Gerber and Edward Lauterbach, "Rudyard Kipling: An Annotated Bibliography of Writings about Him," *English Fiction in Transition*, III, nos. 3-5 (1960). 1-235; VIII, nos. 3-4 (1965). 136-241. C. E. Carrington, *The Life of Rudyard Kipling* (1955), the authorized biography; Rupert Croft-Cooke, *Rudyard Kipling* (1948); Robert Escarpit, *Rudyard Kipling: Servitudes et grandeurs impériales* (Paris, 1955); Francis Léaud, *La Poétique de Rudyard Kipling* (Paris, 1958); J. M. S. Tompkins, *The Art of Rudyard Kipling* (1959); C. A. Bodelsen, *Aspects of Kipling's Art* (Manchester, 1964); Roger L. Green, *The Reader's Guide to Rudyard Kipling's Work* (Canterbury, 1961) and *Kipling and the Children* (1965); Lionel Trilling, "Kipling," *The Liberal Imagination* (1950), pp. 118-128; H. L. Varley, "Imperialism and Rudyard Kipling," *JHI*, XIV (1953). 124-135; Michael Edwardes, "Rudyard Kipling and the Imperial Imagination," *Twentieth Century*, CLIII (1953). 443-454; Noel Annan, "Kipling's Place in the History of Ideas," *VS*, III (1960). 323-348; *Kipling's Mind and Art: Selected Critical Essays*, ed. Andrew Rutherford (Stanford, 1964); *Kipling and the Critics*, ed. Elliot L. Gilbert (1965); Stewart, *Eight Modern Writers*, ch. VI.

**1504** A. W. Yeats, "The Genesis of *The Recessional*," *Univ. of Texas Stud. in English*, XXXI (1952). 97-108.

**1506** Note 49: See also Donald L. Hill, "Kipling in Vermont," *NCF*, VII (1952). 153-170.

# XXXVII. The Irish Literary Renaissance

**1507** *One Thousand Years of Irish Poetry*, ed. Kathleen Hoagland (1947); *Irish Poets of the Nineteenth Century*, ed. Geoffrey Taylor (Cambridge, Mass., 1951); *One Thousand Years of Irish Prose*. Part I: *The Literary Revival*, ed. Vivian Mercier and David H. Greene (1952).—Benedict Kiely, *Modern Irish Fiction: A Critique* (Dublin, 1950); Estella R. Taylor, *The Modern Irish Writers: Cross Currents of Criticism* (Lawrence, Kan., 1954); Herbert Howarth, *The Irish Writers, 1880-1940: Literature under Parnell's Star* (1958). *The Genius of the Irish Theater*, ed. Sylvan Barnet, Morton Berman, and William Burto (1960), an anthology of plays. Peter Kavanagh, *The Story of the Abbey Theatre* (1950); *Ireland's Abbey Theatre: A History, 1899-1951*, ed. Lennox Robinson (1951); Jan Setterquist, *Ibsen and the Beginnings of Anglo-Irish Drama* (2v, Cambridge, Mass., 1951-60); Gerard Fay, *The Abbey Theatre: Cradle of Genius* (1958).

**1508** Yeats: *Collected Plays* (1952); *Poems* (2v, 1949), definitive edition; *Variorum Edition of the Poems*, ed. Peter Allt and Russell Alspach (1957); *Poems*, ed. A. Norman Jeffares (1962); *Selected Poems*, ed. M. L. Rosenthal

(1962); *Essays and Introductions* (1961); *Senate Speeches,* ed. Donald R. Pearce (Bloomington, Ind., 1960); *Explorations,* ed. Mrs. W. B. Yeats (1962); *Autobiography* (1953); *W. B. Yeats and T. Sturge Moore: Their Correspondence 1901-1937,* ed. Ursula Bridge (1953); *Letters to Katharine Tynan,* ed. Roger J. McHugh (1953); *Letters,* ed. Allan Wade (1954).—Wade, *A Bibliography of the Writings of W. B. Yeats* (1951, rev. 1958); George B. Saul, *Prolegomena to the Study of Yeats's Poems* (Philadelphia, 1957) and *Prolegomena to the Study of Yeats's Plays* (Philadelphia, 1958); John Unterecker, *A Reader's Guide to W. B. Yeats* (1959). Richard Ellmann, *Yeats: The Man and the Masks* (1948) and *The Identity of Yeats* (1954); Jeffares, *W. B. Yeats, Man and Poet* (New Haven, 1949, rev. 1962); Monk Gibbon, *The Masterpiece and the Man: Yeats as I Knew Him* (1959); three books by Peter Ure, *Towards a Mythology: Studies in the Poetry of W. B. Yeats* (1946), *Yeats the Playwright: A Commentary on Character and Design in the Major Plays* (1963), and *Yeats* (Edinburgh, 1963); Donald A. Stauffer, *The Golden Nightingale: Essays on Some Principles of Poetry in the Lyrics of William Butler Yeats* (1949); Thomas R. Henn, *The Lonley Tower: Studies in the Poetry of W. B. Yeats* (1950, rev. 1965); Birgit Bjersby, *The Interpretation of the Cuchulain Legend in the Works of W. B. Yeats* (Dublin, 1950); Vivienne Koch, *Yeats: The Tragic Phase: A Study of the Last Poems* (1951); Thomas F. Parkinson, *W. B. Yeats, Self-Critic: A Study of His Early Verse* (Berkeley, 1951), and *W. B. Yeats: The Later Poetry* (Berkeley, 1964); Arland Ussher, *Three Great Irishmen: Shaw, Yeats, Joyce* (1952); Margaret Rudd, *Divided Image: A Study of William Blake and W. B. Yeats* (1953); Virginia Moore, *The Unicorn: Yeats's Search for Reality* (1954); Hazard Adams, *Blake and Yeats: The Contrary Vision* (Ithaca, 1955); Francis A. C. Wilson, *W. B. Yeats and Tradition* (1958) and *Yeats's Iconography* (1960); Giorgio Melchiori, *The Whole Mystery of Art* (1960); George T. Wright, *The Poet in the Poem: The Personae of Eliot, Yeats and Pound* (Berkeley, 1960); Benjamin L. Reid, *W. B. Yeats: The Lyric of Tragedy* (Norman, Okla., 1961); Amy G. Stock, *W. B. Yeats: His Poetry and Thought* (Cambridge, 1961); Morton I. Seiden, *William Butler Yeats: The Poet as Mythmaker* (East Lansing, Mich., 1962); Richard M. Kain, *Dublin in the Age of William Butler Yeats and James Joyce* (Norman, Okla., 1962); Jon Stallworthy, *Between the Lines: Yeats's Poetry in the Making* (Oxford, 1963); Helen H. Vendler, *Yeats's Vision and the Later Plays* (Cambridge, Mass., 1963); Edward Engelberg, *The Vast Design: Patterns in W. B. Yeats's Aesthetic* (Toronto, 1964); Priscilla W. Shaw, *Rilke, Valéry, and Yeats: The Domain of the Self* (New Brunswick, N. J., 1964); Thomas R. Whitaker, *Swan and Shadow: Yeats's Dialogue with History* (Chapel Hill, 1964); Leonard Nathan, *The Tragic Drama of William Butler Yeats* (1965); Suheil B. Bushrui, *Yeats' Verse Plays: The Revisions, 1900-1910* (1965); Donald Torchiana, *W. B. Yeats and Georgian Ireland* (Evanston, Ill., 1966); Alex Zwerdling, *Yeats and the Heroic Ideal* (1965); Balachandra Rajan, *W. B. Yeats: A Critical Introduction* (1965); *W. B. Yeats, 1865-1965: Centenary Essays,* ed. D. E. S. Maxwell and S. B. Bushrui (Ibadan, 1965); *In Excited Reverie: A Centenary Tribute,* ed. Jeffares and K. G. W. Cross (1965); *The Permanence of Yeats: Selected Criticism,* ed. James Hall and Martin Steinmann (1950); *Yeats: A Collection of Critical Essays,* ed. Unterecker (1963); *The Integrity of Yeats,* ed. Denis Donoghue (Cork, 1964); *The World of W. B. Yeats: Essays in Perspective,* ed. Robin Skelton and Ann Saddlemyer (Seattle, 1965); Bayley,

*The Romantic Survival*, ch. viii; Hough, *The Last Romantics*, ch. vi; Stewart, *Eight Modern Writers*, ch. vii (see selected list of chapters and essays on Yeats, pp. 677-679).—*Concordance to the Poems of W. B. Yeats*, ed. Stephen M. Parrish (Ithaca, 1963).

**1510**  Lady Gregory: *Selected Plays*, ed. Elizabeth Coxhead (1962); *Journals, 1916-1930*, ed. Lennox Robinson (1946). Coxhead, *Lady Gregory: A Literary Portrait* (1961); Ann Saddlemyer, *In Defense of Lady Gregory, Playwright* (1965).—Note 14: Sister Marie-Thérèse Courtney, *Edward Martyn and the Irish Theater* (1957); Jan Setterquist, *Ibsen and the Beginnings of Anglo-Irish Drama. 2. Edward Martyn* (Cambridge, Mass., 1960).

**1512**  *Letters from Æ*, ed. Alan Denson (1961). Denson, *Printed Writings by George W. Russell (Æ): A Bibliography* (Evanston, Ill., 1961). "John Eglinton" [William Magee], "The Poetry of Æ," *Dublin Mag.*, n.s. xxvi, no. 3 (1951). 5-9.

**1513**  Synge: *Collected Works* (5v, 1962-      ); *Plays and Poems*, ed. T. R. Henn (1963); *Translations*, ed. Robin Skelton (Dublin, 1961); *Autobiography*, ed. Alan Price (Dublin, 1965).—Jan Setterquist, *Ibsen and the Beginnings of Anglo-Irish Drama. 1. John Millington Synge* (Cambridge, Mass., 1951); David H. Greene and Edward M. Stephens, *J. M. Synge, 1871-1909* (1959); Price, *Synge and the Anglo-Irish Drama* (1961); Donna Gerstenberger, *John Millington Synge* (1964); Roger McHugh, "Yeats, Synge and the Abbey Theatre," *Studies*, xli (1952). 333-340; Norman Podhoretz, "Synge's *Playboy*: Morality and the Hero," *EIC*, iii (1953). 337-344; Ellen Douglass Leyburn, "The Theme of Loneliness in the Plays of Synge," *Modern Drama*, i (1958). 84-90; O'Casey and Synge number of *Modern Drama*, iv (Dec., 1961). There are also short contributions by Greene in *PMLA*, lxii (1947). 233-238, 824-827, and lxiii (1948). 1314-1321.

**1514**  Michael J. O'Neill, *Lennox Robinson* (1964). O'Casey's six autobiographical volumes were collected as *Mirror in My House* (2v, 1956).—Jules Koslow, *The Green and the Red: Sean O'Casey, the Man and His Plays* (1950); Robert G. Hogan, *The Experiments of Sean O'Casey* (1960); David Krause, *Sean O'Casey: The Man and His Work* (1960); Saros Cowasjee, *Sean O'Casey: The Man Behind the Plays* (Edinburgh, 1963); O'Casey and Synge number of *Modern Drama*, iv (Dec., 1961).

**1515**  Note 20: *Collected Poems* (1954); *A James Stephens Reader* (1962) and *James, Seumas and Jacques: Unpublished Writings of James Stephens* (1964), both ed. Lloyd Frankenberg; *Memoirs*, ed. Merle M. Bevington (1954). Birgit Bramsbäck, *James Stephens: A Literary and Bibliographical Study* (Uppsala, 1959); Hilary Pyle, *James Stephens: His Work and An Account of His Life* (1965); Augustine Martin, "James Stephens: Lyric Poet," *Studies*, xlix (1960). 173-182, l (1961). 75-87.

# XXXVIII. Modern Drama

**1516**  On antecedents of the modern period see suppl. to p. 1264 above. *Edwardian Plays*, ed. Gerald Weales (1962); *The Genius of the Later English*

*Theater*, ed. Sylvan Barnet *et al.* (1962). Ernest Reynolds, *Modern English Drama: A Survey of the Theatre from 1900* (1950); John C. Trewin, *Theatre Since 1900* (1951); Albert E. Wilson, *Edwardian Theatre* (1951); Frederick Lumley, *Trends in Twentieth-Century Drama* (1956, rev. 1960); Weales, *Religion in Modern English Drama* (Philadelphia, 1961), and "The Edwardian Theater and the Shadow of Shaw," *Edwardians and Late Victorians* (1960), pp. 160-187; Raymond Williams, "Criticism into Drama, 1888-1950," *EIC*, 1 (1951). 120-138.

**1517**  Maynard Savin, *Thomas William Robertson, His Plays and Stagecraft* (Providence, R. I., 1950).—*The Savoy Operas*, ed. Derek Hudson (2v, 1962-63). C. L. Purdy, *Gilbert and Sullivan, Masters of Mirth and Melody* (1947); William A. Darlington, *The World of Gilbert and Sullivan* (1950); Leslie Baily, *The Gilbert and Sullivan Book* (1952, rev. 1956); Audrey Williamson, *Gilbert and Sullivan Opera: A New Assessment* (1953); Hesketh Pearson, *Gilbert: His Life and Strife* (1957); *Crowell's Handbook of Gilbert and Sullivan*, ed. Frank L. Moore (1962).—Jan Setterquist, *Ibsen and the Beginnings of Anglo-Irish Drama* (2v, Cambridge, Mass., 1951-1960).

**1518**  James O. Bailey, "Science in the Dramas of Henry Arthur Jones," *Booker Memorial Studies* (Chapel Hill, 1950), pp. 155-183.

**1520**  *The Theatre of Bernard Shaw*, ed. Alan S. Downer (1961), ten plays; *Selected Prose*, ed. Diarmuid Russell (1952); *Selected Non-Dramatic Writings*, ed. Dan H. Laurence (Boston, 1965); *Bernard Shaw: A Prose Anthology*, ed. H. M. Burton (1959); *Sixteen Self-Sketches* (1949); *The Quintessence of G. B. S.*, ed. Stephen Winsten (1949); *Shaw and Society: An Anthology and a Symposium*, ed. C. E. M. Joad (1953); *An Unfinished Novel*, ed. Stanley Weintraub (1958); *Shaw on Education*, ed. Louis Simon (1958); *Shaw on Theatre*, ed. E. J. West (1958); *Dramatic Criticism (1895-98)*, ed. John F. Matthews (1959); *How to Become a Musical Critic*, ed. Dan H. Laurence (1961); *Platform and Pulpit*, ed. Laurence (1961); *On Shakespeare*, ed. Edwin Wilson (1961); *The Matter with Ireland*, ed. Dan H. Laurence and David H. Greene (1962); *On Language*, ed. Abraham Tauber (1963); *Religious Speeches*, ed. Warren S. Smith (University Park, Pa., 1963); *The Rationalization of Russia*, ed. Harry M. Geduld (Bloomington, Ind., 1964). *Collected Letters*, ed. Dan H. Laurence (4v, 1965-    ); *Bernard Shaw and Mrs. Patrick Campbell: Their Correspondence*, ed. Alan Dent (1952); *Advice to a Young Critic and Other Letters*, ed. West (1955); *Letters to Granville-Barker*, ed. C. B. Purdom (1957); *To a Young Actress: The Letters of Bernard Shaw to Molly Tompkins*, ed. Peter Tompkins (1960).—Earl Farley and Marvin Carlson, "George Bernard Shaw: A Selected Bibliography (1945-1955)," *Modern Drama*, II (1959). 188-202, 295-325. Archibald Henderson, *George Bernard Shaw: Man of the Century* (1956), the third and final version of this "authorized" biography; St. John Ervine, *Bernard Shaw: His Life, Work, and Friends* (1956); Hesketh Pearson, *Bernard Shaw: His Life and Personality* (1961), combining his 1942 biography and *G.B.S.: A Postscript* (1950); three books by Stephen Winsten, *Days with Bernard Shaw* (1948), *Shaw's Corner* (1952), and *Jesting Apostle: The Life of Bernard Shaw* (1956); *Shaw the Villager and Human Being*, ed. Allan Chappelow (1961), like Winsten's books typical of the large literature of personalia surrounding Shaw's figure; Lawrence

Langner, *G.B.S. and the Lunatic* (1963); Weintraub, *Private Shaw and Public Shaw: A Dual Portrait of Lawrence of Arabia and G.B.S.* (1963); Audrey Williamson, *Bernard Shaw: Man and Writer* (1963); B. C. Rosset, *Shaw of Dublin: The Formative Years* (University Park, Pa., 1964); Eric Bentley, *Bernard Shaw: A Reconsideration* (Norfolk, Conn., 1947; rev. 1957); William Irvine, *The Universe of G.B.S.* (1949); Joad, *Shaw* (1949); Edmund Fuller, *George Bernard Shaw: Critic of Western Morale* (1950); Alick West, *George Bernard Shaw: A Good Man Fallen Among Fabians* (1950); Desmond MacCarthy, *Shaw's Plays in Review* (1951); A. C. Ward, *Bernard Shaw* (1951); Arland Ussher, *Three Great Irishmen: Shaw, Yeats, Joyce* (1952); Arthur H. Nethercot, *Men and Supermen: The Shavian Portrait Gallery* (Cambridge, Mass., 1954); Julian B. Kaye, *Bernard Shaw and the Nineteenth Century Tradition* (Norman, Okla., (1958); Richard M. Ohmann, *Shaw: the Style and the Man* (Middletown, Conn., 1962); C. B. Purdom, *A Guide to the Plays of Bernard Shaw* (1963); Martin Meisel, *Shaw and the Nineteenth-Century Theater* (Princeton, 1963); Homer E. Woodbridge, *George Bernard Shaw* (Carbondale, Ill., 1963); Barbara B. Watson, *A Shavian Guide to the Intelligent Woman* (1964); *G. B. S. 90: Aspects of Bernard Shaw's Life and Work*, ed. Winsten (1946), a symposium; *George Bernard Shaw: A Critical Survey*, ed. Louis Kronenberger (1953); Stewart, *Eight Modern Writers*, ch. IV; *The Shaw Bulletin*, later *The Shaw Review* (1951-    ); *The Independent Shavian*, later *The Shavian* (1963-    ).

**1525** Charles B. Purdom, *Harley Granville-Barker: Man of the Theatre, Dramatist and Scholar* (1955); Margery M. Morgan, *A Drama of Political Man: A Study in the Plays of Harley Granville-Barker* (1961); Alan S. Downer, "Harley Granville-Barker," *Sewanee Rev.*, LV (1947). 627-645.

**1528** Richard A. Cordell, "The Theatre of Somerset Maugham," *Modern Drama*, I (1959). 211-227.—Cynthia Asquith, *Portrait of Barrie* (1954); Roger L. Green, *Fifty Years of "Peter Pan"* (1954), on the play's theatrical tradition.

**1530** Bottomley: *Poems and Plays*, ed. C. C. Abbott (1953); *A Stage for Poetry: My Purposes with Plays* (Kendal, 1948); *Poet and Painter, Being the Correspondence between Gordon Bottomley and Paul Nash, 1910-1946*, ed. C. C. Abbott and Anthony Bertram (1955). A. J. Farmer, "Gordon Bottomley," *Études anglaises*, IX (1956). 323-327.—Muriel Spark, *John Masefield* (1953).

# XXXIX. Other Late-Victorian Poets

**1532** Patmore: *Poems*, ed. Frederick Page (Oxford, 1949); *A Selection of Poems*, ed. Derek Patmore (rev. of 1931 vol., 1949); *The Rod, the Root, and the Flower*, ed. D. Patmore (1950); *Essay on English Metrical Law*, ed. Sister Mary Roth (Washington, D.C., 1961).—Augusto Guidi, *Coventry Patmore* (Brescia, 1946); D. Patmore, *The Life and Times of Coventry Patmore* (1949), a complete revision of his *Portrait of My Family* (1935); Edward J. Oliver, *Coventry Patmore* (1956); John C. Reid, *The Mind and Art of Coventry Patmore* (1957); J. M. Cohen, "Prophet without Responsibility," *EIC*, I (1951). 283-297; Heath-Stubbs, *The Darkling Plain*, pp. 128-140.

**1533** Francis Thompson: *Literary Criticisms* (1948), [reviews of] *Minor*

*Poets* (Los Angeles, 1949), *The Man Has Wings: New Poems and Plays* (1957), and *The Real Robert Louis Stevenson and Other Critical Essays* (1959), all ed. Terence L. Connolly.—Myrtle P. Pope, *A Critical Bibliography of Works by and about Francis Thompson* (1959). Viola Meynell, *Francis Thompson and Wilfrid Meynell: A Memoir* (1952); John C. Reid, *Francis Thompson* (1959); Pierre Danchin, *Francis Thompson: la Vie et l'oeuvre d'un poète* (Paris, 1959); Paul Van K. Thomson, *Francis Thompson* (1961); Danchin, "Francis Thompson (1859-1907): À propos d'un centenaire," *Études anglaises*, XIII (1960). 427-443; Peter Butter, "Francis Thompson," *REL*, II, no. 1 (1961). 87-94.

**1535**   Meynell: *Prose and Poetry, Centenary Volume*, ed. Frederick Page *et al.* (1947); *Essays* (Westminster, Md., 1947) and *Poems* (1948), both ed. Francis Meynell. *Alice Meynell Centenary Tribute, 1847-1947*, ed. Terence L. Connolly (Boston, 1948); "An Idyll of Life and Letters," *LTLS*, Oct. 18, 1947, p. 534.— Johnson: *Complete Poems*, ed. Iain Fletcher (1953). A. Bronson Feldman, "The Art of Lionel Johnson," *Poet Lore*, LVII (1953). 140-160.

**1536**   James Sambrook, *A Poet Hidden: The Life of Richard Watson Dixon, 1833-1900* (1962).—Mary Coleridge: *Collected Poems*, ed. Theresa Whistler (1954). Beatrice White, "Mary Coleridge: An Appreciation," *E&S*, XXXI (1945). 81-94.

**1536-1537**   Hopkins: *Poems*, ed. W. H. Gardner (1948, enlarged ed. 1956), superseding earlier editions; *Sermons and Devotional Writings*, ed. Christopher Devlin (1949, rev. 1959); *Selected Poems*, ed. James Reeves (1953); *A Hopkins Reader*, ed. John Pick (1953); *Poems and Prose*, ed. Gardner (1954). The *Note-Books and Papers*, ed. House, appeared in an enlarged edition (as *Journals and Papers*), ed. Graham Storey (1959), as did the *Further Letters*, ed. Abbott (1956).—Bibliography in Faverty, ch. VIII. Vol. II of Gardner's *Gerard Manley Hopkins* appeared in 1949. *Immortal Diamond: Studies in Gerard Manley Hopkins*, ed. Norman Weyand and R. V. Schoder (1949), an important collection of critical essays by American Jesuits; Sister Marcella Marie Holloway, *The Prosodic Theory of Gerard Manley Hopkins* (Washington, D.C., 1947); W. A. M. Peters, *Gerard Manley Hopkins: A Critical Essay towards the Understanding of His Poetry* (1948); Geoffrey H. Hartman, *The Unmediated Vision* (New Haven, 1954); Alan Heuser, *The Shaping Vision of Gerard Manley Hopkins* (1958); Robert R. Boyle, *Metaphor in Hopkins* (Chapel Hill, 1961); Jean-Georges Ritz, *Le Poète Gerard Manley Hopkins: sa vie et son oeuvre* (Paris, 1964); two identically titled articles by Selma Jeanne Cohen and John K. Mathison, "The Poetic Theory of Gerard Manley Hopkins," *PQ*, XXVI (1947). 1-20, 21-35; James Collins, "Philosophical Themes in G. M. Hopkins," *Thought*, XXII (1947). 67-106; Yvor Winters, "The Poetry of Gerard Manley Hopkins," *Hudson Rev.*, I (1949). 455-476, II (1949). 61-93 (a severe judgment; cf. reply by J. H. Johnston in *Renascence*, II [1950]. 117-125); Marjorie D. Coogan, "Inscape and Instress: Further Analogies with Scotus," *PMLA*, LXV (1950). 66-74; Donald A. Davie, "Hopkins as a Decadent Critic," *Purity of Diction in English Verse* (1952), pp. 160-182; Lois W. Pitchford, "The Curtal Sonnets of Gerard Manley Hopkins," *MLN*, LXVII (1952). 165-169; J. Hillis Miller, "The Creation of the Self in Gerard Manley Hopkins," *ELH*, XXII (1955). 293-319; Walker Gibson, "Sound and Sense in G. M. Hopkins," *MLN*, LXXIII (1958). 95-100; Paull F. Baum, "Sprung

Rhythm," *PMLA*, LXXIV (1959). 418-425; John Wain, "Gerard Manley Hopkins: An Idiom of Desperation," *Proc. Brit. Acad.*, XLV (1959). 173-197; Carl Wooton, "The Terrible Fire of Gerard Manley Hopkins," *Texas Stud. in Lit. and Lang.*, IV (1962). 367-375; Miller, *The Disappearance of God* (1963), ch. VI; Elisabeth W. Schneider, "Sprung Rhythm: A Chapter in the Evolution of Nineteenth-Century Verse," *PMLA*, LXXX (1965). 237-253.

**1537** Note 19: See Philip M. Martin, *Mastery and Mercy: A Study of Two Religious Poems* (1957), on *The Wreck of the Deutschland* and Eliot's *Ash Wednesday*, and John E. Keating, *"The Wreck of the Deutschland": an Essay and a Commentary* (Kent, Ohio, 1963).—Note 20: Among the many explications and analyses of *The Windhover* since 1948 are those of F. N. Lees, *Scrutiny*, XVII (1950). 32-37; Carl R. Woodring, *Western Rev.*, XV (1950). 61-64; F. L. Gwynn, *MLN*, LXVI (1951). 366-370; Archibald A. Hill, *PMLA*, LXX (1955). 968-978; Robert W. Ayers, *MLN*, LXXI (1956). 577-584; Thomas J. Assad, *Tulane Stud. in English*, XI (1961). 87-95; John F. Huntley, *Renascence*, XV (1964). 154-162; F. X. Shea, *VP*, II (1964). 219-239. References to additional commentary on this and other poems of Hopkins may be found in the annual check lists in *The Explicator*.

**1538** Bridges: *Poetry and Prose*, ed. John Sparrow (Oxford, 1955). Jean-Georges Ritz, *Robert Bridges and Gerard Hopkins, 1863-1889* (1960); J. M. Cohen, "The Road Not Taken: A Study in the Poetry of Robert Bridges," *Cambridge Jour.*, IV (1951). 555-564.

**1540** Elizabeth C. Wright, *Metaphor, Sound, and Meaning in Bridges' "The Testament of Beauty"* (Philadelphia, 1951).

**1541** Doughty: Thomas J. Assad, *Three Victorian Travellers: Burton, Blunt, Doughty* (1964); John Holloway, "Poetry and Plain Language: The Verse of C. M. Doughty," *EIC*, IV (1954). 58-70; Barker Fairley, *"The Dawn in Britain* after Fifty Years," *UTQ*, XXVI (1957). 149-164; Heath-Stubbs, *The Darkling Plain*, pp. 188-199.

**1542** Gordon Pitts, "Lord de Tabley: Poet of Frustration," *West Virginia Univ. Phil. Papers*, XIV (1963). 57-73.

The Earl of Lytton, *Wilfred Scawen Blunt: A Memoir* (1961); T. J. Assad, *Three Victorian Travellers* (1964); William T. Going, "Wilfred Scawen Blunt, Victorian Sonneteer," *VP*, II (1964). 67-85.

**1543** George MacBeth, "Lee-Hamilton and the Romantic Agony," *Critical Quar.*, IV (1962). 141-150.

**1544** W. M. Parker, "William Ernest Henley: Twenty-Five New Poems," *Poetry Rev.*, XL (1949). 188-199. Jerome H. Buckley, *William Ernest Henley* (Princeton, 1945); "John Connell" [John Henry Robertson], *W. E. Henley* (1949).

Davidson: *Poems and Ballads*, ed. Robert Macleod (1959); *John Davidson: A Selection of His Poems*, ed. Maurice Lindsay (1961).—John A. Lester, Jr., *John Davidson: A Grub Street Bibliography* (Charlottesville, Va., 1958). John B. Townsend, *John Davidson: Poet of Armageddon* (New Haven, 1961); Paul Turner, "John Davidson: The Novels of a Poet," *Cambridge Jour.*, V (1952). 499-504; Lester, "Friedrich Nietzsche and John Davidson: A Study in Influence,"

*JHI*, xviii (1957). 411-429, and "Prose-Poetry Transmutation in the Poetry of John Davidson," *MP*, lvi (1958). 38-44.

**1545**  Housman: *Complete Poems*, ed. Tom Burns Haber (1959); *The Manuscript Poems of A. E. Housman*, ed. Haber (Minneapolis, 1955); *Selected Prose*, ed. John Carter (Cambridge, 1961).—*A. E. Housman: An Annotated Hand-List*, ed. John Carter and John Sparrow (1952, rev. 1957). George L. Watson, *A. E. Housman: A Divided Life* (1957); Maude M. Hawkins, *A. E. Housman: Man Behind a Mask* (Chicago, 1958); Norman Marlow, *A. E. Housman: Scholar and Poet* (Minneapolis, 1958); Oliver Robinson, *Angry Dust: the Poetry of A. E. Housman* (Boston, 1950); Robert Hamilton, *Housman the Poet* (Exeter, 1953); Edmund Wilson, "A. E. Housman," *The Triple Thinkers* (1948), pp. 60-71; John W. Stevenson, "The Pastoral Setting in the Poetry of A. E. Housman," *So. Atl. Quar.*, lv (1956). 487-500; Christopher Ricks, "The Nature of Housman's Poetry," *EIC*, xiv (1964). 268-284.

**1546**  Note 37: Faith Mackenzie, *William Cory: A Biography, with a Selection of Poems* (1950).

# XL. The Modern Novel

**1547**  General works on twentieth-century English literature, of pertinence to this and the following chapters, include: William York Tindall, *Forces in Modern British Literature* (1947, rev. 1956); B. Ifor Evans, *English Literature Between the Wars* (1948); A. S. Collins, *English Literature of the Twentieth Century* (1951, enlarged 1960); R. A. Scott-James, *Fifty Years of English Literature, 1900-1950* (1951); Raymond Tschumi, *Thought in Twentieth-Century English Literature* (1951); J. Isaacs, *The Assessment of Twentieth-Century Literature* (1951); G. S. Fraser, *The Modern Writer and His World* (1953, rev. 1964); A. C. Ward, *Twentieth-Century English Literature, 1901-1960* (1964); Giorgio Melchiori, *The Tightrope Walkers: Studies of Mannerism in Modern English Literature* (1956); David Daiches, *The Present Age: After 1920* (1958); Graham Hough, *Image and Experience: Reflections on a Literary Revolution* (1960); *The [Pelican] Guide to English Literature*, ed. Boris Ford, Vol. vii: *The Modern Age* (1961, rev. 1964).

Works on the twentieth-century English novel: D. S. Savage, *The Withered Branch: Six Studies in the Modern Novel* (1950); Arnold Kettle, *Introduction to the English Novel*, Vol. ii: *Henry James to the Present Day* (1953); Seán O'Faoláin, *The Vanishing Hero: Studies in Novelists of the Twenties* (1956); Frederick R. Karl and Marvin Magalaner, *A Reader's Guide to Great Twentieth-Century English Novels* (1959); *Modern British Fiction*, ed. Mark Schorer (1961), a collection of critical essays; David Daiches, *The Novel and the Modern World* (Chicago, 1960), a revision of his 1939 volume; Walter Allen, *The English Novel* (1954), chs. vi-vii, and *Tradition and Dream: The English and American Novel from the Twenties to Our Time* (1964); Lionel Stevenson, *The English Novel* (1960), chs. xvi-xvii.

Henry James: *Complete Tales* (12v, 1962-1964), *Complete Plays* (1949), both ed. Leon Edel. Most of the major novels are available in well edited reprints, too numerous to list here. James's journalism and other fugitive writings have been assembled in a number of volumes, including *The Art of Fiction and Other Essays*, ed. Morris Roberts (1948); *The Scenic Art: Notes on Acting and the Drama, 1872-1901*, ed. Allan Wade (New Brunswick, N.J., 1948); *Eight Uncollected Tales*, ed. Edna Kenton (New Brunswick, 1950); *The Painter's Eye: Notes and Essays on the Pictorial Arts*, ed. John L. Sweeney (Cambridge, Mass., 1956); *Parisian Sketches*, ed. Leon Edel and Ilse D. Lind (1957); *Literary Reviews and Essays*, ed. Albert Mordell (1957); *The Art of Travel*, ed. Morton Dauwen Zabel (1958). Anthologies containing some of the better-known stories and criticism are: *American Novels and Stories*, ed. F. O. Matthiessen (1947); *Ghostly Tales* (New Brunswick, 1948), *American Essays* (1956), *The Future of the Novel* (1956), *The House of Fiction* (1957)—all ed. Edel; *The Portable Henry James* (1951) and *Fifteen Short Stories* (1961), both ed. Zabel; *Selected Literary Criticism*, ed. Morris Schapira (1963); *Americans and Europe: Selected Tales*, ed. Napier Wilt and John Lucas (Boston, 1965). *Autobiography*, ed. F. W. Dupee (1956), including *A Small Boy and Others, Notes of a Son and Brother*, and *The Middle Years; Notebooks*, ed. Matthiessen and Kenneth B. Murdock (1947); *Henry James and Robert Louis Stevenson: A Record of Friendship and Criticism*, ed. Janet Adam Smith (1948); *Henry James and H. G. Wells: A Record of Their Friendship*, ed. Edel and Gordon N. Ray (Urbana, Ill., 1958); *Henry James and John Hay: The Record of a Friendship*, ed. George Monteiro (Providence, R. I., 1965). Leon Edel (ed. *Selected Letters*, 1955) is preparing a definitive edition of James's letters.—Edel and Dan H. Laurence, *A Bibliography of Henry James* (1957, rev. 1961); Maurice Beebe and William T. Stafford, "Criticism of Henry James: A Selected Checklist," *Mod. Fiction Stud.*, III (1957-58). 73-96. The fullest lists of current publications on James are found in the quarterly bibliography in *American Lit.* and the annual bibliography in *PMLA*. Edel, *Henry James* (4v, Philadelphia, 1953-    ), the standard biography; *The Legend of the Master*, ed. Simon Nowell-Smith (1947), contemporary records of James's personality; Matthiessen, *The James Family* (1947); Elizabeth Stevenson, *The Crooked Corridor: A Study of Henry James* (1949); Dupee, *Henry James* (1951, rev. 1956); Robert C. LeClair, *Young Henry James: 1843-1870* (1955); Quentin Anderson, *The American Henry James* (New Brunswick, N.J., 1957); Osborn Andreas, *Henry James and the Expanding Horizon* (Seattle, 1948); Edwin T. Bowden, *The Themes of Henry James* (New Haven, 1956); Frederick C. Crews, *The Tragedy of Manners: Moral Drama in the Later Novels of Henry James* (New Haven, 1957); Leo B. Levy, *Versions of Melodrama: A Study of the Fiction and Drama of Henry James, 1865-1897* (Berkeley, 1957); Christof Wegelin, *The Image of Europe in Henry James* (Dallas, 1958); Harold T. McCarthy, *Henry James: The Creative Process* (1958); Alexander Holder-Barrell, *The Development of Imagery and Its Functional Significance in Henry James's Novels* (Bern, 1959); D. W. Jefferson, *Henry James* (1960) and *Henry James and the Modern Reader* (1964); Richard Poirier, *The Comic Sense of Henry James* (1960); Robert Marks, *James's Later Novels: An Interpretation* (1960); Oscar Cargill, *The Novels of Henry James* (1961); J. A. Ward, *The Imagination of Disaster: Evil in the Fiction of Henry James* (Lincoln, Neb., 1961); Dorothea Krook, *The Ordeal of Consciousness in Henry James* (Cambridge, 1962); Walter F. Wright, *The Madness of Art: A Study of Henry James* (Lincoln, Neb., 1962); Maxwell Geismar, *Henry James and the Jacobites* (Boston, 1963); Sister M. Corona Sharp,

*The Confidante in Henry James* (South Bend, Ind., 1963); Joseph Wiesenfarth, *Henry James and the Dramatic Analogy* (1963); Robert L. Gale, *The Caught Image: Figurative Language in the Fiction of Henry James* (Chapel Hill, 1964); Laurence B. Holland, *The Expense of Vision: Essays on the Craft of Henry James* (Princeton, 1964); Krishna Vaid, *Technique in the Tales of Henry James* (Cambridge, Mass., 1964); Edward Stone, *The Battle and the Books* (Athens, Ohio, 1965); *The Question of Henry James,* ed. Dupee (1945); *Henry James: A Collection of Critical Essays,* ed. Edel (1963); *Discussions of Henry James,* ed. Naomi Lebowitz (Boston, 1962); Stewart, *Eight Modern Writers,* ch. III (see also pp. 647-649 for a selected list of chapters and articles in periodicals).

**1551** *The Portable Conrad,* ed. Morton Dauwen Zabel (1947); *Joseph Conrad on Fiction,* ed. Walter F. Wright (Lincoln, Neb., 1964); *Letters to William Blackwood and David S. Meldrum,* ed. William Blackburn (Durham, N. C., 1958); *Conrad's Polish Background: Letters to and from Polish Friends,* ed. Zdzislaw Najder (1964).—Kenneth A. Lohf and Eugene P. Sheehy, *Joseph Conrad at Mid-Century: Editions and Studies, 1895-1955* (Minneapolis, 1957); Maurice Beebe, "Criticism of Joseph Conrad: A Selected Checklist," *Mod. Fiction Stud.,* x (1964). 81-106. Jocelyn Baines, *Joseph Conrad: A Critical Biography* (1960), the best biography, replacing G. Jean-Aubry, *The Sea Dreamer: A Definitive Biography of Joseph Conrad* (1957), which in turn superseded Jean-Aubry's 1927 life. Wright, *Romance and Tragedy in Conrad* (Lincoln, Neb., 1949); Douglas Hewitt, *Conrad: A Reassessment* (Cambridge, 1952); Paul L. Wiley, *Conrad's Measure of Man* (Madison, Wis., 1954); E. H. Visiak, *The Mirror of Conrad* (1955); Thomas Moser, *Joseph Conrad: Achievement and Decline* (Cambridge, Mass., 1957); Robert F. Haugh, *Joseph Conrad: Discovery in Design* (Norman, Okla., 1957); Albert J. Guerard, *Conrad the Novelist* (Cambridge, Mass., 1958); Osborn Andreas, *Conrad: A Study in Nonconformity* (1959); Adam Gillon, *The Eternal Solitary: A Study of Joseph Conrad* (1960); *The Art of Joseph Conrad: A Critical Symposium,* ed. R. W. Stallman (East Lansing, Mich., 1960); *Joseph Conrad: Centennial Essays,* ed. Ludwik Krzyzanowski (1960); Leo Gurko, *Joseph Conrad: Giant in Exile* (1962); Eloise Knapp Hay, *The Political Novels of Joseph Conrad* (Chicago, 1963); Frederick R. Karl, *A Reader's Guide to Joseph Conrad* (Chicago, 1963); Conrad number of *Mod. Fiction Stud.* (Spring, 1964); Stewart, *Eight Modern Writers,* ch. v (see also pp. 662-664 for a selected list of chapters and articles in periodicals).

**1553** *The Nigger of the "Narcissus,"* ed. Morton Dauwen Zabel (1951), Douglas Brown (1960), Albert Guerard (1960, with *The End of the Tether).—Youth,* ed. Zabel (1959, with *The End of the Tether).—Heart of Darkness,* ed. Guerard (1950, with *The Secret Sharer*); ed. Robert Kimbrough (1963), authoritative text with critical essays. *"Heart of Darkness" and the Critics,* ed. Bruce Harkness (San Francisco, 1960); *"Heart of Darkness": Backgrounds and Criticisms,* ed. Leonard F. Dean (1960).—*Lord Jim,* ed. Robert B. Heilman (1957), Zabel (1958), Walter Wright (1958). Tony Tanner, *Conrad: "Lord Jim": A Critical Study* (1963).—*Nostromo,* ed. Robert Penn Warren (1951), F. R. Leavis (1960), Dorothy Van Ghent (1961).

Note 13: In the 1960's there was a considerable revival of critical interest in Ford Madox Ford. *The Bodley Head Ford Madox Ford* (4v, 1962-1963); *Parade's End* (1950), a tetralogy composed of *Some Do Not* (1924), *No More Parades*

(1925), *A Man Could Stand Up* (1926), and *Last Post* (1927); *The Good Soldier,* ed. Mark Schorer (1951); *Critical Writings,* ed. Frank MacShane (Lincoln, Neb., 1964); *Letters,* ed. Richard M. Ludwig (Princeton, 1965).—David D. Harvey, *Ford Madox Ford 1873-1939: A Bibliography of Works and Criticism* (Princeton, 1962). Douglas Goldring, *The Last Pre-Raphaelite* (1948); Richard A. Cassell, *Ford Madox Ford: A Study of His Novels* (Baltimore, 1962); John A. Meixner, *Ford Madox Ford's Novels* (Minneapolis, 1962); Paul L. Wiley, *Novelist of Three Worlds: Ford Madox Ford* (Syracuse, N.Y., 1962); Carol Ohmann, *Ford Madox Ford: From Apprentice to Craftsman* (Middletown, Conn., 1964); R. W. Lid, *Ford Madox Ford: The Essence of His Art* (Berkeley, 1964); Frank MacShane, *The Life and Work of Ford Madox Ford* (1965).

**1554** *Under Western Eyes* (1951), *The Shadow-Line* (1959), and *The Mirror of the Sea* (1960, with *A Personal Record*), all edited by Zabel.—Note 15: *Conrad's "Secret Sharer" and the Critics,* ed. Bruce Harkness (San Francisco, 1962).

**1555** *The Man of Property,* ed. Lionel Stevenson (1949). Helmut E. Gerber *et al.,* "John Galsworthy: An Annotated Checklist of Writings About Him," *English Fiction in Transition,* I, no. 3 (1958). 7-29, VII (1964). 93-100.—R. H. Mottram, *For Some We Loved: An Intimate Portrait of Ada and John Galsworthy* (1956); Dudley Barker, *The Man of Principle: A View of John Galsworthy* (1963); Jan Henry Smit, *The Short Stories of John Galsworthy* (Rotterdam, 1948); J. Gordon Eaker, "Galsworthy and the Modern Mind," *PQ,* XXIX (1950). 31-48; Drew B. Pallett, "Young Galsworthy: The Forging of a Satirist," *MP,* LVI (1959). 178-186.

**1557** *Journals,* ed. Frank Swinnerton (1954), a selection; *Arnold Bennett and H. G. Wells: A Record of a Personal and Literary Friendship,* ed. Harris Wilson (Urbana, Ill., 1960).—Reginald Pound, *Arnold Bennett: A Biography* (1952); Walter Allen, *Arnold Bennett* (1948); Vittoria Sanna, *Arnold Bennett e i romanzi delle Cinque Citta* (Florence, 1953); James Hall, *Arnold Bennett: Primitivism and Taste* (Seattle, 1959); John Wain, "The Quality of Bennett," *Preliminary Essays* (1957), pp. 121-156; James G. Hepburn, *The Art of Arnold Bennett* (Bloomington, Ind., 1963); Kettle, II. 82-89 (on *The Old Wives' Tale*).

**1558** Wells: *Collected Short Stories* (1960); *The History of Mr. Polly,* ed. Gordon N. Ray (Boston, 1960); *The Outline of History,* revised by Raymond Postgate (1961); *Henry James and H. G. Wells: A Record of Their Friendship* ed. Leon Edel and G. N. Ray (Urbana, Ill., 1958); *Arnold Bennett and H. G. Wells: A Record of a Personal and Literary Friendship,* ed. Harris Wilson (Urbana, Ill., 1960).—Vincent Brome, *H. G. Wells: A Biography* (1951); Antonia Vallentin, *H. G. Wells: Prophet of Our Day* (1950); Bernard Bergonzi, *The Early H. G. Wells: A Study of the Scientific Romances* (Manchester, 1961); Ingvald Raknem, *H. G. Wells and His Critics* (Oslo, 1962); Kettle, II. 89-95 (on *Tono-Bungay*).

**1560** Joyce: *Chamber Music,* ed. William Y. Tindall (1954); *Exiles* (1951) and *Dubliners* (1954), both ed. Padraic Colum; *Stephen Hero, with Additional Manuscript Pages,* ed. Theodore Spencer (Norfolk, Conn., 1955); *Critical Writings,* ed. Ellsworth Mason and Richard Ellmann (1959); *The Portable James Joyce,* ed. Harry Levin (1947); *Letters,* ed. Stuart Gilbert (1957).—John J. Slocum and Herbert Cahoon, *A Bibliography of James Joyce, 1882-1941* (1953);

Maurice Beebe and A. Walton Litz, "Criticism of James Joyce: A Selected Checklist," *Mod. Fiction Stud.*, IV (1958-59). 71-99. Ellmann, *James Joyce* (1959), the standard biography; Mary and Padraic Colum, *Our Friend James Joyce* (1958); Stanislaus Joyce, *My Brother's Keeper: James Joyce's Early Years* (1958); Sylvia Beach, *Shakespeare and Company* (1959). Levin's *James Joyce: A Critical Introduction* was revised in 1960 and Kain's *Fabulous Voyager* in 1959. L. A. G. Strong, *The Sacred River: An Approach to James Joyce* (1949); Patricia Hutchins, *James Joyce's Dublin* (1950) and *James Joyce's World* (1957); three books by Tindall, *James Joyce: His Way of Interpreting the Modern World* (1950), *A Reader's Guide to James Joyce* (1959), and *The Joyce Country* (University Park, Pa., 1960); Arland Ussher, *Three Great Irishmen: Shaw, Yeats, and Joyce* (1952); William Powell Jones, *James Joyce and the Common Reader* (Norman, Okla., 1955); Kristan Smidt, *James Joyce and the Cultic Use of Fiction* (Oslo, 1955); Marvin Magalaner and Richard M. Kain, *Joyce, the Man, the Work, the Reputation* (1956); Hugh Kenner, *Dublin's Joyce* (Bloomington, Ind., 1956); William T. Noon, *Joyce and Aquinas* (New Haven, 1957); Kevin Sullivan, *Joyce among the Jesuits* (1958); Matthew Hodgart and Mabel P. Worthington, *Songs in the Works of James Joyce* (Philadelphia, 1959); J. Mitchell Morse, *The Sympathetic Alien: James Joyce and Catholicism* (1959); Magalaner, *Time of Apprenticeship: The Fiction of Young James Joyce* (1960); Samuel L. Goldberg, *Joyce* (Edinburgh, 1962); Kain, *Dublin in the Age of William Butler Yeats and James Joyce* (Norman, Okla., 1962); Helmut Bonheim, *Joyce's Benefictions* (Berkeley, 1964); Joseph Prescott, *Exploring James Joyce* (Carbondale, Ill., 1964); Joseph G. Brennan, *Three Philosophical Novelists: James Joyce, André Gide, Thomas Mann* (1964); Anthony Burgess, *Here Comes Everybody* (1965); *A James Joyce Miscellany,* ed. Magalaner (1st ser., New York, 1957; 2nd and 3rd ser., Carbondale, Ill., 1959, 1962); *James Joyce: Two Decades of Criticism,* ed. Seon Givens (1948, rev. 1963); *James Joyce Rev.* (1957-1959); *James Joyce Quar.* (1963-    ); Stewart, *Eight Modern Writers,* ch. VIII (see also pp. 684-686 for selected list of chapters and articles in periodicals).

**1561**  Robert S. Ryf, *A New Approach to Joyce: "The Portrait of the Artist" as a Guidebook* (Berkeley, 1962); *The Workshop of Daedalus: James Joyce and the Raw Materials for "A Portrait of the Artist as a Young Man,"* ed. Robert E. Scholes and R. M. Kain (Evanston, Ill., 1965); *Joyce's "Portrait": Criticism and Critiques,* ed. Thomas E. Connolly (1962).

A. Walton Litz, *The Art of James Joyce: Method and Design in "Ulysses" and "Finnegans Wake"* (1961); S. L. Goldberg, *The Classical Temper: A Study of Joyce's "Ulysses"* (1961); Robert M. Adams, *Surface and Symbol: The Consistency of James Joyce's "Ulysses"* (1962).—*Word Index to James Joyce's "Ulysses,"* comp. Miles E. Hanley (Madison, Wis., 1951).

**1562**  *A First-Draft Version of "Finnegans Wake,"* ed. David Hayman (Austin, Tex., 1963); Adaline Glasheen, *A Census of "Finnegans Wake": An Index to the Characters and Their Roles* (Evanston, Ill., 1956, enlarged ed. 1963); Frances M. Boldereff, *Reading "Finnegans Wake"* (1959); James S. Atherton, *The Books at the Wake* (1959); Fred H. Higginson, *Anna Livia Plurabell: The Making of a Chapter* (Minneapolis, 1960); *Scribbledehobble: The Ur-Workbook for "Finnegans Wake",* ed. Thomas E. Connolly (Evanston, Ill., 1961); Clive Hart, *Structure and Motif in "Finnegans Wake"* (1962); Bernard Benstock,

*Joyce-Agains Wake: An Analysis of "Finnegans Wake"* (Seattle, 1966); *Twelve and a Tilly,* ed. Jack P. Dalton and Clive Hart (Evanston, Ill., 1966), a collection of essays.—*A Concordance to "Finnegans Wake,"* ed. Hart (Minneapolis, 1963).

**1563** D. H. Lawrence: *Complete Short Stories* (3v, 1955); *Short Novels* (2v, 1956); *Complete Poems,* ed. Vivian de Sola Pinto and Warren Roberts (2v, 1964); selections of poems, ed. Kenneth Rexroth (1947), W. E. Williams (1950), J. Reeves (1951); *Selected Poetry and Prose,* ed. T. R. Barnes (1957); *Selected Literary Criticism,* ed. Anthony Beal (1955); *The Portable D. H. Lawrence,* ed. Diana Trilling (1947); *Sex, Literature, and Censorship,* ed. Harry T. Moore (1953); *The Symbolic Meaning,* ed. Armin Arnold (1962), early versions of *Studies in Classic American Literature; A D. H. Lawrence Miscellany,* ed. Moore (Carbondale, Ill., 1959); *Collected Letters,* ed. Moore (2v, 1962); *Letters,* ed. Richard Aldington (1950), a selection; *The Plumed Serpent,* ed. William Y. Tindall (1951); *Sons and Lovers,* ed. Mark Schorer (1951).—Roberts, *A Bibliography of D. H. Lawrence* (1963); Maurice Beebe and Anthony Tommasi, "Criticism of D. H. Lawrence: A Selected Checklist of Criticism," *Mod. Fiction Stud.,* II (1959-60). 83-98. Moore, *The Life and Works of D. H. Lawrence* (1951, rev. 1964), and *The Intelligent Heart: The Story of D. H. Lawrence* (1954, rev. 1960), the standard biography; *D. H. Lawrence: A Composite Biography,* ed. Edward Nehls (3v, Madison, Wis., 1957-59), a collection of primary source material; Piero Nardi, *La Vita di D. H. Lawrence* (Milan, 1947); Aldington, *Portrait of a Genius, But—* (1950); Witter Bynner, *Journey with Genius: Recollections and Reflections Concerning the D. H. Lawrences* (1951); Eliot Fay, *Lorenzo in Search of the Sun* (1953); *Frieda Lawrence: The Memoirs and Correspondence,* ed. E. W. Tedlock, Jr. (1961); Anthony West, *D. H. Lawrence* (1950); "William Tiverton" [Martin Jarrett-Kerr], *D. H. Lawrence and Human Existence* (1951); Kenneth Young, *D. H. Lawrence* (1952); Mark Spilka, *The Love Ethic of D. H. Lawrence* (Bloomington, Ind., 1955); F. R. Leavis, *D. H. Lawrence: Novelist* (1955); Mary Freeman, *D. H. Lawrence: A Basic Study of His Ideas* (Gainesville, Fla., 1955); Graham Hough, *The Dark Sun: A Study of D. H. Lawrence* (1956); Arnold, *D. H. Lawrence and America* (1958); Richard Rees, *Brave Men: A Study of D. H. Lawrence and Simone Weil* (1958); F. J. Temple, *David Herbert Lawrence, l'Oeuvre et la vie* (Paris, 1960); Eliseo Vivas, *D. H. Lawrence: The Failure and the Triumph of Art* (Evanston, Ill., 1960); Beal, *D. H. Lawrence* (Edinburgh, 1961); Anaïs Nin, *D. H. Lawrence, An Unprofessional Study* (1962), first published in limited edition, 1932; Julian Moynahan, *The Deed of Life: The Novels and Tales of D. H. Lawrence* (Princeton, 1963); Kingsley Widmer, *The Art of Perversity: D. H. Lawrence's Shorter Fictions* (Seattle, 1963); Eugene Goodheart, *The Utopian Vision of D. H. Lawrence* (Chicago, 1963); Ronald P. Draper, *D. H. Lawrence* (1964); Tedlock, *D. H. Lawrence, Artist and Rebel: A Study of Lawrence's Fiction* (Albuquerque, 1964); H. M. Daleski, *The Forked Flame* (1965); George H. Ford, *Double Measure: A Study of the Novels and Stories of D. H. Lawrence* (1965); *The Achievement of D. H. Lawrence,* ed. Frederick J. Hoffman and Harry T. Moore (Norman, Okla., 1953); *D. H. Lawrence: A Collection of Critical Essays,* ed. Spilka (1963); Stewart, *Eight Modern Writers,* ch. IX (see also pp. 692-694 for a selected list of chapters and articles in periodicals).

**1565** Huxley: *Collected Short Stories* (1957); *Collected Essays* (1959); *Point*

*Counter Point,* ed. H. H. Watts (1947); *Antic Hay* and *The Gioconda Smile* (1957) and *Brave New World* and *Brave New World Revisited* (1960), both vols. ed. C. J. Rolo; *The World of Aldous Huxley,* ed. Rolo (1947).—Claire J. Eschelbach and Joyce L. Shober, *Aldous Huxley: A Bibliography, 1916-1959* (Berkeley, 1961). Teddy Brunius, *Aldous Huxley* (Stockholm, 1947); Pierre Jouguelet, *Aldous Huxley* (Paris, 1948); John A. Atkins, *Aldous Huxley: A Literary Study* (1956); S. K. Ghose, *Aldous Huxley: A Cynical Salvationist* (Bombay, 1961); Derek S. Savage, "Aldous Huxley and the Dissociation of Personality," *Sewanee Rev.,* LV (1947). 537-568; Geoffrey Bullough, "Aspects of Aldous Huxley," *ES,* xxx (1949). 233-243; Charles I. Glicksberg, "Aldous Huxley: Art and Mysticism," *Prairie Schooner,* xxvii (1953). 344-353, and "Huxley, the Experimental Novelist," *So. Atl. Quar.,* LII (1953). 98-110; Carlyle King, "Aldous Huxley's Way to God," *Queen's Quar.,* LXI (1954). 80-100, and "Aldous Huxley and Music," *ibid.,* LXX (1963). 336-351; Colin Wilson, "Existential Criticism and the Work of Aldous Huxley," *London Mag.,* V, no. 9 (1958). 46-59; Rudolf B. Schmerl, "Aldous Huxley's Social Criticism," *Chicago Rev.,* XIII, no. 1 (1959). 37-58, and "The Two Future Worlds of Aldous Huxley," *PMLA,* LXXVII (1962). 328-334; A. E. Dyson, "Aldous Huxley and the Two Nothings," *Critical Quar.,* III (1961). 293-309; Charles M. Holmes, "Aldous Huxley's Struggle with Art," *Western Humanities Rev.,* XV (1961). 149-156.

Note 25: *The Bodley Head Saki* (1963); *The Best of Saki,* ed. Graham Greene (1950); *Short Stories,* ed. Christopher Morley (1951).—Robert Drake, " 'Saki': Some Problems and a Bibliography," *English Fiction in Transition,* V, no. 1 (1962). 6-26, and "Saki's Ironic Stories," *Texas Stud. in Lit. and Lang.,* V (1963). 374-388.

Note 26: *Norman Douglas: A Selection from His Works,* ed. D. M. Low (1955); *In the Beginning,* ed. Constantine FitzGibbon (1953), first complete publication.—Cecil Woolf, *A Bibliography of Norman Douglas* (1954). R. M. Dawkins, *Norman Douglas* (1952); FitzGibbon, *Norman Douglas: A Pictorial Record* (1953); Richard Aldington, *Pinorman* (1954); Nancy Cunard, *Grand Man: Memories of Norman Douglas* (1954); "Portrait of Norman Douglas," *LTLS,* July 4, 1952, pp. 429-431.

**1566** Gloria Glikin, "A Checklist of Writings by Dorothy M. Richardson" and "An Annotated Bibliography of Writings About Her," *English Lit. in Transition,* VIII, no. 1 (1965). 1-35. Caesar Blake, *Dorothy Richardson* (Ann Arbor, 1960); Leon Edel, "Dorothy Richardson, 1882-1957," *Mod. Fiction Stud.,* IV (1958). 165-168; Shiv K. Kumar, "Dorothy Richardson and the Dilemma of 'Being versus Becoming,' " *MLN,* LXXIV (1959). 494-501; Grace Tomkinson, "Dorothy M. Richardson, Pioneer," *Dalhousie Rev.,* xxxviii (1959). 465-471; Glikin, "Dorothy M. Richardson: The Personal 'Pilgrimage,' " *PMLA,* LXXVIII (1963). 586-600.—Robert Humphrey, *Stream of Consciousness in the Modern Novel* (Berkeley, 1954); Melvin Friedman, *Stream of Consciousness: A Study in Literary Method* (New Haven, 1955).

**1567** *Virginia Woolf and Lytton Strachey: Letters,* ed. Leonard Woolf and James Strachey (1956).—B. J. Kirkpatrick, *A Bibliography of Virginia Woolf* (1957, rev. 1965); Maurice Beebe, "Criticism of Virginia Woolf: A Selected Checklist," *Mod. Fiction Stud.,* II (1956-57). 36-45. Revised editions of Daiches' and Bennett's studies were published in 1963 and 1964, respectively. Aileen Pippett,

*The Moth and the Star* (Boston, 1955); L. Woolf, *Beginning Again: An Auto-biography of the Years 1911-18* (1964); R. L. Chambers, *The Novels of Virginia Woolf* (Edinburgh, 1947); Bernard Blackstone, *Virginia Woolf: A Commentary* (1949); Vittoria Sanna, *Il Romanzo di Virginia Woolf: Inspirazione e motivi fondamentale* (Florence, 1951); Irma Rantavaara, *Virginia Woolf and Blooms-bury* (Helsinki, 1953) and *Virginia Woolf's "The Waves"* (Helsinki, 1960); James R. Hafley, *The Glass Roof: Virginia Woolf as Novelist* (Berkeley, 1954); Monique Nathan, *Virginia Woolf par elle-même* (Paris, 1956; Eng. trans. 1961), noteworthy for expert use of photographs; Dorothy Brewster, *Virginia Woolf's London* (1959) and *Virginia Woolf* (1962); Jean Guiguet, *Virginia Woolf et son oeuvre: l'art et la quêt du réel* (Paris, 1962; Eng. trans. 1965); A. D. Moody, *Virginia Woolf* (1963); N. C. Thakur, *The Symbolism of Virginia Woolf* (1965); Josephine O. Schaefer, *The Three-Fold Nature of Reality in the Novels of Virginia Woolf* (1965).

Note 29: Katherine Mansfield: *Selected Stories,* ed. D. M. Davin (1953); *Journal* (rev. 1954), *Letters to John Middleton Murry, 1913-1922* (1951), both ed. J. M. Murry.—Antony Alpers, *Katherine Mansfield: A Biography* (1953); Odette Lenoël, *La Vocation de Katherine Mansfield* (Paris, 1946); Sylvia L. Berkman, *Katherine Mansfield: A Critical Study* (New Haven, 1951); Anne-Marie Monnett, *Katherine Mansfield* (Paris, 1960); Saralyn R. Daly, *Katherine Mansfield* (1965); Murry, *Katherine Mansfield and Other Literary Studies* (1959), ch. 11.

**1568**  *H. M. Tomlinson: A Selection from His Writings,* ed. Kenneth Hopkins (1953).

Maugham: *Complete Short Stories* (3v, 1951); *Collected Plays* (3v, 1952); *Selected Novels* (3v, 1953); *The Travel Books* (1955); *The Maugham Reader* (1950); *The Maugham Enigma: An Anthology,* ed. Klaus W. Jonas (1954); *Of Human Bondage,* ed. Richard A. Cordell (1956).—Jonas, *A Bibliography of the Works of W. Somerset Maugham* (1950); Raymond T. Stott, *The Writings of W. Somerset Maugham* (1956, supplement 1961). Helmut Papejewski, *Die Welt-, Lebens- und Kunstanschauung Maughams* (Cologne, 1952); Karl G. Pfeiffer, *W. Somerset Maugham: A Candid Portrait* (1959); Cordell, *Somerset Maugham: A Biographical and Critical Study* (Bloomington, Ind., 1961), superseding his 1937 volume; Laurence Brander, *Somerset Maugham: A Guide* (1963).

**1569**  B. J. Kirkpatrick, *A Bibliography of E. M. Forster* (1965); Helmut E. Gerber, "E. M. Forster: An Annotated Checklist of Writings about Him," *Eng-lish Fiction in Transition,* 11, no. 1 (1959). 4-27; Maurice Beebe and Joseph Brogunier, "Criticism of E. M. Forster: A Selected Checklist," *Mod. Fiction Stud.,* VII (1961). 284-292. James McConkey, *The Novels of E. M. Forster* (Ithaca, 1957); H. J. Oliver, *The Art of E. M. Forster* (Melbourne, 1960); J. B. Beer, *The Achievement of E. M. Forster* (1962); Frederick C. Crews, *E. M. Forster: The Perils of Humanism* (Princeton, 1962); K. W. Gransden, *E. M. Forster* (1962); Alan Wilde, *Art and Order: A Study of E. M. Forster* (1964); David Shusterman, *The Quest for Certitude in E. M. Forster's Fiction* (Bloomington, Ind., 1965); *E. M. Forster: A Tribute, with Selections from His Writings on India,* ed. K. Natwar-Singh (1964).

Leo Robertson, *Compton Mackenzie: An Appraisal of His Literary Work* (1955).—Rupert Hart-Davis, *Hugh Walpole: A Biography* (1952).

**1570**  Jessica B. Young, *Francis Brett Young: A Biography* (1962).
"The Pleasures of Knowing Rose Macaulay," *Encounter*, XII (1959). 23-31, tributes from many leading writers. (She was born in 1887 and died in 1958.)

# XLI. Poetry in the Twentieth Century

**1572**  J. Isaacs, *The Background of Modern Poetry* (1951); Lawrence Durrell, *A Key to Modern British Poetry* (Norman, Okla., 1952); Anthony Thwaite, *Contemporary English Poetry* (1959); J. M. Cohen, *Poetry of This Age, 1908-1958* (1960); M. L. Rosenthal, *The Modern Poets: A Critical Introduction* (1960); H. N. Fairchild, *Religious Trends in English Poetry*, Vol. V: *Gods of a Changing Poetry* (1962); C. K. Stead, *The New Poetic* (1964).

**1573**  "Edwardian Poets," *LTLS*, March 20, 1953, p. 186, on Binyon and Bottomley.

**1574**  De la Mare: *Collected Tales*, ed. Edward Wagenknecht (1949); *Walter de la Mare: A Selection from His Writings*, ed. Kenneth Hopkins (1956); *A Choice of De La Mare's Verse*, ed. W. H. Auden (1963). Leonard Clark, "A Handlist of the Writings in Book Form (1902-1953) of Walter de la Mare," *Stud. in Bibliography*, VI (1954). 197-218. John Atkins, *Walter de la Mare: an Exploration* (1947); Henry C. Duffin, *Walter de la Mare: A Study of His Poetry* (1949); N. J. Endicott, "Walter de la Mare, 1873-1956," *UTQ*, XXVI (1957). 109-121.—*W. B. Yeats and T. Sturge Moore: Their Correspondence, 1901-1937*, ed. Ursula Bridge (1953). Frederick L. Gwynn, *Sturge Moore and the Life of Art* (Lawrence, Kan., 1951).

**1577**  Davies: *Complete Poems* (1963); *The Essential W. H. Davies*, ed. Brian Waters (1951). Richard J. Stonesifer, *W. H. Davies* (1963).

**1578**  Edward Thomas: *Selected Poems*, ed. Robin Skelton (1962). H. Coombes, *Edward Thomas* (1956); Eleanor Farjeon, *Edward Thomas: the Last Four Years* (1958); Coombes, "The Poetry of Edward Thomas," *EIC*, III (1953). 191-200; C. Day Lewis, "The Poetry of Edward Thomas," *Essays by Divers Hands* (Royal Soc. of Lit.), n.s. XXVIII (1956). 75-92; John Burrow, "Keats and Edward Thomas," *EIC*, VII (1957). 404-415; John F. Danby, "Edward Thomas," *Critical Quar.*, I (1959). 308-317.—Squire: *Collected Poems* (1959).

**1579**  *Georgian Poetry*, ed. James Reeves (1962). Christopher Hassall, *Sir Edward Marsh* (1959); Robert H. Ross, *The Georgian Revolt 1910-1922: Rise and Fall of a Poetic Ideal* (Carbondale, Ill., 1965); George MacBeth, "Georgian Poetry: 1912-1922," *London Mag.*, n.s.II (1962). 74-80.
Murry: *Selected Criticism, 1916-1957*, ed. Richard Rees (1960). F. A. Lea, *The Life of John Middleton Murry* (1959); Derek Stanford, "Middleton Murry as Literary Critic," *So. Atl. Quar.*, LVIII (1959). 196-205; J. B. Beer, "John Middleton Murry," *Critical Quar.*, III (1961). 59-66; André Crépin, "John Middleton Murry et le sens allégorique de la vie," *Études anglaises*, XIV (1961). 321-330.

**1580**  Stanley K. Coffman, Jr., *Imagism: A Chapter for the History of Modern Poetry* (Norman, Okla., 1951).
Hulme: *Further Speculations*, ed. Sam Hynes (Minneapolis, 1955; enlarged ed., Lincoln, Neb., 1962). Alun R. Jones, *The Life and Opinions of T. E. Hulme*

(1960); Murray Krieger, "T. E. Hulme: Classicism and the Imagination," *The New Apologists for Poetry* (Minneapolis, 1956), ch. 1.

LeRoy C. Breunig, "F. S. Flint, Imagism's Maître d'École," *CL,* IV (1952). 118-136.

Alister Kershaw, *A Bibliography of the Works of Richard Aldington from 1915 to 1948* (Burlingame, Cal., 1950); *Richard Aldington: An Intimate Portrait,* ed. Kershaw and F. J. Temple (Carbondale, Ill., 1965).

Thomas B. Swann, Jr., *The Classical World of H. D.* (Lincoln, Neb., 1962).

**1581**    John H. Johnston, *English Poetry of the First World War* (Princeton, 1964); Bernard Bergonzi, *Heroes' Twilight: A Study of the Literature of the Great War* (1965).

Brooke: *Poetical Works,* ed. Geoffrey Keynes (1946); *Prose,* ed. Christopher Hassall (1956). Keynes, *A Bibliography of Rupert Brooke* (1954, rev. 1959). Arthur Stringer, *The Red Wine of Youth: A Life of Rupert Brooke* (Indianapolis, 1948); Hassall, *Rupert Brooke: A Biography* (1964).

Owen: *Poems,* ed. Edmund Blunden (1947). D. S. R. Welland, *Wilfred Owen: A Critical Study* (1960); Harold Owen, *Journey from Obscurity: Memoirs of the Owen Family* (Oxford, 1963-    ); Hilda D. Spear, "Wilfred Owen and Poetic Truth," *Univ. of Kansas City Rev.,* XXV (1958). 110-116; Samuel J. Hazo, "The Passion of Wilfred Owen," *Renascence,* XI (1959). 201-208; Rosemary Freeman, "Parody as a Literary Form: George Herbert and Wilfred Owen," *EIC,* XIII (1963). 307-322.

**1582**    Blunden: *Poems of Many Years,* ed. Rupert Hart-Davis (1957); *Edmund Blunden: A Selection of His Poetry and Prose,* ed. Kenneth Hopkins (1950).

Sassoon: *Collected Poems* (1947, enlarged ed., 1961). Geoffrey Keynes, *A Bibliography of Siegfried Sassoon* (1962). Joseph Cohen, "The Three Roles of Siegfried Sassoon," *Tulane Stud. in English,* VII (1957). 169-185.

Graves: *Collected Poems* (1965).—J. M. Cohen, *Robert Graves* (1961); Douglas T. Day, III, *Swifter Than Reason: The Poetry and Criticism of Robert Graves* (Chapel Hill, 1963); Horace Gregory, "Robert Graves: A Parable for Writers," *Partisan Rev.,* XX (1953). 44-54; Ronald Hayman, "Robert Graves," *EIC,* V (1955). 32-43; George Steiner, "The Genius of Robert Graves," *Kenyon Rev.,* XXII (1960). 340-365; D. J. Enright, "Robert Graves and the Decline of Modernism," *EIC,* XI (1961). 319-337; Ronald Gaskell, "The Poetry of Robert Graves," *Critical Quar.,* III (1961). 213-222; Robert Graves number of *Shenandoah,* XIII (Winter, 1962), with essays by W. H. Auden, Enright, G. S. Fraser, and others.

**1584**    Campbell: *Collected Poems* (3v, 1949-1960). Victor M. Hamm, "Roy Campbell: Satirist," *Thought,* XXXVII (1962). 194-210; Harold R. Collins, "Roy Campbell: The Talking Bronco," *Boston Univ. Stud. in English,* IV (1960). 49-63. —Richard Fifoot, *A Bibliography of Edith, Osbert, and Sacheverell Sitwell* (1963). C. M. Bowra, *Edith Sitwell* (Monaco, 1947); *A Celebration for Edith Sitwell,* ed. Jose García Villa (Norfolk, Conn., 1948); Geoffrey Singleton, *Edith Sitwell, "The Hymn to Life"* (1961); Ihab H. Hassan, "Edith Sitwell and the Symbolist Tradition," *CL,* VII (1955). 240-251; Ralph J. Mills, Jr., "The Poetic Roles of Edith Sitwell," *Chicago Rev.,* XIV, no. 4 (1961). 33-64.—Osbert Sitwell's autobiography was continued by *Great Morning!* (1947), *Laughter in the Next Room* (1948), and *Noble Essences* (1950); *Tales My Father Taught Me* (1962) is an appendage. *Collected Stories* (1953). André Guimbretière, "La Satire dans

les nouvelles de Sir Osbert Sitwell," *Études anglaises*, XIII (1960). 346-358.—
There are two distinct editions of the *Selected Works of Sacheverell Sitwell*
(Indianapolis, 1953, and London, 1955). *Selected Poems* (1948). Joseph Warren
Beach, "Rococo: The Poetry of Sacheverell Sitwell," *Poetry*, LXXIV (1949). 217-233.

**1585** Eliot: *Collected Plays* (1962); *Collected Poems* (1963).—Donald Gallup,
*T. S. Eliot: A Bibliography* (1952). Matthiessen's *The Achievement of T. S. Eliot*
appeared in revised and enlarged editions, 1947 and 1958. George Williamson,
*A Reader's Guide to T. S. Eliot* (1953); *T. S. Eliot: A Study of His Writings
by Several Hands*, ed. B. Rajan (1947); *T. S. Eliot: A Symposium*, ed. Richard
March and Tambimuttu (1948); V. H. Brombert, *The Criticism of T. S. Eliot*
(New Haven, 1949); Elizabeth Drew, *T. S. Eliot: The Design of His Poetry*
(1949); Helen Gardner, *The Art of T. S. Eliot* (1949); Kristian Smidt, *Poetry
and Belief in the Works of T. S. Eliot* (Oslo, 1949; rev. London, 1961); Rossell
H. Robbins, *The T. S. Eliot Myth* (1951); Desmond E. S. Maxwell, *The Poetry
of T. S. Eliot* (1952); David Morris, *The Poetry of Gerard Manley Hopkins and
T. S. Eliot in the Light of the Donne Tradition* (Bern, 1953); Grover Smith,
Jr., *T. S. Eliot's Poetry and Plays: A Study in Sources and Meaning* (Chicago,
1956); G. Cattaui, *T. S. Eliot* (Paris, 1957); C. A. Bodelsen, *T. S. Eliot's "Four
Quartets"* (Copenhagen, 1958); *T. S. Eliot: A Symposium for His Seventieth
Birthday*, ed. Neville Braybrooke (1958); Hugh Kenner, *The Invisible Poet:
T. S. Eliot* (1959); Staffan Bergsten, *Time and Eternity* (Stockholm, 1960), on
*Four Quartets;* David E. Jones, *The Plays of T. S. Eliot* (1960); Seán Lucy, *T. S.
Eliot and the Idea of Tradition* (1960); George T. Wright, *The Poet in the
Poem: the Personae of Eliot, Yeats, and Pound* (Berkeley, 1960); Charles Moor-
man, *Arthurian Triptych: Mythic Materials in Charles Williams, C. S. Lewis,
and T. S. Eliot* (Berkeley, 1960); Lewis Freed, *T. S. Eliot: Aesthetics and History*
(La Salle, Ill., 1962); Northrop Frye, *T. S. Eliot* (1963); Eric Thompson, *T. S.
Eliot: The Metaphysical Perspective* (Carbondale, Ill., 1963); Carol H. Smith,
*T. S. Eliot's Dramatic Theory and Practice, from "Sweeney Agonistes" to "The
Elder Statesman"* (Princeton, 1963); Philip Headings, *T. S. Eliot* (1964);
Genesius Jones, *Approach to the Purpose* (1964); *T. S. Eliot: A Selected Critique*,
ed. Leonard Unger (1948); *T. S. Eliot: A Collection of Critical Essays*, ed.
Kenner (1962).

**1588** B. C. Bloomfield, *W. H. Auden: A Bibliography: The Early Years
Through 1955* (Charlottesville, Va., 1964). Francis Scarfe, *W. H. Auden* (1949);
Richard Hoggart, *Auden: An Introductory Essay* (1951); Joseph Warren Beach,
*The Making of the Auden Canon* (Minneapolis, 1957); Monroe K. Spears, *The
Poetry of W. H. Auden: The Disenchanted Island* (1963); John G. Blair, *The
Poetic Art of W. H. Auden* (Princeton, 1965); Bayley, *The Romantic Survival*,
ch. IX; *Auden: A Collection of Critical Essays*, ed. Spears (1964).

# XLII. Anthropology; Travel; History; Criticism

**1589** Arthur Calder-Marshall, *Havelock Ellis* (1959); John Stewart Collis,
*Havelock Ellis* (1959).

**1590** Frazer: Stanley E. Hyman, *The Tangled Bank: Darwin, Marx, Frazer
and Freud as Imaginative Writers* (1962); M. J. C. Hodgart, "In the Shade of

*The Golden Bough," Twentieth Century,* CLVII (1955). 111-119; John B. Vickery, *"The Golden Bough:* Impact and Archetype," *Virginia Quar. Rev.,* XXXIX (1963). 37-57.

**1593** *The Essential T. E. Lawrence,* ed. David Garnett (1951); *The Home Letters of T. E. Lawrence and His Brothers,* ed. M. R. Lawrence (1954); *Letters to T. E. Lawrence,* ed. A. W. Lawrence (1962); *Selected Letters,* ed. Garnett (1952).—Victoria Ocampo, *338171 T. E. (Lawrence of Arabia)* (Paris, 1947; English trans. 1963); Richard Aldington, *Lawrence of Arabia: A Biographical Enquiry* (1955); Flora Armitage, *The Desert and the Stars* (1955); Jean Beraud-Villars, *T. E. Lawrence, or The Search for the Absolute* (1958); Anthony Nutting, *Lawrence of Arabia: The Man and the Motive* (1961); Stanley Weintraub, *Private Shaw and Public Shaw* (1963); Gordon Mills, "T. E. Lawrence as a Writer," *Texas Quar.,* v, no. 3 (1962). 35-45.

**1594** *The Essential R. B. Cunninghame Graham,* ed. Paul Bloomfield (1952). A. F. Tschiffely, *Tornado Cavalier* (1955).

**1595** Hudson: *Works,* Uniform Edition (7v, 1951-1954); *The Best of W. H. Hudson,* ed. Odell Shepard (1949).—Robert Hamilton, *W. H. Hudson: the Vision of Earth* (1946); F. Liandrat, *W. H. Hudson, 1841-1922, Naturaliste: sa vie et son oeuvre* (Lyons, 1946); Richard E. Haymaker, *From Pampas to Hedgerows and Downs* (1954); Ruth Tomalin, *W. H. Hudson* (1954); Carlos Baker, "The Source-Book for Hudson's *Green Mansions,"* *PMLA,* LXI (1946). 252-257; Hoxie N. Fairchild, "Rima's Mother," *PMLA,* LXVIII (1953). 357-370.

**1596** Beatrice Webb: *Our Partnership,* ed. Barbara Drake and Margaret I. Cole (1948); *Diaries, 1912-1924* (1952) and *Diaries, 1924-1932* (1956), both ed. Cole. Cole, *The Webbs and Their Work* (1949).

**1598** *Concerning Andrew Lang,* ed. A. B. Webster (Oxford, 1949). Oscar Maurer, "Andrew Lang and *Longman's Magazine,* 1882-1905," *Univ. of Texas Stud. in English,* XXXIV (1955). 152-178.

Belloc: *One Thing and Another: A Miscellany from His Uncollected Essays,* ed. Patrick Cahill (1955); *Selected Essays,* ed. J. B. Morton (1948); *An Anthology of His Prose and Verse,* ed. W. N. Roughead (1951); *Verse,* ed. Roughead (1954); *Letters,* ed. Robert Speaight (1958). Morton, *Hilaire Belloc: A Memoir* (1955); Speaight, *The Life of Hilaire Belloc* (1957); *Testimony to Hilaire Belloc,* ed. Eleanor and Reginald Jebb (1956); Bernard Bergonzi, "Chesterton and/or Belloc," *Critical Quar.,* I (1959). 64-71.

**1599** John Sullivan, *G. K. Chesterton: A Bibliography* (1958). Hugh Kenner, *Paradox in Chesterton* (1948); Maisie Ward, *Return to Chesterton* (1952); Garry Willis, *Chesterton: Man and Mask* (1961); Elizabeth Sewell, "G. K. Chesterton: the Giant Upside-Down," *Thought,* XXX (1955-1956). 555-576; Jeffrey Hart, "In Praise of Chesterton," *Yale Rev.,* LIII (1963). 49-60.

**1600** Strachey: *Collected Works* (6v, 1948-1952); *Virginia Woolf and Lytton Strachey: Letters,* ed. Leonard Woolf and James Strachey (1956).—Martin Kallich, "Lytton Strachey: An Annotated Bibliography of Writings About Him," *English Fiction in Transition,* v, no. 3 (1962). 1-77. Charles R. Sanders, *Lytton Strachey: His Mind and Art* (New Haven, 1957); Kallich, *The Psychological Milieu of Lytton Strachey* (1961). For Strachey's importance in the history of modern biography, see Richard D. Altick, *Lives and Letters: A History of Literary Biography in England and America* (1965), ch. IX.

**1601**  *Essays, Poems and Tales of H. W. Nevinson,* ed. H. N. Brailsford (1948).

*Gilbert Murray: An Unfinished Autobiography,* ed. Jean Smith and Arnold Toynbee (1960).

Laura Lovat, *Maurice Baring: A Postscript* (1947); David Lodge, "Maurice Baring, Novelist: A Reappraisal," *Dublin Rev.,* CCXXXIV (1960). 262-270.

**1602**  Richard Garnett: see Carolyn G. Heilbrun, *The Garnett Family* (1961).

**1603**  Lily B. Campbell, "Bradley Revisited: Forty Years After," *SP,* XLIV (1947). 174-194, a reappraisal of *Shakespearean Tragedy.*

*A Saintsbury Miscellany: Selections from His Essays and Scrap Books* (1947), including biographical material; *A Last Vintage: Essays and Papers,* ed. John W. Oliver *et al.* (1950). Wellek, *History of Modern Criticism,* IV. 416-428.

Gosse: *Father and Son,* ed. William Irvine (Boston, 1965); *The Correspondence of André Gide and Edmund Gosse, 1904-1928,* ed. Linette F. Brugmans (1959); *Correspondence with Scandinavian Writers,* ed. Elias Bredsdorff (Copenhagen, 1960); *Transatlantic Dialogue: Selected American Correspondence,* ed. Paul F. Mattheisen and Michael Millgate (Austin, Tex., 1965); Osbert Sitwell, *Noble Essences* (1950), ch. II; Mattheisen, "Gosse's Candid 'Snapshots,'" *VS,* VIII (1965). 329-354.

**1604**  Ker: *On Modern Literature: Lectures and Addresses,* ed. Terence Spencer and James Sutherland (Oxford, 1955). J. H. P. Pafford, *W. P. Ker, 1855-1923: A Bibliography* (1950).

# Index

[**Boldface numbers** indicate main reference in the text. Numbers preceded by an **S** in this Index refer to paragraph/page numbers set in boldface in the BIBLIOGRAPHICAL SUPPLEMENT. These paragraph **numbers** correspond to pages of the text.]